to £16.45
- S2A

ECONOMICS

Alain Anderton

D0246208

WITHDRAWN

Causeway Press

NEWARK
LEARNING
CENTRE

NEWARK COLLEGE
FRIARY ROAD
NEWARK-ON-TRENT
NG24 1PB
Tel: 01636 680680

Newark
Learning Centre

Cover design by Susan and Andrew Allen

Cartoons by Brick

Graphics by Caroline Waring-Collins

Photography by Andrew Allen

Acknowledgements

The publishers wish to thank the following for permission to reproduce photographs and copyright material.

Audience Planners p.589; Bank of England p.363; BHS pp.87,88; Body Shop International pp.192,290; British Coal p.262; British Railways Board p.223; Dillons the Bookstore/Andrea Marks public relations pp.40,88; *Employment Gazette* p.547; *Financial Times* pp.53,93,138,179; Ford Motor Company pp.8,101; Health Education Authority p.204; Jeff Titon p.589; *Liverpool Daily Post and Echo PLC* pp.162,277; Liverpool University p.224; Midland Bank PLC p.332; Midland Montague p.361; National Savings p.362; Popperfoto pp.6,225,294,442; Royal Mint pp.350,351; Sally and Richard Greenhill pp.175,226,260; South Yorkshire Transport p.78; *Surveyor* p.343; Susan Allen p. 304; Topham Picture Source pp.111,344; Toyota Motor Corporation pp.108,124; Virgin Group Ltd p.290; Volvo p.10.

The publishers also wish to thank Jim Nettleship for the ideas on p.190 in 'Last days of the beerage'; Ian Traynor for the cartoon on p.595 and Mike Gibbons, photography on pp.45,124 and 344.

All Department of Employment and CSO sources are reproduced with the permission of the Controller of Her Majesty's Stationery Office.

Every effort has been made to locate the copyright owners of material used in this book. Any omissions brought to the notice of the publisher are regretted and will be credited in subsequent printings.

British Library Cataloguing in Publication Data

Anderton, A.G. (Alain G.)
 Economics.
 1. Economics
 I. Title
 330

 ISNBN 0-946183-65-1

Causeway Press Limited
PO Box 13, Ormskirk, Lancs, L39 5HP
© Alain Anderton
1st impression 1991

Typesetting by John A. Collins (Picatype), Ormskirk, L39 1QR; Reidmark, Ormskirk, L39 2AW
Printed and bound by The Alden Press, Oxford.

Contents

Contents

Preface

Teachers and students of economics are critical groups of people. Constantly dissatisfied with the materials that they use, they face the problems of limited resources, a wide variety of needs and a constantly changing world. This book is intended to go some way to resolving this example of the basic economic problem.

The book has a number of distinctive features.

Comprehensive The book contains sufficient material to satisfy the demands of students taking a wide range of examinations including 'A' level and 'AS' level economics.

Flexible unit structure The material is organised not into chapters but into shorter units. This reflects the organisation of a number of GCSE textbooks, and therefore students should be familiar with this style of presentation. The unit structure also allows the teacher greater freedom to devise a course. Economics teachers have a long tradition of using their main textbooks in a different order to that in which they are presented. So whilst there is a logical order to the book, it has been written on the assumption that teachers and students will piece the units together to suit their own teaching and learning needs. Cross referencing has been used on occasions to further aid flexibility. This approach also means that it is relatively easy to use the book for a growing number of courses which encompass part of a traditional 'A' level syllabus, such as modular 'A' level syllabuses, 'AS' syllabuses and professional courses with an economics input.

Accessibility The book has been written in a clear and logical style which should make it accessible to all readers. Each unit is divided into short, easily manageable sections. Diagrams contain concise explanations which summarise or support the text.

A workbook The text is interspersed with a large number of questions. These are relatively short for the most part, and whilst some could be used for extended writing work, most require relatively simple answers. They have been included to help teachers and students assess whether learning and understanding has taken place by providing immediate application of content and skills to given situations. I hope that many will be used as a basis for class discussion as well as being answered in written form.

Applied economics as well as economic theory Many economics courses require teachers and students to have a book covering economic theory **and** an applied economic text. In this book, a systematic approach to applied economics has been included alongside economic theory. Each unit has an applied economics section and some units deal only with applied economics. It should be noted that many of the questions also contain applied economics material and where sufficiently significant, this has been referred to in the index.

Use of data Modern technology has allowed much of the book to proceed from manuscript to book in a very short period. This has meant that we have been able to use statistics which were available in late 1990. Most statistical series therefore go up to 1989, although some (particularly from CSO, *Annual Abstract of Statistics*, CSO, *Social Trends* and OECD, *Historical Statistics*) were only available to 1988. At the same time, experience has shown that too many current stories quickly date a book. Materials therefore been chosen, particularly for the macro-economic section of the book, from throughout the post-war era, with particular emphasis on the turbulent times of the 1970s and 1980s. This approach will help candidates to answer questions which require knowledge of what has happened 'in recent years' or 'over the past decade'.

Investigations/coursework Coursework is increasingly being used as a method of learning and assessment. It is already a feature of some syllabuses. 9 sets of coursework investigations have been included in the book which should give candidates help with how to choose, research and present a piece of coursework even if they do not make full use of a particular suggestion in the book. If some of the comments in the coursework seem repetitive, they have been included because it has been assumed that students will only complete a few of the 18 core suggestions given.

Key terms Many units contain a key terms section. Each section defines new concepts, which appear in capitals in the text of the unit. Taken together, they provide a comprehensive dictionary of economics.

Great care has been taken with how the book has been presented. It is hoped that the layout of the book, the use of colour and the use of diagrams will make learning economics a more rewarding experience.

I have many thanks to make. Dave Gray has been a superb editor and a pleasure to work with. Rosalind Levačić provided invaluable comments on parts of the book, whilst Peter Chapman reviewed the whole book. Ronald Bramham greatly improved the readability of the text and Mike Kidson carried out the unenviable task of proof reading. All mistakes in the book, however, remain my own responsibility. My wife has performed a variety of tasks, not least putting up with the stresses and strains of the production of such a large volume.

The author and Causeway Press would welcome any comments you have to make about the book, whether critical or otherwise. We hope you enjoy using it and that it helps you achieve success in your chosen field.

Summary

1. Nearly all resources are scarce.
2. Human wants are infinite.
3. Scarce resources and infinite wants give rise to the basic economic problem - resources have to be allocated between competing uses.
4. Allocation involves choice and each choice has an opportunity cost.
5. The production possibility frontier (PPF) shows the maximum potential output of an economy.
6. Production at a point inside the PPF indicates an inefficient use of resources.
7. Growth in the economy will shift the PPF outwards.

Scarcity

It is often said that we live in a global village. The world's resources are finite: there is only a limited amount of land, water, oil, food and other resources on this planet. Economists therefore say that resources are SCARCE.

Scarcity means that economic agents, such as individuals, firms, governments, and international agencies, can only obtain a limited amount of resources at any moment in time. For instance, a family has to live on a fixed budget: it cannot have everything it wants. A firm might want to build a new factory but not have the resources to be able to do so. A government might wish to build new hospitals or devote more resources to its foreign aid programme but not have the finance to make this possible. Resources which are scarce are called ECONOMIC GOODS.

Not all resources are scarce. There is more than enough air on this planet for everyone to be able to breathe as much as they want. Resources which are not scarce are called FREE GOODS. In the past many goods such as food, water and shelter have been free, but as the population of the planet has expanded and as production has increased, so the number of free goods has diminished. Recently, for instance, clean beaches in many parts of the UK have ceased to be a free good to society. Pollution has forced seaside local authorities to spend resources cleaning up their local environment. With the destruction of the world's rain forests and increasing atmospheric pollution, it may be the case that the air we

breathe may no longer remain a free good. Factories may have to purify the air they take from the atmosphere for instance. This air would then become an economic good.

Infinite wants

People have a limited number of NEEDS which must be satisfied if they are to survive as human beings. Some are material needs, such as food, liquid, heat, shelter and clothing. Others are psychological and emotional needs such as self esteem and being loved. People's needs are finite. However, no one would choose to live at the level of basic human needs if they could enjoy a higher standard of living.

This is because human WANTS are unlimited. It doesn't matter whether the person is a peasant in China, a mystic in India, a manager in the UK or the richest individual in the world, there is always something which he or she wants but is unable to have. This can include more food, a bigger house, a longer holiday, a cleaner environment, more love, more friendship, better relationships, more self-esteem, greater fairness or justice, peace, or more time to listen to music or meditate or cultivate the arts.

QUESTION 2 Draw up a list of minimum human needs for a 17 year old living in the UK today. How would this list differ from the needs of a 17 year old living in Bangladesh or sub-Saharan Africa?

The basic economic problem

Resources are scarce but wants are infinite. It is this which gives rise to the BASIC ECONOMIC PROBLEM and which forces economic agents to make choices. They have to allocate their scarce resources between competing uses. Economics is the study of this allocation of resources – the choices that are made by economic agents. Every CHOICE involves a range of alternatives. For instance,

QUESTION 1 Some people have objected to water privatisation in the UK on the grounds that water is 'free' and that what is free should not be sold for a profit.

In what senses is water a 'free good' from an economic viewpoint?

should the government spend £10 billion in tax revenues on nuclear weapons, better schools or greater care for the elderly? Will you choose to become an accountant, an engineer or a vicar?

These choices can be graded in terms of the benefits to be gained from each alternative. One choice will be the 'best' one and a rational economic agent will take that alternative. But all the other choices will then have to be given up. The benefit lost from the next best alternative is called the OPPORTUNITY COST of the choice. For instance, economics may have been your third choice at 'A' level. Your fourth choice, one which you didn't take up, might have been history. Then the opportunity cost of studying economics at 'A' level is studying history at 'A' level. Alternatively, you might have had enough money to buy just one of your two favourite magazines - *Melody Maker* or the *New Musical Express*. If you choose to buy the *Melody Maker*, then its opportunity cost is the benefit which would have been gained from consuming the *New Musical Express*.

Free goods have no opportunity cost. No resources need be sacrificed when someone, say, breathes air or swims in the sea.

QUESTION 3 You are given £30 as a birthday present. If you could buy only one item, what would you spend that money on? What is the opportunity cost of purchasing the item?

Production possibility frontiers

Over a period of time, resources are scarce and therefore only a finite amount can be produced. For example, an economy might have enough resources at its disposal to be able to produce 30 units of manufactured goods and 30 units of non-manufactures. If it were now to produce more manufactured goods, it would have to give up some of its production of non-manufactured items. This is because the production of a manufactured item has an opportunity cost - in this case the production of non-manufactures. The more manufactures that are produced, the less non-manufactures can be produced.

This can be shown in Figure 1.1. The curved line is called the PRODUCTION POSSIBILITY FRONTIER (PPF) - other names for it include PRODUCTION POSSIBILITY CURVE, or BOUNDARY and TRANSFORMATION CURVE. The PPF shows the different combinations of economic goods which an economy is able to produce if all resources in the economy are fully and efficiently employed. The economy therefore could be:
- at the point C on its PPF producing 30 units of manufactured goods and 30 units of non-manufactures;
- at the point D, producing 35 units of manufactured goods and 20 units of non-manufactures;
- at the point A, devoting all of its resources to the production of non-manufactured goods;
- at the points B or E or anywhere else along the line.

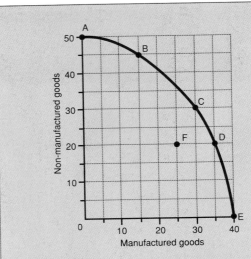

Figure 1.1 *The production possibility frontier ABCDE is a production possibility frontier. It shows the different combinations of goods which can be produced if all resources are fully and efficiently utilised. For instance, the economy can produce no manufactured goods and 50 units of non-manufactures, 30 units of manufactured goods and 30 units of non-manufactures, or 40 units of manufactured goods but no non-manufactures.*

The production possibility frontier illustrates clearly the principle of opportunity cost. Assume that the economy is producing at the point C in Figure 1.1 and it is desired to move to the point D. This means that the output of manufactured goods will increase from 30 to 35 units. However, the opportunity cost of that (i.e. what has to be given up because of that choice) is the lost output of non-manufactures, falling from 30 to 20 units. The opportunity cost at C of increasing manufacturing production by 5 units is 10 units of non-manufactures.

The production possibility frontier for an economy is drawn on the assumption that all resources in the economy are fully and efficiently employed.

If there are unemployed workers or idle factories, or if production is inefficiently organised, then the economy cannot be producing on its PPF. It will produce within the boundary. In Figure 1.1 the economy could produce anywhere along the line AE. But because there is unemployment in the economy, production is at point F.

The economy cannot be at any point outside its existing PPF because the PPF, by definition, shows the maximum production level of the economy. However it might be able to move to the right of its PPF in the future if there is **economic growth**. An increase in the productive potential of an economy is shown by a shift outwards of the PPF. In Figure 1.2 economic growth pushes the PPF from PP to QQ, allowing the economy to increase its maximum level of production say from A to B. Growth in the economy can happen if:
- the quantity of resources available for production increases; for instance there might be an increase in the number of workers in the economy, or new factories and offices might be built;

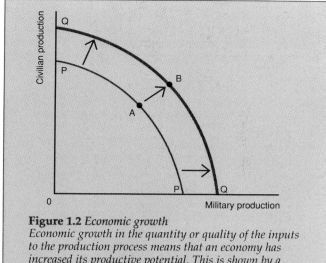

Figure 1.2 *Economic growth*
Economic growth in the quantity or quality of the inputs to the production process means that an economy has increased its productive potential. This is shown by a shift to the right of the production possibility frontier from PP to QQ. It would enable the economy to move production, for instance, from the point A to the point B.

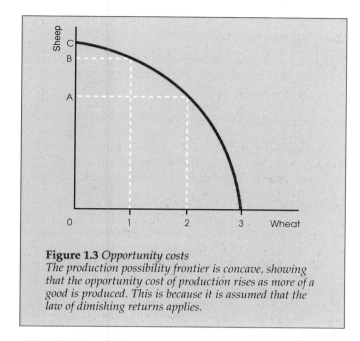

Figure 1.3 *Opportunity costs*
The production possibility frontier is concave, showing that the opportunity cost of production rises as more of a good is produced. This is because it is assumed that the law of dimishing returns applies.

■ there is an increase in the quality of resources; education will make workers more productive whilst technical progress will allow machines and production processes to produce more with the same amount of resources.

The production possibility frontiers in Figures 1.1. to 1.2 have been drawn concave (bowing outwards) rather than as straight lines or as convex lines. This is because it has been assumed that the **law of diminishing returns** affects production. Take for instance the production of wheat in the UK. Comparatively little wheat is grown in Wales because the soil and the climate are less suited to wheat production than in an area like East Anglia. Let us start from a position where no wheat is grown at all in the UK. Some farmers then decide to grow wheat. If production in the economy is to be maximised it should be grown on the land which is most suited to wheat production (i.e. where its opportunity cost is lowest). This will be in an area of the country like East Anglia. As wheat production expands, land has to be used which is less productive because land is a finite resource. More and more marginal land, such as that found in Wales, is used and output per acre falls. The land could have been used for another form of production, for instance sheep rearing. The more wheat is grown, the less output per acre and therefore the greater the cost in terms of sheep production.

In Figure 1.3 only sheep and wheat are produced in the economy. If no wheat is produced the economy could produce OC of sheep. If there is one unit of wheat production only OB of sheep can be produced. Therefore the opportunity cost of the first unit of wheat is BC of sheep. The second unit of wheat has a much higher opportunity cost - AB. But if the economy produces wheat only, then the opportunity cost of the third unit of wheat rises to OA of sheep.

The PPF by itself gives no indication of which combination of goods will be produced in an economy. All it shows is the combination of goods which an economy could produce if output were maximised from a given fixed amount of resources. It shows a range of possibilities and much of economics is concerned with explaining why an economy, ranging from a household economy to the international economy, chooses to produce at one point either on or within its PPF rather than another.

QUESTION 4 Draw a production possibility frontier. The scale on both axes is the same. The economy is currently producing at point A on the frontier which is at the mid point between the vertical axis (showing public sector goods) and the horizontal axis (showing private sector goods). Mark the following points on your drawing.
Point B - a point which shows production following the election of a government which privatises many public sector services but maintains full and efficient employment.
Point C - where unemployment is present in the economy.
Point D - where the state takes over production of all goods and services in the economy.
Now draw two new production possibility frontiers.
PP - which shows the position after a devastating war has hit the economy.
QQ - where there is an increase in productivity in the economy such that output from the same amount of resources increases by 50 per cent in the public sector but twice that amount in the private sector.

Key terms

Scarce resources - resources which are limited in supply so that choices have to be made about their use.
Economic goods - goods which are scarce because their use has an opportunity cost.
Free goods - goods which are unlimited in supply and which therefore have no opportunity cost.
Needs - the minimum which is necessary for a person to survive as a human being.
Wants - desires for the consumption of goods and services.
The economic problem - resources have to be allocated between competing uses because wants are infinite whilst resources are scarce.
Choice - economic choices involve the alternative uses of scarce resources.
Opportunity cost - the benefits foregone of the next best alternative.
Production possibility frontier (also known as the production possibility curve or the production possibility boundary or the transformation curve) - a curve which shows the maximum potential level of output of one good given a level of output for all other goods in the economy.

Applied economics

Military spending

It is difficult to establish exactly how much is spent world-wide on defence, but in its 1988 annual report, the World Bank estimated that 6 per cent of the world's total public spending was used for military purposes. This was more than $900bn in 1985. The cost of the UK Trident project (the sea-launched nuclear missile system) is estimated at £10bn alone. Although the West spends more in terms of hard cash, developing nations spend more as a percentage of GNP (gross national product - a measure of the total income of a country). North Africa and the Middle East allocated 11 to 14 per cent of GNP to defence between 1974 and 1985, East Asia 7 per cent, South East Asia and sub-Saharan Africa less than 4 per cent and Latin America 1.5 per cent.

Military spending has an opportunity cost. Money spent on arms could be spent on civilian projects. For instance, spending on defence in the UK is only a little less than public expenditure on health or education. If there were no defence budget, it would be possible to

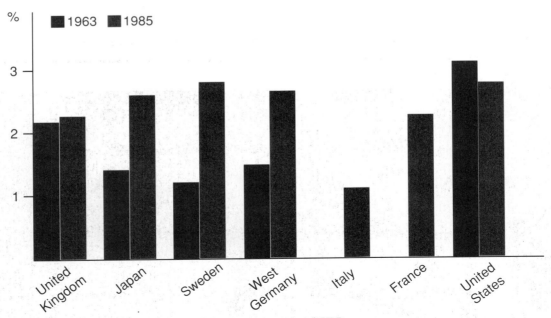

Figure 1.4 *Expenditure on Research and Development as a percentage of GDP*

Table 1.1 *Growth rates, percentages*

	1960-70	1970-1980	1980-1988	1960-88
UK	2.9	2.0	3.0	2.5
Japan	10.3	4.4	3.9	6.5
Sweden	4.4	2.0	2.3	3.0
W. Germany	4.3	2.6	1.8	3.1
Italy	5.5	3.8	2.2	4.0
France	5.5	3.2	1.8	3.7
USA	4.4	2.8	3.4	3.3

Source: adapted from Unctad, *Handbook of International Trade and Development Statistics.*

almost double spending on the National Health Service or education spending.

Military spending can also be seen to have a further opportunity cost. Figure 1.4 shows that 2.3 per cent of GDP (gross domestic product - a measure of total income) was spent in the UK on R & D (research and development) in 1985. This was slightly below the average of the other economies shown. However, the UK spent a significantly higher percentage of the total on defence R & D than any other country apart from the USA. This could well be one factor in explaining why the UK had such a low growth rate of GDP compared to other industrialised economies as shown in Table 1.1. Higher spending on civilian R & D by UK competitors has given them an advantage in developing new products ranging from motorcycles to cameras to photocopiers. Figures 1.4 and 1.5 also show that over the period 1963 to 1985, the share of defence-related R & D grew in the UK at a time when the percentage share of GDP spent on R & D barely changed. In comparison West Germany, with a much higher growth rate than the UK over the period, not only almost doubled its spending on R & D as a percentage of GDP, but also cut the proportion of defence R&D by two-thirds. This could indicate that the opportunity cost of defence R & D may be lower economic growth. Arms today means less consumption tomorrow.

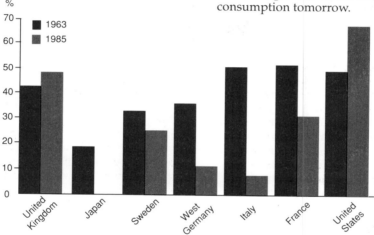

Figure 1.5 *Government defence finance as related percentage of total expenditure on Research and Development*

BETTER GREEN THAN BETTER OFF, SAY MOST AMERICANS

By Alan Friedman in Houston

The American public favours government spending on the environment, even if that results in slower economic growth, according to a survey released yesterday by Cambridge Energy Research Associates (CERA), international energy consultants.

It shows that, if forced to choose between the environment and the economy, 74 per cent of Americans would accept slower growth.

Dr Daniel Yergin, president of CERA, said this showed that 'the environmental consensus will be a major factor in the future American political and business landscape'.

The study also notes that, while 70 per cent of the US public would favour stronger fuel efficiency standards for vehicles to reduce air pollution, 66 per cent oppose a 50 cents-a-gallon tax on petrol.

Source: *Financial Times*, 8.2.1990.

1. **Explain the examples of opportunity cost given in the data.**

2. **Why is the 'environmental problem' an example of the basic economic problem?**

Summary

1. An economy is a social organisation through which decisions about what, how and for whom to produce are made.
2. The factors of production - land, labour, capital and entrepreneurship - are combined together to create goods and services for consumption.
3. Specialisation and the division of labour give rise to large gains in productivity.
4. Markets exist for buyers and sellers to exchange goods and services using barter or money.

What is an economy?

Economic resources are scarce whilst human wants are infinite. An economy is a system which attempts to solve this basic economic problem. There are many different levels and types of economy. There is the household economy, the local economy, the national economy and the international economy. There are free market economies which attempt to solve the economic problem with the minimum intervention of government and command economies where the state makes most resource allocation decisions. Although these economies are different, they all face the same problem.

Economists distinguish three parts to the economic problem.

■ **What** is to be produced? An economy can choose the mix of goods to produce. For instance, what proportion of total output should be spent on defence? What proportion should be spent on protecting the environment? What proportion should be invested for the future? What proportion should be manufactured goods and what proportion services?

■ **How** is production to be organised? For instance, are hi-fi systems to be made in the UK, Japan or Taiwan? Should car bodies be made out of steel or fibreglass? Would it better to automate a production line or carry on using unskilled workers?

■ **For whom** is production to take place? What proportion of output should go to workers? How much should pensioners get? What should be the balance between incomes in the UK and those in Bangladesh?

An economic system needs to provide answers to all these questions.

QUESTION 1 Consider your household economy.
(a) What is produced by your household (e.g. cooking services, cleaning services, accommodation, products outside the home)?
(b) How is production organised (e.g. who does the cooking, what equipment is used, when is the cooking done)?
(c) For whom does production take place (e.g. for mother, for father)?
(d) Do you think your household economy should be organised in a different way? Justify your answer.

Economic resources

Economists commonly distinguish three types of resources available for use in the production process. They call these resources the FACTORS OF PRODUCTION.

LAND is not only land itself but all natural resources below the earth, on the earth, in the atmosphere and in the sea. Everything from gold deposits to rainwater and natural forests are examples of land.

NON-RENEWABLE RESOURCES, such as coal, oil, gold and copper, are land resources which once used will never be replaced. If we use them today, they are not available for use by our children or our children's children. RENEWABLE RESOURCES on the other hand can be used and replaced. Examples are fish stocks, forests, or water. Renewable resources can sometimes be over-exploited by man leading to their destruction.

LABOUR is the workforce of an economy - everybody from housepersons to doctors, vicars and cabinet ministers. Not all workers are the same. Each worker has a unique set of inherent characteristics including intelligence, manual dexterity and emotional stability. But workers are also the products of education and training. The value of a worker is called his or her HUMAN CAPITAL. Education and training will increase the value of that human capital, enabling the worker to be more productive.

CAPITAL is the man-made stock of tools, machines, factories, offices, roads and other resources which are used in the production of goods and services. Capital is of two types. WORKING or CIRCULATING CAPITAL is stocks of raw materials, semi-manufactured and finished goods which are waiting to be sold. These stocks circulate through the production process till they are finally sold to a consumer. FIXED CAPITAL is the stock of factories, offices, plant and machinery. Fixed capital is fixed in the sense that it will not be transformed into a final product as working capital will. It is used to transform working capital into finished products.

Sometimes a fourth factor of production is distinguished. This is ENTREPRENEURSHIP. Entrepreneurs are individuals who:
■ organise production - organise land, labour and capital in the production of goods and services;
■ take risks - with their own money and the financial capital of others, they buy factors of production to produce goods and services in the hope that they will be able to make a profit but in the knowledge that at worst they could lose all their money and go bankrupt.
It is this element of risk taking which distinguishes

entrepreneurs from ordinary workers. There is much controversy today about the role and importance of entrepreneurs in a modern developed economy (☞ unit 55).

Specialisation

When he was alone on his desert island, Robinson Crusoe found that he had to perform all economic tasks by himself. When Man Friday came along he quickly abandoned this mode of production and specialised. SPECIALISATION is the production of a limited range of goods by an individual or firm or country in co-operation with others so that together a complete range of goods is produced.

Specialisation can occur between nations (☞ unit 84). For instance, a country like Honduras produces bananas and trades those for cars produced in the United States. Specialisation also occurs within economies. Regional economies specialise. In the UK, Stoke-on-Trent specialises in pottery whilst London specialises in services.

Specialisation by individuals is called THE DIVISION OF LABOUR. Adam Smith, in a passage in his famous book *An Enquiry into the Nature and Causes of the Wealth of Nations* (1776), described the division of labour amongst pin workers. He wrote:

> *A workman not educated to this business ... could scarce ... make one pin in a day, and certainly could not make twenty. But in the way in which this business is now carried on, ... it is divided into a number of branches ... One man draws out the wire, another straightens it, a third cuts it, a fourth points, a fifth grinds it at the top for receiving the head; to make the head requires two or three distinct operations; to put it on is a peculiar business, to whiten the pins is another; it is even a trade by itself to put them into the paper.*

He pointed out that one worker might be able to make 20 pins a day if he were to complete all the processes himself. But ten workers together specialising in a variety of tasks could, he estimated, make 48 000 pins.

This enormous increase in productivity arises from a variety of sources.
■ Specialisation enables workers to gain skills in a narrow range of tasks. These skills enable individual workers to be far more productive than if they were jacks-of-all-trades. In a modern economy a person could not possibly hope to be able to take on every job which society requires.
■ The division of labour makes it cost-effective to provide workers with specialist tools. For instance, it would not be profitable to provide every farm worker with a tractor. But it is possible to provide a group of workers with a tractor which they can then share.
■ Time is saved because a worker is not constantly changing tasks, moving around from place to place and using different machinery and tools.

QUESTION 2

Table 2.1 *Composition of UK national wealth*

	Per cent	
	1957	1987
Residential buildings	26.1	41.7
Agricultural land and buildings and forestry	2.2	1.8
Other building and civil engineering works	23.7	26.7
Plant and machinery	18.6	13.4
Vehicles including ships and aircraft	2.5	1.5
Stocks and work in progress	11.8	4.7
All tangible assets	85.0	89.7
Intangible non-financial assets	14.8	6.5
Net claims overseas	0.1	3.9
National wealth[1]	100.0	100.0

1. Totals may not add up to the sum of components due to rounding.

Source: adapted from CSO, *Economic Trends* May 1987; National Income Blue Book.

(a) Give examples of fixed and working capital from the data.
(b) Give two examples of goods or services produced by each of the 6 categories of capital distinguished in the data.
(c) Describe how the composition of wealth has changed over time and suggest some reasons as to why this might have occurred.

■ Workers can specialise in those tasks to which they are best suited.

The division of labour has its limits. If jobs are divided up too much, the work can become tedious and monotonous. Workers feel alienated from their work. This will result in poorer workmanship and less output per person. Workers will do everything possible to avoid work - going to the toilet, lingering over breaks and reporting sick for instance. The size of the market too will limit the division of labour. A shop owner in a village might want to specialise in selling health foods but finds that in order to survive she has to sell other products as well.

Over-specialisation also has its disadvantages. In the colonial period, Britain and France allocated crops between different colonies. Ghana, for example, was forced to grow cocoa whilst Kenya grew tea and coffee. Today these countries are over-dependent on one cash crop. Low international prices or a poor harvest will lower incomes, create unemployment and play havoc with long term planning. Similarly in the UK, the North, Wales, Scotland and Northern Ireland have paid a heavy price in terms of income and unemployment for their over-dependence on heavy manufacturing industry. Shipyard, steel and textile workers have all found that the division of labour can exact a heavy price if their skills are no longer wanted. Another problem with specialisation is that a breakdown in part of the chain of production can cause chaos within the system. Small falls in the supply of oil on world markets in the mid-1970s resulted in a major shock to the world economy. Equally, anyone dependent upon rail transport knows that a rail strike can cause chaos.

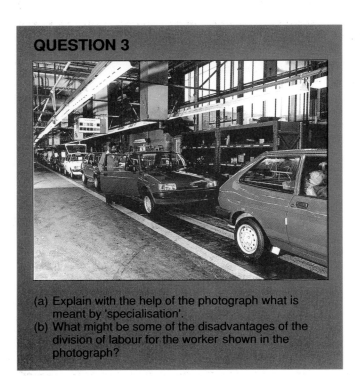

QUESTION 3

(a) Explain with the help of the photograph what is meant by 'specialisation'.
(b) What might be some of the disadvantages of the division of labour for the worker shown in the photograph?

Money and exchange

Specialisation has enabled people to enjoy a standard of living which would be impossible to achieve through self-sufficiency. Specialisation, however, necessitates exchange. Workers can only specialise in refuse collecting, for instance, if they know that they will be able to exchange their services for other goods and services such as food, housing and transport.

Exchange for most of history has meant **barter** - swopping one good for another (☞ unit 65). But barter has many disadvantages and it would be impossible to run a modern sophisticated economy using barter as a means of exchange. It was the development of **money** that enabled trade and specialisation to transform economies into what we know today. Money is anything which is widely accepted as payment for goods received, services performed, or repayment of past debt. In a modern economy, it ranges from notes and coins to money in bank accounts and deposits in building society accounts.

Markets

There must be a buyer and a seller for exchange to take place. Buyers and sellers meet in the market place. For economists, markets are not just street markets. Buying and selling can take place in newspapers and magazines, through mail order or over the telephone in financial deals in the City of London, or on industrial estates as well as in high street shopping centres. A MARKET is any convenient set of arrangements by which buyers and sellers communicate to exchange goods and services.

Economists group buyers and sellers together. For instance, there is an international market for oil where large companies and governments buy and sell oil. There are also national markets for oil. Not every company or government involved in the buying and selling of oil in the UK, say, will be involved in the US or the Malaysian oil markets. There are also regional and local markets for oil. In your area there will be a small number of petrol filling stations (sellers of petrol) where you (the buyers) are able to buy petrol. All these markets are inter-linked but they are also separate. A worldwide increase in the price of oil may or may not filter down to an increase in the price of petrol at the pumps in your local area. Equally, petrol prices in your area may increase when prices at a national and international level remain constant.

How buyers and sellers are grouped together and therefore how markets are defined depends upon what is being studied. We could study the tyre industry or we could consider the market for cars and car components which includes part but not all of the tyre industry. Alternatively we might want to analyse the market for rubber, which would necessitate a study of rubber purchased by tyre producers.

Many Western economists argue that specialisation, exchange and the market lie at the heart of today's economic prosperity in the industrial world. Whilst it is likely that the market system is a powerful engine of prosperity (☞ unit 107), we shall see that it does not always lead to the most efficient allocation of resources (☞ units 35-45).

QUESTION 4

(a) Who are the major buyers and sellers in the UK market for shoes?
(b) What is the relationships between this market and the market for
   (i) sports equipment and
   (ii) leather goods?

Key terms

The factors of production - the inputs to the production process: land, which is all natural resources; labour, which is the workforce; capital, which is the stock of man-made resources used in the production of goods and services; entrepreneurs, individuals who seek out profitable opportunities for production and take risks in attempting to exploit these.

Non-renewable resources - resources, such as coal or oil, which once exploited cannot be replaced.

Renewable resources - resources, such as fish stocks or forests, which can be exploited over and over again because they have the potential to renew themselves.

Working or circulating capital - resources which are in the production system waiting to be transformed into goods or other materials before being finally sold to the consumer.

Fixed capital - economic resources such as factories and hospitals which are used to transform working capital into goods and services.

Specialisation - a system of organisation where economic units such as households or nations are not self-sufficient but concentrate on producing certain goods and services and trading the surplus with others.

The division of labour - specialisation by workers.

Market - any convenient set of arrangements by which buyers and sellers communicate to exchange goods and services.

Applied economics

Howe Bridge Mill

In 1988, Coats Viyella, the international textile group, announced the completion of a £6 million investment programme at its Howe Bridge Mill. The mill spins polyester-cotton yarn for pillow cases and duvet covers sold under the Dorma brand name.

Modern machinery has been installed at every stage of the production process. The bulk of the investment is in open-end spinning machines. These not only combine three functions of the old process - roving, spinning and winding - but are four-and-a-half times more productive than the ring spinning system they have replaced. Almost the only manual work in the production process is moving cans of yarn from machine to machine. As a result, production has increased from 88 000 kg a week to 108 000 kg a week. Employment has fallen from 437 to 274 workers.

Howe Bridge Mill is just one of the many mills and factories owned by Coats Viyella. It specialises in manufacturing polyester-cotton yarn, which is then passed on to a weaving mill for the yarn to be made into pillow cases and duvet covers. The Dorma pillow cases and duvet covers are sold on the market to customers throughout the world. Coats Viyella uses the money it receives from those sales to pay its workers, buy raw materials, and fund investment programmes.

Coats Viyella needed to make the investment because of competition from the Far East. Competition forced the company to re-examine how it was making polyester-cotton yarn. By substituting one factor of production for another, (machines for workers), they have been able to reduce their costs. Unless it can keep its prices down, however, it will find itself with fewer customers and ultimately could close down in the same way that so many Lancashire textile firms have done in the past. Only by using the most modern production techniques can Coats Viyella survive in the international market place.

VOLVO

In 1974, Volvo opened its revolutionary Kalmar production plant. Henry Ford's assembly line method of production had dominated mass car production since 1914. Workers stayed in one place, doing one task on cars which were brought to them on the assembly line. Volvo introduced assembly line production only in 1953 and by the 1960s was finding that it caused high absenteeism and labour turnover without necessarily improving productivity.

At Kalmar, the company went back to traditional ways of building motor cars. Workers were organised into small teams that would organise themselves to build a complete car. Components were brought to the workers whilst the car stayed in one place as it was being built.

In 1989, Volvo opened a new car plant at Uddevalla based upon the lessons learnt at Kalmar. There is a relatively low level of mechanisation and in the assembly area there are no robots. To compensate, workers are trained to perform a wide variety of tasks. Teams of 8 to 10 highly skilled workers build a complete car. There are no supervisors or foremen. Absenteeism rates at Uddevalla and Kalmar average 8 per cent, compared to up to 25 per cent at Volvo's more traditional Gothenburg plant.

Volvo believes that Uddevalla is a model for the future of a car industry where consumers will increasingly demand high craftmanship whilst workers will refuse to perform jobs that are menial and inhumane.

1. **Outline the advantages and disadvantages of Henry Ford's assembly line method of production.**

2. **Explain why Volvo has chosen to organise its car production in a different way.**

3 Economic data

Summary

1. Economic data are collected not only to verify or refute economic models but to provide a basis for economic decision making.
2. Data may be expressed at nominal (or current) prices or at real (or constant) prices. Data expressed in real terms take into account the effects of inflation.
3. Indices are used to simplify statistics and to express averages.
4. Data can be presented in a variety of forms such as tables or graphs.
5. All data should be interpreted with care given that data can be selected and presented in a wide variety of ways.

The collection and reliability of data

Economists collect data for two main reasons.

■ The scientific method requires that theories be tested. Data may be used to refute or support a theory. For instance, an economist might gather data to support or refute the hypothesis that 'Cuts in the marginal rate of income will increase the incentive to work', or that 'An increase in the real value of unemployment benefit will lead to an increase in the number of people unemployed'.

■ Economists are often required to provide support for particular policies. Without economic data it is often difficult, if not impossible, to make policy recommendations. For instance, twice a year (in the Autumn when he presents public expenditure plans and in the Spring when in the Budget he presents his tax plans), the Chancellor of the Exchequer has to make a statement to the House of Commons outlining the state of the economy and the economic outlook for the next 12 months. Without a clear knowledge of where the economy is at the moment it is impossible to forecast how it might change in the future and to recommend policy changes to steer the economy in a more desirable direction.

Collecting economic data is usually very difficult and sometimes impossible. Some macro-economic data - such as the balance of payments figures or the value of national income - are collected from a wide variety of sources. The figures for the balance of payments on current account are compiled from returns made by every exporter and importer on every item exported and imported. Not surprisingly the information is not totally accurate. Some exporters and importers will conceal transactions to avoid tax. Others will not want to be bothered with the paper work.

Other macro-economic data such as the Index of Retail Prices (used to measure inflation) are based on surveys. Surveys are only reliable if there is accurate sampling and measuring and are rarely as accurate as a complete count.

Some macro-economic data are very accurate statistically but do not necessarily provide a good measure of the relevant economic variable. In the UK the unemployment level is calculated each month at benefit offices throughout the country. It is extremely accurate but no economist would argue that the figure produced is an accurate measure of unemployment. There is general agreement that some people who claim benefit for being unemployed are not unemployed and conversely there are many unemployed people who are not claiming benefit.

In micro-economics use is again made of survey data, with the limitations that this implies. Economists also make use of more experimental data, gathering evidence for case studies. For instance, an economist might want to look at the impact of different pricing policies on entry to sports centres. He or she might study a small number of sports centres in a local area. The evidence gathered would be unlikely to decisively refute or support a general hypothesis such as 'Cheap entry increases sports centre use'. But it would be possible to conclude that the evidence **tended** to support or refute the hypothesis.

In economics it is difficult to gather accurate data and for that reason academic economists mostly qualify their conclusions.

QUESTION 1

Table 3.1 *Selected balance of payments statistics for second quarter 1980*

Date of estimate	Visible balance	Invisible balance	Current balance
		£ millions	
October 1980	-378	+85	-293
October 1981	-321	+159	-162
October 1982	-317	+67	-250
October 1983	-273	+109	-164
October 1985	-308	+51	-257
October 1987	-308	-2	-310
October 1989	-179	+55	-125

Source: adapted from CSO, *Economic Trends*.

(a) Comment on how the published estimate of the three current balances for the 2nd quarter of 1980 has changed over the period 1980 to 1989.
(b) Suggest reasons why there might have been these changes.

Real and nominal values

There are many different **measures** in use today such as tonnes, litres, kilograms and kilometres. Often, we want to be able to compare these different measures. For instance, an industrialist might wish to compare oil measured in litres, and coal measured in kilograms. One way of doing this is to convert oil and coal into therms using gross calorific values. In economics, by far the most important measure used is the value of an item measured in **monetary terms**, such as pounds sterling, US dollars or French francs. One problem in using money as a measure is that inflation (the general change in prices in an economy) erodes the purchasing power of money.

For instance, in 1948 the value of output of the UK economy (measured by gross domestic product at factor cost) was £10 398 million. Forty years later in 1988 it was £384 781 million. It would seem that output had increased 37 times - an enormous increase. In fact, output increased by only a fraction of that amount. This is because most of the measured increase was an increase not in output but in prices. Prices over the period rose about 13½ times. Stripping the inflation element out of the increase leaves us with an increase in output of just over 2½ times.

Values unadjusted for inflation are called NOMINAL VALUES. These values are expressed AT CURRENT PRICES (i.e. at the level of prices existing during the time period being measured).

If data are adjusted for inflation, then they are said to be at REAL VALUES or at CONSTANT PRICES. To do this in practice involves taking one period of time as the BASE PERIOD. Data are then adjusted assuming that prices were the same throughout as in the base period.

For instance, a basket of goods costs £100 in year 1 and £200 in year 10. Prices have therefore doubled. If you had £1 000 to spend in year 10, then that would have been equivalent to £500 at year 1 prices because both amounts would have bought 5 baskets of goods. On the other hand, if you had £1 000 to spend in year 1, that would be equivalent to £2 000 in year 10 prices because both would have bought you 10 baskets of goods.

Taking another example, the real value of output in UK 1948 at 1948 prices was the same as its nominal value (i.e. £10 398 million). The real value of output in 1989 at 1948 prices was £29 616 million. It is much lower than the nominal 1989 value because prices were much higher in 1989.

On the other hand, at 1989 prices, the real value of output in 1948 was £152 628 million, much higher than the nominal value because prices in 1989 were much higher than in 1948. Further examples are given in Table 3.2.

Prices can be adjusted to any base year. UK government statistics expressed in real terms are adjusted every 5 years. In 1990, figures are expressed at 1985 prices. In the early 1990s figures will be readjusted at 1990 prices.

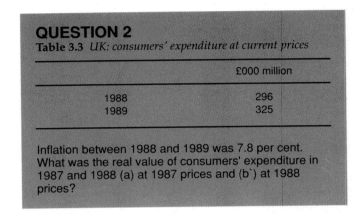

QUESTION 2

Table 3.3 *UK: consumers' expenditure at current prices*

	£000 million
1988	296
1989	325

Inflation between 1988 and 1989 was 7.8 per cent. What was the real value of consumers' expenditure in 1987 and 1988 (a) at 1987 prices and (b`) at 1988 prices?

Indices

It is often more important in economics to compare values than to know absolute values. For instance, we might want to compare the real value of output in the economy in 1985 and 1988. Knowing that the real value of output (GDP at factor cost at 1985 prices) in 1985 was £304 933 million and in 1988 was £340 264 million is helpful but the very large numbers make it difficult to see at a glance what, for instance, was the approximate percentage increase. Equally, many series of statistics are averages. The Retail Price Index (the measure of the cost of living) is calculated by working out what it would cost to buy a typical cross-section or 'basket' of goods. Comparing say £458.92 in one month with £475.13 the next is not easy.

So, many series are converted into INDEX NUMBER form. One time period is chosen as the base period and the rest of the statistics in the series are compared to the value in that base period. The value in the base period is usually 100. The figure 100 is chosen because it is easy to work with mathematically. Taking the example of output again, if 1948 were taken as the base year, then the value

Table 3.2 *Nominal and real values*

Nominal value	Inflation between year 1 and 2	Real values	
		Value at year 1 prices	Value at year 2 prices
Example 1 £100 in year 1	10%	£100	£110
Example 2 £500 in year 1	50%	£500	£750
Example 3 £200 in year 2	20%	£166.66	£200
Example 4 £400 in year 2	5%	£380.95	£400

Note: £100 at year 1 prices is worth £100 x 1.1 (i.e. 1+10%) in year 2 prices. £200 at year 2 prices is worth £200 ÷ 1.2 in year 1 prices.

Table 3.4 *Converting a series into index number form*

		Consumption		
Year	£ millions	Index number if base year is:		
		year 1	year 2	year 3
1	500	100.0	83.3	62.5
2	600	120.0	100.0	75.0
3	800	160.0	133.3	100.0

Note: The index number for consumption in year 2 if year 1 is the base year is (600 ÷ 500) x 100.

of real output in 1948 would be 100, and in 1989 would be 284.8. Alternatively if 1989 were taken as the base year, the value of output would be 100 in 1989 and 35.1 in 1948. Or with 1985 as the base year, the value of output in 1948 would be 40.6 whilst in 1989 it would be 115.6. Further examples are given in Table 3.4.

The construction of one weighted index, the Retail Price Index, is explained in greater detail in unit 92.

QUESTION 3

Table 3.5 *UK Investment 1984-89*

	£ millions (at 1985 prices)
1984	58 058
1985	60 343
1986	61 593
1987	66 923
1988	76 099
1989	79 418

Source: adapted from CSO, *Monthly Digest of Statistics*.

Using a calculator, convert these figures into index number form using as the base year: (a) 1984; (b) 1986; (c) 1988.

The interpretation of data

Data can be presented in many forms and be used both to inform and mislead the reader. To illustrate these points, let us consider the unemployment figures in recent years in the UK economy. One way in which these figures can be presented is in **tabular form** as in Table 3.6. It shows that unemployment rose from 1979 to 1986, after which it started to fall back again.

The data could also be presented in the form of a graph as in Figure 3.1(a). Graphs must be interpreted with

Table 3.6 *UK unemployment.*

	%
1979	4.0
1980	5.1
1981	8.1
1982	9.5
1983	10.5
1984	10.7
1985	10.9
1986	11.2
1987	10.3
1988	8.3
1989	6.4

Source: adapted from CSO, *Annual Abstract of Statistics*; CSO, *Monthly Digest of Statistics*.

some care. Figure 3.1(b) gives a very optimistic picture of unemployment. By excluding the period 1979 to 1985, the reader is left with the impression that unemployment has been falling for some years. By not starting the axis at zero but making the scale discontinuous between zero and 6.0 per cent, the fall in unemployment can be effectively exaggerated. On the other hand, Figure 3.1(c) would deceive the casual observer into thinking that the fall in unemployment since 1986 has been relatively slight. It uses a log scale of the number of unemployed in millions. This compresses values as they increase. Without careful reading of the scale, it would look as if the fall in unemployment between 1986 and 1987 were far less than the rise in unemployment between 1979 and 1980 - which is incorrect.

Data can be also be expressed in verbal form. To present a complete series in words would be tedious and difficult to take in. However, in verbal form we can note that unemployment was nearly twice as high in 1988 as in 1979, that unemployment rose 170 per cent between 1979 and 1986 and that the unemployment fell at a faster rate in 1988 than in 1987.

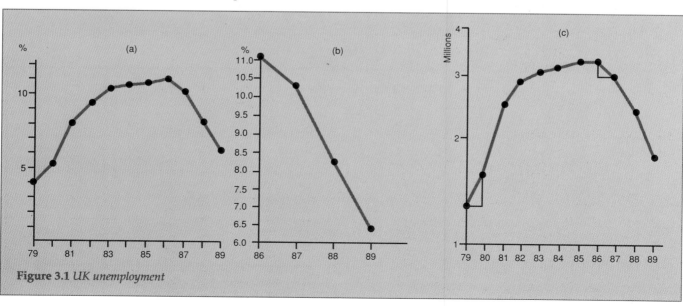

Figure 3.1 *UK unemployment*

QUESTION 4

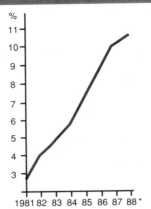

Figure 3.2 *Profitability of UK Companies %*

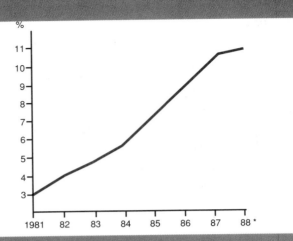

Figure 3.3 *Profitability of UK Companies %*

*Estimate

Note: Rate of return on capital employed by UK industrial and commercial companies excluding North Sea Companies.

Source: adapted from *Economic Progress Report*, The Treasury, June 1989.

Consider each graph in turn. What does each show? Explain why each seems to give a different picture of UK company profitability.

Key terms

Nominal values - values unadjusted for the effects of inflation (i.e. values **at current prices**).

Real values - values adjusted for inflation (i.e. values **at constant prices**).

Base period - the period, such as a year or a month, from which all other values in a series are compared. In an index number series, the base period is given the value of 100.

Index number - an indicator of change in a series of statistics, often used to average a number of statistics, where one figure in a series (the base) is given the value of 100 and all other figures are adjusted in proportion to that value.

Applied economics

Better or worse off?

Are Britain's pensioners becoming better or worse off? Pensioners receive income from a variety of sources including private occupation pensions and income from savings. However, half of all OAPs in 1986 had only one source of income, the state retirement pension. Has their lot improved between 1971 and 1989?

Table 3.7 shows how the state old age pension for a single person has increased over time. A cursory glance at the table would seem to indicate that single pensioners were £37.60 a week better off in 1989 than in 1971. Using the index numbers for easy calculation,

Table 3.7 *State retirement pension for a single person under 80*

	£ per week at current prices	September 1971=100
September 1971	6.00	100
November 1976	15.30	255
November 1981	29.60	493
November 1983	34.05	568
November 1985	38.30	638
November 1987	39.50	658
November 1989	43.60	727

Source: adapted from CSO, *Annual Abstract of Statistics*.

Table 3.8 *State retirement pension for a single person under 80 at constant prices.*

	£ per week at 1987 prices	1987=100
September 1971	29.72	75
November 1976	37.06	94
November 1981	38.73	98
November 1983	40.40	102
November 1985	40.65	103
November 1987	39.50	100
November 1989	38.57	98

Source: adapted from CSO, *Annual Abstract of Statistics*.

pensioners were 627 per cent better off in 1989 than in 1971.

However, these figures are expressed at **current prices**. No allowance has been made for the fact that prices too increased over the period. Table 3.8 shows how pensioners' **real incomes** have changed over the period (i.e. how their pensions adjusted for inflation have changed).

This gives a very different story. The real value of pensions rose markedly between 1971 and 1976 but since then have seen little real growth. Since 1980 in fact, the government has only increased pensions in line with inflation. Because of the way this increase is calculated (this year's increase in pension being based upon last year's inflation rate), it can mean that pensioners are either slightly better off or slightly worse off from one year to the next.

Indexing the value of retirement pensions might seem a reasonable arrangement. However, we know that the nation's income has increased, on average, about 2½% per year over the past 25 years. Indexing state retirement pensions to the rate of inflation means that those pensioners whose sole income is the state pension will receive no share of Britain's ever increasing prosperity.

This can be seen by comparing the value of the retirement pension to average earnings in Figure 3.4. Since the mid-1970s, pensioners whose only income has been the state pension have been getting progressively worse off compared to the average male worker in the UK. Only linking retirement pensions to average earnings can prevent the steady erosion of the relative standard of living of pensioners. If a significant proportion of pensioners are poor today, they will be relatively much poorer in 10 years' time.

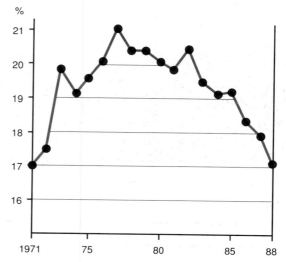

Source: adapted from CSO, *Annual Abstract of Statistics*.

Figure 3.4 *Single person state retirement pension as a percentage of average male earnings*

Figure 3.5 *Pattern of expenditure: changes over time. All households, 1957-1988*

Source: adapted from CSO, *Family Expenditure Survey*.

1. **Outline the main changes in the pattern of household expenditure over the period 1957 to 1988.**
2. **Explain whether or not it is possible to conclude from the data that:**
   (i) **total household expenditure has increased;**
   (ii) **spending on food has fallen in real terms;**
   (iii) **spending on housing has increased at a faster rate than spending on motoring and fares.**

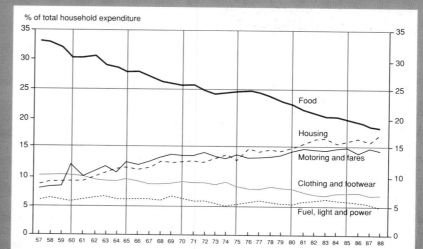

Summary

1. Demand for a good is the quantity of goods or services that will be bought over a period of time at any given price.
2. Demand for a good will rise or fall if there are changes in factors such as incomes, the price of other goods, tastes, and the size of the population.
3. A change in price is shown by a movement along the demand curve.
4. A change in any other variable affecting demand, such as income, is shown by a shift in the demand curve.
5. The market demand curve can be derived by horizontally summing all the individual demand curves in the market.

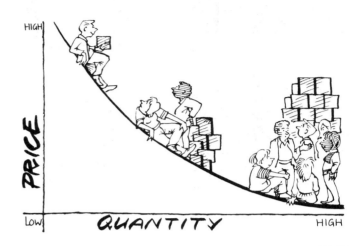

Demand

A market exists wherever there are buyers and sellers of a particular good (☞ unit 2). Buyers **demand** goods from the market whilst sellers **supply** goods on to the market.

DEMAND has a particular meaning in economics. Demand is the quantity of goods or services that will be bought at any given price over a period of time. For instance, approximately 2 million new cars are bought each year in the UK today at an average price of, say, £7 000. Economists would say that the annual demand for cars at £7 000 would be 2 million units.

Demand and price

If everything else were to remain the same (this is known as the **ceteris paribus** condition ☞ unit 111), what would happen to the quantity demanded of a product as its price changed? If the average price of a car were to fall from £7 000 to £3 500, then it is not difficult to guess that the quantity demanded of cars would rise. On the other hand, if the average price were £35 000 very few cars would be sold.

This is shown in Table 4.1. As the price of cars rises, then ceteris paribus, the quantity of cars demanded will fall. Another way of expressing this is shown in Figure 4.1. Price is on the vertical axis and quantity demanded over time is on the horizontal axis. The curve is

Table 4.1 *The demand schedule for cars*

Price (£)	Demand (million per year)
3 500	4.0
7 000	2.0
14 000	1.0
35 000	0.4

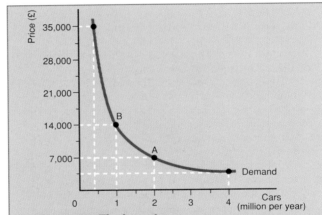

Figure 4.1 *The demand curve*
The demand curve is downward sloping, showing that the lower the price, the higher will be the quantity demanded of a good. In this example, only 0.4 million cars per year are demanded at a price of £35 000 each, but a reduction in price to £3 500 increases quantity demanded to 4 million units per year.

downward sloping showing that as price falls, quantity demanded rises. This DEMAND CURVE shows the quantity that is demanded at any given price. When price changes there is said to be a **movement along** the curve. For instance, there is a movement along the curve from the point A to the point B, a fall of 1 million cars a year, when the price of cars rises from £7 000 to £14 000.

It is important to remember that the demand curve shows EFFECTIVE DEMAND. It shows how much would be bought (i.e. how much consumers can afford to buy and would buy) at any given price and not how much buyers would like to buy if they had unlimited resources.

Economists have found that the inverse relationship between price and quantity demanded - that as price rises, the quantity demanded falls - is true of nearly all goods. In unit 10 we shall consider the few examples of goods which might have upward sloping demand curves.

QUESTION 1 National water metering trials are taking place between 1989 and 1992 in 11 areas of the UK. The trials are designed in part to provide evidence on different patterns of water consumption before every home in the UK is installed with a water meter from 1992 onwards.

Using demand curve diagrams, explain what economic theory would predict would happen to water consumption under the following tariff structures:

(a) water prices were higher in the morning and afternoon than at other times of the day;
(b) water prices were higher in summer than in winter;
(c) the price per unit falls as consumption of water increases.

Demand and income

Price is not the only factor which determines the level of demand for a good. Another important factor is income. Demand for a normal good rises when income rises. For instance, a rise in income leads consumers to buy more cars. A few goods, known as inferior goods, fall in demand when incomes rise (☞ unit 10).

The effect of a rise in income on demand is shown in Figure 4.2. Buyers are purchasing OA of clothes at a price of OE. Incomes rise and buyers react by purchasing more clothes at the same price. At the higher level of income they buy, say, OB of clothes. A new demand curve now exists passing through the point S. It will be to the right of the original demand curve because at any given price more will be demanded at the new higher level of income.

Economists say that a rise in income will lead to an **increase in demand** for a normal good such as clothes. An increase in demand is shown by a SHIFT IN THE DEMAND CURVE. (Note that an **increase in quantity demanded**, would refer to a change in quantity demanded resulting from a change in price and would be shown by a movement along the curve.) In Figure 4.2, the original demand curve D_1 **shifts** to the right to its new position D_2. Similarly, a fall in income will lead to a **fall in demand** for a normal good. This is shown by a **shift** to the left of the demand curve from D_1 to D_3. For instance, at a price of OE, demand will fall from OA to OC.

Two points need to be made. Firstly the demand curves in Figure 4.2 have been drawn as straight lines. These demand curves drawn show a hypothetical (or imaginary) position. They are drawn straight purely for convenience and do not imply that actual demand curves for real products are straight. Secondly, the shifts in the demand curves are drawn as parallel shifts. Again this is done for convenience and neatness but it is most unlikely that a rise or fall in income for an actual product would produce a parallel shift in its demand curve.

QUESTION 2
Table 4.2

Quantity demanded (million units)	Price (£)
10	20
20	16
30	12
40	8
50	4

(a) Draw a demand curve from the above data.
(b) An increase in income results in the quantity demanded changing by 5 million units at every price level. Add this new demand curve to your diagram.
(c) Draw a demand curve which would show the effect of a fall in incomes on the original demand for the good.

The price of other goods

Another important factor which influences the demand for a good is the price of other goods. For instance, in the great drought of 1976 in the UK, the price of potatoes soared. Consumers reacted by buying fewer potatoes and replacing them in their diet by eating more bread, pasta and rice.

This can be shown on a demand diagram. The demand curve for pasta in Figure 4.3 is D_1. A rise in the price of potatoes leads to a rise in the demand for pasta. This means that at any given price a greater quantity of pasta will be demanded. The new demand curve D_2 will therefore be to the right of the original demand curve.

Not all changes in prices will affect the demand for a particular good. A rise in the price of tennis balls is unlikely to have much impact on the demand for carrots for instance. Changes in the price of other goods as well

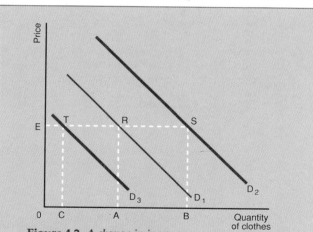

Figure 4.2 *A change in income*
An increase in income will raise demand for a normal good. At a price of OE, for instance, demand will rise from OA to OB. Similarly, at all other prices, an increase in income will result in a level of demand to the right of the existing demand curve. So the demand curve will shift from D_1 to D_2. A fall in income will result in less being demanded at any given price. Hence the demand curve will shift to the left, from D_1 to D_3.

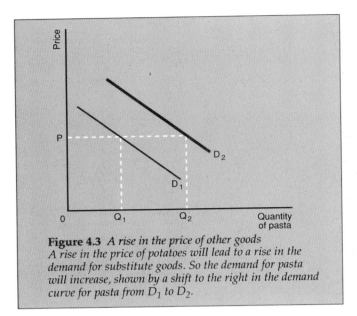

Figure 4.3 *A rise in the price of other goods*
A rise in the price of potatoes will lead to a rise in the demand for substitute goods. So the demand for pasta will increase, shown by a shift to the right in the demand curve for pasta from D_1 to D_2.

QUESTION 3 Between 1973 and 1975, the price of oil quadrupled. Explain, using demand diagrams, what effect you would expect this to have had on the demand for:

(a) oil tankers;
(b) coal;
(c) ice cream;
(d) gas-fired central heating systems.

may have either a positive or negative impact on demand for a good. A rise in the price of tennis rackets is likely to reduce the demand for tennis balls as some buyers decide that tennis is too expensive a sport. On the other hand, the demand for cinema places, alcoholic drink or whatever other form of entertainment consumers choose to buy instead of tennis equipment, will increase. The effect on the demand for one good of changes in price of other goods is considered in more detail in unit 7.

Other factors

There is a wide variety of other factors which affect the demand for a good apart from price, income and the prices of other goods. These include:
- changes in population - an increase in population is likely to increase demand for goods;
- changes in fashion - the demand for items such as wigs or flared trousers or black kitchen units changes as these items go in or out of fashion;
- changes in legislation - the demand for seat belts, anti-pollution equipment or places in old-people's homes have all been affected in the past by changes in government legislation;
- advertising - a very powerful influence on consumer demand which seeks to influence consumer choice.

QUESTION 4

Explain, with the help of a demand diagram, the likely effect on demand for the product in the advert resulting from the marketing campaign of which this advertisement was a part.

A summary

It is possible to express demand in the form of a **functional** relationship. The quantity demanded of good N (Q_n) varies according to (i.e. is a function of) the price of good N (P_n), incomes (Y), the price of all other goods ($P_1,... P_{n-1}$) and all other factors (T). Mathematically, this is:

$$Q_n = f [P_n , Y, (P_1,... P_{n-1}), T]$$

At this stage, this mathematical form of expressing the determinants of demand is a convenient shorthand but little else. The major tools of dealing with demand at this level are either the written word or graphs. At a far more advanced level, the algebraic formula for demand is often the most powerful and useful tool in analysing demand.

QUESTION 5

$$Q_D = 20 - \tfrac{1}{2}P$$

where Q_D is the quantity demanded and P is price. Draw the demand curve given by this equation between prices of £1 and £20.

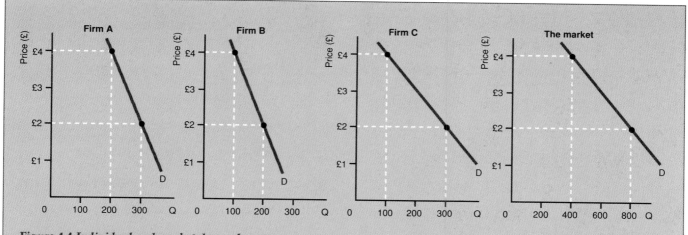

Figure 4.4 Individual and market demand curves
The market demand curve can be derived from the individual demand curves by adding up individual demand at each single price. In this example for instance, the market demand at a price of £2 is calculated by adding the demand of firm A, B and C at this price.

Individual and market demand curves

So far, it has been assumed that demand refers to demand for a product in a whole market (i.e. MARKET DEMAND). However, it is possible to construct individual demand curves and derive market demand curves from them. An INDIVIDUAL DEMAND CURVE is the demand curve of an individual buyer. This could be a consumer, a firm or government.

The determinants of demand for an individual are no different from those of the market as a whole. When price rises, there is a fall in the quantity demanded of the product; when income rises, assuming that the product is a normal good, demand will increase; etc.

Figure 4.4 shows a situation where there are three and only three buyers in a market, firms A, B and C. At a price of £2, firm A will buy 300 units, firm B 200 units and firm C 300 units. So the total market demand at a price of £2 is 300 + 200 + 300 or 800 units. At a price of £4, total market demand will be 200 + 100 + 100 or 400 units. Similarly, all the other points on the market demand curve can be derived by summing the individual demand curves. This is known as **horizontal summing** because the figures on the horizontal axis of the individual demand curves are added up to put on the market demand curve. But the figures on the vertical axis of both individual and market demand curves remain the same.

Key terms

Demand or effective demand - the quantity purchased of a good at any given price, given other determinants of demand remain unchanged.
Demand curve - the line on a price-quantity diagram which shows the level of effective demand at any given price.
Shift in the demand curve - a movement of the whole demand curve to the right or left of the original caused by a change in any variable affecting demand except price.
Individual demand curve - the demand curve for an individual consumer, firm or other economic unit.
Market demand curve - the sum of all individual demand curves.

QUESTION 6
Table 4.3

Price (£)	Quantity demanded of good X (000 units)		
	Firm A	Firm B	Firm C
100	500	250	750
200	400	230	700
300	300	210	650
400	200	190	600
500	100	170	550

There are only three buyers of good X, firms A, B and C.
(a) Draw the individual demand curves for each firm.
(b) Draw the market demand curve for good X.

Applied economics

What price sight?

In April 1989, charges for eye checks were introduced for the first time since the National Health Service was created in 1946. The move was part of a more general policy to increase the proportion of NHS spending paid for directly by the patient and reduce the amount paid for by the taxpayer. The average fee for an eye check following abolition was £11.70, although children and those on low incomes were still entitled to free treatment.

Ministers claimed that there would be no fall in the number of sight tests carried out. They suggested that everyone who was required to pay the fee could afford to do so. Indeed, Mrs Thatcher, the Prime Minister, stated in the House of Commons that people would be upset if they were not allowed to pay for the tests and thus contribute towards the cost of other improvements in the NHS.

However, economic theory suggests that an increase in the price of a good will lead to a contraction in demand. Introducing charges for eye tests should therefore lead to a reduction in the number of eye tests. This indeed is what the initial evidence suggests has happened.

An independent survey of opticians published in June 1990 found that the number of sight tests carried out had dropped from 13.2 million in 1988-9 to 8.9m in 1989-90. About 1.4 million of this 4.3 million drop could be accounted for by the bringing forward of eye tests by those wishing to beat the charges. This left a net fall of 2.9 million to be accounted for by the introduction of charges.

Figure 4.5 shows this contraction of demand. Before the introduction of eye charges, demand was at A. Price was zero and the underlying quantity demanded was 11.8 m (13.2m - 1.4m). After the introduction of eye charges, the underlying demand falls to B. Price is £11.70 and quantity demanded is 10.3m (8.9m + 1.4m: this is a maximum figure because it assumes that all those who brought forward their eye tests, 1.4m people, would have been prepared to pay for an eye test if necessary).

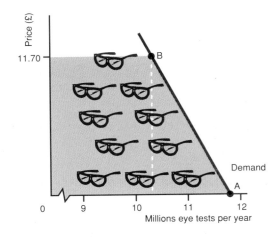

Figure 4.5 *Contraction in demand for eye tests*

THE RECORD MARKET

Data question

In 1989 the Manchester Business School published a study of the UK record market. They argued that a wide range of factors was likely to influence the demand for records. These were the price or discount offered on a record, airplay, television exposure of artists, advertising, artist loyalty, fashion, discotheques, disposable income, numbers of people in different age groups, ownership of audio equipment, seasonality, the music press, and word of mouth.

They concluded that the most important variables determining the demand for all records sold in the UK were the level of advertising, the level of disposable income and the rate of price inflation of all goods and services in the UK.

1. Which factors given in the article do you think would be most important in determining the level of demand for an individual record?

2. Using diagrams, explain what would happen to the demand for all records in the UK, according to the study, if there were:
   (a) an increase in disposable incomes;
   (b) a fall in advertising expenditure on records;
   (c) a fall in the price of a particular album.

Summary

1. A rise in price leads to a rise in quantity supplied, shown by a movement along the supply curve.
2. A change in supply can be caused by factors such as a change in costs of production, technology and the price of other goods. This results in a shift in the supply curve.
3. The market supply curve in a perfectly competitive market is the sum of individual supply curves.

Supply

In any market there are buyers and sellers. Buyers **demand** goods whilst sellers **supply** goods.

SUPPLY in economics is defined as the quantity of goods that sellers are prepared to sell at any given price over a period of time. For instance, in 1987, UK farmers sold 11.94 million tonnes of wheat at an average price of £111 per tonne so economists would say that the supply of wheat at £111 per tonne over the 12 month period was 11.94 million tonnes.

Supply and price

If the price of a good increases, how will producers react? Assuming that no other factors have changed, they are likely to expand production to take advantage of the higher prices and the higher profits that they can now make. In general, quantity supplied will rise if the price of the good also rises, all other things being equal.

This can be shown on a diagram using a **supply curve**. A supply curve shows the quantity that will be supplied over a period of time at any given price. Consider Figure 5.1 which shows the supply curve for wheat. Wheat is priced at £110 per tonne. At this price only the most efficient farmers grow wheat. They supply 110 million tonnes per year. But if the price of wheat rose to £140 per tonne, farmers already growing wheat might increase their acreage of wheat, whilst other non-wheat growing farmers might start to grow wheat. Farmers would do this because at a price of £140 per tonne it is possible to make a profit on production even if costs are higher than at a production level of 110 million units.

A fall in price will lead to a **fall in quantity supplied**, shown by a **movement along** the supply curve. At a lower price, some firms will cut back on relatively unprofitable production whilst others will stop producing altogether. Some of the latter firms may even go bankrupt, unable to cover their costs of production from the price received.

An upward sloping supply curve assumes that:
- firms are motivated to produce by profit - so this model does not apply, for instance, to much of what is produced by government;
- the cost of producing a unit increases as output

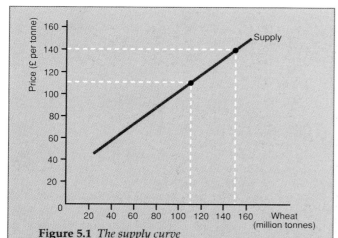

Figure 5.1 *The supply curve*
The supply curve is upward sloping, showing that firms increase production of a good as its price increases. This is because a higher price enables firms to make a profit on the increased output whereas at the lower price they would have made a loss. Here, an increase in the price of wheat from £110 to £140 per tonne increases quantity supplied from 110 million tonnes to 150 million tonnes per year.

QUESTION 1
Table 5.1

Price (£)	Quantity supplied (million units per year)
5	5
10	8
15	11
20	14
25	17

(a) Draw a supply curve from the above data.
(b) Draw a new supply curve assuming that quantity supplied increased by 50 per cent at any given price.

increases (a situation known as rising marginal cost ☞ unit 18) - this is not always true but it is likely that the prices of factors of production to the firm will increase as firms bid for more land, labour and capital to increase their output, thus pushing up costs.

Costs of production

The supply curve is drawn on the assumption that the general costs of production in the economy remain constant (part of the **ceteris paribus** condition. If other things change, then the supply curve will shift.) If the costs of production increase at any given level of output, firms will attempt to pass on these increases in the form of higher prices. If they cannot charge higher prices then profits will fall and firms will produce less of the good or might even stop producing it altogether. A rise in the costs of production will therefore lead to a decrease in supply.

This can be seen in Figure 5.2. The original supply curve is S_1. A rise in the costs of production means that at any given level of output firms will charge higher prices. At an output level of OA, firms will increase their prices from OB to OC. This increase in prices will be true for all points on the supply curve. So the supply curve will **shift** upwards and to the left to S_2 in Figure 5.2. There will have been a **fall in supply**. (Note that a fall in **quantity supplied** refers to a change in quantity supplied due to a change in price and would be shown by a movement along the supply curve.) Conversely a fall in the costs of production will lead to an increase in supply of a good.

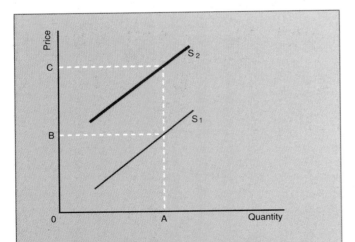

Figure 5.2 *A rise in the costs of production*
A rise in the costs of production for a firm will push its supply curve upwards and to the left, from S_1 to S_2. For any given quantity supplied, firms will now want a higher price to compensate them for the increase in their costs.

QUESTION 2 In 1988-9, average wage settlements in the UK were around 9 per cent. What would be the likely impact of this upon the supply curve of goods and services in the UK?

This is shown by a shift to the right in the supply curve.

Technology

Another factor which affects supply of a particular good is the state of technology. The supply curve is drawn on the assumption that the state of technology remains unchanged. If new technology is introduced to the production process it should lead to a fall in the costs of production. This greater **productive efficiency** will encourage firms to produce more at the same price or produce the same amount at a lower price or some combination of the two. The supply curve will shift downwards and to the right. It would be unusual for firms to replace more efficient technology with less efficient technology. However, this can occur at times of war or natural disasters. If new technical equipment is destroyed, firms may have to fall back on less efficient means of production, reducing supply at any given price, resulting in a shift in the supply curve to the left.

QUESTION 3 Explain, using supply curves, why it cost £10 000 in 1970 for a machine that could do the same as a calculator which cost £100 in 1975 and £6 today.

The prices of other goods

Changes in the prices of some goods can affect the supply of a particular good. For instance, if the price of beef increases substantially there will be an increase in the quantity of beef supplied. More cows will be reared and slaughtered. As a result there will be an increase in the supply of hides for leather. At the same price, the quantity of leather supplied to the market will increase. An increase in the price of beef therefore leads to an increase in the supply of leather. On the other hand, an increase in cattle rearing is likely to be at the expense of production of wheat or sheep farming. So an increase in beef production is likely to lead to a fall in the supply of other agricultural products as farmers switch production to take advantage of higher profits in beef.

Other factors

A number of other factors affect supply. These include:
- the goals of sellers - if for some reason there is a change in the profit levels which a seller expects to receive as a reward for production, then there will be a change in supply; for instance, if an industry such as the book retailing industry went from one made up of many small sellers more interested in selling books than making a profit to one where the industry was dominated by a few large profit-seeking companies, then supply would fall;
- government legislation - anti-pollution controls which raise the costs of production, the abolition of legal barriers to setting up business in an industry, or tax

changes, are some examples of how government can change the level of supply in an industry;

■ expectations of future events - if firms expect future prices to be much higher, they may restrict supplies and stockpile goods; if they expect disruptions to their future production because of a strike they may stockpile raw materials, paying for them with borrowed money, thus increasing their costs and reducing supply;

■ the weather - in agricultural markets, the weather plays a crucial role in determining supply, bad weather reducing supply, good weather producing bumper yields.

QUESTION 4 In 1988, many parts of the USA suffered a prolonged drought. The wheat harvest was dramatically reduced. Many livestock ranchers were forced to sell entire breeding herds because of lack of pasture to feed them.

(a) Using a supply diagram, explain the effect of the drought on the world supply of wheat in 1988.
(b) Using diagrams, explain the effect of the drought on the supply of beef in the USA
   (i) during the drought and
   (ii) in 1989 and 1990.

Individual and market supply curves

The MARKET SUPPLY CURVE can be derived from the INDIVIDUAL SUPPLY CURVES of sellers in the market (this assumes that supply is not affected by changes in the demand curve as would happen under monopoly or oligopoly; ☞ unit 28 for an explanation of why this is so). Consider Figure 5.3. For the sake of simplicity we will assume that there are only three sellers in the market. At a price of £10 per unit, Firm X is unwilling to supply any

goods. Firm Y supplies 3 units whilst Firm Z supplies 2 units. So the market supply at a price of £10 is 5 units. At a price of £20, Firm X will supply 1 unit, Firm Y 5 units and Firm Z 9 units. So the market supply at a price of £20 is 15 units. The rest of the market supply curve can be derived by **horizontally summing** the level of output at all other price levels.

QUESTION 5
Table 5.2

Quantity supplied (million units)			
Firm A	Firm B	Firm C	Price (£)
10	2	0	1
12	5	3	2
14	8	6	3
16	11	9	4
18	14	12	5

Firms A, B and C are the sole suppliers in the market and the market is perfectly competitive.

(a) Draw the market supply curve.
(b) What is supply at a price of (i) £1 and (ii) £3.50?

Key terms

Supply - the quantity of goods that suppliers are willing to sell at any given price over a period of time.
Individual supply curve - the supply curve of an individual producer.
Market supply curve - the supply curve of all producers within the market. In a perfectly competitive market it can be calculated by summing the supply curves of individual producers.

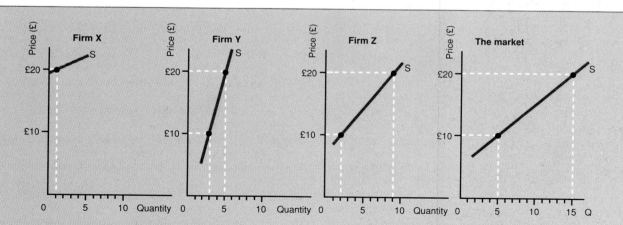

Figure 5.3 *Individual and market supply curves*
The market supply curve is calculated by summing the individual supply curves of producers in the market. Here the market supply at £20, for instance, is calculated by adding the supply of each individual firm at a price of £20.

Applied economics

Hard times for retailers

In 1980-81, the British economy suffered the worst depression since the 1930s. Unemployment rose from 1½ million to 3 million and retailers, not surprisingly, were hard hit. However, the economy then slowly began to recover. Both established retailers, like Burtons, Habitat and Marks and Spencer, and new retailers, like Next, Body Shop and B&Q, experienced booming sales. The higher prices they were able to charge for their products due to the shift in demand led to an expansion of supply. As a consequence there was a movement up the supply curve. Retailers were also able to reduce costs through the use of new technology, improved manning and bulk buying. This led to an increase in supply shown by a shift to the right of the supply curve in the retailing industry.

However the party was to come to an abrupt end for many retailers in 1988. The Chancellor of the Exchequer, Nigel lawson, doubled the rate of interest over a period of 15 months. The housing market collapsed as mortgage interest repayments for home owners soared. High fashion chains like Next and Burtons were badly hit. Their customers tended to be young, in their 20s and 30s. They were likely to have a large mortgage, the cost of which almost doubled in 1988-89, and were also likely to buy goods on credit rather than pay cash. Worst affected were stores in the furniture and soft furnishings industry. These goods were traditionally bought on credit and purchases were linked to moving house.

As a result of the fall in demand, many retailers were forced to reduce their supply of goods to the market place. Some, like Coloroll, went bankrupt. Others, like Next and Habitat, closed shops which had ceased to make a profit. There was a contraction in supply, illustrated by a movement down the supply curve in these sectors of the retailing industry.

Data question

EGYPTIAN COTTON PRODUCTION

Table 5.3 *Egyptian cotton production*

Crop year	1980	1981	1982	1983	1984	1985	1986	1987	1988	1991[1]
Production (million kantars[2])	10.57	9.99	9.21	8.00	7.98	8.71	8.06	7.01	6.19	10.58

1. Target in Egyptian government 5 year plan.
2. 1 kanter is approximately 50kg.

Source: *Financial Times*, 27.4.89.

Cotton was once one of the most important crops for the Egyptian economy. However the industry suffered disruption from nationalisation in the 1960s and 1970s and the Egyptian government continued to starve the industry of money in the 1980s. All cotton grown in Egypt has, by law, to be sold to the government which then sells it on world markets. In the 1980s, Egyptian farmers received only a quarter of the price that the Egyptian government obtained for cotton exports. By 1989, the government realised that production of cotton would fall even further unless action were taken. On 1 March 1989, the price paid to farmers per kantar of cotton was raised by 34 per cent. The government also launched a publicity campaign to persuade farmers to plant their crops on time rather than extend the season for other more profitable crops.

1. (a) What happened to production levels of cotton in Egypt in the 1980s?
   (b) Suggest reasons why this should have occurred.

2. Explain the likely effects of the measures taken by the Egyptian government in 1989. Use diagrams to illustrate your answer.

Summary

1. The equilibrium or market clearing price is set where demand equals supply.
2. Changes in demand and supply will lead to new equilibrium prices being set.
3. A change in demand will lead to a shift in the demand curve, a movement along the supply curve and a new equilibrium price.
4. A change in supply will lead to a shift in the supply curve, a movement along the demand curve and a new equilibrium price.
5. Markets do not necessarily tend towards the equilibrium price.
6. The equilibrium price is not necessarily the price which will lead to the greatest economic efficiency or the greatest equity.

Equilibrium price

Buyers and sellers come together in a market. A price (sometimes called the **market price**) is struck and goods or services are exchanged. Consider Table 6.1. It shows the demand and supply schedule for a good at prices between £2 and £10.

Table 6.1

Price (£)	Quantity demanded (million units per month)	Quantity supplied (million units per month)
2	12	2
4	9	4
6	6	6
8	3	8
10	0	10

■ If the price is £2, demand will be 12 million units but only 2 million units will be supplied. Demand is greater than supply and there is therefore EXCESS DEMAND (i.e. too much demand in relation to supply) in the market. There will be a **shortage** of products on the market. Some buyers will be lucky and they will snap up the 2 million units being sold. But there will be a 10 million unit shortfall in supply for the rest of the unlucky buyers in the market. For instance, it is not possible to buy some luxury cars without being on a waiting list for several years because current demand is too great.

■ If the price is £10, buyers will not buy any goods. Sellers on the other hand will wish to supply 10 million units. Supply is greater than demand and therefore there will be EXCESS SUPPLY. There will be a **glut** or surplus of products on the market. 10 million units will remain unsold. A sale in a shop is often evidence of excess supply in the past. Firms tried to sell the goods at a higher price and failed.

■ There is only one price where demand equals supply. This is at a price of £6 where demand and supply are both 6 million units. This price is known as the EQUILIBRIUM PRICE. This is the only price where the planned demand of buyers equals the planned supply of sellers in the market. It is also known as the MARKET-CLEARING price because all the products supplied to the market are bought or cleared from the market but no buyer is left frustrated in his or her wishes to buy goods.

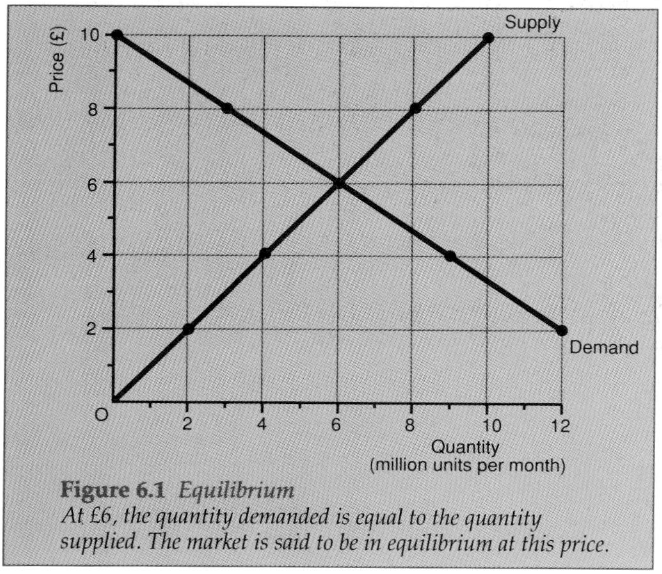

An alternative way of expressing the data in Table 6.1 is shown in Figure 6.1. The equilibrium price is where demand equals supply. This happens where the two curves cross at a price of £6 and a quantity of 6 million units. If the price is above £6, supply will be greater than demand and therefore excess supply will exist. If the price

Figure 6.1 *Equilibrium*
At £6, the quantity demanded is equal to the quantity supplied. The market is said to be in equilibrium at this price.

QUESTION 1
Table 6.2

Price (£)	Quantity demanded (million units)	Quantity supplied (million units)
30	20	70
20	50	50
10	80	30

(a) At what price is there
   (i) excess demand and
   (ii) excess supply?
(b) What is the equilibrium price?

is below £6, demand is greater than supply and therefore there will be excess demand.

Changes in demand and supply

In was explained in units 4 and 5 that a change in price would lead to a change in quantity demanded or supplied, shown by a movement along the demand or supply curve. A change in any other variable, such as income or the costs of production, would lead to:
- an increase or decrease in demand or supply and therefore
- a **shift** in the demand or supply curve.

Demand and supply diagrams provide a powerful and simple tool for analysing the effects of changes in demand and supply on equilibrium price and quantity.

Consider the effect of a rise in consumer incomes. This will lead to an increase in the demand for a normal good. In Figure 6.2 (a) this will push the demand curve from D_1 to D_2. As can be seen from the diagram, the equilibrium price rises from P_1 to P_2. The quantity bought and sold in equilibrium rises from Q_1 to Q_2. The model of demand and supply predicts that an increase in incomes, all other things being equal (the **ceteris paribus** condition) will

lead to an increase both in the price of the product and in the quantity sold. Note that the increase in income **shifts** the demand curve and this then leads to a **movement along** the supply curve.

Figure 6.2 (b) shows the market for black and white televisions. In the early 1970s, both the BBC and Independent Television started to broadcast programmes in colour for the first time. Not surprisingly there was a boom in sales of colour television sets and a slump in sales of black and white ones. In economic terms the demand for black and white sets fell. This is shown by a shift to the left in the demand curve. The equilibrium level of sales in Figure 6.2 (b) falls from OB to OA whilst equilibrium price falls from OF to OE. Note again that a shift in the demand curve leads to a movement along the supply curve.

Prices of both black and white and colour television sets tended to fall in the 1970s and 1980s. The main reason for this was an increase in productive efficiency (☞ unit 33) due to the introduction of new technology enabling costs of production to fall . A fall in costs of production is shown by the shift to the right in the supply curve in Figure 6.2 (c). At any given quantity of output, firms will be prepared to supply more television sets to the market.

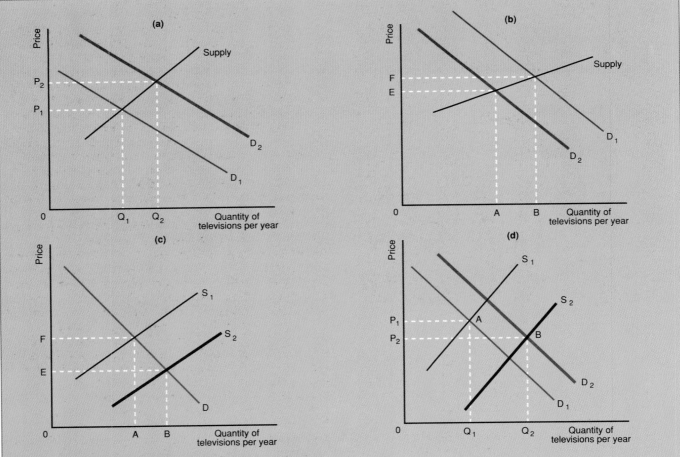

Figure 6.2 *Shifts in demand and supply curves*
Shifts in the demand or supply curves for a product will change the equilibrium price and the equilibrium quantity bought and sold.

The result is an increase in quantity bought and sold from OA to OB and a fall in price from OF to OE. Note that there is a shift in the supply curve which leads to a movement along the demand curve.

So far we have assumed that only one variable changes and that all other variables remain constant. But in the real world, it is likely that several factors affecting demand and supply will change at the same time. Demand and supply diagrams can be used to some extent to analyse several changes. For instance, in the 1970s and 1980s, the demand for colour television sets increased due to rising real incomes (☞ unit 3 for a definition of 'real' values). At the same time, supply increased too because of an increase in productive efficiency. Overall, the price of television sets fell slightly. This is shown in Figure 6.2 (d). Both the demand and supply curves shift to the right. This will lead to an increase in quantity bought and sold. In theory, depending upon the extent of the shifts in the two curves, there could be an increase in price, a fall in price or no change in the price. Figure 6.2 (d) shows the middle of these three possibilities.

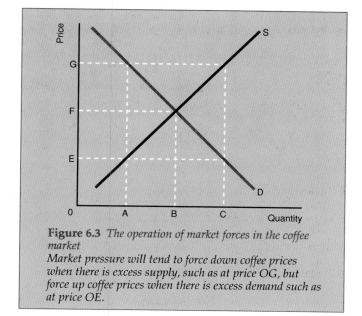

Figure 6.3 *The operation of market forces in the coffee market*
Market pressure will tend to force down coffee prices when there is excess supply, such as at price OG, but force up coffee prices when there is excess demand such as at price OE.

QUESTION 2 During the 1970s the price of metals such as nickel were historically high. This prompted nickel producers to invest in new production facilities which came on stream during the late 1970s and early 1980s. But the world economy went into deep recession during the early 1980s, prompting a collapse in the world price of nickel. Producers reacted by closing facilities. Between 1980 and 1986, the industry lost about 32 500 tonnes of annual capacity compared with an annual demand of between 400 000 and 500 000 tonnes. The world economy started to recover from 1982 but it wasn't until 1987 that a sharp increase in demand from Japanese stainless steel producers, one of the major buyers in the industry, made prices rise. In the last quarter of 1987, nickel could be bought for $1.87 a lb. By March 1988, it had soared to over $9 per lb.

Using demand and supply diagrams, explain why the price of nickel changed when:
(a) new production facilities came on stream in the late 1970s;
(b) there was a world recession in the early 1980s;
(c) the industry closed capacity during the early 1980s;
(d) Japanese stainless steel producers increased purchases in 1987.

Do markets clear?

It is very easy to assume that the equilibrium price is either the current market price or the price towards which the market moves. Neither is correct. The market price could be at any level. There could be excess demand or excess supply at any point in time.

Nor will market prices necessarily tend to change to equilibrium prices over time. One of the most important controversies in economics today is the extent to which markets tend towards market-clearing prices.

The argument put forward by neo-classical free market

economists is that markets do tend to clear. Let us take the example of the coffee market. In this market, there are many producers (farmers, manufacturers, wholesalers and retailers) that are motivated by the desire to make as large a profit as possible. When there is excess demand for coffee (demand is greater than supply), coffee producers will be able to increase their prices and therefore their profits and still sell all they produce. If there is excess supply (supply is greater than demand), some coffee will remain unsold. Producers then have a choice. Either they can offer coffee for sale at the existing price and risk not selling it or they can lower their price to the level where they will sell everything offered. If all producers choose not to lower their prices, there is likely to be even greater pressure to reduce prices in the future because there will be unsold stocks of coffee overhanging the market. Therefore when there is excess demand, prices will be driven upwards whilst prices will fall if there is excess supply.

This can be shown diagrammatically. In Figure 6.3, there is excess demand at a price of OE. Buyers want to purchase AC more of coffee than is being supplied. Shops, manufacturers and coffee growers will be able to increase their prices and their production and still sell everything they produce. If they wish to sell all their output, they can increase their prices to a maximum of OF and their output to a maximum OB, the market-clearing prices and production levels. This they will do because at higher prices and production levels they will be able to make more profit. If there is excess supply, coffee producers will be left with unsold stocks. At a price of OG, output left unsold will be AC. Producers in a free market cannot afford to build up stocks forever. Some producers will lower prices and the rest will be forced to follow. Production and prices will go on falling until equilibrium output and price is reached. This is usually referred to as a **stable equilibrium** position.

These pressures which force the market towards an equilibrium point are often called FREE MARKET

FORCES. But critics of the market mechanism argue that free market forces can lead away from the equilibrium point in many cases. One example of **unstable equilibrium**, the Cobweb theory, is explained in unit 11. In other markets, it is argued that market forces are too weak to restore equilibrium. Many Keynesian economists cite the labour market as an example of this. In other markets, there are many forces such as government legislation, trade unions and multi-national monopolies which more than negate the power of the market.

QUESTION 3

$$Q_D = 20 - \tfrac{1}{2} P$$
$$Q_S = 10 + \tfrac{3}{4} P$$

where Q_D is quantity demanded, Q_S is quantity supplied and P is price (in £).

The current price is £12.
(a) Is there excess demand or excess supply in the market?
(b) Will free market forces tend to lead to a fall or rise in price?

Points to note

Equilibrium is a very powerful concept in economics but it is essential to remember that the equilibrium price is unlikely to be the most desirable price or 'right' price in the market. The most desirable price in the market will depend upon how one defines 'desirable'. It may be, for instance, the one which leads to the greatest economic efficiency, or it may be the one which leads to greatest equity. Alternatively it may be the one which best supports the defence of the country.

Demand can also equal supply without there being equilibrium. At any point in time, what is actually bought must equal what is actually sold. There can be no sellers without buyers. So actual demand (more often referred to as **realised** or **ex post** demand in economics) must always equal actual (or realised or ex post) supply. Equilibrium occurs at a price where there is no tendency to change. Price will not change if, at the current price, the quantity that consumers wish to buy (called **planned** or **desired** or **ex ante** demand) is equal to the quantity that suppliers wish to sell (called planned or desired or ex ante supply).

Therefore only in equilibrium will planned demand equal planned supply.

Key terms

Excess demand - where demand is greater than supply.
Excess supply - where supply is greater than demand.
Equilibrium price - the price at which there is no tendency to change because planned (or desired or ex ante) purchases (i.e. demand) is equal to planned sales (i.e. supply).
Market clearing price - the price at which there is neither excess demand nor excess supply but where everything offered for sale is purchased.
Free market forces - forces in free markets which act to reduce prices when there is excess supply and raise prices when there is excess demand.

Applied economics

The UK car industry

The first half of the 1980s were not good years for motor manufacturers selling to the UK market. As can be seen from Figure 6.4, the recession of 1980-81 led to a fall in car sales and subsequent growth proved to be short lived. The depression in car sales in the early 1980s led to manufacturers slashing prices and a fierce price war developed. This is what economic theory would have predicted. A shift to the left in the demand curve for cars resulted in a downward movement along the supply curve. Fewer cars were sold at a lower price.

The second half of the 1980s was a complete contrast. The market expanded rapidly. In 1987, the 2 million car sales barrier was breached for the first time in UK history. Car manufacturers were able to increase prices regularly and enjoyed record profits. In economic terms, the demand curve shifted to the right, leading to an upward movement along the supply curve. Both prices and sales increased.

Motor manufacturers feared this would all end when interest rates nearly doubled in 1988-89. Yet the UK car market proved remarkably resilient. Both years saw net records set for sales and profits and there was very little price discounting. However, 1990 proved to be a turning point. Sales fell from their 1989 levels as high interest rates finally began to bite. Motor manufacturers, anxious to preserve market share, slowly began to introduce sales incentives (i.e. reduce the price of their cars). A fall in demand led to a downward movement along the supply curve.

In the long term, the outlook for many motor manufacturers is bleak. Japanese investment worldwide and in the EC in particular will lead to gross overcapacity in the industry in the 1990s. This shift to the right in the supply curve will leave the weakest, least profitable companies in an exposed position. Some companies, like the Rover Group, could be forced to leave the industry, a casualty of intense competition resulting from short term disequilibrium in the car market. For consumers, overcapacity (i.e. excess supply) should be good news in the short term. They will be offered a wide range of models at greatly discounted prices as the manufacturers fight it out for survival.

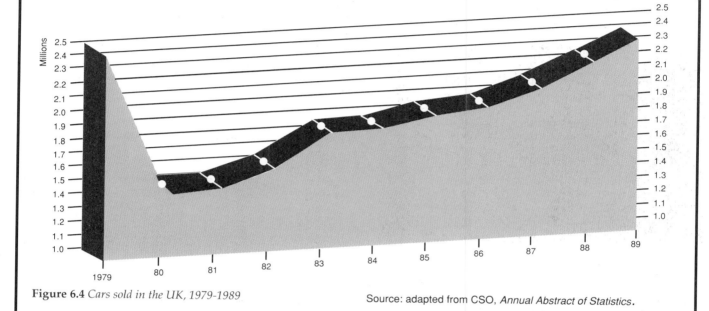

Figure 6.4 *Cars sold in the UK, 1979-1989*

Source: adapted from CSO, *Annual Abstract of Statistics*.

TEA

The world tea market has grown rapidly over the past 3 decades with supply roughly keeping pace with demand. World production of tea has grown from 530 million in 1952 to 1.64 billion kilos in 1988. The share of world production bought by the UK has declined over the period. Partly this is because the British consumer is now drinking more coffee and soft drinks, but more importantly demand has increased substantially in India, the Soviet Union, the Middle East and other developing countries.

In the 1990s demand could well outstrip supply. Demand is forecast to rise by 3-5 per cent per annum. Supply, on the other hand, could well increase more slowly. Yields have increased over time, from 500-1,000 kg per hectare in the early 1950s to over 2,000 per hectare today. However there is some doubt as to whether yields per hectare can carry on increasing at this rate in the future. If supply is to increase substantially, it may only come about through planting of new bushes.

1. Explain what has happened to
    (a) the demand
    (b) the supply and
    (c) the quantity bought and sold
    of tea since the 1950s.

2. How might the world price of tea change in the 1990s? Use diagrams to illustrate your answer.

Summary

1. Some goods are complements, in joint demand.
2. Other goods are substitutes for each other, in competitive demand.
3. Derived demand occurs when one good is demanded because it is needed for the production of other goods or services.
4. Composite demand and joint supply are two other ways in which markets are linked.

Partial and general models

A model of price determination was outlined in unit 6. It was explained that the price of a good was determined by the forces of demand and supply. This is an example of a **partial model**. A partial model is an explanation of reality which has relatively few variables (☞ unit 111). But a more **general model** or wider model of the market system can be constructed which shows how events in one market can lead to changes in other markets. In this unit we will consider how some markets are interrelated.

Complements

Some goods, known as COMPLEMENTS, are in JOINT DEMAND. This means that, in demanding one good, a consumer will also be likely to demand another good. Examples of complements are:

■ tennis rackets and tennis balls;
■ washing machines and soap powder;
■ strawberries and cream;
■ video tapes and video recorders.

Economic theory suggests that a rise in the quantity demanded of one complement will lead to an increase in the demand for another, resulting in an increase in the price and quantity bought of the other complement. For instance, an increase in the quantity demanded of strawberries will lead to an increase in demand for cream too, pushing up the price of cream.

This can be shown on a demand and supply diagram. Assume that new technology reduces the cost of production of washing machines. This leads to an increase in supply of washing machines shown by a shift to the right of the supply curve in Figure 7.1 (a). As a result there is a fall in price and a rise in the quantity demanded of washing machines, shown by a movement along the demand curve. This in turn will increase the demand for automatic soap powder, shown by a shift to the right in the demand curve in Figure 7.1 (b). This leads to a rise in quantity purchased of automatic soap powder and also an increase in its price.

Substitutes

A SUBSTITUTE is a good which can be replaced by another good. If two goods are substitutes for each other, they are said to be in COMPETITIVE DEMAND. Examples of substitutes are:

■ beef and pork;
■ Coca-cola and Pepsi-cola;
■ fountain pens and biros;

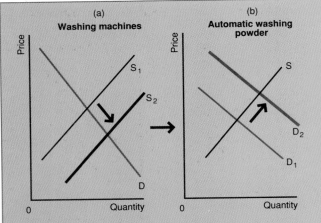

Figure 7.1 *Complements*
An increase in supply and the consequent fall in price of washing machines will lead to a rise in the quantity of washing machines and a rise in demand (shown by a shift in the demand curve) for a complementary good such as automatic washing powder.

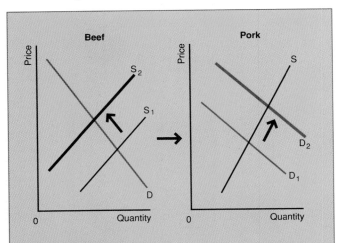

Figure 7.2 *Substitutes*
A fall in the supply of beef leading to a rise in its price will lead to a fall in the quantity demanded of beef and an increase in the demand for a substitute product such as pork.

■ gas and oil (in the long term but not particularly in the short term).

Economic theory predicts that a rise in the price of one good will lead to an increase in demand and a rise in price of a substitute good.

Figure 7.2 shows a rise in the price of beef, due to a fall in its supply. This leads to a fall in the quantity demanded of beef as the price of beef rises. In turn, there will be an increase in the demand for pork as consumers substitute pork for beef. The demand for pork will increase, shown by a shift to the right in the demand curve for pork. This leads to a rise in the price of pork and a rise in quantity purchased.

Many substitute goods are not clearly linked. For instance, a rise in the price of foreign holidays will lead some consumers to abandon taking a foreign holiday. They may substitute a UK holiday for it, but they may also decide to buy new curtains or a new carpet for their house, or buy a larger car than they had originally planned.

QUESTION 1

(a) Explain whether the following are complements or substitutes:
    (i) electricity and gas;
    (ii) tea and milk;
    (iii) bus and train journeys;
    (iv) chocolate bars and crisps.

(b) Show on a demand and supply diagram the effect on the price of electricity of a rise in the price of gas.

Derived demand

Many goods are demanded only because they are needed for the production of other goods. The demand for these goods is said to be a DERIVED DEMAND.

For instance, the demand for steel is derived in part from the demand for cars and ships. The demand for flour is derived in part from the demand for cakes and bread. The demand for sugar is in part derived from demand for some beverages, confectionery and chocolate.

Figure 7.3 shows an increase in the demand for cars. This leads to an increase in quantity bought and sold. Car manufacturers will increase their demand for steel, shown by a rightward shift of the demand curve for steel. The price of steel will then increase as will the quantity bought and sold. Economic theory therefore predicts that an increase in demand for a good will lead to an increase in price and quantity purchased of goods which are in derived demand from it.

QUESTION 2 In December 1988 the Ford Motor Company announced that it had developed a platinum-free catalyst used to reduce car exhaust emissions. The company claimed that it was significantly cheaper than current designs of catalyst which used platinum. The news caused chaos in the platinum market given that about 35 per cent of platinum currently mined is used in car catalysts.

Using a diagram and the concept of derived demand, explain what is likely to have happened to the price of platinum as a result of the Ford announcement.

Composite demand

A good is said to be in COMPOSITE DEMAND when it is demanded for two or more distinct uses. For instance, milk may be used for yoghurt, for cheese making, for butter or for drinking. Land may be demanded for residential, industrial or commercial use. Steel is demanded for car manufacturing and for shipbuilding.

Economic theory predicts that an increase in demand for one composite good will lead to a fall in supply for another. Figure 7.4 shows that an increase in the demand by the chemical industry for oil will push the demand curve to the right, increasing both the quantity sold and

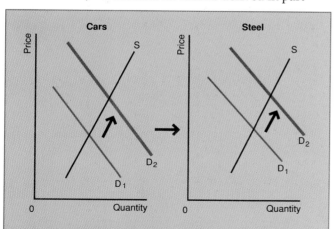

Figure 7.3 *Derived demand*
An increase in the demand for cars will lead to an increase in demand for steel. Steel is said to be in derived demand from cars.

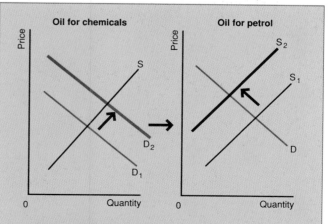

Figure 7.4 *Composite demand*
An increase in the demand for oil from chemical producers will result in a fall in the supply of oil to the petrol market because oil is in composite demand.

the price of oil. With an upward sloping supply for oil as a whole, an increase in supply of oil to the chemical industry will reduce the supply of oil for petrol. This is shown by a shift upwards in the supply curve in Figure 7.4. The price of oil for petrol will rise and the quantity demanded will fall.

Economic theory therefore predicts that an increase in demand for a good will lead to a rise in price and a fall in quantity demanded for a good with which it is in composite demand.

Joint supply

A good is in JOINT SUPPLY with another good when one good is supplied for two different purposes. For instance, cows are supplied for both beef and leather. An oil well may give both oil and gas.

Economic theory suggests that an increase in demand for one good in joint supply will lead to an increase in supply, an increase in the quantity demanded of the other good and therefore a fall in price with which it is in joint supply. Figure 7.5 shows that an increase in demand for beef leads to an increase in both price and quantity bought and sold of beef. More beef production will lead, as a by-product, to greater supply of leather. This is shown by a shift to the right in the supply curve for leather. The price of leather will then fall and quantity demanded bought and sold will increase.

QUESTION 3 The supply of oil from the North Sea is predicted to decline from now until the oil wells are exhausted in the early 21st century. Natural gas is a by-product of most oil wells. Using diagrams, explain the likely effect on the price of natural gas in the UK of these developments.

Key terms

Complement - a good which is purchased with other goods to satisfy a want.
Joint demand - when two or more complements are bought together.
Substitute - a good which can be replaced by another to satisfy a want.
Competitive demand - when two or more goods are substitutes for each other.
Derived demand - when the demand for one good is the result of or derived from the demand for another good.
Composite demand - when a good is demanded for two or more distinct uses.
Joint supply - when two or more goods are produced together, so that a change in supply of one good will necessarily change the supply of the other goods with which it is in joint supply.

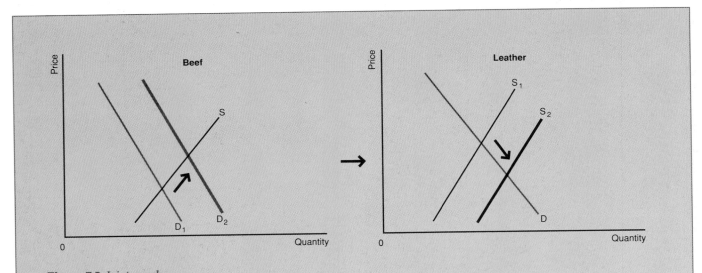

Figure 7.5 *Joint supply*
An increase in the demand for beef, which leads to more beef being produced, results in an increase in the supply of leather. Beef and leather are said to be in joint supply.

Applied economics

A mining proposal

In February 1990, two Canadian companies announced that they were seeking financial backing for a mining project in Chile. They planned to mine a 660 square kilometre area in the Atacama desert in the north of the country. The main product from the operation would be potassium nitrate, a low-volume high-value chemical, in derived demand from the food and tobacco industries, as it is used by a small number of specialist agricultural users for high-value crops such as tobacco, some vegetables and in selected hydroponics.

However the operation would also produce iodine, used industrially in various chemical processes from animal feed supplements to x-rays and also in pharmaceuticals and medicines. Sodium sulphate, used in pulp and paper products, detergents and in print and textile dyes, would also be a significant by-product. Hence potassium nitrate, iodine and sodium sulphate would all be in joint supply.

Mining analysts were sceptical of the proposals. According to the two Canadian companies, output of potassium nitrate from the project would reach 188 000 tonnes within two years. Yet total world demand was only 540 000 tonnes. Hence there would probably be a ruthless price war as the supply curve for the product shifted significantly to the right. It would be difficult to predict how low the price might have to fall to clear the market. The profitability of the project would depend crucially upon the successful sale of the by-products - iodine and sodium sulphate. Yet increased output would put downward pressure on world prices of these two products too as their supply expanded.

Data question

PLATINUM

During 1990 automotive emission control catalysts are expected to overtake jewellery as the major end user of platinum, according to Shearson Lehman Hutton, the financial services group.

By 1994, when western Europe will have car emission control standards as tight as those currently in place in the US, demand for use in the production of catalysts is expected to rise to 1.7m ounces a year from 1.2m ounces in 1989.

A third source of demand for platinum comes from investors, who in 1989 bought 250 000 ounces.

The growth in demand is, however, likely to be matched over the next few years by increased output. Western world mine production is forecast to rise from 2.87m ounces in 1989 to 4.29m ounces in 1994.

Source: adapted from the *Financial Times*, 8.2.1990.

1. What is the difference between 'derived demand' and 'composite demand'? Illustrate your answer with examples from the passage.
2. Using diagrams, suggest what is likely to happen to the price of platinum in the first half of the 1990s.

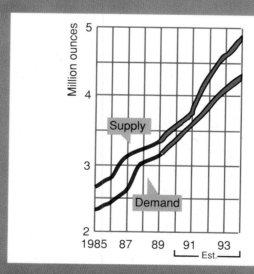

Source: Shearson Lehman Hutton.

Figure 7.6 *Platinum: non-communist world (m ounces)*

Summary

1. Elasticity is a measure of the extent to which quantity responds to a change in a variable which affects it, such as price or income.
2. Price elasticity of demand measures the responsiveness of quantity demanded to a change in price.
3. Price elasticity of demand varies from zero, or infinitely inelastic, to infinitely elastic.
4. The value of price elasticity of demand is determined by the availability of substitutes and by time.

The meaning of demand elasticity

The quantity demanded of a good is affected by changes in the price of the good, changes in price of other goods, changes in income and changes in other relevant factors. **Elasticity** is a measure of **just how much** the quantity demanded will be affected by a change in price or income etc.

Assume that the price of gas increases by 1 per cent. If quantity demanded consequently falls by 20 per cent, then there is a very large drop in quantity demanded in comparison to the change in price. The price elasticity of gas would be said to be very high. If quantity demanded falls by 0.01 per cent, then the change in quantity demanded is relatively insignificant compared to the large change in price and the price elasticity of gas would be said to be low.

Different elasticities of demand measure the responsiveness of quantity demanded to changes in the variables which affect demand. So price elasticity of demand measures the responsiveness of quantity demanded to changes in the price of the good. Income elasticity measures the responsiveness of quantity demanded to changes in consumer incomes. Cross elasticity measures the responsiveness of quantity demanded to changes in the price of another good. Economists could also measure population elasticity, tastes elasticity or elasticity for any other variable which might affect quantity demanded, although these measures are rarely calculated.

Price elasticity of demand

Economists choose to measure responsiveness in terms of percentage changes. So PRICE ELASTICITY OF DEMAND - the responsiveness of changes in quantity demanded to changes in price - is calculated by using the formula:

$$\frac{\text{percentage change in quantity demanded}}{\text{percentage change in price}}$$

Table 8.1 shows a number of calculations of price elasticity. For instance, if an increase in price of 10 per cent leads to a fall in quantity demanded of 20 per cent, then the price elasticity of demand is 2. If an increase in price of 50 per cent leads to a fall in quantity demanded of 25 per cent then price elasticity of demand is ½.

Elasticity is not a concept which many students find easy to understand at first. It is essential to memorise the formulae for elasticity. Only then can they be used with ease and an appreciation gained of their significance.

Table 8.1

Change in price (%)	Change in quantity demanded (%)	Elasticity
10	20	2
50	25	½
7	28	4
9	3	⅓

QUESTION 1
Table 8.2

	Percentage change in	
	quantity demanded	price
a)	10	5
b)	60	20
c)	4	8
d)	1	9
e)	5	7
f)	8	11

Calculate the price elasticity of demand from the data in Table 8.2.

Alternative formulae

Data to calculate price elasticities are often not presented in the form of percentage changes. These have to be worked out. Calculating the percentage change is relatively easy. For instance if a consumer has 10 apples and buys another 5, the percentage change in the total number of apples is of course 50 per cent. This answer is worked out by dividing the change in the number of apples she has (i.e. 5) by the original number of apples she possessed (i.e. 10) and multiplying by 100 to get a percentage figure. So the formula is:

$$\text{percentage change} = \frac{\text{absolute change}}{\text{original value}} \times 100\%$$

Price elasticity of demand is measured by dividing the percentage change in quantity demanded by the percentage change in price. Therefore an alternative way of expressing this is $\Delta Q/Q \times 100$ (the percentage change in quantity demanded Q) divided by $\Delta P/P \times 100$ (the percentage change in price P). The 100s cancel each other out, leaving a formula of:

$$\frac{\Delta Q}{Q} \div \frac{\Delta P}{P} \quad \textbf{or} \quad \frac{\Delta Q}{Q} \times \frac{P}{\Delta P}$$

This is mathematically equivalent to:

$$\frac{P}{Q} \times \frac{\Delta Q}{\Delta P}$$

Examples of calculations of elasticity using the above two formulae are given in Figure 8.1.

Example 1
Quantity demanded originally is 100 at a price of £2. There is a rise in price to £3 resulting in a fall in demand to 75.
Therefore the change in quantity demanded is 25 and the change in price is £1.
The price elasticity of demand is:

$$\frac{\Delta Q}{Q} \div \frac{\Delta P}{P} = \frac{25}{100} \div \frac{1}{2} = \tfrac{1}{2}$$

Example 2
Quantity demanded originally is 20 units at a price of £5 000. There is a fall in price to £4 000 resulting in a rise in demand to 32 units.
Therefore the change in quantity demanded is 12 units resulting from the change in price of £1 000.
The price elasticity of demand is:

$$\frac{P}{Q} \times \frac{\Delta Q}{\Delta P} = \frac{5000}{20} \times \frac{12}{1000} = 3$$

Figure 8.1 *Calculations of elasticity of demand*

QUESTION 2
Table 8.3

	Original values		New values	
	Quantity demanded	Price (£)	Quantity demanded	Price (£)
a)	100	5	120	7
b)	20	8	25	9
c)	12	3	16	6
d)	150	12	200	14
e)	45	6	45	8
f)	32	24	40	2

Calculate the price elasticity of demand for the data in Table 8.3

Elastic and inelastic demand

Different values of price elasticity of demand are given special names.

- Demand is price ELASTIC if the value of elasticity is greater than one. If demand for a good is price elastic then a percentage change in price will bring about an even larger percentage change in quantity demanded. For instance, if a 10 per cent rise in the price of tomatoes leads to a 20 per cent fall in the quantity demanded of tomatoes, then price elasticity is 20÷10 or 2 and therefore the demand for tomatoes is elastic. Demand is said to be **infinitely elastic** if the value of elasticity is infinity (i.e. a fall in price would lead to an infinite increase in quantity demanded whilst a rise in price would lead to the quantity demanded becoming zero).

- Demand is price INELASTIC if the value of elasticity is less than one. If demand for a good is price inelastic then a percentage change in price will bring about a smaller percentage change in quantity demanded. For instance, if a 10 per cent rise in the price of commuter fares on British Rail Southern Region resulted in a 1 per cent fall in rail journeys made, then price elasticity is 1÷10 or 0.1 and therefore the demand for BR commuter traffic is inelastic. Demand is said to be **infinitely inelastic** if the value of elasticity is zero (i.e. a change in price would have no effect on quantity demanded).

- Demand is of UNITARY ELASTICITY if the value of elasticity is exactly 1. This means that a percentage change in price will lead to an exact and opposite change in quantity demanded. For instance a good would have unitary elasticity if a 10 per cent rise in price led to a 10 per cent fall in quantity demanded. (It will be shown in unit 9 that total revenue will remain constant at all quantities demanded if elasticity of demand is unity.)

This terminology is summarised in Table 8.4.

Table 8.4 *Elasticity: summary of key terms*

	Verbal description of response to a change in price	Numerical measure of elasticity	Change in total outlay as price rises[1]
Perfectly inelastic	Quantity demanded does not change at all as price changes	Zero	Increases
Inelastic	Quantity demanded changes by a smaller percentage than does price	Between 0 and 1	Increases
Unitary elasticity	Quantity demanded changes by exactly the same percentage as does price	1	Constant
Elastic	Quantity demanded changes by a larger percentage than does price	Between 1 and infinity	Decreases
Perfectly elastic	Buyers are prepared to purchase all they can obtain at some given price but none at all at a higher price	Infinity	Decreases to zero

1. This is explained in unit 9.

QUESTION 3 Explain whether you think that the following goods would be elastic or inelastic in demand if their price increased by 10 per cent whilst all other factors remained constant: (a) petrol; (b) fresh tomatoes; (c) holidays offered by a major tour operator; (d) a Ford car.

Graphical representations

Figure 8.2 shows a straight line graph. It is a common mistake to conclude that elasticity of a straight line demand curve is constant all along its length. In fact nearly all straight line demand curves vary in elasticity along the line.

At the point A, price elasticity of demand is infinity. Here quantity demanded is zero. Putting Q = 0 into the formula for elasticity:

$$\frac{\Delta Q}{Q} \div \frac{\Delta P}{P}$$

we see that zero is divided into ΔQ. Mathematically there is an infinite number of zeros in any number.

At the point C, price elasticity of demand is zero. Here price is zero. Putting P = 0 into the formula for elasticity, we see that P is divided into ΔP giving an answer of infinity. Infinity is then divided into the fraction $\Delta Q \div Q$. Infinity is so large that the answer will approximate to zero.

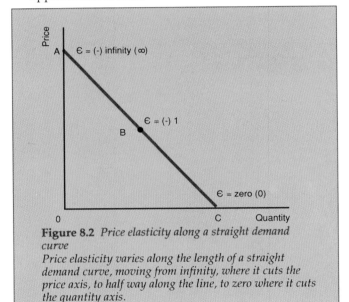

Figure 8.2 *Price elasticity along a straight demand curve*
Price elasticity varies along the length of a straight demand curve, moving from infinity, where it cuts the price axis, to half way along the line, to zero where it cuts the quantity axis.

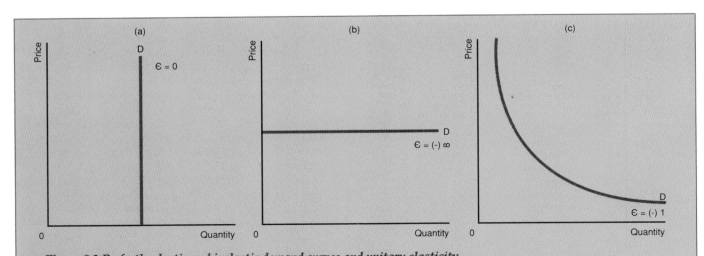

Figure 8.3 Perfectly elastic and inelastic demand curves and unitary elasticity
A vertical demand curve (a) is perfectly inelastic, whilst a horizontal demand curve (b) is perfectly elastic. A curve with unitary elasticity (c) is a rectangular hyperbola with the formula PQ = k where P is price, Q is quantity demanded and k is a constant value.

■ At the point B exactly half way along the line, price elasticity of demand is 1.

Worth noting is that the elasticity of demand at a point can be measured by dividing the distance from the point to the quantity axis by the distance from the point to the price axis, BC ÷ AB. In Figure 8.2, B is half way along the line AC and so BC = AB and the elasticity at the point B is 1.

Two straight line demand curves discussed earlier do not have the same elasticity all along their length. Figure 8.3(a) shows a demand curve which is perfectly inelastic. Whatever the price, the same quantity will be demanded. Figure 8.3(b) shows a perfectly elastic demand curve. Any amount can be demanded at one price or below it whilst nothing will be demanded at a higher price.

Figure 8.3(c) shows a demand curve with unitary elasticity. Mathematically it is a rectangular hyperbola. This means that any percentage change in price is offset by an equal and opposite change in quantity demanded.

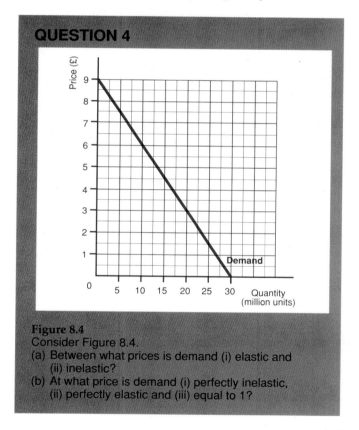

QUESTION 4

Figure 8.4
Consider Figure 8.4.
(a) Between what prices is demand (i) elastic and (ii) inelastic?
(b) At what price is demand (i) perfectly inelastic, (ii) perfectly elastic and (iii) equal to 1?

Two technical points

So far we have written of price elasticity of demand as always being a positive number. In fact any downward sloping demand curve always has a negative elasticity. This is because a rise in one variable (price or quantity) is always matched by a fall in the other variable. A rise is positive but a fall is negative and a positive number divided by a negative one (or vice versa) is always negative. However, economists find it convenient to omit the minus sign in price elasticity of demand because it is easier to deal in positive numbers whilst accepting that

the value is really negative.

A second point relates to the fact that elasticities over the same price range can differ. For example, at a price of £2, demand for a good is 20 units. At a price of £3, demand is 18 units. Price elasticity of demand for a rise in price from £2 to £3 is:

$$\frac{P}{Q} \times \frac{\Delta Q}{\Delta P} = \frac{2}{20} \times \frac{2}{1} = \frac{1}{5}$$

But price elasticity of demand for a fall in price from £3 to £2 is:

$$\frac{P}{Q} \times \frac{\Delta Q}{\Delta P} = \frac{3}{18} \times \frac{2}{1} = \frac{1}{3}$$

The price elasticity for a rise in price is therefore less than for a fall in price over the same range. This is not necessarily a problem so long as one is aware of it. One way of resolving this is to average out price and quantity. In the formulae, P becomes not the original price but the average price (i.e. the original price plus the new price divided by 2) and Q becomes the average quantity demanded (i.e. the original quantity demanded plus the new quantity demanded divided by 2). In the above example, the average price is £(2+3)/2 or £2½. The average quantity demanded is (20+18)/2 or 19. Price elasticity of demand is then:

$$\frac{P}{Q} \times \frac{\Delta Q}{\Delta P} = \frac{2½}{19} \times \frac{2}{1} = \frac{5}{19}$$

As you would expect, this value is in between the two price elasticities of $1/_5$ and $1/_3$.

The determinants of price elasticity of demand

The exact value of price elasticity of demand for a good is determined by a wide variety of factors. Economists however argue that two factors in particular can be singled out: the availability of substitutes and time.

The availability of substitutes The better the substitutes for a product, the higher the price elasticity of demand will tend to be. For instance, salt has few good substitutes. When the price of salt increases, the demand for salt will change little and therefore the price elasticity of salt is low. On the other hand, spaghetti has many good substitutes, from other types of pasta, to rice, potatoes, bread, and other foods. A rise in the price of spaghetti, all other food prices remaining constant, is likely to have a significant effect on the demand for spaghetti. Hence the elasticity of demand for spaghetti is likely to be higher than that for salt.

The more widely the product is defined, the fewer substitutes it is likely to have. Spaghetti has many substitutes, but food in general has none. Therefore the elasticity of demand for spaghetti is likely to be higher than that for food. Similarly the elasticity of demand for boiled sweets is likely to be higher than for confectionery in general. A 5 per cent increase in the price of boiled sweets, all other prices remaining constant, is likely to lead to a much larger fall in demand for boiled sweets than a 5 per cent increase in the price of all confectionery.

Time The longer the period of time, the more price elastic is the demand for a product. For instance, in 1973/4 when the price of oil quadrupled the demand for oil was initially little affected. In the short term the demand for oil was price inelastic. This is hardly surprising. People still needed to travel to work in cars and heat their houses whilst industry still needed to operate. Oil had few good substitutes. Motorists couldn't put gas into their petrol tanks whilst businesses could not change oil-fired systems to run on gas, electricity or coal. However, in the longer term motorists were able to and did buy cars which were more fuel efficient. Oil-fired central heating systems were replaced by gas and electric systems. Businesses converted or did not replace oil-fired equipment. The demand for oil fell from what it would otherwise have been. In the longer run, the demand for oil proved to be price elastic. It is argued that in the short term, buyers are often locked into spending patterns through habit, lack of information or because of durable goods that have already been purchased. In the longer term, they have the time and opportunity to change those patterns.

It is sometimes argued that **necessities** have lower price elasticities than **luxuries**. Necessities by definition have to be bought whatever their price in order to stay alive. So an increase in the price of necessities will barely reduce the quantity demanded. Luxuries on the other hand are by definition goods which are not essential to existence. A rise in the price of luxuries should therefore produce a proportionately large fall in demand. There is no evidence however to suggest that this is true. Food, arguably a necessity, does not seem to have a lower elasticity than holidays or large cars, both arguably luxuries. Part of the reason for this is that it is very difficult to define necessities and luxuries empirically. Some food is a necessity but a significant proportion of what we eat is unnecessary for survival. It is not possible to distinguish between what food is consumed out of necessity and what is a luxury.

It is also sometimes argued that goods which form a relatively low proportion of total expenditure have lower elasticities than those which form a more significant proportion. A large car manufacturer, for instance, would continue to buy the same amount of Tippex even if the price of Tippex doubled because it is not worth its while to bother changing to an alternative. On the other hand, its demand for steel would be far more price elastic. There is no evidence to suggest that this is true. Examples given in textbooks, such as salt and matches, have low price elasticities because they have few good substitutes. In the case of Tippex, its manufacturers would long ago have raised its price substantially if it believed that price had little impact on demand for its product.

QUESTION 5 In 1987, the Courage brewery put up the cost of beer supplied to its pubs. In response the landlord of the Woodman pub in Wednesbury cut the price of a pint of lager by 2p to 72p a pint when other local pubs were putting their prices up to 76p. He calculated that he would need to sell 25 per cent more beer if he were not to make a loss by price cutting.

(a) What would be the elasticity of demand for beer if the landlord of the Woodman pub succeeded in selling 25 per cent more beer?
(b) Using the concept of elasticity, explain whether or not you think he would succeed in avoiding a loss by his strategy.

Key terms

Price elasticity of demand - the responsiveness of changes in quantity demanded to changes in price, measured by the formula:

$$\frac{P}{Q} \times \frac{\Delta Q}{\Delta P}$$

Elastic demand - where the price elasticity of demand is greater than 1. The responsiveness of demand is proportionally greater than the change in price. Demand is infinitely elastic if price elasticity of demand is infinity.
Inelastic demand - where the price elasticity of demand is less than 1. The responsiveness of demand is proportionally less than the change in price. Demand is infinitely inelastic if price elasticity of demand is zero.
Unitary elasticity - where the value of price elasticity of demand is 1. The responsiveness of demand is proportionally equal to the change in price.

Applied economics

The elasticity of demand for oil

Throughout the 1950s and 1960s, oil was a cheap fuel. Indeed the price of oil fell from approximately $1.70 a barrel in 1950 to $1.30 a barrel in 1970 as supply increased at a faster rate than demand. The early 1970s saw a reversal of this trend. Demand increased more rapidly than supply as the world economy boomed and policy makers became increasingly convinced that oil would remain a cheap and efficient energy source. By 1973, the price of a barrel of oil had risen to approximately $3.

In November 1973, politics in the Middle East was to catapult the oil market into the world headlines. The Egyptians launched an attack on Israel on the day of Yom Kippur, the Jewish equivalent to Christmas. Other middle eastern states, such as Saudi Arabia, gave support to their Arab neighbours by threatening to cut off oil supplies to any country which gave support to Israel. With an existing tight market, the result was an explosion in the price of oil. The war was soon over but its economic fall-out was not lost on OPEC, the Organisation for Petroleum Exporting Countries. OPEC, whose members at the time supplied over 60 per cent of world demand for oil, organised a system of quotas amongst themselves, fixing limits on how much each member could produce. By slightly cutting back on pre-1973 production levels, they were able to quadruple the price of oil to $12 a barrel in 1974, as shown in Figure 8.5.

The reason why OPEC could engineer this massive price rise was because the demand for oil was price inelastic in the short run. Oil consumers had invested heavily in capital equipment such as oil-fired heating systems and petrol-driven cars. In the short term, there were no cheap alternative substitutes. Car owners, for instance, did not suddenly change their cars for more fuel efficient models because the price of petrol at the pumps

increased. Hence the quadrupling of the price of oil (a 300 per cent increase) only led to a 5 per cent fall in world demand for oil (i.e. the price elasticity of demand for oil in the short term was 0.016).

In the longer term, consumers were able to replace oil-powered equipment. Cars became far more fuel-efficient. Homeowners insulated their houses. In the UK, the bottom dropped out of the market for oil-fired heating systems. As a consequence, as Figure 8.6 shows, when the demand for oil began to grow again in 1976, it was at a slower rate than in the early 1970s.

In 1978, the Shah of Iran was toppled and was replaced by an Islamic fundamentalist government led by the Ayatollah Khomeini. Iran was a major oil producer and the Islamic revolution and subsequent war between Iran and Iraq severely disrupted supplies from these two countries. OPEC used this opportunity to tighten supply again. With highly inelastic demand, the price rose from $12 a barrel in 1978 to $37 a barrel in 1981. Total world demand, which peaked in 1979 at approximately 63 million barrels per day, fell to a low of 58 million barrels per day in 1982 before resuming its growth.

In August 1990, political events in the Middle East yet again rocked the world price of oil. Iraq's invasion of Kuwait and the subsequent United Nations embargo on trade from Iraq and Kuwait meant that there was a significant fall in oil available for sale on world markets. Within weeks, oil prices rose from approximately $18 a barrel to $30. At this stage, it cannot be said whether this new price will be sustainable in the long run.

It is difficult to calculate the long term elasticity of demand for oil exactly because there are so many other variables affecting the demand for oil, many of which change over time. Figure 8.7 gives some indication of what has happened to the demand for oil if increases in

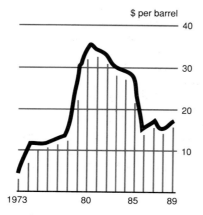

Figure 8.5 *Oil price.: Saudi Light till 1980 and Brent since then*

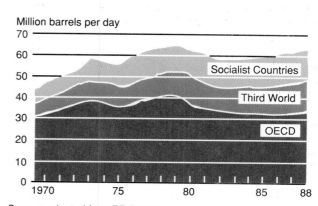

Source: adapted from BP figures.

Figure 8.6 *Consumption: million barrels per day*

income in western economies are discounted. Following the first oil price shock of 1973-4, the demand for oil per $1 000 of income declined from 1973 to 1976. Then it stabilised between 1976 and 1979 as the price of oil stabilised. Demand then fell from 1979 in response to the second oil price shock of 1978-80 and only bottomed out in 1985. Since 1985 demand has slightly increased in response to the fall in oil prices. Hence, as economic theory would predict, the demand for oil is sensitive to its price in the long run.

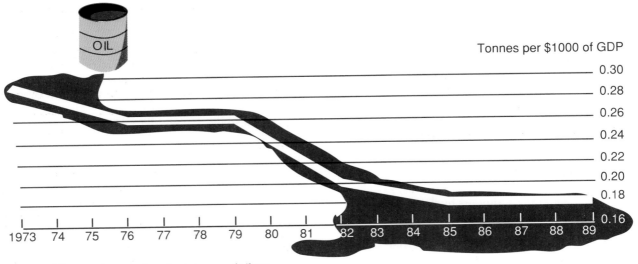

Tonnes per $1000 of GDP

Figure 8.7 *Oil use and economic output: tonnes of oil per $1,000 of GDP in OECD*

Source: adapted IEA, OECD, FT estimates.

DISCOUNTING BOOKS

Most books in the UK are sold under the Net Book Agreement. Bookshops are forced to sell books at a price decided upon by publishers. Terry Maher, the chairman of Pentos which owns Dillons the book shop chain, has long been a critic of the system. In 1989, he took one step towards challenging the system by offering reductions of between 20 and 26 per cent on 8 titles in the important pre-Christmas season. Sales of those titles at Dillons increased five-fold, against a backdrop of a 19 per cent year-on-year increase in book sales generally.

1. (a) Estimate the price elasticity of demand for the 8 titles mentioned in the data.
   (b) Why can your answer only be an estimation?

2. Explain whether you would expect the price elasticity of demand for a 20 per cent reduction in price on one title to be higher or lower than for a 20 per cent reduction in the price of books in general.

Summary

1. Income elasticity of demand measures the responsiveness of quantity demanded to changes in income.
2. Cross elasticity of demand measures the responsiveness of quantity demanded of one good to the change in price of another good.
3. Price elasticity of supply measures the responsiveness of quantity supplied to changes in price.
4. The value of elasticity of supply is determined by the availability of substitutes and by time factors.
5. The price elasticity of demand for a good will determine whether a change in the price of a good results in a change in expenditure on the good.

Income elasticity of demand

The demand for a good will change if consumers' incomes change. INCOME ELASTICITY OF DEMAND is a measure of that change. If the demand for housing increases by 20 per cent when incomes increase by 5 per cent, then the income elasticity of demand would be said to be positive and relatively high. If the demand for food were unchanged when income rose, then income elasticity would be zero. A fall in demand for a good when income rises gives a negative value to income elasticity of demand.

The formula for measuring income elasticity of demand is:

$$\frac{\text{percentage change in quantity demanded}}{\text{percentage change in income}}$$

So the numerical value of income elasticity of a 20 per cent rise in demand for housing when incomes rise by 5 per cent is +20/+5 or +4. The number is positive because both the 20 per cent and the 5 per cent are positive. On the other hand, a rise in income of 10 per cent which led to a fall in quantity demanded of a product of 5 per cent would have an income elasticity of -5/+10 or -½. The minus sign in -5 shows the fall in quantity demanded of the product. Examples of items with a high income elasticity of demand are holidays and recreational activities, whereas washing up liquid tends to have a low income elasticity of demand.

Just as with price elasticity, it is sometimes easier to use alternative formulae to calculate income elasticity of demand. The above formula is equivalent to:

$$\frac{\Delta Q}{Q} \div \frac{\Delta Y}{Y}$$

where Δ is change, Q is quantity demanded and Y is income. Rearranging the formula gives another two alternatives:

$$\frac{Y}{Q} \times \frac{\Delta Q}{\Delta Y} \quad \text{or} \quad \frac{\Delta Q}{Q} \times \frac{Y}{\Delta Y}$$

Examples of the calculation of income elasticity of demand are given in Table 9.1.

Table 9.1 *Calculation of income elasticity of demand*

Original quantity demanded	New quantity demanded	Original income (£)	New income (£)	$\frac{\Delta Q}{Q} \div \frac{\Delta P}{P}$	Numerical value
20	25	16	18	5/20÷2/16	+2
100	200	20	25	100/100÷5/20	+4
50	40	25	30	-10/50÷5/25	-1
60	60	80	75	0/60÷-5/80	0
60	40	27	30	-20/60÷3/27	-3

QUESTION 1
Table 9.2

£

	Original		New	
	Quantity demanded	Income	Quantity demanded	Income
(a)	100	10	120	14
(b)	15	6	20	7
(c)	50	25	40	35
(d)	12	100	15	125
(e)	200	10	250	11
(f)	25	20	30	18

Calculate the income elasticity of demand from the data in Table 9.2.

Cross elasticity of demand

The quantity demanded of a particular good varies according to the price of other goods. In unit 7 it was argued that a rise in price of a good such as beef would increase the quantity demanded of a substitute such as pork. On the other hand, a rise in price of a good such as cheese would lead to a fall in the quantity demanded of a complement such as macaroni. CROSS ELASTICITY OF DEMAND measures the responsiveness of the quantity demanded of one good to changes in the price of another.

For instance, it is a measure of the extent to which demand for pork increases when the price of beef goes up; or the extent to which the demand for macaroni falls when the price of cheese increases.

The formula for measuring cross elasticity of demand for good X is:

percentage change in quantity demanded of good X

_____

percentage change in price of another good Y

Two goods which are substitutes will have a positive cross elasticity. An increase (positive) in the price of one good, such as gas, leads to an increase (positive) in the quantity demanded of a substitute such as electricity. Two goods which are complements will have a negative cross elasticity. An increase (positive) in the price of one good such as sand leads to a fall (negative) in demand of a complement such as cement. The cross elasticity of two goods which have little relationship to each other would be zero. For instance, a rise in the price of cars of 10 per cent is likely to have no effect (i.e. 0 per cent change) on the demand for Tippex.

As with price and income elasticity, it is sometimes more convenient to use alternative formulae for cross elasticity of demand. These are:

$$\text{Cross elasticity of good X} = \frac{\Delta Q_X}{Q_X} \div \frac{\Delta P_Y}{P_Y}$$

or

$$\frac{P_Y}{Q_X} \times \frac{\Delta Q_X}{\Delta P_Y}$$

QUESTION 2 Explain what value you would put on the cross elasticity of (a) gas for electricity; (b) tennis shorts for tennis rackets; (c) luxury cars for petrol; (d) paper for tights.

Price elasticity of supply

Price elasticity of demand measures the responsiveness of changes in quantity demanded to changes in price. Equally, the responsiveness of quantity supplied to changes in price can also be measured: this is called PRICE ELASTICITY OF SUPPLY. The formula for measuring the price elasticity of supply is:

percentage change in quantity supplied

_____

percentage change in price

This is equivalent to:

$$\frac{\Delta Q}{Q} \div \frac{\Delta P}{P}$$

or

$$\frac{P}{Q} \times \frac{\Delta Q}{\Delta P}$$

where Q is quantity supplied and P is price.

The supply curve is upward sloping (i.e. an increase in price leads to an increase in quantity supplied and vice versa). Therefore price elasticity of supply will be positive because the top and bottom of the formula will be either both positive or both negative.

As with price elasticity of demand, different ranges of elasticity are given different names. Price elasticity of supply is:

- **perfectly inelastic** (zero) if there is no response in supply to a change in price;
- **inelastic** (between zero and one) if there is a less than proportionate response in supply to a change in price;
- **unitary** (one) if the percentage change in quantity supplied equals the percentage change in price;
- **elastic** (between one and infinity) if there is a more than proportionate response in supply to a change in price;
- **perfectly elastic** (infinite) if producers are prepared to supply any amount at a given price.

These various elasticities are shown in Figure 9.1.

It should be noted that any straight line supply curve passing through the origin has an elasticity of supply equal to 1. This is best understood if we take the formula:

$$\frac{P}{Q} \times \frac{\Delta Q}{\Delta P}$$

$\Delta Q / \Delta P$ is the inverse of (i.e. 1 divided by) the slope of the line, whilst P/Q, assuming that the line passes through the origin, is the slope of the line. The two multiplied together must always equal 1.

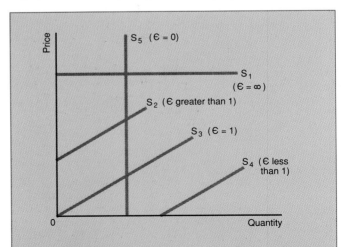

Figure 9.1 *Elasticity of supply*
The elasticity of supply of a straight line supply curve varies depending upon the gradient of the line and whether it passes through the origin.

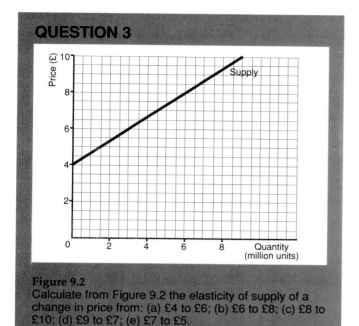

QUESTION 3

Figure 9.2
Calculate from Figure 9.2 the elasticity of supply of a change in price from: (a) £4 to £6; (b) £6 to £8; (c) £8 to £10; (d) £9 to £7; (e) £7 to £5.

Determinants of elasticity of supply

As with price elasticity of demand, there are two factors which determine supply elasticity across a wide range of products.

Availability of substitutes Substitutes here are not consumer substitutes but producer substitutes. These are goods which a producer can easily produce as alternatives. For instance, one model of a car is a good producer substitute for another model in the same range because the car manufacturer can easily switch resources on its production line. On the other hand, carrots are not substitutes for cars. The farmer cannot easily switch from the production of carrots to the production of cars. If a product has many substitutes then producers can quickly and easily alter the pattern of production if its price rises or falls. Hence its elasticity will be relatively high. But if a product has few or no substitutes, then producers will find it difficult to respond flexibly to variations in price. If there is a fall in price, a producer may have no alternative but either to carry on producing much the same quantity as before or withdrawing from the market. Price elasticity of supply is therefore low.

Time The shorter the time period, the more difficult firms find it to switch from making one product to another. During the late 1970s when skateboarding first became a craze, the supply of skateboards was relatively inelastic. Suppliers were overwhelmed with orders and were initially unable to expand production sufficiently to cope with demand. Supply elasticity was therefore low. In the

longer term new firms came into the market, existing firms expanded their production facilities and price elasticity of supply rose. This has also been the case with videos, personal stereos and CD players.

Price elasticity of demand and total expenditure

Price elasticity of demand and changes in total expenditure on a product are linked. Total expenditure can be calculated by multiplying price and quantity:

Total expenditure = quantity purchased x price

For instance, if you bought 5 apples at 10 pence each, your total expenditure would be 50 pence. If the price of apples went up, you might spend more, less, or the same, on apples depending upon your price elasticity of demand for apples. Assume that the price of apples went up 40 per cent to 14p each. You might react by buying fewer apples. If you now buy 4 apples (i.e. a fall in demand of 20 per cent), the price elasticity of demand is 20 ÷ 40 or ½. Your expenditure on apples will also rise (from 50 pence to 56 pence). If you buy two apples (i.e. a fall in quantity demanded of 60 per cent), your elasticity of demand is 60 ÷ 40 or 1½ and your expenditure on apples will fall (from 50 pence to 28 pence).

These relationships are what should be expected. If the percentage change in price is larger than the percentage change in quantity demanded (i.e. elasticity is less than 1, or inelastic), then expenditure will rise when prices rise. If the percentage change in price is smaller than the percentage change in quantity demanded (i.e. elasticity is greater than 1 or elastic), then spending will fall as prices rise. If the percentage change in price is the same as the change in quantity demanded (i.e. elasticity is unity), expenditure will remain unchanged because the percentage rise in price will be equal and opposite to the percentage fall in demand.

QUESTION 4 The following firms wish to increase revenue from sales of their products. Explain whether you think they should increase or decrease price: (a) British Rail on its commuter routes; (b) Mars on Mars Bars; (c) Father Christmas in a big department store at Christmas time; (d) Heinz on their baked beans.

Key terms

Income elasticity of demand - a measure of the responsiveness of quantity demanded to a change in income. It is measured by dividing the percentage change in quantity demanded by the percentage change in income.
Cross elasticity of demand - a measure of the responsiveness of quantity demanded of one good to a change in price of another good. It is measured by dividing the percentage change in quantity demanded of one good by the percentage change in price of the other good.
Price elasticity of supply - a measure of the responsiveness of quantity supplied to a change in price. It is measured by dividing the percentage change in quantity supplied by the percentage change in price

Applied economics

Cross elasticities of demand for food

Many foods are substitutes for each other: tea is a substitute for coffee; oranges are substitutes for apples; butter is a substitute for margarine. Economic theory would suggest that these goods would therefore have a positive cross elasticity of demand. An increase in the price of one good would lead to an increase in demand of the substitute good, whilst a fall in price of one good would lead to a fall in demand of another.

Evidence from the General Household Survey gives some support for this. Table 9.3 shows estimates of the cross elasticity of demand for 10 foods, grouped into four categories. The estimates are based on UK data for 1981-88. The cross elasticities are shown in black.

The cross elasticities of demand of butter for margarine and margarine for butter are 0.06 and 0.08 respectively. So a 10 per cent increase in the price of margarine will lead to a 0.6 per cent increase in the demand for butter, whilst a 10 per cent increase in the price of butter will lead to a 0.8 per cent increase in the demand for margarine.

Of the three fruits in Table 9.3, apples and pears have a relatively high cross elasticity. Pears seem to be a good substitute for apples. A 10 per cent increase in the price of apples leads to a 2.8 per cent rise in the quantity demanded of pears. Interestingly though, apples are less good a substitute for pears since a 10 per cent increase in the price of pears results in only a 0.5 per cent increase in the demand for apples. The data would suggest that apples and oranges are not substitutes at all since their cross elasticities are negative at - 0.22 and - 0.09. Similarly pears and oranges have negative cross elasticities.

One explanation of the negative cross elasticities in Table 9.3 would be in terms of income and substitution effects. For instance, a rise in the price of coffee will lead to more tea being demanded because tea is now relatively cheaper (the substitution effect of the price rise). However, the real income of consumers (what they can buy with their money income) will have declined. Hence they buy less coffee (a drop of 1.4 per cent for every 10 per cent rise in price) but also less tea (the income effect). The data would suggest that this income effect is more significant than the substitution effect in the case of tea when the price of coffee increases.

Table 9.3 also shows (in red) the price elasticities of demand for the 10 food products. The demand for butter, margarine, tea, instant coffee and apples is price inelastic, whilst the demand for beef and veal, mutton and lamb, pork, oranges and pears is price elastic.

Table 9.3 *Estimates of price and cross-price elasticities of demand for certain foods, 1981-1988*

	Elasticity with respect to the price of				Elasticity with respect to the price of		
	Tea	Instant coffee			Beef and veal	Mutton and lamb	Pork
Tea	**-0.33**	-0.01		Beef and veal	**-1.23**	0.04	0.02
Instant coffee	-0.01	**-0.14**		Mutton and lamb	0.10	**-1.75**	-0.11
				Pork	0.05	-0.11	**-1.57**

	Elasticity with respect to the price of				Elasticity with respect to the price of		
	Butter	Margarine			Oranges	Apples	Pears
Butter	**-0.38**	0.06		Oranges	**-1.44**	-0.22	-0.11
Margarine	0.08	**-0.29**		Apples	-0.09	**-0.19**	0.05
				Pears	-0.28	0.28	**-1.70**

Source: adapted from HMSO, *Household Food Consumption and Expenditure.*

Data question

ELASTICITIES

Table 9.4 *Estimates of price elasticities of demand for selected household foods, 1981-1988*

	Estimated price elasticity
Liquid wholemilk and low fat milks	-0.00
Cheese	-1.19
Carcass meat	-1.17
Frozen convenience meat and meat products	-0.96
Fresh potatoes	-0.16
Frozen peas	-0.87
Fresh fruit	-0.77
Bread	-0.16

Source: HMSO, *Household Food Consumption and Expenditure.*

1. **Suggest reasons why some foods in Table 9.4 are more price elastic than others.**

2. **An increase in the price of which foods would be most likely to lead to**
   (i) the greatest and
   (ii) the least change in household expenditure?
   Explain your answer.

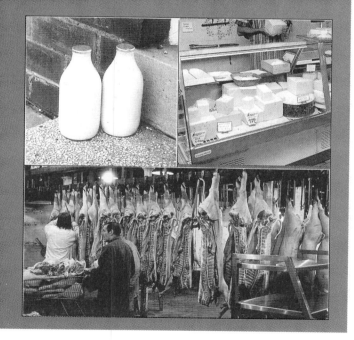

Summary

1. An increase in income will lead to an increase in demand for normal goods but a fall in demand for inferior goods.
2. Normal goods have a positive income elasticity whilst inferior goods have a negative elasticity.
3. A Giffen good is one where a rise in price leads to a rise in quantity demanded. This occurs because the positive substitution effect of the price change is outweighed by the negative income effect.
4. Upward sloping demand curves may occur if the good is a Giffen good, if it has snob or speculative appeal or if consumers judge quality by the price of a product.

Normal and inferior goods

The pattern of demand is likely to change when income changes. It would be reasonable to assume that consumers will increase their demand for most goods when their income increases. Goods for which this is the case are called NORMAL GOODS.

However, an increase in income will result in a fall in demand for other goods. These goods are called INFERIOR GOODS. There will be a fall in demand because consumers will react to an increase in their income by purchasing products which are perceived to be of better quality. Commonly quoted examples of inferior goods are:

■ bread - consumers switch from this cheap, filling food to more expensive meat or convenience foods as their incomes increase;

■ margarine - consumers switch from margarine to butter, although this has become less true recently with greater health awareness;

■ bus transport - consumers switch from buses to their own cars when they can afford to buy their own car.

A good can be both a normal and an inferior good depending upon the level of income. Bread may be a normal good for people on low incomes (i.e. they buy more bread when their income increases. But it may be an inferior good for higher income earners).

Normal and inferior goods are shown on Figure 10.1. D_1 is the demand curve for a normal good. It is upward sloping because demand increases as income increases. D_2 is the demand curve for an inferior good. It is downward sloping, showing that demand falls as income increases. D_3 is the demand curve for a good which is normal at low levels of income, but is inferior at higher levels of income.

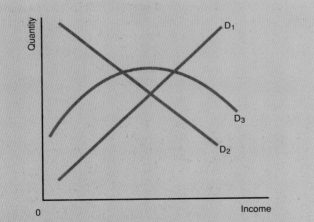

Figure 10.1 *Normal and inferior goods*
On the quantity-income diagram, a normal good such as D_1, has an upward sloping curve, whilst an inferior good such as D_2 has a downward sloping curve. D_3 shows a good which is normal at low levels of income but is inferior at higher levels of income.

QUESTION 1

Table 10.1 *Estimated household food consumption in Great Britain*

	Ounces per person per week		
	1976	1981	1986
Liquid milk	5.05	4.43	4.12
Sugar	12.2	11.08	8.04
Chicken	6.00	7.3	7.3
Canned tomatoes	1.06	1.52	1.82
Bread	33.17	31.23	30.79
Pickles and sauces	1.66	2.01	2.18

Source: CSO, *Annual Abstract of Statistics*.

Household incomes rose between each of the years 1976, 1981 and 1986. Assuming that all other factors remained constant, which of the goods shown in Table 10.1 are normal goods and which are inferior?

Inferior goods and income elasticity

Inferior goods can be distinguished from normal goods by their income elasticity of demand. The formula for measuring income elasticity is:

$$\frac{\text{percentage change in quantity demanded}}{\text{percentage change in income}}$$

A normal good will always have a positive income elasticity because quantity demanded and income either both increase (giving a plus divided by a plus) or both decrease (giving a minus divided by a minus). An inferior good, however, will always have a negative elasticity because the signs on the top and bottom of the formula will always be opposite (a plus divided by a minus or a minus divided by a plus giving a minus answer in both cases).

For instance, if the demand for bread falls by 2 per cent when incomes rise by 10 per cent then it is an inferior good. Its income elasticity is -2/+10 or -0.2.

Giffen goods

A GIFFEN GOOD is a special sort of inferior good. Alfred Marshall (1842-1924), an eminent economist and author of a best selling textbook of his day, claimed that another eminent economist, Sir Robert Giffen (1837-1910), had observed that the consumption of bread increased as its price increased. The argument was that bread was a staple food for low income consumers. A rise in its price would not deter people from buying as much as before. But 'poor' people would now have so little extra money to spend on meat or other luxury foods that they would abandon their demand for these and instead buy more bread to fill up their stomachs. The result was that a rise in the price of bread led to a rise in the demand for bread.

Another way of explaining this phenomenon is to use the concepts of income and substitution effects (☞ unit 13 for a more detailed discussion). When a good changes in price, the quantity demanded will be changed by the sum of the substitution effect and the income effect.

■ **Substitution effect.** If the price of a good rises, consumers will buy less of that good and more of others because it is now relatively more expensive than other goods. If the price of a good falls, consumers will buy more of that good and less of others. These changes in quantity demanded are known as the substitution effect of a price change.

■ **Income effect.** If the price of a good rises, the real income of consumers will fall. They will not be able to buy the same basket of goods and services as before. Consumers can react to this fall in real income in one of two ways. If the good is a normal good, they will buy less of the good. If the good is an inferior good,

they will buy more of the goods. These changes in quantity demanded caused by a change in real income are known as the income effect of the price change.

For a normal good the substitution effect and the income effect both work in the same direction. A rise in price leads to a fall in quantity demanded because the relative price of the good has risen. It also leads to a fall in quantity demanded because consumers' real incomes have now fallen. So a rise in price will always lead to a fall in quantity demanded, and vice versa.

For an inferior good, the substitution effect and income effect work in opposite directions. A rise in price leads to a fall in quantity demanded because the relative price of the good has risen. But it leads to a rise in quantity demanded because consumers' real incomes have fallen. However, the substitution effect outweighs the income effect because overall it is still true for an inferior good that a rise in price leads to an overall fall in quantity demanded.

A Giffen good is a special type of inferior good. A rise in price leads to a fall in quantity demanded because of the substitution effect but a rise in quantity demanded because of the income effect. However, the income effect outweighs the substitution effect, leading to rises in quantity demanded. For instance, if a 10p rise in the price of a standard loaf leads to a 4 per cent fall in the demand for bread because of the substitution effect, but a 10 per cent rise in demand because of the income effect, then the net effect will be a 6 per cent rise in the demand for bread.

The relationship between normal, inferior and Giffen goods and their income and substitution effects is summarised in Figure 10.2.

Giffen goods are an economic curiosity. In theory they could exist, but no economist has ever found an example of such a good in practice. There is no evidence even that Sir Robert Giffen ever claimed that bread had an upward sloping demand curve - it crept into textbooks via Alfred Marshall and has remained there ever since!

Type of good	Effect on quantity demanded of a rise in price		
	Substitution effect	Income effect	Total effect
Normal good	Fall	Fall	Fall
Inferior good	Fall	Rise	Fall because substitution effect > income effect
Giffen good	Fall	Rise	Rise because substitution effect < income effect

Figure 10.2 *Substitution and income effects on quantity demanded of a rise in price for normal, inferior and Giffen goods*

QUESTION 2
Table 10.2

Good	Change in price (pence per unit)	Change in quantity demanded as a result of	
		income effect	substitution effect
Bacon	+10	+10%	-8%
Bus rides	+15	+2%	-5%
Jeans	-100	+1%	+5%
Baked beans	-2	-1%	+4%
Compact discs	-150	+4%	+3%

An economist claims that she has observed the effects detailed in Table 10.2 resulting from a change in price of a product. Which of these products are normal goods, which are inferior and which are Giffen goods?

Upward sloping demand curves

Demand curves are usually downward sloping. However, there are possible reasons why the demand curve for some goods may be upward sloping.

Giffen goods Giffen goods, a type of inferior good, have been discussed above.

Goods with snob appeal Some goods are bought mainly because they confer status on the buyer. Examples might be diamonds, fur coats or large cars. The argument is that these goods are demanded because few people can afford to buy them because their price is high. If large numbers of people could afford to buy them, then the demand (the quantity buyers would buy) would be low. This might be true for some individual consumers, but economists have not found any proof that it is true for markets as a whole. Whilst some might buy diamonds only because they are expensive, the majority of consumers would buy more diamonds if their price fell because they like diamonds. So there must be some doubt as to whether snob appeal does give rise to upward sloping demand curves.

Speculative goods Throughout most of 1987, stock markets worldwide boomed. Share prices were at an all time high and the demand for shares was high too. But in October 1987 share prices slumped on average between 20 and 30 per cent. Overnight the demand for shares fell. This could be taken as evidence of an upward sloping demand curve. The higher the price of shares, the higher the demand because buyers associate high share prices with large speculative gains in the future. However, most economists would argue that what is being seen is a **shift** in the demand curve. The demand curve is drawn on the assumption that expectations of future gain are constant. When share prices or the price of any speculative good fall, buyers revise their expectations downwards. At any given share price they are willing to buy fewer shares, which pushes the demand curve backwards to the left.

Quality goods Some consumers judge quality by price. They automatically assume that a higher priced good must be of better quality than a similar lower priced good. Hence, the higher the price the greater the quantity demanded. As with snob appeal goods, this may be true for some individuals but there is no evidence to suggest that this is true for consumers as a whole. There have been examples where goods that have been re-packaged, heavily advertised and increased in price, have increased their sales. But this is an example of a shift to the right in the demand curve caused by advertising and repackaging rather than of an upward sloping demand curve.

In conclusion, it can be seen that there are various reasons why in theory demand curves might be upward sloping. But few, if any, such goods have been found in reality. The downward sloping demand curve seems to be true of nearly all goods.

QUESTION 3
Before the Stock Market crash of October 1987 which wiped out approximately 25 per cent of the value of shares on the London Stock Exchange, the number of shares traded were considerably more than after the crash. For instance, on 29 September 1987, the FT ordinary share index (a measure of the average price of shares listed on the Stock Exchange) stood at 1853.7 and 731.7 million shares were bought and sold. On 27 September 1990, the Ordinary Share Index had fallen to 1535.7 whilst the number of shares traded was 376.7 million.

To what extent can this data be used as evidence to support the existence of an upward sloping demand curve for shares?

Key terms

Normal good - a good where demand increases when income increases (i.e. it has a positive income elasticity of demand).
Inferior good - a good where demand falls when income increases (i.e. it has a negative income elasticity of demand).
Giffen good - a special type of inferior good where demand increases when price increases.

Applied economics

Income elasticities and inferior goods

Table 10.3 gives estimates of the income elasticity of demand for food in the UK. Food has an income elasticity of 0.0 and therefore could be seen as a necessity. This compares with many other goods or services which have higher income elasticities and could be classed as luxuries. For instance, Deaton (1975) estimated that the income elasticity of demand for wines and spirits was 2.59, for recreational goods was 1.98 and for expenditure abroad was 1.14.

Nine of the foods in Table 10.3 are inferior goods (i.e. have a negative income elasticity).

■ Margarine is a traditional textbook example of an inferior good. As incomes rise, households buy less margarine. Interestingly, though, butter too is an inferior good according to the data. This is likely to be due to recent awareness of the dangers of eating too much fat.

■ Rising incomes enable poorer households to switch from cheap filling foods such as bread, potatoes and liquid milk to a more varied diet of more expensive food products.

■ Processed cheese is likely to be replaced by natural cheese products as incomes rise.

■ Tea has a surprisingly large negative income elasticity. As incomes rise, households substitute a greater variety of drinks for tea which, per cup, is very cheap. One very good substitute is coffee, which has a positive income elasticity.

■ It is more difficult to explain why eggs and bacon should be inferior goods. However, it could be that eggs and bacon are cheap substitutes for more expensive meats, or that the traditional British breakfast is more common in low income households.

The category of food with the highest income elasticity is fruit juices, an expensive but increasingly popular item of expenditure amongst the more affluent households in the economy.

Table 10.3 *Income elasticities of demand for household foods, 1988*

	Elasticity
Milk and cream	0.02
Liquid wholemilk	-0.27
Cheese	0.25
of which	
Natural	0.29
Processed	-0.17
Chicken, uncooked	0.06
Other poultry, uncooked	0.31
Bacon and ham, uncooked	-0.34
Eggs	-0.57
Butter	-0.09
Margarine	-0.49
Fresh potatoes	-0.53
Fresh fruit	0.53
Fruit juices	0.73
Bread	-0.28
Tea	-0.68
Coffee (instant)	0.08
All foods	0.00

Source: adapted from HMSO, *Household Food Consumption and Expenditure*, 1988.

Data question

1. Compare the likely relative incomes of the four types of household in Table 10.4.
2. Explain which of the goods in the data are likely to have (a) the highest and (b) the lowest income elasticities of demand.
3. Are there any inferior goods listed in the data? Explain your answer.

Table 10.4 *Households with durable goods: by economic status of head of household, 1987*

Source: CSO, *Social Trends*.

Great Britain				Percentages and numbers
	Economic status of head of household			
	Working	Unemployed	Economically inactive	All households
Percentage of households with:				
Deep-freeze	85	60	59	74
Washing machine	91	78	72	84
Tumble drier	50	31	22	39
Microwave oven	41	20	15	30
Dishwasher	12	2	3	8
Telephone	90	55	79	84
Television				
Colour	94	82	86	91
Black & white only	5	14	12	8
Video	63	41	19	46
Home computer	27	16	4	18
Sample size (= 100%) (numbers)	5,819	539	3,622	9,980

Summary

1. The cobweb theorem is a dynamic model of price and output determination.
2. It assumes that suppliers base their output decisions on the price received in the previous time period.
3. Cobwebs can be divergent, convergent or stable.
4. The cobweb theorem predicts that markets do not necessarily converge to their long term equilibrium position.

Static market models

A **static** model is one where time is not a variable. Time is said to be an **exogenous variable**, a variable which is not determined within the model. The theory of demand, supply and price outlined in unit 6 is an example of a static model.

However it was pointed out that there is a tendency for people who use this model to make a hidden assumption: that there are market forces at work which will move the market from a point where demand does not equal supply to an equilibrium position where the two are equal. To make this assumption explicit would require a more complicated **dynamic** model of price determination, one where time was an **endogenous variable** (i.e. included in the model).

Economists have devised many dynamic models of the market, but in this unit we will consider only one such model, called the COBWEB THEORY.

The assumptions of the cobweb model

The cobweb theory was devised by an American economist, Mordecai Ezekial, in the 1930s. He used it to try to explain why there were price oscillations in the pig market in Chicago.

He postulated that farmers based their supply decisions upon the price they received in the previous time period. Mathematically this can be expressed as:

$$Q_t = f (P_{t-1})$$

QUESTION 1

Supply is given by the following equation:

$$Q_t = 0.5 P_{t-1} - 10$$

where Q_t is quantity supplied in time period t, and P_{t-1} is price in time period t-1.

What is the level of quantity supplied in 1995 if price in 1994 were:
(a) £60;
(b) £100;
(c) £300;
(d) £250?

This says that the quantity supplied in time period t (Q_t) is a function of (i.e. varies with) the price received in the previous time period t-1 (P_{t-1}).

The cobweb diagram

The market for carrots can be used to illustrate the workings of the cobweb model. It takes time to plant and grow carrots for sale on the market. Because of this time lag, farmers are assumed within the model to base their decision as to how many carrots to grow this season on the price they received last season. So the supply in 1995 would be dependent upon the prices received by farmers in 1994.

In Figure 11.1, the market is in long run equilibrium at a price of P_0 and quantity Q_0. Assume that in year 1 a severe attack of carrot fly destroys much of the crop such that only Q_1 is available for sale. Consumers will pay a price of P_1 for Q_1 of carrots (remember the demand curve shows how much buyers will purchase at any given price). At the beginning of year 2 farmers have to decide how many carrots to grow. According to the cobweb theorem, they will base their decision on last year's prices. Hence, given that the price was P_1 last year and given that the supply curve S remains unchanged, farmers in year 2 will decide to grow Q_2 of carrots. But when they come to

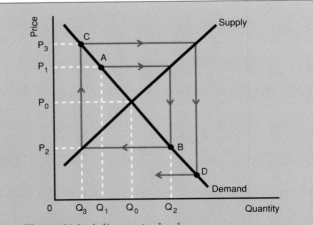

Figure 11.1 *A divergent cobweb*
Output is based upon price received in the previous time period. So short term equilibrium, starting at the point A, moves to B, then to C and then to D, steadily moving away from the stable equilibrium price of P_0.

sell them they will find that buyers are not prepared to buy Q_2 of carrots at a price of P_1. Farmers cannot store carrots for several years. They have to sell them within 12 months or destroy them. Therefore the price of carrots will have to fall to P_2 to clear the market of Q_2 carrots. At the beginning of year 3, farmers will base their planting decision on the very low price of P_2 obtained the previous year. They will therefore only plant Q_3 of carrots and be pleasantly surprised at the end of the year to receive a price of P_3 for them. In year 4, carrot planting will be higher than in any of the previous years and consequently prices will plummet at harvest time.

The path shown in Figure 11.1, from point A through to point D, shows a market which is moving further and further away from the long term equilibrium price of P_0 and quantity Q_0. This is called a **divergent cobweb**. However, cobwebs can also be either **convergent** or **stable**. A convergent cobweb is shown in Figure 11.2.

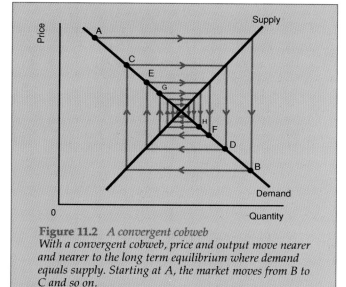

Figure 11.2 *A convergent cobweb*
With a convergent cobweb, price and output move nearer and nearer to the long term equilibrium where demand equals supply. Starting at A, the market moves from B to C and so on.

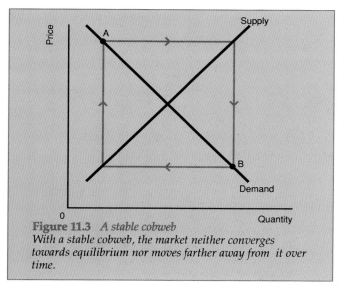

Figure 11.3 *A stable cobweb*
With a stable cobweb, the market neither converges towards equilibrium nor moves farther away from it over time.

Here market forces do act to restore a market to its long run equilibrium position where demand and supply are equal. Figure 11.3 shows a stable cobweb. The market has regular cycles of high prices followed by low prices and there is no tendency for the market either to move nearer the point where demand and supply are equal or to move away from it.

QUESTION 2 Demand and supply are given by the equations:

$$D = 30 - 0.75 P_t$$
$$S = P_{t-1} - 10$$

where D is quantity demanded, S is quantity supplied, P is price and t is time period t.

(a) Draw the demand and supply curves within the quantity range 0 to 30 and the price range 0 to 40.
(b) Will these equations produce a convergent, divergent or stable cobweb?

Realism of the model

The theory does not suggest that a convergent cobweb is any more likely to occur than a divergent or stable cobweb. However, empirical evidence suggests that divergent cobwebs are not common. Farmers operating in free markets do not base their planting decisions solely on the basis of last year's price. If they did, they would soon learn that it was an inaccurate predictor of current prices. They use more sophisticated techniques, using both past prices and estimates of future supplies from other farmers. Even so, these techniques are unlikely to lead to accurate predictions, especially given the vagaries of the weather and other factors which affect output. Cycles do seem to exist but they are for the most part either stable or convergent. Anyway, many agricultural product markets are regulated by the state in industrialised countries, from rice in Japan to wheat in the USA to beef in the European Community. Such regulation destroys any cobweb-type relationship that might have existed in these markets.

Apart from farming, the cobweb theory is likely to be less relevant since most products are capable of being stored from one time period to the next. If prices fall too low, businesses can within limits refuse to supply to the market, store production and sell in some future time period. Therefore price cycles are more likely to be more convergent in other industries than in an industry such as farming where the possibilities of storage are more limited.

Key terms

Cobweb theorem - a dynamic model of price determination which assumes that output decisions are based upon price received in the previous time period.

Applied economics

The British pig cycle

Table 11.1 *UK pig statistics*

	Total number of pigs on UK farms at June each year (millions)	Price deadweight (£ per kg)
1976	7.9	67
1977	7.8	73
1978	7.7	80
1979	7.9	81
1980	7.8	87
1981	7.8	94
1982	8.0	97
1983	8.2	92
1984	7.7	108
1985	7.9	104
1986	7.9	98
1987	7.9	97
1988	8.0	90

Source: CSO, *Annual Abstract of Statistics.*

The UK pig industry suffers from price volatility. As can be seen from Table 11.1, the average deadweight price of pigs per kg ranged from a low of £67 in 1976 to a high of £108 in 1984. Some commentators have argued that there is a 'pig cycle' with peaks and troughs occurring about every five years.

The cycle is caused by the investment decisions of pig farmers. When prices are high, pig farmers invest in their pig herds. High prices generate the profits needed to do this and make farmers optimistic about future prices. It takes about 2 to 3 years for piglets to grow and come to market. Then there is a price slump due to this increased supply. Farmers suffer losses, cut back on investment and may even be forced to slaughter young pigs early in order to stave off bankruptcy. This generates a shortage of pigs, leading to rising prices. The cycle then starts all over again.

Does Table 11.1 give any support to this theory? 1988 was a year of depression for pig prices with the number of pigs on UK farms at a peak of 8 million. This should, according to the theory, have been preceded 2 to 3 years earlier by high prices. Indeed, in 1984-5, record prices were achieved for pigs. The number of pigs on UK farms also increased in 1984-5 from 7.7 to 7.9 million. 1989-90, not shown on the table, saw increased pig prices as many farmers pulled out of pig farming.

However, the data prior to 1985 are more difficult to analyse. With peak prices in 1984-5, the 5 year cycle theory would predict that prices would peak and herds would be at their lowest around 1979-80. Certainly herd sizes fell to a cyclical low in 1980, but prices increased every year between 1976 and 1982. One problem with the data is that it is expressed at current prices rather than at constant prices. A clearer picture might emerge if the inflationary element of price increases were taken out. What can be said is that in 1980 and 1981 there were substantial percentage price rises at current prices compared to the surrounding years. So even this earlier period of data tends to support the theory that there is a cobweb-type cycle in the UK pig industry.

Data question

WHY THE GOOD TIMES MAY NOT LAST LONG

The late 1970s and early 1980s were painful times for the world's leading chemical companies. They had invested heavily in new plant in the first half of the 1970s when the world economy was growing strongly and the price of oil, the basic raw material for many plastics, was cheap. Then came the two oil crises of 1973-4 and 1978-80. The world economy was plunged into recession and oil prices shot up.

However, profits for the chemical companies slowly began to recover in the mid-1980s as the world economy grew and oil prices fell. By the late 1980s, the industry was enjoying record profits and companies such as Dow Chemicals, Phillips Petroleum and BP were announcing ambitious investment plans. Industry analysts warned

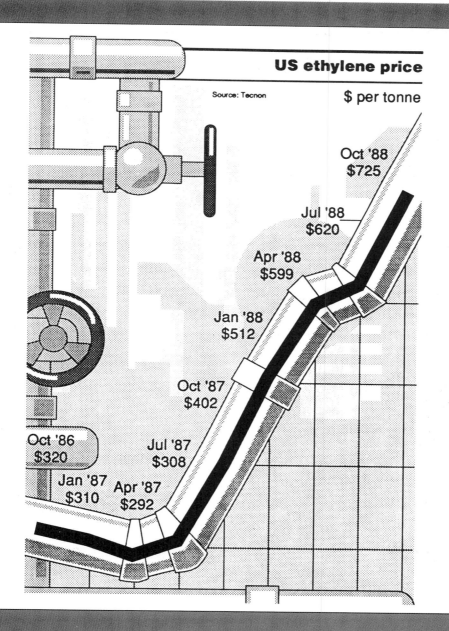

US ethylene price

Source: Tecnon

$ per tonne

Oct '88
$725

Jul '88
$620

Apr '88
$599

Jan '88
$512

Oct '87
$402

Jul '87
$308

Oct '86
$320

Jan '87
$310

Apr '87
$292

Table 11.2 *World production of ethylene*

Million tonnes	US	Western Europe	Japan	Rest of the world*	Total
1985	15.3	13.2	4.4	10.4	43.3
1990 Projection	16.6	14.7	4.7	13.7	49.7
1995 Projection	20.0	17.2	5.3	19.3	61.8

*Not including Communist bloc.

that this boom was almost predestined to be followed by a slump. Even if the world economy continued to grow at a steady pace in the 1990s, the amount of new capacity planned in the late 1980s would lead to a glut of basic chemicals like ethylene in the mid-1990s. The fall in price of basic chemicals would be even larger in the mid-1990s if the world economy were to falter.

Source: *Financial Times*, 6.12. 1988.

1. **How might economic theory explain the behaviour of companies in the world market for basic chemicals such as ethylene?**

Summary

1. Prices of commodities and agricultural products tend to fluctuate more widely than the prices of manufactured goods and services.
2. Governments may impose maximum or minimum prices to regulate a market.
3. Maximum prices can create shortages and black markets.
4. Minimum prices can lead to excess supply and tend to be maintained only at the expense of the taxpayer.
5. Cartels raise prices by restricting output.
6. Buffer stock schemes attempt to even out fluctuations in price by buying produce when prices are low and selling when prices are high.

Price fluctuations

The price of a can of tomatoes fluctuates far less than the price of fresh tomatoes. This illustrates a general point. The free market price of primary products (commodities such as gold and tin, and agricultural products such as wheat and beef) fluctuates far more than the price of either manufactured goods or services.

This is mainly due to supply side influences. The demand for canned tomatoes or fresh tomatoes is likely to remain broadly constant over a twelve month period. However, the supply of these two products will differ. Canned tomatoes can be stored. Therefore the supply too will remain broadly the same over a twelve month period. But the supply of fresh tomatoes varies greatly. In the summer months, supply is plentiful and the price of tomatoes is therefore low. In winter, supply is low and prices are high.

On a year to year basis, the supply of raw agricultural commodities can vary greatly according to crop yields. A bumper crop will depress prices whilst crop failure will lead to high prices. Bumper crops can be disastrous for farmers. In Figure 12.1, if the demand for a product is price inelastic, a large fall in price is needed to sell a little extra produce. This will greatly reduce farmers' revenues.

Equally, a poor crop can be disastrous for individual farmers. Although farm income overall will be higher than average, only farmers who have crops to sell will benefit. Farmers whose crops have been mostly or completely destroyed will receive little or no income.

Manufactures and services also contain greater value added than primary products. The cost of a can of tomatoes is made up not only of the cost of tomatoes themselves but also of the canning process and the can. If fresh tomatoes only account for 20 per cent of the cost of a can of tomatoes, then a doubling in the price of fresh tomatoes will only increase the price of a can by just over 7 per cent.

Demand side influences can, however, also be a source of price fluctuations for commodities. In manufacturing and services, producers devote much effort and money to stabilising demand through branding, advertising and other marketing techniques. However, Zambian copper is little different from Chilean copper. Buyers are free to buy from the cheapest source so demand fluctuates more greatly. In the short term, supply is relatively inelastic. Countries have invested in mines, oil wells and other commodity producing plant and need, often for foreign exchange purposes, to maximise output and sales. Small changes in demand, as shown in Figure 12.2, can produce

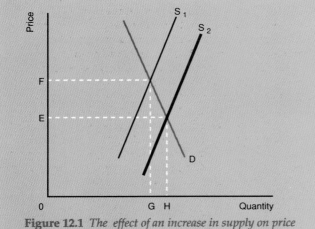

Figure 12.1 *The effect of an increase in supply on price*
If demand and supply are both relatively inelastic, then a small increase in supply from S_1 to S_2 will lead to a large fall in price of FE. Incomes will therefore be greatly reduced.

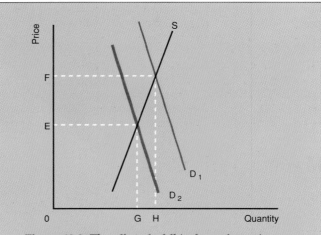

Figure 12.2 *The effect of a fall in demand on price*
If demand and supply are both relatively inelastic, then a small fall in demand from D_1 to D_2 will lead to a large fall in price of FE.

large changes in price. Any slowdown in the world economy is likely to have a larger impact on commodities than on manufactured goods. Manufacturers may react to a small fall in their sales by cutting their stock levels and perhaps delaying the buying of stock by a few months. This results in a large, if temporary, fall in the price of raw materials. Whilst the slowdown persists, prices are likely to remain low. (The converse is also true - in a boom, commodity prices go up far faster than those of manufactures or services.)

Demand and supply influences combine to bring about large fluctuations in the price of commodities. Governments and other bodies have often reacted to this situation by intervening in the market place. Producers also attempt to manipulate prices, and the quantity demanded and supplied for their own benefit.

QUESTION 1 At the beginning of 1987, aluminium stood at $1 200 per tonne. By the second quarter it reached a peak of over $3 600 per tonne. The major cause of this was an increase in world demand at a time when production was stagnant and stocks were falling. At the same time, the cost of cars and aluminium foil, two major products which use aluminium, increased only by a few percent.

Use demand and supply diagrams to explain
(a) why there was such a large increase in the price of aluminium and
(b) why the price of aluminium fluctuated more than that of the products in which it was used.

Government intervention in the market

Governments may intervene in markets by setting minimum prices or maximum prices. Minimum prices may be set to guarantee incomes to producers. For instance, a minimum wage (the wage rate is the price employers have to pay to obtain labour) is designed to prevent employers from paying their workers too low a wage. Minimum prices for wheat or beef, offered by the European Community to farmers, are designed to give farmers minimum returns on their crops. Maximum prices on the other hand may be used to set limits on the returns that producers can make. Or they may be intended to help consumers afford products, often staple necessities such as bread, rice or housing.

Maximum prices

The workings of maximum prices can be illustrated using a demand and supply diagram. In Figure 12.3, the free market price is P_1 and Q_1 is bought and sold. Assume that this is the market for rented accommodation. At a

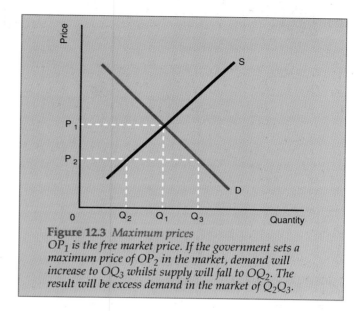

Figure 12.3 *Maximum prices*
OP_1 *is the free market price. If the government sets a maximum price of OP_2 in the market, demand will increase to OQ_3 whilst supply will fall to OQ_2. The result will be excess demand in the market of Q_2Q_3.*

price of P_1 the poorest in society are unable to afford to rent houses and there is therefore a problem of homelessness. The government intervenes by fixing a maximum price for accommodation of P_2. In the very short term, this may well seem to alleviate the problem. Landlords will continue to offer Q_1 of housing whilst the poorest in society will be more able to afford the new lower cost housing. But in the longer term, economic theory predicts that new problems will arise. At a price of P_2, demand will be higher than at P_1, whilst supply will be lower. There will in fact be an excess demand of Q_2Q_3. At the lower price, consumers will demand more housing. On the other hand, landlords will reduce their supply, for instance by selling off their properties for owner occupation, not buying new properties to rent out, or living in their own properties instead of renting them out.

Permanent rent controls will thus reduce the supply of privately rented accommodation to the market whilst increasing its demand. The market may react in a number of ways. In a law abiding society, queues or waiting lists may develop. It may be a matter of luck rather than money whether one is able to get rented accommodation. The state may devise systems to allocate rented accommodation on the basis of greatest need. Landlords may develop a variety of ways in which they can get round the price controls. A black market may develop, illegal and uncontrolled, where rents are fixed at, or greater than, the free market price of P_1. Economic theory therefore predicts that maximum prices may benefit some consumers - those able to obtain the goods which are controlled in price - but will disadvantage those who are prepared to pay a higher price for the good but are unable to obtain it because of a shortage of supply.

If the maximum price were set at P_3, there would be no effect on the market. P_1, the free market price, is below the maximum price and therefore nothing will happen following the introduction of maximum price controls.

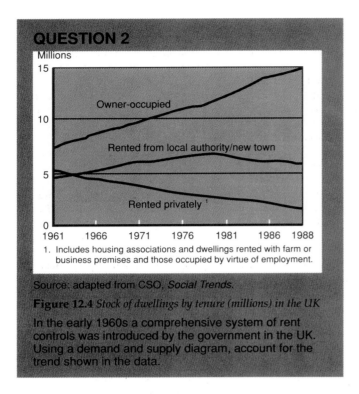

Source: adapted from CSO, *Social Trends*.

Figure 12.4 *Stock of dwellings by tenure (millions) in the UK*

In the early 1960s a comprehensive system of rent controls was introduced by the government in the UK. Using a demand and supply diagram, account for the trend shown in the data.

Minimum prices

Minimum prices are usually set to help producers increase their incomes. Consider Figure 12.5 which shows the market for wheat. The free market price is P_1. The government decides that this is too low a price for farmers to receive and sets a minimum price of P_2. As a result, farmers will now grow Q_1Q_3 more wheat. Consumers will react to the new higher prices by reducing their demand by Q_1Q_2. Total excess supply of Q_2Q_3 will result.

This poses a problem for the government. With maximum prices, the government did not need to intervene when excess demand appeared. The excess demand could remain in the market forever if need be. But this is not true of excess supply. If consumers only buy Q_2 of wheat then farmers can only sell Q_2 of wheat. Q_2Q_3 will remain unbought. Unless the government takes action, there will be strong pressure for farmers to sell this at below the minimum price. Average prices will fall until the market is cleared. The resulting price structure is likely to be very complex, some wheat being sold at the official minimum price of P_2 whilst the rest is sold at a variety of prices, the lowest of which is likely to be below the free market clearing price of P_1. Government action will have been frustrated.

So an effective minimum price structure must be accompanied by other measures. There are two main ways of dealing with this problem. The first is for the government to buy up the wheat that consumers refuse to buy (i.e. buy up the excess supply Q_2Q_3). This in turn creates problems because the government has to do something with the wheat it buys. This has been the

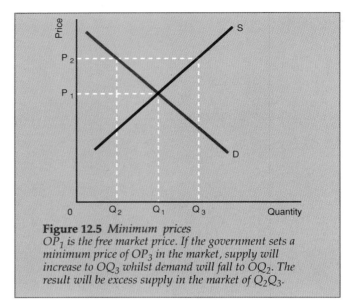

Figure 12.5 *Minimum prices*
OP_1 *is the free market price. If the government sets a minimum price of OP_3 in the market, supply will increase to OQ_3 whilst demand will fall to OQ_2. The result will be excess supply in the market of Q_2Q_3.*

classic problem with the Common Agricultural Policy in the European Community. A variety of solutions, from selling wheat mountains to Third World countries at rock bottom prices, selling it back to farmers to feed to animals, or offering it at reduced prices to those in need in the EC, or simply destroying the produce, have been adopted. All have one drawback - they cost the taxpayer money because the price paid to farmers is inevitably higher than the price received from the sale of the surplus.

The second solution to the problem of excess supply is to restrict production. Governments can either force, or pay, farmers to reduce the size of their herds or leave part of their land uncultivated . At a price of P_2, the government ensures that only Q_2 is supplied to the market. If farmers are paid to set aside land, the taxpayer will have to subsidise the farmer. If farmers receive no compensation, the scheme may defeat its own purposes. As was pointed out in unit 9, it depends upon the price elasticity of demand whether a farmer receives a higher income by selling a smaller quantity at a higher price. Only if the demand is price inelastic will higher prices give farmers higher revenues.

QUESTION 3 The price of table wine in the European Community (EC) during the mid-1980s was supported by the Common Agricultural Policy. Wine growers were able to obtain a minimum price for other wine by selling it to the EC rather than on the open market. In 1988, production of table wine in the EC amounted to 130m hectolitres. Consumption on the other hand was only 98m hectolitres. EC stocks of table wine were about 100m hectolitres.

Using a demand and supply diagram, explain why the EC had such large stocks of table wine in 1988.

Cartels

A CARTEL is an organisation of producers grouped together for their own benefit. The most well known cartel in existence today is OPEC, the Organisation of Petroleum Exporting Countries. Its members are some (but not all) of the most important oil producing countries including Saudi Arabia and Mexico (OPEC is discussed in further detail in the applied section below). Most cartels try to raise prices at the expense of consumers.

As was shown above, any attempt to raise prices above the free market price produces problems of excess supply. A cartel must deal with these problems if it is to survive. Unlike in the agricultural sector, governments are not likely to be willing to buy up any excess supply. So cartels have to devise arrangements to restrict supply. Members are likely to be given production **quotas** (i.e. maximum output figures). There is a great incentive for individual members to sell more than their quota. By increasing their supply, which is likely to be only a fraction of total supply to the market, they can sell more at a price which is likely to be close to the high cartel price. They get the benefits of higher output and higher prices. But if all members cheat in this way, the price will fall. If there is no effective discipline, the price will revert to the free market price.

QUESTION 4 In September 1989, OPEC was suffering from one of its regular bouts of internal disagreement. Current production was 22 million barrels per day (b/d) and oil was selling for $16 per barrel. The new quota ceiling for all OPEC countries was set at 20.5m b/d with a target price of $18 per barrel. However, there were serious doubts as to whether the quota would be kept to. In particular, Kuwait and the United Arab Emirates (UAE) indicated that they would sign the agreement but continued to produce more than allowed by their quota. The UAE, for instance, were given a quota of 1.35m b/d but were currently producing over 2m b/d.

(a) Using diagrams, explain why
   (i) the new quotas, if kept, would raise the price of oil and
   (ii) countries such as Kuwait, which exceed their quotas, benefit from the existence of OPEC.
(b) What would happen to the price of oil if all OPEC producers behaved in the same way as Kuwait and the UAE?

Buffer stock schemes

A BUFFER STOCK SCHEME is a cartel arrangement which combines both the elements of minimum and maximum pricing. In theory it is designed to even out price fluctuations for producers. An intervention price is set. If the free market price is below this, the buffer stock agency will buy in the market until the price is at the intervention price. (It may, as the Common Agricultural Policy does, offer to buy any amount at the intervention price.) If the free market price is above the intervention price, the buffer stock will sell, forcing down the price

towards the intervention price.

Buffer stock schemes are not common. One major reason for this is that a considerable amount of capital is needed to set them up. Money is required to buy produce when prices are too low. There are also the costs of administration and storage of produce purchased. But in theory, the overall running costs of the scheme should be low. Indeed, with skilful buying and selling the scheme may make an operational profit. This is because the scheme buys produce at or below the intervention price but sells at a price above the intervention price.

Buffer stock schemes also have a mixed record of success. Pressure to set up these schemes tends to come from producers who have a vested interest in setting the intervention price above the average market price. If they succeed in doing this, their revenues in the short term are likely to be larger than they would otherwise have been. But the buffer stock scheme will have been buying more produce than it sold. Eventually it will run out of money, the scheme will collapse, and prices will plummet because the accumulated stocks will be sold to pay the debts of the scheme. The glut of produce on the market will result in producers receiving below average prices for some time to come. Successful buffer stock schemes are those which correctly guess the average price and resist attempts by producers to set the intervention price above it.

QUESTION 5 In 1985 the International Tin Council's (ITC) price support scheme collapsed. Countries like the UK, which had agreed to support the Council's purchase of tin when tin prices fell below the intervention price, refused to provide any more money to buy tin to put into stock. Tin prices collapsed and remained weak between 1985 and 1988 as tin stocks, totalling 120 000 tonnes and equivalent to nine months of tin demand, were gradually sold. The main tin producing countries formed themselves into a cartel and agreed production quotas. By 1989, the ITC's stocks were down to 25 000 tonnes and tin prices had risen from $7 200 a lb at the end of 1988 to a peak of $10 000 a lb in 1989.

Using diagrams, explain why
(a)   the ITC's price support scheme collapsed in 1985 and
(b)   the price of tin should have risen in 1989.

Key terms

Cartel - an organisation of producers which exists to further the interests of its members, often by restricting output through the imposition of quotas leading to a rise in prices.
Buffer stock scheme - a scheme whereby an organisation buys and sells in the open market so as to maintain a minimum price in the market for a product.

Applied economics

OPEC

The cartel

OPEC, the Organisation of Petroleum Exporting Countries, was founded in 1960. For the first 13 years of its existence, it remained an obscure and relatively unimportant organisation, but in 1973, with the Arab-Israeli Yom Kippur War, it leapt to world prominence (☞ unit 8). The members of the organisation realised that they could form an effective cartel if they agreed production quotas amongst themselves. By slightly reducing supply in 1974, they were able to quadruple the world price of oil.

The strengths of OPEC

There are a number of reasons why OPEC has been one of the few international cartels which has survived over a long period of time.

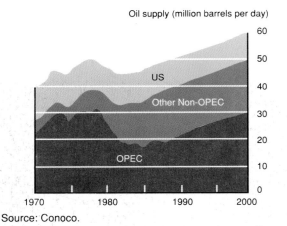

Source: Conoco.

Figure 12.6 *World oil supply projections*

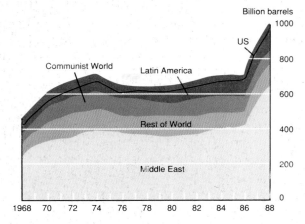

Source: adapted from the *Financial Times*.

Figure 12.7 *Proven reserves of oil*

■ There is no need for any buffer stocks or large amounts of financial capital. If OPEC wishes to reduce supply, member countries simply produce less and leave their oil in the ground.

■ There are a relatively small number of members of OPEC. Member countries are able to exert a high degree of control over the volume of oil lifted within their countries. This contrasts, for instance, with coffee where governments wishing to limit production have to control tens of thousands of small farmers.

■ Oil production is not particularly affected by the vagaries of weather. Hence supply need not fluctuate wildly and randomly from year to year as it does in many agricultural markets.

■ OPEC countries, as Figures 12.6 and 12.7 show, supply a significant proportion of total world output and control an even larger proportion of known oil reserves. Because non-OPEC producers tend to produce at maximum capacity, countries such as the USA and the UK are unable to exert downward pressure on oil prices even if they wanted to.

The weaknesses of OPEC

In real terms, oil prices in July 1990 were little different from those at the start of 1973. The OPEC countries managed to increase substantially their revenues in the mid-1970s and in 1979-80 but these were short lived gains. It is likely that the jump in the price of oil to over $30 a barrel due to the 1990 Iraq Gulf Crisis will prove to be equally short lived.

OPEC since 1973 has suffered from two fundamental weaknesses.

■ The large increases in oil prices in the 1970s led to some fall in demand but, more importantly, an increase in supply from non-OPEC countries. Known world oil reserves, as shown in Figure 12.7, are higher today than they were at the time of the 'energy crisis' in the 1970s. The operation of market forces led to a substantial increase in exploration and subsequently to a significant increase in the supply of oil from non-OPEC countries. This increase in supply has depressed world prices in the 1980s.

■ The increase in non-OPEC supply has also led to enormous strains amongst OPEC members. In any cartel there is an incentive to cheat. If one country can increase its production above its allocated quota, it can sell this extra output at a price almost equal that of the cartel price. However if all countries cheat, then the price will fall rapidly. In the mid-1980s, many OPEC countries exceeded their quotas, driving down the price of oil. Saudi Arabia, the OPEC member with by far the largest oil reserves, was prepared for some time to reduce its liftings in order to prevent too rapid a fall in the price. In 1986, its patience ran out and it began to supply as much oil as buyers would purchase at the market price. World oil prices tumbled to $8 a barrel and analysts predicted that they could fall below the $5 a barrel level. Other OPEC members, realising that they had everything to lose if OPEC broke up, agreed to new quotas and the price rose rapidly to above $15 a barrel. However, cheating has remained a persistent problem in OPEC since 1986 and this was not helped by the sharp political differences between some of the member countries like Iraq, Iran and Kuwait.

The long term future

In the longer term, OPEC is likely to increase its power over the market. As Figure 12.6 shows, it is predicted that the OPEC share of world oil supplies will increase over the next 20 years. The OPEC share of known world oil reserves will also increase. Non-OPEC producers have little scope for increasing production to satisfy rising demand. Indeed only the 5 big OPEC producers - Iran, Iraq, Kuwait, Saudi Arabia and the United Arab Emirates (4 if Iraq has succeeded in holding on to Kuwait) - have such substantial known reserves that they can easily increase production. As oil becomes increasily scarce, its price will rise. OPEC will then have to show considerable economic judgement. The temptation will be to restrict supply sufficiently to produce another huge rise in prices. This will simply encourage exploration in non-OPEC countries and reduce world demand leading to a fall in price in the medium term. On the other hand, it is in the interests of OPEC members to charge as high a price as the market will bear.

Data question

THE COMMON AGRICULTURAL POLICY (CAP)

One of the most important steps taken by the European Community in its early years was to create the Common Agricultural Policy in 1958. Article 39 of the Treaty of Rome cites 5 objectives of agricultural policy:
■ to increase agricultural productivity;
■ to ensure a fair standard of living for farmers;
■ to stabilise markets;
■ to guarantee availability of supplies;
■ to ensure fair prices for consumers.
It was hoped that CAP would achieve this through regulation of the agricultural industry in the Community. For many products, an **intervention price** was established. Farmers could then choose to sell their produce on the open market or to the EC at this minimum fixed price. The EC guaranteed to buy up any amount at the intervention price. Farmers were protected from overseas competition through a complex system of tariffs and quotas.

CAP proved to be far more favourable to farmers than to consumers. The farming community in the EC became very adroit at lobbying their individual governments to vote for high intervention prices at the annual price fixing negotiations in Brussels.

Consumers lost out in two ways. Firstly, they had to pay directly for food which was much higher in price than it would otherwise have been if it had been bought on world markets. Secondly, as taxpayers, they had to pay for the heavy costs of running the CAP.

In theory, the CAP should have been fairly inexpensive to run. If there was a glut of produce on the market in one season, the EC would buy some of it at the intervention price and store it. The next season, when there was perhaps a shortage, the EC could take the produce out of storage and sell it. Prices would not fluctuate by as much as under a market system and the sale of produce would ensure that the major cost of the system would be administration and storage.

In practice, the cost of the CAP rose remorselessly. High intervention prices led to increased production, as economic theory would predict. Supply then began to outstrip demand. Instead of selling produce taken into storage to European consumers at a later date, mountains and lakes of produce developed. This produce then had to be sold, often at a fraction of the

cost of production, to the USSR, Third World countries, and to EC farmers for use as animal feed. Some was even destroyed.

By the mid-1980s, there was general agreement that the system could no longer continue in its original form and in 1987, the threatened cost of CAP was so great that it could only be contained within its legally set budget by deferring some payments to 1988. The simplest solution would have been to reduce intervention prices, increasing demand for food and reducing EC supply. However, the power of the farming lobby was so great that such a solution was politically impossible. Instead, agriculture ministers chose to build on a system of quotas first imposed in the mid-1980s on milk production. Farmers are not allowed to produce, individually in the case of milk and collectively in the case of wheat, more than a fixed amount. If they overproduce they will be fined. A set-aside scheme was also established whereby farmers

would be compensated for setting aside land that would have been used for production.

Many feel that the reforms of the late 1980s are unlikely to solve any of the fundamental problems of CAP. Over-production can only be resolved by lower prices. If farmers need income support, then it is far cheaper to provide it directly through some form of social security system than through high prices paid at the farm gate.

1. Using diagrams, explain why 'mountains' and 'lakes' of produce developed in the EC in the 1970s and 1980s.
2. Who benefited and who lost from this overproduction?
3. Using diagrams, show how quotas or set-aside schemes might reduce surpluses of produce in the EC.

Summary

1. Indirect taxes can be either ad valorem taxes or specific taxes.
2. The imposition of an indirect tax is likely to lead to a rise in the unit price of a good which is less than the unit value of the tax.
3. The incidence of indirect taxation is likely to fall on both consumer and producer.
4. The incidence of tax will fall wholly on the consumer if demand is perfectly inelastic or supply is perfectly elastic.
5. The incidence of tax will fall wholly on the producer if demand is perfectly elastic or supply is perfectly inelastic.

Indirect taxes and subsidies

An **indirect tax** (discussed in greater detail in unit 45) is a tax on expenditure. The two major indirect taxes in the UK are VAT and excise duties.

VAT is an example of an AD VALOREM tax. The tax levied increases in proportion to the value of the tax base. In the case of VAT, the tax base is the price of the good. Most goods in the UK carry a 15 per cent VAT charge. Excise duties on the other hand are an example of a SPECIFIC or UNIT tax. The amount of tax levied does not change with the value of the goods but with the amount or volume of the goods purchased. So the excise duty on a bottle of wine is the same whether the bottle costs £5 or £500, but the VAT is 100 times more on the latter compared to the former. The main excise duties in the UK are on alcohol, tobacco and petrol. They should not be confused with customs duties which are levied on imports.

A SUBSIDY is a grant given by government to encourage the production or consumption of a particular good or service. Subsidies for instance may be given on essential items such as housing or bread. Alternatively they may be given to firms who employ disadvantaged workers such as the long term unemployed or handicapped people. Or they may be given to firms manufacturing domestically produced goods to help them be more competitive than imported goods.

The incidence of tax

Price theory can be used to analyse the impact of the imposition of an indirect tax on a good. Assume that a specific tax of £1 per bottle is imposed upon wine. This has the effect of reducing supply. Sellers of wine will now want to charge £1 extra per bottle sold. In Figure 13.1, this is shown by a vertical shift of £1 in the supply curve at every level of output. However many bottles are produced, sellers will want to charge £1 more per bottle and therefore there is a parallel shift upwards of the whole supply curve from S_1 to S_2.

The old equilibrium price was £3.30, at which price 60 million bottles were bought and sold. The introduction of the £1 tax will raise price and reduce quantity demanded.

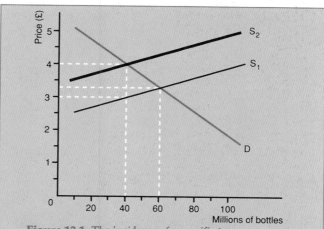

Figure 13.1 *The incidence of a specific tax*
The imposition of an indirect tax of £1 per unit on wine will push up the supply curve from S_1 to S_2. The vertical distance between the two supply curves at any given output is £1. As a consequence equilibrium price will rise from £3.30 to £4. The consumer therefore pays an extra 70p per bottle of wine. The other 30p of the tax is paid by the producer because the price it receives per bottle before tax falls from £3.30 to £3.

QUESTION 1 The price of a gallon of petrol at the pumps is made up as follows:

	£
Petrol cost before tax	0.76
Excise duty	0.98
	1.74
VAT @ 15%	0.26
Price at the pumps	2.00

Calculate the new price of petrol if:
(a) an increase in the cost of crude oil pushed up the cost of petrol before tax from 76p to 96p;
(b) the government increased excise duty from 98p to 138p;
(c) VAT was reduced from 15 per cent to 10 per cent;
(d) the government subsidised the cost before tax by 10p a gallon.
(For each part, assume that the price at the pumps is initially £2.00.)

The new equilibrium price is £4, at which price quantity demanded falls to 40 million bottles.

This result might seem surprising. The imposition of a £1 per bottle tax has only raised the price of a bottle by 70p and not the full £1 of the tax. This is because the INCIDENCE OF TAX is unlikely to fall totally on consumers. The incidence of tax measures the burden of tax upon the taxpayer. In this case the consumer has paid 70p of the tax. Therefore the other 30p which the government receives must have been paid by producers.

QUESTION 2 Most years, the Chancellor raises the duty on a packet of 20 cigarettes in his Budget. The cigarette manufacturers, however, do not always pass on all the increased duty in the form of higher prices. Using a demand and supply diagram, explain why this is so.

Tax revenues

Using Figure 13.1 we can also show the change in total expenditure before and after imposition of the tax as well as the amount of tax revenue gained by the government. The government will receive total tax revenue of £1 x 40 million (the tax per unit x the quantity sold): hence tax revenues will be £40 million. Consumers will pay 70p x 40 million of this, whilst producers will pay 30p x 40 million. Consumers will therefore pay £28 million of tax whilst producers will pay £12 million. Total spending on wine will fall from £198 million (£3.30 x 60 million) to £160 million (£4 x 40 million). Revenues received by producers will fall from £198 million (£3.30 x 60 million) to £120 million (£3 x 40 million).

Ad valorem taxes

The above analysis can be extended to deal with ad valorem taxes. The imposition of an ad valorem tax will lead to an upwards shift in the supply curve. However, the higher the price, the greater will be the amount of the tax. Hence the shift will look as in Figure 13.2. Consumers will pay FG tax per unit whilst the incidence of tax on producers per unit will be HG.

Subsidies

A subsidy on a good will lead to an increase in supply, shifting the supply curve downwards and to the right. This is shown in Figure 13.3. It should be noted that a subsidy of AC will not lead to a fall in price of AC. Part of the subsidy, AB, will be appropriated by producers because of the higher unit cost of production of higher levels of output (shown by the upward sloping supply curve). Prices to consumers will only fall by BC.

QUESTION 3
Table 13.1

Price (£)	Quantity demanded	Quantity supplied
4	16	4
6	12	6
8	8	8
10	4	10
12	0	12

(a) Draw the demand and supply curves from the data in Table 13.1.
(b) What is the equilibrium quantity demanded and supplied?
The government now imposes Value Added Tax of 50 per cent.
(c) Show the effect of this on the diagram.
(d) What is the new equilibrium quantity demanded and supplied?
(e) What is the new equilibrium price?
(f) What is the incidence of tax per unit on (i) the consumer and (ii) the producer?
(g) What is
   (i) the tax per unit and
   (ii) total government revenue from the tax?
(h) By how much will the revenue of producers before tax change?

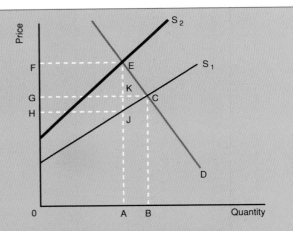

Figure 13.2 *The incidence of an ad valorem tax*
The imposition of an ad valorem tax will push the supply curve upwards from S_1 to S_2. The following gives the key facts about the change:
(a) original equilibrium price and quantity, OG and OB;
(b) new equilibrium price and quantity, OF and OA;
(c) incidence of tax per unit on consumers, GF;
(d) incidence of tax per unit on producers, HG;
(e) tax per unit in equilibrium, HF;
(f) total tax paid by consumers, GKEF;
(g) total tax paid by producers, GHJK;
(h) total tax revenue of government, FHJE;
(i) change in producers' revenue, OBCG - OAJH;
(j) change in consumers' expenditure, OBCG - OAEF.

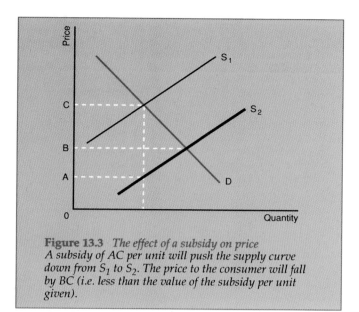

Figure 13.3 *The effect of a subsidy on price*
A subsidy of AC per unit will push the supply curve down from S_1 to S_2. The price to the consumer will fall by BC (i.e. less than the value of the subsidy per unit given).

Taxes and elasticity

The extent to which the tax incidence falls on consumers rather than producers depends upon the elasticities of demand and supply. Figure 13.4 shows a situation where either the supply curve is perfectly elastic or the demand curve is perfectly inelastic. In both cases, the vertical shift in the supply curve, which shows the value of the tax per unit, is identical to the final price rise. Therefore, all of the tax will be paid by consumers.

Figure 13.5, on the other hand, shows two cases where the incidence of tax falls totally on the producer. Producers will find it impossible to shift any of the tax onto consumers if the demand curve is perfectly elastic. Consumers are not prepared to buy at any higher price than the existing price. If the supply curve is perfectly inelastic, then the supply curve after imposition of the tax

will the same as the one before. Equilibrium price will therefore remain the same and producers will have to bear the full burden of the tax.

Generalising from these extreme situations, we can conclude that the more elastic the demand curve or the more inelastic the supply curve, the greater will be the incidence of tax on producers and the less will be the incidence of tax on consumers. So far as the government is concerned, taxation revenue will be greater, all other things being equal, the more inelastic the demand for the product taxed. For instance, if demand were perfectly elastic, the imposition of an indirect tax would lead to quantity demanded falling to zero and tax revenue being zero. At the opposite extreme, if demand were perfectly inelastic, consumers would buy the same quantity after

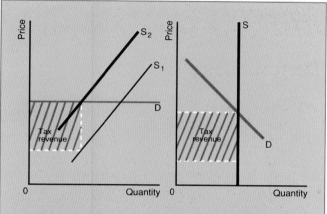

Figure 13.5 *Where the incidence of tax falls wholly on the producer*
If supply is perfectly inelastic or demand perfectly elastic, then it can be seen from the graphs that the incidence of tax will fall wholly on producers.

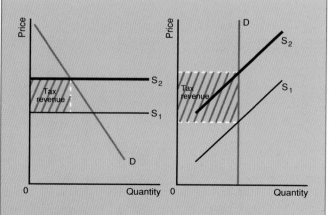

Figure 13.4 *Where the incidence of tax falls wholly on the consumer*
If supply is perfectly elastic or demand perfectly inelastic, then it can be seen from the graphs that the incidence of tax will fall wholly on consumers.

QUESTION 4
Table 13.2

	Price elasticity of demand
Food	- 0.52
Durables	- 0.89
Fuel and Light	- 0.47
Services	- 1.02

Source: John Muellbauer, 'Testing the Barten Model of Household Composition Effects and the Cost of Children', *Economic Journal*, September 1977.

The government wishes to raise VAT on selected goods, all these goods and services being zero-rated at present. Which categories of goods does the data suggest would yield (a) the most and (b) the least revenues? (Assume that at present the average price and the quantity demanded of goods in each category is identical.) Explain your reasoning carefully.

imposition of the tax as before. Hence revenue will be be equal to the tax per unit times the quantity demanded before imposition. If the price elasticity of demand lies between these two extremes, the imposition of a tax will lead to a fall in quantity demanded. The higher the elasticity, the larger will be the fall in quantity demanded and hence the lower will be the tax revenue received by government. Hence, it is no coincidence that in the UK, excise duties are placed on alcohol, tobacco and petrol, all of which are relatively price inelastic.

Key terms

Ad valorem tax - tax levied as a percentage of the value of the good.
Specific or unit tax - tax levied on volume.
Subsidy - a grant given which lowers the price of a good usually designed to encourage production or consumption of a good.
Incidence of tax - the tax burden on the taxpayer.

Applied economics

Unleaded petrol

In his 1988 budget, the Chancellor of the Exchequer raised the tax on a gallon of leaded 4 star petrol by 10p but left the tax on unleaded petrol unchanged. This introduced a 10p price differential between a gallon of leaded 4 star and a gallon of unleaded petrol.

Economic theory would suggest that demand for leaded petrol would fall. Indeed, within just over 12 months of the introduction of the price differential, sales of leaded petrol had fallen by nearly one-quarter. Figure 13.6 shows how this might have come about. The short term supply curve for petrol is perfectly elastic: petrol companies are prepared to supply any amount at a given price of £1.90. Hence the 10p increase in indirect taxes on petrol shifts the supply curve upwards by 10p along its length and the consumer bears all of the increase in price to £2.00. The demand curve for leaded petrol is very price elastic. This is because unleaded petrol is a very good substitute given that so many cars can take unleaded as well as leaded petrol. So an approximate 5 per cent rise in the price of leaded petrol leads to a 25 per cent fall in sales (i.e. the price elasticity of demand is

approximately 5).

If the government had raised all petrol prices, it would have received more revenue. But the Chancellor thought that the small loss in Exchequer finance was worth the environmental gain from the switch to lead free petrol.

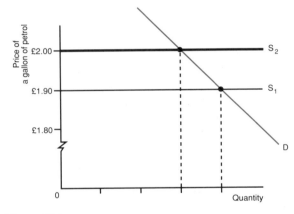

Figure 13.6

FISH AND CHIPS

Data question

In his 1984 Budget, the Chancellor imposed VAT at 15 per cent on take-away food. Before then, take-away food had been exempt from VAT. Within a few months fish and chip shops up and down the country were reporting substantial falls in sales ranging from 10 to 40 per cent. However, more expensive take-away outlets and hamburger chains reported little loss of sales.

1. **With the aid of a diagram, explain why the imposition of VAT should have led to a change in sales for fish and chip shops.**

2. **Using the concept of elasticity, suggest why fish and chip shops should have been more affected than other take-way outlets.**

A. Price fluctuations

Aims

■ To compare the causes of price fluctuations in two commodity markets, one which is a free market, the other where either a cartel or a buffer stock scheme influence price.
■ To evaluate the extent to which a cartel or buffer stock scheme may reduce price fluctuations.
■ To judge whether the introduction of a cartel or buffer stock scheme would stabilise prices in a previously free market.
■ To predict whether the abandonment of a price-fixing arrangement would lead to greater price instability.

Research activity

Choose two goods. Both should be internationally traded commodities such as tin, wheat, coffee or rubber. One should be traded in a free market (such as copper or zinc), the other in a market in which there is one or several cartels or buffer stock schemes which regulate prices (such as oil or wheat).

Find out as much as you can about demand and supply conditions in the markets you have decided to investigate. For instance, which countries are the main producers and consumers? Are there any firms of significant size which either buy or sell in the market? Where are the main markets for buying and selling of the commodity? Do prices fluctuate freely or are prices fixed? Do cartels or buffer stock schemes operate in the market? If so, how? What are the aims of the cartel or buffer stock scheme? What has been its recent history?

Follow the price movements of the two commodities over a period of time. This could be a historical analysis, for instance investigating broad price movements over the past ten years, or investigating detailed price movements over the previous twelve months. Alternatively it could be an ongoing investigation, recording and analysing price movements for a three month period. Record how prices change. Note any factors which might cause either demand for or supply of the commodity to change.

Sources

The *Financial Times* publishes an excellent section on commodity prices every day. There are regular reviews of commodity markets as well. The dates of recent articles can be found using the index to the newspaper published by the *Financial Times*. Other quality newspapers, such as the *Independent*, also have the occasional article, as do quality magazines such as the *Economist*. *The Guardian* and *The Times* both publish indexes too. Alternatively, the *Research Index*, published by Business Surveys Ltd. may be available in the reference library which you intend to use. It covers articles of financial interest in 100 newspapers and periodicals on a monthly basis. The library may also construct its own indexes.

The Central Statistical Office publish statistics relating to agricultural prices in the UK. *The Annual Abstract of Statistics* gives annual prices for selected commodities over a ten year period whilst the *Annual Review of Agriculture* (White Paper) gives prices over the previous 4 years. Monthly figures for the previous twelve months are given in *Agricultural Statistics, England and Wales. Agricultural Market Report*, a weekly publication, gives prices and quantities bought and sold for grains such as wheat for the previous week. For the latest details of sources, consult the *Guide to Official Statistics*.

The EC *Index of Producer Prices of Agricultural Products*, a Eurostat publication, gives agricultural prices across the EC. UNCTAD, the UN and the World Development Bank also publish commodity prices in a number of their publications.

Structuring your report

Introduction Outline the aim of your investigation.
Market background Describe the characteristics of the two markets which you have investigated taking into account those factors described above.
Economic theory Outline briefly a theory of price determination in a free market and in one covered by a cartel or buffer stock scheme (whichever applies to the market you have chosen). Suggest the most likely factors which economic theory might suggest would influence either demand for or supply of the product.
Analysis of price movements Describe the price movements which you have observed over time. To what extent have prices in the market covered by a cartel or buffer stock arrangement fluctuated less than those in the free market? Using the concepts of demand and supply, put forward possible reasons why prices have changed in the two markets. Compare the importance of different factors which influence price between the two markets, and in particular analyse the reasons why the cartel or buffer stock scheme has succeeded or failed in providing greater price stability than in the free market.
Evaluation of alternatives Suggest what would happen to prices if the cartel or buffer stock scheme were abandoned and the market became a free market. Would it be possible for producers in the free market to form a cartel or organise a buffer stock scheme? Would the price-fixing arrangement be durable? What effect might it have on prices in your opinion?
Sources Outline the sources of information you used. What problems did you encounter in gathering relevant data? What data would you have liked to have obtained but could not? To what extent were the data reliable?

When presenting your report, use appropriate diagrams whenever possible. For instance, you could use charts showing price movements over time, or demand and supply diagrams showing shifts in the demand and supply curves which cause changes in price.

Other suggestions

Instead of investigating two commodities, investigate a range of commodities. For instance, agricultural commodities within the EC could be chosen to analyse the effects of the Common Agricultural Policy.

Primary research could be undertaken by recording the price of fresh foods such as tomatoes or potatoes in the shops over a period of time. It would then be important to distinguish the extent to which price movements are the result of changes in commodity prices and which are the result of price changes by retailers and wholesalers. More difficult would be to attempt to calculate elasticities of demand and supply for commodities. Not only would you need to collect data over a period of time relating to price, quantities bought and sold, incomes, etc., but you would also need to assume when making one calculation (e.g. price elasticity of demand) that all other factors remained constant. Since this will not be so in the real world, your estimates of elasticity will only be approximations at best.

Investigate house prices in your area. Remember that houses are non-homogeneous (i.e. no two houses are likely to be the same). Therefore, when explaining how house prices change over time, it is important to compare the prices of similar houses. The Halifax Building Society publishes regularly a house price index giving changes in house prices by region.

B. School or college - provision of a service

Aims

■ To investigate the nature of resource allocation within an educational establishment.
■ To evaluate whether resources could be used more effectively to provide educational services.

Research activity

All economic systems, such as a school or college, have to resolve three basic questions.

What? Identify the range of educational services which your school or college provides. For instance, what courses are offered to what age of client? What, if any, qualifications are available on each course? What else, apart from qualifications, could be seen to be the outcome of attendance at school or college (for example the development of personal skills such as politeness, ability to work in a group, initiative and confidence)? What recreational services are offered to students (e.g. swimming or squash)? What other services, such as meals or shopping facilities, are offered by the school or college? How could the services offered be improved?

How? How is production organised and what factors of production are used? Find out what division of labour there is within the organisation. Having established a broad outline, select certain areas of the school or college to investigate in detail. For instance, how are GCSE courses organised, what is the structure of the social science faculty, or how are meals organised? Why is production organised in this way rather than another? Which services are sold in a market and which are supplied free at the point of sale (within a **command** structure ☞ unit 109). Who pays for services provided free at the point of consumption? How is payment organised? How could the production of services in the school or college be better organised?

For whom? Who receives the services that the school or college provides? There is some controversy over this. For instance, is it individual students, their parents, government, or employers and industry? Would there be any benefits if production of services were switched to suit the needs of one group more than another?

Sources

The school or college is likely to produce a variety of documents which will give some of the information you need to collect. For instance, it may produce a brochure which it sends to prospective students or their parents. By law, schools have to produce an Annual Report giving such information as levels of staffing. There will also be a large number of confidential documents which you **may** be able to obtain, such as organisation of teaching by faculty, the staff handbook and financial budgets.

You will need to interview a number of staff. This is likely to include your economics teachers or lecturers, as well as more senior members of staff such as a deputy head or vice principal. Interview some non-teaching staff as well, such as caretaking staff or kitchen staff. You may also wish to interview an industrialist and a parent to seek their views on what ought to be produced by the school or college. Interviewing a governor may also give valuable information. A questionnaire drawn up before hand is likely to be useful in these interviews. Think what questions you wish to ask, and what form of question is more likely to give you the information you need. Alternatively, you could get an individual to fill in a questionnaire instead of interviewing them. Note though that many people don't bother to fill in questionnaires even if they say they will.

Newspaper articles, from national newspapers such as *The Guardian* and specialist newspapers such as the *Times Educational Supplement*, may give useful background material on a wide range of issues arising from the assignment.

Structuring your report

Introduction Outline the aims of your investigation, detailing the economic concepts such as scarcity, resource allocation and the division of labour which you will use in your report for the purposes of analysis.
What is produced Present your findings on what services are produced by the school or college.
How it is produced Analyse how production takes place. What factors of production are used and what contribution do they make to the production process?
For whom production takes place Discuss who are the recipients of the education service and how they benefit.
How resource allocation could be changed Evaluate how resource allocation could be altered, either to provide the same services but at lower cost, or provide improved services. You must outline how you would judge whether there had been an improvement in services.
Sources Explain how you collected your data for the report. What problems did you encounter in obtaining relevant data? How reliable was the evidence gathered. In particular, how reliable was the evidence from interviews and questionnaires? What data would you have liked to obtain but were unable to?

Use appropriate diagrams and graphs throughout. For instance, you may want to use diagrams showing the hierarchy within the organisation. Or you may want to show spending on a block graph.

Other suggestions

Instead of studying an educational establishment, it would be possible to study one of the following. The aim would remain to find out what, how and for whom production takes place and how, if at all, the allocation of resources could be improved: a small local firm such as a hairdressers; a local hospital; a youth club, or society; an aspect of local authority service provision such as a swimming baths or sports centre; a local cinema.

Summary

1. A consumer gains utility when he or she consumes a good.
2. The law of diminishing marginal utility states that marginal utility will decline as consumption of a good increases.
3. The consumer is in equilibrium when the marginal utility per £ spent is the same for all goods.
4. The paradox of value is explained by the fact that consumers base their spending decisions not on total utility gained but on marginal utility.
5. Consumer surplus is the difference between the total utility measured by the maximum amount that a consumer would be prepared to pay for a number of units of a good and the actual amount paid.

Total and marginal utility

UTILITY is the satisfaction derived from consuming a good. That good could be anything from a pint of beer, to a night out at the cinema or a donation to charity. Consumption may also yield negative utility - **disutility** as it is sometimes called. A spell in prison or a pint of beer which makes you sick would yield disutility.

The TOTAL UTILITY of consuming a good is the utility derived from consuming a given quantity of the good. So we can talk about the total utility of consuming 5 pints of beer, 2 holidays or 6 records. MARGINAL UTILITY is the utility gained from consuming an **extra** unit of the good. So we can talk about the marginal utility of consuming the fifth pint of beer, or the second holiday or the sixth record.

Table 14.1 shows an example of utility gained from consuming beer by an individual. Utility is measured in terms of units of utility (or UUs). As can be seen, the greater the consumption of beer, the greater the total utility. However, total utility peaks when 5 pints are consumed and actually falls when 6 pints are consumed. This is because the marginal utility at this level (the utility gained by consuming the extra sixth unit which makes you feel sick) is negative.

Table 14.1 *Total and marginal utility*

Pints of beer consumed	Total utility (in UUs)	Marginal utility (in UUs)
1	10	10
2	19	9
3	27	8
4	34	7
5	37	3
6	35	-2

Total utility can be derived from marginal utility and vice versa. Marginal utility is the utility gained from consuming one extra unit of a good and is found by measuring the difference between two levels of total utility. The marginal utility of the fifth pint of beer is the difference in the total utility gained from consuming 5 pints and that gained by consuming 4 pints. The marginal utility gained from consuming the second pint is the difference between the total utility gained by 2 pints and the total utility gained by 1 pint. Conversely total utility is the sum of marginal utilities. The total utility gained by consuming 4 pints is the sum of the marginal utility of the first pint, added to the second pint, added to the third pint, added to the fourth pint.

The law of diminishing marginal utility

Economists argue that marginal utility declines as consumption of a good increases. Each unit consumed gives less and less additional utility (although total utility will continue to rise until the marginal unit gives disutility). For instance, it is likely that a second car gives less utility than a first car to a two car family. Equally, consumption of the fifth packet of crisps of the day is likely to yield less utility than consumption of the first. This proposition, known as the **law of diminishing marginal utility**, can be illustrated diagrammatically in Figure 14.1. As consumption rises between O and A, total utility rises but marginal utility per unit falls. If consumption is pushed beyond OA, marginal utility is negative and total utility falls.

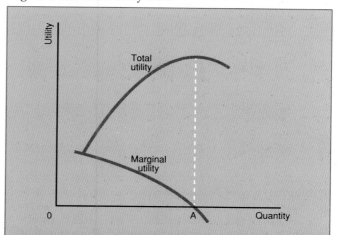

Figure 14.1 *Total and marginal utility*
Marginal utility falls as consumption increases because of the law of diminishing marginal utility. Total utility is at a maximum when marginal utility is zero.

Consumer equilibrium

The law of diminishing marginal utility can be used to explain how a consumer will allocate resources. Three assumptions will be made.

- Consumers seek to maximise their total utility (i.e. consumers will allocate their resources in such a way as to maximise the satisfaction derived from it).
- Their resources are defined as the goods and services that could be bought with their income. They have other resources available to them, such as their time, but these will be ignored.
- Food and drink are the only two goods available for purchase.

Table 14.3

Expenditure £	Utility gained from £1 of income spent on	
	Food	Drink
1st	10	20
2nd	6	10
3rd	3	6
4th	1	2

The marginal utility gained from each pound of spending is shown in Table 14.3. A consumer has a total income of £5 to spend. So she could spend it on, say, £4 of food and £1 of drink, or £2 of food and £3 of drink. She will maximise her utility by buying £2 of food and £3 of drink. For if she spent a fourth pound on drink she would only get 2 extra units of utility but would lose the 6 she gets from spending this same pound on food. If she spent a third pound on food, she would get 3 extra units of utility but would lose the 6 units of utility gained from consuming the third pound of drink.

Generalising this argument, a consumer will maximise total utility when the marginal utility per £1 spent is equal for all goods. If the marginal utility per £1 spent were higher on good X than on good Y, the consumer could increase utility by buying more X and less Y. As more X is bought, the marginal utility will fall whilst the marginal utility of good Y will rise as less is bought. When the two are equal per £1 spent, the consumer will not be able to increase utility by switching from one good to another.

Mathematically this is expressed as:

$$\frac{\text{marginal utility of good X}}{\text{price of good X}} = \frac{\text{marginal utility of good Y}}{\text{price of good Y}}$$

Dividing the marginal utility by the price gives the marginal utility per £ or pence or per whatever unit of money in which the price is denominated. In Table 14.3, the consumer will maximise total utility where the marginal utility of the last pound spent is 6.

Deriving the demand curve

Demand theory states that an increase in the price of a good will lead to a reduction in demand. Marginal utility theory can be used to prove this. Assume that the price of good X increases. The value of the marginal utility of good X ÷ the price of good X will now fall because the figure on the bottom of the fraction (the price) has increased. The marginal utility of good X per £1 spent will now be less than on other goods. The consumer can therefore increase total utility by spending less on good X (which will increase the value of the marginal utility of good X per £1 spent) and spending more on other goods (reducing the value of their marginal utility per £1 spent). In other words, as the price of X rises, the consumer only maximises total utility by buying less of good X. The demand curve for a good is therefore downward sloping.

The paradox of value

We are now in a position to understand one of the problems which perplexed economists for a long time. Adam Smith, for instance, was puzzled as to why consumers paid high prices for goods such as diamonds, which were unnecessary to human existence, whilst the price of necessities such as water was very low. These economists failed to make the distinction between total and marginal utility.

Consumer decisions are made at the margin. The total utility from consuming water will be very high compared to diamonds. But water and diamonds will be consumed to the point where their marginal utilities per pound spent are equal. An ordinary person may consume thousands of gallons of water per year but only buy a diamond once every 20 years. So it is not surprising that the marginal utility of that one diamond is relatively high compared to the marginal utility of, say, the sixty thousandth gallon of water consumed, and that today's consumers are therefore prepared to pay a much higher price for an extra diamond than an extra gallon of water.

Consumer surplus

CONSUMER SURPLUS is generated when a consumer pays less for a good than he or she would be prepared to pay for it. Consider the demand curve shown in Figure

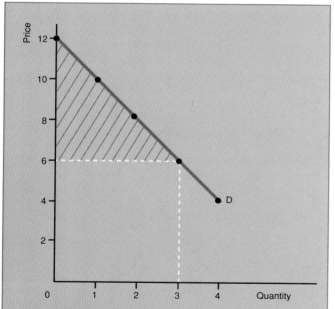

Figure 14.2 *Consumer surplus*
The demand curve shows the price that the consumer would be prepared to pay for each unit. Except on the marginal unit purchased, the price that the consumer is prepared to pay is above the market price that is paid. The difference between these two values is the consumer surplus. It is represented by the shaded area under the demand curve.

14.2. A consumer buys 3 records at a price of £6 each. The demand curve shows that she would have been prepared to pay £10 for the first record purchased. This means that she values the marginal utility of the first record at £10. Therefore she has gained £4 of utility free on her first purchase. This is part of her consumer surplus. On the second record, she valued the record at £8 but only paid £6 for it. Her consumer surplus on this was therefore £2. On the third record she paid exactly the price at which she valued the record. There was no consumer surplus on the third record. Her total consumer surplus is therefore £4 + £2 or £6.

Consumer surplus is the shaded area under the demand curve above the horizontal price line of £6. It is the difference between the total expenditure on the good (price x quantity) and the value of the total utility that the consumer placed on purchase of the good.

If records were banned from sale, how much would the consumer need to be compensated if her utility were to remain the same? She values the 3 records she buys at £24 (£10 + £8 + £6). If she could no longer buy records, she would have £18 (£6 x 3) available to spend on other goods. However, she would need to be compensated by an extra £6 (£24 - £18), the consumer surplus on her purchases, if she is not to lose utility as a result of the ban.

QUESTION 3

A demand curve is given by the equation:

$$Q_D = 100 - 0.5P$$

where Q_D is quantity demanded and P is price.

(a) Draw the demand curve for prices between 0 and £200.
(b) Shade the area of consumer surplus at a price of £60.
(c) Is consumer surplus larger or smaller at a price of £40 compared to £60?

Key terms

Utility - the satisfaction derived from consuming a good.
Total utility - the utility derived from consuming a given quantity of the good.
Marginal utility - the utility gained from consuming an extra good.
Consumer surplus - the difference between what consumers are prepared to pay for a good and what they actually pay.

Applied economics

The economics of altruism

The process of giving, asserts Dr. Barry Bracewell-Milnes in a recent pamphlet* for the Institute for Economic Affairs, 'at least doubles the value of the gift'. This is a rather startling claim. Suppose, out of the goodness of my heart, I give you a crisp £5 note. You are £5 better off; I am £5 worse off. Wealth has been redistributed, but surely not created. After all, there is still only one £5 note.

Dr. Bracewell-Milnes says this accurately describes what happens when money is redistributed through the tax system. In effect, assets are seized and allocated to other individuals. But voluntary giving, he claims, is something else. If I am rational, I will donate a gift only if its value to me in the hands of the recipient exceeds its value to me in my own hands. In other words, I will give you £5 only if the monetary value of the psychic satisfaction I derive exceeds £5.

After my act of giving, you possess a physical act worth £5. I possess psychic satisfaction or "utility" worth more than £5. Hence wealth has been more than doubled. This form of wealth creation, moreover, is both environmentally clean and virtually costless. It is also, the author claims, of considerable economic significance. The annual sum passing by gift and bequest is of the order of £50bn; the wealth created by these transfers therefore exceeds £50bn, possibly by a large margin.

Tax relief for charitable giving is usually justified either on the grounds that charities perform socially useful functions or that they supply services which would otherwise have to be provided by the public sector at taxpayers' expense. The wealth-creating potential of giving, suggests Dr. Bracewell-Milnes, provides a further powerful justification for tax relief. Governments have long accepted the maximisation of incomes (or living standards) as a goal of public policy: why not also encourage personal wealth creation through giving?

In fact, he goes further and argues that if tax rates are low, tax relief should be allowed at a rate in excess of an individual's marginal tax rate.

There is an ingenious reason for this: the extra relief can turn virtuous thoughts into actual deeds. If I do not give £5 to Save the Children it is because the value of the £5 in my hands is greater than its value to me in the hands of the charity. But if I am well disposed to Save the Children, the difference may be quite small. The value to me of £5 in their hands might be, say, £4.90. If tax relief in excess of my marginal rate reduced the cost to me of the gift below £4.90, ineffective altruism would become effective and I would make the donation. Benign thoughts would be translated into possible action: and a little tax relief would have triggered the creation of a much larger amount of psychic wealth.

At this stage, readers may be wondering whether Dr. Bracewell-Milnes is either demented or perpetrating an elaborate hoax. He admits that the wealth created by giving exists only in the minds of givers. How can he expect us to pay attention to anything so nebulous? But wait a moment. The only reason we consume or possess anything is because it 'makes us feel good'. In the last analysis, the utility we derive from consumption or ownership is every bit as cerebral as that from giving.

The problem lies not in the intangibility of the wealth created by giving, but in whether giving actually makes us feel good. The author assumes that all human actions can be explained within the utility-maximising framework of market economics. He assumes that I donate £5 only if this use of my money makes me happier than any alternative use. But this is surely rarely the case. We often give out of a sense of duty, not because this is how we want to spend our money: charities appeal to an aspect of our personalities that is irrelevant to the workings of a market economy. This is sad because it means there is less wealth in the world than Dr. Bracewell-Milnes suspects, but encouraging because it implies we care about more than merely our own happiness.

*The Wealth of Giving. 2 Lord North Street. London SW1.

Source: *Financial Times*, 16.1.90.

Data question

WATER METER TRIALS

In April 1989, 11 areas of the UK became subject to an economic experiment. By the year 2000, the privatised Water Boards will have to find a way of charging households for water which is not based on the rating system. Under the rating system, households are charged a fixed amount for the year, however much water they consume, based upon a notional rental value for the property. The Water Boards would like to move away from a fixed fee system to one where water bills were directly related to water consumed.

As a step towards this change, 11 areas have been chosen to take part in the National Water Metering Trials. The largest area is the whole of the Isle of Wight, covering 53 000 households. There are about 1 000 households in each of the other 10 areas.

Five different tariff structures will be tested.

■ A flat rate tariff - each unit of water costs the same regardless of consumption.

■ A rising block tariff - the more water consumed, the higher the tariff per unit. This is intended to discourage consumption and will be of interest to Water Boards in areas such as the South East and the South West which have difficulty meeting demand in times of drought.

■ A declining block tariff - the more water consumed, the lower the tariff per unit. This will encourage consumption and is of interest to Northumbrian Water which has excess supplies of water.

■ A seasonal tariff - charges will be higher in summer than in winter.

■ Peak demand tariff - tariffs will be higher in the morning and afternoon when demand for water is high, than in the evening when demand is lower.

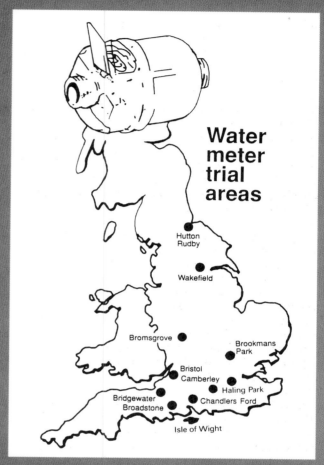

Water meter trial areas

Hutton Rudby
Wakefield
Bromsgrove
Brookmans Park
Bristol
Camberley
Haling Park
Bridgewater
Broadstone
Chandlers Ford
Isle of Wight

Figure 14.3

1. Under the present rating system
   (a) how is the total tariff paid by a household for its water calculated and
   (b) what is the marginal cost to the household of a gallon of water?

2. Using a diagram, explain:
   (a) how much water households would consume under the present rating system;
   (b) how their consumption of water is likely to change under each type of tariff structure being used in the National Water Metering Trials.

Summary

1. A consumer will maximise utility when he or she consumes at the point where the budget line is tangential to his or her highest indifference curve.
2. An increase in price results in a rotation of the budget line. As a consequence, there is a fall in consumption shown on the indifference curve map.

This can be used to explain why the demand curve slopes downward from left to right.
3. Indifference curve analysis can be used to distinguish between the income and substitution effects of a price change.

Indifference curves

One of the fundamental assumptions of economics is that consumers have unlimited wants (☞ unit 1). They would always prefer to consume more rather than less. A consumer would prefer to have 4 pairs of jeans and 6 jumpers rather than 2 pairs of jeans and 3 jumpers for instance. However, what if the consumer were offered either 2 pairs of jeans and 3 jumpers **or** 3 pairs of jeans and 2 jumpers? It is not immediately obvious which she would prefer. Indeed, she might be **indifferent** between the two bundles of goods. She doesn't mind which she has.

An INDIFFERENCE CURVE is a line which links bundles or combinations of goods between which a consumer is indifferent. In Figure 15.1, the consumer is indifferent between the following bundles of goods: 8 ties and 1 shirt, 6 ties and 2 shirts, 4 ties and 4 shirts, and 2 ties and 7 shirts.

The consumer would prefer to have more goods rather than less goods. Hence he would prefer to be to the right of the existing indifference curve. In Figure 15.1, he would prefer to have 8 ties and 2 shirts at B to 8 ties and 1 shirt at A. Similarly, he would prefer to have 6 ties and 4 shirts at D to 4 ties and 4 shirts at C. Indeed, if he prefers B to A, and is indifferent between A and C, he must logically prefer B to C. He must prefer to consume 8 ties

and 2 shirts to 4 ties and 4 shirts.

Similarly, if he consumed any combination of goods to the left of the indifference curve, he would be worse off than if he consumed on the indifference curve shown.

Note that an indifference curve is drawn on the assumption that a consumer can rank alternative combinations or bundles of goods in order of preference, stating which give the highest utility, which the second highest and so on, (although he does not need to place a value on utility as he must in marginal utility theory ☞ unit 14).

QUESTION 1 A student is indifferent between the following combinations of chocolate bars and packets of crisps: 1 chocolate bar and 14 crisps, 2 chocolate bars and 6 crisps, and 5 chocolate bars and 1 packet of crisps.
(a) Draw her indifference curve for these combinations.
(b) Explain whether she would prefer to consume:
  (i) 14 packets of crisps and 3 chocolate bars rather than any of the combinations on her indifference curve;
  (ii) 3 chocolate bars and 4 packets of crisps, or 1 chocolate bar and 8 packets of crisps.

The marginal rate of substitution

Indifference curves slope downward (i.e. they have a negative slope). If the indifference curve were upward sloping it would indicate that the consumer was indifferent between more and fewer goods.

They are also drawn convex to the origin. This is because of the hypothesis of the diminishing marginal rate of substitution. The MARGINAL RATE OF SUBSTITUTION is the amount a consumer has to give up of a good to get one unit of another good and leave the level of utility or satisfaction unchanged. For instance, between points B and C in Figure 15.2, the consumer has to give up 3 lipsticks to gain 2 ribbons if utility is to remain unchanged. Therefore the marginal rate of substitution is 3/2.

The hypothesis of the diminishing marginal rate of substitution states that the more is consumed of a good, the larger the quantities needed to compensate for the loss of consumption of another good to hold utility constant.

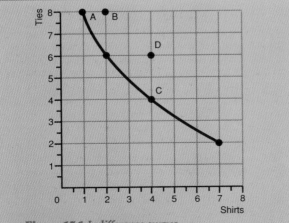

Figure 15.1 *Indifference curves*
The indifference curve shows the combination of ties and shirts between which the consumer is indifferent.

In Figure 15.2, the consumer with a large number of lipsticks is prepared to give up a relatively large number of them to gain one ribbon. But if she has few lipsticks and a large number of ribbons she will want a large number of ribbons to compensate her for the loss of just one lipstick. Hence the marginal rate of substitution of lipsticks for ribbons falls as consumption of lipsticks falls and this is what produces the convex shape of the indifference curve.

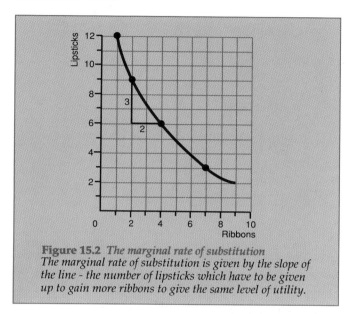

Figure 15.2 *The marginal rate of substitution*
The marginal rate of substitution is given by the slope of the line - the number of lipsticks which have to be given up to gain more ribbons to give the same level of utility.

Indifference maps

The tastes of an individual consumer are represented by a family or set of indifference curves shown on an indifference map. In Figure 15.3, a consumer has an

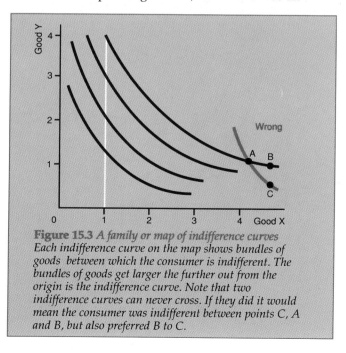

Figure 15.3 *A family or map of indifference curves*
Each indifference curve on the map shows bundles of goods between which the consumer is indifferent. The bundles of goods get larger the further out from the origin is the indifference curve. Note that two indifference curves can never cross. If they did it would mean the consumer was indifferent between points C, A and B, but also preferred B to C.

indifference curve associated with the consumption of 1 unit of good X and 1 unit of good Y she also has a higher indifference curve associated with the consumption of 1 unit of good X and two units of good Y and so on.

Two indifference curves can never cross. In Figure 15.3, the two indifference curves AB and AC show that the consumer is indifferent between consumption at the points A and B, and A and C. Therefore we know that the consumer must be indifferent between points B and C. But we also know that the consumer would prefer B to C because at B the consumer can have more of both goods X and Y. The consumer cannot be indifferent between B and C and prefer B to C. Therefore it is logically impossible for indifference curves to cross.

Budget lines

A student on a fixed budget is able to buy different bundles of goods. But each bundle has an **opportunity cost**. For instance, buying more clothes leaves less to spend on books. This can be shown on a BUDGET LINE.

A budget line shows combinations of goods which a consumer is able to buy. Consider a consumer who has £100 to spend. Suppose she can spend it on only two goods: records costing £5 each, or boxes of chocolates costing £2.50. Table 15.1 shows combinations of records and boxes of chocolates which she could purchase. For instance, she could buy 20 records and no chocolates, or 10 records and 20 boxes of chocolates.

Table 15.1 *Combinations of records priced at £5 and boxes of chocolates priced at £2.50 which a consumer could buy with a budget of £100*

Records		Boxes of chocolates
20	AND	0
15	AND	10
10	AND	20
5	AND	30
0	AND	40

These figures are shown graphically in Figure 15.4. The line is the consumer's budget line, showing the different combinations of records and chocolate boxes that can be bought with £100. Like a **production possibility frontier** (☞ unit 1), consumers can only consume on or within the line. For instance, the consumer could buy 40 boxes of chocolates and no records, or 10 records and 10 boxes of chocolates leaving £25 unspent. But the consumer cannot purchase combinations of goods beyond the frontier. She cannot buy 20 records and 10 boxes of chocolates because that would cost £125, which is more than her budget.

The slope of the budget line indicates relative prices of goods. In Figure 15.4, the slope of the line is given by the change in consumption of boxes of chocolates divided by the change in records (i.e. the vertical change divided by the horizontal change). For every 2 boxes of chocolates purchased, 1 record has to be foregone. The price ratio of chocolates to records is therefore 2:1.

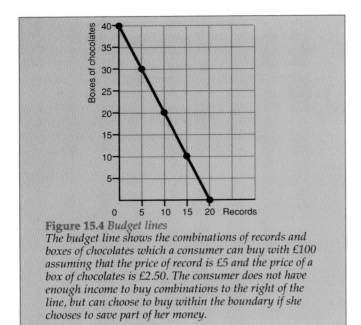

Figure 15.4 *Budget lines*
The budget line shows the combinations of records and boxes of chocolates which a consumer can buy with £100 assuming that the price of record is £5 and the price of a box of chocolates is £2.50. The consumer does not have enough income to buy combinations to the right of the line, but can choose to buy within the boundary if she chooses to save part of her money.

A change in income If income changes, there will be a parallel outward shift in the budget line. For instance, if the consumer in our example is given an income increase of £50, she can buy more of both records and boxes of chocolates. How much more is shown in Figure 15.5 (a). Relative prices have not changed and therefore the slope of the budget line remains the same.

A change in price If prices change, the budget line again will shift but the shift will not be a parallel one. Assume that the price of records increases from £5 to £10 but that the price of a box of chocolates remains unchanged. Common sense says that the consumer will now be able to buy less with her unchanged income of £100. How much less is shown in Figure 15.5 (b). The budget line has

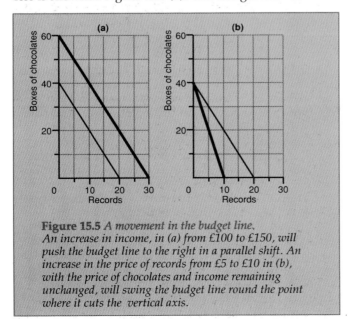

Figure 15.5 *A movement in the budget line.*
An increase in income, in (a) from £100 to £150, will push the budget line to the right in a parallel shift. An increase in the price of records from £5 to £10 in (b), with the price of chocolates and income remaining unchanged, will swing the budget line round the point where it cuts the vertical axis.

pivoted round its point on the horizontal axis. This shows that the same number of chocolate boxes can be bought if no records are consumed, but that fewer records can be bought at every level of chocolate box consumption. If no boxes of chocolates are purchased, only half the number of records can be bought compared to previously. Points to the right of the new budget line become unobtainable. The steeper slope of the line gives the new relative prices of 4:1.

Utility maximisation

Indifference curve analysis can be used to explain what combination of goods a consumer will choose to consume. The budget line shows the combination of goods which a consumer is able to purchase. An indifference map shows the different combinations of goods between which a consumer would choose. Assuming that the consumer will seek to maximise utility, it is true that the consumer will seek to consume on the highest indifference curve possible within the budget line constraint.

In Figure 15.6, the consumer is unable to consume at the point C. This is because he does not have the resources shown by his budget line to do so.

On the other hand, he would prefer to consume at B rather than A because at B he is on a higher indifference

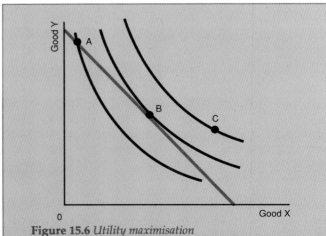

Figure 15.6 *Utility maximisation*
A consumer will maximise utility by consuming on the highest indifference curve possible, subject to the constraint of his or her budget line. This will be at the point B where the indifference curve is tangential to the budget line.

curve. B, where the indifference curve just touches or is **tangential** to the budget line, is the highest possible indifference curve that the consumer can afford to be on.

The consumer will therefore maximise utility where the slopes of the two lines are equal. The slope of the budget line is the relative price of good Y compared to good X. The slope of the indifference curve is the marginal rate of substitution of Y for X. Therefore the consumer will be in equilibrium, maximising utility where relative prices are equal to the marginal rates of substitution.

QUESTION 3
(a) On a diagram, draw a budget line for a consumer and the indifference curve on which she will consume if she maximises her utility. Label the axes 'apples' and 'crisps'.
(b) Mark points on the diagram which show each of the following: (i) A, where the consumer buys only apples; (ii) B, the utility maximising point of consumption; (iii) C, an unattainable level of consumption; (iv) D, an attainable level of consumption but one which does not maximise the consumer's utility; (v) E, where the consumer is indifferent between that level of consumption and the utility maximising level of consumption; (vi) F, where the consumer might prefer to be if she had a higher income.

The downward sloping demand curve

It is now possible to show that the demand curve is downward sloping. In Figure 15.7, the price of good X is falling. This changes the budget line from RS to RT and then to RV. The consumer was initially in equilibrium at the point A, consuming OF of good X. The fall in price of good X, shown by the change in the budget line to RT, will result in a new equilibrium consumption point of B. At this point the consumer will buy OG of good X. When the budget line shifts to RV, consumption will again change to the point C where OH of good X will be bought. We have therefore shown that a fall in price will increase quantity demanded.

A line can be drawn joining together the different equilibrium consumption points as the price of good X changes. This line, ABC on Figure 15.7, is called the **price consumption curve**. Tracing these points onto the demand curve shows that as the price of good X falls, the quantity demanded increases.

Note that if I_2 were drawn such that the point B lies above but to theft of point A, then a fall in price would lead to a fall in quantity demanded. Good X would then be a **Giffen good** (☞ unit 10).

It is also possible to draw an **income consumption curve**. If income rises, budget lines shift outwards. The income consumption curve then links all the associated equilibrium points. From Figure 15.7, it is not difficult to imagine how parallel shifts of the budget line out from RS

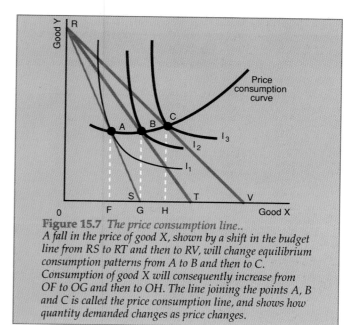

Figure 15.7 *The price consumption line..*
A fall in the price of good X, shown by a shift in the budget line from RS to RT and then to RV, will change equilibrium consumption patterns from A to B and then to C. Consumption of good X will consequently increase from OF to OG and then to OH. The line joining the points A, B and C is called the price consumption line, and shows how quantity demanded changes as price changes.

QUESTION 4
Table 15.2

Indifference curve I_1		Indifference curve I_2		Indifference curve I_3	
Skirts	Dresses	Skirts	Dresses	Skirts	Dresses
16	3	16	5	16	7
8	4	8	6	12	8
6	5	4	8	7	10
1	12	2	12	5	12

Table 15.2 shows three different bundles of goods which form convex indifference curves, I_1 to I_3, for a consumer.
(a) Draw the three indifference curves.
(b) On which indifference curve would the consumer prefer to be?
(c) Which indifference curve shows the lowest level of utility?
(d) What is the marginal rate of substitution on each indifference curve when consumption of skirts falls from 16 to 8?
A consumer has an income of £224. Skirts are priced at £14 whilst dresses are priced at £32.
(e) Draw the consumer's budget line.
(f) What is the utility maximising combination of consumption of skirts and dresses for the consumer?
The price of a dress now falls to £22.40.
(g) Draw the consumer's new budget line.
(h) What will be the new optimum point of consumption for the consumer?
The price of a dress now falls again to £13.50.
(i) What will be the new optimum point of consumption for the consumer?
(j) Draw the price consumption curve for the consumer.

would lead to increased equilibrium consumption of good X. Hence good X would be a normal good. For good X to be an inferior good (i.e. one where an increase in income led to a fall in consumption), the income consumption curve would have to slope upwards and to the left from the point A. Indifference curves I_2 and I_3 would then have to be drawn much higher up and further to the left of their existing positions.

Income and substitution effects

Indifference curves can be used to analyse more deeply the concepts of income and substitution effects first introduced in unit 14. A consumer will buy more or less of a product when its price changes for two reasons.

■ The price of the good relative to all other goods has changed. If price increases, demand will fall because other goods will become relatively cheaper. This is known as the SUBSTITUTION EFFECT of a price change.

■ The real income of a consumer has changed. If price has increased, the consumer will be able to buy a smaller number of goods than before and therefore his or her real income will have fallen. The consumer will react by buying less of the good if the good is **normal**, but more of the good if the good is **inferior**. This is know as the INCOME EFFECT.

Consider Figure 15.8. TR is the original budget line. The consumer is in equilibrium at the point A where he is on his highest indifference curve. The price of food now increases so that the budget line shifts to TS. The new equilibrium consumption point is B. But we can

disaggregate the income and substitution effects of the change.

■ To find the **substitution effect**, we must find a point where the new level of prices is effective but the consumer is no better or no worse off than before. To do this, we draw a line PP which is parallel to the new budget line TS and therefore has the same slope. This line then gives the same relative prices as implied by TS. The consumer will be no better or worse off if he is consuming on his original indifference curve I_1. So drawing the line PP tangential to the indifference curve I_1, we see that the consumer would consume at the point C if prices had changed but income had not. The movement from the point A to the point C is therefore the substitution effect of the price change.

■ To find the **income effect**, we must find the movement between two points where income has changed but the same relative prices are effective. So the movement from C to B is the income effect of the price change.

The good in Figure 15.8 is a normal good because a rise in price leads to a fall in demand both from the substitution effect and from the income effect. Figure 15.9 shows the income and substitution effects of a price rise for an inferior good. The movement from A to C, the substitution effect, shows a decline in demand for food when the price of food increases. The movement from C to B shows an increase in demand for food due to the fall in income. The substitution effect is greater than the income effect and therefore a rise in price leads to an overall fall in demand for food. If the income effect had been greater than the substitution effect (i.e. the indifference curves had been drawn such that B was to the right of A), then food would have been a Giffen good.

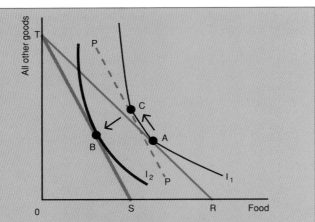

Figure 15.8 *Income and substitution effects for a normal good*
The consumer is originally at the point A. The price of food increases so that the budget line shifts from TR to TS. The substitution effect of the price change is found by drawing a line PP showing the new price relativities tangential to a point on the original indifference curve I_1. At the point C, the consumer is no better or worse off than before but consumes as if food had increased in price. The movement from A to C is therfore the substitution effect of the price change. The movement from C to B is then the income effect of the price change.

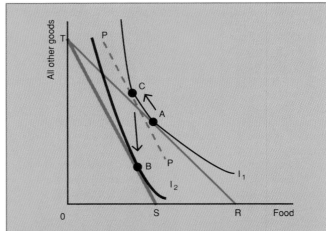

Figure 15.9 *Income and substitution effects for an interior good*
Food in this diagram is assumed to be an inferior good. A rise in the price of food, shown by a shift in the budget line from TR to TS, produces a fall in quantity demanded due to the substitution effect (from A to C) but a rise in quantity demanded due to the income effect (from C to B). The overall effect will still be a fall in quantity demanded because the substitution effect outweighs the income effect.

QUESTION 5 Show on a diagram the income and substitution effects of the change in price resulting from the situation in the photograph. Assume all other prices remain constant.

Key terms

Indifference curve - a line which links combinations of goods between which a consumer is indifferent to consuming.
Marginal rate of substitution - the amount of a good a consumer has to give up to obtain one unit of another good and leave total utility unchanged.
Budget line - a line showing the combinations of goods which a consumer is able to purchase with a given budget.
Substitution effect - that part of the change in quantity demanded of a good when price changes which is caused by the consequent change in relative prices.
Income effect - that part of the change in quantity demanded of a good when price changes which is caused by the consequent change in real income.

Applied economics

Benefits in kind or in cash

Clothing allowances

Who pays for your clothes? Most students aged 16-18 are funded in one of two ways:
- some are given an allowance by their parents (which they may top up with earnings from a part time job) out of which they have to pay for everything from clothes to bus fares to cassettes;
- others have their clothes bought for them by their parents; if they have a part time job, they may choose to buy clothes out of that as well.

Economic theory suggests that the first method of funding is likely to yield the highest utility for the student. To see why, consider Figure 15.10. Parents spend £50 a month on their 17 year old daughter Sophie. On average, each item of clothing costs £10, whilst on average each item of all other goods costs £1. The budget line XY shows that if consumption were at X, with the £50 all spent on clothes, 5 clothes items could be bought.

Alternatively the £50 could all be spent on non-clothes items with consumption at the point Y. Or a mix of clothes and all other goods could be bought. Assume that the parents choose to give £20 a month pocket money to Sophie to spend on all other goods and use the remaining £30 a month to purchase clothes for her. Sophie therefore consumes at the point A on her indifference curve I_1. But she would be better off if she were given all of the £50 and were free to spend it as she wished. She would prefer to consume at B, on the highest indifference curve available to her, I_2. Sophie would choose, if left to herself, to spend less on clothes and more on all other goods.

Hence, Sophie's utility could well not be maximised if spending choices are made for her by her parents. Sophie's spending patterns will reflect utility maximising choices of her parents more than her own.

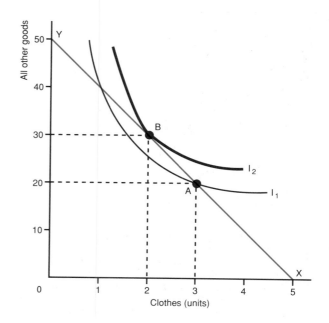

Figure 15.10

Public policy

Indifference curves can be used to analyse public policy issues too. For instance, it is sometimes argued that old age pensioners should be able to travel on public transport at a reduced rate or even free of charge. Figure 15.11 shows possible policy alternatives. With no subsidy, a pensioner's budget line is AB and she consumes at the point P on her highest indifference curve I_1. Government then introduces a subsidy scheme which changes her budget line to AC. She is now better off, consuming on a higher indifference curve I_2 at Q. However, the government could have used the money to increase the state old age pension instead. Whether the pensioner would be better off or worse off than with the alternative of cheap public transport depends on the shape of her indifference curves and the size of the shift in her budget line. In Figure 15.11, the pensioner would be better off with an increase in pension rather than subsidised public transport if her budget line had shifted to DE. She could have consumed on the higher indifference curve I_3 at the point R. On the other hand, if the increase in her old age pension had been relatively small with her budget line shifting only a little to the right from AB, she would have been better off with the subsidy on public transport.

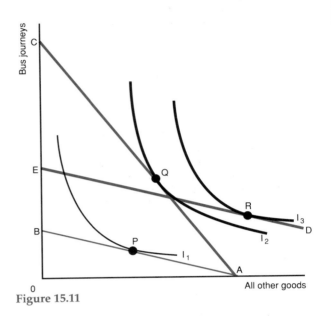

Figure 15.11

Data question

CHEAP PUBLIC TRANSPORT

On March 31 1986, central government forced Sheffield City Council to abandon its policy of cheap public transport. Bus fares rose whilst the local authority grant to the bus service fell. One result was that fewer passenger journeys were made by bus.

1. Using an indifference curve diagram, show why economic theory might predict that a rise in bus fares would lead to a fall in journeys made by public transport.

2. Assuming that local taxes were now lower than before in Sheffield because the transport subsidy had been cut, would Sheffield citizens be better off or worse off as a result of the change in policy?

Business structure

Business organisation

From a legal point of view, there are a number of different ways in which a UK business may be structured.

Sole proprietorships A SOLE PROPRIETORSHIP is a business organisation with only one owner. For tax purposes he or she would be classed as self employed. It is the most common form of business organisation in the UK by number, although sole proprietorships produce comparatively little of total UK output.

The typical sole proprietor is a shopkeeper who owns his or her own shop. Family might be employed to help run the shop. Sole proprietorship is also common in agriculture and manual trades such as plumbing.

Owners of a sole proprietorship have **unlimited liability**. This means that no distinction is made between the assets of the business and the private assets of the owner. If the business goes bankrupt and the assets of the business do not cover the debts, then the owner will be forced to sell his or her own private assets as well.

Sole proprietorships are common because they are very easy to establish or wind down. There are no particular legal formalities to setting up the business apart from those which would apply to any business in the particular industry chosen. Income tax and national insurance contributions have to be paid on profits of the business, but the total tax liability is likely to be far less than if the owner established a limited company. The owner is also likely to be in full control of the company. Sole proprietorships may employ workers, but it would be quite exceptional for a sole proprietor to employ a manager to be in charge of a considerable number of personnel.

The great disadvantage of sole proprietorships is their inability to attract finance. As will be explained in unit 22 it is often difficult for small businesses to raise finance in order to expand.

Partnerships In a PARTNERSHIP, there are usually (though not always) between 2 and 20 shareholders. It is in a far stronger position than a sole proprietorship to raise money to invest in the business. The partners can also work together allowing their complementary skills to benefit the firm.

However, each partner has unlimited liability (except in a limited liability partnership where partners who do not work for the partnership - 'sleeping partners' -

are allowed limited liability). If the partnership breaks up or goes bankrupt, this can expose individual partners to the risk of paying for another partner's mistakes. This is one reason why partnerships are common in family firms, where family members are seen as more trustworthy than outsiders.

Partnerships are also particularly common in certain professions, such as accountancy, the law, medical practices and architectural consultancies, where professional associations advise or insist that professionals should be exposed to unlimited liability as a form of professional discipline.

Joint stock companies A JOINT STOCK COMPANY is one where a number of shareholders own a company and enjoy the benefit of **limited liability**. A joint stock company is a legal entity in itself and can, for instance, be sued.

The great advantage of a joint stock company is that it can attract money for investment in the form of new shares. Shareholders know that if the firm goes bankrupt, the most they stand to lose is the value of their shareholding. This advantage is so great that almost all privately owned large companies and most medium sized companies in the UK are joint stock companies.

There are two types of joint stock company. **A private limited** company is one where shares are not freely available for purchase by the public. This limits their attractiveness to shareholders and therefore larger companies tend to be **public limited companies** (plcs). A plc will have its shares quoted on a stock exchange, such as the London or Birmingham Stock Exchanges. These stock exchanges provide a cheap and efficient way in which owners of shares can sell them. This makes these types of shares far more desirable to shareholders than shares in private limited companies which have no open market. This, together with limited liability, explains why plcs find it easier to attract new shareholder capital than other forms of business organisation.

There are about half a million joint stock companies in the UK with only about 3 per cent being public limited companies. However, nearly all the largest companies in the private sector are plcs.

Various Companies Acts lay down regulations about the information which plcs have to disclose to the public about their operations. For instance, they have to present accounts and name directors of the company and their salaries. Private limited companies do not have to disclose this information. Some owners prefer to keep their companies small to retain control and keep secret the financial affairs of their company. But C&A is the only company of any size in the UK that is not a plc. It is owned by a family originating in Holland who have chosen to keep their financial affairs completely secret by establishing a partnership.

Neo-classical economic theory suggests that firms are motivated by a desire to maximise profits. This may well be true when the owners of a firm also have day to day control of the business. However, in a plc power is often more diffuse. Shareholders elect directors at an Annual General Meeting. Directors then appoint a chairman of the company and a managing director from amongst themselves, who may be one and the same person. The directors are appointed to look after the interests of shareholders. In a plc, the directors must be shareholders themselves. The managing director is responsible for the day to day running of the company and is responsible for appointing all other staff.

In theory, this chain ensures that shareholders remain in overall control of the company. In practice, the shareholding in a company may be very widespread, with no single shareholder owning more than a few per cent of the shares. Many shareholders may know little or nothing about the company apart from its name and share price. Directors are often part time and are likely to know less about the company than its managers. In consequence, managers have far more power in deciding how the company should be run than the theory would suggest. Couple this with the fact that relatively few shareholders bother to vote at, let alone attend, AGMs and it can be understood why many economists believe that ownership of a plc is often very different from control. Where

shareholders do play a key role is when directors are major shareholders themselves. This tends to occur either when a member or members of the original family which started the company are still involved in its day to day running, such as John Sainsbury or Cadbury or when another company has built up a minority stake and is then represented on the board of the company.

Traditionally shareholders have been relatively wealthy private individuals who have owned shares to gain a private income. However, in the post-war period, the pattern of shareholding has been changed. The percentage of shares owned by individuals has declined from over 50 per cent in the 1950s to 20 per cent in 1988. The percentage owned by institutions has correspondingly increased. These institutions are assurance companies, pensions funds and other savings businesses which take money from the individual and use it to invest on their behalf in a variety of assets including shares. Since 1979, the government has actively promoted the idea of 'wider share ownership' and 'a share owning democracy'. It has been government policy to encourage individuals to buy shares in order to own a part of the industrial and commercial wealth of the country. Figure 16.1 shows that the government has achieved some success in this, although most new shareholders are owners of just one or two privatised share issues. Given that shares are a risky form of investment, it is perhaps not surprising that individuals prefer to reduce that risk by saving indirectly in shares through assurance companies, pension funds and unit trusts rather than building up their own portfolios of shares.

Co-operatives There are two main types of co-operatives. Consumer co-operatives, the familiar Co-op shops and superstores, are limited liability businesses which exist to further the interests of their customers. Shareholders each have one vote and are entitled to a fixed dividend on their shares (rather like preference shares in a plc). The remainder of the profits, after tax and investment, is distributed to customers in the form of a purchase dividend which today usually takes the form of stamps.

Worker co-operatives are owned by some or all of the workers of a limited liability business. They may be created by workers to prevent redundancies or create employment. Alternatively they may be set up to produce some good or service which the workers believe should be provided to society, such as religious books or health foods.

Neither form has been particularly successful in the UK over the past 40 years. Consumer co-operatives have suffered a crisis because more and more consumers have preferred to shop at plcs such as Sainsbury's and Tesco's rather than at the Co-op store which should be providing best value for money. Worker co-operatives, on the other hand, have not

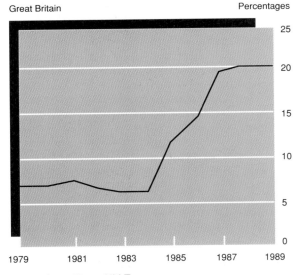

Source: adapted from *HM Treasury*.

Figure 16.1 *Shareholders as a percentage of the adult population (aged 16+)*

proved particularly popular amongst workers. It needs a great deal of initiative and trust amongst a group of workers to set up a co-operative. If it is successful, problems arise because some workers will want to sell their shareholding to non-workers and make a capital gain. Others will want to see the firm expand by introducing new shareholders who may not be workers.

Public corporations Public corporations (or nationalised industries) are a fast-disappearing type of limited liability company owned by the state. Their organisation is discussed in ☞ unit 42.

Establishments, enterprises, companies and firms

'Business' can be defined in a number of different ways. The Central Statistical Office distinguishes between two of these.
■ **Establishments** are individual factories or plants.
■ **Enterprises** are companies or groups of companies with one set of owners.
The basic legal units of business organisation in the UK are:
■ **Companies**
whilst economic theory further distinguishes:
■ **Firms** which are defined as business organisations where decisions are made.
In a small business, all four of these are likely to be one and the same thing. A small business will have one factory or plant. It is an enterprise with one set of owners. It is a company if it has registered as a joint stock company. And it is a firm because it is the unit where economic decisions are made.

In a large business, the four may be very different. A large business is likely to have several establishments or workplaces. It is one enterprise, but there may be a number of different companies within the enterprise. There will be a **parent company** (often called a **holding company**) in which shareholders will own shares. The parent company will then own **subsidiary companies**. There is likely to be a **head office** which will supervise and set targets for the subsidiary companies in the **group**. Head office may also provide financial services and bulk buying facilities so that individual companies can enjoy greater **economies of scale** (☞ unit 20). From an economic viewpoint, the main business decisions are likely to be made at the level of the subsidiary company and therefore the company is the firm rather than the enterprise as a whole.

The size of establishments

The Central Statistical Office publishes information about the size of manufacturing establishments in the

Table 16.1 *Size of establishments by employment and output, 1987*

Number of employees	Total units		Total employment		Total net output	
	Number	% of total	Millions	% of total	£ millions	% of total
1-99	137 459	94.3	1.347	27.6	24 708.4	22.2
100-499	6 779	4.7	1.444	29.7	31 507.1	28.3
500-1 499	1 200	0.8	0.961	19.7	23 746.7	21.3
1 500 +	314	0.2	1.121	23.0	31 339.4	28.2
Total	145 752	100.0	4.874	100.0	111 301.6	100.0

Source: adapted from *Business Monitor*, PA 1002.

UK. In 1987, as Table 16.1 shows, 94.3 per cent employ less than 100 workers. However, small establishments account for relatively little of total employment and output. Table 16.1 shows that establishments with less than 100 employees accounted for only 27.6 per cent of total employment and 22.2 per cent of total output. On the other hand, the 314 establishments with 1 500 or

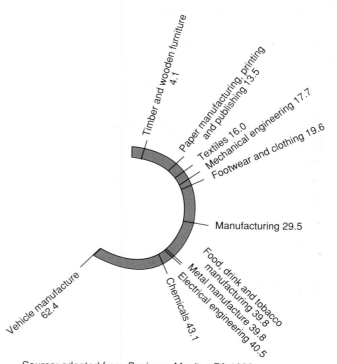

Source: adapted from *Business Monitor*, PA 1002.

Figure 16.2 *Percentage of total employment in selected industries in establishments with 1 000 or more workers*

more employees employed 23.0 per cent of total manufacturing workers and produced 28.2 per cent of total output.

The size of manufacturing plants has risen over time, indicating perhaps the greater exploitation of economies of scale. In 1935, 15 per cent of workers were employed in establishments with 1 500 workers or more. By 1987 this had risen to 23 per cent. However, the proportion of total output produced by different sized establishments has remained broadly the same.

Figure 16.2 indicates that there are greater economies of scale to be gained in some industries than others. Most car production, for instance, takes place in large factories with 1 000 or more workers. At the other end of the scale, establishments in timber and furniture tend to be relatively small.

The size of enterprises

Given that an enterprise may own more than one establishment, it is perhaps not surprising to see in Table 16.2 that small manufacturing enterprises are even less important to total manufacturing output and employment than small establishments. 96.4 per cent of all enterprises employed less than 100 workers but these accounted for only 19.0 per cent of total output. At the other extreme, only 0.3 per cent of enterprises employed 1 500 employees and over. Yet these accounted for 46.5.5 per cent of total employment and 53.9 per cent of total output. The largest 100 manufacturing enterprises have for some time accounted for well over 40 per cent of of total manufacturing output.

Table 16.2 *Size of enterprises by employment and output, 1987*

Number of employees	Total units		Total employment		Total net output	
	Number	% of total	Millions	% of total	£ million	% of total
1- 99	128 327	96.4	1.138	24.6	20 213.5	19.0
100 - 499	3 760	2.8	0.772	16.7	15 769.2	14.8
500 - 1 499	683	0.5	0.566	12.2	13 108.2	12.3
1 500 +	370	0.3	2.151	46.5	57 453.0	53.9
Total	133 140	100.0	4.627	100.0	106 543.9	100.0

Source: adapted from *Business Monitor*, PA 1002.

Key terms

Sole proprietorship - a business with one owner who has unlimited liability.
Partnership - a business with usually between 2 and 20 partners or owners with unlimited liability.
Joint stock company - a company with at least two shareholders who have limited liability.

NUMBER OF LEGAL UNITS, 1988

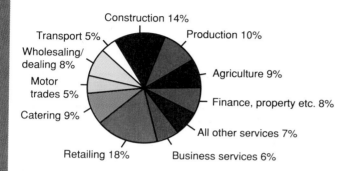

All businesses

- Construction 14%
- Production 10%
- Transport 5%
- Wholesaling/dealing 8%
- Agriculture 9%
- Motor trades 5%
- Finance, property etc. 8%
- Catering 9%
- All other services 7%
- Retailing 18%
- Business services 6%

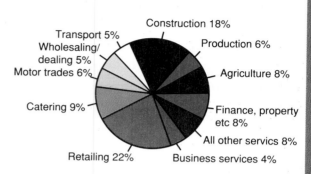

Sole proprietors

- Transport 5%
- Construction 18%
- Wholesaling/dealing 5%
- Production 6%
- Motor trades 6%
- Agriculture 8%
- Catering 9%
- Finance, property etc 8%
- All other servics 8%
- Retailing 22%
- Business services 4%

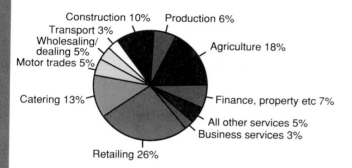

Partnerships

- Construction 10%
- Production 6%
- Transport 3%
- Wholesaling/dealing 5%
- Agriculture 18%
- Motor trades 5%
- Catering 13%
- Finance, property etc 7%
- All other services 5%
- Business services 3%
- Retailing 26%

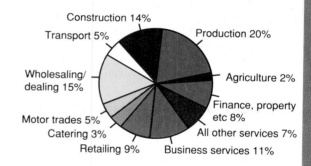

Companies & public corporations

- Construction 14%
- Transport 5%
- Production 20%
- Wholesaling/dealing 15%
- Agriculture 2%
- Motor trades 5%
- Finance, property etc 8%
- Catering 3%
- All other services 7%
- Retailing 9%
- Business services 11%

Figure 16.3 *Number of legal units,* **1988**

Source: adapted from *Business Monitor*, PA 1002.

1. In which sectors of industry are (a) sole proprietorships and partnerships and (b) companies and public corporations most common?
2. Suggest reasons why this might be the case.

Summary

1. A production function shows the relationship between output and different levels and combinations of factor inputs.
2. The short run is defined as that period of time when at least one factor of production cannot be varied. In the long run, all factors can be varied, but the state of technology remains constant. In the very long run, the state of technology may change.
3. If a firm increases its variable inputs in the short run, eventually diminishing marginal returns and diminishing average returns will set in.
4. Constant returns to scale, or economies and diseconomies of scale, may occur in the long run when all factors are changed in the same proportion.

The production function

A farmer decides to grow wheat. In economic terms, wheat is then an output of the production process. To grow wheat, the farmer will have to use different factors of production (☞ unit 2).

■ She will grow the wheat on land.
■ It will be planted and harvested using labour.
■ She will also use capital. If she is a Third World farmer, the capital may be some simple spades, hoes, irrigation ditches and sacks. If she is a First World farmer, she may use tractors, combine harvesters, fertilizers and pesticides.

The land, labour and capital used to produce wheat are the factor inputs to the production process.

A PRODUCTION FUNCTION shows the relationship between output and different levels and combinations of factor inputs. For example, if it needs 50 cows and 1 worker to produce 50 pints of milk a day, then the production function could be expressed as:

$$50Q = L + 50 \, C$$

where Q is the number of pints of milk, L is the number of workers and C is the capital input, the number of cows.

QUESTION 1 C W Cobb and P H Douglas, two American economists estimated, in an article published in 1938, that the production function for US manufacturing industry between 1900 and 1922 was:

$$x = 1.10 \, L^{0.75} C^{0.25}$$

where x is an index of total production per year, L is an index of labour input and C an index of capital input.

Using a calculator with a power function, calculate the increase in the index of production if:
(a) the quantity of labour inputs were increased by (i) 10% and (ii) 20%;
(b) the quantity of capital inputs were increased by (i) 20% and (ii) 30%;
(c) the quantity of both labour and capital inputs were increased by (i) 30% and (ii) 50%.

A production function assumes that the state of technology is fixed or given. A change in the state of technology will change the production function. For instance, the microchip revolution has enabled goods (the outputs) to be produced with fewer workers and less capital (the inputs).

The short run and long run

Economists make a distinction between the short run and the long run. In the SHORT RUN, producers are faced with the problem that some of their factor inputs are fixed in supply. For instance, a factory might want to expand production. It can get its workers to work longer hours through overtime or shift work, and can also buy in more raw materials. Labour and raw materials are then variable inputs. But it only has a fixed amount of space on the factory floor and a fixed number of machines to work with. This fixed capital places a constraint on how much more can be produced by the firm.

In the LONG RUN, all factor inputs are variable. A producer can vary the amount of land, labour and capital if it so chooses. For instance, in the long run, the firm in the above example could move into a larger factory and buy more machines, as well as employ more labour and use more raw materials.

In the long run, existing technologies do not change. In the VERY LONG RUN, the state of technology can change. For instance, a bank would be able to move from a paper-based system with cheques, bank statements and paper memos to a completely electronic paperless system with cards, computer terminal statements and memos.

The way that the short run and the long run are defined in the theory of production means that there is no standard length of time for the short run. In the chemical industry, a plant may last 20 years before it needs replacing and so the short run might last 20 years. In an industry with little or no permanent physical capital, the short run may be measured in months or even weeks. The short run for a market trader, who hires everything from the stall to a van and keeps no stock, may be as short as one day, the day of the market when she is committed to hiring equipment and selling stock.

The short run: diminishing returns

In the short run at least one factor is fixed. Assume for example that a firm uses only two factors of production: capital, in the form of buildings and machines, which is fixed and labour which can be varied. What will happen to output as more and more labour is used?

Initially, output per worker is likely to rise. A factory designed for 500 workers for instance is unlikely to be very productive if only one worker is employed. But there will come a point when output per worker will start to fall. There is an optimum level of production which is most productively efficient (☞ unit 3). Eventually, if enough workers are employed, total output will fall. Imagine 10 000 workers trying to work in a factory designed for 500. The workers will get in each other's way and result in less output than with a smaller number of workers. This general pattern is known as the LAW OF DIMINISHING RETURNS or LAW OF VARIABLE PROPORTIONS.

Total, average and marginal products

The law of diminishing returns can be explained more formally using the concepts of total, average and marginal products.
- TOTAL PRODUCT is the quantity of output produced by a given number of inputs over a period of time. It is expressed in physical terms and not money terms. (Indeed economists often refer to total physical product, average physical product and marginal

physical product to emphasise this point.) The total product of 1 000 workers in the car industry over a year might be 30 000 cars.
- AVERAGE PRODUCT is the quantity of output per unit of input. In the above example, output per worker would be 30 cars per year (the total product divided by the quantity of inputs).
- MARGINAL PRODUCT is the addition to output produced by an extra unit of input. If the addition of an extra car worker raised output to 30 004 cars in our example, then the marginal product would be 4 cars.

Now consider Table 17.1. In this example capital is fixed at 10 units whilst labour is a variable input.
- If no workers are employed, total output will be zero.
- The first worker produces 20 units of output. So the marginal product of the first worker is 20 units.
- The second worker produces an extra 34 units of output. So the marginal product of the second worker is 34 units. Total output with two workers is 54 units (20 units plus 34 units). Average output is 54 ÷ 2 or 27 units per worker.
- The third worker produces an extra 46 units of output. So total output with three workers is 100 units (20 plus 34 plus 46). Average output is 100÷3 or approximately 33 units per worker.

Initially, marginal product rises, but the fifth worker produces less than the fourth. **Diminishing marginal returns** therefore set in between the fourth and fifth worker. Average product rises too at first and then falls, but the turning point is later than for marginal product. **Diminishing average returns** set in between 5 and 6 workers.

The law of diminishing returns states that if increasing quantities of a variable input are combined with a fixed input, eventually the marginal product and then the average product of that variable input will decline.

Table 17.1 *Total, average and marginal products*

Units

Capital	Labour	Physical product as labour is varied		
		Marginal	Total	Average[1]
10	0		0	0
		20		
10	1		20	20
		34		
10	2		54	27
		46		
10	3		100	33
		51		
10	4		151	38
		46		
10	5		197	39
		33		
10	6		230	38
		20		
10	7		251	36
		-17		
10	8		234	29

1. Rounded to the nearest whole number.

It is possible to draw total, average and marginal product curves. The curves in Figure 17.1 are derived from the data in Table 17.1. All three curves first rise and then fall. Marginal product falls first, then average product and finally total product.

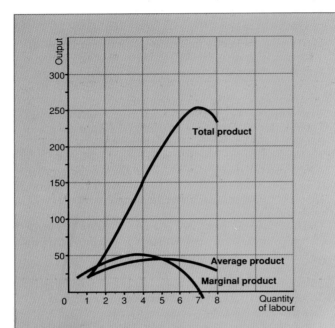

Figure 17.1 *Total, average and marginal product*
The curves are derived from the data in Table 17.1. Note that diminishing marginal returns set in before diminishing average returns. Note too that the marginal product curve cuts the average product curve at its highest point, whilst the total product curve falls when the marginal product curve cuts the horizontal axis.

The long run: returns to scale

The law of diminishing returns assumes that firms operate in the short run. In the long run, firms can vary all their factor inputs. What happens to the output of a firm if, for instance, it were to increase all its inputs by the same proportion? There are only three possibilities.

■ INCREASING RETURNS TO SCALE (or ECONOMIES OF SCALE) occur if an equal percentage increase in inputs to production leads to a more than proportional increase in output. If a firm doubles its land, labour and capital inputs, but as a consequence trebles its output, then increasing returns to scale have occurred. For instance, if as in Table 17.3, 1 unit of capital and 1 unit of all other factors of production are used, then 20 units of output are produced. Doubling the inputs to 2 units of capital and 2 units of all other factors more than doubles output to 50 units. An increase in inputs by 50% from 2 to 3 units of all factors increases output by more than 50% from 50 units to 80 units. Therefore the firm is operating under conditions of increasing returns to scale.

■ CONSTANT RETURNS TO SCALE occur if an equal percentage increase in inputs to production leads to the same percentage increase in output. For example, if a firm doubles its inputs and this leads to a doubling of output, then constant returns to scale occur.

■ DIMINISHING RETURNS TO SCALE (or DISECONOMIES OF SCALE) occur if an equal percentage increase in inputs to production leads to a less than proportional increase in output. So decreasing returns to scale occur if a firm trebles its inputs but only doubles its output.

Table 17.3 *Increasing returns to scale*

		Units of capital		
		1	2	3
Units of all	1	**20**	35	45
other factors	2	30	**50**	65
of production	3	35	63	**80**

QUESTION 4
Table 17.2

		Units
Capital	Labour	Total product
10	1	8
10	2	24
10	3	42
10	4	60
10	5	70
10	6	72

Table 17.2 shows the change in total product as the quantity of labour increases and all other factor inputs remain constant.
(a) Calculate the average and marginal product at each level of labour input.
(b) Draw the total, average and marginal product curves on a graph.
(c) At what level of output do (i) diminishing marginal returns and (ii) diminishing average returns set in?

QUESTION 5
Table 17.4

		Units of labour				
		1	2	3	4	5
Units of all	1	1	2	4	5	6
other factors	2	2	3	6	8	10
of production	3	3	5	9	11	12
	4	5	7	10	12	13
	5	7	9	11	13	14

The table shows the output of a firm given different levels of factor inputs over the long run. Over what range does the firm experience (a) increasing returns, (b) constant returns and (c) decreasing returns to scale?

Key terms

Production function - the relationship between output and different levels and combinations of inputs.

The short run - the period of time when at least one factor input to the production process cannot be varied.

The long run - the period of time when all factor inputs can be varied, but the state of technology remains constant.

The very long run - the period of time when the state of technology may change.

Law of diminishing returns or variable proportions - if increasing quantities of a variable input are combined with a fixed input, eventually the marginal product and then the average product of that variable input will decline. Diminishing returns are said to exist when this decline occurs.

Total product - the quantity of output measured in physical units produced by a given number of inputs over a period of time.

Average product - the quantity of output per unit of factor input. It is the total product divided by the level of output.

Marginal product - the addition to output produced by an extra unit of input. It is the change in total output divided by the change in the level of inputs.

Returns to scale - the change in percentage output resulting from a percentage change in all the factors of production. There are increasing returns if the percentage increase in output is greater than the percentage increase in factors employed, constant returns if it is the same and decreasing returns if it is less.

Applied economics

British Home Stores

British Home Stores (BHS) is a major high street retailer in the UK. Its product is a service. British Home Stores purchases its stock in large quantities from manufacturers around the world. It arranges shipment, storage and then the display of stock in its stores. Consumers are able to buy a range of goods from clothes to lighting and food in small quantities in a pleasant, convenient environment.

The output of BHS is a stream of sales, worth approximately £600 million in 1990. Output is often associated with manufacturing industry, but service industries also produce an output. In this case sales are used as a proxy for the quantities sometimes used to measure output in manufacturing. The inputs in 1990 included over 17 000 staff, 134 stores and their fittings, the merchandise on offer for sale to customers as well as warehouses, offices and computer systems. It would therefore be possible to devise a production function for the operations of BHS, showing how changes in, say, staffing levels or the number of stores would affect total output of the company.

BHS has not been without its problems in the 1980s. Growth in sales and profit in the first half of the 1980s was disappointing, especially when compared to rival chains such as Next and Marks and Spencer. In 1986, BHS was merged with Habitat-Mothercare and came under the direction of Sir Terence Conran, the internationally renowned designer. He felt that many of BHS's problems were due to the dowdy design of the stores and the unimaginative range of goods on sale. In the next two years, many of the stores received

a face-lift whilst more attractive goods were offered for sale. However, sales and profits continued to prove disappointing.

In 1989 the company appointed a new chief executive, David Dworkin, who had had wide experience of retailing in the USA. He rapidly instituted a number of simple but fundamental

changes, one of which had a significant impact on the nature of the production function. Until 1989, the policy at BHS had been wherever possible to keep stock on sale until it was sold at its full price. Only when existing stock had been sold would new stock be brought out from stock rooms and warehouses. If stock proved really difficult to sell, it would be returned to store rooms and kept either for the 'sales' or brought out again in the next season. Dworkin, against the advice of staff, decided that slow selling stock should be reduced in price immediately to clear and allow new ranges to be put on sale. For instance, at Christmas 1989, seasonal stock in the clothes ranges which failed to sell was marked down and the spring ranges which had already arrived at the warehouses and stores were put out on sale.

By April 1990, BHS sales were 20 per cent up on the previous April, and sales of womenswear were 35 per cent ahead. Effectively, in the short run David Dworkin had combined more stock (a variable input) with the same number of stores, warehouses etc. (the fixed inputs) to increase sales (the output). It is not possible to say on the basis of the above data whether BHS then experienced increasing returns or diminishing returns,

although it is likely that average returns were approximately constant given that for every unit of stock brought in, one unit of stock was sold.

Data question

SALES IN BRITISH BOOKSHOPS

Table 17.5

Annual booksales of the shop	Below £118 000	£118 000- £192 000	£192 000- £281 000
Sales per employee	£36 900	£44 600	£48 300
Sales per sq.ft. of shop space	£117	£121	£155

Source: adapted from an economic survey by The Booksellers Association and the Manchester Business School.

1. Assume that the 'output' of a bookshop can be measured by its total sales. What do the data imply about returns to scale in the long run in the British bookshop industry?

18 Costs, revenue and profits

Summary

1. Economists use the word 'cost' of production in a way different to its general usage. Economic cost is the opportunity cost of production.
2. Many costs are imputed - that is they form part of the cost of production but the producer does not directly pay for them.
3. Fixed costs (or indirect or overhead costs) are costs of production which do not vary directly with the level of output. Variable costs (or direct costs) are costs which increase as the level of output increases.
4. Economists distinguish between the total, average and marginal costs of production.
5. Total, average and marginal revenues can be distinguished too.
6. Economic or abnormal profit is the difference between total revenue and total cost. Normal profit is an economic (i.e. opportunity) cost of production.

The economic definition of cost

Economists use the word 'cost' in a very specific sense. The ECONOMIC COST of production for a firm is the opportunity cost of production. It is the value that could have been generated had the resources been employed in their next best use.

For instance, a market trader has some very obvious costs such as the cost of buying stock to sell, the rent for her pitch in the market and the petrol to get her to and from the market. Money will be paid for these and this will be an accurate reflection of opportunity cost. But there are a number of costs which are hidden. Resources which have an opportunity cost but for which no payment is made must have an IMPUTED COST. There are a number of examples that can be used to illustrate imputed cost.

Labour A market trader working on her own account may calculate that she has made £50 'profit' on a day's trading. But this may not include the value of her own time. If she could have earned £40 working in another job for the day, then her economic profit is only £10. Hence, the opportunity cost of her labour must be included as an economic cost of production.

Financial capital A small businessman may start a company with his own money investing, say, £50 000. The economic cost of production must include the opportunity cost of that start-up capital. If he could have earned 10 per cent per annum in an alternative investment, then the economic cost (the opportunity cost) is £5 000 per year.

Depreciation The **physical capital** of a company will deteriorate over time. Machines wear out, buildings need repairs, etc. Moreover, some capital will become obsolete before the end of its physical life. The economic cost of depreciation is the difference between the purchase price and the second hand value of a good. A car, for instance, which lasts for 8 years does not depreciate at 12½ per cent each year. In the first year, cars depreciate on average by 40 per cent. So a company paying £10 000 for a new car which depreciates by 40 per cent over its first year only has an asset worth £6 000 at the end of the year. £6 000 is the monetary value of the opportunity cost of keeping the car rather than selling it at the end of that year.

Goodwill A firm trading over a number of years may acquire a good reputation. It may produce branded goods which become household names. The goodwill of these brands has an opportunity cost. They could be sold to a rival company. Therefore the interest foregone on the potential sale value of these must be included as an economic cost. For instance, Nestlé bought Rowntree Mackintosh in 1988 for £2.3bn. It paid £1.9bn over and above the value of buildings, machinery, etc. This was effectively a payment for the brand names of Rowntree Mackintosh products such as KitKat, Smarties, Polo and After Eight as well as the relationships which the company had with its suppliers and customers. The opportunity cost of this sum (e.g. the interest that could have been received had the money been lent) should have been included as an economic cost for Rowntree Mackintosh.

It can be seen from this discussion that economists differ in their use of the word 'cost' from accountants, tax inspectors, businesses and others. Accountants have developed specific conventions about what is and what is not a cost and what should and should not be included on a balance sheet and an accountant's balance sheet may be very different from that of an economist's.

QUESTION 1 A businesswoman runs her own business. Over the past twelve months she has paid £6 000 for materials and £3 000 in wages to a worker whom she employs. She runs the business from premises which her husband owns. These premises could be rented out for £2 000 a year if she were not occupying them. She has £10 000 worth of her own capital tied up in the business. She is a trained teacher and at present works exactly half time in a school earning £6 000. She could work full time as a teacher if she didn't run her business. The current rate of interest is 10 per cent. The total revenue of her business over the past 12 months was £18 000.

On the basis of these figures, what were her accounting costs and what were her economic costs? Did she make a profit last year?

Fixed and variable costs

Economists distinguish between two types of cost: fixed and variable cost.

A FIXED COST (also called an INDIRECT or OVERHEAD COST) is a cost which does not vary directly with output. As production levels change, the value of a fixed cost will remain constant. For instance, a company may rent premises. The rent on the premises will remain the same whether the company produces nothing or produces at full capacity. If a firm pays for an advertising campaign, the cost will be the same whether sales remain constant or increase. Costs commonly given as examples of fixed costs are capital goods (e.g. factories, offices, plant and machinery), rent and rates, office staff and advertising and promotion.

A VARIABLE (or DIRECT or PRIME) COST is a cost which varies directly with output. As production increases, so does variable cost. For instance, a steel maker will use iron ore. The more steel produced, the more iron ore will be needed, so the cost of iron ore is a variable cost. Raw materials for production are the clearest example of variable costs for most firms. It is not always easy to categorise a cost as either fixed or variable. Many costs are SEMI-VARIABLE COSTS. Labour is a good example. Some firms employ a permanent staff which could be classified as a fixed cost. They might ask the permanent staff to do overtime when necessary, or employ temporary labour. These costs would be classified as variable. But permanent staff could be seen as a variable cost if a firm were willing to hire and fire staff as its output changed. In practice, firms do adjust staff numbers with output, but the adjustment is sluggish and therefore the cost of labour is neither variable nor fixed - it is semi-variable.

In the **short run** (☞ unit 17), at least one factor input of production cannot be changed. So in the short run, some costs are fixed costs whilst others will be variable. In the **long run**, all factor inputs can vary. So in the long run, all costs will be variable costs.

> **QUESTION 2** Rachel Hughes owns a whole food vegetarian restaurant. Explain which of the following costs would be most likely to be fixed costs, variable costs or semi-variable costs for her business: rice, rent, wages of casual staff, interest payments on a loan, electricity, cooking oil, pots and pans, her own wage, VAT.

Total, average and marginal cost

It is important to distinguish between the total, average and marginal costs of production. The TOTAL COST (TC) of production is the cost of producing a given level of output. For instance, if a manufacturer produces 100 units a week and its weekly costs come to £1 million, then £1 million is the total cost of production. Increased production will almost certainly lead to a rise in total

Table 18.1 *Total costs of production*

(1)	(2)	(3)	(4)
Output (per week)	Total variable cost (£)	Total fixed cost (£)	Total cost (columns 2+3) (£)
0	0	200	200
1	200	200	400
2	300	200	500
3	600	200	800
4	1200	200	1400
5	2000	200	2200

costs. If the manufacturer increased output to 200 units a week, it would need to buy more raw materials, increase the number of workers, and generally increase its factor inputs.

This is illustrated in Table 18.1. At an output level of 1 unit per week, the total cost of production is £400. If output were 2 units per week, total costs would rise to £500.

The total cost of production is made up of two components:
■ TOTAL VARIABLE COST (TVC) which varies with output;
■ TOTAL FIXED COST (TFC) which remains constant whatever the level of output.

So in Table 18.1, total variable cost increases from zero to £2 000 as output increases from zero to 5 units per week, whilst total fixed costs remain constant at £200 whatever the level of output. Total variable costs when added to total fixed costs are equal to total cost. Mathematically:

$$TVC + TFC = TC$$

The AVERAGE COST OF PRODUCTION is the total cost divided by the level of output. For instance, if a firm makes 100 items at a total cost of £1 000, then the average cost per item would be £10. If a firm made 15 items at a cost of £30, then the average cost of production would be £2. Mathematically:

$$AC = \frac{TC}{Q}$$

where AC is average cost, TC is total cost and Q is quantity or the level of output.

Average cost, like total cost, is made up of two components.
■ AVERAGE VARIABLE COST (AVC) is total variable cost divided by the level of output.
■ AVERAGE FIXED COST (AFC) is total fixed cost divided by the level of output.

The average costs of production for the example given in Table 18.1 are given in Table 18.2.

MARGINAL COST is the cost of producing an extra unit of output. For instance, if it costs £100 to produce 10 items and £105 to produce 11 items, then the marginal cost of the eleventh item is £5. If it costs £4 to produce 2 items but £10 to produce 3 items, then the marginal cost of the third unit is £6. Mathematically, marginal cost (MC) is calculated by dividing the change in total cost (ΔTC) by the change in total output (ΔQ).

$$MC = \frac{\Delta TC}{\Delta Q}$$

The marginal costs of production for the figures in Tables 18.1 and 18.2 are given in Table 18.3.

Table 18.2 *Average costs of production*[1]

(1)	(2)	(3)	(4)
Output (per week)	Average variable cost (£)	Average fixed cost (£)	Average total cost (columns 2+3) (£)
1	200	200	400
2	150	100	250
3	200	67	267
4	300	50	350
5	400	40	440

1. Rounded to the nearest pound.

Table 18.3 *Marginal costs of production*

(1)	(2)	(3)
Output (per week)	Total cost (£)	Marginal cost per unit of output (£)
1	400	400
2	500	100
3	800	300
4	1400	600
5	2200	800

QUESTION 3
Table 18.4

£

Output	Total fixed cost	Total variable cost	Total cost	Average fixed cost	Average variable cost	Average cost	Marginal cost
0	40						
1		6					
2		11					
3		15					
4			60				
5			66				

Complete Table 18.4, calculating the missing figures.

Total, average and marginal revenues

A firm's revenues are its receipts of money from the sale of goods and services over a time period such as a week or a year. The relationships between total, average and marginal revenue are the same as between total, average and marginal cost.

- TOTAL REVENUE (TR) is the total amount of money received from the sale of any given level of output. It is the total quantity sold times the average price received.
- AVERAGE REVENUE (AR) is the average receipt per unit sold. It can be calculated by dividing total revenue by the quantity sold. If all output is sold at the same price, then average revenue must equal the price of the product sold.
- MARGINAL REVENUE (MR) is the receipts from selling an extra unit of output. It is the difference between total revenue at different levels of output. Mathematically:

$$MR = TR_n - TR_{n-1}$$

where n and n-1 are the last and last but one goods sold respectively. For instance, if a firm sold 9 units for a total of £200 and 10 units for £220, then the marginal revenue from the tenth unit sold would be £20.

QUESTION 4
Table 18.5

Sales (million units)	Average revenue (£)
1	20
2	15
3	12
4	8
5	4

Calculate (a) total revenue and (b) marginal revenue at each level of sales from 1 million to 5 million.

Profit

The PROFIT of a company can be calculated by taking away its total cost from its total revenue:

$$Profit = TR - TC$$

It can also be calculated by finding the average profit per unit, which is average revenue minus average cost, and multiplying that by the quantity sold.

It should be remembered that cost for an economist is different from that for an accountant or business person. As explained above, the economic cost of production is its **opportunity cost**. It is measured by the benefit that could have been gained if the resources employed in the production process had been used in their next most profitable use. If a firm could have made £1 million profit by using its resources in the next best manner, then the £1 million profit is an opportunity cost for the firm. In economics, this profit which is counted as an economic cost is called NORMAL PROFIT.

If the firm failed to earn normal profit, it would cease to produce in the long run. The firm's resources would be put to better use producing other goods and services where a normal profit could be earned. Hence, normal profit must be earned if factors of production are to be kept in their present use.

ECONOMIC PROFIT (also called PURE PROFIT, or ABNORMAL PROFIT or SUPERNORMAL PROFIT) is the profit over and above normal profit (i.e. the profit over and above the opportunity cost of the resources used in production by the firm). It is important to remember that

the firm earns normal profit when total revenue equals total cost. But total revenue must be greater than total cost if it is to earn abnormal profit.

QUESTION 5 A business person leaves her £50 000 a year job to set up a company from which she draws a salary of £30 000. She puts £40 000 of her own savings into the company as start up capital which previously had been invested and had earned a rate of return of 20 per cent per annum. Accountants declare that the costs of the firm over the past twelve months have been £250 000 whilst revenues were £300 000.

(a) What is the accounting profit made by the firm?
(b) What is the firm's economic profit?
(c) What is its normal profit?

Key terms

Economic cost - the opportunity cost of an input to the production process.
Imputed cost - an economic cost which a firm does not pay for with money to another firm but is the opportunity cost of factors of production which the firm itself owns.
Fixed or indirect or overhead costs - costs which do not vary as the level of production increases or decreases.
Variable or direct or prime costs - costs which vary directly in proportion to the level of output of a firm.
Total cost - the cost of producing any given level of output. It is equal to total variable cost + total fixed cost.
Average cost - the average cost of production per unit, calculated by dividing the total cost by the quantity produced. It is equal to average variable cost + average fixed cost.

Marginal cost - the cost of producing an extra unit of output.
Total revenue - the total money received from the sale of any given quantity of output.
Average revenue - the average receipts per unit sold. It is equal to total revenue divided by quantity sold.
Marginal revenue - the addition to total revenue of an extra unit sold.
Profit - the difference between total revenue and total cost.
Normal profit - the profit that the firm could make by using its resources in their next best use. Normal profit is an economic cost.
Economic profit (or pure profit or abnormal profit or supernormal profit) - the profit over and above normal profit (i.e. the profit over and above the opportunity cost of the resources used in production by the firm).

Applied economics

Massey-Fergusson

Massey-Ferguson is a major manufacturer of tractors. The first half of the 1980s was a difficult time for tractor manufacturers worldwide. Increased competition from new producers, particularly the Japanese, combined with falling demand, resulted in a ferocious squeeze upon established tractor manufacturers. By 1987, losses at Massey-Ferguson's tractor plant in Coventry forced management at the company to take drastic action. The

choice was simple: either the plant returned to profitability or it would face almost certain closure.

Part of the reorganisation involved cutting costs, such as component costs, administration and data processing costs. The other part involved cutting labour costs. After three months of negotiations with the trade unions representing the workers, during which time there were walkouts, legal action over a strike ballot and threats of closure of the plant by management, an agreement was reached. 700 workers lost their jobs out of a workforce of nearly 3 000. Workers took a 10 per cent pay cut. The workforce also had to agree to radical new work arrangements which involved workers agreeing to do a range of jobs in the factory as and when required (job flexibility) instead of doing one job only.

Was the cost of labour a fixed or a variable cost for Massey-Ferguson? On the one hand it can be seen as mainly a fixed cost. Admittedly any overtime and bonus payments were linked to output, but in any one week, the basic wage bill of the Coventry plant was the same whether 500 or 1 000 tractors were produced. On the other hand, production of tractors at the plant had

fallen before the 1987 agreement was signed. Management responded to that fall in production by cutting their wage costs. So in that sense, labour costs were a variable cost.

This, however, was not the sort of response which management was likely to repeat on a weekly or monthly basis. The cut in wage costs came from a crisis situation which threatened the existence of the Coventry plant. So labour costs are likely to be best classified as semi-variable. Massey-Ferguson had limited opportunities to vary its wage bill on a week to week basis, but it was only over a much longer period that it could change its fundamental labour cost structures.

Data question

A VILLAGE NICHE

Phil Careless left the army after 24 years of service and decided, with his wife, to buy a village store. They found what they wanted at Stanmer outside Brighton. A six year lease on the store cost £33 000. £4 000 was spent on stock and legal bills, whilst a replica vintage van cost £15 000 secondhand. To pay for this initial expense, the Carelesses realised £34 000 from the sale of their house. Phil commuted one-third of his army pension of £5 100 a year to provide another £25 000 and Barclays Bank provided a £15 000 small business loan. The Carelesses are now living over the shop. The balance sheet for the first two years of operation is shown in Table 18.6.

Note: Gross profit is defined here as profit before deduction of fixed costs.

1. How might an economist measure the economic profit or loss that Phil Careless's business made in
   (a) its first year and
   (b) its second year of operation?

Table 18.6 *Balance sheet for a village store (Stanmer, Sussex)*

First Year:	Income	Expenditure
Army wages (net)	£11,000	
Profit (gross)	£11,000	
Savings	£15,000	
Capital purchases		£18,515
Overheads		£18,000
	£37,000	£36,515
Second Year (estimated):		
Army gratuity	£4,000	
Lump sum from pension	£25,000	
Profit (gross)	£17,000	
Capital purchases		£26,000
Overheads		£10,000
	£46,000	£36,000

Source: adapted in part from the *Financial Times*, 13.5.1989.

UNIT 19

Short run costs - diminishing returns

Summary

1. **The short run average cost is U-shaped because of the law of diminishing marginal returns.**
2. **Diminishing average returns set in when average variable cost begins to increase.**
3. **Diminishing marginal returns set in when marginal cost begins to increase.**
4. **If factor input prices are constant, the average and marginal product curves are the mirror image of short run average and marginal cost curves.**
5. **The marginal cost curve cuts the average variable cost and average cost curves at their lowest point.**

Diminishing returns

It was explained in unit 17 that in the short run a firm was faced with employing at least one factor input which could not be varied. For instance, it might have a given number of machines or a fixed quantity of office space. If it were to increase output by using more of the variable factor inputs, diminishing marginal returns and then diminishing average returns would set in eventually.

Diminishing returns were expressed in terms of physical inputs and physical product (the output of the firm). But it is possible to express physical inputs in terms of costs. For example, a firm which employed 5 workers at a wage of £200 per week, and had no other costs, would have total weekly costs of £1 000. If each worker produced 200 units of output, then the average cost per unit of output would be £1 [£1 000 ÷ (5 x 200)]. The marginal cost of the 200 units produced by the fifth worker would be her wage (£200), and so the marginal cost per unit of output would be £1 (£200 ÷ 200).

Table 19.1

Units			£						
Capital	Labour	Total physical product (output)	Total cost[1] TVC	TFC	TC	Average cost[2] AVC	AFC	ATC	Marginal cost MC
10	0	0	0	1000	1000	0	-	-	
									10.0
10	1	20	200	1000	1200	10	50	60	
									5.9
10	2	54	400	1000	1400	7.4	18.5	25.9	
									4.3
10	3	100	600	1000	1600	6.0	10.0	16.0	
									3.9
10	4	151	800	1000	1800	5.3	6.6	11.9	
									4.3
10	5	197	1000	1000	2000	5.1	5.1	10.2	
									6.1
10	6	230	1200	1000	2200	5.2	4.3	9.6	
									9.5
10	7	251	1400	1000	2400	5.6	4.0	9.6	
									22.2
10	8	260	1600	1000	2600	6.8	3.8	10.0	

1. Assuming that capital costs £100 per unit and labour costs £200 per unit.
2. The three measures of average cost have been calculated to the nearest decimal from total figures. ATC therefore does not always equal AVC+ATC because of rounding.

Short run cost schedules

Having converted inputs into costs, it is possible to express the law of diminishing returns in terms of costs and output. Table 19.1 is an example of how this can be done. It is assumed that the firm can employ up to 8 workers at identical wage rates (i.e. the supply of workers over the range 1 to 8 is **perfectly elastic**). The price of capital per unit is £100 and the price of labour is £200 per unit.

Capital is the fixed factor of production. Therefore whatever the level of production, total fixed cost will be £1 000 (10 units x £100). Total variable cost will increase as more and more labour is added. So the total variable cost of producing 20 units is £200 (1 unit of labour x £200), of 54 units it is £400 (2 units of labour x £200), and so on.

Total cost is total fixed cost plus total variable cost. Once the three measures of total cost have been worked out, it is possible to calculate average and marginal costs (☞ unit 18). Alternatively, it is possible to calculate marginal cost per unit by finding the cost of the additional labour and dividing it by the marginal physical product. In our example, the cost of hiring an extra worker is a constant £200. So the marginal cost of producing, say, an extra 34 units once 20 have been made is £200 (the cost of the second worker). The marginal cost per unit is then £200 ÷ 34. Average variable cost can be calculated in a similar manner.

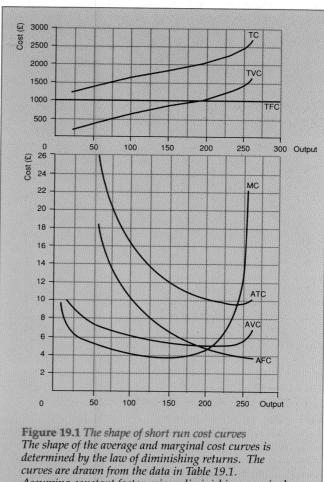

Figure 19.1 *The shape of short run cost curves*
The shape of the average and marginal cost curves is determined by the law of diminishing returns. The curves are drawn from the data in Table 19.1. Assuming constant factor prices, diminishing marginal returns set in at an output level of 145 when the marginal cost curve is at its lowest point. Diminishing average returns set in at the lowest point of the average variable cost curve at an output of 210 units.

QUESTION 1
Table 19.2

Labour	Units Total physical product
1	20
2	45
3	60
4	70

Table 19.2 shows how total physical product changes as the number of units of labour changes with a fixed quantity of capital. The cost of the capital employed is £200. The firm can employ any number of workers at a constant wage rate per unit of labour of £50. What is the value of the following if: (a) 1 unit of labour (b) 2 units of labour; (c) 3 units of labour; (d) 4 units of labour are employed?
(i) Total fixed costs (ii) Total variable costs (iii) Total costs (iv) Average fixed costs (v) Average variable costs (vi) Total average cost (vii) Marginal cost.

Short run cost curves

The cost schedules in Table 19.1 can be plotted on a graph (Figure 19.1) to produce cost curves.

Total cost curves The total fixed cost (TFC) curve is a horizontal straight line, showing that TFC is constant whatever the level of output. The total cost (TC) and total variable cost (TVC) curves are parallel because the vertical distance between the two (the difference between TC and TVC) is the constant total fixed cost. The inflections in the TC and TVC curves are caused by the change from increasing returns to diminishing returns.

Average cost curves The average fixed cost (AFC) curve falls as output increases because fixed costs represent an ever decreasing proportion of total cost as output increases. The average cost (AC) curve and average variable cost (AVC) curve fall at first and then rise. They rise because diminishing average returns set in. The vertical distance between the AC and AVC curves is the value of average fixed cost. This must be true because average cost minus average variable cost is equal to average fixed cost.

Marginal cost curve The marginal cost (MC) curve at first falls and then rises as diminishing marginal returns set in.

Points to note

U-shaped AC and MC curves The MC and AC curves in Figure 19.1 are 'U-shaped'. This is a characteristic, not just of the sample figures in Table 19.1, but of all short run MC and AC curves. They are U-shaped because of the law of diminishing returns. The lowest point on each curve shows the point where diminishing marginal returns and diminishing average returns set in respectively.

Product and cost curves The marginal and average cost curves shown in Figure 19.1 are mirror images of the marginal and average product curves that could be drawn from the same data in Table 19.1. Marginal and average physical product rise when marginal and average cost fall, and vice versa. This is what should be expected. If marginal physical product is rising, then the extra cost of producing a unit of output must fall, and similarly with average physical product and average variable cost. For instance, when the second worker produces 34 units, the third worker 46 units and the fourth worker 51 units, the marginal cost of production must be falling because the increase in output is rising faster than the increase in cost. When marginal physical product is falling, the extra cost of producing a unit output must rise for the same reason. However, the cost and product curves will only be mirror images of each other if there are constant factor costs per unit. If, for instance, we assumed that the unit cost of labour rose as more workers were employed, so that the average wage of three workers was higher than the average wage of two, then the product and cost curves would not be mirror images.

MC curve cuts AC curve at its lowest point In Figure 19.1, the marginal cost curve cuts the average cost curve and average variable cost curve at their lowest points. To understand why this must be so, consider the example of a group of students whose average height is 6 feet. A new student (the marginal student) arrives in the group. If the student is above 6 feet then the average height of the group will now rise. If the student is less than 6 feet, the average height of the group will fall. If the student is exactly 6 feet herself, then the average height of the group

will stay the same. Now apply this to average and marginal cost. If the average cost curve is falling, then the cost of an extra unit of output (the marginal cost) must be less than the average cost. If average cost is rising, it must be true that the cost of an extra unit of output is even higher than the average cost. When average cost is neither rising or falling, marginal cost must the same as average cost. Hence we know that:

■ the average cost curve is above the marginal cost curve when average cost is falling;
■ the average cost curve is below the marginal cost curve when average cost is rising;
■ average cost and marginal cost are equal for all levels of output when average cost is constant; if the average cost curve is U-shaped, this means that marginal cost will be equal to and will cut the average cost curve at its lowest point.

The same chain of reasoning applies to the relationship between the average variable cost curve and the marginal cost curve.

QUESTION 2
Table 19.3

		Units
Capital	Labour	Total product
10	0	0
10	1	8
10	2	24
10	3	42
10	4	60
10	5	70
10	6	72

Table 19.3 shows the change in total product as more labour is added to production and all other factor products remain constant. The price of capital is £1 per unit whilst labour is £2 per unit.

(a) Calculate the following over the range of output from zero to 72 units: (i) total fixed cost; (ii) total variable cost; (iii) total cost; (iv) average fixed cost; (v) average variable cost; (vi) average total cost; (vii) marginal cost.
(b) Plot each of these cost schedules on graph paper, putting the total cost curves on one graph and the average and marginal cost curves on another.
(c) Mark on the graph the point where (i) diminishing marginal returns and (ii) diminishing average returns set in.

Applied economics

Diminishing returns in agriculture

In agriculture, farmers combine land, labour and capital to produce their crops. Land could be said to be a fixed factor of production. Labour and capital, however, are variable. Therefore, in theory, farmers could face diminishing returns. Is there any evidence

to suggest that this is the case?

Table 19.4 shows growth rates of total food production across the world by area during the period 1961 to 1989. The annual rate of growth of food production fell from 3.1 per cent in the 1960s to 2.1 per

Table 19.4 *Annual average growth rate of food production*

	Total food production		
	1961-70	1970-80	1980-89
World	3.1	2.4	2.1
Developed market economies	2.3	2.4	2.1
of which			
US	2.2	2.3	0.2
Canada	2.4	2.4	0.3
UK	1.5	1.6	0.6
Developing countries	2.9	3.0	2.7
Eastern European countries	3.7	1.6	2.1
Socialist countries of Asia	5.3	3.3	4.2

Source: adapted from UNCTAD, *Handbook of International Trade and Development Statistics.*

cent in the 1980s. This might suggest the existence of diminishing returns, but any such conclusion would, in fact, be very debatable for a number of reasons.

■ Whilst regions have seen a fall in the annual rate of growth of production, some increased their rate of growth between decades. The socialist countries of Asia, which includes China, had a higher growth rate of output in the 1980s than they did in the 1970s. The 1980s were also difficult times for agriculture in certain parts of the world due to drought. Sub-Saharan Africa was badly affected throughout the decade, whilst, for instance, the US drought of 1988 saw an overall 7 per cent fall in US food production in that year.

■ The figures say nothing about factor inputs. The proportion of the world's labour force working in agriculture fell from 71 per cent in 1960 to 59 per cent in 1980 in the developing world, whilst in the developed world it fell from 28 per cent in 1960 to 12 per cent in 1980. This meant that the agricultural labour force increased in the Third World but decreased in the First World. In the First World, where diminishing returns should have been found to be greatest because land is being used most intensively, increases in output per worker throughout the period 1961-90 averaged 3 per cent per annum. Fewer workers produced more food.

■ Both in the USA and in the EC, the 1980s saw an attempt by government to restrict the growth of food output. Supply was far outstripping demand in domestic markets where farmers were receiving large subsidies. So the fall in the growth of output in these regions probably had far more to do with government policy than with the law of diminishing returns.

Why is there little clear evidence of diminishing returns in agriculture? Part of the reason must be that land itself is in one sense not a fixed factor of production. Although the total quantity of land is in fixed supply, its productive potential has a great deal to do with the quality of land. The productivity of land can be greatly improved, for instance through drainage, irrigation and the use of fertilizers. Many economists in the past, including Malthus, an early 19th century British economist, have predicted that agricultural production could not keep up with the growth in population. However, so far they have been proved wrong. The average world increase in food production per capita was 2.5 per cent per annum between 1961 and 1989, and in the developed world, the main problem in agriculture is not under-production but over-production.

Data question

CATERING FOR GROWTH

From being a domestic science teacher, Angela's initial foray into the world of business was an outside catering service run from her own home. Later she resigned her teaching post and opened up a coffee shop in Tynemouth to run alongside the catering.

'I had tested the water with my small catering operation and I knew I could make a go of the business,' explains Angela. 'The catering would keep things going while the coffee shop was quiet. We then branched out into making cakes and pies to order - this was a great success.'

As business boomed, so Angela's problems grew. In the third year turnover increased by 26 per cent on the previous year which meant Angela's Kitchen was rapidly becoming unmanageable and there was an urgent need for a move to larger and better placed premises.

Source: *Employment Gazette*, October 1989.

1. **How might Angela's problems illustrate the law of diminishing returns?**

Summary

1. Economic theory suggests that the long run average cost curve is U-shaped.
2. Production is at an optimal level when average cost is lowest.
3. Sources of economies of scale are technical, managerial, purchasing and marketing and financial.
4. Diseconomies of scale may arise due to the inability of management to control large organisations.
5. External economies will shift the average cost curve downwards.
6. The long run average cost curve of a firm is an envelope for the firm's short run average cost curves.

Returns to scale and average cost

In the long run, a firm is able to vary all its factor inputs. It was explained in unit 17 that a firm which increases its inputs by the same proportion would experience:

■ **increasing returns to scale** or economies of scale if output rose by a greater proportion;
■ **constant returns to scale** if output rose by the same proportion;
■ **decreasing returns to scale** or diseconomies of scale if output rose by a lesser proportion.

It is possible to express returns to scale in terms of costs. Assume that a firm can purchase any quantity of a factor input at a constant unit price (i.e. the factor is in perfectly elastic supply ☞ unit 9).

■ If there are increasing returns to scale, the long run average cost of production will fall. For instance, a firm doubles its inputs from a value of £10 million to £2 million. As a result, production increases from 10 million units to 40 million units. Economies of scale are therefore present and the average cost of production falls from £1 per unit (£10m÷10m) to 50p per unit (£20m ÷ 40m).
■ If there are constant returns to scale, the long run average cost of production will be horizontal. A doubling of factor inputs from a value of £10 million to £20 million leads to a doubling of output from 10 million units to 20 million units. Hence the average cost of production remains the same at £1 per unit.
■ If there are decreasing returns to scale, the long run average cost curve will rise as output increases. For instance, a firm would double its average cost if quadrupling its inputs only led to a doubling of output (assuming constant prices).

Empirically, economists have found that firms over initial levels of output are likely to experience economies of scale. As a firm expands in size, its long run average cost tends to fall. Later, constant returns to scale will occur and eventually, a firm may become too large and suffer diseconomies of scale. This pattern is shown in Figure 20.1. At output levels up to OA, the firm will enjoy falling long run average costs and therefore produce under conditions of increasing returns to scale. Between output levels of OA and OB, long run average costs are constant and therefore there are constant returns to scale.

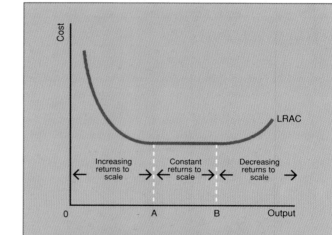

Figure 20.1 *Returns to scale.*
The long run average cost curve is U-shaped because long run average costs:
■ *at first fall over the output range OA showing increasing returns to scale ;*
■ *then are constant over the output range AB showing constant returns to scale ;*
■ *then rise when output exceeds OB showing decreasing returns to scale .*
Over the output range AB , the minimum cost level of production, the firm is said to be at its optimum level of production.

To the right of B, long run average costs rise and decreasing returns therefore set in.

It should be remembered that a cost curve is drawn on the assumption that unit costs of inputs are constant. If unit costs rise, such as a rise in the basic wage rate of labour, then the cost curve will shift upwards (i.e. at any given level of output, it will now cost more to produce that output) and vice versa.

The optimum level of production

Productive efficiency is said to exist when production takes place at lowest cost (☞ unit 33). If the long run average cost curve is U-shaped, then this will occur at the bottom of the curve when constant returns to scale exist. The output range over which average costs are at a minimum is said to be the OPTIMAL LEVEL OF PRODUCTION. In Figure 20.1 the optimal level of production occurs over the range AB.

The output level at which lowest cost production starts is called the MINIMUM EFFICIENT SCALE (MES) of production. In Figure 20.1, the MES is at the point A. If a firm is producing to the left of the MES, then long run average costs will be higher. To the right, they will either be the same (if there are constant returns) or will be increasing (if there are diseconomies of scale).

QUESTION 1
Table 20.1

Output (million units)	Long run average cost (£)
1	10
2	8
3	5
4	5
5	5
6	5
7	6

(a) Over what output range are there (i) diseconomies of scale, (ii) increasing returns to scale and (iii) constant returns?
(b) What is the optimum level of output for the firm?
(c) What is the minimum efficient scale of production?

Sources of economies of scale

Economies of scale - declining long run average costs - occur for a number of reasons.

Technical economies Many firms find that they need equipment but are unable to make maximum use of it. For instance, a small builder may use a cement mixer on average only 3 days a week. If he were able to take on more work he might be able to use it 5 days a week. The total cost of the cement mixer is the same whether used for 3 days or 5 days a week (apart from possible depreciation) but the average cost per job done will be lower the more it is used. This is an example of an **indivisibility**. The larger the level of output, the less likely that indivisibilities will occur.

Technical economies arise too because larger plant size is often more productively efficient. For instance, because an oil tanker is essentially a cylinder, doubling the surface area of the tanker (and therefore doubling the approximate cost of construction) of an oil tanker leads to an approximate three-fold increase in its carrying capacity.

It is generally cheaper to generate electricity in large power stations than in small ones. The average cost of production of a car plant making 50 000 cars a year will be less than one making 5 000 cars a year.

Managerial economies Specialisation (☞ unit 2), is an important source of greater efficiency. In a small firm, the owner might be part time salesman, accountant, receptionist and manager. Employing specialist staff is likely to lead to greater efficiency and therefore lower costs. The reason why small firms don't employ specialist staff is because staff often represent an indivisibility.

Purchasing and marketing economies The larger the firm the more likely it is to be able to buy raw materials in bulk. Bulk buying often enables these firms to secure lower prices for their factor inputs. Large firms are also able to enjoy lower average costs from their marketing operations. The cost of a sales force selling 40 different lines of merchandise is very much the same as one selling 35 lines. A 30 second TV commercial for a product which has sales of £10 million per annum costs the same as a 30 second TV commerical for one which has sales of only £5 million per annum.

Financial economies Small firms often find it difficult and expensive to raise finance for new investment. When loans are given, small firms are charged at relatively high rates of interest because banks know that small firms are far more at risk from bankruptcy than large firms. Large firms have a much greater choice of finance and it is likely to be much cheaper than for small firms.

QUESTION 2
On 16 February 1989, the *Financial Times* reported that some of the smaller Japanese manufacturers of audio equipment were finding it difficult to compete with larger firms in the industry. The competition was so stiff at the upper end of the market that audio manufacturers needed to change their product ranges every 6 months to a year. This favoured the larger manufacturers who had the resources to invest heavily in research and development and employ production systems flexible enough to change models quickly. The smaller manufacturers were also being squeezed at the lower end of the market by high volume, low priced imports from other Far Eastern countries.

To what extent can Japanese audio equipment manufacturers exploit economies of scale?

Diseconomies of scale

Diseconomies of scale arise mainly due to management problems. As a firm grows in size it becomes more and more difficult for management to keep control of the activities of the organisation. There are a variety of ways of dealing with this problem. Some companies choose to centralise operations with a small, tightly-knit team controlling all activities. Sometimes a single charismatic figure, often the founder of the company, will keep tight control of all major decisions. In other companies, management is decentralised with many small subsidiary companies making decisions about their part of the business and head office only making those decisions which affect the whole group. However, controlling an organisation which might employ hundreds of thousands of workers is not easy and there may come a point where no management team could prevent average costs from rising.

Geography too may lead to higher average costs. If a firm has to transport goods (whether finished goods or raw materials) over long distances because it is so large, then average costs may rise. Head office may also find it far more difficult to control costs in an organisation 1 000 miles away than one on its door step.

Movements along and shifts in the long run average cost curve

The long run average cost curve is a boundary. It represents the minimum level of average costs attainable at any given level of output. In Figure 20.2, points below the LRAC curve are unattainable. A firm could produce above the LRAC boundary, but if it were to do this it would not use the most efficient method to produce any given level of output. So a firm could, for instance, produce at the point A, but it would be less efficient than a firm producing the same quantity at the point B.

An increase in output which leads to a fall in costs would be shown by a **movement along** the LRAC curve. However, there are a variety of reasons why the LRAC might **shift.**

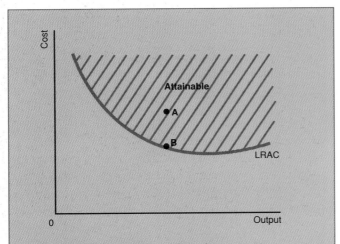

Figure 20.2 *The LRAC as a boundary*
The LRAC curve is a boundary between level of costs which are attainable and those which are unattainable. If a firm is producing on the LRAC curve , then it is producing at long run minimum cost for any given level of output, such as at the point B. If long run production is inefficient, cost will be within the LRAC boundary such as at point A.

External economies of scale The economies of scale discussed so far in this unit have been INTERNAL ECONOMIES OF SCALE. Internal economies arise because of the growth in output of the firm. EXTERNAL ECONOMIES OF SCALE arise when there is a growth in the size of the industry in which the firm operates. For instance, the growth of a particular industry in an area might lead to the construction of a better local road network, which in turn reduces costs to individual firms. Or a firm might experience lower training costs because other firms are training workers which it can then poach. The local authority might provide training facilities free of charge geared to the needs of a particular industry. The government might assist with export contracts for a large industry but not a small industry. External economies of scale will shift the LRAC curve of an individual firm downwards. At any given level of output, its costs will be lower because the industry as a whole has grown.

Taxation If the government imposes a tax upon industry, costs will rise, shifting the LRAC curve of each firm upwards. For instance, if the government increased employers' National Insurance contributions, a tax upon the wage bill of a company, the total cost of labour would rise, pushing up average costs.

Technology The LRAC curve is drawn on the assumption that the state of technology remains constant. The introduction of new technology which is more efficient than the old will reduce average costs and push the LRAC curve downwards.

> **QUESTION 3** In 1989, the government announced a £12 billion road building programme over the following 10 years. The Road Hauliers' Association, representing firms in the road transport business, welcomed the announcement and claimed that if the programme were not implemented the costs of road haulage in the UK would continue to rise due to increased congestion.
>
> Explain, using a diagram, the argument of the Road Hauliers' Association.

The relationship between the short run average cost curve and the long run average cost curve

In the short run, at least one factor is fixed. Short run average costs at first fall, and then begin to rise because of diminishing returns. In the long run, all factors are variable. Long run average costs change because of economies and diseconomies of scale.

In the long run, a company is able to choose a scale of production which will maximise its profits. Assume in

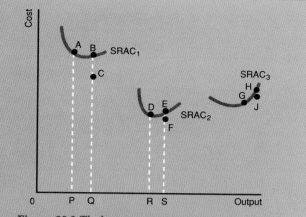

Figure 20.3 *The long run average cost curve*
In the long run, all factors are variable. Points A, D and G show long run cost levels at different levels of production. If the firm in the short run then expands production, average costs may fall or rise to B, E or H respectively. But they will be above the long run costs, C, F and J, for those levels of output because the cost of production with at least one fixed factor is likely to be higher than the cost if all factors were variable.

Similarly, if D and F are long run cost positions, a firm producing at E with plant and machinery designed to produce at D must be less cost effective than a firm operating at F with a factory designed to produce OS of output.

A, C, D, F, G and J are least cost points in the long run. Combining these, as in Figure 20.4, we get a long run average cost curve. For each point on this curve there is an associated short run average cost curve, such as AB. If the firm operates in the short run at the point where the short run cost curve just touches (is tangential to) the long run cost curve, then it is operating where the company thought it would operate when it was able to vary all its factor inputs. If short run output is different from this position, then its short run costs will be higher than if it could have varied all its factors of production. But it could be higher or lower than the tangency point depending upon whether diminishing returns have or have not set in.

The long run average cost curve is said to be the **envelope** for the short run average cost curves because it contains them all.

Figure 20.3 that it decides to produce in the long run at the point A. It buys factors of production such as plant and machinery to operate at this level. Later it wishes to expand production by PQ but in the short run it has fixed factors of production. Expanding production may well lead to lower average costs as it does in Figure 20.3. Diminishing average returns have not set in at the point A. But production must be less cost efficient at B compared to the long run situation where the firm could have varied all its factors of production and produced at C. At B the firm is working with plant and machinery designed to work at optimum efficiency at a lower output level OP. At C, the firm is working with plant and machinery designed to produce at C.

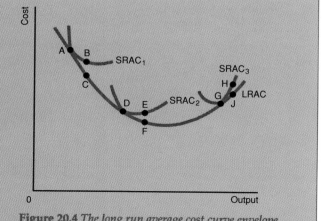

Figure 20.4 *The long run average cost curve envelope*
The long run average cost curve is an envelope for all the associated short run average cost curves because long run average cost is either equal to or below the relevant short run average cost.

QUESTION 4 In 1989, Ford announced that it was to transfer part of the production of its Sierra model from Dagenham in the UK to Genk in Belgium. Dagenham in future would only make the Fiesta model. It blamed the move on high costs of production at Dagenham. Part of the problem lay in the inefficient physical layout of the 50 year old Dagenham plant. At the same time, Toyota was announcing the building of a green field motor manufacturing plant near Derby.

Ford at Dagenham.

Using a diagram, explain why you might expect Toyota to enjoy lower average costs of production at its Derby plant than Ford at its Dagenham plant.

Key terms

Optimal level of production - the range of output over which long run average cost is lowest.
Minimum efficient scale of production - the lowest level of output at which long run average cost is minimised.
Internal economies of scale - economies of scale which arise because of the growth in the scale of production within a firm.
External economies of scale - falling average costs of production, shown by a downward shift in the average cost curve, which result from a growth in the size of the industry within which a firm operates.

Applied economics

Economies of scale

Economic theory suggests that, in the long run, a firm will experience first economies of scale, but eventually diseconomies of scale will set in. The long run average cost curve is therefore U-shaped. However, research in this area tends to support the view that long run average cost curves in practice are not U-shaped but L-shaped. Firms experience economies of scale, but when output reaches the minimum efficient scale of production, average costs do not start to climb but remain constant. For instance, CF Pratten (1971) studied 25 industries, including newspapers, soap, oil, bread and steel and found L-shaped rather than U-shaped long run average cost curves.

Figure 20.5 shows an estimate of economies of scale in three areas of vehicle production: diesel engine production, commercial vehicles and cars. Economies of scale are largest in car production and smallest in diesel engine production. This is what would be expected given the much greater complexity of car production than engine production. Note, however, that the evidence suggests that for cars most economies of scale have been gained with an annual production of 2 million. But the market for commercial vehicles and diesel engines is much smaller and it was not possible to estimate data for production levels over 100 000 units a year. The data would suggest that economies of scale had not been exhausted at these production levels for these two

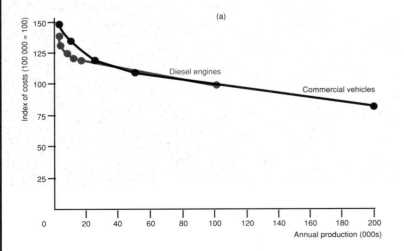
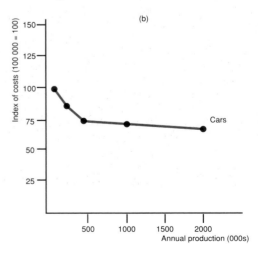

Source: adapted from Garel Rhys, 'Heavy Commercial Vehicles: a decade of change', *National Westminster Bank Quarterly Review'* August 1984; Garel Rhys, 'Economics of the Motor Industry', *Economics*, Volume XXIV, Part 4, no.104, Winter 1988.

Figure 20.5 *Economies of scale in vehicle manufacture*

Table 20.1 *Economies of scale in car production*

	Minimum efficient scale of production volume output per year (millions)
Technical economies	
Casting of engine block	1
Casting of various other parts	0.1-0.75
Power train (engine, transmission, etc.) machining and assembly	0.6
Pressing of various panels	1-2
Paint shop	0.25
Final assembly	0.25
Non-technical economies	
Advertising	1
Sales	2
Risks	1
Finance	2
Research and development	5

Source: Garel Rhys, 'Economics of the Motor Industry', *Economics*, Journal of the Economics Association, Volume XXIV, Part 4, no.104, Winter 1988, p.161.

products and that therefore existing producers had not reached the minimum efficient scale of production.

The sources of economies of scale in car manufacturing are shown in Table 20.1. For instance, the minimum efficient scale of production for the casting of an engine block is 1 million units a year whilst in final assembly it is 250 000 units a year. Economies of scale are greatest in research and development at 5 million units a year. This explains the proliferation of mergers, takeovers and co-operation agreements which have characterised the world motor industry for the past 20 years. A small manufacturer like Rover, for instance, had no choice but either to be taken over by or to collaborate with another major car producer if it was to survive in the long term. It could not mass produce cars profitably at a sufficiently low price on the relatively low volumes it was selling. It opted for collaboration with Honda, another relatively small car manufacturer. Joint ventures are likely to be even more common in the future. With the opening up of markets in Eastern Europe and in Asia, the major car companies will also seek to gain longer production runs by establishing manufacturing facilities in these countries and 'exporting' the fruits of research and development in which there are very large economies of scale to be gained.

Data question

GM AND SAAB

In 1989, General Motors (GM), the world's largest motor manufacturer, took a 50 per cent stake in Swedish luxury car producer, Saab. GM had been seeking to buy a luxury car manufacturer in Europe for some time given that it had found it difficult to establish satisfactory market share at the top end of the car market with its Vauxhall/Opel Senator range. Saab had experienced problems in the late 1980s, resulting in a loss of $294 million in its car division in 1988 and did not have the resources to move successfully into the 1990s. As the Chief Executive of Saab-Scania was quoted as saying in the *Financial Times* (16.12.1989):

'soaring costs for research and development and ever-increasing international competition make it difficult for small volume car makers to survive on their own in a longer perspective'.

GM and Saab plan to develop a range of luxury cars for the international market. Saab will also manufacture GM cars for sale through the GM distribution network in Scandinavia.

1. What economies of scale are likely to result from the agreement between GM and Saab?

Summary

1. An isoquant shows different combinations of inputs which can be used to produce a given level of output.
2. An isocost line shows the combination of factor inputs which a firm can buy with a given budget.
3. The firm will minimise cost where the isoquant curve is tangential to its isocost line.
4. A rise in the price of one factor of production will lead to the substitution of that factor by other factors in the production process.

How to produce

It was argued in unit 2 that the function of an economy was to resolve three fundamental economic questions: what to produce, how to produce it and how to distribute it. This unit considers why a firm might decide to use one production technique rather than another, and why firms might change their production techniques over time as, for instance, the cost of labour increases, or the cost of capital decreases. Much of what follows is very similar to indifference curve analysis (☞ unit 15), and just as in indifference curve analysis the economist is interested in how a consumer can maximise utility, so below it will be explained how a firm can minimise its costs through the efficient allocation of factor inputs.

Isoquants

There is a variety of production techniques which a firm could use to produce 1 million chocolate bars a year. Assume that its land or raw material inputs are constant (so it is producing in the short run), but it can vary the amount of labour and capital it uses. As the firm employs more and more labour, economists would predict that it would need to use less and less capital to produce 1 million chocolate bars. Labour can be **substituted** for capital in the production process.

However, the more labour is used, the greater the amount that needs to be substituted to replace 1 unit of capital. Adding an extra 10 workers to a firm which already has many workers but little capital is unlikely to be as productive as adding 10 workers to a firm producing the same good which has few workers but a great deal of capital.

This is shown in Table 21.1. The chocolate firm can use a lot of labour and little capital (such as 100 units of

Table 21.1 *Units needed to produce 1 million chocolate bars*

Labour	Capital
100	20
70	30
40	44
20	70
12	100

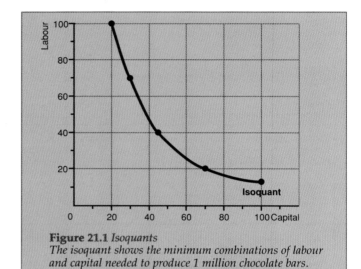

Figure 21.1 *Isoquants*
The isoquant shows the minimum combinations of labour and capital needed to produce 1 million chocolate bars. The curve is constructed from the figures in Table 21.1.

labour and 20 units of capital), or little labour and a lot of capital (such as 12 units of labour and 100 units of capital), or choose some combination in between. Figure 21.1 shows these input combinations in graphical form.

The curve joining the four points shown in Figure 21.1 is known as an ISOQUANT. An isoquant is a line which shows different combinations of inputs needed to produce a given level of output efficiently. Reading off the graph, it would also be possible to produce 1 million chocolate bars a year by using 80 units of labour and 25 units of capital in addition to the points noted in Table 21.1.

The isoquant shows the most efficient form of production possible. It would not be possible to produce 1 million chocolate bars with input combinations below the curve. On the other hand, it is possible to produce above the curve. For instance, 100 units of labour could be combined with 40 units of capital instead of 20, but this input combination would be less **productively efficient** than an input combination on the isoquant.

The isoquant drawn in Figure 21.1 is part of a family of isoquants. Isoquants can be drawn for every production level of chocolate bars. In Figure 21.2, three isoquants are drawn for production levels of 500 000, 1 million and 1.5 million chocolate bars. It takes more inputs to produce 1 million than ½ million chocolate bars, so the isoquant for the former will be farther out from the origin than the latter.

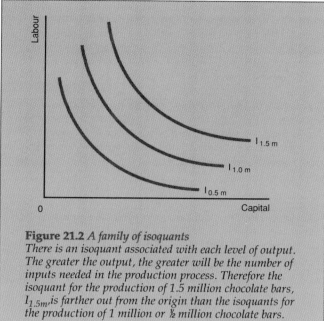

Figure 21.2 *A family of isoquants*
There is an isoquant associated with each level of output. The greater the output, the greater will be the number of inputs needed in the production process. Therefore the isoquant for the production of 1.5 million chocolate bars, $I_{1.5m}$, is farther out from the origin than the isoquants for the production of 1 million or ½ million chocolate bars.

QUESTION 1
Table 21.2

Units per month

	Output per week		
100 units		200 units	
Labour	Capital	Labour	Capital
12	1	12	2
3	3	6	4
1	5	2	9

(a) Draw the two isoquant curves for output levels of 100 units and 200 units per month on graph paper.
(b) A firm wishes to produce 100 units per month. State whether the following input combinations are possible but productively inefficient **or** possible and efficient **or** insufficient to produce that level of output: (i) 5 units of labour and 5 units of capital; (ii) 2 units of labour and 2 units of capital; (iii) 8 units of labour and 2 units of capital; (iv) 4 units of labour and 2 units of capital.

Isocost lines

An ISOCOST LINE shows the combination of factor inputs which a firm can buy with a given budget. For instance, if a firm has a budget of £100 and the price of labour per unit is £1 whilst the price of capital is £2, then the firm can buy 100 units of labour and no units of capital, **or** no units of labour and 50 units of capital **or** some combination in between. The isocost line based upon these numbers is shown in Figure 21.3(a).

The slope of the isocost line reflects the relative prices of inputs. The slope of the line in Figure 21.3(a) is 2,

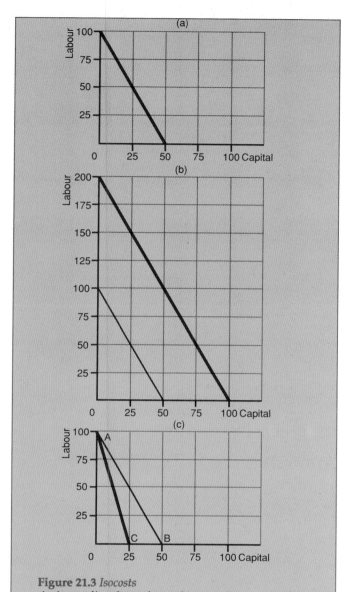

Figure 21.3 *Isocosts*
An isocost line shows the combination of inputs which can be purchased with a fixed budget. Figure 21.3(a) shows the combination of inputs that could be bought with £100 if the price of labour were £1 per unit and the price of capital were £2 per unit. If relative input prices remain unchanged at £1 per unit for labour and £2 per unit for capital, but a firm's budget increases from £100 to £200, then twice the number of inputs can be bought as in Figure 21.3(b). A doubling in the price of capital from £2 to £4 per unit with the price of labour remaining unchanged, given a budget of £100, will result in a swing of the isocost line from AB to AC as in Figure 21.3(c).

showing that 2 units of labour can be bought for every 1 unit of capital not purchased.

If the firm is able to increase its budget, it will be able to buy more labour and capital as in Figure 21.3(b). The budget has increased from £100 to £200, allowing the firm to buy 200 units of labour and no capital **or** no units of labour and 100 units of capital **or** some combination in between. The new line is parallel to the original line because relative prices of labour and capital have not changed. 2 units of labour still cost the same as 1 unit of capital despite the increased budget.

If the relative price of inputs does change, then the slope of the isocost curve will change too. Assume that a firm has a budget of £100, the price of labour is £1 per unit but the cost of capital increases from £2 per unit to £4 per unit. The isocost curve will then shift from AB to AC as in Figure 21.3(c). AB is the same isocost line drawn in Figure 21.3(a). AC shows the new isocost curve with the higher price of capital. At any given level of input usage, the firm can only buy half the amount of capital because the price of capital has doubled.

QUESTION 2

(a) Draw an isocost line for a firm spending £2 400 per month on factor inputs when labour costs £200 per unit per month and capital £300 per unit per month.
(b) Show how the isocost line changes if: (i) the price of capital now increases to £600 per month; (ii) the firm's budget for the purchase of factor inputs increases to £3 000 per month when the cost of capital is £300 per unit per month.

Cost minimisation

By combining isoquants and isocost lines, it is possible to explain which combination of factors a firm will use in its production process. In Figure 21.4, a firm wishes to produce at an output level associated with the isoquant I. AB, CD and EF are three isocost lines. Production on EF is the most costly, AB the least costly. All three show the same relative cost of labour to capital because the lines are

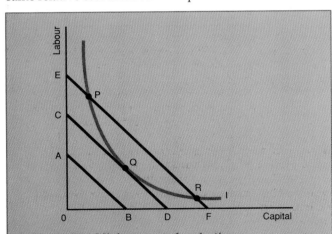

Figure 21.4 *Minimum cost of production*
A firm wishes to produce a level of output given by the isoquant I. It faces relative input prices shown by the identical slopes of the three isocost lines, AB, CD and EF. It is unable to produce on the line AB because the isoquant I does not cut or touch it. It could produce on the isocost curve EF, but it would be cheaper to produce at the point Q on the isocost curve CD. CD is the lowest isocost curve on which the firm can produce.

parallel with each other. If the firm chooses to produce at P or R, it will be more costly than if it produces at Q because Q is on a lower isocost line. It cannot produce on the isocost line AB if it wishes to secure an output level associated with the isoquant I. Q is the least cost point of production because CD is the lowest isocost line on which the firm can be.

A firm will therefore minimise its production costs by choosing that point where the isocost curve is tangential to (just touches) the isoquant. This is the same as saying that cost minimisation will occur where the slope of the isocost line (the relative price of factor inputs) is equal to the slope of the isoquant.

QUESTION 3 Combining the solutions to the previous two sets of questions in this unit,
(a) what is the lowest cost combination of factor inputs if:
  (i) output of the firm is 200 units when its budget is £2400 per month, labour costs £200 per unit per month and capital costs £300 per unit per month;
  (ii) output of the firm is 100 units when its budget is £2400 per month, labour costs £200 per unit per month and capital costs £600 per unit per month;
(b) what is the minimum budget needed to produce 200 units of output per month when labour costs are £220 per unit and capital costs are £170 per unit per month?

Factor substitution

Common sense tells us that if the price of labour increases when the price of capital remains the same, a firm will react by using less labour and more capital. In other words, capital will be **substituted** for labour.

This can be shown using isoquants and isocost lines. In Figure 21.5, an increase in the price of labour pivots the isocost line round from AB to AC. As a result the firm will no longer be able to produce on the isoquant I_1. With a fixed budget, it will be forced to reduce output to the level given by the isoquant I_2. Production will change from the point P to the point Q.

This change is made up of two components, a **substitution effect** and an **output effect**. The substitution effect occurs because the price of labour has become higher relative to capital. The output effect occurs because the firm now has a smaller real budget to spend on inputs. The size of the substitution effect can be seen by assuming that the company is able to produce the same amount as before (i.e. it can still produce on the isoquant I_1) but that it faces the new relative prices. DE is an isocost line which, being parallel to AC, shows the new relative prices but is also the minimum isocost curve which will allow the company to produce on I_1. At the new prices and the old output level, the firm will produce at R. Hence the movement from P to R is the substitution effect of the price change. The movement from R to Q is the output effect. This represents the fall in demand for

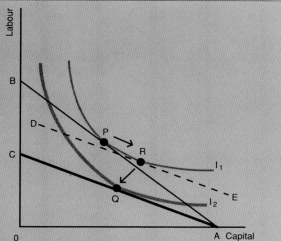

Figure 21.5 *Substitution and output effects.*
A firm producing at the point P on an isocost I_1 is faced with an increase in the cost of labour. As a result its isocost line pivots round A from AB to AC. It will as a result use less labour as production shifts from the point P to the point Q. Part of the reduced demand for labour occurs because of the substitution effect of the price change. If the firm was in a position to produce the same output as before, but faced new relative prices, then it would have shifted production from P to R: this is the substituion effect of the price change. The output effect is shown by the shift from R to Q when, at the new relative prices, the firm suffers a fall in the real value of its budget.

both labour and capital because the firm is now able to produce less due to the fall in the real value of its budget. Figure 21.5 shows that a firm will buy less labour when the cost of labour rises because labour becomes relatively more expensive to other inputs **and** because the firm suffers a real fall in its budget.

QUESTION 4 Modern industrial development has been characterised by a rise in the cost of labour relative to capital. What does economic theory predict would happen to the quantity of labour employed in the production process compared to the quantity of capital? Giving examples, discuss whether this prediction is supported by recent economic history.

Key terms

Isoquant - shows different combinations of inputs needed to produce a given level of output efficiently.
Isocost line - shows the combination of factor inputs which a firm can buy with a given budget.

Applied economics

'Just-in-time' production systems

It can be argued that the most important innovation in the manufacturing process since Henry Ford began building cars on a production line has been 'just-in-time' production systems. Pioneered by Toyota in the 1950s and 1960s, it has become standard practice amongst large Japanese manufacturers and has increasingly been adopted by European and American companies in the 1980s. The concept is simple. Instead of holding stocks of goods at every stage of the manufacturing process, firms reduce or eliminate stocks by telling their suppliers to deliver parts only when they are needed. For a car manufacturer this may mean deliveries of parts three or four times a day.

The advantages are numerous. As Clive Wolman, writing in the *Financial Times* (20.5. 1989), argues: 'Most obviously, just-in-time production leads to a drastic reduction of inventory. This means less working capital, no double handling of components, no laborious checking of materials into and out of storage, and less warehousing space. Just-in-time production allows machines to be placed close to each other - with

no work in progress piling up between - which in turn makes it easier for teams of workers to supervise groups of machines'.

'In fact, the key benefit of the just-in-time approach is its impact on the organisation and motivation of the workforce. In the West, inventory is traditionally used as a buffer to absorb delays - and also mistakes. Just-in-time production is supposed to ensure that any defects and any production delays are immediately exposed. This in turn increases the pressure of responsibility on the individual workers; he or she can no longer bury defective products in a pile of inventory.'

What effect have just-in-time production techniques had on the isoquant curves facing a manufacturing firm such as Toyota? These techniques have led to a shift to the left in the isoquant curves as shown in Figure 21.6. Assume that before the introduction of just-in-time production, a firm produces at the point A on the isoquant I_1. The new techniques allow the firm to produce the same amount using fewer factors of production. The isoquant shifts to I_2 and the firm now produces at B. It has been able to make a substantial reduction in its use of inventories of PQ, but the other advantages of just-in-time production also enable a reduction in the use of all other factors of RS.

In general, technical progress in production will lead to a shift to the left of isoquant curves facing a firm. With a constant budget and no change in the relative prices of factors, this means that firms will be able to produce more, shown by a movement to a higher isoquant curve. This in turn is likely to lead to lower prices, the outcome that would be expected from technical progress.

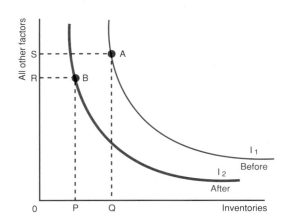

Figure 21.6

PIRELLI GENERAL

Data question

In July 1988, Pirelli General opened a new cable factory on its Aberdare site in South Wales where it has been manufacturing cables since 1971. The fully automated plant replaces a previous factory which was closed in 1985. Of the 80 workers made redundant then, 40 have been re-employed at the new plant.

According to the company, the plant is one of the most advanced computer integrated, flexible manufacturing systems in the country. There are no forklift trucks carrying around components, only computer guided vehicles. The company's offices are designed to be paperless. The production system is run by a suite of IBM computers, which control everything from production schedules to testing the quality of the finished product.

Source: adapted from the *Financial Times* 12.11. 1988.

1. **Using an isoquant diagram, suggest reasons why Pirelli has changed its production techniques.**

Applied economics

Cost, revenue and cash flow

A company's finances can be split into two types. A company, operating on a day to day basis, receives money from sales of goods (its **turnover** or **revenue**) and pays out money (**its costs**), for instance to its workers in wages and to its suppliers.

The difference between the monies received by a company and its outgoings over a period of time is known as the CASH FLOW of the company. Table 22.1 shows the cash flow for a new company over its first

Table 22.1

Month	1	2	3	4	5	6
Receipts (£)	10	20	30	40	50	60
Payments (£)	50	30	10	10	10	10
Cash flow (£)	-40	-10	20	30	40	50

six months of operation. The cash flow is negative for the first two months. Far more is paid out than is received. However, the cash flow for the next four months is positive. Overall, the company is in a strong position, but without financial reserves or an ability to borrow money it would go out of business at the end of the first month.

A company needs financial capital to cope with negative cash flows. In a company starting up, or a company which is growing, negative cash flows are often associated with investment by the company - the purchase of equipment, premises, stock, etc. The rest of this unit will consider ways in which companies can obtain funds for investment.

Sources of funds for companies

Table 22.2 shows how companies in the UK raise funds to finance investment (i.e. additions to their stock of capital).

Retained profit RETAINED PROFIT is by far the most important source of company finance in the UK. Companies split the profits they make three ways. They give some to their shareholders in the form of **dividends**. Some is taken by the government in **tax** (mainly corporation tax). The rest, **retained profit**, is kept by companies to plough back into the business.

Bank borrowing Bank borrowing is the second most important source of company finance. Essentially there are only two types of bank borrowing. An

Table 22.2 *Sources of capital funds for industrial and commercial companies 1979-1989*

£ million

	1979	1981	1983	1985	1987	1988	1989
Retained profit	24 328	20 569	26 771	29 894	33 810	33 618	25 758
Bank borrowing	3 981	6 340	1 552	7 454	12 142	31 066	33 386
Ordinary shares	879	900	1 872	3 407	13 410	3 533	2 340
Debenture and preference shares	-22	523	608	1 586	2 935	4 381	7 034
Other	3 167	2 590	3 733	1 946	6 899	10 567	22 503
Total	32 333	28 971	34 536	44 287	69 196	83 165	91 021

Source: adapted from CSO, *Financial Statistics*.

overdraft facility allows a company to borrow and repay money at will within a specified limit. A **loan** is where money is lent to the company on a certain date and it has to be repaid in regular instalments on specified dates. There are many variations upon these two basic forms of borrowing, and the bigger the sum borrowed the more hybrid might be the borrowing package offered by a bank or group of banks. The largest companies in the world are able to borrow hundreds of millions of pounds at a time to finance their capital needs.

Ordinary shares An **ordinary share** or **equity stake** signifies ownership of a part of a company. Shareholders buy shares because they thus become entitled to a share of the profits (company dividends). Also, they hope that the company will grow in value and this will be reflected in an increased share price. They will then be able to make a **capital gain** by selling their shares for more than they bought them. When a company issues new shares, it creates new part owners of the company, diluting the percentage of the company owned by existing shareholders. Ordinary shareholders carry the greatest risk in a company. All bills, including interest on bank loans, will be paid before shareholders receive a dividend. If the company makes a loss no dividend will be paid, but the interest on a loan or overdraft will still need to be paid.

Preference shares and debentures A **preference share** is a share which carries a fixed rate of dividend (such as 5 per cent), but is less risky than an ordinary share because preference shareholders must be paid in full before ordinary shareholders can receive any dividend. However, as in the case of ordinary shares, a company making a loss or insufficient profit need make no dividend payment to preference shareholders. A **debenture or stock** is a long term loan which, like a share certificate, can be traded on a stock exchange. A company might issue 20 million £1 stock certificates at a fixed rate of interest to be repaid in 20 years' time. During the 20 year lifetime of the stock, individual certificates might be bought and sold. In effect, it is a loan which the lenders can sell to another party in order to regain their money. In unit 67 it will be explained that stocks can fluctuate in price according to the prevailing rate of interest. Large stocks, denominated in a different currency from the domestic currency of the issuing company are called **Eurobonds**. If ICI, for instance, issued stock in French francs, then this would be a Eurobond issue.

Other means of finance Companies may get grants from government or the European Community for locating in a particular area, training workers (such as the Youth Training Scheme), or investing in new technology. They may use **hire purchase** rather than bank loans to finance investment. **Leasing** (i.e. renting) equipment is popular. Some companies sell their debt collection to a specialist finance company - this is called **factoring**. The company is given, for instance, 95 per cent of the value of invoices to be collected. This improves the cash flow of the company, saves on wages of staff who would have to chase up payment and reduces risk because the factoring firm takes on any consequent bad debts. A company may also choose to mortgage its property, or sell buildings to a property company which then leases it back. In the latter case, the company is receiving a large lump sum now but the opportunity cost is that it will have to pay rent on the property in the future.

Choice of finance

Firms seem to have a wide range of finance available to them. In practice their choice is more limited.

Small firms often find it difficult to raise money. They are seen as risky ventures: in the late 1980s, 32 per cent of companies which registered for VAT had ceased trading within three years of starting up. They are too small to be able to tap sources of money in the City of London which have a large minimum start-up fee attached to them. So new share money usually comes either from the people wanting to set up the company or their close relatives and friends. Banks will provide loans at high rates of interest but only after the company has put forward a convincing business plan detailing, amongst other things, how it plans to repay the loan.

Larger firms, (almost all public limited companies in the UK), have a greater choice. Retained profit is important for two reasons. Firstly, the UK taxation system makes it very attractive for companies to retain profit for investment, and for shareholders to receive benefits in the form of rising share prices rather than high dividends. Secondly, retained profit is a low risk form of capital acquisition. If the investment proves unprofitable, the firm will not have the burden of bank interest charges to pay, or have disappointed shareholders wanting their dividends maintained. However, it is important to remember that retained profit has an opportunity cost. The company could have used it, for instance, to repay existing debts or build up a cushion of financial capital which would earn interest. A company which fails to make effective use of its retained profit is likely to see its share price slide, making it a takeover target.

Bank loans are attractive because, although they are often an expensive form of raising finance, they are flexible. It is far easier to arrange a bank loan than to issue new shares for instance. Bank loans can be repaid and the interest burden removed, whilst share capital is unlikely ever to be redeemed and therefore dividends will have to be paid forever. Shareholders in small companies may not wish to see their control over the firm diluted, whilst new share issues in large companies are often unpopular with their existing shareholders because the share price tends to go down after a new share issue.

The Stock Exchange

The media in the UK give a great deal of coverage to stock exchange prices. Most news bulletins on national radio or television, for instance, will give the latest figure for the *Financial Times* Ordinary Share Index, an index which measures changes in the average value of shares quoted on the exchange. However, it can be argued that day to day share price movements have little economic significance and that the Stock Exchange itself is marginal to the workings of the UK economy.

A stock exchange is a market for second hand securities, such as shares issued by companies or stocks issued by governments. A company which wishes to issue new share capital to expand its business is unlikely to sell these new shares on a stock exchange (and is not allowed to on the London Stock Exchange). The shares are offered for sale directly to the public or to investing institutions such as assurance or pension fund companies. Once the sale has been completed, the company may be able to get the shares quoted on a stock exchange. This means that these shares may be bought and sold through the exchange. Quoted companies have to accept the rules and regulations of the stock exchange and be accepted as a suitable company by the exchange.

A stock exchange has two main economic functions. Firstly, it makes it easier for companies to issue new shares because savers who buy the shares know that they can sell the shares through the exchange when they want to. They might have to sell them for a lower price than they bought them, or they might lose all their money because the firm goes bankrupt. But it is far easier to sell shares in a quoted company than to try to find buyers for shares in an unquoted company. Because it is easier to sell second hand shares which are quoted, companies as a whole can raise more money through share issues than they would otherwise have been able to do. However, it should be remembered that, in the UK, only a few per cent of money raised to finance the expansion of firms each year is raised from share issues. Therefore it is debatable as to how important a stock exchange is in the financing of industry.

Secondly, a stock exchange provides a clear mechanism for mergers and takeovers. The argument is that profit is an indicator of economic efficiency. Companies which fail to make the profits expected of them will see their share price fall. A low share price will attract predator firms who will buy up the company and use its assets more efficiently. So an economic system with stock exchanges, where it is easy to buy shares and to obtain important information about the performance of companies, leads to greater economic efficiency than one where it is difficult to buy shares in companies and where firms are able to keep their finances secret. The validity of this argument turns on whether takeovers and mergers are seen as beneficial or harmful to an economy (☞ unit 38).

Many companies see stock exchanges as harmful to their business. Pressure to make large profits in the short term to satisfy shareholders and to keep predator companies at bay leads to the long term interests of the company being sacrificed. The short term interests of a company may coincide with its long term interests. But sometimes an investment which may be excellent in the long term has high short term costs. The desire to please shareholders today may lead to the investment not going ahead, resulting in a loss of economic efficiency both for the company and the economy as a whole.

Key terms

Cash flow - the difference between money received and money paid out over a period of time.

Retained profit - profit kept back by the company to pay for investment.

MONEY TALKS

In the words of Shakespeare "All the world's a stage and all the men and women merely players". We at British Coal Enterprise are playing a leading role in the success of new and developing business.

In the last 4 years we have committed over £50 million towards helping create real jobs. We have committed our support to more than 2300 business projects, involving a total investment of over £350 million and helping create more than 30,000 new job opportunities.

Our plan for 1989 is simple - by utilising additional financial support made available by the government we intend to help create over 10,000 additional new jobs.

We aim to achieve this by offering comparatively low interest finance to help new businesses get off the ground, to finance established businesses in expansion and to assist U.K. and overseas companies to locate into coal mining regions - as long as the projects need our assistance to provide permanent new jobs for the local workforce.

The package is attractive and thankfully lacking in excessive red tape. There is no need to wait until the jobs are created as the cash is available once your project is approved.

Also we can offer free practical and expert support - an on-going involvement with the right kind of guidance and encouragement from people who want you to succeed.

At British Coal Enterprise we want to help create jobs, and if you want to succeed in business we can help one another, because our money talks good business sense.

For further information on how we may help you call us FREE on

☎ FREE **0800 622517**

British Coal Enterprise Ltd., Eastwood Hall, Eastwood, Nottingham. NG16 3EB.

With the best Will in the world, you won't find better support for business enterprise.

British COAL enterprise
Helping Create Jobs

Source: British Coal Enterprise Ltd.

1. **A firm is considering locating a new factory in a coal mining area. How might it best raise the money to finance this expansion?**

2. **To what extent should business finance be left to the private sector?**

Summary

1. In a pure free market, there would be perfect factor mobility and no unemployment.
2. In reality, firms choose to site themselves according to criteria such as closeness to the market, transport costs, the presence of external economies, government policy, the quality of the local environment and historical links with a locality.

A factory needs space for manufacturing (F), offices (O), car parking (C), materials (M), and loading (I). It also needs access to markets via road transport (R), rail trains (T), and if possible room for expansion (E).

Location in a pure free market

The UK has arguably had a North-South divide since the end of the First World War. Unemployment has been higher and wages lower in the North than in the South of the UK. The UK is not alone in having regional divides. In what was West Germany, the South was more prosperous than the North whilst in Italy it is the North which is the more prosperous.

In a pure free market, this situation would be an impossibility. Firms would locate where the costs of production were lowest. In a region of high unemployment, such as the North of England or Northern Ireland, average wage rates would, in theory, be lower than in a full employment region such as the South East. Land and factory values too will be lower. Firms from the South East would therefore migrate to the North and to Ireland. They would invest in these regions, reducing unemployment, pushing up wage rates and property prices. At the same time, workers would migrate from high unemployment regions to low unemployment regions. By increasing the supply of labour in the South East, wages in that region would tend to fall. But there would be upward pressure on wage rates in the high unemployment regions because their supply of labour had fallen. This process would carry on till the costs of production were equal in all these regions.

Barriers to mobility

In practice, free market forces have been too weak to solve the problems of the higher unemployment regions of the UK. In part this is because there are many other influences apart from the cost of labour and capital which influence the location of industry.

Nearness to the market Many industries need to be located near to their market if they are to minimise costs and maximise revenues. At one extreme, many service industries have to be located in the middle of their market. A company selling petrol will not open a new petrol service station in Glasgow, however cheap the land, if it wants to sell petrol to Londoners. Many industries prefer to be sited near to their markets so that they can keep in touch with their customers. Selling parts in London to a firm two miles down the road, all other things being equal, is likely to be easier than selling parts to Scotland or Northern Ireland.

Transport costs No mention was made of transport costs in the pure free market described above. However, transport costs can be a major component of final costs. In general, firms should locate near to their markets if the cost of transport of the finished product is higher than the cost of transport of raw materials. Conversely, firms should locate near their raw materials if the transport of raw materials is more costly than the transport of finished products. Steel production is an example of an industry

QUESTION 1
Table 23.1 *Selected regional statistics: 1989*

	South East	North
Average wage rate	£312.40	£243.50
Unemployment	3.9%	10.0%
Vacancies at Jobcentres	71 700	10 600
Average new house price 1988	£86 700	£45 800

Source: CSO, *Regional Trends.*

Explain how (i) firms in the South East and (ii) workers in the North of England might be affected by the data shown in the table.

which is located near to its raw materials because the cost of transporting iron ore and coal is much higher than the cost of transporting steel itself. Coal fired electricity power generation plants have been located next to coal fields because they need to be near their source of power to minimise transport costs. The early cotton mills in Lancashire and Yorkshire were located in the Pennines with machinery driven by water power.

External economies of scale External economies of scale (☞ unit 20) arise when an increase in the size of the industry results in a reduction in average costs for a firm in the industry. Many external economies arise within a small geographical area. Stoke on Trent, for instance, has a large pool of workers experienced in working for the pottery industry. Local education colleges run special courses for the industry. There are many firms supplying the industry in the local area. Therefore the average costs of pottery in the Stoke area are likely to be lower than in a city such as Swansea. This helps to account for the fact that Stoke on Trent continues to be the centre of the UK pottery industry.

Industrial inertia Industries may locate initally in an area for a sound economic reason. Over a period of time, these factors may lose their importance but firms stay in the same location. This is known as industrial inertia. For instance, the Lancashire textile industry was initially based there because of cheap power, first from water and then coal. Lancashire also has a damp climate which prevented threads from drying out and breaking easily in manufacture. It was also on the west coast facing America and the colonies, the main sources of imports of raw cotton and of exports. Today, these factors are unimportant commercially. A textile company could as well set up in Glasgow or Bath as in Lancashire. However, the textile industry is still strongly represented in Lancashire because there are no economic reasons why most companies should move from their traditional base in Lancashire to another part of the country.

The local environment Decisions to set up or move a medium sized or large business are made by managers and directors. The quality of their lives and the lives of their families will be an important factor in deciding where to locate. Advertisements for particular locations often place great stress on the availability of golf courses, access to the countryside or to a big city, or quality of the housing. One reason why firms don't relocate even when there are big savings to be made from doing so is that the staff of the company are likely to be very antagonistic to moving away from their locality. A firm which loses too many key staff in a move could find itself in serious trouble.

Government policy Both local and central government play an important role in determining the location of industry. Everything from giving grants to firms that locate in unemployment blackspots to advertising campaigns for a local area, or building a new motorway, will change the attractiveness to businesses of a particular location.

QUESTION 2 'The South-East is ... the wealthiest part of Britain, both in terms of output (40 per cent of the gross national product) and income. ... The county of Surrey tops the household income charts ... nearly twice the lowest income in mid-Glamorgan. ... At least 10 towns in the South East have unemployment rates below 3 per cent. ... Companies ... do not decide lightly to move. They want to be sure key employees will go with them. ... In a survey of 100 high growth companies ... 53 per cent said they would not want to move beyond a 10 mile radius. ... In economic terms, the opening of the Channel Tunnel in 1993 will boost the region further.'

(a) Explain, illustrating your answer from the data, why the South East exerts such a strong pull on industrial location in the UK.
(b) Why does the attraction of the South East create problems for companies located there, which in turn lead to the relocation of firms outside the region?

Applied economics

Location of industry by region in the UK

Each region of the UK has a different industrial base. Figure 23.1 shows in outline the relative importance of different primary, secondary and tertiary industries throughout the UK in 1989. A region is shown to specialise in the production of a particular type of good or service if a greater percentage of its total workforce is employed compared to the national average in that industry. For instance, 4.7% of workers in the West Midlands are employed in the metals, minerals and chemical industries compared to a national average of 3.0%. Because the West Midlands percentage is above the national percentage, the region can be said to specialise in these products. The fact that the West Midlands does not specialise in any service industries does not mean that no services are produced in the region: just that local service employment is below the national average.

A clear pattern emerges from the map. The South East of England is predominantly a service economy with some light manufacturing ('other manufacturing'). The three other administrative areas of the UK apart from England - Northern Ireland, Wales and Scotland - have a considerable number of public administration jobs which in England tend to be concentrated in London (part of the South East region). But apart from this, the UK outside of the South East specialises mainly in primary and secondary industries. The West Midlands, for instance, specialising only in the metal and motor industries, has a very narrow industrial base. The North of England specialises in energy and water supply, construction, and metals, minerals and chemicals. Only the South West of England and East Anglia, areas within the South of the 'North-South' divide specialise in a service industry apart from public administration.

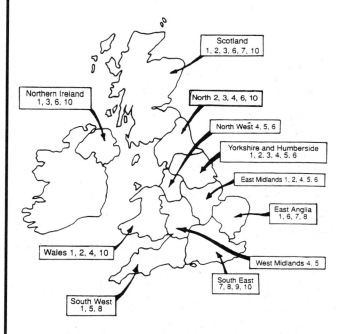

The map shows those regions which have more than the national average percentages of their labour forces employed in a particular sector of industry.

Key

1. Agriculture , forestry and fishing
2. Energy and water supply
3. Construction
Manufacturing
4. Metals, minerals and chemicals
5. Metal goods, engineering and vehicle industries
6. Other manufacturing
Services
7. Distribution, hotels and catering, repairs
8. Transport and communication
9. Banking, finance, business services and leasing
10. Public administration and other services

Source: adapted from *Regional Trends*, CSO.

Figure 23.1 *Specialisation by region in the UK ,1989*

The reasons for geographical specialisation

The pattern of a service rich South, and a more impoverished North relying on primary and secondary industries, has arisen from the economic history of the UK over the past two hundred years. Service industries associated with government have traditionally been located in regional capitals. London, Edinburgh and Belfast, for instance, have been the centre of civil service jobs and employment in the legal profession. These centres have also attracted companies in the financial sector such as banks and insurance companies, both because of the presence of government and because of good transport links with the rest of the country. Headquarters of companies have also come to be centred in these capitals for the same reasons.

Primary industry needs to be located where there are raw materials. The South East, apart from its farm land, has not been a rich source of raw materials. It has been the other areas of the UK which have developed concentrations of coal mining, clay workings, offshore oil, etc.

Secondary industry after the Industrial Revolution sited itself near to its raw material sources, such as coal or iron ore. Therefore, in the main it tended to site itself in the 'North' where such raw materials were relatively abundant. The West of England also developed more industrially than the East because of the pattern of trade in the 19th century. Britain's colonies and the United States of America were our major trading partners. It was cheaper to send goods to these destinations from west coast ports such as Glasgow, Belfast, Liverpool and Bristol than from east coast ports.

In the 19th century, London was a thriving commercial centre but so too were the industrial towns of the Midlands, the North of England, Scotland, Wales and Northern Ireland.

Since the end of the First World War, three important changes have occurred to create the North-South divide. Firstly, as the UK has become more affluent, it has moved progressively to a more service sector based economy. The South East, which specialised throughout the 19th century in the provision of services, has been able to reinforce its comparative advantage. Secondly, the direction of trade has altered. Today Europe is our major trading partner. Therefore the regions of the UK closest to Europe, and particularly the South East, have a transport cost advantage over the rest of the UK. The west of the UK has had to cope with a relative decline in trade. Most of the west coast's docks, for instance, have long since closed to commercial freight traffic and have been converted to service sector use such as yachting marinas, housing or leisure centres.

Thirdly, and perhaps most importantly, the UK has lost much of its comparative advantage in the production of manufactured goods relative to the rest of the world (☞ unit 59). Industry after industry has been hit by foreign competition, from textiles to shipbuilding to car manufacturing. Countries such as Japan, Korea or Germany have taken away British markets and devastated British industry. Manufacturing industry was heavily concentrated in the 'North' of England and hence the North has declined relative to the South.

Since the low point of the early 1980s, there has been some recovery in employment and output in the regions of the UK. Local authorities are keen to diversify their industrial base so that they are no longer dependent upon one industry. Foreign manufacturing investment in the UK, such as that by the Japanese or by the Germans, has been concentrated in Wales and the North of England, helped by government regional grants. However, it is difficult to see how the South East, with its traditional comparative advantage in services and its proximity to Europe, will continue to be anything other than the most prosperous region of the UK.

Data question

HIGHLAND SPIRIT

To most people, the Highlands and Islands conjures up images of desolate mountains swept by driving rain, remote fields populated with cattle, and the odd stone crofter's cottage every few hundred miles - an apparently eccentric choice of location for any but the most cottage - based industry.

There are, it is true, many companies in the Highlands and Islands who have to be located there. An obvious example is Callanish, on the isle of Lewis, which manufactures pharmaceutical grade oils from fish oils, and is therefore located to be near supplies.

But the real eye - opener is the number of modern, high - technology industries who have chosen to locate in the Highlands and Islands in preference to anywhere else in the UK. Although Inverness is a negligible hour and a half by air to London, distance is probably the first factor that springs to the mind of a British business person contemplating on relocation to the North - or even business dealings with it. So what sort of company takes to the Scottish air?

Many Highland manufacturing companies are export - orientated and concentrate on high - value low - volume products.

'Location is absolutely no problem at all. Shipping costs are the same as anywhere else in the UK; shipping companies offer a flat rate, and besides, a shipping cost of £100 on a piece of equipment costing £20,000 is neither here nor there'; says Ross Maxwell, Managing director of Aspen Medical.

The company manufactures electronic instrumentation for medical markets, with particular emphasis on urology and gastroenterology.

As 70 per cent of Aspen's business is export, Ross Maxwell believes 'There is no alternative location anywhere in the UK that makes more sense than the Highlands. The only place more advantageous to our market would place us somewhere between Frankfurt and Luxembourg. A suprising number of our customers choose to visit us here - especially in the summer months.'

The isolation of the region can also be a major plus point. For many companies it is the ideal place to base their research programmes, because privacy is easy to achieve.

Their workers are also those who can benefit most from a lifestyle free from the stresses of city dwelling and conducive to creative thinking.

Even companies whose business is primarily within the UK would argue that it is a misconception that high transportation costs automatically accompany distance from the industrial heartland of the UK. Norfrost, for example, in Caithness (in the far North of Scotland) transports its freezers to England for approximately £2 each, while Zonal, which produces professional recording tape, can send products to London for half the cost as from its sister site in Surrey.

Such facts are part of the reason why this tract of Scotland is more attractive to many companies than the 'silicon valleys' of the South, which have a stronger industrial history but also higher land and labour costs. The Highlands and Islands are attracting new business at the rate of over 500 a year, and boast an unemployment rate considerably lower than in the rest of Scotland (8.7 per cent compared with the Scottish average of 9.9 per cent).

It could be that there is something distinctive in the make-up of the Highlanders, accustomed as they have been to self-sufficiency. The strong tradition of self-employment in the area lingers, with 14.6 per cent of the workforce being self-employed, against the national average of 9.4 per cent.

Source: *Business Today*, February, 1990.

1. What are the possible advantages of locating a firm in the Highlands and Islands of Scotland?
2. Compare the likely costs and benefits to the following of locating near Inverness:
   (a) a specialist manufacturer of underwater television cameras selling 60 per cent of its output abroad;
   (b) an assembly plant for a high volume car manufacturer;
   (c) a computer software company selling worldwide.

Summary

1. Shareholders, managers, workers, government, consumers and others influence decision making in a firm.
2. Neo-classical theory assumes that firms are short run profit maximisers. In the short run, such firms will operate so long as their revenue is greater than their variable cost.
3. The neo-Keynesian theory of the firm assumes that firms are long run profit maximisers.
4. Managerial theories assume that managers maximise their own utility subject to a profit satisficing constraint.
5. Behavioural theories assume that decision making within a firm is not controlled by any one group, such as shareholders, but by all parties involved with the firm.

The main participants

The question of what motivates a firm in its actions can only be answered if there is a clear understanding of who controls the decision making processes. There are a number of possible answers to this in a UK context.

The owners or shareholders It might seem obvious to state that it is the shareholders of a company who control it. This is perhaps true for small businesses where the owner is also the director or manager of the business. The owner of a small local corner shop, for instance, who also runs the shop will make the decisions about the business. However, it is less obvious that owners control the business they own when there are a very large number of shareholders.

Directors and managers Shareholders in a public limited company elect directors to look after their interests. Directors in turn appoint managers who are responsible for the day to day running of the business. Therefore there may be a divorce between ownership and control. The only way in which owners can influence decision making directly is by sacking directors at the Annual General Meeting (AGM) of the company. In practice the company needs to be going bankrupt to stir sufficient shareholders for this to happen. Shareholders can also sell their shares, forcing the share price down and making the company more vulnerable to a takeover bid. If there is a takeover the directors and managers may well lose their jobs and hence there is pressure on managers to perform well.

The workers The workers, particularly through their trade unions, may be able to exert strong pressure on a company. They do not have the power to run the company in the way that shareholders or managers might be able to do. However, they can have an important influence on matters such as wages (and therefore costs), health and safety at work and location or relocation of premises.

The state The state provides an underlying framework for the operation of the company. Legislation on taxation, the environment, consumer protection, health and safety at work, employment practices, solvency and many other issues force companies to behave in a way which they might otherwise not do in an unregulated environment.

The consumer The consumer, through organisations such as the Consumers' Association or various trade organisations, can bring pressure to bear on companies in an attempt to make them change their policies. This form of influence is often rather weak: **consumer sovereignty** (☞ unit 40) is more important. In a free market, consumers cast their spending votes amongst companies. Companies which do not provide the products that consumers wish to buy will go out of business whilst companies which are responsive to consumers' needs may make large profits. According to this argument, it is the consumer who ultimately controls the company. This assumes that consumer sovereignty exists. In practice, firms attempt to manipulate consumer preferences by marketing devices such as advertising. Firms are therefore not the powerless servants which theory implies.

QUESTION 1 In 1988, the Swiss multinational company Nestlé made a bid to take over Rowntree Mackintosh, a British company based in York which produced brands such as KitKat and After Eight. There was strong opposition to the bid. Directors advised shareholders not to sell their shares to Nestlé because they felt that the price offered by the multinational was too low. Managers and workers opposed the bid because they feared that Nestlé would move production and research facilities away from York, and would close down some plants completely in order to rationalise production across Europe. They lobbied Parliament because the Department of Industry had the power to refer the bid to the Monopolies and Mergers Commission. This body would have investigated the bid and could have recommended that the merger was not in the public interest. The government, however, decided not to refer the bid. Nestlé increased its share price offer. Consumers stood by helpless. The Board of Directors of Rowntree Mackintosh recommended that shareholders accept because the new price offered was very good. Enough shareholders sold to ensure that Rowntree Mackintosh passed into Swiss hands.

Which interest groups controlled decision making at Rowntree Mackintosh during the bid by Nestlé?

Short run profit maximisation

In neo-classical economics it is assumed that the interests of owners or shareholders are the most important. Just as consumers attempt to maximise utility and workers attempt to maximise their rewards from working, so shareholders will be motivated solely by maximising their gain from the company. Therefore it is argued that the goal of firms is to maximise profits.

Firms are not always able to operate at a profit. They may be faced with operating at a loss. Neo-classical economics predicts that firms will continue in production in the short run so long as they cover their variable costs. Consider Table 24.1. The company would lose £20 million in any period in which it shut down its plant and produced nothing. This is because it still has to pay its fixed costs of £20 million even if output is zero. Total fixed costs represent the maximum loss per period the company need face. The table shows that the firm is

facing a steadily worsening trading situation. Its costs remain the same throughout, but each period its revenue declines. In period 1, total revenue exceeds total costs. The firm makes a profit of £10 million if production takes place. In period 2, it makes no profit by operating its plant (although it should be remembered that cost includes an allowance for normal profit (☞ unit 18).

However, this is better than the alternative of shutting down and making a £20 million loss. So too is producing in period 3. Although the company makes a loss of £10 million, it will continue to produce because the alternative to not producing is a loss of £20 million. In period 4 the company is on the dividing line between whether to produce or not. In period 5, the company will clearly not produce. Its operating losses would be greater than if the plant were shut down.

So short run profit maximisation implies that a firm will continue to produce even if it is not fully covering its total costs. It will only shut down production when its total revenue fails to cover its total variable cost.

QUESTION 2 A company has fixed costs of £10 million. Its variable costs increase at a constant rate with output. The variable cost of production of each unit is £1 million. Explain whether it will produce (a) 10 units if total revenue is £30 million; (b) 15 units if total revenue is £25 million; (c) 20 units if total revenue is £22 million; (d) 25 units if total revenue is £20 million.

Long run profit maximisation

Neo-Keynesian economists believe that firms maximise their long run rather than their short run profit. This is based upon the belief that firms use COST PLUS PRICING techniques. The price of a product is worked out by calculating the average total cost of operating at full capacity and adding a profit mark-up. The price set and therefore the profit aimed for is based upon the long run costs of the firm.

Short run profit maximisation implies that firms will adjust both price and output in response to changes in market conditions. However, according to neo-Keynesians, rapid price adjustments may well damage the firm's position in a market. Consumers dislike frequent price changes. Price cuts may be seen as a sign of distress selling and large buyers may respond by trying to negotiate even large price reductions. Price increases may be interpreted as a sign of profiteering, with consumers switching to other brands or makes in the belief that they will get better value for money. Price changes also involve costs to the company because price lists need to be changed, sales staff informed, advertising material changed, etc. Therefore it is argued that firms attempt to maintain stable prices whilst adjusting output to changes in market conditions.

This may mean that a firm will produce in the short run even if it fails to cover its variable cost. If it takes the view that in the long run it will make a profit on

Table 24.1

£ million

Period	Total variable cost	Total fixed cost	Total cost	Total revenue	Profit or loss — If production takes place	Profit or loss — If plant is shut down
1	30	20	50	60	+10	-20
2	30	20	50	50	0	-20
3	30	20	50	40	-10	-20
4	30	20	50	30	-20	-20
5	30	20	50	20	-30	-20

production of a particular good, it will prefer to produce at a loss rather than disrupt supplies to the market. Equally, it may cease production in the short run even if it can cover its variable costs. It may prefer to keep prices above the market price in the short run; and sell nothing if it believes that price cutting in the short run would lead to a permanent effect on prices and therefore profits in the long run.

QUESTION 3 A firm has total fixed costs of £900 and variable costs of £1 per unit.
(a) What will be the price per unit if it sets out to manufacture 300 units a week and make a 25 per cent profit over costs?
(b) Demand is not as great as the company hoped. If it maintains its price, what is the minimum number of units that must be sold per week if the company is to break-even?
(c) Demand is 150 units per week. The company is offered an order for an extra 350 units a week if it drops its price on all units sold to £3 per unit. But it believes that demand will slowly increase in the future to the planned 300 units a week if the original price is maintained. Should the firm accept the order?

Managerial theories

Managerial theories of the firm start from the assumption that there is some divorce between ownership and control of companies. The shareholders are assumed to be a different group of people from the managers of the company. Shareholders will wish to see profits maximised. However, it is far from obvious that managers will share this goal. As workers they will attempt to maximise their own rewards. These may include their own pay and fringe benefits, their working conditions, their power within the organisation, their ability to appropriate resources, and the amount of effort they have to make. For instance, a manager may be more interested in which company car he or she will get, whether there is time to play golf on a Wednesday afternoon, or whether there is an extra £1 million available for the budget, than whether the company has maximised its profits at the end of the financial year.

This does not mean to say that making a profit is not important. Managers have to be seen to be efficient enough to justify their salaries. A shareholders' revolt is always a possibility. Some directors may take it upon themselves to promote actively the interests of the owners of the company. There is always the threat of takeover or bankruptcy leading to a loss of jobs, so managers have to make enough profit to satisfy the demands of their shareholders. This is known as PROFIT SATISFICING. But once a satisfactory level of profits has been made, the managers are free to maximise their own rewards from the company.

One theory put forward in the 1950s by William Baumol was that firms would attempt to maximise sales rather than profits. Increased sales and increased salaries for top managers and directors tend to go hand in hand. Another more complicated theory put forward by O. Williamson postulates that managers have a utility function consisting of factors such as salary, size of the workforce directed by the manager, the amount of money under his or her control and the number of perks, such as company cars, that the manager receives (☞ unit 32).

QUESTION 4 It was reported in 1988 that Britain's business travellers were spending nearly £20 billion on travel and entertainment for their companies. American Express, who conducted the survey, believed that many companies did not control such spending sufficiently well. Where spending was controlled, policies might well backfire. For instance, some companies insisted that all air travel should be by economy class only, but senior directors flouted the rule and flew first class. Moreover rules could be so petty that the cost of time spent by executives seeking to outwit the system was greater than any savings made on a more generous allowance system.

Do you think there would be any difference between the attitude of a business person who owned her own business and a manager who worked for a large company towards spending on travel and entertainment? Who, in particular, will seek to minimise cost and maximise profit for the company they are involved with?

Behavioural theories

Behavioural theories of the firm, pioneered by the American economist Herbert Simon, argue that decision making within a company is made not by any one group but by all groups involved in the firm. It is only by studying the relative power of each group and the power structures within the organisation that the way in which a firm behaves can be understood.

For instance, it could be argued that in the 1960s and the 1970s, trade unions were very powerful in large companies. They were influential in increasing the share of revenues allocated to wages and reducing the share that went to shareholders. During the 1980s, government legislation and mass unemployment has seriously weakened the power of unions in the UK. At the same time, shareholders have become more conscious of their right to make profits. The result has been a large increase in the returns to shareholders, which could be seen as being financed by a reduction in the returns to the workers of the firm. Shareholders are more important today in company board rooms and workers less important than they were 20 years ago.

Behavioural theories assume that each group has a minimum level of demands. Shareholders demand that the firm makes a satisfactory level of profits. The government demands that laws be obeyed and taxes paid. Workers will require a minimum level of pay and work satisfaction if they are to stay with the company.

Consumers demand a minimum level of quality for the price they pay for goods purchased. Local environmentalists may be able to exert enough moral pressure on the company to prevent gross over pollution.

QUESTION 5 During the 1960s and 1970s, it was difficult to see who controlled the Fleet Street newspaper industry. Owners of the newspapers were often rich entrepreneurial-type figures who allowed their titles to make little or no profit in return for the prestige and influence over the UK public that ownership gave them. Trade unions had a virtual veto on changes in working practices. Trade unions, not management, controlled shop floor appointments. The ability to call wild-cat strikes which would lose a paper its entire production run for a day ensured that shop floor workers earned wages which bore no resemblance to the wages of workers in other comparable occupations.

Consumers rewarded with more sales those newspapers which included more page 3 pin-ups and less serious political news. Governments, meanwhile, made public noises about deteriorating press standards whilst in private attempting to get the press to toe the current party line. Management were caught in the middle, attempting to balance all the conflicting demands made of them.

New technology and soaring property prices put paid to all this. In the 1980s it became apparent that newspapers could make large profits for their owners. The key to success was to sack as many shop floor workers as possible and replace them with machines. Those kept on would be paid reduced rates. Fleet Street offices could be sold off at vast profit on a soaring property market, the proceeds more than paying for a move to new technology premises elsewhere. The unions resisted, but not even the Wapping riots could prevent the change.

To what extent can behavioural theories of the firm explain the recent history of the Fleet Street newspaper industry?

Other goals

Some firms have clearly distinct aims apart from those mentioned above. Consumer co-operatives aim to help consumers (although there is considerable debate in the UK as to whether they do not, in practice, serve the interests of their workers and management more). Worker co-operatives are often motivated by a desire either to maintain jobs or to produce a particular product, such as health foods. There have been examples of philanthropic owners in the past, such as Rowntree or Cadbury, who have placed great priority on improving the living conditions of their workers. Nationalised industries in the UK prior to 1979 had a whole range of goals from avoiding a loss to maintaining employment to providing a high quality service.

So it is simplistic to argue that all firms aim to maximise profit. However, there is much evidence to suggest that large firms whose shares are freely traded on stock exchanges, and which are vulnerable to takeover, place the making of profit very high on their list of priorities. Therefore it is not unreasonable to make an assumption that, in general, firms are profit maximisers.

Key terms

Cost-plus pricing - the technique adopted by firms of fixing a price for their products by adding a fixed percentage profit margin to the long run average cost of production.
Profit satisficing - making sufficient profit to satisfy the demands of shareholders.

Applied economics

The role of the shareholder

Shareholder power

In the UK and the USA, companies at least pay lip-service to the power of their shareholders. Company chairmen make constant referrals to 'serving the interests of shareholders' or 'maximising shareholder wealth'. However, the power of the shareholder is an indirect one. Annual shareholder meetings of quoted companies are poorly attended, annual shareholder reports are not understood even when read by many shareholders and directors can usually rely upon blocks of votes from key investors to push through any resolutions they recommend. Shareholders' power lies not in being able to influence decisions directly, but in their ability to sell their shares freely. If enough shareholders are disappointed with a company's performance and sell their shares, then the share price will fall and make the company an attractive takeover target. The management of a company taken over could, at worst, face immediate redundancy. So in the UK and the USA, shareholder power is vitally dependent upon free and open stock markets.

In continental Europe and Japan, shareholder power is exercised in a different way. It is far more difficult for companies to be taken over. In Italy for instance, of 200 companies listed on the stock market in 1989, only two were open to a British-style takeover bid. This was because only seven had more than half their shares in public hands and five of those were in practice controlled by families. In Spain, shareholdings are not even disclosed but bank, family and corporate cross shareholdings tie up control of most companies. In France, it is estimated that more than half of the 200 largest quoted or unquoted companies are family controlled and many of the rest have key blocks of shares held either by the government or by single private shareholders. In Germany, three large banks, which for more than a century have financed German industry, have huge stakes. In Japan, companies prevent individual shareholders from becoming too powerful by buying them out or diluting their shareholding by the issue of more shares. There is also a strong tradition of corporate cross holdings.

Short-termism

For many years now, there has been a debate in the UK about whether or not the system of shareholding has a major influence on the behaviour of firms. There are those who argue that the UK system leads to 'short-termism'. Companies are forced to pursue the goal of maximising short term profit for fear that they will otherwise be taken over. This makes it difficult for them to pursue other objectives, particularly investment both in capital equipment and in their workers which have long pay-back periods.

In contrast, on the Continent and in Japan, companies can afford to take a long term view. Ultimately the company will only survive if it makes a profit. But profit should increase if the company grows over time. Hence it is the interests of the company which are paramount. The company is not just the shareholders, but also the workers, the management, the customers, the local citizens etc. Because shareholders do not expect their companies to maximise short term profits, management is free to invest in a way which will maximise the long term growth of the company. Maximising the long term growth of the company, as a by-product, is also likely to maximise the long term gain for the shareholder. It is also likely to maximise long term growth in the economy. It is interesting to note that continental European countries and Japan have enjoyed higher economic growth in the post-war period on average than either the UK or the USA.

If the 'short-termist' view is correct, then it could be argued that firms are short run profit maximisers in the UK and in the USA. In contrast, on the Continent and in Japan, firms are long run profit maximisers. However, long run profit maximisation is an incidental outcome of a process of decision making which is perhaps best explained by behavioural theories of the firm.

JAPANESE GOALS

Japanese companies are not perfect; they get into trouble from time to time just like their Western counterparts. But recent cases indicate that if the pressure on Japanese companies from banks has eased (shareholders never had much say), other pressures, both social and competitive, remain formidably strong in Japan's business community. Okuma Machinery Works, one of the top machine tool makers, became a bit lazy a couple of years ago and profits sagged. The company's trade union complained loudly about nepotism in the executive suite and, with support from the company's lead bank, it forced the Okuma family to relinquish control.

As for diversification, Japanese industrial managers appear to approach it from a healthier viewpoint than some Western companies. Far from seeking to expand their own power and perks, they are more interested in preserving the competitiveness of their core businesses. In return for employees' support for rationalisation and automation plans, managers create new jobs for those displaced, and diversification is a way to go about it.

Source: adapted from the *Financial Times*, 15.2. 1990.

1. **How might economic theory explain the behaviour of (i) the Japanese companies and (ii) their Western counterparts discussed in the data?**

Summary

1. Market structures are the characteristics of a market which determine firms' behaviour within the market.
2. The number of firms within a market may vary from one (as in monopoly), to several (as in oligopoly), to a large number (as in monopolistic competition or perfect competition).
3. Barriers to entry prevent potential competitors from entering a market.
4. Industries may produce homogeneous or differentiated (branded) goods.
5. Perfect knowledge or imperfect knowledge may exist in an industry.
6. Firms may be independent or interdependent.

Market structure

MARKET STRUCTURES are the characteristics of a market which determine firms' behaviour. Economists single out a small number of key characteristics:

- the number of firms in the market and their relative size;
- the number of firms which might enter the market;
- the ease or difficulty with which these new entrants might come in;
- the extent to which goods in the market are similar;
- the extent to which all firms in the market share the same knowledge;
- the extent to which the actions of one firm will affect another firm.

The number of firms in an industry

The number of firms in an industry may vary from one to many. In the UK market for gas, for instance, British Gas is essentially the sole supplier. In agriculture, on the other hand, there are tens of thousands of farms supplying potatoes and carrots to the market in the UK.

- A **monopoly** is said to exist where there is only one supplier in the market.
- In a market dominated by a few large producers, the market structure is **oligopolistic**. In an oligopolistic market there may be a large number of firms, but the key characteristic is that most are small and relatively unimportant, whilst a small number of large firms produce most of the output of the industry.
- In **perfect competition** or in **monopolistic** competition there are a large number of small suppliers, none of which is large enough to dominate the market.

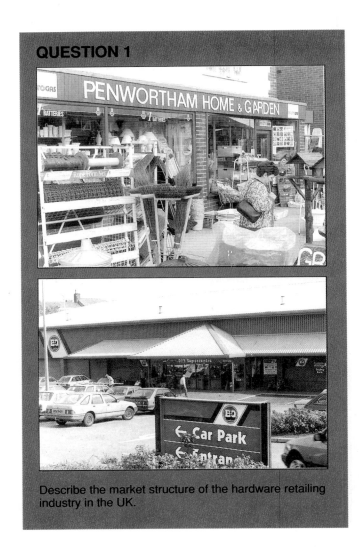

QUESTION 1

Describe the market structure of the hardware retailing industry in the UK.

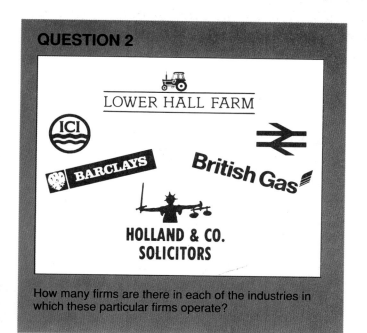

QUESTION 2

LOWER HALL FARM

ICI

BARCLAYS

British Gas

HOLLAND & CO.
SOLICITORS

How many firms are there in each of the industries in
which these particular firms operate?

Barriers to entry

Market structures are not only affected by the number of
firms in an industry and their relative output, but also by
the potential number of new entrants to the market.
Firms in an industry where there are unlikely to be any
new entrants may behave differently from firms in an
industry where there are many strong potential
competitors.

There are a number of BARRIERS TO ENTRY which
prevent potential competitors from entering an industry.

Capital costs Buying a local corner shop is relatively
cheap and therefore the entry cost to most forms of
retailing is low. Buying a car plant or an aluminium
smelter, on the other hand, is extremely expensive. Entry
costs to these industries are very high and only large
companies on the whole can pay them. Capital costs
therefore represent a very important barrier to entry and
vary from industry to industry.

Sunk costs SUNK COSTS are costs which are not
recoverable. For instance, a woman may set up a
gardening business, buying a lawnmower, a van, garden
tools and paying for advertising. If the business folds, she
will be able to get some money back by selling the van,
the tools, and mower, but she won't be able to get any of
the money back from the advertising. The cost of
advertising and the difference between the purchase price
and resale price of the capital equipment would be her
sunk costs. High sunk costs will act as a barrier to entry
because the cost of failure for firms entering the industry
will be high. Low sunk costs, on the other hand, will
encourage firms to enter an industry because they have
little to lose from failure (☞ unit 32, the theory of
contestable markets).

Scale economies In some industries, economies of scale
are very large. A few firms operating at lowest average
cost (the **optimum level of production** ☞ unit 20) can
satisfy all the demand of buyers. This will act as a barrier
to entry because any new firm entering the market is
likely to produce less and therefore have much higher
average costs than the few established producers. In some
industries, it could be that a few firms supplying the
whole industry are still unable to exploit fully the
potential economies of scale. A **natural monopoly** is then
likely to result, with just one firm surviving in the
industry, able to beat off any new entrants because it can
produce at lowest costs.

Natural cost advantages Some producers possess
advantages because they own factors which are superior
to others and which are unique (i.e. have no close
substitutes). For instance, a petrol station site on a busy
main road is likely to be superior to one in a sleepy
country village. A stretch of desert in Saudi Arabia with
oil underneath is superior for oil production to the most
beautiful of the Derbyshire Dales. The Victoria and Albert
Museum will be able to attract more visitors because of its
wide collection than a small provincial town museum.
As a result, they will either be able to produce at lower
cost or be able to generate higher revenues than their
potential competitors.

Legal barriers The law may give firms particular
privileges. Patent laws prevent competitor firms from
making a product for a given number of years after its
invention. The government may give a firm exclusive
rights to production. For instance, it may give broadcast
licences to commercial television companies or it may
make nationalised industries into monopolies by legally
forbidding private firms to set up in the industry, as is the
case the Post Office in the UK.

Marketing barriers Existing firms in an industry may be
able to erect very high barriers through high spending on
advertising and marketing. The purpose of these is to
make consumers associate a particular type of good with
the firm's product, creating a powerful **brand** image. One
example of this from 50 years ago was the success of the
Hoover company with its vacuum cleaner. Even today,
many people still refer to vacuum cleaners as 'hoovers'.
More recently, a personal stereo is often called a
'Walkman', the brand name of Sony who first put it on the
market. In the UK detergent industry, a national launch of
a new brand of soap or washing powder will cost in
excess of £10 million. Soap and washing powders are low
technology products whose costs of production are
relatively low. Marketing barriers, however, make the
industry almost impossible to enter.

Restrictive practices Firms may deliberately restrict
competition through restrictive practices (☞ unit 39). For
instance, a manufacturer may refuse to sell goods to a
retailer which stocks the products of a competitor firm. A
manufacturer may refuse to sell a good, when it has a

monopoly in production, unless the buyer purchases its whole range of goods. Firms may be prepared to lower prices for long enough to drive out a new entrant to the business.

These barriers to entry may be divided into two groups. Some occur inevitably. These are known as **innocent entry barriers**. Most cost advantages fall into this category. However, other barriers are created by firms in the industry **deliberately** to keep out potential competitors. Marketing barriers and restrictive practices are examples of these.

The extent to which there is freedom of entry to a market varies enormously. Manufacturing industries, with high capital costs and with extensive marketing power, tend to have higher barriers than service industries. But many service industries have high barriers too. Banking, for instance, has a high capital cost of entry, legal permission is required, and marketing barriers are high. In the professions, like law, architecture and accountancy, new entrants are kept out by enforcement of minimum qualification levels, qualifications which are

impossible to obtain except through working in the profession itself.

Product homogeneity and branding

In some industries products are essentially identical whichever firm produces them. Coal, steel and potatoes are examples. This does not mean to say that there are not different grades of coal or types of steel, but no producer has a monopoly on the production of any such grade or type. Goods which are identical are called HOMOGENEOUS goods.

Firms find it much easier to control their markets if they can produce goods which are non-homogeneous. Differentiating their product from their competitors, and creating BRANDS allows them to build up brand loyalty. This in turn leads to a reduction in the elasticity of demand for their product. A branded good may be physically no different from its competitors, or it may be slightly different. But branding has value for the firm because consumers think that the product is very different, so different that rival products are a very poor substitute for it. This perception is built up through advertising and marketing and enables firms to charge higher prices without losing very much custom (i.e. demand is relatively inelastic).

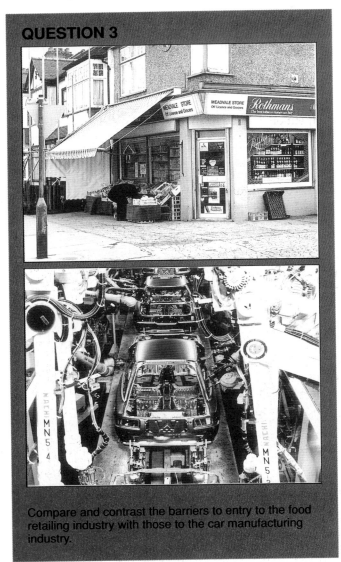

QUESTION 3

Compare and contrast the barriers to entry to the food retailing industry with those to the car manufacturing industry.

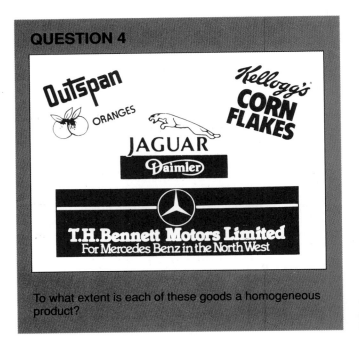

QUESTION 4

To what extent is each of these goods a homogeneous product?

Knowledge

Buyers and sellers are said to have PERFECT INFORMATION or PERFECT KNOWLEDGE if they are fully informed of prices and output in the industry. So if one firm were to put up its prices, it would lose all its customers because they would go and buy from elsewhere in the industry. Hence, there can only be one price in the market.

Perfect knowledge also implies that a firm has access to all information which is available to other firms in its industry. In UK agriculture, for instance, knowledge is widely available. Farmers can obtain information about different strains of seeds, the most effective combinations of fertilizers and pesticides and when it is best to plant and reap crops.

Perfect knowledge does not imply that all firms in an industry **will** possess all information. An inefficient farmer might not bother to gather relevant information which is readily available. In the short term, the farmer might survive, although in the longer term the farm will be driven out of business by more efficient competitors. Equally, perfect information does not imply that all firms know everything about their industry and its future. Farmers do not know if in 6 months' time a drought will destroy their crops. They have to work on the basis of probability. Perfect knowledge only means that all firms have the same access to information.

Firms have imperfect knowledge where, for instance, there are industrial secrets. Individual firms may not know the market share of their competitors or they may be unaware of new technology or new products to be launched by rival companies. Information could then act as a barrier to entry, preventing or discouraging new firms entering the industry.

Interrelationships within markets

There are two possible relationships between firms in an industry. Firms may be **independent** of each other. This means that the actions of any one firm will have no significant impact on any other single firm in the industry. In agriculture, for instance, the decision of one farmer to grow more wheat this season will have no direct impact on any other farmer. It will not affect his next door neighbour. This independence is one reason why perfect knowledge exists to some degree in agriculture. There is no point in keeping secrets if your actions will not benefit you at the expense of your competitors.

If firms are **interdependent** then the actions of one firm will have an impact on other firms. An advertising campaign for one brand of soap bar, for instance, is designed mainly to attract customers away from other brands. Firms are more likely to be interdependent if there are few firms in the industry.

Competition and market structure

The neo-classical theory of the firm recognises a number of market structures derived from the characteristics above. In units 27 to 32 these market structures will be considered in greater detail. Here, however, the key features are summarised. In neo-classical theory, there are three main types of market structure.

- **Perfect competition.** A large number of firms, each producing a homogeneous good, compete in the industry. None of the firms is large enough to have a direct impact on any other firm or on the market price of the good. There is freedom of exit and entry to the industry.
- **Monopoly.** There is only one firm in the industry. Barriers to entry make it impossible for new firms to enter.
- **Imperfect competition** . Exists where there are at least two firms in the industry, and the industry is not perfectly competitive. For instance, non-homogeneous goods may be produced, there may be imperfect knowledge or firms may be interdependent, or some combination of these.

Firms in imperfectly competitive industries can compete in a number of ways. For instance, they can compete on:
- **price** - offering a lower price should attract more orders;
- **quality** - consumers are likely to prefer a better quality good;
- **after-sales service**;
- **delivery date** - a buyer may look elsewhere if a firm cannot deliver quickly and on time;
- **image** - building a strong brand image through advertising and other forms of marketing is likely to be a major factor in determining demand for the product.

In perfect competition, firms are not in direct competition with each other. One firm can expand output without affecting either the price received by or the sales of another firm. Each firm is a price taker facing a perfectly elastic demand curve. However, competition is 'perfect' because any firm which charges a higher price than its competitors, or sells an inferior product, will lose all its sales as perfectly informed consumers buy

---

QUESTION 5 Producers in the 1.5 billion Christmas card market face a variety of different types of competition. At one end of the market are mainly Eastern European producers who compete on price. If you buy a large box of budget Christmas cards in your local supermarket, the likelihood is that it will have been made in a Soviet block country. Slightly more expensive are cards from the large UK producers such as Hallmark Cards and Rust Craft Greetings Cards. They produce better quality cards and market them along with their range of birthday and other greetings cards through a wide range of newsagents. At the top end of the price range are cards produced by a large number of small independent card publishers, exploiting market niches such as joke Christmas cards, fine art cards and pop-art cards. They too are sold mainly through newsagents. Finally, charities offer a wide range of designs, selling at medium prices mainly through mail order.

To what extent do firms in the Christmas card market compete on price?

elsewhere in the market. The discipline of the market is so strong in a perfectly competitive industry that, in the long run, productive inefficiency (production at above minimum cost) cannot exist.

Key terms

Market structures - the characteristics of a market which determine the behaviour of firms within the market.
Barriers to entry - factors which make it difficult or impossible for firms to enter an industry and compete with existing producers.
Sunk costs - costs of production which are not recoverable if a firm leaves the industry.
Homogeneous goods - goods which are identical.
Brand - a named good which in the perception of its buyers is different from other similar goods on the market.
Perfect knowledge or information - exists if all buyers in a market are fully informed of prices and quantities for sale, whilst producers have equal access to information about production techniques.

Applied economics

Market structures in the UK

What is an industry or market?

How many firms are there in an industry or market (here we will assume that the two terms can be used interchangeably)? The answer to this question will depend on how we define the market or industry. For instance, the economy could be split up into three very broad markets classifications, the market for primary goods, the market for secondary goods and the market for tertiary goods. There are a large number of firms operating in each of these markets. At the other extreme, one could ask how many UK firms produce balls for use in professional cricket. This is an extremely narrow market in which there are only two producers.

It should be obvious that the narrower a market is defined, the more likely it is that there will be relatively few producers. In the transport market, there are bus companies, rail companies, airlines, etc. In the air transport market, there will be fewer companies. In the market for air travel to the Isle of Skye there is only one company.

The Standard Industrial Classification

The Central Statistical Office (CSO) conducts regular censuses of production in the UK. The statistics record production levels in different industries using the Standard Industrial Classification 1980. This is a

classification system which subdivides industry into broad divisions. For instance, division 1 comprises energy and water supply industries, divisions 2 to 4 cover manufacturing industries and division 5 is construction. Each division is then further divided into classes. Class 32, for instance, is mechanical engineering whilst class 43 is the textile industry. The CSO classification is one way of grouping firms into individual industries, each class representing an industry.

Concentration ratios

Having classified firms into industries, it is possible to see how many producers there are in the industry. The number of producers is likely to be less important in studying the behaviour of the industry than the economic power of individual producers within the industry. One way of measuring this potential power is to calculate how important are the top few companies in the market. It can be done by looking at their importance in terms of market share in the industry, how many workers they employ or some other measure. This measure is then called a CONCENTRATION RATIO.

A three-firm concentration ratio would be the total share of the market (by output, employment or some other measure) held by the three largest producers in the industry; a four-firm concentration ratio would be the total share of the market held by the four largest producers; etc.

Market concentration in the UK

Table 25.1 shows the five-firm concentration ratios for UK manufacturing industry in 1987. On average the largest five firms in an industry accounted for approximately 40 per cent of net output. However, an industry can be widely defined. For instance, one of the 103 industries included in Table 25.1 is passenger car production (Class 351 under the 1980 Standard Industrial Classification). Within that industry, it could be argued that there are a number of different markets, for instance the small car market, the family-size saloon car market and the luxury car market. The concentration ratio is likely to be higher in each of these markets than in the market for passenger car production as a whole because there will be fewer producers in each market segment. In general, the narrower the definition of the market, the higher the concentration ratio is likely to be.

Figure 25.1 shows concentration ratios for selected

industries in the UK. This ranges from 8.3 per cent in the metal working machine tool industry to 99 per cent in the tobacco industry.

In manufacturing, there has been increasing concentration this century. A slight fall in concentration during the 1970s can be partially explained by the decline in manufacturing industry at the time due to severe international competitive pressure. Many large manufacturers cut back production or left the market altogether, reducing their power within the market place. The take-over boom in the 1980s and continued European economic integration post-1992 is likely to see an upward trend in industrial concentration once again.

Table 25.1 *5 firm concentration ratios: manufacturing industries, 1987*

Percentage of net output of the five largest firms in the industry	Number of industries
0-9	4
10-19	13
20-29	17
30-39	15
40-49	16
50-59	12
60-69	11
70-79	8
80-89	2
90-99	5

Source: adapted from *Census of Production, Summary Tables, Business Monitor* PA 1002.

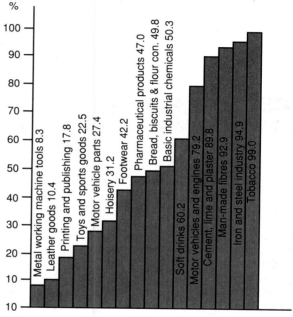

Source: adapted from *Census of Production, Summary Tables, Business Monitor* PA 1002.

Figure 25.1 *Five-firm concentration ratios for selected UK industries 1987*

1. **From the evidence in the table and from your own knowledge, discuss the structure of the car market in the UK.**

Table 25.2 *UK car registrations, January 1990*

	Number of registrations	Percentage of total
Total	206 393	100.00
of which		
Ford	46 697	22.63
Vauxhall	35 791	17.34
Rover	27 847	13.49
Peugeot/Citroen	22 210	10.76
Audi/VW/Seat	15 149	7.34
Nissan	9 680	4.69
Renault	8 561	4.15
Volvo	8 148	3.95
Fiat/Alfa/Lancia	5 656	2.74

Source: Society of Motor Manufacturers and Traders.

26 Short run profit maximisation

Summary

1. Profit is maximised at a level of output where the difference between total revenue and total cost is greatest.
2. At this profit maximising level of output, marginal cost = marginal revenue.
3. An increase in costs will lower the profit maximising level of output.
4. An increase in revenues will raise the profit maximising level of output.

Total cost and total revenue

Profit is the difference between **revenue** (the receipts of the firm) and **costs** (the monies paid out by the firm). A firm will make the most profit (or **maximum** profit) when the difference between total revenue and total cost is greatest.

This is shown in Table 26.1. Total revenue is shown in the second column whilst total cost is in the third column. Profit is the difference between the two. At low levels of production, the firm will make a loss. The BREAK-EVEN POINT, where total revenue equals total cost, is reached at an output level of 3 units. Thereafter the profit made increases as output increases.

There are two levels of output where profit is highest at £27. But it should be remembered that the difference between revenue and cost here is **abnormal** or **economic profit**. Normal profit is included as a cost of production (☞ unit 18). So profit, both normal and abnormal, is at a maximum at an output level of 7 units rather than 6 units because the cost of the seventh unit includes an allowance for normal profit.

Marginal cost and marginal revenue

Marginal cost and marginal revenue can also be used to find the profit maximising level of output. Marginal cost is the addition to total cost of one extra unit of output. Marginal revenue is the increase in total revenue resulting from an extra unit of sales.

Table 26.2 shows the marginal cost and marginal revenue figures derived from Table 26.1. Marginal revenue minus marginal cost gives the extra profit to be made from producing one more unit of output. The firm makes a loss of £10 on the first unit, and £1 on the second. But the third unit of output yields a profit of £11, the fourth £10 and so on. So long as the firm can make additional profit by producing an extra unit of output, it will carry on expanding production. But it will cease extra production when the extra unit yields a loss (i.e. where marginal profit moves from positive to negative). In Table 26.2, this happens at an output level of 7 units. The seventh unit contributes nothing to **abnormal** profit.

However, as explained above, cost includes an allowance for normal profit and therefore the firm will actually produce the seventh unit. The eighth unit yields a loss of profit of £9. The firm will therefore not produce

Table 26.1

Output	Total revenue (£)	Total cost (£)	Profit (£)
1	25	35	-10
2	50	61	-11
3	75	75	0
4	100	90	10
5	125	106	19
6	150	123	27
7	175	148	27
8	200	182	18
9	225	229	-4

Table 26.2

Output	Marginal revenue (£)	Marginal cost (£)	Addition to total profit (£)
1	25	35	-10
2	25	26	-1
3	25	14	11
4	25	15	10
5	25	16	9
6	25	18	8
7	25	25	0
8	25	34	-9
9	25	47	-22

the eighth unit if it wishes to maximise its profit.

Economic theory thus predicts that profits will be maximised at the output level where marginal cost equals marginal revenue.

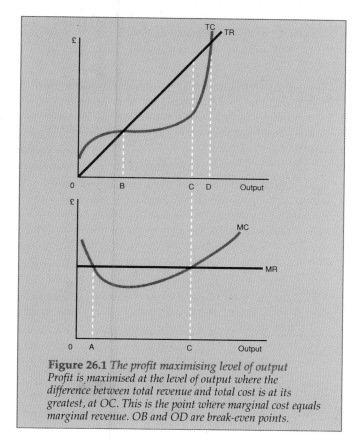

Figure 26.1 *The profit maximising level of output Profit is maximised at the level of output where the difference between total revenue and total cost is at its greatest, at OC. This is the point where marginal cost equals marginal revenue. OB and OD are break-even points.*

QUESTION 1
Table 26.3

Output (million units)	Total revenue (£ million)	Total cost (£ million)
1	10	8
2	20	14
3	30	20
4	40	30
5	50	50
6	60	80

(a) Calculate the total profit at each level of output.
(b) What is the profit maximising level of output?
(c) Calculate the marginal revenue and marginal cost of production at each level of output.
(d) Explain, using the data, why MC = MR at the profit maximising level of output.

Cost and revenue curves

These same points can be made using cost and revenue **curves**. The revenue curves in Figure 26.1 are drawn on the assumption that the firm receives the same price for its product however much it sells (i.e. demand is perfectly price elastic) So the total revenue curve increases at a constant rate.The marginal revenue curve is horizontal, showing that the price received for the last unit of output is exactly the same as the price received for all the other units sold before (☞ unit 28 for a discussion of the alternative assumption that a firm has to lower its price if it wishes to increase sales). The shape of the cost curves are as described in units 19 and 20.

The total revenue and total cost curves show that the firm will make a loss if it produces between O and B. Total cost is higher than total revenue. B is the break-even point. Between B and D the firm is in profit because total revenue is greater than total cost. However, profit is maximised at the output level C where the difference between total revenue and total cost is at a maximum. If the firm produces more than D, it will start making a loss again. D, the second break-even point on the diagram, is the maximum level of output which a firm can produce without making a loss. So D is the sales maximisation point subject to the constraint that the firm should not make a loss.

Now consider the marginal cost and marginal revenue curves. It can be seen that the profit maximising level of output, OC, is the point where marginal cost equals marginal revenue. If the firm produces an extra unit of output above OC, then the marginal cost of production is above the marginal revenue received from selling the extra unit. The firm will make a loss on that extra unit

and total profit will fall. On the other hand, if the firm is producing to the left of OC the cost of an extra unit of output is less than its marginal revenue. Therefore the firm will make a profit on the extra unit if it is produced. Generalising this, we can say that the firm will expand production if marginal revenue is above marginal cost. The firm will reduce output if marginal revenue is below marginal cost.

It should be noted that there is another point in Figure 26.1 where MC = MR. This is at the point A. It isn't always the case that the marginal cost curve will start above the marginal revenue curve at the lowest level of output. However, if it does, then the first intersection point of the two curves, when marginal cost is **falling**, is not the profit maximising point. The MC = MR rule is therefore a **necessary** but not **sufficient** condition for profit maximisation. A second condition has to be attached, namely that marginal cost must be rising as well.

QUESTION 2
(a) From the data in Table 26.3, draw two graphs showing (i) total revenue and total cost curves and (ii) marginal revenue and marginal cost curves. Draw the graphs one underneath the other using the same scale on the output axis.
(b) Mark on each of the graphs (i) the break-even levels of output and (ii) the profit maximising level of output.

Shifts in cost and revenue curves

It is now possible to analyse in greater depth the effects of changes in costs or revenues on output. Assume that costs, such as the price of raw materials, increase. This will mean that the marginal cost of production at every level of output will be higher. The marginal cost curve will shift upwards as shown in Figure 26.2. The profit maximising level of output will fall from OQ_1 to OQ_2. Hence a rise in costs will lead to a fall in output.

On the other hand a rise in revenue will lead to an increase in output. Assume that revenue increases at every given level of output. Perhaps consumers are prepared to pay higher prices because their incomes have increased, or the good has become more fashionable to purchase. This will push the marginal revenue curve upwards as shown in Figure 26.3. The profit maximising level of output will then rise from OQ_1 to OQ_2.

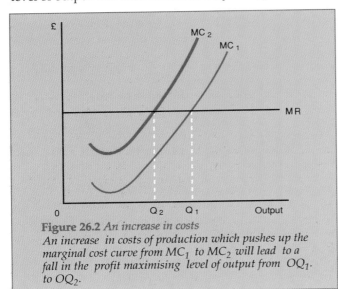

Figure 26.2 *An increase in costs*
An increase in costs of production which pushes up the marginal cost curve from MC_1 to MC_2 will lead to a fall in the profit maximising level of output from OQ_1 to OQ_2.

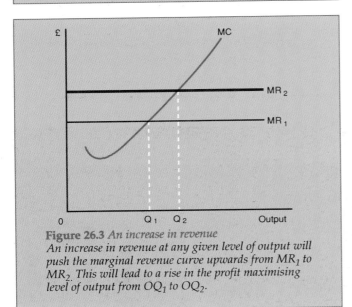

Figure 26.3 *An increase in revenue*
An increase in revenue at any given level of output will push the marginal revenue curve upwards from MR_1 to MR_2. This will lead to a rise in the profit maximising level of output from OQ_1 to OQ_2.

QUESTION 3 Consider the data in Table 26.3. What is the new profit maximising level of output if:
(a) marginal revenue falls to £6 at each level of output;
(b) marginal revenue increases to £20 at each level of output;
(c) marginal cost increases by £4 at each level of output?

Good models

The MC = MR condition is one which is very important in the neo-classical theory of the firm. However, economists know from studies made that most businessmen are not familiar with the economic concepts of marginal cost and marginal revenue, and even fewer could state their current marginal cost of production.

In one sense this is very damning for the neo-classical theory of the firm. It will be explained in unit 111 that one criterion for judging a good model or theory is whether the model is realistic.

However, neo-classical economists would not claim that businessmen decide on their output levels by equating marginal cost and marginal revenue. They would start from the premise that firms attempt to maximise profits. If they don't, then in the real world they tend either to be forced out of business by more efficient firms which are maximising profit or they are taken over and made more efficient. So there are strong pressures forcing businesses towards their profit maximising levels of output. Economists then find it helpful to analyse the profit maximising level of output in terms of marginal cost and marginal revenue.

The MC = MR rule then is not an attempt by economists to explain how businesses arrive at their level of output. Rather, it is a rule which says that if businesses have maximised profit, it must logically be true that marginal cost equals marginal revenue. Parallels can be found in the physical sciences. A cricketer throwing a ball to another player will not analyse the throw in terms of velocity, friction, wind speed etc. But a physicist, using these concepts, could work out the optimum trajectory for the ball. The theory is not worthless because it fails to describe accurately how the player thinks and acts about the throw. Rather the theory helps us to understand the science behind everyday reality.

Key terms

Break-even point - the levels of output where total revenue equals total cost.

Applied economics

The Japanese production miracle, 1985-90

Japanese manufacturing industry has proved to be highly competitive in the post-war era. In part this success has been due to the ability of Japanese industry to cut its costs of production over time. As the marginal cost of production has fallen, so output has expanded. In Figure 26.4, the shift in the MC curve from MC_1 to MC_2, leads to an increase in output from OA to OB.

By the mid-1980s, Japan's exports far exceeded its imports and this, together with speculative buying of the yen and a little help from central banks in Europe and the USA, prompted a sharp rise in the value of Japanese yen against other currencies including the US dollar. At the start of 1985, the exchange rate was 250 yen to the US dollar. By 1988, the yen had doubled in value to 125 yen to the US dollar.

This was potentially disastrous for Japanese firms dependent upon exports. In order to sell the same volume into export markets they could not afford to increase the foreign currency price (the price in US dollars or pounds sterling or French francs) of their products. But if they did not increase their foreign currency prices, they would have to take a cut in the price they received in Japanese yen leading to a fall in their marginal revenue. For instance, a $100 camera in 1985 would have been worth 25 000 yen to a Japanese exporter in 1985 but only 12 500 yen in 1988. A fall in marginal revenue will lead to a fall in the profit maximising level of output. So in theory, the dramatic rise in the value of the yen should have led to a fall in production for many Japanese companies.

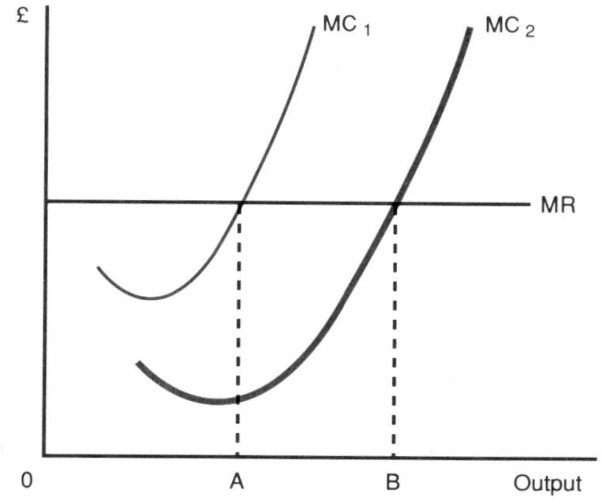

Indeed in 1985 and 1986, profits of many Japanese companies fell. Industries, such as steel and shipbuilding, which competed internationally mainly on price, made record losses. However, Japanese industry did not respond passively to this desperate situation. Companies reacted by sharply cutting costs. Some production was moved overseas to cheaper locations. Workers took wage cuts. Firms redoubled their efforts to find ways of increasing the productivity of labour (i.e. raising the output per worker). So the marginal cost curve of many Japanese companies moved sharply to the right as in Figure 26.4.

Companies also, wherever possible, increased their output of higher value, higher profit items. For instance, in 1985 Sony relied for over 80 per cent of its sales on televisions, video and audio equipment. By 1990 this had fallen to under 70 per cent as it increased its sales of new products such as floppy disks and computer workstations. So Japanese industry managed to shift its marginal revenue curve upwards from its 1985/6 low point.

By 1990, Japanese manufacturing industry was, if anything, stronger than in 1985. Output was at record levels, profits were high and many companies were implementing expansion plans. Japanese companies were once again experiencing year on year falls in marginal cost and rises in marginal revenue, signals for them to continue increasing their output.

Figure 26.4

BRYMBO STEEL WORKS CLOSES

Data question

In May 1990, United Engineering Steels announced the closure of its Brymbo steel works in Wrexham with the loss of 1 125 jobs. The plant had suffered from rising costs of iron ore, electricity and wages. At the same time, the price of steel products fell as high interest rates cut the demand for cars and commercial vehicles. The Brymbo steel works had long been considered a marginal plant.

Starved of investment, it was a high cost production plant.

1. Explain, using the concepts of marginal cost and marginal revenue, why United Engineering Steel decided to close its Brymbo steel works.

Summary

1. In a perfectly competitive market it is assumed that there are a large number of small firms that produce a homogeneous product. Firms are price-takers. There are no barriers to entry or exit and there is perfect knowledge.
2. The demand curve facing an individual firm is perfectly elastic because the firm is a price taker. This means that price = AR = MR.
3. The short run supply curve of the firm is its marginal cost curve above its average variable cost curve.
4. If firms in the short run are making abnormal profits, new firms will enter the industry, increasing market supply and thus reducing price. This will continue until only normal profits are being made.
5. If production is unprofitable, firms will leave the industry, reducing market supply and increasing price. This will continue until only normal profits are being made.
6. In long run equilibrium, AR = AC because no abnormal profits are made.

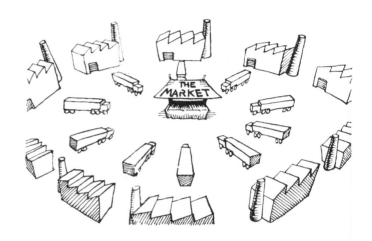

Assumptions

The model of PERFECT COMPETITION describes a market where there is a high degree of competition. The word 'perfect' does not mean that this form of competition produces ideal results or maximises economic welfare: in other words, the word 'perfect' should not have any **normative** overtones (☞ unit 111).

A perfectly competitive market must possess four characteristics.

■ There must be **many buyers and sellers** in the market, none of whom is large enough to influence price. Buyers and sellers are said to be PRICE TAKERS. This type of market has many relatively small firms that supply goods to a large number of small buyers.

■ There is **freedom of entry and exit** to the industry. Firms must be able to establish themselves in the industry easily and quickly. Barriers to entry must therefore be low. If a firm wishes to cease production and leave the market, it must be free to do so.

■ Buyers and sellers possess **perfect knowledge** of prices. If one firm charges a higher price than the market price, the demand for its product will be zero as buyers buy elsewhere in the market. Hence the firm has to accept the market price if it wishes to sell into the market (i.e. it must be a price taker).

■ All firms produce a **homogeneous** product. There is no branding of products and products are identical.

There are relatively few industries in the world which approximate to this type of market structure. One which might is agriculture. In agriculture there are a large number of farmers supplying the market, none of whom is large enough to influence price. It is easy to buy a farm

| QUESTION 1 | |

QUESTION 1
Table 27.1 *Tour operators' market share 1988*

	% by volume
Thomson Travel	28
ILG	17
Horizon	8
Redwing	5
Owners Abroad	4
Airtours	3
Best Travel	3
Yugotours	2
Cosmoair	2
Granada Travel	2
Others	26

(Total: 13.2 million package tours)

Source: *Business Monitor*, MSI.

From your own knowledge and from the above data, discuss the extent to which the package holiday market is perfectly competitive.

and set up in business. Equally it is easy to sell a farm and leave the industry. Farmers on the whole possess perfect knowledge. They know what prices prevail in the market, for instance from the farming press. Finally, farmers produce a range of homogeneous products. King Edwards potatoes from one farm are indistinguishable from King Edwards potatoes from another. In Europe and in many countries round the world, farming is in certain instances not a perfectly competitive market. This is because governments may interfere in the market, buying and selling to fix a price (☞ unit 12).

Demand and revenue

It is an assumption of the model of perfect competition that there is a large number of sellers in the market. Assume that one of these firms decides to double output. Industry supply will increase, pushing the supply curve to the right. However, the increase in supply is necessarily very small because the firm is small. In fact it will be so small that the resulting movement along the demand curve will be impossible to distinguish and the price will not change.

This can be seen in Figure 27.1. The area round the existing equilibrium point has been enlarged. An increase in supply by one firm has shifted the supply curve from S_1 to S_2, reducing equilibrium price by AC and increasing equilibrium quantity demanded and supplied by CB. However, AC is so small that it has no effect on the overall equilibrium price of OF and it is impossible to draw two supply curves thinly enough to show this shift in supply.

In agriculture, for instance, it would be surprising if the decision of one farmer to double wheat output were to have any perceptible influence on equilibrium price. His or her extra output is so insignificant that it cannot affect the market price for wheat. Of course, if all farmers were to double their wheat output, the price of wheat would collapse. But here we are interested only in the effect on price of the production decisions of a single farm.

A firm in perfect competition can therefore expand output or reduce output without influencing the price. Put another way, the firm cannot choose to raise price and expect to sell more of its product. It can lower its price but there is no advantage in this since it can sell its entire output at the higher market price. The demand curve for an individual firm is therefore horizontal (i.e. **perfectly elastic** ☞ unit 18 as in Figure 27.2. Note that if a firm expanded output sufficiently its demand curve would become downward sloping. But then the industry would be made up of one large firm and many small firms and would no longer be perfectly competitive.)

This demand curve is also the firm's average and marginal revenue curve. If a firm sells all its output at one price, then this price must be the average price or average revenue received. If a firm sells an extra or marginal unit, it will receive the same price as on preceding units and therefore the marginal price or revenue will be the same as the average price or revenue.

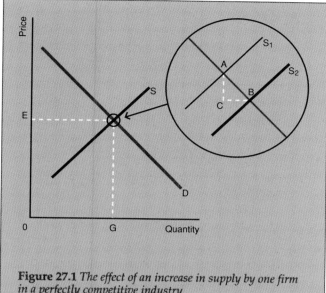

Figure 27.1 *The effect of an increase in supply by one firm in a perfectly competitive industry*
An increase in supply by one firm from S_1 to S_2, will have such a small effect on total supply that equilibrium price will remain at OF.

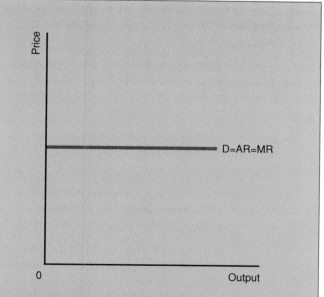

Figure 27.2 *The demand curve facing a firm in perfect competition*
A change in output by the firm will have no effect on the market price of the product. Therefore the firm faces a perfectly elastic demand curve. This is also the firm's average and marginal revenue curve.

Cost and supply curves

In a perfectly competitive market, the supply curve of the firm will be its marginal cost curve.

■ The marginal cost of production is the lowest price at which a firm would be prepared to supply an extra unit of output. For instance, if the marginal cost were £5 when price received were £3, then the firm would be able to make £2 **abnormal profit** (profit over and above the **normal profit** included in cost on that unit). The firm would definitely produce this marginal unit. If marginal cost were £3 when price were £3 it would still produce this marginal unit because it would earn normal profit on it. However, if marginal cost were £2 when price was £3 it would not produce the extra unit because it would make a £1 loss on it.

■ In the short run, a firm will not necessarily shut down production if it makes a loss (☞ unit 24). A firm has fixed costs which it has to pay whether it closes down and produces nothing or whether it continues to operate. Any revenue over and above variable cost will make some contribution towards paying its fixed costs. Therefore it will only close down (i.e. cease to supply) if average revenue or price is below average variable cost.

The firm's short run supply curve will therefore be that part of the marginal cost curve above its average variable cost curve - the thick portion of the marginal cost curve in Figure 27.3 (a).

In the long run there are no fixed costs and the average total cost and average variable cost curves are one and the same. The firm will not produce unless it can cover all its costs. Therefore in the long run, the firm's supply curve is the marginal cost curve above its average cost curve as shown in Figure 27.3 (b).

The supply curve for the industry can be constructed by horizontally summing the individual supply curves of each firm (☞ unit 5).

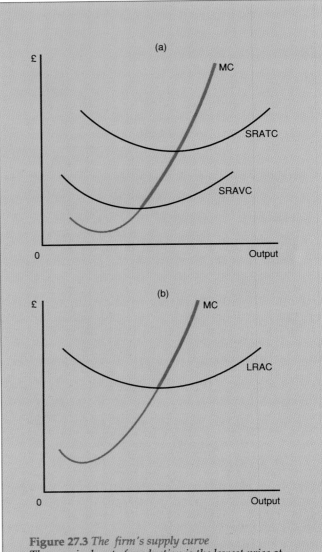

Figure 27.3 *The firm's supply curve*
The marginal cost of production is the lowest price at which a profit maximising firm will sell a marginal unit of production. Therefore the marginal cost curve is the supply curve for the firm. However, in the short run the firm may stay in production providing it can cover its average variable costs. Hence the short run supply curve is the marginal cost curve above average variable cost as in Figure 27.3(a). In the long run a firm will leave the industry if it makes a loss. Hence, the supply curve in the long run is the marginal cost curve above the average cost curve as in Figure 27.3 (b).

Short run equilibrium

In perfect competition it is assumed that firms are short run profit maximisers. So the firm will produce at that level of output where marginal cost equals marginal revenue (the MC= MR rule, (☞ unit 26). The price it charges is fixed by the market because the individual firm is a price-taker.

Figure 27.4 shows one possible short run equilibrium situation. The demand curve is perfectly elastic at a price of OE. The marginal cost curve cuts the marginal revenue curve at H and hence the equilibrium, profit maximising level of output for the firm is OQ. At this level of output, average revenue (QH) is higher than average cost (QG) and so the firm will make an abnormal profit. This is given by the shaded area EFGH and is average profit (EF) multiplied by the quantity produced (FG).

Figure 27.5 gives another possible situation. Here the firm is making a loss at its equilibrium, profit maximising (or in this case loss minimising) level of output OQ where MC = MR. Price OF is lower than average cost and hence the firm makes a total loss of EFGH. The firm will stay in production if this loss is smaller than the loss it would make if it shut down (i.e. so long as average revenue is above average variable cost).

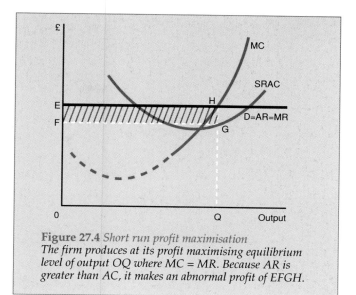

Figure 27.4 *Short run profit maximisation*
The firm produces at its profit maximising equilibrium level of output OQ where MC = MR. Because AR is greater than AC, it makes an abnormal profit of EFGH.

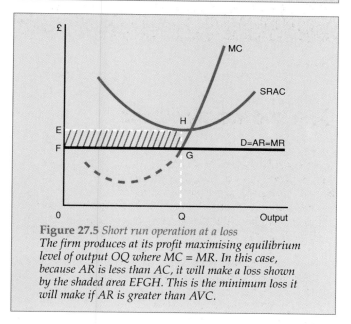

Figure 27.5 *Short run operation at a loss*
The firm produces at its profit maximising equilibrium level of output OQ where MC = MR. In this case, because AR is less than AC, it will make a loss shown by the shaded area EFGH. This is the minimum loss it will make if AR is greater than AVC.

QUESTION 3
Table 27.3

Output	Marginal Cost (£)
2	
	40
3	
	30
4	
	40
5	
	60
6	
	100
7	

A firm has total fixed costs of £100. Total variable cost of production of the first 2 units is £100. Table 27.3 shows the marginal cost of production.

(a) Calculate for levels of output from 2 to 7 units: (i) total variable cost; (ii) total cost; (iii) average variable cost; (iv) average total cost.
(b) Plot the firm's short run supply curve on a graph.
(c) Would a firm cease production (1) in the short run and (2) in the long run if the sales price per unit were: (i) £80; (ii) £70; (iii) £60; (iv) £50; (v) £40; (vi) £30?

Long run equilibrium

In the long run, a perfectly competitive firm will neither make losses nor abnormal profits.

Consider a situation where firms were making losses. In the long term, some firms would leave the industry. It is pointless carrying on production in the long term at a loss. If firms leave the industry, total supply will fall. The more firms that leave the industry, the greater will be the fall in supply and the greater will be the rise in price of the product. Firms will continue to leave the industry until the industry as a whole returns to profitability. This is shown in Figure 27.6. When the supply curve is S_1 the firm is making a loss. Firms leave the industry, pushing the supply curve to the left, with S_2, the price is just high enough for firms to make **normal profit.** If on the other hand a firm were making abnormal profit in the short run, other firms would enter the industry eager to gain high profits. This is shown in Figure 27.7. At a price of P, firms are making abnormal profit. This encourages new entrants to the industry, increasing supply from S_1 until with S_2 the price is just low enough for firms to make a normal profit.

In the long run, then, competitive pressures ensure equilibrium is established where the firm neither makes abnormal profits or losses. This means that in equilibrium, average revenue equals average cost (AR = AC). It should also be remembered that MC = MR because the firm is profit maximising and that AR = MR because the demand curve is horizontal. Putting these three conditions together, it must be true that for a firm in long run equilibrium in a perfectly competitive market:

$$AC = AR = MR = MC$$

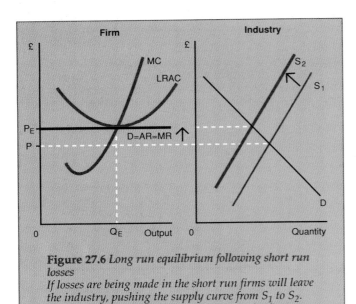

Figure 27.6 *Long run equilibrium following short run losses*
If losses are being made in the short run firms will leave the industry, pushing the supply curve from S_1 to S_2. At S2 there will no longer be any pressure for firms to leave because they will be able to make normal profits on their operations.

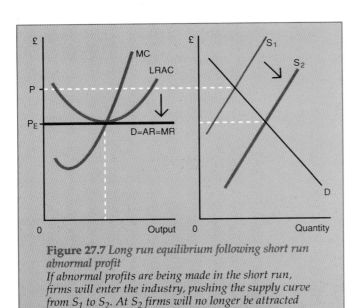

Figure 27.7 *Long run equilibrium following short run abnormal profit*
If abnormal profits are being made in the short run, firms will enter the industry, pushing the supply curve from S_1 to S_2. At S_2 firms will no longer be attracted into the industry because they will only be able to make normal profits on their operations.

QUESTION 4 The international steel market can be seen as a perfectly competitive market. There are a large number of steel producers manufacturing a number of homogeneous products. During the early 1970s, profits were high and new steel producers, particularly in the newly industrialised countries such as South Korea, entered the market. The first oil crisis of 1973-4, however, had a disastrous impact on steel producers. Demand for steel fell as economies went into recession. For the next ten years, many steel companies made little if any profit and many made large losses. In Europe and the USA, plants were closed and firms merged or went out of business. How can the model of perfect competition explain the behaviour of steel firms in the 1970s and 1980s?

Long run cost curves

One interesting point to note is that the model of perfect competition predicts that all perfectly competitive firms will have identical costs in the long run. Assume a firm discovers some new technique of production which enables it to reduce costs and increase profits in the short run. Other firms will respond by copying this technique. They can do this because there is perfect knowledge in the industry and therefore there can be no industrial secrets. Firms will then start to cut prices, hoping to be able to expand their sales. If a firm fails to adopt the new techniques, it will start to make a loss when other firms expand supply and undercut its price. Eventually it will be forced either to leave the industry because it is uncompetitive, or adopt the latest production techniques.

Alternatively, a firm may possess some unique factor of production. It may have an exceptional manager, or find that it is far better sited than other firms. In a perfectly competitive world the manager will be able to demand increases in salary which match the extra profit that she is generating for the firm. If the firm fails to pay this, she will be headhunted by another firm which realises the potential of the manager to create profits. As for the better site, the firm could sell it to another firm in the industry for a much higher price than those sites owned by competitors. Therefore the opportunity cost of the site is much higher than other sites and it is the opportunity cost, not the accounting cost, that is shown in economists' cost curves.

Key terms

Perfect competition - a market structure where there are many buyers and sellers, where there is freedom of entry and exit to the market, where there is perfect knowledge and where all firms produce a homogeneous product.

Price-taker - a firm or other economic agent which is forced to accept the ruling market price for the sale of its product.

QUESTION 5 In 1988, it was reported that Pompes Funébres Générales (PFG), the largest firm of French undertakers, had bought a 29 per cent stake in Kenyon Securities, the third largest quoted undertaking business in Britain. In France a declining mortality rate had hit undertakers hard and PFG was looking for new markets. One reason why the UK is attractive is because there are more cremations in the UK than in France. 70 per cent of the UK market is accounted for by cremations whereas in France the figure is only 4 per cent. Profit margins on cremations are much higher than on burials.

Source: adapted from the Financial Times, 22.6.1988.

Why might PFG be prepared to pay more for its stake in Kenyon Securities than it would have to pay if it attempted to set up a rival undertaking business from scratch in the UK?

Applied economics

Big Bang and its aftermath

Before October 1986, the Stock Exchange was a regulated market (i.e it was not perfectly competitive). Anyone wishing to buy or sell stocks or shares had to buy through a **stockbroker**. The stockbroker charged a fixed commission which was set by the Stock Exchange itself. It meant that a large pension fund buying £20 million worth of shares had to pay the same percentage commission as a small investor buying £500 worth of shares despite the fact that the dealing costs of a £20 million deal were far lower per share.

The stockbroker then had to buy from or sell shares to a **jobber**. The stockbroker had a duty to shop around the jobbers on the Stock Exchange for the best price for the stocks or shares being traded. The jobber made his money by offering to buy shares at a lower price than that which he was prepared to sell.

The number of jobbing firms was fixed by the Stock Exchange Council, itself made up of representatives from jobbing and stockbroking firms who were unlikely to permit large numbers of new entrants to the market because it would have cut into their own businesses. Moreover, the stockbroking and jobbing firms allowed to trade on the Stock Exchange were kept small through Stock Exchange rules about ownership. For instance, no bank could own either a stockbroking or a jobbing firm.

The Conservative government elected in 1979 was committed to liberalising markets, making them more competitive. Stock Exchange rules clearly contravened the Restrictive Practices Act 1976 (☞ unit 39) and the government indicated to the Stock Exchange that if it did not remove restrictions on trading, it would take action to do so itself. In 1983, the Stock Exchange announced a package of changes which was to completely change the London Stock Exchange. As from March 1986, any Stock Exchange firm could be taken over by any other company. As from 27 October 1986, ('Big Bang' as it came to be called), fixed commissions were abolished and stocks and shares could be bought and sold by any licenced company.

The market, it could be argued, became perfectly competitive. For instance, buyers and sellers of stocks and shares were now able to shop around for the best deal. Firms trading in stocks and shares were forced to compete on price.

Before 'Big Bang', stockbroking and jobbing firms had been able to earn abnormal profits, the result of price fixing and barriers to entry to the industry. The 1986 reforms led to a flood of new entrants to the market, attracted by the abnormal profit being made. UK and overseas banks bought up existing stockbroking and jobbing firms, or set up their own securities operations. For instance, the number of jobbing firms dealing in gilt edged stock (loans of the UK government) rose from just 2 to 27 in 1986.

This rise led to a fall in the average and marginal revenue curve in the industry as firms cut their dealing price in order to secure business.

From October 1986 to October 1987, the fall in average and marginal revenue due to price cutting was to some extent offset by booming business. Stock Market prices kept rising and investors were attracted into the market, buying and selling large volumes of stocks and shares. Then came the Stock Market crash of October 1987. 25 per cent of the value of companies quoted on the London Stock Exchange was wiped out. This had two effects. Firstly, since commission charged on dealings was based upon the price of securities, dealers immediately started to lose 25 per cent of their earnings on every share deal. Even more importantly, the Stock Market crash frightened away many investors. Building Society deposits boomed as small investors played it safe. As a result, the volume of business on the Stock Exchange slumped.

The result was that the average revenue curve of dealers in the market fell sharply. For many it fell well below their average cost curves, resulting in large losses. The theory of perfect competition predicts that firms will leave the industry if losses are being made. This is exactly what happened. Throughout 1988, 1989 and 1990, there was a string of announcements of banks closing their dealing operations or scaling them down. Even then, many firms were still making losses or were barely profitable. More firms will have to leave the market in the early 1990s if the remaining firms in the industry are to make a normal profit and the industry is to achieve long run equilibrium.

Analysts leaving the office after being made redundant.

Data question

SALMON FARMING

Salmon has long been a luxury food, commanding high prices due to its scarcity. However, the 1980s has seen an explosion in salmon farming. This has substantially raised output of salmon with a consequent fall in price. For instance, salmon which was fetching $7 to $8 a kilogram in the USA and Japan in 1988 was being sold for between $5 and $5.50 in 1990.

New companies are entering the market all the time. More than 100 salmon farming companies were set up in Chile in the second half of the 1980s. Exports were only 12 000 tonnes in 1989, but this was double the figure in 1988 and it is predicted that Chile could be exporting 22 000 tonnes by 1992.

Chile's increased output is still small fry compared with Norway's production of 120 000 tonnes in 1989. However, some commentators predict that some small producers will soon begin to be squeezed out of the business. Already producers are looking at alternatives to salmon. In Chile some companies have chosen to concentrate on oyster farming and seeweed farming because of the better returns available on these products.

1. To what extent could the salmon market be considered perfectly competitive?
2. Using diagrams, explain why (a) new companies have entered the salmon market in the 1980s and (b) other companies have chosen to produce products other than salmon.

28 The neo-classical theory of monopoly

Summary

1. A monopolist is the sole producer in an industry.
2. The demand curve faced by the monopolist is the market demand curve.
3. The monopolist's demand curve is also its average revenue curve.
4. The marginal revenue falls twice as steeply as the average revenue curve.
5. The profit maximising monopolist will produce where MC = MR and price on its demand curve.
6. The monopolist is likely to be able to earn abnormal profit because average revenue will be above average cost at the equilibrium level of output.
7. A monopolist may be able to price discriminate and further increase abnormal profit.

Assumptions

The neo-classical theory of monopoly assumes that a MONOPOLY market structure has the following characteristics:

■ there is only one firm in the industry - the monopolist;
■ barriers to entry prevent new firms from entering the market;
■ the monopolist is a short run profit maximiser.

There are many industries in the world economy which possess most or all of these characteristics. In the UK for instance, gas, electricity, telecommunications, rail transport and water supply are monopolies. Some of these monopolies are state owned (☞ unit 42) whilst others were state monopolies which have since been privatised without the creation of genuine new competition (☞ unit 43).

Some monopolies, such as the UK water companies, possess considerable market power because there are no good substitutes for their products. British Rail too is a monopolist but its monopoly position is weaker because it faces competition from other forms of transport. In fact the existence of monopoly depends upon how an industry is defined. For instance, British Rail is a monopolist in rail travel, but not in transport. Shell is not a monopoly supplier of petrol to the UK market, but it may have a monopoly in a rural area if it owns the only garage for miles around.

Monopolies can only remain as monopolies if there are high barriers to entry to the industry (☞ unit 25). In the case of a natural monopoly(☞ unit 37), economies of scale are so large that any new entrant would find it impossible to match the costs and prices of the established firm in the industry. Other barriers to entry include legal barriers such as patents, natural cost advantages such as ownership of all key sites in an industry, marketing barriers such as advertising, and restrictive practices designed to force any competitor to leave the market.

QUESTION 1

Table 28.1 *Inland energy consumption of fuels, UK 1988*

	Million therms
Coal and other solid fuels[1]	6 886
Gas	18 665
Electricity[2]	8 724
Petroleum	24 890

1. Includes coal used to produce electricity.
2. Excludes electricity generated from coal.

Source: CSO, *Annual Abstract of Statistics.*

British Coal is currently a monopoly producer of coal in the UK. To what extent is British Coal a monopoly?

Revenue curves

A monopoly firm is itself the industry. Because the industry faces a downward sloping demand curve, so too must the monopolist. It can therefore only increase sales by reducing price, or increase price by reducing sales. It can set either price or output but not both.

The demand curve shows the quantity bought at any given price. For instance, a water company might sell 2 billion gallons of water at 1p per gallon. This price is the same as its average revenue: on average it will receive 1p per gallon. So the downward sloping demand curve facing the firm is also the average revenue curve of the firm.

If average revenue is falling, marginal revenue must be falling too and at a faster rate. For example, assume a firm sells 10 units at £20 each. To sell an eleventh unit, it needs to lower its price, say to £19. Not only will it have to lower its price on the eleventh unit, but it will also have to lower its price on the other 10 units. This is because it cannot charge a higher price to some consumers than others (although we will see later on in this unit that it is possible in limited cases). There is a loss of revenue not just of £1 on the sale of the eleventh unit but a further £10 on the first 10 units. Total revenue increases from £200 (£20 x 10 units) to £209 (£19 x 11 units). So marginal revenue on the eleventh unit is £9 (£209 - £200) whilst the average revenue on selling 11 units is £19 (£209 ÷ 11 which is, of course, the price).

Table 28.2 gives a further example of falling marginal and average revenues. Note that the fall in marginal revenue is twice as large over any given change in quantity as the fall in average revenue. This is true of all

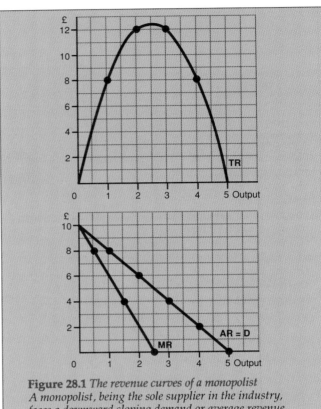

Figure 28.1 *The revenue curves of a monopolist*
A monopolist, being the sole supplier in the industry, faces a downward sloping demand or average revenue curve. Marginal revenue falls at twice the rate of average revenue and becomes zero when total revenue is maximised.

Table 28.2

Quantity	Average revenue or price £	Total revenue £	Marginal revenue £
0			
			8
1	8	8	
			4
2	6	12	
			0
3	4	12	
			-4
4	2	8	
			-8
5	0	0	

straight line average revenue curves. Plotting these figures on a diagram, we arrive at Figure 28.1. The marginal revenue figures, as with all marginal figures, are plotted half way between 'whole' output figures. So the marginal revenue of the fourth unit is plotted half way between 3 and 4 units. It can be seen that at any given level of output, average revenue is twice marginal revenue. Total revenue is maximised when marginal revenue is zero. If marginal revenue (the addition to total revenue) becomes negative then total revenue will automatically fall. Total revenue is zero if average revenue, the price received per unit of output, is zero too.

Equilibrium output

The neo-classical theory of the firm assumes that a monopolist will be a short run profit maximiser. This means that it will produce where MC = MR.

Figure 28.2 adds the traditional U-shaped average and marginal cost curves (☞ units 19 and 20) to the average and marginal revenue curves outlined above.

- ■ **The equilibrium profit maximising level of output** is OA where MC = MR.
- ■ **The price** will be OE. Buyers are prepared to pay OE for this output. We know this because the average revenue curve is also the demand curve and the demand curve shows the maximum price buyers will pay for any given level of ouput.
- ■ **Abnormal profit** of EFGC will be made. The abnormal profit per unit (GF) is the difference between the average revenue received (AF) and the average cost incurred (AG). OA units are sold. Therefore total abnormal profit is OA x FG, or the area EFGC. Note that this is abnormal profit because economic cost includes an allowance for normal profit.

Note also that price is not equal to the intersection of the MC and MR curves (i.e. price is not AB). This is because the firm, although deciding on the level of output by the MC = MR condition, fixes its price on the average revenue or demand curve. Also abnormal profit is not the area EF x FB (i.e. it is not the area between the average revenue curve and the marginal revenue and cost curves). Profit per unit is the difference between average revenue and average cost.

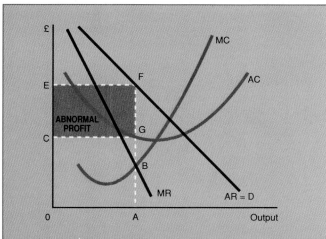

Figure 28.2 *Profit maximising output*
The monopolist will maximise profits by producing where MC = MR at OA. It will base its prices on its average revenue curve, charging OE. It will be able to earn abnormal profit of EFGC because average revenue is greater than average cost at this level of output.

Discriminating monopoly

Some buyers in the market will almost certainly be prepared to pay a higher price for a product than other buyers. In Figure 28.3, the profit maximising output for a monopolist is assumed to be OH and the profit maximising price is therefore OA. OA represents the maximum price that the marginal consumer is prepared to pay. Other consumers are prepared to pay a higher price. For instance, if output were only OK, the marginal consumer would be prepared to pay OB. The area ACF represents the area of consumer surplus (☞ unit 14), the difference between what consumers are prepared to pay in total for a good and what they actually pay. For instance, a rail commuter is likely to be prepared to pay more for a journey at 8 o'clock in the morning to take her to work than would a shopper. A business is likely to be prepared to pay a higher price for a telephone call during office hours than a householder. A millionaire faced with the need for heart surgery will pay more than a poor person with the same complaint.

A monopolist may be able to split the market and PRICE DISCRIMINATE between different buyers. For instance, in Figure 28.3, the monopolist may be able to charge OB for OK of output, and then charge a lower price of OA for KH of output. In this way, the monopolist appropriates ABEG of consumer surplus in the form of higher profit.

There are a number of different ways in which a monopolist may choose to discriminate.

- ■ Time. It may charge a different price at different times of the day or week, as do British Telecom or British Rail.
- ■ Place. It may vary price according to the location of the buyer. The same car can be bought at different prices in different countries of the EC for instance.
- ■ Income. It may be able to split up consumers into income groups, charging a high price to those with

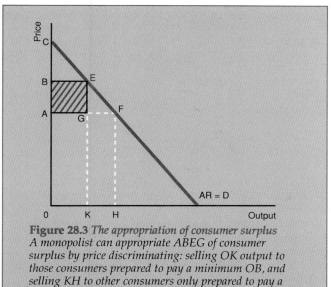

Figure 28.3 *The appropriation of consumer surplus*
A monopolist can appropriate ABEG of consumer surplus by price discriminating: selling OK output to those consumers prepared to pay a minimum OB, and selling KH to other consumers only prepared to pay a minimum OA.

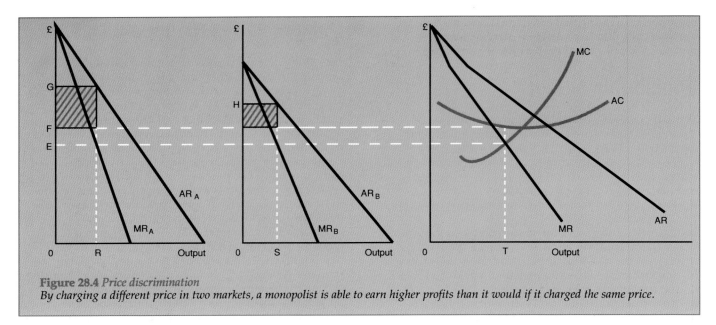

Figure 28.4 *Price discrimination*
By charging a different price in two markets, a monopolist is able to earn higher profits than it would if it charged the same price.

high incomes, and a low price to those with lower incomes. Examples of this can be found in medical practice and amongst lawyers. Hairdressers (who may be local monopolists) offering reduced rates to pensioners are likely to be price discriminating according to income too.

Three conditions must hold if a monopolist is to be able to price discriminate effectively.

■ The monopolist must face different demand curves from separate groups of buyers (i.e. the elasticity of demand of buyers must differ). If all buyers had the same demand curve, then the monopolist could not charge different prices to buyers.

■ The monopolist must be able to split the market into distinct groups of buyers, otherwise it will be unable to distinguish between those consumers prepared to pay a higher price and those prepared to a pay a lower price.

■ The monopolist must be able to keep the markets separate at relatively low cost. For instance, it must be able to prevent buyers in the high priced market from buying in the low price market. If a German car company sells its cars at 25 per cent less in Belgium than in the UK, then it must be able to prevent UK motorists and UK retailers from taking a day trip to Belgium to buy those cars. Equally, it must be able to prevent traders from buying in the low price market and selling into the high price market at a price which undercuts that of the monopolist.

Price discrimination can be analysed using the concepts of marginal cost and marginal revenue. Assume that the monopolist is able to divide its market into two and that the costs of production are identical for both markets.

The firm needs to allocate production between the two markets so that the marginal revenue is identical for each market if it is to maximise profit. To understand why, take a situation where marginal revenue in one market, A, is higher than another market, B. The firm could increase its

total revenue from a given output by switching goods from B to A. Marginal revenue in market B will now rise because it can charge a higher price if it sells less. Marginal revenue in market A will fall because it has to lower price to sell more. For instance, if marginal revenue in market A were £10 when it was £6 in market B, then the firm could gain an extra £4 of revenue by switching the marginal unit of production from market B to market A. It will carry on switching from market B to A until there is no more advantage in doing so, which occurs when the marginal revenues are the same.

In Figure 28.4, the demand curves in markets A and B are drawn first. From these demand or average revenue curves, the marginal revenue curves in each market can then be calculated. The average and marginal revenue curves for the total market can be calculated by summing horizontally the average and marginal revenue curves in each market. The profit maximising monopolist will produce where MC = MR across the whole market, at output level OT. This output (OT) is then split between the two markets (OR and OS) so that the marginal revenue is equal in both individual markets (OE). In each market, a firm's price will be based on the average revenue curve. A price of OG can be charged in market A, and a price of OH can be charged in market B. Average cost of production is OF and the abnormal profit earned in each market is shown by the shaded areas on the diagram. This will be higher than the abnormal profit the firm would have made if it had not discriminated.

Three technical points

Absence of a supply curve in monopoly In perfect competition, the supply curve of the firm is its marginal cost curve above average cost in the long run (☞ unit 27). In monopoly, there is no supply curve which is determined independently of demand.

Look back at Figure 28.2. The firm will produce at output OA because that is the output where MC = MR. Now assume that demand changes in such a way that the marginal revenue curve is much steeper but still passes through the point B. If the MR curve is steeper, so too will be the AR curve. The firm will now be able to charge a much higher price than OE for its product. For each differently sloped MR curve that passes through the point B, the firm will charge a different price to the consumer. The firm is prepared to supply OA output at a variety of different prices, depending upon demand conditions. So no supply curve for the monopolist can be drawn. (Contrast to this to the firm in perfect competition. Falls in demand which reduce prices received by the firm will result in a fall in quantity supplied as the firm moves down its supply curve.)

A monopolist will produce only where demand is elastic Look back to Figure 28.1. It should be obvious that a firm will not produce more than 2½ units of output. If it produces 3 units, it will almost certainly have higher costs than if it produces 2½ units but total revenue will fall. Profit therefore is bound to fall. 2½ units is the output where marginal revenue is zero. It is also the point where price elasticity of demand is unity because we are now half way along the demand or average revenue curve (☞ unit 8). To the left, elasticity is greater than 1, to the right less than 1. Since the firm will only produce to the left of 25½ units, it must produce where demand is elastic. An alternative explanation is to remember that a fall in price (needed to increase quantity sold) will only increase revenue if demand is elastic. Therefore a monopolist would not increase sales to the point where demand became inelastic.

Short run and long run operation So far no distinction has been made between the short run and the long run. A firm will produce in the short run if total revenue is greater than total variable cost (☞ unit 24). In the short run, a monopolist may therefore operate at a loss but it will close down if it cannot cover its variable costs. In the

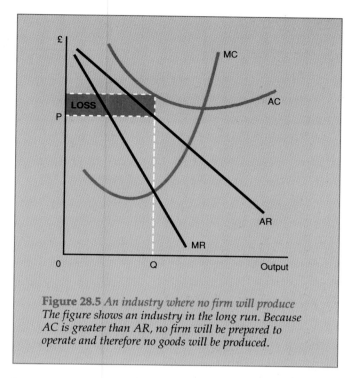

Figure 28.5 *An industry where no firm will produce* The figure shows an industry in the long run. Because AC is greater than AR, no firm will be prepared to operate and therefore no goods will be produced.

long run, a monopolist will not operate if it cannot cover all costs of production. Such a situation is shown in Figure 28.5. To maximise profits or minimise losses, it will produce where MC = MR, but at this level of output average cost is greater than average revenue. Hence this is a loss minimising point of production which will not attract any firms to the industry.

QUESTION 4 Draw two diagrams showing the change in equilibrium output of a profit maximising monopolist if (a) its marginal revenue increases; (b) its marginal cost increases.

Key terms

Monopoly - a market structure where one firm supplies all output in the industry without facing competition because of high barriers to entry to the industry.
Price discrimination - charging a different price for the same good or service in different markets.

Applied economics

British Telecom and its international phone monopoly

British Telecom has long had a monopoly on international calls into and out of the UK. In 1990, the *Financial Times* revealed that the profits on its international service in 1987-8 averaged 58 per cent of net revenue. In industry generally, a 20 per cent profit margin would be considered enough to attract new competition into the market.

International telephone companies gain revenues in two ways. Firstly, they charge their national customers for outgoing calls. For instance, British Telecom charges UK customers a standard rate of £0.71 a minute for calls to the United States. Secondly, the companies form part of an international cartel which regulates transfers of revenue between countries. British Telecom will pay monies to other telephone companies for carrying calls made by British customers, whilst foreign companies pay monies to BT for carrying their international calls to customers in the UK. In 1987-8 British Telecom received £5.6m more than it paid to West Germany, but paid £9.6m more than it received to Pakistan.

Overall, in 1987-8, BT collected £800m from customers for international calls, but paid a net £30m to foreign phone companies, leaving it with net revenue of £770m. The cost of running the international network, including the use of satellites and cables, was £178m, whilst £146m was charged for the use of the domestic network, making a total cost of £324m. Hence on average, UK international callers were being charged over twice the actual cost of making the call.

British Telecom is able to earn abnormal profits on its international operations because of lack of competition. Before 1979, there was no question of the British government licensing companies to compete with BT. With the election of a government committed to competition and free markets, the climate has changed. The 1981 Telecommunications Act allowed new operators to enter the market and subsequently a licence was given to Mercury, a new company, which has since competed with BT for commercial traffic on both national and international routes. However, Mercury is so small that it represents little threat to BT's continued dominance of the UK telecommunications market. It is likely that unless OFTEL (the body which regulates BT) acts firmly, BT will continue to exploit its international telephone market in order to maximise profits at the expense of consumers.

Data question

BRITISH GAS

In October 1988, the Monopolies and Mergers Commission published a report condemning British Gas's pricing policies as an abuse of its monopoly position. The Commission, reporting the results of an 11 month inquiry, found that industrial users consuming more than 25 000 therms per year suffered price discrimination.
■ Customers who were unable to use alternative fuels, such as electricity or oil, were charged a high price for guaranteed supplies of gas.
■ Customers who could substitute other fuels at short notice were charged a low price, although British Gas reserved the right to interrupt their gas supplies if necessary, for instance at peak demand times in winter.
■ British Gas did not publish price lists but negotiated contracts with large industrial customers individually. So there were price differences based upon willingness to pay even between consumers who were unable to use alternative fuels.

Not only did industrial customers pay higher prices than could be justified, but price discrimination served to 'deter new entrants and to inhibit the development of competition'.

In March 1989, British Gas announced a new pricing structure to meet the objections of the Commission. British Gas estimated that the new prices would lead to a fall in its profits of £75 million.

1. **Using diagrams, explain (a) how and (b) why British Gas price discriminated against its large industrial users.**
2. **Why should price discrimination by British Gas 'inhibit the development of competition'?**

Summary

1. Most industries operate in imperfectly competitive markets.
2. The monopolistic competition model makes the same assumptions as that of perfect competition except it is assumed that each firm produces a differentiated product and is therefore a price-maker.
3. In long run equilibrium, each firm will only earn normal profit and therefore AC = AR. Each firm will produce at its profit maximising output where MC = MR.

Imperfect competition

Perfect competition and monopoly are at either end of a spectrum of market structures. There are relatively few industries which conform to the strict characteristics of these two models. Most industries fall somewhere in between. In most industries:

■ competition exists because there are at least two firms in the industry;
■ competition is imperfect because firms sell products which are not identical to the products of rival firms.

The neo-classical theories of perfect competition and monopoly were first developed during the latter half of the 19th century. At the time, it was not unreasonable to suggest that many industries were made up of a large number of small firms producing identical or homogeneous products. In the 20th century fewer and fewer industries can be said to be perfectly competitive. So a number of theories of IMPERFECT COMPETITION have been advanced to explain the behaviour of firms. One important model, the model of MONOPOLISTIC COMPETITION, was developed by Edward Chamberlain, an American economist, in the 1930s, and his work was mirrored by an English economist, Joan Robinson, at the same time.

Assumptions

The theory of monopolistic competition makes almost the same assumptions as that of perfect competition, namely:

■ there are a large number of buyers and sellers in the market each of which is relatively small and acts independently;
■ there are no barriers to entry or exit;
■ firms are short run profit maximisers;
■ there is perfect knowledge in the market.

However, one assumption is different:

■ firms produce differentiated or non-homogeneous goods.

It can be argued that relatively few industries possess these characteristics. One possible example would be retailing in the UK. It has traditionally been fragmented. Even in areas where there are large national chains such as

groceries (Sainsbury's, Tesco, Waitrose, Co-op) or DIY (Do-it-all, B&Q, Texas Homecare), **concentration ratios** (☞ unit 25) are relatively low. Firms possess a certain amount of market power because of the location of stores or brand images, but this power is relatively weak in most cases.

QUESTION 1

Table 29.1 *UK grocers' market shares 1987/1988*

	%
Tesco	14.0
J Sainsbury	13.9
Dee	11.5
Argyll	
Presto etc.	6.1
Safeway	4.6
Asda	7.6
Co-op	12.1
Other	30.2

Source: *Financial Times*, 19.9.1988.

From the data above, and your own knowledge of the grocery industry, discuss the extent to which the grocery market could be described as monopolistically competitive.

The downward sloping demand curve

If a firm produces a product which is slightly different from its competitors, then it has a certain amount of market power. It will be able to raise price, for instance, without losing all its customers to firms which have kept their prices stable. So it is not a **price-taker** like a perfectly competitive firm. However, because there are a large number of firms in the industry producing relatively close substitutes, its market power is likely to be relatively weak. Small changes in price are likely to result in relatively large changes in quantity demanded as consumers switch to close substitutes (i.e. demand is likely to be relatively elastic).

The demand curve facing the firm is therefore downward sloping but elastic (i.e. it will operate on the upper portion of its demand curve). The firm's marginal revenue curve will fall twice as steeply as the average revenue curve (or demand curve), as shown in Figure 29.1.

Long run equilibrium

The firm will produce where MC = MR because it is a profit maximiser. In Figure 29.1, this means that it will produce at an output level of OA. It will charge a price based on its demand or average revenue curve, in this case OB.

The firm in the long run will not be able to earn abnormal profit. This is because there is freedom of entry to the market. If the firm is making abnormal profit in the short run (which would be shown on the diagram by average cost falling below average revenue at output OA), then firms will come into the industry attracted by the high level of profits. This will increase supply, shifting the average revenue curve downwards to the point where average revenue is just equal to average cost. If firms in the industry are making losses in the short run, then firms will leave the industry, reducing supply and shifting the average revenue curve upwards to the point where average revenue is just equal to average cost.

So in monopolistic competition two conditions must hold in long run equilibrium:
■ MC = MR because the firm is a profit maximiser;
■ AC = AR because competitive pressures mean that a firm cannot either make a loss or earn abnormal profit.

This means that at the profit maximising output, the average cost curve is tangential to the average revenue curve.

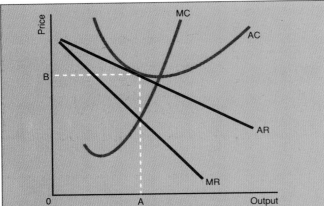

Figure 29.1 *Long run equilibrium for a monopolistically competitive firm.*
A firm will produce where MC=MR. Because there are no barriers to entry, the firm will be unable to earn abnormal profits in the long run. Therefore it must also be true that AC=AR at the equilibrium level of output. This occurs when the AC curve is tangential to the AR curve.

Key terms

Imperfect competition - a market structure where there are several firms in industry, each of which has some ability to control the price they set for their product.
Monopolistic competition - a market structure where a large number of small firms produce non-homogeneous products and where there are no barriers to entry or exit.

Applied economics

The supply of petrol in the UK

The oil wholesaling and retailing industry in the UK could be argued to be monopolistically competitive in character. For instance, there are a large number of firms in the market. According to a Monopolies and Mergers Commission report (1990), the market is supplied by 69 wholesalers. The five largest of these - Esso, Shell, British Petroleum, Texaco and Mobil - accounted for 65.6 per cent of deliveries to retailers in 1988. The retailers in the petrol industry are the garages which sell petrol. Some garages are independent, some are owned by oil wholesalers and leased to tenants, and others are run directly by the wholesalers.

Many wholesalers try to brand their products. However, despite extensive advertising, consumer loyalty to a particular brand of petrol is very weak. Consumers buy petrol on price, the location of petrol stations, the quality of the service offered including opening hours, and the extent of additional facilities on sites, such as shops or car washes. Hence, firms such as Esso face a downward sloping demand curve for their petrol but the elasticity of demand for their product is very high.

There is freedom of entry and exit to the industry. It is possible for new entrants in the wholesale market to gain market share by selling to independent petrol retailers. Equally it is possible for new entrants to buy petrol stations. The Monopolies and Mergers Commission did not find that ownership of forecourts by existing wholesalers was a significant barrier to entry.

It is difficult to say whether the 69 wholesalers in the market are all short run profit maximisers. However, given the openness of the market and the non-technical nature of petrol, it is likely that perfect knowledge exists to a great extent in the industry.

The theory of monopolistic competition predicts that firms will only earn normal profit in the long run. The Monopolies and Mergers Commission found that during the 1980s, total profits on the wholesaling of all petroleum products from refineries 'were positive but not unduly high'. Profits from wholesaling petrol alone were 'no more than moderate'.

The Commission's report pointed out that the level of the competition in the industry could be reduced in the future if there was a substantial decrease in the number of wholesalers in the market or if the large wholesalers came to own substantially more petrol stations, reducing the number of independents. If this came about, the market would cease to be monopolistically competitive and would become an oligopoly.

Data question

NEXT

Next, the fashion retailer, announced a series of sales and closures of its stores in 1989 and 1990. It had expanded rapidly in the 1980s, firstly expanding its chain of women's and men's clothing shops, and then diversifying into mail order, jewellery, childrenswear and household furnishings, as well as buying a chain of newsagents. However, the group was hard hit by the downturn in growth of sales in the late 1980s, the result of the government's high interest rate policy.

To stem losses, it closed 50 small shops in 1989 and announced the closure of 15 large stores for 1990. It sold its newsagent chain as well as Mercado, a carpet wholesaling business. It was also seeking buyers for the Next Jewellery chain of 50 shops and Biba, a West German retail chain.

1. To what extent could Next be said to be operating in a monopolistically competitive market?

2. How would economic theory explain (a) the growth of Next in the 1980s and (b) its strategy of sales and closures in 1989 and 1990?

30 The neo-classical theory of oligopoly

Summary

1. Most markets are oligopolistic.
2. An oligopolistic market is one where a small number of interdependent firms compete with each other.
3. Non-price competition is an important feature of oligopolistic markets.
4. The neo-classical kinked demand curve model assumes that a firm will reduce its price if a competitor starts a price war, but will leave price unchanged if a competitor raises its price.

The importance of oligopoly

Most industries could be said to be imperfectly competitive. A few are monopolistically competitive but the majority are **oligopolistic.** Most industries in the UK, the EC and the USA are dominated by a few suppliers (☞ unit 25). Therefore the theory of OLIGOPOLY is arguably the most important of the theories of the firm. Yet there is no single dominant model of oligopoly within economics. Rather there are a number of competing models which make different assumptions and draw different conclusions. Some of these models will be outlined in this and the next two units but first the characteristics of an oligopolistic market will be described.

Characteristics of oligopoly

For a market to be called 'oligopolistic', it must possess two characteristics.
■ Supply in the industry must be concentrated in the hands of relatively few firms. For instance, an industry where the three largest firms produce 80 per cent of output would be oligopolistic. Note that alongside a few very large producers there may also be a much larger number of very small firms. So an industry with 100 firms, where the three largest firms produced 80 per cent of the output, would still be classed as oligopolistic.
■ Firms must be interdependent. The actions of one large firm will directly affect another large firm. In perfect competition, firms are independent. If one farmer decides, for instance, to grow more wheat, that will have no impact on price or sales of other farmers in the industry. In oligopoly, if one large firm decides to pursue policies to increase sales, this is likely to be at the expense of other firms in the industry. One firm is likely to sell more only by

taking away sales from other firms.
■ In addition, for an industry to remain oligopolistic in the long run, it must be true that there are barriers to entry to the industry. If there were no barriers, firms would enter the industry to take advantage of the abnormal profits characteristic of oligopolies and would reduce the market share of the few large producers in the industry.

QUESTION 1 In the UK market for heavy duty liquid detergents (such as Persil Liquid and Ariel Liquid), two firms had market shares of 43 per cent each in 1987.
    Proctor and Gamble, an American company, has been battling with Unilever, an Anglo-Dutch company, for supremacy in the UK detergent market since the 1920s. Both companies are amongst the largest spenders on television advertising in the UK.

Source: adapted from the *Financial Times, 26.9.1988.*

Using information from the article, explain why the market for liquid detergents is oligopolistic.

Features of oligopolistic markets

Studies of oligopolistic markets have shown that individual firms can exhibit a wide number of different behaviour patterns. However, there are some features which are common to most oligopolistic markets. It is these features which an economic model of oligopoly must be able to incorporate or explain.

Non-price competition In a perfectly competitive market, firms producing homogeneous goods compete solely on price. In the short run, factors such as delivery dates might assume some importance, but in the long term price is all that matters. In an imperfectly competitive market, price is often not the most important factor in the competitive process. Firms decide upon a MARKETING MIX - a mixture of elements which form a coherent strategy designed to sell their products to their market. The marketing mix is often summarised in the '4 Ps'. Firms produce a **product** which appeals to their customers. The product may or may not be differentiated from rivals' products. A **price** needs to be set but this could be above or below the price of competing products depending upon the pricing strategy to be used. For instance, a high price will be set if the product is sold in a quality market. A low price will be set if the firm wishes to sell large quantities of a standard product. **Promotion** (advertising and sales promotion) is essential to inform buyers in the market that the good is on sale and to change their perceptions of a product in a favourable manner. A good distribution system is essential to get the product to the right **place** at the right time for the customer.

Many markets are dominated by **brands**. A branded good is one which is produced by a particular firm and which appears to possess unique characteristics. These may be real characteristics, such as a unique formulation or a unique design. A Mars Bar or a Rolls Royce car for instance are unique products. But often more important than the real characteristics are the imagined characteristics of the product in the mind of the buyer. This image is likely to have been created by advertising and promotion. So it is possible for the same baked beans or the same breakfast cereal to be packaged differently and sold on the same supermarket shelves at different prices. Often the higher priced branded product will sell far better than the lower priced unbranded product despite the fact that the product itself is the same.

Price rigidity Prices in oligopolistic markets seem to change far less than in perfectly competitive markets. Despite changes in underlying costs of production, firms are often observed to maintain prices at a constant level.

L-shaped average cost curves Economic studies (☞ unit 20) have established that in the real world average variable cost curves are often more L-shaped than U-shaped. Over a wide range of output, large firms face the same average variable costs whether they increase or decrease output, as shown in Figure 30.1.

Collusion Oligopolistic firms will often benefit if they collude. This means that they make agreements amongst themselves so as to restrict competition and maximise their own benefits. Before such **restrictive trade practices** (☞ unit 41) were made illegal in the UK by the 1956 Restrictive Trade Practices Act, most large UK manufacturing companies had entered into agreements with other firms.

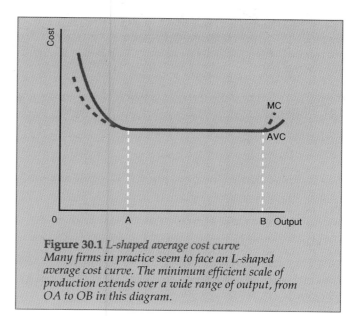

Figure 30.1 *L-shaped average cost curve*
Many firms in practice seem to face an L-shaped average cost curve. The minimum efficient scale of production extends over a wide range of output, from OA to OB in this diagram.

QUESTION 2 In September 1986, Unilever launched Wisk, the first liquid washing detergent, onto the UK national market. New product launches are notoriously difficult to establish in the market and most fail. Wisk was first test marketed in the Midlands for a year before being given its national launch. It proved surprisingly successful. In January 1987, Proctor and Gamble launched its challenge - Ariel Liquid and Liquid Daz. The appearance of the liquid detergents under already familiar and trusted names led to an increase in the size of the market but also to an increase in Proctor and Gamble's market share. In Spring 1988, Proctor and Gamble were claiming a 60 per cent market share. Unilever threw caution to the wind and introduced Persil Liquid with hardly any test marketing. The company claimed that it had captured 20 per cent of the market within one month. In the meantime, both companies were spending large sums of money on advertising and promotion. Heavy television promotion, free watches, cash back and the liberal application of Bogof (Buy one, get one free) were all used in the competitive war.

Source: adapted from the *Financial Times*, 26.9.1988.

Explain, using examples from the detergent industry, how firms in an oligopolistic market compete.

The neo-classical kinked demand curve model

One model of oligopoly was developed in the late 1930s by Paul Sweezy in the USA and R Hall and C Hitch in the UK. Any theory of oligopoly must make an assumption about how one firm will react to the actions of another firm. The kinked demand curve model assumes that there will be an asymmetrical reaction to a change in price by one firm. If the firm increases its price, other firms will not react. The firm which has increased its price will then lose market share. On the other hand, if it reduces its price its competitors will reduce price too in order to prevent an erosion of their market share. The firm will gain little extra demand as a result. The demand curve therefore facing a firm is more elastic for a price rise than for a price fall.

This is shown in Figure 30.2. Price is initially at OP. If the firm increases price to OR it will lose far more sales than it would gain if it reduced price by an equal amount. This occurs because of the different reactions to price increases and decreases by competitors. Therefore the demand curve is kinked around the original price. If the demand curve (i.e. the average revenue curve) is kinked, then this produces a discontinuous marginal revenue curve. At output level OQ, there will be a jump in marginal revenue between a small increase in price and a small decrease in price (an example of this is given in Question 3).

The firm is assumed to be a short run profit maximiser. Therefore if the price is OP and the firm is producing OQ, the marginal cost curve must cut the marginal revenue at output OQ, somewhere between price OV and OW. This means that there are a number of possible marginal cost curves which would produce a price of OP. It could, for instance, be MC_1 or MC_2. Assume that it is MC_1 then a rise in costs to MC_2 would result in no change in price. The oligopolist would absorb the whole of the cost increase by reducing its profit.

This theory provides one explanation of why prices in oligopoly are relatively stable. Changes in costs which shift the marginal cost curve will not change either the profit maximising level of output or the profit maximising price.

However, there are a number of weaknesses in the theory. Firstly there is no explanation of how the original price, P, was arrived at. Secondly, the theory only deals with price competition and ignores the effects of non-price competition. Thirdly, the model assumes a particular reaction by other firms to a change in price of a firm's product. It is unlikely that firms will react in exactly this way all the time. A much wider range of possible reactions needs to be explored.

QUESTION 3

Table 30.1

Output	Average revenue	Total revenue	Marginal revenue £
1	49	49	
			45
2	47		
3	45		
3	45		
			15
4	40		
5	35		
6	30		

(a) Complete Table 30.1, filling in the missing figures.
(b) Plot the average and marginal revenue curves on a graph. Remember that marginal revenue for the second unit of output should be plotted at output level 1½, the third at 2½, etc. Also mark on the graph a vertical line at output level 3 and draw the marginal revenue curves up to the line on either side of it as in Figure 30.2.
(c) Why is the marginal revenue curve discontinuous?

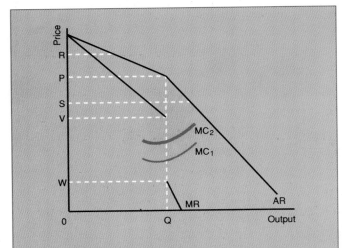

Figure 30.2 *The kinked demand curve model*
With a demand curve kinked round the prevailing price OP, a rise or fall in marginal cost will not affect the profit maximising level of output or price. Hence this model can be used to explain relative price stability in oligopolistic markets.

Key terms

Oligopoly - a market structure where there is a small number of firms in the industry and where each firm is interdependent with other firms. Barriers to entry are likely to exist.
Marketing mix - different elements within a strategy designed to create demand for a product.

Applied economics

The UK burger market

In 1989, the UK burger market was dominated by two large chains, Macdonald's and Wimpy. Macdonald's has 338 stores and according to a market report by Gordon Simons Research (1990), 21 million adults paid a visit to Macdonald's over the year. Wimpy, with 380 stores, had 17 million adult visits. In very poor third place was Burger King with 30 outlets.

The burger market is likely to see changes in the 1990s. In 1989, Grand Metropolitan, the brewing and leisure group and owner of Wimpy, acquired Burger King, Macdonald's main rival in the USA. It made a strategic decision in the UK market to expand its chain of Burger King outlets as an effective competitor to Macdonald's. The quickest and easiest way to do this was to convert existing Wimpy outlets into Burger King stores. About half of all Wimpy outlets would be converted by the end of 1990.

The above data would suggest that the burger market in the UK is oligopolistic.

■ The market is dominated by just two firms (a duopoly ☞ unit 31).

■ Those two firms are interdependent. If Grand Metropolitan succeeds in expanding its market share, it is likely to be at the expense of Macdonald's market share and its profits.

■ There are also substantial barriers to entry to the market. The decision by Grand Metropolitan to expand Burger King by closing half its Wimpy outlets is one indication that acquiring good sites would be a major problem to any new would-be competitor. Marketing barriers too are substantial. In 1989, Macdonald's spent £13.5m on advertising alone.

Till now, Wimpy and Macdonald's in the UK have not competed much on price. Macdonald's have spent a great deal of money building a brand image for their product through marketing campaigns. In the United States, Macdonald's has pursued a similar strategy, although rival burger chains have been far more prepared to cut their prices to gain market share. It could be that Grand Metropolitan too will choose to compete on price in its Burger King outlets in the UK. It would be one possible strategy for gaining substantial market share. However, abnormal profits can only be gained in the longer run if Macdonald's and Burger King refrain from price competition and sell their products at premium prices.

The burger market is part of a much wider £3bn a year market for fast foods. About a quarter of the adult UK population - about 11 million, including half of all 16 to 24 year olds, buy fast food weekly. Until 1989, traditional fish and chips was probably the largest sector within the market, but in 1989 it was overtaken by burgers with estimated sales of £650m. In the longer term, however, the main competition to Macdonald's may not come from other hamburger chains. The fastest growing sector of the fast food market is the pizza market. Moreover, with widespread ownership of microwaves, Macdonald's may become a small player in a market dominated by supermarkets selling imitations of Big Macs, Kentucky Fried Chicken pots and Pizza Hut pizzas. From this perspective, it could be argued that Macdonald's, Wimpy and Burger King operate not in an oligopolistic market but in a monopolistically competitive market.

Data question

GUINNESS PUTS VALUE ON BRANDS

Guinness, the UK drinks group, stepped into the controversy over brand accounting yesterday when it announced plans to put a value of £1.695bn on some recently acquired brands in its 1988 balance sheet. These brands include Johnnie Walker, Gordons Gin, Dewars, Bells, White Horse, Hennessy Cognac, Dom Perignon, Veuve Clicquot, and Christian Dior and Givenchy perfumes.

In arriving at individual brands' values, Guinness said it had looked at profits made by each brand in the year before acquisition, and had applied an appropriate

multiple to it. The multiples were based on multiples ruling the sector at the time of acquisition.

Guinness said it did not foresee any end to the useful life of the brands. However, it will review this - and the carrying value of the brands - every year.

Source: *Financial Times*, 24.2.1989.

1. **Explain, using examples from the data, what is a 'brand'.**
2. **Why do brands have a monetary value?**

Summary

1. Games theory explores the reactions of one player to changes in strategy by another player.
2. Oligopoly is characterised by price stability. One explanation of this is that changing price is a very risky strategy for one firm because it will provoke a reaction by other firms.
3. Non-price competition is common in oligopolistic markets. It is a less risky strategy than price competition.
4. Successful branding enables producers to charge a premium price and earn abnormal profit on a product.
5. Collusion enables oligopolistic firms to move to their most profitable output level.
6. The large number of different market strategies available to oligopolistic firms may result in permanent disequilibrium in the market.

Games theory

Central to any understanding of oligopoly is interdependence. The actions of one large firm in the industry will directly affect all other firms in the industry. It is therefore essential, in any theory of oligopoly, to understand the nature and consequences of those reactions.

One very powerful tool for analysing oligopolistic behaviour is the theory of games. GAMES THEORY has a wide variety of applications, from playing cards through to nuclear deterrence. In a game the players are interdependent. The best move for a player depends upon how the other players will react.

Price stability

One commonly observed feature of oligopoly is price stability. Firms maintain stable prices over a pricing season which may last from 6 months to several years. Price stability may be a rational strategy for oligopolists.

If an oligopolistic firm raises price, it risks losing market share if its competitors do not follow suit. Lower market share could lead to lower profits and, if investment and research and development budgets are cut, a reduced ability to compete in the long run.

If it lowers its price, it risks starting a price war. It could be that the size of the market will expand as consumers buy more of the industry's products. But the benefits in the form of larger sales could well be more than offset by losses in revenue due to lower prices. All firms in the industry could see sharp falls in profits as they battle it out. Eventually, prices will have to rise again to restore

profitability and the firm which started the price war could have lost market share.

So changing prices is a risky strategy. When prices do change, all firms tend to change their prices by the same percentage. For instance, a rise in the interest rate by one large building society tends to lead to a rise in all building society interest rates. A rise in petrol prices by one company is usually matched by the other petrol suppliers.

Games theory can be used to explain this. Consider Table 31.1. There are just two firms in the industry (it is a DUOPOLY). Each firm has two strategies. It can either raise the price of its product or leave it unchanged. The figures in the box represent the change in profits for firm A which would result from each strategy. We will assume that each firm has the same expectations of what would happen to profits as a result of each strategy. We will further assume that the game is a ZERO SUM GAME. This means that any gain by one player is exactly offset by a loss by the other player. For instance, if firm A raises it price and firm B reacts to this by raising price too, then firm A will be the winner. Its profits will increase by £10 million whilst firms B's profits will fall by £10 million. If on the other hand firm B were to react by keeping its price

Table 31.1

		Firm B	
		Raise price	Leave price unchanged
Firm A	Raise price	£10 million	-£2 million
	Leave price unchanged	-£1 million	0

unchanged, firm A would see its profits fall by £2 million whilst firm B would see its profits rise by £2 million.

The game in Table 31.1 has an equilibrium solution. Firm A will decide to leave its price unchanged. This is because if it raises its price, it could gain an extra £10 million in profits if firm B also raised its price. But it knows that firm B would be most unlikely to react in this way because firm B would stand to lose £10 million by adopting that strategy. So firm B would adopt the strategy of leaving its price unchanged. This would result in losses of £2 million for firm A if it raised price. If, on the other hand, firm A kept its price unchanged, the most it would stand to lose is £1 million.

As for firm B, raising price would be a very dangerous strategy because it would lose £10 million in profit if firm A raised price too. Leaving price unchanged would either result in no change in profits or a gain in profits of £2 million.

So both firms will choose to leave their prices unchanged. This is the safest strategy for both firms. The alternative for each firm would lead to losses because of the rival firm's reactions.

Now consider Table 31.2 which shows a game where firms cut prices. The game here is not a zero sum game. The change in profits of firm A of a particular combination of strategies is shown in black, whilst the change in profits for firm B is shown in red. For instance, if both firms cut prices, firm A will lose £10 million in profits whilst firm B will lose £20 million.

It is clear from the table that it is in both firms' interests to leave prices unchanged. If one firm decides to lower its price in order to gain market share, the other firm would suffer a large drop in profits. For instance, firm A would lose £13 million in profits if it left its price unchanged when firm B lowered its price. It would prefer to lower its price too and limit the loss in profits to £10 million. The same is true for firm B. If it dropped its price and firm A did not react, it would increase its profit. But if firm A reacted by dropping its price too, the resulting price war would have disastrous consequences for both sides.

Many economists have argued that firms avoid risk (they are said to be 'risk averse'). Competition is always risky and strategies which aim to reduce market share and profits of competitors especially so. 'The best of all monopoly profits is a quiet life', argued J R Hicks (1935).

QUESTION 1 Petrol prices of the major brands of petrol tend to change at the same time in the UK. The RAC, for instance, commented to an inquiry of the Petrol Retailers Association in 1989 that all the major companies tend to put up their prices if one of the major oil company raises prices. There follows a period when petrol prices slowly come down as the companies jostle for competitive advantage. Then, as one of the major companies puts up its prices again, everyone follows.

Petrol retailing has not been very profitable for the oil majors. Between the time of the first oil crisis in 1973-4 and 1986, most companies lost money on their petrol sales. In 1986 oil prices plunged and the companies used the opportunity to increase their profitability rather than pass the reduction on to motorists in the form of lower petrol prices. Since then the companies have tended to make profits but the return is still less than the UK industrial average.

(a) Use games theory to help explain why the major oil companies tend to move their prices in line with one another.
(b) Why did none of the oil companies take the opportunity in 1986 to slash its price and attempt to gain market share at the expense of its rivals?

Non-price competition

A characteristic of oligopoly is the lack of price competition. Price wars can be very damaging for firms in an oligopolistic industry. So firms choose to compete in other ways apart from price. An advertising campaign, for instance, by firm A is likely to be limited in cost and may increase market share. Other firms in the industry may react by launching their own advertising campaign, but there is a reasonable chance that the advertising campaign of the competitors may not be as good, plus the fact that advertising may expand the market as a whole. The reward for firm A will be a small increase in market share and, presumably, profits. Other firms, however, will not be hit too hard and so will not take drastic measures which might affect the profitability of all firms in the industry. On the other hand, firm A's campaign may back-fire if another firm launches a more successful advertising campaign. But the potential loss is unlikely to be very great.

This suggests that, in oligopoly, firms might not attempt to drive their main rivals out of the market. This would be an extremely risky strategy which might lead to themselves being the victim of such a move. Rather, oligopolists limit competition in order to limit the risks to their own market shares and profits.

Non-price competition is also a very powerful means of deterring potential competitors - firms which might enter the industry. This is discussed further below.

Table 31.2

		Firm B	
		Lower price	Leave price unchanged
Firm A	Lower price	-£10m/-£20m	+£5m/-£27m
	Leave price unchanged	-£13m/+£5m	0

QUESTION 2 In October 1989, Proctor and Gamble, the international detergent manufacturer, launched a new product, Ariel Ultra, with the aid of a £7 million advertising campaign from Saatchi and Saatchi. It was claimed to be an environmentally safe product, using 30 per cent fewer chemicals than conventional powders and was phosphate-free and bio-degradeable. It was 'twice the concentrate' of ordinary powders. Hence it used 30 per cent less packaging and that packaging was made from 80 per cent recycled board.

It was aimed to fend off competition from two directions. Firstly, a small eco-business, Full Moon, had been gaining a significant if small share of the market with Ecover, a washing powder which claimed to be environmentally safe. Proctor and Gamble were determined to meet this challenge head on. Secondly, a major Japanese company, Kao, was known to be intending to launch a concentrate washing powder on the UK market. Ariel Ultra pre-empted this attack.

Why should Proctor and Gamble choose to compete by launching a new brand of washing powder rather than by reducing prices on its existing products?

Branding

Interdependence limits the ability of oligopolistic firms to exploit markets to their own benefit. Ideally oligopolistic firms would like to turn themselves into monopolists with full control of their markets. One way of doing this is by the creation of strong brands. A strong brand has two major advantages for a producer.

■ A strong brand has few good substitutes so far as the buyer is concerned. The firm is therefore able to charge a premium price (a relatively high price for the good) and earn monopoly profit on the good without seeing too great a fall in demand for it.

■ It is very difficult for competitors to challenge the supremacy of the brand. For instance, Kellogg's Corn Flakes, Mars Bars, and Jaguar cars all have stable demands at premium prices in the short run. In the long run, tastes may change or new strong brands may appear. But even then old brands, such as Ovaltine, Horlicks or Ambrosia rice pudding may continue to be highly profitable to their owners, still commanding premium prices at lower sales volumes but with little or no development costs.

Strong brands are difficult to create, which is why many firms prefer to take over other companies and their brands at very high prices rather than attempt to establish new brands. For instance, Nestlé paid £1.9 bn for the brands of Rowntree Mackintosh, a recognition of how much it would possibly cost to establish rival brands from scratch. To establish a new brand, a company usually has to produce an innovative product (innovative could mean anything from changing the colour or smell of a product to a radically new technological breakthrough) and then market it effectively. The failure rate of new brands in

some markets such as food and confectionery can be as high as nearly 100 per cent. With this in mind, it is hardly surprising that a firm would be prepared to pay millions of pounds for an established brand rather than employ research workers to devise new products.

QUESTION 3 Gillette, Wilkinson Sword and Bic between them controlled 94% of the markets in razors, blades and disposables in 1987. Each is a company which uses its company name as a brand name. Gillette is the dominant world supplier with 52 per cent of the UK market and 63 per cent of the US market. Wilkinson Sword has always been a much smaller company with 25 per cent of the UK market and 4 per cent of the US market.

However, Wilkinson Sword has been responsible for two of the most significant technical developments in the safety razor business. In 1961, it launched the PTFE-coated low-friction blade. It took Gillette 2 years to develop a similar product and yet within 12 months had stolen the market lead. In 1970, Wilkinson Sword launched a bonded twin-blade shaving system. Again, Gillette followed with a competing product and seized control of most of the market. The Gillette name and the financial resources to back large marketing campaigns were sufficient to ward off potentially dangerous innovations from a small company like Wilkinson Sword.

Source: adapted from the *Financial Times*, 12.6. 1989.

(a) Explain why the Gillette brand name is extremely valuable.
(b) How might you put a financial value on it?

Collusion

Another way in which an oligopolist can turn itself into a monopoly is by colluding with other firms. In markets which are unregulated by government, there is a strong tendency for firms to collude (i.e. to join together and act as if they were one firm). Cartels and restrictive trade practices (☞ unit 39) were the norm in British manufacturing industry before such practices were made illegal in the 1950s.

Games theory can help us understand why this is the case. Consider Table 31.3. The figures show the profits to be gained by two firms, A and B, depending upon whether they adopt a high or low price strategy. Firm A, whose profit figures are in black, would like to adopt a low price strategy in opposition to a high price strategy by its rival. That would result in profits of £25m. But it can see that firm B would not allow such a situation because its profits would only be £5m. However, a high price strategy for firm A would be worse because it would face making the lowest possible profit, £10m, should firm B choose to adopt a low price strategy. So firm A will choose a low price strategy, hoping that firm B will adopt a high price strategy, but more realistically knowing that it

Table 31.3

		Firm B	
		Low price	High price
Firm A	Low price	£15m/£10m	£25m/£5m
	High price	£10m/£20m	£20m/£25m

too will adopt a low price strategy. Firm A will then make a profit of £15m - the highest minimum profit it can make.

Firm B will adopt a low price strategy too. Although it stands to gain £25m in profit by a high price strategy if firm A too goes for a high price stategy, it risks only making £5m if firm A were to go for a low price. So it will maximise its minimum profit of £10m and go for a low price strategy.

The result is that both firms adopt low price strategies because they fear the reactions of their competitor. They would have been considerably better off if they had both adopted high price strategies. The only way to get into the high price 'box' is for the two firms to come to some form of understanding that they will not adopt low price strategies (i.e. they must collude).

The figures shown in Table 31.3 are an example of what is often called the 'Prisoner's Dilemma'. Substitute profits for prison sentences and prices for pleading guilty or not guilty. If both prisoners kept apart in different cells plead not guilty, then they will be released through lack of evidence. But if one prisoner pleads guilty, then he will get a reduced sentence and the other will get a heavier sentence. If both plead guilty they will get heavy sentences. If they could get together (i.e. collude) they would choose to plead not guilty. But in isolation they cannot trust the other prisoner. So each chooses to plead guilty and they both suffer!

QUESTION 4 In 1989, the European Commission announced that it was investigating possible collusion amongst manufacturers of soda ash, a raw material used mainly in the glass and detergent industries. During the 1980s the demand for and the price of soda ash in European markets had hardly changed. Increasing availability of cheaper substitutes, competition from imports and rising fuel costs had squeezed profitability. What had made the European Commission suspicious was the remarkable similarity in soda ash prices from the main manufacturers including Britain's Imperial Chemical Industries.

Why might soda ash producers have found it in their interests to collude?

Disequilibrium

So far the games considered have had a definite solution. An equilibrium set of strategies has been arrived at which leads to stability within the market. However, there are many games which lead to disequilibrium, where the players are unable to pursue stable strategies. A move by one firm will lead to a change in strategy of the other firm and so on.

Moreover, only two-firm, two-option situations have been discussed. In reality there are likely to be more than two firms in the industry each with more than two policy options open to them. For instance, a six policy zero-sum game for two firms is shown in Table 31.4. There are 36 (6x6) different possible solutions to this game. If there were 3 firms in the industry, the number of possible solutions would rise to 1296 (36x36).

Games theory predicts, then, that there are a large number of different possible outcomes in an oligopolistic setting. Given this very large number, it is perhaps not surprising that economic theory has found it difficult to provide one unified model which would explain price and output decisions in the industry.

Table 31.4

			Firm B					
			Price			Advertising expenditure		
			Raise	Lower	Leave unchanged	Raise	Lower	Leave unchanged
Firm A	Price	Raise	£10m	-£5m	-£10m	£2m	-£1m	-£2m
		Lower	£2m	-£1m	-£4m	-£1m	£2m	£1m
		Leave unchanged	£3m	-£5m	0	£2m	-£4m	0
	Adv. exp.	Raise	-£1m	£7m	£5m	£3m	-£5m	-£1m
		Lower	£2m	-£3m	-£5m	£4m	-£2m	-£1m
		Leave unchanged	£2m	-£2m	0	£3m	-£1m	0

Key terms

Games theory - the analysis of situations in which players are interdependent.
Duopoly - an industry where there are only two firms.
Zero sum game - a game in which the gain of one player is exactly offset by the loss by other players.

Applied economics

A brands-centred business strategy

CPC International is a US food group with annual sales worldwide in 1989 of $5bn. Sales in Europe accounted for 40 per cent of this total. It has grown by acquisition, buying up brands which have significant shares in their markets. For instance, in April 1990 it purchased Marmite, Bovril and the Ambrosia range of rice pudding and similar dairy-based desserts from SmithKline Beecham for £157m. Other CPC products include Hellman's mayonnaise, mustard and ketchup, Napolina pasta sauces, Mazola oil, Banania and Benco breakfast drinks, Yabon desserts and Knorr soups.

How can games theory help us understand CPC's European strategy? Some of the brands just listed are unfamiliar to British consumers. Hellman's mustard, for instance, is sold only in Greece and Spain where it has a significant share of the market. Banania and Benco breakfast drinks are household names in France but are not sold in the UK. Similarly, CPC has no plans to market Bovril or Ambrosia rice pudding in Europe.

The strategy is to avoid competing in markets where its brands cannot be market leaders. Strong brands can be sold at premium prices, earning the company abnormal profits. For instance, Mr Moss, head of CPC Europe Consumer Foods, said of the purchase of Bovril, Marmite and Ambrosia: 'It gives us good volume and three brand leaders with 100 per cent penetration'.

If CPC adopted an alternative strategy of introducing established brands to new national markets, or attempting to build a new brand from scratch, what would be the likely outcome? Selling Marmite in Spain or Yabon desserts in the UK could well lead to large losses in the short term, as the brand is introduced to the market, and in the long term if sales are too low. Equally, establishing a new brand is notoriously difficult and is rarely successful. At best, such strategies are likely to result in the establishment of weak brands generating neither the sales nor the price needed to ensure high profitability. CPC is therefore avoiding the strong competition that would be offered by other firms with strong, established brands. As such, it is a low risk strategy, but a highly successful one as witnessed by the company's strong profit performance and continued expansion.

Data question

THE EUROPEAN HOSIERY MARKET

In the 1980s, the European hosiery market was relatively fragmented with different companies concentrating on their own national markets. However the market is changing. Sara Lee, the US consumer products group and market leader in the US hosiery market, decided to enter the European market through acquisition. In 1988, it bought Dim, the market leader in the French market. In 1989 it bought a minority interest in Fred Vatter of West Germany and took control of Elbeo in the UK, one of Vatter's subsidiaries.

Sara Lee's arrival poses a serious threat to the stability of the established European players. Golden Lady, the large Italian hosiery manufacturer, has already responded. It increased its capacity by 20 per cent last year and will do the same this year. Late last year it acquired Focus on Legs, a privately-owned company, as a marketing base in the UK.

Golden Lady has also changed its export strategy by emphasising branded products, rather than own-label. It is now Europe's biggest hosiery producer and exports half its output.

The other European producers are also becoming more active in other countries, albeit less aggressively than Golden Lady. The two largest UK manufacturers, Pretty Polly and Aristoc, presently export less than 5 per cent of output, but both intend to increase overseas sales, concentrating on value-added products.

Omsa of Italy is increasing its capacity. Le Bourget of France is becoming more active in other countries. Wolford, the leading Austrian producer, is strengthening its position in 'designer' hosiery across Europe.

These changes are fuelled by the fear that, unless the established manufacturers increase sales to other countries, they could be very vulnerable if Sara Lee and Golden Lady were to make inroads into their own markets.

Source: *Financial Times*, 12.1. 1990.

1. Discuss the nature of competition in the European hosiery market.
2. Explain (a) how and (b) why firms are reacting to the threat posed by the entry of Sara Lee into the European market.

Summary

1. The neo-Keynesian theory of the firm assumes that firms are long run profit maximisers which determine prices according to cost-plus pricing principles. Price stability is a feature of this model.
2. Baumol's sales maximisation model assumes that firms aim to maximise sales subject to a profit satisficing constraint.
3. Managerial theories predict that costs and output are likely to be higher than neo-classical theory would suggest.
4. Both managerial and behavioural theories predict that organisational slack is likely to be present.
5. A contestable market is one where there is freedom of entry and exit to the market. This theory concludes that the degree of competition in a market depends not on the number or size of firms in the industry but the potential number of competitors which might enter the market if profits were high enough.

The neo-Keynesian model

R Hall and C Hitch in the 1930s outlined a radically different model of the firm from existing neo-classical models. Their research indicated that firms did not equate marginal cost and marginal revenue in an attempt to maximise short run profits. Rather, firms maximised profits in the long run (☞ unit 24). Firms then determined prices by calculating costs and adding a profit mark-up (hence the term **cost-plus pricing**). Prices are stable because firms take a long term view of the market.

In the model, it is argued that firms respond to changes in demand and cost not by changing price but by changing output. A large inflow of orders will not lead to a rise in price but to an increase in production. If a manufacturer is already producing at normal full capacity, it may attempt to produce at over-full capacity by encouraging its employees to work overtime or extra shifts. In the service sector, a booming supermarket will not increase prices if it proves far more popular than expected. Rather it will allow overcrowding in the short term and in the longer term may open longer hours, open an extension or build a new supermarket close by. Alternatively, a firm may allow waiting lists to develop. (A waiting list may be helpful in some cases to the image of a product because it is a sign that there are customers who think the product is so good that they are prepared to wait to buy it.)

If demand falls or costs rise, a firm will not necessarily respond by reducing price. Rather it will reduce output. If losses threaten to become too high, it will close down production rather than reduce price which may be seen to be damaging to the longer term prospects for the product.

Prices may not change on a daily basis (as for instance for carrots or tomatoes in the agricultural market) but equally, firms' prices are not permanently fixed. The frequency of price changes will vary from industry to industry, but a yearly review of prices is not uncommon in British manufacturing industry.

The size of the profit mark-up will vary too. However, the mark up will tend to be higher where:
- firms in the industry are able to collude, acting as if they were a monopolist;
- there are only a few large firms in the industry, which results in less price competition;
- barriers to entry are high, limiting the possibility of new firms entering the industry;
- there are a large number of small buyers in the market, rather than a few significant buyers who are able to use their buying power to exert downward pressure on prices.

The neo-Keynesian theory of the firm is able to explain relative price stability in the market. However, it is pointed out by neo-classical economists that traditional cost curves should include an allowance for the cost of changing price - in other words, the insight that price changes can be costly can be incorporated within a neo-classical model.

QUESTION 1 Never mind high interest rates and crippling mortgages, Motorfair is pulling in the punters again. And there is a lot to see, even if some of the new cars are beyond the reach of all but the seriously rich.

Even they will have to be patient. The Mercedes SL and Porsche Carrera 4 are in such demand that orders placed now will not be filled for at least two years. Ferrari's 348 is so oversubscribed that the concessionaires will not even take an order.

Source: *Financial Times*. 21.10. 1989.

Explain how the neo-Keynesian theory of the firm would help explain why Mercedes, Porsche and Ferrari don't increase price until supply equals demand in the short run.

Revenue maximisation model

Neo-classical theory assumes that firms are short run profit maximisers. In the early 1950s an American

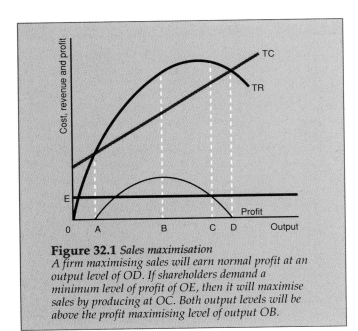

Figure 32.1 *Sales maximisation*
A firm maximising sales will earn normal profit at an output level of OD. If shareholders demand a minimum level of profit of OE, then it will maximise sales by producing at OC. Both output levels will be above the profit maximising level of output OB.

Managerial and behavioural theories of the firm

In both managerial and behavioural theories of the firm (☞ unit 24), it is argued that there is a divorce of ownership and control. In managerial theories, it is assumed that managers control the firm subject to a profit satisficing constraint.

Managerial models tend to make three clear predictions.

- Costs will be higher than neo-classical theory would predict. Higher salaries, expensive company cars and unnecessary levels of staffing have to be paid for.
- Firms will produce at higher levels of output than neo-classical theory would predict. This is because higher output and higher sales will lead to more staff being employed, which is beneficial to the utility of managers. Moreover, higher output levels may be more important in determining salary levels than increased profitability.
- In a recession, management may suffer disproportionally. In the attempt to prevent the company from sliding into loss and possible take over or bankruptcy, managers may be sacked as administration is streamlined and their salaries and perks reduced. In an economic boom, managers may benefit more than most as they are able to increase their own salaries and perks whilst increasing profits too. Shareholders find it difficult to prevent this because they are unable to gauge how much more profit the company could have made if managers had not increased costs unnecessarily.

In behavioural theories, it is argued that it is not just shareholders and managers who determine the behaviour of firms. Other interested parties, such as government, trade unions and other pressure groups like environmentalists, can have an important say too. The eventual outcome will depend upon the relative strength of the various competing parties. In the UK newspaper industry in the 1970s, for instance, it could be argued that trade unions played an unusually dominant role in decision making, which led to exceptionally high wages being paid to their members. In the 1980s, shareholder power became more fashionable. The 1990s might be the decade when environmentalists substantially increase their power within corporate structures. The main supermarket chains in the UK, for instance, now carry a wide range of 'environmentally friendly' products which were not on the shelves ten years ago. A profit maximising assumption is then seen to be simplistic and will necessarily lead to misunderstanding about how firms behave.

economist, W Baumol, put forward an alternative model suggesting that firms might maximise sales revenue rather than profits. He recognised that firms cannot make a loss if they are to survive in the long term, so at least some profit must be made. Managers also need to make enough profit to satisfy their shareholders (☞ unit 24).

In Figure 32.1, total cost and total revenue curves are drawn. The difference between the two is profit, shown by the curve at the bottom of the graph. The firm can operate anywhere between output levels OA and OD without making a loss. It will maximise profit at OB. If shareholders are content to earn just normal profit and managers wish to maximise sales, then the firm will operate at OD. On the other hand, if the minimum acceptable level of profit for shareholders is OE, then output will be at OC. As can be seen from the diagram, the higher the profit satisficing level of output, the lower will be the level of output and the nearer it will be to the profit maximising level of output.

QUESTION 2

(a) A monopolist is a revenue maximiser subject to the constraint that it needs to make normal profits to satisfy its shareholders. Draw a standard neo-classical monopoly diagram (☞ unit 28). Mark on it:
 (i) the profit maximising level of output;
 (ii) the firm's revenue maximising level of output subject to its profit constraint.

(b) Compare the effect on output and price if a monopolist moves from being a profit maximiser to being a sales maximiser.

QUESTION 3 According to a letter by K P McCann in the *Financial Times* 14.12.1989, 'the maximisation of shareholders' wealth (is not) necessarily regarded as an overriding objective in many countries outside the UK. This is especially true in Germany where ... the relative lack of importance attached to the stock markets, social and employment legislation, tax regulations and the approach to financing industry all point to an economic culture which believes that a business is important in many different ways to a country, its economy and its society. The idea that shareholders' interests alone should prevail is not widely accepted.'

Explain why this letter supports a behavioural view of the firm.

QUESTION 4 In 1988, Aveling Barford, the firm which at one time was the biggest construction machinery producer in the UK, went into receivership. It had had a long history of troubles including chronic underinvestment, although incompetent management and powerful trade unions were possibly the two most important contributors to Aveling's demise. Restrictive practices were widespread, even between welders on the thickness of plate they were allowed to work on. The firm has now been bought by a management buy-in team. Only 300 of the 900 workers employed in 1988 have kept their jobs and the aim is double output per man. Management has been ruthlessly streamlined. The company hopes that it will now survive.

(a) What examples of organisational slack are given in the data?
(b) What happened to organisational slack when the company was bought out after going into receivership?

Organisational slack

Both managerial and behavioural theories predict that ORGANISATIONAL SLACK is likely to be present. Organisational slack or X-INEFFICIENCY were terms used by Professor Harvey Leibenstein to describe the tendency of firms in non-competitive markets to produce at higher than minimum cost. So when a manager receives a Jaguar when she would have been content with a Carlton, or when a trade union member receives £500 a week when he would have worked for £300, or when a chargehand chooses to organise production in a traditional way when a far more efficient modern method is available, then organisational slack is present.

Organisational slack exists partly because of a lack of knowledge. Decision makers don't know the exact minimum amount for which a worker might be prepared to work for instance. Perhaps more importantly, organisations are often very conservative. They might order components from a firm they have always dealt with even if they know that the components could be purchased more cheaply elsewhere. Or they might be reluctant to invest in new machinery because all investment is a risk, despite the fact that potentially there are considerable cost savings to be made.

Different interest groups in the firm might be able to exploit their potential power to their advantage, thus increasing organisational slack. Environmental groups, for instance, might force a firm to adopt stricter environmental standards than cost-minimisation would dictate by threatening a media campaign against the firm. Trade unions might threaten to strike, causing short term chaos, unless their demands are met.

In a recession, organisational slack tends to decline. Firms are forced to concentrate on safeguarding profits and, as a result, unnecessary costs tend to be pruned first. Everything, from the size of the company director's car to working practices on the shop floor to the provision of food in the company canteen, is likely to be affected.

The theory of contestable markets

A CONTESTABLE MARKET is one where there is free entry to and exit from the market (i.e. there are no **barriers to entry**). Free entry implies that there are no **sunk costs** of production (☞ unit 25). If a firm leaves a contestable market, it must be able to sell any capital involved or redeploy the capital.

Perfect competition can only arise if there are a large number of buyers and sellers in the market. However, the theory of contestable markets argues that oligopolistic firms can be forced to behave as if they were in a perfectly competitive market if there is freedom of entry and exit.

■ Firms are assumed to maximise profits, producing where MC = MR.

■ In the long run, firms in a contestable market cannot earn abnormal profit (i.e. in the long run AR = AC). If firms in the industry were earning abnormal profit in the short run, then new firms would be free to enter the industry, increasing supply and driving down price to the point where only normal profit was being earned. Equally, if a firm is earning less than normal profit, it will leave the industry in the long run because its owners will wish to reallocate their resources in more profitable ways.

■ In the long run, firms in a contestable market will operate at the bottom of their average cost curve (i.e. they will operate at the optimal level of output where MC = AC). If in the short run, firms in the industry were not doing this, then firms would enter and produce at the most efficient level. Existing firms would have to lower cost if they were to compete successfully.

■ If in the long run AR = AC and MC = AC, then AR or price must equal MC. The theory of contestable markets concludes that firms will price at marginal cost in the long run.

For instance, assume that total market demand is 300 units at a price of £10 whilst lowest average cost for a single producer is £10 at an output of 100 units. Three firms will therefore find it profitable to produce in the industry, but each firm will only earn normal profits because AC = AR. With only normal profits being earned, the industry is in long run equilibrium because there is no incentive for other firms to enter.

However, a problem arises if market demand is, for instance, 300 units but the optimal level of production for each firm is 120 units. If there were only two firms in the industry, each firm would be producing under conditions of decreasing returns to scale if each produced 150 units. There would be an incentive for a new firm to enter the industry and produce at the optimum lowest cost level of output of 120 units. It would be difficult to believe that the two existing firms would not react by reducing output, moving towards the optimal level. But if there were three firms each producing the same output of 100 units, then one firm could expand output and experience greater economies of scale. The other firms in the industry would then be likely to react by expanding their own output. Market price would fall below the minimum average cost of production and firms would make losses, sending back signals that firms should cut their production. There is in fact no level of output which would produce an equilibrium situation.

This is likely to be less of a problem if average cost curves are L-shaped rather than U-shaped. If demand is 300 units, and the minimum efficient scale of production were 120 units, then two firms could produce 150 units each at lowest cost. The theory does not, however, predict whether one firm will produce 120 units and the other 180, or both produce 150 units, or some other combination subject to a minimum of 120 units.

The theory of contestable markets argues that the number of firms in an industry is not important. The key to understanding the behaviour of firms is the extent to which there is potential competition. If an industry is contestable (i.e. there is freedom of entry and exit) then firms in the industry, however few there are, will behave as if competition were very strong and will be unable to exploit the market in the long run. The possibility that a firm outside the industry is able to hit and run, entering the industry in the short run to take advantage of abnormal profits and then leaving it at no cost when the abnormal profit disappears, is sufficient to force existing firms to price at lowest cost.

The theory also gives insights into markets where barriers to entry exist. It is only possible to make abnormal profit in the long run if there are barriers to entry. Some barriers are natural (sometimes called **innocent entry barriers**) but others are deliberately created by existing firms in the industry to keep out potential competitors. Oligopolistic and monopoly firms will attempt to erect barriers so long as the cost of so doing is less than the potential fall in profits if competitors were allowed into the industry.

For instance, it is worth opening a price war with a new entrant if the profit lost in the short term is less than the long term profit loss resulting from the new entrant becoming established in the industry. The ability to fight a price war may depend upon the ability of the existing firm to increase output immediately and so it may need to possess expensive spare capacity. Spending tens of millions of pounds promoting a brand is money well spent if the alternative is fierce competition from other firms. Equally, a firm might find it much easier to ward off potential competition if it offers a range of branded products to buyers rather than just one. It is much easier to enter a market where there are only two or three brands on sale than one where there might be ten or fifteen, even if in both cases only two or three firms operate in the industry.

QUESTION 5 There are only four large British banks - Barclays, Lloyds, Natwest and the Midland. The banking market is therefore arguably oligopolistic in nature and the 'big four' should be earning abnormal profits. However, there is evidence to suggest that the market is far more competitive than might at first seem.

For instance, in the City of London it is relatively costless for a foreign bank to set up a branch employing a few people and deal on the London money markets. The past 30 years have seen an explosion of American, Japanese and other banks with single branches in the City.

Building societies too have been gradually eating away at the retail deposit base of the banks. During the 1960s and 1970s their share of the market grew at the expense of the banks. During the 1980s, building societies have been able to offer cheque book accounts at little extra cost to themselves.

In contrast, the banks have moved into the once building society-dominated world of the mortgage. At various times during the 1980s they have made significant inroads into the new mortgage market, although at other times they have partially withdrawn when new mortgage business ceased to be relatively profitable. The costs of entry and withdrawal have been very low. It is not difficult for a bank manager to switch from selling mortgages to selling personal loans or unit trusts.

How would the theory of contestable markets explain the possible absence of abnormal profits in the British banking and building society industries?

Key terms

Organisational slack or X-inefficiency - inefficiency arising because a firm or other productive organisation fails to minimise its costs of production.

Contestable market - a market where there is free entry to and exit from the market.

Applied economics

Breakfast cereals

Kellogg invented the cornflake in 1891. Since then, the company he founded has expanded from its base in Battle Creek, Michigan, across the breakfast tables of 50 countries around the world. It has created the market for ready-to-eat cereals, changing the breakfast eating habits first of Anglo-Saxons in the USA, the UK, Canada and Australia, and more recently of continental Europeans, Latin Americans and the Japanese. Its worldwide market share is 40 per cent.

There are other major companies in the market but none approach Kellogg in terms of size. In the UK, for instance, Weetabix had a 14 per cent share of the market with its cereal biscuit and Alpen brand muesli in 1987-88. Ranks Hovis McDougal (RHM) had 8 per cent of the market with Shredded Wheat and in addition had a substantial share of the 22 per cent own label supermarket trade. Quaker Oats and Allied Lyons, makers of Ready Brek, dominate the hot cereals corner of the market. But companies like RHM, which have significant shares of the UK market, have little global power in comparison with Kellogg. RHM in 1987-8 had no market share in France or Germany. A company like Banania, with 9 per cent of the French market, had no presence outside France.

Kellogg's formidable market power has been created and sustained through the introduction of new brands and through advertising. Kellogg in 1989 had a range of 48 different products, from its original Cornflakes, through the children's suite of sugary brands such as Frosties, to brands aimed at the adult health and fitness market such as Fruit 'N' Fibre. It is constantly reviewing its portfolio of brands, introducing new products when it can see a new market opening up. Brands are maintained through heavy advertising. In 1988 for instance, Kellogg spent £45m on advertising in the UK, nearly three-quarters of the total for all breakfast cereals. It was also the third largest single advertiser in the UK media.

From the evidence so far presented, it could be argued that the breakfast cereal market worldwide is not contestable. Firms can enter individual national markets perhaps and gain some success, particularly if they are competing for orders in the own label market. But it is difficult to see how any new entrant could gain significant market share.

However, in 1989, Nestlé, the Swiss food group and General Mills, a major US food producer with 23 per cent of the US breakfast cereal market, announced that they intended to do just that. They agreed to set up a joint company, Cereal Partners Worldwide, to market breakfast cereals in the European market. General Mills would continue to produce and market cereals on

Cornbix

Breakfast cereals market share 1987-88

% value	France	Italy	UK	US*	W.Germany
Kellogg	54	48	42	41	42
Quaker	16	18	7	8	-
Nabisco	-	4	8	5	-
Nestlé	12	-	-	-	-
Weetabix	-	6	14	-	-
Banania	9	-	-	-	-
General Mills	-	-	-	23	-
Philip Morris	-	-	-	12	-
Ralston Purina	-	-	-	6	-
CPC	-	-	-	-	8

*cold cereals only

Source: *Euromonitor Market Direction.*

Figure 32.2 *Breakfast cereals market share, 1987-88*

its own in the USA. But in Europe, they would join together with Nestlé supplying marketing and distribution strengths as well as a strong overall brand image, whilst General Mills would supply production expertise and technology. They hoped that together they would also be able to exploit new opportunities in Eastern Europe, the Far East and Latin America.

Whether their strategy will work is debatable. Significantly, they do not intend to work together in the UK market which accounts for nearly three-quarters of European sales. Rather, they are hoping to meet the Kellogg challenge in continental European countries where breakfast cereals are still not established as an obvious breakfast food.

The sunk costs of the plan are relatively small. The joint company intends to use existing Nestlé plants for production and Nestlé was intending to spend substantial sums on product development and advertising on breakfast cereals in the 1990s anyway as part of its attempt to break into this fast growing market. For Nestlé, the attraction of the partnership is access to existing successful US brands such as Cherios. For General Mills, it is a cheap way of entry to the continental European market. It could also be argued that Cereal Partners Worldwide is not a genuine new entrant since both its parent companies compete in individual breakfast cereal markets round the world. The low sunk costs are a reflection of this. Any genuine new entrant on a world market scale would face extremely large sunk costs. So despite this new development, it could be strongly argued that the world breakfast cereal market is not contestable to any great extent.

EUROPEAN AIR TRAVEL

Since its inception, the European air transport industry has operated within a complex set of rules designed to restrict competition and confer monopoly rights on individual national carriers such as British Airways and Air France. This situation has allowed European airline companies to be inefficient and give a poor service to their customers. Inefficiency has resulted not only in high prices but also in low profits, which they can get away with because most of the large European airlines are under state control.

The European Community's single market programme, symbolised by the date 1992, should lead to a fundamental shift in the industry towards greater competition as restrictive practices are swept away. However, already there are signs that European airlines will react to this by attempting to grow in size in order to reduce competition in the market. For instance, British Airways has offered to buy a 20 per cent stake in the Belgian state airline, Sabena, whilst Air France and Lufthansa have announced a cooperation agreement. Taking over competitors, or merging operations, enables airlines to remove competition directly from individual routes. Large airlines also have the resources to use predatory pricing or route saturation (scheduling so many flights on a route that neither the company nor its competitor could hope to make anything other than a loss) against any small competitor which attempts to compete on an

individual route. Large companies have considerable influence with governments and with airports. This enables them to gain landing and take-off rights at the expense of their rivals, rights which in Europe have to be allocated between airlines because of airport congestion.

1. **To what extent is the European air transport market contestable?**
2. **Why should restrictive practices in the air transport industry lead to economic inefficiency?**

INVESTIGATIONS 2

A. Business finance

Aims

- To analyse how a large firm has financed expansion in recent years.
- To evaluate the extent to which this has enabled it to secure its goals.
- To evaluate alternative means of financing for the firm.

Research activity

Choose a large company which either has grown very fast in recent years or one which has got into difficulties over its finances. These could include News International, Poly Peck or Hanson Trust.

Write to the company explaining that you are undertaking an economics 'A' level investigation into its financing. Request its latest Annual Report and Accounts, together with any other material they might think is appropriate for the study. (The company which has got into difficulties is unlikely to be very co-operative to any request greater than that for a copy of the Annual Report.)

Conduct a newspaper search. Using whatever indexes are available in your nearest large reference library, find and read all the newspaper articles about the company in recent years. You are looking for material about the history of the company, its products and the markets in which it operates. More importantly, you will find out the aims of the firm in financing expansion, and how the company obtained finance (for example issuing shares or bank loans). You will also need to evaluate whether the financing was successful or not. The library may have its own index of newspaper articles. It may have indexes published by the newspapers themselves, such as the index to the *Financial Times*, *The Times* and *The Guardian*. Alternatively, it may have the Research Index, a monthly index of financial interest covering 100 newspapers and periodicals and published by Business Surveys Ltd.

Structuring your report

Introduction Explain the aims of your investigation.

Company background Describe the company you have chosen to investigate, the products it sells and the markets in which it operates. Write a brief history of the company.

Analysis of company finance Describe how the company has financed its expansion. Explain the company's aims in obtaining finance for expansion. Discuss the extent to which the chosen means of finance have enabled the firm to achieve its goals.

Evaluation of alternative strategies Outline alternative strategies that the firm could have pursued. Compare and contrast the merits of each for the particular firm in

question. Would these have resulted in a more profitable outcome for the firm? What methods did you use to evaluate the success of alternative strategies (e.g. profitability or security)?

Sources Outline the sources of information you used. What problems did you encounter in gathering relevant data? What data would you have liked to have obtained but could not? To what extent were the data reliable?

Other suggestions

Instead of investigating the financing of expansion by one company, you could compare:
- the growth of a number of companies, perhaps contrasting a successful company with one which has failed;
- companies which have adopted similar financial strategies; for instance, you could compare two or more companies who issued additional share capital at roughly the same time, or you could compare two management buy-outs;
- a small company with a large company; what different sources of finance are available and what problems would they face in financing expansion?

Alternatively, you could investigate the financing of a single small company and examine the problems and successes that it has had in financing itself. Small companies are usually very reluctant to give details of their finances. Therefore a personal contact in the firm, such as a parent or relative, is often the best form of introduction to a potential source of information. Outline its current sources of finance. Discuss how it has financed itself in the past. For instance, how did it find the start-up capital for the company? What are its likely future financing needs and how best could it obtain that finance?

B. Market structure

Aims

- To investigate the market structure of a particular industry and the resultant behaviour of firms within the market.
- To discuss the extent to which the structure of the industry and the behaviour of firms within it conforms to an economic model of the firm.

Research activity

Choose an industry which you wish to investigate (e.g. the airline industry, bus transport, crisps and other snacks, telecommunications, soap powders or grocery retailing). Find out about the market structure of the industry. For instance, how many firms are there in the industry? What barriers to entry and exit exist? Do firms produce homogeneous or branded products and what range of products are sold? Is there perfect knowledge in the industry? Are firms interdependent? Is the aim of firms to maximise profits?

At the same time, make observations about the nature and outcome of competition within the industry. For instance, are firms price takers? Can a firm price discriminate between different consumers? Are prices similar? Is competition mainly price competition or is it based on other factors such as advertising or branding? Do firms earn abnormal profits? Do price movements within the industry appear to be co-ordinated? Are there recent examples of firms entering or leaving the industry and, if so, why did this occur? This information should allow you to identify the type of market structure within which the firm operates.

Sources

You are likely to start your research in one of three ways.
- You might read an interesting newspaper or magazine article about a particular industry.
- You might have a personal interest in and knowledge of the products of a particular industry, for instance through a part time job or a hobby (e.g. skateboard production, cinemas, grocery retailing, or chocolate manufacture!).
- You may have a contact, such as a relative, working in the industry from whom you can gather preliminary information.

To acquire further information, you will need to undertake a newspaper search. Using indexes for the *Financial Times* and other quality newspapers such as *The Times*, as well as magazines such as the *Economist*, find and read all recent articles about the industry and the activities of firms within the industry.

If the firms in the industry are plcs, write to as many as possible outlining your investigation and requesting any relevant information. Ask specifically for the firm's Annual Report and Accounts and samples of advertising literature. There could well be a trade magazine/journal/ newspaper for the industry. Individual firms may be able to indentify its name and send you past copies or give you a contact address. Alternatively your nearest large public reference library may be able to help. There may be a controlling or regulatory body (such as OFTEL or ABTA) to which you could write for information.

Information about output, employment levels and imports and exports of different industries can be obtained from the *Annual Abstract of Statistics* published by the Central Statistical Office. A more detailed analysis can be found in the relevent *Business Monitor* for the industry, published by the Department of Industry. You may be able to gather primary evidence by obtaining an interview with a company in the industry, or by making direct observations about sales and marketing techniques.

Structuring the report

Introduction Outline the aims of your investigation.

Economic theory Outline briefly what economists mean by 'market structure' and put forward a model of behaviour of the firm which you judge is applicable to the industry you have chosen to investigate.

Analysis of market structure Outline the main features of the market structure of the industry you have chosen to investigate. Discuss the extent to which the structure conforms to the model of the firm you have already described.

Evaluation To what extent does the behaviour of firms conform to your chosen model of the firm?

Sources Outline the sources of information you used. What problems did you encounter in gathering relevant data? What data would you have liked to have obtained but could not? To what extent were the data reliable?

Other suggestions

Instead of investigating one industry, you could investigate contrasting industries, such as a monopoly (e.g. the water industry) and a perfectly competitive industry (e.g. parts of agriculture).

Alternatively, you could concentrate on particular characteristics of industries and test a variety of hypotheses. For instance:
- does the opening of competition to a previously monopolised industry lead to (a) greater choice and (b) lower prices?
- do prices in oligopolistic markets tend to be stable when compared to competitive industries?
- do more firms enter and leave competitive industries than imperfectly competitive industries?
- do restrictive practices lead to fewer firms going bankrupt?

Summary

1. Productive efficiency exists when production is achieved at lowest cost.
2. Allocative efficiency is present if the marginal cost of production equals price in all markets in an economy.
3. Dynamic efficiency concerns how resources are allocated over time so as to promote technical progress and economic growth.
4. To judge whether there is an optimal allocation of resources in an economy, it is necessary to make value judgements about the allocation of resources.

Efficiency

The market mechanism allocates resources, but how well does it do this? One way of judging this is to consider how **efficiently** it resolves the three fundamental questions in economics of how, what and for whom production should take place (☞ unit 1). Efficiency is concerned with how well resources, such as time, talents or materials are used to produce an end result. In economic terms, it is concerned with the relationship between scarce inputs and outputs. There are a number of different forms of efficiency which need to be considered.

Productive efficiency

PRODUCTIVE EFFICIENCY exists when production is achieved at lowest cost. There is productive inefficiency when the cost of production is above the minimum possible given the state of knowledge. For instance, a firm which produces 1 million units at a cost of £10 000 would be productively inefficient if it could have produced that output at a cost of £8 000.

Productive efficiency will only exist if there is TECHNICAL EFFICIENCY. Technical efficiency exists if a given quantity of output is produced with the minimum number of inputs (or alternatively, if the maximum output is produced with a given number of units). For instance, if a firm produces 1 000 units of output using 10 workers when it could have used 9 workers, then it would be technically inefficient. However, not all technically efficient outputs are productively efficient. For instance, it might be possible to produce 1 000 units of output using 9 workers. But it might be cheaper to buy a machine and employ only 2 workers.

Allocative efficiency

ALLOCATIVE or ECONOMIC EFFICIENCY is concerned with whether resources are used to produce the goods and services that consumers wish to buy. For instance, assume that consumers place equal value on consumption of shoes and jumpers. However, the last 1 million pairs of shoes produced in the economy cost 10 times as much to manufacture as an extra 1 million jumpers would have done (i.e. the economy could have produced either 1 million pairs of shoes or 10 million jumpers). It would have been more allocatively efficient if 1 million jumpers had been produced rather than the 1 million pairs of shoes because:
■ consumers value the jumpers as much as the shoes;
■ either an extra 9 million jumpers or 900 000 pairs of shoes or some combination of the two could have been produced **as well as** the 1 million jumpers (assuming constant costs of production).

This argument can be developed using demand and cost curves. Demand and marginal cost have a particular significance in WELFARE ECONOMICS, the study of how an economy can best allocate resources to maximise the utility or economic welfare of its citizens.
■ The demand curve shows the value that consumers place on the last unit bought of a product. For instance, if a utility maximising consumer bought a pair of tights at £2, then the pair of tights must have given at least £2 worth of value (or **satisfaction** or

QUESTION 1
Table 33.1

Output	Units	
	Minimum input levels	
	Labour	Capital
10	4	1
20	8	2
30	11	3
40	14	4
50	16	5

Which of the following combinations are (i) technically efficient and (ii) productively efficient if the minimum cost of a unit of labour is £100 and of a unit of capital is £500?
(a) 8 units of labour and 2 units of capital to produce 20 units of output at a cost of £1 800. (b) 15 units of labour and 4 units of capital to produce an output of 40 units at a cost of £3 500. (c) 4 units of labour and 1 unit of capital to produce 10 units of output at a cost of £1 000.

utility ☞ 14 unit). If total demand for a product is 100 units at a price of £10, then the value placed by consumers on the hundredth unit must have been £10. The value placed on each of the other 99 units bought is likely to be above £10 because the demand curve is upward sloping. The marginal (or extra) value of a good to the consumer (i.e. the marginal utility) is given by the price shown on the demand curve at that level of output.

■ The marginal cost curve shows the cost to firms of producing an extra unit of the good. 'Cost', we will assume here, is the cost of production to society as well as to firms. (We will see in unit 35 that the **private cost** of production of the firm may differ from the **social cost** because of **externalities**, and that this has important implications for allocative efficiency.)

In Figure 33.1, two markets are shown. In the wheat market, current output is OB. The market price is £1 per unit, but farmers receive £3 per unit, for instance because the government subsidises production. In the gas market, output is OE. Price is £6 but gas suppliers receive only £4, for instance because the government imposes a £2 tax per unit.

In the wheat industry, price is below marginal cost (P < MC). This means that the value that consumers place on the product is less than the cost to society of producing the product. Consumers value the last unit produced at OB at £1 (shown on the demand curve). The cost to society of producing the last unit is £3 (shown on the marginal cost curve). Therefore consumers value the last unit of wheat purchased at £2 less than it cost to produce.

In the gas market, price is above marginal cost (P > MC). This means that the value consumers place on the last unit produced is more than the cost to society of its production. Consumers value the last unit produced at OE at £6 whilst its cost to society is only £4. Hence consumers value the last unit of gas purchased at £2 more than it cost to produce.

This suggests that scarce resources would be more efficiently allocated if less wheat and more gas were produced in the economy, but how much wheat and gas should be produced? If price is equal to marginal cost in both markets (P = MC), then consumers value the last unit consumed of both wheat and gas as much as it costs to produce those commodities. If the price of wheat in Figure 33.1 were £2 and gas £5, then it would be impossible to reallocate resources between the two industries to the advantage of consumers.

Hence allocative efficiency will exist if price is equal to marginal cost in each industry in the economy. This is a very important conclusion but we shall see in unit 34 that this conclusion needs to be very heavily qualified.

If P=MC in all industries (such as wheat and gas in the above example), it is impossible to make any one better off without making someone else worse off. The allocation of resources is then said to be PARETO EFFICIENT (after Vilfredo Pareto, an Italian economist, who first put forward this condition in 1909 in a book entitled *Manuel D'Economie Politique*). If an allocation of resources is said to be Pareto inefficient, then it must be possible to make some or all people better off without making anybody worse off.

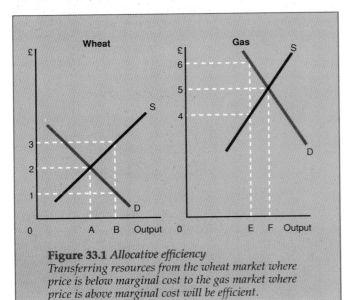

Figure 33.1 *Allocative efficiency*
Transferring resources from the wheat market where price is below marginal cost to the gas market where price is above marginal cost will be efficient.

QUESTION 2
Table 33.2

Millions			£ per unit	
	Goods		Services	
Quantity	Price	Marginal cost	Price	Marginal cost
1	10	2	10	4
2	8	4	9	5
3	6	6	8	6
4	4	8	7	7
5	2	10	6	8

The table shows the relationship between quantity demanded and price and between output and marginal cost for the only two commodities produced in an economy.
(a) The economy produces 3 million units of goods and 4 million units of services. Why is this an allocatively efficient level of production?
(b) Explain, using a diagram, why there would be a loss of economic efficiency if the allocation of resources changed such that:
(i) only 2 million units of goods were produced and the resources released were switched to the production of services;
(ii) only 2 million units of services were produced and the resources released were switched to the production of goods.

Dynamic efficiency

Both productive and allocative efficiency are **static** (☞ unit 111) aspects of efficiency. They are concerned with how resources are used at a point in time. However, it is also important to ensure that there is an efficient allocation of resources over a period of time. DYNAMIC EFFICIENCY is concerned with the efficient allocation of resources over a period of time. For instance, would there be greater efficiency in the economy if more resources were devoted to consumption or to investment? It could be argued that the Japanese economy is more dynamically efficient than the UK economy because it has grown at almost twice the rate of the UK economy in the post-war era. Moreover, Japanese firms seem to introduce new production techniques and develop new products at a much faster rate than comparable UK firms. This could explain why so many UK industries have seen their markets taken away from them by Japanese competitors.

Efficiency and the production possibility frontier

The various concepts of efficiency can be illustrated using a **production possibility frontier** (☞ unit 1). A production possibility frontier shows combinations of goods which could be produced if all resources were fully used (i.e. the economy were at full employment). If there were productive inefficiency in the economy, production would take place within the boundary, for instance at points A, B or C in Figure 33.2. With all resources fully employed, it would be possible to move, for instance, from A to D if costs were minimised.

A, B and C are also Pareto inefficient. This is because it is possible to increase output for both John and all other people without making anyone worse off by moving to a point north east of these combinations. So production at D is more efficient than A, production at E is more efficient than at B etc.

On the other hand, D, E and F are Pareto efficient. At any of these points it is not possible to produce more for John without reducing production for all other people. This is true for all points on the production possibility frontier. Hence, all points on the PPF are Pareto efficient.

All points on the PPF also satisfy the P=MC condition. So points on the frontier are both productively and allocatively efficient.

Note that it is only possible to make Pareto efficiency statements about points which are north east and south west of each other. For instance, F is Pareto efficient whilst C is not. But K cannot be compared with F because at K all other people are better off than at F but John is worse off.

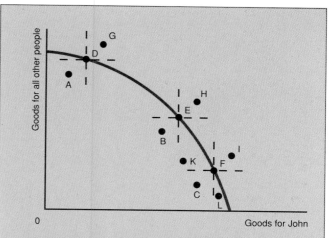

Figure 33.2 *Pareto efficient points of production*
Points on the production possibility frontier, such as D, E and F are Pareto efficient because it is not possible to produce more goods for John without reducing the production of goods for other people. Points G, H and I are unattainable whilst points A, B and C are Pareto inefficient because it is possible to increase production and produce more goods for both John and all others.

QUESTION 3 Many scientists have predicted that the destruction of the Brazilian rain forests will add to the 'greenhouse effect', in turn leading to a rise in world temperatures and a rise in sea levels. Much of the destruction is being carried out by ranchers who wish to clear land to rear cattle. They can then earn a profit by selling the beef to First World countries such as the USA and the UK.

Using a production possibility frontier (putting 'beef' on one axis and 'rain forest' on the other), discuss whether a ban on the felling of trees in the Brazilian rain forests would lead to Pareto efficiency.

The optimal allocation of resources

All points on the production possibility frontier are productively and allocatively (i.e. Pareto) efficient. Therefore in one sense all points on the frontier represent an OPTIMAL ALLOCATION OF RESOURCES. It is not possible to make one person better off without making another worse off. In making this judgement, we are implicitly assuming that it is not possible to say that one distribution of resources is better than another. However, this gives little help to policy makers who believe that one distribution of resources is superior to another. For instance, in Figure 33.3, points A and B are both Pareto efficient and therefore in one sense represent an optimal allocation of resources. However, the government may believe that society would be better off if there were less rather than more defence spending so that the economy would be better off at B rather A. It is making a value judgement about what constitutes economic welfare.

This value judgement can be expressed in terms of **social welfare** functions. These are the equivalent of indifference curves (☞ unit 15) for society as a whole,

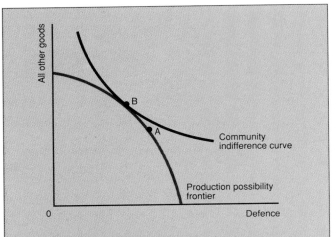

Figure 33.3 *The optimal allocation of resources If it is assumed that it is not possible to make comparisons about welfare between individuals, then all points on the production possibility frontier give an optimal allocation of resources. However, if value judgements are made, then a community indifference curve can be constructed and a single optimal allocation of resources, B, can be found.*

giving relative welfare values of different combinations of output. A social welfare function (called here a **community indifference curve**) is shown in Figure 33.3. An optimal allocation of resources exists when the highest level of social welfare is achieved on the production possibility frontier of the economy, where the community indifference curve is tangential to the production possibility frontier at B. But a social welfare function necessarily reflects the value judgements of the economist or politician who constructs it.

Key terms

Productive efficiency - is achieved when production is at lowest cost.
Technical efficiency - is achieved when a given quantity of output is produced with the minimum number of inputs.
Allocative or economic or Pareto efficiency - occurs when no one can be made better off by transferring resources from one industry to another. Allocative efficiency will exist in an economy if price = marginal cost in all industries.
Welfare economics - the study of how an economy can best allocate resources to maximise the utility or economic welfare of its citizens.
Dynamic efficiency - occurs when resources are allocated efficiently over time.
Optimal allocation of resources - occurs when resources are efficiently used in such a way as to maximise the welfare or utility of consumers.

Applied economics

The Common Agricultural Policy (CAP)

When the European Community was first formed, there was a commitment to free trade between member countries. This found its first major expression in 1958 in the Common Agricultural Policy, a Community-wide policy which aimed to harmonise the agricultural policies of the original six member countries (☞ the data question in unit 12 for an explanation of how CAP functions). One of the implicit aims of CAP was to increase efficiency in the market for agricultural products. To what extent has this been achieved?

Productive efficiency has certainly increased. The number of small, relatively inefficient, farms has declined over time whilst the percentage of output from large farms with lower overall costs has increased. Not only has productive efficiency increased, but the production possibility frontier for agricultural goods has moved outwards due to mechanisation, fertilizers, new strains of animals and

crops and more productive farming methods in general.

However, European agriculture is not fully productively efficient. There are still far too many small farmers producing on marginal land, such as in Wales or the French Alps. In 1983, the average size of a farm in Spain was 12.9 hectares (of utilised farming area) and in Italy it was 5.6 hectares, compared to 64.4 hectares in the UK. Small farmers are unable to exploit the economies of scale enjoyed by large farms and consequently their costs of production are much higher.

But it could be argued that the difference in productivity between farms in Europe is not as important an issue as the difference in the cost of production between the EC and the rest of the world. World prices for many agricultural commodities, such as wheat or butter, are considerably below those maintained by the complex system of tariffs, quotas and intervention prices in the EC. Table 33.3 shows an IMF calculation of the cost of agricultural support policies in different industrialised economies. Part of the cost is born by taxpayers because governments pay subsidies or minimum prices to support farmers. Part is born by consumers because they have to pay higher prices than they would if world prices prevailed in their economies. The producer subsidy equivalent shows the subsidy that would be required to maintain farmers' incomes at the current level if all support policies were removed. For

Table 33.3 *Costs of agricultural support policies of selected industrial countries*

(Annual average 1984-86)

	Direct cost to:			Producer subsidy equivalent[2]
	Taxpayers[1]	Consumers	Total	
	(in billions of US dollars)			(In percent)
United States	49.1	17.1	66.3	28.3
Canada	3.0	2.7	5.7	39.1
Australia	0.6	0.7	1.3	14.5
New Zealand	0.4	0.1	0.5	22.5
Japan	7.4	34.9	42.3	68.9
Austria[3]	0.6	1.0	1.6	35.3
European Community	25.2	42.0	67.2	40.1
Total	86.3	98.5	184.9	38.4

1. Taxpayer cost is net of budgetary receipts from tariff and includes data for all levels of government except local government. Cost assumes no change in other tax rates.
2. The subsidy that would be required to maintain producers' incomes at the current level if all support policies were removed; measured as a percent of the gross value to agricultural producers.
3. 1984-85.

Source: Issues and Development of International Trade Policy, IMF Occasional Paper No. 63 by Margaret Kelly and others (1988), based on data from the OECD.

instance, in the EC a 40 per cent subsidy would be needed, indicating that for every £60 of income farmers would receive for their produce at world prices, they would need an extra £40 to bring them up to their present level of income of £100. Put another way, on average EC consumers are paying 1.66 times more (100÷60) for agricultural produce than they would if markets were free. The UK National Consumer Council, in a 1988 report, estimated that the average EC family of two adults and two children paid £728 a year more for their food than they would if trade were free.

The agricultural market is also allocatively inefficient in terms of the MC = price criterion. The marginal cost of production far exceeds the price consumers are prepared to pay. For instance, it was estimated in The World Development Report 1986 that EC farmers are paid up to three times the world price for wheat, barley, butter and sugar (which was nothing compared to Japanese farmers who were paid 14 times the world price for their sugar). Allocative efficiency could therefore be increased by shifting resources out of agriculture into other industries.

If the cost of CAP is so large, why is nothing done about it? Eliminating EC farm subsidies would be very likely to increase allocative efficiency but there would be losers as well as winners. By the dismantling of CAP, EC farmers would almost certainly be made worse off but consumers would be made considerably better off. Though politically, the farming lobby in the EC is very powerful, over the past ten years there has been a growing realisation that its demands for ever increasing prices, resulting in mountains and lakes of unsold produce and an EC agriculture budget which takes up 75 per cent of total EC spending, must be refused. But it is difficult to see how politically it will be possible even in the long term to lower prices in the EC such that price is nearer marginal cost than at present.

Data question

EDUCATION

A study by Howard Glennerster and William Low (1990) showed that household spending on private education, ranging from shorthand to music classes to private schools, rose during the 1970s and 1980s. For every 1 per cent increase in their income, households spent 1.05 per cent more on education in 1960-65, 1.06 in 1970-5 but reached 1.16 between 1980 and 1986. At the same time, state spending on education fell. For every 1 per cent increase in national income in the 1960s, the state increased education spending by 1.5 per cent. In the period 1980 to 1986, this figure fell to below 0.9 per cent.

1. (a) How did consumers change their allocation of income on private education according to the data?
   (b) How does this compare with the way in which the state chose to allocate resources to education on the behalf of consumers?

2. What impact has the change in the rate of growth of state spending on education had on economic efficiency?

Summary

1. The market is a mechanism for allocating resources.
2. In a free market, consumers, producers and owners of the factors of production interact, each seeking to maximise its returns.
3. Prices and profits play a key role, signalling how resources should be allocated or reallocated within the market.
4. In the absence of market failure, a free market will achieve an optimal allocation of resources.
5. There are many examples of market failure, including imperfect competition and monopoly, externalities and missing markets.
6. The General Theory of the Second Best shows that, in an imperfect market economy, a move towards marginal cost pricing in one industry may not lead to a Pareto improvement.

The role of the market

Adam Smith, in his book *An Enquiry into the Nature and Causes of the Wealth of Nations*, attacked the economic system of his day. It was a system founded upon protectionism, economic restrictions and numerous legal barriers. He presented a powerful case for a free market system in which the 'invisible hand' of the market would allocate resources to everyone's advantage. There are three main types of actor or agent in the market system. Consumers and producers interact in the **goods markets** of the economy. Producers and the owners of the factors of production (land, labour and capital) interact in the **factor markets** of the economy.

The main actors in the market

The consumer In a pure free market system it is the consumer who is king. Consumers are free to spend their money however they want and the market offers a wide choice of products. It is assumed that consumers will allocate their scarce resources so as to maximise utility (☞ units 14 and 15).

The firm In a pure free market, firms are servants of the consumer. They are motivated by making as high a profit as possible. This means maximising the difference between revenues and costs.
- **Revenues.** If they fail to produce goods which consumers wish to buy, they won't be able to sell them. Consumers will buy from companies which produce the goods they want. Successful companies will have high revenues, unsuccessful ones will have low or zero revenues.
- **Costs.** If they fail to minimise costs, then they will fail to make a profit. Other more efficient firms will be able to take their market away from them by selling at a lower price.

The price of failure - making insufficient profit to retain resources and prevent factor owners from allocating their resources in more profitable ways - will be the exit of the firm from its industry. On the other hand, in the long run firms cannot make abnormal profit. If they did, new competitors would enter the industry attracted by the high profits, driving down prices and profits and increasing output.

Owners of the factors of production Owners of land, labour and capital - rentiers, workers and capitalists - are motivated by the desire to maximise their returns. A landowner wishes to rent her land at the highest possible price. A worker wishes to hire himself out at the highest possible wage, all other things being equal. A capitalist

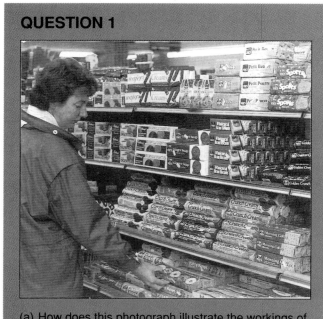

QUESTION 1

(a) How does this photograph illustrate the workings of the market system?
(b) What happens in a market system if a brand of biscuits fails to sell in sufficient quantities?

wishes to receive the highest rate of return on capital. These owners will search in the market place for the highest possible reward and only when they have found it will they offer their factor for employment. Firms, on the other hand, will be seeking to minimise cost. They will only be prepared to pay the owner the value of the factor in the production process.

The allocation of resources

In the market mechanism, everyone is assumed to be motivated by pure self interest. Consumers are motivated by the desire to maximise their utility.

Producers wish to maximise profits. Workers, rentiers and capitalists seek to maximise the returns from the factors that they own. What Adam Smith argued was that this apparently chaotic system of billions of separate transactions would not only allocate resources, but it would allocate resources in an efficient way. It wasn't necessary for government or any other body to order that resources should go in this way or that. The hidden hand of the market would do the job, and it would do it far better. The following three examples show how the market can reallocate resources when market conditions change.

Example 1 Assume that lobbying from animal welfare groups changes consumers tastes. In the market for fur coats, fewer fur coats will be purchased. In the short run, companies in the fur trade are likely to cut prices to boost demand but this will depress profits. In the long run, some firms will leave the fur industry, reducing supply. This in turn will affect the factor markets. For instance, the demand by firms in the fur industry for workers, equipment and animals will fall. So wages of fur workers may fall. The price of hunting permits or of land for fur farms may fall too. Some workers will leave the industry attracted by higher wages elsewhere whilst land will be put to other uses. Meanwhile, consumers will have increased their spending on other goods, for instance on imitation furs. In the short term the price of imitation furs will rise. Increased profits will attract new firms into the industry, thus boosting supply. This will increase the demand for factors of production used in the making of imitation furs. Their prices will tend to rise.

Example 2 A new production process is invented which reduces the cost of manufacturing shoes. Initially, firms will be able to make abnormal profit - revenues will be the same but costs will be lower. However, new firms will be attracted to the industry by high profits. Extra supply will lead to price reductions. The price of shoes will go on falling until no abnormal profit can be made. Competition has forced firms to offer the lowest price possible to consumers. Meanwhile the new low prices will have increased the demand for shoes. So more factors of production will be demanded by the shoe industry and their price will tend to rise.

Example 3 There is a large increase in the number of young workers in the population. This increased supply of young workers will force their wages down. Firms will employ more young workers at lower wages. This should reduce the costs of firms, which in turn will be passed on to the consumer in the form of lower prices. The market mechanism has once again ensured that the consumer benefits from this change.

QUESTION 2 In 1989, there were about 15 000 companies with a workforce of over 350 000 making shoes in the European Community. But the European shoe industry was in deep trouble. Imports of shoes from Asian countries, particularly South Korea and Taiwan, had increased the import penetration ratio (the percentage of imports sold in relation to total shoe sales) from 27 per cent to 42 per cent over the period 1986 to 1988. Over that period, there were 13 000 job losses in Italy, 10 000 in France and 7 500 in West Germany.

There were two main causes of these problems. Emerging Asian economies had invested heavily to increase their footwear manufacturing capacity. At the same time, the value of the dollar had fallen. The effect of this was to make it less profitable for both European producers and the new Asian producers to sell to the large US market. European exports fell whilst the Asian manufacturers switched shoes intended for sale in the US market to the European market. Only Portugal amongst the European nations managed to maintain its sales and that was because the Portuguese shoe industry is a low wage industry.

Using demand and supply diagrams, explain how the market mechanism reallocated resources within the shoe market over the period 1986 to 1989.

Prices and profits

Prices and profits play a key role in the market mechanism. They are the signals which allocate resources within the market. When prices rise, buyers react by buying less, whilst sellers react by wanting to sell more. Profits too act as signals for firms. Abnormal profits will lead to increased supply as firms move into the industry. Losses will lead to firms leaving the industry. If governments or other agencies intervene to control prices and profits, distorted signals will be sent out. The result will be the misallocation of resources to the detriment of the consumer.

The market and economic efficiency

It would seem from what has been said above that the market is likely to promote **economic efficiency**

(☞ unit 33). Indeed, it is possible to show that if all markets are **perfectly competitive** (☞ unit 27), resources in the economy will be efficiently allocated.

■ In long run equilibrium in a perfectly competitive market, firms will produce at the bottom of their average cost curves. Therefore there will be productive efficiency.

■ For there to be allocative efficiency, the cost to society of producing an extra unit of output must equal the value placed on consumption of that good by the individual (the price = marginal cost condition outlined in unit 33). In a perfectly competitive market, firms maximise profits by producing where marginal cost = marginal revenue. Marginal revenue is equal to price because the perfectly competitive firm is a price taker. Therefore marginal cost = price. On the other hand consumers maximise their utility by equating the marginal utility of each good consumed per £1 spent. Hence price is an accurate reflection of the value of the good (the marginal utility) to the individual.

It is also true that allocative efficiency in the sense of Pareto efficiency will exist in an economy where all markets are perfectly competitive. Because firms are producing at least cost, the economy must be on its production possibility frontier and therefore the allocation of resources must be Pareto efficient.

Market failure

If all markets in an economy are perfectly competitive, then two conditions must hold.

■ There must be perfect competition in all goods markets. Consumers must be able to allocate their resources in a way which will maximise their utility. They must possess perfect knowledge for instance. There must be enough consumers in any market to prevent undue pressure being exerted on producers to their advantage. Production too must be organised under conditions of perfect competition. Each industry must comprise a large number of small producers all of whom are price takers. There must be freedom of entry and exit to every industry and all firms must possess perfect knowledge.

■ All factor markets must be perfectly competitive. There must be perfect mobility of labour for instance. There must be no trade unions which act as monopoly suppliers of labour. Neither must there be any monopoly employers, such as the UK government with teachers and nurses. Capital must flow freely between industries and regions according to the levels of profit being made.

No real economy is like this. Imperfections exist in all sectors of modern industrialised economies as they do in developing economies which **prevent** the efficient allocation of resources through the market mechanism. This MARKET FAILURE is the subject of units 35 to 45.

Here we will provide a summary of the different types of market failure.

■ **Imperfect competition** (☞ units 37 - 40 and 42 - 43). The free market model assumes that there are a large number of buyers and sellers in all markets and that there is no concentration therefore of market power. The reality is often very different. Power is often very concentrated in market economies. Most goods markets are oligopolistic, dominated by a few large firms. Consumers, far from being kings, can often be seen as pawns in the games that firms play to maximise their own gains. In factor markets, monopoly suppliers such as trade unions are often present. So too are monopoly buyers such as governments. This can (but does not necessarily) lead to inefficiency.

■ **Externalities** (☞ unit 35). Prices and profits should be accurate signals, allowing the actors in the market mechanism to allocate resources efficiently. In reality, prices and profits can be very misleading. This is because actual prices and profits do not reflect the true prices and profits to society of different economic activities. For instance, in Brazil it makes commercial sense to cut down huge areas of rain forest to provide grazing land for cattle sold to the West as meat for hamburgers. This could lead to global economic catastrophe in the long run. The market is putting out the wrong signals.

■ **Missing markets** (☞ unit 40 and 44). The market, for a variety of reasons, fails to provide certain goods and services. Some goods, called public goods, such as defence, will not be provided by a market. Other goods, called merit goods, will be underprovided by the market. Health care and education are two examples of merit goods. Part of the reason for underprovision is because the market mechanism is often poor at dealing with risk and with providing information to agents in the market.

Even if a market were efficient, it would not necessarily lead to a socially desirable distribution of resources between individuals. Both efficiency and **equity** (☞ units 41 and 45) contribute to the level of economic welfare. For instance, Pareto efficiency exists when an economy operates on its production possibility frontier. But there are an infinite number of points on the frontier. Which is the one which is most desirable? That question cannot be answered without some view about the distribution of resources within an economy (i.e. without a **social welfare function** ☞ unit 33). Most would agree that an economy where one person enjoyed 99 per cent of the resources whilst the other 100 million people were left with 1 per cent would be unlikely to provide a higher level of welfare than one where the distribution of resources was more equal. Most (but not all) would agree that it is unacceptable in today's Britain to allow people to die of hunger on our streets. The question of what distribution is desirable or is judged to maximise total welfare is a value judgement.

QUESTION 3

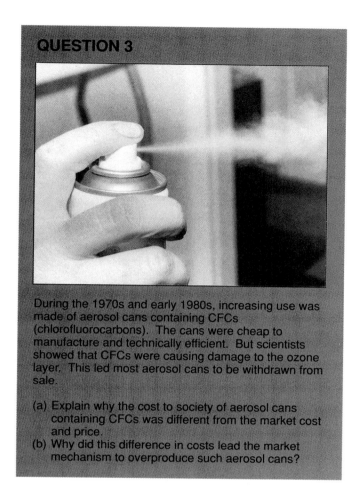

During the 1970s and early 1980s, increasing use was made of aerosol cans containing CFCs (chlorofluorocarbons). The cans were cheap to manufacture and technically efficient. But scientists showed that CFCs were causing damage to the ozone layer. This led most aerosol cans to be withdrawn from sale.

(a) Explain why the cost to society of aerosol cans containing CFCs was different from the market cost and price.
(b) Why did this difference in costs lead the market mechanism to overproduce such aerosol cans?

The theory of the second best

An economy will be economically efficient if all markets are perfectly competitive. Therefore it might seem like commonsense to argue that economic efficiency will be increased in an economy where there are many instances of market failure if at least some markets can be made perfectly competitive and market distortions removed.

In the late 1950s, Richard Lipsey and Kelvin Lancaster (1956-7) published an article entitled 'On the General Theory of the Second Best'. They assumed an economy where some firms were not pricing at marginal cost. They then showed that a move towards marginal cost pricing by one firm might lead to an an increase in efficiency, but equally it could lead to a decrease in efficiency. The radical conclusion was that introducing marginal cost pricing could lead to efficiency losses rather than efficiency gains.

For instance, consider Figure 34.1. It shows two industries. The food industry is assumed to be monopolistic. Output is set at OA where MC = MR (the profit maximising condition) and price is then set at OP on the average revenue or demand curve. The entertainment industry is perfectly competitive. Output is at OF where marginal cost equals price. Assume that resources were transferred from the entertainment

industry to the food industry such that output in the food industry rose to OB whilst output in the entertainment industry fell to OE. The welfare gain in the food industry, shown by the difference between demand and marginal cost, is the shaded area on the graph. This is larger than the welfare loss in the entertainment industry, shown by the shaded triangle. Hence in this case there is a net welfare gain if there is a move away from perfect competition in the entertainment industry.

It can be shown that, in general, efficiency can be increased by transferring resources from industries where price is far in excess of marginal cost to industries where it is less so or where demand is less than marginal cost. Efficiency is likely to be achieved where the difference between price and marginal cost is the same throughout an economy.

This is a very important conclusion. Every economy suffers from market failure. It will never be the case that marginal cost can equal price across all sectors of the

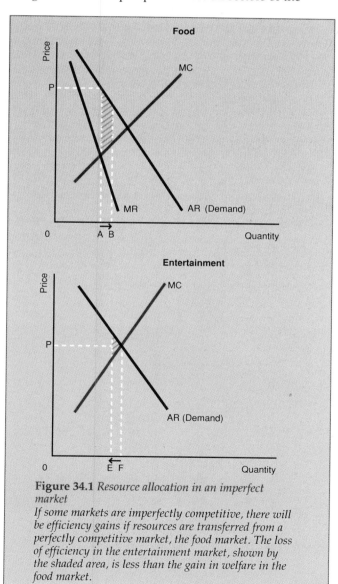

Figure 34.1 *Resource allocation in an imperfect market*
If some markets are imperfectly competitive, there will be efficiency gains if resources are transferred from a perfectly competitive market, the food market. The loss of efficiency in the entertainment market, shown by the shaded area, is less than the gain in welfare in the food market.

economy. Therefore simple rules or slogans such as 'competition good, monopoly bad' are unlikely to lead to good economic policy making. What the theory of the second best suggests is that distortions within an economy need to be evened out as far as possible. Eliminating them in some markets but allowing them to remain high in others could well lead to less efficiency overall than decreasing them in markets where they are high but actually increasing them in markets where distortions are low.

Key terms

> **Market failure** - where resources are inefficiently allocated due to imperfections in the working of the market mechanism.

Applied economics

The metamorphosis of Chelsea Girl

Chelsea Girl, owned by Lewis Shops Group, was a chain of fashion stores aimed at girls in their teens and early twenties. It grew large in the swinging '60s and was profitable and well run in the 1970s and 1980s. However, current demographic trends are against retailers who cater for the teenage market. The number of females aged 15-19, for instance, fell from 2.3 million in 1981 to 2.1 million in 1989 and is projected to fall to 1.7 million by 1996. On the other hand, the baby-boomers of the 1950s and 1960s are working their way through the population so that the number of 30-34 year olds, say, whilst staying roughly constant throughout the 1980s at 1.9 million is projected to increase to 2.1 million by 1996. Hence, in the 1990s, there will be a relatively greater increase in demand for fashion clothes by middle aged women than by teenagers.

The way in which the market mechanism deals with this change in consumer preferences is shown by what happened to Chelsea Girl. If Chelsea Girl had continued trading as a chain of just under 200 stores, it would have faced difficult trading conditions. Profit might have increased, but it is unlikely that it would have increased by as much as the profit of those chains catering for the older market. So, Lewis Shops Group, a family-run private company, decided to 'reposition' itself in the market.

In 1988, the group launched 'River Island', aimed at more up-market buyers in the 20-35 age range. By early 1990, with 75 shops, the concept had proved itself successful. Lewis Shops Group then decided to convert all their Chelsea Girl outlets into River Island shops. Mr Leonard Lewis, managing director, said he believed that the River Island name was 'ideally positioned to capitalise upon the emerging lifestyle and demographic trends of the new decade'.

Profit acted as a signal for a firm to leave the teenage fashion market and move to the fashion market for a slightly older group. The market mechanism has reallocated resources within the economy in response to changing consumer preferences.

UK TOURISM BENEFITS AT THE EXPENSE OF FOREIGN HOLIDAYS

Summer 1989 was a very poor year for Britain's package tour operators. Increasing dissatisfaction with the standards of packaged holidays abroad, together with very high interest rates which made the cost of borrowing expensive, led to a sharp fall in the number of foreign holiday tours booked. The British tourist industry, on the other hand, did record business. In August 1989,

Thomson Holidays, the largest firm in the market, announced that it was to cut 500 000 foreign holidays from its 1990 holiday programme.

1. **Explain how, according to the data, the market mechanism led to a reallocation of resources in 1989/90.**

35 Externalities

Summary

1. Externalities are created when social costs and benefits differ from private costs and benefits.
2. Externalities can lead to economic inefficiency if the marginal social cost of production is not equal to price.
3. Externalities can also redistribute real income within the economy.
4. Government can limit the effects of externalities through, for instance, regulation, extending property rights and taxing the externality.

Private and social costs and benefits

A chemical plant may dump waste into a river in order to minimise its costs. Further down the river, a water company has to treat the water to remove dangerous chemicals before supplying drinking water to its customers. Its customers have to pay higher prices because of the pollution.

This is a classic example of EXTERNALITIES or SPILLOVER EFFECTS. Externalities arise when private costs and benefits are different from social costs and benefits. A PRIVATE COST is the cost of an activity to an individual economic unit, such as a consumer or a firm. For instance, a chemical company will have to pay for workers, raw materials and plant and machinery when it produces chemicals. A SOCIAL COST is the cost of an activity not just to the individual economic unit which creates the cost, but to the rest of society as well. It therefore includes all private costs, but may also include other costs. The chemical manufacturer may make little or no payment for the pollution it generates. The difference between private cost and social cost is the externality or spillover effect. If social cost is greater than private cost, then a negative externality is said to exist.

However, not all externalities are negative. A company may commission an architect to design a building which is not just functional but also beautiful. The value of the pleasure which the building gives to society over its lifetime may well far exceed any extra cost involved to the company. Hence, if social benefit is

greater than private benefit, a positive externality is said to exist.

This is often the case with health care provision. Although one individual will benefit from innoculation against illness, the social benefit resulting from the reduced risk of other members of society contracting the illness will be even greater. Positive extemalities could also result from education and training. An individual may benefit in the form of a better job and a higher salary but society may gain even more from the benefits of a better trained workforce.

Activities where social benefit exceeds private benefit

QUESTION 1

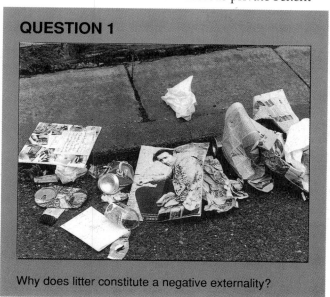

Why does litter constitute a negative externality?

are often inadequately provided by a market system. In many cases this results in either state provision or a government subsidy to encourage private provision.

Market failure

The price mechanism allocates resources. Prices and profits are the signals which determine this allocation. However, a misallocation of resources will occur if market prices and profits do not accurately reflect the costs and benefits to society of economic activities.

For instance, in the case of the chemical plant above, the price of chemicals does not accurately reflect their true cost to society. The private cost of production to the manufacturer is lower than the social cost to society as a whole. Because the price of chemicals is lower than that which reflects social cost, the quantity demanded of chemicals and therefore consumption of chemicals will be greater than if the full social cost were charged. On the other hand, if the water company is pricing water to consumers, it will have to charge higher prices to consumers than would have been the case without the chemical pollution. Demand for water and consumption of water will therefore be less than it would otherwise have been without the externality.

The greater the externality, the greater the market failure and the less market prices and profits provide accurate signals for the optimal allocation of resources.

Allocative efficiency

Externalities can be illustrated within the framework of welfare economics introduced in units 33 and 34. It was argued that allocative efficiency would exist, subject to very strict conditions, if price were equal to the marginal cost of production.

■ The demand curve is effectively the marginal benefit curve, showing the value that consumers place on consuming an extra unit of the good.

■ The marginal cost curve is the cost of producing an extra unit of output.

Allocative efficiency will be achieved where the marginal cost of production is equal to the marginal benefit received by consumers.

Price equals marginal cost in long run equilibrium in a perfectly competitive industry. In Figure 35.1, the marginal private cost of production (MPC) is equal to demand at a price of OE. So in a perfectly competitive market, OB will be produced.

However, allocative inefficiency will exist if private cost or benefit differs from social cost or benefit. In Figure 35.1, the marginal social cost of production (MSC) is assumed to be higher than the marginal private cost. Production should only be at OA if price is set equal to marginal social costs. Overproduction of AB leads to allocative inefficiency. The efficiency loss to society is given by the difference between the cost to society of production of AB (shown by the marginal social cost

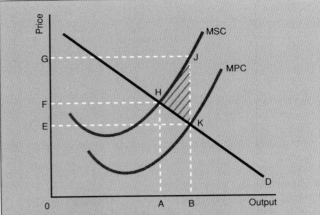

Figure 35.1 *Social cost arising from an externality*
If an industry is perfectly competitive, long run production will take place where price = marginal private cost (MPC) at output OB. This, subject to certain conditions, is also the allocatively efficient level of production. But if there is a negative externality leading to marginal social cost being higher than MPC, then output should be lower to maximise efficiency. The externality causes overproduction of AB.

curve) and the value placed by society on consumption of AB (shown by the demand curve). This difference is the shaded triangle HJK. The greater the difference between marginal social cost and marginal private cost, the greater will be the net social cost shown by the area of the triangle.

It should be noted that the social cost arising from a negative externality is likely to be less under conditions of imperfect competition. For instance, a monopolist will produce less than the level of output where MC = price. It could even be the case that the monopolist will so reduce output that production is to the left of OA in Figure 35.1 (i.e. there will be no social cost due to the externality, but there will be an efficiency loss due to underproduction by the monopolist).

Distributional effects

Externalities don't just create potential inefficiencies. There are also distributional implications. For instance, in the example under Market Failure above, there is a redistribution of income from consumers of water, who pay too high a price for water, to consumers of chemicals who pay less than the social cost of production.

Assume that the price of chemicals is raised by a tax on output to reflect the marginal social cost of production. This should correct the market failure present in the market for chemicals. However, the water company downstream is still having to pay to clean up the pollution created by the chemical company. Only if the chemical company pays the water company will there also be efficiency in the market for water. In this case it would seem to be relatively simple for an arrangement to be made for the water company to charge the chemical company for the latter's dumping of chemical waste in the river.

But there is likely to be no such simple remedy for local residents and local anglers. Their welfare may be diminished by the polluted river. How do you decide who to compensate in the local community and how much compensation should you give? One answer which economists have suggested involves local residents and local anglers and the chemical company paying the other party an amount which is equal to the welfare loss. If citizen A is willing to pay £5 a year, and citizen B £10 a year and all other citizens £9 985, then the value of a clean river to the local community is £10 000. That is how much:

- either the chemical company should give in compensation to the local community;
- or the local community should pay to the chemical company to stop them polluting the river.

There are a number of problems with this approach in practice. Firstly, economics cannot provide an answer to the question of 'who compensates whom?' Should the chemical company pay the local residents, or should the local residents pay the chemical company? It is also impossible in most cases to find out who exactly loses as a result of an externality.

However, it is important to remember that externalities can give rise not only to inefficiencies but also to a redistribution of income. Externalities have implications both for economic efficiency and equity.

QUESTION 3 In March 1989, the Confederation of British Industry published the results of survey on traffic congestion in the UK. It calculated that traffic chaos in London alone was costing British industry £15 billion a year. Costs included lost production hours, late arrival of staff, increased fuel consumption and vehicle maintenance. It claimed that every British household has to spend at least £5 more a week than it needs to on goods and services to meet the costs to business of congestion on London's road and rail systems.

(a) Who is creating the negative externalities on London's roads - industry or the private motorist?
(b) Who should pay to correct this market failure (e.g. the taxpayer, business, the consumer, the private motorist) and how should the money be transferred?

Government policy

Pollution could be seen as the most politically sensitive externality today. Therefore, we will concentrate our discussion here on ways in which governments can control pollution. There are three main ways in which governments can reduce pollution externalities.

Regulation This method is currently used in the UK. The government lays down maximum pollution levels or forbids pollution-creating activities altogether. For instance, there are regulations which set a limit on harmful emissions from car exhausts and it is illegal for households to burn ordinary coal in urban areas.

This solution will only result in an efficient allocation of resources in the economy if the government equates the marginal cost of compliance with regulations with the marginal social benefit resulting from lower pollution. Consider Table 35.1. It shows the marginal private costs and marginal social benefits of compliance with three levels of pollution controls. If the pollution controls are too rigorous, the marginal cost to the company of complying with the regulations over and above the optimal level (£30m) will exceed the marginal social benefits resulting from less pollution (£10m). On the other hand, if the pollution controls are too lax, the cost to the company of better pollution control (£5m) will be less than the value to society of lower pollution (£30m). The

Table 35.1

Pollution control	Marginal cost to company of compliance with each level £m	Marginal social benefit £m	
Level 3	30	10	Too rigorous
Level 2	20	20	Optimal
Level 1	5	30	Too lax

optimal level of pollution control is one where an extra £20m of spending by the company to cut pollution from level 1 to level 2 is equal to the £20m social benefit gained.

So regulation will only optimise allocative efficiency if government can accurately assess costs and benefits and if they are prepared to make regulations accordingly. If pollution controls are too lax, firms have no incentive to reduce pollution levels below the minimum legal requirement even though there would be a net social benefit as a result. If pollution controls are too strict, there is a net social cost as firms are forced to pay out far more in equipment to control pollution than the value of the social benefit.

Extending property rights If a chemical company lorry destroyed your home, you would expect the chemical company to pay compensation. If the chemical company polluted the atmosphere so that the trees in your garden died, it would be unlikely that you would gain compensation, particularly if the chemical plant were in the UK and the dead trees were in Germany.

Externalities arise because property rights are not fully allocated. Nobody owns the atmosphere or the oceans, for instance. Governments can extend property rights. They can give water companies the right to charge companies which dump waste into rivers or the sea. They can give workers the right to sue for compensation if they have suffered injury or death as a result of working for a company. They can give local residents the right to claim compensation if pollution levels are more than a certain level. This is known as **internalising the externality** - eliminating the externality by bringing it back into the framework of the market mechanism.

This solution has the advantage that the cost of the externality should be accurately assessed so that costs and benefits are equalised. It should also lead to redistribution of income from losers to gainers from the externality. The problem is that it is very difficult to extend property rights in many cases. Who, for instance, should pay and who should be compensated for the depletion of the ozone layer?

Taxing the externality The solution which commands the widest support from economists is taxation. Government becomes responsible for assessing the cost to society of pollution. It then sets tax rates on polluters so that the tax is equal to the value of the externality (i.e. the marginal benefit to the producer of pollution is equal to the marginal cost it has to pay in the form of a pollution tax). This means that companies are rewarded by lower taxes if they reduce pollution. So there are incentives within the system for companies to control pollution.

This is easier to organise than a system of extended property rights. However, the citizens and firms which suffer from the pollution are not compensated. Hence this solution leads to a different distribution of resources compared to a pollution free world.

The problem with all of these solutions is that there is often a lack of data to assess the value of the externality

(☞ unit 36). How much is the death of German forests worth? What is the value to society of a 20 per cent reduction in acid rain? How much loss has been suffered by an individual who has had a motorway built within 200 metres of her house? Moreover, when externalities cross national boundaries, there is often an extreme reluctance for anyone to admit responsibility.

There are many 'Greens' who would argue that market failure in this area is so great that it is likely to lead to the destruction of the world eco-system and to existence as we know it. They are arguing that externalities today are enormous. If they are right, then internalising all externalities would produce an economic system which would bear little resemblance to our present world economy.

QUESTION 4 In December 1989, the Institute of International Affairs published a report which advocated controlling emissions of carbon dioxide, the main contributor to the greenhouse effect, through 'marketable carbon permits'. Each country would be allocated permits for carbon dioxide emissions according to the size of its population. These could then be traded internationally. Developing countries would be likely to have a surplus of permits whilst developed countries would not have enough. So developing countries would sell some of their permits to developed countries. The money received could only be used for 'development and pollution abatement programmes and related transfers of technology and technical expertise'.

(a) Explain why this system would be likely to lead to a reduction in emissions of carbon dioxide worldwide.
(b) Suggest why it might be difficult to implement such a programme.

Key terms

Externality or spillover effect - the difference between social costs and benefits and private costs and benefits. If net social cost (social cost minus social benefit) is greater than net private cost (private cost minus private benefit), then a negative externality exists. If net social benefit is greater than net private benefit, a positive externality exists.
Private cost and benefit - the cost or benefit of an activity to an individual economic unit such as a consumer or a firm.
Social cost and benefit - the cost or benefit of an activity to society as a whole.

Applied economics

The economics of global warming

The environmental problem

During the 1980s, there was a growing awareness that levels of greenhouse gases (carbon dioxide, chlorofluorocarbons, methane and nitrous oxide) in the atmosphere were rising and that this might pose a serious problem for the future of the planet. 'Global warming', a rise in world temperatures, comes about because greenhouse gases act as a blanket, trapping heat within the earth's atmosphere.

The possible rise in temperatures shown in Figure 35.2 might be welcomed by many sun-lovers in the UK. However, it has grave consequences for many parts of the world. Firstly, it could change the location of the world's deserts and adversely affect some of the major food growing areas in the world. Temperature rises of just one or two degrees centigrade are enough to change fertile land into a barren wilderness. The recent drought problems of sub-Saharan Africa and in particular the Ethiopian famines of the 1980s together with the 1988 US drought were seen by some as evidence of existing global warming.

The second possible consequence of global warming is a rise in the sea level due to a melting of the polar ice caps. The minimum predicted rise in temperature of 3 degrees centigrade in Figures 35.2 and 35.3 would lead to a rise in sea levels of 30cm. This would be enough to flood areas such as the east coast of England, the Bangladesh delta and the Maldive islands.

The economic problem

Global warming is an example of the economic problem. On the one hand, there are infinite wants which are the cause of the ever increasing use of natural resources which create the emissions of greenhouse gases. On the other hand, resources are scarce. If we want more cars, more food and more services, we have to accept that this may damage the environment. The opportunity cost of economic growth could be the loss of the climate we know today.

There is a growing consensus amongst developed nations of the world that the future cost of global warming is likely to be greater than the benefits derived from increased consumption of the goods and services that cause it. There has been a growing call for the growth of greenhouse emissions to be stabilised if not reduced.

Unfortunately greenhouse emissions are usually externalities. An individual firm in a free market, for instance, will choose to dump gases into the atmosphere rather than seek more costly alternatives to disposal. It is society as a whole who will pay the

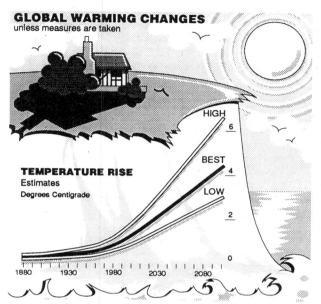

Figure 35.2 *Temperature rise, estimates in degrees centigrade*

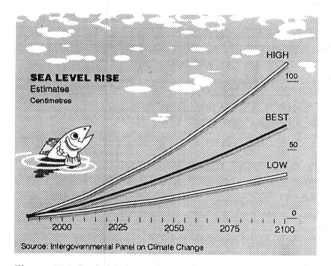

Figure 35.3 *Sea level rise, estimates in centimetres*

eventual price for the resulting contribution to the process of global warming. Equally, it will be in the interests of an individual country to allow all other countries to reduce their greenhouse gas emissions whilst it takes no action. It can then enjoy the benefits of a safe environment whilst allowing others to pay the cost (this is an example of the **free-rider problem** ☞ unit 44).

Possible solutions

There are a number of possible solutions to the problem. One is for all countries round the world to freeze their emissions of greenhouse gases. Whilst this might be acceptable to developed countries, it is completely unacceptable to developing countries such as India and China. They would pay a large price in terms of lower economic growth to solve a problem which has been created in the first place by the high standards of living of First World countries.

A more imaginative solution would be to use the power of the market to reduce emissions. It has been suggested that there ought to be a tax on emissions in First World countries. The proceeds of that tax would then be used to subsidise the introduction of environmentally friendly technologies in Third World countries. This is unlikely to be an acceptable solution politically. First World countries have shown little enthusiasm in the past for transferring large amounts of aid to Third World countries.

Another imaginative solution would be for an international body to be created which would sell licences allowing individual firms to emit greenhouse gases. The number of licences issued would be fixed in such a way as to limit current emissions. In the most radical market version of this, the licences would be sold to the highest bidders. They would be the companies and organisations which placed the highest value on being able to continue producing harmful emissions, possibly because they were least able to reduce them without incurring substantial costs. The revenues obtained would be used to pay an inspectorate to police the system and additional revenues could be used, for instance, to support Third World development or be returned to national governments participating in the scheme.

The most likely outcome of the current debate is that the major industrialised nations of the world will agree to limit their own emissions but Third World countries will choose to ignore calls for restraint. In the short term, this should have a significant effect. This is because six countries - the USA, the Soviet Union, Japan, West Germany, the UK and Poland - account for more than half the world's carbon dioxide emissions. In the longer term, the larger Third World countries must be drawn into an agreement if disaster is to be averted.

ACID RAIN

In the 1960s and 1970s, it became increasingly apparent that central European and Scandinavian forests were being destroyed by some unknown agent. Research showed that the problem was acid rain. An increase in the acidity of precipitation was killing off trees in huge numbers. Acid rain was caused by pollution of the atmosphere. Because winds tend to blow from the west, across the Atlantic to Scandinavia and central Europe, countries such as the UK suffered far less from this problem than Sweden for instance. Gases such as sulphur dioxide produced in the UK's coal fired electricity power stations would drift across the North Sea and be deposited in continental Europe. For many years the UK government denied the existence of the problem, but in the late 1980s it was forced to agree to a number of measures to reduce acid rain emissions.

1. Why were emissions such as sulphur dioxide an externality for the UK in the 1970s and most of the 1980s?

2. Assess the different ways in which the UK government could limit acid rain emissions in the UK.

36 Cost-benefit analysis

Summary

1. Cost-benefit analysis is a technique which attempts to evaluate the social costs and benefits of an economic decision.
2. Social costs and benefits may differ from private costs and benefits.

3. It is often difficult and sometimes impossible to place a price on externalities.
4. Cost-benefit analysis is often used to assess public sector investment projects.

Market failure

In a free market, decisions are based upon the calculation of **private costs and benefits**. However, there are many markets where significant **externalities** exist (☞ unit 35). This means that there are significant costs or benefits which are unlikely to be taken account of by the private economic decision maker.

COST-BENEFIT ANALYSIS is a procedure which takes into account all costs and all benefits (i.e **social costs and benefits**). Its purpose is to give guidance in economic decision making. It is used particularly by governments to evaluate important investment projects.

Costs and benefits

It is relatively easy to place a value on private costs and benefits. For instance, British Rail wishes to build a high speed rail link between London and the Channel Tunnel. It will be able to calculate the financial cost of constructing the link. This is the private cost to British Rail. It will also be able to calculate the revenues to be earned from fares. These will be its private benefits. If the private benefits exceed private costs the link will be profitable and British Rail will go ahead and construct the link.

However, there will be other costs and benefits associated with the project. These are the externalities of the link. For instance, residents near the link will suffer from pollution, including noise pollution. The ports of Dover and Folkestone, together with the cross Channel ferry companies, are likely to see a fall in their trade, with possible effects on unemployment. There may be considerably more road congestion around rail terminals leading to longer journey times for non-Tunnel users. Travellers from London to Paris may save time on their journeys compared to rail/boat or air journeys, a time saving perhaps not reflected in an increase in the price of their tickets. Traffic may be taken off the road if travellers find the rail link attractive, easing road congestion for non-Tunnel users.

These externalities are very important costs and benefits which would be completely ignored by British Rail if it operated in a pure free market. In a cost-benefit analysis British Rail would attempt to place a value on these externalities in order to calculate the social cost and social

benefit of the project and proceed only if social benefit exceeded social cost.

QUESTION 1 Leigh Interests is currently Britain's largest waste treatment group. Its headquarters at Walsall in the West Midlands have been the subject of much controversy in recent years. The local council and local residents would like to see the treatment plant and a large landfill site for industrial (including solid toxic) waste closed down. The treatment plant, close to housing estates, deals with some of the most hazardous by-products of industry such as arsenic, cyanide, mercury and antimony. Some of the liquid waste most difficult to deal with is blended together in tanks and then piped into a disused coal mine. Permission to do this was granted after a public inquiry in 1978 because impermeable clay surrounding the mine makes seepage impossible.

Source: adapted from the *Financial Times*, 3.2.1989.

(a) What are the likely private costs and benefits to Leigh Interests of processing waste at its Walsall plant?
(b) What might be the externalities caused by the plant?

Problems with placing a value on externalities

The value of many externalities is difficult to estimate. For instance, assume that, as a result of the building of the link, 5 million travellers every year save on average 30 minutes each on their journey times between London and Paris. In a cost-benefit analysis, a value would need to be placed on the 2½ million hours saved. However, it is unclear what value should be given to each hour since there is no obvious market in which a price is set for the time. A high cost estimate would assume that the time should be valued as if the travellers could have earned money during that time. This might give an estimate of £9 per hour at an average annual wage for the typical link user of £18 000. On the other hand, it could be assumed that the traveller places almost no value on the time saved. It could be just 50p per hour. Comparing these two estimates, we get a high estimate of £22.5 million and and a low estimate of £1.25 million.

Even more difficult is how to place a value on a human life. Assume that the rail link takes traffic off the roads and as a result 5 fewer people are killed in road accidents each year. The value of a life today in a court case involving accidents is mainly determined by the expected earnings of the deceased. For instance, if a company director earning £500 000 per annum were killed in a road crash, together with her chauffeur earning £10 000 per year, then all other things being equal (age, family circumstances etc.) the family of the company director would receive far more compensation than the family of the chauffeur. These values, however, are open to much debate.

Other intangibles, such as pollution and illness, are very difficult to value in money terms.

Even the values placed on private costs and benefits may be difficult to estimate. For instance, British Rail may charge £15 for a single journey from London to the Tunnel. But that may not necessarily reflect the cost to British Rail of the journey. It may include a large element of monopoly profit, or it may be subsidised by British Rail in the hope that passengers arriving in London will then travel onwards from London on British Rail. It may therefore be necessary for the cost-benefit analysis to estimate a **shadow price** for the journey - a price which more accurately reflects the cost to British Rail of providing the service.

QUESTION 2 Almost the whole of the M25 is operating above its design standard of 85 000 vehicles per day. The busiest sections are carrying more than 130 000. According to the Freight Transport Association, an average lorry spends 90 hours a year stuck on the M25. 14 500 lorries per day use the busiest sections.

Source: adapted from the *Financial Times* 29.10.1988.

How would you estimate a value for traffic congestion on the M25?

Benefit across time

Calculations are further complicated by the fact that costs and benefits will occur at different points in time. A Channel Tunnel rail link, for instance, could still be carrying passengers in the year 2100 and beyond. Many of our major rail links today in the UK were first built over 100 years ago.

A value has to be given to future costs and benefits. Economic theory suggests that £1 of benefit in 20 years' time is worth considerably less than £1 of benefit today (☞ unit 53). This is because £1 today could be saved or invested. Each year that passes it should be worth more. For instance, if the rate of interest, (or rate of return, or rate of discount) is 10 per cent per annum then £1 today is

worth £1.10 in one year's time, £1.21 in two years' time, £1.33 in three years' time, £10.83 in 25 years' time and £117.39 in 50 years' time (these figures are calculated using compound interest). It must therefore be true that a benefit of £117.39 available in 50 years' time is only worth £1 today if the rate of return is 10 per cent per annum.

So in cost-benefit analysis, all future costs and benefits need to be revalued using a rate of discount. There are two ways of doing this (☞ unit 53). Either a rate of discount is assumed and all costs and benefits are calculated as if they occurred today. This is known as calculating present values. Saying that £117.39 available in 50 years' time is worth £1 today is an example of this technique. Alternatively the internal rate of return on the project can be calculated. So if we knew that £1 had been invested today and the one and only benefit were £117.39 which would be paid in 50 years' time, then we would know that the rate of return on the project would be 10 per cent per annum.

QUESTION 3 A motorway could be built to last either 25 years or 50 years. It has been estimated that it would cost £100 million to build it for 25 years and £200 million for 50 years. In 25 years' time the cost of repair to make it last another 25 years would be £900 million.

(a) If the rate of discount (or rate of interest or rate of return) were 10 per cent, would it cheaper to build it to last for 25 years and repair it, or build it to last for 50 years?
(b) Your answer would be different if the rate of discount were 5 per cent. Explain why.

Note: you might find it helpful to read unit 53 if you have difficulty with this question.

A critique of cost-benefit analysis

Cost-benefit analysis is a procedure where:
- all costs and benefits, both private and social are identified;
- then a value is placed on those costs and benefits, wherever possible in monetary terms.

The technique is used mainly where it is assumed that market failure is present. Calculating all costs and benefits would seem to be a more rational way of evaluating an important investment project than relying upon projections of private profit or even having no facts and figures to consider.

However, cost-benefit analysis can be a very imprecise procedure. It is difficult to place a value on certain important costs and benefits and the results depend crucially upon the rate of discount of future costs and benefits used.

So the results of cost-benefit analysis should be used with caution. The assumptions made in the analysis should be explicit. Ideally a range of results should be calculated showing what would happen to costs and benefits if different assumptions were made. Social costs and benefits which cannot be valued in monetary terms should be clearly stated.

If this is done, cost-benefit analysis can be a useful tool in the evaluation of investment projects. But it should be recognised that it is only one piece of evidence amongst many and it could well be that other considerations, such as political considerations, prove ultimately to be more important.

Applied economics

Key terms

Cost-benefit analysis - a procedure, particularly used by governments to evaluate investment projects, which takes into account social cost and benefits.

London transport

London enters the 1990s with one of the most primitive transport systems in the developed world. Demand for transport within the capital is estimated to rise significantly by the year 2 000, but almost no new capacity is planned to cope with this rising demand. The result can only be more chaos, longer journey times and greater costs for London's long-suffering travellers.

Much of the blame for this situation can be laid at the door of successive governments who have failed to invest sufficiently in London's transport system. For instance, in January 1989, the Department of Transport published the Central London Rail Study. The study proposed that two new underground rail links be built, one going east-west linking Paddington and Marylebone with Liverpool Street, the other going north-south linking Euston and King's Cross with Victoria, as shown in Figure 36.1. These would be built to take British Rail through-trains, so that instead of commuters from Watford having to change at Euston to catch an underground train to get, say, to Tottenham Court Road, they could travel there directly. The estimated capital cost of the two tunnels was £2bn. In 1990, the government announced that it would build one tunnel, the east-west link, but not the other, the north-south link. However, many believe that building the east-west link, whilst extremely important in contributing to a future reduction in congestion, is insufficient because of the significant externalities

present. The social benefits of the proposed lines are far greater than the private benefits.

For instance, passengers on other lines in Central London would benefit directly because there would be less congestion on those lines. This would mean faster journey times and their journeys would be more pleasant. At street level, some passengers would be attracted off the roads and onto the underground system. Car journey times might be faster. Businesses such as British Telecom and the Post Office might save millions of pounds at present wasted because of workers and their vehicles stuck in traffic jams. On a cost-benefit basis, the Central London Rail Study estimated that far from making a loss, the economic benefits would exceed the costs by 60 per cent.

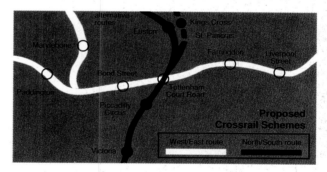

Figure 36.1 *Proposed crossrail schemes*

THE CHANNEL TUNNEL

Data question

The Channel Tunnel is the single most important civil engineering project in the UK and in France today. Its projected cost exceeds £7 billion. During its construction, it has had a major impact on employment, housing and the environment in Kent and in the Pas de Calais. But in the longer term, the effects on jobs, the location of industry and the environment will be far greater.

Opponents of the Tunnel link include the cross Channel ferry companies and inhabitants of Kent and South London

who are most likely to be affected by increased traffic and by the pressures of industrialisation in the region. Interestingly, whilst there is much opposition to the Tunnel in Kent, it is being welcomed wholeheartedly in Northern France where it is seen as an important catalyst for development in a region which has suffered above average unemployment in the post-war period.

1. Assess the costs and benefits of the Channel Tunnel scheme.

Summary

1. Neo-classical theory suggests that monopoly has higher prices and lower output than perfect competition.
2. This is only likely to be true for a multi-plant monopolist. A natural monopolist may have far lower costs than if the industry were split up into competing units.
3. A monopolist might have higher costs because it needs to maintain barriers to entry. It may also suffer from X-inefficiency.
4. On the other hand, monopolies may be far more innovative than perfectly competitive firms.
5. Government may attempt to correct market failure caused by monopoly. It may tax abnormal profit away, subsidise production, set maximum prices, nationalise the industry, break it up or reduce entry barriers.

Perfect competition vs monopoly

Traditional neo-classical economic analysis has tended to support the view that competition increases efficiency. One argument used is that allocative efficiency will be reduced if a perfectly competitive industry becomes a monopoly.

Multi-plant monopolists In a perfectly competitive industry there is a large number of small producers each operating at the bottom of the average cost curve. Each firm has therefore exploited all potential economies of scale. If new firms enter the industry because of price increases, their cost curves will be identical to the cost curves of existing firms. Equally, firms leaving the industry will have the same cost curves as those firms remaining.

If the industry became a monopoly, the new firm would be made up of a large number of small factories or plants. The monopolist would not attempt to merge these plants because they were already at their most efficient size under perfect competition. Hence the monopolist will become a MULTI-PLANT MONOPOLIST.

If, in the long run, the multi-plant monopolist wished to expand output, it would do so not by expanding an existing plant but by building a new one. It would operate the plant at its most efficient scale, at the bottom of the plant's average cost curve. If it wanted to contract output in the long run it would close down a plant rather than maintain the same number of plants each producing at less than the most efficient scale of production. Hence, the long run average cost curve for a multi-plant monopolist is horizontal. It can increase or reduce output

in the long run at the same minimum average cost.

Allocative efficiency The demand curve for the monopolist is downward sloping (☞ unit 28). The marginal cost curve will be the same as the average cost curve if the AC curve is horizontal (for the same reasons that AR = MR if average revenue is constant ☞ unit 27). Hence, the cost and revenue curves facing the multi-plant monopolist are as shown in Figure 37.1.

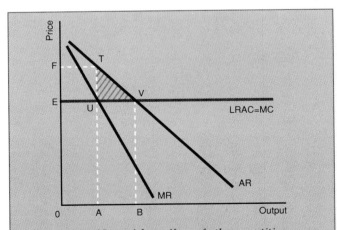

Figure 37.1 *Net social cost if a perfectly competitive industry becomes a monopoly*
If the industry were producing under conditions of perfect competition, price and output would occur where price = MC, at output OB and price OE. If the industry were a monopoly, output would be where MC = MR at OA whilst price would be on the demand curve at OF. Price is higher and output lower in the monopoly

If the industry were perfectly competitive, it would produce where demand equals supply (i.e. where price is equal to marginal cost). If it is a monopoly, the firm will produce at its profit maximising position where MC = MR, and price on its demand or average revenue curve. Hence, under perfect competition output will be at OB whilst price will be at OE. If the industry were a monopoly, long run output will fall to OA and price will rise to OF. This leads to the conclusion that output will be lower and price will be higher in monopoly than under perfect competition. The multi-plant monopolist is **allocatively inefficient.**

The net social cost (or welfare cost) can be shown on the diagram. It is assumed that there are no externalities. The demand curve shows the marginal social benefit received by consumers of the product (☞ unit 35). The marginal cost curve is the marginal social cost curve, the cost to society of producing an extra unit of output. Consumers were prepared to pay OF for the extra unit at OA whilst it would only have cost OE to produce. Therefore the net social cost (the difference between social benefit and social cost) on the last unit of output is EF. Similarly the vertical distance between the demand curve and the average cost curve shows the net social cost of each unit not produced between OA, the monopoly output, and OB, the output under perfect competition. Hence the net social cost to society of multi-plant monopoly production compared to production under conditions of perfect competition is the shaded triangle TUV.

The net social cost might be even greater than this triangle for two reasons.

■ The monopolist might have to create and maintain barriers to entry to keep potential competitors out of the industry. For instance, it might have to spend large sums of money on advertising or other promotions. This will increase its average and marginal cost in the long run. Output will then be even lower and price even higher than if it operated under the same cost conditions as perfect competition.

■ The firm may be able to shelter behind barriers to entry and as a consequence inefficiency may result. **X-inefficiency** is the term used to describe inefficiencies which occur in large organisations which are not under pressure to minimise cost. Average costs will therefore be higher than under perfect competition, resulting in even lower output and even high prices.

Natural monopoly

So far it has been assumed that the monopolist is a multi-plant monopolist. However, many monopolies are NATURAL MONOPOLIES. Natural monopolies occur in industries where not even a single producer is able to exploit fully the potential economies of scale. Hence, the dominant firm in the industry, the firm with the largest output and the lowest cost, is always able to undercut competitors in price and force them out of the industry if it so chooses.

This is shown in Figure 37.2. The monopolist will produce where MC = MR at output OB and earn abnormal profit by pricing at OF. However, it would be a nonsense to talk about making the industry more competitive. Splitting the industry into two for instance, with each firm producing OA (half of OB), would increase the average cost of production from OE to OG. More competition in the industry would result in a loss of welfare, not a gain. It should also be noted that producing at the Pareto-efficient level of output where price = MC would result in a loss for the firm. At output OC, average revenue is less than average cost. This has

QUESTION 1 In May 1989, OFTEL, the Office of Telecommunications, announced that private companies would be allowed to compete in the market for private payphones. Up to that time, only British Telecom (BT) were legally entitled to supply and install private payphones in pubs, shops, restaurants, hotels and other outlets.

At the time BT were charging a quarterly rental ranging from £24.50 to £81, plus a connection fee plus the cost of calls. The renter was able to keep the premium rate charged to the users of the payphones.

OFTEL's announcement was immediately followed by an announcement by Southwestern Bell Telecom, a US company, that it would sell payphones for £215 plus VAT. The company claimed that the number of payphones would rise from 300 000 to 350 000 within a year, and it was aiming to supply more than half of the extra payphones.

(a) Using a diagram, explain the likely effect on the price and output of payphones resulting from the break up of BT's payphone monopoly.
(b) Is OFTEL's decision likely to affect economic efficiency?

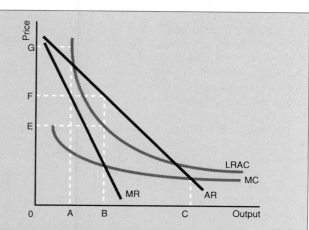

Figure 37. 2 *Natural monopoly*
In a natural monopoly, economies of scale are so large that not even a single producer could fully exploit them. Competition would be highly inefficient, raising the average cost of production. The profit maximising level of output for the monopolist is OB, but output where price = MC would be greater at OC.

important implications for the running of nationalised industries (☞ unit 42).

Natural monopolies tend to occur in industries where fixed costs are very large. For instance, it would be inefficient to have two railway companies with two sets of tracks in the same area running between two towns. In gas, electricity, water and telephones, it would be inefficient to have two or more sets of lines or pipes to every household so that they had the choice of which company to buy from. The Channel Tunnel is a natural monopoly too. It would make no economic sense to build a second tunnel until the first is being used to full capacity.

QUESTION 2 In 1989 discussions about the building of a Channel Tunnel rail link between London and the Tunnel took place between British Rail, the Department of Transport and a number of private consortia. The cost of construction of a dedicated rail link with rolling stock was estimated at up to £4 billion. No agreement was reached because the plans were unprofitable. British Rail still hopes that the line will be built but it is likely that a less expensive option will be decided upon.

(a) How do the data illustrate that a railway company is likely to be a natural monopolist?
(b) Would economic efficiency be increased if a natural monopoly were replaced by a number of competing firms?

Innovation

So far, the analysis has been **static**. Perfect competition and monopoly have been compared at a point in time. However, there are also important **dynamic** considerations. The Austrian economist, Joseph Schumpeter (1883-1950), argued that monopoly might be far more efficient over time than perfect competition.

In perfect competition, there are a large number of small firms operating in the market. No one firm will have large enough funds available for research and development. Small firms in general find it more difficult to raise finance for growth and expansion than large firms (☞ unit 26), and banks are likely to be unsympathetic if borrowed money is to be used on risky research projects. Moreover, perfect knowledge is assumed to exist in the market. The invention of one firm will quickly be adopted by other firms, so there is little or no incentive to undertake research and development.

Patent laws and copyright laws can protect the inventions of small firms providing some encouragement to innovate. However, it is noticeable that in the few perfectly competitive industries which might be argued to exist, innovation is often provided not by individual firms but by government funded or government organised research institutions. In agriculture, for instance, major advances in crop strains in the Third World have been developed by state-funded universities and research

institutes. This is an example of government correcting **market failure.**

A monopolist, safe behind high entry barriers, can react in two ways. It may choose to take the easy life. Sleepy and inefficient, it exploits the market and earns enough profits to satisfy shareholders. Research and development, which imply potential change, are unlikely to be a high priority for this type of firm.

Schumpeter, however, argued that the reverse was likely. The monopolist would have the resources from its abnormal profits to spend on research and development. Remember that in the UK, for instance, about 70 per cent of all investment is funded from retained profit (☞ unit 22). The monopolist would also have the incentive so to spend. It would be able to exploit any new products or new techniques of production to its own advantage, safe from competitors behind its high entry barriers. Productive efficiency would increase because costs would fall. Allocative efficiency would increase because the monopolist would bring new products to the market.

Moreover, a monopolist is never safe from competition. In the 18th century, the canal seemed unassailable as a form of industrial transport. Yet during the 19th century, the monopoly of canals, and the monopoly profits of canal owners, were destroyed by the coming of railways. In the 20th century, the same process turned railways into loss making concerns as railway monopolists saw their markets taken away by the motor car and lorry. Schumpeter called this 'the process of creative destruction'. High barriers mean that potential competitors have to produce a substitute product which is radically better than the old. It is not good enough to add some fancy packaging or change the colour of the product or add a few gadgets. Therefore monopoly encourages fundamental rather than superficial progress. So Schumpeter argued that a system of monopoly markets was far more likely to produce efficiency over a period of time than perfect competition.

QUESTION 3 The big news in 1989 was Sony's video Walkman; in 1990 VHS will be fighting back in the personal video market.

VHS has been the world's favourite format for years. But most manufacturers agree that the cassettes are much too bulky for movies on the move. VHS inventor JVC is developing something called Concept C, using smaller cassettes which play on a normal machine with an adaptor. Recently, Panasonic - the giant electronics corporation which owns JVC - has produced the world's first VHS-C tape capable of running for 90 minutes.

This now puts many of the top box-office movies within reach for viewing both home and away. In the meantime, Sony's latest version of the video Walkman boasts a 4-inch LCD screen and plays tiny Video 8 tapes lasting up to three hours in long play.

How do the data illustrate the principle of creative destruction?

Imperfect competition

So far, monopoly has been contrasted with perfect competition. The same arguments can be used to consider the social costs or benefits of imperfect competition. In imperfect competition output is likely to be lower and price higher than in perfect competition and hence there is a net social cost. Abnormal profits are likely to be made, again imposing net social costs.

In perfect competition and in many cases of monopoly, the consumer is offered only a homogeneous product. On the other hand, imperfect competition is characterised by the selling of a large number of different branded goods. Welfare is likely to be increased if consumers can choose between many, if fairly similar, products rather than being faced with no choice at all.

Schumpeter's arguments about innovation apply to imperfect competition too. Oligopolists, for instance, are more likely to innovate than perfectly competitive firms.

The verdict?

It can now be seen that it is not possible to come to any simple conclusions about the desirability of competition in the market. Competition is by no means always 'best'. On the one hand, multi-plant monopolists and many imperfectly competitive firms may exploit the market, earning abnormal profits at the expense of consumers, reducing output and increasing price. This leads to a welfare loss. On the other hand, natural monopolies are far more efficient than any alternative competitive market structures. There may or may not be a link between monopoly and innovation.

Government policy

Governments have a range of possible COMPETITION POLICIES which can be used to improve economic efficiency.

Taxes and subsidies Abnormal profit can simply be taxed away. This may improve equity within the economic system, transferring the resources which the monopolist has expropriated from consumers back to taxpayers. Unfortunately, this will not improve allocative efficiency. A tax on profits will not affect either marginal cost or marginal revenue. Therefore the monopolist will continue to produce at less than the efficient level of output.

However, it is possible to shift the marginal cost curve downwards by providing a **subsidy**. At any given level of output, the government could subsidise production, reducing marginal cost. If the government wishes the monopolist to produce where MC = price, it will need to find out the level of output where the marginal cost curve cuts the average revenue curve before a subsidy is given. On Figure 37.3, this occurs at output level OB where MC_1 = AR. The size of the subsidy required on the last

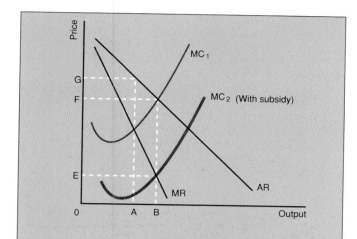

Figure 37.3 *Subsidising a monopolist to improve efficiency*
A profit maximising monopolist will produce at OA where MC = MR and price is OG. Output under perfect competition would be at OB, where price = MC. A subsidy of EF on the last unit of output would shift the marginal cost curve downwards from MC_1 to MC_2. The monopolist would now produce at the perfect competition level of output. The government could recoup the subsidy by a tax on profits.

unit of output is EF. This shifts the marginal cost curve to MC_2. The monopolist produces OB because this is now the level of production where MC = MR, and society benefits because production is at a level where the true cost to society, MC_1 is equal to price. The government can recoup that subsidy by taxing away the profits made by the monopolist.

This seems an ideal solution. Unfortunately there are a number of practical problems. Firstly, giving subsidies to private sector monopolists is likely to be politically impossible for any government. It is difficult enough for governments to subsidise nationalised industries (☞ unit 42). Secondly, the policy requires an accurate knowledge of cost and revenue curves. When the policy is first imposed there is some chance that a reasonable guess can be made. However, taxes and subsidies distort the market so that in the long term it becomes very difficult to guess where hypothetical points on the curves might be. Thirdly, it has already been discussed in detail whether allocative efficiency would increase by moving to a price = MC level of output in one industry (☞ unit 34). Imposing taxes and subsidies assumes that there is clear understanding of what the efficiency maximising level of output and price might be.

Price controls An obvious method of controlling monopolists would be to impose price controls on their goods. The maximum price that a monopolist could charge would be set equal to the marginal social cost: in Figure 37.4 where MC = price. To the left of output OA, the average revenue curve is horizontal because the government has imposed a maximum price of OB. To the right, the free market average revenue curve reappears. If

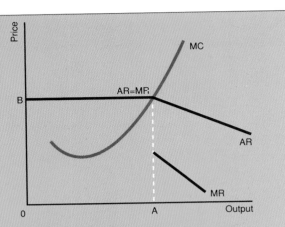

Figure 37.4 *Price controls in a monopoly industry*
Price controls change the shape of the average and marginal revenue curves. A maximum price of OB will produce a kinked average revenue or demand curve . To the left of OA, the average revenue curve is horizontal, showing the maximum price of OB that the firm is allowed to charge.. To the right the average revenue falls because the free market price is below the maximum price. The monopolist will now produce at OA, the output level of a perfectly competitive industry where MC = price. This is because OA is now the profit maximising level of output (i.e. where MC = MR for the monopolist).

the monopolist wishes to sell more than OA, it has to lower its price. Marginal revenue is equal to average revenue if average revenue is constant (☞ unit 27). There is then a discontinuity at OA for the marginal revenue curve. The monopolist will produce at OA because that is now the level of output where MC = MR. The policy works because the government has effectively turned the marginal revenue curve from being downward sloping to being horizontal up to the efficiency maximising level of output.

This type of policy is being used to control privatised industries in the UK (☞ unit 43). However, it suffers from the same defects as subsidies. It is difficult to know where the cost and revenue curves lie and what is the allocatively efficient level of output.

Nationalisation The private monopolist is assumed to maximise profit. This leads to an inefficient level of output. Another way of controlling monopoly is to change the goals of the firm. This could be achieved by nationalising the industry. The industry is then charged with maximising social welfare and not private profit. The advantages and problems of this solution are discussed in detail in units 42 and 43.

Breaking up the monopolist The monopolist can be broken up into competing units by government. This might be an effective solution for a multi-plant monopolist with a large number of plants where the **minimum efficient scale of production** (☞ unit 20) is very low. But most monopolists or oligopolists have

relatively high minimum efficient scales. The welfare gain from splitting a monopolist into a duopoly, for instance, might be negligible. In the case of natural monopolies, breaking up a monopolist would almost certainly lead to welfare losses. Breaking up cartels is more likely to increase welfare.

Reducing entry barriers It is impossible for governments to reduce entry barriers to industries which are natural monopolies. However, many multi-plant monopolists and oligopolists earn abnormal profit because they artificially maintain high entry barriers and keep potential competitors out. Governments can reduce entry barriers by a variety of means (☞ unit 39).

QUESTION 4 In 1981, the Monopolies and Mergers Commission recommended that British Posters Ltd be broken up. At the time, British Posters controlled 80 per cent of Britain's 170 000 roadside poster sites, hiring the sites from their owners and then marketing them to potential advertisers. The Commission found that British Posters' monopolies 'have led to a higher level of prices than would have obtained in a more competitive market'. Advertisers also complained that British Posters was inflexible. They were not offered a choice of sites. Sites next to each other were differently priced. Clients were forced to accept lengthy contracts which sometimes meant that a product was being advertised long after it had been withdrawn from the market.

(a) How did British Posters exploit its monopoly position?
(b) To what extent would the break up of British Posters into several competing companies lead to greater economic efficiency?

Key terms

Multi - plant monopolist - a monopoly producer working with a number of factories,offices or plants.
Natural monopoly - where economies of scale are so large relative to market demand that the dominant producer in the industry will always enjoy lower costs of produce than any other potential competitor.
Competition policy - government policy to influence the degree of competition in individual markets within the economy.

Applied economics

Competition policy

The legislative framework

It was widely recognised during the inter-war years that there was a lack of competition in domestic British industry which could have operated against the interests of the consumer. In 1948, the government passed the Monopolies and Restrictive Practices (Inquiry and Control) Act designed to curb anti-competitive practices. It set up what is now the Monopolies and Mergers Commission. In 1956, the restrictive practices part of its work was given over to the Restrictive Practices Court (☞ unit 39). The 1973 Fair Trading Act established the present day structure of referrals for handling anti-competitive practices.

■ A Director General of Fair Trading is appointed by the government. He or she is responsible for co-ordinating competition and consumer protection policy and advising the Secretary of State for Trade and Industry. Either the Director General or the Secretary of State has the power to refer monopolies for investigation to the Monopolies and Mergers Commission.

■ The Monopolies and Mergers Commission is an administrative tribunal which investigates potential monopoly situations. A firm is defined as possessing a monopoly if it has at least 25 per cent of the market. This could be either a national market or a local market. The result of an inquiry by the Commission is given in a Report. This explains the Commission's findings and lists its policy recommendations.

■ The Secretary of State for Trade and Industry is the minister responsible for competition policy. He or she receives reports of the Monopolies and Mergers Commission. The Secretary of State may decide not to act, effectively rejecting the Commission's recommendations. Most likely the Secretary of State will ask the Director General of Fair Trading to negotiate a voluntary agreement with the firms concerned. This is designed to curb the malpractices found by the Commission. If the firms refuse to co-operate, he or she has the power to issue an order forcing them to comply.

The 1948 Act only covered firms in the private sector of the economy. The 1980 Competition Act made it possible for the Monopolies and Mergers Commission to investigate public sector monopolies too. The Act also gave the Director General of Fair Trading powers to curb anti-competitive practices such as refusal to supply without the need for a full referral to the Commission.

The EC has the power to investigate monopolies under Article 86 of the Treaty of Rome. The European Commission is responsible for investigating and applying policies. To date, the Commission has been more concerned with mergers and restrictive trade practices than monopolies.

The effectiveness of policy

In the USA, monopolies are illegal because it is presumed that monopoly will always act against the public interest. The basis of UK law is different. Monopoly is permissible unless government is convinced that it acts against the public interest.

The 1973 Fair Trading Act defined the public interest as 'the desirability (a) of maintaining and promoting effective competition between persons supplying goods and services; (b) of promoting the interests of consumers ... in respect of the prices charged and ... their quality and the variety of goods and services supplied; (c) of promoting, through competition, the reduction of costs and the development and use of new techniques and new products, and of facilitating the entry of new competitors into existing markets; (d) of maintaining and promoting the balanced distribution of industry and employment; (e) of maintaining and promoting activity in markets outside the United Kingdom.'

This definition, and the similar one in the 1948 Act, whilst comprehensive, have frequently been criticised as being too vague. Moreover, it has been difficult to ensure continuity of interpretation of the criteria. The Monopolies and Mergers Commission is made up of a constantly changing pool of members who sit on the Commission in a part time capacity. No two reports are compiled by the same group of people. Hence it has not been difficult to detect differences in emphasis and interpretation between different investigations.

When clear recommendations have been made by the Commission, the government has favoured a voluntary approach to their enforcement. Critics argue that this can lead to firms negotiating very favourable terms with governments anxious to avoid upsetting the industrial lobby. In major cases, such as the breweries, political considerations can be seen to be more important than economic ones. Where changes are enforced, firms lobby over time for the release of the undertakings they have made. Governments can prove weak in the face of this type of pressure.

The whole process of investigation by the Monopolies and Mergers Commission has been accused of being unwieldy and time consuming. Since 1948, the Commission has produced only about

200 reports, of which slightly more than 25 per cent have related to monopoly supply situations. Most of the latter have found evidence of anti-competitive practices. During the 1980s much of the energy of the Commission has been devoted to investigating industries which are under government control and ownership. One part of government has been appointed watchdog over another part. Some see this as an admission that government cannot control its own activities. It has also diverted resources away from investigations of the private sector of the economy.

So the experience of the past 40 years is that an industry is unlucky if it finds itself being investigated and even unluckier if it has to change its competitive practices in any serious way. More frequent investigations, regular monitoring of industries found to be operating against the public interest, and more serious penalties for offending firms, are seen by some to be essential if monopoly control is to have teeth.

Data question

THE LAST DAYS OF THE BEERAGE

The Monopolies and Mergers Commission report on the brewing industry showed how some much needed competition could be introduced. The aim would be to increase consumer choice and lower the price of a pint of beer. The MMC described the brewing industry as a 'complex monopoly'. It gave a number of reasons for this statement.

■ Beer rose in price by 15% in real terms between 1979 and 1987. This was twice the rise in prices charged by restaurants.
■ The price of continental and American style lagers is unduly high in Britain.
■ The price of soft drinks in pubs is excessively high.
■ In some towns and villages all the pubs are owned by the same brewer.

The British brewing industry is different from any other in the world in that it has a high degree of vertical integration. The brewers produce, distribute and sell beer. They own pubs through which they sell their own beer.

At present the six biggest brewers produce 75 per cent of Britain's beer and own 75 per cent of 'tied' pubs. In March, the Monopolies and Mergers commission recommended that no brewer should own more than 5 000 each, and that tied tenants should sell at least one 'guest' beer, and should be able to buy other drinks from the most competitive suppliers.

1. Explain what is meant by:
   (a) 'a complex monopoly';
   (b) 'a high degree of vertical integration'.
2. What potential benefits to the consumer might result from the MMC's investigation into the brewing industry?
3. Analyse the effects on the industry of increased competition.

Summary

1. Small firms in an industry exist because economies of scale may be limited, barriers to entry low and the size of the market may be very small.
2. A healthy small firm sector in the economy may lead to increased economic efficiency if it increases competition, reduces prices and increases future efficiency.
3. Firms may grow internally or through mergers, amalgamation or takeover.
4. Mergers may be horizontal, vertical or conglomerate.
5. Firms grow in order to exploit potential economies of scale, control their markets or reduce risk through diversification.
6. Firms may choose to grow by amalgamation for instance because it is cheaper to buy a firm than grow internally.
7. Evidence suggests that many mergers fail to increase economic efficiency.

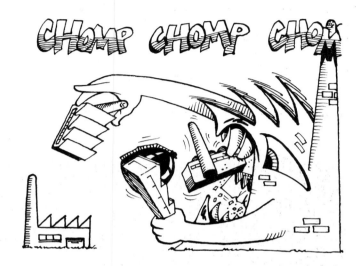

The size of firms

Although production in the UK is dominated by large firms (☞ unit 16), there are many industries where small firms play a significant role.

Large firms exist for two main reasons.

■ Economies of scale in the industry may be significant. Only a small number of firms, producing at the minimum efficient scale of production, may be needed to satisfy total demand. The industry may be a natural monopoly where not even one firm can fully exploit potential economies of scale.

■ Barriers to entry may exist which protect large firms from potential competitors.

Conversely, small firms survive for the opposite reasons.

Economies of scale may be very small relative to the market size A large number of firms in an industry may be able to operate at the minimum efficient scale of production. Small firms may also be able to take advantage of the higher costs of larger firms in the industry caused by diseconomies of scale.

The costs of production for a large scale producer may be higher than for a small company In part, this may be due to productive inefficiency: a large firm operating within its average cost curve boundary. For instance, larger firms may be poorly organised in what they see as small unimportant segments of the market (called market **niches**). Or X-inefficiency may be present

(☞ unit 32). Equally, the average cost curve of a large producer may be higher in certain markets than for a small producer. For instance, a large firm may be forced to pay its workers high wages because it operates in formal labour markets (☞ unit 50). A small firm may be able to pay relatively low wages in informal labour markets. Indeed owners of small companies can work exceptionally long hours at effective rates of pay which they would find totally unacceptable if in a normal job. Or a small producer, like a corner shop sole proprietorship, may be prepared to accept a much lower rate of return on its capital employed than a large company.

Barriers to entry may be low The cost of setting up in an industry, such as the grocery industry or the newsagents market, may be small. Products may be simple to produce or sell. Finance to set up in the industry may be readily available. The product sold may be relatively homogeneous. It may be easy for a small firm to produce a new product and establish itself in the market.

Small firms can be monopolists A monopolist offers a product for sale which is available from no other company. Many small firms survive because they offer a local, flexible and personal service. For instance, a newsagent may have a monopoly on the sale of newspapers, magazines, greetings cards, toys and stationery in a local area. Consumers may be unwilling to walk half a mile extra to buy greetings cards at a 10 per cent discount or travel 10 miles by car to a local superstore to buy a £2 toy at a 25 per cent reduction. Or the newsagent may double up as a grocery store and off-licence, opening till 10 o'clock at night and all day Sunday, again offering a service which is not offered anywhere else in the locality. A small shop could be the only place locally where informal credit is offered, or where it is possible to buy a single item instead of a pack of six. Equally in the case of some products such as cricket balls or croquet mallets, the size of the market is so small that one or two very small firms can satisfy total demand.

QUESTION 1

(a) Why can small firms survive successfully in the hotel industry?
(b) What economic forces might favour hotel chains in the future?

Efficiency and size

There is no direct correlation between the size of a firm and economic efficiency. Some economists argue that small firms are a major source of economic efficiency in the economy.

■ The small firms of today are the large firms of tomorrow. Historically in the UK and the USA, today's top largest 100 firms bear little relation to the list of the largest 100 firms 50 years ago. It is important to have as large a number of small firms as possible so that a few can become the large firms of tomorrow.
■ Small firms provide the necessary competition to prevent large firms from exploiting their markets. Large firms would be less efficient and their prices higher if they were not aware that small firms could enter the market and take away parts of their market. In some markets, economies of scale are small relative to market size. The alternative to a large number of small firms would be multi-plant oligopolists or monopolists which would erect barriers to entry to the industry and then make abnormal profit. Prices would then be higher and output lower, leading to a loss of efficiency.

There are, however, a number of arguments which suggest that large firms can be more efficient. Large firms may be necessary to exploit economies of scale. They are more likely to be in a position to undertake research and development. Moreover, the size of firms

QUESTION 2 Anita Roddick's Body Shop was one of the success stories of the 1980s. Providing a range of environmentally sound products, it grew steadily in the face of competition from established multiples such as Boots and from the large scale advertising and promotion of giants such as Revlon and Unilever.

In what sense might it be said that Body Shop contributed to greater economic efficiency in the UK economy in recent years?

and the number of firms in an industry is not necessarily an indication of competition or the lack of it. As the **theory of contestable markets** (☞ unit 32) shows, what is important is not size or number of firms operating in the industry but the degree of potential competition. Barriers to entry are the key indicator of likely inefficiency, not size of the firm.

The growth of firms

Firms may grow in size in two ways:
- by **internal growth**;
- through MERGER, AMALGAMATION or TAKEOVER.

Internal growth simply refers to firms increasing their output, for instance, through increased investment or an increased labour force. A merger or amalgamation is the joining together of two or more firms under common ownership. The boards of directors of the two companies, with the agreement of shareholders, agree to merge their two companies together. A takeover implies that one company wishes to buy another company. The takeover may be amicable. Company X makes a bid for company Y. The board of directors considers the bid and finds that the price offered is a good price for the shareholders of the company. It then recommends the shareholders to accept the offer terms. However, the takeover may be contested. In a hostile takeover the board of directors of company Y recommends to its shareholders to reject the terms of the bid. A takeover battle is then likely to ensue. Company X needs to get promises to sell at the offer price of just over 50 per cent of the shares to win and take control.

Types of merger

Economists distinguish between three types of merger.
- A HORIZONTAL MERGER is a merger between two firms in the same industry at the same stage of production: for instance, the merger of two building societies, or two car manufacturers or two bakeries.
- A VERTICAL MERGER is a merger between two firms at different production stages in the same industry. **Forward integration** involves a supplier merging with one of its buyers, such as a car manufacturer buying a car dealership, or a newspaper buying newsagents. **Backward integration** involves a purchaser buying one of its suppliers, such as a drinks manufacturer buying a bottling manufacturer, or a car manufacturer buying a tyre company.
- A CONGLOMERATE MERGER is the merging of two firms with no common interest. A tobacco company buying an insurance company, or a food company buying a clothing chain would be conglomerate mergers.

QUESTION 3 Place each of the following mergers into one of the three categories above:
(a) Nestlé with Rowntree Mackintosh (1988); (b) Ford with Jaguar cars (1989); (c) Lloyds Bank buying a number of estate agents (from the mid-1980s onwards); (d) British Aerospace with Austin Rover (1988); (e) British American Tobacco with Farmers Group (a US insurance group) (1988); (f) Hanson Trust with Consolidated Gold Fields (1989).

The reasons for growth

Profit maximising companies are motivated to grow in size for three main reasons.
- A larger company may be able to exploit economies of scale more fully. The merger of two medium sized car manufacturers, for instance, is likely to result in potential economies in all fields, from production to marketing to finance. Vertical and conglomerate mergers are less likely to yield scale economies because there are unlikely to be any technical economies. There may be some marketing economies and more likely there may be some financial economies.
- A larger company may be more able to control its markets. It may therefore reduce competition in the market place in order to be better able to exploit the market.
- A larger company may be able to reduce risk. Many conglomerate companies have grown for this reason. Some markets are fragile. They are subject to large changes in demand when economies go into boom or recession. A steel manufacturer, for instance, will do exceptionally well in a boom, but will be hard hit in a recession. So it might decide to **diversify** by buying a company with a product which does not have a cyclical demand pattern, like a supermarket chain. Other industries face a very uncertain future. It became fashionable in the 1970s and early 1980s for tobacco companies to buy anything which seemed to have a secure future, from grocery stores to insurance companies.

Reasons for amalgamation

Why do profit maximising companies choose to grow through amalgamation rather than through internal growth?

Cost One answer is that it is often cheaper to merge than to grow internally. For instance, a company may wish to expand and calculates that it will cost £50 million if it does so internally. It then looks to the stock markets and sees that a firm which already has the capabilities required is valued at £25 million. Even after paying the likely premium on the share price involved in takeover bids, it would be cheaper to buy the existing firm than undertake new investment. The ratio between the value of assets of a firm and its stock market price is called the **valuation ratio**. In theory, the larger the difference between asset values and stock market prices, the greater the incentive for firms to grow through takeovers rather than grow internally.

The position is often complicated because it is very difficult to place a value on the assets of a firm. In particular, it has become clear in recent years that intangible assets, particularly brands, can be more valuable than all the factories, offices, stock and other physical assets put together. A strong brand represents a guaranteed income for the foreseeable future. It is also a block on which to build. However large the company, it cannot guarantee to establish a new brand in the market place. Companies can invest money for years in the attempt to build a brand, and fail.

Asset stripping Not all companies in the merger market are necessarily interested in growing in size. Some companies specialise in asset stripping. The predator company will look for companies which have high asset values but low stock market prices. Companies being stalked may well have inefficient management who are unable to manage the company to earn the profit expected by shareholders and the stock market in general. Once a company is taken over, it will be broken up in the most profitable manner to the asset stripper. For instance, parts of the company may be sold as going concerns to other companies. Parts may be closed down. A factory site may be far more profitable sold off as building land than as a working factory. The predator company will then keep the rest to add to its portfolio of companies. A successful asset stripper will often aim to sell off some of the parts of the company for more than it paid for the whole. The part of the company which the predator might keep is then a useful addition to the profit made on the whole deal.

Rewards to management So far, it has been assumed that companies are motivated to grow because of profit. But there is much evidence to suggest that profits of merged companies are often no more and sometimes less than the combined profits of the two individual firms would have been. **Managerial and behavioural theories** of the firm (☞ units 24 and 32) can explain this by pointing out that the goal of a firm is not necessarily to maximise profit. The managers of the firm have a vested interest in seeing a firm grow because their rewards (their pay, bonuses, company cars, prestige and influence) tend to increase with the size of the firm. The managing director of a company which doubles its size overnight is likely to receive a substantial pay rise in the not-too-

distant future.

Moreover, the financial markets have a strong incentive to encourage takeovers and mergers. Banks, merchant banks and other financial institutions can make very large profits from organising takeovers.

QUESTION 4 In August 1989, Hanson Trust purchased Consolidated Gold Fields (ConsGold) for £3.3 billion. By the end of the year, the company had raised at least £1.03 billion in sales of parts of ConsGold including:
- ARC America, the US part of the quarry and stonecrushing products group, for £417 million;
- 30 per cent of Gold Fields of South Africa to the Rembrandt tobacco/mining/banking group for £368 million;
- the other 8 per cent of its stake in Gold Fields of South Africa and the rest of ConsGold South African mining interests for £240 million.

The ARC group in Britain is valued at between £1.2 billion and £1.8 billion. It is well placed to benefit from Britain's road modernisation programme and Hanson may well choose to keep it rather than sell it.
(a) Suggest why Hanson Trust purchased ConsGold.
(b) Who might benefit and who might lose as a result of the takeover?

Mergers and efficiency

There is much controversy as to whether mergers increase economic efficiency. Productive efficiency will increase if average costs of production after the merger fall because of economies of scale. Allocative efficiency will increase if the merged company provides a wider range of goods, better quality products, etc.

On the other hand, mergers tend to reduce competition in the market. The loss of efficiency which might arise was discussed in detail in unit 37.

Moreover, asset stripping is very controversial. Supporters of this view argue that the asset stripper performs a useful economic function. The value to society of a company can be calculated by the sum of its component parts. If greater profit can be made by demolishing a factory, sacking the workforce and selling the land for shops, houses or offices than by keeping the factory operational, then the asset stripper is performing a useful social role by doing so. The asset stripper is reallocating resources according to the signals of the market. The problem is that market prices may not be an accurate reflection of true social value. Short run profit maximisation by one company may well not lead to an economically efficient outcome for society.

Key terms

Merger, amalgamation, integration or takeover - the joining together of two or more firms under common ownership.
Horizontal merger or integration - a merger between two firms in the same industry at the same stage of production.

Vertical merger or integration - a merger between two firms at different production stages in the same industry.
Conglomerate merger - a merger between two firms producing unrelated products.

Applied economics

Mergers legislation

The legislative background

The 1948 Monopolies Act did not cover merger activity. However, it came to be recognised that monopolies against the public interest could be created by merger activity. The Monopolies and Mergers Act (1965) gave the Monopolies and Mergers Commission the duty to investigate mergers referred to it by the Secretary of State for Trade and Industry. It had to produce a report with recommendations within 6 months. The Secretary of State could then accept or reject the advice of the Commission. Currently the Secretary of State can refer any merger where the assets acquired are more than £30 million. In 1984, the government stated that the main consideration for referral would be whether the merger would potentially affect competition.

Since 1965, only a minute fraction of all UK mergers have been referred to the Monopolies and Mergers Commission. In 1988, for instance, only 14 out of 306 qualifying mergers were referred. The 306 did not include the many mergers which fell below the £30 million threshold.

The effectiveness of mergers control

Mergers have in part been responsible for the growing concentration of British industry. It is argued (☞ unit 39) that the merger boom which has been a feature of the UK economy since the 1960s was, at least to start with, a response to the abolition of restrictive trade practices by the 1956 Act. Unable to collude together to rig the market in their favour, firms resorted to taking over other firms to gain sufficient control of the market to gain monopoly profits.

Merger policy in the UK has done little to prevent this increasing concentration. Many have argued that:
■ too few cases are referred to the Monopolies and Mergers Commission;
■ there is little rationale behind the choice of which potential mergers are referred;

■ this lottery is made worse by the inconsistency of the stance taken by a Monopolies and Mergers Commission staffed by different people at different times.

Critics would argue that a much tougher line needs to be taken. In particular, companies should need to prove more than just that a merger would not be against the public interest. Merging companies should be forced to prove that the merger is likely to be in the public interest.

Mergers and economic efficiency

Evidence suggests [see, for instance, G Meekes (1977) or K G Cowling (1980)] that most mergers do not lead to any efficiency gains. Many in fact lead to losses of economic efficiency. There are a number of ways in which this could be measured.
■ Profits of the combined company decline from what they might otherwise have been. This is often anticipated in the stock market where the share price of a company taking over another falls when the takeover is announced.
■ Turnover falls. Mergers may well lead to 'rationalisation' of plant and other facilities. In the process the capacity of the firm falls, leading to a loss of turnover. This destruction of capacity may not be compensated for by an increase in capacity elsewhere in the economy, pushing the production possibility frontier backwards towards the origin.
■ Employment falls. Rationalisation often involves reducing the workforce. These workers may then be added to a pool of long term unemployed people.

If mergers fail to improve efficiency, why has the UK been gripped by merger mania in recent years? Shareholders, workers and consumers may be left with a welfare loss following a merger. But according to managerial theories of the firm, they are not in control of companies. It is managers who control industry and it is managers who stand most to gain from takeovers. Their salaries are likely to increase even if the new combined company is less efficient than the two former companies. Moreover, the whole process is encouraged by the City which earns fat fees from mergers. The bigger the merger, the fatter the fee paid. In this view, top managers and the City gain whilst ordinary people, whether they be workers, consumers or shareholders, lose.

BRISTOL BUS MERGER MAY HAVE TO BE REVERSED

A TAKE OVER agreed by two Bristol bus companies last year may have to be reversed after a Monopolies and Mergers Commission report that it may be expected to act against the public interest.

The takeover took place in April 1988 when Badgerline, which operates near Bristol and runs services into the city centre, bought Midland Red West, in a deal worth £10.5m.

Midland Red West operates services through western parts of the Midlands. As a result of its own acquisition of the Bristol company, City Line, in 1987, Midland Red West also operates services in Bristol.

The commission said in its report published yesterday that there had been no material loss of competition in commercial services as a result of the Badgerline takeover. It identified serious 'detriments' to competition in the provision of contract services.

Those are services companies consider insufficiently profitable to operate, but which local councils subsidise and put out to tender.

The first 'detriment,' the commission said, was the expectation of an increase in the anti-competitive practice whereby Badgerline dropped some commercial services, and, if it failed to win the tendered contracts for the subsidised services replacing them, started up again in opposition to the successful candidate.

The second was the loss of City Line as an independent competitor for the county of Avon's contract services. That would weaken competition tendering and reduce Avon's ability to support socially necessary bus services.

The commission said Sir Gorden Borrie, director general of Fair Trading, should seek undertakings from Badgerline on its behaviour over Avon's contract services.

Source: *Financial Times*, 9.3.1989.

1. **Briefly outline the sequence of takeovers which led to the Monopolies and Mergers Commission investigation.**
2. **Why might the takeover described in the data 'have to be reversed'?**

Price fixing and collusion

Summary

1. Collusion enables individual producers to share monopoly profits with other producers.
2. Cartels may collapse. Individual members have an incentive to cheat on the agreement. Non-cartel members may increase their market share at the expense of cartel members.
3. Restrictive trade practices are likely to lead to a loss of economic efficiency.

Collusion

During the 19th century and for most of the 20th century, British industry was dominated by collective agreements. Firms COLLUDED to restrict competition. By colluding, firms could gain some monopoly power over their markets. As a result, they became price-makers rather than price-takers.

Consider Table 39.1. It shows the cost and revenues for an industry. If the market were perfectly competitive, then long run output would be 6 million units. This is because no firm in the industry could earn abnormal profit. If it did, competitor firms would be attracted into the industry, increasing supply and driving down prices and profits until abnormal profit were eliminated.

However, individual firms could earn abnormal profit if they combined together to force up price, restrict output and keep potential competitors out of the industry. The profit maximising level of output for the industry as a whole is 3 million units. If each firm in the industry agreed to half its current output, £9 million of abnormal profit could be shared between the colluding firms.

The problems facing cartels

A **cartel** is a group of producers which has agreed to restrict competition in the market. Possibly the most famous cartel today is OPEC, the Organisation of Petroleum Exporting Countries. Restricting competition is not necessarily easy.

■ An agreement has to be reached. This is likely to be easiest in oligopolistic industries where only a few firms dominate the market: the larger the number of firms, the greater the possibility that at least one key participant will refuse to collude. It is also likely to be easiest in stable mature industries where no single firm has recently been able to gain advantage by pursuing aggressive competitive strategies. For instance, collusion is far more likely in a mature industry like steel manufacturing or cement making than in a rapidly changing industry like the computer industry.

■ Cheating has to be prevented. Once an agreement is made and profitability in the industry is raised, it would pay an individual firm to cheat so long as no other firms do the same. For instance, it would pay a small cartel producer with 10 per cent of the market to expand production to 12 per cent by slightly undercutting the cartel price. The profit it would lose by the small cut in price on the 10 per cent is more than offset by the gain in profit on the sale of the extra 2 per cent. However, if every producer does this, the market price will quickly fall to the free market level and all firms will lose the privilege of earning abnormal profit.

■ Potential competition must be restricted. Abnormal profits will encourage not only existing firms in the industry to expand output but also new firms to enter the industry. Firms already in the industry which don't join the cartel may be happy to follow the policies of the cartel in order to earn abnormal profits themselves. To prevent this, cartel firms could agree to drive other firms which compete too aggressively out of the market. Cartel firms could also agree to increase barriers to entry to the industry.

Table 39.1

Million units			£ millions
Output	Average revenue	Average cost (including normal profit)	Total abnormal profit
(a)	(b)	(c)	(b - c) x a
1	10	5	5
2	9	5	8
3	8	5	9
4	7	5	8
5	6	5	5
6	5	5	0

QUESTION 1 A firm in perfect competition joins a cartel. The cartel succeeds in doubling the market price but all members of the cartel have to reduce output by 20 per cent.

(a) Draw a diagram for an individual firm in perfect competition marking on it the long run equilibrium output of the firm.
(b) Show what happens to the firm's equilibrium output and price after it has joined the cartel.
(c) Explain why the firm benefits from the cartel.

QUESTION 2 Between 1962 and 1989, the International Coffee Agreement (ICA) created a cartel in the international coffee industry. Prices were kept artificially high as individual countries were given quotas restricting their sales of coffee onto world markets. The agreement broke down in 1989 because of the opposition of Brazil and Columbia. Brazil had seen its world market share decline from 40 per cent in 1962 to 24 per cent in 1988 as less efficient producers, particularly African countries, entered the market or increased production as a result of high prices. Prices during 1989 dropped by 50 per cent with Brazil vowing to drive high cost producers out of the market.

(a) Suggest reasons why Brazil should have taken steps to break up the ICA.
(b) What problems about cartels does the breakdown of the ICA illustrate?

Restrictive trade practices and efficiency

RESTRICTIVE TRADE PRACTICES are strategies used by producers to restrict competition in the market. Cartels use them to enforce their collective agreements and to deter competitors. Individual firms use them to establish or reinforce monopoly positions. A wide variety of practices could have been and have been used, including minimum prices, market sharing agreements, resale price maintenance, refusal to supply firms which stock competitors' products, discriminatory pricing and sharing information. Examples are given in the applied section below.

The arguments for and against the restriction of competition have already been given in units 33,34,37 and 38. Restrictive trade practices tend to raise price and reduce output. There is therefore a loss of economic efficiency. There is also a redistribution of income from consumers to shareholders of companies because of abnormal profit. Choice may also be restricted. On the other hand, restrictive trade practices may enable companies to earn sufficient profit to engage in research and development to the benefit of consumers. They may also encourage potential competitors to bring new products to the market which are so attractive that the monopoly of an established producer is competed away.

QUESTION 3 In 1989, the European Commission forced seven of Europe's largest industrial gas suppliers to scrap restrictive sales agreements. The companies were accused of abusing their dominant market position by obliging customers to buy exclusively from them over fixed periods, use their storage equipment, promise not to resell their gases, and provide details of competitors offering lower prices. They had set up joint subsidiaries to squeeze out competition in France, Belgium, Luxembourg, the Netherlands and West Germany. Some companies had also insisted on compulsory advance cash deposits and had obscurely defined price rises.

Explain how each of the restrictive practices mentioned in the data could be used by gas suppliers to increase their profitability.

Key terms

Collusion - collective agreements between producers which restrict competition.
Restrictive trade practices - strategies used by producers to restrict competition in the market.

Applied economics

Restrictive trade practices - the legislative background

The Monopolies Commission, set up in 1948, quickly found that British industry was riddled with restrictive trade practices. In 1955 the Commission published a report on collective discrimination which detailed many such practices. The government of the day responded by passing the Restrictive Trade Practices Act in 1956.

The 1948 Monopolies Act made the fundamental assumption that monopolies were against the public interest only if this could be proved by the state. The 1956 Act took the opposite route. Restrictive trade practices would be illegal unless the companies involved could prove that the practices were in the public interest.

A court of law, the Restrictive Practices Court, was established. All firms which engaged in restrictive practices had to register these with the Registrar of Restrictive Trading Agreements. The agreements would then be brought before the Court which would either uphold them or order their abandonment.

The Act laid down eight 'gateways' through which companies could attempt to uphold their restrictive practices. Companies had to show the agreement was necessary:

- to protect the public against injury;
- because its abandonment would deny to the public specific and substantial benefits;
- to counter anti-competitive practices by other producers;
- to negotiate 'fair terms' with others;
- because otherwise there would be 'serious and persistent' effects on unemployment;
- to prevent a fall in exports;
- to uphold another agreement accepted by the Court.

Finally, an agreement would be allowed if it was not anti-competitive.

Even if the agreement met one of these criteria, then it would still be declared illegal (or 'struck down') if it was not shown that the benefits to the public outweighed the costs.

Subsequent acts widened the net of the 1956 Act. In 1964, the Resale Prices Act 1964 made it illegal for firms to enforce resale price maintenance (RPM) unless it could be shown to be in the public interest. RPM was a practice whereby a manufacturer could force a retailer to sell its product at a particular price, usually a minimum price. It meant that goods such as television sets or cigarettes from one manufacturer were sold at identical prices in all shops in the UK. Information agreements, where firms agreed to circulate price lists or market share figures amongst themselves, were made illegal in 1968. The 1976 Restrictive Practices Act included service industries as well as goods industries. The 1980 Competition Act gave powers to the Monopolies and Mergers Commission to investigate uncompetitive practices in monopoly situations.

Articles 85 and 86 of the Treaty of Rome cover restrictive practices. Price-fixing and market-sharing agreements are illegal unless it can be proved that they are of benefit to the public. The European Commission is responsible for investigating illegal Community-wide practices.

Three examples of restrictive trade practices

In many industries, the 1956 Restrictive Trade Practices Act brought to an end a tradition of collusive agreements. But there is evidence to suggest that they continued, illegally, in the the UK building trade. For instance, in February 1989 the Office of Fair Trading took four ready-mixed concrete companies to the Court, alleging that the companies concluded price-fixing and market-sharing agreements in parts of Oxfordshire during 1983 and 1984. This was after the Office of Fair Trading had uncovered 146 price fixing

and market-sharing agreements involving a large part of the ready-mixed concrete industry in the mid-1970s.

The book trade is covered by one of the few restrictive practices which the Restrictive Trade Practices Court upheld (i.e. made legal). Under the Net Book Agreement, publishers are allowed to set a minimum price for which a book may be sold. In effect, the prices of most books are the same whether bought in a small local bookseller's, a supermarket or a large book chain. Publishers and small booksellers are, for the most part, in favour of the agreement. They argue that without the agreement consumers would buy from the cheapest source. These would be large book chains like W H Smith, or non-traditional booksellers like supermarkets or garage shops which have the financial power to buy cheaply in bulk. The small local bookseller would be forced out of business and many communities would be left without a bookshop. Consumers would also suffer from a smaller choice of books. Publishers would concentrate on producing fewer books which would be marketed more heavily, for instance, by cutting their price. Opponents of the agreement argue that the small local bookseller will survive because most books are bought on impulse or as a present and convenience of purchase is therefore very important. Equally, the number of books sold will increase if the prices of some books are cut because the demand curve for books is downward sloping.

At an EC level, the European Commission investigated the plastics and chemical industries throughout the 1980s. In 1986, 15 companies, including ICI, were fined for price-fixing and market-sharing in polypropylene between 1977 and 1983. Over that period, there was substantial oversupply in the industry and it seemed that the companies involved formed a cartel to prevent a price war which would have resulted in huge losses and some firms leaving the market.

The effectiveness of UK policy

There is general agreement that restrictive practices legislation has been effective in changing the climate of competition in the UK. Before 1956, most of manufacturing and much of the service sector contained restrictive practice agreements which operated to the advantage of the producer and to the detriment of the consumer. Since 1956, about 5 000 agreements have been registered with the Court. These represent a fraction of the number of agreements that were in operation. Almost all of the 5 000 were abandoned voluntarily before being brought before the Court.

However, the Office of Fair Trading and the European Commission continue to unearth agreements made in secret. Illegal restrictive trade practices are still present within some sectors of the economy.

Perhaps more importantly, there is much evidence to suggest that the merger boom in UK industry which started in the 1960s is a direct response to restrictive practices legislation. After 1956, firms could not collude to give themselves monopoly profits. There followed a period of intense competition. Some companies went out of business. Others were taken over. The result was increased concentration ratios throughout much of British industry. This process continued to the point where industry, as a whole, was able once again to enjoy the level of monopoly profits it earned before the abolition of restrictive agreements. For instance, P E Hart and R Clarke (1980 and 1984) estimated the average three firm concentration ratio in a sample of 42 industries increased from 29 per cent in 1951 to 32 per cent in 1958 but jumped to 41 per cent in 1968. Since then there has been little change. If this is true, restrictive practices legislation will have had little impact on efficiency in UK industry because collusion has been replaced by monopoly.

Data question

BLACK & DECKER REJECTS RULING

By Christopher Parkes, Consumer Industries Editor

Black & Decker, the power-tool maker, has refused to bow to a ruling from the Office of Fair Trading that its policy of cutting off supplies to retailers which sell its products at reduced prices is anti-competitive.

The issue is now likely to be taken up by the Monopolies and Mergers Commission, which will judge whether Black & Decker's long-established practice is against the public interest. Had the company pledged to scrap its policy, the matter would have been closed without referral to the Monopolies Commission.

The OFT gave its ruling on a sample charge, brought by Woolworth Holdings, parent of B & Q, Britain's largest do-it-yourself retailer. Black & Decker had threatened to stop supplies of Workmate benches offered at promotional prices, and of heat guns, which, it claimed, were being sold as 'loss-leaders' for £17.95 against the £19.95 price recommended by the manufacturer.

Retailers have been at odds for years with their biggest supplier of power-tools. They said yesterday that there had been a noticeable 'softening' of Black & Decker's policy during the period of the investigation, starting last September.

The OFT discovered in investigating that eight retailers had either been threatened with a cut in supplies or had experienced a cut. The most significant, according to Black & Decker, concerned the Argos catalogue shop chain, owned by BAT Industries. Its 1987 January catalogues included 11 alleged loss-leaders, which aroused protests from other retailers who complained.

Black & Decker withheld supplies and only started shipping to Argos again when they raised prices in May.

The OFT said yesterday that while it was permissible under the Resale Prices Act for a manufacturer to refuse to supply a retailer who sold its products as loss-leaders, this could be anti-competitive under the Competition Act when applied by a company with Black & Decker's market share.

Last year, the US-based group accounted for 66 per cent of the £114m British market for power-tools and work-benches.

It said yesterday it would welcome an opportunity to show the Monopolies Commission that its policy worked in consumers' interests.

The company told the OFT in evidence that its policy was aimed at ensuring fair competition between retailers, by applying standard terms to all.

It argued that widespread price-cutting among the multiple chains would drive smaller retailers out of the power-tool business, reduce the number of service points and lead ultimately to higher prices.

However, the OFT did not accept that competition was increased by having a larger number of retailers stocking Black & Decker products when those retailers are not free to compete on price.

It also concluded that the effect of the policy was that average prices were higher than they would otherwise be.

Source: *Financial Times*, 9.3.89.

1. Describe the 'anti-competitive' practices of Black & Decker.
2. Why might these practices be (a) harmful and (b) beneficial to the interests of consumers and retailers?

Summary

1. Consumer sovereignty exists when consumer choices determine the allocation of resources in the economy.
2. Consumer sovereignty can only fully exist if there is perfect information in the market.
3. Consumers are less likely to possess perfect information if they make infrequent purchases, if goods are technically complex, if time and risk are elements of the purchase and if the product is heavily advertised.
4. Advertising can be informative or persuasive. The former increases knowledge in the market. The latter is intended to manipulate consumer preferences.
5. Governments can increase consumer sovereignty by passing laws and increasing the availability of information in the market.

Consumer sovereignty

CONSUMER SOVEREIGNTY exists when resources are allocated according to the wishes of consumers (☞ unit 34). This will occur in a perfectly free market. Consumer spending is comparable to votes in an election. The companies which receive the most votes will be able to purchase the factors of production needed to produce the goods demanded by consumers. Firms which receive no votes will go out of business.

QUESTION 1 Many consumers are prepared to use their purchasing power to campaign for a cleaner environment, according to a survey by Leo Burnett, the advertising agency.

The survey of 2,000 adults showed that 72 per cent believed individuals can make a difference to environmental problems while 70 per cent said they would discriminate in favour of 'green' products.

A total of 42 per cent were prepared to pay a premium for 'environmentally friendly' goods whilst 20 per cent were willing to boycott products they believed to be environmentally harmful, and 40 per cent were prepared to boycott products tested on animals.

Asked which retailers were actively helping to protect the environment, 32 per cent said The Body Shop, 25 per cent J Sainsbury and 25 per cent Boots The Chemists.

Source: *Financial Times*, 15.11.1989.

(a) How can consumers 'campaign for a cleaner environment'?
(b) How does this illustrate the concept of consumer sovereignty?

Perfect information

Total consumer sovereignty only exists if there is perfect knowledge or perfect information in the market place (☞ unit 25). If consumers are to allocate their resources in a way which will maximise their utility, they need to know about the products they are buying. In many cases, consumers are well placed to make consumption decisions. For instance, a consumer is likely to be the best judge of whether to buy bananas or apples. However, there are many markets where consumers have less than perfect knowledge.

In many markets, like those for cars, television sets or solicitors, consumers make infrequent purchases. If they buy, and find for whatever reason that they don't like the product, then it is very expensive to make a fresh choice. When they come to replace an item the product range may have changed completely. This is different from markets like food where consumers are making frequent purchases. In the food market, consumers can experiment at little cost and find the products they prefer. So in general, the less frequent the purchase, the less likely it is that consumers will have built up sufficient knowledge of the product to make a optimal choice.

Consumers may not be capable of making rational choices because of the technical nature of the product. For instance, consumers for the most part are unable to tell which make of freezer has the best insulation, which television set has the most durable components, or which solicitor might do the best conveyancing job on a house purchase.

Time and risk too pose problems. Consumers often find it difficult to project forward. Healthy 25 year olds may see little point in providing for health care or paying into a pension scheme. Yet when they have a serious accident or come to retire they may think that their utility would have been greater over time if they had made different spending decisions.

There are other reasons why consumers are sometimes not the best judge of what they should buy. Some goods, such as drugs (including alcohol and tobacco), are addictive, so the consumer is unable to make a rational choice about present and future consumption. Often these same goods also create externalities, such as increased crime or road accidents, not to mention the cost of medical treatment. Society, through government, may choose to limit or ban the sale of these goods because it does not wish to pay the cost of the externality.

Finally, consumer choices are deliberately manipulated by producers through advertising and other forms of marketing.

Informative and persuasive advertising

Between 1 and 2 per cent of UK national income is spent each year on advertising. On some products, such as some brands of soap powder, 25 per cent of the cost to the consumer is advertising cost. Advertising is a cost to the producer (a cost which of course will ultimately be borne by the consumer). Therefore producers must be convinced that advertising increases demand for their products if such large sums are spent on advertising each year.

Neo-classical economic theory predicts that advertising could be beneficial for a firm. Figure 40.1 shows the cost and revenue curves for a profit maximising monopolist. Before advertising, it faces a demand or average revenue curve of AR_1 and average and marginal cost curves of AC_1 and MC. A successful advertising campaign will push the firm's demand curve to the right to AR_2. The advertising campaign will cost money. It is debatable as to whether advertising is a fixed or variable cost, but here we will assume that it is a fixed cost. Hence the marginal cost curve will stay the same but average total cost will rise to AC_2. (The analysis is fundamentally no different if advertising is treated as a variable cost which consequently raises marginal cost too.) It can be seen that monopoly profits rise from ABCD to EFGH. The extra revenue generated as a result of the advertising campaign has been greater than the cost of the advertising campaign and the extra costs of production.

Two types of advertising can be distinguished. INFORMATIVE ADVERTISING is advertising which increases consumer knowledge about a product. Small ads in local newspapers, for instance, inform potential buyers that a product is for sale. Consumers may need to be made aware that a new product has come onto the

QUESTION 2

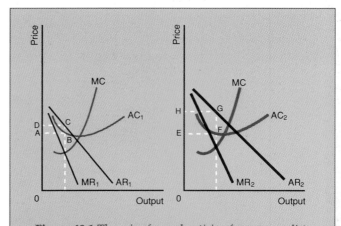

Why might consumers find it difficult to make rational choices about each of these products?

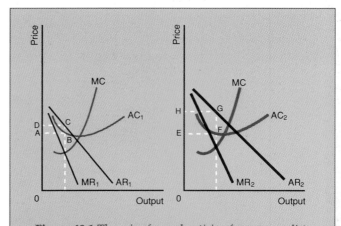

Figure 40.1 *The gains from advertising for a monopolist An advertising campaign which increases demand will increase abnormal profit from ABCD to EFGH despite an increase in average costs.*

market through a national advertising campaign. Firms may wish to inform consumers in local telephone directories that they supply services. In general, economists would argue that this type of advertising increases consumer sovereignty because it enables consumers to make a more rational choice of what to buy. It gives them more information about what is available in the market place.

PERSUASIVE ADVERTISING is advertising intended to manipulate consumer preferences. Most television advertisements or large advertisements in magazines and newspapers are persuasive. These advertisements may contain some information, but the main aim is to persuade consumers that a particular product is more desirable than competitors' products. At best, persuasive advertising may tip the balance for a consumer who is undecided between alternative products. At worst, persuasive advertising makes consumers buy products they would otherwise not have bought.

Government policy

It is difficult to assess the extent to which consumer sovereignty exists in a modern industrialised economy. J K Galbraith, in his book *The New Industrial State*, argued that consumer sovereignty was largely lacking in markets dominated by oligopolistic and monopoly industries (i.e. most of manufacturing industry and much of the service industry). Producers were able through advertising and promotion to channel consumer spending. Of course consumers won't buy just any product because it is advertised. But they will buy product X rather than product Y if the producer can find the right combination of jingle, story, sex symbol or other image to associate with the product.

On the other hand free market economists argue that even if consumer knowledge is imperfect, the alternatives which involve the state deciding what is desirable or undesirable leads to a far less efficient allocation of resources.

Governments have a wide range of choice of policies to correct possible market failure arising from imperfect consumer knowledge.

Governments can try to prevent sellers from misinforming the consumer. Much of consumer protection legislation is designed to protect the consumer from unfair practices on the part of sellers. For instance, the Trade Descriptions Act 1968 made it illegal for retailers to sell goods with misleading descriptions. Government can also encourage or force sellers to provide information which they might otherwise prefer not to give. Contents of manufactured food, or 'best before' dates are two such examples.

The government can help consumers fight more effectively for redress against often better financed sellers. Making it cheaper to take a firm to court, for instance, through a Small Claims Court system, makes consumers far more powerful.

The government can also provide information itself to the consumer, or encourage independent bodies to do so. Bodies such as the British Standards Institute and local Trading Standards Departments help in this area.

More controversial are bans on advertising. Alcohol and tobacco advertising is already limited in the UK. It would be possible to introduce much wider controls on advertising, particularly to control persuasive advertising. However, governments have chosen not to, partly because of a scepticism (not shared by industry) about the effectiveness of such advertising. Moreover, advertising creates tax revenue and pays for commodities such as television services which otherwise might have to be paid for by government or by consumers. The consumer lobby

QUESTION 3

DOUBLE GLAZING UNIT 1125 m/m x 840 m/m. Unused. Incorrect size ordered, £20 ono. Tel. Rainford 3129.
M & S CROCKERY Autumn leaves pattern, 1 teapot, 6 dinner plates. £15. Tel. 526 2828.
FOUR YELLOW PLEATED/FRINGED wall light shades & matching 12" shade £8. Tel. 531 8799 after 6.
SILVER CROSS hard bodied pram includes sun canopy, fly net and shopping tray, immaculate £25.

BRASS CANOPY for fireplace, size 20 ins deep x 30 ins wide, price £5 ono. Tel. Parbold 2749.
JUST RIGHT for this cold weather, lovely teddy-bear fur coat shawl collar, cuffs, full length, size 18, colour brown. Tel. 02576/2749 £15 ono.
MOTHERCARE FIREGUARD can be extended, £15. Tel. 574497.
BRITAX BABYSURE car seat, birth to 20lbs, reclines and fits front or rear seatbelts, good condition, easy release buckle £20. Tel.

To what extent do these advertisements increase consumer sovereignty?

is also far weaker than industrial lobbies because consumers are fragmented whilst large firms may spend considerable sums of money persuading government of their case. As Galbraith pointed out, governments can be 'captured' by industry and manipulated to serve the interests of business against the interests of the consumer.

Ultimately it may be felt that consumers are not in the best position to decide how resources should be allocated and that collective provision is necessary. Health care, education and pension provision are some of the markets where governments have decided that market failure cannot be corrected by the market mechanism. This will be explored in more detail in unit 44.

Key terms

Consumer sovereignty - exists when the economic system permits resources to be allocated according to the wishes of consumers.
Informative advertising - advertising which increases consumer knowledge about a product.
Persuasive advertising - advertising intended to manipulate consumer preferences.

QUESTION 4

Teach her a lesson. Cut out the coupon.

Teaching children about smoking isn't easy. You don't need us to tell you that.

However, our free 'Smoking and Pollution' pack should make for interesting lessons.

It's aimed at eleven to twelve year old children. It looks into the harmful effects of smoking, not just to individuals but to the environment as well.

And it comes in the form of three booklets. One for teachers, one for pupils, and one for parents.

How many 'Smoking and Pollution' packs would you like?

To what extent does this advertisement extend or limit consumer sovereignty?

Applied economics

Advertising in the UK

Advertising is big business in the UK. As Figures 40.2 and 40.3 show, advertising expenditure was over £7.5 billion in 1989, representing 1.75 per cent of GDP. It represents spending of approximately £130 per head, or £520 for a family of four per year. If advertising were banned, consumers would have to pay for commercial television and they would have to pay higher prices for newspapers and magazines. Even so, the advertising industry uses up a significant proportion of resources in the economy, resources which have an opportunity cost.

Producers use advertising because they know that it influences consumer preferences. For instance, the Guardian Royal Exchange ran an advertising campaign in the financial press in 1989 which boasted of its successes in its television campaigns. It claimed: 'Freedom is the UK's leading brand of universal life insurance'. In the three months that followed national

TV advertising, sales doubled year on year. Mars, when it launched Ice Cream Mars, spent £500 000 on television and press advertising in addition to monies spent on a nationwide poster campaign. This was considered a very modest sum to spend on launching a new product. The drinks industry in the UK spends over £200 million on advertising and a top beer brand, like Carling Black Label, is likely to be supported by advertising of over £5 million a year. Pedigree, the top pet food manufacturer in the UK, spent over £30 million in 1989 advertising its products.

The advertising industry is subject to controls. The Advertising Standards Authority (ASA), an 'independent' body paid for by the advertising industry, can request companies to halt particular advertising campaigns if they are not 'legal, decent, honest and truthful'. However, there is so much room for disagreement about what, for instance, might be

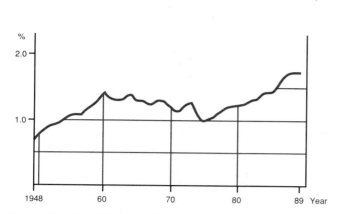

Source: *The Advertising Association.*
Figure 40.2 *Advertising expenditure as % of GDP at factor cost.*

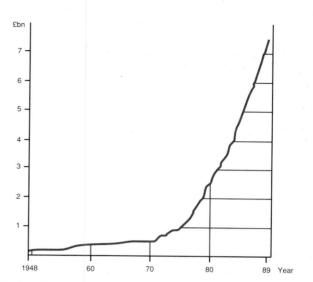

Source: *The Advertising Association.*
Figure 40.3 *Advertising expenditure*

meant by 'truthful' that in practice the ASA is of marginal importance in the control of advertising.

Of more significance for the advertising industry is the growing call worldwide for controls or bans on advertising of certain products. All countries in the European Community, for instance, already ban tobacco advertisements on television and in 1990 Brussels issued a draft directive which would restrict tobacco advertising on posters, in newspapers and in magazines. The advertising community fear that if this directive is ratified, it will be followed by severe restrictions on the advertising of goods ranging from alcohol, to children's toys to over-the-counter pharmaceutical products such as branded aspirin.

In California, a state referendum in November 1988 raised the tax on a packet of cigarettes from 10 cents to 35 cents with the stipulation that part of the revenue raised should be used to educate the public on the dangers of smoking. The Tobacco Institute, the Washington lobbying group for the tobacco industry, commented that: 'California is making smokers pay for their own harassment'. In general, however, expenditure on anti-smoking or anti-drinking campaigns is insignificant in comparison with the advertising expenditures of the tobacco and drinks industries.

There is a growing recognition in the UK that advertising can be harmful to the public interest because it promotes harmful products. But the advertising lobby is so strong politically that we are unlikely to see greater controls on alcohol and tobacco advertising in the UK in the foreseeable future.

Data question

TOBACCO AND THE ROLE OF ADVERTISING IN A MATURE MARKET

From Mr A.D.C. Turner.
Sir, Lucy Kellaway, in her article ('Fighting to the last gasp', February 8) about tobacco advertising ban proposals emanating from Brussels, asks why, if there is no link between advertising and consumption of tobacco, would the tobacco industry wish to advertise?

The answer remains as it has been over many years of a declining UK market; namely that the 300 brands of cigarettes currently on sale must advertise to retain, or gain, market share. A total ban would simply see an immediate freezing of the brand share picture with total consumption not necessarily being related.

European Commission officials appear to have little or no understanding of the role of advertising as it pertains to a mature product category.
A.D.C. Turner,
Deputy Chief Executive,
Tobacco Advisory Council,
Glen House, Stag Place , SW1.

Source: *Financial Times*, 13.2.1990.

1. **Explain, with the help of a diagram, the relationship between advertising and the total consumption of cigarettes according to Mr Turner.**
2. **Why do tobacco companies advertise?**
3. **Should the European Community introduce much tighter controls on tobacco advertising?**

Summary

1. Two types of equity or fairness can be distinguished - horizontal equity and vertical equity.
2. A Lorenz curve can be used to show the degree of inequality in income in society.
3. Absolute poverty occurs when human beings are unable to consume sufficient necessities for survival. Relative poverty occurs when people are poor relative to the rest of society.
4. A different distribution of income and wealth is likely to result if a perfectly competitive market becomes imperfectly competitive.
5. There can be a conflict between efficiency and equity, although redistributive government policies need not necessarily result in greater inefficiency.

Horizontal and vertical equity

If all markets in an economy were perfectly competitive, production would be Pareto efficient (i.e. it will not be possible to make one person better off without making another person worse off ☞ units 33 and 34). However, efficiency is different from EQUITY or fairness. The market mechanism may allocate resources efficiently but not necessarily equitably. To understand why, it is necessary to define equity.

Horizontal equity HORIZONTAL EQUITY is the identical treatment of identical individuals. Inequitable treatment can occur in a number of different situations in our society today. An Asian applicant for a job may be turned down in preference to a white applicant even though they are the same in all other respects. A woman may apply to a bank for a business loan and be refused when a male applicant for exactly the same project may have been successful. A 55 year old may be refused a job in preference to a 25 year old despite identical employment characteristics. An 18 year old may gain a place at university in preference to another solely because her father is much richer.

Vertical equity Everybody is different, from the colour of their hair to the size of their toes and from their intellectual capacities to their social background. VERTICAL EQUITY is the different treatment of people with different characteristics in order to promote greater equity. For instance, if equity were defined in terms of equality, vertical equity would imply that everybody should have the opportunity to receive the same standard of education and the same standard of health care whatever their job, race, income or social background.

Equity and equality

Equity or fairness is a different concept from equality. There can be an equitable distribution of resources in the economy (in the sense of horizontal or vertical equity) without there necessarily being an equal distribution of resources. However, many economists do use degrees of equality or inequality as a criterion to judge the extent to which equity exists in an economy.

One common way of displaying inequalities in income

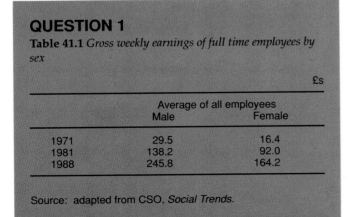

QUESTION 1

Table 41.1 *Gross weekly earnings of full time employees by sex*

£s

	Average of all employees	
	Male	Female
1971	29.5	16.4
1981	138.2	92.0
1988	245.8	164.2

Source: adapted from CSO, *Social Trends.*

(a) To what extent has horizontal equity between males and females increased over time in the UK?
(b) Suggest reasons why there has been this change.
(c) To what extent do you think this trend is likely to continue in the future?

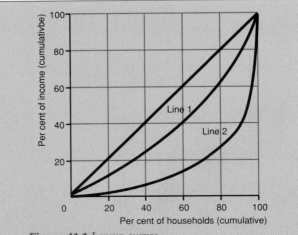

Figure 41.1 *Lorenz curves*
A Lorenz curve shows the degree of inequality of income in a society. The farther from the 45° line is the curve, the greater the degree of inequality.

is to use a LORENZ CURVE. On the horizontal axis in Figure 41.1, the cumulative number of households is plotted, whilst the vertical axis shows cumulative income. The straight 45° line shows a position of total equality. For instance, the line shows that the bottom 20 per cent of households receive 20 per cent of total income whilst the bottom 80 per cent of households receive 80 per cent of income. Hence, each 1 per cent of households receives 1 per cent of income and there is complete equality of income.

Line 1 shows an income distribution which is relatively equal. The bottom 20 per cent of households receive 10 per cent of income. This means that they receive half the average income. The top 10 per cent of households (between 90 and 100 on the horizontal axis) receive 20 per cent of income (from 80 to 100 on the vertical axis). So they receive twice the average income.

Line 2 shows a very unequal society. The bottom 50 per cent of the population receive only 10 per cent of income. Therefore half of all households receive one-fifth (10 ÷ 50) of average income. The top 10 per cent of income earners on the other hand earn 60 per cent of all income (from 40 to 100 on the vertical axis). That means the top 10 per cent earn 6 times the average income.

These two examples taken together show that the farther the Lorenz curve is from the 45° line, the greater the income inequality in society.

Inequality is sometimes discussed in terms of ABSOLUTE and RELATIVE POVERTY. Absolute poverty occurs when human beings are not able to consume sufficient **necessities** to maintain life. Human beings who are homeless or malnourished suffer from absolute poverty. Absolute poverty can be eradicated from society. In the UK today there are some suffering from absolute poverty, such as homeless young people, but the vast majority of the population have a sufficiently high income not to be poor in this sense. The largest concentrations of absolute poverty today are to be found in the Third World.

Relative poverty is always present in society. The poor in this sense are those at the bottom end of the income scale. There is no exact measure of this, like the poorest 10 per cent or 20 per cent of society. But Adam Smith gave one measuring rod of relative poverty when he wrote that necessities were 'whatever the custom of the country renders it indecent for creditable people, even of the lower order, to be without.'

The impact of imperfectly competitive markets

Imperfectly competitive markets will result in a different distribution of income and wealth than perfectly competitive markets. Consider Figure 41.2. It shows the cost and revenue curves for an industry (☞ unit 37). If the industry were perfectly competitive, production would take place where price = MC at output level OB. If the industry now became a multi-plant monopolist, output would be at OA where MC = MR. EFG is the allocative loss to society. It is sometimes called a **deadweight loss** because the loss is not recoverable. However, there is also a transfer of income from consumers to the monopoly producer represented by the rectangle CDEF. Under perfect competition, the consumer would only have paid OCFA for the output OA. Under monopoly, consumers are forced to pay ODEA.

In a free market system, monopolies are owned by private shareholders. In the nineteenth century, these private shareholders would, for the most part, have been private individuals. Undoubtedly some, such as the Rockefellers and the Vanderbilts, grew extremely rich from monopoly profits. Today, monopolies are more likely to be owned by pension funds, assurance companies and a host of other financial institutions which

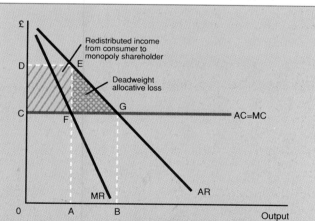

Figure 41.2 *Allocative and distributive effects of monopoly*
If the industry is perfectly competitive, it will produce at OB where price = MC. If it were a multi-plant monopolist, it would produce at OA where MC = MR. EFG is the deadweight allocative loss to society. CDEF is the total 'tax' of the monopolist on the consumer. It results in a redistribution of income from consumer to shareholder.

QUESTION 2

Table 41.2 *Distribution of original income, 1976 and 1986*

	Quintile groups of households				
	Bottom fifth	Next fifth	Middle fifth	Next fifth	Top fifth
1976	0.8	9.4	18.8	26.6	44.4
1986	0.3	5.7	16.4	26.9	50.7

Source: adapted from CSO, *Social Trends*.

(a) Construct two Lorenz curves from the data above.
(b) Has the distribution of income become more or less equal between 1976 and 1985?

channel savings through the money and capital markets on behalf of wealthy and not so wealthy individuals. In the nineteenth century, elections particularly in the USA could be won or lost on this monopoly profit issue. Today, it is a less important issue because monopoly profits are distributed more widely through the economic system. However, it should still be remembered that monopolies effectively impose a tax on consumers, the revenue being received by shareholders.

Equity vs efficiency

Governments intervene in the market to redistribute income because it is widely accepted that the distribution of income thrown up by the workings of free market forces is unacceptable. In a pure free market, efficiency is maximised because all production takes place where price = MC (☞ unit 34). If a government then intervenes in the market, say by subsidising food for the poor, imposing taxes of any kind to pay for government expenditure, subsidising housing or providing welfare benefits, it introduces a distortion in the market. Hence, government intervention leads to allocative inefficiency.

In practice there are no pure free market economies. Economies are riddled with market imperfections, such as oligopolistic and monopoly industries, monopoly unions and externalities. The theory of the second best shows that introducing another distortion, such as welfare payments to the poor, may in fact lead to greater economic efficiency. The theory suggests that efficiency will be greatest if the distortion is spread thinly across many markets rather than concentrated on a few markets. For instance, it is likely that large housing subsidies combined with no subsidies to any other goods would lead to less economic efficiency than small subsidies spread across all goods in the economy. Equally, low levels of unemployment benefit available to all unemployed workers in the economy are likely to lead to

greater economic efficiency than high levels of unemployment benefit available only to male manual employees.

Key terms

Equity - fairness.
Horizontal equity - the identical treatment of identical individuals or groups in society.
Vertical equity - the different treatment of individuals or groups which are dissimilar in characteristics.
Lorenz curve - shows the extent of inequality of income in society.
Absolute poverty - absolute poverty exists when individuals do not have the resources to be able to consume sufficient necessities to survive.
Relative poverty - poverty which is defined relative to existing living standards for the average individual.

Applied economics

The distribution of income and wealth in the UK

Income is distributed unevenly in the UK. Table 41.3 gives three measures of distribution of income between households. Original income is the gross income of households from sources such as wages and salaries, private pensions and investment income. Disposable income is gross income after income tax and National Insurance contributions have been paid but including state welfare benefits such as unemployment benefit, family credit and the state old age pension. Final income is disposable income minus indirect taxes such as VAT, but including the value of state services such as education and the National Health Service.

The statistics give an indication of the extent of inequality in income. For instance, in 1986, the bottom

20 per cent of households (mostly pensioner households and those with unemployed adults) received only 0.3 per cent of total original income generated in the UK. That means that each household received just 0.015 (0.3 ÷ 20) of average income in the UK. In comparison, the top 20 per cent of households received 50.7 per cent of total UK orginal income. On average each of these households received 2.54 times (50.7 ÷ 20) the average income.

In a welfare state, it should be expected that the distribution of disposable income and final income would show less inequality than original income. Taxes should fall most heavily on the better off

Table 41.3 *Distribution of income*

	Bottom fifth	Next fifth	Middle fifth	Next fifth	Top fifth
	Quintile groups of households				
Original income					
1976	0.8	9.4	18.8	26.6	44.4
1986	0.3	5.7	16.4	26.9	50.7
Disposable income					
1976	7.0	12.6	18.2	24.1	38.1
1986	5.9	11.0	17.0	23.9	41.7
Final income					
1976	7.4	12.7	18.0	24.0	37.9
1986	5.9	11.4	17.0	23.9	41.7

Source: adapted from CSO, *Social Trends*.

whilst benefits should be received mainly by the poorer sections of society. Table 41.3 shows that to some extent this is true in the UK. The share of disposable income of the bottom 20 per cent of households was 5.9 per cent in 1986 (compared to 0.3 per cent of original income). That means that the average household in the bottom 20 per cent received 0.295 (5.9 ÷ 20) of the average income. The share of the top 20 per cent of households was 41.7 per cent giving the average household 2.09 times the average income in the UK. Figures for final income (disposable income minus indirect taxes such as VAT plus the value of benefits in kind such as education and the NHS) differ little compared to disposable income.

It should be remembered that there will be considerable variation in income within each of the quintile groups (groups of 20 per cent). For instance, in the bottom quintile there will be some households whose final income will be markedly less than the average for the group. On the other hand in the top quintile there will be a few who will earn hundreds of times the national average income. Equally, the statistics say nothing about how many people live in a household. A one person household in the bottom quintile may have a higher income per person than a six person household in the middle quartile.

For most of this century, the long term trend has been for income differentials to narrow. Since 1979, this trend has been reversed, mainly due to government policy which has shifted the burden of taxation away from the better off whilst at the same time freezing or reducing most state benefits. This will be discussed more fully in unit 104.

The distribution of wealth

The distribution of wealth in the UK is far less equitable than the distribution of income. Table 41.4 shows that in 1987 the top 1 per cent owned 18 per

Table 41.4 *Distribution of wealth*

Percentage of marketable wealth owned by:	1911	1954	1971	1981	1987
Most wealthy 1%	69	43	31	21	18
Most wealthy 5%	-	-	52	40	36
Most wealthy 10%	92	79	65	54	50
Most wealthy 25%	-	-	86	77	74
Most wealthy 50%	-	-	97	94	93
Least wealthy 50%	-	-	3	6	7

Source: adapted from CSO, *Social Trends*.

cent of marketable wealth in the UK. That meant that the richest 1 per cent of the population owned 18 times the national average. Perhaps even more surprising is that half the population owned just 7 per cent of the nation's wealth. Each person on average in the bottom 50 per cent owned a mere 0.14 of the average wealth per person in the UK. The single most important divide today between 'rich' and 'poor' is home ownership. Approximately one-third of marketable wealth according to *Social Trends* is now made up of the value of owner occupied houses.

Horizontal equity

Horizontal inequity exists in the UK in a number of different ways. One measure is the relative earnings of males and females. As Table 41.1 showed, there is a wide disparity between the relative earnings of males and females. Part of this can be explained by factors such as different education and training experiences, different age compositions of the male and female workforce and the loss of work experience by women during the crucial years when they might leave the workforce to raise children. However, despite equal pay legislation, it is unlikely that all of the difference in pay between males and females can be explained in this way and therefore horizontal inequity can be said to exist between males and females.

Table 41.5 *Distribution of household income by region, 1987-8*

	Average income per week per household (£)
South East	338.6
South West	273.7
UK	270.0
East Anglia	256.8
North West	245.8
West Midlands	244.7
East Midlands	241.3
Scotland	234.2
Yorkshire and Humberside	232.8
Wales	227.5
Northern Ireland	224.8
North	220.1

Source: adapted from CSO, *Regional Trends*.

Another measure of horizontal inequity is the North-South divide in the UK. Table 41.5 shows average income per week per household in the UK in 1987-8. The South East had the highest income whilst the North of England had the lowest. The difference in real income is likely to be less than that implied by Table 41.5 because of lower prices for instance for houses in areas outside the South. However, a whole number of measures, including ownership of goods, indicate that the picture of a North-south divide painted by Table 41.5 does exist.

Absolute and relative poverty

Absolute poverty is rare in the UK, although evidence suggests that it has been growing since 1979. The main indicator of absolute poverty in the UK is homelessness. There are no reliable estimates of the numbers of people who live 'rough' on the streets of our cities, but at end 1988 there were 32 000 people according to government figures who were living in temporary accommodation such as hostels and refuges. If there is little absolute poverty in the UK, there is, by the definition of the term, relative poverty. The extent of relative poverty is difficult to gauge. One common measure is to see how many people are living at or below the minimum income set by government for the receipt of means tested benefits. Table 41.6 shows numbers claiming a variety of different benefits. Supplementary pensions are paid to the retired. Supplementary allowances were paid to those out of work, whilst family income supplement was a benefit targeted at the low paid in work. Housing benefit could be claimed by all three of the groups just mentioned. Each claimant of benefit is likely to have dependants, so the total number of people of poverty is

much higher than the number receiving benefit. Many benefits also have low take-up rates. In 1984 for instance, the take-up rate of family income supplement was only about 65 per cent. The result is that on the government's own estimates produced by the DHSS, there were 6 million people in poverty in 1979, 8.8 million in 1983 and over 11 million today.

There are those who point out that using benefit levels to define poverty has the perverse effect of increasing poverty when benefits are raised whilst reducing poverty when benefits are lowered. It is also pointed out that relative to our Victorian ancestors, nearly all in society today enjoy a very high standard of living. However, relative poverty is most commonly defined in terms of poverty relative to the average in the society of the day. The evidence shows that there has been an increase in relative poverty since 1979.

Table 41.6 *Number of people in receipt of selected social security benefits*

		Millions
	1979-80	1988/9
Supplementary pensions and supplementary benefit/income support[1]	2.92	4.22
Family income supplement/ family credit[1]	0.08	0.29
Housing benefit	1.43	4.03

1. Major reforms of the benefit system in April 1988 saw supplementary pensions and supplementary benefits replaced by income support whilst family income supplement was replaced by family credit.

Source: CSO, *Social Trends*.

POVERTY

Poverty is back on Britain's political agenda. It is not the people you can see sleeping rough on London's pavements that has made it so but a single speech by the Secretary of State for Social Security, Mr John Moore. In the speech, he argued that it is a mistake to define poverty as an income below 140 per cent of welfare support payments. He went on to say that 'a certain kind of politician' uses this 140 per cent definition to keep 'the fires of resentment and envy ...

forever stoked ... Their purpose in calling "poverty", what is in reality simply inequality, is so they can call western material capitalism a failure'.

Source: adapted from the *Financial Times*, 6.5.1989.

1. **To what extent might poverty in the UK be the result of inequity in society?**

Summary

1. Nationalised industries and public corporations are state owned companies.
2. A wide variety of arguments was advanced to support the nationalisation programme of the late 1940s, including lower costs, greater allocative efficiency, greater motivation of the workforce and a more equitable distribution of resources.
3. Economic theory suggests that nationalised industries should price at marginal social cost.
4. Investment should be undertaken when 'social profit', subject to a test rate of discount, can be achieved.

Nationalisation

NATIONALISED INDUSTRIES (most of which are PUBLIC CORPORATIONS, to give them their legal title) are currently a fast-disappearing type of business organisation in the UK. A nationalised industry is an industry which is owned by the state. Nationalisation occurs when the state acquires the assets of companies from the private sector.

Between 1950 and 1980 nationalised industries played an important role in the UK economy. In the early 1980s, nationalised industries accounted for 10 per cent of national output, 7 per cent of total employment and 17 per cent of total investment. Nationalised industries included coal, rail, steel, electricity, gas, bus transport, airlines, postal services, water and telecommunications. In addition, the state owned many companies which competed in markets with private sector firms, such as motor vehicles, broadcasting, brewing, airline manufacturers and engine manufacturers. Since 1980 there has been a large scale sale of these industries and companies to the private sector - the process called **privatisation.**

The arguments for nationalisation

For much of this century the nationalisation of private sector assets has been seen by many economists to have important advantages. The large scale nationalisation programme of Clement Attlee's Labour government between 1945 and 1951 reflected a widespread belief that nationalisation would promote both economic efficiency and greater equity. A number of arguments were put forward in support of the nationalisation of industries such as gas, electricity, rail, steel and coal.

Lower costs Nationalised industries would be more **productively efficient** than equivalent firms in the private sector. Most of the post-war privatisation programme involved the purchase of a number of private firms in an industry. For instance, before 1947 there were a number of private railway companies operating throughout the UK. It was argued that **economies of scale** could be achieved by merging the competing firms into one, dispensing with duplication of production resources. Moreover, competition with expenditure on advertising and promotion was seen as wasteful. The elimination of such marketing costs would result in even lower total costs of production. To a great extent, these arguments rely upon the fact that industries which were nationalised were **natural monopolies** (☞ unit 37).

Better management Supporters of nationalisation often held a very poor view of private sector management. They argued that private firms were often run in a very amateurish way by managers or owners more interested either in enjoying a quiet life or short run profit than in the welfare of the company and the economy. Nationalisation was seen as a chance to appoint efficient modern management which would run the industries to maximise net social benefit. In some of the industries, particularly coal, there was an appalling record of industrial disputes. It was hoped that nationalisation would make labour relations more harmonious because workers would see the industry as 'their' industry and management would no longer see workers as enemies.

Control of monopolies Many of the nationalised firms, such as railway companies and gas suppliers, were local monopolists. Nationalisation was seen as the easiest and most effective way of controlling these monopolies and preventing them from reducing social benefit by raising prices and lowering output.

Maximisation of net social benefit and not private profit Significant **externalities** were seen to be present in the industries which were nationalised. For instance, in the coal industry it was felt that private companies had too little regard for the welfare of their workers. The safety and lives of coalminers were sacrificed for the sake of private profit. Nationalised industries were given the task of maximising net social benefit even if this meant sacrificing private profit.

Greater control of the economy State ownership of some of the most important industries in the economy (sometimes called control of the **commanding heights** of the economy) was seen as essential if the government was to manage an unstable market economy. The 1930s, for instance, were seen as an example of the inability of free market forces to bring stability and prosperity to an economy. Nationalisation was effectively a move towards a more centrally planned type economy. In the 1970s, a number of key UK companies, such as Rolls Royce and British Leyland (now the Rover Group), were taken into public ownership because they went bankrupt under private management. It was felt that the state had to intervene to prevent free market forces from destroying companies which played a key role in assuring the long term prosperity of the country.

A fairer distribution of resources Private firms are in business to make private profit for their owners. Before 1945 most firms were owned by the people who ran them. The family firm was the most typical business organisation. It was therefore easy for workers to see the difference in income of owners and workers. Coal miners, for instance, could compare the standard of living of their children, with barely enough to eat, badly clothed, perhaps not having a pair of shoes and sleeping several to a room, with the comparatively luxurious life-style of the mine owner's children. Capitalist profit was seen as expropriation of money which had been earned by the workers. Nationalisation was an opportunity to seize those profits and use them for the benefit of everybody in society, both workers and consumers, not just a few capitalists.

There are a number of assumptions made in these arguments which are of direct relevance to the current privatisation debate.

■ The public sector is seen as more efficient than the private sector. In particular, public sector management is seen as better at allocating the economy's resources than private sector management.

■ The private sector is seen as exploitative of workers and consumers. State control is needed to neutralise monopoly power and the pursuit of private profit at the expense of the public interest.

■ Profit is seen more as an indication of monopoly power than as a signal which allocates resources efficiently within the economy.

Overall, there was a presumption that state allocation of resources was as good as if not better than private sector allocation - or to mimic George Orwell (in 'Animal Farm'), 'public sector good, private sector bad'.

QUESTION 1 Amalgamation under public ownership will bring great economies in operation and make it possible to modernize production methods ... Public ownership ... will lower charges, prevent competitive waste, open the way for co-ordinated research and development... Only if public ownership replaces private monopoly can industry become efficient.'

Source: Labour Party Manifesto, 1945.

Explain the economic arguments which lie behind the views expressed in the Labour Party Manifesto of 1945.

How should public corporations be run? Economic theory can make major contributions to two aspects of this question. Firstly, it can suggest the price a nationalised industry should set for its products. Secondly, it can help determine whether a nationalised industry should invest or not in a particular project.

Pricing

At what price should a nationalised industry sell its product if it is instructed to maximise net social benefit? In unit 33 it was shown that, subject to very strict conditions, efficiency will be maximised if the price of a good is equal to its marginal cost (known as marginal cost pricing). However, there are a number of problems with this simple rule.

Externalities (☞ unit 35). The marginal private cost of production to the nationalised industry may not reflect the marginal social cost of production. For instance, the electricity industry may burn coal which releases carbon into the atmosphere and contributes to the greenhouse effect, a railway may cause noise pollution, or a new coal mine may ruin a beauty spot for local residents. Equally, the price which consumers are prepared to pay for the product may not reflect its social benefit. For instance, a new underground railway line in London may relieve congestion on London roads. That relief is a benefit which is not reflected in the price that underground travellers pay. Or a railway line to an isolated community may prevent the community disintegrating and adding to congestion problems elsewhere in the region. Hence, nationalised industries should not price at marginal private cost. Cost should be adjusted to include both positive and negative externalities. Price should then be set to equal marginal social cost.

Imperfectly competitive markets In practice, markets are not perfectly competitive. A large number of markets exist where price does not equal marginal cost. The **theory of the second best** (☞ unit 34) shows where this is the case, economic efficiency is likely to be greater if individual nationalised industries do not price at marginal cost. For instance, if prices are 10 per cent higher than marginal cost in all other markets in the economy, then net social benefit is likely to be maximised if the nationalised industry price is set at 10 per cent higher than marginal cost.

Profits and losses Marginal cost pricing could lead to a nationalised industry making an accounting loss. In Figure 42.1, a profit maximising firm would produce at OA where MC = MR and would earn abnormal profit. However, a nationalised industry adopting marginal cost pricing techniques will produce at OB, charging a price of OE. At this level of output, average cost (BG) is higher than average revenue (BH) and hence the firm will make a loss of EFGH. Industries where this is most likely to

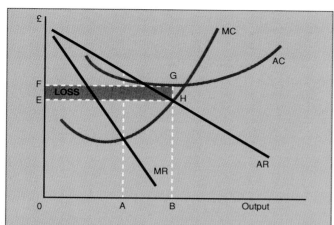

Figure 42.1 *Marginal cost pricing may lead to losses*
A nationalised industry which could earn abnormal profit (at the profit maximising level of output OA) would make a loss of EFGH if it produces at OB where price = MC. Whether or not marginal cost pricing does lead to a loss depends on the relationship between costs and revenues in the industry.

nationalised industries are monopolies. They are likely to have the power to **price discriminate**. So, for instance, British Rail charges peak time commuters a higher price than customers travelling at off peak times. The electricity boards charge less for electricity during the night than during the day. British Telecom, when it was a nationalised industry, charged less for calls made between 6 p.m. and 8 a.m.

QUESTION 2 In 1989/90 Network SouthEast, which operates London British Rail commuter services, was given a subsidy by central government of approximately £90 million. Commuters were charged higher prices than off-peak travellers.
(a) What economic justification might there be for central government to subsidise London commuter services?
(b) Why is economic efficiency likely to be greater if commuters are charged more rather than the same as off-peak travellers?

---

happen is where fixed costs are very large and variable costs (and therefore marginal costs) are relatively small. This is true of industries such as railways, electricity generation and gas supply.

Marginal cost pricing will not necessarily lead to a nationalised industry making a loss. But it will make less profit than a similar profit maximising firm in an imperfectly competitive industry. This could pose political problems. Low profits or losses make it seem as if the nationalised industry is inefficient compared to private sector companies. This makes it politically difficult to finance these losses from tax revenues. Moreover, using tax revenues to finance losses introduces a further distortion to the market system which in turn may lead to a loss of welfare. There may also be undesirable distributional effects. For instance, if taxes are raised on the poor to pay for losses of nationalised industries whose products are bought mainly by the better off, then welfare may be lowered.

Differentiated products Nationalised industries are unlikely to make one single product. Rather, they will produce a wide variety of products. The marginal cost pricing rule then requires that nationalised industries know the marginal cost of each product - a calculation which in practice can be very difficult to make with any accuracy.

One important aspect of marginal cost is time. Railways, electricity producers and telephone companies, for instance, have to provide a service at peak times. At other times of the day much of this equipment will lie idle. Therefore the long run marginal cost of providing a service for the customer buying at peak times is higher than at other times.

Marginal cost pricing therefore suggests that peak users should be charged more than other customers. This is known as **peak load pricing.** In some markets, this would be impossible to implement, but many

Investment

Private sector companies invest because they hope to make a profit. There are a number of different ways of calculating the return on an investment project (☞ unit 53). One way is to calculate the average rate of return over the lifetime of a project. This is similar to calculating the interest rate on a bank or building society account. For instance, a 10 per cent annual rate of return means that over the lifetime of the project, the investing firm will make a 10 per cent profit each year. The higher the rate of return the more likely it is that a firm will invest.

A nationalised industry therefore should invest in those projects which have the highest rate of return. When calculating this, nationalised industries should not only include the private costs and benefits of the project. Because they are charged with maximising net social benefit, they need to take externalities into account too (i.e. they need to base their investment decisions on cost-benefit analysis ☞ unit 36). For instance, a new tube line in London might lose money - the private rate of return would therefore be negative. But it might have a very high social rate of return if, as is likely, it considerably reduces congestion on the roads and reduces surface pollution.

Nationalised industries should not, however, undertake all investment projects which show a positive rate of return. Investment by a nationalised industry has an opportunity cost. The resources could be used elsewhere in the economy, for instance in consumption or private sector investment. If the economy had to choose between a private sector investment project which yielded 10 per cent and a nationalised industry project which yielded 2 per cent, then the private sector project would be better.

So nationalised industry rates of return should be comparable to those in the private sector. If the private sector will only invest if the rate of return is more than 10 per cent, then 10 per cent should be the minimum for nationalised industries.

There are two reasons why the minimum rate of return on nationalised industry investment is likely to be relatively low. Firstly, nationalised industry investment is likely to be low risk investment. Nationalised industries tend to operate in markets with little or no competition. Demand is secure. In the private sector, risk is rewarded by higher returns. Secondly, the opportunity cost of nationalised industry investment could be the consumption foregone by taxpayers who have had to pay higher taxes to finance the investment. The opportunity cost of consumption for consumers is likely to be the after tax return they can secure in a bank or building society. This is far less than, for instance, the cost of overdrafts or loans for firms wanting to borrow money to invest. As a consequence, governments in the UK have set the minimum rate of return for nationalised industry investment between 5 and 10 per cent in the post-war era.

Key terms

> **Nationalised industries and public corporations -** state owned industries or companies.

Applied economics

Nationalised industries in the UK

History

The state is responsible for organising the production of many goods and services. Some, such as defence and education, have traditionally been financed through taxes and have been provided free at the point of sale. However, there has also been a long tradition of the state selling goods and services in the same way that a private company might. For instance, a public postal service was established in 1840 which has grown to be today's Post Office. In 1912, the Post Office first provided a national telephone service. During the 1920s and 1930s, successive UK governments established the British Broadcasting Corporation, the London Passenger Transport Board (now London Transport), the British Overseas Airways Corporation (now part of British Airways) and the Central Electricity Generating Board. Local authorities also provided many goods and services such as public baths, bus transport and gas.

Up to the Second World War, government enterprises were set up on an ad hoc basis where it was felt that state provision would be better than private provision in that particular case. However, the Labour

government elected to office in 1945 believed strongly that nationalisation was in general likely to be beneficial. Clement Attlee's government nationalised coal, rail, steel, the Bank of England and road transport. It created the gas boards and electricity boards that existed for the next 40 years. The Labour Party after 1951 remained committed to further nationalisation but it was not a high priority. The two remaining firms which passed into public ownership were both firms which went bankrupt and were taken over in the national interest - Rolls Royce in 1971 by the Conservative government of Edward Heath and British Leyland cars in 1975 by Harold Wilson's Labour government.

Organisation

Most nationalised industries, legally, are public corporations, bodies intended to be similar to public limited companies in organisation. The shareholder, the government, appoints a board of directors and a chairman. The board is then responsible for the day-to-day running of the corporation.

QUESTION 3 In March 1989, British Rail announced a proposed route for a dedicated rail link between London and the Channel Tunnel. Initially, British Rail had hoped to run the whole of the link overground. However, strong protests from residents along the route led to British Rail proposing to put about two thirds of the link underground.

British Rail are required to show a rate of return of 7 per cent before investment can proceed. Without the environmental improvements, British Rail might have achieved that figure if it were to run commuter trains as well as Channel Tunnel traffic along the track. However, putting most of the track underground increased the cost from an estimated £1.7 billion to £3.5 billion. The government refused to subsidise the link. Later that year, British Rail abandoned its plans for a dedicated rail link and announced that it hoped to build the overground part of the original line from the Channel Tunnel to Swanley in Kent and then use existing British Rail lines to London. Fierce opposition to these new proposals is now expected from residents in London close to the overland track.

(a) Explain why raising the cost of the Channel Tunnel rail link should lower its rate of return.
(b) Why might the extra private cost to British Rail of building a link underground in London be offset by gains to London residents?
(c) What arguments might be put forward for (i) central government or (ii) the residents of Kent to subsidise the dedicated underground rail link?

The power of the board, however, is checked in a number of ways. Firstly, the Act of Parliament which created the corporation is likely to have placed certain obligations on it. White Papers are occasionally issued which set guidelines for pricing and investment policies. Parliament scrutinises the activities of corporations through a number of select committees. Each corporation has a consumer council which represents the interests of consumers and acts as a consumer watchdog. Since 1980, the Monopolies and Mergers Commission (☞ unit 37) has had the power to investigate the activities of public corporations. Finally and most importantly, the board is responsible to a government minister who in practice has a decisive influence on every important decision made by a corporation.

The legislative background

The post-war nationalisation Acts which created most of the nationalised industries which were to operate for the next 40 years laid down only that the industries should break even year-on-year. In 1961, financial targets for nationalised industries were introduced. Nationalised industries and the government would agree upon a projected profit or loss figure for the year.

But it was not until 1967 that a White Paper established that nationalised industries should price at marginal cost and should adopt net present value techniques for investment decisions which would include not only private costs and benefits but all externalities too. The minimum rate of return (or the

discount rate) on public sector investment projects was set at 8 per cent (later raised to 10 per cent). This was held to be comparable to higher risk private sector rates of return of 15-16 per cent. It was recognised that nationalised industries had a duty to provide goods or services at a loss if social benefits exceeded social costs (i.e. there were positive externalities). However, these would be made explicit and the government undertook to provide nationalised industries with a grant to cover the loss made. British Rail today, for instance, receives subsidies from both central and local government for running local passenger services.

Various problems which arose from the 1967 rules led to a new White Paper in 1978. It replaced the 10 per cent discount rate on investment projects with a 5 per cent (raised to 8 per cent in 1989) real rate of return (RRR) to be achieved on new investment. The 1978 White Paper also gave higher priority to the targeting system introduced in 1961. Each industry had to set a financial target for itself for the next 3-5 years based upon factors such as projected efficiency gains, social considerations and the rate of inflation. Non-financial performance indicators had to be set too. For instance, the industry might set targets for quality of service.

Since 1979, the emphasis has shifted from considerations of social cost and social profit to private costs and benefits. Instead of seeing nationalised industries as important agencies to correct private sector market failure, the government has viewed them as a significant contributor to market failure in the UK. Nationalised industries have been given much stricter financial targets in an attempt to increase the private profitability of the industries. This can be justified on

the grounds that some nationalised industries' consumers have been subsidised by taxpayers in the past (i.e. price has been set at less than marginal cost) - a distortion in the market resulting in too great a consumption of nationalised industries' products and too little consumption of other private sector goods and services. Stricter financial limits would increase efficiency because at least part of the increased profit would have to come from reduced costs. Levels of profit comparable to the private sector were also needed if nationalised industries were to be successfully privatised.

Nationalisation: success or failure ?

It could be argued that the tide of economic opinion in the 1980s has swung against nationalised industries. Nationalised industries in the post-war era failed to live up to many of the hopes of the politicians who argued so fervently for nationalisation half a century ago.

Nationalised industries have come to be seen by some as highly inefficient. The absence of competition means that there is no incentive for them either to produce at lowest cost or to produce arrange of goods and services which consumers want to buy. The management of nationalised industries, far from being efficient technocrats, have been portrayed as lazy and inefficient bureaucrats more interested in their own rewards than in the consumer (☞ unit 24). Economies of scale may not be significant in most of the nationalised industries - they could be split up into several competing firms and still attain the minimum efficient scale of production. Where nationalised industries are natural monopolies, government regulation of private sector companies, as happens in the USA, will lead to a far better allocation of resources than a system of state owned industries.

There is an element of truth in these criticisms. However, much of the alleged inefficiency of public corporations can be seen not as naturally inherent in nationalisation, but as a reflection of the political processes in the UK. Every government since 1945 has used nationalised industries as a tool to manage the economy. For instance, during the 1960s and 1970s, governments forced nationalised industries to keep price increases down as part of their anti-inflation policies. Not unexpectedly, nationalised industries then earned little profit or went into the red. Critics were able to claim that nationalised industries must be less efficient than more profitable private sector counterparts.

Nationalised industries were also used to create jobs or prevent unemployment. Investment was directed not to areas which would maximise profit but to areas where new investment would secure the votes of local citizens for the government.

Top management in the industries were paid less than their private sector counterparts. Not surprisingly, nationalised industries found it difficult, if not impossible, to recruit the quality of personnel needed to run the industries.

Perhaps more damaging has been the squeeze on investment spending. Since the mid-1960s, successive governments have attempted to control the growth of public expenditure. Nationalised industry investment has been an easy option for cutting spending relatively painlessly. But failure to invest has resulted in long term problems. Dangerous overcrowding on the London underground, polluted water and railway accidents are just a few of the legacies left to citizens today of the failure to invest sufficiently in the past.

Since 1979 there has been a transformation within the nationalised industries. The government has made it clear that private profit is the most important long term goal of the industries. It has appointed a number of highly paid executives recruited from the private sector to turn around unprofitable corporations. It has been remarkably successful in its objectives, so successful that it has managed in a ten year period to sell off over half of the nationalised industries to the private sector.

According to this view, the 'problem' of nationalised industries lies not with nationalised industries per se but with government itself. The experience of the 1980s shows that nationalised industries can be turned into profit maximising concerns if the government so wishes and is prepared to give the industries sufficient freedom. If making large profits is equated with economic efficiency, then nationalised industries can do this as well as any private sector company. But economic theory suggests that private profit and economic efficiency are not necessarily compatible.

GOVERNMENT PREVENTS BR BUYING NEW STOCK

By Kevin Brown, Transport Correspondent.

BRITISH Rail is being prevented from buying new and much-needed rolling stock by the government's strict rules on investment, the statutory railway watchdog claimed yesterday.

The Central Transport Consultative Committee, set up to represent passengers after nationalisation of the railways in 1948, said it was becoming increasingly concerned about the 'misery of overcrowding' on some BR lines.

'The key to conquering the problem of overcrowding lies in the provision of sufficient additional capacity,' the committee says in its annual report.

'It is therefore essential that BR continues to come forward with investment proposals for new rolling stock and related schemes where overcrowding exists, and that government gives speedy authorisation to such projects.'

The committee says BR 'feels unable' to make a sound financial case for additional vehicles on one group of routes operated by its provincial sector, even though passengers are suffering severe overcrowding.

In another case, the number of new vehicles approved by ministers for an expansion scheme on the Network South - East sector was less than the number requested by BR.

The committee says the government's sole criterion in evaluating investment proposals is whether the project will achieve the 8 per cent rate of return on capital required of all nationalised industry investments.

' The government's insistence that BR has to justify the cost of every scheme in purely financial terms, often by an assessment of potential savings resulting from the scrapping of old assets, is deterring BR from seeking new investment in rolling stock, even where this is known to be necessary to tackle overcrowding,' the committee says. Mr Mike Patterson, secretary of the CTCC, said BR was finding it impossible to meet agreed targets for service quality and reducing overcrowding because of the constraints on investment caused by the government's financial regulations.

He urged the government to relax the rules to allow investment to go ahead where it was needed to improve the quality of services.

Mr Lennox Napier, chairman, said the committee deeply regretted the decline of the public service operating grant - intended to cover loss-making passenger services - which had now reached an ' irreducible minimum.'

The grant has fallen by 51 per cent in real terms over the last five years, and is forecast to fall from £590m this year to £470m by 1992.

The committee claims there is a clear link between the decline of the subsidy and problems on routes such as those in East Anglia and South Wales, where BR wants to withdraw evening services.

Source: *Financial Times*, 26.7.1989.

1. What are the 'government's strict rules on investment'?
2. Why might they conflict with providing a high quality service to British Rail passengers?
3. To what extent should a nationalised industry like British Rail be forced to generate a profit on its operations?

43 Privatisation

Summary

1. Privatisation can take a variety of forms including the sale of state assets to the private sector, deregulation and the contracting out of previously state provided services to the private sector.
2. Arguments in favour of privatisation include lower costs, greater choice, better quality products, greater innovation and greater economic freedom.
3. Privatisation has also been used to promote wider share ownership and to reduce taxes and government borrowing.
4. Privatisation is likely to increase economic efficiency more if competition is introduced.
5. Governments can control privatised monopolies either through creating new competition or through regulation.

Privatisation

PRIVATISATION has come to be associated with the sale of large nationalised industries to the private sector. British Steel, British Gas and British Telecom are examples of public corporations which have been sold off. Such sales are just one part of a wider programme aimed at transferring resources from the public sector to the private sector. Other aspects of privatisation include the following.

■ Sales of parts of nationalised industries to the private sector. For instance, Jaguar cars (now part of the Ford Motor Company) was part of British Leyland (now owned by British Aerospace) before it was sold off.
■ Sales of individual assets of government bodies. For instance, local authorities are now forced to allow council house tenants to buy their own homes if they wish. Government departments have been encouraged to sell surplus land and buildings.
■ The creation of private sector competition to state monopolies. Regulations, often created at the time of nationalisation, prevented effective competition in industries such as telecommunications, coal and gas. Abolishing these regulations has enabled competitors, such as Mercury, to enter markets previously supplied exclusively by public sector concerns.
■ Compulsory competitive tendering. Many services, often local authority services, have been provided by public sector employees in the past. Dustbins have been emptied by council refuse collectors, schools cleaned by council cleaners and hospital sheets washed by health service employees. The government has now forced its own departments, local authorities, and other government bodies, to put these services out to tender. Workers who previously provided the service have been sacked, although most have regained their jobs working for the private sector company which gained the contract.

The arguments for privatisation

The advocates of privatisation claim that it will lead to important gains in economic efficiency. At the heart of the argument is the claim that the unrestricted operation of competition and market forces will increase economic welfare.

Costs will be lower Nationalised industries and other state bodies have no incentive to produce at lowest cost. Public sector employees will not be sacked if costs are high. The taxpayer will pick up the bill for losses made. In the private sector, high cost firms are driven out of business by low cost firms. Private sector managers have every incentive to minimise costs - if they don't, they could well lose their jobs.

Choice will be greater Public sector organisations have no incentive to produce goods which consumers want to buy. Many are monopoly producers and therefore consumers have to buy from them whether they like it or not. As 'lazy' monopolists, they tend to produce a restricted range of goods or services in high volumes. In the private sector, competition will drive companies which fail to provide the goods consumers want to buy out of business. The result is a proliferation of choice as companies attempt to find new products which will increase their market share and reduce the market share of their competitors.

Quality will be higher Consumers have no choice about the quality of a wide range of services from refuse collection to train services. Public sector monopolists have no need to be responsive to consumer complaints about poor quality goods or services. In the private sector, the discipline of the market ensures that companies which provide shoddy goods and services go out of business as consumers switch their spending to other companies.

Innovation will be greater Protected from market

QUESTION 1 Explain what type of privatisation each of the following would be:
(a) staffing prisons with private security guards; (b) the sale of British Coal; (c) the sale of land owned by British Rail; (d) allowing all types of private coal mines to operate.

competition, state organisations have no incentive to innovate. In the private sector, faced with competition, companies have to innovate or see their market taken away from them.

Greater economic freedom Market forces allocate resources so that they are used in the most efficient manner. Consumer spending decisions in a free market act like votes in a democratic election, indicating consumer preferences. Monopoly state organisations, on the other hand, lack the knowledge of consumer preferences to make efficient allocative decisions on their behalf. Moreover, governments interfere in the market place and misallocate resources for short term political objectives. Governments are the enemy of economic freedom because they have such overwhelming political power. Therefore, governments should have as little control over the economy as possible. Only the operation of free market forces, the counterpart of democratic systems of government, will ensure the optimal allocation of resources.

QUESTION 2 'In privatising British Telecom, we stimulated competition by licensing Mercury as a competing network. We have also liberalised other aspects of telecommunications - permitting anyone to provide value added and data services and to run their own branch system; introducing competition in paging, cellular, other mobile radio and satellite services; allowing 'telepoint' services and personal communications networks to develop; and giving choice to the public over the telephone apparatus they buy. The result is a dramatic improvement in the variety and quality of services available to the public and of course a growing and flourishing telecommunications service sector able to compete in the international market place.'

Source: Nicholas Ridley, Secretary of State for Trade and Industry writing in the *Financial Times*, 6 November 1989.

How, according to Nicholas Ridley, has privatisation increased economic efficiency?

Other objectives of privatisation

The main justification for privatisation is that it results in a more efficient allocation of resources within the market. However, the privatisation programme in the UK during the 1980s has also been used to pursue a number of other objectives.

Firstly, privatisation has been used to increase share ownership. It has been argued that wider share ownership is desirable. In the past, share ownership has been too narrow. Only a few relatively rich people have chosen to invest their savings in shares. The result has been a divide between workers and capitalists, with some workers seeing share owners as parasites who skim off the profits which arise from the efforts of workers.

In a wide share owning democracy, the distinction between worker and capitalist is not present because workers are also capitalists. Workers will be better able to appreciate the risks that capitalists take with their assets and will be able to see, for instance, that wage increases are not necessarily economically desirable. The wealth of the country will be more evenly spread and this too can be seen as desirable.

In pursuit of this goal, the UK government has deliberately marketed privatisation issues to the general public. Share allocations and the staging of payments have been weighted in favour of the small investor.

Another objective of the government has been to reduce both public sector borrowing and taxation. Increasing the profitability of nationalised industries, reducing the costs of services provided by government, and the selling off of state assets, all contribute to achieving these goals.

QUESTION 3 Privatisation share issues have tended to favour the small investor. For instance, applicants for the minimum number of shares (often 100 shares) have often been allocated all of the shares they applied for. Shareholders applying for more than the minimum have had their applications scaled down - the larger the number of shares applied for, the larger the scaling down.

Why has the government chosen to allocate shares in privatisation issues in this way?

Privatisation and efficiency

Most economists suggest that the welfare gains from privatisation are likely to be less than those claimed by its advocates. In order to understand the likely gains in efficiency, it is important to distinguish between different types of privatisation.

Some companies were already in competitive markets before privatisation. British Leyland (now Rover) and Jaguar were in a competitive market with other European and world car manufacturers. British Aerospace faced competition from domestic and foreign aircraft manufacturers. British Airways too was in a world market. Before privatisation, it could be argued that management of these companies did not have to be as competitive and efficient as their private sector counterparts because they knew that the government would always finance any losses made. Selling them to the private sector subjected them to the discipline of market forces and the advantages described above of lower costs, better quality etc. were achieved. It should be noted that in practice the major changes in these companies occurred whilst the companies were being prepared for privatisation and not after privatisation. It was under state ownership, not private ownership that these companies were 'transformed'.

The main arguments in favour of privatisation centre round the benefits of competition. However, the big companies which have been privatised are not in competitive markets at all. British Telecom, British Gas, and the water boards are, for the most part, natural monopolies. Public sector monopolies have been replaced by private sector monopolies. In these newly privatised industries there are no competitive pressures to reduce costs, raise quality or innovate. Traditional neo-classical welfare economics suggests that private sector monopolies lead to a loss of economic efficiency and welfare (☞ unit 37).

QUESTION 4 In 1989 the Adam Smith Institute, a free market think tank, published 'The Burning Question', a report on fire services in the UK. It advocated that local authorities should be forced to contract out their fire services to private firms. Existing fire services could be sold off to the highest bidder - possibly to existing workers or management through management buy-outs.

The report claimed that the present service was inefficient. 'Costs are constantly rising; restrictive labour practices limit management initiative; there is little innovative use of equipment or manpower. The economist would recognise these as classic symptoms of an over-regulated, non-competitive industry.'

(a) How might competitive tendering in the fire service increase productive efficiency?
(b) To what extent do you think allocative efficiency might be impaired if this happened?

The control of privatised monopolies

Given that privatisation has created private sector monopolies, government has been faced with the problem of how to prevent them exploiting their monopoly powers. Two different types of solution have been implemented.

The creation of competition Competition can be created either by splitting the monopoly up into several competing firms or by allowing private sector firms to enter the industry. The problem with splitting up an industry is that present and former public sector monopolies such as the railways and gas are not multi-plant monopolists: that is, they do not produce an identical product at different plants round the country. They are, for the most part, natural monopolies whose plant would be extremely costly to duplicate.

The electricity industry has been privatised to form three types of units. Local area boards are natural monopolists distributing electricity. The national grid is a natural monopoly too. In contrast, an element of competition was introduced into power generation by the creation of two rival companies, National Power and Powergen. The last posed as many problems as it solved because economic theory suggests that duopolies can be as inefficient as monopolies. Moreover, the duopoly

would face a monopoly buyer (**a monopsonist** - the area boards) which would have extremely unpredictable results on economic welfare. One possibility would be that the area boards could force the power generators to charge such low prices that the power generators would not invest in new plant. In the long term, this would result in a shortage of electricity.

As for allowing new competitors to enter the industry, experience with British Telecom suggests that effective competition takes a great deal of time to establish itself. Moreover, competition only takes place in the most profitable areas of the market. In the less profitable areas of the market, the monopolist is not challenged to increase efficiency by the threat of genuine competition.

Neither of these possibilities addresses the issue of how to force a private sector monopolist to take account of externalities.

Regulation Regulation seems a more promising solution. As privatisation has proceeded, regulatory regimes have been tightened in recognition of the welfare problems associated with monopolies. The privatised monopolies have been forced to provide certain public services, such as public telephones, even if these result in losses for the firm. In the case of water, strict quality standards have been imposed on the privatised water authorities which have also been forced to permit increased competition in the industry. British Telecom, for instance, has been forced to allow Mercury to use British Telecom lines.

To prevent monopoly pricing and encourage cost reductions, privatised monopolies are set maximum prices. These are usually linked to the rate of inflation. So British Telecom might be allowed to raise prices over the next five years at the rate of inflation minus 2 per cent for instance. The price in theory should be set low enough to prevent the monopoly earning abnormal profit. But it has an incentive to increase productive efficiency over and above the targets set by government because it is allowed to keep the resulting extra profits.

The problem with regulation is that it is very difficult for the regulating authority to know what level of competition or what level of prices will result in economic efficiency. Moreover, the government has set up independent regulatory bodies for each industry. From US experience, it is known that **regulatory capture** can occur. This is where the regulating body becomes more interested in furthering the interests of the monopolist it

QUESTION 5 When British Telecom was privatised in 1984, it was allowed to increase charges at an annual rate of the increase in the Retail Price Index (RPI) minus 3 per cent. In 1989, the rate of increase was changed to RPI minus 4.5 per cent.

(a) Why has British Telecom not been allowed to set prices at whatever level it wishes?
(b) Suggest reasons why OFTEL, the regulatory body of British Telecom, changed the value of the RPI - X formula in 1989.

is supposed to control than in protecting the consumer. This tends to occur over a lengthy period of time. It will only be in 10 or 20 years that it will be possible to judge whether the regulatory bodies established in the 1980s and 1990s will have protected the consumer or become the puppets of monopolists.

Applied economics

Privatisation

Background

The large scale nationalisation of industries by Clement Attlee's Labour government between 1945 and 1951 was followed by a period of consensus. A Conservative government de-nationalised the steel industry in 1952 but there was broad acceptance that coal, railways, gas, electricity and other industries should remain in the public sector. The Conservative government of Edward Heath, elected in 1970, promised a radical change in the role of the private sector but it became bogged down in anti-inflationary policy. It privatised Thomas Cook and Carlisle breweries but was responsible for taking the bankrupt Rolls Royce into state ownership in 1971.

Privatisation was not even specifically mentioned in the 1979 Conservative Party manifesto. Yet within 10 years, many public sector companies had been sold off to the private sector. Table 43.1 shows the timetable for the sale of state owned assets to the private sector from 1979. Initially, relatively small companies with healthy profits were put up for sale. These were in markets where there was already competition. The first public monopoly to be privatised was British Telecom in 1984. By 1991, the only substantial companies left in public hands were coal, the railways and the Post Office. These three industries were more difficult to sell for a variety of reasons discussed below.

Competitive tendering has proceeded more slowly. However, by 1989, local authorities had been forced to put services such as refuse collection and school cleaning out to tender. Tendering for cleaning and other services was common in the NHS. There are some in the Conservative Party who believe that both central and local government should become mainly buyers of goods and services on behalf of the public. They argue that governments should collect taxes and use the money to shop around for privately produced goods and services. For instance, local authorities would buy everything from library services to places in old people's homes. Central government would buy operations from hospitals, put criminals in privately run prisons and pay private companies to issue social security payments.

Examples of deregulation include allowing private bus companies to compete first on long distance routes and then on local services, ending the monopoly of

qualified opticians on the sale of spectacles and solicitors on conveyancing, and allowing building societies to compete in the banking market. In the 1990s, a Conservative government would bring far reaching changes to the legal profession.

Efficiency gains

There is little evidence at present to suggest that the sale of state owned assets to the private sector has resulted in either gains or losses in economic efficiency. Advocates of privatisation point to the increased profitability of privatised companies and an improvement in the quality of their products. Unfortunately this proves little. For instance, the basis of British Steel's profitability today rests upon the changes made to the company when it was in public ownership. The most dramatic changes in many privatised companies occurred in the run-up to privatisation as government gave management a very clear brief - to increase profitability.

Similarly, there is little firm evidence to date which

Table 43.1 *Sale of state owned companies to the private sector*

Date begun

1979	*British Petroleum	1986	British Gas
	*ICL	1987	British Airways
	*Ferranti		Rolls Royce
	Fairey		Leyland Bus
1981	British Aerospace		Leyland Truck
	*British Sugar		Royal Ordnance
	Cable and Wireless		British Airport Authority
	Amersham International	1988	British Steel
1982	National Freight Corporation		British Leyland
	Britoil	1989	British Water Authorities
1983	*Associated British Ports	1990	Electricity Area Boards
	British Rail Hotels	1991	Electricity Generation
1984	British Gas Onshore Oil		
	Enterprise Oil		To be privatised
	Sealink Ferries		British Coal
	Jaguar Cars		British Rail
	British Telecom		Post Office
	British Technology Group		

* Partly owned by government at the time of sale.

would suggest that contracting out has brought large scale efficiency gains. On the one hand, the cost of services such as refuse collection and cleaning has declined in some areas. Therefore it could be said that there has been an increase in productive efficiency. However, one important source of savings in costs has come from paying lower wages to workers. Councils have sacked workers and they have been re-employed by private sector companies at lower wage rates. Productive efficiency has increased but it is not possible to say that Pareto efficiency has been achieved because there has been a transfer of income from workers (who tend to be very lowly paid in these industries) to taxpayers (who tend to be better off). It could be argued that costs have been reduced simply by reducing the quality of the service. Schools are cleaned less often, food portions at old peoples' homes are reduced and refuse collection services are cut back.

It is difficult at this early stage to evaluate potential efficiency gains from privatisation. It will perhaps only be in 10 years' time that a full evaluation will be possible.

The costs of privatisation

Privatisation has been attacked on a number of fronts. Critics, as explained above, have been very doubtful about any efficiency gains from the sale of state owned assets.

Another criticism relates to the cost of the sales, including advertising, underwriting fees and large payments to the banks handling issues. More importantly, in its desire to sell publicly owned companies quickly and to spread share ownership, the government has offered companies for sale at below the market price. Shares in most privatisation issues open to the public have risen in value on the first day of trading. It is difficult to establish at what price companies could be sold for. However, British Telecom shares traded at a 90 per cent premium immediately whilst more recently water shares registered an immediate 50 per cent average gain. The only privatisation issue where shareholders lost money immediately was British Petroleum in 1987.

Critics have also accused the government of 'selling the family silver'. Assets which belong to the nation as a whole have been sold off at bargain basement prices. In one sense this is false. The companies exist and produce goods and services whether they are in public or private hands. The nation does not lose the assets of the company through privatisation (although the argument is more complicated in the case of shares sold to foreigners).

On the other hand, the redistribution of wealth in the economy does have important implications.

- If privatisation receipts have been used to reduce the need for the government to borrow, then taxpayers in the future will save on paying interest on that borrowing. Offset against that are the potential profits of the companies, which could have been used to pay for public spending and thus reduce taxes.
- If the privatisation proceeds have been used to reduce taxes in the year of receipt, then taxpayers

receive a once and for all bonus.
- In the run up to privatisation, companies have been 'fattened up'. In monopoly industries, such as gas and telephones, substantial increases in tariffs were made in the years prior to sale. It is possible that profits would have been lower and charges lower if privatisation had not taken place. If this true, there has been a redistribution of income from consumers

(of gas, telephone services etc.) to taxpayers.
- Any profits made are now distributed to private shareholders rather than to taxpayers via the government. Advocates of privatisation point out that before 1979, public corporations tended to be a net drain on the Exchequer. Taxpayers on the whole subsidised the consumers of the public corporations.

PRIVATISATION OF BRITISH RAIL?

A leaked confidential memorandum revealed possible government thinking about the privatisation of British Rail. The memorandum stated that BR's assets are probably worth between £10bn and £15bn, but sale proceeds might be quite modest because purchasers would be more concerned with earnings potential than asset values, particularly if any strings were attached to disposal of assets. Instead the greater benefits of privatisation would include a radical change of culture among BR members and staff, greater flexibility over fares and pay, access to private capital for investment and a closer relationship between customers and suppliers. The paper observes that none of BR's business is yet earning enough to survive in the private sector. InterCity and bulk freight might be viable by the mid-1990s, but Network SouthEast and the rest of the freight business are unlikely to be sufficiently profitable much before the end of the decade, and the provincial passenger sector will always make losses.

Source: adapted from the *Financial Times*, 12.9.1990.

1. **Discuss the possible advantages of privatisation of British Rail.**
2. **To what extent would British rail be an attractive proposition to private buyers?**

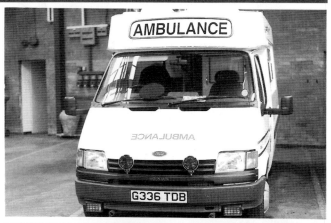

Summary

1. There will inevitably be market failure in a pure free market economy because it will fail to provide public goods.
2. Public goods must be provided by the state because of the free rider problem.
3. Merit goods are goods which are underprovided by the market mechanism. Demerit goods, such as drugs, are overprovided.
4. Part of public expenditure is devoted to achieving a more equitable distribution of income.
5. The desirability of state provision of goods and services can be judged using the criteria of productive and allocative efficiency and of equity.

Market failure

A pure free market system is most unlikely to produce an efficient and equitable distribution of resources. In theory, a free market system would be Pareto-efficient only if every market were perfectly competitive, (☞ unit 34). However, modern industrialised economies are dominated by oligopolistic and monopoly producers; externalities are widespread in many markets; and the free market system produces instability, seen in fluctuations in the level of economic activity. Equally, there are goods which the market system is unlikely to produce at all, or which it is likely to underproduce or overproduce. The market system may also lead to an inequitable distribution of resources in the economy (☞ unit 41). Therefore it is argued that government needs to regulate the private market system, to take responsibility for the production of goods which the free market underproduces and to redistribute income in a way that will result in a more equitable distribution of income.

Public goods

Nearly all goods are **private goods** (not to be confused with goods produced in the private sector of the economy). A private good is one where consumption by one person results in the good not being available for consumption by another. For instance, if you eat a bowl of muesli, then your friend can't eat it; if ICI build a plant on a piece of land, that land is not available for use by local farmers.

A few goods, however, are PUBLIC GOODS. These are goods which possess two characteristics:

- **non-rivalry**- consumption of the good by one person does not reduce the amount available for consumption by another person;
- **non-excludability** - once provided, no person can be excluded from benefiting (or indeed suffering in the case of a public good like pollution).

There are relatively few examples of pure public goods, although many goods contain a public good element. Clean air is a public good. If you breath clean air, it does not diminish the ability of others to breath clean air. Moreover, others cannot prevent you from breathing clean air. Defence is another example. An increase in the population of the UK does not lead to a reduction in the defence protection accorded to the existing population. A person in Manchester cannot be excluded from benefiting even if she were to object to current defence policy, prefer to see all defence abolished, and refuse to pay to finance defence.

Goods which can be argued to be public goods are:

- defence;
- the judiciary and prison service;
- the police service;
- street lighting.

Many other goods, such as education and health, contain a small public good element.

The free rider problem

Public goods need to be provided by the state because these goods would otherwise be under-provided in a pure market economy. This is because of the FREE RIDER problem. A public good is one where it is impossible to prevent people from receiving the benefits of the good once it has been provided. So there is a very little incentive for people to pay for consumption of the good. A free rider is someone who receives the benefit but allows others to pay for it. For instance, citizens receive benefits from defence expenditure. But individual citizens could increase their economic welfare by not paying for it.

In a free market, national defence is unlikely to be provided. A firm attempting to provide defence services would have difficulty charging for the product since it could not be sold to benefit individual citizens. The result would be that no one would pay for defence and therefore the market would not provide it. The only way round this problem is for the state to provide defence and force everyone to contribute to its cost through taxation.

QUESTION 1

Explain why lighthouses might be classed as a public good.

Merit and demerit goods

Even the most fervent advocates of free market economics agree that public goods are an example of market failure and that the government should provide these public goods. However, more controversial are merit and demerit goods.

A MERIT GOOD is one which is underprovided by the market mechanism (i.e. one which some people think should be provided in greater quantities). The problem with this definition is that there is no indication of what criteria we might use to judge whether a good is 'underprovided'. In general, criteria of efficiency and equity are used, but there might be others.

Health, education and insurance are the main merit goods provided today by government in the UK. Health and insurance are two examples where consumers find it difficult to make rational choices because of time. If left totally to market forces, the evidence suggests that individuals would not give themselves sufficient health cover or cover against sickness, unemployment and old age. Young people tend to be healthy and in work. Many find it difficult to appreciate that one day they will be ill and out of work. However, the cost of health care and pensions etc. is so great that young people can only afford them if they save for the future. If they don't, they find when they are older that they do not have sufficient resources to pay for medical services, or the insurance needed to cover them against loss of earnings due to illness or retirement. Therefore it makes sense for the state to intervene and to force young people in particular to make provision against sickness, unemployment and old age.

In the case of education, the main beneficiary (the child or student) is unlikely to be the person paying for the education. Therefore there could be a conflict of interest. It could be in the interest of the parents to pay as little as possible for the child's education but in the interest of the child to receive as high quality an education as possible. Others in society also have an interest. A child, for instance, who cannot read or write is an economic liability in the UK of the 1990s. He or she is more likely than not to have to receive support from others rather than contribute to the nation's welfare. There are many other examples of goods with a merit good element. Lack of industrial training, for instance, is seen as a major problem in the UK. Individual firms have an incentive not to train workers not only because it is so costly but also because their trained workers can then be poached by competitors. Rather, they go into the market place and recruit workers who have been trained at other firms' expense. This is an example again of the free rider problem. It would perhaps be more desirable if the state were to organise industrial training and levy a tax on all firms to pay for this.

A DEMERIT GOOD is one which is over-provided by the market mechanism. The clearest examples of demerit goods are drugs - everything from hard drugs such as LSD to alcohol and tobacco. Consumption of these goods produces large negative **externalities**. Crime increases, health costs rise, valuable human economic resources are destroyed, and friends and relatives suffer distress. Moreover, individuals themselves suffer and are unable to stop consuming because drugs are addictive. Therefore it can be argued that consumers of drugs are not the best judges of their own interests.

Governments intervene to correct this market failure. They have three main weapons at their disposal: they can ban consumption as with hard drugs; they can use the price system to reduce demand by placing taxes on drugs; or they can try to persuade consumers to stop using drugs, for instance through advertising campaigns.

QUESTION 2 There are major worries today about the lack of training given to young workers in the UK. In Germany, for instance, the vast majority of youngsters will receive education and training either in school or in a firm at least up the age of 18.

Suggest reasons why education and training for youngsters aged 16-18 might be considered a merit good in the UK today.

Equity

It would be extremely improbable that a free market system would lead to a distribution of resources which every individual would see as equitable. It is therefore argued by some economists that the state has a duty to reallocate resources.

QUESTION 3

The number of people who were homeless increased considerably during the 1980s. What economic arguments could be used for and against the view that society has an obligation to provide every citizen with a home to live in?

It could be argued that, in the UK today, there is some consensus that citizens should not die for lack of food, or be refused urgent medical treatment for lack of money.

In the UK, over 30 per cent of all public spending is devoted to social security payments. Some of these payments come from the National Insurance fund and therefore could be seen as merit goods. But benefits such as family credit are an explicit attempt to redistribute income to those in need. It could also be argued that the free provision of services such as health and education leads to a more equitable distribution of resources.

The effectiveness of government attempts to redistribute income are evaluated in more detail in unit 104.

State provision of public and merit goods

The **privatisation** debate in the UK can be separated into two parts.
- Which goods are public and merit goods and therefore need to be provided by the public sector? How should the state organise the provision of these goods? This is the issue which will be discussed in the rest of this unit.
- Does the state have a role in providing goods which are not public or merit goods? For instance, should the state have any role in the provision of coal or railway services? This was the debate discussed in detail in unit 43.

There are a variety of ways in which public and merit goods can be provided by the State. All methods involve the state taxing individuals and paying for the provision of these services.
- The state can produce the goods itself. In the UK this is done in health and education, for instance.
- The state can contract private companies to provide the goods or services. This system is currently being implemented in many areas of local authority services such as refuse collection and school cleaning.
- The state can provide resources or income to individuals and then force them to use that income to buy goods and services. It has been suggested, for instance, that all schools be privatised and that each child be given a voucher for education. The parents of the child would then be free to spend that voucher at the private school of their choice. The voucher would be worth a sum equivalent to the minimum required to provide an adequate education. If a school charged higher fees than the value of the voucher, then parents of children attending the school would have to top up the fees with their own money.

Which is the most desirable form of provision is a complex issue. However, there are three key considerations.

Productive efficiency There can be large **economies of scale** available if a service is provided for the total population. For instance, it should be more costly for two refuse collection companies in competition to collect refuse on a housing estate than just one. Therefore providing every household with a voucher for refuse collection to spend with the company of their choice is likely to be far more costly than either direct provision of the service by the local authority or a system of tendering to a private contractor. The same might apply to health care provision. The amount spent on the National Health Service (NHS) is about two-thirds of that in France and Germany and almost half that of the USA as a percentage of national income. It could be argued that this is because the NHS provides lower quality health care than in other countries. But there is evidence to suggest that there are significant economies of scale in the NHS which are not found in the private health care systems of continental Europe and the USA. There are likely to be far fewer economies of scale and therefore services are likely to be far more costly under voucher-type schemes than under a system of direct provision.

Alternatively, it is sometimes claimed that **diseconomies of scale** are present in organisations like the NHS. They are such large bureaucracies that management is unable to control costs and utilise resources efficiently. **X - inefficiency** (☞ unit 32) raises costs as workers within the organisation manipulate the system for their own advantage. Only the break-up of the organisation and the creation of strong competition in the market place can lower costs and eliminate inefficiency. If this were true, it would be a strong argument in favour of a voucher-type system.

Allocative efficiency State production or tendering systems are unlikely to create much **consumer choice**. In the NHS, for instance, there are very limited opportunities for patients to exercise choice about which doctor to see, or when to have an operation, or which hospital to go to. Moreover consumers have no choice about how much money should be spent on the NHS except indirectly through the ballot box every five years.

Choice is likely to be greatest under voucher-type systems, where the consumer is able to shop around and where there are a number of producers in the market. Choice would be enhanced if consumers could top up vouchers with their own money. For instance, one school might charge just the state voucher for its pupils, whilst a competing school might charge the state voucher plus £100 a term, presumably for a 'better' education. Parents could then choose which type of education to buy for their children.

However, choice may not be so great as it might seem. Consumers of education or health are likely to want to buy from their nearest supplier. Therefore, weak local monopolies are likely to emerge, particularly in rural areas. Choice implies that consumers are able to make rational choices. But there may be little **consumer sovereignty** (☞ unit 40) in the market. Producers may use their market power to distort information supplied to consumers. Consumers may also have extremely limited understanding of the services they are being asked to buy for themselves.

Distribution of resources Voucher-type systems are likely to encourage better-off consumers to top up their vouchers and buy what they perceive to be a superior product. But it could be argued that consumption of services such as health and education are a basic right in a modern industrialised economy and that all people should be treated equally (horizontal equity ☞ unit 41). Therefore it is inequitable for a rich person to receive better health care than a poor person, and for the child of a rich person to receive a better education than the child of a poor person. The two alternative forms of provision are likely to produce a more equitable distribution of resources. The National Health Service aims to provide the same quality of health care for everyone, regardless of income.

QUESTION 4 It has been suggested that all people reaching the age of 16 should be given an education voucher. This could be spent at any age between 16 and 60. A person might choose to spend it on a university or polytechnic course, or it might be used for vocational training at a training institute.

Education in schools and colleges of further education up to the age of 18 would continue to be free. Students attending university or college would be charged full fees and receive no grant. They would use their voucher to pay for their education.

Discuss the relative merits of funding education and training in this way.

Key terms

Public good - a good where consumption by one person does not reduce the amount available for consumption by another person and where once provided, all individuals benefit or suffer whether they wish to or not.

Free rider - a person or organisation which receives benefits that others have paid for without making any contribution themselves.

Merit good - a good which is under-provided by the market mechanism. A demerit good is one which is over-provided by the market mechanism.

Applied economics

Public Expenditure in the UK

Public expenditure totals

The public sector in the UK comprises central government, local government and government enterprises such as public corporations. Table 44.1 shows that central government is responsible for 71 per cent of total public spending. Compared to other countries, the size of Britain's public sector is unexceptional. As shown in Table 44.2, it is greater as a proportion of GDP than the free market economies of the United States or Japan, broadly similar to our EC partners, but much lower than a mixed economy such as Sweden.

Public expenditure totals can be divided by function, as illustrated in Table 44.1.

■ The largest single item of public expenditure is social security. This covers **transfer payments** such as unemployment benefit and family credit from government to individuals. The largest single component of this is the state retirement pension.

■ Spending on health and personal social services is the second largest category of expenditure. Most of this is accounted for by the cost of the National Health Service. Personal social services are mainly the social services departments of local authorities.

■ Education and science covers local government spending on primary and secondary schools, and colleges of further education. Central government pays for higher education and research grants. Defence spending is expenditure on the army, navy and airforce.

■ Other environmental services includes spending on street lighting, parks, refuse collection and sanitation.

■ Transport is mainly spending on roads.

■ Housing is expenditure by councils on council houses and grants to Housing Associations.

■ Industry, energy, trade and employment includes central government loans and grants to nationalised industries such as the Post Office. Employment spending includes expenditure on the Employment Training Scheme and the Youth Training Scheme.

■ Law, order and protective services covers spending on the police, the judiciary, prisons and the fire service.

■ Other expenditure includes expenditure on overseas aid, agriculture, forestry and fishing, the Arts, libraries, embassies abroad and interest payments on the National Debt.

Table 44.1 *Public expenditure by function*

United Kingdom	£ billion
	1988-89 estimated outturn
Function	
Defence	18.1
Overseas services, including overseas aid	3.0
Agriculture, fisheries, food and forestry	2.2
Industry, energy, trade and employment	6.4
Arts and libraries	1.1
Transport	5.6
Housing	3.0
Other environmental services	5.4
Law, order and protective services	8.1
Education and science	21.2
Health and personal social services	25.4
Social security	46.3
Other expenditure	4.1
Privatisation proceeds	-5.7
Planning total	144.4
Of which expenditure by:	
Central government	109.9
Local authorities	40.6
Nationalised industries	0.2
Other public corporations	0.5

Source: adapted from CSO, *Social Trends*.

Table 44.2 *Government expenditure as percentage of GDP*

	1960 - 67	1968 - 73	1974 - 79	1980 - 88
Sweden	34.8	44.3	54.4	62.8
France	37.4	38.9	43.3	50.4
Average EC	33.9	37.1	43.2	48.4
Italy	31.9	36.0	42.9	48.4
Germany	35.7	39.8	47.5	47.9
UK	34.7	39.5	44.6	45.7
Canada	29.3	34.7	39.2	45.1
US	28.3	31.0	32.6	36.0
Japan	18.7	20.5	28.4	33.2

Source: adapted from OECD, *Historical Statistics*.

Trends in public expenditure

Total government spending in real terms has tended to rise over time. Figure 44.1 shows that it has also risen as a percentage of GDP. Public expenditure, not unexpectedly, peaked on the latter measurement during both World Wars. Since 1979 it has been government policy to reduce public expenditure as a percentage of GDP. Initially, the Conservative government hoped that public expenditure in real terms would fall. However, commitments to higher spending on defence and law and order, together with the worst recession since the 1930s, initially led to a rise in public spending. Since the mid 1980s, government has found it politically impossible to reduce spending on the National Health Service or to cut pensions in

real terms. Coupled with growing anxiety about the state of Britain's roads, the environment and the education service, it is likely that spending will continue to rise during the 1990s. Having failed to cut public spending in real terms, the government has now redefined its objective in terms of cutting public spending as a percentage of GNP. Since the mid-1980s, they have succeeded to some extent in achieving this. If this policy objective is to be achieved in the 1990s, it will come about because public expenditure grows more slowly than GNP.

Changes in the components of public spending in recent years are shown in Figure 44.2. There have been large falls in public sector investment - in housing and nationalised industries - and in government grants for private sector investment - expenditure on industry.

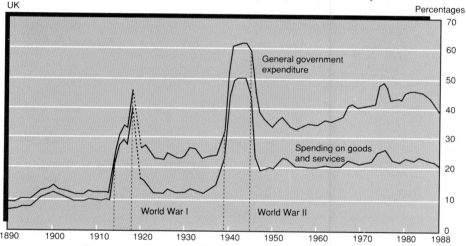

Figure 44.1 *General goverment expenditure as a percentage of GDP*

Source: CSO, *Social Trends.*

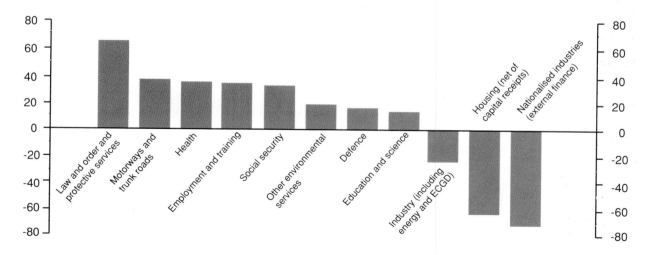

Figure 44.2 *Changes in government expenditure by function in real terms. Financial years 1978-79 to 1989-90, % change*

Source: adapted from The Treasury, *Economic Progress Report*, February 1990.

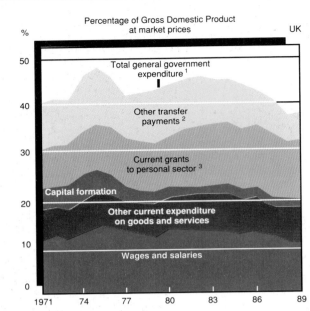

Percentage of Gross Domestic Product at market prices

UK

- Total general government expenditure [1]
- Other transfer payments [2]
- Current grants to personal sector [3]
- Capital formation
- Other current expenditure on goods and services
- Wages and salaries

1. Combined central government and local autority sector.
2. Mainly subsidies, debt interest, other central government and local authority grants and loans.
3. Social security payments, educational grants, etc.

Source: adapted from CSO, *Social Trends*; CSO, United Kingdom National Accounts (Blue book).

Figure 44.3 *Total general government expenditure by economic category[1]*

The latter also includes subsidies to industry. The largest percentage increase in spending has been on the police and the prison service. Note that GDP over the period 1978 to 1989 increased in real terms by 28 per cent. So in areas like health and roads, the proportion of GDP being spent on these areas has barely increased, whilst there has been a fall in the proportion of GDP being spent on defence and education. An alternative way of looking at public spending is shown in Figure 44.3. Current grants and other transfer payments include social security payments and interest on the National Debt. If these are excluded, then it can be seen that over half of total government spending is made up of wages and salaries. Services such as education, health, defence and law and order are labour intensive. This explains why control of public sector pay is essential if government is to reduce the share of public spending in the economy. Note too the considerable squeeze on capital formation during the 1980s. Spending on everything from new roads to council houses and new schools has fallen as a percentage of GNP, if not in real terms. Critics of the government would point to problems of homelessness, overcrowding on Britain's roads and railways and deteriorating school buildings as evidence of the failure of government to invest in the social infrastructure of the UK.

Are public services improving?

There are major problems in assessing whether there has been a growth in public services in recent years. Taking the National Health Service as an example, there are three key factors which need to be considered.

The cost of the service Data are often presented 'at constant prices'. This means that figures are adjusted for the general rate of inflation in the economy (measured by the GDP deflator rather than the Retail Price Index). However, increases in real expenditure on services do not necessarily mean that the volume of services has increased. This is because inflation in the public sector is likely to be higher than inflation in the economy as whole. The public sector is far more labour intensive than the private sector. There is also far less scope for increases in productivity. Earnings on average increase about 2 per cent more than the increase in inflation each year. Hence the NHS has to pay more in real terms each year to buy the same number of doctors, nurses, etc.

The needs of the patients The population structure is slowly changing. In particular, there is a growth in the number of over 75 year olds. This age group is a particularly heavy user of NHS facilities. If public spending on the NHS is kept constant, the level of service to the average patient will inevitably decline.

Expectations and technology Each year, consumers expect to be able to buy better products. They expect to see more advanced cars, eat a wider range of food and go to more exotic places for their holidays. They also expect to receive better health care. Advances in medicine mean that more and more illnesses are capable of treatment. But if these illnesses are to be treated, then extra money must be found to pay for them. Consumers also expect better facilities - everything from potted plants in waiting rooms, to private hospital rooms, to being able to choose the timing of medical treatment. These cost money.

Our expectations are for spending on the NHS to rise each year well above the rate of inflation. But this is not happening. The result is growing dissatisfaction with the National Health Service. Overall, it is probably right to claim that the quality of care in the National Health Service has improved since 1979. The problem is that consumers are dissatisfied with the pace of change. J K Galbraith, in his book *The Affluent Society*, talked about 'private affluence and public squalor'. Opinion polls consistently show that consumers and taxpayers wish to spend more of their income on a better National Health Service. Government policy to curb public spending will frustrate those desires. The result is ever increasing market failure. This is likely to be true not just of health services but also of services such as transport and education.

HALF-BAKED PROPOSALS BASED ON NEO-LIBERTARIAN FANTASIES

Michael Prowse
on the Welfare State.

Suppose Neville Chamberlain had refused to appease Hitler and the Second World War had been avoided. The social solidarity created by total war would not have occurred; the Labour Party would probably not have won a landslide victory in 1945. What kind of Welfare State would the UK have created? Would nearly all hospitals be publicly owned? Would most pupils be state-educated?

These may appear to be irritatingly hypothetical questions. But they do have relevance because a vocal element of the Conservative Party would like to see the socialist legacy of the 1940s completely erased during the 1990s. They favour a return to 19th century *laisser faire* and Samuel Smiles's self-help.

The tendency is best represented by the No Turning Back group of the right-wing Tory MPs.

The group's latest pamphlet, Choice and Responsibility: the Enabling State, urges the government to intensify the assault on the 'very concept of individual dependence on state provision of health care, education and social security.'

In a strange way, the pamphlet invites ridicule. It seriously suggests that Britain should draw inspiration from Hong Kong and Singapore and seek a future as a' kind of free port linking Europe and the world...'

It describes the achievements of the Thatcher government as virtually unparalled in British political history.

It defends privatisation as a general policy on the grounds that British Airways offers a better service.

Factual errors are even more alarming. The MPs claim that: 'In 1979 the British government spent a higher proportion of Gross Domestic Product than any of those who are now our European Community partners. Now we spend less.'

The truth is rather different. The Tories did not inherit a European Leviathan from Labour. OECD figures show that in 1979 public spending as a percentage of GDP was lower in Britain than in West Germany, Ireland and the Netherlands. In most cases the gap was considerable.

Yet in spite of its inaccuracy, hyperbole and naivety, the No Turning Back group's pamphlet poses valid questions.

The Welfare State of the 1940s has no God-given right of existence. Reforms which genuinely offer the prospect of better quality at lower prices deserve serious consideration.

The MPs, however, appear to start from the assumption that state welfare can be justified only by arguments about social justice - arguments which in their view are thoroughly misguided. They seem wholly unaware that there are many technical reasons why heavy state involvement in welfare is necessary.

To take one example, the No Turning Back group advocates a big extension of private insurance to cover the risk of unemployment. But it is no accident that private markets have not evolved in this field even in the US.

Private insurance only works well in the absence (among other preconditions) of 'moral hazard': when policy holders can not influence the likelihood, timing of magnitude of claims.

But the way a person behaves can greatly influence the risk of redundancy and the duration of unemployment. A subsidiary problem is that the risks insured are not independent: claims are likely to be unacceptably bunched because unemployment rises and falls according to the nation's, macro - economic health.

Similar technical problems exist in most other parts of the Welfare State.

Public sectors throughout the developed world play a large role in health care, education, pensions and so forth not because they are gripped by an outdated Marxist ideology but because they can often perform these tasks more efficiently than private markets.

Welfare states can and will evolve, but the search for increased efficiency is probably best pursued within a public sector context.

European considerations, which the No Turning Back group wilfully ignores, only reinforce this conclusion. It is simply not credible to argue that Britain has a future as Europe's free market Hong Kong. Economic and political integration within the European Community is bound to accelerate. The UK thus needs to create education, health and social security systems that mesh easily with those on the Continent - which are invariably public sector run.

Half-baked proposals based on the neo-libertarian fantasies of US think - tanks (which are largely ignored in Washington) no longer serve a useful service. If the No Turning Back group wants to make a serious contribution it should send fact-finding missions to the capitals which count - Bonn, Paris, and Brussels.

Source: *Financial Times*, 24.9.1990.

1. Outline the arguments put forward in favour of dismantling the Welfare State.
2. Why might services such as unemployment insurance, health care and education be less efficiently provided by private markets rather than the state?
3. What might be the implications of the UK becoming a 'kind of free port linking Europe and the world'?

45 Taxation

Summary

1. Governments need to raise taxes to pay for public spending. Taxes are also used to correct market failure, to redistribute income and wealth and to manage the economy.

2. Taxes can be direct or indirect, proportional, progressive or regressive.
3. The canons of taxation are a set of principles by which taxes can be evaluated.

The reasons for taxation

Governments use taxation for a number of purposes.

To pay for government expenditure Governments need to raise finance for their expenditure programmes (☞ unit 44). They can borrow a limited amount of money for this, but most of the finance must come from taxation if inflation is to be avoided.

To correct market failure such as externalities Governments can intervene in individual markets by changing taxes and thus changing demand. For instance, tobacco consumption can be reduced by raising taxes on cigarettes, pollution can be controlled by imposing pollution taxes, or sales of books can be increased by exempting them from VAT. Used in this way, taxation becomes a way of increasing economic efficiency.

To manage the economy as a whole Taxation can have an important influence on the **macro-economic** performance of the economy (☞ unit 77). Governments may change tax rates in order to influence variables such as inflation, unemployment and the balance of payments.

To redistribute income A government may judge that the distribution of resources is inequitable. To redistribute income, it may impose taxes which reduce the income and wealth of some groups in society and use the money collected to increase the income and wealth of other groups.

QUESTION 1 Each year in the Budget, the Chancellor of the Exchequer announces whether or not he will change the level of excise duties on tobacco. In most years, this is increased at least in line with inflation, although in some years, particularly election years, it is not increased at all. Why might the government change the level of excise duty on tobacco each year?

Direct and indirect taxes

Taxes are classified into two types. A DIRECT TAX is a tax levied directly on an individual or organisation. For instance, income tax is a direct tax because individual income earners are responsible for paying it. The poll tax or community charge is a direct tax because individuals over 18 pay it directly to the local authority. Corporation tax, a tax on company profits, is a direct tax too because companies have to pay it directly to the Inland Revenue.

An INDIRECT TAX is a tax on a good or service. For instance, value added tax is an indirect tax because it is a 15 per cent tax on most goods and services. Local Authority rates were an indirect tax on the notional rent of a property as is the new Uniform Business Rate for businesses.

QUESTION 2 Explain which of the following taxes are direct taxes and which are indirect:

(a) income tax; (b) National Insurance contributions; (c) inheritance tax; (d) corporation tax; (e) capital gains tax; (f) poll tax; (g) VAT; (h) excise duties.

Progressive, regressive and proportional taxes

Another way of classifying taxes is to consider their **incidence** (☞ unit 13) as a proportion of income. A PROGRESSIVE TAX is a tax where the proportion of income paid in tax rises as the income of the taxpayer rises. For instance, income tax would be progressive if a worker earning £ 4 000 a year were to pay 5 per cent of income in tax, but 25 per cent on income of £ 40 000.

A REGRESSIVE TAX is a tax where the proportion of income paid in tax falls as the income of the taxpayer rises. An extreme example of a regressive tax is the poll tax. The amount paid in poll tax is identical for most poll tax payers. A person earning £8 000 per year and paying £400 a year in poll tax would pay exactly the same amount as a person earning £40 000. But the proportion of tax paid would be different - 5 per cent of income for the person earning £8 000 a year (£400 ÷ £8 000), but only 1 per cent for the person earning £40 000 a year (£400 ÷ £40 000).

A PROPORTIONAL TAX is one where the proportion paid in tax remains the same as the income of the taxpayer changes (although the actual amount paid increases as income increases). VAT is an example of a broadly proportional tax. Whilst lower income earners spend a higher proportion of their income on zero-rated goods and services, higher income earners tend to save more of their income. Hence, the average rate of VAT paid by individuals tends to be a little less than 15 per cent.

The distinction between progressive, regressive and proportional taxes is made because it is important in the study of the distribution of income and wealth. The more progressive the tax, the greater the link with ability to pay the tax and the more likely it is to result in a redistribution of resources from the better off in society to the less well off.

QUESTION 3 From 5 October (1989) the system of National Insurance contributions will be simplified so that:
- those with earnings below £43 per week will continue to pay nothing:
- those with earnings at or above £43 per week will pay 2 per cent on the first £43 (i.e. 86p) and 9 per cent on the rest up to the upper earnings limit of £325.

Source: The Treasury, *The Budget in Brief*, 14.3.1989.

(a) Calculate the total amount of National Insurance contributions a worker would have to pay if her weekly earnings were: (i) £20; (ii) £42; (iii) £44; (iv) £143; (v) £243; (vi) £500.
(b) Are National Insurance contributions progressive, regressive or proportional over the weekly income range: (i) £20 to £40; (ii) £42 to £44; (iii) £44 to £143; (iv) £143 to £243; (v) £243 to £500?

The canons of taxation

Taxation has been a source of much controversy since the first tax was introduced. Adam Smith wrote at length on the subject of taxation in his book *An Enquiry into the Nature and Causes of the Wealth of Nations*, published in 1776. He argued that a good tax was one which had four characteristics:
- the cost of collection should be low relative to the yield of the tax;
- the timing of collection and the amount to be paid should be clear and certain;
- the means of payment and the timing of the payment should be convenient to the taxpayer;
- taxes should be levied according to the ability to pay of the individual taxpayer.

There have been examples in history where taxes did not possess these canons. For instance, at certain periods in Roman history tax collecting was privatised. The Roman government sold the right to collect taxes in a province to the highest bidder. This individual would buy the right, hoping to charge more in taxes than he paid to the Roman authorities. With luck he might make 100 per cent profit

on the contract - in this case the cost of collection would hardly be low. He would terrorise the province, forcing anyone and everyone to pay as much tax as he could exact from citizens. No attempt was made to make means of payment or timing suitable to the taxpayer. It was not clear on what basis citizens were being taxed, and there was no attempt to link taxes to ability to pay, since it was the poor who were the most easily terrorised whilst better off citizens were left alone for fear that they might complain to Rome!

Economists today have argued that in addition to Adam Smith's canons, a 'good' tax should be one which:
- leads to the least loss of economic efficiency, or even increases economic efficiency;
- is compatible with foreign tax systems, and in the case of the UK, particularly with EC tax regimes;
- automatically adjusts to changes in the price level - this is particularly important in a high inflation economy.

In the applied economics section at the end of this unit, the extent to which one tax, the poll tax, can be considered a good tax will be discussed.

QUESTION 4
Table 45.1 *Revenue and cost of collection for selected taxes, 1986-7*

	Revenue	Administration costs		Compliance costs	
	£ bn	£m	%	£m	%
Income tax, capital gains tax & National Insurance contributions	65.1	997	1.53	2 212	3.4
VAT	21.4	220	1.03	791	3.69
Excise duties	16.5	42	0.25	33	0.20
Average central government	122.3	1 369	1.12	3 409	2.33

Source: adapted from the *Financial Times*, 20 .12.1989

Revenue is defined as the total revenue received by the government from the tax. Administrative costs are the costs to the government of collecting the tax (in £m and as a percentage of the revenue raised in tax). Compliance costs are an estimate of the cost of collection which is borne by private firms and individuals (again in £m and as a percentage of the revenue raised in tax). For instance, businesses have to spend time and therefore money accounting for the VAT they charge customers.

To what extent is VAT a 'good tax'?

Taxation, efficiency and equity

A tax is likely to lead to a fall in supply and a consequent reduction in the quantity demanded of the product or

service being taxed. For instance:
- VAT and excise duties on a product push the supply curve to the left which in turn leads to a fall in the quantity demanded of the product (☞ unit 13);
- Income tax is likely to lead to a fall in the supply of labour to the market (☞ unit 99);
- Corporation tax is likely to lead to a fall in the supply of entrepreneurs to the market (☞ unit 55).

Taxes therefore distort markets. This may be beneficial in some markets, particularly if there are important negative externalities present and the tax brings private costs and benefits into line with social costs and benefits (☞ unit 35).

In other markets, taxes may lead to a loss of efficiency. For instance, if all markets were perfectly competitive, then the economy would be Pareto efficient (☞ unit 34). The introduction of a tax on one commodity, such as petrol, would then lead to a loss of efficiency in the economy because marginal cost would no longer equal price in that market. In practice, there are so many examples of market failure that it is impossible to come to any simple conclusions about whether a tax does or does not lead to efficiency losses. However, the **theory of the second best** suggests that taxes which are broadly based are less likely to lead to efficiency losses than narrow taxes. Low rates of tax spread as widely as possible are likely to be less damaging to economic welfare than high rates of tax on a small number of goods or individuals. For instance, a single rate VAT is likely to result in greater efficiency than a tax solely on petrol which raises the same revenue. Or an income tax which all earners pay is likely to lead to lower efficiency losses than an income tax paid solely by manufacturing workers.

It should be remembered that taxes are raised mainly to pay for government expenditure. Even if the imposition of taxes does lead to a loss of efficiency, this loss should be outweighed by the gain in economic efficiency resulting from the provision of **public** and **merit** goods by the government.

Taxes are also raised to ensure a redistribution of resources within the economy. There will be an increase in economic welfare if the welfare gains from a more desirable distribution of resources outweigh the welfare losses from the greater inefficiency arising from taxation.

QUESTION 5 The government levies a 100 per cent tax on the purchase price of gas.
(a) What are the likely economic consequences of this?
(b) Will it lead to greater or less efficiency in the economy as a whole?

Key terms

Direct tax - a tax levied directly on an individual or organisation, such as income tax or poll tax.
Indirect tax - a tax levied on goods or services, such as value added tax or excise duties.
Progressive, regressive or proportional taxes - taxes where the proportion of income paid in tax rises, falls or remains the same respectively as income rises.

Applied economics

Taxation in the UK

The main taxes in the UK

Figure 45.1 shows the breakdown of government revenue in 1989-90. All but 5 per cent is gained from taxation. The main UK taxes are as follows.

Income tax This is the single most important source of revenue for government. It is a tax on the income of individuals. Each person in the UK is allowed to earn a certain amount before paying tax. This amount is called a **tax allowance**. One tax allowance which everyone gets is the **personal allowance**. In 1990/91, a person could earn £3 005 a year 'tax free'. An additional allowance of £1 720 is also given to one person of a married couple. The two other main allowances are payments to pension schemes and mortgage interest relief on mortgages up to £30 000 a year.

Income earned over the value of allowances (the **tax threshold**) is liable to tax (and is called **taxable income**). The current basic rate of tax is 25 per cent. Taxable income over £20 700 is taxed at 40 per cent, the higher rate of tax. Table 45.2 gives an example of how the income tax of an individual would be calculated.

For very low income earners, the **marginal rate of tax is** 0 per cent (i.e. they can earn an extra £1 without paying income tax). For most of those who earn more than the value of their allowance over the year, the marginal rate of tax is 25 per cent. For high income earners (those earning more than £20 700 plus allowances), the marginal rate is 40 per cent. However, the average rate of tax is less than this. Look again at Table 45.2. This person is earning £50 000 before tax. She pays just £11 800 in tax. Therefore her average rate of tax is only 23.6 per cent. But her marginal rate is 40 per cent because she paid 40p in tax on the last £1

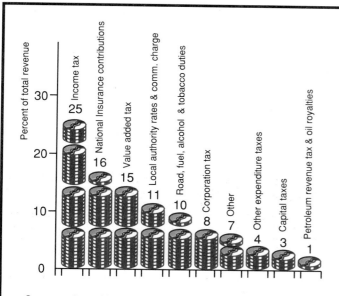

Source: adapted from The Treasury, *The Budget in Brief*, 20.3.1990.

Figure 45.1 *Government revenue 1989/90*

Table 45.2

		£
Income before tax		50 000
Allowances		
Personal allowance	4000	
Interest on mortgage	3000	
Pension payments	6000	
Total	13 000	13 000
Taxable income		37 000
Tax		
20 000 at 25%	5000	
17 000 at 40%	6800	
Total tax paid	11 800	11 800

earned. The average rate of tax is always less than the marginal rate for taxpayers. This is because all income earners can earn a portion of their income 'tax free' and the next £20 000 approximately is taxed at only 25 per cent.

Income tax from employed workers is collected by employers through the PAYE (pay as you earn) system. Employers then pay it to the Inland Revenue.

National Insurance contributions (NICs) All taxes apart from NICs are paid into one central fund (called the **Consolidated Fund**) and are used to pay for government spending. However, there is a separate National Insurance Fund out of which are paid National Insurance benefits such as state pensions and unemployment benefit. The National Insurance Fund is financed from National Insurance contributions. Strictly speaking, contributions are not taxes because they are a form of insurance premium. However, they have come to be seen, and used by, government as a form of tax. NICs are paid by workers. In 1990/91 employed workers paid contributions of 9 per cent of earnings between £46 and £350. In addition, employers have to pay employers National Insurance contributions on a sliding scale from 0 to 10.45 per cent of earnings. For instance, they have to pay 10.45 per cent of the weekly earnings of any worker earning more than £175 per week.

Corporation tax Corporation tax is a tax on company profits. The top rate of tax is 35 per cent on profits over £1 million per annum. However, companies can claim numerous allowances, including investment

allowances. As a result the average rate of tax on company profits is considerably less than the marginal rate for most companies.

Capital gains tax This is a tax on real capital gains - the difference between the buying price and selling price of an asset adjusted for inflation. Most goods and services are exempt, including the buying and selling of a person's main home. It is paid mainly on stocks and shares. Individuals can make capital gains of up to £5 000 per year free of tax. Thereafter capital gains are included with income and taxed at the appropriate rate of income tax (i.e. either 25 per cent or 40 per cent).

Inheritance tax This is a tax on the value of assets left on death by an individual. The first £128 000 (in 1990-91) of any inheritance is tax free. Thereafter, it is taxed at 40 per cent. There are numerous exemptions. For instance, any money left by one spouse to another is completely tax free. There is also no tax on gifts made during the lifetime of an individual provided that they are made 7 years before death.

Excise duties These are not to be confused with customs duties, taxes on imported goods. Excise duties are taxes levied on fuel, alcohol, tobacco and betting. They are calculated not on value (as with VAT) but on the volume sold. So excise duty is paid per litre of petrol or per bottle of wine for instance.

Value added tax (VAT) This is a tax on expenditure. There are two rates of tax. Essential commodities such as food, children's clothing and electricity are tax exempt (i.e. there is a zero rate). All other goods and services are taxed at 15 per cent. VAT is collected by business and is imposed on the value added to a product by that business.

Petroleum revenue tax and oil royalties These are taxes on the output of North Sea oil.

Local authority rates/poll tax In April 1990, local authority rates, a tax on property, were replaced by the poll tax (or community charge) and business rates in England and Wales. These taxes are the only tax imposed by local government as opposed to central government and are dealt with below.

International comparisons

Figure 45.2 gives an international comparison of taxes. It has been argued in the past that Britain is highly taxed and that this has contributed to low economic growth rates. Figure 45.2 shows that taxes excluding National Insurance contributions (social security contributions) are indeed higher as a percentage of national income than, for instance, in France and Germany. However, Britain is less highly taxed than these countries if National Insurance

contributions are included. Internationally the UK never has been a particularly high tax economy even when National Insurance contributions have been taken into consideration.

Changes in tax

Since 1979 there have been significant changes in the burden of tax, as Tables 45.3 and 45.4 show.

A shift from income tax to VAT In the 1979 Budget, the standard rate of VAT was increased from 8 per cent to 15 per cent. The extra revenue generated was used to finance cuts in income tax, in particular a cut in the top rate of income tax from 83 per cent to 60 per cent. Throughout the 1980s, government has made its top priority cuts in income tax rather than indirect tax. In 1988 the top rate of tax was reduced again from 60 per cent to 40 per cent and over the period 1979 to 1989 the standard rate of income tax was cut from 33 per cent to 25 per cent.

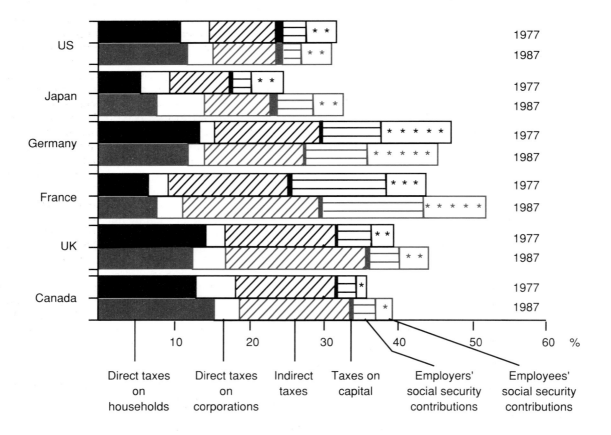

Figure 45.2 *International tax comparisons: taxes as a percentage of GDP*

Source: adapted from OECD, *Historical Statistics*.

Table 45.3 *Central government income*

	Per cent	
	1979	1989
Taxes on income		
Paid by persons	31.0	26.6
Paid by corporations	7.5	12.7
Taxes on expenditure		
Customs and excise (Including VAT)	27.9	30.6
Other indirect taxes	7.2	3.3
Social insurance contributions		
Paid by employees	6.9	8.4
Paid by employers	10.5	10.0
Rent, interest, dividends, royalties and other current income	7.4	5.8
Taxes on capital	1.5	2.3
Total[1]	100.0	100.0

1. Figures may not add up to 100 because of rounding.

Source: adapted from CSO, National Income and Accounts Blue Book.

Table 45.4 *Local authority income*

	Per cent	
	1979	1989
Grants from central government	51.6	49.1
Rates/community charge	29.4	37.9
Other	19.0	13.1
Total	100.0	100.0

Source: adapted from CSO, National Income and Accounts Blue Book.

A reduction in the incidence of taxes on capital
Capital gains tax has become progressively less of a burden. Possibly the two most important measures which accomplished this were the index linking of capital gains (where capital gains were calculated in real terms and not money terms for the purpose of tax) and the abolition of tax liabilities for all capital gains made before 1982. Inheritance tax, introduced in 1986, replaced capital transfer tax. The latter taxed not only transfers of money on death but also lifetime gifts. Anybody wishing to avoid inheritance tax is now able to give away their money during their lifetime. Whilst the incidence of tax has fallen, individuals have become more wealthy during the 1980s. In particular, many more than before have inherited houses from relatives which have been subject to inheritence tax. Hence, tax revenues and the proportion of tax derived from taxes on capital have increased between 1979 and 1989.

A shift in the burden of National Insurance contributions Whilst National Insurance contributions paid by employees have increased as a percentage of tax revenue, those paid by employers have declined. It could be argued that part of the reduction in income tax has effectively been paid for by the overall increase in National Insurance contributions.

Increased local authority taxes As Table 45.4 shows, central government has reduced its grants to local authorities between 1979 and 1989 as a percentage of total local authority income. It could be argued that this has meant that central government has been able to cut its taxes, particularly income tax, and has forced local authorities to increase their taxes.

The tax system has become more regressive
Income tax is generally considered to be progressive because the average rate of tax tends to rise as increase increases. National Insurance contributions (NICs) of employees are less progressive because the lower rate band at the bottom of the scale is, very small. Moreover, the marginal rate of employees' NICs on income over £350 is zero, so over this limit contributions become regressive. VAT is proportional or possibly regressive. Although low income earners spend a greater proportion of their income on zero rated goods and therefore pay less VAT, the better off save a larger proportion of their income, again exempting this portion of income from VAT. Excise duties are regressive because petrol, alcohol and tobacco form a larger proportion of the income of low income earners than high income earners. Local authority rates were regressive. The poll tax which replaced the rates is extremely regressive.

The changes introduced since 1979 have served to shift the burden of taxation from the better off to those worse off. Cuts in higher rate income tax have made income tax less progressive. Increases in National Insurance rates have had the same effect. The increase in the rate of VAT from 8 to 15 per cent in 1979 is likely to have made the tax more regressive. The poll tax has changed local authority taxation from being mildly regressive to being extremely regressive.

Poll tax (the community charge) and the canons of taxation

Poll tax, or the community charge, is a tax on people. It is levied on almost all adults aged 18 and over. People on low incomes pay a reduced rate (20 per cent of the full rate). Everyone else, irrespective of income, pays the same amount.

Poll tax replaced the domestic rating system. Rates were a tax on property. Broadly speaking, the larger the property, the higher the rates. The amount of tax was based on the rateable value of a property. This was assessed on a notional rental value. The last revaluation of rateable values occurred in 1973. Therefore by the time rates were abolished in 1990, there were a large number of anomalies in the system. In particular, older houses which were less fashionable and commanded lower rents in 1971, had lower rateable values than new houses. But by 1990 there was little price difference or rental difference between these two types of property.

Business premises were rated too. In 1989/90, all business properties were re-rated and a new business rate system introduced. There were two major differences between the new and old business rate systems.

- Every business had a new rateable value. Businesses which paid more tax under the new system were those businesses which had seen large increases in the values of their property during the 1970s and 1980s. In practice, this meant businesses in the South of England and shops and offices in town centres. The gainers were those who had not enjoyed such large increases in property values. This meant businesses outside the South of England and manufacturing industry.
- Under the new system, the level of business rates was fixed not by local authorities as previously, but by central government. A business in London would pay exactly the same rate in the pound as a business in Newcastle. Local authorities lost control over their ability to decide how much to raise in taxes from businesses in their area.

Poll tax can be evaluated in the light of Adam Smith's canons of taxation.

Cost of collection The cost of collecting the poll tax is estimated to be about twice as much as collecting domestic rates. One reason is because there are twice as many adults as owners of dwellings in the UK. That means twice the number of taxpayers. The second reason is that it was difficult to evade rates. You can't disappear over night with property! But it is possible to evade poll tax by providing false information to local authorities. The cost of policing the system is therefore much higher.

Certainty and convenience The poll tax should be as certain and convenient for taxpayers as the rating system. But it should be remembered that roughly twice the number of people as before will now have the inconvenience of arranging payment of the tax.

Ability to pay Apart from the safety net at the bottom, all poll tax payers will pay the same amount. Therefore, for an estimated 80 per cent of adults, there will be no link at all between tax and ability to pay.

The rates system was mildly regressive but, on average, the higher the income the more paid in rates.

There are other points which are considered when evaluating how 'good' is a tax.

Economic efficiency Rates were a tax on property. Abolishing rates meant that there was no longer any tax on property. The cost of owning a house, therefore, fell relative to all other goods, and economic theory would suggest that the demand for houses would then rise. This rise in demand would lead to an increase in house prices, all other things being equal. (Given the depressed housing market in the South of the late 1980s, this would result in lower falls in house prices than would otherwise be the case.) The lowest estimates put the rise in price of houses at 15 per cent.

One of the major problems confronting the UK economy today is a lack of regional labour mobility, partly caused by rigidities in the housing market. People in the North are unable to move south because of high property prices, whilst those in the South are afraid to move north in case they ever have to move south again and pay southern house prices. Increases in property prices will make this situation even worse. It will also further encourage people to buy property rather than financial assets like stocks and shares. Indirectly this is likely to lead to greater investment in new housing and less investment in manufacturing and service industries, which may adversely affect our international competitiveness.

Compatibility with foreign tax systems No other industrialised country has a poll tax. All have taxes on residential property.

The poll tax, or community charge, does not meet most criteria for a 'good' tax. Why then has it been introduced? Partly, the reasons were political but there were also some economic arguments. Central government has been trying to get local authorities to reduce their expenditure since 1979. The government argued that local authority services were inefficient and gave poor value for money. Because most local electors did not pay rates, they were able to vote for political parties which promised high spending without suffering any financial consequences. Under the poll tax, though, all adults pay a local authority tax and therefore if citizens vote for a high spending party, they should know that this could mean high poll tax bills for themselves.

The system was geared to amplify the effects of local authority 'overspending' on poll tax payers. Each year, government decides upon a **standard spending assessment** for each local authority. This is the amount which the government thinks a local authority needs to spend to provide services in its area. The government then bases its grant to local authorities on that figure. Roughly, for every £1 that the government says a local authority ought to spend, 50p is financed from a central government grant, 25p from the business rates (controlled by government) and 25p from the poll tax. If the local authority decides to spend £1.10 instead of the £1 fixed by the government, the extra 10p has to be paid by poll tax payers. Instead of paying 25p, they pay 40p - an increase of 40 per cent. In its first year in operation, 1990-91, nearly all local authorities spent more than the standard spending assessment fixed by central government. As a result, poll tax bills were much higher than government predicted. Opinion polls showed that citizens placed the blame for this not on their local authorities but on central government.

So in Autumn 1990, the government announced a £3bn increase in grants to local authorities for 1991-92 and a return to the system of **capping** which had operated under the rating system. The government would prevent any local authority spending more than a small percentage over the standard spending assessment. But these measures effectively removed any idea that voters should be made financially accountable for their decisions in the ballot box.

In defence of the poll tax, there was also a secondary argument about the equity (or fairness) of the taxation system. Some argued that taxes should be linked not with ability to pay but to use of service. They equated local authorities with supermarkets. In a supermarket, a can of baked beans is the same price to a rich person as to a poor person. So why should the better off pay more for local authority services than the poor? However, evidence suggests that higher income earners benefit more from local authority services than low income earners. Their children are far more likely to stay on in education post - 16. They own more cars and therefore make more use of the roads. They dispose of more rubbish in their bins each week. They are more likely to use public libraries.

In December 1990, less than 8 months after its introduction in England and Wales, the government announced that it was to conduct a fundamental review of local authority finance, with the implication that the poll tax would be replaced by the sort of local taxes found everywhere else in the industrialised world - property taxes, income taxes or sales taxes.

1. To what extent are income tax and National Insurance contributions progressive taxes?

2. Suggest reasons why the percentages paid in tax and NICs have changed during the 1980s.

Table 45.5 *Percentage of income paid in income tax and National Insurance contributions (NICs) by a married couple*

			Per cent
	1980-81	1984-85	1989-90
Half average earnings			
Tax	8.5	6.9	6.5
NIC	6.7	9.0	6.7
Average earnings			
Tax	19.2	18.5	15.8
NIC	6.7	9.0	8.3
Twice average earnings			
Tax	24.6	24.2	20.4
NIC	4.8	7.1	6.1

Source: adapted from CSO, *Social Trends*.

INVESTIGATIONS 3

A. Externalities

Aims

- To examine a local example of externalities.
- To investigate the private and social costs and benefits of an activity which gives rise to externalities.
- To identify the methods of internalising externalities and evaluate their costs and benefits.

Research activity

Choose a local example of an activity which results in externalities. For example, you could investigate the externalities resulting from the building of a new road or the repair or alteration of an existing road. Alternatively you could investigate a local airport or the building of a new factory in the area. In making your choice consider carefully how much information you will be able to obtain.

Identify the nature of the activity which leads to the occurrence of externalities. For instance, if you are investigating the location of a new factory, find out what is produced and the process which is used.

Identify the externalities which result and who suffers and who benefits. Quantify the externalities if possible.

If negative externalities result, find out what restrictions exist to control them. What suggestions have, if any, been put forward to limit further production of negative externalities?

Sources

Primary evidence can be gathered by direct observation. For instance, if you investigate noise pollution from a local road, it might be possible to measure noise levels at various distances from the road at various times of the day. You could also design a questionnaire for local residents, pedestrians, motorists and local business people. Question them about the externalities which result from the road. Further information could be found by interviewing business people who benefit or suffer as a result of the road and the traffic on it.

Some research into the scientific and technical causes of pollution resulting from road traffic and how it could be reduced is likely to be needed. Approach your science department for help with this.

Government publications, such as *Social Trends* and the *Digest of Environmental Protection and Water Statistics*, published by the Central Statistical Office, might give regional and national figures for road use and traffic pollution. The *CSO Guide to Official Statistics* will give you more detailed sources by type of pollution. The Environmental Department of your local council might be able to give figures or other information on a local basis. If the road has been built recently, then surveys may have been taken. Local meetings may have been held on the potential benefits and problems of the road. You may also

be able to find articles in the local newspaper, back copies of which should be available either at your local public reference library or at the offices of the newspaper. Environmental pressure groups such as Friends of the Earth and Greenpeace may have relevant data. They may also have policy documents on the reduction of negative externalities caused by road transport.

Structuring your report

Introduction Outline the aims of your investigation. Briefly describe the type and source of the externalities you have found.

Investigation Describe your research methods. What problems did you encounter? Present the results of your information in a suitable form. Analyse the extent to which your results were accurate.

Analysis Using the economic concepts of social costs and benefits and externalities, classify your findings. What, if any, controls exist on the negative externalities present? Explain what impact these controls may have had.

Evaluation Are negative externalities greater than positive externalities? Are social costs greater than social benefits? What criteria did you use to judge these? Justify your use of criteria. Would it be possible to increase positive externalities and reduce negative externalities? What would be the cost of this? What role should the government, either central or local, play in this issue?

Other suggestions

Identify the private and social costs and benefits of a particular course of action. For instance:
- your decision to go to university or polytechnic, or perhaps leave education after 'A' levels to get a job;
- the decision by your local authority to increase or reduce spending on education in the next financial year;
- a decision by your parents to buy you a car.

Evaluate the extent of the externalities created and suggest policies which could help reduce any negative externalities which arise.

B. Local authority finance

Aims

- To investigate different local authority financing systems.
- To compare the workings of the rating system with the community charge and any other subsequent or proposed system of local authority finance.

■ To evaluate each system according to recognised economic criteria.

Research activity

Explore how the local authority rating system worked in England and Wales before 1989, and find out examples of rates and rateable values in **your** local authority and at least one other. Do the same for the poll tax or community charge and the uniform business rate introduced in 1989. What changes to local authority finance have occurred since that time, or have been proposed? Find out what advantages and disadvantages are said to exist for each type of tax system (such as local authority income tax or transfer of education to central government) and the arguments used to support those opinions.

Sources

Economics and tax textbooks will provide some background to the different local authority tax systems which have operated over the past ten years. For details of current or recent proposals for reform of local authority finance, conduct a newspaper and magazine search in a local large public reference library. Using indexes, find and read recent articles in quality newspapers such as the *Financial Times* and the *Independent* as well as magazines such as the *Economist*. Photocopy anything which you find particularly useful. Local newspapers are also likely to have given wide coverage to local authority finance, but remember to take into account that there is considerable bias in both national and local newspapers.

Rateable values for properties still exist because they form the basis for water rates. So, by asking parents and friends, it should be possible to obtain a range of rateable values for differing properties. It should also be possible, again by interviewing relations and friends, to find out how much in rates was paid on a variety of properties before 1989 and the levels of community charge paid per person after April 1989.

By contacting the Treasurer's Department of your local authority, you may be able to find out a variety of figures which would help you to compare the rating system with the community charge system. For instance, how many taxpayers were there under each system? What was the cost of collection? What were the problems with taxpayers who either didn't pay or paid late? If you conduct a personal interview, you may also be able to find out the views of the interviewee about changes in the system of local authority finance.

Conduct a survey amongst adults who are or were liable for the community charge. Find out their views about the previous rating system, the community charge and any possible replacement for the tax. The wider the range of people interviewed, the better. For instance,

attempt to interview people who differ by income, age, the area in which they live and their known political views.

Structuring the report

Introduction Outline the aims of your investigation.

Local authority tax systems Describe, giving examples from your survey work, the operation of the rating system, the community charge system and any system which might replace the present system. Compare the basis on which people, households and firms were taxed. Identify the major problems claimed to be inherent in each system.

Analysis Using the concepts of progressive and regressive taxation, assess the incidence of tax on different groups. Analyse the extent to which each system in practice affects or affected incentives (e.g. incentives to work, incentives to save, incentives to improve property).

Evaluation Using the canons of taxation, evaluate alternative local authority financing systems. Give as evidence the results of any interviews you may have conducted.

Sources Outline the sources of information you used. What problems did you enounter in gathering relevant data? What data would you have liked to have obtained but could not? To what extent did the data gathered show evidence of bias? To what extent was the evidence gathered from interviews typical of the views of people in the UK as a whole?

Other suggestions

It would be possible to evaluate any change in taxation. For instance:
■ should National Insurance contributions become part of the income tax system;
■ should there be an increase in VAT to finance a reduction in income tax rates;
■ should excise duties on tobacco, alcohol and petrol be raised and the revenue gained be used to lower VAT;
■ should the UK harmonize VAT rates with the rest of the European Community;
■ should the UK introduce a wealth tax?

For each of these, it would be possible to research possible arguments and opinions by using newspapers, periodicals and books as well as through interviews. It is important to examine the arguments for and against the change, expose any bias in arguments used and come to an overall conclusion.

Summary

1. In the long run, the demand curve for labour is downward sloping because capital can be substituted for labour.
2. In the short run, the downward sloping demand curve for labour can be explained by the law of diminishing returns.
3. The marginal revenue product curve of labour is the demand curve for labour. This is true whether the firm operates in a perfectly competitive or imperfectly competitive market.
4. The elasticity of demand for labour is determined by time, the availability of substitutes, the elasticity of demand for the product and the proportion of labour costs to total costs.

The downward sloping demand curve

Firms need workers to produce goods and services. The demand curve for labour shows how many workers will be hired at any given wage rate over a particular time period. A firm, for instance, might want to hire 100 workers if the wage rate were £2 per hour but only 5 workers if it were £200 per hour.

Economic theory suggests that the higher the price of labour, the less labour firms will hire.
- In the long run, other things remaining equal, firms can vary all factors of production. The higher the wage rate, the more likely it is that firms will substitute machines for workers and hence the lower the demand for labour.
- In the short run, firms are likely to have an existing stock of capital . They will have to produce with a given amount of factory or office space and with a fixed amount of plant, machinery and equipment. The more workers that are added to this fixed stock of capital, the less likely it is that the last worker employed will be as productive as existing employees. Hence the wage rate would have to fall to encourage the employer to take on an extra worker.

So the demand curve for labour is likely to be downward sloping both in the long run and the short run. Why do the long run and short run demand curves slope downward and what determines the elasticity of demand for labour?

The long run demand for labour

In the long run, all factors of production are variable. A firm has complete freedom to choose its production techniques. In the Third World, where labour is cheap relative to capital, firms tend to choose labour intensive methods of production. In the First World, labour is relatively expensive and hence more capital intensive techniques of production are chosen. So in the First World, far more use is made of tractors and other machinery, whilst in the Third World, far more workers per acre are employed.

A full explanation of this using **isoquants** and **isocost** lines was developed in unit 21.

QUESTION 1

Table 46.1 *Real gross capital per employee in the UK (£ thousands at 1985 prices)*

	Real gross capital per employee	
	1979	1987
Agriculture, forestry and fishing	76	87
Energy and water supply	224	336
Manufacturing	34	51
Construction	12	15
Distribution, hotels and catering, repairs	16	21
Transport and communication	80	87
Banking, finance, insurance etc.	43	59
Other services etc. (various industries)	31	34
Average all industries	58	74

Source: adapted from CSO, *National Income Accounts; Annual Abstract of Statistics.*

(a) How has real capital per employee changed over the period 1979 to 1987?
(b) Real average earnings rose 23 per cent between 1979 and 1987. There was little difference in this rise between industries. Assuming that the real cost of capital did not increase over this period, would a firm setting up in 1987 be likely to have used a more or less capital intensive technique of production than if it had set up in 1979? Give reasons for your answer.

The short run demand for labour

In the short run, at least one of the factors of production is fixed. Assume that all factors are fixed except labour. The **law of diminishing returns** states that marginal output will start to decline if more and more units of one variable factor of production are combined with a given quantity of fixed factors. One common example is to imagine a plot of land with a fixed number of tools where extra workers are employed to cultivate the land. Diminishing returns will quickly set in and the eleventh worker, for instance, on a one acre plot of land will contribute less to total output than the tenth worker.

This is shown in Table 46.2. Labour is assumed to be a variable factor of production whilst all other factors are fixed. As extra workers are employed, total output, or TOTAL PHYSICAL PRODUCT increases. However, MARGINAL PHYSICAL PRODUCT, the number of extra units of output a worker produces, starts to decline after the employment of the second worker. So diminishing marginal returns set in with the third worker. Assume that the firm is in a perfectly competitive industry and therefore faces a horizontal, perfectly elastic demand curve. This means that the firm can sell any quantity of its product at the same price per unit. In Table 46.2, it is assumed that the price of the product is £10. MARGINAL REVENUE PRODUCT can then be calculated because it is the addition to revenue from the employment of an extra worker. For instance, the first worker produces 8 units and so, at a price per product unit of £10, her marginal revenue product is £80 (£10 x 8). The marginal revenue product of the second worker is £90 (£10 x the marginal physical product).

It is now possible to calculate how many workers a firm will employ. The contribution to the payment of fixed costs and the earning of profit of each worker is the difference between the marginal revenue product of the firm and the cost to the firm of the worker. Assume that the firm is able to employ any number of workers at a wage rate of £70. The contribution of the first worker is £10, her marginal revenue product minus her wage (£80 - £70). The contribution of the second worker is £20 (£90 - £70). It can be seen from Table 46.2 that the first three

workers each make a positive contribution. The fourth worker neither increases or decreases total profit for the firm. The firm would definitely not employ a fifth worker because her employment would result in a loss of £10 to the firm. Her wage of £70 would exceed her marginal revenue product of £60. So marginal revenue product theory suggests that the firm will employ a maximum of 4 workers because this number maximises total profit (or minimises the loss) for the firm.

If the wage rate were to fall to £50, the firm would employ more workers. The fourth worker would now definitely be employed because her contribution would be £20. The fifth worker too would contribute a positive £10. The firm might also employ a sixth worker although her contribution is zero. Marginal revenue product theory therefore suggests that the lower the wage, the more workers will be employed.

QUESTION 2
Table 46.3

Number of workers employed	Total physical product per week
1	10
2	24
3	36
4	44
5	50
6	53

Table 46.3 shows the total physical product per week for a small firm as employment varies. The price of the product sold is £10 per unit.
(a) Calculate total revenue product at each level of employment.
(b) Calculate marginal revenue product as employment increases.
(c) Explain how many workers the firm should employ if the weekly wage per worker were: (i) £60; (ii) £30; (iii) £120; (iv) £100.

The demand curve for labour

Figure 46.1 shows a firm's marginal revenue product curve for labour. It is downward sloping because marginal revenue product declines as output increases (as shown in Table 46.2). If the wage rate is OF, the firm will employ OB units of labour. If the wage rate rises, the firm will cut back employment to OA. If, on the other hand, wage rates fall to OE, then the firm will take on extra workers and increase the labour force to OC. The marginal revenue product curve therefore shows the number of workers the firm will employ at any given wage rate. But this is the definition of the firm's demand curve for labour. Therefore the marginal revenue product curve is also the firm's demand curve for labour.

This is true for all factors of production. Figure 46.1 shows the familiar price/quantity diagram. The price of labour is the wage rate. Quantity is the quantity of labour

Table 46.2

					Per week	
1	2	3	4	5	6	7
Labour input	Total output	Marginal physical product	Price of product	Marginal revenue product (3 x 4)	Wage rate per worker	Contribution (5 - 6)
(workers)	(units)	(units)	£	£	£	£
1	8	8	10	80	70	10
2	17	9	10	90	70	20
3	25	8	10	80	70	10
4	32	7	10	70	70	0
5	38	6	10	60	70	-10
6	43	5	10	50	70	-20

employed. The downward sloping marginal revenue product curve gives us the familiar downward sloping demand curve.

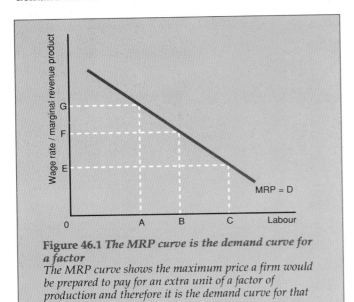

Figure 46.1 *The MRP curve is the demand curve for a factor*
The MRP curve shows the maximum price a firm would be prepared to pay for an extra unit of a factor of production and therefore it is the demand curve for that factor.

Perfect and imperfect competition

So far it has been assumed that the employer is supplying goods in a perfectly competitive market. This is because it has been assumed that the firm can supply any quantity of goods to the market at the same price per unit (i.e. the firm faces a horizontal demand curve). The marginal revenue product curve falls because of diminishing returns.

However, if the employer supplies goods in an imperfectly competitive market, then it faces a downward sloping demand curve for its product. If it expands output, price per unit sold will fall. Consider Table 46.2 again. The fall in marginal revenue product would be even greater than that shown if the price of the product did not remain at £10 per unit, but fell as output expanded. So the marginal revenue product curve for an imperfectly competitive firm falls not only because of diminishing returns but also because the price or average revenue of the product sold falls too as output expands.

Whether the firm is perfectly or imperfectly competitive, it is still true that the demand curve for labour is the marginal revenue product curve of labour.

Determinants of the elasticity of demand for labour

The elasticity of demand for labour is a measure of the responsiveness of the quantity demanded of labour to changes in the price of labour (i.e. the wage rate; units 8 and 9 for a full discussion of elasticity). For instance, if elasticity of demand for labour were 2 and wage rates increased 10 per cent then, all other things being equal, the demand for labour would fall by 20 per cent. If demand for labour fell by 1 per cent when wage rates rose by 100 per cent, all other things being equal, then elasticity of demand for labour would be 0.01 (i.e. highly inelastic).

Time The longer the time period for adjustment, the easier it is to substitute labour for other factors of production or vice versa. In the short term, a firm may have little choice but to employ the same number of workers even if wage rates increase rapidly. Workers will have contracts of employment. There may be severe financial penalties in the form of redundancy payments if workers are sacked. Or a firm may not wish to lose skilled staff because they would be difficult to replace. In the longer term, the firm can buy new labour saving machinery and carry out changes in its methods of work which will reduce the labour employed. Hence the longer the time period, the higher will tend to be the elasticity of demand for labour.

Availability of substitutes The easier it is to substitute other factors for labour, the greater will be the response by firms to a change in real wage rates. So the better the substitutes, the higher will tend to be the elasticity of demand for labour.

Elasticity of demand for the product Labour is a **derived demand** (☞ unit 7). It is only demanded because the goods that it produces are demanded. For instance, if there is a collapse in demand for coal, then there will also be a collapse in the demand for coal miners. This means that the elasticity of demand for labour in an industry is directly correlated with the elasticity of demand for the product made in the industry. If the elasticity of demand

QUESTION 3 The firm in Table 46.4 produces in an imperfectly competetive market. As output increases, the price falls as follows:

Table 46.4

Number of units sold per week	Price per unit £
10	£15
24	£14
36	£12
44	£11
50	£10
53	£9

(a) Calculate (i) the total revenue product and (ii) the marginal revenue product of labour as employment increases.
(b) How many workers would the firm employ if the weekly wage were: (i) £20; (ii) £40; (iii) £60; (iv) £80; (v) £100; (vi) £120?

for the product is low, as for instance for gas or electricity, then a sudden rise in wages which pushes up gas or electricity prices will have little effect on demand for gas or electricity. There will be little effect on employment in the industry and hence the demand for labour will be low. If, on the other hand, elasticity of demand for the product is high, elasticity of demand for labour will be high. British Steel, for instance, faces highly elastic demand for many of its products. A rise in wages not matched elsewhere in the industry is likely to increase British Steel prices and lead to a loss of orders and therefore jobs.

The proportion of labour cost to total cost A rise in costs will reduce the supply of a product, shifting the supply curve upwards and to the left. This will lead to a reduction in quantity demanded. The bigger the shift, the larger the reduction in demand. If a group of workers gain a 50 per cent pay rise but these workers only account for one per cent of the total cost of production, then the supply curve of the product will hardly shift. There will be little fall in demand and hence little loss of employment in the firm. If however this group of workers accounted for 50 per cent of the costs of the firm, then a 50 per cent pay rise would have a dramatic effect on the supply curve and lead to a large decrease in quantity demanded of the product. This in turn would lead to a large fall in employment. Hence, the larger the proportion of labour cost to total cost, the higher the elasticity of demand for labour.

QUESTION 4 In August 1989, the *Daily Mirror* reported that Harrods had been forced to lay off 15 of its senior staff due to a fall in sales. Many chains had been forced to close outlets and sack workers. In a survey of 310 shopping chains, four in ten retailers told the Confederation of British Industry that they were selling less than 12 months previously. Blame for the fall in sales was put mainly on very high interest rates which had sent mortgage repayments rocketing.

Explain whether you would expect the elasticity of demand for labour in the retailing industry to be relatively high or low.

Key terms

Total physical product – the total output of a given quantity of factors of production.
Marginal physical product - the addition to output of an extra unit of a variable factor of production.
Marginal revenue product - the value of the physical addition to output of a variable factor of production. In a perfectly competitive product market where marginal revenue equals price, it is equal to marginal physical product times the price of the good produced.

Applied economics

Performance-related pay

During the 1980s, there was a trend in British industry towards performance-related pay. Managers' pay was increasingly linked to measures of their value to the company. Performance-related pay had been quite common at one time on the shop floor. Many manual workers were on a piece-rate system. The more they produced, the higher their wages at the end of the week. If they produced nothing, they received no pay. Equally, many sales people have been rewarded mainly on sales commission rather than basic pay.

Such systems can be seen as an attempt by employers to pay workers according to their revenue product. For instance, if one worker produces twice as many steel bars as another per week, it might seem logical to pay that worker twice as much. It also enables companies to decide whether or not to retain staff. For instance, if a foreign exchange dealer is paid £25 000 a year, but only generates £15 000 a year surplus for his bank, then he should be sacked. Equally, if a company has five workers, all equally productive, but the output of one worker is sold at a

loss, then one worker should be sacked.

Such payment systems can be very controversial. During the 1980s, there was an increase in the relative pay of managers to shop floor workers. A number of company executives hit the front pages of newspapers because they were awarded pay increases vastly in excess of anything awarded to workers in their companies. Lord Hanson, for instance, head of Hanson Trust, became the most highly paid company director in the UK in 1989 with a salary of £1.534 million. This was a 24 per cent increase on the previous year. Sir Ralph Halpern, head of Burton the retailers and a keen advocate of performance-related pay, earned £899 000 in 1989. This however was a drop of £97 000 from the previous year due to a deterioration in Burton's performance.

These very high salaries have been justified on the grounds that individual chief executives have added that much extra value to their companies over the year. Without their particular talents, the company would have had lower profits, or lower sales, or a generally poorer trading position. However, as trading conditions in the UK worsened in the late 1980s, some chief executives continued to be given large salary increases. Michael Shapinker, writing in the *Financial Times* on 7 December 1989, asked: 'Is the pay of Britain's top executives based on rational principles, in which rewards are linked clearly and fairly to performance, or is the guiding motivation nothing more than the desire to be rich?'

Data question

LAST MONTH KYLIE MINOGUE EARNED £620,000

How her cash comes in

LAST MONTH

Kylie album:	U.K. sales 330,000	£297,000
	Australian sales 175,000	£157,000
	European sales 104,000	£93,600
Locomotion single:	U.K. sales 190,000	£56,715
	German sales 51,000	£15,300

TOTAL (not including Neighbours fees, merchandising commissions, public appearance fees, and interest in investments) £619,615

THIS YEAR

Last month's income	£619,615
I Should Be So Lucky worldwide sales 1,750,000	£525,000
Got To Be Certain worldwide sales 495,000	£148,500
TOTAL	£1,293,115

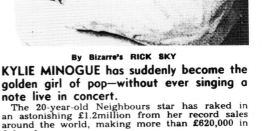

By Bizarre's RICK SKY

KYLIE MINOGUE has suddenly become the golden girl of pop—without ever singing a note live in concert.

The 20-year-old Neighbours star has raked in an astonishing £1.2 million from her record sales around the world, making more than £620,000 in July alone.

Source: *The Sun*, 5.8.1988.

1. **Suggest, with reasons, a likely value for the elasticity of demand (i) in the short run and (ii) in the long run for the services of Kylie Minogue.**

Summary

1. The supply curve for an individual worker is backward sloping at high levels of income.
2. Backward sloping supply curves result because the negative income effect of a wage increase outweighs the positive substitution effect.
3. The supply curve of labour to a firm, to an industry and to the economy as a whole is likely to be upward sloping.

The supply curve for an individual worker

A supply curve shows the quantity that will be supplied to the market at any given price. For an individual worker, the quantity supplied is the number of hours worked over a time period such as a year. Neo-classical theory starts by assuming that a worker can decide how many hours to work per week and how many weeks' holiday to take per year. The price of labour is the wage per time period (i.e. the wage rate). The wage rate that determines supply is the **real wage rate** (the money or nominal wage rate divided by the price level). This is because the worker decides how many hours to work by relating it to what the wage will buy. For instance, a worker might take a job if a week's wages of £300 were to buy a television set, but she would be likely to turn it down if £300 were to only buy a newspaper.

Figure 47.1 shows a backward bending supply curve for labour. Between wages rates O and B a rise in real wage rates will lead to an increase in working hours supplied. For instance, the worker will offer to work DF extra hours if real wage rates increase from A to B . However, a rise in real wage rates above OB, for instance from B to C, will lead to a desire for shorter working hours.

To understand why this might be the case, consider a part time factory worker. Initially she is low paid, as are nearly all part time workers. The firm she works for then doubles her real wage rate. She is likely to respond to this by wanting to work longer hours and perhaps become a full time worker. Further increases in real wage rates might persuade her to work overtime. However, there are only 24 hours in a day and 365 days in a year. Eventually it is likely that increases in wage rates will make her want to reduce her working week or increase her holidays. She will value increased leisure time more than extra money to spend. Put another way, she is choosing to buy leisure time by forgoing the wages she could otherwise have earned and the goods she could otherwise have bought. This is an example of the concept of opportunity cost.

This process can be seen at work over the past 100 years in the UK. Real wage rates have risen considerably but hours worked have fallen. The typical Victorian working week was 60 to 70 hours with few or no holidays. Today, average hours worked per week are down to about 40 hours with a typical holiday entitlement of 4 weeks per year. Workers have responded to increases in wage rates by supplying less labour.

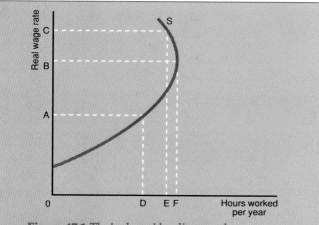

Figure 47.1 *The backward bending supply curve*
The supply curve for an individual worker is assumed to be this shape because at high levels of income the worker will prefer to work shorter hours rather than receive the extra income he or she could have earned.

QUESTION 1

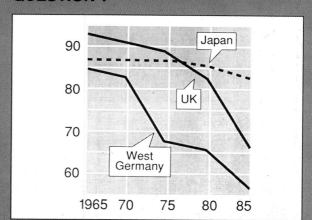

Source: adapted from OECD.

Figure 47.2 *Labour force: participation rates of men aged 55-64 (%)*

Real wage rates in Japan, the UK and West Germany increased in the twenty years from 1965 to 1985. Does the data support the idea that the supply curve of labour for an individual worker is backward sloping?

Note that when wage rates increase, workers are likely to be able to both increase earnings **and** reduce hours worked. For instance, if real wage rates increase by 20 per cent from £10 per hour to £12 per hour, then workers can cut their hours worked by 10 per cent from 40 hours to 36 hours per week and still see an increase in earnings from £400 per week (40 x £10) to £432 per week (36 x £12). Real wage rate increases in the neo-classical model give workers a choice between increased earnings or increased leisure time or some combination of the two.

Income and substitution effects

The backward bending supply curve occurs because of the interaction of **income and substitution effects.** (A thorough understanding of unit 15 would be helpful for what follows.) If a consumer is in equilibrium, the utility gained from the goods bought with the money earned from the last hour worked will exactly match the utility gained from the last hour of leisure time. If leisure time were more valuable, the consumer could increase utility by working less and having more leisure time.

An increase in real wage rates is likely to lead to a positive substitution effect. The number of goods that can be bought with the money earned from the last hour worked will increase. The utility derived from the last hour worked will now be greater than the last hour of leisure. So the worker will substitute work for leisure until the two once again become equal.

However, it is unclear what the income effect of a rise in real wage rates will be. A rise in real wage rates leads to a rise in the worker's income at the existing level of hours worked. A worker may respond to this rise by working longer hours, working shorter hours or working the same number. The backward bending supply curve implies that the income effect will initially be positive at lower levels of income, but become negative at higher levels of wage rates. The argument is that leisure is a luxury good. At some point on the income scale, workers value extra leisure more than extra goods. It is pointless being able to buy tennis or squash equipment if you don't have the time to play. Having the time to go on holiday in the car is likely to be more valuable to the average family than working enough extra hours to be able to buy a third car.

In Figure 47.3, the substitution and income effects of a real wage rate rise are initially both positive. So higher real wage rates lead to an increase in hours worked. Eventually the worker's income becomes so high that the income effect of a rise in real wage rates becomes negative. Assume, for example, that this occurs at the real wage rate of OA. Between OA and OB, the substitution effect is positive and the income effect is negative, but the substitution effect outweighs the income effect. Hence a rise in real wage rates will still lead to an increase in hours worked. However, at wage rate levels higher than OB, the negative income effect is greater than the positive substitution effect. A rise in real wage rates leads to a fall in the number of hours worked.

In Figure 47.4, indifference curves are combined with budget lines to show the impact of a rise in real wages.

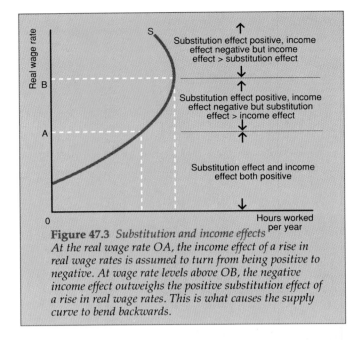

Figure 47.3 *Substitution and income effects*
At the real wage rate OA, the income effect of a rise in real wage rates is assumed to turn from being positive to negative. At wage rate levels above OB, the negative income effect outweighs the positive substitution effect of a rise in real wage rates. This is what causes the supply curve to bend backwards.

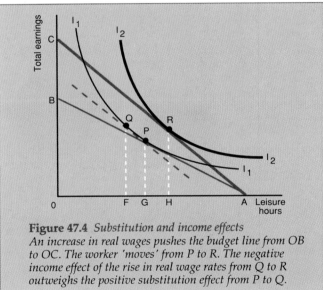

Figure 47.4 *Substitution and income effects*
An increase in real wages pushes the budget line from OB to OC. The worker 'moves' from P to R. The negative income effect of the rise in real wage rates from Q to R outweighs the positive substitution effect from P to Q.

Total earnings (i.e. the real wage rate x the number of hours worked) is on the vertical axis. The number of leisure hours available to the worker is on the horizontal axis. The budget lines AB and AC show the various combinations of earnings and leisure that the worker may enjoy. The greater the number of hours worked, the greater will be total earnings but the less will be time available for leisure. I_1I_1 and I_2I_2 are indifference curves showing the worker's indifference between earnings and leisure.

An increase in real wages will lead to an increase in total real earnings assuming that leisure time remains unchanged. This increase is shown by a change in the budget line from AB to AC. The worker will now move from equilibrium at P to equilibrium at R. This shows that the worker will receive higher earnings **and** work fewer hours because leisure time increases. The income effect of the increase in real wage rates must therefore have been negative and have outweighed the substitution effect. The substitution effect can be measured by drawing a third budget line tangential to I_1I_1 but parallel to the new budget line AC. The movement from P to Q is the substitution effect. It shows that as a result of the increase in real wage rates, the worker will demand FG fewer hours of leisure (i.e. he or she will work FG extra hours). But this is outweighed by the income effect from Q to R. As a result of the rise in income, the worker will choose to 'buy' FH extra hours of leisure (i.e. work FH fewer hours). FH is greater than FG and therefore overall the worker will work GH fewer hours as a result of the increase in real wages.

Figure 47.4 shows a situation where a rise in real wages leads to a reduction in working hours. However, it is equally possible to draw a diagram showing that a rise in real wages will lead to an increased number of hours worked (by drawing I_2I_2 higher up the budget line AC such that position R is horizontal to the left of P).

QUESTION 2 In 1986, the results of a government commissioned report on the incentive effects of cuts in income tax were published. The report, by Professor C V Brown of Stirling University, found no evidence that tax cuts encourage people in employment either to work harder or to work longer. Lower taxes did encourage women, particularly in part time jobs, to work longer because they would keep more of their earnings. But for males on average earnings, the boost to existing income provided by lower taxes tended to be more important than the incentive (i.e. substitution) effect of the tax cut.

Source: adapted from the *Financial Times*, 16.12.1986.

Using indifference curve diagrams, explain the typical effects found by Professor Brown of income tax cuts on (a) a male worker on average earnings and (b) a female part time worker.

Supply of labour to a firm

In a perfectly competitive market there are many buyers and sellers (☞ unit 27). In a perfectly competitive factor market, there are many firms hiring many individual workers. This means that an individual firm will be able to hire an extra worker at the existing wage rate.

Figure 47.5 (a) shows the supply curve of labour facing the firm. The firm is small and wants to expand its workforce from 20 workers to 21 workers. Figure 47.5 (b) shows the supply curve of labour for the industry to be upward sloping, as will be argued below. 100 000 workers are currently employed in the industry. The movement up the industry supply curve from 100 000 workers to 100 001 workers is so small that the firm can employ the extra worker at the ruling industrial wage rate. Therefore the supply curve facing the firm is horizontal

(i.e. perfectly elastic).

Many industries, however, are either oligopolies or monopolies. Firms in these industries are therefore likely to be significant employers of particular types of labour. For instance, the government employs over 90 per cent of all UK teachers. British Rail employs nearly 100 per cent of engine drivers in the UK. If a firm is a **monopsonist** (i.e. is the sole buyer) in its labour market, then the supply curve of labour to the firm will also be the supply curve of labour to the industry. It will be upward sloping, showing that the firm has to offer increased wages if it wishes to increase its labour force.

The cost of employing an extra worker (the marginal cost) will be higher than the wage rate it has to pay the extra worker. This is because it not only has to pay a higher wage rate to the worker but it must also pay the higher wage rate to all its other workers. In Table 47.1 for instance, the firm has to increase the wage rate as extra workers are employed. The wage rate needed to attract 3 workers to the industry is £30 per worker. However, the marginal cost of the third worker is £50; £30 for the third worker plus an extra £10 paid to each of the first two workers.

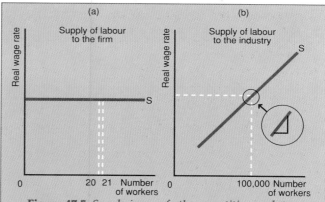

Figure 47.5 *Supply in a perfectly competitive market*
The supply curve of labour facing a firm in a perfectly competitive factor market is perfectly elastic. The firm can hire new workers at the existing wage rate because their employment has an insignificant impact on the total supply of labour in the market.

Table 47.1

Units of labour supplied	Cost per unit (£)	Total cost (£)	Marginal cost (£)
0	-	0	
			10
1	10	10	
			30
2	20	40	
			50
3	30	90	
			70
4	40	160	

The supply curve of labour to the firm and the firm's marginal cost of labour derived from the data in Table 47.1 are shown in Figure 47.6. The marginal cost curve for labour for the monopsonist employer is higher than the supply curve of labour.

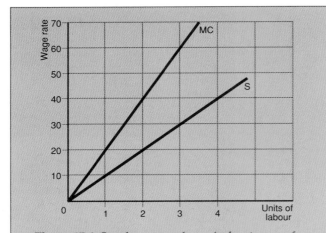

Figure 47.6 *Supply curve and marginal cost curve of labour facing a monopsonist employer*
The supply curve for labour facing a monopsonist employer is upward sloping. The marginal cost of hiring extra workers is more than the wage rate because the higher wage rate paid to the marginal worker needs to be paid to all existing workers.

QUESTION 3

Table 47.2

Number of workers employed	Wage per week per worker (£)
100	200
200	220
300	240
400	260

The table shows the wage rates per week a firm has to offer to recruit workers.
(a) Draw (i) the supply curve of labour and (ii) the marginal cost curve of labour facing the firm. (Remember that the marginal cost of, for instance, the 100 workers employed between 300 and 400 is drawn at the 350 point.)
(b) How would the supply curve and marginal cost curve differ if the firm could recruit any number of workers at a wage rate of £200 per week?

The supply curve of labour for an industry

An industry can increase the number of hours worked by its labour force in two ways:
■ it can increase the number of hours worked by its existing labour force;
■ it can recruit new workers.

As explained above, a rise in real wage rates all other things being equal may or may not increase the supply of labour by individual workers in the industry. However, it is likely to attract new workers into the industry. These new workers may be from other industries or they may be workers who previously did not hold a job, such as housewives or the unemployed. Therefore the supply curve of labour for an industry is likely to be upward sloping, the ability of firms to recruit new workers outweighing any possible disincentive effect on existing workers. The higher the industry real wage rate, the more workers will want to enter that particular industry. The elasticity of supply of labour to an industry will depend upon a number of factors.

The availability of suitable labour in other industries An engineering company wanting to recruit unskilled workers will be able to 'poach' workers relatively easily from other industries because there is a large pool of unskilled workers spread throughout industry. The National Health Service will have more difficulty recruiting brain surgeons because nearly all brain surgeons in the UK are already employed by the NHS. So the elasticity of supply of a pool of workers spread across many industries is likely to be higher than that of a group of workers concentrated in the recruiting industry.

Time Elasticity of supply is likely to be lower in the short run than in the long run. For instance, the NHS might not be able to recruit large numbers of brain surgeons tomorrow. But it could expand supply considerably over a 20 year period by training more of them.

The extent of under-employment and unemployment The higher the level of unemployment, the higher is likely to be the elasticity of supply. With high unemployment, firms are more likely to be able to recruit workers at the existing real wage rate from the pool of the unemployed.

QUESTION 4
There is a widespread prediction that during the 1990s employers will have increasing problems recruiting labour, particularly young workers. As a result many have urged companies to recruit more people aged 50 and over.

Why is the elasticity of supply of workers aged 50+ for jobs like shelf stackers or checkout assistants at a supermarket likely to be higher than jobs like managers of supermarkets?

Supply of labour to the economy

The supply of labour to the economy as a whole might seem to be fixed (i.e. perfectly inelastic). However, this is unlikely to be the case.
■ In the UK, only about three-quarters of people aged 16-64 are in employment. The rest tend to be in education, at home looking after children, unemployed or have taken early retirement. This

pool of people are potential workers and some would enter the workforce if real wages rose.

■ Some of the retired could be brought back to work if there were sufficient incentives for them.
■ Immigration too could expand the domestic supply of labour. Immigration was used by the UK to solve labour supply problems in the 1950s.

So the supply of labour to the economy as a whole is likely to be upward sloping too. There is some evidence to suggest that it might also be backward sloping. There has been an increase over the past ten years in early retirement. This has been due to many factors, but one is that males particularly have been able to earn sufficiently high wages during their working life to make early retirement with a reduced pension attractive. Workers are choosing to reduce the number of hours worked over their lifetime.

QUESTION 5

Table 47.3 *Pay and employment of women*

	1971	1981	1988
Real average earnings of females (at 1988 prices)	£97.16	£131.43	£164.20
Total UK female employment (millions)	8.4	9.3	10.3

Source: adapted from CSO, *Social Trends* and *Economic Trends Annual Supplement*.

(a) Do the data support the theory that the supply curve for labour in an economy is upward sloping?
(b) What other factors apart from earnings might affect the supply curve of female labour in an economy?

Key terms

Population of working age - defined in the UK as men aged 16 to 64 and women aged 16-59.
Labour force - those in work or officially counted as unemployed.
Workforce in employment - the numbers of workers with a job.
Activity rates - the percentage or proportion of any given population in the labour force.
Net migration - immigration minus emigration.

Applied economics

The supply of labour in the UK

The UK labour force

In 1990 the population of the UK was approximately 57.5 million people. Not all were available for work. Those below the age of 16 were in full time education whilst women over 60 and men over 65 were officially counted as retired. The rest, those aged 16-60/65, are known as the POPULATION OF WORKING AGE. Figure 47.7 shows that the numbers in this age group have increased in recent decades from 32.5 million in 1971 to over 35 million in 1990.

Not all those of working age are members of the LABOUR FORCE or WORKFORCE. Many women choose to leave employment to bring up children. Young people too may stay on in education after the age of 16 whilst there is a growing trend for the over-50s to take early retirement. So the labour force is smaller than the population of working age.

The labour force is made up of two groups. By far the largest group, the WORKFORCE IN EMPLOYMENT, comprises those workers with a job. However, there is a signficant minority of the labour force who are unemployed. Figure 47.7 shows that the labour force (those in work plus the unemployed) has tended to increase over time, from 25 million in 1971 to 27.5 million in 1990. The growth in the workforce in

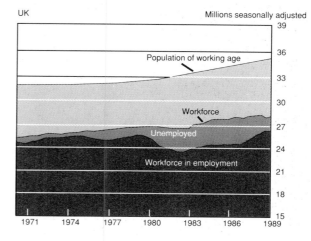

Source: adapted from CSO, *Social Trends*.

Figure 47.7 *Working population, workforce and workforce in employment*

employment has been less smooth. Two major recessions, between 1975 - 1977 and 1980 -1983 resulted in large increases in unemployment and falls in the workforce in employment. The recession of 1980-1983 was so deep that there was even a fall in the labour force from 26.8m in 1980 to 26.6m in 1983. Workers, particularly women, became discouraged from looking for work and disappeared from official counts of the unemployed. A change in the way in which unemployment was calculated in 1982, which excluded any unemployed worker not able to claim benefit for being out of work, also led to many women disappearing from the official count of the labour force. As jobs became more plentiful from 1983 onwards, they returned to work, resulting in a rise in the labour force from 26.6m in 1983 to 27.8m in 1986 at a time when unemployment rose slightly from 3.1m to 3.3m.

Male and female employment

The labour force over the past 20 years has grown at a faster rate than the population of working age. Table 47.4 shows that whilst the total population of working age has grown by 2.5 million workers over the period 1971 to 1988, the labour force has grown by 2.7 million. The totals, however, mask a much larger change in the composition of the labour force. There has been virtually no growth in the male labour force over the period. Almost all the growth has come from an increase in the number of women working, from 9.3 million in 1971 to 11.8 million in 1988.

Table 47.4 *Civilian labour force and population of working age*

Great Britain				Millions
	Civilian labour force			Population of working age
	Males	Females	Total	
Estimates				
1971	15.6	9.3	24.9	31.7
1976	15.6	10.1	25.7	31.9
1979	15.6	10.4	26.0	32.6
1981	15.6	10.6	26.2	32.9
1983	15.3	10.6	25.9	33.3
1984[1]	15.5	11.0	26.4	33.6
1984[2]	15.5	11.1	26.6	33.6
1985	15.6	11.2	26.8	33.7
1987	15.7	11.6	27.3	34.1
1988	15.8	11.8	27.6	34.2
Projections				
1991	16.0	12.2	28.2	34.4
2000	15.9	12.7	28.6	34.7

Note: 1. GB labour force definitions up to 1984.
      2. ILO/OECD definitions from 1984.
Source: CSO, *Social Trends.*

Within the female total, the growth in employment has come mainly from women aged 25-44 as indicated in Table 47.5. This table shows selected ACTIVITY RATES. These are the percentage of any given population in the labour force (i.e. employed or unemployed). 52.4 per cent of females aged 25-44 were part of the labour force

Table 47.5 *Economic activity rates by age and sex*

Great Britain		Percentages
	1971	1988
All males aged 16+	80.5	74.2
All females aged 16+	43.9	51.1
Females aged		
16-19	65.0	72.9
20-24	60.2	71.5
25-44	52.4	70.9
45-54	62.0	70.5
55-59	50.9	52.8
60+	12.4	6.6

Source: adapted from CSO, *Social Trends.*

in 1971, but by 1988 this figure was 70.9 per cent. Male activity rates have been declining, mainly due to the trend towards early retirement.

Employment by age

Not only has the balance of the labour force changed between the sexes, it has also changed by age. Since 1971 there has been a significant increase in the proportion of 25-54 year old workers in the labour force. The numbers and percentage of workers over 55 have declined because of increased early retirement. The numbers of 16-24 year old workers have fluctuated. In the ten years between 1975 and 1985, there was a significant increase in the numbers in this category. Some economists believe that this was a prime cause of the increase in unemployment over that period, and particularly the increase in youth unemployment. The economy was unable to provide jobs for a growing number of young workers entering the labour market for the first time. However, the numbers of young people entering the labour market peaked in the mid-1980s and have begun to decline. This fall is expected to bottom out in the second half of the 1990s. The fall in the number of young workers in the 1990s is likely to bring substantial benefits to young people. Not only will they find it far easier to find jobs than their counterparts in the 1980s, but the fall in supply of young people will tend to push up their wage rates.

Change in the size of the labour force

There are factors other than the increased participation of women and the growth of early retirement amongst men which affect the size of the labour force.

■ If immigration is larger than emigration, then the workforce is likely to increase. During the 1950s, the UK encouraged immigration from New Commonwealth countries to fill an acute labour shortage. Since the 1961 Immigration Act,

NET MIGRATION (immigration minus emigration) has tended to be negative. More people have left the country than have entered. However, the numbers emigrating and immigrating and the net migration figure are so small that migration has not had a significant impact upon the size of the labour force in the 1970s and 1980s.

- The numbers of workers in the labour force say nothing about hours worked per week or per year. The long term trend is for workers to work fewer hours per week and for their holiday entitlement to increase. Offset against this is the trend towards more and more women moving from part time jobs to full time jobs.

The quality of the labour force

Greater production can be achieved by using more labour. However, the size of the UK labour force is likely to change only slowly over the next 50 years. Of more significance are likely to be changes in the quality of the labour force. Rising educational standards, as shown for instance by greater numbers gaining high grades at GCSE, 'A' levels and higher education awards, would suggest that the labour force is becoming potentially more productive over time. However, many economists, such as Sig Prais of NIESR (the National Institute for Economic and Social Research), argue that the UK is being left behind by countries such as France and West Germany in providing education and training for its workers. This has significant implications for the UK's future relative standard of living (☞ unit 63).

Data question

1. How has holiday entitlement changed over the period shown in the data?

2. Real incomes rose by over one-third in the period 1971 to 1988. Using an economic theory with which you are familiar, explain how this might account for changes in holiday entitlement over the period.

Source: adapted from CSO, *Social Trends*.
Figure 47.8 *Percentage entitled to annual paid holidays of duration*

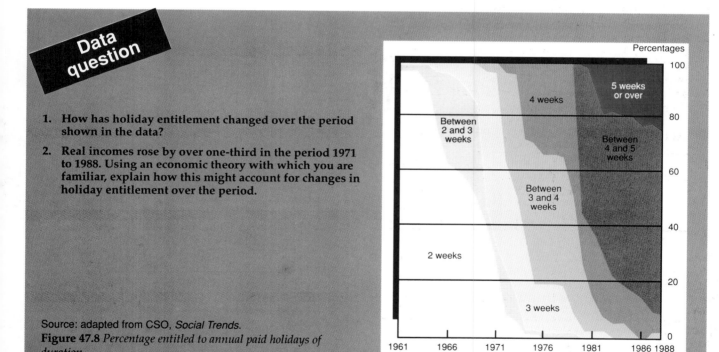

Summary

1. The wage rate of labour is determined by the demand for labour and the supply of labour.
2. In an economy where labour is homogeneous and all markets are perfect, wage rates would be identical for all workers.
3. Wage differentials are caused partly by market imperfections and partly by differences in individual labour characteristics.
4. In a perfectly competitive market, individual firms face a horizontal supply curve and will hire labour up to the point where the wage rate is equal to the marginal revenue product of labour.
5. In an imperfectly competitive market, either the firm is a monopsonist or there is a monopoly supplier of labour, such as a trade union, or both. A monopsonist drives down wage rates and employment levels, whilst a monopoly supplier increases wage rates.

How wage rates are determined

Prices are determined by demand and supply. So the price of labour, the real wage rate, is determined by the demand for and the supply of labour.

The demand curve for labour in an industry is the marginal revenue product curve of labour (☞ unit 46). This is downward sloping, indicating that more labour will be demanded the lower the real wage rate. The supply curve of labour to an industry is upward sloping (☞ unit 47), indicating that more labour will be supplied if real wage rates increase. This gives an equilibrium real wage rate of OA in Figure 48.1. OB units of labour are demanded and supplied.

The demand and supply curves for labour can shift for a variety of reasons, giving new equilibrium real wage rates and levels of employment in the industry. The demand curve for labour will move to the right showing an increase in the demand for labour if the marginal revenue product of labour increases. This might occur if:

■ productivity improves, perhaps due to changing technology or more flexible working practices, increasing output per worker;
■ there is a rise in the selling price of the product, increasing the value of the output of each worker;
■ the price of capital increases, leading to a substitution of labour for capital.

The supply curve might move to the right, showing an increase in supply, if:

■ there is an increase in the number of workers in the population as a whole, perhaps because of changing demographic trends, or because government alters tax and benefit levels increasing incentives to work;

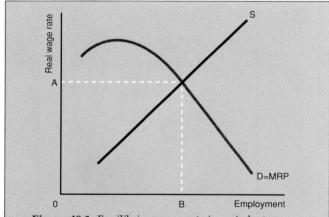

Figure 48.1 *Equilibrium wage rate in an industry*
The equilibrium real wage rate is OA whilst the level of employment in equilibrium is OB.

QUESTION 1

(a) On a diagram, draw a demand and supply curve for labour in the record production industry.
(b) Mark on the diagram the equilibrium wage rate and the equilibrium level of employment.
(c) Show how the demand curve or the supply curve might shift if there is:
  (i) a fall in labour productivity;
  (ii) an increase in wage rates in all other labour markets in the economy;
  (iii) a fall in demand for records;
  (iv) an introduction of new labour saving technology;
  (v) a fall in the number of 16-25 year olds in the population as a whole.

■ wages or conditions of work deteriorate in other industries making conditions relatively more attractive in this industry.

A labour market where all workers are paid the same

Consider an economy which has the following labour market characteristics.
■ Labour is homogeneous (i.e. all workers are identical, for instance in age, skill and sex).
■ There is perfect knowledge in the labour market. A worker in Scotland is as aware of job opportunities in London as a Londoner.
■ There is perfect mobility of labour. Workers can move at no cost between jobs in the same industry, between different industries and between geographical areas. Equally, there are no costs to firms in hiring and firing workers.
■ All workers and employers are price takers. There are no trade unions or monopsonist employers.
■ There are no barriers which prevent wages rising and falling to accommodate changes in the demand for and supply of labour.
■ Firms aim to maximise profit and minimise costs of production, whilst workers aim to maximise their wages.

In this perfect labour market, all workers would be paid the same wage rate. To show that this must be true, consider two markets where wage rates are different. In the Welsh steel industry, wages are higher than in the catering market in London. London catering workers would know this because there is perfect knowledge in the market. They would apply for jobs in Welsh steel firms. They would be prepared to work for less than existing Welsh steel workers so long as the wage rate was higher than their existing wage rate as caterers. Welsh steel makers, seeking to minimise cost, would then either sack their existing workers and replace them with cheaper London catering workers, or offer to continue employing their existing workforce but at a lower wage. Meanwhile, London catering firms would be threatened with a loss of their workers. To retain them they would need to put up their wage rates. Only when the two wage rates are equal

would there be no incentive for London catering workers to become Welsh steel workers.

Why wage rates differ

In the real world, wage rates differ. One important reason is because labour is not homogeneous. Each worker is a unique factor of production, possessing a unique set of employment characteristics such as:
■ age - whether young, middle aged or old;
■ sex - whether male or female;
■ ethnic background;
■ education, training and work experience;
■ ability to perform tasks - including how hard they are prepared to work, their strength and their manual or mental dexterity.

For instance, a manager of a company is likely to be paid more than a cleaner working for the same company. On the one hand, the marginal revenue product of the manager is likely to be higher. Her education, skills and work experience are likely to provide greater value to the company than the cleaner. On the other hand, the supply of managers is lower than the supply of cleaners. Most workers in the workforce could be a cleaner, but only a few have sufficient qualities to be managers. Greater demand and less supply lead to higher wage rates for managers than cleaners.

Wage rates also differ because workers do not necessarily seek to maximise wages. Wages are only part of the net benefit workers gain from employment.

QUESTION 3

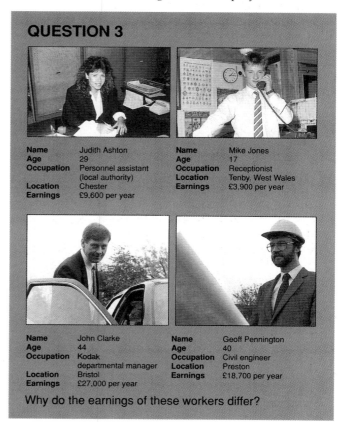

Name	Judith Ashton
Age	29
Occupation	Personnel assistant (local authority)
Location	Chester
Earnings	£9,600 per year

Name	Mike Jones
Age	17
Occupation	Receptionist
Location	Tenby, West Wales
Earnings	£3,900 per year

Name	John Clarke
Age	44
Occupation	Kodak departmental manager
Location	Bristol
Earnings	£27,000 per year

Name	Geoff Pennington
Age	40
Occupation	Civil engineer
Location	Preston
Earnings	£18,700 per year

Why do the earnings of these workers differ?

Workers whose jobs are dangerous, unpleasant, tedious, where there is little chance of promotion, where earnings fluctuate and where there are few or no fringe benefits, will seek higher wages than workers whose jobs possess the opposite characteristics. Market forces will tend to lead not to equality of wage rates but to equality of net benefits to workers.

Labour is not perfectly mobile. Hence there can be unemployment and low wages in Scotland whilst employers offering much higher wages are crying out for labour in London. Part of the reason why there is a lack of mobility is the absence of perfect knowledge within the labour market. Workers in Scotland may be unaware of job opportunities in the South of England. There are also many other imperfections in the market which prevent wage rates rising or falling in response to market pressures (☞ unit 50).

Perfectly competitive labour markets

In a perfectly competitive factor market, there are a large number of small firms hiring a large number of individual workers. For the individual firm operating in such a market:
- the demand curve for labour, the marginal revenue product curve of labour, is downward sloping (☞ unit 46);
- the supply curve of labour is perfectly elastic and therefore horizontal (☞ unit 47); the firm can hire any number of workers at the existing industry wage rate.

How many workers should this type of firm employ? If a worker costs £200 per week, but increases revenue net of all other costs by only £150, then he should not be employed.

Putting this theoretically, the firm will hire workers up to the point where the marginal cost of labour is equal to

the marginal revenue product of labour. If the marginal cost were higher than marginal revenue product, for instance at OC in Figure 48.2, the firm would make a loss on the output produced by the marginal worker and hence it would cut back on employment of labour. If the marginal revenue product of labour were higher than the marginal cost of labour, for instance at OA, then it would hire more workers because these workers would generate a profit for the firm.

Hence, in Figure 48.2 the equilibrium level of employment by the firm is OB. This is the point where the marginal cost of labour (the supply curve) is equal to the marginal revenue product of labour (the demand curve). The equilibrium real wage rate is OW. This is the ruling equilibrium wage rate in the industry as a whole.

QUESTION 4

Table 48.1

Number of workers employed	Total revenue product (£ month)
1	700
2	1300
3	1800
4	2200

The data show the monthly total revenue product of a profit maximising manufacturing company in a perfectly competitive industry.
(a) Plot the marginal revenue product curve on graph paper (remembering to plot the MRP half way between whole numbers on the employment axis).
(b) What would be the maximum number of workers the firm would employ if the monthly wage per worker were: (i) £600; (ii) £400; (iii) £425; (iv) £800; (v) £525?

Imperfectly competitive labour markets

An imperfectly competitive labour market is one where:
- either the firm is a dominant or monopoly buyer of labour;
- or the firm is faced by a monopoly supplier of labour, which is most likely to be a trade union.

If the firm is the sole buyer of labour, it is called a **monopsonist**. The state, for instance, employs over 90 per cent of teachers in the UK and therefore is essentially a monopsonist. A monopsonist is able to exploit market power and therefore common sense would suggest that the monopsonist would use this power to force down wage levels.

The marginal cost of employing an extra unit of labour is higher for the monopsonist than the average cost or wage. This is because the firm has to raise wage rates to attract extra labour into the industry. So the cost of employing an extra unit of labour is not just the higher

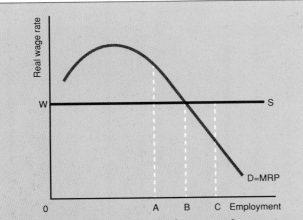

Figure 48.2 *Equilibrium employment and wage rates for a firm in a perfectly competitive factor market*
In a perfectly competitive factor market, the supply curve for labour facing the firm is horizontal. The equilibrium real wage rate, OW, is set by the industry as a whole. The firm will then employ OB workers in equilibrium.

wage paid to that unit but also the extra wages that now need to be paid to all the other workers in the industry (☞ unit 47).

In Figure 48.3, the demand and supply curves for labour are drawn. The firm will employ workers up to the point where the marginal cost of an extra worker is equal to the

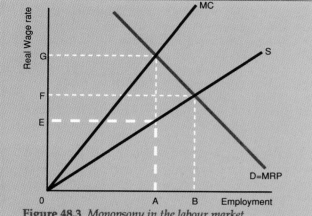

Figure 48.3 *Monopsony in the labour market*
A monopsonist will hire labour to the point where MC = MRP (i.e. up to the point OA). It will then pay labour the lowest wage rate possible which is OE. If the industry had been perfectly competitive then both the equilibrium wage rate OF and the equilibrium level of employment OB would be higher than under monopsony.

worker's marginal revenue product. Therefore the monopsonist will employ OA workers, the intersection of the marginal cost curve and the marginal revenue product or demand curve. The firm does not then need to pay a real wage rate of OG to each worker. It only needs to pay a real wage rate of OE to attract OA workers to the industry.

If the market were perfectly competitive, employment would be OB and the equilibrium wage rate would be OF. So economic theory suggests that a monopsonist drives down wages and reduces employment levels compared to a perfectly competitive factor market. Note that this is similar to the perfect competition/monopoly analysis in a goods market where it is argued that a monopolist reduces output and raises prices compared to a perfectly competitive market.

The effect of a monopoly supplier of labour will be considered in the next unit on trade unions.

QUESTION 5 In the labour market for teachers fn the UK, weak monopoly trade unions face a strong monopsonist employer, the government.
(a) Draw a diagram to show this situation.
(b) Explain whether the equilibrium wage rate is likely to be higher or lower than if the market for teachers were perfectly competitive.

Applied economics

Wage determination

Wage structure by occupation

Economic theory would suggest that wage rates would be the same if all labour was homogeneous and all jobs possessed the same characteristics. In the real world workers are not identical. They differ, for instance, in where they are prepared to work, their hours of work and their levels of human capital (☞ unit 2). Jobs differ too. In particular the marginal revenue product curve for each type of job is different.

For example, the average earnings of professional workers in management and administration were £404.20 a week in April 1989. This compares with manual workers in the farming and fishing industries who earned an average £160.40 a week (Table 48.2). Neo-classical economic theory suggests that such differences are due to differences in the demand for and supply of different types of labour.

On the supply side, there are potentially far more workers with the ability and training to become

manual workers than non-manual workers. The manager could become the office cleaner, but the office cleaner could not necessarily become a successful manager. Not all workers are prepared to take on any particular job. Occupations which are unpleasant or dangerous, or where earnings can fluctuate greatly, are likely to attract fewer workers than others where the non-pecuniary advantages are much greater. Hence, earnings in construction and mining are likely to be higher than average, all other things being equal, because of the danger of the job. In general, the larger the potential supply of labour to an occupation, the lower is likely to be the level of earnings.

On the demand side, non-manual jobs are likely to carry a higher marginal revenue product than manual jobs. Without an effective manager, a company may lose thousands and perhaps millions of pounds of potential revenue or suffer high costs of production. But the company could get by without an effective office cleaner. Hence professional workers in

Table 48.2 *Earnings by occupation, full time adult men, April 1989*

	Average gross weekly earnings
Non-manual	
Professional and related in management and administration	£404.20
Professional and related in education, welfare and health	£317.80
Literary, artistic and sports	£331.80
Professional and related in science, engineering and technology	£324.30
Managerial	£317.00
Clerical	£211.90
Selling	£241.50
Security	£275.50
Manual	
Catering, cleaning, hairdressing	£170.70
Farming, fishing and related	£160.40
Materials processing (excluding metals)	£218.60
Making and repairing (excluding metals and electrical)	£223.50
Processing, making and repairing (metal and electrical)	£244.20
Painting, repetitive assembling, product inspection	£209.30
Construction, mining	£217.70
Transport operating	£210.50
Miscellaneous	£198.50
Total non-manual	£326.60
Total manual	£217.80
Total all occupations	£269.50

Source: Department of Employment, *New Earnings Survey*.

management and administration are paid more highly than workers in catering, cleaning and hairdressing because their revenue product is greater.

So far we have assumed that labour markets are perfectly competitive and that they are in equilibrium. In practice, many of the differences in wages between occupations may be accounted for by trade unions or monopsony employers. For instance, print workers in the 1980s saw their trade union power decline as employers, such as Times Newspapers, won a number of key industrial disputes.

Alternatively the market may be in disequilibrium. In the 1980s, for instance, earnings in the shipbuilding industry in the UK have been depressed as the industry has declined. On the other hand, earnings in occupations related to computers have been buoyant as the industry has expanded.

Wage structure by gender

Females have traditionally earned considerably less than men. Economic reasons can be put forward for this. In the past, women were denied the same educational opportunities as men and were thus unable to acquire the same level of human capital.

Equally, they were denied access to all but a narrow range of jobs.

Today, possibly the most important factor causing inequality in earnings between the sexes in the UK is the unequal burden of child care. It is still almost universal for women to take primary responsibility for bringing up children. Many women still choose to abandon their careers to return home and look after their children. When they do return to work, many take up low paid, part time work which fits in to their primary role as child-carers.

Taking a break in a career is enormously costly in terms of human capital. Those who continue in employment will not only receive formal training, but will build up informal knowledge and understanding of new work methods, new technology, new products, etc. On average, earnings of both men and women rise by about 3 per cent a year when in work. The skills of the woman who left work 10 years ago in comparison will be outdated. A woman's earning potential drops by 3 per cent a year for every year a woman is out of the labour force (M J Artis, 1989). The time when women choose to leave their careers is also important. It is traditional for workers to make their most important career progressions between the ages of 20 and 40, precisely the time when many women are out of the workforce. Employers respond to the less stable work patterns of women by offering less training to female employees. There is also evidence to suggest that, despite legislation, women are passed over in promotion.

Table 48.3 shows the relative pay of men and women. During the 1970s, the gap between male and female earnings narrowed. This was almost certainly the result of the Equal Pay Act 1970 and the Sex Discrimination Act 1975. The 1970 Act made it illegal to pay women less than men if they were doing the same job. The 1975 Act guaranteed women equality of opportunity. However, the evidence suggests that this was a once and for all gain. There has been almost no change in the relative pay of women during the 1980s. Indeed, a number of measures passed by Parliament during this decade, such as reduced job security for part time workers, has increased the power of employers and is therefore likely to have, if anything, depressed women's wages.

A number of other factors will affect the pay of women. Many occupations, such as nursing, are

Table 48.3 *Wage relativities by gender: ratio of female to male gross weekly earnings, full time employees*

	1971	1976	1981	1988
Manual employees	.53	.62	.62	.62
Non-manual employees	.52	.61	.61	.60
All employees	.57	.66	.67	.67

Source: adapted from CSO, *Social Trends*.

dominated by females. The proportion of women working in manufacturing is far smaller than in service industries. Women are less likely to be members of trade unions. However, even taking all these factors into account, Blanchflower and Oswald (1989) found that a typical 23 year old woman in 1981 earned 23 per cent less per hour than her male counterpart. This is caused simply by discrimination.

Wage structure by region

Figure 48.4 shows that wages vary between regions. They are highest in the South East of England and lowest in Northern Ireland. There are a number of factors which may account for this variation.

- ■ There is a difference in occupational structures between regions. The South East has the highest concentration of service sector jobs in the UK (☞ unit 23) and therefore has a disproportionate number of non-manual workers in its labour force.
- ■ Demand for labour in the South East has tended to outstrip supply in the post-war era leading to upward pressure on wages. This was particularly noticeable in the late 1980s.
- ■ Staying-on rates in education at 16 are higher in the South East than elsewhere suggesting that young workers are gaining more human capital than their counterparts in the rest of the country.
- ■ The cost of living is also higher in the South East, shifting the supply curve of labour upwards as workers demand higher wages for the same work than their counterparts in other areas of the country.

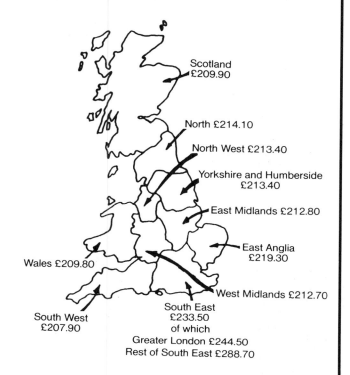

Source: adapted from Department of employment, *New Earnings Survey.*

Figure 48.4 *Regional earnings. Average gross weekly earnings for full time manual males on adult rates, April 1989*

CITY PAY LEAVES WOMEN TRAILING

More than four in every five of the most highly paid jobs in the City are held by men and very few women hold jobs commanding a salary of above £70 000 according to a new study of pay rates in the capital. There are substantially more men than women working in the City, but their stranglehold on the top jobs is still grossly out of proportion the survey concludes. Only in the 'newer' areas of business, such as investment banking, have women made a mark among the higher paid.

Salaries for men and women start to diverge in the mid-twenties and continue to move further apart as their ages increase. At a time when women might be assessing choices such as marriage and a family, employers were also looking at their salaries and were tending to peg them back behind their male counterparts. Taking time

out to have children had particularly severe consequences for high-powered women in the City since financial businesses were so fast moving. Women also tend to be less aggressive in the annual salary round.

Source: adapted from an article by Lisa Buckingham, *The Guardian*, 1.6.1990.

1. **Outline the arguments used in the passage to explain the relative low pay of women working in the City.**

2. **How might the gap between earnings of male and female City workers be narrowed?**

Summary

1. Trade unions exist to further the interests of their own members.
2. Neo-classical economic theory predicts that trade unions increase wages but create unemployment in perfectly competitive industries.
3. Theory also predicts that a monopsonist buyer of labour will employ more workers and pay them a higher wage rate when bargaining with a union than in a situation where it is bargaining with a large number of individual employees.
4. Trade unions will be more powerful the larger the trade union membership, the less elastic the demand for labour and the greater the profitability of the employer.
5. Trade unions will reduce efficiency in a perfectly competitive economy, but they may increase efficiency if the economy is imperfectly competitive.
6. Trade unions may reduce costs of production for firms if they facilitate change and perform some of the tasks, such as personnel management, which management would otherwise have to undertake.

Trade unions. Do they raise their members' wages or cause unemployment? Or do they do both?

Collective bargaining

A trade union is an organisation of workers who combine together to further their own interests. Within a company organisation, an individual worker is likely to be in a relatively weak bargaining position compared to his or her employer. The employer possesses far greater knowledge about everything from safety standards to the profitability of the firm than an individual worker. Moreover, the loss of an individual worker to a firm is likely to be far less significant than the loss of his or her job to the employee.

So workers have organised themselves in unions to bargain collectively. Instead of each individual worker bargaining with the firm on a wide range of wage and employment issues, workers elect or appoint representatives to bargain on their behalf. From an economic viewpoint, trade unions act as monopoly suppliers of labour.

Trade unions play a very controversial role in the economy. Critics argue that trade unions, by forcing up wages and resisting changes in working practices, create unemployment. Neo-classical economic theory supports this view, assuming that factor markets are perfectly competitive. However, as will be argued below, it also suggests that trade unions increase employment if a trade union represents workers in a firm which is the sole buyer of labour.

Competitive industries

Trade unions act to further the interests of their members. One of the key ways in which they do this is to press for

higher wages. In economic terms, they attempt to fix a minimum price for the supply of labour. This produces a kinked supply curve.

In Figure 49.1 the non-union demand and supply curves for labour in an industry are D and S_1 respectively. A union agreement to raise wages from the free market wage of OA to the unionised wage rate of OB means that employers in the industry cannot hire workers below a

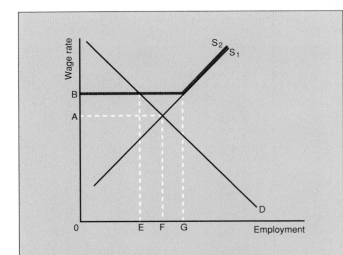

Figure 49.1 *Trade unions in a competitive market*
The entry of a trade union to a competitive factor market is likely to 'kink' the supply curve of labour. OB is the union negotiated wage rate in an industry. Employment will fall from OF to OE whilst wages rates will rise from OA to OB.

wage rate of OB. The supply curve therefore is perfectly elastic (i.e. horizontal) over the employment range OG. The union agreement does not prevent employers paying higher wages than the negotiated wage. Employers would need to pay higher wage rates if they wished to hire more workers than OG. Above OG the new supply curve S_2 is the same as the old supply curve S_1. The new equilibrium wage rate is OB, the wage rate that the union negotiated. However, employment in the industry falls from OF (the equilibrium in a non-unionised market) to OE.

Neo-classical micro-economic theory therefore suggests that trade unions increase wages for their members, but also cause unemployment in the industry. Wages would be lower and employment higher if the industry were non-unionised.

Trade unions vs monopsony employers

Many trade unions operate in factor markets where there are monopsony employers. A sole seller of labour (the trade union) faces a sole buyer of labour (the monopsonist).

Economic theory suggests that a trade union will increase both wages and employment compared to a factor market where a monopsony employer negotiates with a large number of individual employees. Figure 49.2 (a) shows the wage and employment levels in an industry with a monopsonist and many individual employees (☞ unit 48 for a full explanation of the graph). Employment is OA and the equilibrium wage rate is OE. Figure 49.2 (b) shows the entry of a trade union to the industry. Assume that the trade union forced the wage rate up to OF. This produces a kinked supply curve. The monopsonist cannot pay a wage rate lower than OF because of its union agreement. However, it is free to pay higher wage rates if it wishes to employ more than OB workers. This produces a kink in the marginal cost of labour to the firm. Up to OB, the marginal cost of labour is the same as the union negotiated wage rate. The employer can hire an extra unit of labour at that wage rate. If it employs more than OB workers, the wage rate will rise, resulting in a jump in marginal cost at OB. The monopsonist has a profit incentive to hire extra workers so long as the marginal revenue product of labour, shown by the demand curve, is greater than the marginal cost of labour. Hence it will employ OB workers.

Why should a monopsonist buy more labour at a higher wage rate from a union than it would otherwise? It should be remembered that a firm bases its decision on on how much labour to hire not on the wage rate (the average cost of labour) but on the marginal cost of labour. It can be seen from Figure 49.2 that the marginal cost of unionised labour is lower between employment levels A and B than it would have been if labour had been non-unionised. In the former case it is flat at OF, whilst in the latter it is rising steeply above OF.

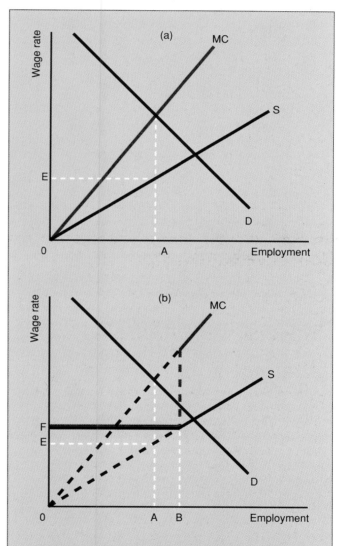

Figure 49.2 *A trade union vs a monopsonist employer A monopsonist facing a large number of employees in an industry will force wage rates down to OE and restrict employment to OA. The entry of a trade union to the industry which sets a minimum wage of OF will 'kink' the supply curve of labour and produce a discontinuity in the marginal cost curve for labour. The monopsonist has a profit incentive to hire extra workers so long as the marginal revenue product of labour, shown by the demand curve, is greater than the marginal cost of labour. Hence it will employ OB workers.*

QUESTION 2

Table 49.1   £

Units of labour employed	Wage rate per worker		Marginal cost of employing 1 extra worker		Marginal revenue product of labour
	With no trade union	With a trade union	With no trade union	With a trade union	
2	4	8	4	8	16
3	5	8	6	8	14
4	6	8	8	8	12
5	7	8	10	8	10
6	8	8	12	8	8
7	9	9	14	14	6
8	10	10	16	16	4

The table shows wage rates, marginal employment costs and MRPs facing a monopsonist employer of labour.

(a) (i) What is the maximum number of workers the firm would employ if the labour force were non-unionised?
     (ii) What would be the equilibrium wage rate?
(b) What is the maximum number of workers the firm would employ if workers belonged to a trade union and it had negotiated a minimum wage rate of £8?
(c) Explain why trade unions might increase rather than decrease the level of employment in an industry.

The power of trade unions

There are a variety of factors which make trade unions more or less powerful.

Trade union membership and militancy A union which has 100 per cent membership an industry is likely to be stronger than a union which only represents 10 per cent of potential members. It could be argued that the National Union of Railwaymen is far more powerful in the railway industry than the Transport and General Workers Union is in the hairdressing industry. Equally, unions are more likely to call for industrial action if union members are militant. The more militant the union membership, the more costly a dispute is likely to be for an employer. For instance, the nursing unions are very weak because the dominant union, the Royal College of Nursing, won't take strike action.

The demand curve for labour is relatively inelastic A rise in wage rates will have far less impact upon employment in the industry if the demand for labour is relatively inelastic than if it is elastic. Hence, there will be far less cost to the union of a wage rate increase in terms of lost membership and to its members in terms of lost employment (☞ unit 46 for a discussion of why the demand for labour might be inelastic).

Profitability of the employer A trade union is unlikely to be able to negotiate large wage increases with an employer on the verge of bankruptcy. It is likely to be in a stronger position with a highly profitable firm. This implies that trade unions will be stronger in monopolistic and oligopolistic industries, where firms are able to earn abnormal profit, than in perfectly competitive industries where only normal profit can be earned in the long run.

QUESTION 3

How would economic theory account for the strength and weakness of union power in these industries?

Efficiency

Neo-classical economic theory suggests that trade unions operating in competitive industries reduce employment levels and raise wage rates. If all industries but one were perfectly competitive then a trade union in that one industry would mean that the economy as a whole was not Pareto efficient (☞ unit 33).

However, most industries in the UK are imperfectly

competitive. A trade union facing a monopsonist will redress the balance of power in the industry and lead to a level of employment and a wage rate which will be nearer to the free market price of labour. It could well be that the presence of a trade union increases economic efficiency in an imperfectly competitive market. Hence the effect of trade unions on economic efficiency depends on the structure of markets in an economy.

A further important argument needs to be considered. Some economists have suggested that trade unions raise economic efficiency because they lower costs of production to the firm. The trade union performs many of the functions of a personnel department within a firm. It deals with workers' problems and obviates the need for the firm to negotiate pay with each and every worker. More importantly, it can be a good vehicle for negotiating changes in working practices. A firm may wish to implement changes which will lead to less pleasant working conditions for its workers. Perhaps it wishes to increase the speed of the assembly line, or force workers to undertake a variety of tasks rather than just one. It may find it difficult to implement these changes on a non-unionised workforce because some workers may take

unorganised industrial action or do their best to disrupt any changes being introduced. A union may help the firm to persuade workers that changes in working practices are in their own interest. The union will usually demand a price for this co-operation - higher wage rates for its members. But it still leads to an increase in economic efficiency because the firm is able to make higher profits whilst workers receive higher wage rates. According to this view, trade unions increase productivity in the economy.

Key terms

Trade union mark-up - the difference between wage rates in a unionised place of work and the wage rate which would otherwise prevail in the absence of trade unions.
Closed shop - a place of work where workers must belong to a recognised trade union.

QUESTION 4 It could be argued that there has been a revolution in working practices in the UK during the1980s. Many companies have reorganised the way in which workers perform tasks. One way of increasing flexibility is to organise the workforce into multi-skilled work groups, or 'hit squads' able to carry out a range of tasks as required. Examples include a deal made in 1988 at Ind Coope Burton Brewery, Burton-on-Trent which provided for the formation of teams within which allocation of work is based on competence. In return, team members were awarded higher pay. Also in 1988 an agreement was signed at an industry level between the British Printing Industry Federation and the National Graphical Association (NGA) trade union which provided for workers to 'carry out any of the duties within and between origination and printing room departments in accordance with the needs of production'. Another way of increasing flexibility is to make production line workers responsible for their own quality control instead of employing supervisors . For example, at Cameron Iron Works welders have been given theoretical and practical training and now do their own inspection.
Source: Adapted from the *Employment Gazette*, August 1989.

(a) How might the changes described in the data increase efficiency?
(b) What are the possible advantages and disadvantages to workers of the changes outlined?

Applied economics

Trade unions

Trade unions in the UK have existed for over 200 years. In the early 19th century, trade unions were outlawed for being anti-competitive. By the early 20th century there were 2 million trade union members and, as Figure 49.3 shows, this rose to a peak of over 13 million in 1979. In the 1980s there has been a sharp fall in the number of trade union members. There are a number of possible explanations for this radical change in union membership in the 1980s.
■ The recession of 1980-2 led to an increase in unemployment of nearly 2 million. The unemployed tend to allow their union membership to lapse. It is interesting to note, however, that the rise in employment in the late 1980s has not lead to

a corresponding rise in trade union membership.
■ The 1980s saw a radical restructuring of British industry. Employment in manufacturing, a sector which was very highly unionised, fell significantly. The new jobs that were created tended to be in the service sector of the economy, traditionally far less unionised than manufacturing.
■ The 1980s was a decade in which the government showed a marked hostility to trade unions. This affected the willingness of workers to join unions and increased the confidence of those employers attempting to reduce or eliminate trade union activity in their workplaces.

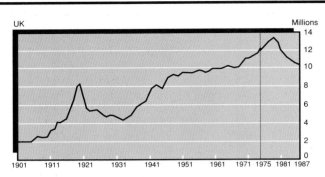

Note: discontinuity in 1975.

Source: adapted from CSO, *Social trends*.

Figure 49.3 *Trade union membership*

The trade union mark-up

Economic theory suggests that trade unions will increase wage rates for their members by shifting the supply curve of labour upwards. Studies of the UK economy tend to confirm that such a MARK-UP, the difference between actual wage rates in unionised labour markets and the wage rate which would otherwise prevail in the absence of trade unions, is indeed present. Figure 49.4 is one estimate of the union mark-up over time. The trend suggests that the size of the mark-up is cyclical (☞ unit 83). When the economy is in boom and unemployment is falling, non-union wages tend to rise faster than union wages. Hence the mark-up falls. When the economy is in recession and unemployment is rising, non-union wages tend to rise more slowly than union wages. Hence the mark-up tends to rise.

The union mark-up varies from industry to industry. M Stewart (1983) found that the mark-up ranged from 18 per cent in shipbuilding to 2 per cent in electrical engineering. The results are shown in Table 49.2.

Sources of trade union power

It can be seen from Figure 49.4 that the mark-up has tended to rise over time from about 2.5 per cent in the

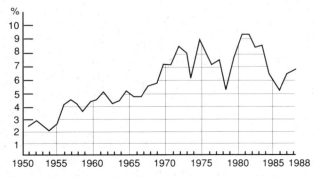

Source: Layard and Nickell (1986).

Figure 49.4 *Estimated mark-up of union over non-unionised wages*

Table 49.2 *Estimate of the trade union mark-up by industry 1975*

Industry	Mark-up (%)
Shipbuilding and marine engineering	18.2
Paper, printing and publishing	11.4
Other manufacturing industries	10.9
Metal goods not elsewhere specified	10.7
Clothing and footwear	10.1
Chemicals and allied industries	9.6
Vehicles	9.6
Timber and furniture	9.1
Instrument engineering	8.6
Food, drink and tobacco	6.6
Metal manufacture	5.4
Mechanical engineering	4.1
Bricks, pottery, glass and cement	2.4
Electrical engineering	2.0

Source: *M. Stewart* (1983).

early 1950s to between 5 and 10 per cent in the 1980s. What factors might determine the size of this union mark-up and why does the union mark-up vary from industry to industry?

Union density Union density refers to the proportion of the workforce which belongs to a trade union. Figures 49.3 and 49.4 show that over the 1950s, 1960s and 1970s trade union membership has risen at the same time as the union mark-up. So the size of the mark-up may be linked to the percentage of workers belonging to a trade union. Indeed, the industries with a high union mark-up shown Table 49.2, such as shipbuilding and printing, have traditionally been highly unionised. Many firms within these industries are CLOSED SHOPS. In a closed shop, all workers have to belong to a recognised trade union. Closed shops are commonly assumed to increase trade union power at the expense of the employer.

Union militancy The willingness of trade unions to take industrial action may be another factor influencing the size of the union mark-up. Industrial action may take a variety of forms, including strikes, work-to-rules, and overtime bans. The greater the willingness of unions to strike, the more costly industrial action will be to employers and therefore the more likely it is that they will concede high pay rises. In practice, it is difficult to measure the degree of union militancy and therefore it is difficult to gauge the degree of correlation between such militancy and the change in the union mark-up.

The legislative background Unions have to work within a legal framework. Unions in the UK gained the right to organise in 1824 with the repeal of the Combination Acts. Their right to strike without being sued for damages by an employer was enshrined in the Industrial Disputes Act of 1906. During the 1960s, however, there was a growing feeling that trade unions and their members were using their power in a way which was damaging to the economy as a whole. The

Labour government of 1964-1970 shelved plans to introduce trade union reforms in the face of trade union opposition, but Edward Heath's Conservative government of 1970-1974 did take action. The Industrial Relations Act (1971) was highly controversial, met substantial opposition from the trade union movement and failed to reduce their power effectively. It was repealed in 1974 when a new Labour government came into office and trade union rights were extended by various pieces of legislation in the following two years. The 1980s, arguably, saw a transformation in the climate of industrial relations in the UK. The Conservative government, instead of introducing large scale legislative reform, passed a number of acts each of which restricted union power at the margin. By 1990:

- secondary picketing had been made illegal;
- trade unions had to hold a secret ballot and gain a majority of the votes cast to call an official strike;
- social security benefits were withdrawn from the dependants of striking workers;
- union officers had to be elected by secret ballots;
- closed shop agreements were restricted and greater opportunities were given for employees to opt out of closed shops.

Power within the union movement shifted. Before 1979, small groups of workers who were willing to take unofficial strike action and certain militant trade union leaders tended to dominate at least the newspaper headlines. The reforms of the 1980s made it more costly and more difficult for workers to take widespread unofficial action. The power of trade union leaders to call strikes was curbed because workers now had to be balloted on strike action. Moreover, the democratisation of union voting procedures made it much more difficult for militant trade union leaders to get elected to key posts within trade unions.

The government also shrewdly distanced itself from the prosecution of trade unions. Previous legislation had concentrated on criminal law, where offenders were prosecuted by the state and could be fined or imprisoned. Government always risked creating trade union 'martyrs'. Much of the union legislation of the 1980s concentrated on civil law. Employers were given powers to sue trade unions for breaches of the law. For instance, if a trade union calls a strike without holding a secret ballot, it is the employer affected which sues the trade union for damages. The government has no power to prosecute the union.

This means that trade unions risk losing considerable sums of money if they do not comply with the law, but individual trade union members cannot gain public sympathy by being sent to prison as they could in theory under the 1971 Industrial Relations Act.

Not only has the government considerably reduced the ability of trade unions and their members to take industrial action, it also, during the 1980s, took a strong stance with public sector trade unions. The most important trade union defeat in the public sector was the breaking of the miners' strike in 1984-5.

Furthermore, the government completely cut off the trade union movement from decision making at a national level. This contrasted with the 1960s and 1970s when governments, both Labour and Conservative, would often consult trade union leaders before making important decisions.

It is perhaps not surprising then that the trade union mark-up has not increased during the 1980s and some groups of workers, such as miners and print workers, have almost certainly seen a substantial reduction in their mark-up.

Data question

EMPLOYMENT LAWS HAVE LITTLE EFFECT ON BRITISH PERFORMANCE

The government's employment legislation of the 1980s forced unions to tighten their internal organisation and made them more cautious about calling strikes, but had little effect on Britain's economic performance. These are the conclusions of Professor William Brown and Mr Sushil Wadhwani in a review article. They found that legislation has a limited impact on both unemployment and labour efficiency. They argued further that high unemployment gave employers the freedom to manage labour better and the incentive to do so by increased competition in product markets, but it is implausible to think that legislation on its own stimulated better labour management.

The authors say the legislation has so far failed in increasing employment in union companies by reducing the 'union mark-up' of wages in those companies compared with non-unionised competitors. Employers who recognised unions have tended to reduce employment by reorganising working practices instead. The 'union mark-up' has remained constant, partly because employers distributed some savings in the form of higher wages for their employees.

Source: adapted from the *Financial Times*, 28.2.1990.

1. **Explain, using a diagram, why reducing the union mark-up might increase employment.**
2. **Why, in the opinion of the authors, has employment legislation failed to reduce the union mark-up?**

Summary

1. In a perfectly competitive labour market, there is no unemployment, no discrimination and market forces allocate workers to their highest paid occupations.
2. In practice, there are many examples of market failure in labour markets.
3. One major cause of labour market failure in the UK is the lack of mobility of labour, in turn caused principally by failure in the housing market and by a lack of skills amongst workers.
4. In segmented labour markets, the formal sector is unlikely to make short term adjustments to unemployment and hence labour markets may be prevented from clearing.
5. Trade unions and monopsonist employers, such as government, can reduce employment in the market. So too can government policy.
6. Governments attempt to correct labour market failure in a variety of ways, including minimum wage legislation and equal pay legislation. These may lead to an increase in wages for some workers but it may also lead to unemployment for others.

Efficiency, equity and market failure

An economy where all markets are perfectly competitive is Pareto efficient (☞ unit 33). All labour markets will clear. Everyone who wants a job at the going wage rate is able to obtain one and therefore there is no unemployment. There is perfect factor mobility and therefore there can be no regional or sectoral unemployment. The market mechanism will allocate workers to their highest value occupations, ensuring that total output in the economy is maximised.

In a real modern industrialised economy, few markets are perfectly competitive. There are many instances of market failure and this is true not just in the goods market (☞ unit 34) but also in labour markets. Market failure can be judged against a number of criteria of efficiency including:
■ full employment - the extent to which the market mechanism provides jobs for those who wish to work;
■ maximum labour productivity - the extent to which the potential, the talents and the skills of workers in jobs are fully utilised in an economy.

Market failure can also be judged against different criteria of equity:
■ equal opportunities - the extent to which all groups in society including women, the young, the elderly and those from ethnic minorities are not discriminated against in the labour market;
■ wage differentials - the extent to which individual workers receive a 'fair' wage for the work they do.

Causes of labour market failure

There are a considerable number of ways in which labour markets are imperfect.

Mobility of labour In a perfect labour market, there is complete mobility of labour. Workers are free at no cost to themselves, to move jobs between industries and between regions. In practice, there are major obstacles to mobility.
■ Many workers have job-specific skills. For instance, a teacher could not easily become a manager. A manager could not easily become a concert pianist. A concert pianist could not easily become a chef. When industries, such as the steel industry or the shipbuilding industry shrink as they did in the 1970s and 1980s in the UK, redundant skilled workers in these industries find it difficult to find any employment except unskilled, low paid jobs. Industrial training by firms and by government favours young workers. So older workers find it difficult to move from industry to industry, even if they so wish.
■ Knowledge is imperfect in the labour market, particularly in occupations where there is a long tradition of labour immobility. There are high SEARCH COSTS for workers and employers in finding out about employment opportunities. These search costs include time spent looking for jobs, or job applicants, and money costs such as travel, postage and advertisements. The higher the search costs, the less likely a search will take place and the less labour mobility there will be.
■ Workers are not just workers. They belong to families and local communities. They take a pride in their area or in the skills they have acquired over a long period of time. Many people prefer not to move round the country in pursuit of a job or a career. They prefer to remain unemployed or stay in a job which is not particularly rewarding rather than move.
■ A major obstacle to labour mobility in the UK is the housing market. Over 60 per cent of all homes are now owner-occupied. Moving house is very expensive. Moreover, the gap between house prices in the South of England and the rest of the UK is so large that many outside the South cannot afford to buy property in London and the South East. Even if they can, they have to trade down in terms of the property they can afford to buy. Not surprisingly, many workers are deterred from moving from North to South in the UK. The rented housing market is even less flexible. The private rented sector is now very small and provides almost no family size accommodation at affordable

rents. The public sector (council houses) and voluntary sector (mainly Housing Associations) both have long waiting lists for their accommodation. It is allocated almost exclusively to local residents in need. So whilst relatively high income earners can afford to be mobile, those on average or below average incomes find it difficult, if not impossible, to move geographically. The unemployed, those who need to be most mobile, find they are restricted from moving to jobs in other areas because they cannot get housing.

QUESTION 1 In 1988, the *Financial Times* reported that construction workers in the Crawley and Gatwick areas of Sussex had difficulties finding accommodation. The housing charity Shelter estimated that over 100 workers were sleeping rough or in cars. Typical was a construction worker who came South after being unemployed in Huddersfield for 9 months. He slept in his car. Despite the fact that he could afford the £45 a week rent for a room, he had been unable to find a vacancy. He would have liked to bring down his wife and daughter to join him, but a furnished house would be too expensive. According to Shelter, the cost would be between £500 and £600 a month. Shelter described the rented housing stock in the area as 'run-down and expensive '.

How does this story illustrate the problems of the mobility of labour in the UK today?

Segmented labour markets Some economists have argued that labour markets are segmented so that there is little movement of labour from one market to another. One version of this argument is the DUAL LABOUR MARKET HYPOTHESIS. In the formal, primary or planning sector of the economy, workers, often unionised, are employed by large employers such as oligopolistic or monopoly firms or by government. Workers in the formal sector tend to be better qualified and better paid. In the informal, secondary, or market sector, workers, mainly non-unionised, are employed by small firms or are self-employed. These workers tend to be low-skilled or unskilled workers on low pay.

In the formal sector, workers are seen as important assets by their employers. They are trained and are expected to pursue a life-long career in their occupation. They are seen as reliable, dependable and loyal. In return for these qualities, firms are prepared to give a complete remuneration package, including not just pay, but also benefits such as pension schemes, sickness benefit and paid holidays. At times, this package may be far in excess of the equilibrium wage rate (i.e. the firm could employ workers at far lower wages). However, reducing wages to take advantage of short term weaknesses in the labour market would be counter-productive in the long run. It might lead to lower morale, greater uncertainty and lower productivity amongst existing staff. If workers are brought in from outside the company, it may take time for new staff to become familiar with often complex work routines and there may be friction between these

outsiders and existing company staff. Reducing wages in the short term may also deter young people, who see that wages can be volatile, from entering the industry.

In the informal sector, workers are expected to be mobile. Job security is low. Training is minimal. Workers are not expected to stay with their employers and hence little is provided in the form of extra benefits, such as sickness benefits or pension schemes.

If the economy is in fact divided into these two sectors, there are important implications for unemployment and discrimination. Market economists argue that unemployment in an industry can only be a short term phenomenon because wages will fall to clear the market. However, employers do not react to unemployment by cutting wages in the formal sector of the economy. On the contrary, workers may continue to receive pay rises in line with their career expectations. In the informal sector, there will be wage cuts which will expand employment. Overall it will take much longer for the economy to return to full employment because only the informal sector behaves in the way economic theory suggests. What is more, the process of adjustment will lead to widening income differentials. Whilst workers in the formal sector will be receiving pay rises, those in the informal sector will receive wage cuts. So the burden of adjustment falls disproportionately hard on those most likely to receive low wages.

For a variety of reasons discussed below, women and those from ethnic minorities tend to form a much larger percentage of the workforce in the informal sector of the economy than the formal. Hence, this dual economy reinforces discrimination against these groups.

QUESTION 2

Table 50.1 *Average earnings and unemployment 1980 and 1981*

	1980	1981
Average earnings 1980=100		
Banking, finance and insurance	100	114
Hotels and catering	100	112
Retail Price Index	100	118
Unemployment (millions)	1.6	2.5

Source: adapted from Department of Employment, *Employment Gazette*; CSO, *Economic Trends Annual Supplement*.

How might the theory of segmented labour markets help to explain the difference in the earnings increase between the sectors shown in the data?

Trade unions and monopsony employers It is argued that trade unions and monopsony employers create unemployment in the market. A full explanation of this was given in units 48 and 49.

Government policy Government policies, ranging from taxation on cigarettes to interest rate policy to health and safety legislation, affect the labour market in a variety of ways. Each individual policy lessens market failure or leads to an increase in market failure. Many aspects of the debate on this issue are discussed in units on supply-side economics, but it is important to realise that government policies designed specifically to deal with labour market failure may well themselves create further labour market failure.

Correcting market failure

Governments have adopted a variety of policies in an attempt to improve both efficiency and equity in the labour market. However, some economists believe that the problems created by these policies are worse than the problems they were originally designed to counter.

Minimum wage legislation One way of tackling low pay is for the government to enforce minimum wage rates on employers. In the UK, wages councils have the power to fix minimum wages in a number of industries noted for their low pay.

This would seem to be an ideal solution to the problem of poverty amongst workers. However, economic theory predicts that the policy will have undesirable secondary effects. Figure 50.1 shows the demand and supply curves for labour in an industry. The equilibrium wage rate is OE whilst the equilibrium level of employment is OB. The government now imposes a minimum wage of OF, forcing industry wage rates to rise to OF. Firms demand AB less labour whilst BC more workers wish to gain jobs in the industry. The result is AC unemployment.

Existing workers have not necessarily benefited. OA workers have gained higher wages. But AB workers have lost their jobs as a result of the legislation. What is more, the workers who have lost their jobs are likely to be the least employable. Firms will have fired their least productive employees.

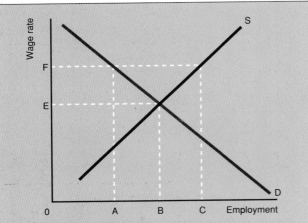

Figure 50.1 *Minimum wage legislation*
A minimum wage of OF will result in higher wage rates in the industry. However, AB workers will lose their existing jobs whilst a total of AC unemployment will be created.

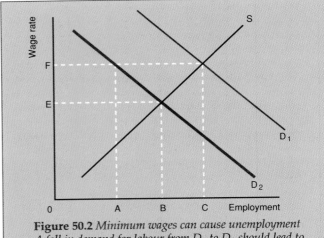

Figure 50.2 *Minimum wages can cause unemployment A fall in demand for labour from D₁ to D₂ should lead to a fall in wage rates from OF to OE. However, a minimum wage of OF will prevent this and will cause unemployment of AC to arise.*

Minimum wage legislation can also prevent the market from clearing when there is an increase in unemployment. In Figure 50.2, D_1 and S are the original demand and supply curves respectively. Assume that the minimum wage is set at OF. Then the equilibrium market wage rate is equal to the minimum wage rate and there is no unemployment. Now assume that the economy goes into recession. Demand for the industry's product falls and so the demand for labour in the industry falls (remember, labour is a derived demand). The new demand curve is D_2. If the market had been free, wage rates would have fallen to OE and any transitional unemployment in the market would have disappeared. But with a minimum wage of OF, unemployment of AC is created. So it is argued that minimum wage legislation can cause unemployment.

Equal pay legislation Equal pay legislation is designed to raise the wage rates of groups of workers who perform work of equal value to other workers doing the same job who are at present paid higher wages. In the UK, equal pay legislation has been applied particularly to women and to workers from ethnic minorities.

Economic theory suggests that equal pay legislation will have the same effect as the imposition of a minimum wage. Equal pay legislation is designed to raise the wages of workers who are discriminated against. In the UK, there is evidence to suggest that it has been partially successful in achieving this (☞ applied economics below). However, raising wages will reduce the demand for and increase the supply of labour. If the market was in equilibrium to start with, then the introduction of legislation will cause unemployment amongst those groups whom it is designed to benefit. There is a direct trade-off between higher pay and fewer jobs.

Health and safety legislation and other employment protection measures Government has passed many acts designed to improve the living standards of workers. For instance, health and safety legislation is designed to protect workers against accidents at work. These measures have the effect of raising the cost to firms of employing labour. Not only do firms have to pay workers a wage, but the legislation also forces a rise in labour-related costs. For instance, machines have to be made safe and minimum and maximum work temperatures have to be maintained. This shifts the supply curve upwards and to the left. At any given level of employment, workers will only work for a given wage rate plus the cost of protection measures, in turn leading to a fall in employment. Hence it is argued by free market economists that measures designed to protect the employee usually lead to a fall in employment.

The extent to which government legislation giving workers extra rights leads to a rise in unemployment depends crucially upon two factors.

■ Firstly, if the demand for labour is relatively inelastic, the fall in employment will be less than if it is relatively elastic. Indeed if the demand for labour is perfectly inelastic, a rise in wages will have no effect on the demand for labour. One conclusion that could be drawn from the argument above is that the demand for labour is relatively less elastic in the formal sector of the economy than in the informal sector. So minimum wage legislation or equal pay legislation will have a much greater impact on jobs in the informal sector than in the formal sector. This would correspond with evidence which suggests that semi-skilled and unskilled workers have suffered disproportionately from unemployment in the 1970s and the 1980s in the UK.

■ Secondly, what might be true for a single industry might not be true for the economy as a whole. For instance, minimum wage legislation in the hairdressing industry might result in unemployment amongst hairdressers. But minimum wage legislation across all industries might have little or no effect on unemployment. In economics, it is not possible to conclude that the economy as a whole will behave in the same way as an individual market.

QUESTION 3 Jobs are also hit by excessive pay increases, and inflexible pay arrangements. Excessive pay increases add to costs and put pressure on prices. The result is to reduce the level of output that can be profitably produced and to reduce a company's international competitiveness.

At present there are 26 wages councils. They cover 2.5 million workers, or 11 per cent of the country's workforce and 376 000 establishments. The main trades affected are retailing, catering and clothing manufacture. Each council can set a minimum rate of pay for all workers in the sector it covers. There is a strong case for abolition. A system of national statutory rates of pay is inconsistent with the need for flexible pay determination. Wages councils prevent employers from developing pay systems wholly in accordance with the best interests of their businesses.

Source: Department of Employment, *Employment News*, December 1988, No 171.

(a) Explain, using a diagram, an economic theory which would support the conclusions of the extract.
(b) Will economic efficiency and equity be promoted by allowing employers to develop 'pay systems wholly in accordance with the best interests of their businesses'?

Key terms

Search costs - costs, such as money and time, spent searching for a job.
Dual labour market hypothesis - the hypothesis that the labour market is split into two sectors: the formal sector with a relatively skilled, highly paid and stable workforce and the informal sector with a relatively unskilled, low paid and unstable workforce.

Applied economics

Wages councils

The work of wages councils

Wages councils date back to 1909 when the Liberal government of the day established a number of trade boards to set minimum wages in industries with a history of low pay. In 1990, there were 26 wages councils which set minimum pay levels for 2.5 million workers working in about 400 000 establishments. Industries covered by wages councils include retailing, catering, garment manufacture and hairdressing. There is a disproportionate number of women and part time workers in industries covered by wages councils. Part

time women workers are particularly vulnerable to exploitation by employers. The minimum wage levels set by councils are enforceable in law. There is an inspectorate which visits places of work to ensure that workers are paid these minimum rates of pay.

Since 1979, the government has repeatedly stated that it sees wages councils as a major distortion in the labour market, thus impairing the efficiency of the market mechanism. In 1988 it issued a White Paper signalling its intention to abolish the councils in the near future. However, there was considerable opposition to this not only from trade unions and charities representing the interests of the low paid, but also from many employers and employers' organisations.

Minimum pay

Wages councils were established to raise the pay of low paid workers. However, there is considerable debate as to whether wage councils have protected the interests of low paid workers in recent years.

- They have not set minimum wages much in excess of the market level according to J R Shackleton (1985). Whilst individual workers might have gained some protection from employers who would otherwise have paid far less than the free market rate, low paid workers as a whole have not benefited from substantially higher wage rates.
- Income differentials between workers have widened during the 1980s. For instance, S. Nickell (1985) estimated that the pay of workers covered by wages councils fell by 8 per cent relative to average earnings in the decade 1975 to 1985.
- There is widespread evasion by employers of wages councils' orders. According to a Low Pay Unit report (1989) about 28 per cent of establishments visited in 1988 were found to be underpaying their employees. This was an increase from 26 per cent in 1987. The number of inspectors was cut from 120 in 1985 to 71 in 1989. Only 19 582 establishments out of total of 379 253 were visited in 1988 and employers were rarely fined, inspectors preferring

to issue warnings or to advise. Hence there is little financial incentive for employers to make themselves familiar with wages councils' orders. Indeed, in l989 the Federation of Self Employed and Small Businesses stated in its response to the government White Paper on abolition that there was widespread evasion of orders. This meant that those companies which paid their workers the minimum wage were at a competitive disadvantage with other firms.

Unemployment

If wages councils have done little to increase the wages of low paid workers, then it is unlikely that they are a major source of unemployment in Britain. Professor Patrick Minford suggested in 1985 that unemployment would fall by 300 000 if wages councils were abolished. This assumed that wages councils raised pay by about an average of 10 per cent for workers covered by orders. However, other estimates for job gains have suggested far lower numbers and H Neuberger (1984) estimated that only 8 000 jobs would be created across the whole economy if wages councils were abolished.

Overall, the balance of evidence suggests that wages councils create little unemployment, but equally that they have failed to raise the wages of the low paid substantially. Economic theory predicts that the more they raise the relative wages of low paid workers, the higher the price paid in terms of unemployment.

Data question

SEGMENTED LABOUR MARKETS

In a government-funded study of the labour market, published by Nuffield College Oxford (1990), researchers found the traditional insider-outsider model of segmented labour markets inadequate. They distinguished different types of workers based upon a sample of 1 022 adults in Nottingham.

- Primary workers formed 40 per cent of the sample. They tended to be well paid, were of higher social class, and 78 per cent male.
- Stickers were 62 per cent women. Although they were paid less and had lower skill levels than the primary group, they also were the most satisfied.
- Young and mobile workers were only 5 per cent of the sample but they were 80 per cent male. These were workers who had the highest expectation of getting a better job. On average they were 30 years old.
- Female descenders were losers. Half had moved to a lower paid job when they last transferred employment. They frequently changed jobs and had

the lowest pay. 96 per cent were women and had the highest amount of domestic interference in their career. Many were part time.

- Male descenders were losers too. They had all changed jobs in the past to one of a lower social class rating, and most had been sacked or made redundant at some time.

1. In a perfectly competitive national labour market, workers are able to move freely from job to job. What barriers to mobility are suggested by the data?

2. Why were primary workers the highest paid workers in the sample?

3. What government policies might be introduced to help female workers transfer from the 'stickers' and 'female descender' categories to the 'primary worker' group?

Applied economics

Population change in the UK

The population of the UK has increased this century from 38 million in 1901 to a current figure of about 58 million. There are three ways in which a country's population can increase.

The numbers being born can rise As Figure 51.1 shows, there has been a considerable fluctuation in the number of births this century. The two World Wars saw sharp falls in the number of births. Other periods of economic uncertainty or recession - the 1920s and 1930s, and the late 1960s and early 1970s - were also associated with falls in births. The period of sustained economic growth from 1950 to the mid-1960s saw an increase in births - the so-called post-war baby boom. Subsequently the number of births did not begin to increase again until the late 1970s.

The BIRTH RATE, the numbers of live births as a proportion of the total population, is determined by two factors. Firstly, the larger the number of women of child bearing age, the higher the birth rate is likely to be. For instance, the bulge in births in the 1950s and mid-1960s produced an increase in the numbers of

women of child-bearing age from the late 1970s onwards. Hence this provides a partial explanation for the increase in the birth rate from the late 1970s. Secondly, the birth rate is determined by the FERTILITY RATE, the numbers of live births as a proportion of women of child-bearing age.

What determines the fertility rate is difficult to say. One reason why fertility rates were much higher in the pre-First World War era was the high infant mortality rate. Because so many children died, women needed to have a large number of children if some of these were to survive into adulthood. Today few children die and therefore parents are fairly confident that if they have two children, then those two will survive into adulthood.

Increased use of contraception and abortion too are likely to have affected the fertility rate. However, it should be remembered that contraception and abortion only became widely practised in the 1960s with the introduction of the pill and the legalisation of abortion. So they are unlikely to be major determinants of the changes in the birth rate seen in the first half of this century.

The economics of child rearing is likely to provide a

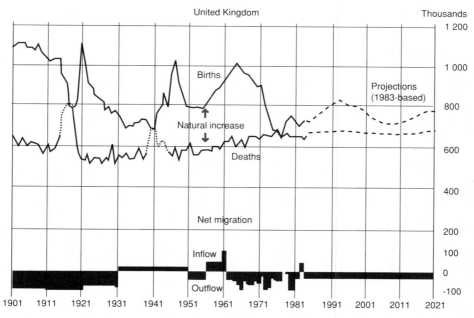

Note: The dots on this line cover the periods 1914-18 and 1939-45 which include deaths of non-civilian and merchant seamen who died outside the country.
Source: adapted from CSO, *Social Trends*.

Figure 51.1 *Population changes and projections*

more significant explanation of the trend in all developed countries to lower fertility rates. The opportunity cost of rearing children has steadily increased. In many Third World countries, children are economic assets for the parents. They can be put to work at an early age and custom often demands that children have a duty to look after parents in their old age - having children is the equivalent of investing in a pension scheme. In developed countries, the average leaving age for children from full time education is slowly increasing. More and more children need to be supported through to the age of 21. Children are expensive to keep. There is little tradition in the UK of financial support of parents in old age. What's more, the opportunity cost for women of staying at home to rear children has increased. Women have been able to obtain higher and higher wages and leaving employment for any length of time has a devastating effect on a woman's long term earnings potential (☞ unit 48). In countries such as West Germany, the birth rate today is so low that the population is actually falling.

The number of deaths can fall Figure 51.1 shows that the number of deaths has been increasing since the Second World War. This is due to increased numbers in the population. However, the DEATH RATE, the proportion of deaths to the total population, has been falling as life expectancy has increased. Better food, improved housing, safer working conditions as well as medical advances have been the cause of this trend towards greater longevity.

Net migration can be positive Net migration is the difference between immigration and emigration. If it is positive, it means that more people enter the country than leave to settle abroad. Figure 51.1 shows that the UK has tended to suffer a loss of population through migration over time. However, the numbers involved are relatively small. In the 1980s, net migration tended to be positive. In 1985, the year with the largest positive net migration figure, 174 000 people left the country whilst 232 000 came to settle in the UK. Of this 232 000, nearly half, 110 000, were existing British citizens returning to the UK after residing for a period abroad. The change in total population resulting from migration was a mere 0.01 per cent.

The changing age structure of the population

The death rate has changed only slowly over time, and has tended to fall. However, the birth rate in the UK this century has fluctuated significantly and it is this fluctuation which has caused major changes in the age structure of the population. Table 51.1 summarises the most important changes which have occurred since 1971 and are projected to occur by the year 2025. Four major changes can be singled out.

Children The number of pupils in schools, shown by the population aged 5-15, declined during the 1970s and 1980s. This resulted in widespread closure of schools. However, the increase in the birth rate from 1978 will lead to an increased demand for school places in the 1990s before falling again in the next century. This means that there is likely to be an increased demand for goods such as school buildings, children's books and clothing, and teachers during the last decade of this century.

Table 51.1 *Selected social and economic needs of population groups by age*
UK

Indices 1991 = 100

	1971	1981	1986	1991	2001	2011	2025	Social and economic needs of different age groups of the population
People aged								
Under 1	110	89	92	100	93	87	93	Maternity services, Health visiting, Preventive medicine.
1-4	118	87	93	100	102	91	97	Day care, Nursery education.
5-15	125	116	103	100	113	107	104	Compulsory education.
16-19	101	125	119	100	95	110	93	Further and higher education, Training, Employment.
15-44 (females)	86	95	100	100	95	91	89	Maternity services.
20-49	86	90	95	100	96	94	90	Employment, Housing, Transport.
50-59/64[1]	111	106	102	100	117	126	133	Pre-retirement training, Early retirement.
60/65[2]-74	99	103	101	100	95	108	123	Retirement, Pensions.
75-84	70	86	95	100	104	101	126	Retirement pension, Health care, Home helps, Sheltered housing, Retirement homes.
85 and over	55	68	81	100	132	150	154	

Notes: 1. 59 for females, 64 for males.
2. 60 for females, 65 for males

Source: adapted from CSO, *Social Trends*.

Young workers The number of school leavers and young workers aged 16-19 grew substantially in the 1970s. This is likely to have been a significant factor in the growth of youth unemployment in that decade. However, in the 1990s, the numbers of young workers is predicted to fall significantly - the so-called 'demographic timebomb'. Employers will be faced with a shortage of youngsters on the job market. As a result youth unemployment is likely to disappear and the pay of young workers relative to average earnings will rise. Given rising demand for young workers with qualifications, those leaving school or college with 'A' levels or graduates leaving higher education are particularly likely to benefit.

The 'baby-boomers' The generation of workers born in the post-war baby boom is now moving through the age structure of the population. In the 1970s and early 1980s as they entered the workforce, they suffered unemployment. In the 1990s and the early part of the next century, they will constitute a growing proportion of the labour force as the number of young people entering the workforce declines. This has important implications for employers. Increasingly they will have to look to older people to fill vacancies. Already employers in the South East, the area of greatest labour shortage, are showing greater willingness to promote older workers and to attract mature females back into jobs. The 'baby-boomers' are also likely to be of increasing significance to sellers of goods and services. The 1960s and 1970s were decades when young people represented an important and growing market for firms. However, the numbers of young people are now in decline. Therefore firms will increasingly have to switch their products to appeal to middle-aged people - 'the baby-boomers'.

The elderly A growing proportion of the population is now retired. In 1971, there were 7.4m aged 65 and over, 13.3 per cent of the total population. This grew to 8.5m in 1981 and by 1991 is projected to reach 9.0m, 15.7 per cent of the total population. The 1990s will see little change in the numbers of over 65s, but in the first decade of the next century the numbers are projected to rise to 9.6m in 2011 and 10.9m in 2021 as the baby-boomers retire. As Table 51.1 shows, these overall numbers mask significant changes in the composition of the elderly population. In the 1990s, there will be little change in the total figure. But the number of 75 year olds and over (born before or immediately after the First World War) will increase whilst the numbers of 65-74 year olds (the generation born in the 1920s and 1930s) will decrease.

This has significant implications for the state. Those aged 75 and over tend to be on very low incomes and therefore need income support. Many are unable to look after themselves and therefore need care in the community or in institutions such as old people's homes. They are particularly expensive for the National Health Service (NHS). Therefore NHS, social security and social services budgets will have to increase in real terms in the 1990s if the standard of living of the elderly is to be maintained at its present levels. Even in the next century, the number of 75 year olds and over will continue to increase, imposing strains upon government finance. However, the balance of population amongst the elderly will start to change as the baby-boomers begin to retire. In the 2020s and 2030s, the baby-boomer 65-75 year olds, retiring on good pensions and having been brought up accustomed to post-war affluence, are likely to be a powerful force in society and in the market place.

An international comparison

In the developing world, most countries have a relatively young population compared to the UK. Their problems are those of paying for the education of their children and the provision of jobs as these children move into the workforce. In the developed world, the major problem that countries now face is the ageing of the population. Table 51.2 shows the change in the percentage of the population aged 65 and over in selected OECD countries. Of the 7 countries shown, the UK will be least affected by the 'greying' of its population. Over the 70 year period from 1980 to 2050, the percentage of the population over retirement age is projected only to double. In Japan, it will nearly quadruple and in West Germany and France it will increase nearly 2½ times. The OECD predicts that by the year 2050, more than one-fifth of the population of West Germany and France will be over the age of 80 and one-third will be above 65.

As argued above, this has considerable implications for government spending and the economy. For instance, currently health spending is more than four times as high per capita on the over-65s as on the under-65s in OECD countries. For the over-75s, the proportion rises to nearly 6 times.

However, it also has implications for the standard of living of workers in the population. The higher the DEPENDENCY RATIO, the proportion of dependants (i.e. non-workers) to workers in the population, the lower will be the after-tax incomes of workers if dependants are to receive a given income. For instance, workers will see their share of national income fall over the next 70 years in France and West Germany if pensioners are to increase their incomes at the same rate as workers.

One response to this is for the government to cut expenditure on state pensions. In the early 1980s, the UK government, faced with projections that state pensions would take an ever increasing percentage of the total budget in the next century, reduced future benefits to workers in the State Earnings Related Pension Scheme (SERPS). In the late 1980s, the government encouraged workers to opt out of SERPS altogether by offering National Insurance rebates to

Table 51.2 *Projections of the elderly population, % of population aged 65 and over*

	Canada	France	W.Germany	Italy	Japan	UK	US
1980a	9.5	14.0	15.5	13.5	9.1	14.9	11.3
1985a	10.4	13.0	14.8	12.9	10.2	15.1	11.9
2000	12.8	15.3	17.1	15.3	15.2	14.5	12.1
2020	20.0	21.2	23.5	20.7	22.9	18.7	17.2
2040	29.2	29.7	34.1	29.1	29.2	26.4	25.3
2050	33.0	34.0	36.2	31.0	33.1	28.7	29.0

Note: a = actual
Source: OECD

those who left SERPS and instead took out a personal pension scheme. The combined effect of these two changes will mean that total expenditure on state pensions should be lower in future. Future workers who would have had to pay taxes and National Insurance contributions to pay for the pensions of today's workers will now be better off.

The danger with this approach is that those who are contracted into SERPS will be worse off and also that workers who contracted out will not make adequate payments into their private pension scheme. This will tend to increase income inequalities as, already today, pensioners are the largest single group on low incomes.

Key terms

Birth rate - the numbers of live births as a proportion of the total population.
Fertility rate - the numbers of live births as a proportion of women of child-bearing age.

Death rate - the number of deaths as a proportion of the total population.
Dependency ratio - the proportion of dependants (i.e. non-workers) to workers in the population.

GRADUATE LABOUR MARKET IN THE 1990s

In a report (1989) by the Institute of Manpower Studies, 'The Graduate Labour Market in the 1990s', it is suggested that the 1990s could prove a difficult time for UK employers. During the decade, there could be a 30 per cent rise in the demand for new graduates but, due to demographic trends, there could be almost no rise in supply. Moreover, the composition of graduates is likely to change. There will be a rising proportion of female and mature graduates, as well as more graduates who entered higher education without traditional A-level qualifications. There will also be a continuation of the fall in the numbers of engineering and technology graduates.

1. How will the graduate labour market change in the 1990s (i) in the UK and (ii) in Europe?
2. How might UK employers respond to this change in the labour market?

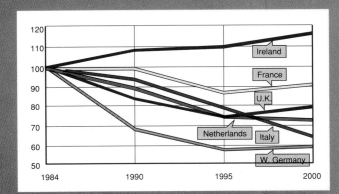

Source: adapted from IMS.

Figure 51.2 *15-19 year olds in Western Europe*

Summary

1. The functional distribution of income is the share of national income received by each factor of production.
2. A factor receives economic rent if its earnings are above its transfer earnings. Quasi rent is rent earned only in the short run.
3. Economic rent will be greater, the more inelastic the supply curve.
4. A change in economic rent will not affect the allocation of resources.

The functional distribution of income

The factors of production are classified into **land**, **labour**, **capital** and **entrepreneurship** (☞ unit 2). The owners of factors of production receive a reward for renting out their factors. Landowners receive rent, labour receives wages, capitalists receive interest and entrepreneurs earn profits.

The FUNCTIONAL DISTRIBUTION OF INCOME shows the share of national income received by each factor of production. This is different from the **personal distribution of income** described in unit 41. An individual or household may receive income from several factors of production. For instance, a pensioner may have a part time job, receive rent from a property which she owns and receive dividends from shares.

The functional distribution of income depends in part upon the price that each factor of production is paid. Neo-classical economic theory suggests that the price of a product is determined by the forces of demand and supply. For instance, the wage rate of labour will be determined by the demand for labour and the supply of labour (☞ unit 48). Rent on land will be determined by the demand for land and the supply of land. The laws of demand and supply are as applicable in factor markets as they are in the goods markets.

The exact shape of the demand and supply curves for land, labour and capital are discussed at length in the units which precede and follow this unit. However, they are broadly the same shape as in a goods market (i.e. the demand curve is downward sloping whilst the supply curve is upward sloping).

Demand and supply analysis can be used to show the functional distribution of income. In Figure 52.1, the equilibrium wage rate in the labour market is OC. OA workers are employed and therefore the total wage bill is OA x OC (the number of workers employed x the wage rate per worker). The value to the employer of OA workers is given by the area OEBA, the sum of the marginal revenue product of each worker employed up to OA workers (the marginal revenue product of each worker is the vertical distance between the MRP curve and the horizontal axis).

Total revenue received by the employer is OEBA. OCBA is paid in wages. Therefore BCE is the amount left, after wages have been paid, to reward the other factors of production employed by the firm. Out of BCE it has to pay rent, interest and profits to the owners of land and capital and to entrepreneurs.

Figure 52.1 shows the market for labour. The same analysis would apply if the market for land or capital were shown.

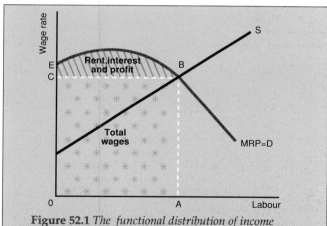

Figure 52.1 *The functional distribution of income Total revenue for the firm is the sum of the marginal revenue product of each worker (i.e. OEBA). The total wage bill for the firm is OCBA. Therefore BCE is left to distribute in the form of rent, interest and profit.*

Economic rent

David Ricardo, writing in the early part of the 19th century, developed a theory of economic rent which today can be applied to all factors of production. During the Napoleonic Wars, land rents rose steeply at the same time as the price of corn. Many argued that the rise in the price of corn was due to landowners increasing rents on agricultural land. Ricardo, however, argued that it was the rise in the price of corn that resulted in farmers demanding more land for corn production and thus bidding up the price of land. Rent, he argued, was price

QUESTION 1

Table 52.1 *The functional distribution of income in the UK*

at current prices

	1968 £m	1968 % of total	1978 £m	1978 % of total	1988 £m	1988 % of total
Income from employment and self-employment	29 086	76	112 382	74	292 392	73
Profits	6 640	17	27 991	18	77 458	19
Property rents	2 152	6	10 036	7	27 464	7

Note: Percentages do not add up to 100 because of rounding and because the input charge for consumption of non-trading capital is not shown on the table.

Source: CSO, *United Kingdom National Accounts (Blue Book)*.

(a) Describe the changes in the functional distribution of income in the UK between 1968 and 1988.
(b) Using diagrams, explain the following arguments which might account for the data in Table 52.1:
(i) wage rates have risen because the increasing use of capital has made workers more productive;
(ii) the rate of return on capital has not fallen over time because innovation and technical progress have pushed the marginal efficiency of capital schedule to the right; (iii) property rents have increased over time because the supply of land is very inelastic.

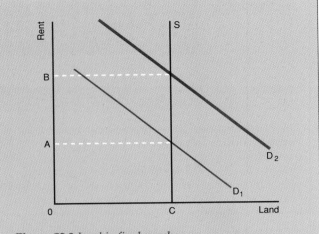

Figure 52.2 *Land in fixed supply*
If the supply of land is perfectly inelastic, any increase in its demand will raise rents but will have no effect on allocation of land as a resource in the economy.

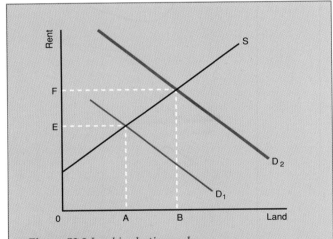

Figure 52.3 *Land in elastic supply*
If the supply of land is not perfectly inelastic, then an increase in its demand will affect not only its price but also the allocation of land within the economy.

determined and not price determining.

In Figure 52.2, the supply of land is shown to be perfectly inelastic. There is only a fixed amount of land available for corn production. An increase in the derived demand for land to rent, due to an increase in the price of corn, will push the demand curve for land from D_1 to D_2 and the price or rent on land will increase from OA to OB.

A change in the rent on land in Figure 52.2 caused by a change in demand would have no effect on the allocation of resources in the economy. Because the supply is perfectly inelastic, land would be used to grow corn whether the price was almost zero or much higher than OB.

However, supply is not perfectly inelastic for most factors of production. For instance, the land used for growing corn in our example above could have alternative uses, such as growing vegetables or grazing animals. A change in the price of the factor will then have an allocative effect. In Figure 52.3, an increase in demand from D_1 to D_2 will lead to an increase of AB units of the factor being used.

The theory of economic rent distinguishes between two elements in the payment made to a factor of production.
■ The TRANSFER EARNINGS of the factor. This is the **minimum** payment needed to keep the factor in its present use. If a worker is paid £200 a week, but

could only earn £150 a week in her next best paid occupation, then her transfer earnings would be £150 per week. Transfer earnings are the **opportunity cost** of employing the factor. A change in transfer earnings will affect the allocation of resources. If the worker could now earn £250 a week in her next best paid occupation, economic theory would predict that all other things being equal she would leave her present £200 a week job and take the more highly paid job.
■ The ECONOMIC RENT of the factor. Economic rent is the payment over and above the minimum needed to keep the factor in its present use (i.e. it is the difference between its current payment and its transfer earnings). Economic rent will not affect the allocation of resources. If the transfer earnings of a worker were £150, she would remain in her present job whether she

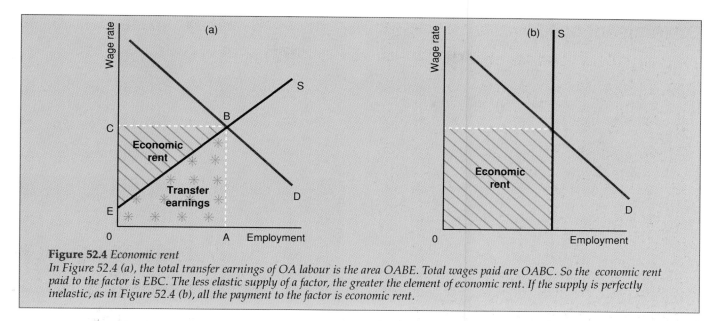

Figure 52.4 *Economic rent*
In Figure 52.4 (a), the total transfer earnings of OA labour is the area OABE. Total wages paid are OABC. So the economic rent paid to the factor is EBC. The less elastic supply of a factor, the greater the element of economic rent. If the supply is perfectly inelastic, as in Figure 52.4 (b), all the payment to the factor is economic rent.

earned £200 a week or £250 a week.

The theory of economic rent can be explained using a demand and supply diagram. In Figure 52.4 (a), the equilibrium wage rate of labour is OC. However, only the last worker employed has transfer earnings of OC. The first worker would be prepared to work for a wage rate of OE. We know this because the supply curve shows the minimum wage rate for which workers would be prepared to work. As successive workers are employed, so the transfer earnings of the marginal worker (the last worker employed) increase. The transfer earnings of the first worker are OE whilst those of the last worker are AB (i.e. it is the vertical distance between the horizontal axis and the supply curve). So the total transfer earnings of all the workers employed, OA, is the area OABE.

The total earnings of OA workers is the area OABC (total number of workers OA times the wage rate per worker OC). The difference between the total payment to a factor and its transfer earnings is its economic rent. Hence the economic rent of labour in Figure 52.4 (a) is the area EBC.

Economic rent will be greater the more inelastic the supply curve. If, as in Figure 52.4 (b), supply is perfectly inelastic, then all the factor payment is economic rent and the transfer earnings of the factor are zero. Transfer earnings are zero because the factor will be supplied whether the payment received is zero or infinity (as shown by the vertical supply curve). Similarly, if demand is perfectly elastic (i.e. the demand curve is horizontal), all the factor payment is transfer earnings and economic rent is zero. Whatever quantity bought, a higher price would result in demand for the factor falling to zero. The factor cannot earn any more than the minimum needed to keep it in its present use.

Quasi-rent

Sometimes, economic rent can be earned in the short run, but not in the long run. Economic rent which can only be

QUESTION 2

The Liverpool Echo (6 August 1990) reported that John Barnes reputedly earned over £200 000 in the 1989/90 football season.

Explain why footballers are often said to receive high economic rents.

earned in the short run is called QUASI-RENT. For instance, a firm may buy a piece of machinery which is so specialised that it has no alternative uses. Then its transfer earnings are zero and hence all the payments received from the use of the machine are quasi-economic rents. In the long run, the machinery must be replaced completely or not at all, and hence part or all of the earnings of this piece of capital will be transfer earnings. In the long run the machine will need at least to cover its economic cost or it will not be replaced.

Government policy

The amount of economic rent earned by a factor of production will not affect the allocation of resources within the economy. Hence, it is theoretically possible for the government to tax economic rent from a factor without altering economic efficiency in the economy (it was argued in unit 45 that taxes might have an adverse effect on economic efficiency). For instance, the UK government places heavy taxes upon North Sea oil production, but attempts to levy them in such a way as not to discourage the development of marginal fields (i.e. oil fields which are only just profitable and which would not be developed if costs, including taxes, were higher).

Those who argue in favour of taxing economic rents usually want to see a redistribution of income from rich to poor. They argue that it offends against principles of equity that owners of some factors of production should receive high payments whilst others should receive little or nothing. Why should footballers or popstars earn hundreds of thousands of pounds a year when many workers earn a wage which is less than one per cent of

that figure? Why should a farmer suddenly acquire a windfall gain of £1 million because his land has been given residential planning permission by the local council?

The problem with a tax on economic rents is that it is very difficult to tax just economic rent and not tax transfer earnings. As soon as transfer earnings are taxed, there will be allocative effects and there may be a loss of efficiency in the economy.

Key terms

Functional distribution of income - shows the share of national income received by each factor of production.
Transfer earnings - the minimum payment needed to keep a factor of production in its present use. It is the opportunity cost of the factor.
Economic rent - the payment made to a factor over and above its transfer earnings in the long run.
Quasi-rent - economic rent earned only in the short run.

QUESTION 3

(a) Explain why this field in Lancashire might be worth £2 500 as farming land but £220 000 as building land.
(b) Should farmers be allowed to keep any capital gain on land following the decision by a local authority to grant planning permission for building on the land?

Applied economics

Education in crisis

The post-war baby boom peaked in the mid-1960s. From 1970 onwards, school rolls started to fall, firstly in primary schools and then in secondary schools. By the late 1970s there was a surplus both of school buildings and of teachers.

The supply of teachers in the short term is relatively inelastic, as shown in Figure 52.5. Teachers possess few skills which are readily transferable to other occupations with comparable salaries. With 3 million unemployed in the early 1980s, teachers found it difficult to move occupationally.

If the supply of teachers is inelastic, a significant proportion of teachers' pay must be made up of

economic rent. In Figure 52.5, OACD is economic rent whilst the transfer earnings of teachers amount only to ABC. This, combined with falling demand for teachers, has meant that employers have been able to depress the wages of teachers relative to other workers without creating a crisis of supply in teaching (i.e. without leading to any large scale reallocation of labour resources).

However, the 1990s may prove to be very different. On the demand side, the birth rate started to rise again from the late 1970s onwards, increasing the number of teachers needed in the classroom from the mid-1980s. Recent changes in education policy, such as the

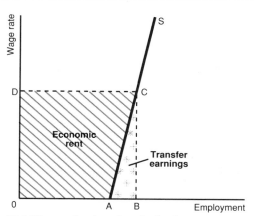

Figure 52.5 *The supply of teachers in the short term*

introduction of the national curriculum, have increased the demand for teachers too. On the supply side, local authorities have found it increasingly difficult to attract new teachers into the profession, particularly in areas such as science, mathematics and technology. Recruitment can only get worse in the early 1990s as the number of young people entering the labour market falls dramatically.

There are a large number of possible ways in which local authorities could attempt to avert the crisis.

■ The employers could attempt to shift the supply curve to the right. Recently, local authorities have actively encouraged women, who left the profession to bring up children, to return to teaching. Many of the London boroughs have actively recruited trained but unemployed and inexperienced young graduates from countries such as Ireland, Holland, Germany and Australia. In 1990, the government mounted a national advertising campaign to recruit teachers. It has also offered, through its licenced teachers scheme, to employ and train people who want to become teachers but do not have the qualifications traditionally required for entry into teaching.

■ An alternative policy option is to raise teachers' pay relative to other workers. Because teachers' pay is mainly economic rent, a large change in pay, upwards of 25 per cent, will be needed to alter significantly the allocation of labour resources.

■ Another possibility is to turn to more individualised pay bargaining. An inner London borough may have difficulty in recruiting enough teachers in all schools and in all subjects. An appropriate response there would be to raise the pay of all teachers. However, in Devon it could be that there is no shortage of history teachers but there is a shortage of infant headteachers. An appropriate policy response would be to reduce the pay of history teachers until the last teacher employed earned no economic rent (i.e. was paid just enough to prevent him or her leaving). But the pay of infant headteachers should be increased to the point where the last headteacher employed earns no economic rent. Taken to its logical conclusion, employers could negotiate with each teacher individually. If employers succeeded in paying each individual teacher just the value of his or her transfer earnings, considerable savings could be made in education budgets.

Teaching unions argue that the only way forward is to increase the pay of all teachers. Employing poorly qualified or foreign staff, however enthusiastic, is unlikely to provide the high standards of education now expected by parents. Individualised pay bargaining would cause bitter resentment amongst staff. Teachers who were relatively immobile (in practice these would be women who saw their career as less important than their husband's career) would be paid less than their more mobile colleagues (in practice these would be disproportionately male) for doing the same job. In general, paying teachers less is unlikely to solve any of the deep-rooted problems of low morale and widespread teacher shortages in education today.

Data question

1. What is likely to have happened over the 1980s to the amount of economic rent earned by home owners?
2. Using a diagram, explain why this change is likely to have occurred.

Table 52.2

	Percentage change, 1980 - 1989
Prices	
House prices	260
All prices (measured by the Retail Price Index)	84
Factors affecting demand for housing	
Real disposable income of households	22
Net advances by banks, building societies and other lenders for mortgages	392

Source: adapted from the *Financial Times* 28.2.90 and CSO, *Economic Trends Annual Supplement*.

Asset prices and the rate of interest

Summary

1. Interest payments increase the value of money over time. Conversely, the value of money available in the future is less than its value today when it is discounted back to its present value.
2. The higher the rate of interest or rate of discount and the longer the time period, the less valuable today is a fixed sum that is payable in the future.
3. The present value of capital goods which yield a stream of benefits in the future can be calculated using the rate of discount.
4. A firm should invest if the present value of the capital is equal to or more than the current cost of the capital.
5. The higher the rate of interest or discount, the lower the present value of capital and hence the less investment there will be.

Present and future values

A saver places £100 in a building society. The advertised rate of interest is 10 per cent per annum. At the end of one year, her £100 will have grown to £110 ({£100 + [£100 x 10 per cent]} **or** £100 x 1.1). At the end of two years, it should have grown to £121 (£110 x 1.1 **or** £100 x 1.1 x 1.1). At the end of three years, it should have grown to £133.10 (£121 x 1.1 **or** £100 x 1.1 x 1.1 x 1.1). If the rate of interest had been 20 per cent, £100 would have grown to £120 at the end of the first year, £144 at the end of the second year and £172.80 at the end of the third year.

This illustrates an important point. Money grows over time if it is deposited or lent with interest. Put another way, a fixed sum of money payable in the future is worth less than that fixed sum paid today. £100 placed in the building society grew to be worth more than £100 at the end of three years. Therefore a fixed sum of £100 available in three years' time is worth less than £100 available today. How much less depends upon a number of factors.

The rate of interest or rate of discount The higher the RATE OF INTEREST or RATE OF DISCOUNT, the less valuable is a fixed sum of money available at a future point in time. For instance, at a rate of interest of 10 per cent, £133.10 in three years' time would be worth exactly £100 today. If the rate of interest were 20 per cent, £172.80 in three years' time would be worth £100 today.

The length of time The farther into the future that the money is available, the less valuable it is today. For instance, at a rate of interest of 10 per cent, £133.10 in three years' time is only worth £100 today. If £100 were available in 25 years' time, it would only be worth £9.23 today at 10 per cent per annum (i.e. £9.23 saved today at 10 per cent per annum would grow to be worth £100 in 25 years' time).

Rental payments and asset prices

Firms use factories, offices, machines and stocks to produce goods and services. If a firm wants to buy a piece of machinery, it has to decide the maximum price that it is prepared to pay for it. The machinery will give a stream of benefits to a company over a long period of time. The firm therefore has to assess what the future benefits are worth today, because it is today that it has to pay the money for the machinery. This is where the discussion above about present and future values can provide some answers to the question: what price should be put on an asset?

A firm can acquire the use of capital in two ways:
■ it can buy capital outright;
■ it can rent or lease capital.

The purchase price of capital and the RENTAL VALUE or YIELD are two different ways of measuring the price of capital. (Note that labour can also have two prices. If people could be bought and sold under a system of slavery, then it would be possible to buy labour outright. However, in a modern economy this is illegal; the only way to buy labour is to rent it. The rental value of labour is the wage rate. In the case of land, it can either be purchased outright, or rented.)

Economic theory suggests that firms should calculate the price they are prepared to pay for a piece of capital by **discounting** future yields.

Example 1 A firm wishes to buy a machine today. The machine will last for one year, has no scrap value and will give a yield of £110 in one year's time (i.e. after all other costs, including an allowance for normal profit, have been taken away, £110 of revenue is left in one year's time). The amount the firm will pay for the machine will depend upon the rate of interest or rate of discount. Assume that it is 10 per cent. Then the firm will pay a maximum of £100 (the maximum purchase price from the company's viewpoint). This is because £110 in one year's time is the same as £100 today if the rate of interest is 10 per cent.

Example 2 A firm wishes to buy a lorry today for use over a two year period. The lorry will give a yield of £5 500 at the end of the first year, £12 100 at the end of the second year and then can be sold to another company for £24 200. The rate of interest or rate of discount is 10 per cent. Then the present value of £5 500 available in one year's time is £5 000. The present value of £12 100 available in two years' time is £10 000, and the value of £24 200 in two years' time is £20 000. So the total present value is £35 000 and the firm would be prepared to pay up to £35 000 for the lorry.

QUESTION 2
Table 53.1

Year	Value at £100, at a compound rate of interest of 10 per cent [1]	Net yield from a machine
0	£100	0
1	£110	£110 000
2	£121	£121 000
3	£133	£133 000
4	£146	£292 000
5	£161	£483 000
6	£177	£885 000
7	£195	£780 000
8	£214	£642 000
9	£236	£472 000
10	£259	£259 000

1. Rounded to the nearest £1.

A firm is considering the purchase of a machine. The machine produces the yield each year shown in Table 53.1. At the end of 10 years, the machine wears out and has no scrap value. What is the maximum price the firm should pay for the machine if the rate of discount is 10 per cent?

Discounting

The relationship between the two prices of capital, the rental value of yield and the asset price can be expressed more formally.

It has already been explained how a given money payment in the future is worth less today. How much less is determined by the rules of compound interest. For instance:

■ £110 in one year's time is worth only £100 today at 10 per cent - this is calculated by dividing the yield, £110, by (1 + the rate of interest);
■ If £121 is available in two years' time, then it is worth £121 ÷ (1 + r) in one year's time and £121 ÷ (1 + r) ÷ (1 + r) today where r is the rate of interest. This is equivalent to £121 ÷ $(1 + r)^2$.

In general if a benefit is available in n years' time, then it needs to be divided by $(1 + r)^n$ to calculate its present value. For instance:

■ £100 available in 25 years' time is worth only £100 ÷ $(1 + r)^{25}$ today;
■ £1 million available in 50 years' time is worth only £1 million ÷ $(1 + r)^{50}$ today. At a rate of interest of 10 per cent per annum, that is worth just £8 519 today!

The PRESENT VALUE of capital is equal to the discounted sum of future yields (and hence is sometimes also called the DISCOUNTED CASH FLOW). This can be expressed mathematically:

$$\text{Present value (PV)} = \frac{A_1}{(1+r)} + \frac{A_2}{(1+r)^2} + \cdots + \frac{A_n}{(1+r)^n}$$

PV is the present value. A is the amount of rental value or yield received by the firm from owning the capital. r is the rate of interest or rate of discount, and 1, 2, ... n are time periods such as years. The formula is saying that the present value of capital can be calculated by adding the discounted rental values the capital produces in each year. The following examples illustrate this point.

■ A company invests in a machine which at the end of the first year gives a yield of £110, at the end of the second year a yield of £121 and at the end of the third year a yield of £133.10. The machine then wears out and has no scrap value. If the rate of discount is 10 per cent, the present value of the machine is the sum of the discounted yields of £110, £121 and £133.10. From the explanation above, each of the three figures discounted back to the present is worth £100. So the present value of the machine is £300.
■ A company buys a machine which at the end of the first year yields £12 million, at the end of the second year yields £28.8 million, at the end of the third year yields £17.28 million and at the end of the fourth year yields £20.736 million. It then wears out and has no scrap value. If the rate of discount is 20 per cent, the present value is equal to:

$$\frac{£12m}{(1+0.2)} + \frac{£28.8m}{(1+0.2)^2} + \frac{£17.28m}{(1+0.2)^3} + \frac{£20.736m}{(1+0.2)^4}$$

$$= £10m + £20m + £10m + £10m = £50m$$

So the present value of yields which in the future will be worth £78.816 million is just £50 million discounted back to the present at a discount rate of 20 per cent. The present value of the machine is therefore £50 million.

QUESTION 3 A firm buys a machine which yields £1 000 a year each year for 5 years and then wears out. The machine has no scrap value. What would be the present value of the machine in the year of purchase if the discount rate were:
(a) 2 per cent; (b) 5 per cent; (c) 10 per cent; (d) 20 per cent; (e) 30 per cent?

Rate of return

The two ways of expressing the price of capital - the present value of capital and the yield or rental value - are related by the rate of interest or rate of discount. So far, a rate of interest and rental values have been given and the present value calculated. However, it is possible to calculate the RATE OF RETURN or PERCENTAGE YIELD if the present value and the rental values are given. For instance, if a firm buys a machine today for £100 and it gives a yield of £110 in one year's time and has no value thereafter, what is the rate of return? The answer is 10 per cent.

The rate of return or percentage yield is the amount of yield or rental value divided by the asset price of capital. In the equation above, if the present value (PV) and the amount of yield (A) are known, then a rate of return (r) can be calculated.

When should a company buy capital?

A company uses a rate of discount of 10 per cent. It is offered a machine which will provide a yield of £110 in one year's time and be of no value thereafter. From the above discussion, we know that the present value of the machine is £100. So the company is prepared to pay up to £100 for the machine. Therefore:
- if the price of capital is less than or equal to the present value of capital, a firm will buy capital (i.e. it will invest);
- if the price of capital is greater than the present value of capital, the firm will not buy capital.

The present value of capital depends upon the rate of interest or rate of discount used. A firm could use any rate of discount it wished. However, economic theory suggests that firms should link the rate of discount with rates of interest available in financial markets. The opportunity cost of money used to buy capital is the interest foregone from saving it with a bank or other financial institution. For instance, if a firm could gain 10 per cent per annum in a bank, it should not invest in capital if the rate of return on capital is only 5 per cent. Another way of looking at this is to consider that many firms borrow money to finance the purchase of capital. The rate of discount on capital must be at least as high as the rate of interest that has to be paid to borrow money. In fact, it has to be higher because there is risk attached to buying capital whereas there is little or no risk if the money is saved with a bank. The risk is that the goods or services produced by the capital won't sell, or won't sell at the estimated price, or other factors such as a machine breakdown might affect the profitability of the capital. The higher the risk, the higher the rate of discount (made up of the rate of discount on a riskless investment plus a **risk premium**). The higher rate of return is compensation to the owners of capital for taking risks.

So another way of deciding whether to invest is to compare the rate of return on a project with current rates of interest.
- If the rate of return on a piece of capital is higher than the current market rate of interest, then a company should buy the capital.
- If the rate of return is less than the current market rate of interest, the company should not buy capital but instead place the money on the financial markets.

QUESTION 4 In 1990 Ratners, the UK jewellery chain, paid $62.1m for Weisfield's, a US speciality jewellery chain. It borrowed some of the money for the purchase in the US.
(a) What was the profit in $ that it expected to make from the deal over the next 5 years if it wished to make a rate of return of 20 per cent per annum on the purchase? Assume that the sale value of Weisfield's did not change over the period.
(b) Would Ratners have paid $62.1m for Weisfield's if it had wished to make a rate of return of (a) 10 per cent and (b) 30 per cent per annum? Explain your answer.

Key terms

Rate of interest or rate of discount - the opportunity cost of capital, the rate used to discount future income back to present value.
Rental value or yield - the price paid for the use of a factor of production over a period of time.
Present value or Discounted Cash Flow - the purchase price of capital. It is the maximum price that would be paid for an asset which gave a stream of benefits or rental values over time.
Rate of return or percentage yield - the amount of yield or rental value divided by the value of capital. It is expressed as a percentage.

Applied economics

The Channel Tunnel rail link

When the Channel Tunnel contract was awarded to a consortium which proposed a rail link rather than a road link, it seemed inevitable that the overland rail links from the Channel to London and Paris would be upgraded. Indeed the French soon announced ambitious plans to build a new dedicated link to join a new high speed line between Paris and Brussels. Passengers travelling from the British coast to Paris or Brussels will be able to travel at high speeds from the day the Channel Tunnel opens in 1993.

But on the British side, trains will rumble along track built over a century ago, winding their way through the Kent countryside and into London. The trains will be scheduled in between existing Southern Region commuter trains. Cynics have pointed out that it will be like travelling by Concorde between Paris and the British coast and then changing to a horse and cart.

In 1988, British Rail announced a variety of possible routes for a dedicated rail link. There was uproar in Kent as local communities fought hard not to have the link through their back yard. BR responded by proposing to put much of the link underground, but this increased the cost from £1.25bn to £3bn. The link was now commercially unviable because BR was required by government to make an 8 per cent return on any investment and this it would not do.

In 1989 the government invited private sector companies to put forward proposals for a private rail link. A consortium of BR, Trafalgar House and BICC produced plans for a rail link that would cost £2.6bn. But the private sector companies stated that they would not proceed unless they could make a 20 per cent rate of return on their investment. To do this, the government would either have to give a grant for the link, which it was forbidden to do under Section 42 of the Channel Tunnel Act, or subsidise the link in a less obvious fashion. One idea was that the government should put £500m into the line and £400m into proposed new railway terminals at Kings Cross in London and Ashford in Kent in return for BR being allowed to run commuter trains along the route. This would raise the rate of return on the project to the 20 per cent needed because the grants would be revenues for the consortium in the years 1993 to 1998.

The second idea was that the consortium should take over the running of cross channel passenger services, not from 1998 when the new line would be built, but from 1993 when trains would still be using the antiquated 19th century lines from Folkstone. The profit that the consortium would make would then offset some of the construction costs of the new line. Again, because there would be revenues for the consortium between 1993 and 1998, the rate of return would rise to 20 per cent.

In June 1990, the government rejected all these proposals, stating that if the dedicated link was not commercially viable, then it should not be built. The market must decide how scarce resources are allocated. British Rail, which was never very happy about working with a private sector consortium, will now press ahead with its own plans. By the year 2 000, it will probably have built some new track in Kent, but will choose to upgrade existing track through South London. Capital costs will be lower and it will thus be able to achieve the 8 per cent rate of return needed.

However, local residents in South London will suffer much greater noise pollution than if the link had been put in a tunnel. Journey times will be longer, encouraging travellers to fly by plane or go by car, increasing the demands for new roads and additional airport facilities and increasing pollution from these forms of transport. BR might be able to make an 8 per cent return, but these higher social costs (☞ unit 35) will almost certainly mean that the social rate of return on this half-way house scheme will be far less than if BR had built a dedicated line.

THE CHANNEL TUNNEL

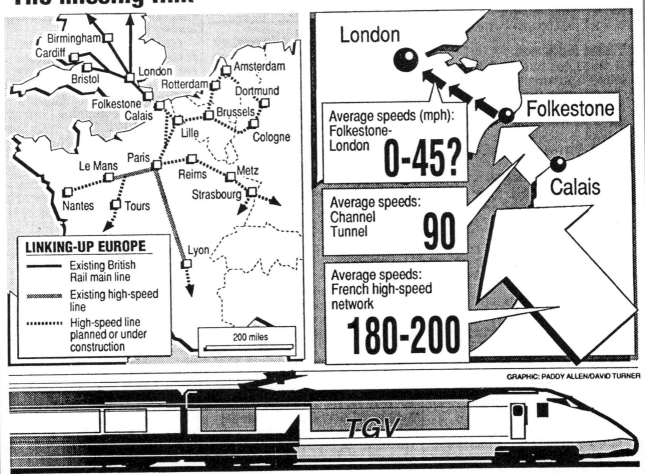

The missing link

LINKING-UP EUROPE
— Existing British Rail main line
∼∼∼ Existing high-speed line
⋯⋯ High-speed line planned or under construction

200 miles

Average speeds (mph): Folkestone-London **0-45?**

Average speeds: Channel Tunnel **90**

Average speeds: French high-speed network **180-200**

GRAPHIC: PADDY ALLEN/DAVID TURNER

Source: *The Guardian*, 16.6.90.

Between 1988 and 1990, the estimated cost of building the Channel Tunnel rose from approximately £5 billion to £8 billion. Not until the Tunnel opens in 1993 will Eurotunnel begin to receive revenues from the project.

1. Explain why the increase in the cost of building the tunnel led to a fall in the estimated rate of return on the project.

2. What would happen to the estimated rate of return if traffic through the Tunnel was much higher in 1993 than currently forecast?

3. Why would the rate of return on the project change if the rate of interest on money borrowed to finance the building of the Tunnel fell?

Summary

1. The demand curve of capital for a firm is the marginal efficiency of capital (MEC) schedule.
2. The MEC schedule will shift if, for instance, there are changes in the cost of production, the price of output, in risk or in the 'animal spirits' of businessmen.
3. The supply of capital can be equated with the supply of loanable funds to the market (i.e. the supply of savings).
4. The loanable funds theory states that the rate of interest is determined by the demand for and supply of loanable funds.
5. The price of land is determined by the demand for and supply of land.
6. The supply of land for a particular use, such as agricultural use or residential use, is likely to be inelastic but not perfectly inelastic.

The marginal efficiency of capital

The **law of diminishing** returns states that the marginal product of a factor, such as capital, will eventually decline if increasing quantities of that factor are combined with fixed quantities of other factors. For instance, the marginal physical product of capital for a firm will eventually decline if it uses more and more machines with a fixed quantity of workers and raw materials.

Marginal physical product can be changed into a monetary figure in a number of ways. In labour market theory, it is usual to calculate the marginal revenue product of labour (☞ unit 46). Capital theory usually expresses the marginal productivity of capital in terms of the **percentage yield** or **rate of return** on capital (i.e. the yield or rental value of capital divided by the value of capital). For instance, if a machine gives a return of £200

per year when the value of the machine is £1 000, then the rate of return on the machine is 20 per cent (£200 ÷ £1 000 expressed as a percentage).

This yield or rate of return on the last unit of capital employed is called the MARGINAL EFFICIENCY OF CAPITAL. Because of the law of diminishing returns, the marginal efficiency of capital declines as a firm's stock of capital increases.

The demand for capital

The marginal revenue product curve for labour is the demand curve for labour. Similarly, the marginal efficiency of capital curve is the demand curve for capital.

To understand why, remember that a demand curve shows the quantity that will be demanded at any given price over a period of time. Quantity in this case is quantity of capital. The price of capital is measured by the rate of return on capital. Figure 54.1 shows the falling

QUESTION 1
Table 54.1

Number of machines	Marginal physical product	Marginal revenue product of capital	Marginal efficiency of capital
	(units of output)	(£)	(%)
1	30		
2	25		
3	20		
4	15		
5	10		
6	5		

Table 54.1 shows the marginal physical product of capital (i.e. the extra output gained by employing an extra machine using the same amount of land and labour). Complete the table by calculating:
(a) the marginal revenue product of capital if each unit of output could be sold for £10;
(b) the marginal efficiency of capital if each machine could be bought for £1 000.

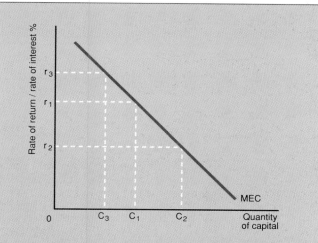

Figure 54.1 *The marginal efficiency of capital schedule*
The MEC schedule is downward sloping because of diminishing returns. It is the demand curve for capital because it is the line which equates the rate of return on capital with the cost of capital, the rate of interest.

marginal efficiency of capital schedule facing a firm.

A firm will demand capital if it can make a profit by buying or renting capital (i.e. if the rate of return on capital is equal to or greater than the cost of capital). There are two senses in which the cost of capital can be equated with the rate of interest.

■ The firm has the money to buy capital goods. In which case, it could save that money with a financial institution such as a bank and earn interest. The **opportunity cost** of buying capital is then the interest foregone on the money spent. The firm will only invest (i.e. buy capital goods) if the rate of return on capital, including a risk premium, is greater than the return on money placed with a financial institution.

■ The firm has to borrow the money to finance capital expenditure. The cost of borrowing money is the interest that has to be paid on the loan. The firm will only invest if the rate of return on capital (which will include an allowance for normal profit) is equal to or greater than the cost of borrowing the money.

If the rate of interest is r_1 in Figure 54.1, then the firm will demand C_1 of capital. It would not demand C_2, for instance, because the rate of return on C_2 would only be r_2. The rate of return, r_2, would then be less than the rate of interest, r_1, and the firm would lose money relative to the best alternative. Nor would it demand C_3 of capital as the rate of return on C_3 is r_3, which is above the rate of interest r_1. It could therefore profitably expand its capital stock to C_1. This is the equilibrium amount of capital demanded if the rate of interest is r_1 because it is the point where the cost of capital (the rate of interest) is equal to the return from capital (the rate of return).

QUESTION 2
(a) Draw the marginal efficiency of capital schedule from the data in Table 54.1.
(b) How many machines would the firm buy if the rate of interest were: (i) 30 per cent; (ii) 20 per cent; (iii) 10 per cent?

Shifts in the demand curve for capital

There are a number of factors which could cause the MEC schedule or the demand curve for capital to shift. A shift upwards and to the right in the curve would show that the rate of return or marginal efficiency of capital on the existing capital stock of firms had increased. Equally, it would show that firms now demand more capital at the same rate of interest. Capital is therefore more profitable than before. This could be caused by a number of factors.

A fall in the cost of production If there were a fall in the cost of production, then the yield on capital would rise. For instance, a fall in the cost of building factories or buying new machines will increase the rate of return on marginal capital. Hence, at a given rate of interest, more capital will be bought.

An increase in the price of output If the firm can sell its product for a higher price, then the rate of return on capital will increase.

A reduction in risk All investment is risky. Capital is bought to produce a stream of services in the future and the future is always uncertain. A firm will include an allowance for risk when it calculates the potential rate of return on an investment project. The higher the risk, the higher the rate of return needed to persuade a firm to invest. Hence, if a firm downgrades the risk associated with the purchase of capital, it will be prepared to undertake more investment at the same market rate of interest.

Animal spirits John Maynard Keynes argued that investment was crucially dependent upon the animal spirits of investors. He argued that firms swung from pessimism to optimism about the future and vice versa. The more optimistic firms are about the future, the higher the rate of return they expect from new capital and hence the further to the right will be the MEC schedule.

QUESTION 3 Demand for earth-moving equipment and other construction machinery has begun to decline sharply after several years of steep increases on the back of the surge in building.

Total sales of 14 of the main types of machinery used in the UK are expected to fall to just under 19 500 units this year from 22 800 last year, according to the Corporate Intelligence Group, an industry analyst.

High interest rates, the fall in house building starts and the forecasts of static construction are cited by Corporate Intelligence as reasons for the fall in sales.

Source: adapted from the *Financial Times*, 4.10.1989.

Using a diagram, explain why there was a change in demand for earth-moving equipment and other construction machinery in 1989.

The supply of capital

The demand for capital can be seen as the demand by firms to borrow money for investment, an increase in their capital stock, at any given rate of interest. Similarly, the supply of capital can be defined as the quantity of money available to firms for investment purposes at any given rate of interest.

Interest is the reward for lending money. Saving takes place for a number of reasons: one is that savers will have more money to spend in the future if they save now (i.e. current consumption has an opportunity cost in terms of future consumption). The higher the rate of interest, the more can be earned in the future and the more attractive saving money becomes today. The more money that is saved, the more there is available for firms to borrow.

Hence, the supply curve of funds available for firms to borrow to invest is upward sloping as in Figure 54.2. An increase in the rate of interest from A to B will increase the supply of funds available for investment in capital from E to F.

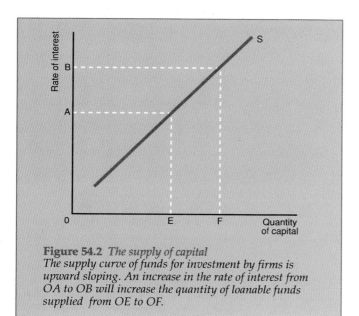

Figure 54.2 *The supply of capital*
The supply curve of funds for investment by firms is upward sloping. An increase in the rate of interest from OA to OB will increase the quantity of loanable funds supplied from OE to OF.

Determination of the rate of interest

Prices are determined by the forces of demand and supply. The price of capital is the rate of interest. Hence the rate of interest must be determined by the demand for and supply of capital. The demand for capital is the demand for investment goods. The higher the rate of interest, the lower will be investment demand and hence the lower will be the demand for borrowed or loanable funds to finance the investment. The supply of capital can be equated with the supply of loanable funds to the market (i.e. the volume of saving). The higher the rate of interest, the more money will be saved, which can then be lent out to firms to borrow for investment.

The LOANABLE FUNDS THEORY of the rate of interest argues that the rate of interest is determined by the demand and supply for loanable funds (i.e. the demand for and supply of capital). The theory is a

QUESTION 4 For each of the following, explain using a diagram:
(a) whether it will affect the demand for or supply of loanable funds;
(b) the effect it will have on the equilibrium rate of interest.
(i) Government gives tax relief on savings;
(ii) government cuts tax concessions on pension schemes; (iii) businessmen become more optimistic about the economy; (iv) wages increase at a faster rate than the price of capital; (v) firms increase the price of their products.

simplification because consumers and governments borrow money too. A more complete explanation of interest determination is given in unit 70.

Land

The price of land is determined by the demand and supply of land. As with capital, the price of land can be expressed in two ways:
■ the purchase price of land;
■ the rental value of land.
It might seem that land is in fixed supply and therefore its supply is infinitely price inelastic. There is only a finite amount of land on this planet. The supply of land can be increased through land reclamation, for instance, but the resulting addition to the stock of land can only be very small.

However, there are many markets for land and the land can be switched from one use to another. For instance, industrial land can be used for housing. Housing land can be used for shops. Agricultural land can be used for industrial purposes. Hence the supply of land, although likely to be inelastic, is not perfectly inelastic.

Figure 54.3 shows the demand and supply curves for land used for housing. An increase in the population will increase the demand for housing land from D_1 to D_2. The result will be a rise in the price of housebuilding land and an increase in quantity supplied. In the UK, this extra land is likely to be found by taking agricultural land and using it for house building.

Using agricultural land for housing purposes is controversial in the UK. The government, through Green Belt policies, has limited the supply of agricultural land for housing. This has had the effect of making the supply of land for housing far more inelastic than it would otherwise have been. It has also pushed up the price of building land from what it would have been without the

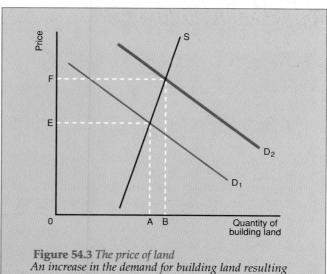

Figure 54.3 *The price of land*
An increase in the demand for building land resulting from an increase in the population will increase land prices from OE to OF.

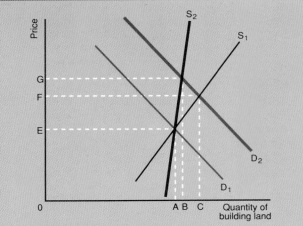

Figure 54.4 *Green belt regulations*
*The effect of green belt regulations is to make the free
market supply curve S₁ more inelastic. With a 'Green
Belt supply curve' for building land, S₂, an increase in
the demand for housing will result in a large increase
in the price of land of EG and only a small increase,
AB, in the quantity of building land.*

Green Belt policies. This is shown in Figure 54.4. Initially,
the market is in equilibrium with price at OE and
quantity bought and sold OA. An increase in population,
leading to a shift in the demand curve from D_1 to D_2,
would lead to an increase in the price of land by EF.
However, if the government has imposed limits on the
sale of agricultural land for building purposes, the supply
curve is not S_1 but S_2. The result is that the increase in the
price of land is not EF but EG. Moreover, instead of an
extra AC land being released for building purposes, only
AB more is sold. Fewer houses are likely to be built,
resulting in either homelessness or overcrowding in the
existing stock of houses.

QUESTION 5 In 1990, the Environment Secretary,
Mr Chris Patten, rejected a proposal to build a new
village of 3 200 homes at Great Lea near Reading.
The scheme included a regional shopping centre, with
new roads and a railway station close to an exit from
the M4 motorway near Wokingham. The new village
would have been built on agricultural land. This
rejection was one of a number of rejections of new
village schemes in the South of England.

(a) Explain, using diagrams, what the effect would
    have been on (i) the price of land for residential
    building and (ii) the price of agricultural land if
    schemes such as Great Lea had been given
    planning permission.
(b) Discuss who might benefit from and who might
    lose from the refusal to grant planning permission
    for the village at Great Lea.

Key terms

Marginal efficiency of capital - the rate of return
on the last unit of capital employed. It is measured
by dividing the rental value or yield by the cost of
the last unit of capital employed.
Loanable funds theory - the loanable funds theory
of interest rate determination argues that the rate of
interest is determined by the demand for and
supply of loanable funds, in particular, for purchase
of capital.

Applied economics

Capital

The stock of capital

If an economy grows over time, it is almost certain that
this will be reflected in the growth of its capital stock.
Table 54.2 shows the composition of the stock of
physical capital in the UK in 1988. The most important
category of physical capital is 'Other buildings and
works'. This comprises buildings such as factories,
offices and warehouses. 'Dwellings' are private homes,
either owner occupied or rented from landlords such as
local councils. Examples of 'plant and machinery' are
machine tools, industrial computers and photocopiers
as well as large plant such as chemical works.
'Inventories' are stocks of goods held by companies in
the production process and are included in the capital

stock because, like a machine, they will be used to
produce further goods and services in the future.

Marginal efficiency of capital theory

Marginal efficiency of capital theory suggests that the
stock of capital will increase if industry becomes more
profitable. At any given rate of interest, there will be
more investment if the rate of return on that
investment has increased. This is shown by a shift to
the right in the MEC schedule. On the other hand, a
fall in the rate of return on capital will lead to a fall in
investment.

Figures 54.5 and 54.6 give some support to this
theory. During the late 1960s and early 1970s, the real

Table 54.2 *UK physical capital*

	Gross capital stock by type of asset at 1985 replacement cost. £bn at 1985 prices.
Road vehicles	50.9
Trains, ships and aircraft	15.3
Plant and machinery	470.5
Other buildings and works	562.6
Dwellings	537.6
Total	1 637.9

Source: adapted from CSO, UK National Accounts.

rate of return on capital fell in the UK. This subsequently led to a fall in the level of investment as a percentage of GDP from 1968 to 1981. The rate of return on capital picked up again in the mid-1970s and having fallen again in the 1979-81 recession, rose to levels not seen since the 1960s. This increase in the rate of return could be argued to have led to the increase in investment from 1981.

However, the figures are not conclusive as:

■ the correlation between the real rate of return and investment as a percentage of GDP is not particularly close;

■ nothing is said about other factors which will have affected investment and which changed over the period, such as the rate of interest;

■ whilst increases in demand in the economy, which would affect the MEC schedule, have been taken into account by dividing investment by GDP, it could be argued that a more sophisticated demand variable is needed.

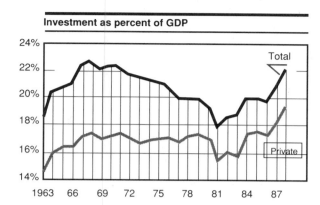

Source: Political Quarterly.
Figure 54.5 *Investment as per cent of GDP*

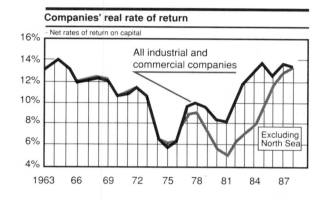

Source: 1989 Financial Statement.
Figure 54.6 *Companies' real rate of return*

BASE METAL PRICES 'NOT HIGH ENOUGH TO ENCOURAGE EXPLORATION'

The Financial Times reported on 14 November 1989 that the prices of base metals would have to increase significantly before mining companies would be willing to bear the cost of exploring for new deposits.

Mr James Jack, chief consulting geologist at Boliden International Mining, said that every dollar spent on grassroots exploration was questioned by managements. 'Success in exploration can depend today as much on the introduction or withdrawal of tax incentives as on assay values' he suggested. The lack of base metal exploration might lead to metal shortages in the future, he predicted.

1. **Exploration creates capital. Explain using diagrams why James Jack argues that base metals exploration is related to (a) the price of base metal and (b) tax incentives.**

Summary

1. Entrepreneurship involves the organisation of production, risk taking and innovation.
2. Owner managers of small firms are likely to combine all these three functions and therefore are most likely to be classified as entrepreneurs.
3. Managers too can be seen as entrepreneurial if they take risks on behalf of their companies and if they are responsible for innovation.
4. Shareholders too risk their capital and therefore could be seen as entrepreneurial.
5. Pure or abnormal profit is the reward for entrepreneurship.
6. An 'enterprise culture' may increase economic welfare if entrepreneurs are responsible for a disproportionate share of innovation, job creation and wealth creation in the economy.
7. An entrepreneurial spirit can be created in large firms if pay and other rewards of managers are linked to their performance.

Entrepreneurs? - Anita Roddick (Body Shop International PLC) and Richard Branson (The Virgin Group LTD).

The nature of entrepreneurship

There is no standard definition of an **entrepreneur** in economic theory. However, different economists have identified three possible elements of the entrepreneurial function.

The organisation of production The entrepreneur is the factor of production which brings together the other factors in the production process. Land and capital are inert objects. Workers wait for the instructions of their bosses. It is the entrepreneur who buys land and capital, hires labour and then organises all three factors to produce goods and services for sale. The entrepreneur can then be seen as the key to production in the economy. It could be argued that if there were no entrepreneurs, there would be no production.

Risk Production is a risky process. In many industries, land, labour and capital have to be purchased before there is any certainty that the finished product will be sold. For instance, a car manufacturer is likely to make cars without there being any firm orders for their sale. If it makes too many cars, they will have to be stockpiled for sale at a later date. Too big a stockpile and too few orders could result in the bankruptcy of the firm. Hence firms face uncertainties and have to take risks.

The American economist, F H Knight, working in the inter-war period, defined such risk in terms of unquantifiable risk. Some risks are quantifiable and can therefore be insured against. For instance, a firm can insure itself against the risk of fire damage or theft. However, other risks, such as whether a new product will sell, or whether a new production technique will lead to a reduction in costs, are unquantifiable and therefore cannot be insured against.

Entrepreneurs are those who take unquantifiable risks and suffer the consequences if they get it wrong.

Innovation New products are being launched all the time but evidence suggests that only a few will be successful. New production techniques are also being constantly pioneered with varying degrees of success. Joseph Schumpeter, the Austrian economist working in the inter-war years, argued that the entrepreneur is someone who innovates within an organisation.

Entrepreneurs

Most economists would accept that the owner manager of a newly set up company that produced an innovative product could be described as an entrepreneur. This is a person who combines all three of the characteristics described above. She organises production because she is the manager of the company. She takes risks because she has put money into the firm to start it and is producing an innovative product which could well fail. She is an innovator because her product is new to the market.

However, this type of person is only likely to be found in the small firm sector of the economy where an individual is likely to:
- have sufficient capital to be able to finance the setting up of the firm;
- have total control over the organisation of production;
- be exposed to considerable risk if the enterprise fails.

So entrepreneurship has tended to be associated with new, small firms. However, economists have suggested that other workers could be classed as entrepreneurs, or have an entrepreneurial function.

Managers A manager of a company may have no shares in the company for which she works (i.e. she is not an owner or part owner of the company). Hence she does not risk her capital in the business. She could still be regarded as an entrepreneur if she were involved in one of two areas.
- According to Knight's definition above, she would be an entrepreneur if she took decisions which involved an uncertain outcome. For instance, it would be entrepreneurial behaviour if a manager gave the go-ahead for the launch of a new flavour of yoghurt. The flavour might be very successful or it might not. Hence the outcome of the decision is uncertain. Managers of large companies can, in this view, be as entrepreneurial as owner-managers of small companies.
- According to Schumpeter's definition, she would be an entrepreneur if she took decisions which led to innovation. So again, managers of large companies

can be seen to be entrepreneurial if they are responsible for pushing their companies into new areas.

Individual managers can be entrepreneurial, but so can groups of managers. If managers work together as a team and innovate or take risks, then the group is entrepreneurial. Hence, large Japanese companies, which often have a tradition of group decision making, can be just as entrepreneurial as the lone businessman who sets up and runs his own business.

Capitalists Millions of individuals in the UK today directly own shares in companies. Does this make them into entrepreneurs? In one sense it does. A few shareholders are 'Aunt Sallys' - friends, relations or business acquaintances of individuals who want to set up their company. These shareholders risk their money to back an individual or an idea which attracts them. They are backing change and may even be in a position to give advice to the person setting up the company. On a wider front, all shareholders in both small and large companies carry the risk of the success or failure of the enterprise. If the company fails, shareholders lose their money. On the other hand, shareholders are unlikely to be involved in organising production. Nor are they involved in innovation in the firm. So some economists argue that capitalists are in some senses entrepreneurs, whilst others disagree.

Profit - the reward for entrepreneurship

In traditional economic theory, profit is seen as the reward for entrepreneurship. Profit is the revenue left over after the other factors of production have been paid. If the entrepreneur is successful, there will be a large residue after wages, interest and rents have been paid. If the entrepreneur is unsuccessful, profits will be negative and the firm could go bankrupt.

Not all profit is the reward to entrepreneurship. **Normal profit** (☞ unit 22) is the opportunity cost of factors such as labour and capital which receive no money payment for their use. Only **abnormal profit** or **pure profit** can be seen as the payment which entrepreneurs receive.

Entrepreneurship and economic welfare

Over the past 15 years, there has been a resurgence of interest amongst policy makers in entrepreneurs and their activities. A number of arguments have been put forward as to why entrepreneurs play such an important role in the economy.

■ Innovation. It is claimed that entrepreneurship is essential for innovation. Indeed Schumpeter defined entrepreneurship in terms of this key role in the economy. Without innovation, the economy would stagnate. There would no improvement in living standards. Innovation is therefore vital if economic welfare is to increase.

■ Job creation. Successful entrepreneurs create jobs. In particular, there has been much interest in the ability of small firms to create jobs and help ease the unemployment problems of the 1970s and 1980s.

■ Wealth creation. Entrepreneurs create wealth by their activities. The small firms of today will become the large successful firms of tomorrow.

On the other hand, it is argued that entrepreneurs, whilst they can play a part in raising economic welfare, are not essential in this process. There is little evidence to suggest that small firms, often seen as more entrepreneurial than large firms, contribute disproportionately to job creation or wealth creation. If any form of innovation is classified as 'entrepreneurial',

then entrepreneurs are essential in an economy. But innovation can lead to failure as well as success. It is noticeable that the UK and the USA, economies where the small firm entrepreneur has been seen by many as a folk hero, have had lower economic growth rates than economies such as Japan and Germany where greater stress is placed on team work and co-operation. On the other hand, perhaps the difference between the USA and Japan is that in the USA it is the individual which classically undertakes entrepreneurial activity whilst in Japan it is a team of workers which is entrepreneurial.

Creating an 'enterprise culture'

It is common to equate entrepreneurship with the small business sector of the economy. Many of the claimed advantages of the 'entrepreneurial spirit' are in fact the possible advantages of having an active small business sector in an economy. On this view, the entrepreneur is the owner manager of a small company. Hence government can best support the creation of an enterprise culture by measures which will support the creation and expansion of small firms in the economy. An evaluation of policies taken over the past 15 years by government is contained in the applied economics section below.

Economic theory, however, suggests that the entrepreneurial spirit need have nothing to do with small firms. Both innovation and risk taking can be as much if not more the concern of large firms as small firms. How then can a more entrepreneurial spirit be created in large firms?

In recent years, there has been a move towards paying managers by results. Some managing directors, for instance, are paid a basic salary but can earn far more if their company achieves a range of objectives. These could include increases in sales, increases in profits, increases in the share price of the company or reductions in the cost of production. Extra payments may come in the form of cash or shares in the company. The idea is to make managers who are employees of the firm accept more risk. If the firm does well, the managers will do well. If the firm does badly, so too do the managers.

QUESTION 3 It was reported in 1990 that small businesses employing fewer than 20 people had contributed the most to job creation in the late 1980s despite employing little more than one fifth of all workers. A study by the Dunn and Bradstreet credit rating group found that of companies listed by the group, those employing between 5 and 19 staff generated 295 000 jobs between 1985 and 1987, whilst there was a loss of 106 000 jobs among companies employing more than 1 000 workers. Total net job creation over the period was put at 307 000 - only half the official government estimate of the increase in private sector employment over the same period.

(a) Why might entrepreneurs contribute disproportionately to the growth of welfare in an economy?
(b) Why might the findings of the report not be totally accurate?

QUESTION 4 In the late 1980s, Burton's, the retailing chain, was at the forefront of offering performance related pay to its executives. In 1987 it decided to offer about 80 senior employees share option schemes worth four times annual earnings which they would be able to exercise if Burton's real earnings per share growth exceeded 30 per cent within a five year period.

How might this scheme make executives more entrepreneurial?

Applied economics

The enterprise culture

The growth of self-employment in the UK

The self-employed have traditionally constituted only a small percentage of the total labour force in the UK. Figure 55.1 shows that the number of self-employed workers was approximately 1.8 million or about 7.4 per cent of the workforce throughout the 1970s. However, there was a growth of self-employment during the 1980s so that by 1989, the number of self-employed was 3.2 million, and they formed 11.3 per cent of the labour force.

Did this substantial increase in the numbers of self-employed reflect a dramatic shift towards an enterprise culture in the UK? Superficially these figures might seem to indicate that more people were becoming entrepreneurs, setting up their own businesses and taking risks with the aim of making profits. However, some economists believe this was not the case. The growth in self-employment occurred at a time when the UK economy was suffering the severest and most-prolonged recession since the 1930s. They argue that it was unemployment and recession which led to an increase in the numbers of self-employed.

- Some of those made redundant received substantial redundancy payments and therefore had financial capital to set up their own business.
- Some of the unemployed could see no way in which they would get a job in the near future. Self-employment was a way out of this situation, earning money and regaining self-respect.
- Industry itself encouraged the growth of self-employment. In a recession, employers are reluctant to take on new staff because there might be no work for them in six months' or a year's time. Instead, recession and uncertainty provide a powerful incentive to employers to contract work out. For instance, there was a sharp decline in the number of employees of major construction companies in the 1980s. Construction companies increasingly used casual labour or contracted small firms to do jobs.

The substantial shift in employment from manufacturing to service industry during the 1980s is also likely to have been a factor in the growth of self-employment. Far less capital is required to set up a service sector business than a manufacturing business. Hence there are far lower financial barriers to entry for a would-be entrepreneur in the tertiary sector than in the secondary sector of the economy.

Government policy

Although high unemployment and structural changes in the UK economy were important factors in the growth of self-employment in the 1980s, it is also true that the decade was one where government economic policy created a climate favourable to entrepreneurial activity.

- Taxes were cut to increase incentives. The highest rate of tax on earned income fell from 83 per cent to 40 per cent between 1979 and 1988. The main rate of corporation tax fell from 52 per cent to 35 per cent and the small companies rate was reduced from 42 per cent to 25 per cent. The burden of administering VAT was lightened, for instance by allowing small companies to make just one VAT return a year.
- The government has attempted to reduce the amount of 'red tape' imposed on small businesses. In a 1988 White Paper, *Releasing Enterprise*, the government stated that 150 proposals for reducing bureaucratic burdens on business had either been introduced or were to be introduced.
- Small companies have found it easier to obtain financial capital to start up and expand. The

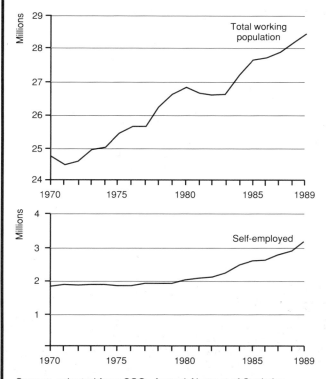

Source: adapted from CSO, *Annual Abstract of Statistics*.

Figure 55.1 *Self-employment and the total working population, UK*

government has encouraged the major banks to lend more to the small business sector. It has also encouraged the growth of the venture capital industry, firms which specialise in putting in share capital to new or expanding businesses. The government introduced the Loan Guarantee Scheme. This is a scheme whereby firms can borrow money from banks and if the firm defaults on its loan, the government will repay the bank any money outstanding. Individual taxpayers were encouraged to invest in firms through the Business Expansion Scheme (BES), a scheme whereby all profits and capital gains made on investment in a BES company were tax free after five years.

■ In 1988, the Department of Trade and Industry (DTI) launched the Enterprise Initiative. This initiative offered free or subsidised training and consultancy for small businesses in areas such as marketing, new technology and production.

■ The unemployed were encouraged to set up their own enterprises through the Enterprise Allowance Scheme. Participants needed to produce a business plan and they were given help to do this through initial enterprise training provided by the Training Agency. They were then given £40 a week for one year to help them establish their own business. Between 1983 and 1989, nearly 500 000 participated in the scheme and of those who completed the initial year, 65 per cent were still trading after three years.

Data question

THE RISE AND FALL OF SOCK SHOP

Sock Shop typifies the success and problems of the entrepreneur in the 1980s. It was founded by Sophie Mirman with her husband Richard. Ms Mirman originally worked for Marks and Spencers and then for Tie Rack. She spotted a gap in the market when she couldn't find a pair of white woolly tights to match a dress. She checked out that Marks and Spencers had only 12 per cent of the hosiery market, and with a belief that women were fed up with fighting their way through crowded department stores every time their tights laddered, she opened her first shop in Knightsbridge Underground station. The design, size and typical locations of the shops were based on the successful Tie Rack formula. They were small, bright, cheerful, and situated wherever there was a large volume of passing customers.

Like so many entrepreneurs, the Mirmans had problems obtaining finance. They were refused venture capital by banks who thought the idea was unworkable. Eventually with £1 000 each in capital, they raised the money for the Knightsbridge shop with the backing of the Government Loan Guarantee Scheme.

The shop was an instant success. By 1987 they had 47 shops, the company had been floated on the Unlisted Securities Market with a capital value of over £50 million and the Mirmans were millionaires.

Then came disaster. Sock Shop expanded into the USA but the shops became the targets of hit and run raids by youths. Eventually, the company had to employ a security guard for each shop which made the venture unviable. By 1990, they pulled out, having lost millions of pounds. In the UK, the long hot summer of 1989 resulted in dramatic

falls in the sales of tights and socks. Sock Shop moved into loss and in 1990 administrators were appointed under the Insolvency Act. The Mirmans, along with the rest of the shareholders, lost all their money.

Within nine months, the Mirmans had bounced back, opening a children's toy and clothes shop in London. Their entrepreneurial spirit was still very much alive, despite one spectacular failure.

1. **Why might the Mirmans be called 'entrepreneurs'?**
2. **In what ways might the Mirmans have contributed to the economic welfare of the UK?**

INVESTIGATIONS 4

A. Demographic changes

Aims

- To describe the changes in the numbers of 16-21 year olds in the UK population over the period 1970 to 2020.
- To analyse the possible effects of these changes on employment opportunities, rates of pay and unemployment for 16-21 year olds compared to other workers.
- To evaluate what response, if any, government should make to these changing demographic trends in the future.

Research activity

Start by finding out the age structure or estimated age structure of the population over the period 1970 - 2020. In particular, you need to find the numbers of 16 to 21 year olds in the population over the period. If possible, break down the UK figures by sex and by region. Also establish what proportion of 16-21 year olds are in full time education, what proportion are in work and what proportion are unemployed. Then find out what has happened to the relative pay of young workers aged 16-21 compared to the rest of the population in recent years. Also, find figures for unemployment rates of 16-21 year olds compared to the average for all workers over the period.

Conduct a newspaper and magazine search to find out what predictions have been made recently about young people and their role in the labour market. What impact is this likely to have on older workers and the increased trend towards early retirement? How might government respond to this?

Sources

The CSO *Guide to Official Statistics* gives sources for all government published statistics. General statistics about the population are contained in CSO, *Social Trends*, *Annual Abstract of Statistics* and *Regional Trends*. Large public reference libraries may well also stock OPCS *Monitor Population Projections*, *Population Trends* and *Regional Population Projections*.

CSO, *Social Trends* and CSO, *Annual Abstract of Statistics* also give numbers in full time and part time education. More detailed figures can be obtained from CSO, *Education Statistics for the United Kingdom*. Activity rates are given in CSO, *Social Trends*. A more detailed breakdown can be obtained from occasional articles published in the *Department of Employment Gazette*, a monthly magazine.

Relative earnings can be obtained on a yearly basis from the Department of Employment, *New Earnings Survey*. The *Department of Employment Gazette* also publishes regular articles on earnings which may have relevant material. For your newspaper and magazine search, use one or more indexes. The *Financial Times*, *The Times*, *The Guardian* and the *Economist* all publish indexes for past issues. The library may also carry other indexes such as the *Research Index*, published by Business Surveys Ltd., which covers articles of financial interest in 100 newspapers and periodicals on a monthly basis.

Structuring your report

Introduction Outline the aims of your investigation.

Changing demographic trends Describe the change in the numbers of 16-21 year olds in the population. Contrast this with other changes in the population. Outline the distribution of young people between work and education. Describe the changes in the ratio of females to males in the 16-21 age range. If possible, present regional as well as national data. Use charts, tables or diagrams to present or illustrate your findings.

Effects on earnings and employment What would economic theory suggest would happen to earnings of 16-21 year olds and to youth unemployment as a result of the demographic changes you have already described? Outline what has happened to these variables since 1970 and what has been suggested will happen in the future. What other effects on industry and employment might result from changing demographic trends, particularly the ratio of females to males and the ratio of 16-21 year olds to total population in regions of the UK? To what extent is the evidence you have gathered consistent with the predictions of economic theory?

Government response Outline what measures the government could take to deal with any problems likely to result from changing numbers of 16-21 year olds in the population in the future. Evaluate the likely effectiveness of such policies.

Sources Outline the sources of information you used. What problems did you encounter in gathering relevant data? What data would you have liked to have obtained but could not? To what extent were the data reliable?

Other suggestions

Instead of considering the economic effects of changes in the numbers of 16-21 year olds in the population, it would be possible to investigate the likely economic effects of changes in the numbers of any group in the population. For instance, what are the likely effects of the 'greying' of the population or what is likely to happen to the size of the working population over the next 20 years and what effects will this have?

Alternatively, survey the local job market. What rates of pay can 16-21 year olds gain in different occupations? To what extent can economic theory account for these differences in pay rates? This investigation could involve primary research, for instance a survey of 16-21 year olds in the local area. Local business people could be interviewed on their views about the effects of changing demographic trends on local business. A survey of local newspapers may also provide information about local rates of pay.

B. Entrepreneurship

Aims

- To gather data through the use of interviews and desk research.
- To present the findings of that research in a clear and logical manner.
- To assess the extent to which those interviewed could be considered to be 'entrepreneurs'.
- To evaluate the importance of entrepreneurship in the economy.
- To compare and contrast research findings with the predictions of economic theory.

Research activity

This investigation involves interviewing two entrepreneurs. Your first task is to find a number of people who might be worth approaching. They might own their own companies or be self-employed. Alternatively, they might work for a company in a role which could be seen as an obvious starting point. You may also have a part time job employed by an entrepreneur and therefore have a suitable contact there. National figures, such as Alan Sugar or Richard Branson, are most unlikely to give interviews.

Select two potential entrepreneurs and make an approach either personally or by letter. You need to outline the purpose of your investigation, when and where you propose the interview might take place and give some examples of questions you are likely to ask. You may decide to ask the person to come to your school or college and the whole group can participate in the interview. Alternatively, you may go to the place of work or home of the individual. You could perhaps link this with a work experience placement.

Before the interview, draw up a questionnaire. Think carefully about what information you must have if the investigation is to have substance. What supplementary questions will you need to ask if your original question does not draw forth a sufficiently detailed answer? Equally, think about what information the entrepreneur may well be unwilling to divulge (e.g. sales figures and profit figures).

In the interview, be confident and remain in control of the interview. Do not be afraid to ask the interviewee to explain or elaborate on an answer. It is usually easiest if you tape record the interview and make notes on it afterwards. However, if you use a tape recorder, you **must** obtain consent before the interview.

The second part of your research is to collect material about entrepreneurs and entrepreneurship in general. Read what textbooks and other materials have to say about the characteristics of entrepreneurs and the role of entrepreneurs in the economy. Conduct a newspaper and magazine search on entrepreneurs, the role of small businesses in the economy and on individuals who might be called 'entrepreneurs'. To conduct your search, it is easier if you use an index. The quality newspapers and magazines, such as the *Financial Times*, publish their own indexes. Otherwise, use any index which your local large public library might have available, such as the *Research Index*, published by Business Surveys Ltd., which covers articles of financial interest in 100 newspapers and periodicals on a monthly basis.

Structuring your report

Introduction Outline the aims of your investigation. Explain briefly the meaning and role of 'entrepreneurship' in economic theory.

A description of the two entrepreneurs interviewed Introduce the two entrepreneurs you interviewed - their names, their occupation, whether or not they owned their own company, etc. Outline the main questions you asked (you may wish to include the whole questionnaire as an appendix) and briefly summarise the responses.

Application and analysis To what extent could the two people interviewed be considered to be entrepreneurs? Compare their role with the role of the entrepreneur in economic theory. Compare too their activities with those of other 'entrepreneurs' whom you have discovered from your newspaper and magazine search.

Evaluation Consider the extent to which entrepreneurs perform a useful role in a market economy like that of the UK. Illustrate your answer from the material gathered during the interviews and your newspaper and magazine search. To what extent is entrepreneurship essential for economic success?

Other suggestions

A wide variety of people could be interviewed to illustrate the role of workers in an economy and the rewards to other factors of production.

- One or more trade unionists could be interviewed to consider the role of trade unions in today's Britain. To what extent do they protect their workers' interests? Does a trade union mark-up exist? Do trade unions cause unemployment?
- A manager could be interviewed. What is the role of a manager in an organisation? To what extent are managers entrepreneurial? To what extent could management be seen as part of the inefficiency of production (X-inefficiency ☞ unit 32).
- Workers in two contrasting markets could be interviewed to evaluate the extent of economic rent. What do they consider to be their transfer earnings? What factors might affect their level of economic rent?
- The process of wage determination could be investigated by interviewing a number of employees in different occupations. What factors determine their wage rates/earnings and how does this correlate with the predictions of economic theory?

Summary

1. In a simple circular flow model of the economy, households spend all their earnings on goods produced by firms which in turn pass back all earnings to households. There is no government and no foreign trade.
2. Income, output and expenditure are defined as being equal in the circular flow model.
3. If it is assumed that households save as well as spend, whilst firms produce not only goods for consumption but also investment goods, then saving becomes a leakage from the circular flow whilst investment is an injection.
4. Actual injections must equal actual withdrawals.
5. In the real world, it is the financial system which links investment and savings.
6. In an economy with government, public spending is an injection whilst tax revenues are a withdrawal from the circular flow.
7. In an open economy where there is foreign trade, exports are an injection whilst imports are a withdrawal.

A simple economy

Macro-economics is the study of the workings of the whole economy. An economy is a complicated structure and not surprisingly there is much disagreement amongst economists about exactly how it works. Just as in micro-economics, where the model of demand, supply and the market provides a basic framework for the analysis of many problems, so in macro-economics there is an accepted general model of economic behaviour. This is the CIRCULAR FLOW OF INCOME model.

In a pure **subsistence economy**, there is no trade between individuals. People consume only the goods and services that they themselves produce. In a more sophisticated market economy, producers and consumers become separated.

■ **Households** own the wealth of the nation. They own the land, labour and capital used to produce goods and services. They supply these factors to firms in return for rents, wages, interest and profits - the rewards to the factors of production. They then use this money to buy goods and services.

■ **Firms** produce goods and services. They hire factors of production from households and use these to produce goods and services for sale back to households.

The flow from households to firms is shown in Figure 56.1. The flow of money round the economy is shown in red. Households receive payments for hiring their land, labour and capital. They spend all that money on the goods and services produced by firms (consumption). An alternative way of putting this is to express these money payments in **real** terms (☞ unit 3 explains the distinction between real and monetary values). The real flow of products and factor services is shown in black. Households supply land, labour and capital and in return receive goods and services.

This model of the economy is a very simple one because it has been assumed that:

■ Households spend all of their income on goods and

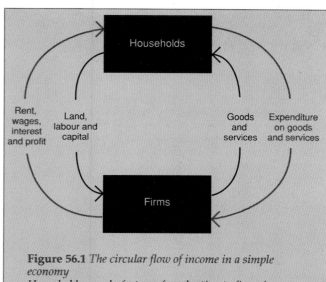

Figure 56.1 *The circular flow of income in a simple economy*
Households supply factors of production to firms in return for rent, wages, interest and profit. Households spend their money on goods and services supplied by firms.

QUESTION 1

Table 56.1

	£bn
Rent	5
Wages	75
Interest and profit	20

The figures in Table 56.1 represent the only income payments received by households. There are no savings, investment, government expenditure and taxes or foreign trade in the economy. Construct a circular flow of income diagram showing the income and expenditure of households and firms.

services produced by firms whilst firms spend all of their revenues on factors of production owned by households;

■ there is no government sector and hence there is no government spending or taxes;

■ the economy is CLOSED (i.e. there is no foreign sector).

Income, output and expenditure

The amount of money flowing round the system gives a value to the level of economic activity. As can be seen from Figure 56.2, this can be measured in three different ways. Going from right to left, the level of economic activity can be measured as the value of:

■ national expenditure (E) - spending by households on the goods and services produced by firms;

■ national output (O) - the output of firms (i.e. the value of what they produce);

■ national income (Y) - the income paid by firms to households.

In national income accounts, the three are identical because they are defined in such a way as to be identical:

$$O \equiv E \equiv Y$$

■ National income is defined as income generated from the production of national output.

■ National expenditure is defined as the expenditure needed to purchase national output.

This is true not just in the simplest circular flow model but in all circular flow models.

Savings and investment

In the simple model above, it was assumed that households spent all of their income. In practice not all household income is spent. Some of it is saved.

Saving (☞ unit 60) is called a LEAKAGE or WITHDRAWAL from the circular flow of income and expenditure because the money saved leaves the circular flow. Withdrawals lower the level of economic activity in the system.

Firms too do not spend all of their money on existing factors of production. They spend money on **investment goods**. These are goods such as machines, factories, offices and other capital equipment used to produce other goods and services. As well as this **fixed capital**, there is **circulating capital** (also called stocks, stocks and work in progress or inventories). These are goods which have been produced by firms but have not been sold to consumers. They could, for instance, be coal at a steel mill, steel at a car plant, or cars in a dealer's showroom. Investment expenditure is an INJECTION to the circular flow. Injections increase the level of economic activity in the system.

Savings and investment are shown in Figure 56.3. Money saved leaks from the circular flow, whilst money spent on goods and services flows round the system. Those firms manufacturing investment goods receive payments for those goods. Real goods and services and the services of real factors of production flow round the system in the opposite direction.

In the real world, savings in the economy are linked to investment through the financial system. For instance, households save money and deposit their savings in a

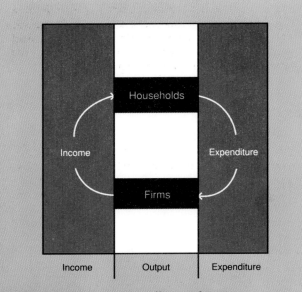

Figure 56. 2 *Income , expenditure and output*
The value of the flow of money round the system can be measured at three different points - as income , output or expenditure. These three must be identical because they measure the same flow.

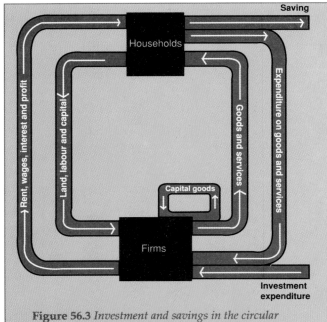

Figure 56.3 *Investment and savings in the circular flow*
Investment is an injection to the circular flow whilst saving is a leakage.

bank. The bank then lends out the money to firms to finance their investment programmes.

Injections must equal withdrawals

So far nothing has been said about the size of the flows round the economy. In the simplest model, the circle is closed. Hence, the flow of money round the system will be constant and the economy will be in **equilibrium** (i.e. there will be no tendency to change within the system).

But if investment and saving takes place, money enters and leaves the system. Commonsense suggests that the two will be equal at some point. Consider what would happen if they were not. If investment spending were greater than saving, the amount of money entering the system would be greater than the amount leaving. Every time money went round the circular flow it would increase, leading eventually to an infinite amount of money and a corresponding infinite level of production in the system. If on the other hand, savings were greater than investment, there would be a net drain of money from the system. Eventually there would be no money left in the system and all production would stop.

To understand why injections must equal withdrawals, it is necessary to introduce two **identities**. An identity is something which is true by definition. For instance, a quadruped must always have four legs by definition. Therefore 'quadrupeds are four legged animals' is an identity. Identities are shown by the symbol ≡.

It was assumed above that households either spend their income or save it. Hence by definition, income must equal consumption expenditure plus savings:

$$Y \equiv C + S$$

where Y is income, C is consumption expenditure and S is savings.

It was also assumed that there were only two components of total spending on goods and services in the economy. Households bought goods and services, whilst firms spent money on investment goods. Hence by definition, total expenditure must equal consumption expenditure plus investment:

$$E \equiv C + I$$

where E is total expenditure and I is investment.

Income and expenditure are two ways of measuring the same flow round the economy. Y and E are therefore always the same value. Hence:

$$C + S \equiv C + I$$

and it must therefore be true that:

$$S \equiv I$$

In the circular flow model, withdrawals (in this case savings) must always be equal to injections (in this case investment). This is true of **actual** savings and **actual** withdrawals. In unit 74, we shall see that economic agents may **plan** to save and invest different amounts but that their plans may be frustrated because **actual** injections and withdrawals must always be equal.

QUESTION 2
Table 56.2

£bn

	Consumption	Saving	Investment	National income
(a)	70	30		
(b)	20			25
(c)	50		10	
(d)		250		800
(e)			8	48

The table shows actual consumption, saving, investment and national income in a simple closed economy with no government. Fill in the missing figures in the table for each line a to e.

The government sector

Governments exist in all national economies. Governments raise money through taxes to finance their expenditure on services such as defence and education.

Taxes represent a withdrawal of money from the circular flow. Government takes money from households and firms in a variety of taxes. Government spending, on the other hand, is an injection to the circular flow. Government spending puts money back into the flow.

In a closed economy, (i.e. one where there is no foreign trade), there are thus two injections and two withdrawals. Investment and government spending are injections and savings and taxes are withdrawals. It was argued above that actual injections must always equal actual withdrawals. Hence, it must be true that:

$$I + G \equiv S + T$$

Note that it need not be true that $I \equiv S$ if there is a government sector. Investment could be greater than savings if taxes were greater than government spending. What must be true however is that total injections (I + S) must always equal total withdrawals (S + T).

Foreign trade

Nations trade with each other. Consumers spend money on imported goods. This is money which leaves the domestic circular flow of income to be given to foreigners. Imports are therefore a withdrawal from the circular flow. On the other hand, foreigners spend money on goods and services produced domestically. This is therefore represented as an injection into the circular flow.

In an OPEN ECONOMY (i.e. a country with foreign dealings) with a government sector, there are now three injections and three withdrawals:

■ the injections are investment, government spending and exports;

■ the withdrawals are savings, taxes and imports.

Actual injections must equal actual withdrawals. Hence:

$$I + G + X \equiv S + T + M$$

where X is exports and M is imports.

It is now possible to draw a circular flow diagram for this economy. Figure 56.4 does not attempt to show exactly how the injections and withdrawals fit into the circular flow. Such a diagram would be extremely complicated. For instance, taxes can be paid not only by households and firms but also by foreigners on exports and imports. Computer models of the circular flow for the UK can use hundreds of different equations to describe the interactions within the economy.

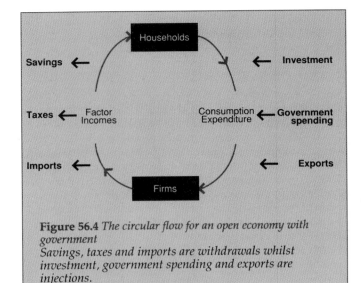

Figure 56.4 *The circular flow for an open economy with government*
Savings, taxes and imports are withdrawals whilst investment, government spending and exports are injections.

Key terms

Circular flow of income - a model of the economy which shows the flow of goods, services and factors and their payments round the economy.
Closed economy - an economy which has no economic trade with foreign countries. There are therefore no exports or imports.
Leakage or withdrawal - national income which is not spent on current consumption and therefore leaves the circular flow of income. Savings, taxes and imports are usually considered to be leakages.
Injection - national expenditure in addition to consumption expenditure in the circular flow of income. Investment, government spending and exports are usually considered to be injections.
Open economy - an economy with economic trade with foreigners.

QUESTION 3

Draw a circular flow diagram for the UK economy. Where would you place on it: (a) the purchase by a UK firm of new machinery manufactured domestically; (b) the deposit of money by a household into a bank; (c) the payment of wages by a firm; (d) the purchase by a UK household of a car manufactured in Germany; (e) the purchase of theatre tickets by American tourists in London; (f) the purchase by a UK household of a meal in Glasgow; (g) the payment of profits to Japan from a Japanese owned factory in Wales?

The Channel Tunnel project

The Channel Tunnel is currently the largest civil engineering project in the UK. Its impact on the economy can be traced through the circular flow of income mechanism. (For the sake of simplicity we will assume below that Eurotunnel and its builders are British, although in fact it is an Anglo-French company).

The Channel Tunnel is classified as investment. As such, it is an injection, (flow 1), into the circular flow, as shown in Figure 56.5. Part of the money is used directly by Transmanche-Link, the construction company of Eurotunnel, to pay direct costs of production. Part is used to pay other firms employed by Transmanche-Link for subcontracting work (flow 2). Both Transmanche and its subcontractors will spend money on imported goods and services, a leakage from the circular flow of the UK economy (3). They will also spend money on the wages of workers (4), whilst other monies will be spent on interest, profits and dividends for shareholders etc. (5). Taxes on earnings, a withdrawal from the circular flow, will be deducted at source and paid to the government (6). Households then receive income net of tax.

In Figure 56.6, the flow of income is traced back from households to firms. Households will save part of the money (7), a leakage from the circular flow. The rest will be used to purchase consumer goods (8). Some consumer goods will be imported (9). Most consumer goods will be subject to VAT or other indirect taxes (10). Money given over to taxation or imports will leak out of the UK circular flow. The rest will flow back to the UK firms supplying the consumer goods. They in turn will use the money to pay for materials from other firms, to pay their workers, their shareholders, etc. and so the money will flow back round the left hand side of the circular flow shown in Figure 56.5.

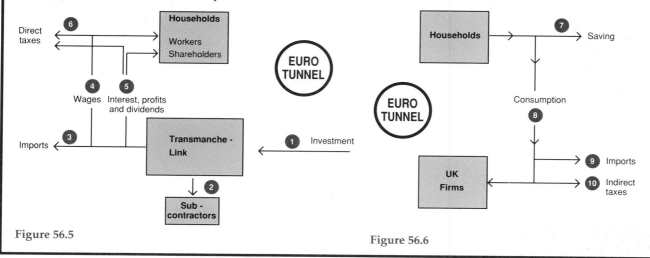

Figure 56.5

Figure 56.6

Data question

£80M SEASIDE SPECTACULAR

A major new initiative costing £80 million and creating 1 500 new jobs was unveiled in Southport today. The proposal by London and Manchester-based developers **Sibec** was announced at a press conference hosted by Sefton Borough Council. But planning permission is still to be given to the scheme, which would cover 10 acres of land and provide 'unique high street theatre experience'.

The proposal will go before the council next month. If granted, work should start early next year.

Sibec chief executive Mike Birchall said the development would reflect the historic themes of previous buildings on the site - the Winter Gardens and the Lord Street railway station.

He said the 600 000 sq.ft. complex will include modern shop units arranged around a naturally lit glazed mall space with restaurants, food courts and halls, a children's world and other family attractions.

There would also be provisions for a major department store, several medium sized stores and 80 smaller shop units.

Victorian

There would be car parking for 1 000 vehicles and 250 staff cars.

The intention, he said, was to to retain the Victorian frontage of the building, which has been used recently as a bus station on Lord Street.

A new 150 bedroom hotel would be a prominent feature of the scheme, designed in crescent form above the shopping centre overlooking the seafront.

Expand

He said: 'The development would transform Southport into one of the most important retail locations in the North West, attracting shoppers from a wide area.'

Sibec expects the hotel to expand the town's tourist trade and, together with establishing Southport as an important business location, will provide a significant long-term boost for the local economy.

He said the anticipated £40 million building contract would commence in mid-1988 with the two level shopping and leisure galleries of the new Winter Gardens in 1991.

He said: ' It will quickly establish itself as the most unique and exciting centre in Western Europe.'

Source: *Liverpool Echo*, 4.7.1987.

1. **Explain how the proposed development might affect the circular flow of income of the UK economy in future years.**

Summary

1. National income can be measured in three different ways: national income, output and expenditure.
2. National income is equal to wages, rents, interest and profit.
3. National output is equal to the sum of the output of individual industries. It is important to avoid double counting in the output method.
4. National expenditure is equal to consumption, investment, government spending and exports minus imports.
5. National income is equal to domestic income plus net property income from abroad.
6. Expenditure at factor cost is equal to expenditure at market prices minus indirect taxes plus subsidies.
7. The difference between gross and net national income is capital consumption.
8. Transfer payments such as National Insurance benefits should not be included in national income.
9. The value of the real increase in stocks must be included in national expenditure.

Income, output and expenditure

The circular flow model, discussed in the previous unit, forms the basis for national income accounting. In the model, there are three ways of measuring the same flow of money round an economy. Actual income, output and expenditure must always be identical. Income, output and expenditure are **flows** of money which pay for goods, services and factors over a period of time, and are made up of a number of different components.

Income Income is payment received for the hire of factors of production. Therefore income is made up of wages received by workers, rents received by the owners of land and property, and profits and interest received by the owners of capital and entrepreneurs.

Output Output measures the value of the output of industry. There are two ways of calculating this. One way is to measure the value of the final output of industry. **Final output** is the goods and services which are either purchased by consumers or used as capital goods by industry. For instance, a can of baked beans bought in a supermarket would be an example of final output. The purchase of the can and the beans by the food manufacturer would be an example of **intermediate output**. Adding together the value of the beans, the can, and the final product bought in the supermarket would give the wrong answer to the question: what is the value of what has been produced? If the can of baked beans cost 40p in a shop, and the can itself cost 4p whilst the beans cost 7p, the value of output is still 40p and not 51p.

An answer of 51p would be an example of **double counting**. This occurs when an item is counted more than once. It produces an inflated figure for whatever is being measured. Double counting is avoided if only the final output of industry is computed. Another way to avoid double counting is to calculate VALUE ADDED. Instead of counting the value of the final output of a product, it is possible to calculate the value added at each stage of

Table 57.1

	Value added	Total value of output
Raw materials (beans, can, etc.) bought by a baked bean manufacturer	20p	20p
Baked bean manufacturer 'makes' the product and sells to the supermarket	15p	35p
Supermarket sells to the customer	5p	40p
Final output	40p	40p

production. For instance, if the manufacturer sells a can of baked beans to the supermarket for 35p and the supermarket sells it to the consumer for 40p, then the value added by the supermarket is 5p. As can be seen from Table 57.1, the sum of the value added at each stage of production must equal the value of final output.

Expenditure There are various types of spending in the economy:
■ consumption - spending by households on goods and services;
■ investment - spending by producers on capital goods;
■ government spending - on services such as defence and education;
■ exports - spending by foreigners on domestic goods.
Expenditure on consumption, investment and public sector services includes spending on imported goods. There is no corresponding domestic output for import expenditure and therefore imports must be taken away from total expenditure if expenditure is to equal the value of output produced in the domestic economy.

Figure 57.1 summarises the three ways of calculating national income. Net exports in the expenditure column is the difference between exports and imports. In practice, calculating national income is extremely complex. We will now discuss some of the most important details of this calculation.

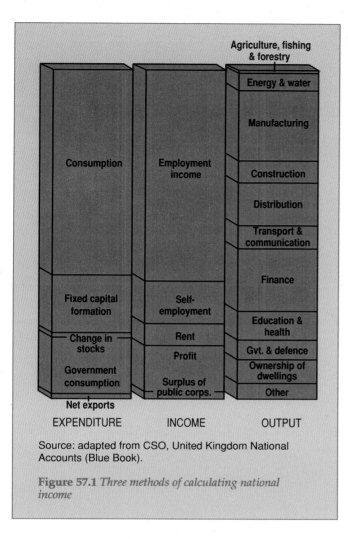

Source: adapted from CSO, United Kingdom National Accounts (Blue Book).

Figure 57.1 *Three methods of calculating national income*

Domestic income to national income

In a real economy, foreigners own some domestic resources. For instance, the Japanese car manufacturer Nissan owns a car plant in Sunderland and Japanese banks have lent money to British firms. On the other hand, UK citizens and companies own assets abroad. These assets give rise to corresponding income. Nissan repatriates profits to Japan, whilst Japanese banks earn interest on their loans. British assets abroad give a flow of incomes from abroad to the UK.

So DOMESTIC INCOME is distinguished from NATIONAL INCOME in national income accounts. Domestic income is the nation's income before income paid and received from abroad has been included. National income is income which includes not only domestic income but also incomes earned and paid abroad.

In the UK national income statistics, this income is called NET PROPERTY INCOME FROM ABROAD. So:

Domestic income + net property income from abroad = national income

QUESTION 2
In 1989 in the UK:
■ property income from abroad was £74 601m;
■ domestic product (i.e. domestic income) was £438 774m;
■ property income paid abroad was £70 019m.

What was the value of national product or income?

At market prices to factor cost

If you were to buy some eye shadow at £1.15 the price would include 15 per cent Value Added Tax (VAT). The actual value of the output is therefore £1. This is the amount that the retailer receives after paying 15p to the government. This £1 is used to pay factor incomes - wages, rents, etc. So £1 and not £1.15 passes round the circular flow of income.

Some goods are **subsidised**. For instance, in 1975 the government subsidised the price of bread. This meant that the amount paid by consumers for bread was less than the value of the output of bread. The difference between what the consumer paid and what the producer received was the subsidy. The amount flowing round the circular flow in this case is the expenditure on bread plus the subsidy paid by government. This is equal to the value of total output of bread and of total incomes received from bread production.

The value of expenditure including indirect taxes such as VAT and subsidies is called expenditure AT MARKET PRICES. Expenditure excluding taxes and subsidies is called expenditure AT FACTOR COST. To go from market prices to factor cost, it is necessary to take away

QUESTION 1 The following are extracts from the national income accounts of a country.
Table 57.2

	£ million
Wages and salaries	35
Investment	10
Output of manufacturing industry	10
Government expenditure	15
Rents	5
Interest and profits	10
Exports	15
Consumers' expenditure	20

(a) Calculate national income by the income method assuming that all the necessary information on incomes is contained in the data.
(b) What must be the value of national expenditure?
(c) What must be the value of imports?
(d) Why is it not possible to calculate national income by the output method from the data given?

indirect taxes and add subsidies. So:

Expenditure at factor cost = expenditure at market prices - indirect taxes + subsidies

Gross national income to net national income

Gross and net have different precise meanings in different contexts. In national income accounting, the difference between gross income and net income is depreciation. Over a period of time, the capital stock of a country - factories, offices, machines, roads, hospitals etc. - wears out. This is called DEPRECIATION or CAPITAL CONSUMPTION.

Depreciation should be excluded from national income. To see why, consider an individual who spends £12 000 over a year. £2 000 of that was drawn from her savings. Her income therefore must have been £10 000 and not £12 000. The capital stock of a country is like an individual's wealth. If it has been run down to provide money for spending, then the value of that depreciation or capital consumption must be taken away to arrive at a true value of income.

Another way of seeing this is to consider gross and net investment. Gross investment is the total value of investment expenditure over a period of time. Part of that investment simply replaces capital goods which have worn out over the period. This is the value of depreciation. The rest, net investment, is the increase in the capital stock. Net investment rather than gross investment shows how much the productive potential of the country has increased over time. So:

Gross national income - capital consumption = net national income

Transfer payments

There are some incomes which have no corresponding output. These are called TRANSFER PAYMENTS. For instance:
- the government pays National Insurance and social security benefits to individuals, but the recipients produce nothing in return;
- students receive student grants from government, but

again produce nothing which can then be sold;

■ children receive pocket money and allowances from their parents;

■ an individual selling a second hand car receives money, but no new car is created.

Transfer payments should be excluded from calculation of national income. So transfer incomes need to be excluded from the income method whilst government National Insurance and social security payments need to be excluded from national expenditure. Government spending in national income accounting is therefore total government spending minus government transfer payments.

Stocks

A company might produce £10 million worth of goods but only sell £9 million to consumers. Output is therefore £10 million, but only £9 million is received in consumer expenditure. The other £1 million of goods will have been added to the firm's STOCKS or INVENTORIES. These are goods which a firm has produced or bought from another firm but is waiting to sell them. A company may also buy stocks of raw materials. These stocks are awaiting transformation into new goods and services.

In national income accounts, changes in stocks are treated as expenditure by the firm. In the above example, the company has been forced to buy from itself the £1 million of goods that it had hoped to sell. Equally, if it had bought raw materials and held them in stock, this would have been classified as expenditure.

Note that it is **changes** in stocks and not stocks themselves that are treated as expenditure in national income accounts. Income, expenditure and output are money or real flows over a period of time. The corresponding flow is the change in stocks and not stock levels.

There is a further complication resulting from inflation. Profits of companies include an allowance for stock appreciation. For instance, a company may have held 100 units of raw material in stock throughout the period. Their total value may have increased because of inflation. But this increase in value has no corresponding output - there are still 100 units in stock at the end of the period even if their value has increased. Therefore stock appreciation must be deducted from national income if income is to equal output.

Measures of national income

It is now possible to explain a number of the different measures of national income given by national income accounts.

■ Gross domestic product at factor cost (GDP at factor cost). This is a measure of domestic income, or output or expenditure (remember the three must be equal) before net property income from abroad has been added (or subtracted if it is negative) and before depreciation has been deducted.

■ Gross national product at factor cost (GNP at factor cost). This is a measure of national income (or output or expenditure) which includes net property income from abroad but does not include capital consumption.

■ NATIONAL INCOME. Strictly speaking this is net national product at factor cost. It is equal to national expenditure and national output. It is the most complete measure of national income currently calculated by government. Note that 'national income' is the term used in economic theory to refer to all three measures of the flow of money round the circular flow.

GDP and GNP tend to be quoted in articles and publications more often than national income. The reason is because figures for depreciation are usually not given in month by month estimates of current national income. It is also difficult to estimate and tends not to fluctuate very much as a percentage of national income. So GDP and GNP and their changes are good indicators of changes in net national product. GDP is often used in preference to GNP because it is a better indicator of output and employment trends in the domestic economy. Moreover, net property income from abroad is very small for the UK, and the GDP and GNP figures tend to move in the same direction.

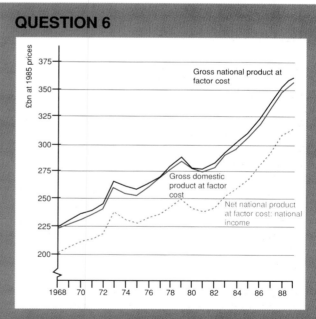

QUESTION 6

Source: adapted from CSO, CSO, *United Kingdom National Accounts (Blue Book).*

Figure 57.2 *GDP,GNP and NNP at factor cost (average estimates), 1968 - 1989*

(a) What is the difference between GDP, GNP and national income?

(b) Account for the extent to which these three measures of national income change at the same rate over time.

Key terms

Value added - the difference between the price paid for inputs by one producer to another and the value of the output of the producer.
Domestic and national income - domestic income is income which excludes the value of incomes generated by assets owned overseas and of domestic assets owned by foreigners. National income includes these.
Net property income from abroad - the difference between income received from overseas assets and that paid on domestic assets owned by foreigners.
Market prices and factor cost - national income at market prices includes taxes on expenditure and subsidies. Factor cost excludes these.
Depreciation or capital consumption - the cost of replacing the capital stock which has been used up or

has depreciated over the time period.
Transfer payments - income payments for which there is no corresponding output. They are excluded from national income accounts.
Stocks or inventories - goods held by a firm either for future production or sale.
Gross domestic product at factor cost - a measure of national income before property income from abroad and depreciation have been accounted for.
Gross national product - a measure of national income including net property income from abroad but before depreciation.
National income - net national product at factor cost.
Gross domestic fixed capital formation - gross investment (i.e. before depreciation).

Applied economics

The national income accounts of the United Kingdom

Income, expenditure and output

The current UK national income statistics calculate gross domestic product at factor cost by each of the income, output and expenditure methods. National income is then derived from the figure obtained.

In practice, estimates of gross domestic product at factor cost calculated by the expenditure method differ from those calculated by the income method and both differ from figures for the output method. This is hardly surprising. National income statistics are calculated from millions of individuals' returns. Inaccuracies are inevitable. Returns can also be falsified or not submitted to evade taxes such as income tax and VAT. So a figure for a **statistical discrepancy or residual error** is included in the calculation of each method of national income. It is the difference between the actual estimate of gross domestic product at factor cost as calculated by one method and the average estimate of GDP calculated by the three methods. For instance, if GDP by the income method were £98, by the output method were £99 and by the expenditure method £103, then the average estimate of GDP would be £100 [(£98 + £99 + £103)÷3]. So the statistical discrepancy for income would be +£2, for output +£1 and for expenditure -£3.

Gross domestic product by the expenditure method

Table 57.5 shows how GDP by the expenditure method

is calculated. National expenditure is made up of consumption, investment, government spending and net exports.
- The table shows that consumers' expenditure is by far the largest single item.
- Government expenditure is split into two parts. Investment by government on roads, new hospitals, new schools etc. is included in the figure for investment. General government final consumption measures non-investment expenditure such as wages and salaries, and purchases on consumable items from toilet paper to school textbooks to petrol.
- Investment is called GROSS DOMESTIC FIXED CAPITAL FORMATION in national income accounts. It is investment both by the private and the public sectors.
- The addition to stocks is also part of expenditure as explained above.

The total of these components of expenditure is called **total domestic expenditure**. Exports are added to arrive at **total final expenditure**. However, imports must be taken away because there is no corresponding output figure for imports. This gives a figure for **gross domestic product at market prices**. The statistical discrepancy in 1989 was positive, indicating that the estimate for domestic expenditure was less than the average of the three methods. To go from market prices to factor cost (see above), it is necessary to take away indirect taxes like VAT and excise duties and add subsidies. The figure now arrived at is **GDP at factor cost**.

Table 57.5 *GDP by the expenditure method , 1989*

	£ millions
Consumers' expenditure	328 453
General government final consumption	99 426
Gross domestic fixed capital formation	100 472
Value of physical increase in stocks and work in progress	3 102
Total domestic expenditure	531 453
Exports of goods and services	123 396
Total final expenditure	654 849
less imports of goods and services	142 527
Gross domestic product at market prices	512 322
Statistical discrepancy	920
less taxes on expenditure	80 136
plus subsidies	5 668
Gross domestic product at factor cost	438 774

Source: adapted from CSO, *United Kingdom National Accounts (Blue Book).*

GDP by the income method

Incomes in the circular flow are factor incomes - wages, profits and rents. Table 57.6 shows the breakdown of domestic income.
- Wages paid to workers are split into two categories. Income from employment is the measure of salaries and wages paid to employed workers. The earnings of the self-employed are classified separately.
- Profits too are split into two categories. Gross trading profits of companies refers to the profits earned by private sector businesses. Gross trading surpluses of public corporations and general government enterprises refers to the profits made by state owned companies ranging from British Rail to local authority swimming pools.
- Rent is the payments received by individuals from the lease of property. Government too owns property. The imputed charge for consumption of non-trading capital is an estimate of how much the state would have had to pay in rent if the property had been owned within the private sector.

These added together make up **total domestic income**. The value of the monetary increase in the value of stocks must now be deducted (see above). Adjusting the figure with the statistical discrepancy gives the value of GDP at factor cost.

Table 57.6 *GDP by the income method, 1989*

	£ millions
Income from employment	284 399
Income from self-employment	53 126
Gross trading profits of companies	65 639
Gross trading surpluses of public corporations and general government enterprises	6 768
Rent	31 568
Imputed charge for consumption of non-trading capital	3 840
Total domestic income	445 340
less stock appreciation	17 598
less statistical discrepancy	1 032
Gross domestic product at factor cost	438 774

Source: adapted from CSO, *United Kingdom National Accounts (Blue Book).*

GDP by the output method

Table 57.7 shows the breakdown of domestic output. The figures are for the value added by each industry rather than final output. In some industries, such as defence and education, little or nothing is traded in the market place. Therefore there can be no price set upon the products. So the value of the output of these

Table 57.7 *GDP by the output method , 1989*

	£ millions
Agriculture, forestry and fishing	6 561
Energy and water supply	22 619
Manufacturing	97 380
Construction	30 274
Distribution, hotels and catering, repairs	62 133
Transport and communication	30 074
Banking, finance, insurance and business services	86 628
Ownership of dwellings	25 482
Public administration and national defence	29 571
Education and health services	42 547
Other services	29 715
Total	462 984
Adjustment for financial services	- 25 242
Statistical discrepancy	+ 1 032
Gross domestic product at factor cost	438 774

Source: adapted from CSO, *United Kingdom National Accounts (Blue Book).*

industries is assumed to be equal to the value of the inputs. For instance, the output of the defence industry is assumed to be equal to the salaries paid to personnel, equipment bought over the time period, etc.

From GDP to GNP

Gross domestic product measures income, output and expenditure generated from resources in the UK. But the UK owns assets abroad and foreigners own assets in the UK. So property income received from abroad needs to be added to GDP whilst property income paid abroad must be subtracted from GDP giving a figure for net property income from abroad. Table 57.8 shows the movement from GDP to GNP.

From GNP to national income

Gross national product at factor cost is an estimate of national income before consumption has been deducted. Table 57.8 arrives at net national product at factor cost or national income by deducting capital consumption.

Statistical problems

During the second half of the 1980s, there was major criticism of the quality of official government statistics. During the early 1980s, government had cut resources devoted to the collection of economic statistics, partly in an 'efficiency' drive and partly to relieve business of government 'red tape'. The 1980s also saw deregulation of much of the financial sector of the economy and it became much more difficult to monitor the flows of money round the financial system.

The result has been growing discrepancies between the three measures of national income. For instance, in the first nine months of 1987, income was £2 billion greater than expenditure according to the statistics. Over the same period in 1989 it was £9 billion greater. The difference between output and expenditure is

Table 57.8 *From GDP at factor cost to national income, 1989*

	£ millions
Gross domestic product at factor cost	438 774
Net property income from abroad	4 582
Gross national product at factor cost	443 356
less capital consumption	56 186
National income	387 170

Source: adapted from CSO, *United Kingdom National Accounts (Blue Book).*

currently about 4 per cent, the equivalent of about 2 years' growth of the economy.

The national accounts are balanced by using a 'residual error' or 'statistical discrepancy', sometimes called a 'black hole' of statistics. Some of the most significant discrepancies are:
- the balancing item on the balance of payments - figures for exports and imports and for flows of money in and out of the UK are notoriously unreliable;
- company profits and investment - profits are over-recorded whilst investment is under-recorded;
- personal savings - savings are calculated as the difference between income and expenditure; since both income and expenditure statistics are large and inaccurate it is perhaps not surprising that savings estimates can be grossly inaccurate;
- purchases of securities by the private sector - these have been overestimated by the government.

Without more resources and with greater demands made upon individuals and firms to provide information it is unlikely that the quality of official statistics will improve. Without accurate statistics, it is very difficult, if not impossible, for government and industry to plan for the future.

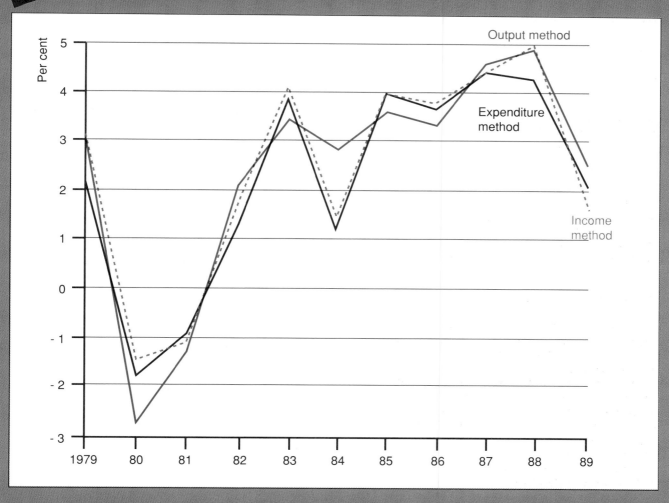

RATE OF CHANGE OF GDP

Data question

Figure 57.3 *Rate of change of GDP*

1. (a) To what extent are the growth rates in
   expenditure, income and output the same over the
   period 1979 to 1989? (b) Explain why you would
   expect them to be the same in any one year.

Source: adapted from CSO, *United Kingdom National Accounts
(Blue Book).*

2. Suggest reasons why there are these discrepancies
   between the three measures of growth of national
   income.

Summary

1. National income statistics are used by academics to formulate and test hypotheses. They are used by policy makers to formulate economic policy both on a micro-economic and macro-economic level. They are often used as a proxy measure for the standards of living and to compare living standards between countries and within a country over time.
2. National income statistics can be inaccurate because of statistical errors, the existence of the black economy, of non-traded sectors, and difficulties with valuing public sector output.
3. Problems occur when comparing national income over time because of inflation, the accuracy and presentation of statistics, changes in population, the quality of goods and services and changes in income distribution.
4. Further problems occur when comparing national income between countries. In particular, an exchange rate has to be constructed which accurately reflects different purchasing power parities.

Why is national income measured?

National income is a measure of the output, expenditure and income of an economy. National income statistics provide not only figures for these totals but also a breakdown of the totals. They are used in a number of different ways.

■ Academic economists use them to test hypotheses and build economic models of the economy. This increases our understanding of how an economy works.

■ Government, firms and economists use the figures to forecast changes in the economy. These forecasts are then used to plan for the future. Government may attempt to direct the economy (☞ for instance unit 77 on fiscal policy), making changes in its spending or its taxes at budget time. Groups such as trade unions or the CBI will make their own recommendations about what policies they think the government should pursue.

■ They are used to make comparisons over time and between countries. For instance, national income statistics can be used to compare the income of the UK in 1950 and 1990. Or they can be used to compare France's income with UK income. Of particular importance when making comparisons over time is the rate of change of national income (i.e. the rate of economic growth).

■ They are used to make judgements about economic welfare. Growth in national income, for instance, is usually equated with a rise in living standards.

The accuracy of national income statistics

National income statistics are inaccurate for a number of reasons.

Statistical inaccuracies National income statistics are calculated from millions of different returns to the government. Inevitably mistakes are made - returns are inaccurate or simply not completed. Currently the statistical discrepancy between the different measures of income can run at up to 4 per cent, equivalent to nearly two years of economic growth in the UK over the past 40 years (☞ unit 57 for a fuller discussion of this point). The statistics are constantly being revised in the light of fresh evidence. Although revisions tend to become smaller over time, national income statistics are still being revised ten years after first publication.

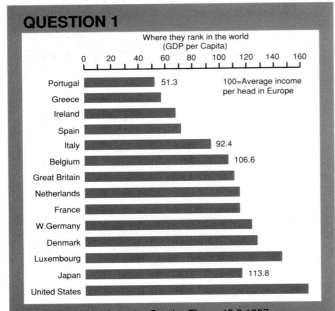

QUESTION 1

Where they rank in the world
(GDP per Capita)

Portugal — 51.3   100=Average income per head in Europe
Greece
Ireland
Spain
Italy — 92.4
Belgium — 106.6
Great Britain
Netherlands
France
W.Germany
Denmark
Luxembourg
Japan — 113.8
United States

Source: adapted from the *Sunday Times*, 15.3.1987.

Figure 58.1 *Where they rank in the world (GDP per capita)*

(a) What statistics do governments need to collect in order to be able to calculate GDP per capita?
(b) How might (i) an economist and (ii) a government use these statistics?

The black economy Taxes such as VAT, income tax and National Insurance contributions, and government regulations such as health and safety laws, impose a burden on workers and businesses. Some are tempted to evade taxes and they are then said to work in the **black, hidden or informal economy**. In the building industry, for instance, it is common for workers to be self-employed and to under-declare or not declare their income at all to the tax authorities. Transactions in the black economy are in the form of cash. Cheques, credit cards, etc. could all be traced by the tax authorities. Tax evasion is the dominant motive for working in the black economy but a few also claim welfare benefits to which they are not entitled. The size of the hidden economy is difficult to estimate, but in the UK estimates have varied from 7 to 15 per cent of GDP (i.e. national income statistics underestimate the true size of national income by at least 7 per cent).

Home produced services In the poorest developing countries in the world, GNP per person is valued at less than £100 per year. It would be impossible to survive on this amount if this were the true value of output in the economy. However, a large part of the production of the agricultural sector is not traded and therefore does not appear in national income statistics. People are engaged in subsistence agriculture, consuming what they themselves produce. Hence the value of national output is in reality much higher. In the UK, the output of the services of housewives and househusbands is equally not recorded. Nor is the large number of DIY jobs completed each year. The more DIY activity, the greater will be the under-recording of national output by national income statistics.

The public sector Valuing the output of much of the public sector is difficult because it is not bought and sold. This problem is circumvented by valuing non-marketed output at its cost of production. For instance, the value of the output of a state school is the cost of running the school. This method of valuation can yield some surprising results. Assume that through more efficient staffing, the number of nurses on a hospital ward is reduced from 10 to 8 and the service is improved. National income accounts will still show a fall in output (measured by a drop the two nurses' incomes). In general, increased productivity in the public sector is shown by a fall in the value of output. It looks as though less is being produced when in fact output remains unchanged.

QUESTION 2 In 1986, Stephen Smith of the Institute of Fiscal Studies estimated that the size of the black economy in the UK was between 3 and 5 per cent of GDP. In his book *Britain's Shadow Economy*, he distinguished between the self-employed, who concealed between 16 and 20 per cent of their income from the Inland Revenue, and the bulk of the population on PAYE, where tax evasion was difficult. The problem of tax evasion was concentrated in a few areas, especially small businesses selling labour-intensive services to private customers.

(a) Explain why the black economy is concentrated particularly amongst the self-employed.
(b) In the 1980s the number of self-employed workers rose as a percentage of the population, as did the proportion of output of services in the economy. What are the implications of this for the size of the black economy in the UK?

Comparing national income over time

Comparing the national income of the UK today with national income in the past presents problems.

Prices Prices have tended to increase over time. So an increase in national income over the period does not necessarily indicate that there has been an increase in the number of goods and services produced in the economy. Only if the rate of increase of national income measured in money terms (the nominal rate of economic growth) has been greater than the increase in prices (the inflation rate) can there be said to have been an increase in output. So when comparing over time, it is essential to consider **real** and not **nominal** changes in income (☞ unit 3).

The accuracy and presentation of statistics National income statistics are inaccurate and therefore it is impossible to give a precise figure for the change in income over time. Moreover, the change in real income over time will also be affected by the inflation rate. The inevitable errors made in the calculation of the inflation rate compound the problems of inaccuracy. The method of calculating national income and the rate of inflation can also change over time. It is important to attempt to eliminate the effect of changes in definitions.

Changes in population National income statistics are often used to compare living standards over time. If they are to be used in this way, it is essential to compare national income **per capita** (i.e. per person). For instance, if the population doubles whilst national income quadruples, people are likely to be nearer twice as well off than four times.

Quality of goods and services The quality of goods may improve over time due to advances in technology but they may also fall in price. For instance, cars today are far better than cars 80 years ago and yet are far cheaper. National income would show this fall in price by a fall in national income wrongly implying that living standards had fallen. On the other hand, pay in the public sector tends to increase at about 2 per cent per annum faster than the increase in inflation. This is because pay across the economy tends to increase in line with the rate of economic growth rather than the rate of inflation. Increased pay would be reflected in both higher nominal and real national income but there may well be no extra goods or services being produced.

Defence and related expenditures The GDP of the UK was higher during the Second World War than in the 1930s, but much of GDP between 1940 and 1945 was devoted to defence expenditure. It would be difficult to argue that people enjoyed a higher standard of living during the war years than in the pre-war years. So the proportion of national income devoted to defence, or for instance to the police, must be taken into account when considering the standard of living of the population.

Consumption and investment It is possible to increase standards of living today by reducing investment and increasing consumption. However, reducing investment is likely to reduce standards of living from what they might otherwise have been in the future. As with defence, the proportion of national income being devoted to investment will affect the standard of living of the population both now and in the future.

Externalities National income statistics take no account of **externalities** (☞ unit 35) produced by the economy. National income statistics may show that national income has doubled roughly every 25 years since 1945. But if the value of externalities has more than doubled over that time period, then the rate of growth of the standard of living has less than doubled.

Income distribution When comparing national income over time, it is important to remember that an increased national income for the economy as a whole may not mean that individuals have seen their income increase. Income distribution is likely to change over time, which may or may not lead to a more desirable state of affairs.

QUESTION 3
Table 58.1

	Nominal GDP £ bn	Index of Retail Prices (1985 = 100)	Population (millions)
1948	12.1	8.3	48.7
1958	23.2	13.0	51.7
1968	44.2	17.5	55.2
1978	168.9	52.8	56.2
1988	469.6	113.0	57.1

Source: adapted from CSO, *Annual Abstract of Statistics*; CSO, *Economic Trends Annual Supplement*.

(a) For each year, calculate the value of real GNP per head of the population.
(b) To what extent is it possible to judge from the data whether living standards increased over the period 1948-1988?

Comparing national income between countries

Comparing national income between economies is fraught with difficulties too. Income distributions may be different. Populations will be different and therefore it is important to compare per capita income figures. National income accounts will have varying degrees of inaccuracy, caused for instance by different sizes of the informal economy in each country. National income accounting conventions will differ.

There is also the problem of what rate of exchange to use when comparing one country's national income with another. The day to day market exchange rate can bear little relation to relative prices in different countries. So prices in some countries, like Switzerland or West Germany, can be much higher at official exchange rates than in France or Italy. Therefore if national income statistics are to be used to compare living standards between countries it is important to use an exchange rate which compares the cost of living in each country. These exchange rates are known as **purchasing power parities**. For instance, if a typical basket of goods costs 10 francs in France and £1 in the UK, then national income should be converted at an exchange rate of 10 francs to the £1 - even if the market exchange rate gives a very different figure.

Even this is not accurate enough. In some countries, consumers have to purchase goods which in others are free. For instance, Sweden spends a greater proportion of its national income than Italy on fuel for heating because of its colder climate. But this extra expenditure does not give the Swedes a higher standard of living. Again, countries are different geographically and one country might have higher transport costs per unit of output than another because of congestion or having to transport goods long distances. In practice, it is almost impossible to adjust national income figures for these sorts of differences.

QUESTION 4

Table 58.2 *Output and living standards, 1985*

Country	Currency units per £		GDP	Population
	Market exchange rates	Purchasing power parities		
USA	1.28	1.75	$3940 bn	239.4m
Sweden	11.00	14.40	864 bn Krona	8.3m
W Germany	3.70	4.40	Dm 1870 bn	61.6m
France	11.50	12.80	FF 4500 bn	54.6m
UK	1.00	1.00	£350 bn	56.5m
Portugal	218.00	116.00	3480 bn Escudos	10.0m

Source: adapted from The Treasury, *Economic Progress Report*, March-April 1987.

(a) Rank in order the countries in the table according to (i) GDP and (ii) GDP per head. To do this you need to convert GDP and GDP per head into pounds sterling using the purchasing power parity exchange rate.
(b) Would your rank order have been different if you had converted GDP at market exchange rates rather than purchasing power parity exchange rates? If so, explain why.

Applied economics

The Italian economy

In 1987, the four largest industrial powers in the world, measured by GNP, were the USA, Japan, West Germany and France. In Italy, politicians in the coalition government were claiming the credit for having dislodged the UK from fifth position. However, were they right?

Comparing the national income of the UK and Italy is not easy. For a start, Italy has a sizeable black economy. In the UK, estimates of the black economy range from 7 to 15 per cent of GNP. In Italy, it is 20 to 30 per cent. 'Moonlighting' is endemic. Many state employees, who finish work at 2.00 p.m. each day, have a second job which they do not declare to the tax authorities. This is also true of workers in the liberal professions such as medicine, law and accountancy. At the other end of the social scale, organized crime employs workers at very low wages in industries ranging from textiles to construction, much of which is kept hidden from the tax authorities.

Italy also probably has a larger proportion of income which is not traded than the UK. Southern Italy is one of the poorest regions in the EC and many families rely upon farming for their living. Some of that agricultural output will be consumed directly by the farmers without being taken to market.

When comparing GNP between countries, a rate of exchange has to be used. In 1987, Italian politicians were using market exchange rates, rather than purchasing power parity rates to prove their point. The two were very similar at the time, although as opposition politicians in Italy pointed out, Italy's lead over the UK had arisen to some extent because of the 12½ per cent devaluation of the pound against the lira in 1986.

Even if GNP per head had been higher in Italy than in the UK in 1987, this would still not show conclusively that living standards were higher in Italy. There is a much wider divide between the rich and poor in Italy than in the UK. In 1987, 25 per cent of school age children in Naples were not enrolled in schools and truancy rates amongst the remaining 75 per cent were very high. One commentator (J Gahagan 1987) suggested that 10 000 workshops in the city would collapse without the use of this child labour. Women as well as children are exploited in the black economy, working in conditions which are often damaging to health. Income and wealth in Italy are heavily concentrated in the North of the country, just as in the UK it is the South which is the more prosperous area.

Italy too probably has a poorer environmental record than the UK. For instance, the Adriatic has been severely affected by algae, a product of dumping from Italian chemical plants. In the South, in Sicily and Calabria, a 1981 census showed that 85 per cent of new buildings had been constructed illegally without planning permission. The result has been whole areas of urban development without proper roads, sewers, lighting or social amenities.

These facts tend to suggest that even if GNP per capita were higher in Italy than in the UK, it would not necessarily mean that the average Italian citizen was better off than the average citizen of the UK.

Data question

COLLECTION OF ECONOMIC STATISTICS TO BE REVISED

Mr John Major, the Chancellor, yesterday announced a sweeping revision of the government's collection of economic statistics in an attempt to solve 'severe problems' in some areas. The revision may require 100 more staff and follows last year's reorganisation of the Central Statistical Office (CSO) which was needed to keep statistics in line with the 'deregulated economy'.

Mr Major said in his speech to the Confederation of British Industry last night that the current high levels of inflation might have been avoided if government statistics had not contained 'growing gaps and inconsistencies'. He said: 'On the basis of the information available, in common with other countries, policy was directed at avoiding a crisis in confidence and a recession in the wake of the stock market crash (in October 1987). Having avoided that recession, as we now know, policy should have been tighter to bear down on strengthening inflationary pressures. At the time we were not exactly overwhelmed with calls for higher interest rates and statistics we had to hand did not reflect the buoyancy of the economy.'

The changes to statistical coverage involve three areas:

- Services. More information is to be collected on external trade in services on a quarterly basis. Inquiries will also be made every quarter on turnover. The aim is to improve the output measure of gross domestic product.
- Capital expenditure, stockbuilding and profits will all be monitored more closely.
- Balance of payments. More enquiries will be made about direct external investment by British companies and also about dealings with domestic and overseas residents.

Source: adapted from the *Financial Times*, 18.5.1990

1. What inaccuracies in the collection of national income statistics are highlighted by the passage?
2. Explain why it is important for national income statistics to be reliable. Illustrate your answer with examples from the passage.

Applied economics

The structure of the economy

The UK economy is structured into three main sectors. In the PRIMARY SECTOR of the economy, raw materials are extracted and food is grown. In the UK national income accounts, the primary sector corresponds approximately to agriculture, forestry and fishing, and parts of energy and water supply. In the SECONDARY SECTOR of the economy, raw materials are transformed into goods. The secondary sector approximates in the UK national income accounts to manufacturing, construction and the rest of energy and water supply not included in primary industry. The TERTIARY SECTOR produces services, such as transport, distribution services, financial services and education.

Figure 59.1 shows shares of output in 1988. Manufacturing accounted for approximately 22 per cent of output, whilst services were 64 per cent. Agriculture was relatively insignificant at a little over 1 per cent, whilst energy and water accounted for 5 per cent of total output. Figure 59.1 also gives a breakdown of manufacturing and service output.

Changes in economic structure

There have been significant changes in the structure of the UK economy over time. Before the industrial revolution of 1750-1850, output was concentrated in the rural sector of the economy. Production was heavily weighted towards the production of food or household services. In the 19th century, manufacturing grew as a percentage of total output. By 1950, as Figure 59.2 shows, the share of manufacturing output in total output was 34 per cent whilst the share of services was 49 per cent. Since then, the share of manufacturing has declined whilst that of services has increased.

Not only has manufacturing declined in relative terms, but it has also declined in absolute terms over certain periods in the past 20 years. Figure 59.3 shows the index of output of manufacturing and services, and of GDP. Whilst GDP and services show a general upward trend, manufactures have seen severe declines of 6 per cent between 1973 and 1976, and 14 per cent between 1979 and 1981. It wasn't until 1988 that manufacturing output reached the same levels as those achieved in 1973 and manufacturing output in 1989 was

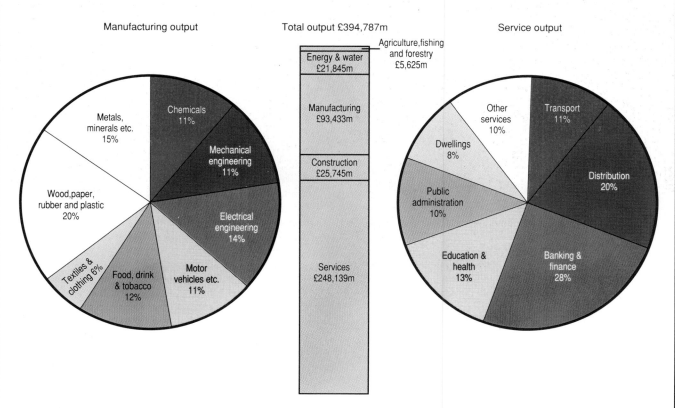

Figure 59.1 *Share of output, 1988*

Source: adapted from CSO, *Annual Abstract of Statistics*.

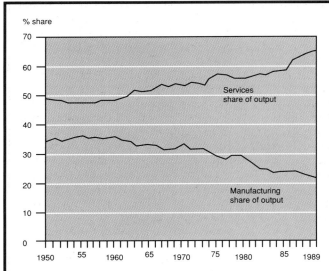

Note: Shares for period 1950-1969 are only approximate as data for this period consistent with last years available.
Source: adapted from CSO, *United Kingdom National Accounts (Blue Book)*.

Figure 59.2 *Manufacturing and service sector output as a share of GDP*

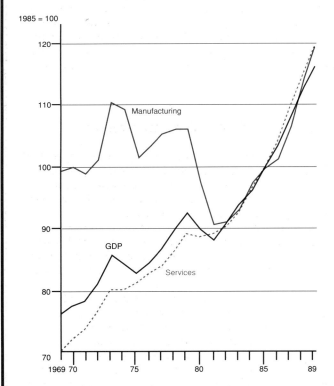

Source: adapted from CSO, National Income and Accounts (Blue Book).

Figure 59.3 *GDP, manufacturing and service output, 1985=100*

only 20 per cent higher than in 1969, compared to a 70 per cent increase in the output of services.

Certain manufacturing industries have done better than others. Table 59.1 shows the 15 groupings of industry in the Standard Industrial Classification. 1985 has been chosen as the base year, and therefore output is given an index number of 100. It can be seen that only 4 industries (chemicals, electrical and instrument engineering, other transport equipment, and food) produced more in 1979 than in 1985. Even by 1989, output was lower in 7 out of 15 industries compared to 1979. Industries which have particularly shrunk are man-made fibres, textiles and metal goods.

Table 59.1 *Manufacturing output by industry at constant factor cost*

			1985 = 100
	1979	1981	1989
Metals	118.2	95.1	124.8
Other minerals and mineral products	114.2	91.6	119.5
Chemicals	93.0	84.2	119.5
Man-made fibres	176.4	109.4	114.7
Metal goods nes	122.6	93.3	112.6
Mechanical engineering	117.4	96.2	110.1
Electrical and instrument engineering	79.2	72.7	126.7
Motor vehicles and parts	132.6	95.1	125.2
Other transport equipment	99.8	111.7	131.6
Food	95.9	94.6	105.4
Drink and tobacco	109.0	104.0	107.4
Textiles	123.6	93.8	97.4
Clothing, footwear and leather	108.5	88.1	100.2
Paper, printing and publishing	109.4	95.9	131.9
All other manufacturing (including timber, furniture, rubber and plastics)	113.9	89.5	132.5
All manufacturing	105.9	90.9	119.2

Source: adapted from CSO, *Annual Abstract of Statistics*; CSO, *Monthly Digest of Statistics*.

Employment and productivity

Not surprisingly, the change in the share of output of manufacturing and service sectors of the economy has produced changes in the structure and pattern of employment. In 1970, 7.9 million workers were employed in manufacturing out of a total workforce of 25.3 million. By 1988, employment in manufacturing had fallen to 5.1 million out of a total workforce of 25.9 million. A rise in manufacturing output of 14.1 per cent was accompanied by a 35.4 per cent fall in employment.

Labour productivity (output per worker) must therefore have risen substantially over the period. Productivity in manufacturing rose an average 3.0 per cent per year in the 1960s, 1.6 per cent in the 1970s and 5.2 per cent between 1981 and 1988. Productivity in the whole economy, however, has risen less fast than in manufacturing. Productivity growth was 2.4 per cent in the 1960s, 1.3 per cent in the 1970s and 2.5 per cent between 1981 and 1988. This must mean that productivity growth in services has been below that of manufacturing.

The causes of de-industrialisation

The process of decline in manufacturing industry is known as DE-INDUSTRIALISATION. There is no standard definition of the term but it has at times been used to describe:
- the absolute decline in output of manufacturing industry;
- a significant decline in the share of manufacturing output in total output;
- the absolute decline in the numbers of workers employed in manufacturing;
- the relative decline in the proportion of all workers employed in manufacturing.

In the case of the UK, the past 20 years have seen an absolute decline in employment and relative falls in both employment and output of manufacturing industry.

It has been argued that de-industrialisation is inevitable in developed economies. Over time, consumers choose to spend an ever greater proportion of their income on services rather than manufactures (i.e. services have an income elasticity of demand greater than 1 whilst manufactures have an income elasticity of demand of less than 1). Table 59.2 would give some support to this hypothesis. It shows that manufacturing output as a share of GDP has fallen in all G7 economies (the 7 largest industrial economies in the world). Equally, whilst employment grew in manufacturing industries of the G7 countries in the 1960s and 1970s, it tended to fall in the 1980s. However, the UK suffered the largest fall in manufacturing output amongst the 7 countries between 1960 and 1988. Also, the UK was the only country to show a consistent fall in

employment over the whole period. If all G7 countries are in the process of de-industrialisation, the UK has de-industrialised at a much faster rate than its international competitors.

Moreover, the change in UK consumer expenditure should have favoured UK manufacturers. UK consumer spending on goods rose 29.2 per cent in real terms between 1979 and 1988, whilst UK manufacturing output rose only 7.8 per cent. The failure of British manufacturing industry to satisfy domestic demand has led to a significant increase in imports of manufactured goods into the country. Not only that, but this has been paralleled by disappointing export performance in manufactures. (This important shift in the structure of foreign trade is discussed in more detail in unit 84.)

From this, it could be argued that the much of the blame for British de-industrialisation must be put on British manufacturing itself. It has failed to compete successfully on world markets and the result has been a declining share of world exports, and declining output. Although productivity in UK manufacturing has increased, it has not increased at a sufficiently high rate. The 1980s has seen some improvement in this position, but at this stage it is difficult to say whether this 'supply side miracle' (☞ unit 99) will be sustained in the 1990s.

A whole variety of arguments have been put forward to explain why British manufacturing industry has proved so uncompetitive. Many of these arguments are equally used to suggest why the UK has such as low growth rate (☞ unit 63). They range from a failure to invest, to 'short-termism' in the City, to over-powerful trade unions, to a failure by government to support industry.

Does de-industrialisation matter?

There are three main reasons which would suggest that Britain's de-industrialisation is of crucial significance. Firstly, the very rapid pace of de-industrialisation has meant that the market economy has found it impossible to redeploy all the resources released from manufacturing into service industries. The result has been high structural unemployment (☞ unit 97) with traditional manufacturing regions of the UK suffering higher rates of unemployment than the service-based South (☞ unit 23).

Secondly, the UK has suffered from balance of payments problems. Unlike in Germany and Japan, both countries with very strong manufacturing industries and persistent balance of payments surpluses, imports have regularly exceeded exports. The response of the UK government has tended to be to reduce spending in the economy, for instance by raising taxes or by raising interest rates. The resulting recession causes a fall in manufacturing output. This reinforces the problems that manufacturing industry has in competing on world markets.

Table 59.2 *Manufacturing output and employment in the G7 countries, 1960-1988*

| | Manufacturing | | | | | | |
| | Output as a percentage of GDP | | | Annual percentage growth in employment | | | |
	1960	1979	1988[1]	1960-67	1968-73	1974-79	1980-88
United States	28	23	19	1.9	1.0	1.5	0.0
Japan	35	29	29	4.0	2.5	-0.4	0.8
Germany	40	34	31	-0.2	0.9	-1.8	-1.0
France	29	26	21	1.1	1.6	-1.1	-2.0
United Kingdom	32	25	21	-0.3	-1.1	-1.2	-2.7
Italy	29	28	23	0.8	0.4	0.3	-1.2
Canada	n.a.	19	17	2.5	2.2	1.9	0.5

1. Figures for UK and US are for 1987 and for Canada 1986.
Source: adapted from OECD, *Historical Statistics*.

Thirdly, manufacturing is important for growth in living standards. Whenever the UK has grown at a rate comparable to countries such as Japan or Germany over the past 40 years, it has tended to run into balance of payments problems because too many imports have been bought. The only way to solve that is either to increase exports or make domestically produced goods more attractive to UK consumers. Either way, UK manufacturing needs to become more competitive. The failure to compete, it can be argued, means that the UK is permanently trapped into a low growth mode, forever getting poorer compared to industrially successful countries such as Germany and Japan.

Key terms

Primary industry - extractive and agricultural industries.
Secondary industry - production of goods, mainly manufactures.
Tertiary industry - production of services.

De-industrialisation - the process of decline of industry, particularly manufacturing industry, measured for instance by declines in absolute levels of employment and output, or declines in relative share of employment or output in the economy of manufacturing industry.

Data question

SOUTH-EAST IS THE 'FIRST REGION TO BE DE-INDUSTRIALISED'

The South-East of England has become Britain's first de-industrialised region, according to a study published today. Services have replaced manufacturing as the backbone of the region's economy, it says. The area now relies more on services for exports than it does on goods, and the finance and business sectors have overtaken manufacturing as the main producer of regionally tradable goods and services.

The annual survey of Regional Economic Prospects, by Cambridge Econometrics, has discovered a shift in economic activity away from the cities and into rural areas. Half of all foreign industrial companies moving to Britain since 1983 chose to set up in rural areas in the South. Wales has been the chief beneficiary of this shift and is projected to have the fastest growth in manufacturing over the next 10 years.

In the South-East, employment trends have changed rapidly. In 1980, manufacturing employed twice as many people as the financial sector, but by 1989 the financial sector employed 10 per cent more people than manufacturing.

Source: adapted from the *Financial Times*, 15.1.1990.

1. **What is meant by 'de-industrialisation'? Illustrate your answer with examples from the passage.**
2. **Using evidence from the data, explain the possible economic consequences of de-industrialisation for the UK economy.**

Summary

1. The consumption function shows the relationship between planned consumption and its determinants, such as disposable income.
2. Planned consumption plus planned saving is equal to disposable income.
3. The average propensity to consume (APC) is the proportion of total disposable income spent. The marginal propensity to consume (MPC) is the proportion of a change in income which is spent.
4. The simple Keynesian consumption function assumes that planned consumption is a function of disposable income and the MPC is less than one.

Defining consumption and saving

Households plan to buy a variety of goods and services (a breakdown is given in the applied economics section below). Household spending is called CONSUMPTION. The main limit for most households on spending is their DISPOSABLE INCOME. This is their income, including state benefits such as unemployment benefit and child benefit after deductions of income tax, National Insurance contributions and other direct taxes. For most working households, this is take-home pay plus state benefits.

Households do not necessarily spend all their disposable income. What is not spent is saved. SAVING is defined as that portion of income which is not spent. So by definition (shown by the ≡ sign):

$$Y \equiv C + S$$

where Y is disposable income, C is consumption (of both domestically produced and imported goods) and S is saving.

The consumption function

There are a number of factors which determine how much a household plans to spend out of a given income. The relationship between planned consumption and these factors is called the CONSUMPTION FUNCTION. Similarly, the SAVINGS FUNCTION is the relationship between planned saving and its determinants. In this unit we will concentrate on looking at the relationship between planned consumption, planned saving and income. In the next unit, we will consider the other determinants of planned consumption and saving.

Empirical evidence suggests that consumption and saving tend to increase as income increases. This is not surprising. If your income increased, it would be likely that you would spend and save more.

Columns 1 and 2 in Table 60.1 show a hypothetical consumption function. As income increases, so does the level of planned consumption. This is plotted in Figure 60.1. The consumption function is upward sloping. Note that at low levels of income, households spend more than they earn. It is assumed that they prefer to borrow money or draw on their stock of savings rather than allow their spending to fall below a certain level (i.e. they **dissave**).

It is then possible to calculate saving. If income is £400 and planned consumption is £360, then planned saving must be £40. If income is £300 and planned consumption £280, then planned saving must be £20. At an income level of £100, planned dissaving of £20 takes place. This is summarised in columns 1-3 and illustrated in Figure 60.2.

Table 60.1 *Consumption, saving and income*

(1) Income Y	(2) Planned consumption C	(3) Planned saving S	(4) Average propensity to consume C ÷ Y	(5) Change in income ΔY	(6) Change in planned consumption ΔC	(7) Marginal propensity to consume ΔC ÷ ΔY
0	40	-40	-			
				100	80	0.8
100	120	-20	1.2			
				100	80	0.8
200	200	0	1.0			
				100	80	0.8
300	280	20	0.93			
				100	80	0.8
400	360	40	0.9			

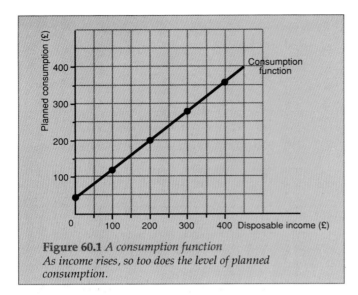

Figure 60.1 *A consumption function*
As income rises, so too does the level of planned consumption.

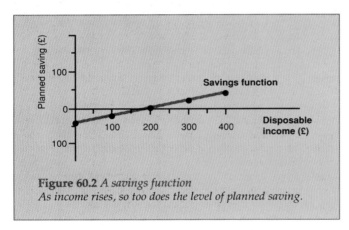

Figure 60.2 *A savings function*
As income rises, so too does the level of planned saving.

QUESTION 1 Consumption is equal to £100 plus ¾ of income.
(a) Calculate the level of consumption at income levels of (i) £200; (ii) £400; (iii) £600; (iv) £800; (v) £1 000.
(b) What is the level of saving at each of these levels of income?
(c) Plot both the consumption and savings functions on a graph.

Average and marginal propensities

It is often important in macro-economics to use the concepts of the average and marginal propensities to consume and save.

Average propensity to consume The AVERAGE PROPENSITY TO CONSUME or APC is defined as the proportion of total income which is spent. It is calculated by dividing total planned consumption by total income:

$$APC = \frac{C}{Y}$$

where C is total planned consumption and Y is total disposable income. Column 4 in Table 60.1 shows how the average propensity to consume changes as income increases.

Marginal propensity to consume The marginal unit is the additional unit. So the MARGINAL PROPENSITY TO CONSUME (MPC) is the proportion which is spent out of a change in (or additional amount of) income. For instance, if you earned an extra £10 and spent £9 of that, then your marginal propensity to consume would be 0.9. Or if you had to take a cut in wages of £5 per week and as a result cut your spending by £3, then your marginal propensity to consume would be 0.6 (3÷5). The MPC is calculated by dividing the change in planned consumption by the change in income.

$$MPC = \frac{\text{change in planned consumption}}{\text{change in income}} = \frac{\Delta C}{\Delta Y}$$

where the Greek letter Δ (delta) means 'change in'. So ΔC means 'change in planned consumption' whilst ΔY means 'change in income'. Columns 5 to 7 in Table 60.1 illustrate the calculation of the marginal propensity to consume.

Average and marginal propensities to save These are defined in the same way as the average and marginal propensities to consume. The AVERAGE PROPENSITY TO SAVE (APS) is the proportion of total income which is saved:

$$APS = \frac{S}{Y}$$

where S is planned saving. The MARGINAL PROPENSITY TO SAVE is the proportion of a change in income which is saved:

$$MPS = \frac{\Delta S}{\Delta Y}$$

Because disposable income must be either spent or saved (because Y = C + S), it must be true that the proportion of income spent plus the proportion saved equals 1. For instance, if an individual spent 0.8 of their income, she must have saved 0.2. So:

$$APC + APS = 1$$

Equally, if an individual spent 0.6 of her annual pay rise, she must have saved 0.4 of it. So:

$$MPC + MPS = 1$$

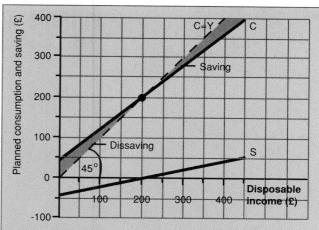

Figure 60.3 *Consumption and savings functions*
The point where the consumption function crosses the 45° line is the break even point. Savings are zero and income equals consumption. The level of autonomous consumption is £40. The slope of the line gives the value of the MPC and the MPS.

A graphical presentation

It is possible to illustrate many of the points made above using graphs. Figure 60.3 shows the consumption and saving functions from Table 60.1.

A 45° line is drawn on the graph. This line shows all points where planned consumption is equal to income. If the consumption function lay along this line, the average propensity to consume would be exactly 1 (i.e. all income would be spent).

The consumption function starts where income is zero and consumption is £40. This is called the level of AUTONOMOUS CONSUMPTION. It is consumption unrelated to the level of income. Whatever the level of income, consumption will always be at least £40. It is the irreducible minimum which will be consumed. Since income must equal consumption plus savings by definition, then a consumption level of £40 when income is zero must mean that saving is - £40. Hence - £40 is where the savings function starts on the vertical axis. Consumption then increases as income increases. This consumption is known as INDUCED CONSUMPTION because it is induced or caused by income.

At an income level of £200, the consumption function passes through the 45° line. The 45° line shows all points where consumption and income are equal. So at an income of £200, consumption is £200 and saving must be zero. Therefore this is the level of income where the savings function cuts the horizontal axis.

At levels of income up to £200, consumption is greater than income and dissaving takes place. At income levels over £200, consumption is less than income and saving is positive. The vertical distance between the consumption function and the 45° line is the level of saving. For instance, at an income level of £300, consumption is £280. So saving must be £20 and this is shown by the savings

function. The shaded area on the diagram, then, is either saving (to the right of the point where the consumption function cuts the line) or dissaving (to the left).

The average propensity to consume is found by dividing total planned consumption by total income. For instance, at an income level of £100, consumption is £120 and so the APC is 1.2. At an income level of £200, consumption is £200 and so the APC is 1.0. At an income level of £400 it is 0.9 (360÷400). For a straight line consumption function which does not pass through the origin, the APC therefore falls as income increases.

The marginal propensity to consume is found by dividing the change in planned consumption by the change in income. For instance, the MPC between an income level of £300 and £400 is 0.8. The change in planned consumption is measured by the vertical distance between two points on the consumption function (for instance from £280 to £360) and the change in income by the horizontal distance (for instance from £300 to £400). Mathematically this is also the slope or gradient of the line. So the marginal propensity to consume between two points is the slope of the consumption function between those two points. In Figure 60.3, the MPC is in fact the same at all points along the line (0.8). You can see this at a glance if you know that the slope of a straight line graph is constant.

The same applies to the average and marginal propensities to save. The average propensity to save increases as income increases (if the APC is falling, the APS must be rising). The MPS is constant, shown by the straight line of the savings function. It is equal to 0.2.

The gradient of the 45° line is 1. Any change in income is exactly matched by a change in consumption. The slope of the consumption and savings functions is shallower than the 45° line, showing that they must be less than 1. So if we draw a consumption function which, starting from the consumption axis, passes through the

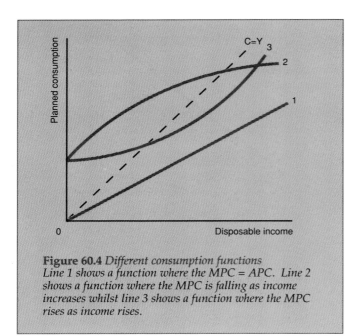

Figure 60.4 *Different consumption functions*
Line 1 shows a function where the MPC = APC. Line 2
shows a function where the MPC is falling as income
increases whilst line 3 shows a function where the MPC
rises as income rises.

45° line, we are stating that the MPC is less than 1.

Figure 60.4 shows a number of different consumption functions. Consumption function 1 is a straight line graph passing through the origin. Because it passes through the origin, it means that there is no autonomous consumption. Total planned consumption divided by total income (the APC) measures the slope of the line. So

the APC is equal to the MPC at all levels of income.

Consumption function 2 is not a straight line and so the gradient of the curve or the MPC is constantly changing. In this case, the slope is getting progressively shallower and therefore the MPC is falling as income increases. Consumption function 3, on the other hand, shows a function where the MPC is increasing as income increases.

The value of the APC and the MPC

The straight line consumption function drawn in Figure 60.3 shows a function where:
- the average propensity to consume is greater than 1 at low levels of income but less than 1 at higher levels of income;
- the marginal propensity to consume is constant and less than 1.

This is broadly the **Keynesian** view of the consumption function (based upon the work of John Maynard Keynes). In the next unit, we will consider this in more detail, explain alternative views and in the applied economics section look at empirical evidence concerning the consumption function.

Important notes

Planned and actual Throughout this unit, it has been explained that the consumption function refers to the relationship between **planned** consumption and income. Planned consumption may differ from actual consumption if plans are frustrated. For instance, households may plan to increase their levels of saving but find that they suffer a fall in income or face unexpected price increases which force them to abandon their plans. PLANNED CONSUMPTION is sometimes also called DESIRED or EX ANTE consumption. ACTUAL CONSUMPTION is sometimes called REALISED or EX POST consumption. We can also make the distinction between planned and actual saving, planned and actual investment, and planned and actual expenditure.

Saving and savings Saving is that part of income which is not spent. It is a **flow** concept because saving takes place over a period of time. Saving is added to a **stock** of savings. A household's stock of savings is the accumulation of past savings. For instance, you might have £100 in the bank. This is your stock of savings. You might then get a job over Christmas and save £20 from that. Your saving over Christmas is £20. Your stock of savings before Christmas was £100 but afterwards it was £120. The savings function explains the relationship between the flow of savings and its determinants. It attempts to explain why you saved £20 over Christmas. It does not explain why you have £100 in the bank already.

Income and disposable income It was explained early on in this unit that the consumption function linked planned consumption with disposable income. However, later in the unit, we talked simply about 'income' rather

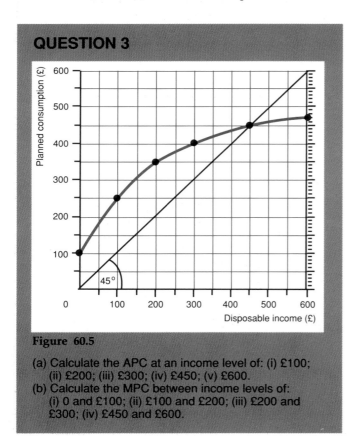

QUESTION 3

Figure 60.5

(a) Calculate the APC at an income level of: (i) £100; (ii) £200; (iii) £300; (iv) £450; (v) £600.
(b) Calculate the MPC between income levels of: (i) 0 and £100; (ii) £100 and £200; (iii) £200 and £300; (iv) £450 and £600.

than disposable income. National income and disposable income are the same in a simple economy where there is no government and no foreign trade. However, they are not the same if there is government because disposable income is income adjusted for taxes and benefits. This is important to remember in more advanced theory.

Real and not nominal values The theory of the consumption and savings function links real consumption and real saving with real income. Changes in the price level, as will be explained in the next unit, can shift the consumption and saving functions.

Aggregate flows Utility theory (☞ units 14 and 15) is used to explain individual consumer behaviour. The theory of the consumption function is a **macro-economic theory** explaining the behaviour of **all individuals** in an economy. Some individuals may reduce spending when income increases but the theory of the consumption function predicts all households taken together will increase their spending.

Key terms

Consumption - total expenditure by households on goods and services over a period of time.
Disposable income - household income over a period of time including state benefits less direct taxes.
Saving (personal) - the portion of households' disposable income which is not spent over a period of time.
Consumption function - the relationship between planned consumption of households and the factors which determine it.
Savings function - the relationship between planned saving and the factors which determine it.
Average propensity to consume - the proportion of total income spent. It is calculated by $C \div Y$.
Marginal propensity to consume - the proportion of a change in income which is spent. It is calculated by $\Delta C \div \Delta Y$.
Average propensity to save - the proportion of a change in income which is saved. It is calculated by $S \div Y$.
Marginal propensity to save - the proportion of a change in income which is saved. It is calculated by $\Delta S \div \Delta Y$.
Autonomous consumption - consumption which is not determined by changes in income.
Induced consumption - consumption expenditure which is related to income.
Planned, desired or ex ante consumption - the amount households intend to spend.
Actual, realised or ex post consumption - the amounts households succeed in spending.

Applied economics

Consumption and saving in the UK

The composition of consumption

Total consumption expenditure over the period 1949 to 1989 nearly trebled. However, as Figure 60.6 shows, there were significant differences in the rate of growth of the components of total expenditure. Spending on food, for instance, only increased by a third whilst spending on durables such as cars, furniture and carpets increase nearly eleven times. In general, expenditure on necessities such as food and energy products increased at a lower rate than expenditure on luxuries such as durable goods or services. It is interesting to note that expenditure on alcoholic drink and tobacco fell between 1979 and 1989. Within this total, expenditure on beer remained roughly constant, whilst expenditure on other alcoholic drinks rose. The overall fall was caused by the decline in expenditure on tobacco, almost certainly the result of increased awareness of the health risks associated with the consumption of the product.

Consumption and income

Keynesian theory suggests that income is the major determinant of consumption. The evidence in Figure 60.7 would tend to support this theory. Over the period 1948 to 1989, real personal disposable income has increased 205 per cent whilst real consumers' expenditure has increased 191 per cent.

Keynesian theory would also suggest that the average propensity to consume declines over time as incomes rise. Figure 60.8 gives some support to this. The APC between 1950 and 1959 averaged 0.96 whilst by the 1970s this had fallen to 0.90. However, the APC rose considerably during the 1980s to a peak of 0.96 in 1988. This would suggest that other factors are important in determining consumption apart from income.

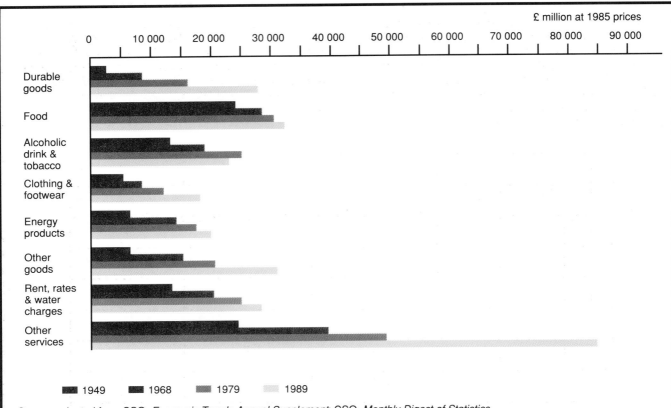

£ million at 1985 prices

1949 1968 1979 1989

Source: adapted from CSO, *Economic Trends Annual Supplement*; CSO, *Monthly Digest of Statistics*.

Figure 60.6 *Composition of consumer expenditure, 1949-1989*

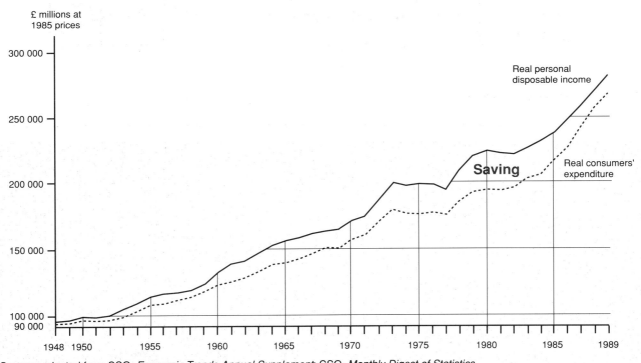

Source: adapted from CSO, *Economic Trends Annual Supplement*; CSO, *Monthly Digest of Statistics*.

Figure 60.7 *Consumption ,saving and personal disposable income*

The level of savings is calculated by taking away consumers' expenditure from personal disposable income. Saving figures fluctuate far more than consumption in percentage terms in part because they are the difference between two very large totals, and also because there are statistical inaccuracies in the calculation of income and consumption. In theory, the combined statistical errors could lead to a maximum 20 per cent discrepancy in the figure for savings in any time period. The personal savings ratio, the APS, is the mirror image of the APC. It rose during the 1950s, 1960s and 1970s but has fallen back in the 1980s. In the applied economics section in unit 61, the possible reasons for the changes in the APC and APS are discussed.

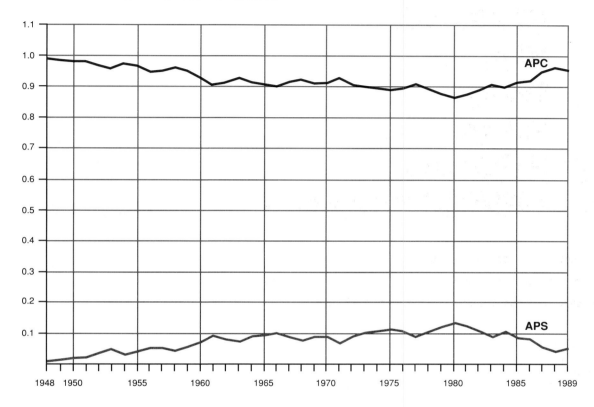

Figure 60.8 *Average and marginal propensities*

CONSUMER SPENDING RISE SHOWS STRENGTH OF ECONOMIC GROWTH

The strength of consumer spending during the summer was highlighted yesterday by official figures showing a sharp rise in the three months to September. The Central Statistical Office said consumer spending rose by 2.2 per cent in real terms compared with the previous three months. It was the biggest quarterly increase since the second quarter of 1979. The CSO said the latest increase reflected buoyant retail sales and particularly high spending on F-registration cars.

The jump underlined the extraordinary strength of economic growth in the third quarter of this year. GDP rose 4.7 per cent in the three months to September. Spending has also been fuelled since June by the tax cuts announced in this year's Budget feeding through to pay packets.

Source: adapted from the *Financial Times*, 22.10.1988; CSO, *Monthly Digest of Statistics*.

1. **Using a diagram, explain how a Keynesian model of consumption would explain the rise in consumer spending described in the data.**

61 The consumption and savings functions

Summary

1. A movement along the consumption function line shows the effect on consumption of a change in income. A shift in the line is caused by a change in variables other than income which determine the autonomous level of consumption.
2. Increases in wealth will lead to an increase in consumption.
3. Expected inflation tends to lead to a rise in saving and a fall in consumption. The effect of households attempting to restore the real value of their stock of savings more than outweighs the effect of households bringing forward their purchases of goods.
4. The rate of interest and the availability of credit particularly affect the consumption of durable goods.
5. A change in the structure of the population will affect both consumption and saving. The greater the proportion of adults aged 35-60 in the population, the higher is likely to be the level of saving.
6. Keynesians hypothesise that consumption is a stable function of current disposable income in the short run.
7. The life cycle hypothesis and the permanent income hypothesis both emphasise that consumption is a stable function of income only in the very long run. In the short run, other factors such as the rate of interest and wealth can have a significant impact upon consumption and savings.

The consumption function

The simple Keynesian consumption function (☞ unit 60) explained the relationship between planned consumption and disposable income. This can be expressed in the equation:

$$C = a + bY$$

where:
- a is the **autonomous element** which does not vary with disposable income;
- bY is the **induced element** which varies directly with disposable income (b is the marginal propensity to consume;
- C is planned consumption;
- Y is income.

A change in income is shown by a **movement along** the consumption function, for instance from point A to point B in Figure 61.1. A change in the autonomous element of consumption will lead to a **shift** in the function. In Figure 61.1, the consumption function shifts upwards from C_1 to C_2. This has been caused by an increase in autonomous consumption from a_1 to a_2.

There are a number of factors apart from income which determine the level of planned consumption in the economy (i.e. which determine the level of autonomous consumption).

Wealth

The wealth of a household is made up of two parts. **Physical wealth** is made up of items such as houses, cars and furniture. **Monetary wealth** comprises items such as cash, money in the bank and building societies, stocks and shares, assurance policies and pension rights.

If the wealth of a household increases, consumption will increase. This is known as the WEALTH EFFECT. There are two important ways in which the wealth of households can change over a short time period.

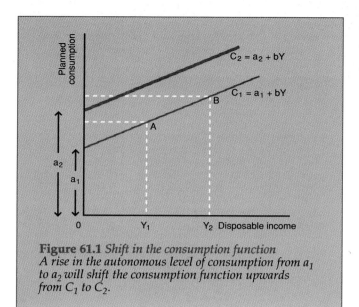

Figure 61.1 *Shift in the consumption function*
A rise in the autonomous level of consumption from a_1
to a_2 will shift the consumption function upwards
from C_1 to C_2.

- A change in the price of houses. If the real price of houses increases considerably over a short period of time, as happened in the UK from 1985 to 1988, then households feel able to increase their spending. They do this mainly by borrowing more money secured against the value of their house.
- A change in the value of stocks and shares. Households react to an increase in the real value of a household's portfolio of securities by selling part of the portfolio and spending the proceeds. The value of stocks and shares is determined by many factors. One of these is the rate of interest. If the rate of interest falls, then the value of stocks will rise (☞ unit 67). So consumption should be stimulated through the wealth effect by a fall in the rate of interest.

QUESTION 1 In January 1988, Dixons the electrical retailing chain, reported lower profits on its UK retailing operations. Like-for-like sales from mid-October 1987 to the end of the calendar year were 8 per cent down on the same period a year previously. Mr Stanley Kalms, the chairman, put the blame firmly on the October stock market crash. The crash of October 1987 had wiped out about 25 per cent of the value of the UK stock market.

(a) Why might consumption be affected by changes in the value of shares on world stock markets?
(b) Suggest reasons why a group like Dixons was badly affected whilst a retailer like Tesco or Sainsbury's saw no change in its sales over the same period.

Inflation

Inflation, a rise in the general level of prices, has two effects on consumption. Firstly, if households expect prices to be higher in the future they will be tempted to bring forward their purchases. For instance, if households know that the price of cars will go up by 10 per cent the next month, they will attempt to buy their cars now. So expectations of inflation increase consumption and reduce saving.

However, this seems to be more than outweighed by the effect of inflation on wealth. Rising inflation tends to erode the real value of money wealth. Households react to this by attempting to restore the real value of their wealth (i.e. they save more). This reduces consumption.

Overall, rising inflation tends to reduce consumption. The negative effect on consumption caused by the erosion of real wealth more than offsets the positive effect on consumption caused by the bringing forward of purchases.

The rate of interest

Households rarely finance expenditure on **non-durables** such as food or entertainment by borrowing money. However, much of the money to buy **durables** such as cars, furniture, kitchen equipment and hi-fi equipment comes from credit finance. An increase in the rate of interest increases the monthly repayments on these goods. This means that, effectively, the price of the goods has increased. Households react to this by reducing their demand for durables and thus cutting their consumption.

Many households also have borrowed money to buy their house. Increased interest rates lead to increased mortgage repayments. Again, this will directly cut spending on other items and perhaps, more importantly, discourage households from borrowing more money to finance purchases of consumer durables.

It has already been explained above that a rise in the rate of interest reduces the value of stocks on stock markets and thus reduces the value of household wealth. This in turn leads to a fall in consumption.

The availability of credit

The rate of interest determines the price of credit. However, the price of credit is not the only determinant of how much households borrow. Governments in the past have often imposed restrictions on the availability of credit. For instance, they have imposed maximum repayment periods and minimum deposits. Before the deregulation of the mortgage market in the early 1980s in the UK, building societies rationed mortgages. They often operated queueing systems and imposed restrictive limits on the sums that could be borrowed. When these restrictions are abolished, households increase their level of debt and spend the proceeds. Making credit more widely available will increase consumption.

QUESTION 2 Consumers have proved impervious to the effects of high interest rates, according to the latest City interpretations of the present trend of high borrowing costs and buoyant spending.

This is a marked shift in behaviour from the mid-1970s, when high rates of inflation were associated with negative real interest rates and subdued consumer spending.

Credit control and inflation forced home owners to save in order to meet interest payments. Those with funds on deposit had to save more to offset the erosion of the real value of their money.

In the 1980s the absence of credit controls has allowed consumers to accumulate debt, not savings, say economists from the London Business School and Shearson Lehman Hutton, the securities house.

A January Gallup survey indicated that the 1980s trend was set to continue. The 1990s had begun with a 'worrying bounce' in consumer confidence. It also showed that people were more willing to buy consumer durables.

Other City analysts are less certain. Flemings Research says that the engine of the consumer boom - vehicles, durables, luxury goods and services - has had its fuel supply cut off by high interest rates.

Source: *Financial Times*, 29.1.1990.

With the aid of a diagram, explain the different influences upon consumption and saving during the 1970s and 1980s.

Expectations

Expectations of increases in prices tend to make households bring forward their purchases and thus increase consumption. Expectations of large increases in real incomes will also tend to encourage households to increase spending now by borrowing more. So when the economy is booming, autonomous consumption tends to increase. On the other hand, if households expect economic conditions to become harsher, they will reduce their consumption now. For instance, they might expect an increase in unemployment rates, a rise in taxes or a fall in real wages.

The composition of households

Young people and old people tend to have higher APCs than those in middle age. Young people tend to spend all their income and move into debt to finance the setting up of their homes and the bringing up of children. In middle age, the cost of homemaking declines as a proportion of income. With more income available, households often choose to build up their stock of savings in preparation for retirement. When they retire, they will run down their stock of savings to supplement their pensions. So if there is a change in the age composition of households in the

economy, there could well be a change in consumption and savings. The more young and old the households, the greater will tend to be the level of consumption.

QUESTION 3 Japan's population is ageing at a much faster rate than that of the UK. In 1990, for every person aged 65+ there were 4.4 workers in the UK but 6.2 workers in Japan. A far greater proportion of Japanese workers is middle aged and soon they will be retiring in large numbers. It is estimated that by the year 2010 there will only 3.4 workers per person aged 65+ in Japan whilst the ratio in the UK will have risen slightly to 4.5. In 1990, the UK personal savings ratio was under 5 per cent. In contrast, the Japanese personal savings ratio was over 20 per cent.

(a) What might account for the difference in savings ratios between Japan and the UK?
(b) What is likely to happen to the savings ratios in the two countries over the next 20 years?

Autonomous savings

Factors which affect consumption also by definition must affect saving (remember, saving is defined as that part of disposable income which is not consumed). In recent years, there has been a considerable change in the average propensity to save in the UK. The main factors which seem to have affected savings over the period seem to have been interest rates, the level of inflation and changes in the composition of households.

The Keynesian consumption function

The Keynesian consumption function lays stress upon the relationship between planned current consumption and current disposable income. Other factors, particularly the availability of credit, can have an important impact upon expenditure on consumer durables. However, in the short term at least, income is the most significant factor determining the level of consumption. Changes in wealth and changes in the rate of interest (the two can be interrelated as argued above) have little impact upon short term consumption. This means that the consumption function is relatively stable. It is not subject to frequent large scale shifts.

A straight line consumption function will give a constant marginal propensity to consume (☞ unit 60), but it could be argued that the MPC falls as income rises (i.e. the consumption function is curved and not straight). Keynes himself was worried that increasing prosperity would lead to a stagnant economy. As households became better off, they would spend less and less of their increases in income. Eventually their demand for consumer goods would be completely satiated and without increases in spending, there could be no more increases in income.

The evidence of the past 40 years has proved Keynes wrong. There does not seem to be any indication that households are reducing their MPCs as income increases. However, this view has also led Keynesians to argue that higher income earners have a lower MPC (and therefore save a higher proportion of their income) than low income earners. Therefore, redistributing income from the poor to the rich will lower total consumption. The reverse, taking from the rich to give to the poor, will increase total consumption. But as we shall now see, this too seems to be contradicted not only by the evidence but also by alternative theories of the consumption function.

QUESTION 4
Table 61.1

£ billion at 1985 prices

	Consumption	Income
1948	92.4	93.2
1949	93.9	95.5
1958	113.7	118.7
1959	118.6	124.7
1968	151.0	164.0
1969	152.0	165.6
1978	186.8	210.0
1979	194.9	222.0
1988	259.9	271.3
1989	269.8	284.3

Source: adapted from CSO, *Economic Trends Annual Supplement*; CSO, *Monthly Digest of Statistics.*

(a) Calculate (i) the APC and (ii) the MPC for 1949, 1959, 1969, 1979 and 1989.
(b) How have the values of the APC and MPC changed over time? How might economic theory account for this?

The life cycle hypothesis

Franco Modigliani and Albert Ando suggested that current consumption is not based upon current income. Rather, households form a view about their likely income over the whole of their lifetimes and base their current spending decisions upon that. For instance, professional workers at the start of their careers in their early 20s may earn as much as manual workers of the same age. But the APC of professional workers is likely to be higher. This is because professional workers expect to earn more in the future and are prepared to borrow more now to finance consumption. A professional worker will expect, for instance, to buy rather than rent a house. The mortgage she takes out is likely to be at the top end of what banks or building societies will lend. The manual worker, on the other hand, knowing that his earnings are unlikely to increase substantially in the future, will be more cautious. He may be deterred from buying his own home and, if he does, will take out a small rather than large mortgage.

During middle age, households tend to be net savers. They are paying off loans accumulated when they were younger and saving for retirement. During retirement they spend more than they earn, running down their savings.

The permanent income hypothesis

Developed by Milton Friedman, this in many ways develops the insights of the life cycle hypothesis. Friedman argued that households base their spending decisions not on current income but on their PERMANENT INCOME. Broadly speaking, permanent income is average income over a lifetime.

Average income over a lifetime can be influenced by a number of factors.
■ An increase in wealth will increase the ability of households to spend money (i.e. it will increase their permanent income). Hence a rise in wealth will increase actual consumption over a lifetime.
■ An increase in interest rates tends to lower both stock and share prices. This leads to a fall in wealth, a fall in permanent income and a fall in current consumption.
■ An increase in interest rates also leads to future incomes being less valuable. One way of explaining this is to remember that a sum of money available in the future is worth less than the same sum available today (☞ unit 53 for a full explanation). Another way is to consider borrowing. If interest rates rise, households will need either to earn more money or cut back on their spending in the future to pay back their loans. Therefore, the real value of their future income (i.e. their permanent income) falls if interest rates rise.
■ Unexpected rises in wages will lead to an increase in permanent income.

Friedman argued that the long run APC from permanent income was 1. Households spend all their income over their lifetimes (indeed, Friedman defined permanent income as the income a household could spend without changing its wealth over a lifetime). Hence, the long run APC and the MPC are stable.

In the short run, however, wealth and interest rates change. Measured income also changes and much of this change is unexpected. Income which households receive but did not expect to earn is called **transitory income**. Initially, transitory income will be saved, as households decide what to do with the money. Then it is incorporated into permanent income. The MPC of the household will depend upon the nature of the extra income. If the extra income is for instance a permanent pay rise, the household is likely to spend most of the money. If, however, it is a temporary rise in income, like a £10 000 win on the pools, most of it will be saved and then gradually spent over a much longer period of time. Because the proportion of transitory income to current income changes from month to month, the propensity to consume from current income will vary too. So in the short run, the APC and the MPC are not constant. This contradicts the Keynesian hypothesis that current consumption is a stable function of current income.

Key terms

Wealth effect - the change in consumption following a change in wealth.
Permanent income - the income a household could spend over its lifetime without reducing the value of its assets. This approximates to the average income of a household over its lifetime.

Applied economics

The UK consumption and saving functions

In the applied economics section in unit 60, it was explained that the APC has been reasonably constant over the post war-period, declining slightly in the 1950s, 1960s and 1970s, but proving more volatile in the 1980s. Because savings are so small in relation to consumption and income, the APS has fluctuated in percentage terms considerably more than the APC. These fluctuations have been particularly significant in the 1980s. There are a number of possible explanations why the APC rose and the APS fell over the period 1980 to 1988 before falling and rising respectively in 1989 as shown in Figure 61.2.

Wealth Between 1980 and 1988, average house prices increased at record rates. After this period, the property market in the South of England collapsed. The rise in property prices resulted in a substantial increase in the wealth of the private sector. Individuals responded by borrowing against the increased value of their properties leading to a rise in the APC and therefore a fall in the APS. Important but probably less significant was the impact of the bull market in shares between 1980 and 1987 which again led to large increases in the wealth of individuals.

Inflation Inflation erodes the value of real wealth. Hence it is argued that high inflation will increase the APS as households save more to restore the real value of their wealth. Inflation peaked in 1980 at 18 per cent before falling to 3 per cent in 1986 as shown in Figure 61.2. This fall in inflation may help account for the fall in the APS. The subsequent rise in inflation from 1987 may account for the upturn in the APS in 1989.

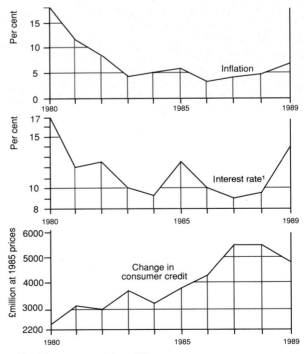

1. Bank base rates at June 30.
Source: adapted from CSO, *Economic Trends Annual Supplement; Monthly Digest of Statistics.*

Figure 61.2 *The consumption and savings functions*

The rate of interest It is difficult to see any correlation between the rate of interest and the savings ratio in Figure 61.2. Neo-classical theory suggests that rises in the rate of interest should lead to an increase in saving and a reduction in borrowing. High interest rates from 1988 onwards were certainly an important factor in bursting the property market bubble and hence might have had an indirect effect on consumption and saving.

The availability of credit The deregulation of mortgage lending in the mid-1980s undoubtedly enabled consumers to unlock part of the rising value of their houses through higher borrowing. Figure 61.2 shows this growth of consumer credit in the 1980s.

1989 showed a fall in this change, possibly caused by the higher interest rates of the late 1980s. This fall again could partially explain the fall in the APC and the rise in the APS.

The age of the population The life cycle hypothesis suggests that consumption and saving patterns change over an individual's lifetime. For instance, 45-64 year olds will be the significant savers in the economy as they put aside money for their retirement. The number of 45-64 year olds in the population declined from 12.3m in 1981 to 12.2m in 1989 at a time when the total population increased from 55.1m to 57.2m. This too might help explain the fall in the APS.

Data question

MISERY IN STORE

When a top store like Harrods is forced to lay off 15 of its senior staff, business has to be bad. Just how bad is being hammered home by Britain's shopkeepers this week. In a survey of 310 shopping chains, four in ten retailers told the Confederation of British Industry that they were selling less than a year ago.

The heatwave and transport strikes have both hit hard. But the big squeeze has come from soaring interest rates which have pushed the monthly payments on a £30 000 mortgage up by £57 to £278 since last July.

Harrods spokesman Andrew Wiles said: 'People have not been buying things like furniture, carpets, hi-

fi - expensive items for the home'. Rumbelows is said to have lost more than £10 million following a sharp downturn in sales since last Christmas. It is closing 30 of its 430 shops immediately and a further 30 to 50 are threatened with the axe unless sales improve.

Source: *The Daily Mirror*, 16.8.1989.

1. Explain why the stores mentioned in the data experienced falling sales in 1989.
2. To what extent do you think supermarket chains, such as Sainsbury's or Gateway, experienced a similar fall in sales?

Summary

1. Investment is the purchase of capital goods which are then used to create other goods and services. This differs from saving, which is the creation of financial obligations.
2. The marginal efficiency of capital theory suggests that investment is inversely related to the price of capital - the rate of interest.
3. Factors which shift the MEC or investment demand schedule include changes in the cost of capital goods, technological change, and changes in expectations or animal spirits.
4. The accelerator theory suggests that investment varies with the rate of change in income.
5. The past and current profitability of industry too may be more important than future rates of return on capital in determining current investment.

A definition of investment

Economists use the word INVESTMENT in a very precise way. Investment is the addition to the **capital stock** of the economy - factories, machines, offices and stocks of materials, used to produce other goods and services.

In everyday language, 'investment' and 'saving' are often used to mean the same thing. For instance, we talk about 'investing in the building society' or 'investing in shares'. For an economist, these two would be examples of saving. For an economist, investment only takes place if real products are created. To give two more examples:

■ putting money into a bank account would be saving; the bank buying a computer to handle your account would be investment;

■ buying shares in a new company would be saving; buying new machinery to set up a company would be investment.

A distinction can be made between **gross** and **net** investment. The value of the capital stock depreciates over time as it wears out and is used up. This is called **depreciation** or **capital consumption**. Gross investment measures investment before depreciation, whilst net investment is gross investment less the value of depreciation. Depreciation in recent years in the UK has accounted for about three-quarters of gross investment. So only about one-quarter of gross investment represents an addition to the capital stock of the economy.

Another distinction made is between investment in **physical capital** and **human capital**. Investment in human capital is investment in the education and training of workers. Investment in physical capital is investment in factories etc.

Investment is made both by the public sector and the private sector. Public sector investment is constrained by complex political considerations. In the rest of this unit, we will consider the determinants of private sector investment in physical capital.

Marginal efficiency of capital theory

Firms invest in order to make a profit. The profitability of investment projects varies. Some will make a high **rate of return** (☞ unit 53), some will yield a low rate of return and others will result in losses for the company. The rate of return on an investment project is also known as the **marginal efficiency of capital** (☞ unit 54).

At any point in time in the economy as whole, there exists a large number of possible individual investment projects. Table 62.1 shows an economy where there are £4bn of investment projects with an MEC of 20 per cent

QUESTION 1

From the photograph, give examples of: (a) past investment in physical capital; (b) past investment in human capital; (c) saving; (d) capital consumption.

Table 62.1 *Planned investment and the marginal efficiency of capital*

Marginal efficiency of capital (% per year)	Planned investment (£bn per year)
20	4
15	8
10	12
5	16

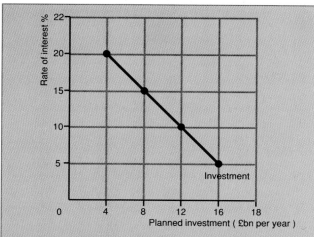

Figure 62.1 *The planned investment schedule*
A fall in the rate of interest will make more investment
projects profitable. Planned investment will rise if the rate of
interest falls.

and above, £8bn with an MEC of 15 per cent and above
and so on. How much of this investment takes place will
depend upon the rate of interest in the economy. If the
rate of interest is 20 per cent, then firms having to borrow
money will make a loss if they undertake any project with
an MEC of less than 20 per cent. Hence, planned
investment will be £4bn. If, on the other hand, the rate of
interest is 5 per cent, then all investment projects with an
MEC of 5 per cent or more will be profitable. Hence,
planned investment will be £16bn. So the conclusion of
marginal efficiency of capital theory is that planned
investment in the economy will rise if the rate of interest
falls. This relationship, using the figures from Table 62.1,
is shown in Figure 62.1.

In our explanation above, the rate of interest was
assumed to be the rate of interest at which firms have to
borrow money. However, most investment by firms in
the UK is financed from **retained profit** (☞ unit 22). This
does not alter the relationship between the rate of interest
and investment. Firms which keep back profits have a
choice about what to do with the money. They can either
invest it or save it. The higher the rate of interest on
savings, such as placing the money on loan with banks or
other financial institutions, the more attractive saving the

money becomes and the less attractive becomes
investment. Put another way, the higher the rate of
interest, the higher the **opportunity cost** of investment
and hence the lower will be the amount of planned
investment in the economy.

Factors which shift the planned investment schedule

Cost of capital goods If the price of capital goods rises,
then the expected rate of return on investment projects
will fall if firms cannot pass on the increase in higher
prices. So increases in the price of capital goods, all other
things being equal, will reduce planned investment. This
is shown by a shift to the left in the planned investment
schedule in Figure 62.2.

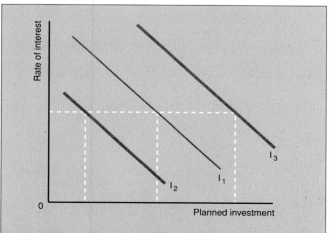

Figure 62.2 *Shifts in planned investment*
An increase in the cost of planned capital will reduce the
rate of return on investment projects. Therefore at any
given rate of interest, planned investment will fall. This is
shown by a shift to the left in the planned investment
schedule. Changes in technology which make capital more
productive raise the level of planned investment, shown by a
shift to the right of the schedule.

Technological change Technological change will make
new capital equipment more productive than previous
equipment. This will raise the rate of return on
investment projects, all other things being equal. Hence,
technological change such as the introduction of
computer aided machinery will raise the level of planned
investment at any given rate of interest. This is shown by
a shift to the right in the planned investment schedule.

Expectations Businesses have to form views about the
future. When calculating the possible rate of return on
future investment, they have to make assumptions about
future costs and future revenues. If managers become
more pessimistic about the future, they will expect the
rate of return on investment projects to fall and hence
planned investment will be reduced. If, on the other

hand, they become more optimistic their expectations of the rates of return on investment projects will tend to rise. Hence planned investment will rise and this will be shown by a shift to the right in the investment schedule. Keynes called the expectations of businessmen their 'animal spirits'. He believed that expectations were crucial in determining changes in investment, and that these expectations could change suddenly.

Government policy Government can play a crucial role in stimulating private sector investment. This will be discussed in more detail in units 98 and 99.

QUESTION 3 Assume Figure 62.2 shows the planned investment schedule for the UK. Is it more likely to shift to I_2 or I_3 if: (a) there is a rise in the real prices of commercial property; (b) the government announces a billion pound programme to encourage the use of micro-computers in industry; (c) the economy grew much faster than expected last year and forecasts show this set to continue; (d) the price of computers and computer aided tools falls; (e) the New York Stock Exchange crashes?

The accelerator theory

The ACCELERATOR THEORY of investment suggests that the level of planned investment varies with the rate of change of income or output rather than with the rate of interest.

To see why this might be the case, consider Table 62.2. A firm producing toys needs one machine to produce £1m of output per year. The machines last 20 years and for the purpose of this example we will assume that none of the firm's machines need replacing over the time period being considered (so we are considering net and not gross investment). Initially in year 1 the firm has £10m worth of orders. It already has 10 machines and therefore no investment takes place. In year 2, orders remain unchanged and so again the firm has no need to invest. However, in year 3 orders increase to £12m. The firm now needs to invest in another two machines if it is to fulfil orders. Orders increase to £15m in year 4. The firm needs to purchase another 3 machines to increase its capital stock to 15 machines. In year 5, orders remain unchanged at £15m and so investment returns to zero. In year 6, orders decline to £14m. The firm has too much

capital stock and therefore does not invest.

In this example investment takes place when there is a change in spending in the economy. If there is no change in spending, then there is no investment. What is more, the changes in spending lead to much bigger changes in investment. For instance, the increase in spending of 25 per cent in year 4 (from £12m to £15m) resulted in an increase in investment of 50 per cent (from 2 machines to 3 machines). In reality, it should be remembered that about 75 per cent of gross investment is replacement investment which is far less likely than net investment to be affected by changes in income. Even so, the accelerator theory predicts that investment spending in the economy is likely to be more volatile than spending as a whole.

The simplest form of the accelerator theory can be expressed as:

$$I_t = a (Y_t - Y_{t-1})$$

where I_t is investment in time period t, $Y_t - Y_{t-1}$ is the change in income during year t and a is the accelerator coefficient or CAPITAL-OUTPUT RATIO. The capital-output ratio is the amount of capital needed in the economy to produce a given quantity of goods. So if £10 of capital is needed to produce £2 of goods, then the capital-output ratio is 5. The theory therefore predicts that changes in the level of investment are related to past changes in income.

This accelerator model is very simplistic. There are a number of factors which limit the predictive power of the model.

- The model assumes that the capital-output ratio is constant over time. However, it can change. In the long term, new technology can make capital more productive. In the shorter term, the capital-output ratio is likely to be higher in a recession when there is excess capacity than in a boom.
- Expectations may vary. Businesses may choose not to satisfy extra demand if they believe that the demand will be short lived. There is little point in undertaking new investment if the extra orders will have disappeared within six months. On the other hand, businesses may anticipate higher output. Despite constant income, they may believe that a boom is imminent and invest to be ahead of their rivals.
- Time lags involved are likely to be extremely complicated. Changes in investment are likely to respond to changes in income over several time periods and not just one.
- Firms may have excess capacity (i.e. they can produce more with current levels of capital than they are at present doing). If there is an increase in income, firms will respond not by investing but by bringing back into use capital which has been mothballed or by utilising fully equipment which had been underutilised.
- The capital goods industry will be unable to satisfy a surge in demand. Some investment will therefore either be cancelled or delayed.

Despite these qualifications, evidence suggests that net

Table 62.2

Year	Annual output £m	Number of machines required	Investment in machines
1	10	10	0
2	10	10	0
3	12	12	2
4	15	15	3
5	15	15	0
6	14	14	0

investment is to some extent linked to past changes in income. However, the link is relatively weak and therefore other influences must be at work to determine investment.

Profits

About 70 per cent of industrial and commercial investment in the UK is financed from retained profit. Some economists argue that many firms do not consider the opportunity cost of investment. They retain profit but rarely consider that it might be better used saved in financial assets. They automatically assume that the money will be spent on investment related to the activities of the firm. The rate of interest is then much less important in determining investment. Investment becomes crucially dependent upon two factors.

■ The amount of retained profit available. So the poor investment record of companies in the UK in the 1970s, for instance, was a direct reflection of their inability to generate profits needed to plough back into their operations.

■ The availability of suitable investment projects. If firms do not have suitable investment projects to hand, they will bank the cash or pay it out to shareholders in dividends. New technology or new products can act as a spur to investment on this view.

Key terms

Investment - the addition to the capital stock of the economy.
Accelerator theory - the theory that the level of planned investment is related to past changes in income.
Capital-output ratio - the ratio between the amount of capital needed to produce a given quantity of goods and the level of output.

Applied economics

Investment in the UK

The composition of investment

Gross investment is called **gross domestic fixed capital formation** (GDFCF) in UK official statistics. Figure 62.3 shows the composition of investment in 1979 and 1989. Significant changes in this composition are apparent from the data. Whilst investment in private sector housing has grown, public sector housing investment, mainly council housing, has fallen (in line with government policy to promote wider home ownership). Expenditure on vehicles, ships and aircraft has remained static and therefore their share of total investment has fallen over the period. On the other hand, investment expenditure on plant and machinery and other new buildings and works has increased.

Table 62.3 shows how the composition of investment has changed by industry. Between 1979 and 1988, gross investment grew faster than GDP, raising the percentage of GDP allocated to investment from 20 per cent to 22 per cent. However, within this total, there are striking differences. Manufacturing investment has barely changed over the ten year period, in contrast with significant increases in many service industries. Banking and finance in particular saw a large increase. Even if we take the period 1981 to 1988, starting at the bottom of the severe recession of the early 1980s, manufacturing investment increased by only 56 per cent, considerably less than the average for service

Table 62.3 *GDP and gross domestic fixed capital formation by industry*

	£ million, at 1985 prices			% change
	1979	1981	1988	1979 - 88
GDP at factor cost	248 057	275 073	347 695	+22
Total GDFCF of which	56 450	48 298	77 302	+37
Agriculture, forestry and fishing	1 358	1 043	889	-35
Extraction of mineral oil and natural gas	3 010	3 196	1 870	-38
Manufacturing	10 136	6 579	10 271	+1
Distribution, hotels and catering, repairs	4 547	3 760	7 467	+64
Communication	1 749	1 749	3 690	+111
Banking, finance, insurance and business services	3 573	4 229	11 078	+210

Source: adapted from CSO, *United Kingdom National Accounts (Blue Book)*.

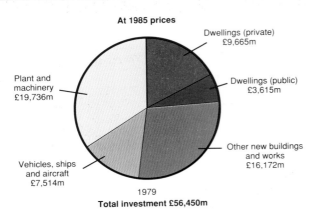

At 1985 prices

Dwellings (private)
£9,665m

Dwellings (public)
£3,615m

Plant and
machinery
£19,736m

Other new buildings
and works
£16,172m

Vehicles, ships
and aircraft
£7,514m

1979
Total investment £56,450m

Dwellings (private)
£11,140m

Dwellings (public)
£2,881m

Plant and
machinery
£32,733m

Other new buildings
and works
£22,388m

Vehicles, ships
and aircraft
£7,876m

1989
Total investment £79,418m[1]

1. Figures do not add up to the total because of a statistical adjustment.
Source: adapted from CSO, *Economic Trends Annual Supplement*; CSO *Monthly Digest of Statistics*.

Figure 62.3 *Gross domestic capital formation by type of asset 1979 and 1989*

sector industries. This difference in investment performance is a significant factor in explaining the process of **deindustrialisation** (☞ unit 59) in the UK in the 1980s.

The determinants of investment

Economic theory suggests that there may be several determinants of private sector investment. The accelerator theory suggests that investment is a function of past changes in income. Neo-classical theory argues that the rate of interest is the important determinant, whilst other theories point to the current level of profits as significant.

The evidence tends to support the idea that the level of investment is determined by a number of variables. In Table 62.4, there is some superficial correlation between investment and changes in income, profits and the rate of interest. However, it should be remembered that these variables may move together through the business cycle (☞ unit 83) and that changes in investment may in themselves affect the three variables in the data.

Table 62.4 *Determinants of investment*

	£ million, at 1985 prices			Per cent
	Private sector investment	Annual change in GDP	Company profits	Interest rate1
1979	40 268	7 650	47 934	13.0
1980	38 577	-5 976	38 614	13.8
1981	35 990	-3 000	34 333	14.7
1982	38 892	4 862	36 925	12.9
1983	39 085	10 080	44 263	10.8
1984	43 872	5 107	47 384	10.7
1985	47 987	11 514	52 572	10.6
1986	49 210	10 107	47 056	9.9
1987	55 542	13 853	56 846	9.5
1988	65 429	15 410	63 014	9.4
1989	67 713	7 235	58 707	10.0

1. British government securities: long dated 20 years: average of working days.
Source: adapted from CSO, *Economic Trends Annual Supplement*; CSO, *Monthly Digest of Statistics*.

INVESTMENT IN THE ALUMINIUM INDUSTRY

According to a report by Alan Bird Associates (1990), the low price of aluminium in late 1989, following a 2½ year fall in price, could seriously jeopardise investment in the industry. If low prices of about $1 500 a tonne were maintained in the medium term, marginal smelters would be closed and there would be a wave of cancellations of new projects.

However, aluminium producers believed that prices

would rise. Current consumption exceeded production and producers were drawing upon their stocks to satisfy demand. Consumption was expected to grow by at least 2-3 per cent per annum in the early 1990s.

1. **Explain, using diagrams, what factors might determine investment in the aluminium industry.**

Summary

1. Economic growth is the change in potential output of the economy shown by a shift to the right of the production possibility frontier. Economic growth is usually measured by the change in real national income.
2. Economic growth is caused by increases in the quantity or quality of land, labour and capital and by technological progress.
3. It is sometimes argued that growth is unsustainable because of the law of diminishing returns. Because land in particular is fixed in supply, diminishing returns will set in. However, most natural resources are not in fixed supply and historical evidence suggests that all factors are variable over time.
4. If all factors of production are variable over time, economies of scale could well be present. Advances in technology in particular may allow economies to grow at even faster rates in the future.

Definition

Economies change over time. One way of measuring this is the rate of change of national income. National income is a measure of how much an economy produces over time. Economists define economic growth as the rate of growth of national income. In practice, national income can be measured in many ways, but growth statistics tend to be presented in terms of either a change in GDP or GNP. Growth must be measured in **real** terms because it is the change in the volume of goods and services that we are attempting to measure and not their monetary value.

The production possibility frontier

Production possibility frontiers (PPFs) can be used to discuss economic growth. The PPF shows the maximum or **potential** output of an economy (☞ unit 1). When the economy grows, the PPF will move outward as in Figure 63.1. A movement from A to C would be classified as economic growth. However, there may be unemployment in the economy. With a PPF passing through C, a movement from B (where there is unemployment) to C (full employment) would be classified as **economic recovery** rather than economic growth. Hence, an increase in national income does not necessarily mean that there has been economic growth. In practice it is difficult to know exactly the location of an economy's PPF and therefore economists tend to treat all increases in GNP as economic growth.

Figure 63.1 can also be used to show the conflict between investment and consumption. One major source of economic growth is investment. All other things being

equal, the greater the level of investment the higher will be the rate of growth in the future. However, increased production of investment goods can only be achieved by a reduction in the production of consumption goods if the economy is at full employment. So there is a trade off to be made between consumption now and consumption in the future. The lower the level of consumption today relative to the level of investment, the higher will be the level of consumption in the future.

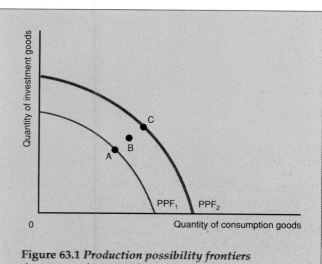

Figure 63.1 Production possibility frontiers
A movement from A to C would represent economic growth if there were a shift in the production possibility frontier from PPF₁ to PPF₂. A movement from B to C would represent economic recovery if the production possibility frontier were PPF₂.

QUESTION 1

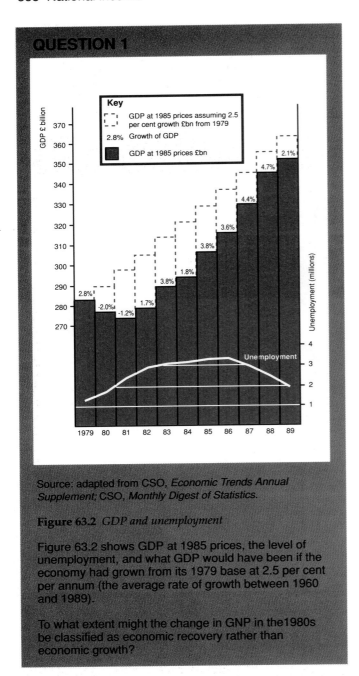

Source: adapted from CSO, *Economic Trends Annual Supplement*; CSO, *Monthly Digest of Statistics*.

Figure 63.2 *GDP and unemployment*

Figure 63.2 shows GDP at 1985 prices, the level of unemployment, and what GDP would have been if the economy had grown from its 1979 base at 2.5 per cent per annum (the average rate of growth between 1960 and 1989).

To what extent might the change in GNP in the 1980s be classified as economic recovery rather than economic growth?

The causes of economic growth

National output can be increased if there is an increase in the quantity or quality of the inputs to the production process. Output can also be increased if existing inputs are used more efficiently. This can be expressed in terms of a **production function** (☞ unit 17):

Output = f (land, labour, capital, technical progress, efficiency)

The remainder of this unit will concentrate on the ways in which the quantity and quality of the factors of production can be increased and on what determines technical progress.

Land

Different countries possess different endowments of land. Land in economics is defined as all natural resources, not just land itself. Some countries, such as Saudi Arabia, have experienced large growth rates almost solely because they are so richly endowed. Without oil, Saudi Arabia today would almost certainly be a poor Third World country. Other countries have received windfalls. The UK, for instance, only started to exploit its oil resources in the mid 1970s. Today oil contributes about 3 per cent of GNP. However, most economists argue that the exploitation of raw materials is unlikely to be a significant source of growth in developed economies, although it can be vital in developing economies.

Labour

Increasing the number of workers in an economy should lead to economic growth. Increases in the labour force can result from three factors.

■ Changes in demography. If more young people enter the workforce than leave it, then the size of the workforce will increase. In most western developed countries the population is relatively stable. Indeed many countries will experience falls in the number of young people entering the workforce over the next ten or twenty years because of falls in the birth rate during the late 1960s and 1970s.

■ Increases in participation rates. Nearly all men who wish to work are in the labour force. However, in most Western countries there exists a considerable pool of women who could be brought into the labour force if employment opportunities were present. In the UK, for instance, almost all of the increase in the labour force in the foreseeable future will result from women returning to or starting work.

■ Immigration. A relatively easy way of increasing the labour force is to employ migrant labour.
  Increasing the size of the labour force may increase output but will not necessarily increase economic welfare. One reason is that increased income may have to be shared out amongst more people, causing little or no change in income per person. If women come back to work, they have to give up leisure time to do so. This lessens the increase in economic welfare which they experience.

Increasing the quality of labour input is likely to be far more important in the long run. Labour is not **homogeneous** (i.e. it is not all the same). Workers can be made more productive by education and training. Increases in **human capital** (☞ unit 2) are essential for a number of reasons.

■ Workers need to be sufficiently educated to cope with the demands of the existing stock of capital. For instance, it is important for lorry drivers to be able to read, typists to spell and shop assistants to operate tills. These might seem very low grade skills but it requires a considerable educational input to get most of the population up to these elementary levels.

■ Workers need to be flexible. On average in the UK, workers are likely to have to change job three times during their lifetime. Increasingly workers are being asked to change role within existing jobs. Flexibility requires broad general education as well as in-depth knowledge of a particular task.

■ Workers need to be able to contribute to change. It is easy to see that scientists and technologists are essential if inventions and new products are to be brought to the market. What is less obvious, but as important, is that every worker can contribute ideas to the improvement of techniques of production. An ability of all workers to take responsibility and solve problems will be increasingly important in the future.

wealth in the future. Investment can also be wasted if it takes place in industries which fail to sell products. For instance, investment in shipbuilding plants during the late 1970s and early 1980s provided a poor rate of return because the shipbuilding industry was in decline. Investment must therefore be targeted at growth industries.

QUESTION 2

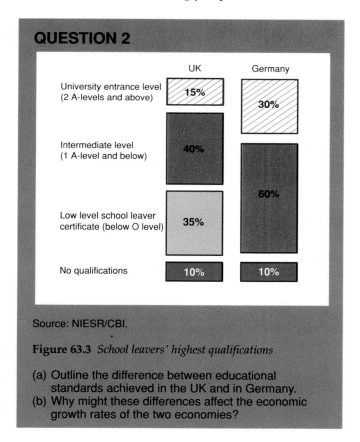

Source: NIESR/CBI.

Figure 63.3 *School leavers' highest qualifications*

(a) Outline the difference between educational standards achieved in the UK and in Germany.
(b) Why might these differences affect the economic growth rates of the two economies?

QUESTION 3

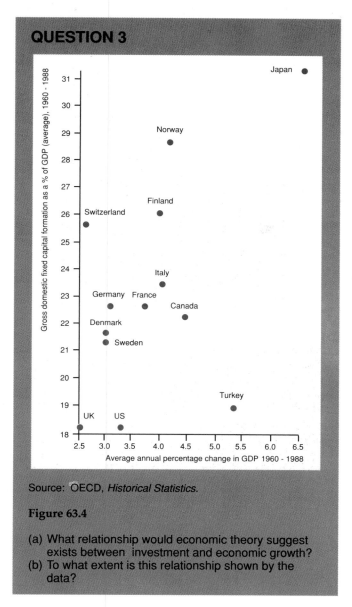

Source: OECD, *Historical Statistics*.

Figure 63.4

(a) What relationship would economic theory suggest exists between investment and economic growth?
(b) To what extent is this relationship shown by the data?

Capital

The stock of capital in the economy needs to increase over time if economic growth is to be sustained. This means that there must be sustained investment in the economy. However, there is not necessarily a correlation between high investment and high growth. Some investment is not growth-related. For instance, investment in new housing or new hospitals is unlikely to create much

Technological progress

Technological progress increases economic growth in two ways.

■ It cuts the average cost of production of a product. For instance, a machine which performed the tasks of a simple scientific calculator was unavailable 100 years ago. 50 years ago, it needed a large room full of expensive equipment to do this. Today it is available for a few pounds.

■ It creates new products for the market. Without new products, consumers would be less likely to spend increases in their income. Without extra spending, there would less or no economic growth.

Diminishing returns and economies of scale

Some economists have argued that growth is unsustainable because of diminishing returns. The **law of diminishing returns** states that if increasing amounts of factors of production are combined with at least one fixed factor, eventually marginal product and then average product will decline. For instance, if more and more painters are put into a room with the same amount of paint and paintbrushes, then very quickly the productivity of each painter added will be less than the last one. Land and labour can be seen as fixed factors. Adding more and more capital will lead to diminishing returns.

Another way of looking at this is to use the concept of the **marginal efficiency of capital** (☞ units 54 and 62). Figure 63.5 shows an economy with a fixed number of investment projects. The more investment projects undertaken, the lower will be the rate of return earned on each project. Eventually the stock of investment projects which yield any positive rate of return will be exhausted. The economy cannot grow any further.

However, it is most unlikely that any factor is fixed. Although the quantity of labour, for instance, might remain unchanged, the quality of labour should increase over time. Equally, land is not fixed. The agricultural industry has had no problems over the past 200 years in steadily increasing the yield per acre in the UK. It has done this partly by increasing the quality of the land input through the use of crop rotation techniques and fertilisers. Evidence suggests that all factors are variable

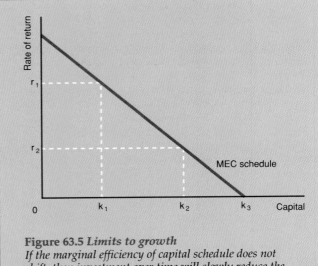

Figure 63.5 Limits to growth
If the marginal efficiency of capital schedule does not shift, then investment over time will slowly reduce the stock of available investment projects. Eventually at k_3 there will be no investment projects left with a positive rate of return and economic growth will stop.

over time.

If this is true, then there may well be economies of scale present. For instance, growth during the inter-war period was higher on average than in Victorian England. Growth since the Second World War has been even higher. Economies of scale could arise, for instance, from the more widespread application of technology across markets. Equally, there is an exponential growth in scientific and technical knowledge. This suggests that the pace of change in production and development of new products will increase at an ever faster rate, allowing countries to enjoy ever faster growth rates. If this is true, then countries which devote a larger proportion of their national income to Research and Development are likely to grow faster than those which lag behind.

Applied economics

Britain's growth rate

Britain's low growth rate

Worries about Britain's growth rate date back over a century. In Edwardian times, for instance, it was not difficult to see the economic advance of Germany and France and compare it with the poor economic performance of the UK economy. Britain's poor growth performance has persisted in the post-war era. As Table 63.1 shows, the UK had the lowest average annual rate of growth between 1960-1988 amongst the seven largest industrial economies of the world (the **Group of Seven** or G7). Having said that, relative UK growth improved in the 1980s and the economy ranked fifth out of seven in this decade. Economists disagree about the causes of the UK's relatively low growth rate

and below only a few major arguments are considered. (A different approach, considering the argument from a free market and interventionist perspective is outlined in unit 103.)

Labour

A number of arguments have been put forward to suggest why the UK lags behind in terms of labour productivity. For instance, one very common argument is that class structures in the UK are much more firmly entrenched than in other countries leading to a 'them and us' attitude. Workers on the one hand see businesses and management as both exploitive and incompetent. They join together in trade unions to

Table 63.1 *Average annual growth rate in GDP, G7 countries 1960-88*

	Year to year percentage changes				
	1960-67	1968-73	1974-79	1980-88	1960-88
United States	4.5	3.2	2.4	2.8	3.3
Japan	10.2	8.7	3.6	4.1	6.5
Germany	4.1	4.9	2.3	1.7	3.1
France	5.4	5.5	2.8	1.9	3.7
United Kingdom	3.0	3.4	1.5	2.2	2.5
Italy	5.7	4.5	3.7	2.4	4.0
Canada	5.5	5.4	2.7	2.8	4.4
Average G7	5.0	4.4	2.7	2.8	3.7

Source: adapted from OECD, *Historical Statistics.*

seek protection from their natural 'class' enemies and have to struggle to secure decent wages and working conditions. Management on the other hand see workers as lazy and greedy, unable to work effectively without proper supervision. Evidence to support this hypothesis ranges from the existence of separate canteen facilities and toilets in places of work to the fact that many top jobs in the country go to people who were educated in privileged public or selective schools, and not in state comprehensive schools with everyone else.

Figures can be produced which suggest that the UK fails to educate and train its workers to a sufficiently high standard. Table 63.2 shows that the UK government spends far less on adult training than her competitors. This is not compensated for by private sector training in the UK. A whole range of statistics, from the numbers staying on in full time education, to results of standardised maths tests, indicate that the UK performs poorly in education and training in comparison with many other industrialised countries, particularly Japan.

An explanation put forward in the 1960s to explain Britain's poor growth record relates to the proportion of workers employed in agriculture. It was argued that continental European countries had grown at a faster rate than the UK because they were able to transfer

Table 63.2 *Publicly-funded training for employed adults in G7 countries.*

	Total expenditure (% of GDP)	Expenditure per trainee (US $)
Japan	0.02	1 000
Germany	0.07	3 500
France	0.04	1 000
United Kingdom	0.01	400
Canada	0.04	2 300
Italy	na	
US	na	

Source: adapted from OECD.

workers from low productivity agriculture to higher productivity manufacturing and service industries. The average proportion of agricultural workers in the total civilian working population was 18.1 per cent in the EC in 1960-7 compared to 4.2 per cent in the UK. By 1980-88, the proportions had fallen to 8.7 per cent and 2.5 per cent respectively, indicating a large shift of workers out of agriculture into other sectors.

Capital

Just as above average increases in levels of human capital are likely, all other things being equal, to lead to above average growth rates, so too are above average increases in levels of physical capital. Table 63.3 shows how the UK has been bottom in the G7 countries throughout the period 1960-88 in terms of investment as a percentage of GDP. The highest investment country, Japan, has equally had the highest level of growth over the period. Whilst there is no direct correlation between investment and economic growth, economic theory would suggest that the low levels of investment in the UK must be a significant factor in explaining the UK's poor growth performance.

A large number of explanations have been advanced as to why the UK invests so little compared to other countries. One relates to the 'short- termism' of the City of London. In continental Europe and Japan, shareholders take a long term view of investment in firms. In both the UK and the US, shareholders are alleged to be interested only in the size of the next dividend payment and the price of the shares in the company today. This results, so it is argued, in UK firms pursuing strategies which maximise short term profits but discourage long term investment, for instance in Research and Development (☞ unit 22). Another argument is that the UK's poor investment record is linked to its low rate of personal saving (☞ unit 103). Whilst it is true that the UK has a lower rate of personal saving than many of its industrial competitors, it is also true that it has a relatively high rate of corporate saving. Companies in the UK have traditionally kept back a significant proportion of their profits for investment purposes.

Table 63.3 *Growth fixed capital formation as a percentage of GDP*

					Per cent
	1960-67	1968-73	1974-79	1980-88	1960-88
United States	18.0	18.4	18.7	17.8	18.2
Japan	31.0	34.6	31.8	29.2	31.4
Germany	25.2	24.4	20.8	20.5	22.7
France	23.2	24.6	23.6	20.4	22.7
United Kingdom	17.7	19.1	19.4	17.2	18.2
Italy	24.9	24.0	24.0	21.4	23.5
Canada	22.6	22.1	21.9	20.6	21.3

Source: adapted from OECD, *Historical Statistics.*

NO MANUFACTURING EXCUSES FOR BRITAIN

Does manufacturing matter? Yes, but it is important to remember that the manufacturing industry we are talking about bears as much relation to the traditional industrial climate of Britain as a Tiger Moth to a Boeing 747. Mass market-wise, we are talking of products that are technologically senile before they emerge, products that may survive three years and products made by people-managed machines, rather than people. Above all, we are talking about products that involve add-on and inbuilt services which, through new automation techniques, can be mass-produced yet tailor-made for the individual as well.

Such products, from the video recorder to the multi-task factory robot, barely existed 10 years ago. Now they account for 42 per cent of the exports from OECD countries and Britain's share so far is small - although British inventiveness and design skills have devised a number of those that are now in the hands of our competitors. Classic 1980s cases of Britain throwing away global research leads through timid investment and lack of a national co-ordinating strategy are the personal computer, the Transputer microchip, and the second-generation industrial robot.

Even if we accept that the UK has no hope of rediscovering a role in mass production, we still need a revolution in management thinking and City investment to succeed at the specialist margins. Price competition isn't the answer. The emphasis must be on increasing added value, based on customised products using multi-technologies.

The track record of the 1980s is appalling. There were scores of British innovations, struggling to emerge. These were scorned by huge industrial combines and finally picked up at bargain basement prices by our amused competitors just as they were ripening. Other second-division nations, from Sweden to Singapore, dodge these predatory pitfalls through long term national strategies, either evolved formally or wheeler-dealed with companies and banks that put patriotism before short term profit. If they can do it, why can't we?

Source: adapted from *The Guardian*, 5.1.1990.

1. Suggest reasons why 'manufacturing matters'.

2. What arguments are put forward in the article that might explain why the UK has had a relatively poor growth performance over the past 40 years?

Summary

1. National income is often used as the main indicator of the standard of living in an economy. A rise in GDP per head is used as an indication of economic growth and a rise in living standards.
2. However, there are many other important components of the standard of living including political freedom, the social and cultural environment, freedom from fear of war and persecution, and the quality of the environment.
3. Economic growth over the past 100 years has transformed the living standards of people in the western world, enabling almost all to escape from absolute poverty.
4. Economic growth is likely to be the only way of removing people in the Third World from absolute poverty.
5. Economic growth has its costs in terms of unwelcome changes in the structure of society.
6. Some believe that future economic growth is unsustainable, partly because of growing pollution and partly because of the exploitation of non-renewable resources.

National income and economic welfare

National income is a measure of the income, output and expenditure of an economy. It is also often used as a measure of the **standard of living**. However, equating national income with living standards is very simplistic because there are many other factors which contribute to the economic welfare of individuals.

Political freedoms We tend to take civil liberties for granted in the UK. But most governments in the world today are totalitarian regimes which rule through fear. In many countries, membership of an opposition party or membership of a trade union can mean death or imprisonment. The freedom to visit friends, to travel and to voice an opinion are likely to be more valuable than owning an extra television or being able to buy another dress.

The social and cultural environment In the UK, we take things such as education for granted. We have some of the world's finest museums and art galleries. We possess a cultural heritage which includes Shakespeare and Constable. The BBC is seen as one of the best broadcasting organisations throughout the world. But we could all too easily live in a cultural desert where the main purpose of television programming might be to sell soap powders and make a profit. Alternatively the arts could be used as political propaganda rather than exist in their own right.

Freedom from fear of violence If a person doesn't feel safe walking the streets or even at home, then no number of microwave ovens or videos will compensate for this loss. Equally, fears of war, arbitrary arrest, imprisonment or torture make material possessions seem relatively unimportant.

The working environment How long and hard people have to work is vital in evaluating standards of living. One reason why the average worker is far better off today than 100 years ago is because his or her working year is likely to be about half the number of hours of his Victorian counterpart's. Equally, the workplace is far safer today than 100 years ago. Industrial accidents were then commonplace and workers received little or no compensation for serious injuries or even death.

The environment Environmental issues are currently at the forefront of people's consciousness. There is a clear understanding that production activities can seriously damage the environment and that in future we may well have to stop consuming certain products if we are to safeguard the environment.

QUESTION 1

Table 64.1

	1971	1988
Minutes necessary to work[1] to pay for		
1 pint fresh milk	5	3
20 cigarettes	22	19
Average daily flow of motor vehicles on UK roads	1 790	2 800
Total attendances at England football league matches	29m	19m
Number of offences notified to police in England and Wales	1.7m	3.7m
Persons divorcing per thousand married people	9.3	24.0
Accidental deaths GB	19 246	12 968
Percentage of dwellings with no inside toilet GB	15	2
Membership of Friends of the Earth	1 000	65 000
Number of clients seen by the Samaritans	87 000	417 000

1. Married couple with husband only working.

Source: adapted from CSO, *Social Trends* 1990.

To what extent do the data indicate that citizens of the UK had higher living standards in 1988 than in 1971?

The growth debate

The rate of economic growth has accelerated historically. Even five hundred years ago, most people would have seen little change in incomes over their lifetime. During Victorian England, the economy grew at about one per cent per annum. Over the past thirty years, the UK economy has grown at an average of just over 2 per cent. But the recent growth performance of the UK, whilst excellent by historical standards, has been low compared to the growth rates of other countries. Japan, after growing at up to 10 per cent per annum in many years after 1945, is still growing at 4-5 per cent. France, Germany and Italy are growing at about 3 per cent per annum.

Growth at these rates over the past 50 years has led to undreamt of prosperity for the citizens of the industrialised world. Consider Table 64.2. It shows by how much £1 will grow over time at different rates. At one per cent growth, income will roughly double over the lifetime of an individual. At 2 per cent, it will quadruple over a lifetime. At 3 per cent, the current growth rates of many continental European countries, it is doubling every twenty five years. At 5 per cent, it only takes about 14 years to double national income. At 10 per cent, it only takes about 7 years to double income.

If recent growth rates are a guide to the future, the average British worker in 30 years' time will earn in real terms twice what he or she is doing today. When they are in their seventies, they can expect workers to earn four times as much as their parents did when they were born.

These increases in income have led to the elimination of **absolute poverty** (☞ unit 41) for most citizens in industrialised countries.

■ Life expectancy has doubled over the past 300 years and infant mortality rates have plummeted.

Table 64.2 *Economic growth rate of £1 over time*

Year	Growth rates				
	1%	2%	3%	5%	10%
0	100	100	100	100	100
5	105	110	116	128	161
10	110	122	130	163	259
25	128	164	203	339	1 084
50	164	269	426	1 147	11 739
75	211	442	891	38 83	127 189
100	271	724	1 870	13 150	1 378 059

QUESTION 2

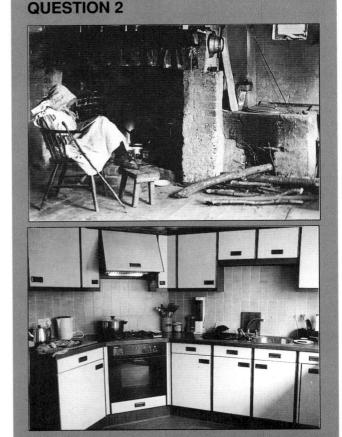

The photographs show a modern kitchen and a kitchen at the turn of the century. To what extent do they show that economic growth has been desirable?

- People have enough to eat and drink. What we eat and drink is nearly always fit for human consumption.
- Housing standards have improved immeasurably.
- Nearly everyone can read and write.

Future increases in income are generally desirable. Very few people would prefer to have less income rather than more income in the future (remember economics assumes that people have **infinite wants**). So economic growth has generally been considered to be highly desirable. Moreover, two-thirds of the world's population do not live in the affluent West. Many who live in the Third World suffer absolute poverty. The only way to eliminate malnutrition, disease, bad housing and illiteracy in these countries is for there to be real economic growth.

Arguments against growth

Despite the apparent benefits, the goal of economic growth has become increasingly questioned in recent years.

One argument is that the increase in national income has been largely fictitious. Three hundred years ago much of the output of the economy was not traded. Women were not on the whole engaged in paid work. Much of the supposed increase in income has come from placing monetary values on what existed already. Much of the increase in income generated by the public sector of the economy comes not from increased production but from increased wages paid to public sector workers who produce the same amount of services. Whilst there is some truth in this, it cannot be denied that material living standards have increased immeasurably over the past three hundred years. People not only consume more goods and services, they have on average far more leisure time.

Another argument is that modern industrialised societies have created large negative **externalities**. For instance, growth has created a large pool of migrant workers, wandering from job to job in different parts of the country. They become cut off from their roots, separated from their families. The result is alienation and loneliness, particularly of the old and the collapse of traditional family values. Crime rates soar, divorce rates increase, stress related illnesses become commonplace and more and more has to be spent on picking up the pieces of a society which is no longer content with what it has.

Supporters of this view tend to look back to some past 'golden age', often agricultural, when people lived mainly in villages as parts of large extended families. However, historical evidence suggests that such a rural paradise never existed. Life for many was short and brutish. Drunkenness was always a problem. Family life was claustrophobic and did not allow for individuality. Most people were dead by the age when people today tend to divorce and remarry.

Perhaps the most serious anti-growth argument is that growth is unsustainable. Consider again Table 64.2. If Western European countries continue to grow at an average 3 per cent per annum then in 25 years' time national income will be twice as large as it is today; in fifty years' time, when an 18 year old student will be retired, it will be over 4 times as large; in 75 years' time, when on current life expectancy figures that student would be dead, it will be nearly 9 times as large; and in 100 years' time it will be nearly 19 times as large. If the average wage in the UK today is £12 000 per annum, then in 100 years' time it will have risen to £355 300 per annum in real terms.

Each extra percent increase in national income uses up **non-renewable resources** such as oil, coal and copper. In the late 1970s, the Club of Rome, a forecasting institute, produced a report called 'The Limits to Growth'. The report claimed that industrialised economies as we know them would collapse. They would be caught between a growth in pollution and a decline in the availability of scarce resources such as oil, coal and timber. Oil was projected to run out in the next century and coal by the year 2 400. In the 1980s, the world was gripped by reports that man was destroying the ozone layer and raising the world's temperature through the greenhouse effect. The planet cannot support growth rates of even 1 or 2 per cent per year. Growth must stop and the sooner the better.

Economic theory suggests that the future may not be as bleak as this picture makes out. In a market economy, growing scarcity of a resource such as oil results in a rise in price. Three things then happen. Firstly demand, and therefore consumption falls: the price mechanism results in conservation. Secondly, it becomes profitable to explore for new supplies of the resource. Known world oil reserves today are higher than they were in 1973 at the time of the first oil crisis! Thirdly, consumers switch to substitute products whilst producers are encouraged to find new replacement products. After the massive rise in oil prices in 1973-4, the world car makers roughly halved the fuel consumption per mile of the average car over a period of ten years through more efficient engines. Brazil developed cars which ran on fuel made from sugar.

Governments too respond to pressures from scientists and the public. The activities of industry are far more regulated today in the western world than they were 30 years ago.

What is worrying, however, is that the market mechanism and governments are frequently slow to act. Governments and markets are not good at responding to pressures which might take decades to build up but only manifest themselves suddenly at the end of that time period. Some scientists have predicted that global warming is now already irreversible. If this is true, the problem that we now face is how to change society to cope with this. There is no clear consensus as to how we could reverse economic growth, consume less, and cope with the coming catastrophe, without creating an economic nightmare with mass starvation.

One point to note is that supporters of the anti-growth lobby tend to be people who are relatively well off. Cutting their consumption by 25 per cent, or producing products through expensive environmentally friendly alternative technologies might not create too much hardship for them. However, leaving the mass of people in the Third World today at their present living standards would mean that they would continue to live in absolute poverty with starvation and death an ever present threat. In the Third World, the struggle for survival is far more important than any environmental concern. Green politics tend to be the preserve of the affluent western middle classes.

Applied economics

The standard of living in the UK since 1900

GDP is often used as the major economic indicator of welfare. Table 64.3 shows that, on this basis, living standards in the UK have risen considerably this century. Between 1900 and 1931, GDP rose 23 per cent and between 1900 and 1989 rose 397 per cent. Population has increased too, but even when this has

Table 64.3

Year	GDP (£bn)	Population (millions)	GDP per head (£)
1901	71.4	38.2	1869
1911	82.3	42.1	1969
1921	72.8	44.0	1655
1931	88.0	46.0	1913
1951	135.9	50.2	2702
1961	178.3	52.7	3383
1971	238.1	55.5	4254
1981	274.3	55.8	4916
1989	354.9	57.1	6215

Source: adapted from CH Feinstein, *National Income, Expenditure and Output in the United Kingdom, 1855-1965* (Cambridge University Press); CSO, *United Kingdom National Accounts (Blue Book)*.

been taken into account, the rise in income per person is impressive.

It is possible to chart a multitude of other ways in which it can be shown that the standard of living of the British family has improved. For instance, 14.2 per cent of children in 1900 died before the age of 1. Today the comparable figure is 0.9 per cent. In 1900, the vast majority of children left school at 12. Today all children stay on till the age of 16, whilst one-third of 17 year olds choose to stay in full time education beyond the statutory school leaving age. In 1900, few people were able to afford proper medical treatment when they fell ill. Today, everyone in the UK has access to the National Health Service.

Table 64.4 illustrates another way in which we are far better off today than a family at the turn of the century. It shows the weekly budget of a manual worker's family in a North Yorkshire iron town, estimated by Lady Bell in her book *At The Works*. The family lived off 7½ home-made loaves of 4lb each

thinly scraped with butter, 4lb of meat and bacon, weak tea, a quart of milk and no vegetables worth mentioning. In 1988, whilst average consumption for five people of bread was only 9.4 lb a week, meat consumption was 11.4lb, vegetable consumption excluding potatoes was 8.7lb and butter, margarine and lard was 2.1lb. Today's diet is far more varied and more ample. Malnutrition, not uncommon in 1900, is virtually unknown in the UK today. The budget in Table 64.4 also says a great deal about the very restricted lifestyle of the average family in 1908. Then, a family would consider itself lucky if it could take a day trip to the seaside. In comparison, 60 per cent of all adults took a holiday of 4 days or more in 1988, and 16 per cent took two or more holidays a year.

Table 64.4

Family budget in 1908
Income 18s 6d family of three

	s.	d.
Rent	5	6
Coals	2	4
Insurance	0	7
Clothing	1	0
Meat	1	6
1 stone flour	1	5
Quarter stone bread meal	0	4½
1lb butter	1	1
Half lb lard	0	2½
1lb bacon	0	9
4 lb sugar	0	8
Half lb tea	0	9
Yeast	0	1
Milk	0	3
1 box Globe polish	0	1
1lb soap	0	3
1 packet Gold Dust	0	1
3 oz tobacco	0	9
Half stone potatoes	0	3
Onions	0	1
Matches	0	1
Lamp oil	0	2
Debt	0	3
Total	18	6

21 million holidays were taken abroad. In 1908, houses were sparsely furnished. The main form of heating was open coal fires: central heating was virtually unknown. Very few houses were wired for electricity. Table 64.4 shows that the typical house was lighted by oil. All the electrical household gadgets we take for granted, from washing machines to vacuum cleaners to televisions, had not been invented. The 1lb of soap in the 1908 budget would have been used to clean clothes, sinks and floors. Soap powders, liquid detergents and floor cleaners were not available. 'Gold Dust' was the popular name for an exceptionally caustic form of shredded yellow soap notorious for its ability to flay the user's hands. Compare that with the numerous brands of mild soaps available today.

Workers worked long hours, six days a week with few holidays, whilst at home the housewife faced a life of drudgery with few labour-saving devices. Accidents were frequent and old age, unemployment and sickness were dreaded and even more so the workhouse, the final destination for those with no means to support themselves.

Ecologically, the smoke-stack industries of industrial areas such as London, the Black Country and Manchester created large scale pollution. The smogs which are found in many cities such as Mexico City and Los Angeles today, were common occurrences in turn-of-the-century Britain. The urban environment was certainly not clean 90 years ago.

Socially and politically, women, who formed over half the population, were not emancipated. In 1900, they did not have the vote, their place was in the home, they were often regarded as biologically inferior to men, and they were debarred from almost all public positions of influence and authority. In many ways, the standard of living of women has improved more than that of men this century because of the repressive attitude held towards women 90 years ago.

Overall, it would be very difficult to look back on 1900 and see it as some golden age. For the vast majority of those in Britain today, the 1990s are a paradise in comparison. However, whilst there might be little absolute poverty today, it could be argued that there is considerable relative poverty. It could also be argued that the poorest today are probably still worse off than the top 5 per cent of income earners in 1900.

Data question

MEASURING ECONOMIC WELFARE

In 1972, William Nordhaus and James Tobin suggested a way of measuring economic welfare. GDP measures output of the economy. In contrast, their proposed Measure of Economic Welfare (MEW) is a measurement of consumption. MEW is calculated by:

- measuring GDP in the traditional way;
- deducting from it expenditure on consumer durables but adding back the value of services given by consumer durables over the year;
- deducting expenditures which give no positive utility but are needed for a property-owning capitalist economy to function effectively - examples are the police, defence, road maintenance and private expenditure such as commuting to work;
- deducting negative externalities such as pollution and congestion;
- adding the value of work which is not marketed such as DIY;
- adding the value of leisure time.

1. Why is GDP only a partial measure of the standard of living?
2. What problems might be encountered in trying to place a monetary value on MEW?

INVESTIGATIONS 5

A. Consumer expenditure

Aims

- To gather appropriate data to investigate the relationship between consumer expenditure, the components of consumer expenditure and their determinants.
- To put forward hypotheses about the relationships between these economic variables.
- To correlate the data collected to establish whether there are any statistical relationships.
- To use these findings to make recommendations concerning business strategies.

The task

You are to assume that you are a private consultancy company. You have been approached by several companies which are seeking to expand their businesses.

- Company X is a company which has a cyclical demand for its product. It wishes to diversify and buy a company which has a relatively stable demand for its product when the economy goes into recession and incomes either grow more slowly or actually fall.
- Company Y is seeking to diversify and is interested in buying a furniture manufacturing company with the use of borrowed funds. It is worried about the extent to which an increase in interest rates, which would push up the costs of its borrowing, would affect the furniture business.
- Company Z is a conglomerate, producing a range of goods and services. It is thinking of increasing its investment expenditure in the next couple of years and wants to know whether you think it ought to proceed given the outlook for the economy in the medium term.

Your task is to give advice to each of these companies and make recommendations about their courses of action.

Research

Obtain figures for consumer expenditure (total and component categories), personal disposable income and the rate of interest (such as base rate and deposit account rate for selected retail banks) on a quarterly and yearly basis from *Economic Trends Annual Supplement* (data go back to 1948). Update the figures from the latest edition of *Economic Trends*. A more detailed breakdown of consumer expenditure can be obtained from CSO, *Annual Abstract of Statistics*, but only annual figures are given over the past 10 years. CSO, *Monthly Digest of Statistics* gives quarterly figures but only for the previous 12 quarters.

Establish from textbooks what relationship you would expect to see between consumption expenditure and these other variables. What other variables might also influence total consumption or individual components of consumption?

You may have access to a computer data base such as SECOS. A powerful computer package will enable you to correlate data over time much more easily than if you have to do it by hand.

You could use newspaper and magazine articles to support your recommendations. Use articles which deal with the factors affecting consumption or the effect of changes in consumption on the economy.

Structuring your report

Introduction Outline the aims of your investigation.

Economic theory Explain various theories of the consumption function. Distinguish between different types of consumption and suggest why some component categories might be influenced more by one variable than another.

Presentation of evidence Using tables, graphs and any other appropriate diagrams, outline your findings. For instance, what are the trends in consumer expenditure? To what extent is total consumption determined by disposable income? What other factors, if any, determine consumption? To what extent is expenditure on food determined by interest rates?

Recommendations What recommendations would you make to each of the three companies? Your comments must be supported by evidence.

Sources Outline the sources of information you used. What problems did you encounter in gathering relevant data? What data would you have liked to have obtained but could not? To what extent were the data reliable?

Other suggestions

It is possible to investigate a number of macro-economic relationships using data from *Economic Trends Annual Supplement* and the *Annual Abstract of Statistics*, together with *Economic Trends* and the *Monthly Digest of Statistics* (all published by CSO).

- The relationship between saving and its determinants such as income and the rate of interest.
- The relationship between investment and determinants such as past changes in income and the rate of interest.
- The relationship between imports and income.

B. Economic growth

Aims

- To gather data about living standards at a point in time in the past and compare them with living standards today.
- To record and present data about living standards.
- To evaluate the extent to which living standards have changed over time, and the effect that this may have had on the economy.

Research

Your task is to compare living standards in the UK between some point in the past and today. Firstly, choose a year with which you wish to compare today's Britain. Your choice will depend upon a number of factors.

- More statistical data is available for post-war Britain than pre-war Britain.
- Picking a census year (e.g. 1951) will increase the amount of secondary evidence available.
- On the other hand, you may wish to use particular secondary sources which you are perhaps using in a history course. This could mean that you wish to compare today's Britain with, say turn-of-the-century England.
- Your choice of date may also be influenced by family records or the age of relatives and friends that you may wish to interview.

Decide upon a list of factors which you judge are important in comparing living standards. For instance, you could consider real national income, real disposable income per head, real consumption, real food consumption, ownership of televisions or cars, working hours, unemployment levels, pollution levels, crime levels, and degree of political freedom. These are just a few examples of many factors which you may wish to take into account. You will need to take into account the effects of inflation and possibly also the distribution of income when carrying out your investigation.

Government CSO statistics can provide basic data for many variables in the post-war period. *Economic Trends Annual Supplement, Annual Abstract of Statistics* and *Social Trends* are good starting points. A large public reference library should carry back copies of these publications. Census data is available for census years (every ten years going back from 1991).

Other secondary sources may be available from historical publications. For instance, anecdotal evidence about past living standards can be gained from past copies of local newspapers. Looking through a month's issues of a local newspaper from, say, 1931, would give an indication of the economic concerns of people in the area at the time. Adverts would give some indication of the types of goods available. Consult the history department in your school or college to find out what might be available in school. Your local large public reference library will also indicate what books, periodicals and other materials that it has which will help you in your research.

Primary evidence can be obtained by interviewing older relatives or friends. Establish before the interview what year you wish the interviewee to talk about. He or she may be able to find written or visual material (e.g. a diary or photographs) which could be shared with you. It is helpful to record the interview using a tape recorder, so permission to do that **must** be obtained beforehand. Draw up a list of questions which you wish to ask. During the interview, where necessary, ask supplementary questions if the interviewee has failed to give enough detail.

Structuring your report

Introduction Outline the aims of your investigation. Explain briefly how living standards might be compared over time and what problems arise in making any comparison.

Presentation of results Outline your findings. Use charts, tables, diagrams, quotes from source material and photographs and drawings wherever appropriate.

Evaluation Discuss the extent to which living standards are higher today than in your chosen year. Outline areas where you found it difficult if not impossible to make a comparison, perhaps because of lack of data, or perhaps because it is not possible to place a value on the change that has taken place. To what extent have changes in living standards been beneficial? What criteria did you use to evaluate this?

Sources Outline the sources of information you used. What problems did you encounter in gathering relevant data? What data would you have liked to have obtained but could not? To what extent were the data, particularly any primary data collected, reliable?

Other suggestions

- Instead of comparing just two points in time, it would be possible to compare a number of years, perhaps covering three or four generations in a single family. Alternatively, you may have access to information about living standards in another country today. To what extent are the French or the Germans better off than the British today?
- You could also compare living standards in different parts of the country or living standards of different 'groups'. You will need to consider whether the factors used to judge standards of living over a period of time are applicable to this type of study or whether they are different.

Summary

1. Money has four functions: as a medium of exchange, a unit of account, a store of value and a standard for deferred payment.
2. Characteristics of good money include acceptability, portability, durability, divisibility, and limited supply.
3. In a modern economy, cash and sight deposits are the assets which best fulfil the function of a medium of exchange. These are known as narrow monies.
4. Near monies, assets which are good units of account and stores of value and can easily be converted into assets which are a medium of exchange, include time deposits in banks and building societies. Broad money is narrow money plus near money.
5. Money substitutes, such as credit cards, are items which act as a medium of exchange but are not stores of value.
6. The money supply is the total amount of money circulating in the economy.

Is this the only form of money?

The functions of money

Most people today in Britain, if asked 'what is money?' would reply 'notes and coins'. What is it about notes and coins that make them money, and is there anything else which possesses these same properties? If something is to be money, it must fulfil four FUNCTIONS (i.e. it must do four things).

A medium of exchange This is the most important function of money. Money is used to buy and sell goods and services. A worker accepts payment in money because she knows that she will be able to use that money to buy products in the shops.

There is no money in a BARTER economy. Exchange is conducted directly by swopping one good with another. For instance, a farmer might pay a dozen eggs to have his horse shod or a woman might trade a carpet for a cow. This requires a **double coincidence of wants**. If the blacksmith didn't want eggs, then he might refuse to shoe the farmer's horse. If the woman with a carpet was offered a horse instead of a cow, again she might refuse to trade. Barter requires that each party to the transaction wants what the other has to trade. This is costly and difficult, if not impossible, and therefore trade is discouraged. Without trade there can be no specialisation. Without specialisation, there can be little or no increase in living standards. So barter is associated with primitive types of economy.

Money separates the two sides of a barter transaction. The farmer can sell his eggs for money. The blacksmith will accept money for shoeing the farmer's horse because he knows that he will be able buy the goods that he wants with the money.

Unit of account Money acts as a measure of value. If a dress costs £30 and a skirt costs £15, we know that the value of one dress equals the value of two skirts. At times of very high inflation, such as in Germany in 1923, money ceases to act as a unit of account. Prices change by the hour. A dress costing £30 in the morning might only buy one skirt in the evening. High inflation therefore destroys the ability of money to perform this function. It is very difficult under a barter sytem to establish an agreed unit of account as people's opinions of the value of certain items differ greatly.

A store of value A worker who receives wages is unlikely to spend the money immediately. She may defer spending because it is more convenient to spend the money later. She will do this only if what she can buy in the future is approximately equal to what she can buy today. So money links the present and the future. It acts as a store of value. High inflation destroys this link because money in the future is worth far less than money today. In the German hyperinflation of 1923, people started to refuse payment in German money because it would lose so much value by the time they had spent it.

A standard for deferred payment If a person lends money today, she will only do so if she thinks that she will be able to buy roughly the same amount of goods when it is paid back. In trade, a company which accepts an order at a fixed price today for delivery and payment in a year's time will only do so if it is confident that the money it receives will have a value which can be assessed today. So again money must link different time periods when it comes to borrowed as well as saved money.

When money ceases to have this function, credit and borrowing collapse and this is very damaging to investment and economic growth in an economy.

QUESTION 1

Explain which of these items might be considered 'money' and which would not.

The characteristics of money

Pigs, silver, gold, teeth, and even wives have been used as money in the past. Some cultures today still use animals as currency. However most, if not all, of these have been unsatisfactory because of their characteristics. Ideally, money should be:

- acceptable to all - it is inconvenient if a type of money is only accepted in some shops but not others for instance;
- portable - pigs, for instance, are not easy to carry around and this limits the trade which is conducted using pigs as a medium of exchange;
- durable - pigs die and wives get old; ideally money

should be durable over time;
- divisible - whole live pigs can't be used to buy the small things in life because they are too valuable; money must be capable of being split into small denominations;
- limited - if ordinary stones are used as money, prices of goods are likely to be very high in terms of stones because they are so easy to obtain;
- difficult to forge - forgeries make money worth less and can lead to its becoming unacceptable in exchange.

QUESTION 2 To what extent do each of the assets in the previous question possess the characteristics of a good money?

Forms of money in a modern economy

In a modern economy there are a number of assets which can be classified as money.

Cash Cash means notes and coins. Cash is a **token money**. It has little or no intrinsic value (unlike gold which would be classified along with items such as pigs and cigarettes as **commodity money**). It is issued either by government or with the permission of government. Government reinforces the acceptability of cash by making it **legal tender**. This means that it must be accepted by law as a means of payment.

During much of the 19th century, bank notes were **convertible**. This meant that it was possible to go into a bank and convert the notes into something of real value: in this case, gold. However, more notes were issued than their value in gold. The value of notes and coins printed over and above the value of gold in bank vaults was called the **fiduciary issue.** Today UK bank notes are not convertible into gold and therefore all notes are **fiat** money, money made legal tender by government decree.

Cash is not perfect money. In the UK it is an almost perfect medium of exchange. But inflation affects three of the functions of money - those of a unit of account, a store of value and a standard of deferred payment. In 1975 for instance, UK inflation was nearly 25 per cent. Anyone holding £1 at the beginning of the year could only buy 75 pence worth of goods with it at the end of the year. The higher the rate of inflation, the less it can be said that cash is a 'good' money.

Money in current accounts Banks and building societies in the UK offer customers current account facilities. Current accounts (called SIGHT DEPOSIT ACCOUNTS in economic theory) have two distinguishing features. Firstly, cash can be withdrawn on demand from the account if it is in credit. So deposits can be immediately converted into money if the account holder so wishes. Secondly, account holders are provided with a cheque book. Cheques can be used to purchase goods and services. Cheque book money therefore is a medium of exchange. It is not perfect because people and firms can refuse to accept cheques in a transaction. Moreover, little or no interest is offered on accounts and so current account deposits lose value over time with inflation, damaging their store of value function. But deposits in current accounts are nearly as good a form of money as cash.

Near monies NEAR MONIES are assets which fulfil some but not all of the functions of money. In particular, they act as units of account and stores of value but cannot be used as mediums of exchange. However, they are convertible into a medium of exchange quickly and at little cost. (The ease with which an asset can be converted into money without loss of value is termed LIQUIDITY. The more liquid an asset, the more easily it is convertible into money.) In the UK, the most obvious type of near monies is TIME DEPOSITS with banks and building societies. Unlike current accounts, they pay interest. They are therefore used more for saving and less for making transactions than current accounts. Depositors need to give notice if they wish to withdraw from the account (hence the term 'time' deposit). Alternatively, many accounts offer instant access if an interest rate penalty is paid (i.e. the saver loses money for the privilege of instant withdrawal).

Non-money financial assets All financial assets can be converted into money. However, for most assets the potential penalties for doing this are great. There can be a long waiting time for withdrawal and there can be considerable loss of money from conversion. This impairs their functions as units of account and stores of value. Economists do not classify these assets as money. Shares, for instance, are easily sold, but it can take up to a month to receive the money from the sale. Shares can also change value rapidly and are therefore not a good store of value (when share prices fall) or a standard for deferred payment (when share prices rise).

Money substitutes

Money is not the only means of payment for goods and services. Charge cards and credit cards have become increasingly important over the past 20 years as a medium of exchange. But they are not stores of value. This is because possession of a card does not show that the cardholder has money in the credit card account. The card only represents an ability to borrow money instantly. So credit cards are not money but they are MONEY SUBSTITUTES (i.e. they are used instead of money).

QUESTION 3 Emma Higgins has £250 in a building society share account. She owns a £100 000 house but owes £50 000 in the form of a mortgage loan. Her current account at her bank is in credit by £200 and she has an overdraft facility of £300. In her purse she has £20 in cash. She has recently purchased £50 worth of goods using her credit card. Her credit card limit is £1 000.

Explain how much money Emma Higgins possesses.

The money supply

The MONEY SUPPLY is the total amount of money circulating in the economy. It has been argued above that there is no financial asset which perfectly possesses all the functions of money. So financial assets can be placed on a spectrum as in Figure 65.1. At the left of the spectrum is the asset which comes closest to fulfilling most of the functions of money today - cash. At the other end are assets which are extremely illiquid, such as shares in companies not traded on a stock exchange. In between there is a range of assets. As we move right assets possess fewer and fewer of the functions of money.

It is now clear that the cut off point between those assets which are money and those which are not is to

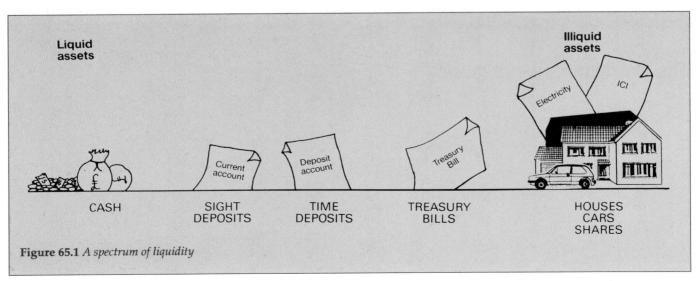

Figure 65.1 *A spectrum of liquidity*

Liquid assets

Illiquid assets

CASH   SIGHT DEPOSITS   TIME DEPOSITS   TREASURY BILLS   HOUSES CARS SHARES

some extent arbitrary. In the UK, there are a number of official definitions of the money supply. There are two broad types of money supply definition.
- NARROW MONEY - money which can be used as a medium of exchange.

- BROAD MONEY - narrow money plus near monies. Current money supply definitions used in the UK are described below in the applied economics section.

Key terms

Functions of money - money must be a medium of exchange, a store of value, a unit of account and a standard for deferred payment.

Barter - swopping one good for another without the use of money.

Sight deposit accounts - Accounts with financial institutions where deposits are repayable on demand and where a cheque book is issued. In the UK, they are more commonly called current accounts.

Near money - an asset which cannot be used as medium of exchange in itself but is readily convertible into money and is both a unit of account and a store of value.

Liquidity - the degree to which an asset can be converted into money without capital loss.

Time deposit accounts - accounts where interest is paid but savers are not able to withdraw without either giving notice or paying an interest rate penalty.

Money substitutes - those which can be used as a medium of exchange but which are not stores of value. Examples are charge cards or credit cards.

Money supply - the total amount of money in circulation in the economy.

Narrow money - money which is primarily used as a medium of exchange.

Broad money - narrow money plus near monies.

Applied economics

The money supply in the UK

There is no single definition of money because no financial asset possesses all the characteristics or fulfils all the functions of money perfectly. A variety of different financial assets possess some of the functions to some degree, and hence it is possible to provide a number of definitions of the money supply. In the United States, over 40 definitions are used, but there are only 4 main measures currently calculated by the Bank of England. Figure 65.2 shows the relationships between different measures of the money supply.
- M0 is the narrowest definition of the money supply. It is equal to the notes and coins in circulation together with the balances held by banks with the Bank of England for operational reasons (☞ unit 66).
- M1, another narrow definition of the money supply, is defined as notes and coins in circulation plus money in current accounts at banks. Current accounts (or **sight** deposits) allow instant withdrawal. Because of this and the fact that cheque books are given, money in current accounts, like notes and coins, is used mainly as a medium of exchange. M1 ceased to be calculated in 1989 as will be explained below.
- M2 takes note of the fact that, in the second half of the 1980s, there was a trend for building societies to

offer current accounts in competition with the banks. Adding these 'retail' deposits of building societies to M1 provides a wide ranging measure of monies used mainly as a medium of exchange. M2 is classified as broad money in official statistics.
- M3, a measure of broad money, like M1, is no longer calculated and illustrates one of the many problems of money supply definitions. M3 was defined as narrow money, M1, plus monies in deposit accounts at banks (i.e. bank time deposits), together with private sector holdings of certificates of deposit (akin to savings certificates ☞ unit 66) issued by banks. In 1989, the Abbey National Building Society became a public limited company and ceased legally to be a building society. As one of the largest building societies in the UK, this presented a major problem to statisticians at the Bank of England. Theoretically, the deposits held with the Abbey National should have been transferred from the building society category to the bank category. But this would have produced a £32bn jump in the value of M3 and a smaller but still significant jump in the value of M1. Given that it seemed likely that a number of building societies would follow the lead set by the Abbey National, the Bank of England decided to discontinue the

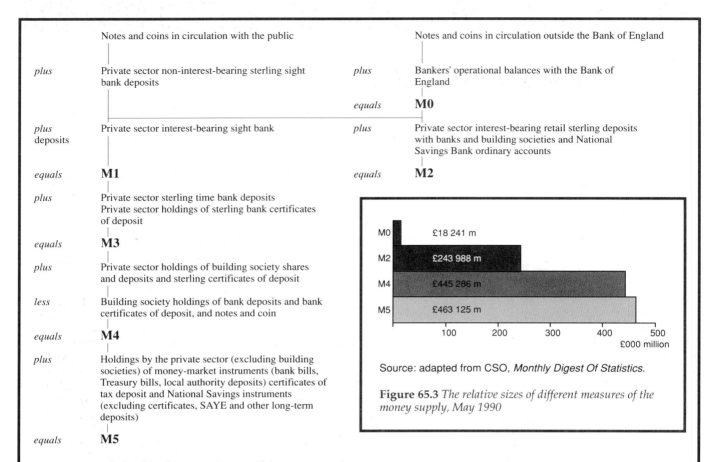

Notes and coins in circulation with the public

plus Private sector non-interest-bearing sterling sight bank deposits

plus Private sector interest-bearing sight bank deposits

equals **M1**

plus Private sector sterling time bank deposits
Private sector holdings of sterling bank certificates of deposit

equals **M3**

plus Private sector holdings of building society shares and deposits and sterling certificates of deposit

less Building society holdings of bank deposits and bank certificates of deposit, and notes and coin

equals **M4**

plus Holdings by the private sector (excluding building societies) of money-market instruments (bank bills, Treasury bills, local authority deposits) certificates of tax deposit and National Savings instruments (excluding certificates, SAYE and other long-term deposits)

equals **M5**

Notes and coins in circulation outside the Bank of England

plus Bankers' operational balances with the Bank of England

equals **M0**

plus Private sector interest-bearing retail sterling deposits with banks and building societies and National Savings Bank ordinary accounts

equals **M2**

Figure 65.2 *Relationships between measures of the money supply*

M0 £18 241 m
M2 £243 988 m
M4 £445 286 m
M5 £463 125 m

100 200 300 400 500
£000 million

Source: adapted from CSO, *Monthly Digest Of Statistics*.

Figure 65.3 *The relative sizes of different measures of the money supply, May 1990*

calculation of M1 and M3.
- M4 is approximately equal to narrow money, M1, plus monies in deposit accounts at the banks and building societies.
- M5 is M4 plus a range of financial assets such as Treasury Bills, local authority deposits and various National Savings instruments which can easily be converted into money and are held by the private sector. M5 is the broadest measure of the money supply officially calculated in the UK.

Figure 65.3 shows the relative size of each of the 4 measures of the money supply currently calculated. Note that M0 is a fraction of the size of M5. This has very important consequences for the control of the economy, and in particular the control of inflation because it is relatively easy for consumers to convert some of their money in time deposits into money that could be used to purchase goods and services in the economy.

PEPSI'S EXPANSION IN THE SOVIET UNION

In 1989, Pepsi, the US drinks group, concluded a deal with the Soviet Union to supply ingredients to make Pepsi Cola. The Soviets would build 85 tankers for two companies, one Norwegian, the other from the Bahamas, for almost $4 billion. About a quarter of the money would then be used by the Soviets to pay Pepsi for its supplies. The deal is in addition to a long running contract whereby Pepsi exchanges its soft drinks for vodka. In 1988, 840 million bottles of Pepsi were sold in the Soviet Union.

1. **Why might Pepsi sales to the Soviet Union be seen as 'barter' sales?**
2. **What problems might Pepsi encounter in the future with the two barter arrangements described in the data?**

Summary

1. Commercial banks are financial intermediaries that borrow and lend money.
2. Banks have the power to create money because they need only retain a fraction of the cash which is deposited with them. The rest can be loaned out, leading to an increase in the money supply.
3. A new £1 deposited in the banking system will lead to an increase of £1 times the credit multiplier in the volume of bank credit and therefore the money supply.
4. The credit multiplier is 1 divided by the reserve ratio.
5. The monetary base of the economy is the name given to the stock of money which banks or other financial intermediaries need to have in order to be able to create credit.

The commercial banks

Commercial banks, such as the Midland Bank or Barclays Bank, are **financial intermediaries**. They link customers together, just as supermarkets link shoppers with food manufacturers. They provide a wide range of financial services including money transmission services. But their main activity is the borrowing and lending of money. They borrow from customers who place money in a variety of different accounts. They then lend money to individuals, businesses and governments. They make a profit by charging a higher rate of interest on loans than they pay on the money they have borrowed.

Credit creation in a single bank system

In the process of borrowing and lending money, banks have the ability to create money. To explain why, some simplifying assumptions need to be made.
- There is only one bank in the economy.
- The public already holds enough money to satisfy its needs and any new money it receives will be deposited with the bank.
- The bank, by law, has to hold 10 per cent of its deposits in cash.

When a customer deposits cash with the bank, the bank will not keep that money in its vaults. It knows that customers, on average, do not demand all of their money back all at once. On any one day, the bank might have to pay back say 10 per cent of deposits made by the public.

The public will also be depositing money with the bank on that day, so it only needs to keep less than 10 per cent of its customers' total deposits in cash on a day to day basis. The more its customers use cheques and money substitutes like credit cards, the less it will need to keep in cash. In the UK today, the major banks only keep between 1 and 2 per cent of total deposits in the form of cash. The ratio between the amount of cash a bank has to keep and its **total liabilities** (the money the bank owes to its customers) is called the **cash ratio**. The cash ratio is an example of a RESERVE RATIO. With a cash ratio, cash is the reserves in the banking system (other assets such as gold could equally be used as reserves). We have assumed above that the reserve ratio is 10 per cent. Today's banking system is called a FRACTIONAL RESERVE BANKING SYSTEM because banks only keep a fraction of total deposits as reserves.

Table 66.1 shows the balance sheet of the one bank in the economy. Liabilities (what the bank owes) are placed on the left hand side whilst assets (what the bank owns) is put on the right. A 'balance sheet' is so called because the liabilities must equal the assets. Customers have deposited £100m with the bank. Thus the bank has liabilities of £100m to its customers. The bank will not keep this in its vaults. It knows that it only needs to keep £10m in cash to satisfy the day to day requirements of its customers. It can lend out the other £90m. This will earn interest and make profit for the bank.

Now assume that the government prints an extra £10m in notes. It gives these to the general public in the form of a tax rebate. It was assumed above that the public was already satisfied with its holdings of cash. So it will deposit all of the £10m with the bank. The new balance

Table 66.1 *Balance sheet of a single bank*

£ million

Liabilities		Assets	
Deposits	100	Cash	10
		Loans	90
	------		-------
Total	100		100

Table 66.2 *Balance sheet following the deposit of £10m cash*

£ million

Liabilities		Assets	
Deposits	110	Cash	20
		Loans	90
	------		-------
Total	110		110

Table 66.3 *Balance sheet following the loan and redeposit of £9m*

£ million

Liabilities		Assets	
Deposits	119	Cash	20
		Loans	99
	------		-------
Total	119		119
	------		-------

Table 66.4 *Final balance sheet following an additional £10m cash in the economy*

£ million

Liabilities		Assets	
Deposits	200	Cash	20
		Loans	180
	------		-------
Total	200		200
	------		-------

sheet will look as in Table 66.2. The bank assets are now £20m in cash and £90m in loans. But it does not need to hold £20m in cash. With a cash ratio of 10 per cent, it only needs to hold £11m in cash (£110m x 10per cent). It could lend out the extra £9m. When it lends out the £9m, the money will probably be spent and returned as a new deposit to the bank (remember the public already holds all the cash it wants to hold). The new balance sheet will look as in Table 66.3. Loans have increased to £99m. The bank still has £20m in cash because, although it lent out £9m in cash, the cash was redeposited with the bank. Liabilities have increased by £9m to £119m.

The bank now holds £20m in cash but only has liabilities of £119m. Its cash ratio is well above 10 per cent. It only needs to hold £11.9m in cash. So it will lend out a further £8.1m (£20m - £11.9m). This will be spent and redeposited with the bank, allowing it to further increase its loans. This process will carry on until the bank achieves a cash ratio of 10 per cent. This is shown in Table 66.4. Total assets and liabilities are £200m. Therefore with cash of £20m, its cash ratio is 10 per cent. £180m have been lent out to customers. This represents an equilibrium position for a bank seeking to maximise profits.

It cannot lend out any more because, although the amount of cash it would have would remain the same (customers keep on returning cash lent out to the bank), its assets and liabilities would be too great in relation to its holdings of cash. For instance, with £20m cash and £400m in liabilities, its cash ratio would fall to 5 per cent, below the legal minimum. The cash ratio therefore sets a limit on a bank's ability to borrow and lend money.

Note that an extra £10m in cash has led to a growth of £100m in deposits at the bank. Deposits in the bank are part of the money supply (☞ unit 65). So the bank has created an extra £90m (£100m - £10m) of money in the system. This money does not belong to the bank. It belongs to customers. But the bank is happy to help create this money for its customers because it can make a profit by lending it out at higher rates of interest than it borrows it for.

The credit multiplier

In the above example, an injection of £10m in cash to the banking system led to a final increase of £100m in the money supply. So the initial £10m was multiplied ten fold. The value of this multiplier is given a variety of names. It is called the CREDIT MULTIPLIER, or MONEY MULTIPLIER, or BANK MULTIPLIER or BANK DEPOSIT MULTIPLIER. The increase in the money supply is given by the formula:

$$(C) + (C \times 0.9) + (C \times 0.9 \times 0.9) + ...$$

where C is the initial cash injection to the bank and 0.9 is the fraction of any new cash which can be lent out by the bank. This is shown in diagrammatic form in Figure 66.1 where it is assumed that £10 cash is injected into the banking system and there is a 10 per cent reserve ratio.

The above is a geometric progression and the value of the final increase can be calculated more easily by multiplying the initial cash injection by the credit multiplier, the formula for which is:

$$\text{Credit multiplier} = \frac{1}{\text{reserve ratio}}$$

For instance, if banks have to keep 10 per cent of their

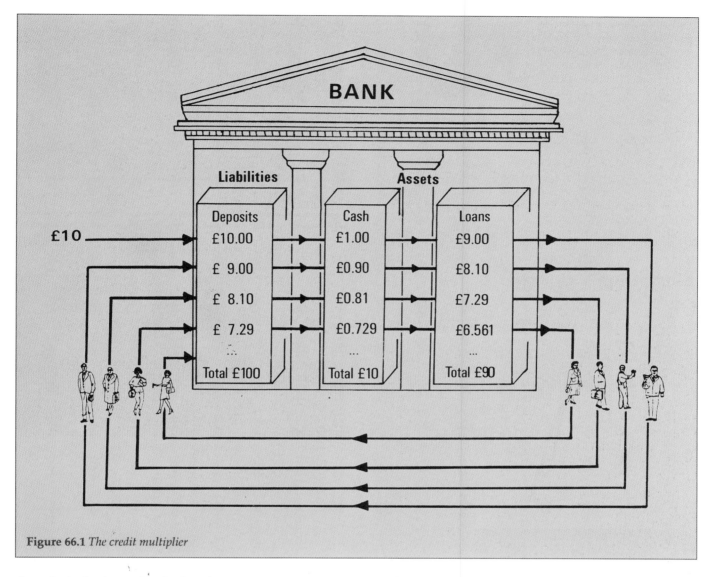

Figure 66.1 *The credit multiplier*

deposits in the form of cash, then the reserve ratio is 10 per cent or 0.1. The credit multiplier is then 1÷ 0.1 or 10. A £10 increase in cash in the system increases the money supply by £10 x 10 or £100.

The larger the reserve ratio, the smaller will be the value of the credit multiplier. For instance, if the banks have to keep 20 per cent of the assets in cash, then the reserve ratio is $^1/_5$. The credit multiplier is therefore 1÷ $^1/_5$ or 5. If banks have to keep only 1 per cent in cash, then the credit multiplier is 1÷ $^1/_{100}$ or 100.

In practice, the credit multiplier is smaller than the above formula would suggest. This is because the public do not redeposit all the cash that they receive when banks lend out money. They keep back some of it mainly to use in day to day transactions. The larger the proportion of cash lent out by banks that the public keeps rather than redepositing, the smaller will be the value of the money multiplier. Note that the reserve ratio is a minimum ratio. If banks by law have to maintain a 10 per cent cash ratio, then it would be illegal for them to have a 6 per cent cash ratio, but legally they could have a 12 per cent or 20 per

cent cash ratio if they so wished. However, in practice, banks are likely to wish to maintain the lowest reserve ratio possible because reserve assets, such as cash, yield little or no financial return.

QUESTION 2 There is only one bank in an economy. All money loaned out by the bank is redeposited with the bank. Cash is the only reserve asset required to be held by banks. By how much will the money supply increase if the reserve ratio and the initial sum of new cash deposited in the bank are: (a) 10 per cent and £500m; (b) 20 per cent and £100m; (c) 25 per cent and £200m; (d) 50 per cent and £1000m; (e) 5 per cent and £1bn; (f) 1 per cent and £120m?

The monetary base

So far we have assumed that reserve assets have been cash. But they need not be cash. Two hundred years ago when gold was the equivalent of cash, and bank notes were the equivalent of modern day cheques, it was gold that was the reserve asset. The banks had to keep back a certain amount of gold to satisfy the day to day transactions demands of their customers. During the 1960s and 1970s in the UK, the government insisted that banks keep a certain proportion of their assets in financial assets such as Treasury Bills, commercial bills and money at short notice with the discount houses. These assets were called 'reserve assets'.

RESERVE ASSETS are sometimes also called HIGH POWERED MONEY. The money is 'high powered' because its possession enables the banks to create extra money. Equally, reserve assets are sometimes called the MONETARY BASE of the economy. They are the base of the system because it is on this base that banks are able to build the credit pyramid.

A multi-bank system

We can now drop the last of our simplifying assumptions. It has been shown that in a single bank system, an increase in reserve assets, such as cash, will lead to a multiple increase in the money supply. The bank has created money. The overall conclusion is no different if there is more than one bank in the system.

Assume that there are two banks. One bank receives a new cash deposit of £10m. The reserve ratio is 0.1 and so the bank keeps £1m in cash and lends out the £9m. We cannot say into which bank the £9m will be redeposited. That will depend on which customers receive the £9m and the market shares of the respective banks. We can say that £9m will be redeposited in the banking system as a whole. We can also predict that the two banks between them will keep £0.9m and lend out £8.1m. By the time the

process has finished, the banking system as a whole will have created £90m of bank money to add to the £10m cash. But depending upon competition in the banking industry, different banks will have created different amounts within that total.

Key terms

Reserve ratio or reserve asset ratio - the ratio between the assets which the bank has to keep to meet either customer or legal requirements and the total amount deposited with the bank.
Fractional reserve banking system - a system in which banks only keep a fraction or proportion of total customer deposits in reserves and lend out the rest.
Credit multiplier, or money multiplier or bank multiplier or bank deposit multiplier - the number of times a change in reserve assets will change the money supply.
Reserve assets, high powered money or the monetary base - those assets which banks have to keep either because they are needed to satisfy customers' requirements (like cash) or because the government insists upon them during times of regulation.

Applied economics

UK banks and the creation of money

The UK clearing banks

The four largest clearing banks in the UK are Lloyds, Barclays, Midland and National Westminster. Traditionally, one of their main functions has been to borrow money from customers who make deposits in **current accounts** or **deposit accounts**. The banks lend out that money in the form of overdrafts or loans. Sometimes the clearing banks are called **high street banks** or **retail banks**. Both of these names refer to the fact that the clearing banks get a large proportion of their total funds from millions of customers through a network of branches in the UK.

'Clearing banks' are so-called because these banks clear cheques. For instance, a customer of Barclays bank may write out a cheque to a customer of Lloyds. The Lloyds customer will accept the cheque because

she knows that Barclays bank is prepared to transfer money to Lloyds upon receipt of the cheque. On any one day, millions of cheques need to be cleared. This is done through a number of regional clearing houses including the principal **clearing houses** in London. Banks send cheques to clearing houses to be sorted. Then balances are transferred between banks. For instance, if Lloyds has £500 million worth of cheques drawn on Barclays bank and Barclays Bank has £750 million worth of cheques drawn on Lloyds Bank then Lloyds will transfer £250 million to Barclays.

Balance sheets

The major UK clearing banks today are financial conglomerates, offering a complete range of financial services to their customers, but their traditional business has been the borrowing and lending of money. The ways in which banks borrow and lend money can be seen from their **balance sheets**. Table 66.6 shows the combined balance sheet of UK clearing banks in June 1990. The balance sheet can be divided into two: the assets of banks in pounds sterling and in foreign currencies, and their liabilities.

Almost all liabilities (i.e. money that the banks owe to their customers or clients) are deposits of one type or another. 'Notes outstanding' are notes issued by the Scottish and Northern Ireland banks. Like the Bank of England, they have the legal power to issue £5, £10, £20 and £50 pound notes. They are a liability to these banks because holders of these notes can return them to the issuing bank and demand payment in another form such as English bank notes. Certificates of deposit are long term bonds issued by the banks mainly to raise finance for long term loans to companies or governments. Items in suspense and transmission etc. are items such as monies received but unaccounted for and monies being transferred between accounts.

The assets of the banks (i.e. what the bank owns) range in liquidity and profitability. In general the less liquid the asset the more profitable it is (☞ unit 70). So banks try to keep as much of their assets as is prudent in the form of advances. The rest of their balance sheet is made up of more liquid assets which provide a buffer in case of a run on the bank.

- Cash. Less than 1 per cent of assets is kept in the form of cash. Banks know that that is all they need to satisfy the everyday transaction needs of their customers.
- Balances with the Bank of England. The banks have to keep ½ per cent of their **eligible liabilities** (broadly the sterling resources of the banks) in a non-interest bearing account with the Bank of England. These could be used to control the money supply through monetary base control (☞ unit 72). In practice they are used as a cheap source of finance by the Bank of England and to settle the day to day clearing needs of the banks.
- Market loans. Banks lend money **at call and short notice**. This means that the money can be recalled very quickly should the need arise. Call money is money which can be recalled immediately. Banks lend money to other banks in the **inter-bank market**. They also lend money to **discount houses** in the discount market (☞ unit 68).
- Certificates of deposit (CDs). Banks borrow money by issuing **certificates of deposit** but they also hold them for liquidity reasons. An equivalent would be homeowners who owe a building society £30 000 on a mortgage and have £1 000 with the same building society in a share account. They don't use the £1 000 to pay off the mortgage today because they may need to withdraw £500 next week.
- Local authority loans. Banks lend money to local

Table 66.6 *Retail banks: balance sheet, June 1990*

	£ million
Liabilities	
Sterling liabilities	
Notes outstanding	1 428
Deposits: UK private sector	212 056
Certificates of deposit and other short term paper	16 631
Other	56 155
Foreign currency deposits	61 421
Sterling and other currency liabilities: items in suspense and transmission, capital and other funds	61 517
Total liabilities	409 208
Assets	
Sterling assets	
Notes and coins	2 948
Balances with Bank of England	1 116
Market loans: Secured money with discount houses	8 567
Other UK banks	32 257
UK bank CDs	4 094
UK local authorities	291
Overseas	5 616
Bills: Treasury Bills	2 565
Eligible bank bills	8 766
Other	294
Advances: UK public sector	462
UK private sector	223 891
Overseas	4 870
Banking department lending to central government (net)	1 441
Investments: British government stocks	2 452
Other	9 886
Other currency assets	
Market loans and advances	62 154
Investments	10 893
Other	26 646
Total assets	409 208

Source: adapted from *The Bank of England Quarterly Bulletin*..

authorities who use the money to finance capital projects such as the building of sports centres or road building.
- Bills. These are short term loans (normally maturing within 91 days of issue). Bills offered for sale by the government are called **Treasury Bills**. When issued by firms they are known as **commercial bills**. Local authorities also issue bills to finance their day to day activities.
- Bonds. Banks buy bonds issued not only by the government (called gilt-edged stock) but also by individual firms.
- Advances. Advances are the single most important asset of banks. Advances earn banks the highest

rate of interest and therefore they try to maximise the level of advances subject to constraints of liquidity and prudence.

The credit multiplier

To what extent can the clearing banks create money (i.e. what is the value of the credit multiplier for the clearing banks)? They must keep at least ½ per cent of their eligible liabilities (eligible liabilities in June 1990 were only £234 440m) with the Bank of England. In addition, they need to keep a proportion of their liabilities in the form of cash to satisfy day to day withdrawals by their customers. The cash ratio has fallen over time as greater use has been made of cheques, credit cards and debit cards for transactions purposes. As can be seen from the balance sheet in Table 66.6, the clearing banks kept approximately 1 per cent (4064 ÷ 409 208) of their assets as cash plus deposits at the Bank of England. So it might seem that the current credit multiplier for clearing banks is approximately 100 (1 ÷ 0.01). (Note that this is the credit multiplier for money in the UK and for overseas money dealt with by the retail banks. It is possible but more complicated to calculate a credit multiplier for sterling assets alone.)

However, banks take into consideration two other factors when deciding upon how much to lend. Firstly, they need to keep a proportion of their assets in forms which are more liquid than advances. If there were ever a run on a bank (i.e. suddenly a large number of customers wanted their money back because they were afraid that the bank would go bankrupt), the bank would want to liquidate some of its assets very quickly to obtain cash to reassure customers. (Of course, if all customers wanted all their money back from a bank immediately, it would necessarily go bankrupt however sound its balance sheet.) So the clearing banks keep a proportion of their assets in liquid financial assets such as Treasury Bills.

Secondly, banks will not lend if the risk is greater than the return on a loan. For instance, it would be foolish to lend money to someone who on average had a 50 per cent chance of complete default on a loan if the bank could only charge 5 per cent interest a year on it. In general, the riskier the loans that a bank is prepared to make, the higher the rate of interest. Hence, the higher the interest rate, the greater will be the desire of banks to lend to the limit set by the credit multiplier.

Data question

M1

Table 66.7 Money stock, (notes and coins in circulation and M1) and bank lending

	£ million	
	1980	1988
Notes and coins in circulation	9 631	14 756
M1	30 436	105 048
Bank lending to the private sector	11 303	66 936

Source: adapted from CSO, *Annual Abstract of Statistics*; CSO, *Economic Trends Annual Supplement*.

Until 1989, the Bank of England published figures for notes and coins in circulation and M1, a measure of the money supply. Notes and coins in circulation are held partly by individuals and companies and partly by banks and other financial institutions. M1 was the sum, approximately, of notes and coins in circulation and money in current accounts at banks.

1. Why would economic theory suggest that a change in notes and coins in circulation might lead to a change in M1 and bank lending?
2. Suggest reasons why notes and coins in circulation have changed at a different rate than M1 over the 1980s.

Summary

1. Bonds are loans which can be bought and sold second hand on world bond markets.
2. The price of (second hand) bonds rises when interest rates fall and falls when interest rates rise.
3. A bill is a loan which pays no interest. Lenders make a return by buying the bill at a discount (i.e. for less than its maturity value).
4. Owners of shares are part owners of companies who are entitled to receive a share of the profits of the company in dividends.

Bonds

BONDS are a form of loan. If a company decides to borrow money through an issue of bonds, it will sell the issue on the market. The purchaser will usually receive a piece of paper - the bond itself. On the bond, there should be three pieces of information.

■ The nominal price of the bond - usually the price at which the bond was originally sold.
■ The nominal rate of interest payable - this is the rate of interest on the nominal price of the bond, fixed for the term of the bond. The bond will also state the frequency of payment of interest.
■ The date on which the nominal value or price of the bond will be repaid.

If the nominal price were £100 and the nominal rate of interest 5 per cent per annum, then £5 interest would be paid each year for the lifetime of the bond. £100 would be repaid when the bond **matured**.

There are a variety of types of bonds and of borrowers. Government borrows money through the issue of bonds. UK government bonds are called GILT EDGED STOCK. Particular bond issues are referred to by their nominal interest rate and date of maturity. For instance, Treasury 10 per cent 2004 is stock which will be repaid in the year 2004 and in the meantime pays 10 per cent interest on the nominal price of the stock (usually £100 per bond). CONSOLS (or consolidated stock) are IRREDEEMABLE bonds. This means that there is no date for repayment on the bond certificate (and it is most unlikely that the UK government will ever pay back the loan given that the nominal rate of interest on the bonds is a mere 2½ per cent). However, consols have value because the government promises to pay the holders interest each year. Consols were issued in the past when interest rates were much lower. A 2½ per cent consol, for instance, with a nominal value of £100, would give a yearly income of £2.50.

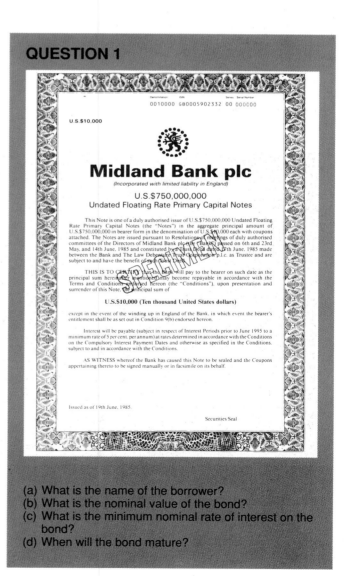

QUESTION 1

(a) What is the name of the borrower?
(b) What is the nominal value of the bond?
(c) What is the minimum nominal rate of interest on the bond?
(d) When will the bond mature?

Companies issue bonds, usually called STOCKS or DEBENTURES, to finance investment. In the UK, these are relatively unimportant as a source of finance today, mainly because firms are unwilling to borrow at current high fixed interest rates over long periods of time.

EUROBONDS are bonds issued by companies and governments which are **denominated** in a currency other than that of the borrower. For instance, ICI might borrow money to finance expansion in Germany by issuing eurobonds denominated in deutschmarks. These Eurobonds could be bought by, say, a French bank, a British company or an American individual.

A key feature of a bond is that it is is negotiable. Buyers of bonds need not wait until the loan matures to get their money back. Bonds can be bought and sold second hand, but the market price of a bond will not necessarily be the same as the nominal value of the bond.

The price of bonds

Economic theory suggests that the higher the rate of interest, the lower will be the price of existing bonds. For consols, for example, a doubling of the rate of interest will halve the market value of the bond.

To understand why this is the case, consider irredeemable stock which has been issued at £100 nominal price and with a nominal interest rate of 2½ per cent per annum. This bond therefore yields £2.50 interest each year. Assume the market rate of interest on comparable assets now rises to 5 per cent. On £100 saved, £5 interest would be paid. So savers would not pay £100 for a bond which yielded only £2.50 interest. In fact, they would be prepared to pay a maximum £50 for this bond [{£2.50÷£50} x 100 = 5 per cent]. If the market rate of interest rose again, this time to 10 per cent, a saver would only pay £25 for a £100 bond which gave only £2.50 interest per year (because £2.50 is 10 per cent of £25). Put as a formula:

$$\text{Market price} = \frac{\text{nominal interest rise}}{\text{market interest rate}} \times \text{normal price}$$

Most bonds are not irredeemable. However, the same inverse relationship between market price and the rate of interest applies to redeemable bonds.

The economic principle is that the farther away in time the payment of the loan, the greater will be the influence of the rate of interest on price. For instance, a £100 government stock repayable tomorrow with a nominal interest rate of 5 per cent when the market rate is 10 per cent will be worth almost £100 (plus any interest due). The same stock repayable in 25 years' time would be worth only about £60. In the first case, whatever the rate of interest on the bond, the government has guaranteed to pay £100 tomorrow and therefore the stock is worth almost £100 today. In the second case, the value of the bond is made up of two parts:

■ the first is the discounted value (☞ unit 53) of £100 available in 25 years' time - this is only worth about £10;

■ the second is the value of a piece of paper which pays the owner £5 interest a year - this is worth £50 at a market rate of interest of 10 per cent.

So the market value of the bond is about £60.

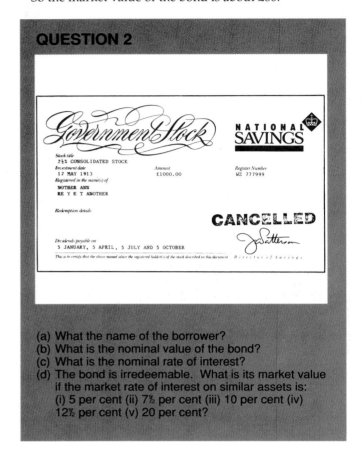

QUESTION 2

(a) What the name of the borrower?
(b) What is the nominal value of the bond?
(c) What is the nominal rate of interest?
(d) The bond is irredeemable. What is its market value if the market rate of interest on similar assets is:
(i) 5 per cent (ii) 7½ per cent (iii) 10 per cent (iv) 12½ per cent (v) 20 per cent?

Bills

A BILL is a loan on which no interest is paid. For instance, the government might issue a Treasury Bill of £100 for repayment in 3 months' time. No one will lend the government £100 free for three months. So the government has to sell the bill at a **discount**. Assume that the current market rate of interest on similar assets is 12 per cent per annum. Then the bill at the start of the three month period will be worth **approximately** £97. The £3 difference in price between £100 and £97 represents the interest or return on the bill. (£3 interest for three months is the equivalent approximately of £12 interest for 12 months, and hence the rate of 12 per cent per annum.) The nearer to the point of redemption, the nearer will be the market value of the bill to its redemption value.

The UK government issues bills, called **Treasury Bills**. Companies too issue a large volume of bills in the UK. These are called **commercial bills**. Bills are used for short term borrowing, typically over 3 or 6 months unlike bonds which are used for long term borrowing.

QUESTION 3

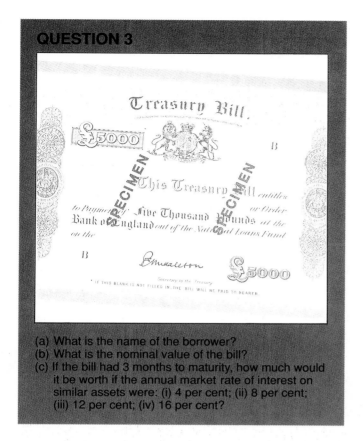

(a) What is the name of the borrower?
(b) What is the nominal value of the bill?
(c) If the bill had 3 months to maturity, how much would it be worth if the annual market rate of interest on similar assets were: (i) 4 per cent; (ii) 8 per cent; (iii) 12 per cent; (iv) 16 per cent?

QUESTION 4

THORNTONS PLC

Offer
by
S. G. Warburg & Co. Ltd.
and
Granville & Co. Limited
of
16,973,980 Ordinary Shares of 10p each
at 125p per share payable in full on application

Source: *Financial Times*, 9.5.1988.

(a) What is the name of the company selling new equity in itself?
(b) Name the two merchant banks which are organising the sale of the new equity.
(c) How many shares are being issued?
(d) What is the nominal price of each share?
(e) How much money will the issuing company receive from the sale (before payments of fees relating to the sale)?

Shares

SHARES entitle the owner to a proportion of the profits of a company. This proportion of profit is called a **dividend**. The prices of shares move erratically over time. Some economists argue that share price movements are completely random and hence it is impossible to pick winners and losers amongst shares.

However, changes in the rate of interest are likely to change share prices. There are two ways of explaining this. Firstly a rise in interest rates will make interest bearing assets relatively more attractive. At the margin, shareholders will sell their shares and buy bonds or put their money in the bank or building society. Secondly, shares will give a stream of dividend payments into the future. When interest rates rise, the present value of those future dividends falls (☞ unit 53). Hence buyers are only prepared to pay a lower price for the shares.

Key terms

Bond or stock - a type of long term borrowing where the loan can be traded during its lifetime.
Irredeemable stock - bonds which have no time limit on repayment of the loan. They are held because they give a guaranteed interest payment.
Bills - a form of short term loan where no interest is paid but a return is made by buying the bill at a lower price than its final redemption value.
Share - ownership of part of a company which entitles the shareholder to dividends, a share of the profits of the company.

Applied economics

Bills, bonds and shares, September-October 1990

In August 1990, the invasion of Kuwait by Iraq produced an immediate military and diplomatic response from the West. The threat of war in the Middle East sent share prices tumbling. On the London Stock Market, the FT Ordinary Share Index fell to a low of 1510.4 on 24 September. Within two weeks, however, the threat of war had receded a little and markets were more optimistic. By 18 October, the FT Ordinary Share Index had risen to 1618.1, a gain of 7.1 per cent. The yield on shares ({dividends ÷ the share price} x 100) therefore automatically fell because of the rise in share prices, from an average of 6.21 per cent on 24 September to 5.92 per cent on 18 October.

In early October, the UK joined the European Exchange Rate Mechanism and the government cut its intervention interest rate by 1 per cent. Bank base rates immediately fell from 15 to 14 per cent. This fall in interest rates spread to the bond market. The market price of $2\frac{1}{2}$ per cent £100 consols undated stock rose from £22$^{13}/_{32}$ on 24 September to £22$^{13}/_{16}$ on 18 October as the yield or market rate of interest on this stock fell from 11.16 per cent to 10.96 per cent.

The price of Treasury Bills rose too as the rate of interest on three month Treasury bills fell from 14$^{5}/_{16}$ per cent to 13$^{3}/_{8}$ per cent. The price of commercial bills rose similarly with the rate of interest on 3 month fine trade bills (bills issued by the most creditworthy companies) falling from 14$^{31}/_{32}$ per cent to 13$^{15}/_{16}$ per cent.

Data question

BRITISH GOVERNMENT SECURITIES: LONG DATED 20 YEARS

Table 67.1 *British government securities: long dated 20 years*

Average of working days

	Percentage yield
1981	14.74
1982	12.88
1983	10.80
1984	10.69
1985	10.62
1986	9.87
1987	9.47
1988	9.36

Source: adapted from CSO, *Economic Trends Annual Supplement.*

1. Using economic theory, explain what happened to the price of long dated government stock between 1981 and 1988.

68 Money and capital markets

Financial intermediaries and markets

Banks, building societies and other financial institutions are financial intermediaries. They are like supermarkets, acting as middlemen between buyers and sellers. In return for the services they provide, they charge in order to make a profit.

Most of the work of financial institutions involves borrowing and lending money. For instance, banks borrow money from some individuals and firms and then lend it back to others. Building societies borrow money from some individuals and lend it back again to the same or other individuals mainly to finance house purchases. Pension funds collect money from individuals and companies and use that money to buy stocks, shares, property and other assets. Financial institutions also provide services such as accounting services, advice on tax, and organisation of mergers and takeovers.

The markets where financial institutions buy and sell money amongst themselves and their clients are known as money markets and capital markets.

Banks

Banks can be divided into two types. **Retail banks** collect deposits from and lend money to a large number of customers. Retail banks in the UK are the clearing banks such as Lloyds and the Midland Bank. **Wholesale banks** survive by trading only in very large sums of money with a relatively small number of clients. Retail banks have branches throughout the UK whilst a wholesale bank, like the US bank, Chase Manhattan, may only have one branch, almost

certainly in London.

The activities and balance sheets of the UK retailing banks were described in unit 66. **Foreign** or **overseas banks** have long had branches in the City of London, but there was an explosion in their number in the 1960s. Foreign banks set up in the City of London for two reasons. Firstly they wanted to be able to offer a service to their clients with interests in the UK. For instance, a Japanese company with a factory in the UK may prefer to deal with a Japanese bank in London than with a UK bank. Secondly, foreign banks need to be physically located in London, one of the most important financial centres of the world, if they are to do business concerned with the London markets efficiently and effectively for their international clients.

Many foreign banks with a branch in London are concerned only with satisfying the needs of the customers in their own countries. A few, however, have established themselves as a major force in the City of London, fighting for custom in financial markets against established UK banks and other financial institutions.

Finance houses

Finance houses, or secondary banks as they are sometimes known, are banks which traditionally have specialised in leasing and hire purchase contracts. By offering higher rates of interest than the banks, they have been able to attract larger single savings deposits from individual customers. They also borrow a significant proportion of their funds from the money markets in London.

Today these banks are tending to offer a wider range of financial services to customers by opening branches in high streets. For instance, today they now offer life assurance and pension fund contracts.

Merchant banks

Traditionally, merchant banks such as Rothschild and Morgan Grenfell were banks which specialised in the finance of trade and commerce (hence the name 'merchant'). One important service they offer is the accepting of commercial bills (or bills of exchange). A company might issue a bill payable in three months' time to another company from which it has bought materials. The receiving company then sells the bill in the London discount market to obtain the money now, but it will have to sell it at a discount (☞ unit 67). It would, however, get a better price for the bill if it was accepted by an accepting house (a merchant bank which belonged to the Accepting Houses Committee). Accepting a bill means that the accepting house will guarantee payment of the bill even if the issuing company goes bankrupt. It is essentially a form of insurance for which the accepting houses charge a fee.

Today merchant banks offer a broad range of services. One of their main activities is the organisation of share issues for companies wishing to sell new shares (hence they are sometimes called issuing houses). They are also prominent in takeover battles. Companies will often hire a merchant bank to assist in a takeover or in defence against another predator company. Merchant banks act as financial advisers, managing the portfolios of wealthy individuals, trusts and pension funds. Many are unit trust managers. They borrow and lend money internationally too, but this is not a major part of their business.

The Bank of England

The Bank of England is the **central bank** of the UK. Owned by the government, it is responsible for carrying out government monetary policy. It has a number of major functions.
- It is responsible for the issue of notes and coins. These are issued on demand to the banking system.
- It supervises the financial system of the UK. For instance, it attempts to prevent fraud and dishonest trading by financial institutions.
- It advises the government on and implements monetary policy (☞ units 72 and 73).
- It manages the Exchange Equalisation Account, the account used to buy and sell foreign currency in order to maintain a given level of sterling in the foreign exchange markets (☞ unit 101).
- It acts as banker to the government, managing the National Debt, and arranging for the issue of new loans to cover any financial shortfall by the government.
- It acts as banker to the banking system. All banks have to keep ½ per cent of their liabilities with the Bank of England and these balances are used to settle accounts between individual banks after all cheques have been cleared (☞ unit 66). The Bank of England also provides liquidity to the banking system if banks are short of cash and other liquid assets. They do this through discount houses.

Discount houses

Discount houses are a peculiarly British institution. In 1990, there were only ten members of the London Discount Market Association and even the largest discount house is very small compared to a clearing bank or merchant bank. But they play a role in the London money markets which is far more important than their size would suggest.

Traditionally the discount houses have borrowed money at very short notice. Banks, for instance, lend money overnight (known as **money at call**). These funds represent very short term operating surpluses of the banks. The discount houses have then used this money to buy bills, such as Treasury Bills. Discount houses **have** to lend short term because they borrow short term.

On some days banks lend surplus funds to the discount houses. On other days, they need to withdraw their funds to maintain the liquidity needed to pay customers who withdraw money from their bank accounts. What would happen if, for instance, Barclays Bank needed money to pay customers who demanded payment, but it didn't have enough? This means that Barclays has too little cash and too few operating balances at the Bank of England, and too many of its assets tied up in advances, government stock, bills or loans to the discount houses. Barclays would react by withdrawing money from the discount houses, or recalling money at call with other banks. They might also be forced to sell other liquid assets such as Treasury Bills. There would be no problem if other banks had surplus funds. They would buy the bills and make deposits with the discount houses. But if all the banks faced the same liquidity crisis, they would all be trying to withdraw money from the discount houses and sell assets without there being enough buyers. In particular, the discount houses would not be able to sell the Treasury Bills and commercial bills they hold to repay the money Barclays had deposited with them. The whole of the banking system could go into bankruptcy. In the past, in the 19th century for instance, there were spasmodic bouts of bankruptcies amongst banks. Most went bankrupt because of mismanagement but some fell victim to crises of confidence. Everybody wanted their money back and the bank could not pay them immediately.

The Bank of England has a responsibility for

ensuring the smooth working of the UK financial system. It does not want to have financially sound banks going bankrupt because of a minor liquidity crisis. So it has created a safety valve within the system. The discount houses have the unique privilege of being able to go to the Bank of England and either sell bills or borrow money, giving bills as security. This allows them to obtain short term money to give to the banks, thus preventing a crisis. However, the Bank of England reserves the right to charge a penal rate of interest, called Bank Rate before 1971 and Minimum Lending Rate between 1971 and 1981. This penal rate is higher than the market rate of interest which means that the discount houses lose money if they are **forced into the Bank**.

The Bank of England in turn uses the discount market for **monetary policy** (☞ units 72 and 73). If there were no Bank of England intervention, a shortage of money in the market would drive up its price (i.e. interest rates would rise). Banks would have to offer higher rates of interest in order to be able to get the cash they needed to prevent themselves going bankrupt. If there is a surplus of funds in the money markets, borrowers of money will be able to reduce the interest rates they offer to pay. On any one day there will almost certainly be either a surplus or a shortage of funds in the money markets, implying that there should be sharp changes in interest rates on a day to day basis. The Bank of England for a long time has seen interest rate fluctuations as undesirable. It therefore intervenes on a day to day basis, supplying money when there is a shortage of funds in the market and selling bills when there is a surplus, so that money market interest rates remain constant over time.

When the Bank of England wants to change short term interest rates, it lets the market know its wishes. The market cannot ignore the Bank because the Bank can charge a penal rate on its transactions with the market, which would then stand to lose a great deal of money.

Building societies

Building societies have traditionally borrowed money from small savers and lent money out to finance house purchases. During the 1980s, there was a revolution in the way in which building societies operated. The Building Societies Act 1986 freed the building societies from previous regulations which limited their ability to offer a wide range of financial services. Today many of the larger building societies are transforming themselves into financial institutions which look increasingly like banks. They have begun to offer services ranging from current accounts to credit cards to pensions. During the 1990s, the competition in the market for retail financial services is likely to be extremely fierce.

Assurance and pension companies

Assurance companies and pension funds provide long term saving plans. They take money from a large number of small savers who usually pay regular premiums into life assurance or pension plans. Today the money that is paid in is used principally to buy shares. Assurance companies and pension funds - so-called **institutional investors** - now dominate shareholdings in the UK. Whether this is desirable or not is debateable (☞ unit 22).

Money markets

There are a large number of different money markets in the UK. They are all interlinked because funds from one market will flow into others if the interest rate differential changes (e.g. if interest rates stay the same in the first market but rise in the others). The main borrowers and lenders in each market are the financial institutions described above.

The discount market Until the early 1960s, the discount market was the main money market in London. As described above, the clearing banks lent money to discount houses overnight or very short term. The money could be withdrawn rapidly if the banks needed extra liquidity because it was deposited at call or at very short notice. The Bank of England guaranteed liquidity in the market by acting as a **lender of last resort**.

Parallel or secondary markets There are five other important sterling markets in London. The largest of these is the **inter-bank market**. In the late 1960s, the newly-arrived foreign banks in London began to lend money at call or short notice amongst themselves instead of to established discount houses. They did this because they were able to get higher rates of interest on money lent. Very quickly, UK banks also began to borrow and lend on the inter-bank market. The oldest parallel money market, started in 1955, is the **local authority market** where local authorities borrow money directly from City institutions. In the **inter-company market**, dating back to 1969, large companies cut out the middleman (the banks and other financial institutions) and borrow and lend between themselves. Finance houses borrow money from other financial institutions through the **finance house market**. Lastly, there is significant trade on the **sterling certificate of deposit market** in certificates of deposit (☞ unit 66) issued in sterling by banks.

Eurocurrency markets The London sterling money markets are completely dwarfed in size by the eurocurrency markets operated from London. Eurocurrency transactions are transactions in any currency apart from the currency of the country where the transaction takes place. In London, this means any transaction in any currency apart from sterling. A complete range of money market instruments or assets is found on eurocurrency markets. For instance, it is possible to borrow and lend money through loans, overdrafts and bonds (called Eurobonds). Governments, industrial companies and financial institutions use the markets for borrowing and lending. Transactions start in millions of dollars. This is very different from the retailing operations of the UK high street banks where money can be borrowed and lent in extremely small quantities.

Capital markets

On the London money markets, organisations borrow and lend money for their immediate short term use. **Capital markets** are markets where firms finance long term development or where government borrows money long term. The financial instruments used by firms and government to do this have been described elsewhere.

■ Companies issue debentures and shares (☞ units 22 and 67).
■ The UK government issues government stock (☞ unit 67).

Traditionally, the major capital market in the UK has been the London Stock Exchange. The Stock Exchange is primarily a secondary market where existing (i.e. second hand) securities such as a shares and gilts have been traded. It has functioned as a primary market to the extent that the UK government has sold new stock on the market, but it is not a primary market for shares. New shares are usually offered for sale to financial institutions or to the public directly by the company issuing the shares. Traditionally these sales have been organised with the help of merchant banks or stockbrokers. To guarantee that all the shares will be sold, the issue can be underwritten. This means that one or a number of financial institutions will buy any shares left unsold at a fixed price. In return for this guarantee, the company has to pay an underwriting fee, payable whether or not the underwriters have to buy any shares.

Data question

NEW LIFE FOR AN OLD CONCEPT

For several decades London's eight discount houses have been regarded as the banking equivalent of an endangered species - a gentle adornment to the City's banking habitat, but one steadily dwindling in numbers, and which is likely to disappear altogether before long.

Though the discount houses are small organisations, with capital of under £1 200m and fewer than 250 staff in all, their work involves handling vast amounts of money, between them perhaps annually 20 times the gross national product. They also deal in gilts (to hedge themselves against long term interest rate risks) and in discounted trade bills - hence the name.

Discount houses deal directly with the Bank of England in the sterling money market, and are the valve through which liquidity passes from the central bank to the commercial banks. No other major industrial country's central bank handles these

tasks in this way and this has led many to view the discount houses as anachronisms.

This summer, however, the Bank of England has given the discount houses a surprise. Far from removing them, it is inviting the establishment of new ones. There is unlikely to be a rush of applications since the rewards, by City standards, are modest. For instance, Union Discount, the largest discount house, reported pre-tax profits of £11.0m on a balance sheet of £3.2bn last year. One problem of operating at a time of rising interest rates was pointed out by Graeme Gilchrist, the managing director of Union Discount. 'The danger is all on the up side. You have always got paper and can't get out of the market, so you get caught even if you know that rates are going to go up.'

The existing discount houses have been diversifying to boost profits. Union Discount, for instance, has ventured into leasing, asset

management and equity market-making. Whether any company will wish to set up a new discount house given their current situation is debateable.

Source: adapted from the *Financial Times*, 26.9.1988.

1. **What is the role of discount houses in the London money markets?**

2. **Explain why discount houses 'get caught even if you know that rates are going to go up'.**

3. **Suggest reasons why (a) the Bank of England wishes to encourage the setting up of more discount houses and (b) there is unlikely to be a large number of companies wishing to establish discount houses.**

Summary

1. Households and firms hold their wealth in money, in non-money financial assets or in physical assets.
2. The opportunity cost of holding money is the benefits foregone from holding other financial or physical assets.
3. The traditional Keynesian approach distinguishes three motives for holding money: a transactions demand, a precautionary demand and a speculative demand. The total demand for money is a function of both income and the rate of interest.
4. A more modern Keynesian approach sees money being held in a portfolio of financial assets. The demand for money is dependent upon the opportunity cost of holding that money.
5. A monetarist approach sees money being held in a portfolio of both financial and physical assets.
6. The major difference between Keynesian and monetarist approaches is that in the former the demand for money is far more interest elastic than in the latter.

A portfolio of assets

Households and firms hold their wealth in a variety of different assets. Two main types of assets can be distinguished:
- **financial assets**, either monetary assets, such as cash and deposits in current accounts at banks, or non-money assets such as stocks and shares;
- **physical assets**, such as houses, buildings, cars, furniture, machinery, computers and inventories.

When economists talk about the 'demand for money', they do not refer to how much money people would like to have in a world where they were infinitely rich. What they mean is how much households and firms choose to hold in the form of money as opposed to holding either non-money financial assets or physical assets.

There is therefore an **opportunity cost** to a household if it holds £300 in cash. It could instead buy shares, and receive dividends and possibly capital gains. It could put money into a pension plan and increase the value of pension payments at some time in the future, or it could buy a new television and enjoy the services which it provides. Hence the price of holding money is the benefits foregone from holding another type of asset.

> **QUESTION 1** How much money do you hold now (in your pocket or at home)? What is the opportunity cost to you of holding that money?

A traditional Keynesian theory of the demand for money

Traditional Keynesian theory identifies three reasons or motives why households and firms hold money rather than other types of assets.

The transactions demand Money is needed to buy goods and services. Cash or cheques are used to pay for everything from a newspaper to a meal or a supermarket bill. This is known as the TRANSACTIONS DEMAND FOR MONEY. The amount of money needed depends upon the level of real expenditure in the economy. The most important determinant of this is the level of real income. The higher the level of real income, the more households and firms will have to spend and hence the higher the level of expenditure.

The transactions demand for money is also dependent upon the level of inflation. Shoppers will need twice the amount of money to buy the same trolley load of goods if the price of supermarket goods doubles over a period of time.

The precautionary demand We live in a world of uncertainty. Tomorrow the car might break down or an important creditor go bankrupt. So households and firms tend, if possible, to hold more money than is needed just for transactions purposes. The higher the level of income, the greater the bill is likely to be from something going wrong. For instance, the cost of repairing an expensive car is likely to be greater than that of a cheap car. So the PRECAUTIONARY DEMAND FOR MONEY is a function of (i.e. varies with) income.

The speculative demand for money One reason why people change the amount of money they choose to hold is because they wish to speculate on the stock market. This component of the total demand for money is called the SPECULATIVE DEMAND FOR MONEY. Assume that the only alternative to holding money is to hold bonds. Remember that the price of bonds is inversely related to the rate of interest. The higher the price of bonds, the lower the rate of interest and vice versa (☞ unit 67).

Now assume that the markets think that interest rates are high. If they are considered 'high', the market is likely to think there is more chance of them falling than going even higher. Hence the market will expect bond prices to rise rather than fall in the future.

How will market speculators react to this? It is possible to make a capital gain by buying bonds when their prices are low and selling them when they are higher. Hence speculators will buy bonds when interest rates are high hoping that interest rates will fall and therefore bond prices will rise. Bonds will be bought with money. So a high demand for bonds means a low speculative demand for money.

When interest rates are very low, they are likely to rise in the future. Hence, speculators are likely to sell bonds for money. Thus the demand for money is likely to be high when interest rates are low.

This theory predicts that the speculative demand for money will be low when interest rates are high (people preferring to buy bonds), but high when interest rates are low.

Figure 69.1 combines the three motives for holding money. The demand for money curve is called the LIQUIDITY PREFERENCE SCHEDULE. It shows the relationship between the demand for money and the rate of interest. OA of money is demanded whatever the rate of interest. This is the amount demanded for transactions and precautionary purposes. At an interest rate of r_1, OC of money is demanded. OA is demanded for transactions and precautionary purposes. AC is demanded for speculative purposes. When interest rates rise to r_2, the demand for money falls. The transactions and precautionary demands remain the same at OA. But the speculative demand falls to AB.

The transactions and precautionary demands for money will increase if real income in the economy rises or if there is inflation. This, shown in Figure 69.2, has the effect of pushing the liquidity preference schedule to the right. If the transactions and precautionary demands increase from OA to OB, then the liquidity preference schedule will shift from LP_1 to LP_2.

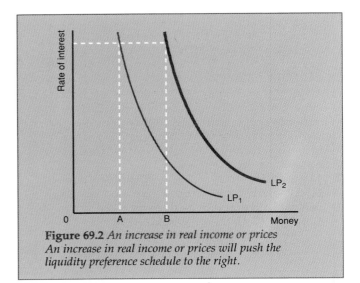

Figure 69.2 *An increase in real income or prices* An increase in real income or prices will push the liquidity preference schedule to the right.

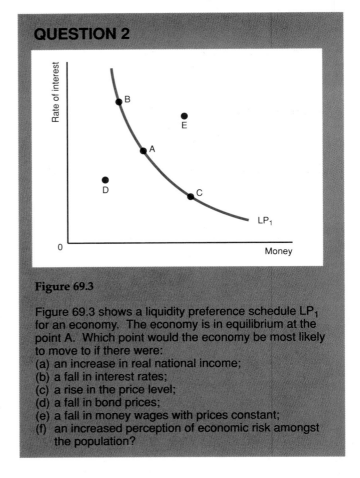

QUESTION 2

Figure 69.3

Figure 69.3 shows a liquidity preference schedule LP_1 for an economy. The economy is in equilibrium at the point A. Which point would the economy be most likely to move to if there were:
(a) an increase in real national income;
(b) a fall in interest rates;
(c) a rise in the price level;
(d) a fall in bond prices;
(e) a fall in money wages with prices constant;
(f) an increased perception of economic risk amongst the population?

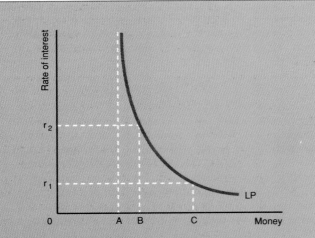

Figure 69.1 *The Keynesian liquidity preference schedule*
OA is the transactions and precautionary demand for money. Both are determined by real income and the price level, independently of the rate of interest. The demand for money above OA is the speculative demand which is inversely related to the rate of interest.

A modern Keynesian approach

The theory of a speculative demand for money is now widely rejected by economists. The idea that bonds are the only alternative to holding money is simplistic in a world where there are so many different money market instruments. Moreover, the theory assumes that there is some 'normal' rate of interest against which speculators can judge whether interest rates are high or low. The experience of the past 20 years suggests that no such normal interest rate exists.

The modern Keynesian approach is based upon ideas first published in 1958 by the American economist Professor James Tobin. Asset holders can hold their wealth in a wide range of financial assets, from cash to bonds to shares. Each type of asset provides a different mix of benefits. In particular:

- money can be used immediately for making transactions;
- non-money assets should yield a return in the form of interest, dividends or capital gain.

The opportunity cost of holding money is then the yield foregone on holding non-money assets. The opportunity cost of holding non-money assets is the advantage of liquidity: being able to spend the money when you like.

It is now possible to explain what happens to the demand for money as different variables change.

A rise in nominal income This is likely to lead to an increase in the number of transactions in the economy. Hence the demand for money will increase.

An increase in prices Households and firms now need more money to complete each transaction. Hence the demand for money will rise.

An increase in interest rates An increase in interest rates increases the opportunity cost of holding money. Therefore, the demand for money will fall and the demand for interest bearing assets will rise. For instance, if the rate of interest on building society money is 2 per cent, there is no great incentive to put money into interest bearing accounts. But when the interest rate is 10 per cent, people are much more aware of the advantages of getting interest on their assets. They are prepared to spend time moving savings around from current accounts (some of which don't pay interest) to interest bearing accounts and back again to maximise interest payments.

An increase in risk Many assets are risky. The rate of return can be positive but it can also be negative. For instance, the prices of shares over long periods of time have tended to increase. In October 1987, world stock markets saw a 25 per cent fall in share price. If the annual rate of return (including capital gains) on shares averaged 5 per cent, many would decide that they didn't want to invest in shares because it was too risky. But if the rate of return on shares increased to 30 per cent per year, then more people would be prepared to buy shares because the rewards would be much greater. Tobin argued that households and firms would trade off higher interest for less risk. But the higher the rate of interest, the greater would be the opportunity cost of holding assets in the form of riskless money. So the higher the rate of interest, the less the demand for money. The higher the risk on non-money assets, the lower will be their demand and the

higher the demand for money.

The portfolio balance approach of Tobin yields the same overall conclusions as the traditional Keynesian approach: the demand for money varies directly with nominal income and inflation but inversely with the rate of interest.

It is also possible within the approach to analyse why narrow definitions of the money supply (notes and coins and money in bank current accounts) have grown more slowly over time than broader measures of the money supply (which also include interest bearing deposit accounts with banks and building societies). During the 1970s and 1980s there has been a large expansion in the use of credit cards, a **money substitute**. The convenience of use of credit cards and the availability of free credit has proved so attractive that the use of narrow money for transactions purposes has fallen as a ratio of the total volume of transactions made. On the other hand, interest rates have increased considerably. Customers have found it worthwhile to lose a certain amount of liquidity to gain high interest. Hence there has been a switch out of cash and current account money into interest bearing accounts.

QUESTION 3 Following the October 1987 stock market crash, the net sales of UK unit trusts fell sharply. At the same time, net inflows of money into building society accounts increased sharply. Explain why this happened.

A monetarist approach

Keynesian theory assumes that financial assets are good **substitutes** for each other. For instance, a good alternative to holding cash is to put the money into a bank account; a good alternative to bank account deposits are stocks and shares. But it is assumed that physical assets, such as houses or furniture, are not good substitutes for financial assets.

In monetarist theory it is argued that physical assets are a good substitute for financial assets. For instance, if the rate of interest falls, both Keynesians and monetarists would predict that asset holders will sell some of their interest bearing assets. These are now no longer so attractive as before. Keynesian theory would suggest that the assets will be converted into money (i.e. the demand for money will rise). Monetarist theory suggests that part will be converted into money but part will be spent. Asset holders will use the opportunity of the sale of interest bearing financial assets to buy physical assets such as furniture, cars or houses.

This debate about whether physical assets are a good substitute for financial assets is important when considering the shape of the liquidity preference schedule. In Figure 69.4, the initial rate of interest is r_1 and the quantity demanded of money is OA. Interest rates now fall to r_2. According to Keynesian theory, asset holders will reduce their holdings of interest bearing financial assets and increase their holdings of money as shown by the curve LP_k. But according to monetarist theory, part of the fall in demand for interest bearing financial assets will be used to buy physical assets and consumption goods. Hence the liquidity preference schedule is LP_m and the increase in the demand for money is only AB and not AC as under Keynesian assumptions.

Monetarists argue that the liquidity preference schedule is far more interest inelastic than Keynesians believe, and that large falls in interest rates are needed to increase the demand for money to any extent. According to monetarists, the dominant demand for money is the transactions demand. The speculative demand is small.

This leads to another conclusion. The transactions demand for money is relatively stable because income is relatively stable. But the speculative demand is dependent upon perceptions of risk. If, as after the stock

market crash of October 1987, there is an increased perception of risk, then the liquidity preference schedule will shift to the right. If the demand for money is essentially a transactions demand, then the demand for money schedule will be relatively stable. If on the other hand risk and speculation play an important part in determining the demand for money, then the liquidity preference schedule will shift frequently as perceptions of risk change.

Keynesians, then, argue that the demand for money is interest elastic and unstable. Monetarists argue the converse: that the demand for money is interest inelastic and stable.

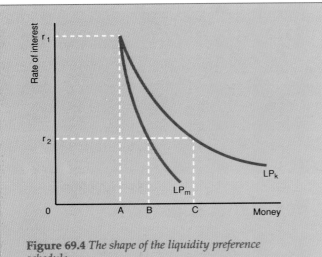

Figure 69.4 *The shape of the liquidity preference schedule*
Monetarists argue that physical assets are a good substitute for financial assets. Hence they argue that the demand for money curve is far more interest inelastic than Keynesians argue.

Key terms

The demand for money - the total amount of money which households and firms wish to hold at a point in time.
The transactions demand for money - the demand for money to make purchases of goods and services.
The precautionary demand for money - the demand for money to safeguard against unforeseen events.
The speculative demand for money - the demand for money arising from speculation in financial assets such as bonds.
Liquidity preference schedule - the demand for money curve, showing the relationship between the quantity of money demanded and the rate of interest.

Applied economics

The demand for money in the UK

Economic theory suggests that the demand for money is a function of several variables, including income and the rate of interest. Statistics for different measures of income and the rate of interest are readily available but how can the demand for money be measured?

At any point in time, the demand for money must equal the supply of money, so it is possible to measure the demand for money by measuring the money supply. There are a number of definitions of the money supply and hence a number of different demands for money can be measured too.

The transactions demand for money is perhaps best

measured using either M0 (notes and coins in circulation) or M1 (M0 plus money in bank current accounts). Figure 69.5 shows the ratio of money to income since 1969. If income were the sole determinant of the transactions demand for money, then the ratio of M0 or M1 to income would be constant over time. However, the ratios broadly fell in the 1960s and 1970s. For M0, it continued to fall in the 1980s, but for M1 it increased.

One reason why the M0-income ratio has fallen over time is the increased use of other means of payment apart from cash. With cheques, credit cards and debit

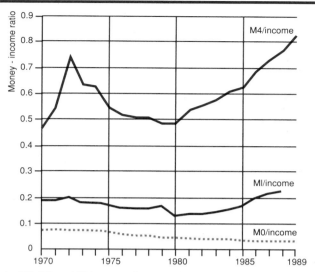

1. M0, M1 and M4 outstanding at end year ÷ GDP at current market prices for the year.
Source: adapted from CSO, *Economic Trends Annual Supplement; Monthly Digest of Statistics.*

Figure 69.5 *The ratio of money to income[1]*

cards, consumers have been reducing their holdings of cash in relation to their rising incomes. Similarly, the fall in the M1-income ratio in the 1970s can be explained in part by a shift in means of payment from cheques to credit cards and also by increased use by individuals of interest bearing time deposit accounts at banks and more importantly building societies. In the 1980s, banks have responded to competitive pressures by introducing interest-bearing current accounts. The rise in the M1-income ratio is perhaps a reflection of increased use of these accounts as customers have switched back some of their monies into interest bearing current accounts.

As economic theory would suggest, there is far less correlation between broad money, M4, and income than, for instance, between M1 and income because

income is only one of several variables which affect the demand for broad money. The M4-income ratio varies from 0.47 to 0.83 in Figure 69.5. One variable influencing the demand for broad money is the rate of interest. Figure 69.6 is a scatter diagram showing the relationship between the rate of interest and the M4-income ratio. Whilst the correlation is not particularly good, it would suggest that the higher the rate of interest, the lower the M4-income ratio - the relationship predicted by economic theory.

Income and the rate of interest are not the only variables which affect the demand for money according to economic theory. However, factors such as wealth and risk are more difficult to measure than income and the rate of interest and, overall, economists have found it difficult to establish a demand for money function which works well over long periods of time.

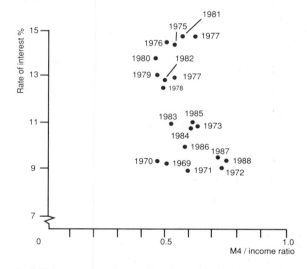

1. British government securities, long dated 20 years.
Source: adapted from CSO, *Economic Trends Annual Supplement; Monthly Digest of Statistics.*

Figure 69.6 *The demand for money and the rate of interest[1]*

Data question

1. Explain why economic theory suggests that there is a relationship between the demand for money and (a) income and (b) the rate of interest.

2. To what extent do the data in Table 69.1 support this theory?

Table 69.1 *Money stock M2, income and the rate of interest*

	M2[1]	GDP[2]	Rate of interest[3]
1983	120 764	260 401	10.80
1984	134 786	279 386	10.69
1985	147 500	305 872	10.82
1986	168 914	324 331	9.87
1987	187 315	355 651	9.47
1988	217 206	396 438	9.36
1989	238 438	434 724	9.56

1. Amounts outstanding at end year.
2. Gross domestic product at factor cost.
3. British government securities, long dated 20 years.

Source: adapted from CSO, *Economic Trends Annual Supplement.*

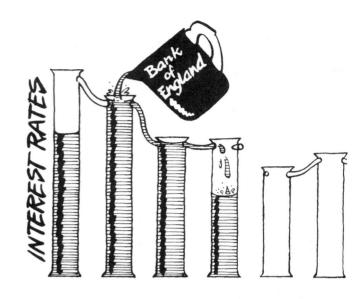

Summary

1. The price of money is the rate of interest.
2. The rate of interest is determined by the demand for and supply of money.
3. An increase in the demand for money or a fall in the supply of money will increase the rate of interest. A fall in the demand for money or an increase in the supply of money will lead to a fall in the rate of interest.
4. Different interest rates exist in different money markets. Interest rates tend to move together in the same direction over long periods of time.
5. Factors which cause interest rates to differ in the same market include time, risk and administrative cost.
6. The real rate of interest is the nominal rate adjusted for inflation.

Determination of the rate of interest

Economic theory suggests that, just as the price of a good is determined by the forces of demand and supply (☞ unit 6), so too is the price of money. So what is the price of money? It is how much needs to be paid if money is borrowed - it is the **rate of interest.**

Figure 70.1 shows the demand and supply curves of money. The demand curve for money is usually called the **liquidity preference schedule** (☞ unit 69). It is downward sloping because the higher the rate of interest, the more households and firms will wish to hold non-money assets such as bonds or shares. The money supply is drawn as a vertical line, showing that the supply of money remains constant whatever the rate of interest.

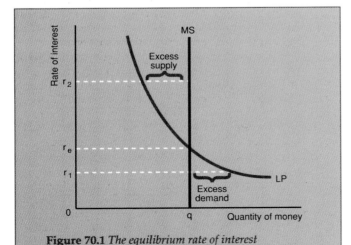

Figure 70.1 *The equilibrium rate of interest*
r_e *is the equilibrium rate of interest - the rate of interest where the demand for and supply of money are equal.*

This assumes that the central bank can and does control the supply of money in the economy independently of its price (☞ unit 72). The money supply is then said to be **exogenous**. It would make no difference to our conclusions here if the money supply were assumed to be upward sloping and therefore **endogenous**, with the money supply determined by the rate of interest rather than by the decisions of the central bank. The equilibrium rate of interest r_e occurs where the demand for money equals the supply of money.

Economic theory suggests that if the rate of interest is above or below this level then it will tend towards its equilibrium value.

■ Assume that the rate of interest is r_1 (i.e. there is an excess demand for money). Households and firms want to hold more money than they are currently holding. They will react by selling some of their non-money assets and converting them into money. If they sell bonds, the price of bonds will fall. If bond prices fall, interest rates automatically increase (☞ unit 67). Similarly, if they sell shares the price of shares will tend to fall and interest rates will consequently rise. If money is defined in narrow terms such as M0, then households could increase their holdings of money by withdrawing some from building society accounts. Building societies will now have a shortfall of deposits and will react by putting up their interest rates to attract more savings. So excess demand for money will push up interest rates, leading to a movement back along the liquidity preference schedule. This will continue until households and firms are in equilibrium where the demand for money equals the supply of money.

■ Now assume the converse: that there is excess supply of money such as would exist at a rate of interest of r_2. Households and firms hold more money than they wish, so they will attempt to put it into the building society, or buy bonds, shares or other types of assets. This will lead to a fall in interest rates back towards the equilibrium interest rate r_e.

Shifts in the money demand and supply curves

What happens if the demand or supply of money changes (i.e. there is a **shift** in either the money demand or supply curves)?

Assume that the liquidity preference schedule shifts to the right as in Figure 70.2. This means that more money is demanded at any given rate of interest. This could be caused by an increase in income, an increase in the price

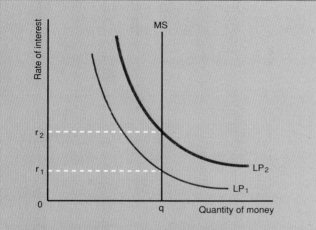

Figure 70.2 *An increase in the demand for money. An increase in the demand for money, shown by a shift in the liquidity preference schedule to the right, will increase the rate of interest from r_1 to r_2.*

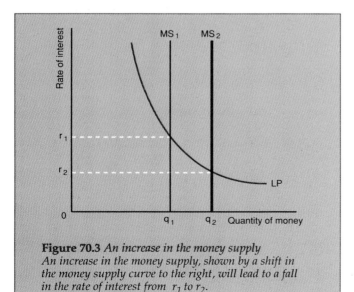

Figure 70.3 *An increase in the money supply An increase in the money supply, shown by a shift in the money supply curve to the right, will lead to a fall in the rate of interest from r_1 to r_2.*

level (we are assuming that the LP curve shows the demand for nominal balances) or an increase in the perceived risk of holding non-monetary assets such as bonds or shares (☞ unit 69). The rate of interest will consequently increase from r_1 to r_2. So an increase in liquidity preference shown by a shift to the right in the LP curve will increase interest rates, but not change the supply of money which is fixed by the authorities. Conversely, a fall in the demand for money will lead to a fall in interest rates.

Now assume that the government increases the supply of money. This is shown by a shift to the right in the supply curve in Figure 70.3. The result will be a fall in the rate of interest from r_1 to r_2. Conversely a fall in the money supply will lead to an increase in interest rates.

> **QUESTION 1** Draw a diagram showing the liquidity preference schedule and the money supply curve. Show the likely effect on the equilibrium rate of interest if there is:
> (a) a fall in the money supply;
> (b) an increase in the price level;
> (c) increased use of credit cards in payment for goods and services;
> (d) a fall in national income at current prices;
> (e) an increase in notes and coins in circulation in the economy;
> (f) a fall in speculative activity in the bond market at any given rate of interest.

Different markets, different rates of interest

So far, it has been implicitly assumed that there is one market for money and one equilibrium rate of interest in the economy. This is a very useful simplification in macro-economic theory. However, in reality there are many markets for money and many rates of interest in an economy. For instance, in the discount market (☞ unit 68) banks and discount houses borrow and lend money from each other. In the local authority bill market, local authorities borrow and lend money from banks and other financial institutions. In the mortgage market, building societies and banks lend money to households purchasing property. If all these markets were perfect, and all loans and borrowing were identical, then the rate of interest in all markets would be the same. But there are many barriers between markets and loans are not identical. Hence interest rates differ. One major barrier between different money markets is imperfect knowledge. For instance, when banks offer higher rates of interest on their accounts than building societies, the building societies will not suffer major drains of funds. This is partly because customers find it inconvenient to change money from one account to another. But also many customers are unaware of differences in interest rates. Equally, in some markets borrowers and lenders are locked into fixed term contracts. These are likely to be short - anything up to say 6 months. This means that money cannot flow into another market to take advantage of higher interest rates.

Barriers to the flow of money between markets exist but on the whole they are not high enough to insulate markets completely. When interest rates increase in the City of London, the major banks will almost certainly increase their interest rates too. The effect will ripple out into the rest of the economy. Building societies may not respond initially but they will suffer a drain of funds in the medium term if they do not increase their interest rates. So interest rates tend to move in the same direction over a period of time.

There are a number of factors which can cause interest rates to differ in the same market.

■ Time. The longer the period of the loan, the higher tends to be the rate of interest. If money is lent out for just 24 hours, the lender has complete flexibility either to stop lending the money or to switch money to another market. If it is lent out for 25 years, there is no such flexibility. So higher interest is necessary to compensate lenders as the length of the term of a loan increases.

■ If the market expects interest rates to fall in the near future, then longer term loans could attract a lower rate of interest than shorter term loans. For instance, if current interest rates are 12 per cent for overnight loans, but you expect them to fall to 10 per cent in a month's time, then you might be prepared to lend money for three months at somewhere between 10 and 12 per cent.

■ Risk. Lending money to an unemployed worker is likely to be far more risky than lending it to the Midland Bank. So the greater the risk of default on the loan, the higher will be the rate of interest.

■ Administrative cost. Lending out £100 million in lots of £100 at a time is likely to be far more administratively costly than lending out £100 million to one customer. So the higher the administration cost, the higher will tend to be the rate of interest.

QUESTION 2

Table 70.1 *Selected interest rates and yields, 6 April 1990*

Source	Period of loan	%
Inter-bank money markets	overnight	14 $^{13}/_{16}$
	one year	15 $^{1}/_{2}$
Treasury Bills	one month	14 $^{21}/_{32}$
	three months	14 $^{9}/_{16}$
Gilt edged stock (high coupon)	5 years	12.83
Company debentures (average)	5 years	15.56

Suggest reasons why the interest rates in Table 70.1 differ from each other.

Nominal and real interest rates

When a building society offers a rate of interest of 10 per cent, it is offering a NOMINAL RATE OF INTEREST. The interest is unadjusted for inflation. But each year, prices in the economy are likely to rise. £100 placed in the building society today will, excluding any interest payments, buy fewer goods and services in a year's time. The REAL RATE OF INTEREST is the rate of interest adjusted for inflation. For instance, the real rate of interest would be 5 per cent if the nominal rate of interest were 10 per cent and the rate of inflation were 5 per cent. With a nominal rate of interest of 12 per cent and a rate of inflation of 8 per cent, the real rate of interest would

QUESTION 3

Table 70.2 *Building society interest rates and the rate of inflation*

Year	Average rate of interest paid on shares %	Inflation rate %
1980	10.3	18.0
1981	9.2	11.9
1982	8.8	8.6
1983	7.3	4.6
1984	7.7	5.0
1985	8.7	6.1
1986	7.8	3.4
1987	7.5	4.2
1988	7.0	4.9

Source: adapted from CSO, *Annual Abstract of Statistics*.

(a) Calculate the annual real rate of interest on building society accounts from the data in the table.
(b) In which years was the real rate of interest negative?
(c) What would have to be true if the real rate of interest were higher than the nominal rate of interest?

be 4 per cent.

Real interest rates can be negative as well as positive. In 1975 with the UK inflation rate at 25 per cent and nominal interest rates about 7 per cent, the real rate of interest was **minus** 18 per cent. Anyone saving at 7 per cent would have lost 18 per cent of the purchasing power of their money during 1975. Why do people save when real interest rates are negative? One reason is that much saving is highly illiquid. People can't liquidate assurance or pension fund contracts easily or without cost for instance. Another reason is that people need to save if only because they do not wish to spend all their income when they receive it on pay day. What's more, savers might have lost 18 per cent. But people who kept their money in cash lost 25 per cent!

Key terms

Nominal interest rates - interest rates unadjusted for inflation.
Real interest rates - nominal interest rates adjusted for inflation.

Applied economics

The rate of interest in four money markets

The rate of interest in each money market in the UK is determined by the demand for and supply of money in that market. It is possible to identify the main borrowers and lenders in most money markets. For instance, in the UK domestic **mortgage market**, banks and building societies are the two most important suppliers of money. People wanting to borrow money to buy a house demand money. The rate of interest on a mortgage loan is low compared to, say, an ordinary overdraft or bank loan. This is mainly because a mortgage loan is secured on a property. If a borrower defaults on the loan, the bank or building society can force the borrower to sell the property and pay back the loan with the money raised. So a mortgage loan is regarded as being relatively free of risk by lenders.

Banks have traditionally been the main source of **loans and overdrafts**, although secondary banks and building societies have recently entered the market too. The demand for money comes from individuals and companies who want to borrow to finance everything from repairs to a car, to a new kitchen or a new factory. Interest rates tend to be set according to risk of default. Large companies can usually get lower rates of interest on loans than small companies, whilst individuals are charged much higher rates than on a mortgage loan. It could be argued that loans through credit cards form part of this market too. Interest rates on credit cards tend to be above overdraft and personal loan rates for individuals. Not only is the risk of default higher on a credit card than on a personal loan but there are much greater administrative costs in handling credit card loans than in handling personal loans and overdrafts.

In a City money market, such as the **discount market** or **local authority market**, individual transactions tend to be for far greater sums of money. In the discount market, the government demands money by issuing Treasury Bills (☞ unit 67) and money is supplied for

their purchase mainly by discount houses and banks. In the local authority market, local authorities demand money whilst banks and other financial institutions supply funds. Table 70.3 shows interest rates in these two markets at a point in time. Treasury Bills carried a lower rate of interest than local authority deposits because central government was considered a marginally better risk than local authorities. In the local authority market, the rate of interest was greater for one month deposits (i.e. deposits repayable in one month's time) than for 7 day deposits as economic theory would suggest . However, for both Treasury Bills and local authority deposits, the rate of interest then fell for three month deposits. This was because the markets thought there was a possibility that interest rates would fall in the near future. More lenders were prepared to supply money on fixed interest 3 month contracts than would otherwise have been the case and hence interest rates were lower than would have been predicted given one month rates.

Table 70.3 *Interest rates, 29.10.1990*

				Per cent
	Overnight	7 day's notice	One month	Three months
Treasury Bills			$13^{21}/_{32}$	$13^{3}/_{8}$
Local authority deposits	$13^{7}/_{8}$	$13^{7}/_{8}$	$13^{15}/_{16}$	$13^{3}/_{4}$

Source: adapted from the *Financial Times*, 30.10.1990.

INTEREST RATES

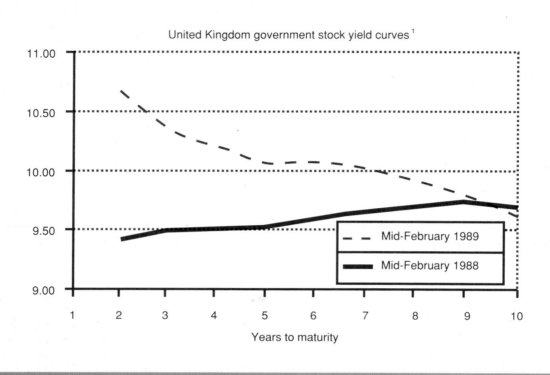

In 1987, for the first time since the late 1960s, the government moved from being a net borrower in the gilts market to repaying debt. This slowly created a shortage of gilts at the long end of the market.

A yield curve shows the percentage yield (effectively the market rate of interest) on government stock of different maturities. For instance, in mid-February 1988, the yield on government stock which would mature in two years' time (i.e. the government would repay money borrowed in 1990) was nearly 9.5 per cent. The yield on government stock with 10 years to maturity was higher at 9.7 per cent.

Source: United Nations, *Economic Survey of Europe*, 1988-1989.

Figure 70.4 *Yield curves for UK government stock*

1. **Explain which of the two yield curves would be considered to be a 'normal' yield curve according to economic theory?**
2. **Suggest why the other yield curve has the shape it does.**

Summary

1. Money is neutral if changes in the supply of money only affect the price level of the economy.
2. The Fisher equation of exchange states that $MV \equiv PT$.
3. The quantity theory of money states that changes in M, the money supply, are the sole determinants of changes in P, the price level.
4. Monetarists argue that V is constant in the short term and changes only slowly in the long run.
5. They also argue that the money supply must grow over time to match any increase in T, the level of real income; if the growth in T were greater than the growth in M, there would be a fall in prices.
6. Keynesian economists dispute whether V is constant in the short run. They also suggest that increases in prices may well lead to increases in the money supply.

The neutrality of money

In 1960, the President of France, General Charles de Gaulle, cut the value of all French money by a factor of 100. He passed a law which decreed that on the 1 January 1960, 100 Francs would be called 1 Franc. So a 1 000 Franc note was reduced in value to 10 Francs. 10 000 Francs in a French bank account was only worth 100 Francs. A company which had borrowed 100 million Francs would only have to repay 1 million Francs. This change in the value of the Franc had little or no effect on the **real economy**. Because all monetary values were changed on the same day, relative values remained unchanged. Prices were only 1 per cent of their former level, but so too were wages. The company which had its loan cut by a factor of 100 still had to earn 100 times more in Francs to pay off the loan. The owner of a 1 000 Franc note saw its value reduced 100 fold, but then prices were reduced by the same factor. The note bought exactly the same quantity of goods and services as before.

This is an example of the neutrality of money. Money is said to be NEUTRAL if changes in the money supply only affect the level of prices in the economy. But economists disagree about the extent to which money is neutral. Some economists argue that changes in the money supply can have important effects on the real economy, in particular on variables such as national income and unemployment, whilst others argue that it is neutral.

The equation of exchange

The EQUATION OF EXCHANGE distinguishes between the real and the money side of the economy. The most famous formulation of the equation was made by Irving Fisher, an American economist who worked during the first half of this century. The FISHER EQUATION is:

$$MV \equiv PT$$

M is the total amount of money in the economy (i.e. the money supply). V is the VELOCITY OF CIRCULATION of money (sometimes also called the INCOME VELOCITY). V is the number of times the money supply changes hands over a period of time, such as a year. P is the average price of each transaction made in the economy. T is the total number of transactions made over a period of time.

The equation of exchange is an identity (i.e. it is true by definition ☞ unit 57). Assume that there is £100 of money (M) in circulation in the economy. On average, each £1 changed hands 4 times (V) during the year. So we know that £400 must have been spent during the year (M x V). If the average price of each transaction was £2 (P), there **must** have been 200 separate transactions (T) over the period. Similarly, if 100 transactions (T) take place over a year and each transaction was for an average of £5 (P), then the total amount spent was £500. If there was only £50 of money in circulation (M), that money **must** have changed hands on average 10 times during the year. So the velocity of circulation of money (V) must have been 10.

QUESTION 1 The money supply M is £200, V is 10 and T is 100.
(a) What is the value of P?
(b) The money supply now doubles. If V and T remain constant, what is the new value of P?
(c) At the new money supply level, T now increases from 100 to 150. What will happen to the price level if there is no change in the money supply and V remains constant?

Different formulations

There are a number of other ways of expressing the equation of exchange.

■ T, the number of transactions in the economy over a period of time, can be equated with real national income, the physical volume of output in the economy. Hence:

$$MV \equiv PY$$

where Y is real national income.

■ P times Y, the average price of each transaction times the level of real national income, is equal to y, the level of nominal national income, or national income at current prices. So:

$$MV \equiv y$$

■ If MV ≡ PY and we divide both sides of the identity by V, then:

$$M \equiv \frac{PY}{V}$$

■ If 1÷V is called k, we then have:

$$M \equiv k\,PY$$

■ Alternatively, if Y÷V is called a, we have:

$$M = aP$$

We will now use these different formulations to explain the quantity theory of money.

The quantity theory of money

The QUANTITY THEORY OF MONEY is one of the oldest economic theories, dating back at least 500 years if not more. The theory states that increases in prices are caused solely by increases in the money supply. As Milton Friedman put it in his 1968 book *Dollars and Deficits*, 'inflation is always and everywhere a monetary phenomenon'.

It is necessary to make a number of key assumptions if we are to make the transition from the equation of exchange, which is an identity and therefore always true, to the quantity theory of money. The simplest way of doing this is to assume that k, the inverse of the velocity of circulation of money, and Y, the real level of national income, are both constant. Then:

$$M = aP$$

where a is the constant kY (or Y÷V). If M increases, then so must P. In the crudest form of monetarism, M and P will change by the same percentage. So a 10 per cent increase in the money supply will increase prices by 10 per cent. Money is therefore neutral.

Advocates of the quantity theory of money are called MONETARISTS and the belief that inflation is caused solely by increases in the money supply is called MONETARISM. Why do monetarists argue that V and Y can be assumed to be constant?

The velocity of circulation The velocity of circulation of money is the average number of times a unit of money changes hands over a period of time. For instance, a £10 note may change hands 50 times a year.

One factor which determines the velocity of circulation is the way in which households receive money and make purchases.

■ The velocity of circulation of broad money will tend to fall if there is a change from paying workers once a week to once a month. Households will now hold money for longer periods of time to cover expenditure later in the month.

■ The increased use of **money substitutes,** such as credit cards, will also reduce the velocity of circulation of money itself. Instead of making many separate money transactions, the card holder will make one transaction at the end of the month to the credit card company. On the other hand, increased use of cheques and debit and credit cards will tend to lead to an increase in the velocity of circulation of notes and coins (M0). Households and firms increasingly do not keep cash as savings at home, but use it for transactions purposes. Cash card machines mean that households keep less and less cash as a proportion of income and spend it very quickly.

Another factor which is important in determining the value of V is the extent to which money is used for speculation. If there is a large **speculative demand for money** (☞ unit 69), then V can vary as asset portfolios are switched in and out of money. Keynesians argue that when the rate of interest rises, households and firms desire to hold less money because the opportunity cost of holding money will have risen. The opportunity cost is the interest or return they could have obtained if they had placed their money in, say, a building society account or in stocks or shares. When the rate of interest rises, less money will be held to make the same number of transactions. Households and firms will make their smaller stock of money work harder (i.e. the velocity of circulation will rise).

So the debate about the value of the velocity of circulation of money is the same debate as the one about the determinants of the demand for money. Monetarists argue that the speculative demand for money is relatively unimportant because money is held mainly for transactions purposes. In the long run V can change as institutional factors change, but the change will be slow. In the short run, V is broadly constant because the demand for money is a stable function of income. Keynesians on the other hand argue that changes in the rate of interest lead to significant changes in **liquidity**

preference (i.e. the demand for money) and therefore the velocity of circulation is volatile in the short run.

National income Real national income tends to rise slowly over time. The annual growth rate of the UK economy over the past 40 years has averaged about 2½ per cent. If M = kPY, and k is constant, then the money supply can grow by the rate of growth of real income without generating a rise in prices. Monetarists indeed argue that the money supply should be expanded in line with real growth, otherwise prices will fall. Falling prices can be just as undesirable as inflation. But any expansion of the money supply over and above the rate of growth of real income will be inflationary, according to monetarists.

QUESTION 2

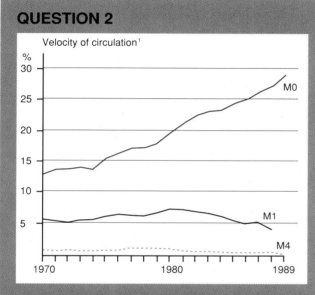

1. GDP at current market prices ÷ money stock outstanding at end of year.
Source: adapted from CSO, *Economic Trends Annual Supplement*; CSO; *Annual Abstract of Statistics*; CSO, *Monthly Digest of Statistics.*

Figure 71.1 *Velocity of circulation*

Figure 71.1 shows three different measures of the velocity of circulation of money. Line 1 shows the velocity of circulation of notes and coins M0. Line 2 shows the velocity of circulation of narrow money M1. Line 3 shows the velocity of circulation of broad money M4.
(a) To what extent is the velocity of circulation of money constant over time?
(b) Suggest reasons why the velocity of circulation may have changed over the period shown.

The money supply and inflation

The quantity theory of money, according to monetarists, shows that price increases are the result of increases in the money supply. This conclusion is dependent upon the assumptions that the velocity of circulation of money is constant and that income (and therefore transactions and output) changes only slowly over time. Keynesians, on the other hand, argue that the demand for money is unstable and therefore the velocity of circulation of money is unstable too. A rise in M could be offset by an decrease in V rather than leading to a change in the price level.

Keynesians also point out that monetarists assume that causality runs from M to P. But logically it could equally be true that price increases could lead to an increase in the money supply. There are two ways in which this might occur.

- Assume that the money supply is **endogenous** (i.e. it cannot be controlled by the central bank but instead is created by the banking system). A rise in wages will lead to increased demand for money from the banks. Firms will need more money to pay their workers, whilst workers will increase their demand for money because their incomes have gone up. An increased demand for money will push up interest rates and banks will find it more profitable to create money. Therefore the money supply will expand.
- If the money supply is **exogenous**, (i.e. its size is controlled by the central bank), it is not necessarily true that the central bank will choose to restrict the growth of the money supply. It may well allow the money supply to expand rather than accept the consequences of restricting its growth. This policy is known as **accommodating** (☞ unit 93) the factors, causing the increase in demand and therefore supply of money.

The quantity theory of money equation also suggests that an increase in the money supply **could** lead to an increase in real income. If M = kPY, and k and P are assumed to be constant, then an increase in M will lead to an increase in Y. Some monetarists (such as Patrick Minford and others from the Rational Expectations school of thought) argue that an increase in M will feed through so quickly to an increase in P that Y will not be affected at all (i.e. there will no time lag between an increase in M and an increase in P). Other monetarists, such as Milton Friedman, argue that, in the short term, much of the increase in the money supply will indeed initially lead to an increase in real income. This link between increases in M and increases in Y is known as the monetary **transmission mechanism** (☞ unit 81). But, they argue, in the longer term, real income will revert to its previous level whilst all of the increase in the money supply will have fed through to an increase in prices (i.e. there is a time lag between increases in the money supply and increases in the price level).

Economists are agreed that very large increases in the money supply will inevitably lead to high inflation. If the money supply increases by 200 per cent over a year, it would be impossible for either V or Y to change sufficiently for P to be unaffected. The monetarist-Keynesian debate centres round the effects of relatively small increases in the money supply. Are money supply increases of 5 or 10 or even 20 per cent necessarily inflationary?

QUESTION 3

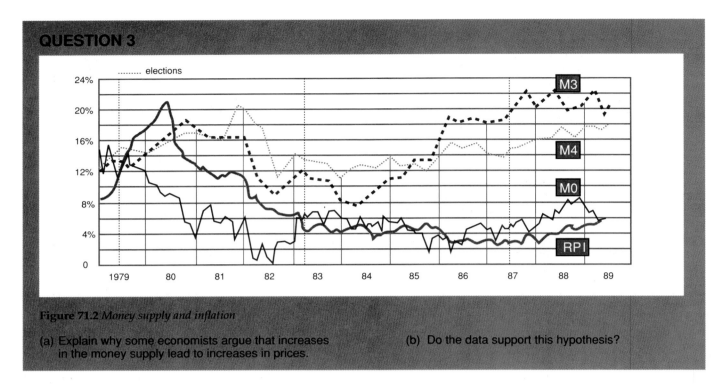

Figure 71.2 *Money supply and inflation*

(a) Explain why some economists argue that increases in the money supply lead to increases in prices.

(b) Do the data support this hypothesis?

Key terms

Neutrality of money - the theory that a change in the quantity of money in the economy will affect only the level of prices and not real variables such as unemployment.

The equation of exchange - the identity $MV \equiv PT$ where M is the money supply, V is the velocity of circulation of money over time, P is the price level and T is the number of transactions over time.

The velocity of circulation of money - the number of times the stock of money in the economy changes hands over a period of time.

The quantity theory of money - the theory, based on the equation of exchange, that increase in the money supply, M, will lead to increases in the price level P.

Monetarists - economists who believe that the quantity theory of money shows that inflation is always and everywhere caused by excessive increases in the money supply.

Applied economics

Inflation and the money supply

The quantity theory of money suggests that inflation is caused by increases in the money supply over and above the rate of real growth in the economy. If this were true, it would be possible to see a strong correlation between money supply growth and the rate of change of prices across a number of countries.

Figure 71.3 is a scatter diagram, giving data for 11 countries. On the horizontal axis is the percentage growth of the money supply, M1, over the ten year period 1978 to 1988. On the vertical axis is the percentage change in prices over the same period. As

can be seen, if a line of 'best fit' is drawn, there does seem to be some correlation between the two variables: the higher the percentage increase in the money supply, the higher the rate of inflation.

It is interesting to note that the one country in the sample which deviates significantly from the mean is the UK. Its rate of growth of the money supply is associated with far less inflation than might be expected from the experience of other countries. Indeed during the 1980s in Britain, there was a steady disillusionment with what is sometimes called 'crude' monetarism (Dennis Healey, Chancellor of the Exchequer from 1976 to 1979 called it 'punk' monetarism!). M1 and M3, targeted by the government in its attempt to control inflation, grew at a far faster rate than inflation. In the early 1980s, whilst inflation fell, the rate of growth of the money supply remained high.

Monetarists today would argue that this arose mainly because of financial deregulation. For instance:

■ exchange controls were abolished in 1979;
■ controls on bank lending were removed in 1980;
■ competition in the banking sector was increased, by allowing building societies to offer banking services under the Building Society Act 1986 for example;
■ the London Stock Market was deregulated in 1986.

This led to individuals and companies increasing their demand for money (i.e. controls had rationed the amount of money available to them). This increase in money holdings relative to all other variables led to a fall in the velocity of circulation of money, previously thought by monetarists to be broadly constant over time. However, the increase in money holdings was a one-off effect and increases in the money supply from the mid-1980s onwards were not absorbed by falls in V. As a result, inflation increased from 1988 to 1990.

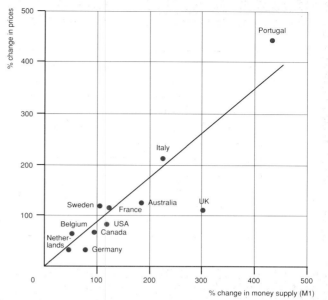

Source: adapted from OECD, *Main Economic Indicators 1960-1988.*

Figure 71.3 *Inflation and the percentage change in the money supply for 11 major economies., 1978 - 1988*

MONEY, PRICES, TRANSACTIONS AND VELOCITY OF CIRCULATION

Data question

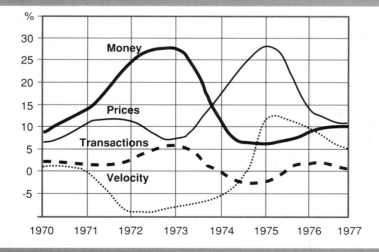

Figure 71.4

Figure 71.4 shows the relationships between the money supply, prices, real output (transactions) and the velocity of circulation of money between 1970 and 1977. It was during this period that many economists and politicians became 'monetarist' in their thinking.

1. Describe the relationship shown between the variables in Figure 71.4.
2. To what extent does it support a monetarist view of inflation?

72 Monetary policy

Summary

1. Policy goals are established by government. Policy instruments are used to achieve these goals. Intermediate targets are used to monitor the success of government intervention in the economy.
2. One policy instrument is monetary base control, the control of high powered money in the economy.
3. Open market operations can affect the money supply through the purchase and sale of government stock.
4. Manipulating interest rates can affect the demand for money.
5. Other policy instruments include credit controls and controls on the growth of bank lending.

Goals, targets and instruments

Governments today set general **policy goals** such as full employment, price stability, a balance of payments equilibrium and high economic growth. All too often the economy is in crisis. Perhaps there is unemployment, inflation or the balance of payments is in deficit. The government may then choose to act to steer the economy back to a more desirable position. It will use a variety of **policy instruments** to achieve this aim, such as changes in interest rates.

How can the government judge whether it has succeeding in achieving its policy goals? Unemployment levels and the number of vacancies notified to Jobcentres could be used to judge whether the economy is at full employment. Unemployment levels and notified vacancies would then be called **intermediate targets** - targets to aim for in attempting to reach the policy goal of full employment.

The money supply and the rate of interest are examples of intermediate targets too. It is widely believed, for instance, that excessive increases in the money supply lead to inflation (☞ unit 71). Hence it is important to target the rate of growth of the money supply. MONETARY POLICY is defined as the attempt by government or a central bank to manipulate the money supply, the supply of credit, interest rates or any other monetary variables to achieve the fulfilment of policy goals.

In this unit we shall consider what policy instruments government might use to control monetary variables. In the next unit, we will consider how effective such control might be. Before we proceed, it is important to note two points.

■ Some monetary variables such as the rate of interest may be used by government as a policy instrument as well as being an intermediate target. This is one of the problems of policy which can make it difficult for government to control the economy effectively.
■ There are various definitions of the money supply ranging from M0 (notes and coins plus bank deposits at the Bank of England) to M5 (the main constituents of which are M0, bank current account deposits, bank deposit account deposits, building society deposits and National Savings deposits). The Bank of England has total control over the issue of notes and coins in the UK. However, less than 1 per cent of M5 is made up of notes and coins. So if it wishes to control anything other than M0, it has to control the amount of money in the banking system and in the wider financial system too.

Monetary base control

Banks have the power to create money (☞ unit 66). But there is a limit to the amount of money that can be created. This is set by the amount of **high powered money** within the system and by the **reserve ratio**. For instance, banks might need to keep 1 per cent (i.e. 0.01) of their total deposits in the form of cash because customers withdraw some cash on a day to day basis from bank branches. Cash is then the high powered money within the system. The money multiplier is $1 \div 0.01$ or 100. So if the banks held £1 billion in cash, they could create a maximum of £100 billion in deposits. The money supply would then consist of any cash in circulation with the public plus £100 billion of bank deposit money.

One possible way in which a central bank can influence the size of the money supply is if it alters the size of the reserve ratio. Suppose in our example that the central bank issued a directive ordering banks in future to keep 2 per cent of their deposits in the form of cash. With only £1 billion in cash, banks could then only hold £50 billion in deposits. The money supply would have fallen by £50 billion (£100 billion - £50 billion). So increases in the reserve ratio will reduce the money supply, whilst falls in the reserve ratio will increase it.

The central bank can also restrict the supply of reserve assets to the banks. Suppose the central bank forced banks to deposit £½ billion of notes with it. They are then not allowed to include these deposits as part of their reserve assets. The banks will therefore see their holdings of reserve assets fall from £1 billion to £ ½ billion. They will be forced to cut the amount of deposits held by the public from £100 billion to £50 billion (1 per cent of £50 billion equalling the £½ billion in cash the banks now hold). So restricting the availability of reserve assets to the banks will lead to a fall in the money supply. This type of monetary control was used extensively by the Bank of England in the 1960s and 1970s and was known as the SPECIAL DEPOSITS SCHEME.

QUESTION 1 The money supply is £110 billion. Of this, £10 billion is cash held by the general public and £100 billion is bank deposits. The central bank has decreed that banks must keep 10 per cent of their total liabilities in the form of cash. So the banking system has £10 billion worth of cash in bank vaults and £90 billion worth of loans on its books.

(a) Which asset is high powered money?
(b) What is the reserve ratio?
(c) What is the value of the credit multiplier?
(d) The central bank increases the reserve ratio to 25 per cent. Assuming that there is no change in the amount of cash held by the general public, what will be (i) the new level of bank assets and liabilities and (ii) the new level of the money supply?
(e) What would the answers be in (d) if the reserve ratio were 5 per cent?
(f) Assume that the reserve ratio stays at 10 per cent. The central bank orders all other banks to deposit 1 per cent in cash of their total assets in a special account at the central bank.
  (i) If the general public maintain their cash holdings of £10 billion, what will be the effect on the money supply of this directive?
  (ii) If the banking system could persuade the general public to deposit an extra £1 billion in cash in bank accounts, what would be the effect on the money supply?

Open market operations

The central bank has the unique power to create bank notes or destroy them at almost no cost to itself (the cost being that of printing and distributing the notes). Assume that the central bank prints £1 million in notes and uses the money to buy financial securities such as government bonds (☞ unit 67) from the general public. The public now hold fewer bonds but they hold £1 million more in bank notes. They are likely to deposit most of these in banks. Assume for simplicity that they deposit all the cash in the banking system. If the reserve ratio is 1 per cent and cash is the reserve asset, then £1 million of extra cash deposited in the banks will enable them to create £100 million of extra money through the credit multiplier process.

The reverse is also true. If the central bank sells £1 million of financial securities, the public are likely to pay for these by withdrawing £1 million from the banking system by issuing cheques to the central bank. The central bank will then present the cheques to the banks for payment in cash. The banking system will now lose £1 million of cash and therefore of reserve assets. With a reserve ratio of 1 per cent (i.e. a credit multiplier of 100), the banking system has to reduce assets and liabilities by £100 million.

This process of buying and selling financial securities in exchange for high powered money (cash in our example) is known as OPEN MARKET OPERATIONS. In practice

credit multipliers are nowhere near as large as in our examples, but open market operations are still likely to produce a multiple increase or contraction of the money supply.

QUESTION 2 Cash is defined as the reserve asset. The central bank imposes a 5 per cent reserve ratio on the bank system.

(a) What is the credit multiplier?
(b) By how much will the money supply change if the central bank sells the following amounts of government bonds to the general public:
  (i) £1 billion; (ii) £250 million; (iii) £500 million?
(c) By how much will the money supply change if the central bank buys the following amounts of government bonds from the general public:
  (i) £2 billion; (ii) £200 million; (iii) £600 million?

The discount rate

Banks can go bankrupt whilst still being perfectly sound financially. They only keep enough cash or other liquid assets to meet their day to day needs. They lend out the rest longer term. If all the customers of a bank wanted their money back today, the bank would be unable to pay and therefore it would be technically bankrupt. To prevent this from happening, central banks act as lenders of last resort. When there is a shortage of cash in the financial system, the central bank will buy securities for cash. In the UK, discount houses are the channel through which the Bank of England acts as lender of last resort (☞ unit 68).

Banks will suffer no financial penalties for running short of liquid assets such as cash if the central bank is prepared to buy financial assets at their current market value. The current market value of assets such as Treasury Bills, commercial bills, and government stock is determined by the rate of interest (☞ unit 67). The higher the rate of interest, the lower the market value of outstanding bills and bonds. So if the **discount rate**, (the interest rate which the central bank uses to calculate the price it will pay for bills and bonds), is equal to the current market rate of interest the banks will not lose money if they are forced to sell assets to the central bank.

But the higher the central bank sets the discount rate above market rates of interest, the greater will be the loss that banks face if they are forced to sell assets to the central bank when short of cash. So the higher the discount rate above market rates, the greater will be the banks' desired ratio of cash to total assets (i.e. their reserve ratio). With cash holdings constant, they can only increase this ratio by reducing their total assets and thus reducing the money supply.

Increases in the discount rate are also likely to increase bank **base rates** as well as other interest rates in the economy. An increase in interest rates will reduce the demand for money (☞ unit 73). In equilibrium, the demand for money is equal to the supply of money. So in theory an increase in interest rates, with the demand curve for money (the liquidity preference schedule ☞ unit 69) unchanged, can only be sustained if the money supply has fallen too. To achieve higher interest rates, the central bank must be prepared to buy and sell financial assets such as bills and bonds on a day to day basis at the constant higher rate of interest. What the central bank cannot do is to choose both an interest rate level and a money supply level. Either it fixes the money supply and allows the rate of interest to find its equilibrium level or it fixes the rate of interest and allows the money supply to adjust.

QUESTION 3 On 27 January 1990, the *Financial Times* reported that the Bank of England had announced an increase in sales of Treasury Bills. It proposed to increase its tender (i.e. its sales) of Treasury Bills on Friday February 2 to £500 of 13 week bills and £200 million of 26 week bills in order to offset excess liquidity in the money market.

The increased tender was to counteract the downward movement of money market rates which follows the seasonal pattern of Exchequer flows, including corporate tax payments. Tax payments are concentrated in the winter months and they tend to reduce the money supply as taxpayers withdraw money from their bank accounts to pay the government. By February the money supply is increasing as tax payments tail off.

(a) If the Bank of England had not sold extra Treasury Bills, the rate of interest in the money markets would probably have fallen. Explain why.
(b) How could the Bank of England have increased money market interest rates?

Funding

In the traditional sense of the term, FUNDING refers to the replacement of short term debt by long term debt. Funding was used in the 19th and early 20th centuries in the UK to manage the National Debt (☞ unit 76), the money which governments had borrowed in the past normally to finance wars. In modern monetary policy, changing the structure of the Debt can affect intermediate targets.

■ Reducing the amount of short term debt, such as Treasury Bills, and increasing the amount of long term debt by a corresponding amount will lower short term interest rates (because there is less demand now for loanable funds) and increase long term interest rates (because there is now a greater demand for long term funds). In the early 1980s, the Bank of England adopted a policy similar to this where it issued more long debt than it needed and used the money from the sales of that debt to buy mainly commercial bills. This policy was called **over-funding** and was designed to increase long term interest rates and reduce the rate of

growth of broad money.
■ Replacing short term debt with long term debt can also be an instrument of monetary base control. If short term debt is counted by the Bank of England as part of the reserve assets of the banking system (i.e. part of high powered money in the economy), then a reduction in short term debt will lead to a contraction in the money supply.

Since the mid-1980s, the Bank of England has adopted a policy of full funding. This simply means that if the government borrows money, it does so through the issue of long term term stock and it does not 'print' the money. If, as has been true in the later 1980s, the government is paying back the National Debt because tax receipts and other revenues are higher than government spending, then the government buys back an equivalent amount of government stock from the market with money (i.e. public borrowing or debt repayment has a neutral effect on the money supply).

Rules and regulations

Central banks have used a variety of other techniques in an attempt to control the money supply. For instance, in the 1970s UK banks were subject to limits on growth of their deposits. Called the **supplementary special deposit scheme** (and nick-named the 'corset'), the Bank of England imposed interest rate penalties on excessive deposit growth. Throughout the post-war period up to 1981, governments used hire purchase controls to limit the amount of hire purchase credit in the economy. During the late 1960s, banks were told to give special priority to firms wishing to borrow money for exports. This was an example of how monetary policy was used to favour certain sectors of the economy at the expense of others.

Key terms

Monetary policy - the attempt by government or a central bank to manipulate the money supply, the supply of credit, interest rates or any other monetary variables, to achieve the fulfilment of policy goals such as price stability.
Special deposits - forced loans by banks to the Bank of England which reduce the reserve assets of the banks and therefore lead to a fall in the money supply.
Open market operations - the buying and selling of financial securities in exchange for high powered money in order to increase or decrease the size of the money supply.
Funding - the replacement of short term debt by long term debt.

Applied economics

UK monetary policy, 1950-1979

1950 - 1971

Before 1971, the two main intermediate targets of UK monetary policy were the rate of interest and the growth in credit. The rate of interest was considered significant because it could affect the level of investment in the economy and, more importantly, influence the value of the pound on foreign exchange markets. The amount of credit offered by banks and finance houses affected the total demand for goods and services in the UK, including the demand for imports.

The Bank of England exercised control over interest rates through operations in the discount market, setting a bank rate (the discount rate explained above) which then influenced all other money market interest rates.

The volume of credit was in part controlled through the imposition of **lending ceilings**. These were an example of **quantitative** controls. The Bank of England set limits on the growth of bank lending. There was a **qualitative** element in that restrictions on lending were made far tighter for personal customers than for businesses. A company wanting to borrow money for a factory to produce exports, for instance, would be far more likely to be granted a loan than an individual wanting to borrow to buy a car. There were also controls on **hire purchase**. Credit cards were only introduced in the late 1960s, and hire purchase was a very important way in which ordinary people borrowed money. The Bank of England set maximum repayment periods and minimum deposits in an attempt to regulate the demand for hire purchase.

In theory, the Bank of England had the power to use monetary base control. Banks had to keep 8 per cent of their liabilities in cash and 28 per cent in other liquid assets such as Treasury Bills and commercial bills. By limiting the amount of cash held by the banks or by reducing the supply of liquid assets, the Bank of England could have induced a multiple contraction in the money supply. Indeed, in 1960, the Bank moved one step towards this when it introduced the **special deposits** scheme (see above). However, except possibly in 1969, the banks were not in practice constrained in their lending by the scheme.

1971-1976

In the 1960s, as the number of banks and other financial institutions in the UK grew, it became increasingly apparent that a significant number of borrowers were avoiding the lending ceilings imposed on the main clearing banks by borrowing money from

financial institutions not subject to Bank of England controls (this is known as **disintermediation** ☞ unit 73). The Bank responded by changing its approach to monetary policy. In 1971, in a document entitled *Competition and Credit Control*, it declared that it would control credit in future not through lending ceilings (a form of rationing) but via the price mechanism. The rate of interest would be used to restrict credit and control the growth of the money supply. Lending ceilings and hire purchase restrictions were abolished, although the special deposits scheme was retained. The 8 per cent cash ratio and 28 per cent liquid assets ratio were replaced by a 12½ per cent reserve asset ratio (reserve assets were a variety of liquid assets such as Treasury Bills, but not cash) with banks agreeing to keep 1½ per cent of their assets as balances with the Bank of England. Bank rate was renamed minimum lending rate (MLR), although its function remained the same as before.

Competition and Credit Control proved to be a failure. Its introduction was followed by an explosive increase in the money supply. M4 increased by 70 per cent between 1971 and the end of 1973. Part of the failure was due to the fact that borrowers who had been limited in their borrowing before 1971 increased their borrowings. Perhaps more importantly, it was introduced at a time when the Conservative government of Edward Heath and his Chancellor Anthony Barber was preparing to spend its way out of a recession. Interest rates needed to be kept low if investment and consumer spending were to be encouraged. But low interest rates encouraged record borrowing. In December 1973, the Bank of England was forced to reintroduce hire purchase controls. It also introduced the **supplementary special deposits scheme**, the 'corset', which penalised banks exceeding lending limits by forcing them to deposit money with the Bank of England at a zero rate of interest.

Essentially, *Competition and Credit Control* failed because the government was unwilling to impose sufficiently high interest rates to curb the credit boom. Instead it reverted to the quantitative controls of the 1950s and 1960s.

1976-1979

Before 1976, the intermediate targets of monetary policy had been the rate of interest and the volume of credit. In 1976, the Labour Chancellor of the Exchequer, Denis Healey, introduced a new intermediate target, growth of the money supply M3. In the first half of the 1970s, many economists had become convinced that changes in the money supply caused changes in inflation (the belief known as **monetarism** ☞ unit 71). Therefore, control of the money supply was essential if governments were to reduce inflation.

It was not intended that monetary policy should actively be used to achieve the target set. Rather, the target was to be used as an indicator when planning the level of government borrowing or setting interest rates. In practice, since 1976 the money supply has always tended to grow at a faster rate than the target set by the government.

The Labour government of 1974-9 used a range of monetary policy instruments to constrain credit and the growth of the money supply. Quantitative controls in the form of the corset were in use, as were restrictions on hire purchase. There was also much greater awareness that the way in which the Public Sector Borrowing Requirement (PSBR) was financed and its size could have an important impact on the growth of the money supply and on interest rates. The Bank of England was no longer allowed to print the money needed by government to cover the PSBR (printing money would otherwise have led to an increase in the money supply). This was achieved by ensuring that new government debt was sold only to the non-bank sector. It was also recognised that the size of the PSBR would have an impact on interest rates. The lower the PSBR, the lower could be the rate of interest.

Data question

CREDIT CONTROLS

In 1989, the opposition Labour Party argued that credit controls were an alternative to high interest rates as a means of controlling the growth of the money supply. The government, however, rejected the idea. Mr Richard Ryder, Economic Secretary to the Treasury, speaking to a retail banking conference, claimed that British credit controls in the 1970s had created spectacular growth in the 'evasion industry'. If controls were reintroduced today, they would be even less effective because of the sophistication of financial markets and the absence of exchange controls.

'However rigorously and determinedly the authorities applied controls to the domestic financial system, it would be impossible to stop loans to consumers, or to shops wishing to lend to consumers, being booked off shore,' he said.

Source: adapted from the *Financial Times*, 31.10.1989.

1. **What are 'credit controls' and how can they restrict the growth of the money supply?**

2. **Why might they be ineffective?**

3. **Explain how, according to economic theory, credit controls could be used as an alternative to high interest rates by a government wishing to reduce the growth of the money supply.**

Summary

1. There is much controversy about the ability of central banks to control the money supply.
2. Attempts to control the growth of bank lending have resulted in disintermediation.
3. Monetary base control could well result in highly volatile short term interest rates. The central bank would also need to have a firm control on the assets which form the monetary base of the economy. Even then monetary policy may be rendered ineffective because of disintermediation.
4. Controlling the money supply through the control of interest rates assumes that the demand for money is stable. Keynesian economists would question this assumption.
5. It is not possible to control simultaneously the money supply, the rate of interest, the level of government borrowing and the exchange rate because all are interlinked.
6. Economists differ as to whether the money supply is exogenous or endogenous.

Monetary policy

The economic theory outlined in unit 72 would suggest that the central bank has a battery of policy instruments with which to control either the money supply or the rate of interest. In practice, monetary policy is extremely complex and it is far from clear whether the central bank has any real control over monetary variables. Why is this?

Disintermediation

A student wishing to buy a magazine has two alternatives if the one she wants is not available at the local shop. Either the student could give up the search altogether, or she could try another shop. Bank loans can be seen to be like the magazine. Assume the central bank is attempting to control the money supply by restricting the growth of bank lending. Potential borrowers then have two choices. Either they don't borrow, in which case the central bank has achieved its policy objective, or they find another way of borrowing the money.

In practice, both are likely to occur. For instance, the operation of the supplementary special deposits scheme (the 'corset' ☞ unit 72) probably led to some reduction in bank lending. But it also encouraged banks and their customers to find new ways of borrowing and lending money which would not appear on the officially controlled balance sheets of the banks. At the time, banks got firms to lend directly to each other. The bank put the two sides in contact with each other and provided

insurance cover to the lender in case of default by the borrower. The bank charged a fee for its work - equivalent to the profit it would have earned if it had received a deposit and then lent out the money in the normal way.

This process is an example of DISINTERMEDIATION and it results in the measured money supply being lower than the actual supply of money. When the corset was abolished in 1980, there was a significant jump in M3 as money which had been driven underground by monetary control measures returned to the official system.

Disintermediation becomes easier, the more alternative forms of borrowing and lending are available. The abolition of **exchange controls** (☞ unit 87) in 1979 meant that there was nothing to prevent a firm which had been refused a loan in London from borrowing the money in New York or Frankfurt. Equally, the abolition of many of the legal restrictions in the financial markets in the 1980s (known as **deregulation**), including 'Big Bang' and the freeing of building societies to provide many banking services, has made it even more difficult for the Bank of England to prevent disintermediation taking place.

Disintermediation is an example of GOODHART'S LAW. Professor Charles Goodhart argued that if the authorities attempted to manipulate one variable which had a stable relationship with another variable, then that relationship would change or break down as behaviour adapts to manipulation. Controlling bank lending won't reduce the money supply - but it will lead to a breakdown in the former stable relationship between bank lending and monetary growth as borrowers borrow outside the banking system.

Monetary base control

Many monetarists have argued that the only effective way of controlling the money supply is through monetary base control. But there are a number of problems with this. Firstly, the central bank is likely to define the monetary base in very narrow terms. High powered money is likely to be defined as cash, or bank balances with the central bank. On any one day, banks are likely to find themselves with too much high powered money or too little. Because the stock of high powered money is relatively small, these surpluses or deficits are likely to lead to large day to day fluctuations in short term interest rates. If the banks are short of high powered money, they will need to borrow the money and this will push up interest rates; and vice versa. Sharp fluctuations in short term money market interest rates will be unsettling for the financial markets as a whole. The Bank of England in the post-war era has always placed a great emphasis upon the stability of day to day short term interest rates. So monetary base control would conflict with this objective.

Secondly, there is doubt about the ability of the central bank to control the stock of high powered money. Assume that the central bank declares that banks must keep 1 per cent of their assets in cash. The central bank then reduces the amount of cash in circulation, hoping to reduce the money supply by bringing about a multiple contraction in bank assets and liabilities. The banks may

respond by tempting their customers to place more of the cash in circulation with the banks. For instance, they could increase interest rates, hoping to make deposits of cash more attractive, or they could make it easier or less costly to use money substitutes such as credit cards. There is only one type of high powered money which cannot be manipulated in this way - balances by the banks with the central bank. If the central bank were to use this as a policy weapon, banks would have every incentive to devise deals which did not show up on their balance sheets (i.e. engage in disintermediation).

The demand for money

The main thrust of UK monetary policy in the post-war era has been the control of interest rates rather than the money supply. Even after 1976 when the Bank of England first announced money supply targets, interest rates were used to shift the money supply curve. This is shown in Figure 73.1. Assume that the central bank wishes to reduce the money supply from MS_1 to MS_2. To achieve this it would raise interest rates from r_1 to r_2 on the assumption that there could be a movement back up the liquidity preference schedule (i.e. there would be a reduction in the quantity of money demanded) and therefore the money supply would have to fall to achieve equilibrium. But this assumes that the central bank knows the shape of the liquidity preference schedule. If it is more interest inelastic than it thinks, then an increase in interest rates will not reduce the money supply by as much as the central bank hoped. Moreover, if the liquidity preference schedule is unstable, there will be frequent shifts of the schedule, making interest rate policy unpredictable in its effects. This is often argued by Keynesian economists.

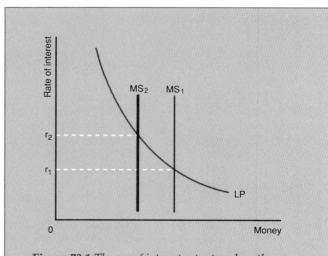

Figure 73.1 *The use of interest rates to reduce the money supply*
An increase in the rate of interest from r_1 to r_2 will be accompanied by a fall in the supply of money if the liquidity preference schedule is stable.

QUESTION 3 Britain's loan boom goes on and on. Few things highlight the Chancellor's dilemma more starkly than the apparently unstoppable rise in lending by UK banks and building societies. Even though interest rates are now at 15 per cent, their highest point in eight years, lending is still increasing. This week's figures showed new loans up by nearly 20 per cent on a year ago.

There is no easy answer as to why this should be so. Personal borrowing was rather flat, indicating that households were feeling the pinch of high interest rates. Corporate sector borrowing was much more buoyant. Partly this reflects the continued strength of industrial activity. Order books are less full than they were, but the latest manufacturing index is still up, for example. On the other hand, conditions are getting tighter and part of the borrowing represents 'involuntary borrowing' - when companies have to turn to their banks to top up the depleted cash flow from declining sales.

Source: adapted from the *Financial Times*, 21.10.1989.

(a) Explain why economic theory would suggest that high interest rates should curb the growth of borrowing and therefore the money supply.
(b) Does the evidence from the data support this link between interest rates and borrowing?

Policy constraints

Even if the central bank could control the money supply, it might not choose to do so because of other policy constraints.

The money supply and the rate of interest The central bank cannot fix both the money supply and the rate of interest. The higher the rate of interest, the lower must be the money supply assuming the demand for money is constant. So the government cannot, for instance, operate a tight monetary policy and have low interest rates.

The money supply, the rate of interest and the PSBR Since the Second World War, governments have traditionally spent more money than they have raised in taxes. The result is that they have had to borrow money. In the UK, this borrowing is known as the **public sector borrowing requirement** (☞ unit 76). Governments have two ways of raising this money, assuming that they are not going to borrow it from foreigners. The first is to borrow the money from the general public (known as the **non-bank sector**). This has no effect on the money supply but it does affect the rate of interest. If the government wishes to increase the amount, it will have to compete for funds with consumers and firms. This extra demand for borrowed funds will increase their price (i.e. the rate of interest will rise). Conversely, a fall in the PSBR will reduce total demand for borrowed funds and thus the rate of interest will fall. So the government cannot choose both the level of the PSBR and the rate of interest if

genuine borrowing takes place.

The government has a second option when financing the PSBR. It could choose to print the money. In a modern economy, it does this by selling government debt to the **banking sector**. Tables 73.1 and 73.2 show how this is achieved. Before, in a one bank economy, the bank has £100 of deposits from customers and, with a 10 per cent cash ratio, keeps £10 in cash and lends the rest out in loans (☞ unit 66). The government now sells the bank £10 of stock which the bank pays for with cash. The government spends the cash and it reappears in the

Table 73.1

			£
Deposits	100	Cash	10
		Loans	90
		Government stock	0
Total	100		100

Table 73.2

			£
Deposits	110	Cash	11
		Loans	89
		Government stock	10
Total	110		110

banking system in the form of new deposits. Deposits therefore increase to £110. As assets, the bank has £10 of government stock. If it is to maintain a 10 per cent cash ratio, it has to reduce its loans to £89 and keep an extra £1 in cash to increase its cash holdings to £11. The important figure is the one for total deposits because these appear in the money supply. They have increased from £100 to £110. Hence, the central bank has effectively 'printed' the money it needed through the banking system. Note that if it had sold government stock to the non- bank sector, bank customers who bought the stock would initially have withdrawn cash from the bank to pay for it. There would then have been an equal and opposite movement as other customers who had received extra cash from the government deposited this in the bank. Overall, the balance sheet of the bank would have remained the same.

There is a long history of governments resorting to the printing presses to finance spending. This method has the advantage that the government does not need to raise taxes. It also means that interest rates do not need to rise. Indeed, they are likely to fall because the money supply will rise. So the government cannot choose both the level of the PSBR and the money supply if it resorts to the printing presses to finance borrowing.

The money supply, the rate of interest and the exchange rate The **exchange rate** is the rate at which one currency can be exchanged for another (☞ unit 87). It is a market price, and therefore the exchange rate is determined by the forces of demand and supply. Governments can intervene to try and fix the exchange rate at a particular level by either buying or selling currency. For instance, if the Bank of England wanted to make the value of the pound fall against other currencies, then it could sell pounds for currencies such as dollars and deutschmarks. But the pounds it sells must come from somewhere. If the Bank prints the money, it will raise the money supply. If it borrows the money from the public, it will raise the demand for loans and hence raise the rate of interest.

Alternatively the value of the pound can be changed by changing interest rates. A rise in interest rates in the UK will attract an inflow of funds to the country increasing the demand for the currency and hence raising its price. The rise in interest rates can only be engineered through a fall in the money supply. So the Bank of England again faces a trade-off in its policy objectives.

The money supply, the rate of interest, the PSBR and the exchange rate are all interlinked. If the government fixes a value for one, it cannot fix a value for others. Hence a government may choose not to control the money supply in order to control other variables such as the rate of interest.

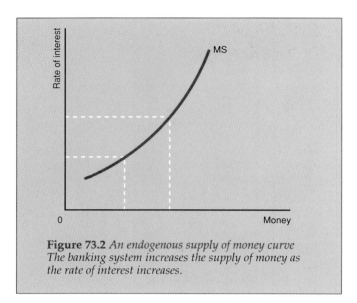

Figure 73.2 *An endogenous supply of money curve The banking system increases the supply of money as the rate of interest increases.*

is then said to be **endogenous** (i.e. determined within the system). The money supply curve is then drawn upward sloping as in Figure 73.2. The higher the rate of interest, the higher the price the banks will receive for the creation of money. Therefore the higher the rate of interest, the higher will be the amount of money supplied to the market.

Monetarists tend to argue that central banks can control the money supply. They often cite the US Federal Reserve Bank and the German Bundesbank as examples of strong central banks which have achieved monetary stability.

They argue that the failure of a central bank to control its money supply is a failure of will often caused by political interference from government more interested in controlling other variables such as the exchange rate than in controlling the money supply. The Bank of England is often cited as an example of such a central bank. If the central bank does control the money supply then the money supply curve is vertical as in Figure 73.1. It shows that whatever the rate of interest, the central bank fixes the amount of money in circulation.

QUESTION 4 In 1987 and early 1988, the value of the pound against other currencies rose. The Chancellor of the Exchequer, Nigel Lawson, believed that this would prove damaging to the economy and he attempted to limit this rise by cutting interest rates. Bank base rates fell from 11 per cent at the start of 1987 to a low of 7½ per cent in mid-1988. However, there were worrying signs that inflation was beginning to increase. The government sharply increased interest rates to 15 per cent by the end of 1988 to brake the rise in the money supply. At the same time, the foreign exchange markets lost confidence in the pound, the value of the pound fell and the Chancellor had to raise interest rates again in 1989 to prevent the pound from falling further.

Using illustrations from the passage, explain the policy conflict between control of the money supply, control of interest rates and exchange rate control.

Money supply: exogenous or endogenous?

Keynesians tend to argue that central banks can, at best, only loosely control the money supply, and then only in the short term. In the long term it is the financial system which determines the money supply. The money supply

Key terms

Disintermediation - in the financial system, the process of bypassing established financial intermediaries to achieve the same result as would have occurred if a financial intermediary had been used.
Goodhart's law - if the authorities attempt to manipulate one variable which had a stable relationship with another variable before, then the relationship will change or break down.

Applied economics

UK monetary policy, 1979-1990

The Conservative administration that came into office in June 1979 was, to start with at least, monetarist in its views. Its most important policy goal was the reduction of inflation and it believed that inflation was caused by excessive increases in the money supply. It therefore attached far more importance to money supply targets than the previous Labour administration. Money supply targets (the **intermediate target** of monetary policy, along with the PSBR) were written by the Chancellor of the Exchequer Geoffrey Howe into the **Medium Term Financial Strategy**, first published with the 1980 budget. A reduction in the money supply was to be achieved by:

■ setting interest rates high enough to lower the demand for money;
■ financing the PSBR without printing money by selling government debt to the non-bank sector;
■ allowing the exchange rate to float, to prevent the buying and selling of foreign currencies from affecting the money supply.

Interest rates, the PSBR and the exchange rate therefore became the **monetary instruments** of government policy.

High interest rates were achieved through increasing Minimum Lending Rate in the discount market. Within five months of coming into office, the government increased MLR from 12 per cent to 17 per cent.

The government attempted to cut the PSBR by reducing government expenditure and raising taxes. Cuts in the PSBR were seen as essential, partly because it was feared that the PSBR would in practice be financed through printing money (despite the sale of new debt to the non-bank sector), and partly because cuts in the PSBR were essential if interest rates were to be reduced from their record levels.

The absence of government intervention in the foreign exchange market resulted in an increase in the value of the pound. The effective exchange rate index increased from 107 in the second quarter of 1979 to 127 in the first quarter of 1981, an appreciation of 19 per cent in less than two years.

Unfortunately for the government, its policy instruments proved neither adequate or suitable to the task of constraining the money supply within pre-set targets. In the early 1980s, the money supply grew at approximately twice the rate set by the government. In part, this can be explained by the government's desire to deregulate financial markets. In 1979, the government abolished **exchange controls**, controls on the amount of sterling that could be taken abroad for investment purposes. The corset was abolished in June 1980, leading to a sudden jump in the money supply as hidden money returned to the official banking system.

There were therefore no quantitative controls on bank lending left. This led to an increase in bank borrowing, and therefore the money supply, as individuals and companies increased their borrowings to their 'free market' level. Increases in debt as a proportion of income rose throughout most of the 1980s fuelled by further measures such as the deregulation of building societies in 1985.

In part, however, it came to be realised that there was no simple connection between the rate of interest, increases in the money supply (however measured) and the rate of inflation. One explanation of this is that controlling the money supply through interest rates assumes that the demand for money is a stable function of income - which it cannot have been in the early 1980s.

By the mid-1980s, the government had effectively abandoned attempts to control the growth of the money supply, and in November 1985 abandoned M3 as an intermediate target.

The government was divided about whether or not the exchange rate should be used as a new intermediate target (☞ unit 102 for a further discussion about what follows). The Chancellor of the Exchequer, Nigel Lawson, believed that fixing the value of the pound against the deutschmark would prevent increases in inflation resulting from devaluations of the pound. He also believed that a fixed value of the pound would impose a discipline on government and industry. To prevent devaluation, the UK inflation rate would have to fall to the level of the German inflation rate. Governments therefore would be forced to set sufficiently high interest rates to reduce growth of the money supply and therefore the level of inflation. Industry could not expect government to finance inflationary pay awards by increasing the money supply and then devaluing the pound to restore UK industrial competitiveness on world markets. Others, led by the Prime Minister Margaret Thatcher, believed that the UK should use interest rates as the main policy weapon to reduce the money supply and bring down inflation, and allow the exchange rate to find its own level.

In 1987, the Chancellor indicated that the pound would 'shadow' the deutschmark. For a variety of reasons, the pound almost immediately began to rise against the deutschmark, and the Chancellor reacted by bringing down interest rates. By mid-1988, it became clear that inflationary pressures were building up again in the UK economy. The government decided to combat inflation by raising interest rates. But raising interest rates would also lead to a rise in the value of the pound against the deutschmark. The Chancellor lost the argument about pegging the exchange rate and bank base rates were increased from 7.5 per cent in May 1988 to 15 per cent by October 1989 whilst the value of the pound increased from 3.00 deutschmarks in the second half of 1987 to nearly 3.25 deutschmarks in the first quarter of 1989. But by October 1990, the government, due to pressure from its EC partners, reversed its policy of allowing the pound to float and joined the European Exchange Rate Mechanism, thus putting stability of the exchange rate as an intermediate target once again.

By 1990, what instruments of monetary policy were used by the Bank of England?

- The Bank of England controlled interest rates through open market operations in the discount market. It fixed short term interest rates in the discount market and then allowed all other interest rates in the economy to be determined by market forces around that rate. On the whole, money and capital markets are so inter-linked that increases in discount market rates will lead to increases in most interest rates in the economy and vice versa.
- It controlled the exchange rate through the buying and selling of foreign currency (☞ unit 101).
- It neutralised any effect on the money supply of government borrowing (or between 1987 and 1990, government debt repayment) by fully funding the PSBR or PSDR.

Monetary base control or quantitative controls (rules and regulations) were not used. Open market operations were confined solely to the discount market, and were used not directly to control the supply of money but to control short term interest rates.

FUNDING AND MONETARY POLICY

The government's main aim is to carry out the financing of the PSBR in a way that supports the objective of monetary policy, maintaining steady downward pressure on inflation.

In a simple economy this would mean literally printing no more (or fewer) notes and minting no more (or less) coins than are needed to keep the economy functioning smoothly. In an economy with a complex financial system, which is closely linked to overseas financial systems, policy is inevitably more complicated. There is a wide range of financial assets with more or less money-like attributes, and changes in the structure of the government's debt will affect their availability. The aim of policy is to manage the government's debt (and financial assets) so as to avoid adding to the volume of liquid and money-like assets in the economy in a way that adds to inflationary pressures.

This policy is expressed in the 'full fund' rule. The rule is intended to ensure that over each financial year the government's borrowing operation will have a neutral impact on the growth of sterling liquidity in the economy, as measured by the growth of M4.

The principle underlying the rule is as follows. If the government put money into the economy, by spending more than they receive, then they take the same amount of money out again by funding. None of the deficit is financed by issuing extra notes and coin. But it is also necessary to neutralise the effect on broad money. Government debt or National Savings will normally be paid for by withdrawing deposits at banks and building societies, hence affecting the level of M4. But this will not apply when purchases are made by banks and building societies themselves. So purchases (or sales) of public debt by these institutions are excluded from the total of funding which counts under the full fund rule.

The full fund has been achieved over each financial year since the present policy was adopted in 1985. In the early 1980s, however, the authorities pursued a policy of systematic overfunding continued over several years. The government sold more gilts than were needed for a full fund and the net proceeds were used to acquire a large stock of financial assets in the form of short term commercial bills. The intention at the time was to use funding policy to try to depress the growth of liquidity. But the operation, and in particular the growth in the Bank of England's holding of commercial bills (the so-called 'bill mountain'), set up distortions in the financial system that were undesirable in themselves and began to undermine the credibility and operation of policy. The policy was discontinued in October 1985.

Source: HM Treasury, *Economic Progress Report*, no.200, February 1989.

1. Explain what is meant by the 'full fund rule'.
2. What effect does the rule have on the rate of growth of the money supply?
3. In the early 1980s, the government overfunded the national debt. Using diagrams, explain the likely effect of this on (i) long term interest rates in the gilts market and (ii) short term interest rates in the discount market.
4. Why in theory might the change in short term interest rates, resulting from overfunding, have depressed the growth of liquidity?

INVESTIGATIONS 6

A. Interest rates

Aims

- To gather data about the structure of interest rates in the UK over a period of time.
- To investigate the characteristics of the money markets in which those interest rates are set.
- To analyse what determines the structure of UK interest rates.
- To analyse why interest rates change over time.

Research

You need to find out about the current structure of interest rates and how and why it can change. Either research a past period (e.g. the past three months or the past five years) or follow the money markets now for a period of time (such as a month or three months). Interest rates are the price of money in a particular money market. For each interest rate you follow, find out who are the buyers and sellers (i.e. the borrowers and lenders) in each market. You may be able to obtain information from local branches of banks, building societies and other financial institutions.

A wide variety of interest rates are quoted on a daily or weekly basis in the *Financial Times*. Other quality newspapers and periodicals, such as *The Times* and *The Independent*, carry a more limited range of interest rates. If you attempt to explain how and why interest rates have changed over a period of years rather than a few months, then statistical publications such as *Economic Trends*, *Economic Trends Annual Supplement*, *Financial Statistics* and the *Annual Abstract of Statistics*, all published by CSO, will be easier to use than daily newspapers.

Quality newspapers and magazines, such as the *Financial Times* and the *Economist*, are the best source of material which might explain why interest rates have changed in the short term. If you are looking back over a period of time rather than attempting to explain why interest rates are changing at the moment, then use an index to help you conduct a newspaper and magazine search. Newspapers such as the *Financial Times* and *The Times* publish their own indexes. The public library you use may construct its own index, or it may carry an index such as the *Research Index* (Business Surveys Ltd.) which covers articles of financial interest from 100 newspapers and periodicals on a monthly basis.

Structuring your report

Introduction Outline the aims of your investigation.

Presentation of research findings Using tables, graphs, charts or whatever might be appropriate, describe the structure of interest rates in the UK and how they have changed over the period of time you have chosen to research. Describe the borrowers and lenders in each money market about which you have gathered data and the characteristics of the market.

Analysis Suggest reasons why interest rates are structured as they are. For instance, why are bank deposit rates below bank base rates? Why are interest rates on credit card loans higher than inter-bank rates? What barriers are there between money markets which prevent all interest rates from being identical?

Then analyse why interest rates have changed over the period you have chosen. What has caused these changes in interest rates? To what extent have all interest rates changed in the same direction or at the same speed or the same magnitude? For instance, a change in bank base rates may only have been followed by a change in building society mortgage rates two weeks later. Credit card interest rates may have remained the same, however. Suggest reasons to account for these different types of change.

Sources Outline the sources of information you used. What problems did you encounter in gathering relevant data? What data would you have liked to have obtained but could not? To what extent were the data reliable?

Other suggestions

- Instead of investigating interest rates, describe and analyse changes in the prices of bills and bonds in the money markets. Daily information about bill and bond prices is given in the *Financial Times* together with an excellent summary describing and explaining price movements. Investigate the factors which may have affected bond and bill prices. To what extent is there a relationship between the rate of interest and the price of bills and bonds?
- Investigate changes in the velocity of circulation of money. Monthly figures for nominal GDP and the money supply are issued by CSO and the Bank of England. Why have changes taken place? To what extent are movements in the different measures of the velocity of circulation similar and why? To what extent can velocity of circulation be said to be stable?

B. Monetary policy

Aims

- To chart changes in the money supply over a period of time.
- To analyse why those changes have taken place and in particular to consider the influence of monetary policy on changes in the money supply.
- To analyse the effects of monetary policy on the wider economy.

Research activity

Your research needs to be concentrated on three areas.
- How has the money supply changed over the past few months?
- How has the government attempted to influence the growth of the money supply if at all (i.e. how has it conducted its monetary policy)?
- What are the possible current effects of monetary policy on variables such as inflation, expenditure and the balance of payments?

Before you start, review material about definitions of the money supply, the types of monetary policy available and the implementation and effectiveness of monetary policy from any books or other materials available to you.

Money supply figures (for the range of measures from M0 to M5) are announced monthly and are widely reported in the quality financial press.

Alternatively, they are published in *Economic Trends*, the *Monthly Digest of Statistics* and *Financial Statistics* all published by CSO. The quality financial press will also suggest reasons to account for the magnitude of the announced money supply figures. Use an index such as the *Financial Times* index, or the *Research Index* (published by Business Surveys Ltd) which covers articles in 100 newspapers and periodicals on a monthly basis, to help you find such articles.

The *Financial Times* publishes daily reports about Bank of England intervention in the discount market to steady interest rates. It also publishes major articles, along with other quality newspapers and periodicals, on the effects of interest rate changes after a major change in interest rates by the Bank of England. Again, use indexes to find these articles.

Structuring your report

Introduction Outline the aims of your investigation.

Changes in the money supply Describe, using charts, graphs or any other appropriate form of diagram, how the money supply has changed in recent months. Explain the different definitions of the money supply and indicate any observed relationship between them.

Analysis of money supply changes Suggest why the money supply has changed. To what extent has this been due to government monetary policy? How did you evaluate this? How has the Bank of England intervened to influence the rate of growth of the money supply? What measures of the money supply changed the greatest? Which measures show greatest correlation between the money supply and monetary policy? Explain why you think this is the case.

Analysis of the effects of monetary policy How is current monetary policy influencing the economy? Consider its possible effects on inflation, expenditure, unemployment, growth and the balance of payments.

Sources Outline the sources of information you used. What problems did you encounter in gathering relevant data? What data would you have liked to have obtained but could not? To what extent were the data reliable and unbiased?

Other suggestions

- Instead of considering the past few months, it would be possible either to take a longer time period (e.g. the past 5 years) or to follow changes in the money supply as they happen over say a three month period, or to investigate a period in the past.
- You could concentrate your investigation upon the effects of monetary policy upon the economy. This would involve monitoring the effects of changes in the money supply on other economic variables such as unemployment, inflation, consumption, saving, investment, exchange rates and the balance of payments.

Summary

1. In the simplest Keynesian model of national income determination, there is no government or foreign trade, wage rates are constant and money is neutral.
2. Aggregate demand (or planned expenditure) is then equal to planned consumption plus planned investment.
3. The equilibrium level of national income occurs where planned expenditure is equal to actual income.
4. The equilibrium level of national income is unlikely to be equal to the full employment level of income.
5. Equilibrium national income also occurs where planned investment equals planned saving.
6. Equilibrium income can be shown either on a 45° line diagram (the income-expenditure approach) or on a Keynesian cross diagram (the injections - leakages approach).

National income determination

In an individual market in the economy, price and output are determined by the forces of demand and supply. For instance, if demand for a product increases, the demand curve will shift to the right. There will then be an increase in both the equilibrium output and the equilibrium price in the market.

Similarly in macro-economics, economic theory suggests that **national** output will be determined by total demand and total supply in the whole economy. The theory of national income determination is complex and so we will start in this unit by explaining one part of it, a simple theory of aggregate demand. The theory was developed following the publication in 1936 of one of the most famous books in economics, *The General Theory of Employment, Interest and Money*. It was written by possibly the greatest economist of this century, John Maynard Keynes. The book was an attempt to explain the economic causes of the Great Depression of the 1930s. This depression had seen millions put out of work, a considerable increase in poverty and a fall in the output of industry. Keynes argued that this was caused by a lack of spending or demand in the economy. Keynes' followers, called **Keynesians**, elaborated a theory which showed how changes in aggregate demand in the economy determine the level of national income.

Simplifying assumptions

In order to keep the analysis as simple as possible, a number of assumptions need to be made.
- The economy has no government sector. This means that total personal disposable income, the determinant of consumption, is equal to national income.
- The economy is closed (i.e. there is no foreign trade). Hence GNP and GDP are equal because there is no net property income from abroad (☞ unit 57).
- There is no depreciation of the capital stock and hence

national income and GNP are equal.
- Wages and prices in the economy will remain constant as demand changes at all levels of income below FULL EMPLOYMENT. Full employment is the level of output at which all the factors of production in the economy are fully utilised at given factor prices. For instance, every worker who wants a job at the current wage rate is in employment.
- Money is neutral so that changes in real variables which affect monetary variables such as the money supply don't feed through to further changes in real variables.

Much of the rest of this book will be spent looking at what happens when we relax these assumptions but to start with we will build a simple model of income determination.

Aggregate demand

AGGREGATE DEMAND (also often called AGGREGATE EXPENDITURE or PLANNED EXPENDITURE) is defined as the amount of desired expenditure in the economy at any level of income. Total spending in the economy is made up of consumption expenditure, investment, government expenditure and net exports (☞ unit 57). In our simple model of the economy, there is no government and no foreign trade. So aggregate demand or planned expenditure (E) is equal to planned consumption (C) plus planned investment (I):

$$E = C + I$$

Table 74.1 shows an example of how aggregate demand would change as income (Y) increases. Planned consumption is assumed to be a function of income (☞ unit 60). As income increases, so does the level of consumption. The formula for the consumption function in the table is $C = 100 + 0.5Y$. Planned investment is assumed to be determined solely by changes in the rate of interest. So investment remains the same as income

Table 74.1 *Aggregate demand*

£

Actual income Y	Planned consumption C	Planned investment I	Planned expenditure E (i.e. C + I)
0	100	100	200
100	150	100	250
200	200	100	300
300	250	100	350
400	300	100	400
500	350	100	450
600	400	100	500

increases (i.e. investment is **autonomous** or **exogenous**). Aggregate demand or planned expenditure is calculated by simply adding planned consumption to planned investment.

QUESTION 1 C = 200 + 0.75Y and I is a constant £600. Calculate the value of planned expenditure if income is: (i) 0; (ii) £800; (iii) £1 600; (iv) £2 400; (v) £3 200; (vi) £4 000.

Equilibrium income

Figure 74.1 shows the data from Table 74.1 plotted on a graph. The consumption function is drawn first. When income is zero, consumption is 100. This is the level of **autonomous** consumption (i.e. that part of planned consumption expenditure which does not vary with income). Consumption then rises as income rises. The rise in consumption is less than the rise in income because

the **marginal propensity to consume** is less than 1 (in this case it is 0.5).

Planned investment is then added to the planned consumption line. The C + I line is parallel to the C line because planned investment remains constant as income changes. The level of planned investment is the vertical distance between the two lines. The 45° line on the diagram shows all points where planned expenditure equals actual income.

It is now possible to find the equilibrium level of income. The EQUILIBRIUM LEVEL OF NATIONAL INCOME is the level of income where there is no tendency for it to change. It occurs when the plans of neither households nor firms are frustrated. This is true only when planned expenditure equals actual income (i.e. at an income level of £400 where the planned expenditure line or aggregate demand schedule crosses the 45° line). To understand why this is true, consider what would happen if planned expenditure were not equal to actual income.

Planned expenditure more than actual income
Assume that the level of income and therefore the level of output is £200 (actual or realised national income must equal national output and national expenditure according to national income definitions). Reading from the graph or table, the level of planned expenditure is therefore £300. A combination of two things is now likely to occur. Firstly, households and firms will attempt to buy consumption and investment goods and find that firms will turn away their orders. The output of firms is not great enough to satisfy the level of demand in the economy. Secondly, firms will destock. They will have goods in stock which they were not planning to sell at that point in time. They will sell these stocks in an attempt to satisfy demand. But these sales are unplanned or undesired. They will then increase output to increase their stocks back to their planned or desired level. So destocking and unfulfilled orders will act as a signal to firms to increase production. Firms will have an incentive to increase output so long as planned expenditure is greater than actual income or output.

Planned expenditure less than actual income Assume that the level of income and therefore output is £600. Reading from the graph or table, we can see that the level of planned expenditure is then £500. If output is greater than expenditure, firms will not be able to sell all their production. They will have to make unplanned increases to their stock levels. They will react by cutting production, using up their existing stocks. They will only stop this when their stock levels are back to their desired level and when planned expenditure equals actual output.

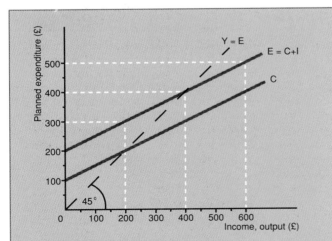

Figure 74.1 *The 45° line diagram*
Equilibrium income is established where the aggregate demand schedule crosses the 45° line (i.e. where planned expenditure equals actual income).

QUESTION 2
Plot on a graph the planned expenditure line derived from your answers to Question 1. What is the equilibrium level of income?

Equilibrium employment and full employment

One of the key predictions of the simple Keynesian model of income determination is that the economy may well settle down to an equilibrium level of output which is not the full employment level of output. On Figure 74.1, it is not possible to determine which is the full employment level of output. The economy will tend towards an equilibrium level of income of £400. But what if the full employment level of income were £600? There is no mechanism within the system to increase the equilibrium level of income to the full employment level. Hence the economy can be stable and there can be large scale unemployment.

Keynes argued the depression of the 1930s showed that mass unemployment could persist over long periods of time. We shall see later (☞ unit 79) that some economists believe the contrary: that unemployment cannot persist in the long run because wages will fall to clear the labour market. However, in the simple Keynesian model, we have assumed that wage rates are constant and therefore the wage rate mechanism cannot lead to a fall in unemployment.

Another approach

Another way of determining the equilibrium level of national income is to use the concepts of injections and leakages from the circular flow of income. In our simple model there is only one injection - investment. There is also only one leakage - savings (savings are that part of income which is not consumed because Y = C + S). Actual investment and actual savings must always be equal (for a proof of this ☞ unit 56). Keynes pointed out savers and investors are two different sets of economic agents. Investors are firms whilst savers are households (although firms too save). So there is no reason why the planned saving should equal planned investment.

National income is in equilibrium when planned investment is equal to planned savings. To understand why, consider what would happen if they were different.

Planned investment greater than planned savings
Income is equal to consumption (or that part of income which is not saved) plus investment. In Table 74.2, it can be seen that if income is £100 and consumption £150, then there must be dissaving of £50. On the other hand if income is £600 and consumption £400, then saving must be £200. If planned investment is greater than planned savings, firms must be planning to spend more than that which households want to save. So planned consumption plus planned investment must be greater than actual income. For instance, in Table 74.2, at an income level of £200, households plan to save nothing and spend £200, whilst firms plan to invest £100. So total planned expenditure is £300. With planned expenditure greater than actual income either firms will be forced to turn

Table 74.2 *Aggregate demand*

£

Actual income Y	Planned consumption C	Planned saving S	Planned investment I	Planned expenditure E (i.e. C + I)
0	100	-100	100	200
100	150	-50	100	250
200	200	0	100	300
300	250	50	100	350
400	300	100	100	400
500	350	150	100	450
600	400	200	100	500

away orders or they will make unplanned reductions in their stock levels. Either way, firms will now want to increase output and therefore national income will rise.

Planned investment less than planned savings If this is the case, then planned spending will be less than actual output. For instance, in Table 74.2 at an income level of £600 households plan to save £200 but firms plan to invest only £100. Total planned expenditure will be £500 (£400 by households and £100 by firms) but income or output will be £600. Firms will therefore be producing more than they can sell. Unplanned stocks will start to build up. Firms will respond by cutting back production. Output and therefore income will fall.

So if planned investment is greater than planned savings, income will tend to rise. If I is less than S, income will tend to fall. Only when planned investment and planned savings are equal will there be no tendency for income to change.

The Keynesian cross diagram

The bottom graph in Figure 74.2 illustrates the points that have just been discussed. Actual income and output are put on the horizontal axis. Planned investment and saving are put on the vertical axis. The saving function is upward sloping, showing that saving increases as income increases. The investment line is horizontal, showing that planned investment remains constant whatever the level of income. The equilibrium level of output is £400 where planned investment equals planned saving. If planned savings is greater than planned investment to the right of the equilibrium point, there will be a tendency for output and income to fall. If planned investment is greater than planned savings to the left of the equilibrium point, there will be a tendency for output and income to rise.

The top graph in Figure 74.2 is a copy of Figure 74.1. Placing the two together shows that the two ways of establishing equilibrium income are equivalent. Both the income-expenditure approach and the injections-leakages approach give exactly the same result.

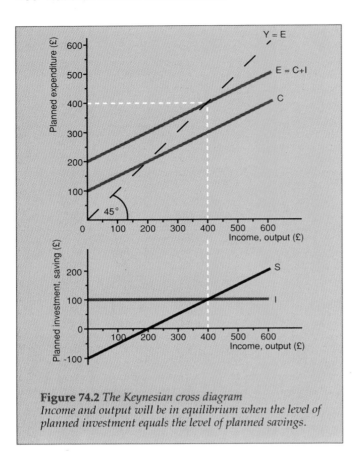

Figure 74.2 *The Keynesian cross diagram*
Income and output will be in equilibrium when the level of planned investment equals the level of planned savings.

QUESTION 3

S = -200 + 0.25Y and I is a constant £600.

(a) Calculate the level of planned savings at incomes level of: (i) 0; (ii) £1 200; (iii) £2 000; (iv) £3 200; (v) £4 000.
(b) Plot the values of planned saving and planned investment on a Keynesian cross diagram.
(c) What is the equilibrium level of national income?

Key terms

Full employment level of income - the level of output in an economy where all factors of production are fully utilized at given factor prices.
Aggregate demand or expenditure - the desired expenditure in the economy at any level of income.
Equilibrium level of national income - that level of income or output where there is no tendency to change. This only occurs where planned expenditure equals actual income (i.e. where the aggregate demand schedule crosses the 45° line).

Applied economics

Stocks and income, 1979 - 1982

In the Keynesian model of income determination, national income will be in equilibrium if planned expenditure equals actual income. The national income accounts of the UK do not give figures for planned expenditure - they only record actual expenditure. However, the accounts do give some clues as to how changes in planned expenditure lead to changes in actual income.

Table 74.3 shows the value of the physical increase in stocks and work in progress and GDP, both at constant market prices, between 1979 and the first quarter of 1983. Increases in stocks are classified as part of total investment in the Keynesian model. So a fall in stock levels, fixed investment remaining equal, would lead to a fall in investment expenditure.

In June 1979, a new Conservative government came

into office committed to reducing inflation. To achieve this, it sharply increased interest rates and allowed the level of the pound to rise to record levels. Both of these factors contributed to a fall in the level of stocks which firms wished to hold (i.e. there was a fall in planned expenditure on new stock). Economic theory would suggest that this fall in planned investment would cause a fall in planned expenditure. The economy would then be in disequilibrium. With planned expenditure less than actual income, firms could not sell all their output. They would respond by cutting their output and stocks even further until once again planned expenditure equalled actual income.

The data in Table 74.3 can be explained in terms of this model. In 1977 and 1978, the quarterly increase in stocks averaged approximately £800m. The first two

Table 74.3 *Quarterly GDP and change in stocks, 1977-1983*

£ million at 1985 prices

| | | At market prices | |
		Value of physical increase in stocks and work in progress	Gross domestic product
1977	Quarterly	854	77 849
1978	average	717	80 645
1979	Q1	1 067	78 672
	Q2	764	82 721
	Q3	1 627	83 228
	Q4	-130	85 485
1980	Q1	-643	80 492
	Q2	139	78 569
	Q3	-524	81 904
	Q4	-2 343	82 756
1981	Q1	-1 223	79 181
	Q2	-1 112	77 850
	Q3	188	80 478
	Q4	-1 053	82 738
1982	Q1	919	79 990
	Q2	560	78 644
	Q3	-482	81 285
	Q4	-2 278	84 552
1983	Q1	445	84 415

Source: adapted from CSO, *Economic Trends Annual Supplement.*

quarters of 1979 saw similar expenditure. However, in the third quarter, there was an exceptional increase in stocks of £1.6bn, an indication perhaps that planned expenditure was now greater than actual income. There then followed two years of destocking. This fall in planned expenditure resulted in a fall in actual income and output, from £85bn in the fourth quarter of 1979 to a low of £78bn in the second quarter of 1981. By 1983, the process of destocking had run its course and for the rest of the 1980s, stockbuilding was on the whole positive, as was the change in GDP.

INVESTMENT AND GDP, 1986 - 1989

Table 74.4 *Increase in real investment[1] and GDP, 1986 -1989*

| | Percentage change | |
	Investment	GDP
1986	2.3	3.6
1987	9.3	4.4
1988	18.1	4.7
1989	2.6	2.1

1. Gross domestic fixed capital formation plus physical increase in stocks and work in progress.
Source: adapted from CSO, *Monthly Digest of Statistics*; CSO, *United Kingdom National Accounts (Blue Book).*

In the second half of the 1980s, the UK enjoyed a mini-investment boom as Table 74.4 shows. There was also an increase in the rate of economic growth.

1. What do the data suggest happened to planned expenditure in the UK in the second half of the 1980s?
2. Using a Keynesian model of income determination, explain the effect of this change in planned expenditure on actual income. Illustrate your answer from the data.

75 The multiplier and the paradox of thrift

Summary

1. An increase in planned investment or the autonomous level of consumption will lead to an increase in planned expenditure.
2. An increase in planned expenditure will lead to a multiple increase in national income.
3. The value of the multiplier is given by the formula $1 \div MPS$.
4. The paradox of thrift states that an increase in planned saving will lead not to an increase in actual saving but to a fall in income.

Assumptions

In unit 74, it was shown that national income would be in equilibrium when planned expenditure equalled actual income. A number of important simplifying assumptions were made: the economy was closed and without a government sector; wages and prices were stable; the economy was at less than full employment so that national income could increase or decrease as aggregate demand changed; money was neutral.

In this unit, we will continue to make these assumptions. The purpose of this unit is to show how aggregate expenditure might change in our simple model and what happens to national income if it does so.

Changes in aggregate expenditure

What happens if consumers spend more money at any given level of income, or businesses increase their investment expenditure? We know that aggregate demand (AD, also called aggregate expenditure or planned expenditure E) is equal to planned consumption (C) plus planned investment (I). So a change in either C or I will lead to a change in E. Common sense suggests that if consumers and businesses plan to spend more money, then the income of the economy will rise. This is indeed what the Keynesian model predicts.

Traditional Keynesian economics assumes that consumption is relatively stable but investment can be volatile, fluctuating with the **animal spirits** (or confidence in the future) of businessmen. Assume that firms plan to spend more on investment goods at every level of income. Then aggregate expenditure will rise. This is shown by the shift in the aggregate expenditure line in the 45° line diagram in Figure 75.1 from E_1 to E_2. The two lines are parallel because it has been assumed that planned investment rises by the same amount whatever the level of income. It can be seen that the equilibrium level of national income rises from Y_1 to Y_2. Hence an increase in planned investment will lead to an increase in the equilibrium level of income.

Exactly the same conclusion can be arrived at using the Keynesian cross diagram in Figure 75.1. An increase in planned investment pushes up the planned investment line from I_1 to I_2. The result is that equilibrium income rises from Y_1 to Y_2.

A fall in planned investment will have the opposite effect. A fall will lead to a shift downwards in the aggregate expenditure line and hence a fall in equilibrium income.

A change in the **autonomous** component of consumption (☞ unit 60) will lead to similar changes in national income. If households plan to spend a constant amount more at every level of income, the aggregate expenditure line will shift upwards, raising the

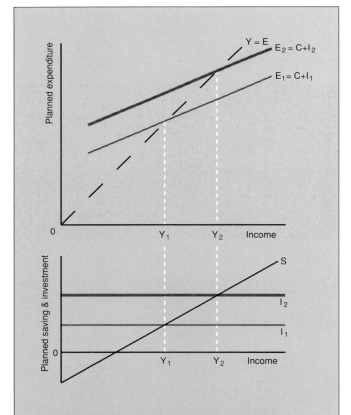

Figure 75.1 *An increase in aggregate expenditure*
A rise in planned investment at every level of income will push the aggregate expenditure line up from E_1 to E_2. Consequently the equilibrium level of income will rise from Y_1 to Y_2.

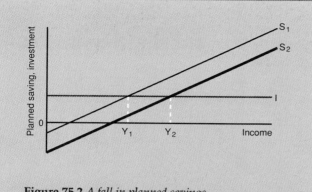

Figure 75.2 *A fall in planned savings*
An increase in planned consumption at every level of income must mean that households have decided to reduce planned saving at every level of income. This is shown by a shift downwards in the savings function from S_1 to S_2, resulting in a rise in equilibrium income from Y_1 to Y_2.

equilibrium level of national income. Figure 79.2 shows the same point using the Keynesian cross diagram. An increase in the autonomous element of planned consumption will lead to a fall in the autonomous element in planned savings. The shift downwards in the savings function from S_1 to S_2 shows that, at any given level of income, households now plan to save less. Equilibrium income consequently rises from Y_1 to Y_2. A fall in planned consumption will have the opposite effect, decreasing the level of equilibrium income in the economy.

QUESTION 1 C = 50 + 0.8Y, S = -50 + 0.2Y and I is a constant £50.
(a) Plot the planned expenditure line on a 45° line diagram for income levels up to £1 000 and find the equilibrium level of income.
(b) I now rises to £100. Draw the new planned expenditure line on your diagram and find the new equilibrium level of income.
(c) What would the equilibrium level of income be if investment fell to £10?

The multiplier

So far we have shown that an increase in planned expenditure in the economy will lead to an increase in national income. But how large will that increase in income be? Imagine what would happen if firms decided that they wanted to increase their investment spending by borrowing more money from banks, for instance. Firms use the money to buy investment goods from other firms, which would then pay their workers, buy materials from other firms and pay bigger dividends to company shareholders etc. These households then spend the money again and so it returns to firms, who in turn pay it back to households in wages, profits and interest (this of

course is the **circular flow of income**). The initial amount of money will keep circulating round the economy, each time increasing the level of national income. This suggests that an initial increase in planned expenditure will lead to an even greater increase in national income.

Indeed, this is what the simple Keynesian model predicts. A rise in aggregate demand will lead to a multiple increase in the equilibrium level of expenditure. Look at Figure 75.3. Aggregate expenditure rises from E_1 to E_2. Assume that the rise comes entirely from an increase in planned investment. The increase in investment is RS, the vertical distance between E_1 and E_2. But the increase in aggregate demand and national income is RT and PQ respectively. (RT and PQ are the same because this is shown by the 45° line.) An increase in investment has led to an even greater increase in income. This is known as the MULTIPLIER EFFECT.

Take a situation where households spend 0.9 of any increase in their income (i.e. the marginal propensity to consume is 0.9) and save the rest (i.e. the marginal propensity to save is 0.1). Firms increase their planned investment expenditure by £100, as shown in the circular flow of income diagram in Figure 75.4. The £100 of investment expenditure at stage 1 of the multiplier process will flow back to households in the form of wages, rents, interest and profits. They will then spend the money - but not all of it because we have assumed that they save one tenth of any increase in income. So at stage 2, £90 is spent and £10 is saved. The money is spent on goods and services produced by firms. That money will then be paid out by firms back to households in the form of wages etc. At stage 3 of the process, households spend 0.9 of the £90 they receive and save the remaining £9. The £81 goes back to firms who return it to households and so on. Each time the money passes round the circular flow, one tenth leaks from the system in the form of saving whilst nine tenths continues to circulate. The final increase in national income can be found by adding the extra investment expenditure (£100) to the extra

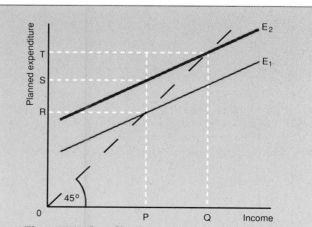

Figure 75.3 *Crowding in*
An increase in planned investment expenditure of RS crowds in extra consumption expenditure of ST leading to a final increase in planned expenditure of RT and in income of PQ.

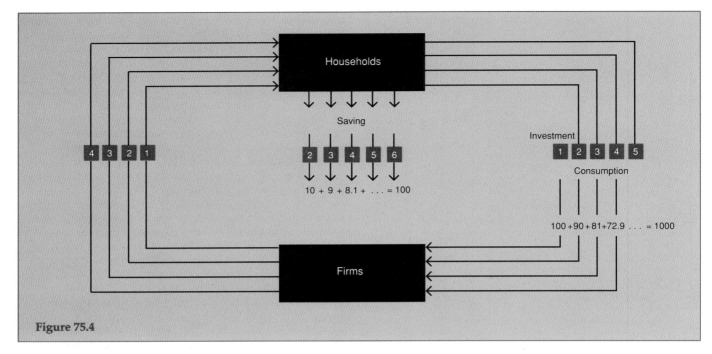

Figure 75.4

consumption expenditure (£90 + £81 + £72.9 + ...). The total comes to £1 000.

Our example shows that an increase in planned investment will lead to an increase in planned consumption as well. The two together go to make up the increase in planned expenditure. An increase in investment expenditure of RS in Figure 75.3 CROWDS IN consumption expenditure of ST, leading to a final increase in aggregate expenditure of RT.

The size of the multiplier depends upon how much or how little of an increase in expenditure leaks from the circular flow of income. It should be evident that the final increase in income would be much smaller in Figure 75.4 if households saved not one tenth of their income but one half.

> **QUESTION 2** Draw a circular flow diagram showing the effect of an increase in planned investment expenditure of £1 000 assuming that the marginal propensity to save is 0.5.

The value of the multiplier

The value of the multiplier can be calculated using a formula:

$$\text{Multiplier (k)} = \frac{1}{\text{MPS}}$$

where MPS is the marginal propensity to save. In our simple economy, households can only save or spend any

increase in their income. Therefore the marginal propensity to save plus the marginal propensity to consume must be equal to 1.

$$\text{MPS} + \text{MPC} = 1$$

Hence the MPS is equal to 1 minus the MPC. This gives an alternative formula for the multiplier:

$$\text{Multiplier (k)} = \frac{1}{1 - \text{MPC}}$$

In the example in Figure 75.4, the MPS was 0.1. The value of the multiplier was 1 ÷ 0.1 or 10. An increase in planned investment expenditure of £100 therefore led to a £1 000 increase (£100 x 10) in national income. Exactly the same answer would be obtained if we used the alternative formula. The MPC was 0.9. Therefore the value of the multiplier was:

$$\frac{1}{1 - 0.9} \text{ or 10.}$$

Sometimes the multiplier is called the INVESTMENT MULTIPLIER, although we have already seen that there would be a multiplier effect if there were a change in autonomous consumption. The multiplier is also sometimes called the KEYNESIAN MULTIPLIER after John Maynard Keynes who first made the concept popular. It is also called the REAL MULTIPLIER to distinguish it from the **credit multiplier**, used to calculate the increase in the money supply following an increase in high powered money held by the banking system (☞ unit 66), and the **money multiplier** which shows the relationship between increases in the money supply and increases in income (☞ unit 81).

The Keynesian cross diagram

The Keynesian cross diagram can also be used to show the effect of different multipliers. In Figure 75.5, national income is initially Y_1. If the savings function is S_1, then an increase in planned investment from I_1 to I_2 will lead to a final increase in equilibrium income of Y_1Y_2. There are two ways of calculating the multiplier from the diagram.

■ The ratio of the increase in income to the increase in investment is $Y_1Y_2 \div I_1I_2$ (i.e $\Delta Y \div \Delta I$). So this is the value of the multiplier.

■ The marginal propensity to save is given by the slope of the savings function (☞ unit 60). So the MPS is $BD \div AB$. The value of the multiplier is $1 \div MPS$ and hence it is equal to $AB \div BD$. Since $AB = Y_1Y_2$ and $BD = I_1I_2$, this is equivalent to the first way of

calculating the multiplier.

If the savings function, however, is S_2 and not S_1, the final increase in equilibrium income Y_1Y_3 is even larger. The slope of the savings function S_2 is shallower than S_1, and therefore the MPS is lower. This indicates that the lower the value of the MPS, the higher the value of the multiplier. This is the conclusion arrived at above when we considered Figure 75.4.

The paradox of thrift

If people plan to save more, is this good or bad for the economy? Savings are usually considered to be good. But the simple Keynesian model suggests that this might not be so. If people plan to save more, they must plan to spend less. Less spending means less demand for goods and therefore lost orders for firms. Income will fall and unemployment will rise. This is part of the phenomenon known as the PARADOX OF THRIFT.

Let us develop this idea more formally. Assume that households plan to save more. An increase in saving at all levels of income will lead to an upward shift in the savings function, shown in Figure 75.6. Equilibrium income will fall from OA to OB. But the new level of planned savings is exactly the same as the old level. This surprising conclusion is the paradox of thrift. In our simple Keynesian model, increases in planned saving lead ultimately not to increases in actual saving but to falls in income.

The reason is because an increase in planned saving will not be matched by an increase in planned investment. Planned investment remains unchanged because we have assumed at this stage that there is no link between the plans of households to save and the plans of firms to invest. But if households have planned to save more, they must also have planned to spend less. Less consumption means lower orders for firms. Firms will cut back production and lay off workers. So the income of

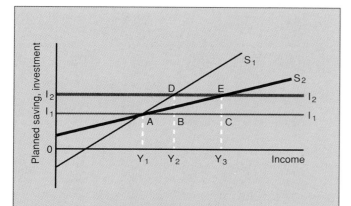

Figure 75.5 *The multiplier*
The value of the multiplier is given by $1 \div MPS$. The MPS is the slope of the savings function. So the value of the multiplier for savings function S_1 is $AB \div DB$ and for S_2 is $AC \div CE$. The lower the value of the MPS, the higher the value of the multiplier.

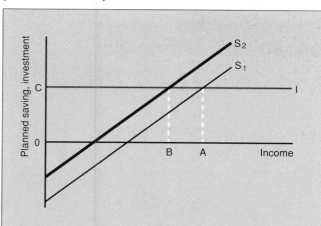

Figure 75.6 *The paradox of thrift*
An increase in planned saving, shown by the shift in the savings function from S_1 to S_2, leads to actual saving remaining unchanged at OC. But equilibrium income falls from OA to OB.

households will fall. This will carry on until once again consumption, savings and investment are in equilibrium.

Another way of understanding this is to see that an increase in planned saving must mean that households now plan to save a greater proportion of their income than before. For instance, they might plan to increase savings from 0.1 of their income to 0.2 of their income. The level of savings in the Keynesian model cannot change if there is no change in the level of investment. Hence, the only way that households can succeed in doubling their savings ratio is if their income is halved.

It is important to remember that we have assumed so far that the economy is at less than full employment. The paradox of thrift tells us that if there is unemployment in the economy, extra saving and less consumption can only make matters worse. The cure for unemployment is not less spending but more spending.

However, if the economy were to be at full employment, the story might be very different. If we relax another of our assumptions - that there is no direct link between investment and savings because savers and investors are two distinct groups in the economy - then a rise in saving (and therefore a fall in consumption) might allow investment to rise. This is likely to lead to increases in national income in the future (i.e. lead to economic growth). Indeed the discussion of the causes of economic growth in unit 63 suggested that one of the reasons for the UK's low growth rate has been her low savings ratio.

QUESTION 4 $S = -200 + 0.25Y$ and $I = 1\ 000$.
(a) On a Keynesian cross diagram, plot the values of S and I between income levels of 0 and 6 000.
(b) What is the equilibrium level of income? Households now change their saving habits and decide to plan to save half of any increase in their income.
(c) What is the new savings function?
(d) Plot the new savings function on your graph.
(e) What is the new level of equilibrium income?
(f) By how much has equilibrium income changed?

Key terms

Multiplier effect - an increase in investment or any other autonomous expenditure will lead to an even greater increase in income.
Crowding in - the process whereby an increase in an autonomous expenditure such as investment creates other expenditures such as consumption.
The multiplier, investment multiplier, Keynesian multiplier or real multiplier - the figure used to multiply a change in autonomous expenditure, such as investment, to find the final change in income. It is the ratio of the final change in income to the initial change in autonomous expenditure.
The paradox of thrift - increases in planned saving lead to a fall in national income with actual saving remaining unchanged.

Applied economics

Savings and income in the UK, 1971-1989

The paradox of thrift suggests that an increase in the propensity to save will lead to a fall in national income. Testing this hypothesis in the context of the UK economy is not easy because changes in the propensity to save are not the only factors which affect GDP. As will be explained in later units, changes in other real variables such as exports and government spending, and monetary variables such as the rate of interest, can lead to significant changes in national income too.

However, do recent statistics give any support to the hypothesis of the paradox of thrift? Table 75.1 shows the personal savings ratio (the APS expressed as a percentage) and the rate of change of real GDP. The correlation between the two sets of figures is relatively

low, possibly indicating that savings is indeed only one factor in determining changes in income, or that there are complex time lags between changes in the savings ratio and changes in income. However, it is interesting to note that two peaks in the APS, in 1975 and 1980, coincided with negative economic growth rates for those years. There was a fall in the APS in each year between 1984 and 1988, a period during which the growth of GDP rose. In contrast, 1989 saw a rise in the APS and a fall in the rate of economic growth. So the data, superficially at least, do not completely contradict the hypothesis that rises in the propensity to save lead to falls in national income and vice versa.

Table 75.1 *The APS and growth in GDP*

Year	Personal saving ratio	Annual growth in real GDP	Year	Personal saving ratio	Annual growth in real GDP
1971	7.3	1.7	1981	12.8	-1.2
1972	9.1	2.8	1982	11.6	1.7
1973	10.1	7.4	1983	9.8	3.8
1974	10.7	-1.5	1984	10.2	1.8
1975	11.6	-0.8	1985	9.5	3.8
1976	10.9	2.6	1986	8.2	3.6
1977	9.6	2.6	1987	5.7	4.4
1978	11.1	2.9	1988	4.2	4.7
1979	12.2	2.8	1989	5.1	2.1
1980	13.5	-2.0			

Source: adapted from CSO, *Economic Trends Annual Supplement*: CSO, *United Kingdom National Accounts (Blue Book)*; CSO, *Monthly Digest of Statistics*.

Data question

JOB CREATION AT MOSSMORRAN

During the 1980s, Exxon and Shell built a £1 billion chemical plant at Mossmorran in Fife, Scotland, to manufacture ethylene from North Sea oil. In 1989, the two companies announced a £200 million proposal to expand the facility. A report, commissioned from economists at St Andrew's University, claimed that for every one job created directly at Mossmorran, two had been created elsewhere in the economy in industries ranging from retailing to government services. Of the extra 1 500 jobs indirectly created by the investment, about half had been in the local Fife economy and about half elsewhere in Scotland. The two companies hoped that the report would be a powerful argument in persuading the local planning authorities to grant permission for the proposed extension to the plant.

1. **Explain how the data illustrate the investment multiplier principle.**
2. **(a) What might be the effect on national income and employment if the proposed extension to the plant were to be given the go-ahead?**
   (b) What sort of jobs might be created?

Government and the national income

Summary

1. Each year, governments present budgets showing their intended spending plans, their intended tax receipts and the amount they intend to borrow.
2. The budget deficit in the UK is called the public sector borrowing requirement (PSBR). When the government runs a surplus, it is said to have a public sector debt repayment (PSDR).
3. Aggregate demand in an economy with government is equal to C + I + G.
4. The economy is in equilibrium when planned C + I + G is equal to actual income. Alternatively, it is in equilibrium when planned injections I + G equal planned withdrawals S + T.
5. An increase in planned government expenditure will lead, via the multiplier process, to an increase in income. The value of the multiplier is equal to $1 \div (MPS + MPT)$.
6. An increase in tax rates will lead to a fall in national income.

The budget

Government is currently responsible for about 40 per cent of national expenditure in the UK. The main areas of public spending are social security, the National Health Service, defence, education and roads. It finances this expenditure mainly from taxes such as income tax and VAT.

In the post-war era, governments have rarely balanced their budgets (i.e. they have rarely planned to match their expenditure with their receipts). Most years, they have run BUDGET DEFICITS, spending more than they receive. As a result, in most years governments have had to borrow money. In the UK, the borrowing of the public sector (central government, local government and other state bodies such as nationalised industries) over a period of time is called the PUBLIC SECTOR BORROWING REQUIREMENT (PSBR).

Since the mid-1980s, the UK government has received more than it has spent. A traditional budget deficit has been turned into a BUDGET SURPLUS. The UK budget surplus is called the PUBLIC SECTOR DEBT REPAYMENT (PSDR). As the name implies, a budget surplus allows the government to pay off part of its accumulated debt. This debt, called the NATIONAL DEBT, dates back to the founding of the Bank of England in 1694.

Most governments present annual budgets when they announce their plans for spending and taxation for the next year. In the UK, announcements about taxation and spending are separated. In 'the Budget', the Chancellor of the Exchequer announces his plans for taxation for the following financial year, which runs from 5 April to the 4 April the following year. The Budget takes place in March. Plans for public spending are announced in November in what is called 'the Autumn Statement'.

Aggregate demand

In the simple Keynesian model of income determination developed in units 74 and 75, a number of assumptions were made:
- the economy was closed and there was no government activity;
- the economy was below full employment;
- wages and prices were stable;
- money was neutral.

In this unit, the simplifying assumption that there is no government economic activity will be dropped but the other assumptions will be kept.

In the simplest model of the economy, aggregate expenditure or aggregate demand is equal to planned consumption plus planned investment. With a public sector, there is a further component of expenditure: planned government expenditure (G). So the new aggregate expenditure equation is:

$$E = C + I + G$$

It is important to understand what constitutes and what determines C, I and G when the activities of government are added to the model.

Investment Planned investment, as in the simple model, is assumed to be autonomous. It is determined by firms independently of the level of income.

Government spending Planned government spending in this model is not equal to public expenditure. Public expenditure includes **transfer payments** (☞ unit 57). These are transfers of income from taxpayers to the recipients of benefits such as the unemployed, students and pensioners. In the circular flow model, expenditure must not only create income but there must also be a corresponding output. Expenditure on, say, unemployment benefits produces no corresponding flow of output of real goods and services. So any spending on transfer payments by government is excluded from the definition of G, government spending, used in our model. What is included, however, is spending on goods and services such as hospitals, schools, the police and the army. An assumption is made within the model that G is autonomous (i.e. it is not determined by the level of income). It is assumed that G is determined by political rather than economic considerations. So when national income rises, the government may or may not choose to change the level of government spending.

Consumption Planned consumption is a function of **disposable income** (☞ unit 60):

$$C = f(Y_d)$$

Disposable income is income after tax but includes transfer payments. In our model, we need to express planned consumption as a function of national income. In the simplest model with no government, disposable income and national income are the same, so no adjustment needs to be made. In a model with government, disposable income (Y_d) is equal to national income (Y) minus net taxes (T). 'Net taxes' in turn is defined as the difference between taxes paid and transfer payments (such as child benefit or unemployment benefit) received. So:

$$Y_d = Y - T$$

Since consumption is a function of disposable income it must be a function of national income minus net taxes:

$$C = f(Y - T)$$

QUESTION 1 A government spends money in just two ways. £5 000 million is spent on its army. £2 000 million is spent on welfare payments to citizens of the country. It raises £6 000 million in taxes and national income is £34 000.
(a) In the circular flow of income model, what would be the value of (i) G and (ii) T where G is government spending and T is net taxes?
(b) What is the value of disposable income?
(c) What is the value of consumption expenditure if $C = 1\ 000 + 0.6Y_d$?

Equilibrium income

In equilibrium, planned expenditure equals actual income (☞ unit 74). So in an economy with government, there is equilibrium when planned consumption plus planned investment plus planned government spending equals

income:

$$Y = C + I + G$$

Figure 76.1 shows this using the 45° line diagram and the Keynesian cross diagram. In the 45° line diagram, the consumption line is drawn upward sloping. This shows that consumption increases as income increases. Investment is autonomous. Whatever the level of income, planned investment expenditure is PQ. Hence the C + I line is parallel to the C line. Planned government expenditure too is autonomous, remaining constant at a level of QR whatever the level of income. Hence the C + I + G line is parallel to the other two lines. Planned expenditure is equal to actual income where the C + I + G line crosses the 45° line. Hence the equilibrium level of national income is OS.

The Keynesian cross diagram shows injections and leakages in the economy. Income is in equilibrium when planned injections equals planned withdrawals. The two injections are investment and government spending. Both are autonomous and therefore the I + G line is horizontal, showing that neither changes as income changes. Both S and T are assumed to increase with income. At higher levels of income, households plan to save more and they have to pay more in taxes such as

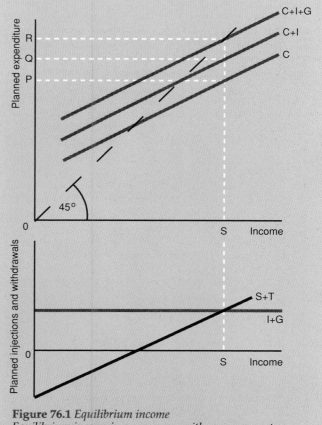

Figure 76.1 *Equilibrium income*
Equilibrium income in an economy with a government sector will occur where planned expenditure, C+ I + G, equals actual income at OS. The same result can be obtained by equating planned injections I + G with planned leakages S + T.

income tax and VAT which in practice are linked to income. Equilibrium income is OS where planned injections equal planned leakages.

Changes in government spending

An increase in government spending will raise the level of aggregate expenditure. More spending in the economy will in turn raise the level of equilibrium income (☞ unit 74 for an explanation of how exactly this occurs). This is shown in Figure 76.2. A rise in planned government spending from G_1 to G_2 will lead to an upward shift in the aggregate expenditure schedule, from $C + I + G_1$ to $C + I + G_2$. Equilibrium national income will now rise from OS to OT.

The increase in government spending in Figure 76.2 was PQ. However, the final increase in planned expenditure was PR. QR consumption expenditure has been crowded in through the multiplier effect. Remember that the multiplier is the ratio of the final change in income to the initial change in planned expenditure:

$$\text{Multiplier} = \frac{\Delta Y}{\Delta J}$$

where ΔY is the change in income and ΔJ is the change in the two injections I and G. We can also express the multiplier in another way as:

$$\text{Multiplier} = \frac{1}{\text{MPS} + \text{MPT}}$$

where the MPS is the marginal propensity to save and the MPT is the marginal propensity to tax. The MPS can be defined as the proportion of a change in income that is saved. The MARGINAL PROPENSITY TO TAX is defined as the proportion of a change in income that is taken in taxes by government. For instance, if the government collects an extra £20 in tax when national income increases by £100, then the MPT is 0.2.

The multiplier can again be expressed in terms of the marginal propensity to consume.

$$\text{Multiplier} = \frac{1}{1 - \text{MPC}}$$

The MPC in this formula is the marginal propensity to consume out of **national income**. This is not the same as the marginal propensity to consume out of disposable income which is found in the consumption function. In the next section we will see how the two MPCs are related mathematically.

The multiplier is used to calculate the change in equilibrium income resulting from a change in either planned investment or planned government spending. For instance, if the multiplier is 2 and planned government spending increases by £500 million, then equilibrium national income will rise by £1 000. If the multiplier were 3, a fall in G of £1 000 million would lead to a fall in equilibrium income of £3 000 million.

Equally, if we know that the marginal propensity to save is 0.3 and the marginal propensity to tax is 0.2, then the value of the multiplier is $1 \div (0.3 + 0.2)$ or 2. So a change in G of £300 million will lead to a change in equilibrium income of £600 million.

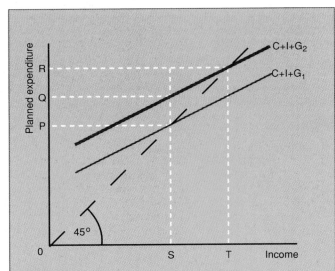

Figure 76.2 *An increase in government spending*
An increase in government spending will shift the aggregate expenditure line up from $C + I + G_1$ to $C + I + G_2$. The result is an increase in the equilibrium level of income from OS to OT.

Changes in taxation

A change in tax rates is a little more difficult to analyse than a change in government spending. Assume that taxes change in proportion to income. So we are assuming that taxes are like income tax where an increase in national income will lead to an increase in tax revenue for the government.

We know that consumption is a function of disposable income. Assume the formula for the consumption function is:

$$C = a + b Y_d$$

where a is autonomous consumption and b is the marginal propensity to consume. It has been explained above that Y_d, disposable income, is equal to Y - T. So:

$$C = a + b (Y - T)$$

Taxes are proportional to income. If there is no autonomous element in taxation and taxes are assumed to be net of benefits, then taxes are equal to the marginal propensity to tax (t) times income:

$$T = tY$$

Substituting this in the previous equation we get:

$$C = a + b (Y - tY)$$

or

$$C = a + b (1 - t) Y$$

For instance, if the marginal propensity to consume out of disposable income (b) is 0.9 and the marginal propensity to tax (t) is 0.2, then the marginal propensity to consume out of national income is 0.9 x (1 - 0.2) or 0.72.

This example shows that the marginal propensity to consume out of disposable income is higher than the marginal propensity to consume out of national income. This is what should be expected. Disposable income is smaller than national income because of taxes. So the proportion spent out of disposable income is bound to be higher than the proportion spent of national income.

Figure 76.3 shows the relationship between the two consumption functions. C_1 shows the relationship between consumption and disposable income. C_2 shows the relationship between consumption and national income. The marginal propensity to consume is the gradient of the line. So C_1 is steeper than C_2 because the marginal propensity to consume out of disposable income is higher than the marginal propensity to consume out of national income.

It is now possible to see what happens if the government increases rates of tax so that more tax is paid at every level of income. An increase in the marginal propensity to tax will lower the marginal propensity to consume out of taxed income. This can be shown by a

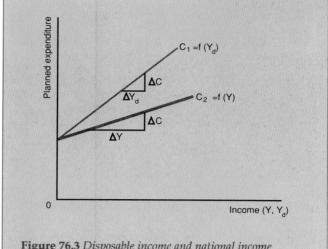

Figure 76.3 *Disposable income and national income*
The MPC out of disposable income is higher than the MPC out of national income. Hence C_1 is steeper than C_2.

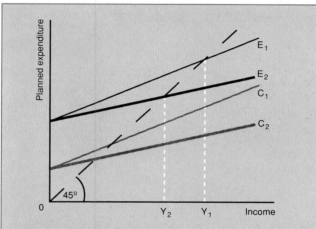

Figure 76.4 *A rise in tax rates*
A rise in tax rates and revenues will lead to a fall in the consumption line from C_1 to C_2 and hence a fall in aggregate expenditure from E_1 to E_2 due to a fall in planned consumption. As a result, equilibrium income will fall from Y_1 to Y_2.

swing downwards in the consumption function from C_1 C_2. If we now add planned investment and government spending, we arrive at the aggregate expenditure lines in Figure 76.4. A rise in tax rates has led to a fall in aggregate expenditure from E_1 to E_2. The result is that equilibrium national income falls from Y_1 to Y_2.

This is the result that would be expected. A rise in tax rates will lead to an increase in tax revenues for the government. Consumers are therefore spending less money. Hence national income will fall. On the other hand, a fall in tax rates will put money into consumers' pockets. They will increase their consumption expenditure, raising the level of national income.

QUESTION 4 During 1988 it became apparent that the economy was overheating. National income was growing at too fast a rate and inflation was beginning to rise. Many economists in 1988 and 1989 suggested that the government should raise taxes in order to slow the growth of the economy. Using a diagram, explain why a rise in taxes might lead to a reduction in national income.

Key terms

Budget deficit or Public Sector Borrowing Requirement (PSBR) - a deficit which arises because government spending is greater than its receipts. Government therefore has to borrow money to finance the difference.
Budget surplus or Public Sector Debt Repayment (PSDR) - a government surplus arising from government spending being less than its receipts. Government can use the difference to repay part of the National Debt.
The National Debt - the accumulated borrowings of government.
The marginal propensity to tax - the proportion of a change in income that is taken in taxes by government.

Applied economics

The Barber boom, 1972-74

Keynesian economic theory suggests that increasing government expenditure or reducing taxes (i.e. increasing the Budget deficit) will lead to an increase in national income. The Barber boom of 1972-74 is an example of how such an increase could be achieved.

When the Conservatives under Edward Heath took over government from Harold Wilson and his Labour administration in 1970, the economy was on the point of moving into recession, although this was not realised at the time by the government. In 1971, the Chancellor, Anthony Barber, adopted a broadly neutral fiscal stance with small cuts in public spending being matched by cuts in tax revenues. But by the Autumn of that year, it was clear that unemployment was rising and growth falling as can be seen from Figure 76.5. In 1970, unemployment stood at approximately 600 000, but by the winter of 1971, it had risen to nearly 1 million. The government decided that such high unemployment was unacceptable. In November 1971, plans were announced to increase public spending. In March 1972, Anthony Barber unveiled a budget which proved to be highly reflationary. The 1972 budget cut income taxes by an estimated £960m and purchase tax (replaced by VAT in 1973) by £135m. The aim was to increase the annual rate of economic growth to 5 per cent and cut unemployment to 500 000.

Very quickly, the shift upwards in the aggregate expenditure line led to increases in the rate of growth of the economy and falls in unemployment. By the first quarter of 1973, the rate of growth over the previous twelve months was 10.4 per cent, a totally unsustainable figure. The March 1973 budget was

broadly neutral but in May 1973, the government announced major cuts in public expenditure on road building and local authority spending, followed in

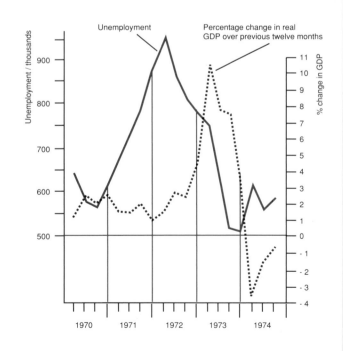

Source: adapted from CSO, *Economic Trends Annual Supplement*, 1981 and 1990.

Figure 76.5 *Growth and unemployment, 1970-1974*

December 1973 by further cuts. The rate of growth of GDP fell and in 1974 became negative. Unemployment began to rise again. The boom came to an end when the government, attempting to deal with rocketing inflation rates, record balance of payments deficits and the effects of the first oil crisis, refused to further boost the economy with more tax cuts and increases in public expenditure.

Data question

FISCAL POLICY, 1975 - 1977

The Labour government which took office in February 1974 barely had a majority in Parliament and therefore was unwilling to increase taxes and cut public expenditure to tackle soaring inflation and a large balance of payments deficit. In November 1974, another general election took place and this time the Labour Party secured a workable majority. In the 1975 Budget, it cut planned public expenditure and increased taxes, both by over £1 000 million. Further cuts in public expenditure were announced in 1976. The PSBR fell from £10 161 million in 1975 to £8 899 million in 1976 and £5 419 million in 1977. As a result, the rate of growth of GDP at current prices fell from 26.2 per cent in 1975 to 18.4 per cent in 1976 to 16.6 per cent in 1977. However, the government relaxed its fiscal stance in 1978, and the PSBR increased to £8 340 million.

1. **Using a Keynesian model of income determination, explain why the rate of growth of GDP at current prices fell between 1975 and 1977.**
2. **What would the model have predicted would happen to the rate of growth of GDP in 1978?**

Summary

1. If the economy is below full employment, a deflationary gap is said to exist. The government can fill this by an increase in spending or a reduction in taxes.
2. If the economy is at full employment, increased government spending or lower taxes cannot, by the definition of full employment, increase output. Instead it will raise prices, and an inflationary gap is then said to exist.
3. Keynesian theory suggests that there is a balanced budget multiplier. Increasing government spending and taxes by the same amount will lead to a rise in national income.
4. Government expenditure and tax revenues which change automatically as income changes are automatic stabilisers. They brake the fall of national income when the economy moves towards a depression and limit the rise of income when the economy is in boom.
5. Active fiscal policy is the term used to describe the deliberate manipulation of government expenditure and taxes to influence the economy.
6. Active fiscal policy has limitations. There are time lags involved in the implementation of policy, economic data on which to base decisions are inadequate, and economic theory itself is not sufficiently well developed for governments to be able to fine tune the economy to meet precise targets.

Assumptions

In the simple Keynesian model of the economy first outlined in unit 74, a number of important simplifying assumptions were made. One was that wages and prices were stable. Another was that the economy operated at below full employment. Hence, when aggregate demand or expenditure rose, prices remained constant whilst output and income expanded.

These two assumptions will now be modified. We will still assume that income can change without causing a change in prices so long as the economy operates below **full employment**. But any increase in aggregate demand when the economy reaches full employment will result not in a rise in output but in a rise in prices. For instance, in the early 1930s when there was mass unemployment in the UK, an increase in spending in the economy would have raised output and put people back to work. But ten years later, with Britain at war, with no unemployment and factories working at full stretch, an increase in spending would not have led to extra output. The economy could not produce any more because it was at full employment. What would have happened, but for a

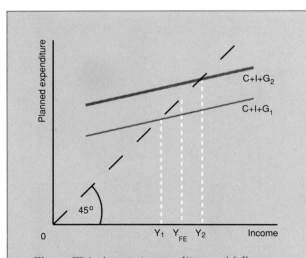

Figure 77.1 *Aggregate expenditure and full employment*
If Y_{FE} is the full employment level of income, then a rise in government spending from G_1 to G_2 will lead to a rise in real output and income of Y_1Y_{FE} and a rise in prices to bring Y_{FE} up to Y_2.

system of rationing, would have been severe inflation, as indeed happened during the First World War under similar circumstances.

This can be shown in Figure 77.1. The economy is initially in equilibrium at income Y_1. The full employment level of income is Y_{FE}. Government now increases its spending from G_1 to G_2, raising the level of planned expenditure from $C + I + G_1$ to $C + I + G_2$. The new equilibrium level of income is Y_2. There will be a rise in **real** output and income from Y_1 to Y_{FE}. But Y_{FE} by the definition of full employment is the maximum level of output for the economy. Therefore the rise in output and income from Y_{FE} to Y_2 cannot be a rise in real output. It must be a rise in nominal output (i.e. output at current prices) caused solely by an increase in prices.

Inflationary and deflationary gaps

An INFLATIONARY GAP is said to exist when planned expenditure is greater than the full employment level of income (i.e. when there are inflationary pressures in the economy). In Figure 77.2, the equilibrium level of income, Y_E, is greater than the full employment level of income, Y_{FE}. If inflation is to be avoided, income needs to fall by $Y_E Y_{FE}$. This will be achieved if planned expenditure falls from E_1 to E_2. This fall could, for instance, come from a fall in government expenditure. The size of the fall needed is AB. Note that this is less than the fall in national income. This is because a fall in autonomous expenditure, such as G or I, will lead to a multiple fall in income through the multiplier effect. AB is then the size of the inflationary gap.

A DEFLATIONARY GAP exists when planned expenditure is less than the full employment level of income (i.e. when there is unemployment in the economy). There must be an increase in autonomous

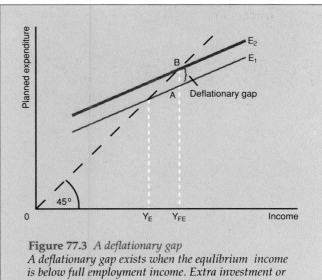

Figure 77.3 *A deflationary gap*
A deflationary gap exists when the equlibrium income is below full employment income. Extra investment or government spending is needed of AB if the gap is to be closed.

expenditure such as investment or government spending if planned expenditure is to rise to equal full employment income. In Figure 77.3, the rise needed is AB. Again, AB is less than $Y_E Y_{FE}$ because of the multiplier effect. A rise in government spending of AB will **crowd-in** extra consumption expenditure to give the final rise of $Y_E Y_{FE}$ in income.

In the simple Keynesian model, it is possible then for government to intervene to stabilise the economy at its full employment level. If the economy is at below full employment, it should increase its budget deficit to fill the deflationary gap. If the economy is threatening to go beyond full employment, it should reduce its budget deficit or run a surplus to remove the inflationary gap.

QUESTION 1 C = 1 000 + 0.6Y, where C is consumption and Y is national income. Government spending is a constant 10 000 and investment is 5 000.
(a) On a 45° line diagram, plot the aggregate expenditure line from income levels of 0 to 50 000.
(b) What is the equilibrium level of income?
(c) If the full employment level of income is 30 000, what is the size of the inflationary gap?
(d) If the full employment of income is 50 000, what is the size of the deflationary gap?

The balanced budget multiplier

So far we have shown that increases in government spending or reductions in tax will raise the level of national income whilst falls in G or rises in T will lead to a fall in Y. But what if the Chancellor in his budget raised both G and T by the same amount? Keynesian theory predicts that this would be likely to increase aggregate demand.

Assume that the Chancellor raises government

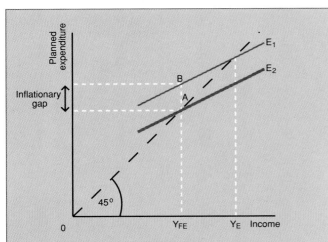

Figure 77.2 *An inflationary gap*
An inflationary gap exists when full employment income is below equilibrium income. Without a fall in planned autonomous expenditure of AB, the economy will suffer inflation.

spending by £1 000m and the value of the multiplier is 2. This will lead to an increase in the equilibrium level of income of £2 000 million. On the other hand, an increase in taxes of £1 000 million will reduce the equilibrium level of income. However, income will fall by less than £2 000 million. This is because households will not reduce their expenditure by that much. Part of the higher taxes will be financed from reduced consumption. But part will come from reduced saving. Saving is a leakage from the circular flow. The more households fund the extra taxes by reducing their saving rather than their consumption, the smaller will be the impact on equilibrium income (i.e. the higher the marginal propensity to save and the lower the marginal propensity to consume out of taxed income, the less the impact of increased taxes on national income).

Imports are also a leakage (☞ unit 74). The more households cut back on the consumption of imported goods and the less on domestically produced goods, the less will be the impact of an increase in taxes on domestic income.

Furthermore, not all government spending is on domestically produced goods. For instance, the government may purchase nuclear missiles from the United States. The multiplier will be lower, the higher the proportion of government spending on foreign goods.

What this all means in practice is that governments can manipulate their expenditure and taxation to change the size of the balanced budget multiplier. For instance, spending extra money on house building which has a very high domestically produced component and financing it by taxing the better off, who have above average propensities to save and import, according to Keynesians, will raise national income. Spending extra money on defence equipment, which has a higher import content, and taxing the poor who have a low propensity to save, will increase national income far less.

Automatic stabilisers

The government sector of the economy can act as an important stabiliser of demand without there being any change in government policy. Assume that the economy is at full employment and that firms plan to increase their investment spending. Increased planned expenditure will lead to a rise in income. However, a rise in income will increase tax revenues from taxes such as income tax and VAT which vary with income and output. This will help reduce at least part of the inflationary impact of the extra investment spending.

On the other hand, assume that the firms plan to invest less. Equilibrium income falls, creating unemployment. Tax revenues fall because of reduced income. But government could now be obliged to pay out more in unemployment benefits, thus increasing household income from what it would otherwise have been. Government spending or tax revenues which automatically change as income changes are called AUTOMATIC or BUILT-IN STABILISERS. The smaller the proportion of national income which is accounted for

by these, the greater the impact on income of changes in autonomous expenditures. In the 1920s and 1930s, UK government expenditure accounted for a much lower proportion of national income than it did in the early 1980s. This is possibly one of the reasons why the depression of the 1930s was more severe than the depression of the early 1980s.

ACTIVE or DISCRETIONARY FISCAL POLICY, on the other hand, is the deliberate manipulation of government expenditure and taxes to influence the economy. The deliberate decision by government to cut tax rates, leading to a fall in tax revenues, would be an example of active fiscal policy. On the other hand a cut in tax revenues which followed from a fall in national income would be an example of an automatic stabiliser.

QUESTION 2 Explain whether the following are likely to be examples of automatic stabilisers or active fiscal policy:
(a) the rise in VAT rates from 8 per cent to 15 per cent in 1979;
(b) the cut in the highest rate of income tax on earned income from 83 per cent to 60 per cent in 1979;
(c) the rise in payments of unemployment benefit from £680 million in 1979/80 to £1 328 million in 1980/81;
(d) the one per cent fall in the real value of taxes on income during 1980;
(e) the abolition of earnings related unemployment benefit in January 1982.

Fiscal policy and gaps

The Keynesian model of income determination was developed from the mid-1930s onwards against the backdrop of the Great Depression. During the depression of the 1930s, millions of workers all over the world lost their jobs. In both the USA and Germany, unemployment levels reached 25 per cent. The economic orthodoxy of the time advocated balanced budgets and argued that government could do little directly to influence the level of income and employment for reasons that we shall return to later on in this book (☞ unit 105). John Maynard Keynes, a Cambridge economist, argued in his book *The General Theory of Employment, Interest and Money*, that the forces which might return an economy to full employment were either very weak or did not exist at all. An economy could remain with very high unemployment over long periods of time. He said that firms were unlikely to close a deflationary gap at times of high unemployment because they would be extremely pessimistic about the future. Hence the government needed to take the lead. Extra government spending or lower taxes would stimulate the economy, crowding in consumption expenditure. Businessmen would become more optimistic and the level of investment would rise too. The government should budget for a sufficiently high deficit to close the deflationary gap.

This view became the economic orthodoxy of the 1950s and 1960s. When the economy was suffering from a rise in unemployment, government would increase the budget deficit. When the economy was at full employment and aggregate demand was threatening to rise even further (a situation known as OVER-HEATING), government would reduce the budget deficit, perhaps even to a budget surplus situation, thus closing the inflationary gap.

In the 1944 White Paper *Employment Policy* (Cmnd 6527), it was stated that: 'The Government accepts as one of their primary aims and responsibilities the maintenance of a high and stable level of employment after the war'. In fact unemployment levels in the 1950s and 1960s tended to fluctuate between 1 and 2 per cent. As time went on, economists and politicians felt more and more that the economy could be FINE-TUNED to a very precise level of unemployment through the use of fiscal levers. This process was called DEMAND MANAGEMENT of the economy - the use of government policy to manage the level of aggregate demand in the economy. But even in the 1950s and 1960s it was recognised that there were limitations to fine-tuning.

QUESTION 3 In early 1959, the Treasury forecast that the economy would grow over the year, but not sufficiently to bring the economy to full employment. How do you think the government of the day reacted to this in its March budget?

The limitations of demand management policies

Conflicting policy objectives Governments in the 1950s and 1960s found it impossible to maintain a **stable** level of low unemployment. The economy tended to move from boom to mild recession - what came to be known as the STOP-GO CYCLE. When unemployment was low, economic growth tended to be high. However, inflation tended to rise and the balance of payments slipped into deficit. It was particularly the balance of payments which worried governments at the time. So when the balance of payments moved into deficit, the government would reduce the budget deficit and the economy would move into mild recession. Then the balance of payments would move into surplus, the government would apply the fiscal levers again, expanding the economy and the cycle would start all over again.

Time lags Assume that the government announces a £500 million increase in civil servant salaries and a £500 million increase in road building. If the multiplier were 2, this would lead to a £2 000 million increase in equilibrium income in the Keynesian model. However, it may take some years for the full increase to work through the economy. The increase in civil servant salaries will work through relatively quickly. Civil servants will increase their spending within a few months of receiving the pay increase. The road building programme may take years

even to start. So a government needs to be careful to take account of lags in spending when using fiscal policy to fill or remove deflationary or inflationary gaps. If a government wishes to reflate or deflate the economy quickly, it needs to change those taxes and those items of expenditure which will have an immediate impact on aggregate demand. Changing income tax rates, social security payments and public sector wages will all act quickly to change demand. Long term capital projects, such as road building or hospital building, are inappropriate for short term changes although they may be ideal in a serious longer term depression such as that which occurred during the 1930s and early 1980s.

In the past, governments have been accused of even destabilising the economy through the use of active fiscal policy. Government would reflate the economy just at a time when the economy was moving into boom of its own accord, just as it arguably was in 1972 when the Chancellor reflated the economy. The combination of extra private sector spending and extra public sector spending would then create an inflationary gap. The more inherently stable the economy, the more potential damage there would be from wrong timing in active fiscal policy. Hence some economists argue that the inability to predict time lags accurately makes it impossible to use fiscal policy to fine-tune the economy.

Inadequacy of economic data Active fiscal policy assumes that the Chancellor knows the current state of the British economy. But statistics are notoriously unreliable. Unemployment statistics and inflation statistics are not revised after publication, but national income statistics and the balance of payments statistics are frequently revised. Moreover, the 'black holes' in these statistics (the 'residual errors', 'balancing items' or 'statistical discrepancies' ☞ unit 58) have become increasingly large over time. If the balance of payments is in deficit, the Chancellor will not know how much of this is due to a genuine deficit and how much is due to inaccurate recording of statistics. Fine-tuning then becomes very difficult. The Chancellor could well reflate the economy even though it was at full employment because he had been misled by statistics showing a recession.

Inadequate economic knowledge Active fiscal policy assumes that we know how the economy behaves. However, there is scepticism that economics will ever be able to predict changes in variables to the last few per cent. This is important because so many of the variables which governments wish to control are very small numbers. For instance, the government may wish to reduce economic growth by half. To do so, they might have to cut the rate of growth of national income from 3 per cent to 1½ per cent. But active fiscal policy is unlikely ever to be sufficiently sensitive to achieve exactly that 1½ per cent fall.

The inadequacy of the model An increased budget deficit will fill a deflationary gap. A reduced budget deficit will close an inflationary gap. These are the conclusions of the simple Keynesian model of income determination. But it should be remembered that the model makes a large number of assumptions. In the 1950s and 1960s, it seemed to many that these were reasonable assumptions to make. In the 1970s and 1980s, these assumptions seemed far less reasonable. Much of the rest of this book will be devoted to exploring why the simple Keynesian model needs to be modified if it is to be used to explain the very unusual economic events of the past two decades, or whether other models are more applicable.

QUESTION 4 In 1988 and 1989, the government sharply increased interest rates to curb rising inflation and a growing balance of payments deficit. In 1989, the current account deficit was nearly £20 000 million. However, the balancing item, the net amount of transactions which went unrecorded, stood at + £15 024 million.

Suggest why the large balancing item may have hindered the government in its attempt to formulate economic policy.

Key terms

Inflationary gap - exists when planned expenditure is greater than the full employment level of income. It is the fall in autonomous expenditure needed to reduce income to its full employment level.

Deflationary gap - exists when planned expenditure is less than the full employment level of income. It is the rise in autonomous expenditure needed to increase income to its full employment level.

Automatic or built-in stabilisers - mechanisms which reduce the impact of changes in the economy on national income.

Active or discretionary fiscal policy - the deliberate manipulation of government expenditure and taxes to influence the economy.

Over-heating - the economy over-heats when planned expenditure is greater than full employment income (i.e. when there are strong inflationary tendencies at full employment income).

Fine-tuning - the attempt by government to move the economy to a very precise level of unemployment, inflation, etc. It is usually associated with fiscal policy and demand management.

Demand management - government use of fiscal and other policies to manipulate the level of aggregate demand in the economy.

Applied economics

A deflationary gap, 1979-1982

The Barber boom of 1972-4 (☞ unit 76) was caused by government increasing public spending and reducing taxes to fill a deflationary gap which emerged in the UK economy during 1971. It was the last time that a UK government was to use the insights of the simple Keynesian model to direct policy. By the mid-1970s, it was generally recognised that increasing the PSBR would have important consequences for inflation even if the economy were below full employment. The Conservative administration which came into office in 1979 saw the control of inflation as their main priority. They believed that increasing government expenditure would lead only to inflation and no long term fall in unemployment. In pursuit of their policies, they cut public expenditure, raised tax revenues, raised the rate of interest and allowed the exchange rate to rise substantially.

Table 77.1 shows the effect of this on national income and employment. Between 1979 and 1981:
■ Increases in interest rates led to sharp falls in stock

levels held by companies. They also contributed to a sharp decline in private sector investment.
■ Exports fell slightly as exporters found it difficult to sell abroad due to the high value of the pound.
■ Government expenditure fell. This change was entirely made up of falls in public sector investment since public sector current consumption in fact rose slightly.

Overall, actual I + G + X at constant market prices fell by £5 367 million in 1980 and £9 837 million in 1981 before increasing again by £6 177 million in 1982.

In the simple Keynesian model, falls in injections to the circular flow, I + G + X, lead to a fall in national income and a rise in unemployment. As can be seen from Table 77.1, this is indeed what happened. GDP at factor cost fell by £5 106 million in 1980 and £2 451 million in 1981 before increasing in 1982 by £3 580 million. Unemployment more than doubled between 1979 and 1982.

Keynesian economists at the time bitterly opposed

government policies. They argued that the government needed to close the widening deflationary gap by increasing government spending and reducing taxes. In 1981, to their dismay, the Chancellor Geoffrey Howe sharply increased taxes in his March Budget. A letter to *The Times* shortly afterwards, signed by 364 UK economists, protested vigorously at what they saw as the folly of government policy. In fact, by 1982 exports and investment had begun to rise, and there was a slight increase in government expenditure too. This pushed up the aggregate demand line and increased GDP, but not sufficiently to prevent a further large increase in unemployment. For the rest of the 1980s, the government refused to use demand management techniques of a fiscal nature to influence either unemployment or inflation. However, the experience of the early 1980s suggests that changes in government spending and taxation may influence the level of income in the economy, at least in the short term.

Table 77.1 *Expenditure, income and unemployment 1979-82*

£ millions at 1985 prices

	1979	1980	1981	1982
Consumption expenditure	194 895	195 060	195 173	197 051
Private sector investment	40 268	38 777	35 990	38 892
Change in stocks and work in progress	3 328	- 3 3 71	- 3 200	- 1 281
Government expenditure[1]	85 896	85 765	83 591	83 981
Exports	88 943	88 966	88 307	89 048
Total final expenditure[2]	414 074	408 872	399 148	407 203
less imports	83 956	81 134	78 878	82 721
less taxes plus subsidies	46 610	45 305	44 246	44 895
GDP at factor cost[3]	283 564	278 458	276 007	279 587
Unemployment (millions)	1.3	1.6	2.5	2.9

1. General government final consumption plus public corporation investment plus general government investment.
2. Totals slightly differ from the sum of components because not all investment expenditure has been allocated between sectors by CSO.
3. Totals different from sum of components because of the method used to re-base on 1985 prices.

Source: adapted from CSO, *Economic Trends Annual Supplement*; CSO, *United Kingdom National Accounts (Blue book).*

Data question

MAKE TAX MORE FLEXIBLE

From Mr. Michael Artis

Sir, The Chancellor's Budget shows that fiscal policy is being used as an instrument of demand management in the interests of curbing inflation; otherwise, the Chancellor could have continued with his strategy of cutting income tax, accepting the consequences for interest rates. That he did not do so suggests either that there is another target of policy besides that of reducing inflation or that there are limits to the use of interest rates.

In either circumstance, what is the point in restraining the use of fiscal policy to once-a-year Budget adjustments? It is not difficult to imagine disturbances (no bigger than the 1p minimum income tax cut that the Chancellor has foregone in this Budget) in which sole reliance on the interest rate will produce unacceptable consequences either for interest rates themselves or for the exchange rate or for both.

Mr. Lawson could add to his reforming reputation by providing for a more flexible response of fiscal policy, reintroducing the regulator (power to vary indirect taxes between Budgets) and providing for temporary income tax surcharges and rebates. These need not interfere with this strategy of reducing taxation.

M.J. Artis,
Professor of Economics,
University of Manchester.

Source: letter in *Financial Times*, 18.3.1989.

1. **Explain what Professor Artis means when he writes of 'a more flexible response of fiscal policy'.**
2. **Discuss, using diagrams, how fiscal policy can be 'used as an instrument of demand management in the interests of curbing inflation'.**

Aggregate demand in an open economy

Summary

1. Exports are exogenously determined in a simple Keynesian model of the economy but imports are assumed to be a function of income.
2. Aggregate demand in an open economy is equal to C + I + G + X - M.
3. The economy is in equilibrium when planned expenditure C + I + G + X - M is equal to actual income.
4. An increase in planned exports will lead to a multiple increase in income.
5. The value of the multiplier is given by the formula 1 ÷ (MPS + MPT + MPM).
6. An increase in imports caused by an increase in the marginal propensity to import will lead to a fall in national income.

Exports and imports

Countries trade with each other because they need the goods and services other countries produce. Goods and services purchased from abroad are called IMPORTS, whilst domestically produced goods and services sold abroad are called EXPORTS. A TRADE DEFICIT occurs if the value of imports is greater than exports. If the value of exports is greater than imports, then there is said to be a TRADE SURPLUS.

The value of exports is determined by a large variety of factors. In the simple Keynesian model of the economy, with fixed exchange rates, it is assumed to be determined by the level of income of foreigners. The higher their income, the more goods and services they will buy, including imported goods. This means that exports are **autonomous** or **exogenous**. They are not determined by factors within the domestic economy.

Imports, however, are assumed to be **endogenous**. If domestic income rises, households and firms will buy more goods, including imported goods. If you were to receive an increase in income of £20 a week, you might increase your spending by £15 on domestically produced products and £5 on imported products. Hence imports are assumed to be a function of income.

Just as it is possible to calculate the marginal propensity to save and the marginal propensity to tax, so it is possible to calculate the MARGINAL PROPENSITY TO IMPORT (MPM). This is defined as the proportion of a change in income which is spent on imported goods. It is calculated by dividing the change in imports (ΔM) by the change in income (ΔY):

$$\text{Marginal propensity to import (MPM)} = \frac{\Delta M}{\Delta Y}$$

So in our example above, the MPM of an increase in your income of £20 is 0.25 (5 ÷ 20).

Figure 78.1 illustrates the points made above. Exports are autonomous and therefore remain constant at a level of OB whatever the level of income. Imports increase as

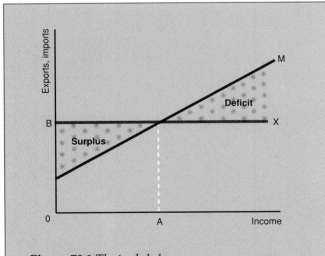

Figure 78.1 *The trade balance*
As income increases, the trade balance moves from being in surplus at income levels below OA to being in deficit.

income increases. At income levels below OA, there is a trade surplus. At income OA the trade balance is zero. At income levels above OA, there is a trade deficit.

Aggregate demand in an open economy

In an economy with no government and no foreign trade, aggregate demand or aggregate expenditure is equal to planned consumption plus planned investment. In unit 76, a government sector was introduced and aggregate demand was redefined as C + I + G. Planned consumption was said to be consumption out of taxed income.

In an economy with government and foreign trade, aggregate demand is commonly defined as:

$$E = C + I + G + X - M$$

Planned exports, X, are an addition to aggregate expenditure. C, I and G are planned spending on goods and services produced both at home and abroad. The goods produced abroad, although they raise domestic spending, have no corresponding impact on either domestic output or domestic income. Hence to find the level of demand within the economy which is equal to national income and national output it is necessary to take away imports. We could do this by redefining C, I and G as expenditures solely on domestically produced goods. For instance, C would be total consumption minus the consumption on imported goods. Aggregate expenditure would then be equal to C + I + G + X. However, it is more usual to leave our definitions of C, I and G unchanged, place imports M into a separate category and then take M away from C + I + G + X.

Equilibrium income

The economy is in equilibrium when planned

expenditure equals actual income; or when planned injections equal planned withdrawals (☞ unit 74). So in an open economy (i.e. where there is foreign trade) with government, national income is in equilibrium when either:

$$Y = C + I + G + X - M$$

or when:

$$I + G + X = S + T + M$$

Figure 78.2 shows these conditions diagrammatically. In the 45° line diagram, equilibrium is achieved where the aggregate demand or expenditure line crosses the 45° line (☞ unit 74 for an explanation of why this should be so). In the Keynesian cross diagram, there are three injections (planned investment, government spending and exports) and three withdrawals (planned saving, imports and taxes). Each of the three injections is assumed to be autonomous. Investment is determined by the decisions of businesses, government spending by government and exports by foreigners. None of these is assumed to change as income changes. Hence the I + G + X line is horizontal. Saving, taxes and imports, on the other hand, are endogenous variables. They increase as income increases. Hence the withdrawals line, S + T + M, is upward sloping. Equilibrium is achieved at Y_E where planned injections equal planned withdrawals.

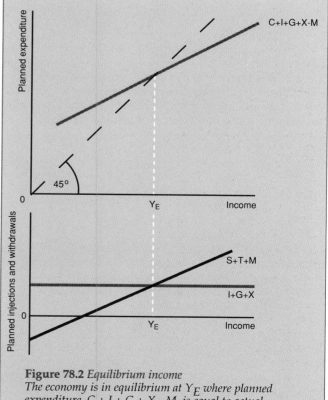

Figure 78.2 *Equilibrium income*
The economy is in equilibrium at Y_E where planned expenditure, C + I + G + X - M, is equal to actual income. Alternatively equilibrium is achieved in the Keynesian cross diagram where planned injections, I + G + X equal planned withdrawals, S + M + T.

A change in exports

An increase in exports will lead to an increase in aggregate expenditure in the economy. Hence the equilibrium level of national income will rise. This is shown in Figure 78.3. A rise in exports of PQ leads to an increase in equilibrium national income of ST. PQ is less than ST and therefore there has been a multiplier effect. Increased export expenditure of PQ has crowded in extra consumption expenditure of QR.

The formula for the multiplier in an open economy with government is:

$$\text{Multiplier} = \frac{1}{\text{MPS} + \text{MPT} + \text{MPM}}$$

(i.e. it is the inverse of the sum of the marginal proportion leaked from the circular flow of income). The larger the value of the marginal propensity to import, the lower will be the value of the multiplier. For instance, if the MPS

were 0.1, the MPT 0.2 and the MPM 0.1, the value of the multiplier would be 2.5 [1 ÷ (0.1 + 0.2 + 0.1)]. If the MPM rose to 0.2, the multiplier would fall to 2 [1÷ (0.1 + 0.2 + 0.2)].

So if the multiplier were 2.5 and exports rose by £1 000 million, equilibrium income would rise by £2 500 million crowding in an extra £1 500 million of spending. If the multiplier were 2 and exports fell by £500 million, equilibrium income would fall by £1 000 million.

A change in imports

Imports are a function of income. So the level of imports and therefore the level of planned expenditure will change as income changes. This change in planned expenditure is shown by a movement along the planned expenditure line in the 45° line diagram. However, if there is a rise in the level of planned imports at any given level of income because the marginal propensity to import has risen, the planned expenditure line will shift downwards from E_1 to E_2 as shown in Figure 78.4. The line will pivot round rather than make a parallel shift

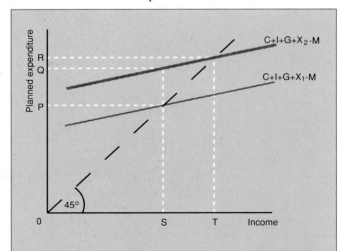

Figure 78.3 *A rise in exports*
A rise in planned export expenditure of PQ will shift the aggregate expenditure line upwards from $C + I + G + X_1 - M$ to $C + I + G + X_2 - M$.

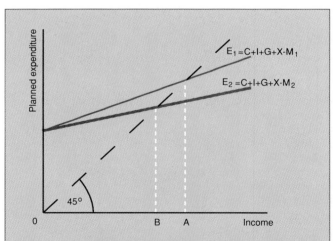

Figure 78.4 *A rise in the propensity to import*
An increase in the propensity to import will lead to a fall in the aggregate expenditure line from $C + I + G + X - M_1$ to $C + I + G + X - M_2$. This will reduce the level of equilibrium income from OA to OB.

because the size of the change in planned imports increases as income increases. It can be seen that the equilibrium level of national income falls. This is what would be expected. If households and firms plan to increase their spending on imports, they must also be planning to spend less on domestic goods. A fall in demand for domestic goods will lead to lower output and lower incomes within the domestic economy.

Note that there could be a rise in the **average** propensity to import without a rise in the **marginal** propensity to import. If, for instance, a country revalued its currency, then imports would become cheaper and at every level of income, planned imports would then be greater. A change in the average propensity to import (APM) would be shown by a parallel shift in the planned expenditure

line, shifting it upwards if the APM were to fall, and downwards if it were to rise.

Key terms

Exports - goods and services produced domestically and sold to foreigners. Payments for exports come into the country.
Imports - goods and services purchased from foreign producers. Payments for imports leave the country.
Trade surplus and deficit - there is a surplus if the value of exports is greater than imports, and a deficit if exports are less than imports.
Marginal propensity to import (MPM) - the proportion of any change in income which is spent on imported goods.

QUESTION 4 In 1980, the value of the pound rose strongly so that by the end of the year the trade weighted index (an average value of the pound against other currencies) was 30 per cent above its value at the beginning of 1979. As a consequence, UK goods became much less competitive against foreign produced goods and therefore there was a rise in the average propensity to import. National income fell by approximately 2 per cent.

Explain, using a 45° line diagram and assuming all other things are equal, why the change in the average propensity to import in 1980 should have affected the level of national income.

Applied economics

The value of the multiplier

In an open economy with government intervention and trade, the proportion of leakages to national income is likely to be relatively high and hence the value of the multiplier is likely to be low.
 M C Kennedy (1989) has estimated that the value of the multiplier for the UK is approximately 1.33. To make this estimate it is necessary to calculate the value of the marginal propensity to consume (MPC), since the multiplier is equal to:

$$\frac{1}{1 - MPC}$$

where MPC is the change in consumption of domestically produced goods (net of taxes) as a proportion of a change in national income. Kennedy assumed that national income is measured by GDP.

We start by calculating personal income from GDP. Assume that GDP increases by £100m. GDP calculated

by the income method can be divided into employment income, approximately 80 per cent of the total, and profit, approximately 20 per cent of the total. Of the £100m increase in GDP, £80m is therefore employment income and £20m can be assumed to be profit. Of the £20m profit, £7m will be undistributed profits and £7m will be paid in corporate taxes, leaving £6m to be distributed to shareholders to form part of their income. The increase in income will increase employment and thus reduce unemployment benefits. Kennedy estimated this fall in transfer payments to households to be £4m. Thus, a £100m rise in GDP will lead to a £82m (£80m + £6m - £4m) rise in personal income.

This £82m rise is an increase in personal income. To calculate personal disposable income it is necessary to take away direct taxes on income. The standard rate of income tax is 25 per cent, whilst National Insurance contributions for the average income earner are approximately 7 per cent. Marginal tax rates are therefore 32 per cent, leaving 68 per cent of an increase in personal income in the hands of consumers. Hence, personal disposable income from the above £82m is approximately £56m (£82m x 0.68).

Of the £56m, approximately 0.9 will be spent on the basis of recent national income figures, according to Kennedy. So consumer spending is £50m (£56 x 0.9). Not all of that represents factor income from spending on goods because indirect taxes are levied on purchases. The average rate of tax on goods (VAT plus excise duties) is 0.18. Factor income from expenditure on goods is therefore £41m (£50m x 0.82).

Factor income generated by expenditure on goods is split between domestically produced goods and imported goods. Kennedy estimated the marginal propensity to import to be 0.39. Of the £41m spent, only £25m [£41 x (1 - 0.39)] will represent purchases of domestically produced goods net of tax.

The marginal propensity to consume out of GDP is therefore 0.25. The value of the multiplier is then 1.333 [1÷ (1- 0.25)]. This means that if exports, for instance, increase by £100m, the final increase in GDP is £133m. £100m represents the extra expenditure on exports. The £33m is an increase in consumer spending on domestically produced goods net of all taxes.

Kennedy points out that this estimate assumes the economy is at less than full employment. Increases in I, G or X can lead to an increase in national income because there are unutilised resources of labour and capital. He also assumes that interest rates remain constant and there is a policy of monetary accommodation (☞ unit 93). Lastly he assumes that the exchange rate does not change.

Data question

PROPENSITY TO IMPORT AND NATIONAL INCOME

Table 78.2 shows imports as a percentage of national income (measured by total final expenditure), averaged over five year periods from 1950.

1. **What has happened to the average propensity to import for the UK between 1950 and 1989?**
2. **Using a Keynesian model of income determination, analyse the effect of this change of the propensity to import on equilibrium national income in the UK.**

Table 78.2 *Imports as a percentage of total final expenditure*

	%
1950 - 1954	14.0
1955 - 1959	14.7
1960 - 1964	15.6
1965 - 1969	16.6
1970 - 1974	19.0
1975 - 1979	19.4
1980 - 1984	20.6
1985 - 1989	21.4

Source: adapted from CSO, *Economic Trends Annual Supplement*; CSO, *Monthly Digest of Statistics*.

Summary

1. There is equilibrium in the labour market when the demand for and supply of labour are equal.
2. Unemployment can be divided into two categories: voluntary unemployment and involuntary unemployment. Workers can be officially registered as unemployed even when the labour market is in equilibrium and there is full employment in the economy.
3. Classical economists argue that involuntary unemployment can only exist in the short term, if at all. If there is involuntary unemployment in the labour market, wages will fall until equilibrium is restored.
4. Keynesian economists argue that if unemployment exists rigidities in the labour market will prevent the labour market from clearing quickly if at all. These rigidities include geographical immobility, segmented labour markets and trade unions.
5. Classical economists stress the importance of supply side policies because they believe that unemployment is essentially voluntary. Keynesian economists stress the importance of demand side policies because they believe that large scale unemployment tends to be involuntary.

Labour market equilibrium

Equilibrium in the labour market is achieved when the demand for labour is equal to the supply of labour (☞ unit 48). The demand for labour in an economy is determined by the **marginal revenue product** of labour. As more and more workers are combined with a fixed stock of land and capital, the marginal revenue product of labour (the addition to output of the extra worker) declines (an example of the **law of diminishing returns**). Hence the demand curve for labour is downward sloping.

The supply curve for labour in an economy is likely to be upward sloping. As real wage rates increase, more adults, particularly women, are attracted into the workforce. In the very short term, employers can also persuade existing workers to work overtime if they offer higher rates of pay.

Figure 79.1 shows the equilibrium level of employment in the economy. Employment is OE whilst the equilibrium wage rate is OW. At this equilibrium wage rate, every worker who wishes to work has got a job. So it would seem that the economy is at full employment. However, some economists argue that there can still be millions of people officially registered as unemployed despite there being **full employment** in the economy. Why is this?

The natural rate of unemployment

It is important to remember that the count by government of the number of workers unemployed in an economy does not correspond precisely to any theoretical concept of unemployment used by economists. For instance, economists in the UK are divided about whether the UK

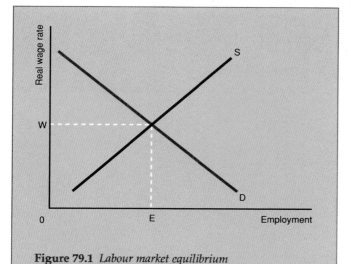

Figure 79.1 *Labour market equilibrium*
The labour market is in equilibrium when the demand for labour is equal to the supply of labour.

unemployment statistics published every month are an underestimation or an overestimation of the true level of unemployment (☞ unit 96). If there are 2 million registered as unemployed this month, who are these 2 million people? One way of answering this question is to split the unemployed into two types. Some workers are VOLUNTARILY UNEMPLOYED. They are workers who choose not to accept offers of employment at the current wage rate (i.e. they turn down jobs that are offered to them). Other workers suffer from INVOLUNTARY UNEMPLOYMENT. These unemployed workers are prepared to take jobs at the current wage rate but are unable to find employment. There are many reasons why workers choose to voluntarily remain unemployed.

■ For instance, some workers are between jobs. They might already have a new job starting at some point in the future and instead of accepting short term work, choose to have time off, or they might be waiting and looking for the right job to come along.

■ Alternatively, some workers cannot find jobs which pay significantly more than the benefits they would receive from being unemployed. The UK benefit system favours those with dependants. Young single unemployed workers receive considerably less in benefits when unemployed than older married men with a number of children. Hence, it is particularly older married men who choose to stay unemployed.

In Figure 79.2, two supply curves for labour are drawn. $S_{(Workers)}$ shows the number of workers who are prepared to accept a job at any given wage rate. $S_{(Labour\ force)}$ is $S_{(Workers)}$ plus those who claim they wish to work but are not prepared to work at the given wage rate. The equilibrium wage rate is OW. The equilibrium level of unemployment is OE. But official statistics show that there is EF unemployment in the economy. This unemployment is voluntary. The percentage of the labour

QUESTION 1 Which of the following would be classified as (i) voluntarily unemployed and (ii) involuntarily unemployed?
(a) An office worker made redundant two weeks ago who is looking for a job with better pay than the one he left.
(b) An unemployed coal miner, out of work for six months, who has placed 100 applications for a wide variety of jobs but has failed to get any of them.
(c) An unemployed home help who would be prepared to work for £2 an hour even though the local 'going rate' for home cleaning is £2.50 an hour.
(d) An unemployed ex-physics teacher, who resigned from his school three months ago because he hated his job, but hasn't been able to find a job outside of teaching which would pay as much.
(e) One of 2 000 shipyard workers made redundant three months ago in a town where the unemployment rate is treble the national average.

force which chooses to remain unemployed when the labour market is in equilibrium is known as the NATURAL RATE OF UNEMPLOYMENT.

Labour market disequilibrium

Periodically, free market economies suffer **recessions** and **depressions**. In a recession, the growth of output may fall. In a depression, the actual level of output may fall. Recessions and depressions are accompanied by a fall in the demand for labour. Figure 79.3 shows this shift to the left in the demand for labour curve from D_1 to D_2. The old equilibrium real wage rate was OE. For equilibrium now to be restored, the real wage rate needs to fall to OF. One of the most important controversies today in economics is whether this fall will take place and if it does, how quickly it will do so.

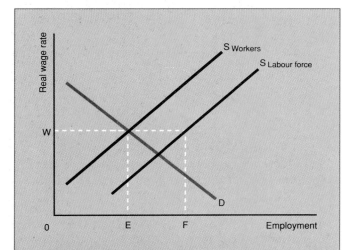

Figure 79.2 *Voluntary employment*
Voluntary unemployment exists when a part of the labour force refuses to work at the going wage rate. Equilibrium full employment exists at OE. At OW the equilibrium wage rate, EF workers choose not to work. The natural rate of unemployment is therefore EF÷OF.

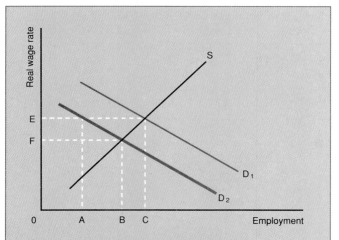

Figure 79.3 *A fall in the demand for labour*
A fall in the demand for labour from D_1 to D_2 will result in short term unemployment of AC. However, the equilibrium level of unemployment will fall from OC to OB in the longer term as a result of a fall of EF in real wage rates. This will restore the economy to full employment.

The classical view At one extreme are some classical, monetarist or supply side economists. They argue that the market for labour is like the market for bananas. Excess supply of bananas will bring about a rapid fall in price to clear the market. So too in the labour market. Unemployed workers will realise that they will have to accept cuts in pay if they are to get another job. Those in work will know that there is a pool of unemployed workers waiting to take their jobs if they do not show at least restraint in their wage claims. Firms know that they can pick up workers at low rates of pay. Hence in an effort to maximise profitability by minimising costs they will not be prepared to pay their existing workforce such high real wage rates. The RATIONAL EXPECTATIONS school of thought, led in the UK by Professor Patrick Minford of Liverpool University, argues that labour market clearing will be instantaneous. Firms and workers are assumed to have perfect knowledge. If there is a shift to the left in the demand curve for labour, both sides know that economic forces will be at work to restore equilibrium through a reduction in the real wage rate. Therefore if unemployment exists, it can only be because workers have refused to accept real wage cuts and have chosen to become unemployed (i.e. the unemployment is voluntary and the economy is at full employment).

A traditional Keynesian view At the other extreme are some Keynesian economists who argue that unemployment will persist until there is an opposing expansion of demand for labour. They argue that real wages will never fall sufficiently to clear the labour market completely. It is of little consequence if the unemployed are labelled 'voluntary unemployed'. Unemployment is an evil whatever it might be called. To understand why real wage rates are unlikely to fall, it is necessary to think clearly about the nature of the labour market in a modern industrialised economy like the UK. In Victorian England, it might have been true that firms hired and fired at will, taking on unemployed workers who were prepared to work for lower wages whilst sacking those who refused to take pay cuts. It might also be true that workers were forced to submit to the iron law of the market place, taking real wage cuts when the demand for labour fell. But conditions are very different in a modern industrial economy (☞ unit 50 for a fuller explanation of the following points).

- Medium to large employers have little to gain by forcing down wages in the short term. Such action is likely to demotivate the existing workforce and lead to a loss of employee loyalty and goodwill. Employees represent valuable assets of the firm. They have received training and are familiar with working practices. Hiring new labour is a costly process if workers leave because of dissatisfaction with the firm. So such employers are likely to take a long term view of the labour market. Even in the deep recession of the early 1980s, many UK employers such as the banks continued to award real wage increases to their workforce despite having hundreds and sometimes thousands of applicants for each job vacancy.

- Trade unions act to protect the interests of their members. Trade union members are almost all in jobs. Therefore they are not particularly concerned with the plight of the unemployed (just as firms are not in business to help alleviate unemployment). Trade unions will naturally not only resist real wage cuts but will press for higher real wages. Can a trade union be said to have achieved its objectives if the workforce of a firm shrinks through natural wastage by a few per cent and those who keep their jobs gain real wage increases?

- Minimum wage legislation (administered in the UK through Wages Councils) restricts the ability of employers to cut wage rates.

- The economy comprises a large number of different labour markets. Labour is immobile geographically in the UK particularly because of the distorted housing market. Labour is immobile occupationally because of the ever increasing division of labour within the economy and the failure of both firms and government to provide the level of training which would make workers mobile.

According to this view, a modern labour market is inevitably imperfect. Real wage rates may conceivably fall sufficiently in the long run to bring the economy back to full employment but then, as Keynes said, 'in the long run we are all dead'. It is little comfort to a 45 year old made redundant today to know that in 15 years' time the economy will have returned to full employment and he may then have a chance of getting a low paid job.

QUESTION 2

Sir,

The Prime Minister, Mr John Major, has argued that 'if wage rises stay high, that will necessarily affect jobs'. Unfortunately, those most likely to obtain large wage increases are, almost by definition, those least likely to become unemployed. Given the skill shortages in Britain, skilled workers demand that their pay should at least rise in line with the cost of living. Their employers, similarly, have no option but to concede. Some will be forced into insolvency as a result, but of the workers who consequently lose their jobs, the ones who have obtained the largest pay increases are also the ones most likely to obtain other employment on the same or better terms. In the process, those least to blame for wage inflation and least able to obtain alternative employment will be cast on the human scrap heap.

Source: an extract from a letter by Brian Reading, the *Financial Times*, 18.12.1990.

(a) Outline the economic reasoning behind Mr John Major's statement quoted in the letter.
(b) Why, according to Brian Reading, will skilled workers be less affected by unemployment than other workers if wage rates rise quickly? What effect will this have on the levels of involuntary unemployment in the UK?

A moderate Keynesian/neo-classical view In between these two views are those of many economists from both Keynesian and monetarist/neo-classical backgrounds who argue that in the short term, a fall in demand for labour will result in unemployment. But in the longer term, say a period of 4-6 years, the economy will tend to revert to full employment. According to this view, rigidities in the labour market are strong. However, over time employers in the formal sector of the economy will push down real wage rates from what they would otherwise have been. Even if this is only one per cent per year, it amounts to over 5 per cent over a five year period. Moreover, there is a significant small business economy where wages are more flexible. Some of those made unemployed will become self-employed accepting a lower wage in the process.

Demand vs supply side causes of unemployment

The Keynesian view of unemployment tends to emphasise demand side factors. Unemployment occurs because there is a fall in the demand for labour. They dispute the argument of classical economists that wages will fall to clear the market. They argue that the labour market fails to return to equilibrium because of imperfections in the labour market.

The classical/monetarist/supply side view of unemployment tends to emphasise supply side factors. The labour market will return to equilibrium rapidly following a disturbance through falls in real wage rates. If there is measured unemployment, it is voluntary unemployment. Workers choose to stay unemployed rather than attempting to become mobile.

This debate about the causes of unemployment is crucial to any policy debate about how to cure unemployment. Keynesians tend to favour increasing the level of aggregate demand to close a deflationary gap in the economy (☞ unit 77). Supply side economists favour using **supply side policies** to reduce the natural rate of unemployment in the economy (☞ unit 98-99).

> **QUESTION 3** At a Conservative Party Conference in the early 1980s, Norman Tebbit, then Secretary of State for Employment, having accepted the problems of high unemployment, told the Conference how his father, when faced with unemployment in the Great Depression of the 1930s, had 'got on his bike' to look for work and did not stop looking until he had found a job. Between 1979 and 1982, unemployment rose from 1.3 million to 2.9 million.
>
> Outline the view of unemployment which Norman Tebbit put forward in his speech to the Conservative Party Conference.

Key terms

Voluntary unemployed - workers who choose not to accept employment at the existing wage rate.
Involuntary unemployment - unemployment which exists when workers are unable to find jobs despite being prepared to accept work at the existing wage rate.
The natural rate of unemployment - the proportion of the workforce which chooses voluntarily to remain unemployed when the labour market is in equilibrium.

Applied economics

The natural rate of unemployment

There is considerable controversy as to the extent of voluntary unemployment in the UK economy. Layard and Nickell (1985 and 1986) have attempted to estimate the natural rate in the UK over the period 1955 to 1983. They assumed that in the decade from 1955 to 1966 the actual rate of unemployment was the same as the natural rate of unemployment. This was because the inflation rate was stable. If inflation fluctuates, then the actual rate of unemployment, the short term rate, is likely to be different from the long term natural rate.

Table 79.1 shows Layard and Nickell's estimates of the natural rate in subsequent time periods, using two different models of the labour market. Whichever model is used, the broad trends are the same. Over the period 1955 to 1983, the natural rate of unemployment rose. From 1967 onwards, sometimes it was above the actual rate of unemployment and sometimes it was below it.

They put forward a number of reasons why the natural rate should have risen during the 1950s, 1960s and early 1970s.

- Trade unions became more militant, forcing wages above the equilibrium wage rate.
- Unemployment benefit rose in proportion to average wages making it more attractive for workers to remain unemployed.
- Employment taxes were raised, particularly employer's National Insurance contributions.
- There was a growing mismatch between the demand and supply of labour. Net job losses tended to be concentrated in areas outside the South of England, were in manufacturing and affected males more than females. Conversely new jobs tended to be in the South, were in service industries and were traditional female jobs.
- Incomes policies, used by government to influence inflation (☞ unit 95), affected unemployment levels over the period.
- Increases in import prices, particularly during the

Table 79.1 *Actual and natural rates of unemployment, males only, UK, 1955-66 to 1980-83*

	1955-66	1967-74	1975-79	1980-83
Natural unemployment rate (model 1)	1.96	4.12	7.80	10.72
Natural unemployment rate (model 2)	1.96	4.03	8.61	11.20
Actual unemployment	1.96	3.78	6.79	13.79

Table 79.2 *Factors contributing to the increase in male unemployment, 1956-83*

	Contribution to the change in unemployment	
	1956-66 to 1975-79	1975-79 to 1980-83
Demand factors	0.7	6.6
Supply factors		
Trade union militancy	2.4	0.8
Employment taxes	0.6	0.4
Mismatch	0.4	0.5
Unemployment benefit	0.5	- 0.1
Incomes policy	- 0.4	0.5
Import prices	0.9	- 0.9
Total change	5.1	7.8

two oil price shocks of 1973-4 and 1979-80, led to high wage demands by workers anxious to protect their real standards of living. These increases in wages are likely to have made British industry less competitive overseas, resulting in a loss of jobs in industries exposed to international competition.

■ A lack of aggregate demand in the economy meant that too little money was being spent to maintain employment levels. Table 79.2 gives Layard and Nickell's estimates of the contribution of these various factors to changes in unemployment over the period. In the 1960s and 1970s, they argue that supply side factors were more important than demand factors. The two most important determinants of increased unemployment were increased trade union militancy and the loss of international competitiveness arising from higher import prices. However, in the periods 1975-9 to 1980-83, by far the most important factor was a lack of demand in the UK.

If high unemployment is caused by a lack of demand, neo-classical economic theory would suggest that real wage rates would fall. Workers would 'price themselves back into jobs'. Published figures for the 1980s show little evidence of this. In every year with the exception of 1981, the average increase in money wages was above the increase in prices (i.e. there was a rise in real wage rates). There are a number of ways of explaining this.

■ Layard and Nickell may have over-estimated the importance of demand-side factors. Patrick Minford from Liverpool University, for instance, would argue that almost all the unemployment in the 1980s was caused by supply side factors and therefore the actual unemployment rate differed little from the natural rate.

■ At the other extreme, some economists argue that the labour market works so imperfectly that demand unemployment does not result in falls in real wage rates. Those workers with jobs are able to resist real wage cuts even with millions unemployed.

■ A further explanation is to suggest that there is no such thing as the natural rate of unemployment. The natural rate hypothesis suggests that when the actual rate of unemployment is above the natural rate, then there will be real wage cuts and the rate of inflation will fall as will the actual rate of unemployment. In the first half of the 1980s however, there were no real wage cuts and the rate of unemployment rose. From 1987 onwards, unemployment did fall but this was arguably due to an expansion of demand by the government rather than the result of the operation of free market forces in the labour market. These figures are used by some economists to argue that a natural rate does not exist.

Data question

PAY RESTRAINT REQUIRED TO PREVENT UNEMPLOYMENT

During the second half of 1989 and throughout 1990, the Conservative government issued continued warnings that the sharp rise in wage costs per unit of output then being experienced by the UK economy would lead to an increase in unemployment. In December 1989, for instance, the then Employment Secretary, Norman Fowler said: 'moderation in pay remains a key requirement if we are to remain competitive in world markets and not put next year's employment prospects at risk.'

1. **Using a diagram, explain how economic theory would support the view of the government.**

Summary

1. The aggregate supply curve shows the level of output in the whole economy at any given level of average prices.
2. In the short run, it is assumed that money wage rates are constant. Firms will supply extra output if the prices they receive increase. Hence, in the short run, the aggregate supply curve is upward sloping.
3. An increase in firms' costs of production will shift the short run aggregate supply curve upward, whilst a fall in costs will shift it downwards.
4. In the long run, wage rates may go up or down. Classical economists argue that if wages are perfectly flexible, unemployment will be eliminated by a fall in real wage rates. With full employment in the economy, the long run aggregate supply curve must be vertical at an output level equal to the full employment level of income.
5. Keynesian economists argue that real wages may not fall far enough to eliminate unemployment even in the long run. The long run aggregate supply curve is then horizontal or upward sloping at levels of output below full employment income but becomes vertical at full employment.
6. Shifts in the long run aggregate supply curve are caused by changes in the quantity or quality of factors of production or the efficiency of their use.

The short run aggregate supply curve

In unit 9, it was argued that the supply curve for an industry was upward sloping. If the price of a product increases, firms in the industry are likely to increase their profits by producing and selling more. So the higher the price, the higher the level of output. The supply curve being talked about here is a **micro-economic** supply curve. Is the **macro-economic** supply curve (i.e. the supply curve for the whole economy) the same?

The macro-economic supply curve is called the AGGREGATE SUPPLY CURVE, because it is the sum of all the industry supply curves in the economy. It shows how much output firms wish to supply at each level of prices.

In the short run, the aggregate supply curve is upward sloping. The short run is defined here as the period when money wage rates and the prices of all other factor inputs in the economy are fixed. Assume that firms wish to increase their level of output. In the short run, they are unlikely to take on extra workers. Taking on extra staff is an expensive process. Sacking them if they are no longer needed is likely to be even more costly, not just in direct monetary terms but also in terms of industrial relations

within the company. So firms tend to respond to increases in demand in the short run by working their existing labour force more intensively, for instance through overtime.

Firms will need to provide incentives for workers to work harder or longer hours. Overtime, for instance, may be paid at one and a half times the basic rate of pay. Whilst basic pay rates remain constant, earnings will rise and this will tend to put up both the average and marginal costs per unit of output. In many sectors of the economy, where competition is imperfect and where firms have the power to increase their prices, the rise in labour costs will lead to a rise in prices. It only needs prices to rise in some sectors of the economy for the average price level in the economy to rise. So in the short term, an increase in output by firms is likely to lead to an increase in their costs which in turn will result in some firms raising prices. But the increase in prices is likely to be small because, given constant prices (e.g. wage **rates**) for factor inputs, the increases in costs (e.g. wage **earnings**) are likely to be fairly small too. Therefore the short run aggregate supply curve is relatively price elastic. This is shown in Figure 80.1. An increase in output from Q_1 to Q_2 leads to a moderate rise in the average price level of $P_1 P_2$.

If demand falls in the short run, some firms in the economy will react by cutting their prices to try and stimulate extra orders. But the opportunities to cut prices will be limited. Firms will be reluctant to sack workers and their overheads will remain the same, so their average cost and marginal cost will barely be altered. Again, the aggregate supply curve is relatively price elastic.

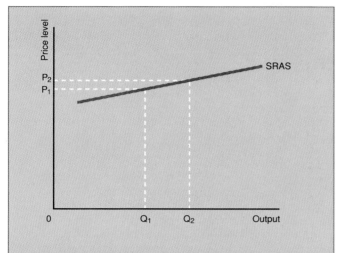

Figure 80.1 *The short run aggregate supply curve*
The slope of the SRAS line is very shallow because, whilst it is assumed that in the short run wage rates are constant, firms will face some increased costs such as overtime payments when they increase output.

QUESTION 1 During 1963, output in the UK economy boomed. GDP rose by 5.5 per cent. Using an aggregate supply curve, show the likely effect of this on prices assuming that money wage rates did not rise during the period.

Shifts in the short run aggregate supply curve

The SHORT RUN AGGREGATE SUPPLY CURVE shows the relationship between aggregate output and the average price level, assuming that money wage rates in the economy are constant. But what if wage rates do change, or some other variable which affects aggregate supply changes? Then, just as in the micro-economic theory of the supply curve, the aggregate supply curve will shift. The following are three of the factors which might cause SUPPLY SIDE SHOCKS, factors which cause the short run aggregate supply curve to shift.

Wage rates An increase in wage rates will result in firms facing increased costs of production. Some firms will respond by increasing prices. So at any given level of output, a rise in wage rates will lead to a rise in the average price level. This is shown in Figure 80.2 by a shift in the short run aggregate supply curve from SRAS₁ to SRAS₂.

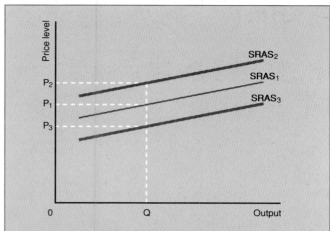

Figure 80.2 *Shifts in the short run aggregate supply curve*
The short run aggregate supply curve is drawn on the assumption that costs, in particular the wage rate, remain constant. A change in costs is shown by a shift in the curve. For instance, an increase in wage rates would push SRAS₁ up to SRAS₂ whilst a fall in wages rates would push the curve down to SRAS₃.

Raw material prices The prices of many commodities, such as copper and rubber, fell in the the early 1980s. A general fall in the prices of raw materials will lower industrial costs and will lead to some firms reducing the prices of their products. Hence there will be a shift in the short run aggregate supply curve downwards. This is shown in Figure 80.2 by the shift from SRAS₁ to SRAS₃.

Taxation An increase in the tax burden on industry will increase costs. Hence the short run aggregate supply schedule will be pushed upwards, for instance from SRAS₁ to SRAS₂ in Figure 80.2.

QUESTION 2 Output in 1982 was broadly the same as in 1978, yet wage rates had increased by approximately 50 per cent over the period. Using a diagram, show the likely effect of this on the short run aggregate supply curve.

The long run aggregate supply curve

In the short run, it was assumed that wage rates were fixed. Most groups of workers today in the UK economy renegotiate their wage rates annually. The short run could be seen as a period of months rather than years. So what is the shape of the aggregate supply curve in the longer run?

The answer to this question depends upon the response of workers to unemployment. Classical or supply side economists see the labour market as functioning perfectly. Unemployment represents a disequilibrium position in the market. Real wages, the price of labour, will therefore fall until demand exactly equals supply. At this equilibrium point there will be no unemployment. The classical viewpoint therefore argues that in the long run firms will always employ all workers who wish to work at the equilibrium wage. Similarly, the markets for the other factors of production, land and capital, will be in equilibrium at their full employment level. Hence in the long run firms will supply the maximum potential output of the economy. This is true whatever the level of prices. Therefore the LONG RUN AGGREGATE SUPPLY CURVE is vertical and is at the full employment level of output. This is shown in Figure 80.3. It should be remembered that classical economists believe that there will be some workers who choose to remain unemployed at the full employment level of output. The percentage of the workforce who are voluntarily unemployed is the **natural rate of unemployment** (☞ unit 79). So even at full employment, the official government unemployment statistics may show there to be unemployment in the economy.

Keynesian economists argue that, even if unemployment exists, workers who have got jobs will carry on negotiating and receiving higher pay rises as the economy grows. There will be little tendency for real wages to fall allowing the labour market to clear (they are **sticky downwards**). Keynesian economists argue that, even in the long run, the labour market may not clear. Unemployment could be a long run feature of an economy. Three possibilities then present themselves.

■ If the economy is in massive recession, an increase in output is unlikely to increase prices. Workers will be too frightened of losing their jobs to negotiate pay rises even if an individual firm is expanding. Here the aggregate supply curve would be horizontal because firms could expand production without experiencing a rise in costs.

■ If unemployment is relatively low, workers will be in a position to bid up wages in response to increased demand. Here the aggregate supply curve is upward sloping. The nearer full employment, the more workers will be able to obtain wages increases.

■ If the economy is at full employment, firms by definition won't be able to take on any more labour, however much they offer. The economy cannot produce more than its full employment output. Hence at full employment the aggregate supply curve will be vertical.

These three possibilities are shown in Figure 80.4. At levels of output between O and A, mass unemployment exists. The aggregate supply curve is therefore horizontal. Between output levels A and B, the economy is experiencing some unemployment, so the aggregate supply curve is upward sloping. At the full employment level of output, B, the supply curve becomes vertical.

Note that both classical and Keynesian economists agree that at full employment, the long run aggregate supply curve is vertical. Whatever prices are charged, industry cannot increase its output. But Keynesian economists argue that, in the long run, the economy may operate at less than full employment, in which case the aggregate supply curve is horizontal or upward sloping.

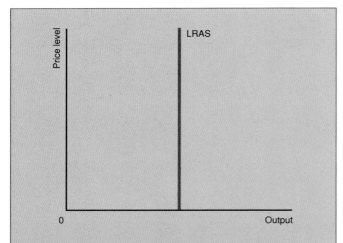

Figure 80.3 *The classical long run aggregate supply curve*
Classical economics assumes that in the long run wages and prices are flexible and therefore the LRAS curve is vertical. In the long run, there cannot be any unemployment because the wage rate will be in equilibrium where all workers who want a job (the supply of labour) will be offered a job (the demand for labour). So, whatever the level of prices, output will always be constant at the full employment level of income.

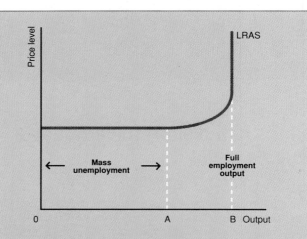

Figure 80.4 *The Keynesian long run aggregate supply curve*
Many Keynesian economists argue that, even in the long run, unemployment may persist because wages don't necessarily fall when unemployment occurs. When there is mass unemployment, output can be increased without any increases in costs and therefore prices. As the economy nears full employment, higher output leads to higher prices. At full employment, the economy cannot produce any more whatever prices firms receive.

QUESTION 3 Money wage rates in an economy increase by 50 per cent in the long run but full employment output remains unchanged. Show the effect of this on the long run aggregate supply curve for the economy.

Shifts in the long run aggregate supply curve

The long run aggregate supply curve is likely to shift over time. If we assume that it is vertical, then we are saying that the economy is always at full employment in the long run. This means that the position of the aggregate supply curve is determined by the potential output of the economy. Economic growth occurs because the quantity or quality of the factors of production available to an economy increase or because existing resources are used more efficiently.

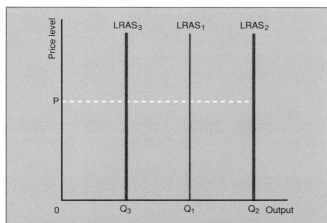

Figure 80.5 *A shift in the long run aggregate supply curve*
An increase in the productive potential in the economy pushes the long run aggregate supply curve to the right, for instance from $LRAS_1$ to $LRAS_2$. A fall in productive potential, on the other hand, is shown by a shift to the left of the curve, from $LRAS_1$ to $LRAS_3$ for instance.

Figure 80.5 shows how a growth in potential output is drawn on an aggregate supply diagram. Assume that the education and skills of the workforce increase. This should lead to labour becoming more productive, in turn leading to an increase in the productive potential of the economy at full employment. The long run aggregate supply curve will then shift from $LRAS_1$ to $LRAS_2$, showing that at a given level of prices, the economy can produce more output. A fall in potential output, caused for instance by a fall in the size of the labour force, would be shown by a leftward shift in the curve, from $LRAS_1$ to $LRAS_3$.

QUESTION 4 The economy was arguably at full employment in both 1964 and 1973. Show the effect on the long run aggregate supply curve of the increase in real GDP over that period from £136 billion in 1964 to £187 billion in 1973 (at 1980 prices).

Key terms

Aggregate supply curve - the relationship between the average level of prices in the economy and the level of total output.
Short run aggregate supply curve - the upward sloping aggregate supply curve which assumes that money wage rates are fixed.
Long run aggregate supply curve- the aggregate supply curve which assumes that wage rates are variable, both upward and downwards. Classical or supply side economists assume that wage rates are flexible. Keynesian economists assume that wage rates may be 'sticky downwards' and hence the economy may operate at less than full employment even in the long run.
Supply side shocks - factors such as changes in wage rates or commodity prices which cause the short run aggregate supply curve to shift.

Applied economics

The case of oil

In 1973, a barrel of oil cost $2.90. A year later the price had risen to $9. This price rise was possibly the most important world economic event of the 1970s. The trigger for the rise came from a war - the Yom Kippur war - when Egypt attacked Israel and was subsequently defeated. The Arab nations, to show

support for Egypt, decreed that they would cut off oil supplies from any country which openly supported Israel. Because the demand for oil in the short run is highly price inelastic, any small fall in the supply of oil is enough to bring large increases in prices. After the war finished, the oil producing nations through their organisation OPEC (the Organisation of Petroleum Exporting Countries) realised that it was possible to maintain a high price for oil by limiting its supply (i.e. by operating a cartel). Since then OPEC has operated a policy of restricting the supply of oil to the market.

Oil prices rose rather more slowly between 1974 and 1978. But between 1978 and 1982 the price of a barrel of oil rose from $12 to $30. Again, a political event was a major factor in triggering the price rise. The Shah of Iran, ruler of an important oil producing country, was deposed by Muslim fundamentalists led by the Ayatollah Khomeini. The revolution plunged Iran into economic chaos and the new rulers, fiercely anti-Western, showed little interest in resuming large scale exports of oil. A small disruption in oil supplies, a situation exploited by OPEC, was again enough to send oil prices spiralling.

The rise in oil prices had an important effect on the aggregate supply curve of the UK economy. It increased the costs of firms. So at any given level of output, firms needed to charge higher prices to cover their costs. This means that the short run aggregate supply curve shifted upwards as shown in Figure 80.6. This is supported by evidence from the UK economy. There is little doubt that the rise in oil prices helped push up UK prices by 16 per cent in 1974, 25 per cent in 1975, 17 per cent in 1979 and 15 per cent in 1980.

It could also be argued that the long run aggregate

curve was pushed back to the left by the oil price rises (from LRAS$_1$ to LRAS$_2$ in Figure 80.6). The rise in oil prices meant that some capital equipment which was oil intensive became uneconomic to run. This equipment was mothballed and then scrapped, leading to a once-and-for-all loss in the productive potential of the economy.

Higher prices and lost output arguably led the UK to experience the most difficult economic circumstances since the Second World War.

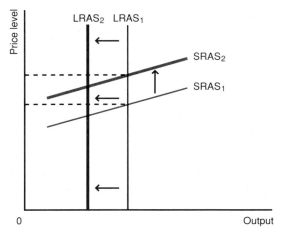

Figure 80.6

AGGREGATE SUPPLY

Interest rates fell from January 1985 to May 1988. It could be argued that one of the effects of these falls in interest rates (bank base rates fell from 14 per cent to 7.5 per cent over the period) was a rise in investment. Annual growth in gross fixed investment by the private sector rose from 2.3 per cent in 1986 to 13.9 per cent in 1987 and 19.2 per cent in 1988. The fall in interest rates also reduced the inflation rate because the cost of mortgages fell. This fed through to lower wage demands in 1987. The annual rate of increase of earnings fell from 7.9 per cent in 1986 to 7.8 per cent in 1987. However, strong demand in the economy helped increase average earnings by 8.7 per cent in 1988.

1. **Using a classical model of the economy, explain the possible effect of the fall in interest rates between 1985 and 1988 on:**
   (a) the short run aggregate supply curve and
   (b) the long run aggregate supply curve.
2. **Compare and contrast the explanation above with the Keynesian view in the short and long run.**

Summary

1. The aggregate demand curve is downward sloping. It shows that an increase in the price level will increase interest rates (via an increase in the demand for money) and lead to a fall in consumption and investment, and equilibrium income.
2. A movement along the aggregate demand curve shows how equilibrium income will change if there is a change in the price level.
3. A shift in the aggregate demand curve will result from a change in either a real variable such as investment, or a monetary variable such as the money supply.
4. Classical or supply side economists argue that an increase in the government's budget deficit will not increase aggregate demand because of crowding-out.
5. Keynesians argue that the aggregate demand curve is very steep (i.e. changes in the price level have little effect on equilibrium output). Classical economists argue that the aggregate demand curve is much shallower (i.e. increases in the price level will significantly depress the equilibrium level of output).

The aggregate demand curve

Aggregate demand is the total of all planned expenditures, $C + I + G + X - M$. The AGGREGATE DEMAND CURVE shows the relationship between the price level and equilibrium real national income. It shows different price and real output levels at which planned spending (i.e. aggregate demand) equals actual output given equilibrium in the money markets. In micro-economics, the demand curve for a product is downward sloping. As price increases, quantity demanded falls. The aggregate demand curve, the demand curve for the economy as a whole, shows the same relationship. If the price level in the whole economy increases, the equilibrium level of spending (and therefore income and output) will fall. To understand why a change in the price level will affect equilibrium income, it is necessary to put together a number of pieces of economic theory outlined in previous units.

Assume that there is an increase in the price level (i.e. there is inflation). What will happen?

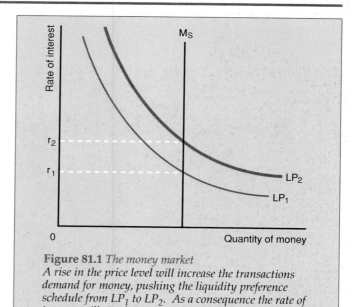

Figure 81.1 *The money market*
A rise in the price level will increase the transactions demand for money, pushing the liquidity preference schedule from LP_1 to LP_2. As a consequence the rate of interest will rise from r_1 to r_2.

The money market An increase in the price level will increase the transactions demand for money (☞ unit 69). If prices have risen, consumers and firms will need more money to buy the same number of goods. Therefore they will hold (i.e. demand) more money and reduce their holdings of non-monetary assets. In Figure 81.1, this is shown by a shift to the right in the liquidity preference schedule from LP_1 to LP_2. As a result, the equilibrium rate of interest will rise from r_1 to r_2. So an increase in the price level, ceteris paribus, results in an increase in interest rates.

Consumption and investment An increase in interest rates will affect both consumption and investment. A rise

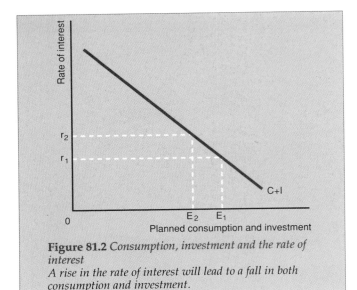

Figure 81.2 *Consumption, investment and the rate of interest*
A rise in the rate of interest will lead to a fall in both consumption and investment.

in the cost of borrowing will reduce spending on consumer durables such as cars and furniture. A rise in interest rates will also tend to reduce the wealth of individuals because the prices of stocks and shares are inversely related to the rate of interest (☞ unit 67). A reduction in wealth will reduce consumption (the **wealth effect** (☞ unit 61). Investment will fall because there will be a movement back up the marginal efficiency of capital schedule (☞ unit 62). Hence there is an inverse relationship between the rate of interest and the level of consumption and investment as shown in Figure 81.2.

The 45° line diagram A rise in interest rates will cause a fall in planned autonomous consumption (i.e. consumption not related to income) and in planned investment. So a rise in interest rates will lead to a fall in

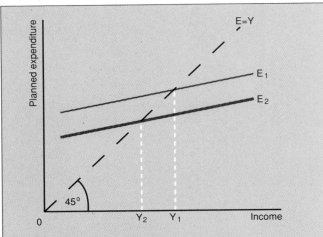

Figure 81.3 *The 45° line diagram*
A fall in the level of planned consumption and investment will lead to a fall in the planned aggregate expenditure line from E_1 to E_2. This in turn leads to a fall in the equilibrium level of national income and output from Y_1 to Y_2.

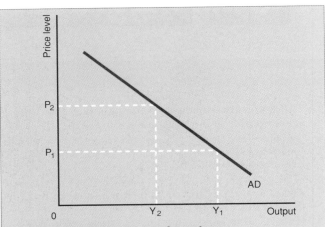

Figure 81.4 *The aggregate demand curve*
A rise in the price level will lead, via a rise in interest rates, to a fall in the equilibrium level of national income and therefore national output. Hence the aggregate demand curve is downward sloping.

the planned aggregate expenditure line on the 45° line diagram (☞ units 74 and 75). This is shown in Figure 81.3. The fall in planned expenditure will result in a fall in the equilibrium level of income from Y_1 to Y_2.

The aggregate demand curve What we have seen is that a rise in the price level feeds through to a fall in the equilibrium level of real national income and therefore of real national output. This is shown in Figure 81.4. A rise in the price level from P_1 to P_2 results in a fall in output from Y_1 to Y_2. The price level is put on the vertical axis whilst equilibrium output is put on the horizontal axis. The aggregate demand curve is downward sloping showing that as prices rise, the equilibrium quantity of goods and services demanded in the economy, and therefore real output, falls. Conversely, a fall in the price level will lead to a rise in the equilibrium level of real income and output.

QUESTION 1 In 1980, inflation rose to a peak of 18 per cent. At the same time real output (GDP at factor cost) fell both in 1980 and in 1981. How might economic theory account for this?

Movements along and shifts in the AD curve

The aggregate demand curve shows the relationship between the price level and the equilibrium level of real income and output. A change in the price level results in a **movement along** the AD curve. (Note, in contrast, that a change in the price level will **shift** the aggregate expenditure line on the 45° line diagram.)

Shifts in the aggregate demand curve will occur if there is a change in any other relevant variable apart from the price level. We can distinguish two types of factor which cause the aggregate demand curve to shift: changes in **real** variables such as consumption and investment; and changes in **monetary** variables such as the money supply and the rate of interest.

QUESTION 2 Which of the following will result in a movement along the aggregate demand curve and which will result in a shift in the curve?
(a) An increase in investment.
(b) A fall in inflation.
(c) A fall in autonomous consumption.
(d) A change in the money supply.
(e) A rise in prices.

QUESTION 3 Explain, using a diagram, the likely effect of the following on the aggregate demand curve for the UK.
(a) The increase in investment expenditure between 1988 and 1990.
(b) The cuts in planned government expenditure by the Labour government between 1976 and 1978.
(c) The large cuts in taxes in the Barber budget of 1972.
(d) The large fall in the Public Sector Borrowing Requirement under a Conservative government in 1981.
(e) The fall in the savings ratio during the 1980s from its peak of 14.2 per cent in 1980.

Changes in real variables

An increase in planned autonomous expenditure in the economy will increase aggregate demand. An increase in planned investment, government spending or exports will lead to an upward shift in the planned aggregate expenditure line on the 45° line diagram. This in turn leads to a shift to the right of the aggregate demand curve shown in Figure 81.5. Keynesian theory suggests that the increase in aggregate demand will be greater than the initial increase in autonomous expenditure because of the multiplier effect (☞ unit 75).

Equally a change in marginal propensities will change the level of aggregate demand. If households plan to spend a lower proportion of their income and save more, then aggregate demand at any given level of prices will fall (the **paradox of thrift**). Hence the aggregate demand curve will shift to the left. On the other hand, aggregate demand will rise and the AD curve will shift to the right if the government lowers the marginal propensity to tax by reducing tax rates.

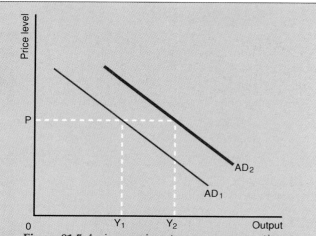

Figure 81.5 *An increase in autonomous consumption An increase in planned investment, government spending or exports will result in a multiple increase in the level of planned expenditure and hence push the aggregate demand curve to the right from AD_1 to AD_2.*

Changes in monetary variables

Changes in monetary variables can also shift the aggregate demand curve. Assume that there is an increase in the money supply. Disequilibrium in the money market will now be present. The money supply will be greater than the demand for money (i.e. households and firms, including financial institutions such as banks, will be holding more money than they desire). Two things will happen according to the theory of the demand for money.

- Money will be exchanged for physical assets. Households and firms will change their portfolio of assets to hold less money and more goods. In simple language, this means that households and firms will spend more money.
- Money will be exchanged for non-monetary financial assets. Households and firms will buy more stocks and shares etc. Greater demand will increase the price of financial assets but it will therefore reduce the rate of interest (remember the price of bonds for instance is inversely related to the rate of interest ☞ unit 67). A fall in the rate of interest will increase the level of consumption and investment in the economy (i.e. households and firms will spend more money).

So an increase in the money supply will result both directly and indirectly in a rise in level of aggregate demand in the economy. This is known as the MONETARY TRANSMISSION MECHANISM: the mechanism through which a change in the money supply affects the real economy. Some monetarist economists even calculate **money multipliers** (not to be confused with credit multipliers used in creation of credit theory). The money multiplier is the number of times an increase in the money supply is multiplied to give the final increase in national income. Many monetarists argue that the money multiplier is large. Hence, small changes in the money supply produce large shifts in the aggregate demand curve. Keynesians on the other hand argue that the money multiplier is very small. They argue that physical assets are a poor substitute for financial assets such as money. Therefore an increase in the money supply will mainly affect holdings of financial assets such as stocks and shares and have little effect on holdings of physical assets. Secondly, they argue that consumption and investment are relatively insensitive to the rate of interest (☞ units 61 and 62). Hence quite large changes in the rate of interest will have little impact upon planned aggregate expenditure.

Economists agree that an increase in the money supply, through the transmission mechanism, will shift the aggregate demand curve to the right whilst a decrease will push it to the left. They disagree about the size of the shift that will occur (i.e. they disagree about the size of the money multiplier).

> **QUESTION 4** In the second half of the 1980s in the UK, there were significant increases in the money supply, particularly in broad money terms. Many economists have argued that these increases were due to the deregulation of financial markets that occurred at the time. In the late 1980s, both the real growth rate and the nominal growth rate of the economy increased. Using a diagram, explain how economic theory might explain the impact of financial deregulation on prices and output in the economy.

Government finance and the money supply

In the simple Keynesian model, an increase in government spending and/or a fall in the level of taxation would increase the level of national income. An increased budget deficit or reduced budget surplus would **crowd in** (☞ unit 75) extra private sector consumption spending. Monetarist, classical or supply side economists, however, would dispute this conclusion.

Assume a government raises its budget deficit in the hope of reflating the economy. This deficit is likely to be financed in one of two ways (it could also be financed by borrowing from abroad or the sale of state assets to the private sector).

■ The government could borrow the money from the non-bank sector. This will lead to a fall in aggregate demand. Government demand for extra loanable funds will raise the demand for loanable funds in the market. Interest rates will rise, choking off some of the demand for funds from the private sector. If the supply of loanable funds is perfectly inelastic (i.e. constant whatever the rate of interest), then extra government borrowing will be exactly offset by reduced private sector borrowing. Private sector borrowing would eventually have been used to finance private sector spending. So, at the most extreme, an extra £1 of government spending will lead to a fall of £1 in private sector expenditure. This is known as the CROWDING OUT effect. Higher public spending or lower taxes crowds out private sector spending.

■ The government could print the money (in a modern economy, usually done by the sale of debt to the bank sector ☞ unit 73), thus raising the money supply. Aggregate demand will now rise through the transmission mechanism. But as we shall see in unit 82, classical economists argue that such a rise will be short lived. Inflation will occur and aggregate demand will start to fall.

So classical economists argue that the expansionary effect of increased budget deficits is partially or completely offset by changes in monetary variables which deflate the economy. 100 per cent crowding out occurs if an increased budget deficit has no effect on aggregate demand.

Keynesian economists would not deny that the size of the Keynesian multiplier is likely to be less than that implied in the simple model because of the existence of monetary effects. However, they argue that crowding in still occurs (i.e. an increase in the budget deficit of £1 leads to a more than £1 rise in national income). Higher interest rates will increase the supply of loanable funds to the market thus allowing both private and public sector borrowing to increase. There is also a **balanced budget multiplier effect** (☞ unit 77) likely to be present.

The shape of the aggregate demand curve

Economists not only disagree about the size of any likely shift in the aggregate demand curve but also about its shape. The shape will determine the extent to which individual government policies can affect the level of equilibrium income.

The Keynesian view Keynesians argue that the aggregate demand curve is steep. To understand why this is, it is necessary to go through each stage of the derivation of the curve again. In the money market, the demand for money is relatively interest elastic. Keynesians argue that the speculative demand for money is a significant element of the total demand for money (☞ unit 69). The supply of money, too, is interest elastic. Central banks are unable to control the money supply to any significant extent. The money supply is endogenous and its size is determined by the banking sector of the economy (☞ unit 73). A rise in the price level which pushes the liquidity preference schedule to the right will therefore have relatively little impact upon the equilibrium rate of interest. Keynesians also believe that consumption is determined mainly by income and not by the rate of interest. As for investment, it is determined by a number of factors including past changes in income but the rate of interest is a very weak influence. Hence changes in interest rates have little impact upon consumption and investment and the C + I line shown in Figure 81.6 is almost vertical. The conclusion is that a rise in prices has little effect upon real expenditure and hence the aggregate demand curve is almost vertical.

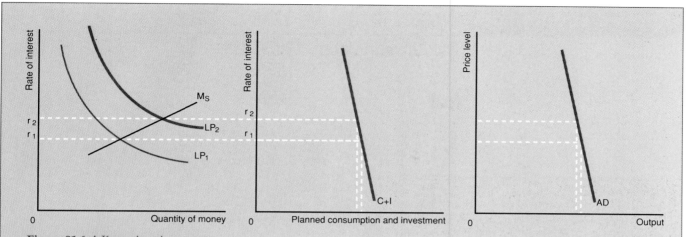

Figure 81.6 *A Keynesian view*
With both the demand and supply of money relatively interest elastic, a rise in the price level which shifts the liquidity preference schedule to the right will have little impact on interest rates. Given that consumption and investment are both inelastic, a rise in interest rates will have little effect on aggregate demand. Hence the aggregate demand curve is almost vertical

The classical view Classical economists argue that the demand for money is relatively interest inelastic. In the money market, the demand for money is fundamentally a transactions demand for money whilst the money supply is vertical because it is exogenously determined by the central bank. A relatively small change in the price level can therefore have a large impact on interest rates as Figure 81.7 shows. Consumption and investment can both be significantly affected by changes in the rate of interest. Hence the C + I line is much shallower than on Keynesian assumptions. As can be seen, a rise in the rate of interest from r_1 to r_2 will lead to a significant fall in the level of consumption and investment. The conclusion is that a rise in prices will have a significant impact upon real expenditure and hence the aggregate demand curve is relatively shallow.

Key terms

Aggregate demand curve - shows the relationship between the price level and equilibrium national income. As the price level rises the equilibrium level of national income falls.
The monetary transmission mechanism - the mechanism through which a change in the money supply leads to a change in national income and other real variables such as unemployment.
Crowding out - the process by which increased government spending reduces the level of private expenditure, leaving aggregate demand little changed.

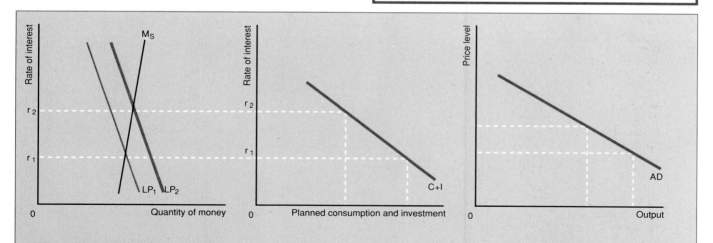

Figure 81.7 *A classical view*
Both the demand and supply of money are interest inelastic. A small change in the price level which produces a small shift in the liquidity preference schedule will give a large change in the rate of interest. Given that consumption and investment are both relatively interest inelastic, this means that the aggregate demand curve is relatively shallow.

Applied economics

The Lawson boom, 1987-1989

Economic theory would suggest that a change in interest rates will affect the level of aggregate demand in the economy. A fall in interest rates will shift the AD curve to the right as was shown in Figure 81.5 above, whilst a rise in interest rates will shift the AD curve to the left. All other things being equal, these shifts in the AD curve will lead to a rise in domestic expenditure (GDP) if interest rates fall and a fall in expenditure if interest rates rise.

Statistics from the second half of the 1980s should give evidence to support or refute this hypothesis. It is argued that fiscal policy at the time was broadly neutral (i.e. changes in taxation and government expenditure had little effect on aggregate demand). However, the government and Nigel Lawson the Chancellor of the Exchequer, used monetary policy to achieve various policy objectives. Figure 81.8 shows changes in bank base rates, the key short term interest rate in the economy, between 1985 and 1989. In the main, bank base rates fell between February 1985 and May 1988 from 14 per cent to 7.5 per cent. The government then tightened monetary policy. Within 6 months, base rates had risen to 13 per cent before climbing even further to 15 per cent by October 1989.

Figure 81.8 also shows the percentage year on year changes in GDP between 1985 and 1989. 1985-1988 were years of high growth, averaging approximately 4 per cent per annum, well above the 2½ per cent trend rate of growth in the post-war period. The annual growth rate peaked in the last two quarters of 1987 and the first quarter of 1988 at 5 per cent. Then it began to decline markedly. By the third quarter of 1989, it had

fallen to 1.5 per cent, with forecasts of 0.75 per cent for 1990 and 0.5 per cent for 1991.

Many people believe that the growth of GDP and the growth of the UK economy in the mid-1980s was directly related to the reduction in interest rates. Furthermore, although the economy had begun to slow a little before the sharp rises in interest rates from May 1988, the rises in interest rates are likely to have been a significant factor in causing the rate of growth of aggregate demand, and therefore GDP, to fall well below trend levels by 1990-91.

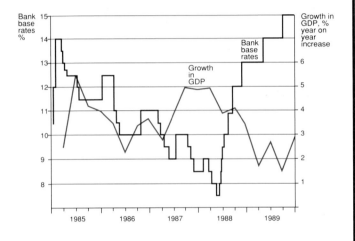

Source: adapted from CSO, *Economic Trends Annual Supplement*.

Figure 81.8 *Bank base rates and economic growth, 1985-1989*

FALL IN DEMAND

In May 1988, bank base rates stood at 7.5 per cent. Within six months they had risen to 13 per cent and by October 1989 they stood at 15 per cent. The increases in interest rates were designed to reduce growth in consumer expenditure in order to squeeze inflation out of the economy. Table 81.1 shows how expenditure on consumer durables was affected by these changes.

1. **What possible effect did high interest rates have on expenditure on consumer durables according to the data?**
2. **Explain, using a diagram, how this will have affected aggregate demand in the UK economy.**

Table 81.1 *Percentage change in expenditure on consumer durables, 1988 - 1989*

		Year on year percentage change
1988	Q1	12.6
	Q2	2.4
	Q3	-1.6
	Q4	- 2.8
1989	Q1	- 1.1
	Q2	4.5
	Q3	- 0.6
	Q4	0.6

Source: adapted from CSO, *Monthly Digest of Statistics*.

Summary

1. The economy is in equilibrium when aggregate demand equals aggregate supply.
2. In the classical model, where wages are completely flexible, the economy will be in long run equilibrium at full employment. In the Keynesian model, where wages are sticky downwards, the economy can be in long run equilibrium at less than full employment.
3. In the classical model, a rise in aggregate demand will in the short run lead to an increase in both output and prices, but in the long run the rise will generate only an increase in prices. In the Keynesian model, a rise in aggregate demand will be purely inflationary if the economy is at full employment, but will lead to an increase in output if the economy is below full employment.
4. A rise in long run aggregate supply in the classical model will both increase output and reduce prices. Keynesians would agree with this in general, but would argue that an increase in aggregate supply will have no effect on output or prices if the economy is in a slump.
5. Factors which affect aggregate demand may well affect aggregate supply and vice versa, although this may occur over different time periods. For instance, an increase in investment is likely to increase both aggregate demand and aggregate supply.

Equilibrium output in the short run

Units 80 and 81 outlined theories of aggregate supply and aggregate demand. It is now possible to develop a theory of equilibrium national output which incorporates not just a theory of real aggregate demand, as does the simple Keynesian model, but also aggregate supply and money.

Both Keynesian and classical economists agree that in the short run the aggregate demand curve is downward sloping whilst the aggregate supply curve is upward sloping. The equilibrium level of output in the short run occurs at the intersection of the aggregate demand and aggregate supply curves. In Figure 82.1, the equilibrium level of income and output is OQ. The equilibrium price level is OP.

Equilibrium output in the long run

The main disagreement amongst economists is about long run equilibrium in the economy. Classical economists argue that in the long run the aggregate supply curve is vertical, as shown in Figure 82.2. Long run equilibrium occurs where the long run aggregate supply curve (LRAS) intersects with the aggregate demand curve. Hence equilibrium output is OQ and the equilibrium price level is OP. Associated with the long run equilibrium price level is a short run aggregate supply curve (SRAS) which passes through the point where LRAS = AD. The long run aggregate supply curve shows the supply curve for the economy at full employment (☞ unit 80). Hence there can be no unemployment in the long run according to classical economists. If there is measured unemployment,

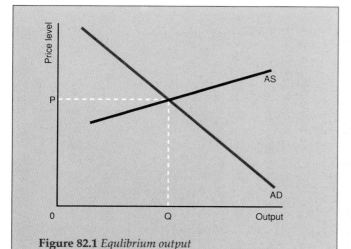

Figure 82.1 *Equilibrium output*
The equilibrium level of national output is set at the intersection of the aggregate demand and supply curves at OQ. The equilibrium price level is OP.

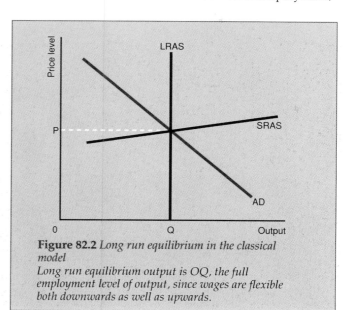

Figure 82.2 *Long run equilibrium in the classical model*
Long run equilibrium output is OQ, the full employment level of output, since wages are flexible both downwards as well as upwards.

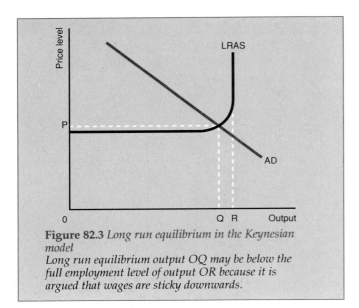

Figure 82.3 *Long run equilibrium in the Keynesian model*
Long run equilibrium output OQ may be below the full employment level of output OR because it is argued that wages are sticky downwards.

it is because workers are choosing not to take up work. They are **voluntarily unemployed** and the percentage of the workforce in this position is known as the **natural rate of unemployment**.

Keynesian economists argue that the long run aggregate supply curve is as shown in Figure 82.3. The economy is at full employment where the LRAS curve is vertical at output OR - a point of agreement with classical economists. However, the economy can be in equilibrium at less than full employment. In Figure 82.3 the equilibrium level of output is OQ where the AD curve cuts the LRAS curve. The key point of disagreement between classical and Keynesian economists is the extent to which workers react to unemployment by accepting real wage cuts.

Classical economists argue that a rise in unemployment will lead rapidly to cuts in real wages. These cuts will

QUESTION 1

What would be the effect on equilibrium income in the long run if the workers in the photograph were (a) successful and (b) unsuccessful with their demands?

increase the demand for labour and reduce its supply, returning the economy to full employment quickly and automatically. Economists like Patrick Minford, of the rational expectations school of thought, argue that this short term disequilibrium is corrected so quickly that the short run can be disregarded. Keynesian economists, on the other hand, argue that money wages are sticky downwards. Workers will refuse to take money wage cuts and will fiercely resist cuts in their real wage. The labour market will therefore not clear except perhaps over a very long period of time, so long that it is possibly even not worth considering.

Having outlined a theory of equilibrium output, it is now possible to see what happens if either aggregate demand or aggregate supply change.

A rise in aggregate demand

Assume that there is a rise in aggregate demand in the economy with long run aggregate supply initially remaining unchanged. For instance, there may be an increase in the wages of public sector employees paid for by an increase in the money supply, or there may be a fall in the marginal propensity to save and a rise in the marginal propensity to consume. A rise in aggregate demand will push the AD curve to the right. The classical and Keynesian models give different conclusions about the effect of this.

The classical model A rise in aggregate demand, which shifts the aggregate demand curve from AD_1 to AD_2 in Figure 82.4, will move the economy from A to B. There will be a movement along the short run aggregate supply curve. Output will rise from OL to OM and this will be accompanied by a small rise in the price level from ON to

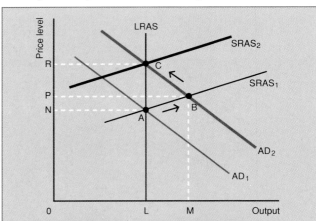

Figure 82.4 *The classical model in the short and long run*
A rise in aggregate demand shown by a shift to the right in the AD curve will result in a movement along the SRAS curve. Both output and prices will increase. In the long run, the SRAS curve will shift upwards with long run equilibrium being re-established at C. The rise in demand has led only to a rise in the price level.

OP.

But the economy is now in long run disequilibrium. The full employment level of output is OL, shown by the position of the long run aggregate supply curve. The economy is therefore operating at over-full employment. Firms will find it difficult to recruit labour, buy raw materials and find new offices or factory space. They will respond by bidding up wages and other costs. The short run aggregate supply curve is drawn on the assumption that wage rates and other costs remain constant. So a rise in wage rates will shift the short run aggregate supply curve upwards. Short run equilibrium output will now fall and prices will keep rising. The economy will only return to long run equilibrium when the short run aggregate supply curve has shifted upwards from $SRAS_1$ to $SRAS_2$ so that aggregate demand once again equals long run aggregate supply at C.

The conclusion of the classical model is that increases in aggregate demand will initially increase both prices and output (the movement from A to B in Figure 82.4). Over time prices will continue to rise but output will fall as the economy moves back towards long run equilibrium (the movement from B to C). In the long term an increase in aggregate demand will only lead to an increase in the price level (from A to C). There will be no effect on equilibrium output. So increases in aggregate demand without any change in long run aggregate supply are purely inflationary.

The Keynesian model In the Keynesian model, the long run aggregate supply curve is shaped as in Figure 82.5. Keynesians would agree with classical economists that an increase in aggregate demand from, say, AD_4 to AD_5 will be purely inflationary if the economy is already at full employment at OD. The increase in aggregate demand has created an **inflationary gap**.

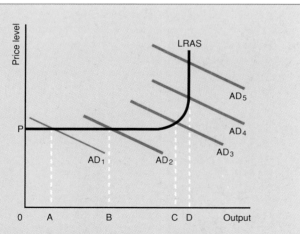

Figure 82.5 *The Keynesian model*
If the economy is already at full employment, an increase in aggregate demand in the Keynesian model creates an inflationary gap without increasing output. In a depression, an increase in aggregate demand will increase output but not prices. If the economy is slightly below full employment, an increase in aggregate demand will increase both output and prices.

But if the economy is in deep depression, as was the UK during the early 1930s, an increase in aggregate demand will lead to a rise in output without an increase in prices. The shift in aggregate demand from AD_1 to AD_2 will increase equilibrium output from OA to OB without raising the price level from OP as there are unused resources available.

The third possibility is that the economy is a little below full employment, for instance at OC in Figure 82.5. Then a rise in aggregate demand from AD_3 to AD_4 will increase both equilibrium output and equilibrium prices.

In the Keynesian model, increases in aggregate demand may or may not be effective in raising equilibrium output. It depends upon whether the economy is below full employment or at full employment.

QUESTION 2 In his Budget of 1981, with unemployment at 3 million and still rising, the Chancellor of the Exchequer Geoffrey Howe raised the level of taxes and significantly reduced the budget deficit in order to squeeze inflationary pressures. In a letter to *The Times*, 364 economists protested at what they saw as the perversity of this decision.

(a) Geoffrey Howe was influenced by classical economic thinking. Using a diagram, explain why he believed that his policy (i) would help reduce inflation and (ii) not lead to any increase in unemployment.
(b) The economists who wrote the letter to *The Times* could broadly be described as Keynesian. Using a diagram, explain why they believed that it was folly to increase taxes at a time when the economy was in the grip of the worst recession since the 1930s.

A rise in long run aggregate supply

A rise in long run aggregate supply means that the potential output of the economy has increased (i.e. there has been genuine economic growth). Rises in long run aggregate supply which are unlikely to shift the aggregate demand curve might occur if, for instance, incentives to work increased or there were a change in technology.

The classical model In the classical model, an increase in long run aggregate supply will lead to both higher output and lower prices. In Figure 86.6 a shift in the aggregate supply curve from $LRAS_1$ to $LRAS_2$ will increase equilibrium output from OL to OM. Equilibrium prices will also fall from ON to OP. Contrast this conclusion with what happens when aggregate demand is increased in the classical model - a rise in prices with no increase in output. It is not surprising that classical economists are so strongly in favour of **supply side** policies (units 98 and 99 - this is why they are often referred to as 'supply side' economists).

The Keynesian model In the Keynesian model, shown in Figure 82.7, an increase in aggregate supply will both

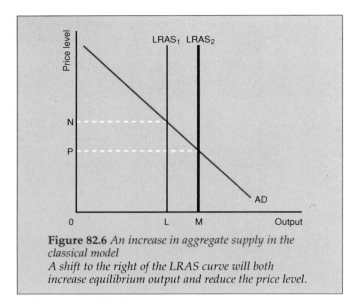

Figure 82.6 *An increase in aggregate supply in the classical model*
A shift to the right of the LRAS curve will both increase equilibrium output and reduce the price level.

important controversies in the history of economics. During the 1930s, classical economists argued that the only way to put the millions of unemployed during the Great Depression back to work was to adopt supply side measures - such as cutting unemployment benefits, reducing trade union power and cutting marginal tax rates and government spending. John Maynard Keynes attacked this orthodoxy by suggesting that the depression was caused by a lack of demand and suggesting that it was the government's responsibility to increase the level of aggregate demand. The same debate was replayed in the UK in the early 1980s. This time it was Keynesians who represented orthodoxy. They suggested that the only quick way to get the millions officially unemployed back to work was to expand aggregate demand. In the Budget of 1981, the Thatcher government did precisely the opposite - it cut its projected budget deficit, reducing aggregate demand and argued that the only way to cure unemployment was to improve the supply side of the economy.

QUESTION 3 Consider the economy today. Using diagrams, explain what effect an increase in aggregate supply would have on (a) output and (b) prices according to (i) classical or supply side economists and (ii) Keynesian economists.

increase output and reduce prices if the economy is at full employment. With aggregate demand at AD_1, a shift in the aggregate supply curve from $LRAS_1$ to $LRAS_2$ increases full employment equilibrium output from Y_E to Y_F. If the economy is at slightly less than full employment, with an aggregate demand curve of AD_2, then the shift to the right in the LRAS curve will still be beneficial to the economy, increasing output and reducing prices. But Keynesians disagree with classical economists that supply side measures can be effective in a depression. If the aggregate demand curve is AD_3, an increase in aggregate supply has no effect on equilibrium output. It remains obstinately stuck at Y_D. Only an increase in aggregate demand will move the economy out of depression.

It is now possible to understand one of the most

Increasing aggregate demand and supply

In micro-economics, factors which shift the demand curve do **not** shift the supply curve as well and vice versa. For instance, an increase in the costs of production shifts the supply curve but does **not** shift the demand curve for a good (although there will of course be a **movement along** the demand curve as a result). But in macro-economic aggregate demand and aggregate supply analysis, factors which shift one curve may well shift the other curve as well. For instance, assume that firms increase their planned investment. This will increase the level of aggregate demand. But in the long run it will also increase the level of aggregate supply. An increase in investment will increase the capital stock of the economy. The productive potential of the economy will therefore rise. We can use aggregate demand and supply analysis to show the effects of an increase in investment.

An increase in investment in the classical model will initially shift the aggregate demand curve in Figure 82.8 to the right from AD_1 to AD_2. There will then be a movement along the short run aggregate supply curve from A to B. There is now long run disequilibrium. How this will be resolved depends upon the speed with which the investment is brought on stream and starts to produce goods and services. Assume that this happens fairly quickly. The long run aggregate supply curve will then shift to the right say from $LRAS_1$ to $LRAS_2$. Long run equilibrium will be restored at C. Output has increased

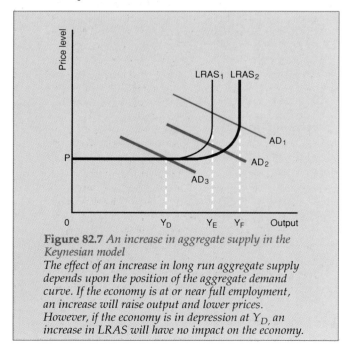

Figure 82.7 *An increase in aggregate supply in the Keynesian model*
The effect of an increase in long run aggregate supply depends upon the position of the aggregate demand curve. If the economy is at or near full employment, an increase will raise output and lower prices. However, if the economy is in depression at Y_D an increase in LRAS will have no impact on the economy.

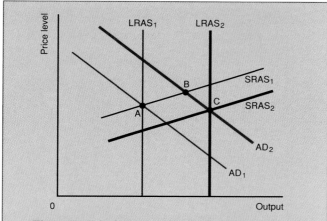

Figure 82.8 *An increase in investment expenditure An increase in investment will increase aggregate demand from AD$_1$ to AD$_2$, and is likely to shift the long run aggregate supply curve from LRAS$_1$ to LRAS$_2$. The result is an increase in output and a small fall in prices.*

and the price level fallen slightly. There will also be a new short run aggregate supply curve, SRAS$_2$. It is below the original short run aggregate supply curve because it is assumed that investment has reduced costs of production.

Not all investment results in increased production. For instance, fitting out a new shop which goes into receivership within a few months will increase aggregate demand but not long run aggregate supply. The long run aggregate supply curve will therefore not shift and the increased investment will only be inflationary. Equally, investment might be poorly directed. The increase in aggregate demand might be greater than the increase in long run aggregate supply. Here there will be an increase in equilibrium output but there will also be an increase in prices. The extent to which investment increases output and contributes to a lessening of inflationary pressure depends upon the extent to which it gives a high rate of return in the long run.

QUESTION 4 Employers in the economy give a 10 per cent wage rise to their workers. Using a classical model of the economy, show the effect of this: (a) on aggregate demand; (b) on short run aggregate supply; (c) on output and prices in the long run.

Applied economics

Stagflation, 1974-76 and 1979-1981

In a simple Keynesian model, rising inflation is associated with falling unemployment and vice versa. The experience of the 1950s and 1960s tended to support the hypothesis that there was this trade off between the two variables. However, in 1974-1975 and 1979-1981 there was both rising rising inflation **and** rising unemployment: this combination of stagnation and inflation came to be called **stagflation**.

The stagflation of both these periods can be explained using an aggregate demand and supply model of the economy. The rise in oil prices in each period was an external supply side shock to the UK economy. It had the effect of raising the short run aggregate supply curve (☞ unit 80) from SRAS$_1$ to SRAS$_2$ in Figure 82.9. The economy shifted from A to B. As can be seen from the diagram, prices rose and output fell.

In the first oil crisis, inflation rose from 9.1 per cent in 1973, to 15.9 per cent in 1974, and 24.1 per cent in 1975, before falling back to 16.5 per cent in 1976. Real GDP on the other hand fell by 1.5 per cent in 1974 and 0.8 per cent in 1975, before resuming an upward path in 1976.

In the second oil crisis, inflation rose from 8.3 per cent in 1978, to 13.4 per cent in 1979, and 18.0 per cent in 1980, before falling back again in 1981. Real GDP fell by 2 per cent in 1980 and 1.2 per cent in 1981.

The classical model would suggest that, all other things being equal, the economy would fall back to A from B. Full employment would be restored at the old price level. The above figures indicate that this did not happen. This was because the aggregate demand curve shifted to the right at the same time as the short run aggregate supply curve was shifting to the left. This led to continued inflation as output rose from 1976 and again from 1982. The rise in aggregate demand in the first period was partly due to the then Labour government increasing the budget deficit, as well as increases in the money supply (the inflation was **accommodated** ☞ unit 93). In the second period, taxation rose and government spending fell during the downturn in the economy, although the money supply increased again. This difference in fiscal stance is a partial explanation of why the rise in unemployment was lower and the rise in inflation higher in the first period than in the second period. It can be argued that the shift to the right in the aggregate demand curve was greater in the mid-1970s than the early 1980s.

In Figure 82.9, the economy is now at C. In reality, the AD and AS curves are constantly shifting to the right, producing new equilibrium price levels and output levels in each time period, so the economy would not remain at C for long. But could the economy stay at C in theory? According to classical economists, the answer is no. At C, given there is unemployment real wages will fall, shifting the SRAS curve down and leading to a new equilibrium with lower prices and higher output. Keynesians would argue that C could well be an equilibrium position for a number of years because the labour market is not a perfect market. Extreme Keynesians would argue that the labour market does not clear in the face of unemployment and therefore the economy could remain at C even in the long run. Did the economy in practice move back to a full employment level? The second oil price shock followed quickly after the first and therefore it is difficult to answer this from the experience of the 1970s. However, unemployment did fall between 1976 and 1979, indicating perhaps a movement towards full employment. Following the second oil price shock, unemployment continued to

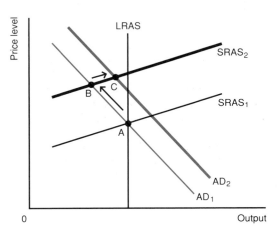

Figure 82.9

increase until the third quarter of 1986. Then it fell rapidly, halving by late 1989. Whether the economy had moved back onto its long run aggregate supply curve is debatable. If it had, then the natural rate of unemployment must have been considerably higher in 1989 than it was, say, in the early 1970s, a somewhat surprising conclusion given the array of labour market measures implemented in the 1980s.

THE TREASURY'S ROTTWEILER GOES FOR THE JUGULAR

Victor Keegan

The government's total reliance on high interest rates is at last biting into the economy. Unfortunately, like a Rottweiler off the leash, it has gone straight for the jugular - manufacturing investment.

In case the Chancellor, Mr Major, has not taken it on board, manufacturing investment fell by 12 per cent in the last quarter of 1989, bringing the decline in the second half of the year to a staggering 20 per cent. This is not a cyclical adjustment. It is a total collapse. If this represents British industry's response to the challenge of a single European market in 1992, then we may as well throw in the towel now. For the record, Japan has

been boosting manufacturing investment by 25 per cent a year in real terms. Over there, manufacturing matters.

Source: *The Guardian*, 26.2.1990.

1. Using diagrams, explain the effect of high interest rates in 1989 and 1990 on (a) aggregate demand, (b) aggregate supply and (c) equilibrium national output in the UK.

2. Suggest why Victor Keegan implies that (a) 1992 and (b) Japanese manufacturing investment are of significance for the UK economy.

Summary

1. Business cycles have been a feature of capitalist economies in the 19th and 20th centuries.
2. The business cycle has four phases - boom, recession, slump and recovery.
3. The multiplier-accelerator theory states that cycles are caused by the interaction of the Keynesian multiplier and the accelerator theory of investment.
4. The inventory cycle theory argues that cycles are caused by regular fluctuations in the levels of stocks in the economy.
5. Long wave cycles have been explained by changes in building in the economy and by changes in technology.
6. Monetarists believe that trade cycles are caused by changes in the money supply.

Characteristics of cycles

It has long been observed in economics that income and employment tend to fluctuate regularly over time. These regular fluctuations are known as BUSINESS CYCLES or TRADE CYCLES.

Figure 83.1 shows the various stages of a traditional cycle, such as occurred during the 19th century, during the 1930s or during the 1970s and 1980s in the UK.

■ **Peak or boom.** When the economy is at a peak or is in a boom, national income is high. It is likely that the economy will be working at beyond full employment. **Overheating** is therefore present (although the economy could be at less than full employment according to Keynesians if there are bottlenecks in certain industries in the economy). Consumption and investment expenditure will be high. Tax revenues will be high. Wages will be rising and profits increasing. The country will be sucking in imports demanded by consumers with high incomes and businesses with full order books. There will also be inflationary pressures in the economy.

■ **Recession.** The economy moves into recession. Output and income fall, leading to a fall in consumption and investment. Tax revenues begin to fall and government expenditure on benefits begin to rise. Wage demands moderate as unemployment rises. Imports decline and inflationary pressures ease.

■ **Trough or slump.** At the bottom of the cycle, the economy is said to be in a trough or slump. Economic activity is at a low in comparison with surrounding years. Mass unemployment exists, so consumption, investment and imports will be low. There will be few inflationary pressures in the economy and prices may be falling (there will be **deflation** in the strict sense of the term).

■ **Recovery or expansion.** The economy moves into a recovery or expansion phase. National income and output begin to increase. Unemployment falls. Consumption, investment and imports begin to rise. Workers feel more confident about demanding wage increases and inflationary pressures begin to mount.

During the 1950s and 1960s, the UK saw much milder trade cycles, as shown in Figure 83.2. National income did not fall but there were regular fluctuations in the rate of economic growth. A recession occurred when the rate of economic growth fell. Recovery or expansion was

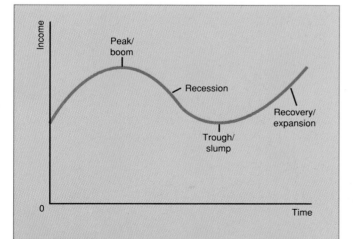

Figure 83.1 *The traditional business cycle*
The economy moves regularly from boom through recession to slump before recovering again.

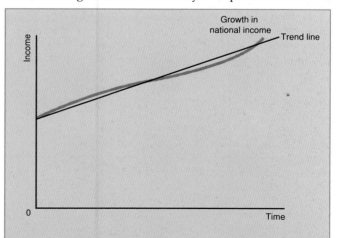

Figure 83.2 *The UK trade cycle of the 1950s and 1960s*
Peaks and troughs occurred when economic growth is high or low respectively.

present when the growth rate picked up again. The economy was in boom when economic growth was at its highest compared to surrounding years. There were troughs too when growth was particularly low but they were not really 'slumps' in the traditional sense. In the post-war period in the UK, the business cycle has tended to last four or five years from peak to peak. This contrasts with longer seven to nine year cycles in the 19th century. Some economists have claimed that there are longer 50 year KONDRATIEV CYCLES, so named after the Russian economist who first put forward the idea.

Business cycle models

Business cycle models can be divided into two types. **Exogenous models** argue that business cycles are started by a shock to the economic system, such as wars, revolutions, gold discoveries or large movements of population. It could be argued that the four-fold increase in the price of oil in 1973/4 gave a significant supply side shock to world economies. These effects rippled through time until economies returned to equilibrium.
Endogenous theories argue that trade cycles are caused by factors which lie within the economic system. Even if there were no supply side shocks, the economy would fluctuate regularly over time, although the fluctuations might be quite mild.

Business cycle models can be explained using aggregate demand and supply analysis. For whatever reason, the aggregate demand or short run aggregate supply curve shifts, moving the economy off the equilibrium long run aggregate supply curve. The business cycle is the path taken by the economy as it returns towards long run equilibrium, or fluctuates around that long run equilibrium position. The aggregate demand and short run aggregate supply curves are in constant motion to produce this path.

The multiplier-accelerator model

One Keynesian explanation of the business cycle is the MULTIPLIER-ACCELERATOR MODEL. The **accelerator theory** of investment says that investment is a function of past changes in income (☞ unit 62). If national income is growing, so too will investment. This increase in investment will lead to a multiple increase in national income via the **multiplier effect** (☞ unit 75). This leads to a further increase in investment. Hence the economy keeps on growing. On the other hand, if income falls, so too will investment, feeding through via the multiplier process to a further fall in income. Investment then falls again. The economy is on a downward path.

So far we have a possible explanation of why an economy might grow or contract over time but there is as yet no explanation of the trade cycle in it. There are two ways of using the multiplier-accelerator model to construct a business cycle model. The first is to construct a far more complicated accelerator model than, for instance, the $I_t = k (Y_t - Y_{t-1})$ theory developed in unit 62. Some formulations of the accelerator model will produce regular cycles. Whether these formulations are realistic can only be gauged when they are tested against real data.

The other way is to postulate the existence of **ceilings** and **floors** in the cycle. An annual growth rate of 5 to 6 per cent has proved unsustainable for the post-war UK economy. The economy moves to full employment and then beyond full employment. There simply isn't any more labour to be hired to sustain the boom. This puts a brake on the economy. As the rate of increase in output slows down, so the rate of growth of investment falls, producing the downturn in the economy. Similarly, national income will not keep falling to zero. At some point firms have to increase investment to replace worn-out machinery. Consumers will increasingly resist falls in their consumption and will be prepared to call on savings or borrow money to prevent their living standards falling even further. This is the turning point for the economy. Output will begin to rise, pulling up consumption expenditure and encouraging investment expenditure.

The inventory cycle

Another Keynesian explanation of the business cycle is the INVENTORY CYCLE hypothesis. **Inventories** is another name for stocks of raw materials and finished products held by producers. For instance, a car

manufacturer will hold stocks of steel, car components and finished cars.

Some economists argue that there is an inventory cycle of business activity in the economy. Changes in inventories cause regular fluctuations in the level of national income. For instance, assume that the government increases its expenditure in real terms. Firms will initially meet part of the extra demand by supplying goods from existing stocks. So they will need to increase their production levels, firstly to replace those stocks and secondly to meet the continued extra demand from government. This leads to an increase in national income via the multiplier process. Eventually firms will have replenished their stocks to their desired levels. They will then reduce their orders from other firms to the level needed to satisfy long term demand. But this reduction in orders will produce a downturn in the economy via the multiplier process. The economy will only pick up once firms have so run down their stocks that they are forced to increase their orders again.

Long wave cycles

A number of economists have argued that long wave cycles exist. Like the multiplier-accelerator theory and the inventory cycle theory, these theories emphasise that cycles are caused by changes in real variables.

In the inter-war period, Kuznets claimed that there was a 15-20 year building cycle. Economic fluctuations were caused by regular long cycles in building and construction.

Again in the inter-war period, a Russian economist Kondratiev suggested that 50 year cycles existed. These were caused by lumpiness in the pace of technological change. The idea was further developed by the Austrian economist, Schumpeter, who identified waves of technological progress. For instance, in the mid-nineteenth century the development of the railways was a major boost to world demand. In the early part of this century, it was the motor car and electricity that provided the stimulus to technological advance. In the post-war period up to 1970, it was the development of chemicals, plastics, nuclear power and a wide range of electrical consumer goods. Today, the world economy is making a start on exploiting the micro-chip and biotechnology.

These waves of innovation produce characteristic cycles. Take the micro-chip revolution: in the 1970s and early 1980s, microchips began to make an impact on products and output. Initially, some new products came onto the market (like calculators). But the biggest impact was on existing products. Costs were cut by incorporating micro-chips into existing machines. This led to a shake out of employment because the new machines could produce more output with less labour. The world economy moved to slump in the early 1980s (exactly 50 years after the Great Depression). Now we can expect to see many more genuine new products appearing on the market. What these will be is difficult to guess but they should lead to a recovery in the world economy. By the year 2010, the micro-chip revolution will reach maturity and the economy will be at the top of its 50 year boom. Exciting new products will begin to be more difficult to invent. So economic growth rates will begin to fall. The economy will then be in its recession phase. By 2020-30, the economy will be again approaching a slump which should occur in the 2030s. Once again new technologies will emerge, but they will only help lift the world economy from recession by the 2040s.

A monetarist explanation

Milton Friedman has suggested that trade cycles are essentially monetary phenomena, caused by changes in the money supply. In their important book *A Monetary History of the United States, 1867-1960*, Milton Friedman and Anna Schwartz argued that US business cycles were preceded by changes in the money supply.

The argument put forward is that changes in the money supply lead to changes in real variables such as unemployment and national income before finally leading to an increase in prices. The path to an increased price level is not a smooth one but is cyclical. The oscillations in the cycle become more and more damped as time goes on. Of course they can become more amplified again if there is another excessive increase in the money supply.

The link between changes in the money supply and changes in income is known as the **transmission mechanism** (☞ unit 81). Assume that there is a once and for all increase in the money supply when the economy is in long run equilibrium. The money supply is now greater than the demand for money. Economic agents, such as banks, firms and consumers, will adjust their portfolio of assets. Some of the excess supply will be used to buy physical assets - goods and services. The rest will be saved, reducing interest rates and thus encouraging the borrowing of money again to buy physical assets. The increase in consumption and investment will result in an increase in income. The economy is now in boom. Prices will begin to rise. This, together with increased real spending, will increase the demand for money. It is most unlikely that the economy will return to equilibrium with the demand and supply for money being equal. What will happen is that the demand for money will carry on increasing so that the demand for money exceeds the supply of money. Once this happens, economic agents will start to adjust their portfolios in the opposite direction. They will cut back on purchases of physical and financial assets. Interest rates will rise. Investment and consumption will begin to fall. The economy is now

in recession with falling income. This reduces the demand for money, bringing it back past the equilibrium point to the bottom of the cycle where once again supply is greater than demand for money. There will be a further bout of portfolio adjustment and aggregate demand will start to rise, bringing the economy into the recovery phase of the cycle. This will carry on, although Friedman argues that without further shocks the oscillations will become smaller and smaller over time.

QUESTION 4 Monetarists argue that the business cycle can be explained by changes in the money supply. For instance, Friedman and Schwartz (1963) argue that the Great Depression of the 1930s in the USA was caused by a drastic fall in the supply of money. They write: 'An initial mild decline in the money stock from 1929 to 1930, accompanying a decline in Federal Reserve credit outstanding, was converted into a sharp decline by a wave of bank failures beginning in late 1930.' Those failures produced (a) widespread attempts by the public to convert deposits into currency and hence a decline in the deposit-currency ratio, and (b) a scramble for liquidity by the banks and hence a decline in the deposit-reserve ratio.

(a) How and why, according to Friedman and Schwartz, did the US money supply contract from 1929?
(b) Suggest how this contraction in the money supply then led to depression.

Key terms

Business or trade cycle - regular fluctuations in the level of economic activity.
Kondratiev cycles - long 50 year trade cycles caused by the 'lumpiness' of technological change.
Multiplier-accelerator model - a model which describes how the workings of the multiplier theory and the accelerator theory lead to changes in national income.
Inventory cycle - fluctuations in national income caused by changes in the level of inventories or stocks in the economy.

Applied economics

The UK business cycle in the post-war period

The duration of the business cycle in the UK in the post-war era has averaged 4 to 5 years from peak to peak. As Figure 83.3 shows, during the 1950s and 1960s, booms and recessions were very mild. Recessions meant declines in the rate of growth of output rather than falls in output. However, the 1970s and 1980s have seen much greater swings, and the recession of 1979-1981 was the severest since the Great Depression of the 1930s.

In the 1950s, 1960s and early 1970s, booms in the economy (1954/5, 1959/60, 1964, 1968 and 1973) were associated with low unemployment, high inflation and a current account deficit on the balance of payments. It is noticeable from Figure 83.3 that unemployment shifted upwards in the late 1960s. The fall in unemployment that could have been expected in the boom of 1968 did not take place. This represented an upward shift in the **natural rate** of unemployment in

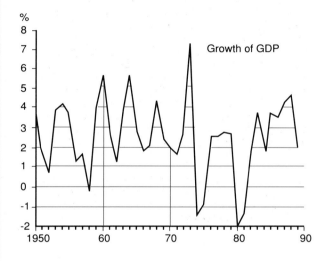

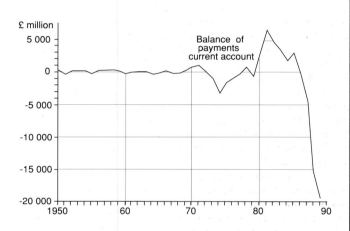

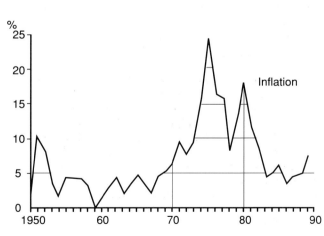

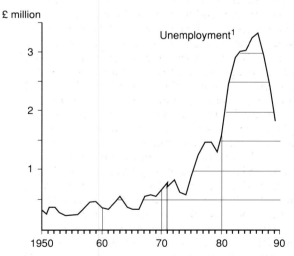

1. There were over 20 revisions to the way in which unemployment was measured in the 1980s. The figures here from 1971 are calculated on the basis of the 1982 definition of unemployment when the count was changed from those registered at Jobcentres for work to those registered as in receipt of benefits for being unemployed. Despite this, there are further discontinuities in the series in 1982, 1983 and 1985.

Source: adapted from CSO, *Economic Trends Annual Supplement*; CSO, *Monthly Digest of Statistics*.

Figure 83.3

the economy (☞ unit 79).

The recession of 1974-5 was unusual in that it coincided with a severe supply side shock to the economy. The quadrupling of oil prices pushed the current account on the balance of payments into record deficit, whilst it led to an increase in the inflation rate. This produced the phenomenon of **stagflation** in 1974. There was rising inflation, a worsening balance of payments, rising unemployment and a fall in output. Within a couple of years, however, more traditional patterns reasserted themselves. The boom of 1978-79 saw faster growth, falling unemployment coupled with rising inflation and a deteriorating current account.

The recession of 1979-1981 was even more severe than that of 1974-5 and again there was stagflation. Unemployment more than doubled and output fell by 4.2 per cent. Manufacturing industry was very badly affected, experiencing a 14.6 per cent fall in output from peak to trough. At the same time, inflation increased from 13.4 per cent in 1979 to 18.0 per cent in 1980 before falling back to 11.9 per cent in 1981. The balance of payments current account moved strongly into surplus. The recession of 1979-81 was untypical

when compared to recessions of the 1950s and 1960s in many ways. The second oil crisis of 1978-1979 fuelled inflation and created a downturn in the international economy which fed through to lower demand for UK exports. At the same time, North Sea oil was beginning to have a major impact on the balance of payments and led to a rise in the exchange rate, again dampening demand for UK non-oil exports. The government also, for the first time in the post-war era, reduced aggregate demand as the economy went into recession, firstly by increasing domestic interest rates and secondly by cutting public spending and raising taxes.

Perhaps not surprisingly, the economy took some time to recover. There was no recession, as past trends would have predicted, in the mid-1980s. However, the economy in 1990 was heading into a traditional recession after a boom in 1988-89 which saw record falls in unemployment, a rise in inflation, strong growth in output and a fast deteriorating current account position. The business cycle seems to have made its reappearance right on cue.

A BOOM IN GOING BUST

The mood among insolvency experts around Britain is buoyant. Business is better than it has been since the mid-1980s. The number of receiverships so far this year - double that of the first quarter of 1989 - suggests a leap in corporate failure comparable to that of the bad years of the early 1980s, or the recession of 1974.

Source: adapted from the *Financial Times*, 17.4.1990.

1. **Explain the relationship between the business cycle and (a) company liquidations and receiverships and (b) formation of new companies.**

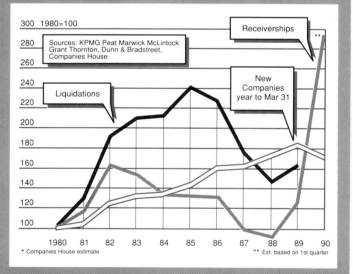

Figure 83.4

A. Aggregate demand and aggregate supply: changes in output and the price level

Aims

- To outline a model of output and price determination.
- To describe current trends in output and prices in the economy.
- To use the model of output and price determination to account for these current trends.
- To evaluate government policies which might be used to resolve the current problems of inflation and lack of sufficient growth of output in the economy.

Research activity

Your first task is to review the aggregate demand and aggregate supply model of output and price determination. Make a list of the variables which affect aggregate demand and aggregate supply and could therefore cause either price or output to change.

Then consider how output and prices in the economy are currently changing, and have been changing over the past, say, 12 months (you may wish to investigate a longer or shorter period). What are the possible causes of these changes? For instance, if output is growing, what variables are likely to be causing this growth? If inflation is falling, what is causing the fall in inflation?

Finally, find out what economic policies commentators (both economic and political) are suggesting that the government should pursue to remedy the current inflation and insufficient growth problems of the economy.

Sources

There is likely to be ongoing commentary about the state of the economy and what policies the government should now pursue on the television and the radio. Quality newspapers and magazines, such as the *Financial Times*, *The Independent* and the *Economist*, will routinely carry articles about changes in output and prices, and government policy. You may also wish to research past copies of these publications. Use indexes to help you with your search, such as those published by the newspapers or magazines for their own publications. Alternatively, use an index which covers a variety of publications, such as the *Research Index*, published by Business Surveys Ltd., which covers articles of financial interest in 100 newspapers and periodicals on a monthly basis. Your choice will depend upon what indexes your local large public reference library carries.

Statistics for a wide variety of economic variables for the previous twelve months are available in publications such as the *Monthly Digest of Statistics*, *Economic Trends* and *Financial Statistics*, all published by CSO.

Remember that most statistics are subject to later revision.

Structuring your report

Introduction Outline the aims of your investigation.

A model of price and output determination Explain briefly the AD/AS model of price and output determination. State which variables can cause prices and output to change.

Application of the model Describe the current state of the economy. Use your research findings to explain how and why prices and output have changed, according to the AD/AS model. For instance, to what extent have changes in interest rates affected output? What influence have exports had on aggregate demand? To what extent was the last government Budget neutral?

Evaluation of government policy options Outline some of the possible policies government could adopt to deal with any current inflationary and output problems of the economy. Evaluate the extent to which each proposed policy could achieve the objectives claimed for it. What policies do you think the government should pursue in the light of your evaluation?

Other suggestions

The above investigation is an ambitious one. It would be possible to reduce its length by just considering the impact of one or two variables on output and prices. For instance:
- what impact have recent changes in investment had on output;
- is there any evidence to suggest that the paradox of thrift can explain recent changes in output;
- assess the impact of the last government Budget on output and prices;
- what has been the effect of recent changes in exports and imports on output and prices?

In each case, it would be possible to carry out the investigation following the steps outlined in detail above.

B. The business cycle

Aims

- To outline a model of the business cycle.
- To investigate the characteristics and causes of the business cycle in post-war Britain.
- To use evidence to suggest which stage of the business cycle the UK economy is currently passing through.
- To analyse the contribution of government to stabilising the cycle or to creating fluctuations in the level of economic activity.

Research

Start by reviewing how economic theory characterises the business cycle and what it suggests might be the causes of the cycle. Make a list of those variables which change through the various stages of the cycle. Make another list of those variables, changes in which are argued to cause regular economic fluctuations.

Then, using CSO, *Economic Trends Annual Supplement*, chart the business cycle for the UK economy since 1948. Using recent newspaper articles, or publications such as the *Monthly Digest of Statistics* or *Economic Trends*, find figures for recent changes in output, prices, stocks, etc. in order to assess whether the UK economy is currently in the boom, slump, recession or recovery phase of the cycle.

In particular, consider recent figures for government spending and taxation. According to economic theory, these should act as automatic stabilisers over the cycle. If the economy is currently in recession, for instance, is there any evidence to suggest that tax receipts are slowing down or even falling; are social security payments related to unemployment rising? Investigate too, particularly by listening to the news on radio or television, or by reading the quality press, whether the government is using government spending and taxation to create a favourable economic climate for when it next has to call a general election. What evidence is there that this has been the case in the past?

Structuring your report

Introduction Outline the aims of your report.

The business cycle Using economic theory, describe the various phases of the typical business cycle. Explain how variables such as prices, investment, consumption and taxes change over the cycle. Use charts and diagrams wherever appropriate.

The UK business cycle Using the data you have gathered, describe the UK business cycle in the post-war period. Identify peaks and troughs in the economy. Show how different variables have changed in the cycle. Suggest whether changes in any one variable have been particularly important in creating a boom or recession in the economy at any point in time. Again, use charts and diagrams wherever appropriate.

The current phase of the business cycle In what phase of the business cycle is the economy at the time of your investigation? Explain your reasoning carefully, backing up your arguments with evidence that you have gathered.

Causes of the business cycle Identify possible causes of the business cycle in the UK economy. You may be able to identify causes which are common throughout post-war British economic history. Alternatively, you may choose to concentrate on the possible causes of one or two booms or recessions in particular trade cycles.

The business cycle and the government To what extent are government spending and taxation acting as automatic stabilisers in the current phase of the cycle? To what extent is government overriding these automatic stabilisers for its own political gains and therefore creating a political stop-go cycle? What are likely to be the consequences of such manipulation for the economy after a general election?

Other suggestions

Instead of considering the whole post-war period, you could choose to focus in on a particular fluctuation in the business cycle. For instance, you could investigate the nature and causes of the 1972-1976 phase of the business cycle.

Alternatively, you could concentrate your investigation on how one variable changes over the cycle.
- How has investment changed in the post-war period?
- Are the changes cyclical in nature?
- How has the money supply changed over the cycle?
- How has the current account on the balance of payments changed?

You could investigate the Kondratiev long wave cycle. Outline what he suggested was the cause of long wave cycles. Does the economic evidence from the UK support or refute his hypothesis?

Summary

1. If one country has lower costs of production for a good than another country, then it is said to have an absolute advantage in the production of that good.
2. International trade will take place even if a country has no absolute advantage in the production of any good. So long as it has a comparative advantage in the production of one good, international trade will be advantageous.
3. Transport costs will limit any welfare gain from international trade. However, economies of scale in production will increase the gains from trade.
4. The terms of trade, (the ratio of export prices to import prices), will determine whether trade is advantageous for a country.
5. David Ricardo thought that comparative advantage existed because of differences in labour costs between countries. In the Heckscher-Ohlin model, comparative advantage is explained by differences in factor endowments.
6. The theory of comparative advantage argues that international trade takes place because of differences in the price of products. However, much world trade is the result of non-price competition between countries. Design, reliability, availability and image are some of the factors which determine purchases of foreign goods.
7. In the theory of preference similarity, it is argued that trade takes place because consumers demand more choice than can be provided by domestic producers.

Absolute advantage

Adam Smith, in his famous example of a pin making factory, explained how specialisation enabled an industry to increase the production of pins from a given quantity of resources (☞ unit 2). In an economy, specialisation exists at every level, from the division of labour in households to production at international level.

Consider Table 84.1. Assume that there are only two countries in the world, England and Portugal. They produce only two commodities, wheat and wine. Labour is the only cost, measured in terms of man hours to produce 1 unit of output. Table 84.1 shows that it costs more in man hours to produce a unit of wine in England than in Portugal. Portugal is said to have an ABSOLUTE ADVANTAGE in the production of wine. It can produce both goods but is more efficient in the production of wine. On the other hand, it costs more in man hours to produce wheat in Portugal than in England. So England has an absolute advantage in the production of wheat. It is clear that it will be mutually beneficial for England to specialise in the production of wheat and for Portugal to specialise in the production of wine and for the two countries to trade.

The same conclusion can be reached if we express relative costs in terms of absolute output. If Portugal could produce either 5 units of wheat or 10 units of wine, or some combination of the two, the relative cost of wheat to wine would be 2:1 as in Table 84.1. If England could produce either 9 units of wheat or 6 units of wine, the relative cost would be 3:2 as in Table 84.1. Hence, Portugal could produce wine more cheaply and England wheat more cheaply.

QUESTION 1 The UK can produce either 10 cars or 100 television sets or some combination of the two if it uses all its resources. France can produce either 9 cars or 108 television sets or some combination of the two if it uses all its resources. Constant returns to scale are assumed.

Which country has an absolute advantage in the production of (i) cars and (ii) television sets?

Comparative advantage

David Ricardo, working in the early part of the 19th century, realised that absolute advantage was a limited case of a more general theory. Consider Table 84.2. It can be seen that Portugal can produce both wheat and wine more cheaply than England (i.e. it has an absolute advantage in both commodities). What David Ricardo saw was that it could still be mutually beneficial for both countries to specialise and trade.

In Table 84.2, a unit of wine in England costs the same amount to produce as 2 units of wheat. Production of an extra unit of wine means foregoing production of 2 units

Table 84.1

| | Cost per unit in man hours | |
	Wheat	Wine
England	10	15
Portugal	20	10

Table 84.2

| | Cost per unit in man hours | |
	Wheat	Wine
England	15	30
Portugal	10	15

of wheat (i.e. the opportunity cost of a unit of wine is 2 units of wheat). In Portugal, a unit of wine costs 1½ units of wheat to produce (i.e. the **opportunity cost** of a unit of wine is 1½ units of wheat in Portugal). Because relative or comparative costs differ, it will still be mutually advantageous for both countries to trade even though Portugal has an absolute advantage in both commodities. Portugal is relatively better at producing wine than wheat: so Portugal is said to have a COMPARATIVE ADVANTAGE in the production of wine. England is relatively better at producing wheat than wine: so England is said to have a comparative advantage in the production of wheat.

Table 84.3 shows how trade might be advantageous. Costs of production are as set out in Table 84.2. England is assumed to have 270 man hours available for production. Before trade takes place it produces and consumes 8 units of wheat and 5 units of wine. Portugal has fewer labour resources with 180 man hours of labour available for production. Before trade takes place it produces and consumes 9 units of wheat and 6 units of wine. Total production between the two economies is 17 units of wheat and 11 units of wine.

Table 84.3

| | Production before trade | | Production after trade | |
	Wheat	Wine	Wheat	Wine
England (270 man hours)	8	5	18	0
Portugal (180 man hours)	9	6	0	12
Total	17	11	18	12

If both countries now specialise, Portugal producing only wine and England producing only wheat, total production is 18 units of wheat and 12 units of wine. Specialisation has enabled the world economy to increase production by 1 unit of wheat and 1 unit of wine. The theory of comparative advantage does not say how these gains will be distributed between the two countries. This depends upon the wheat/wine exchange rate, a point

Table 84.4

| | Output | | | |
	Good X		Good Y	
Country A	20	OR	40	
Country B	50	OR	100	

discussed below.

The theory of comparative advantage states that countries will find it mutually advantageous to trade if comparative costs of production differ. If, however, comparative costs are identical, there can be no gains from trade. Table 84.4 shows the maximum output of two countries, A and B of two products, X and Y. The Table shows that country A, for instance, can either produce 20 units of good X or 40 units of good Y or some combination of both. The comparative costs or the opportunity cost of production is identical in both countries: one unit of X costs two units of Y. Hence there can be no gains from trade.

QUESTION 2
Table 84.5

| | Cost per unit in man hours | |
	Meat	Bread
UK	5	10
France	3	4

(a) Which country has comparative advantage in the production of (i) meat and (ii) bread?
(b) The UK has a total of 300 man hours available for production whilst France has a total of 200. Before any trade took place, the UK produced and consumed 38 units of meat and 11 units of bread. France produced and consumed 20 units of meat and 35 units of bread. How much more could the two countries produce between them if each specialised and then traded?

The assumptions of the theory of comparative advantage

The simple theory of comparative advantage outlined above makes a number of important assumptions.
- There are no transport costs. In reality, transport costs always exist and they will reduce and sometimes eliminate any comparative cost advantages. In general, the higher the proportion of transport costs in the final price to the consumer, the less likely it is that the good will be traded internationally.
- Costs are constant and there are no economies of scale. This assumption helps make our examples easy to understand. However, the existence of economies of scale will tend to reinforce the benefits of international specialisation. In Table 84.3 the gains from trade will be more than 1 unit of wheat and 1 unit of wine if England can lower the cost of production of wheat by producing more and similarly for Portugal.
- There are only two economies producing two goods. Again this assumption was made to simplify the explanation. But the theory of comparative advantage applies equally to a world with many economies producing a large number of trade goods. Table 84.6

Table 84.6

| | Cost per unit in man hours | | | |
	Wheat	Wine	Wheat	Wine
England	10	15	20	50
Portugal	15	10	30	60
Chile	20	20	50	70

shows that Chile has no absolute advantage in any product. However, it has a comparative advantage in the production of copper. Portugal has a clear comparative advantage in the production of wine whilst England has a comparative advantage in the production of apples. Exactly what and how much will be traded depends upon consumption patterns in all three countries. For instance if neither Portugal or Chile consume apples, England will not be able to export apples to these countries.

■ The theory assumes that traded goods are homogeneous (i.e. identical). Commodities such as steel, copper or wheat are bought on price. But a Toyota car is different from a Rover car and so it is far more difficult to conclude that, for instance, the Japanese have a comparative advantage in the production of cars.

■ Factors of production are assumed to be perfectly mobile. If they were not, trade might lead to a lowering of living standards in a country. For instance, assume the UK manufactured steel but then lost its comparative advantage in steel making to Korea. UK steel making plants are closed down. If the factors of production employed in UK steel making are not redeployed, then the UK will be at less than full employment. It might have been to the UK's advantage to have kept the steel industry operating (for instance by introducing quotas) and producing something than producing nothing with the resources.

■ There are no tariffs or other trade barriers (☞ unit 85).

■ There is perfect knowledge, so that all buyers and sellers know where the cheapest goods can be found internationally.

QUESTION 3
Table 84.7

| | Cost per unit in man hours | | | |
	Tapes	Sweaters	Beefburgers	Chocolate
England	20	10	8	20
Portugal	30	8	12	30
Chile	40	8	4	25

(a) Which country has an absolute advantage in the production of (i) tapes; (ii) sweaters; (iii) beefburgers; (iv) chocolates?
(b) Which country has a comparative advantage in the production of (i) tapes; (ii) sweaters; (iii) beefburgers; (iv) chocolates?

The terms of trade

In Table 84.3 it was shown that England and Portugal could benefit from trade. Whether trade takes place will depend upon the TERMS OF TRADE between the two countries. From the cost data in Table 84.2, England could produce 2 units of wheat for every $\frac{1}{2}$ unit of wine. It would not export wheat to Portugal at a price for instance of 2 units of wheat for $3\frac{1}{2}$ units of wine because it could produce wine at a cheaper price domestically. It will only trade if it receives more than a unit of wine for every 2 units of wheat. Portugal on the other hand can produce 2 units of wheat for every $1\frac{1}{3}$ units of wine. It will only trade if it can give England less than $\frac{1}{3}$ units of wine for 2 units of wheat. Hence trade will only take place if the terms of trade are between 2 units of wheat for 1 unit of wine and 2 units of wheat and $1\frac{1}{3}$ units of wine (i.e. between 2:1 and 2:1$\frac{1}{3}$).

This is shown in Figure 84.1. The cost ratios of wine for two units of wheat are drawn. England will only gain from trade if the international price of wine for wheat is to the right of its existing domestic cost line. Portugal on the other hand will only gain if the international price is to the left of its domestic cost line. Hence trade will only be mutually advantageous if the terms of trade are somewhere between the two lines, the area shaded on the graph.

The terms of trade is defined as the ratio between export prices and import prices:

$$\text{Index of terms of trade} = \frac{\text{Index of export prices}}{\text{Index of import prices}}$$

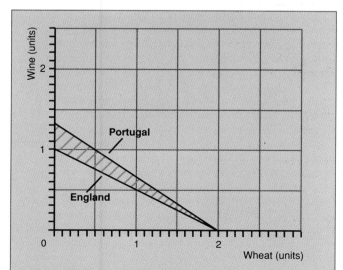

Figure 84.1 *The terms of trade*
England will find it advantageous to trade only if its terms of trade are at least 1 unit of wine for every two units of wheat exported. Portugal will only trade if it can receive at least 2 units of wheat for every 1$\frac{1}{3}$ units of wine exported. Therefore the terms of trade between the two countries will lie somewhere in the shaded area on the graph.

It is an **index** (☞ unit 3) because it is calculated from the weighted average of thousands of different export and import prices.

QUESTION 4 Look again at the data in Table 84.5.
(a) Show on a graph the price ratios of meat for bread in the two countries before trade.
(b) Would both countries find it mutually advantageous to trade if the international trade price ratio were 1 unit of meat for: (i) 4 units of bread; (ii) 3 units of bread; (iii) 1½ units of bread; (iv) 1 unit of bread; (v) ½ unit of bread; (vi) 2 units of bread; (vii) 1⅓ units of bread?

Why comparative advantage exists

David Ricardo believed that all costs ultimately could be reduced to labour costs. This belief is known as the **labour theory of value**. Hence the price of a good could accurately be measured in terms of man-hours of production. Following on from this, he argued that differences in comparative costs reflected differences in the productivity of labour.

There is an element of truth in this idea. The theory suggests that high labour productivity countries would have a comparative advantage in the production of sophisticated high technology goods whilst low labour productivity countries would have a comparative advantage in the production of low technology goods. Looking at the pattern of world trade, it is true for instance that developing countries export low technology textiles whilst developed countries export high technology computer equipment.

However, neo-classical price theory suggests that labour is not the only source of differing opportunity costs of production. For instance, the price of a piece of agricultural land can increase several times overnight if planning permission is given for residential building. This increase in value has little to do with man-hours of production. Prices and costs are, of course, linked to quantities of labour inputs, but they are also linked to forces of scarcity which can drive prices up or down.

Heckscher and Ohlin, two Swedish economists working in the inter-war period, suggested that different costs were the result not just of different labour endowments between countries but also of different capital and land endowments. If an economy, such as India, has a large quantity of unskilled labour but little capital, then the price of capital relative to labour will be high. If, on the other hand, an economy like the USA has a large stock of capital relative to labour, then capital will be relatively cheap. Hence India will have a comparative advantage in the production of goods which can be made using unskilled labour. The USA will have a comparative advantage in the production of goods which require a relatively high capital input. Saudi Arabia is much more richly endowed with oil than France. France, on the other hand, has a rich abundance of skilled labour and capital

equipment in the defence industry. Hence the theory would suggest that Saudi Arabia will specialise in producing oil, France in producing defence equipment and that the two countries will trade one product for the other.

QUESTION 5
Table 84.8 *Total labour costs in the world motor industry, 1988*

	Deutschmarks/hour
W Germany	38.49
US	37.59
Sweden	36.59
Japan	33.41
Belgium	32.10
Netherlands	30.41
Italy	27.77
France	24.85
UK	22.57
Spain	21.95

Source: adapted from VDA (motor industry association of West Germany).

During the late 1980s, a number of key investments in production plants were made by Japanese car manufacturers in Europe. These plants tended to be sited in the UK. The Japanese manufacturers intended to produce not only for the UK domestic market, but also to export cars throughout the European Community. How might the theory of comparative advantage help explain the decisions about location of plants made by Japanese car manufacturers?

Non-price theories of trade

The theory of comparative advantage provides a good explanation of world trade in commodities such as oil, wheat or copper. Countries with relatively rich endowments of raw materials or agricultural land specialise in the production of those commodities. It also provides a good explanation of the pattern of trade between First and Third World countries. Third World countries tend to export commodities and simple manufactured goods whilst importing more technologically sophisticated manufactures and services from the First World. However, the theory does not account for much of that half of world trade which occurs between the rich developed economies of the world.

Commodities are **homogeneous** products. There is nothing to choose between one grade of copper from Chile and the same grade from Zambia. Therefore the main determinant of demand is price. Manufactured goods and services tend to be **non-homogeneous**. Each product is slightly different. So when a consumer buys a car, price is only one amongst many factors that are considered. Reliability, availability, image, colour, shape and driving performance are just as important, if not more so. There is a wide variety of cars to choose from on the market, some produced domestically but many produced abroad. **Preference similarity theory** suggests that many manufactured goods are imported not because they are relatively cheaper than domestic goods but because some consumers want greater choice than that provided by domestic manufacturers alone. Domestic manufacturers, however, should have a competitive edge because they should be more aware of the needs of their domestic customers. This limits the extent to which foreign manufacturers can penetrate the home market.

Key terms

Absolute advantage - exists when a country is able to produce a good more cheaply in absolute terms than another country.

Theory of comparative advantage - countries will find it mutually advantageous to trade if the opportunity cost of production of goods differs.

Comparative advantage - exists when a country is able to produce a good more cheaply relative to other goods produced domestically than another country.

Terms of trade - the ratio of export prices to import prices.

Applied economics

UK trade flows

Table 84.9 *UK exports and imports*

	Exports		Imports	
				£ million
	Goods	Services	Goods	Services
1955	3 023	1 748	3 386	1 590
1965	4 913	2 858	5 173	2 675
1975	19 183	15 001	22 440	13 270
1980	47 147	41 249	45 792	39 809
1985	77 991	80 583	81 119	74 290
1989	92 526	108 399	115 638	104 354

Source: adapted from CSO, *Economic Trends Annual Supplement*; CSO, *Monthly Digest of Statistics*.

The UK exports and imports both goods and services. During the 1950s and 1960s, as can be seen from Table 84.9, the UK exported and imported more goods than services. However, by 1989, exports of services were greater than those of goods, whereas the UK continued to import more goods than services. This might seem to indicate that the UK has increased its comparative advantage in services and experienced a fall in comparative advantage in goods. But the situation is more complicated than this.

Table 84.10 gives a breakdown of visible trade (trade in goods) by commodity. There are very striking trends shown here.

■ Exports of fuels, approximately 95 per cent of which are oil, have increased. This is due to North Sea oil which first came on stream in 1976. By 1985, due to

record production and high oil prices, fuel exports accounted for 21.5 per cent of visible exports. By 1989, this had fallen to only 6.6 per cent as North Sea oil production and the price of oil fell. Imports of oil, on the other hand, have declined as a percentage of total imports.

■ Imports of food and raw materials have declined

Table 84.10 *Exports and imports by commodity (% of total value)*

		1955	1965	1975	1985	1989
Food, beverages and tobacco	Exports	6.0	6.6	7.1	6.3	7.0
	Imports	36.9	29.7	18.0	10.6	9.5
Basic materials	Exports	3.9	4.0	2.7	2.7	2.5
	Imports	29.0	19.3	8.4	6.0	5.4
Fuels	Exports	4.9	2.7	4.2	21.5	6.6
	Imports	10.6	10.6	17.5	12.8	5.2
Total food and raw materials	Exports	14.8	13.3	14.0	30.5	16.1
	Imports	76.5	59.6	43.9	29.4	20.1
Semi-manufactured	Exports	36.9	34.6	31.2	25.6	28.7
	Imports	17.9	23.8	23.9	24.8	26.6
Finished manufactured	Exports	43.5	49.0	51.0	41.2	52.8
	Imports	5.3	15.4	29.9	44.0	52.1
Total manufactures	Exports	80.4	83.6	82.2	66.8	81.5
	Imports	23.2	39.2	53.8	68.8	78.7
Unclassified	Exports	4.8	3.1	3.8	2.7	2.4
	Imports	0.3	1.2	2.7	1.8	1.2

Source: adapted from CSO, *Annual Abstract of Statistics*; CSO, *Monthly Digest of Statistics*.

Table 84.11 *Invisible trade, UK*

£ million

		1955	1965	1975	1985	1989
Total	Exports	1 748	2 858	15 001	80 583	108 399
	Imports	1 590	2 675	13 270	74 290	104 354
of which						
Sea transport						
	Exports	540	749	2 651	3 271	3 870
	Imports	570	748	2 561	3 727	3 840
Civil aviation						
	Exports	37	162	780	3 078	3 758
	Imports	40	134	675	2 925	3 840
Travel						
	Exports	111	193	1 218	5 442	6 877
	Imports	125	290	917	4 871	9 290
Financial and other services						
	Exports	358	551	2 889	12 379	15 150
	Imports	187	311	1 501	4 742	5 806
Interest, profits and dividends of the private sector						
	Exports	517	968	6 298	51 578	72 653
	Imports	343	378	5 182	48 114	65 164

Source: adapted from CSO, *Economic Trends Annual Supplement.*

from 76.5 per cent of total imports to 20.1 per cent in 1989. In the Victorian age, Britain was known as the 'workshop of the world', importing raw materials and exporting manufactured goods. A fall in percentage imports of raw materials would suggest that the UK has lost comparative advantage in the production of manufactured goods.

■ This loss of comparative advantage in manufactured goods is clear from import figures for manufactures. In 1955, manufactures accounted for only 23.2 per cent of imports. By 1989, this had risen to 78.7 per cent.

The possible reasons for the decline in UK manufacturing have already been discussed in unit 59. Some manufacturing industries have suffered more than others. Industries such as the UK motorcycle industry have been wiped out by foreign competition. Others, such as the motor vehicle industry, have moved from surplus to deficit in the 1980s, part of a more general trend for UK engineering. Textiles and metals have suffered more than most, whilst the picture has been more promising for a few industries such as chemicals and pharmaceuticals.

The theory of comparative advantage is often expressed in terms of relative costs of production. Whilst it is clear that our loss of competitiveness in industries such as textiles has been due to higher relative costs, this is less obvious in industries such as car manufacture. Here, poor quality, unreliability, poor design and long delivery dates have been possibly more important in losing markets than high relative prices.

The loss of UK competitiveness in manufactured goods could be argued to be unimportant if

manufactures can be replaced by services. However, service exports and imports are not all traded services. As Table 84.11 shows, the single most important 'service export' today is interest, profits and dividends. These are the earnings from money invested or lent abroad and brought back to the UK. They are the equivalent of interest on a building society account. During the 1970s and 1980s, the UK built up large stocks of foreign investments, but equally foreigners have built up stocks of investments in the UK, from which they take interest, profits and dividends and become imports or debits for the UK. Interest profits and dividends in 1989 accounted for approximately 25 per cent of all foreign trade. It is as if a household paid 25 per cent of its income in interest on a mortgage, whilst receiving 25 per cent of its income from interest on money saved.

Traded services - sea transport, civil aviation, travel (tourism) and financial and other services - are only approximately 20 per cent of the value of traded goods. So, despite the fact that the UK has a significant comparative advantage in the provision of financial services, there is no way in which the UK could in the foreseeable future compensate for significant losses in comparative advantage in manufactures by gaining further comparative advantage in traded services. Manufacturing matters!

So far, the composition of UK trade has been discussed. But Table 84.12 shows how the direction of trade has changed over time. In 1955, the UK was still to a great extent following trading patterns established

Table 84.12 *Visible trade by area*

		Percentage of total[1]	
		1955	1989
EC	Exports	15.0	50.3
	Imports	12.6	52.6
Rest of Western Europe	Exports	13.9	8.7
	Imports	13.1	12.7
North America	Exports	12.0	15.3
	Imports	19.5	12.6
Other developed countries	Exports	20.5	5.8
	Imports	14.2	7.7
Developing countries	Exports	36.9	16.6
	Imports	37.9	12.0
of which			
Oil exporting	Exports	5.1	6.3
	Imports	9.2	17.3
Centrally planned economies	Exports	1.7	1.9
	Imports	2.7	1.9

1. Figures may not add up to100 because of rounding.

Source: adapted from CSO, *Annual Abstract of Statistics;* CSO, *Monthly Digest of Statistics.*

during the Victorian era, buying raw materials from developing countries and selling them manufactured goods. North America was as important a trading partner as EC countries. By 1989, UK trade had shifted dramatically. Over half of exports and imports were now with EC countries. Markets in the Third World were relatively unimportant. Note too that trade with Japan, classified under 'other developed countries', is very small in relation to the total. Over the next ten years, with further economic integration planned by the EC, the percentage total of trade with the EC is likely to continue rising.

Data question

FORD PRODUCTION

During the 1980s, Ford increasingly imported cars from its continental plants to feed growing consumer demand in the UK. In 1989, it announced that production of the Sierra would be stopped at its Dagenham plant and transferred to Genk in Belgium. In future, Dagenham would produce only Fiestas.

1. **How might the theory of comparative advantage be used to explain Ford's actions?**

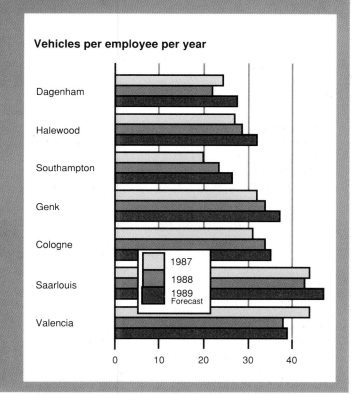

Vehicles per employee per year

Source: adapted from the *Financial Times*.

Figure 84.2 *Vehicles per employee per year*

Summary

1. Although the gains from trade can be large, all countries choose to adopt protectionist policies to some extent.
2. Tariffs, quotas, voluntary export agreements and safety standards are some of the many ways in which countries limit free trade in goods and services.
3. The infant industry argument is one argument used to justify protectionism. It is claimed that young industries need protection if they are to survive the competition of larger more established industries in other countries. When the industry has grown sufficiently, barriers can be removed.
4. It is claimed that protectionism can save jobs. However, there is a great danger that the erection of barriers for this purpose will lead to retaliation by other trading nations, resulting in an overall welfare loss.
5. Protection against dumping will only lead to a gain in long run welfare for a nation if the dumping is predatory.
6. One valid argument in favour of protectionist policies is if the importing country is a monopsonist. The imposition of tariffs will lead to a fall in the price of imports, leading to a gain in welfare for the nation at the expense of foreign suppliers and an improvement in the terms of trade.

Free trade

The theory of comparative advantage (☞ unit 84) shows that trade between countries will be mutually beneficial if relative costs of production differ. Evidence suggests that the gains from trade can be large. They are often most significant in product areas where **economies of scale** are sizeable and transport costs are relatively low.

Specialisation enables total world production to be very much higher than if there were no international trade. But it is important to realise that not everyone benefits from free trade. Some countries or some individuals may gain at the expense of others. Free trade over time will inevitably involve changes in world income distribution. In the rest of this unit we consider how governments can restrict trade and why they might wish to do so.

Methods of protection

There are a large number of ways in which a country may choose to erect TRADE BARRIERS.

Tariffs A TARIFF is a tax on imported goods. It is sometimes called an IMPORT DUTY or a CUSTOMS DUTY. Tariffs can be used by governments to raise

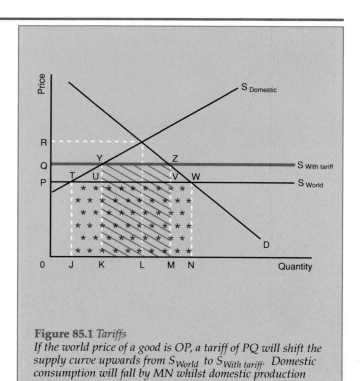

Figure 85.1 *Tariffs*
If the world price of a good is OP, a tariff of PQ will shift the supply curve upwards from S_{World} to $S_{With\ tariff}$. Domestic consumption will fall by MN whilst domestic production will rise by JK. Imports will fall from JN to KM.

revenue to finance expenditure. However, they are most often used in a deliberate attempt to restrict imports. A tariff, by imposing a tax on a good, is likely to raise its final price to the consumer (although occasionally a foreign supplier will absorb all the tariff to prevent this from happening). A rise in the price of the good will lead to a fall in demand and the volume of imports will fall. A tariff should also help domestic producers. Some consumers will switch consumption from imported goods to domestically produced substitutes following the imposition of a tariff. For instance, if the UK imposed a tariff on sugar cane imports, British produced sugar beet would become more competitive and demand for it would rise.

This is shown in Figure 85.1. D is the domestic demand for a good. S Domestic is the domestic supply curve of the product. With no foreign trade, equilibrium output would occur where domestic demand and supply were equal at OL. However, with foreign trade, world producers are assumed to be prepared to supply any amount of the product at a price of OP. Consumers will now buy imported goods because the world price OP is below the domestic price of OR. Domestic supply will fall back along the supply curve to OJ. Demand for the good will rise to ON. Imports must be JN if demand is ON and domestic supply is OJ.

Now assume that the government of the country imposes a tariff of PQ per unit. The price to domestic consumers will rise to OQ. Domestic producers will not pay the tariff. Therefore they find it profitable to expand production to OK. Higher prices cause demand to fall to OM. Hence imports will only be KM. Expenditure on imports will fall from JTWN (price JT times quantity bought JN) to KYZM. Of that area KYZM, KUVM will be the revenue gained by foreign firms. The rest, UYZV, is the tax collected on the imports and will therefore go to the government.

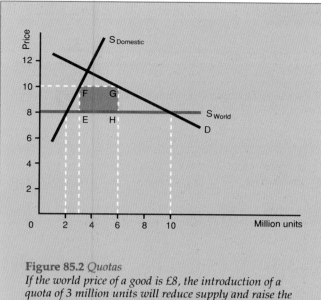

Figure 85.2 *Quotas*
If the world price of a good is £8, the introduction of a quota of 3 million units will reduce supply and raise the domestic price to £10. Domestic consumption will fall from 10 million units to 6 million units whilst domestic production will rise from 2 million units to 3 million units. Importers of the 3 million units subject to quota will make a windfall gain. Before the imposition of the quota they could only get a price of £8 per unit. After the imposition of the quota they can charge £10 per unit.

Quotas A QUOTA is a physical limit on the quantity of a good imported. It is an example of a **physical control**. Imposing a limit on the quantity of goods imported into a country will increase the share of the market available for domestic producers. However, it will also raise the price of the protected product.

This is shown in Figure 85.2. The world supply price of a product is £8. Domestic demand shown by the demand curve D is 10 million units. Of that, 2 million is produced domestically. The remaining 8 million is imported. Now assume that a quota of 3 million units is imposed on imports. Because output is now 4 million units less than it would otherwise have been, price will rise to £10. Domestic production will rise to 3 million units. Domestic consumption is 6 million units. The rise in price has led to a reduction in demand of 4 million units. It should be noted that quotas, unlike tariffs, can lead to gains by importers. It is true in Figure 85.2 that foreign firms have lost orders for 4 million units. But those firms which have managed to retain orders have gained. They used to sell their units for £8. They can now get £10. This is a windfall gain for them, shown on the diagram by the rectangle EFGH.

Other restrictions There are a considerable number of other trade barriers which countries can erect against foreign imports. In the 1970s and 1980s, there has been widespread use of **Voluntary Export Agreements**. These are a type of quota which is enforced by importers. For instance, the UK had an agreement with Japanese car manufacturers that they should not take more than 10 per

QUESTION 1 $Q_D = 100 - \frac{1}{2}P$, $Q_S = 50 + \frac{1}{2}P$
where Q_D is quantity demanded domestically, Q_S is quantity supplied domestically and P is the price of the product.
(a) On graph paper draw the domestic demand and supply curves defined by the two equations between quantities of 0 to 100.
(b) What is the equilibrium price and quantity demanded and supplied domestically?
(c) The country starts to trade internationally. The international price for the product shown is 20. The country can import any amount at this price. What is: (i) the new level of demand; (ii) the new level of domestic supply; (iii) the quantity imported?
(d) The government, alarmed at the loss of jobs in the industry, imposes a tariff of 20 per unit. By how much will: (i) domestic demand fall; (ii) domestic supply rise; (iii) imports fall?

cent of the UK car market. Another widespread barrier is non-competitive purchasing by governments. They are major buyers of goods and services and most governments round the world have a policy of buying only from domestic producers even if this means paying higher prices. Meeting different safety standards can lead to higher costs of production for importers. Simple tactics like lengthy delays at customs posts can also deter imports.

QUESTION 2 The European Commission has brightened the outlook for Europe's lamp post manufacturers by forcing the Spanish government to lift a key trade restriction. The action follows a complaint from a French company, which pointed out that when it attempted to tender for the supply of lamp posts for a Spanish motorway it was rebuffed. It was informed that its product did not conform to local technical requirements.

The Commission stepped in to the dispute by invoking Article 30 of the Treaty of Rome - which guarantees the free circulation of goods - and asked the Madrid government to amend its regulations. This has since been done.

Source: adapted from the *Financial Times*, 1.9.1989.

(a) What type of protection is illustrated in the passage?
(b) What arguments might be used by Spanish lamp post manufacturers to justify the restriction?
(c) What arguments might be used by the European Commission to justify its abolition?

Arguments used to justify protection

The theory of comparative advantage states that there are major welfare gains to be made from free trade in international markets. However, protectionism has always been widespread. What arguments can be put forward to justify protectionist policies?

The infant industry argument This is one of the oldest arguments in favour of protection. Industries just starting up may well face much higher costs than foreign competitors. Partly this is because there may be large economies of scale in the industry. A new low volume producer will find it impossible to compete on price against an established foreign high volume producer. Once sufficiently large, tariff barriers can be removed and the industry exposed to the full heat of foreign competition. Secondly, there may be a learning curve. It takes some time for managers and workers in a new industry to establish efficient operational and working practices. Only by protecting the new industry can it compete until the 'learning' benefits come through.

Some countries, such as Japan, have successfully developed infant industries behind high trade barriers. It is also true that many countries such as the UK have financial systems which tend to take a short view of investment. It is difficult, if not impossible, to find backers for projects which might only become profitable in 10 or even 5 years' time.

However, infant industries in general have not grown successfully behind trade barriers. One problem is that government needs to be able to identify those infant industries which will grow successfully. Governments have a poor record of picking such 'winners'. Secondly, industries protected by trade barriers lack the competitive pressure to become efficient. Infant industries all too often grow up to be lame duck industries. They only carry on operating because they have become skilled at lobbying government to maintain high trade barriers. Thirdly, it is usually more efficient to use other policy weapons if a government genuinely wishes to encourage the development of a new industry. Specific subsidies, training grants, tax concessions, or even the creation of state enterprises, are likely to be better ways of creating new industry.

Job protection Another argument with a very long history is the idea that protectionism can create or at least preserve jobs. During the 1970s, the share of the UK car market taken by domestic car manufacturers shrank drastically. It would have been possible to erect trade barriers against foreign imported cars to preserve jobs in the motor car industry. However, there are two major problems with this policy. Firstly, although the policy may benefit manufacturers and their workers, consumers are likely to have less choice and pay higher prices. Much of the gain for producers is an internal transfer of resources from domestic consumers. Moreover, foreign countries could retaliate by imposing trade restrictions on exports, leading to a loss of jobs in the domestic economy. If they do, then all countries participating in the trade war will suffer. Production will be switched from lower cost to higher cost producers, resulting in a loss of welfare for consumers. The gains from trade resulting from comparative advantage will be lost.

QUESTION 3 In an independent report, commissioned by the Department of Trade and Industry from Professor Aubrey Silberston of Imperial College London, it is argued that British consumers would benefit by £980m a year if import quota restrictions under the Multi-Fibre Arrangement (MFA) were abolished. The MFA protects UK clothing manufacturers from Third World competition. Clothes prices in the shops would fall by 5 per cent. However, 33 000 jobs would disappear in the UK clothing industry. This loss is small compared to the loss of 175 000 jobs that has already occurred in the 1980s.

(a) How would UK clothing manufacturers justify the continuation of the Multi-Fibre Agreement?
(b) What is the opportunity cost of the continuation of the agreement?

Dumping DUMPING can be defined in a number of ways. Broadly speaking it is the sale of goods below their cost of production, whether marginal cost, average total cost, or average variable cost. Foreign firms may sell products 'at a loss' for a variety of reasons.

- They may have produced the goods and failed to find a market for them, so they are dumped on one country in a distress sale. Knickers from China and shoes from Brazil are two examples of this from the 1980s.
- In the short run, a firm may have excess capacity. It will then sell at a price below average total cost so long as that price at least covers its variable cost (☞ unit 27). Steel and chemical manufacturers tended to sell below total cost during the second half of the 1970s and first half of the 1980s because there was so much excess capacity in those industries as a result of the two oil crises.
- Low prices could represent a more serious long term threat to domestic industry. A foreign producer may deliberately price at a loss to drive domestic producers out of business. Once it has achieved this, it can increase prices and enjoy monopoly profits. Japanese companies have been accused of doing this in, for instance, the European semi-conductor market or in the European video recorder market.

Goals of long term domination by a foreign producer might justify trade barriers, although it might be more efficient to subsidise domestic industries. It is more difficult to say whether short term distress dumping leads to a loss of domestic welfare. On the one hand, domestic producers and their workers may suffer a loss of profits and lost wages. The impact on employment should be limited if dumping is only a short term phenomenon. On the other hand, consumers gain by being able to buy cheap goods, even if only for a limited period.

Cheap labour Countries which have plentiful sources of cheap labour are often accused of 'unfair competition'. High labour cost countries find it difficult if not impossible to compete against products from these countries and there is pressure from threatened industries to raise trade barriers. However, cheap labour is a source of comparative advantage for an economy. There is a misallocation of resources if domestic consumers are forced to buy from high wage domestic industries rather than low wage foreign industries. Resources which are used in high cost protected industries could be used elsewhere in the economy to produce products for which the country does have a comparative advantage in production.

The terms of trade One argument in favour of tariffs for which an economic case can be made is the optimal tariff argument. In Figure 85.1 it was assumed that a country could import any amount at a given price because it was a relatively small buyer on the world market. However, if a country imports a significant proportion of world production, then it is likely to face an upward sloping supply curve. The more it buys, the higher the price per unit it will have to pay. At the extreme, the country may

be a **monopsonist** (i.e. the sole buyer of a product).

If the country faces an upward sloping supply curve, the marginal cost of buying an extra unit will not only be the cost of the extra unit but also the extra cost of buying all other units. For instance, a country buys 10 units at £1. If it buys an eleventh unit, the price rises to £11. The cost of the eleventh unit is therefore £11 plus 10 x £1 - a total of £21. The decision to buy the eleventh unit will be made by individual producers and consumers. The cost to them of the eleventh unit is just £11 - the other £10 extra is borne by the producers and consumers who bought the other 10 units.

Therefore the marginal cost to the economy as a whole of buying an extra unit of imports is greater than the marginal cost to the individual. But it is the individual which makes the decision about whether to buy or not. If the marginal cost of purchase is lower for the individual than for the economy as a whole, more imports will be bought than if the individual had to pay the whole cost of purchase (i.e. the cost including the increased price of previously purchased units). This would suggest that a tariff which increased prices to the point where the cost to the individual purchaser was equal to the cost borne by society as a whole of that decision would increase economic welfare.

Imposition of a tariff will reduce demand for imported goods, and this in turn will lead to a fall in the price of imported goods (☞ unit 13 - a tariff is a tax which shifts the supply curve for imported goods to the left, resulting in a fall in equilibrium price received by suppliers). Hence the **terms of trade** (the ratio between export prices and import prices ☞ unit 84) will rise in favour of the importing country. The importing country will be able to buy goods more cheaply. But it is important to remember that this gain will be at the expense of the exporting country. If, for instance, the UK imposed a tariff on tea, the price of tea might fall. The UK will gain but only at the expense of India and Sri Lanka. Also, if the exporting country retaliates by imposing its own tariffs, both countries could be worse off than before.

Other arguments A number of other arguments are put forward in favour of trade barriers. It is sometimes argued that a country needs a particular domestic industry for defence purposes. A country may wish to preserve a particular way of life, such as preventing depopulation of remote rural areas heavily dependent upon a particular agricultural product. It may be felt that some imports are too dangerous to be sold domestically. 'Danger' could range from unsafe electrical products, to toxic waste to drugs. Alternatively, a country may decide that it is too dependent upon one industry. Some small Third World countries depend crucially upon one cash crop such as cocoa, bananas or sugar cane for their economic well being. These commodities are subject to large fluctuations in price on world markets. Falls in price can give rise to large falls in living standards in these economies. Diversifying, even if the newly established industries are uneconomic by world standards, could provide a valuable insurance policy against commodity price fluctuations. Trade barriers are one means of sheltering these industries from foreign competition.

In all of this, however, it is important to question whether trade barriers are the best means of achieving the desired objective. Economists tend to argue that other policies, such as subsidising industries, are likely to be more efficient than trade protection.

Key terms

Trade barriers - any measure which artificially restricts international trade.
Tariff, import duty or customs duty - a tax on imported goods which has the effect of raising the domestic price of imports and thus restricting demand for them.
Quota - a physical limit on the quantity of an imported group.
Dumping - the sale of goods at less than cost price by foreign producers in the domestic market.

Applied economics

GATT and protectionism

The Great Depression of the 1930s led countries to adopt policies which 'exported' unemployment. In order to save and create jobs in their domestic markets, they devalued their currencies and erected trade barriers. But because all countries were engaging in the same practices, all that happened was that total trade fell and countries suffered lower standards of living.

After the Second World War, there was a general recognition that these protectionist policies had been self-defeating. The Bretton Woods system of exchange rates (☞ unit 101) banned competitive devaluations, whilst 23 countries in 1947 signed the General Agreement on Tariffs and Trade (GATT). Under GATT rules, member countries were not allowed to increase the degree of protection given to their domestic producers. Also, under the **most-favoured nation** clause of the agreement, a country which offered a cut in tariffs to one country had to offer it to all member countries.

GATT rules prevent protection increasing, but do nothing to reduce protectionism. For this reason, GATT has, over the years, organised a series of negotiations (called 'rounds') aimed at reducing tariffs and quotas. By the end of the last Tokyo round of negotiations in 1979, the average tariff on industrial goods had fallen to 4.7 per cent. Since 1986, an eighth round, the Uruguay round of negotiations, has been taking place. Its main aim is to reduce protectionism in agriculture, textiles and service industries.

Since the mid-1970s, GATT's work has been made increasingly difficult by two distinct trends. Firstly, a few countries have been drawing closer together and offering tariff reductions to some countries but not others in contradiction to the most-favoured nation clause. In particular, the EC countries have embarked upon an ambitious programme, under the '1992'

banner, to remove a large number of obstacles to free trade without offering the same trading opportunities to non-EC countries. The USA and Canada also signed an agreement in 1988 which effectively removed most trade barriers between the two countries but did not extend the agreement to cover all trading partners. If this were to carry on, it would be possible to see a world comprised of several large trading blocks, each with common external tariffs and free trade within the block. This would contradict the vision of GATT, which is to remove trade barriers between **all** countries.

Secondly, there have been growing trade imbalances. Japan and Germany have consistently exported more than they have imported, resulting in trade deficits for other countries. The USA in particular experienced large current account deficits on its balance of payments during the 1980s, importing far more than it has exported. A number of traditional US industries, such as textiles, car manufacturing and steel, have been badly affected by foreign competition and there have been growing calls for measures to be taken against 'unfair' foreign competition.

It is very difficult to define 'unfair' competition. The whole basis for trade is that it is relatively cheaper to produce goods in some countries than others. It would be foolish for the UK to complain that textiles made by cheap labour in Far Eastern countries represent 'unfair' competition for domestic manufactures given that the source of Far Eastern comparative advantage in textiles lies in its cheap labour. On the other hand, it can be true that countries or companies disrupt markets through **dumping**, which GATT defines as the sale of a product in an export market at a cheaper price than is charged in the domestic market.

Both the USA and EC have increasingly taken action against what they see as dumping. In the EC, up to 100 anti-dumping suits are investigated each year, and suits have been brought against Japanese manufacturers of photocopiers, printers and video tape recorders. But under GATT rules, the USA and EC should take the issue to GATT and allow GATT to judge on it. Countries don't do this, partly because GATT judgements often take years, by which time the damage has been done, and partly because they are uncertain of winning the case. In many instances, anti-dumping suits have more to do with protecting inefficient domestic producers which have lobbied their governments hard, than with unfair trading practices of, say, Japanese companies which may simply be offering the best products at the cheapest prices.

BITTER FRUITS OF PROTRACTED PROTECTIONISM

Sir,

EC Commissioner Martin Bangemann has made it clear that the European car market will not be protected after 1992. While he admits than an open market could make life difficult for well-protected and ill-prepared manufacturers, he also believes that it is the manufacturers who are to blame for the market's apparent lack of competitiveness vis-a-vis Japan.

The EC is as much to blame as the manufacturers. For many years the Commission, enthusiastically supported by the industry, has been putting the blame solely on an almost unlimited variety of so-called unfair Japanese trading practices.

What Commissioner Bangemann does not explain is that, in order to reduce European production costs to a competitive level, another 260 000 or 300 000 jobs will have to go. Protectionism has caused European car prices to be an estimated 15-20 per cent higher than they would otherwise be under free market conditions.

What is to be expected is that the Japanese will offer to restrict their share of the European market to around 10 per cent as it stands today. By doing so, and by allocating the quotas between themselves in a cartel, they can ensure that prices will remain high.

The result is that Toyota is sitting on a war chest of liquid assets totalling $10.3bn - enough to buy Peugeot SA three times over. These are the bitter fruits of protracted protectionism, ironically intended to protect and strengthen national industries in the face of foreign competition.

Source: Vic Heylen, Antwerp, Belgium. Letter in the *Financial Times*, 14.7.1989.

1. **What does the author of the letter see as the main justifications made in the past for protection of the EC motor industry?**
2. **To what extent has protectionism achieved its goals in this market?**

The balance of payments account

Summary

1. The balance of payments accounts are split into two parts. The current account records payments for the exports and imports of goods and services. The capital account records saving, investment and speculative flows of money.
2. The current account is split into two parts: trade in visibles and trade in invisibles.
3. The balance of payments accounts must always balance. However, component parts of the accounts may be positive or negative. If there is a surplus on the current account, then outflows on the capital account must be greater than inflows.
4. In practice, the balance of payments does not balance and for this reason a balancing item is included in the accounts.
5. A current account surplus is often seen as a sign of a healthy economy, whilst a current account deficit is seen as a cause for worry. But current account deficits are not necessarily bad as they may be a sign of borrowing which could finance expansion.
6. A current account deficit is most unlikely to be financed by government. The balance of payments deficit and the government deficit, the PSBR, are two completely different entities.

The balance of payments

The BALANCE OF PAYMENTS ACCOUNT is a record of all financial dealings over a period of time between economic agents of one country and all other countries. Balance of payments accounts can be split into two components:
■ the CURRENT ACCOUNT where payments for the purchase and sale of goods and services are recorded;
■ the CAPITAL ACCOUNT where flows of money associated with saving, investment, speculation and currency stabilisation are recorded.

Flows of money into the country are given a positive (+) sign on the accounts. Flows of money out of the country are given a negative (-) sign.

The current account

The current account on the balance of payments is itself split into two components.

Visible trade VISIBLE TRADE is trade in goods, from raw materials to semi-manufactured products to manufactured goods. **Visible exports** are goods which are sold to foreigners. Goods leave the country, whilst payment for these goods goes in the opposite direction. Hence visible exports of, say , cars result in an **inward** flow of money and are recorded with a positive sign on the balance of payments account. **Visible imports** are goods which are bought by domestic residents from foreigners. Goods come into the country whilst money flows out. Hence visible imports of, say, wheat are given a minus sign on the balance of payments. The difference between visible exports and visible imports is known as the BALANCE OF TRADE.

Invisible trade INVISIBLE TRADE is trade in services.

A wide variety of services is traded internationally, including financial services such as banking and insurance, transport services such as shipping and air travel, and tourism. Also included are transfers of money resulting from the loan of factors of production abroad. For instance, a British teacher working in Saudi Arabia and sending back money to his family in England would create an invisible import for Saudi Arabia and an invisible export for Britain. Similarly, a Japanese company repatriating profits made from a factory based in Britain back to Japan would create an invisible import for the UK and an invisible export for Japan. The easiest way to distinguish between invisible exports and imports (or **invisible credits** and **invisible debits** as they are known in the official UK balance of payments account) is to consider flows of money rather than flows of services. The British teacher in Saudi Arabia is sending money back to the UK. An inflow of money means that this is classified as an export. The Japanese company repatriating profits is sending money out of the UK. An

QUESTION 1 A country has the following international transactions on current account: exports of manufactured goods £20bn; imports of food £10bn; earnings from foreign tourists £5bn; interest, profits and dividends paid to foreigners £4bn; purchase of oil from abroad £8bn; earnings of nationals working overseas which are repatriated £7bn; sale of coal to foreign countries £2bn; payments by foreigners to domestic financial institutions for services rendered £1bn.

(a) Which of these items are: (i) visible exports; (ii) visible imports; (iii) invisible exports; (iv) invisible imports?
(b) Calculate: (i) the balance of trade; (ii) the balance on invisible trade; (iii) the current balance.

outflow of money means that this is classified as an import. The difference between invisible exports and invisible imports is known as the BALANCE ON INVISIBLE TRADE or NET INVISIBLES.

The CURRENT BALANCE is the difference between total exports (visible and invisible) and total imports. It can also be calculated by adding the balance of trade to the balance on invisible trade.

The capital account

Almost all transactions on the capital account of the balance of payments are private sector transactions. They can crudely be split into two types.

■ Short term money flows, sometimes called flows of HOT MONEY, are mainly speculative. Financial institutions, companies and speculators seek to make a profit by buying and selling currencies. A speculator may decide that the value of the dollar will rise over the next week. He buys dollars today, places it perhaps on loan with instant access in New York to earn interest, and then sells dollars in a week's time to take advantage of the next speculative bet. Short term money flows are crucially dependent upon expectations of currency movements and upon interest rates in competing financial centres. If the financial markets expect the pound to fall tomorrow, then they sell today. If interest rates in New York rise, there will be an inflow of hot money into New York to take advantage of the higher interest rates.

■ Long term money flows are mainly associated with long term investment and saving. For instance, a Japanese company may set up a car plant in the UK. To finance its building and operation, it sends money from Japan to the UK. Alternatively, a Japanese pension fund may decide that it needs to broaden its international portfolio. So it buys shares on the Paris Stock Exchange, thus creating an outflow of money from Japan and an inflow of money into France.

Just as on the current account, flows of money into the country on the capital account are given a plus sign whilst outflows of money are given a minus sign. For instance, Japanese investment in the UK would be given a positive

sign on the balance of payments whilst a UK company lending money to a foreign company would be given a minus sign.

The balance of payments must always balance

The balance of payments account must always balance. To understand why, consider a situation where a country experiences a CURRENT ACCOUNT DEFICIT (i.e. imports are greater than exports and outflows of money are greater than inflows). The money to finance the net outflow of money must come from somewhere. Foreigners could lend the money or invest in the country; or the country could run down its savings abroad by selling its assets and bringing the money back home. Either way, in this instance the deficit on the current account will be matched by a surplus (a net inflow of money) on the capital account, reducing the balance on the whole of the balance of payments to zero.

There is a third way in which a current account deficit could be financed. The central bank of the country could sell some of its GOLD AND FOREIGN CURRENCY RESERVES. Central banks hold gold and reserves of other currencies in order to be able to intervene on the foreign exchange markets to alter the value of their own country's currency. The sale of some of its reserves for domestic currency will produce an inflow of domestic money which will be recorded on the balance of payments account.

The balancing item

In theory, it must be true that the addition of the current and capital accounts with the change in gold and foreign currency reserves must be equal to zero: the balance of payments account must balance. In practice this never happens because there is significant under-recording of transactions on the current and capital accounts. Part of the problem is that the accounts are calculated from millions of different returns from firms engaged in exporting and importing or foreign exchange transactions. Completing a form takes time and therefore costs money to the firm. Costs can be cut by not sending in the legally required information to the government. It is also true that some transactions are not recorded to avoid tax or avoid police detection. The balance of payments must always balance. Hence, a **balancing item** is included in the balance of payments to make the accounts balance. As more information about transactions in any one time period become available, the balance of payments accounts are changed, including the value of the balancing item. In theory, the size of the balancing item on each revision should go down as more 'missing' items are found.

QUESTION 2 Would the following be given a plus or a minus sign on the balance of payments account of the United Kingdom?
(a) Investment overseas by UK residents.
(b) Foreign currency lending abroad by UK banks.
(c) Borrowing from banks abroad by general government.
(d) Portfolio investment in the UK by overseas residents.
(e) Deposits with and lending to banks abroad by the UK non-bank private sector.

QUESTION 3

Table 86.1 *UK Balance of payments*

	1980	1982	1984	1986	1988	1989
Visible trade						
exports	47 147	55 330	70 265	72 656	80 772	92 526
imports	45 792	53 422	75 432	82 019	101 587	115 638
Invisible trade						
credits	88 396	66412	77 665	77 463	88 419	108 399
debits	85 601	62 714	70 542	68 145	82 636	104 354
Capital account						
Net transactions excluding official reserves	- 3 639	- 4 010	- 8 808	- 7 214	- 8 226	- 1 396
Balancing item	995	- 2 017	5 944	10 150	9 495	15 024

Source: adapted from CSO, *Economic Trends Annual Supplement*; CSO, *Monthly Digest of Statistics*.

The table shows all the transactions on the UK balance of payments apart from changes in the gold and foreign currency reserves.

(a) For each year, calculate the addition to (which would be shown by a minus figure) or drawings on (shown by a plus figure) the official reserves held by the Bank of England.

(b) (i) What has happened to the balancing item as a proportion of visible exports over time?
(ii) Calculate the current balance if half the balancing item were allocated to the current account balance.
(iii) In the late 1980s, the current account position deteriorated sharply, according to official figures. Would this still be true if half the balancing item were missing current account transactions?
(iv) In the early 1980s, the government cut the amount of money spent on the collection of official statistics. Why might this have affected the size of the balancing item?

Balance of payments disequilibria

Whilst it is true that the balance of payments as a whole must balance, individual components of the account are most unlikely to balance. Often the phrase 'a balance of payments deficit' is used in the news. This usually refers to a deficit on the current account although sometimes it is a deficit on the balance of trade only which is being talked about.

Deficits on current account and therefore surpluses on the capital account are generally considered to be undesirable, whilst surpluses on current account and associated deficits on capital account are considered a sign of economic strength. The main reason for this is that a deficit on current account indicates the country is importing more than it is exporting. Expenditure is therefore higher than income. The deficit is financed either by borrowing from abroad or by running down savings. In any one year, it matters little whether a country is a net borrower internationally. However if the current account deficit is large and persists over a long

period of time, the country will get deeper and deeper into debt. Eventually other countries will refuse to lend any more. The debtor country will have to move back to a current account balance. Not only that but lenders are likely to insist upon repayment of debt. The current account will have to move into surplus to allow this. The 1970s and 1980s have seen a large number of Second and Third World countries such as Poland and Brazil first borrowing large sums and then becoming effectively bankrupt because they have been unable to pay back their debts (for a more detailed discussion of the Third World debt crisis ☞ unit 91). What has happened is analogous to a household consistently spending more than it is earning and therefore getting into deeper and deeper debt problems.

Current account surpluses are seen as desirable for two reasons. Firstly it is assumed that exports create jobs whilst imports destroy jobs. Therefore the more exports and the fewer imports for an economy, the healthier the economy will be. This crude argument is a fallacy. An economy can just as well be at full employment with a current account deficit as with a surplus. What is true, however, is that two very successful post-war economies - Japan and West Germany - have tended to run persistent current account surpluses. But these surpluses are the result of economic strength rather than their cause.

Secondly, current account surpluses are seen as desirable because they are associated with capital account deficits. A capital account deficit means that the country is a net saver internationally. A persistent deficit on capital account is likely to result in growing international wealth. This wealth should generate interest, profits and dividends which can be repatriated to provide an income for the country.

However, current account deficits which necessitate net borrowing from abroad are not necessarily undesirable. The USA ran large persistent current account deficits in the 1980s. But this was not particularly worrying to many because the deficit was only a small fraction of US national income. Moreover, there is little point in producing without consuming. There is no point in building up a stock of savings unless at some point it is used for spending.

There is also a long tradition of countries borrowing money to finance investment. To take the analogy of a firm, few firms would consider it good business practice never to borrow money. There are times when it is essential to borrow if good investment opportunities are not to be lost. Similarly, the United States in the 1830s and 1840s was a net borrower of international capital and therefore ran a current account deficit. It used the money to finance its economic development. One reason why Third World countries borrow so much money is because the money is, in theory at least, to be used for development purposes. Once factories and offices and farms have been established, they then export a share of the increased output to pay back the foreign debt.

Economic theory and economic history therefore suggest that current account deficits are not always undesirable. Some of today's most affluent economies have run current account deficits for a lengthy period of time in the past. However, there is risk associated with this - the risk that the country will not be able to repay and be forced into the hands of its creditors as are so many Third World countries today.

Government deficits and balance of payments deficits

One very common fallacy is to equate current account deficits with government deficits. Most transactions on the balance of payments are made by private individuals and firms. If the country is a net borrower, it is more than likely that this is because private individuals and firms have borrowed more from foreigners than they have lent to foreigners. There is a relationship between government borrowing (the PSBR ☞ unit 76) and the current account deficit but the relationship is complicated, and it could well be the case that the public sector might be in surplus domestically when the current account was in deficit. So the current account deficit is **not** a government deficit in any sense.

Key terms

The balance of payments account - a record of all financial dealings over a period of time between economic agents of one country and all other countries.
Current account - that part of the balance of payments account where payments for the purchase and sale of goods and services are recorded.
Capital account - that part of the balance of payments account where flows of savings, investment and currency are recorded.
Visible trade - trade in goods.
Balance of trade - visible exports minus visible imports.
Invisible trade - trade in services.
Balance on invisible trade or net invisibles - invisible exports minus invisible exports.

Current balance - the difference between total exports (visible and invisible) and total imports. It can also be calculated by adding the balance of trade to the balance on invisible trade.
Hot money - short term flows of money across the foreign exchanges.
Current account deficit or surplus - a deficit exists when imports are greater than exports; a surplus exists when exports are greater than imports.
Gold and foreign currency reserves - gold and foreign currency owned by the central bank of a country and used mainly to change the foreign exchange value of the domestic currency by buying and selling currency on the foreign exchanges.

Applied economics

The UK balance of payments

The balance of payments account of the UK can be split into two broad categories.
■ Transactions on current account include visible and invisible trade.
■ Transactions on capital account include flows of money for borrowing, saving and investment. Currently, inflows of money on capital account are called **transactions in liabilities**. They are a liability for the UK because they represent increased borrowing by UK citizens or companies, purchase by foreigners of UK assets or dissaving by the UK when money is brought home following the sale of UK owned assets abroad. Outflows of money on capital account are called **transactions in assets** since money leaving the UK which is

recorded on the capital account creates assets (or reduces liabilities) abroad for the UK.

Flows of money into the country must equal outflows of money (i.e. the balance of payments must always balance). So in Figure 86.1, inflows of money to the UK in 1989 (exports plus transactions in liabilities) must equal outflows of money from the UK (imports and transactions in assets). In 1989, the balancing item was positive, indicating that recorded inflows of money were less than recorded outflows.

Another way of expressing this is to consider the balances on the two parts of the account. As shown in Figure 86.2, the current balance (exports minus imports - equal to the balance of trade plus the balance on invisible trade) plus net transactions on the capital

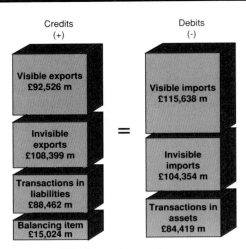

UK Balance of payments

Source: adapted from CSO, *Monthly Digest of Statistics*.

Figure 86.1 *Inflows and outflows on the balance of payments, 1989*

account plus the balancing item must equal zero. Not included in Figure 86.2 are transactions with the IMF (allocation of SDRs and subscriptions to the IMF), because in 1989 there were none.

Since the end of the Second World War, there have been a number of consistent trends on the UK balance of payments.

- The balance of trade has been negative, as can be seen from Figure 86.3. Visible exports have tended to be less than visible imports.
- The balance on invisible trade has been positive. Invisible credits (exports) have been greater than invisible debits (imports).
- The current balance has tended to move from surplus to deficit in a cyclical manner. Figure 86.4 shows that, during the 1950s and 1960s, the current account moved into deficit about every 5 years, coinciding with booms in the economy (☞ unit 83). The two oil crises of the 1970s and the revenue from North Sea oil disturbed this simple relationship in the decade following 1974, but the boom of 1987-89 produced the expected current account deficit.

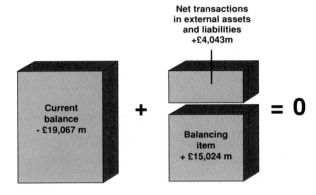

Source: adapted from CSO, *Monthly Digest of Statistics*.

Figure 86.2 *The balance of payments, 1989*

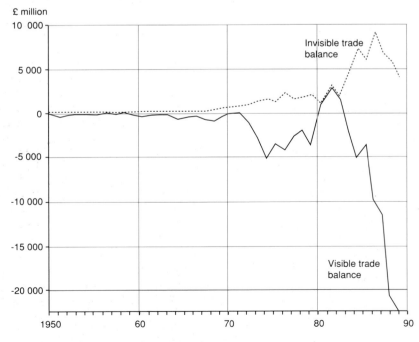

Source: adapted from CSO, *Economic Trends Annual Supplement* ; CSO, *Monthly Digest of Statistics*.

Figure 86.3 *The balance of trade and the invisibles balance, UK*

■ The capital account must move in the contrary direction to the current account, because the balance of payments always balances. A current account surplus necessitates a capital account deficit. Note in Figure 86.5 the considerable net outflows of capital in the early 1980s. These helped to increase the wealth of the UK abroad considerably. In contrast, the net inflows of capital in the late 1980s have reduced the UK's net wealth.

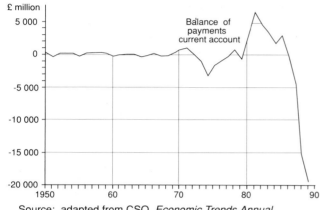

Source: adapted from CSO, *Economic Trends Annual Supplement* ; CSO, *Monthly Digest of Statistics*.

Figure 86.4 *Current balance, UK*

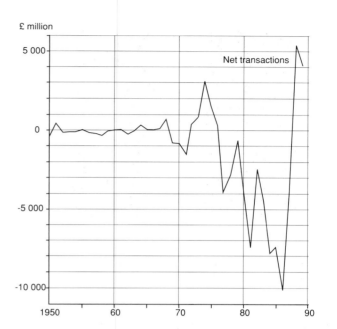

Source: adapted from CSO, *Economic Trends Annual Supplement* ; CSO, *Monthly Digest of Statistics*.

Figure 86.5 *Net transactions in external assets and liabilities, UK*

THE COLOUR OF BRITISH MANUFACTURING

Have you bought a British colour television set recently? It is a common belief that the British colour television industry has been wiped out and that all sets are now imported. In fact, UK-based manufacturers of colour televisions achieved an impressive trade surplus of £58 million last year after a deficit of £12 million in 1988. The British-owned colour television industry has been wiped out. But it has been replaced by foreign - mainly Japanese-owned facilities which are now in the flush of the secondary stage of development.

The first stage (detrimental to the trade figures) was when UK consumers bought direct imports of televisions shipped from Japan. The secondary stage started when overseas companies set up here to supply the home market directly and also to the UK as a base supplying Europe. This gives a direct boost to the trade balance by simultaneously reducing imports and boosting exports. However, the tertiary stage - when profits and other capital payments are remitted back to the host country - has a strongly negative effect on the balance of payments. Remember, the long term aim of foreign investors is a cash drain from the country they operate in.

This is an example of a fascinating long-term structural change in the UK economy. Whether we gain or lose from all this in the long run may well depend on the most fascinating phenomenon of all - the extent to which superior Japanese production and managerial techniques have a catalytic effect on Britain. Decades ago, Japan copied superior Western production techniques to conquer the world. Can Britain copy the Japanese and redress the balance?

Source: adapted from *The Guardian*, 28.2.1990.

1. **Explain how the three 'stages' outlined in the article affect the balance of payments.**
2. **What would be the possible effect on the UK balance of payments if inward investment by the Japanese did indeed lead to a 'catalytic effect' on British owned industry in the UK?**

Summary

1. The exchange rate is the price at which one currency is convertible into another.
2. The equilibrium exchange rate is established where demand for a currency is equal to its supply.
3. The equilibrium exchange rate will change if there is a change in the value of exports or imports, the value of net long term foreign investment, or the volume or direction of speculative flows.
4. On a day to day basis in a free exchange market, speculation tends to be the dominant influence

upon the price of a currency.
5. In the longer term, economic fundamentals relating to exports, imports and long term capital flows tend to determine the exchange rate.
6. The purchasing power parity theory of exchange rates states that exchange rates will in the long run change in line with relative inflation rates between economies.
7. Speculation tends to lead to short term exchange rate instability.

The exchange rate

Different countries use different types of **money** or **currency**. In the UK, goods and services are bought and sold with pounds sterling, in France with the French franc, and in Germany with the German deutschmark.

The rate at which one currency can be converted (i.e. bought or sold) into another currency is known as the EXCHANGE RATE. For instance, a French company may wish to purchase pounds sterling. If it paid 10 million francs to purchase £1 million, then the exchange rate is 10 francs to the pound. A UK household may wish to buy US dollars to take on holiday to Florida. If they receive $2 000 in exchange for £1 000, then the exchange rate is $2 to the pound, or 50p to the dollar.

Exchange rates are normally expressed in terms of the value of one single currency against another single currency: pounds for dollars for instance, or deutschmarks for yen. However, it is possible to calculate the exchange rate of one currency in terms of a group or **basket** of currencies. The EFFECTIVE EXCHANGE RATE (a measure calculated by the International Monetary Fund) and the TRADE WEIGHTED EXCHANGE RATE INDEX (or the EXCHANGE RATE INDEX as it is often called) are two different calculations of the average movement of the exchange rate on the basis of weightings (☞ unit 3) determined by the value of trade undertaken with a country's main trading partners.

To illustrate how the trade weighted index is calculated, assume that the UK trades only with the USA and France. 70 per cent of UK trade is with the USA and 30 per cent is with France. The value of the pound falls by 10 per cent against the dollar and by 20 per cent against the franc (which, incidentally, means the franc has gone up in value against the US dollar). The trade weighted index will

now have changed. The fall in the dollar contributes a 7 per cent fall in the exchange rate (10 per cent x 0.7) whilst the fall in the franc contributes a 6 per cent fall (20 per cent x 0.3). The average fall is the sum of these two components (i.e. 13 per cent). If the trade weighted index started off at 100, its new value will be 87.

QUESTION 1
Table 87.1

Original value of the trade weighted index	Change in exchange rate %		New value of the trade weighted index
	Country X	Country Y	
100	+10	+20	
100	+20	+10	
100	-10	+10	
100	+10	-10	
100	- 6	- 6	

Country A trades only with two countries. 60 per cent of its trade is with country X and 40 per cent with country Y.
(a) Complete the table by calculating the new value of the trade weighted index for country A following changes in its exchange rate with countries X and Y.
(b) What would be the values of the trade weighted index if country A had 90 per cent of its trade with country X and 10 per cent with country B?
(c) Calculate the new values of the trade weighted index in (a) if the original value of the trade weighted index were not 100 but 80.

Equilibrium exchange rates

Foreign exchange is bought and sold on the FOREIGN EXCHANGE MARKETS. Governments may buy and sell currencies in order to influence the price of a currency. Here we will assume that governments do not intervene and that currencies are allowed to find their own price levels through the forces of **demand** and **supply**. There are then three main reasons why foreign exchange is bought and sold.

- International trade in goods and services needs to be financed. Exports create a demand for currency whilst imports create a supply of currency.
- Long term capital movements occur. Inward investment to an economy creates a demand for its currency. Outward investment from an economy creates a supply.
- There is an enormous amount of speculation in the foreign exchange markets.

The equilibrium exchange rate is established where the demand for the currency is equal to its supply. Figure 87.1 shows the demand and supply of pounds priced in dollars. The market is in equilibrium at an exchange rate of $2 = £1. £1 000 million are bought and sold each day.

The demand curve is assumed to be downward sloping. If the price of the pound falls against the dollar, then the price of British goods will fall in dollar terms. For instance, if the exchange rate falls from $2 = £1 to $1 = £1, then a £1 000 British cost will fall in price for Americans from $2 000 to $1 000. Americans will therefore buy more British goods and demand more pounds to pay for them. So a fall in the price of the pound will lead to an increase in quantity demanded of pounds, giving rise to the downward sloping demand curve. Similarly the supply curve is upward sloping because a fall in the value of the pound will increase the price of foreign imports for the British, leading them to reduce their purchases of foreign goods and therefore of foreign exchange.

All other things being equal, a fall in the value of the pound from, say, $2 to $1 is likely to make the pound look cheap and this may attract speculative buying of the pound and discourage speculative selling. This would then produce downward sloping demand curves and upward sloping supply curves for the pound sterling. However, in general on the capital side, it is unclear how buyers and sellers will react to rises and falls in the price of a currency. Given this, the justification for downward sloping demand curves and upward sloping supply curves for foreign exchange tends to rest on arguments about the buying and selling of currency for export and import payments.

Figure 87.2 shows that the exchange rate will change if either the demand or supply curve shifts. Equilibrium is at price OB and output OQ.

- If British exports to the USA increase, American firms will need to buy more pounds than before to pay for them. Hence an increase in the value of UK exports will increase the demand for pounds, shifting the demand curve from D_1 to D_2. The exchange rate will therefore rise from OB to OC.
- If imports from the USA increase, British firms will need to buy more dollars than before to pay for them. They will buy these dollars with pounds. Hence an increase in the value of UK imports will increase the supply of pounds. The supply curve will shift to the right from S_1 to S_2. The equilibrium value of the

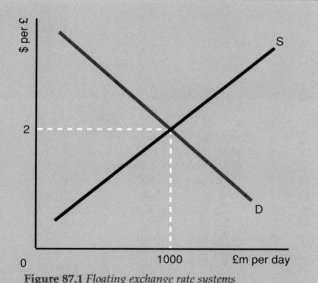

Figure 87.1 *Floating exchange rate systems*
In a free exchange rate market, the price of a currency is determined by demand and supply. Equilibrium price is $2 to the pound whilst equilibrium quantity demanded and supplied is £1 000 million per day.

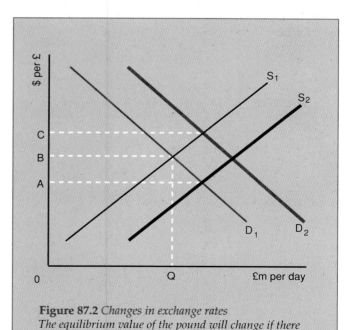

Figure 87.2 *Changes in exchange rates*
The equilibrium value of the pound will change if there is a change in either the demand for or supply of pounds (or both).

pound will fall from OB to OA.

- ■ If the rate of interest in the London money markets increases, US savers will switch funds into the UK. This is likely to be short term money or **hot money** (☞ unit 88) which flows from financial centre to financial centre attracted by the highest rate of return. An increase in inflows on the capital account of the balance of payments will increase the demand for pounds, shifting the demand curve from D_1 to D_2, and increasing the value of the pound from OB to OC.

- ■ If there is an inflow of funds for long term investment in the UK, again the demand for pounds will rise. For instance, Japanese investment in car plants in the UK will raise the demand for pounds (and increase the supply of yen) shown by the shift in the demand curve from D_1 to D_2, raising the value of the pound from OB to OC.

- ■ Speculation is the single most important determinant today of the minute by minute price of the pound. If speculators believe that the value of the pound is going to fall against the dollar, they will sell pounds and buy dollars. An increase in the supply of pounds on the market, shown by the shift in the supply curve from S_1 to S_2, will lead to a fall in the price of the pound from OB to OA.

It is difficult to assess the level of speculative activity on the foreign exchange markets. Less than 5 per cent of daily foreign exchange transactions in London is a result of a direct buying or selling order for exports and imports or long term capital flows. However, each order tends to result in more than one transaction as foreign exchange dealers cover their exposure to the deal by buying and selling other currencies. Even if every order were to result in an extra three transactions, this would still only account for at most 20 per cent of transactions, which would suggest that speculative deals form the majority of trading on a daily basis.

Thus, in the short term, the value of a currency is dominated by speculative activity in the currency. However, there is evidence to suggest that in the longer term, the value of a currency is determined by **economic fundamentals** - by exports, imports and long term capital movements.

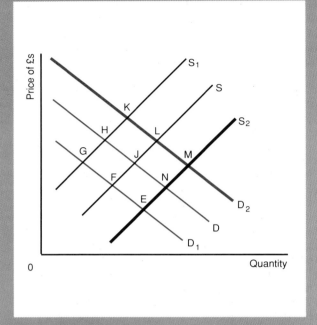

QUESTION 2 Figure 87.3 shows the demand and supply of pounds. D and S are the original demand and supply curves respectively.

Figure 87.3

(a) At which point (E to N) is the market in equilibrium?
(b) To which point will the market be most likely to move in the short term if there is: (i) an increase in exports; (ii) an increase in imports; (iii) a fall in interest rates in the London money markets; (iv) a rise in takeovers of US companies by British companies; (v) a belief that the value of the deutschmark will rise in the near future; (vi) the discovery of a huge new oil field in the North Sea; (vii) bad summer weather in the UK which sharply increases the number of foreign holidays taken; (viii) a series of prolonged strikes in the UK engineering sector of the economy?

The purchasing power parity theory of exchange rates

If purchasing power parity exists, then a given amount of currency in one country, converted into another currency at the current market exchange rate, will buy the same bundle of goods in both countries. For instance, if £1 = $2, and consumers only buy jeans, then purchasing power parity will exist if a £20 pair of jeans costs $40 in the USA. It won't exist if a pair of jeans priced at £20 in the UK is priced at $50 or $30 in the USA. If there are

only two goods in the economy, food and clothing, then purchasing power parity will exist if an identical bundle of food and clothes costs £100 when it costs $200 in the USA, or £500 when it costs $1 000 in the USA.

The PURCHASING POWER PARITY (PPP) THEORY states that exchange rates in the long term change in line with different inflation rates between economies. To understand why exchange rates might change in line with inflation rates, assume that the balance of payments of the UK is in equilibrium with exports equal to imports and capital outflows equal to capital inflows, but it is suffering from a 5 per cent inflation rate (i.e. the prices of goods are rising on average by 5 per cent per year). Assume also that there is no inflation in the rest of world. At the end of one year, the average price of UK exports will be 5 per cent higher than at the beginning. On the other hand, imports will be be 5 per cent cheaper than domestically produced goods. At the end of the second year, the gap will be even wider.

Starting from a PPP rate of $2 = £1, this change in relative prices between the UK and the rest of the world will affect the volume of UK exports and imports. UK exports will become steadily less price competitive on world markets. Hence sales of UK exports will fall. Imports into the UK on the other hand will become steadily more price competitive and their sales in the UK will rise. The balance of payments on current account will move into the red.

A fall in the volume of UK exports is likely to lead to a fall in the value of exports (this assumes that exports are **price elastic** ☞ unit 8) and therefore the demand for pounds will fall. A rise in the value of imports will result in a rise in the supply of pounds. A fall in demand and a rise in supply of pounds will result in a fall in its value.

So the purchasing power parity theory argues that in the long run exchange rates will change in line with changes in prices between countries. For instance, if the annual UK inflation rate is 4 per cent higher than that of the USA over a period of time, then the pound will fall in value at an average annual rate of 4 per cent against the dollar over the period. In the long run, exchange rates will be in equilibrium when **purchasing power parities** are equal between countries. This means that the price of typical bundles of traded goods and services are equal.

The causes of inflation are complex. However one fundamental reason why economies can become less price competitive over time is LABOUR PRODUCTIVITY (i.e. output per worker). If output per worker, for instance, increases at a rate of 2 per cent per annum in the UK and 5 per cent per annum in Japan, then it is likely that the UK will become less competitive internationally than Japan over time. Wage costs are the single most important element on average in the final value of a product. In the UK, approximately 70 per cent of national income is made up of wages and salaries. Hence changes in labour productivity are an important component in changes in final costs.

Other factors affecting competitiveness

Price is an important factor in determining purchasing decisions, but it is not the only consideration. Other factors include design, quality, reliability or availability for instance. Over long periods of time, countries can become increasingly uncompetitive internationally in one or more of these factors. Indeed it is often argued that the UK has suffered this fate over the past century. What then happens is that the economy finds it more and more difficult to export whilst the **marginal propensity to import** (☞ unit 78) increases. There is therefore a continual downward pressure on the exchange rate. The debate about what makes a country internationally

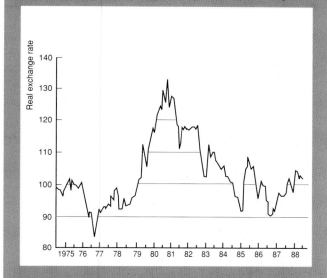

QUESTION 3   Figure 87.4 shows the real exchange rate of sterling between 1975 and 1988. 1975 is taken as the base year (i.e. 1975 = 100). If purchasing power parities were the sole determinant of the exchange rate, the real exchange rate would remain constant at 100 over time (assuming that the exchange rate was in long run equilibrium in 1975).

Note: The real exchange rate has been calculated by dividing the effective exchange rate by the average (weighted) price index of the UK's trading partners relative to the UK Retail Price Index.
Source: adapted from Prest and Coppock's *The UK Economy*, edited by M J Artis, Weidenfeld and Nicolson.

Figure 87.4 *Sterling's real exchange rate*

(a)   To what extent has the real exchange rate deviated from its purchasing power parity value?
(b)   The mid-1970s saw a collapse in confidence in the British economy as record levels of inflation gripped the country. By 1977, inflation was abating and it was becoming increasingly clear that the North Sea would provide the UK with substantial exports of oil over at least the next decade. How might these two factors explain the deviation of the real exchange rate from its PPP level in the years between 1975 and 1982?

uncompetitive is the same as the debate about why a country grows at a slower rate than other countries (☞ unit 63).

Long term capital movements

During much of the 19th century, the USA was a net capital importer. It financed its development in part by borrowing money from Europe. Countries which are in a position to borrow money will have a higher long term exchange rate than they would otherwise have done. For instance, during the 19th century, Europeans demanded dollars to invest in the USA. This rise in demand led to a rise in the value of the dollar. Similarly, net long term lending by a country will tend to depress the exchange rate.

Speculation

Day to day exchange rate movements today are affected by speculation or short term flows of capital. Thirty years ago this was different, as nearly all countries imposed a variety of EXCHANGE CONTROLS upon their currency movements. At the most extreme, currency could only be bought and sold through the central bank. In more liberal regimes, purchases could be made on the open market, but individuals and firms often had to seek permission from the central bank to trade in currency. Exchange controls have now largely been swept away in the major industrialised trading nations of the world. Vast sums of money are committed internationally and flows of just a fraction of these across exchanges can lead to large currency fluctuations.

Classical or monetarist economists in the 1960s and 1970s predicted that speculation would dampen exchange rate fluctuations and help stabilise currencies. They argued that the exchange rate in the long term was fixed by economic fundamentals such as the balance between exports and imports. Economic fundamentals only change slowly over time and therefore market expectations of future exchange rates will only change slowly over time too. If the market believes that in two year's time the value of the pound against the dollar will be $2 = £1, and today the value of the pound is $3 = £1, then speculators will sell pounds, driving down the value of the pound towards its longer term value.

The evidence of the 1970s and 1980s suggests that this is not true. In the above example, it is just as likely that the value of the pound will go up as down even if speculators agree that in the long term the pound is overvalued at today's prices. The reason is that speculation by its very nature is short term. Speculators are not very interested in the price of sterling in 2 years' time. They are far more interested in the price of sterling in the next 30 minutes. Large sums of money can be made by buying and selling in the very short term.

It is impossible to pin-point exactly what drives short term exchange rate markets. Certainly markets tend to react in a predictable way to news about changes in economic fundamentals. A bad set of trade figures, for instance, which points to a future fall in the exchange rate, tends to lead to selling pressure today. A rise in domestic interest rates will tend to increase today's exchange rate as speculators anticipate future capital inflows to take advantage of the higher rates of interest. But many exchange rates are inexplicable. Speculators 'lose

confidence' or 'gain confidence'. They are very influenced by the opinions of other speculators. Some individuals in the market may be extremely influential. A word spoken in a television interview or written in an article may spark off feverish buying or selling.

Some economists argue that there is no pattern at all to exchange rate movements: that they are on a random walk and the market is totally chaotic.

Even though speculation can be highly destabilising in the short term, economists tend to believe that economic fundamentals prevail in the long term.

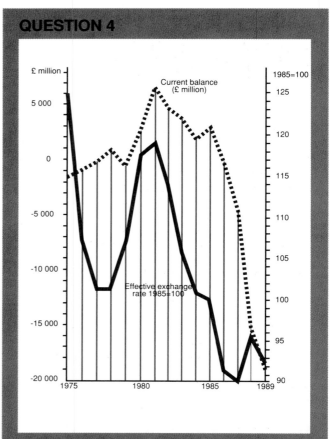

QUESTION 4

Source: adapted from CSO, *Economic Trends Annual Supplement*; CSO, *Monthly Digest of Statistics*.

Figure 87.5 *Effective exchange rate (1985 = 100) and the current balance*

(a) Explain what economic theory predicts is likely to happen to the exchange rate if the current account position deteriorates.
(b) Speculative activity should anticipate changes in economic fundamentals such as changes in the current account position. Do the data provide any evidence for suggesting that currency speculators have correctly anticipated changes in the UK current account position?

Key terms

Exchange rate - the price at which one currency is exchanged for another.
Effective exchange rate and trade weighted exchange rate index - measures of the exchange rate of a country's currency against a basket of currencies of a country's major trading partners.
Foreign exchange markets - the markets, organised in major financial centres such as London and New York, where currencies are bought and sold.
Purchasing power parity theory - the hypothesis that long run changes in exchange rates are caused by differences in inflation rates between countries.
Labour productivity - output per worker.
Exchange controls - controls on the purchase and sale of foreign currency by a country, usually through its central bank.

Applied economics

The exchange rate, 1978-1981

Between 1978 and 1981, the effective exchange rate (EER) of the pound rose by over twenty five per cent before falling back a little, as can be seen in Table 87.2. There are a number of possible reasons why there should have been such a significant change in the EER.

One important factor was the change in the oil balance on the balance of payments. 1976 had seen the first production of North Sea oil and by the early 1980s production had reached its highest level. The effect was to transform a traditional deficit on trade in oil (with the UK importing all her oil requirements) to a substantial surplus. As Table 87.2 shows, there was a £5 000 million turnaround in the oil balance. The effect of increased production was magnified by the second oil crisis of 1978-9 which increased the price of oil from approximately $15 a barrel in 1978 to $36 a barrel in 1981. Increased exports result in greater demand for pounds and hence a higher value of the pound. So the positive change in the oil balance helped increase the EER.

Despite the positive change in the oil balance, the current balance (total exports minus imports) deteriorated in 1978-9. This was because the economy was enjoying a boom, and imports were being sucked into the country to satisfy domestic demand. However, by the early part of 1980, the economy was spiralling downwards into deep recession, which was to see a fall of 5 per cent in GDP and nearly 20 per cent in manufacturing output before the bottom in mid-1981. That led to a sharp fall in imports which, together with the effect of North Sea oil, led to a record current account surplus in 1981. This move from deficit in 1979 to record surplus in 1981, a turnaround of approximately £7 000 million on an annual basis, must have contributed to the rise in sterling between 1979 and 1981.

A further factor which is likely to have put upward pressure on the pound was the rise in interest rates. Between 1978 and 1980, bank base rates rose from 6½ per cent to 17 per cent. This increased the interest rate differential between London and other financial centres round the world, attracting speculative flows of money into sterling. Falls in interest rates in 1980 and 1981 were followed by falls in the exchange rate in 1981.

Speculation too must have played a part in sending the EER to record levels. In 1978, there was still grave international concern about the competitiveness of the

Table 87.2 *Factors affecting the exchange rate, 1979-1981*

		Effective exchange rate 1985 = 100	Interest rate[1] %	Change in official reserves[2] £million	Current account balance £million	Oil balance £million	Net external assets £billion
1978	Q1	105.0	6½	-46	-146		
	Q2	99.2	9	-2 026	509	-2 129.1	12.0
	Q3	100.1	10	54	151		
	Q4	99.6	12½	-311	422		
1979	Q1	101.6	13½	955	-658		
	Q2	106.9	12	68	4	-1 070.7	11.0
	Q3	111.9	14	152	310		
	Q4	107.7	14	-166	-205		
1980	Q1	113.1	17	457	-96		
	Q2	115.5	17	140	-125	60.5	16.8
	Q3	118.3	16	-223	1143		
	Q4	123.6	16	-83	1 873		
1981	Q1	127.1	14	319	2 888		
	Q2	122.7	12	-1 448	1 932	2 871.9	31.1
	Q3	114.1	12	-1 167	510		
	Q4	112.2	15	-123	1 309		

1. Bank base rate at 15 February, 15 May, 15 August, 15 November.
2. Additions to reserves (+), falls in reserves (-).

Source: adapted from CSO, *Economic Trends Annual Supplement*; CSO, *Annual Abstract of Statistics*; CSO, *United Kingdom National Accounts (Blue Book)*.

UK economy and the pound. By 1979, the pound was being seen as a petro currency. It didn't take much to look at what was happening to the oil balance to realise that the UK was likely to be in substantial surplus on current account in the early 1980s. Substantial surpluses would be likely to increase the EER, and therefore speculators bought pounds, which had the effect of further raising the EER.

There were two factors which helped prevent the rise in the pound between 1979 and 1981 being even greater than it was. Firstly, in November 1979, the government abolished exchange controls. These had limited the outflow of money on the capital account, reducing outflows from their free market levels.

Following abolition, there was a substantial outflow of capital from the UK, reflected in the increase in net external assets of the UK shown in Table 87.2.

Secondly, the Bank of England intervened in the foreign exchange markets, on the whole buying foreign currency in exchange for pounds (i.e. the supply of pounds increased). The fact that the Bank of England was intervening like this can be seen from the increase in the official foreign currency reserves of the UK during this period. When the exchange rate began to fall in 1981, the Bank of England reversed its policy. It began to buy pounds with foreign currency. This helped break the fall in the pound, but official foreign currency reserves fell.

IMPORT PENETRATION RATIOS

Table 87.3 *Import penetration ratios, UK*

	1971	1978	1988
Manufacturing industries	17.1	26.0	35.1

Source: adapted from CSO, *Annual Abstract of Statistics*.

Import penetration ratios measure the percentage of imports to domestic consumption of the production. For instance, a penetration ratio of 25 in Table 87.3 would indicate that 25 per cent of manufactures sold in the UK were imported.

1. What has happened to import penetration ratios of manufactures between 1971 and 1988?
2. Suggest possible reasons why there has been this change over time.
3. Explain the likely effect of this trend on the exchange rate of the pound.

Summary

1. In a common market, there is free movement of goods and services, and factors of production. Goods and services imported from outside the common market face a common external tariff.
2. Free trade involves harmonisation in a wide range of areas, including product standards and taxation.
3. The formation of a common market will lead to trade creation and trade diversion. The greater the trade creation and the less the trade diversion, the greater will be the welfare benefits to member countries.
4. Dynamic gains from membership include economies of scale in production. Competition is likely to increase in the short run but mergers and takeovers are likely to lessen competition amongst firms in the long run.
5. Common market spending and taxation will lead to a redistribution of resources between member countries. Inevitably some countries will gain and others will lose from the common market budget.
6. Common markets may be the first step towards complete monetary and political union between member countries.

A common market

A COMMON MARKET or CUSTOMS UNION is a group of countries between which there is free trade and which impose a COMMON EXTERNAL TARIFF on imported goods from outside the market. In theory, free trade between member countries involves goods and services as well as the factors of production.

■ Land. There should be free trade in natural resources. In Europe, for instance, a British company should be free to buy land in Paris, whilst a French company should be free to own a licence to exploit North Sea oil.

■ Labour. Workers should be free to work in any member country. For instance, an Italian should be able to work in London on exactly the same terms as a worker born in Birmingham.

■ Capital. Capital should flow freely between countries. Of particular importance is **financial capital**. A Scottish firm should be free to borrow money in Paris to set up a factory in Italy, just as a London based firm could borrow money from a Scottish bank to invest in Wales.

Imports from outside the common market present a problem. For instance, assume that the UK imposes a tariff of 10 per cent on imports of foreign cars whilst France imposes a tariff of 20 per cent. With free trade between France and the UK, foreign importers would ship cars intended for sale in France to the UK, pay the 10 per cent tariff, and then re-export them 'tariff-free' into France. There are two ways to get round this problem.

■ One way is to impose a common external tariff. All member countries agree to change their tariff structures so as to impose the same tariff on imported items. In our example, France and the UK would have to change or HARMONIZE their tariffs on cars to an agreed European Community figure.

■ The other way is for member countries to impose tariffs on re-exports. In our example France could impose a 10 per cent tariff on the original import price of cars for non-member cars.

This second solution is a feature of FREE TRADE AREAS. A free trade area differs from a common market partly because of its different approach to dealing with non-member imports. It also differs because member countries are not committed to working towards closer economic integration. In a free trade area, the sole objective is free trade between member countries.

In a common market, the goal is to establish a single market in the same way that there is a single market within an individual economy. Ultimately this involves a large number of changes including:

■ no customs posts between countries; just as goods and people are free to travel between Manchester and London, so they should be free to travel between London and Milan;

■ identical product standards between countries; the existence of individual national safety standards on cars, for instance, is a barrier to trade just as it would be if cars sold in London had to meet different safety requirements from cars sold in Bristol;

■ harmonisation of taxes; if the tax on the same car is £2 000 more in the UK than in France, then UK residents will buy their cars in France and take them back to England, distorting the pattern of trade; equally if direct taxes on income are an average 15 per cent in France and 30 per cent in the UK, some UK workers may be tempted to go and work in France;

■ a common currency; having to buy foreign exchange is a barrier to trade, especially if there are exchange rate movements; hence there should a single common market currency just as there is a single currency in the UK.

QUESTION 1 In 1989, the European Commission told the French government that it would be taken to court if it did not reduce a subsidy of £2 billion given to the Renault car company.

Explain why this subsidy to the Renault car company did not conform to the rules of a common market.

Trade creation and trade diversion

The **theory of comparative advantage** (☞ unit 84) shows that free trade between countries is likely to increase total world production. When a small number of countries form a common market, there will be gainers and losers.

TRADE CREATION is said to take place when a country moves from buying goods from a high cost country to buying them from a lower cost country. For instance, country A might have imposed a 50 per cent tariff on imported cars. As a result, all cars sold in country A were produced domestically. It now joins a customs union. The common external tariff is 50 per cent but cars from member countries can be imported free of the tariff. Country A now buys some cars from common market countries because they are lower priced than those previously produced domestically. Consumers in country A have benefited because they are able to buy cars from a cheaper source.

TRADE DIVERSION takes place when a country moves from buying goods from a low cost producer to buying them from a higher cost producer. For instance, before entry to the European Community, the UK had low or zero tariffs on imported foodstuffs. It bought from the lowest cost producers round the world such as New Zealand and the USA. After entry, the UK had to impose the much higher EC common external tariff. As a result it

became cheaper to buy food from other EC countries such as France and Italy. France and Italy are higher cost producers than the USA and New Zealand for many food items.

In general the higher the tariffs imposed by a country before entry to a common market, the more likely it is that trade creation rather than trade diversion will take place. It is also true that the net gains will tend to be larger, the greater the volume of trade between the countries in the common market.

Economies of scale

Gains from trade creation are **static** gains. They occur once and for all following the creation of, or entry to, a common market. Membership of a common market may also result in **dynamic** gains or losses: gains or losses which occur over a period of time. One important such gain comes from **economies of scale** (☞ unit 20). In a common market, the potential size of the customer market is inevitably larger than in a national market. For instance, the European Community has 300 million inhabitants compared to 57 million for the UK. This means that important economies of scale can be achieved by national companies if they carve out a market for themselves throughout the common market. This is no easy task given that each country is likely to have different consumer preferences. However, there are some products, such as basic chemicals, which are demanded by all countries. Other products, such as cars, are relatively easily sold across national boundaries. Yet other products, such as cosmetics, may need different packaging for different countries, but the basic product is the same.

Economies of scale will be achieved over a period of time as companies expand internally or merge with other foreign companies. The size of the potential gains will be greater, the more homogeneous the tastes of consumers within the market. For instance, the gains are likely to be higher for a market comprising France and the UK than of the UK and Iran. Economies of scale bring benefits to

QUESTION 2

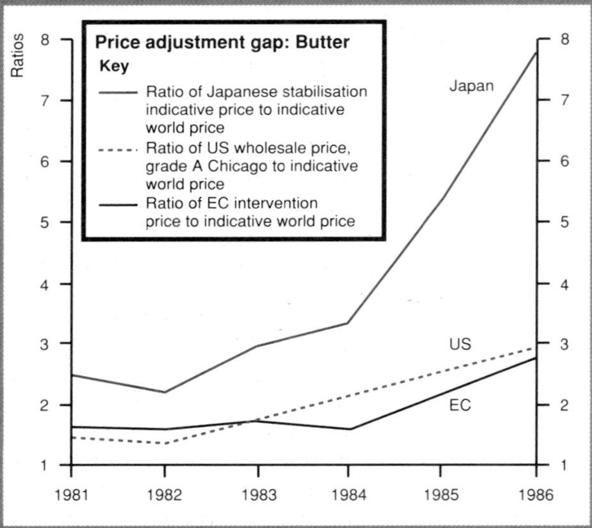

Figure 88.1 *National and world prices*

The chart shows the ratio between the production price of butter in Japan, the US and the EC, and the world production price.

Assume that Japan and the USA formed a customs union in 1986. Explain whether there would be trade creation or trade diversion if the guaranteed production price of butter in both countries: (i) rose to Japanese levels; (ii) were at US levels; (iii) fell to the price guaranteed in the EC.

QUESTION 3 The Cecchini Report, published in 1988, argued that there would be a 5.3 per cent increase in national income of the European Community following the creation of a single market in 1992. One major gain would arise from economies of scale. For instance, there were 50 tractor manufacturers in the EC fighting over a market similar in size to that served in the US by just 4 manufacturers. Similarly in the US there were 4 producers of domestic appliances compared to 300 in the EC.

Source: adapted from the *Financial Times*, 17.11.1988.

(a) Why is there scope for increased economies of scale in the EC following 1992?
(b) (i) What benefits might consumers receive from increased economies? (ii) What might be the costs to workers?

consumers because average costs of production fall, and therefore prices are likely to fall too.

Competition

Another possible dynamic gain arises from increased competition between firms. A common market should eliminate restrictions on trade between member countries. Domestic industries will therefore face greater competition than before from firms in other member countries. Competition will encourage innovation, reduce costs of production and reduce prices. There will therefore be gains in productive and allocative efficiency (☞ unit 33).

Although there is likely to be greater competition in the short run, evidence suggests that this competition will be reduced in the long run. Competition will drive the least efficient firms out of the market, as the theory of perfect competition predicts. Other firms will seek to maintain monopoly profits by re-establishing control over their markets. They will do this by merging with or taking over foreign firms within the common market. Over time, the oligopolistic nature of competition in domestic markets will be recreated on a common market level. This may benefit the consumer through economies of scale but it certainly will not bring the benefits that free market economists suggest.

The Austrian school of Economics argues that competition is not necessarily beneficial to the consumer. Large international monopolies, earning considerable abnormal profit, will have the resources to devote to research, development and investment. If they fail to develop products that satisfy consumer wants, their monopoly will be lost through the process of creative destruction. Competitors will break their monopoly by creating new products. This constant development of new products is far more beneficial to consumer welfare than a few per cent off the price of existing products which might result from a perfectly competitive environment.

Transfers of resources

Common markets may differ in the size and power of their institutions. The European Community has a sizeable bureaucracy, a parliament and a large budget. Money is paid into a Community budget by member countries. The money is used to pay for administration and the implementation of Community-wide policies. In the case of the European Community, about 70 per cent of the budget has traditionally been allocated to one area of policy - the **Common Agricultural Policy** (☞ unit 33). Any budget of any size opens up the possibility that some member countries may pay more into the budget than they receive. There may therefore be a net transfer of resources from one country to another within a common market. These represent static losses and gains (i.e. once and for all losses and gains).

Perhaps more importantly, there can also be transfers of real resources from country to country. Countries in the common market which are particularly dynamic and successful are likely to attract inflows of labour and capital. Countries which have lower growth rates are likely to suffer net capital outflows and lose some of their best workers to other economies. This is likely to heighten regional disparities, making the richer nations relatively even richer.

The process may be magnified if the successful countries are at the geographical centre of the common market whilst the less successful countries are on the fringe. Transport and communication costs tend to be lower for companies sited at the centre and higher for those at the periphery. Hence central countries tend to have a competitive advantage over fringe countries.

Neo-classical economic theory suggests that free market forces would equalize the differences between regions. An unsuccessful region will have cheap labour and cheap land. Firms will be attracted into the region to take advantage of these. In practice, this effect seems to be very weak. Cheap labour economies can easily become branch economies. Firms set up branches in these regions, employing cheap labour to perform low productivity tasks. Tasks which have high value added are completed at headquarters in higher cost areas. The result is growing economic divergence, with poorer regions losing the most skilled of their labour force to the richer regions and being left with less dynamic and less skilled workers to do less well paid jobs.

Monetary and political union

An internal common market where there are different currencies in each country imposes costs upon producers. Therefore a common market implies a move to a common currency. A common currency implies common monetary and fiscal policies. The economic implications of

QUESTION 4 A study by Richard Baldwin of the Centre for Economic Policy Research published in 1989, suggested that the gains from the 1992 programme could produce an increase of between 3.5 and 19.5 per cent in Europe's real standard of living. The central argument of the study is that, as well as increasing the efficiency of the existing capital stock, 1992 will encourage both European and other companies to make fresh investments in Europe, further boosting output and growth.

Although the boost would wear off in time, some economists argue that increased returns on capital lead to accelerated technological innovation, increasing economic growth still further.

Source: adapted from the *Financial Times*, 9.11.1989.

(a) What dynamic gains are suggested by the Baldwin study?
(b) Why should 'increased returns on capital' lead to 'accelerated technological innovation'?

monetary union are discussed further in unit 102.

A common market may eventually lead to political union. Political union inevitably involves a loss of national sovereignty. Decisions which previously were made at national level will now be made at community level. This may have economic implications in that a member country will lose the ability to direct its economic affairs to its own advantage. On the other hand, it can be argued that any country which is very **open** (i.e. exports a high proportion of its national product) has already lost most of its ability to direct its own economic affairs because so much of its economy depends upon the spending and saving decisions of foreigners.

Key terms

Common market - a group of countries between which there is free trade in products and factors of production, and which imposes a common external tariff on imported goods from outside the market.
Common external tariff - a common tariff set by a group of countries imposed on imported goods from non-member countries.
Harmonization - establishing common standards, rules and levels on everything from safety standards to tariffs, taxes and currencies.
Free trade area - a group of countries between which there is free trade in goods and services but which allows member countries to set their own level of tariffs against non-member countries.
Trade creation - the switch from purchasing products from a high cost producer to a lower cost producer.
Trade diversion - the switch from purchasing products from a low cost producer to a higher cost producer.

Applied economics

1992

In 1957, six European countries (France, West Germany, Italy, the Netherlands, Belgium and Luxembourg) signed the Treaty of Rome. It committed the six to free trade between themselves, whilst imposing a common external tariff on goods coming from outside the European Economic Community (EEC or Common Market as it came to be known). The UK refused to join, seeing its interests in trade with countries of the Commonwealth. The higher growth rates of the six and the increased share of UK trade with EEC countries soon convinced the UK that it should join, but in 1962 its application was turned down for political reasons. It was not until 1973 that it was finally allowed to join, along with Eire and Denmark. The 9 were later joined by Greece, Spain and Portugal in the 1980s to make up the 12 country membership in 1990.

The Common Agricultural Policy was the first major initiative of the original 6 member countries and has remained a controversial issue ever since (☞ unit 33). In the 1990s, the European Community as it is now called is likely be preoccupied with the Delors plan for monetary union (☞ unit 102). This will raise questions about the appropriate political institutions needed as the 12 move towards some form of political union. However, perhaps the most important issue in the early 1990s is the 1992 process.

Although the removal of tariff and quota barriers between member countries in 1957 promoted free trade, there still existed substantial barriers to trade.

Firstly, barriers existed in trade in services. For instance, UK insurance companies could not sell most types of insurance in France or Spain. There were legal restrictions on road haulage by foreign transport in domestic markets. Different regulations prevented UK companies borrowing in France, in spite of the fact that French companies might be able to borrow in London. Secondly, different standards presented a major obstacle to trade in goods. For instance, a tractor manufacturer had to produce a different tractor for sale in each member country because each imposed different safety regulations. Thirdly, governments tended to buy only from domestic companies (government purchases are known as 'public procurement'). The French government would only buy computers from a French manufacturer, whilst the UK tended to buy military equipment from UK companies. Lastly, everything from customs posts, import and export forms to different VAT rates and corporation taxes imposed heavy administrative costs on companies trading across country boundaries.

In 1985, member countries signed the Single European Act, which committed the members to removing all such obstacles by 31 December 1992. It is unlikely that the deadline will be met. For instance, 3 000 European standards for products ranging from ventilation equipment to construction products need to be agreed upon. However, in one sense this is relatively unimportant because what is not at issue is that a single European market will be created in the

1990s.

The benefits of a single European market were put forward in the Cecchini report published by the European Commission in 1988 and are summarised in Table 89.1. Removal of border controls, technical regulations and other adminstrative hurdles could increase Community GDP by up to 2.7 per cent. Exploitation of greater economies of scale because producers will now be able to sell across the whole European market rather than in just their domestic markets will add up to 2.1 per cent of GDP. The resulting increase in competition, particularly in the area of public procurement, would increase GDP by up to 1.6 per cent.

These one-off gains would amount to between 4.2 and 6.4 per cent of GDP. However, the dynamic gains might be even greater. In a study by Richard Baldwin (1989), it was estimated that the gains could be up to four times as great as the Cecchini report estimated. This was because the static boost in GDP would lead to an investment boom as more capital was needed to produce the extra output created by the 1992 process. This once and for all increase in investment could add another 15 per cent to GDP on top of the extra 5 per cent (a middle estimate of the 4.2 and 6.4 per cent gain) which might be expected from the static gains.

In all this process, there will be gainers and losers. Inefficient national companies which had been protected from international competition by relying

Table 88.1 *EC gains from the internal market*

	% of GDP
Removal of barriers affecting trade	0.2 - 0.3
Removal of barriers affecting overall production	2.0 - 2.4
Total gains from removing barriers	2.2 - 2.7
Exploiting economies of scale more fully	2.1
Gains from intensified competition reducing business ineffectiveness and monopoly profits	1.6
Total gains from market integration	2.1 - 3.7
Total gains	4.3 - 6.4

Source: European Commission.

upon public procurement contracts would have either to become more efficient or go bankrupt. Either way, it is likely to lead to a loss of jobs. However, overall the Cecchini report estimated that a total of between 1.75 and 5 million extra jobs would be created in the Community in the medium term.

Few economists have argued that 1992 will not bring substantial benefits. The gains from 1992 after all are simply an application of the gains predicted by the theory of comparative advantage (☞ unit 84). Where economists do disagree is where the European Community should go from here.

Data question

CHALLENGE OF ENCOURAGING MOBILITY OF SKILLED LABOUR

A single European labour market is a distant prospect. Whilst employers regard labour costs and skills as an important part of an investment decision, and some workers are willing to move between regions and countries to seek the best work, the European Community is far from being a clearing market which matches demand for skills with supply.

The number of nationals working in another European country is fewer than the 15m people who are counted as unemployed within the EC. The largest movements of labour within Europe have involved the low-paid and low-skilled moving out of peripheral regions such as southern Italy to find work.

If the Single European Act encouraged the movement of workers with higher skill levels, that would be one of its most radical achievements. But the European Commission's effort to construct a social programme to match the economic one could have contradictory effects on mobility.

On the one hand, directives intended to allow the transfer across borders of financial entitlements tied to pay such as pensions and social security benefits, the harmonisation of worker qualifications and minimum standards and entitlements in fields such as working

hours and work contracts, are clearly aimed at improving workers' geographical mobility. On the other hand, the Social Charter's emphasis on minimum wages and conditions of work, together with EC disapproval of companies seeking out low cost labour regions such as Spain and Portugal for factory investment, will discourage firms from seeking out lower cost labour, either by moving workers to the work or moving work to the workers.

Moreover, those who most need to be mobile - the unemployed - are either too old to want to uproot themselves, or they lack the skills that European employers short of labour need. One estimate was that in the EC 3m are unemployed due to a lack of geographical mobility, and 1.5m because they are not mobile enough within professions and industries.

Source: adapted from the *Financial Times*, 2.7.1990.

1. Why should the mobility of labour be a concern to a free trade area like the EC?
2. Why is labour relatively immobile between countries in the EC?
3. How could the EC promote greater labour mobility?

89 First World and Third World

Applied economics

Classification

The world can be divided into groups of countries.

■ FIRST WORLD countries are a small group of rich industrialised countries: the Unites States, Canada, Australia, New Zealand, Japan and Western Europe. Sometimes they are called Western countries, because for the most part they lie in the western hemisphere. Sometimes they are included in the 'North' (from the phrase 'North-South divide'), because for the most part they are in the northern hemisphere. They are also known as DEVELOPED COUNTRIES, indicating that they have reached an advanced stage of economic development.

■ SECOND WORLD countries are the communist and former communist countries of Eastern Europe and the USSR. They too are included in the 'North' and are usually classified as 'developed', although their GDP is far lower than that of the average First World country.

■ THIRD WORLD countries are a large group of poor countries in Asia, Africa and Latin America. Most are situated in the southern hemisphere, and hence are known as the 'South' (as in the phrase 'North-South' divide). Sometimes they are called DEVELOPING COUNTRIES (DCs), indicating that their economies are still developing in contrast with the 'developed' economies of the First World. They are also called LESS DEVELOPED COUNTRIES (LDCs), again contrasted with the 'developed' countries of the North.

Third World countries differ greatly amongst themselves and hence they are often sub-divided into further groups. For instance, sometimes the poorest are called Fourth World countries or low income countries, whilst the richer Third World countries are known as middle income countries. South Korea, Singapore, Taiwan and others are called newly industrialised countries (NICs), indicating that their economies now have a strong, Western-style, industrial base. Third World countries are also grouped by region, such as sub-Saharan African countries, or South East Asian countries.

Characteristics

Third World countries are all very different from each other, and therefore in some ways it is dangerous to lump them together and talk about 'the characteristics of Third World countries'. However, most share some basic problems.

Low per capita income As Table 89.1 shows, approximately three-quarters of the world's population live in the Third World. Yet the total GDP of all developing countries is less than one-third that of First World countries. As a result, the average GDP per capita of $555 in the Third World is only 5 per cent of the average of $9 467 for First World countries. GDP figures in dollars need to be used with care. The collection of GNP statistics in the Third World is unreliable, a significant proportion of output is

Table 89.1 *Population and output*

	Population 1989 (millions)	Gross domestic product 1985 ($billions at 1980 prices)
World	5 201	n.a.
First World	807	7 640
Second World	402	n.a.
Third World	3 992	2 217
Western hemisphere	439	822
West Asia	127	343
South and East Asia	1 633	606
Africa	594	305
Mediterranean	79	141
China	1 120	n.a.

Source: adapted from United Nations, *World Economic Survey*, 1990.

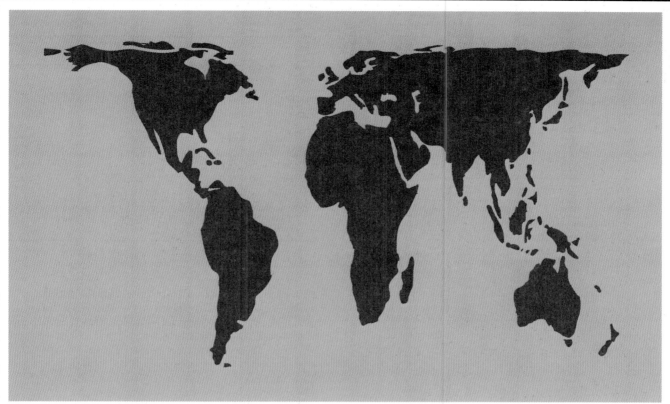

The Peters projection shows the countries of the world with their correct relative areas. It helps to explain why 75 per cent of the world's population live in developing countries.

Figure 89.1 *The Peters Projection*

subsistence agriculture not included in GNP, and figures are converted into dollars using market foreign exchange rates rather than purchasing power rates (☞ unit 58). In practice, it may be misleading to say that average income is likely to be over 15 times as great in First World compared to Third World countries. However, the fact that Third World citizens have considerably lower incomes than their counterparts in the First World is indisputable.

Lack of human capital Because Third World countries are poor, their governments are unable to afford to provide Western standards of education. In 1987 for instance, as shown in Table 89.2, only just over half of children aged 5-11 in Africa were receiving primary education. One result of lack of education is illiteracy, again particularly significant in Africa. With low levels of **human capital** (☞ unit 2), developing countries are less likely to achieve the high levels of output of First World countries.

Lack of physical capital Third World countries have far less physical capital per capita than First World countries. This includes not just factories, offices and machines but also infrastructure capital such as roads and railways as well as schools and hospitals. Lack of human capital and physical capital means that labour productivity in the Third World is a fraction of that in the First World.

High population growth There is a correlation between low incomes, high mortality rates and high population growth. Table 89.3 shows that the rate of population growth is much higher in developing countries than in developed countries. It is projected that by the year 2025, 84 per cent of the world's population will live in the Third World compared to 76 per cent today and 68 per cent in 1950. Increases in

Table 89.2 *Education and literacy, 1987*

	Percentage	
	Children of primary school age receiving education	Literacy rate adults aged 15+
First World	100.0	n.a.
Africa	54.4	46.2
Asia	87.9	63.8
Latin America	83.2	84.1

Source: adapted from United Nations, *World Economic Survey*, 1990.

Table 89.3 *Population and mortality rates*

	Percentage	Per thousand	Billions		
	Population growth 1981-91	Under 5 mortality rate1987	Population size		
			1950	1989	2025
First World	0.5	n.a.	0.83	0.81	1.35
Third World	2.4	121.0	1.76	4.00	7.23
Africa	3.1	168.4	0.22	0.59	1.58
Asia	2.4	80.1	1.37	2.97	4.89
Latin America	2.1	69.1	0.17	0.44	0.76

Source: adapted from United Nations, *World Economic Survey*, 1990.

population mean that Third World countries need to grow at a faster rate than First World countries if the rate of growth per capita is to be maintained.

Low living standards Low income and low output inevitably lead to low expenditure and therefore low living standards. Per head of the population, citizens in the Third World eat less food, consume less energy, have far fewer consumer durables such as cars or refrigerators, and spend less on health care than their counterparts in developed countries.

Economic development

Developing countries, as Table 89.4 shows, have grown on average at a faster rate than developed countries in the 1970s and 1980s. However, some regions of the world have grown faster than others. Asian countries grew particularly fast in the 1970s, although West Asia (countries such as Vietnam and Cambodia) saw a fall in its GDP in the 1980s. Growth in Africa has proved disappointing over the two decades, and in sub-Saharan Africa growth rates have been negative in the 1980s. What factors, then, cause a country to grow at a faster rate than its neighbours? (This has already been discussed within a UK context in unit 63.)

Economic growth only arises if there is an increase in the quantity or productivity of the factors of production. Countries have little control over their endowment of land. However, labour productivity can be improved through education and training, whilst the capital stock of a country can be increased through investment. How these changes can be achieved is part of development economics.

Factors over which countries have little control A few 'developing' countries, such as Saudi Arabia, have higher per capita incomes than the USA. It is not difficult to understand that countries which are endowed with valuable natural resources are more likely to grow at a faster rate than resource-poor countries. Climate might play a part in determining

Table 89.4 *Growth of GDP*

	Per cent per annum	
	1971-1980	1981-1990
Developed market countries	3.1	2.6
Eastern and the Soviet Union	5.2	2.5
Developing countries	5.6	3.2
Africa	4.9	0.5
Western hemisphere	5.5	1.0
South and East Asia	5.8	7.0
West Asia	6.5	- 0.2
Mediterranean	5.3	3.2
World	3.9	2.9

Source: adapted from United Nations, *World Economic Survey*, 1990.

growth rates. Climate affects agricultural output, as has been seen with drought in sub-Saharan Africa in the 1980s. It can also produce natural disasters such as hurricanes, which can lead to significant loss of physical capital. Wars can be devastating. In Africa, for instance, recent droughts in Ethiopia and Mozambique have been turned into famines by disruption to the economy due to civil wars.

There are also cultural differences between countries. In the West, it is assumed for the most part that economic growth and increased living standards are desirable. However, growth inevitably involves change. In some cultures, stability is valued more highly than the gains from change. Not everyone dreams of owning a car, drinking Coca-Cola and holidaying in the Bahamas. The more a culture values tradition, the less likely it is to want to change the way its members behave. Equally it is sometimes argued that some societies are more disciplined than others. In some societies, individuals on the whole share common goals and common agendas. In others, individuals or small groups, such as families or tribes, have very different goals one from another so that there is a lack of social cohesion.

It can then be argued that Asian countries such as Japan and South Korea have grown faster than Western European countries and African countries because of the cultural attitudes found amongst the populations of those countries and regions.

Agriculture and industry Over the past 300 years, developed economies such as the UK have changed from being primarily agriculturally based economies, to being manufacturing economies, to being service-dominated economies. Therefore it could be argued that countries would increase their growth rates by reducing the share of agricultural production through rapid industrialisation. Indeed, industrialisation could be paid for by taxing the agricultural sector of the economy and using the taxes to invest in state industries or subsidise private industry. Alternatively, low maximum prices could be fixed for agricultural produce, so low that it would discourage investment in the agricultural sector of the economy and therefore encourage investment in manufacturing industry. This was the strategy pursued by the Soviet Union in the 1930s and 1940s, and was actively promoted in the Third World by the USSR in the 1950s and 1960s as a development strategy.

Evidence suggests, however, that such a development strategy yields disappointing results. Low agricultural prices or high taxes on the agricultural community will lead to a fall in supply of agricultural produce. Many countries pursuing this strategy have ceased to be self-sufficient in food, and scarce foreign exchange earnings have had to be used to import food. The dynamism and energy of rural economies have been reduced, leading to lower economic growth. Peasants have left the land in large numbers to migrate to cities, creating enormous social problems and an urban population which is often underemployed. Industrialisation has proved difficult, with many projects yielding low rates of return or even negative rates of return. There are many steel mills, chemical plants and car factories in Third World countries which have never operated efficiently.

In the 1970s and 1980s, there has been growing recognition that growth rates would be increased if free market mechanisms were allowed to allocate scarce investment to projects which promised the highest rate of return. This could be an industrial project, but equally it could be agricultural. Countries, such as Zimbabwe, which have allowed farmers to receive free market prices for their produce, have not only become self-sufficient in food but have also become net agricultural exporters. A booming rural economy has then provided the necessary demand for manufactured products which local industry needs if it too is to be successful.

The role of government Economic planning, pioneered by the Eastern Bloc countries and the Soviet Union, was highly influential in the 1950s and 1960s. The market mechanism, it was felt, would not lead to either balanced or high growth. The state needed to intervene to override the market mechanism and ensure that investment and other scarce resources were efficiently organised. In the 1970s and 1980s, it has become increasingly apparent that planned economies suffer many disadvantages. Central to the planning model is the assumption that governments act in a way which leads to the greatest welfare of their citizens. In practice, governments tend to maximise their own utility and that of their supporters (in the same way that it can be argued that managers don't profit maximise but maximise their own utility subject to a profit-satisfising constraint ☞ unit 24). Buying military hardware, building palaces or subsidising food for urban dwellers have often become far more important policy objectives of Third World governments than increasing the standard of living of all the inhabitants of a country.

Rolling back the frontiers of the state - privatisation - has now come to be seen as an important way in which the energy and dynamism of individual citizens can be released, and for living standards to improve. The examples of some of the NICs, like Singapore, would seem to support the view that free market economies can lead to high economic growth. Equally, there are some countries like Japan and South Korea where the state has arguably played a crucial role in guiding the process of development. So whilst it is generally accepted that the planning policies of the 1950s and 1960s in many developing countries were misguided, equally there is still great debate about the extent to which and how governments should intervene in the economy.

Development and inequality Early development economists argued that growing inequality was perhaps a price that had to be paid for economic development in the Third World. On the one hand, Keynesian economics suggested that the average propensity to save was greater for high income earners than low income earners. Therefore, if investment equals savings in an economy, one way to boost investment was to increase savings by increasing the share of national income taken by the better off in society. On the other hand, industrialisation would create a dual sector economy. In the high growth developing sector of the economy, the 'modern' industrialised sector, incomes would rise faster than in the low growth 'backward' rural sector of the economy.

One billion people, about one-third of the population of the Third World, lived on less than $370 per annum in 1990. Development strategies which ignore the needs of so many people could be argued to be inappropriate. International agencies such as the World Bank have increasingly devoted resources to promoting projects which will be of direct benefit to the poor. Instead of building steel plants, dams and chemical works, the traditional development projects of the 1950s and 1960s, aid agencies and governments have been encouraged to increase spending on low cost housing, providing basic water supplies and sanitation facilities, primary education and funding health care based on preventative rather than curative techniques. For instance, the provision of clean water directly increases the standard of living of those drinking it. It prevents the loss of human capital through illness or death. It also means that less need be spent on medicines which, anyway, are often ineffective against waterborne diseases such as cholera. So far as employment is concerned, strategies which encourage the growth of many small labour-intensive firms are likely to be of far greater benefit to most than the establishment of a few capital-intensive plants.

All this means is that the use of appropriate technology is essential in development. As E F Schumacher argued in his book *Small is Beautiful*, hoes might contribute far more to economic development in the Third World than tractors, and bicycles might be a far more appropriate technology than motor cars. **Intermediate technology**, technology which is cheap, simple to operate and easy to maintain, perhaps more advanced than existing technologies in a Third World country but not the 'high-tec' found in developed economies, can be used to benefit the majority of citizens in the Third World, not just a small elite.

Trade, borrowing and aid Policies towards trade, foreign borrowing, multi-national companies and foreign aid will have a significant impact on growth rates of an individual country. These will be considered in greater detail in the next unit.

Key terms

Developed and developing or less developed countries - developed countries are the rich industrialised nations of Europe, Japan and North America, whilst developing or less developed countries are the other, poorer, less economically developed nations of the world.
First World countries - the rich, developed, nations of Western Europe, Japan and North America.
Second World countries - the communist and formerly communist nations of Eastern Europe and the Soviet Union.
Third World countries - the developing nations of the world in Africa, South America and Asia.

Data question

KARACHI SQUATTERS BUILD 'PARALLEL STATE' WHERE GOVERNMENT NEVER GOES

You are now entering the Middle Ages, said Doctor Sahib as he drove past the memorial to Pakistan's founder, round a series of truckclogged roundabouts into the slums of north-west Karachi - areas with names familiar only as sites of frequent ethnic riots.

Curfew is the government's only contribution to life beyond the green line that marks off Orangi, probably the world's largest squatter camp, from the marble palaces which house the politicians and businessmen, and the neat villas of the civil servants.

Some 40 per cent of Karachi's population of 9m live in illegal settlements. The World Bank published a report on Orangi - home to more than a million people from all over the subcontinent - as an insight into how people cope when local government breaks down.

This shanty town, begun in 1965 to accommodate floods of migrants from India and the Biharis from Bangladesh, is a microcosm of Pakistan. It has every kind of problem - poverty, disease, ethnic tension, drugs, mafia and guns. It has Mohajirs, Baluchs, Pathans, Punjabis, Biharis and local Sindhis all competing for scarce jobs in a city where the streets are paved with garbage and not gold.

Inside Orangi's 8,000 acres there is no government - residents are provided with no water, no power, no sewerage, no health care, no transport and no education.

However, once the poorest part of Pakistan with typhoid and malaria cases in every one of its 90,000 houses, Orangi today is a hive of industry, even exporting textiles abroad and bricks to affluent Karachi suburbs.

The transformation is mostly due to the dedication of one elderly man. Akhtar Hammed Khan, known fondly as Doctor Sahib though he has no medical qualifications, persuaded the people that 'the government was never going to give them anything but promises - if they wanted to live like humans they would have to do it themselves'.

They did. With the help of Mr Khan and the Bank of Credit and Commerce International which set up the Orangi Pilot Project (OPP), providing just more than a penny a head, they constructed houses and drains, and soon learnt the value of self-help.

Waterborne diseases, medicine which had eaten up 40 per cent of their incomes, were reduced drastically. Today there are schools, mobile health clinics, women's work centres, a bus service and even a bank lending money for enterprise projects.

Residents laid their own water pipe to a nearby dam. Electricity is bought from entrepreneurs who have invested in a generator, or pirated from overhead cables, often with the palm-greased connivance of the authorities.

'This is the key to how the nation survives', says Mr Khan as he drives through an area of intense hammering, piles of tyres and vehicle parts. 'The government has provided the men in these shacks with nothing, but today this [four-mile] stretch is the hub of Pakistan's entire transport industry. They can fix anything'.

Now in his eighties and resembling a human grasshopper - all sticklike limbs and enthusiasm - Mr Khan has himself become something of a subcontinent fixit. His Comilla project in Bangladesh is used worldwide as a model for self-reliant rural development, but he was forced to leave when the government, feeling his success

undermined their role, labelled him a CIA agent.

Orangi is divided into lanes. Each elects a president responsible for collecting money and organising labour for laying drains and building septic tanks, advised by OPP's band of fervent young people who have developed a manhole cover and latrine costing a fraction of those previously available.

Since the project began in 1980, more than half have built drains. The concept has been so successful that 180 self-help organisations have formed, covering everything from sport to religion.

People are growing rich in Orangi. The average monthly family income is still only Rs1000 (£29), but since 1987, OPP, which has an annual budget of Rs3m, has given Rs2.5m in loans to entrepreneurs, from kite makers to rubbish collectors, knitters to rubber band manufacturers. Sweatshops are disappearing and, encouraged by OPP, women are casting off the veil and running work centres, producing tea towels and clothes for export.

The mushrooming of illegal squatter settlements such as Orangi began in the mid-1960s. State land was sold by powerful middlemen to migrants without due authorisation, thus leaving government with no obligation to provide facilities.

The names of some lanes reflect the efforts of each ethnic group to retain its cultural identity. Thus the

Pathans live on higher ground and keep their women veiled and hidden, while the Mohajirs are the most vocal and have the most schools. They make what the World Bank describes as an 'uneasy mix of co-operation and discord'. This exploded in 1986 when parts of Orangi became a battlefield where 150 people died in a few hours. Since then, the government slaps on daytime curfew at the slightest sign of unrest. Even when quiet, there is a night curfew.

The violence is linked to the growth of a vicious underground drug mafia exploiting ethnic tensions. This, along with some fundamentalist religious groups angered by the OPP's liberation of women, is threatening to overwhelm community development organisations.

Local authorities in Pakistan's largest city are uneasy too at the growth of this rival economy which the World Bank describes as a parallel state, parasitic on the legal one. It is one of Pakistan's few success stories.

Source: *Financial Times*, 12.1.1990.

1. **What are the characteristics of a 'Third World' country? Illustrate your answer from the data.**
2. **Using the experience of Orangi as an example, explain what factors stimulate economic development in the Third World.**
3. **To what extent is state intervention necessary in the development process?**

Applied economics

Patterns of world trade

World output is very unevenly distributed. As Table 90.1 shows, in 1987 developed market economies produced 69.1 per cent of world output and yet only 16 per cent of the world's population lived in these countries. Developing countries produced only 18.1 per cent of world output and yet their population was 52.9 per cent of the world's total. ('Developing countries' as defined here excludes Communist China, which accounted for approximately 20 per cent of the world's population in 1987.) Within the Third World, oil exporting countries and newly industrialised countries ('manufactures exporters') enjoyed a far higher per capita GDP than other developing countries. One-third of the world's population, mainly found in Africa and Asia, live in low income countries.

Given this unequal distribution of world output, it is not surprising that most world trade is centred on First World economies. Figure 90.1 shows the direction of world exports in 1964 and 1987. In 1987, 77.6 per cent of world exports were from developed economies to other developed economies. Developing countries only accounted for 21.6 per cent of exports from developed countries.

Perhaps more surprising is the direction of Third

World trade. It might be expected that Third World countries would trade mainly amongst themselves. In 1987, however, 65.8 per cent of exports from developing countries went to the First World. Exports from developing countries to other developing countries accounted for only 26.4 per cent of Third World exports. Inter-Third World trade has been growing. In 1964, only 21.2 per cent of Third World exports went to other Third World countries.

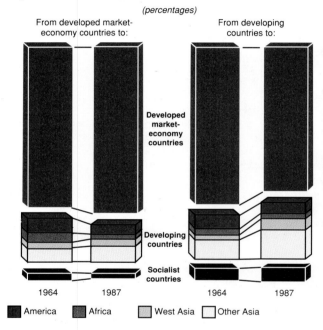

Source: adapted from UNCTAD, *Statistical Pocket Book*.

Figure 90.1 *Direction of trade: exports*

Composition of world trade

World trade in services is difficult to measure. Moreover, services are less tradeable than goods. So official statistics tend to concentrate on trade in primary commodities and manufactures. The share of exports taken by manufactures varies between 70 and nearly 100 per cent in developed countries. The traditional pattern, based upon the colonial trading system established in the 18th and 19th centuries, has been for developed countries to import raw materials, particularly from the Third World, and transform them into manufactured goods, some of which are then exported back to the Third World to pay for those raw materials.

Table 90.1 *Share in world GDP and population*

Country group	Share in world GDP			Share in world population		
	1970	1980	1987	1970	1980	1987
Developed market-economy countries	74.3	70.0	69.1	19.0	17.2	16.0
Developing countries[1]	16.1	18.9	18.1	47.6	50.5	52.9
By major category						
Oil exporters	6.1	7.4	6.0	8.7	9.7	10.4
Manufactures exporters	4.1	5.3	5.5	5.2	5.3	2.2
Remaining countries	5.9	6.2	6.6	33.8	35.5	37.1
By region						
America	6.1	7.3	6.6	7.6	8.1	8.4
Africa	2.9	2.9	2.6	9.1	10.1	11.1
West Asia	2.8	3.4	2.8	2.7	3.0	3.3
Other Asia	3.9	4.7	5.7	27.6	28.7	29.4
By income group						
High income	9.7	11.8	10.8	9.7	10.3	10.7
Middle income	3.1	3.6	3.5	8.4	9.2	9.9
Low income	3.3	3.4	3.8	29.5	31.0	32.3
Least developed countries	0.7	0.7	0.7	7.0	7.6	8.1

1. Excluding China.
Source: adapted from UNCTAD, *Statistical Pocket Book*.

Table 90.2 *Trade of developing countries by main product categories (percentages)*

A. Exports (f.o.b.)

Sector	Primary commodities				Manufactures						Total
	Petroleum		Other		Textiles		Machinery, etc.		Other		
Country group	1965	1987	1965	1987	1965	1987	1965	1987	1965	1987	1965-1987
Developing countries	31.4	27.8	54.2	23.4	4.9	12.5	1.1	17.0	5.2	18.2	100.0
By region											
America	29.9	23.4	64.6	47.7	0.8	3.2	0.6	12.8	3.8	12.5	100.0
Africa	20.2	56.8	71.9	30.2	1.6	6.0	0.5	1.0	5.4	5.5	100.0
West Asia	83.1	77.5	14.0	7.8	0.9	5.0	0.6	3.4	1.3	5.8	100.0
Other Asia	6.6	8.6	53.5	17.3	15.8	20.2	2.6	25.9	9.8	26.4	100.0
Least developed countries	4.9	5.3	86.9	70.7	5.1	14.2	0.1	1.6	3.0	6.9	100.0

B. Imports (f.o.b.)

Sector	Primary commodities						Manufactures				Total
	Food		Petroleum		Other		Machinery, etc.		Other		
Country group	1965	1987	1965	1987	1965	1987	1965	1987	1965	1987	1965-1987
Developing countries	16.9	9.8	8.9	11.6	11.7	10.3	30.8	34.2	28.6	29.1	100.0
By region											
America	13.1	8.4	13.8	16.5	11.6	8.6	32.4	37.3	27.4	25.9	100.0
Africa	17.1	16.1	6.1	8.1	8.3	8.4	34.4	34.7	32.3	29.8	100.0
West Asia	18.2	14.1	7.9	7.7	11.7	7.5	29.9	33.7	30.3	32.5	100.0
Other Asia	19.9	7.3	6.8	11.4	14.5	12.1	28.2	34.5	27.3	30.3	100.0
Least developed countries	22.0	20.0	11.5	16.0	8.0	7.6	22.0	33.7	36.5	22.7	100.0

Source: adapted from UNCTAD, *Statistical Pocket Book*.

Table 90.2 shows that this pattern is slowly changing. In 1965, primary commodities accounted for 85.6 per cent of Third World exports whilst imports of manufactures accounted for 59.4 per cent. By 1987, this had changed to 51.2 per cent and 63.3 per cent respectively.

Table 90.2 highlights some significant points concerning the composition of Third World trade. Oil accounts for a significant proportion of Third World exports. However, oil exports are very unevenly distributed. In the poorest countries of the world (the least developed countries), they accounted for only 5.3 per cent of exports in 1987. In West Asia (which includes Saudi Arabia, Iran and Iraq), they accounted for 77.5 per cent. Textiles are a very important manufactured export, particularly for many Asian countries such as India and Bangladesh. The most significant manufactured import is machinery. Approximately one-third of Third World imports represent investment goods.

Commodity prices

Many Third World countries, particularly smaller countries, are crucially dependent upon the export of one commodity - oil, cocoa, coffee, bananas or sugar cane for instance. Therefore the international price of the commodity has a significant impact upon GNP and the standard of living of the economy. Table 90.3 shows the average annual change in prices for selected primary commodities between 1960 and 1988. The table shows that the current dollar price of commodities rose slightly during the 1960s and rose sharply in the 1970s, but commodity prices have fallen in the 1980s.

However, the current dollar price of a commodity is not the most significant figure for a developing country. What is most important is the trend in prices in terms of what it can buy with the dollar. Inflation in developed countries means that dollar prices of commodities need to keep rising if what a developing country can buy with its dollars is to remain the same. The constant dollar price shows the change in commodity prices adjusted for changes in prices of First World manufactured exports to the Third World. It is a measure of the **terms of trade** (average export prices divided by average import prices ☞ unit 84).

Table 90.3 *Trends in monthly market prices for selected primary commodities*

Commodity	In current dollars			In constant dollars[1]			Commodity	In current dollars			In constant dollars[1]		
	1960-1971	1972-1980	1981-1988	1960-1971	1972-1980	1981-1988		1960-1971	1972-1980	1981-1988	1960-1971	1972-1980	1981-1988
Food							Palm kernels	-0.2	10.5	-11.3	-1.7	-0.5	-14.2
Wheat	-1.4	5.8	-7.7	-3.0	-5.0	-10.6	Palm kernel oil	3.0	11.6	-7.7	1.4	0.6	-10.7
Maize	0.7	7.0	-7.4	-0.9	-4.0	-10.4	Palm oil	-0.3	9.5	-9.5	-1.8	-1.5	-12.4
Rice (free market)	1.0	5.7	-11.0	-0.6	-5.3	-14.0	Linseed oil	-0.9	6.1	-8.4	-2.4	-4.8	-11.4
Bovine meat	8.1	7.2	-1.8	6.5	-3.8	-4.8	**Agricultural raw materials**						
Sugar (free market)	-4.4	3.3	-14.3	-5.9	-7.6	-17.3	Cotton	1.6	8.5	-4.7	0.0	-2.5	-7.7
Bananas (free market)	-1.3	10.5	-1.2	-2.9	-0.5	-4.2	Wool	-8.5	7.1	-0.2	-10.1	-3.9	-3.2
Pepper	4.5	8.2	22.6	2.9	-2.8	19.5	Sisal	-10.7	6.6	-3.8	-12.2	-4.4	-6.7
Soybean meal	1.5	5.0	-4.9	-0.1	-6.0	-7.9	Jute	-0.3	2.4	-0.2	-1.8	-8.5	-3.2
Fish meal	0.9	5.5	-4.5	-0.6	-5.5	-7.5	Hides and skins	2.5	8.5	1.2	1.0	-2.5	-1.8
Tropical beverages							Tropical timber	0.4	10.8	1.4	-1.2	-0.2	-1.6
Coffee	1.5	17.6	1.0	-0.1	6.5	-1.9	**Minerals, ores and metals**						
Cocoa	4.9	19.4	1.0	3.3	8.3	-2.0	Rubber	-4.4	14.6	-2.5	-5.9	3.6	-5.5
Tea	-3.3	11.0	-2.5	-4.8	0.0	-5.5	Phosphate rock	0.4	11.6	-6.3	-1.2	0.6	-9.2
Vegetable oilseeds and oils							Manganese ore	-3.5	10.2	-4.3	-5.0	-0.8	-7.3
Soybeans	1.0	5.3	-5.0	-0.5	-5.6	-8.0	Aluminium	2.6	14.5	2.1	1.1	3.4	-0.9
Soybean oil	1.4	7.5	-6.1	-0.2	-3.5	-9.0	Iron ore	1.5	7.9	-1.6	-0.1	-3.1	-4.5
Sunflower oil	2.6	5.4	-8.4	1.0	-5.5	-11.4	Copper	5.4	4.1	-0.9	3.9	-6.9	-3.9
Groundnuts	3.4	6.6	-9.9	1.8	-4.4	-12.9	Lead	2.6	13.4	-4.5	1.1	2.4	-7.4
Groundnut oil	3.6	7.9	-6.8	2.0	-3.1	-9.8	Zinc	1.8	1.9	-1.0	0.2	-9.1	-4.0
Copra	0.7	10.9	-6.5	-0.8	-0.2	-9.5	Tin	2.1	18.2	-12.2	0.5	7.1	-15.1
Coconut oil	2.9	9.5	-6.8	1.3	-1.5	-9.7	Tungsten	21.5	17.3	-17.8	19.9	6.2	-20.8

1. Constant 1980 dollars (current dollars divided by the United Nations index of export unit value of manufactured goods exported by developed market-economy countries).

Source: UNCTAD, *Statistical Pocket Book.*

Table 90.3 shows that in constant dollar terms, the prices of commodities have been falling for the past three decades and in the 1980s, the price of all commodities fell apart from pepper.

The overall effect of this is shown in Figure 90.2. The peaks in commodity prices in the 1970s were partly due to the rise in oil prices in 1973-4 and 1978-1980. But the general trend in commodity prices at constant dollar prices has been downward. Third World countries today have to export more commodities to get the same number of manufactured goods from the First World than they did in 1970.

One solution to the problem of falling prices is for developing countries to form **cartels** to stabilize or even raise prices. One such cartel, OPEC, has been highly successful since 1973 in achieving at least some of its objectives. However, countries have found it difficult to organise cartels for the sale of most commodities and when cartels have been formed, they have often had to be abandoned at a later date. As was explained in unit 12, cartels fail because:

■ high prices encourage overproduction and cheating on the part of participant countries;
■ it is difficult to persuade all producers to join the cartel;
■ most commodity schemes (unlike OPEC) require the commodity to be produced and then stored if there is oversupply at the minimum price - a costly

process;
■ producers are encouraged to set too high a minimum price, which results in overproduction, and eventually the money to buy up surplus produce runs out.

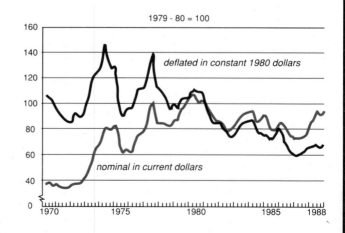

Source: adapted from UNCTAD, *Statistical Pocket Book.*

Figure 90.2 *Monthly index of free market prices of principal commodities exports of developing countries*

Import substitution vs export led growth

A reliance on primary commodities for the main source of exports has proved to be disastrous for many developing countries. Not only have real prices fallen over the past 30 years, but there have been very sharp fluctuations in price of commodities. Third World countries therefore need to diversify. During the 1930s, when the world economy was rocked by the Great Depression in the USA and Europe, many Third World countries, like most First World countries, opted for a policy of **protectionism**. It was argued that the best way to protect jobs and promote the growth of domestic industry was to keep foreign goods out. This then led many Third World countries to believe that their own development could best be promoted through a policy of **import substitution**, the deliberate attempt to replace imported goods with domestically produced goods by adopting protectionist measures.

Whilst import substitution policies might create jobs in the short run, as domestic producers replace foreign producers, economic theory would suggest that in the long run output and growth of output will be lower than it would otherwise have been. This is because import substitution denies the country the benefits to be gained from **specialisation**. The theory of comparative advantage (☞ unit 84) shows how countries will gain from trade. Moreover, protectionism leads to dynamic inefficiency. Domestic producers have no incentive from foreign competitors to reduce costs or improve products. The predictions of economic theory are supported by evidence (for instance, Little, Scitovsky and Scott 1970). Countries which have adopted import substitution strategies have tended to experience lower growth rates than other countries, particularly if they are small countries (the larger the country, the more opportunities there are for specialisation within the country).

The opposite strategy to import substitution is that of **export-led growth**. Rather than becoming less dependent upon world trade, it is argued that growth can be increased by becoming more dependent. Removing trade barriers will force domestic industry either to close or to become as efficient as any world producer. Resources will be reallocated to those industries that produce goods in which the country has a comparative advantage in production. In a developing country, these are likely to be labour intensive, low technology industries. Countries wishing to diversify from exporting commodities can give short term selective assistance to their manufacturing industries. The newly industrialised nations of Brazil and Mexico, and particularly Hong Kong, South Korea and Singapore, have enjoyed above-average growth by adopting such a strategy.

Success has caused its own problems. Cheap imports of textiles, shoes, televisions, toys and a number of other manufactures have led to job losses and factory closures in the First World. During the 1980s, there have been increasing calls in the USA and in Europe for protectionist measures to be taken or strengthened against this 'unfair' competition. Not surprisingly, Third World countries feel that First World countries are more interested in satisfying the vested interests of some in their economy than in helping the Third World develop quickly.

Data question

IVORY COAST STRUGGLES WITH MILLSTONE OF LOW COMMODITY PRICES

Mr Michael Candessus, director general of the International Monetary Fund, has described the Ivory Coast's economic crisis as 'deep and serious'.

Central to the crisis has been the sharp drop in world prices for Ivory Coast's main exports, cocoa and coffee.

Between 1986 and 1989 the real prices of these two exports declined by 48 and 55 per cent respectively, exposing the government's failure to diversify an economy over-dependent on these two crops.

Government critics argue that diversification should have been funded from receipts in the boom years of the mid-to late-1970s and relatively successful mid-1980s. In 1985 cocoa and coffee receipts were worth $1.5bn (£88m); they fell to $776m in 1988 and estimates for last year show little change.

Despite a fall in imports, the balance of payments deficit has more than doubled in the past two years to $1.2bn. As receipts fell, the debts mounted, forcing the government into rescheduling agreements to cope with its $14bn external debt.

But the crisis has been compounded by the government's efforts to cushion cocoa and coffee growers by subsidising producer prices, building up a debt which was being carried by the banks. This created a crisis in the banking sector, only now being resolved.

The scale of the problem was revealed last July. Bank assets were put at $236m, while loans had reached $363m. Recent estimates put the proportion of bad debts at up to 30 per cent, with arrears standing at $145m.

Faced by the urgent need to restructure the economy and reschedule the external debt, the government agreed on a recovery programme supported by a $224m stand-by facility from the Fund, consisting of three main elements: agricultural reforms; reducing the state's dominance of the industrial and manufacturing sectors; and cuts in public spending.

The main plank of the reform platform was put in place last year. The export crop subsidies had cushioned the growers - who with their families account for two-thirds of the Ivory Coast's 11m population - from falling prices.

But with the prices stagnant or falling, the cost proved too high to sustain and by 1989 the state coffee and cocoa marketing board, Caistab, had accumulated a deficit of $440m.

Last September Caistab announced that it intended to pay off its deficit by the end of 1990. Cocoa producers saw a 50 per cent reduction to 200 CFA francs a kilo while the producer price for coffee fell from 150 CFA francs to 100 CFA francs a kilo.

Meanwhile the industrial outlook remains bleak, in part because of the sector's weak base. Of 5,400 companies started between 1980-87, only 13 per cent were involved in manufacturing. Over 60 per cent were involved in trade.

The sector has also been dominated by inefficient government-owned companies. In 1987, 71 per cent of industrial output was in state hands. This combination of trade-based companies and high level of state control illustrates the challenge the Ivory Coast faces if it wants to develop an industrial and manufacturing base which can compete with foreign competitors, both in the domestic market and in West Africa.

The third main plank in the platform of reform involves radical improvements in the state bureaucracy.

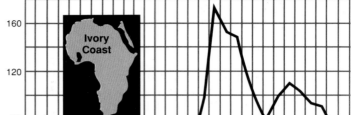

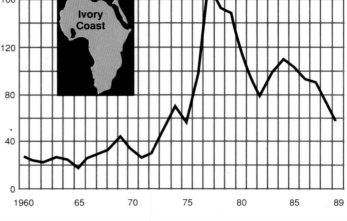

Source: adapted from Gill and Duffus Cocoa statistics.

Figure 90.3 *World cocoa prices*

Inefficient collection of land taxes and business fees, which account for 40 per cent of municipal revenue, are expected to be improved with $25m of the World Bank loans being spent on administrative reforms.

A 10 per cent special entry tax on most imports has also been introduced in a bid to increase revenues by ending widespread tax exemption on imports. Central government costs will also be reduced. A cabinet reshuffle in October led to the number of ministries being cut from 39 to 29.

By the end of this year cuts in government spending are expected to lead to savings of $993m, with the aim of turning the public sector deficit into a 5 per cent surplus by 1992.

Western donors have welcomed these

moves, but the critical question remains whether they can be sustained while commodity prices remain weak and austerity bites.

Source: adapted from the *Financial Times* 10.1.1990.

1. **Briefly outline the problems faced by the Ivory Coast described in the passage and the measures taken to resolve those problems.**
2. **What are likely to be the economic effects of the IMF measures on individual people and firms in the Ivory Coast?**
3. **To what extent could the Ivory Coast influence the price of cocoa and coffee in its favour?**

The colonial experience

From the 16th century onwards, European powers acquired colonial empires throughout most of what we call the Third World today, as well as in North America and Australasia. Colonies were acquired for a variety of reasons, but one major factor was economic gain. In the colonial model of the 19th century, European countries supplied capital to their colonies. They built roads, railways and factories, and invested in agriculture. So there were net **capital flows** to the Third World. However, these capital flows were more than outweighed by the repatriation of **interest, profits and dividends** from Third World colonies back to Europe. After all, there was little point in owning a colony if the colonial power had to pay for the privilege of ownership. Hence, colonial powers could be said to have **exploited** their colonies.

Multi-national companies

When the European powers gave their colonies independence, they often left behind multi-national companies. Indeed, since independence, many multi-national companies such as Coca-Cola have set up in new Third World countries. A multi-national company is one whose shareholders are in mainly one country whilst its operations are in several countries. The aim of a multi-national company is to earn profits for its shareholders. Third World countries should therefore not be surprised that multi-national companies aim in the long term to repatriate more profits to their home country than they invest in the country.

This net drain of resources represents a loss of economic welfare for the Third World economy. However, multi-national companies can also increase economic welfare. Their activities may lead to large increases in exports or falls in imports because of import substitution. This increases the amount of foreign earnings available (net of repatriated profits). It also creates jobs and income in the economy. The activities of multi-national companies may also lead to increased human capital, as local workers are trained in new tasks, and to a transfer of technology if the country can acquire the know-how associated with new capital installed by the multi-national. On the other hand, multi-national companies may be destructive of the local environment and attempt to manipulate the local political process for their own interests.

Multi-national companies are just one way in which resources are transferred between First World and Third World and back again. Foreign aid and commercial loans are two others.

The justification for foreign aid

Following the devastation of the Second World War, the Americans gave Marshall Aid to Europe to help in reconstruction. This became a model for later economic development for the Third World. The argument was persuasive.

- The citizens of Third World countries, because they were so poor, would have a very high propensity to consume and a very low propensity to save. Hence, savings would be likely to be below the level of investment needed to generate high economic growth in the economy. Inflows of foreign capital, for instance supplied through foreign aid programmes, would help fill this **savings gap**.
- Foreign exchange would be extremely scarce. Export revenues would be limited and would be likely to be insufficient to cover imports of machinery and other capital equipment as well as imports of essential raw materials. Foreign aid would help cover this **trade gap**.

Types of foreign aid

Foreign aid can take a variety of forms.

Grants The most generous form of aid is a grant. A donor country might, for instance, give a sum of money to a Third World country for a development project, it might offer free technical expertise, or it might offer free university education for foreign students in the donor country.

Loans Aid might take the form of a loan. The loan might be at commercial rates of interest, in which case the donor country is giving little if anything to the Third World borrower. Alternatively, the loan might be a **soft loan**, a loan which carries a lower rate of interest than the commercial rate of interest.

Tied aid Grants or loans might only be available if the recipient country was prepared to purchase goods and services with the money from the donor country. For instance, during the 1980s the UK government devoted some of its aid budget to backing British exports. UK loan aid was available if a Third World country awarded a contract to a British company.

Bilateral and multilateral aid Bilateral aid is given directly from one country to another. A UK loan to

Kenya would be an example. Multilateral aid describes the situation when donor countries give money to an international agency, such as UNICEF (the United National Children's Fund), and the agency then disperses the aid. The most important multilateral aid agency is the International Bank for Reconstruction and Development (IBRD), more commonly known as the World Bank. Most bilateral aid is tied in one form or another whilst multilateral aid is generally not tied.

An evaluation of foreign aid

Foreign aid has undoubtedly helped millions in the Third World achieve a better standard of living. However, foreign aid has been increasingly criticised by those in both the First World and in the Third World.

■ It is implicitly assumed in the economic argument presented above that Third World governments desire to maximise the economic welfare of their citizens. However, this is not the case in most Third World countries. Governments serve the interests of a narrow range of groups in society, often better-off urban dwellers. Foreign aid monies can be diverted into serving the needs of these groups rather than achieving genuine economic development, particularly for the poor in the Third World.

■ 'Fashions' in foreign aid projects change over time. In the 1950s, large scale projects, such as dams and steel mills, were seen as important in economic development. Many of these projects failed to yield a sufficiently high rate of return. Many large scale manufacturing plant projects failed because of lack of infrastructure and lack of skilled workers and management. In the 1990s, aid to help large numbers of small scale enterprises, particularly in rural areas, is now fashionable. Equally, aid projects are likely to have to pass an environmental audit to prevent large scale ecological disasters which have occurred on some previous aid projects. The question that arises is whether Western aid agencies, even now, know what are the best strategies for development.

■ Foreign aid which takes the form of subsidised food or consumer goods is likely to be positively harmful to long term Third World development. Food aid in a famine situation can be helpful. However, long term food aid, by increasing the supply of food on the local market, depresses local prices and therefore discourages local production of food. This increases the dependence of the country on imported food, uses up scarce foreign exchange and results in lower living standards for farmers.

■ Tied foreign aid, especially in the form of loans, may result in Third World countries getting a worse 'buy' than if they shopped around internationally for the cheapest product.

■ Loans need to be repaid with interest. The repayment of loans has resulted in enormous problems for Third World countries, and it is to this issue that we will now turn.

The Third World debt crisis

Aid has not been the only source of financial capital for Third World countries. They have been free to borrow from banks and on First World money markets. In the 1960s and early 1970s, developing countries used commercial sources of finance to some extent. However, the first oil crisis of 1973-4 proved ruinous for most Third World countries.

Non-oil producing countries were faced with sharply increased bills for imports of oil. An easy way to solve the problem in the short run was to borrow the money to finance increased oil prices.

Oil producing countries, on the other hand, were faced with a sudden inflow of foreign currency. In the very short term, there was no way they could spend this money. In the longer term, countries such as Mexico and Nigeria used the extra revenues to finance investment projects. Others, such as Saudi Arabia and Kuwait, have remained net exporters of capital ever since, building up financial assets in the developed world.

In 1974 and subsequent years, large numbers of petro-dollars (dollars used to pay for oil) were deposited by oil producing countries in Western banks. The banks needed to lend these out again if they were to make a profit. First World countries responded to the first oil crisis by deflating their economies, with the aim of squeezing inflation and reducing balance of payments deficits. They didn't want to borrow the money. So banks turned to the Third World. Countries are good risks, it was argued, because governments cannot go bankrupt. Loans to Third World countries were marketed aggressively by the banks in the second half of the 1970s.

The 1980s proved disastrous both for Third World countries and for banks. In 1980, Ronald Reagan was elected President of the United States. Quickly, he cut taxes whilst leaving government spending totals unchanged. The result was a huge increase in the US government budget deficit. To finance the deficit, the government had to issue enormous amounts of new government stock, which sent US interest rates soaring. Sharply increased interest rates then increased the value of the dollar, as foreign investors demanded dollars to invest in the US. This hit Third World countries hard:

■ increased interest rates meant that repayments on their debt increased sharply;

■ the increased value of the dollar meant that they had to sell far more exports to pay back $1 worth of debt.

In 1982, Mexico precipitated the Third World debt crisis by **defaulting** (i.e. not paying) on part of its loans. The size of the problem can be seen from Table 91.1. Third World debt increased over ten fold between 1973

Table 91.1 *External debt of developing countries[1]*

	$bns
1973	97
1982	662
1986	1 070
1990[2]	1 280
of which	
Latin America	500
Africa	300
Asia	360

1. Excluding oil-dominant economies such as Saudi Arabia and Kuwait.
2. Estimated.

Source: adapted from UNCTAD.

and 1990. Particularly affected were Latin American countries, with Mexico and Brazil having the largest external debts. Africa has suffered badly too because many African economies are amongst the poorest in the world.

Another way of measuring the size of the problem is to consider the ratio of debt to exports. By the mid-1980s, as can be seen from Figure 91.1, the countries with debt-servicing difficulties owed over three year's worth of exports in debt. This would be the equivalent of a household owing three times its annual income in the form of a mortgage. The average debt-service ratio was approximately 20 per cent (i.e. 20 per cent of export earnings in a year was used to repay long term loans together with interest owed). For Latin American countries, the debt-service ratio was over 40 per cent.

Table 91.2 shows the effects of the Third World debt crisis on net flows from the Third World. In the early 1980s, Third World countries on the whole were net importers of capital. Borrowing was greater than repayments of net debt plus interest. Since then, Third World countries have been net exporters, sending funds

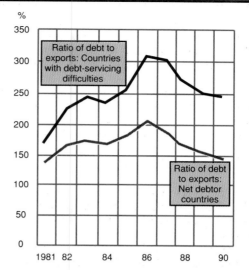

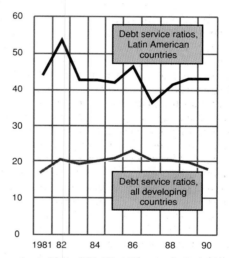

Source: adapted from IMF, *World Economic Outlook*.

Figure 91.1 *Debts and exports*

Table 91.2 *Net transfer of financial resources of groups of developing countries, 1980-1989[1] (billion dollars)*

	1980	1981	1982	1983	1984	1985	1986	1987	1988	1989[2]
Surplus energy exporters	-91.4	-44.6	2.0	26.4	17.8	11.5	28.7	11.8	15.8	5
Capital importing economies of which	31.9	49.1	31.0	-5.9	-33.0	-24.4	-16.5	-47.8	-40.8	-36
Africa[3]	–	14.8	13.9	7.7	1.9	-1.5	5.4	- 0.2	3.9	3
Latin America and the Caribbean	11.4	14.0	3.4	-25.6	-35.2	-31.4	-15.0	-19.3	-22.4	-28
Four recent surplus economies in Asia[4]	6.9	3.9	- 0.3	-4.1	-8.3	-10.9	-22.7	-28.5	-23.4	-16
Other Asia and Europe	13.7	16.4	14.0	16.1	8.5	19.3	15.8	0.2	1.0	4
All developing countries	-59.5	4.5	33.0	20.5	-15.2	-12.9	12.1	-36.0	-24.9	-32

1. Expenditure basis (negative of balance on payments of goods, services and private transfers, excluding investment income).
2. Preliminary estimate.
3. Excluding Libyan Arab Jamahiriya and South Africa.
4. Hong Kong, Republic of Korea, Singapore and Taiwan Province of China.

Source: adapted from United Nations, *World Economic Survey 1990*.

back to the First World as during the colonial period. Latin America in particular has been very badly affected. In 1989, for instance, $28 billion more was sent abroad in interest payments and repayment of existing debt than was loaned to the continent from developed countries.

The effect of the debt crisis on countries most affected has been to reduce growth rates and often to make growth rates negative. Africa, for instance, was probably poorer in 1990 than in 1980. In order to repay debt and interest, countries have been forced to increase exports and reduce imports. Usually this has been accomplished by pursuing deflationary policies, cutting back on government expenditure (such as education and health) and reducing investment programmes. In the process, it is often the poorest who have been most affected.

OVERPRICING OF AFRICAN IRON AND STEEL IMPORTS

Alexander Yeats (1990) found that African countries consistently paid more than the cheapest world price for iron and steel products between 1962 and 1987. He suggested a number of reasons why this might be the case.

■ African countries relied on a small number of suppliers rather than shopping around for the best deal internationally.
■ They kept commercial contacts with relatively few countries. The most important was usually the ex-colonial power. Hence, the former colonial power became a monopoly supplier to the Third World country.
■ The smaller the country the less likely it was to 'shop around'.
■ Countries were often locked in to suppliers because of tied bilateral aid.
■ To qualify for preferential access for their exports of iron and steel goods to the EC under the Lomé Convention, African countries had to buy the iron and steel from the EC.
■ Multi-national companies forced their African subsidiaries to buy iron and steel from Europe at high international prices. This is a hidden way of repatriating profits from Third World countries.

1. **How did European steel producers gain monopoly powers over African countries in the post-colonial period and what effect did this have on prices paid for steel imports by these Third World countries?**
2. **Suggest ways in which African countries could buy their steel more cheaply whilst at the same time not reducing their ability to export to the EC.**

Table 91.3 *Overpricing of iron and steel products to former African colonies by selected European countries*

| | Average premium charged to former colonies | | | |
	Belgium	France	Portugal	United Kingdom
1962-63	20.7	36.9	12.7	4.0
1966-67	25.7	21.0	25.6	14.4
1970-71	15.2	16.7	43.7	13.0
1974-75	26.4	8.1	42.9	9.9
1978-79	37.0	26.1	26.8	15.1
1982-83	25.5	8.6	69.7	36.5
1986-87	31.5	66.5	72.6	53.0

Source: 'Do African countries pay more for imports?' by Alexander Yeats, IMF, *Finance and Development*, June 1990, Volume 27 number 2.

A. The Common Agricultural Policy

Aims

- To describe the operation of the Common Agricultural Policy.
- To assess its impact on an individual farmer in the UK, and on an individual family.
- To evaluate proposed reforms of CAP, with particular reference to an individual farmer and an individual family.
- To argue the case for a particular set of reforms, considering them both from the viewpoint of economic efficiency and equity.

Research activity

This is likely to be best done as a group task. A group could undertake the research and then individuals could write reports based upon the group's findings.

Your first task is to find a farmer who is willing to be interviewed. One of your teaching group may have a parent, or other relation or friend who is a farmer. Alternatively, write off to the local branch of the NFU (National Farmers' Union).

Prepare a questionnaire. You want to find out what effect the Common Agriculture Policy has on the farmer, what could be the effect of proposed reforms and what reforms the farmer thinks are necessary. For instance, what crops does the farmer grow which are covered by price regulation under CAP? What livestock is reared which is subject to intervention pricing or quotas? What is the effect of set-aside on the farmer's activities? What does the farmer think about proposals to cut farm subsidies? Does the farmer think that he or she should be paid an allowance for 'keeping the country tidy'?

Agree with the farmer upon a place and a time for the interview. This could be in school or college, or it could be at the farm. Before the interview, outline the sort of questions that you will be asking at the interview. State that the more facts and figures that he or she can give, the better you will be able to understand the effect of CAP on farming. You may wish to record the interview rather than taking notes at the time. Permission to do so **must** be asked in advance.

Before the interview, familiarise yourself as much as possible about the operations of CAP and proposed reforms. For instance, go to your local public library and undertake a newspaper and magazine search for any articles about CAP published over the last 6 months. Use an index to help you with your search. The librarian will be able to tell you what indexes are available in the library. Follow the news on radio and television. Listen in particular to the daily radio broadcast on Radio 4, Farming Today, at 6.10 a.m.

At the same time as you are working through the process of interviewing a farmer, consider the impact of CAP on your own family and other consumers throughout the EC. How much does it cost taxpayers to fund CAP? How much extra does the average family have to pay in higher food prices because it has to buy expensive EC food rather than food from outside the EC available at lower world prices? If possible, find one of the reports completed on the cost of CAP. These include:

- National Consumer Council (1985), *Consumers and the CAP* (HMSO); OECD (1986), *The World Development Report* (Oxford University Press);
- Canberra Centre for International Economics (1988), *Macroeconomic Consequences of Farm Support Policies* (CIE).

A summary of some material is contained in The Treasury, *Economic Progress Report* (February 1988).

Structuring your report

Introduction Outline the aims of your investigation.

The Common Agricultural Policy Explain briefly how the Common Agricultural Policy works. Outline, also briefly, any proposed reforms of CAP currently being discussed.

Effects of CAP on an individual farmer Explain your research findings. Assess the impact of CAP on the prices received for produce by the farmer, the influence CAP has on levels of output, and the effect of CAP on costs, revenues and profits of the farm.

CAP and the consumer What is the impact of CAP on the taxpayers and consumer in the EC? How much lower could the annual food bill of your family be if CAP were abolished and food were available at world prices?

Analysis of proposed reforms What effect would proposed reforms have on the individual farm surveyed? For instance, what would be the effect on prices, output, revenues and profits? What would be the effect on the taxpayer and the consumer?

Evaluation of reforms Outline what you think would be an equitable and efficient reform of CAP. When coming to a conclusion, consider the impact of your proposals on the farmer you have interviewed, as well as on the average family.

Sources Outline the sources of information you used. Evaluate critically the reliability of the information given by the interviewee. What data would you have liked to have obtained but could not?

Other suggestions

Instead of considering the impact of the CAP on farmers and on individuals, it would be possible to consider the impact of the 1992 process on a firm and on individual families. Find out as much as possible from books, newspapers and magazines about the Single European Market before interviewing a local business person. Evaluate the costs and benefits to the firm, to a household as a consumption unit, and to a household as a provider of factors of production, particularly labour.

Alternatively, consider the impact of the moves towards a single European currency. What effect has British entry to the ERM already had on a particular business and a particular family? What are likely to be the consequences if Stage 2 and Stage 3 of the Delors plan are implemented?

B. Comparative advantage

Aims

- To undertake a household survey.
- To present the findings of the survey.
- To apply economic theory in order to analyse and account for patterns of world trade.
- To evaluate reasons for the lack of international competitiveness of UK industry.
- To assess how British industry and the UK government could improve the competitiveness of industry.

Research activity

Your first task is to survey the contents of your house. Select 50 items at random and for each write down its country of origin. Then choose 10 goods from your list. These should represent a variety of different goods, rather than be a bundle of similar goods. No more than 25 per cent of the goods should be of British origin. Include if possible the family car.

You now need to find reasons why the goods you have selected from your survey are produced in a particular country. Use the theories of trade that you have learned (such as the theory of comparative advantage) to formulate a hypothesis for each good about the reasons for its origin. Then attempt to find evidence to support or refute the hypothesis. For instance, does the country of origin enjoy the benefit of cheap labour, or abundant reserves of a particular raw material? Has the country a reputation for high quality design or manufacture of the good? Do trade statistics show that the country is a particularly strong exporter of the good?

A wide variety of statistics about world trade and world economies are available in publications from the UN (United Nations), GATT (General Agreement on Trade and Tariffs), UNCTAD (United Nations Conference on Trade and Development), the IMF (International Monetary Fund), OECD (Organisation for Economic Co-operation and Development) and the World Bank (IBRD, the International Bank for Reconstruction and Development). Large public reference libraries tend to take a variety of these publications but exactly what is available varies from library to library. Ask the librarian for help in locating what they carry in stock.

CSO publish several publications detailing UK trade. The standard reference source is *UK Balance of Payments (Pink Book)*. Some statistics are published in the *Annual Abstract of Statistics* (updated monthly in the Monthly Digest of Statistics) whilst detailed figures are given in *Overseas Trade Statistics of the UK*.

In addition, quality newspapers and magazines publish occasional articles about world trade in particular commodities. It should be relatively easy to find articles about world trade in cars, clothes or shoes for instance. Use whatever indexes are available in your local large public reference library. For instance, the *Financial Times* and the *Economist* produce indexes to their publications, whilst the *Research Index*, published by Business Surveys Ltd., covers 100 newspapers and magazines on a monthly basis.

Structuring your report

Introduction Outline the aims of your report.

Trade theory Describe briefly one or more theories of trade. Identify the main factors which are likely to explain why world trade takes place. In the light of these factors, state the hypotheses you formulated about the reasons for the origin of each good.

Your survey Describe the survey you conducted and present its findings. Classify the countries of origin for the 50 goods (e.g. UK, EC, Third World, Far East).

Analysis of survey results To what extent does evidence support or refute your original hypotheses? In some cases, you will have found it more difficult to gather evidence than in others. Don't be afraid of stating this. Equally, don't be afraid of saying that the evidence refutes your original hypothesis. In some cases, it may be unclear as to why a particular country should have produced a particular product.

Evaluation On the basis of your analysis, state what you think British firms need to do if they are to regain market share in the domestic market and gain increased market share abroad? What policies should governments pursue to help them achieve this?

Sources Outline the sources of information you used. What problems did you encounter in gathering relevant data? What data would you have liked to have obtained but could not? To what extent were the data reliable?

Other suggestions

Instead of looking at a number of different goods for a number of different countries, it would be possible to concentrate on the reasons for trade for a particular economy, such as Hong Kong, Singapore, Japan or France. Describe the trade flows from the country and then assess the extent to which theories of trade can account for these particular patterns.

Alternatively, it would be possible to consider changing patterns of trade for a particular good or commodity. For instance, how has world trade in cars changed over the past 30 years? Can economic theory account for this changing pattern of trade?

You could also choose a particular good and consider how its UK production and trade have changed over time. What factors might account for the changes you have found?

Summary

1. Inflation is a general sustained rise in the price level.
2. Inflation is measured by calculating the change in a weighted price index over time. In the UK this index is called the Retail Price Index.
3. A price index only measures inflation for average households. It also cannot take into account changes in the quality and distribution of goods over time.
4. Inflation is generally considered to give rise to economic costs to society. These include shoe-leather and menu costs, psychological and political costs, and costs which arise from the redistribution of income in society. Some economists believe that inflation also results in higher unemployment and lower growth in the long term.
5. Unanticipated inflation tends to give rise to higher economic costs than anticipated inflation.

The meaning of inflation

INFLATION is defined as a sustained general rise in prices. The opposite of inflation - DEFLATION - is a term which can have two meanings. Strictly speaking it is defined as a fall in the PRICE LEVEL. However it can also be used to describe a slowdown in the rate of growth of output of the economy. This slowdown or **recession** is often associated with a fall in the **rate of inflation**. Before the Second World War, recessions were also associated with falls in prices and this is the reason why deflation has come to have these two meanings.

A general rise in prices may be quite moderate. CREEPING INFLATION would describe a situation where prices rose a few per cent on average each year. HYPER-INFLATION, on the other hand, describes a situation where inflation levels are very high. There is no exact figure at which inflation becomes hyper-inflation, but inflation of 100 or 200 per cent per annum would be deemed to be hyper-inflation by most economists.

Measuring inflation

The inflation rate is the change in average prices in an economy over a given period of time. The price level is measured in the form of an **index** (☞ unit 3). So if the price index were 100 today and 110 in one year's time, then the rate of inflation would be 10 per cent.

Calculating a price index is a complicated process. Prices of a representative range of goods and services (a **basket** of goods) need to be recorded on a regular basis.

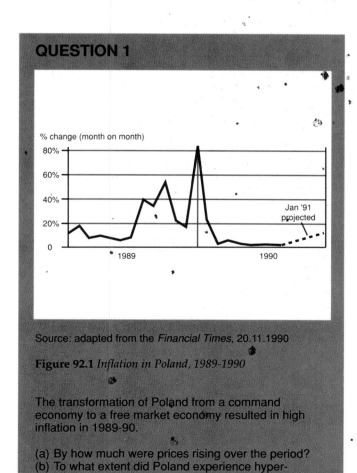

QUESTION 1

% change (month on month)

Jan '91 projected

1989   1990

Source: adapted from the *Financial Times*, 20.11.1990

Figure 92.1 *Inflation in Poland, 1989-1990*

The transformation of Poland from a command economy to a free market economy resulted in high inflation in 1989-90.

(a) By how much were prices rising over the period?
(b) To what extent did Poland experience hyper-inflation between 1989 and 1990?

In the UK, the most widely used measure of the price level is the Retail Price Index. In theory, each month, on the same day of the month, surveyors are sent out to record 175 000 prices for 600 items. Prices are recorded in different areas of the country as well as in different types of retail outlets, such as corner shops and supermarkets. These results are averaged out to find the average price of goods and this figure is converted into **index number form.**

Changes in the price of food are more important than changes in the price of tobacco. This is because a larger proportion of total household income is spent on food than tobacco. Therefore the figures have to be **weighted** before the final index can be calculated. For instance, assume that there are only two goods in the economy, food and cars, as shown in Table 92.1. Households spend 75 per cent of their income on food and 25 per cent on cars. There is an increase in the price of food of 8 per cent and of cars of 4 per cent over one year. In a normal average calculation, the 8 per cent and the 4 per cent would be added together and the total divided by 2 to arrive at an average price increase of 6 per cent. But this provides an inaccurate figure because spending on food is more important in the household budget than spending on cars. The figures have to be weighted. Food is given a weight of $3/4$ (or 0.75 or 750 out of 1 000) and cars a weight of $1/4$ (or 0.25 or 250 out of 1 000). The average increase in prices is 8 per cent multiplied by $3/4$ added to 4 per cent multiplied by $1/4$ (i.e. 6 per cent + 1 per cent). The weighted average is therefore 7 per cent. If the RPI were 100 at the start of the year, it would be 107 at the end of the year. In order to calculate a weighting, it is necessary to find out how money is spent. In the case of the Retail Price Index, the weighting is calculated from the results of the Family Expenditure Survey. Each year, a few thousand households are asked to record their expenditure for one month. From these figures it is possible to calculate how the average household spends its money. (This average household, of course, does not exist except as a statistical entity.)

Table 92.1

Commodity	Proportion of total spending	Weight	Increase in price	Contribution to increase in RPI
Food	75%	750	8%	6%
Cars	25%	250	4%	1%
Total	100%	1 000		7%

The accuracy of price indices

It is important to realise that any price index is a weighted average. Different rates of inflation can be calculated by changing the weightings in the index. For instance, the Retail Price Index calculates the average price level for the average household in the UK. But it is possible, again using data from the Family Expenditure Survey, to calculate price indices for pensioner households or one parent households. One major difference between these households and the average household is that they spend a larger proportion of their income on food. So a 10 per cent rise in the price of food compared to a 5 per cent rise in the price of all other items will result in a higher rate of inflation for pensioners and one parent households than the average household. In fact each individual household will have a different rate of inflation. The Retail Price Index only measures an average rate of inflation for all households across the UK.

The household spending patterns upon which the index is based also change over time. For instance, food was a far more important component of the Retail Price Index 30 years ago than it is today because spending on food was then a higher proportion of total spending. The index cannot indicate changes in the quality of goods. Cars might increase in price because their specification improves rather than because there has been an inflationary price rise. The weights for the Retail Price Index are changed annually to take account of changes in spending patterns. But this does not get round the fact that the average 'basket' or 'bundle' of goods purchased in 1950 and upon which the RPI for 1950 was calculated was very different from the average bundle of goods purchased in 1990.

QUESTION 3

Table 92.3 *Index of Retail Prices*

	Average annual percentage change				
	1976-1981	1981-1986	1987	1988	1989
General index	13.4	5.5	4.2	4.9	7.8
Pensioner index, two person household	12.8	5.3	2.6	3.8	5.5

Source: adapted from CSO, *Economic Trends Annual Supplement.*

(a) Explain why the change in the General Index of Retail Prices may differ from the change in the Pensioner Index.

(b) A two person pensioner household where the pensioners retired in 1976 receives pensions linked to the General Index of Retail Prices. In which years would they on average have seen (i) an increase and (ii) a decrease in their real purchasing power? Explain why this occurs.

The costs of inflation

Inflation is generally considered to be a problem. The higher the rate of inflation the greater the economic cost. There are a number of reasons why this is the case.

Shoe-leather costs If prices are stable, consumers and firms come to have some knowledge of what is a fair price for a product and which suppliers are likely to charge less than others. At times of rising prices, consumers and firms will be less clear about what is a reasonable price. This will lead to more 'shopping around', which in itself is a cost.

High rates of inflation are also likely to lead to households and firms holding less cash and more interest bearing deposits. Inflation erodes the value of cash, but since nominal interest rates tend to be higher than with stable prices, the opportunity cost of holding cash tends to be larger, the higher the rate of inflation. Households and firms are then forced to spend more time transferring money from one type of account to another or putting cash into an account to maximise the interest paid. This time is a cost.

Menu costs If there is inflation, restaurants have to change their menus to show increased prices. Similarly, shops have to change their price labels and firms have to calculate and issue new price lists. Even more costly are changes to fixed capital, such as vending machines and parking meters, to take account of price increases.

Psychological and political costs Price increases are deeply unpopular. People feel that they are worse off, even if their incomes rise by more than the rate of inflation. High rates of inflation, particularly if they are unexpected, disturb the distribution of income and wealth as we shall discuss below, and therefore profoundly affect the existing social order. Change and revolution in the past have often accompanied periods of high inflation.

Redistributional costs Inflation can redistribute income and wealth between households, firms and the state. This redistribution can occur in a variety of ways. For instance, anybody on a fixed income will suffer. In the UK, many pensioners have received fixed pensions from private company pension schemes which are not adjusted for inflation. If prices double over a five year period, their real income will halve.

Any group of workers which fails to be able to negotiate pay increases at least in line with inflation will suffer falls in their real incomes too. For instance, the UK government has kept a tight rein on public sector pay during the 1980s. In some years, public sector workers, faced by a monopsony employer, have been forced to accept cuts in their real pay because their pay increase has been less than the rate of inflation. Overall, public sector pay has not kept pace with private sector pay resulting in a change in pay differentials between the two sectors.

If **real** interest rates (☞ unit 70) fall as a result of inflation, there will be a transfer of resources from borrowers to lenders. With interest rates at 10 per cent and inflation rates at 20 per cent, a saver will lose 10 per cent of the real value of saving each year whilst a borrower will see a 10 per cent real reduction in the value of debt per annum.

Taxes and government spending may not change in line with inflation. For instance, if the Chancellor fails to increase excise duties on alcohol and tobacco each year in line with inflation, real government revenue will fall whilst drinkers and smokers will be better off in real terms assuming their incomes have risen at least by as much as inflation. Similarly, if the Chancellor fails to increase personal income tax **allowances** (the amount which a worker can earn 'tax free') in line with inflation, then the burden of tax will increase, transferring resources from the taxpayer to the government.

Unemployment and growth Some economists, mainly monetarists, have claimed that inflation creates unemployment and lowers growth. Inflation increases costs of production and creates uncertainty. This lowers the profitability of investment and makes businessmen less willing to take the risk associated with any investment project. Lower investment results in less long term employment and long term growth.

There is also a balance of payments effect. If the exchange rate does not fully adjust to **purchasing parity** levels (☞ unit 87), exports will become less competitive and imports more competitive. The result will be a loss of jobs in the domestic economy and lower growth.

Anticipated and unanticipated inflation

Much inflation is **unanticipated**: households, firms and government are uncertain what the rate of inflation will be in the future. When planning, they therefore have to estimate as best they can the expected rate of inflation. It is unlikely that they will guess correctly and hence their plans will be to some extent frustrated. On the other hand, inflation may be **anticipated**. Inflation may be a constant 5 per cent per year and therefore households, firms and government are able to build in this figure to their plans.

Unanticipated inflation imposes far greater costs than anticipated inflation. If inflation is anticipated, economic agents can take steps to mitigate the effects of inflation. One way of doing this is through INDEXATION. This is where economic variables like wages or taxes are increased in line with inflation. For instance, a union might negotiate a wage agreement with an employer for staged increases over a year of 2 per cent plus the change in the Retail Price Index. The annual changes in social security benefits in the UK are linked to the Retail Price Index.

Economists are divided about whether indexation provides a solution to the problem of inflation. On the one hand, it reduces many of the costs of inflation although some costs such as shoe leather costs and menu costs remain. On the other hand, it reduces pressure on government to tackle the problem of inflation directly. Indexation eases the pain of inflation but is not a cure for it.

Key terms

Inflation - a general rise in prices.
Deflation - a fall in the price level.
Price level - the average price of goods and services in the economy.
Creeping inflation - small rises in the price level over a long period of time.
Hyper-inflation - large increases in the price level.
Indexation - adjusting the value of economic variables such as wages or the rate of interest in line with inflation.

Applied economics

The Retail Price Index

In April 1990, the House of Commons Public Accounts Committee investigated the compilation of the Retail Price Index (RPI), following the publication of a report earlier in the year by the National Audit Office (NAO). The report had highlighted a number of problems in the collection of the statistics which form the basis for the calculation of the RPI.

Responsibility for collecting statistics lies with 175 employment service offices round the country. In theory, 175 000 prices are collected each month but in practice only about 95 000 prices were recorded. Of nine offices surveyed in detail by the NAO, eight of them collected between 42 and 84 per cent of the theoretical maximum. The ninth, Camden, was on strike and therefore provided no data. There were a number of reasons why prices were not collected. In Camden, for instance, only one-third of prices were collected regularly because of lack of staff. For the remaining two-thirds, price data was copied forward from price collection forms for the previous month. In general, almost 30 per cent of specific items for which prices were collected at the beginning of the year become unavailable in the course of the year. There was a high turnover of staff collecting the statistics, and staff had no formal training in their task.

The House of Commons Public Accounts Committee was also interested in the complicated way in which housing is included in the the RPI. Increases in the price of houses are not included in the RPI, but changes in the rate of interest on mortgages to finance home buying are included. This means that an increase in the mortgage interest rate will increase the RPI, whilst a reduction in the mortgage rate will lead to a fall in the RPI. If increasing interest rates is used as a way of reducing inflation in the longer term (☞ unit 95), this has the paradoxical effect of increasing the inflation rate in the short term. Many economists have therefore argued that mortgage interest payments should not be included in the RPI.

Equally, occasionally the government changes taxes or changes tax rates. For instance, in 1979, the government cut income tax rates but paid for this by increasing the standard rate of VAT from 8 to 15 per cent. This added approximately 5 per cent to the RPI (5 per cent rather than 7 per cent because items such as food and electricity are not subject to VAT), even though on average people were no better or worse off than before. In 1989 in Scotland and 1990 in England and Wales, the domestic rating system was replaced by the poll tax or community charge and this too increased the RPI.

Some economists argue that these sorts of price changes should be excluded from the RPI. By removing them, an 'underlying' rate of inflation can be calculated which these economists believe is a far better indicator of trends in prices than the RPI. Figure 92.2 shows one such calculation of the underlying rate of inflation for the UK between 1982 and 1990. Note that the 'underlying' rate of inflation can be both above and below the 'all items' RPI. When it is below it, as throughout 1989 and 1990, this tends to indicate that there have been significant recent increases in the mortgage rate. When it is above the underlying rate, there will have been recent cuts in the mortgage rate, 'artificially' depressing the rate of growth of the existing RPI.

On the other hand, the RPI is intended to reflect changes in prices for the average household. To exclude changes in mortgage rates would mean that the RPI no longer served this function, unless some other proxy measure were used to record changes in mortgage repayments by households.

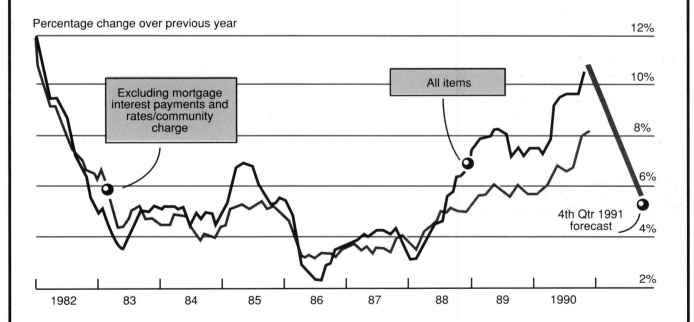

Source: Autumn Statement, 1990.

Figure 92.2 *Retail price inflation*

HALIFAX BUILDING SOCIETY RATES

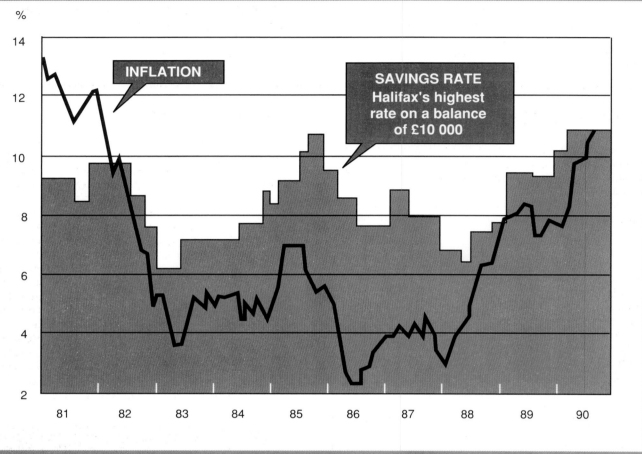

Figure 92.3

1. Outline the changes in the real rate of interest on a £10 000 deposit with the Halifax Building Society between 1981 and 1990.

2. Explain who might have benefited and who might have suffered as a result of these changes.

Summary

1. Monetarists argue that inflation is caused by excessive increases in the money supply.
2. Some Keynesians believe that excess demand in the economy is the principal cause of inflation - the demand-pull theory of inflation.
3. Other Keynesians argue that inflation is primarily cost-push in nature.
4. If inflation is caused by shifts in the aggregate demand or aggregate supply curves, it can only persist if it is either validated or accommodated by an increase in the money supply.

The monetarist explanation

Monetarists argue that the sole cause of inflation is a rise in the money supply. As Milton Friedman put it, 'inflation is always and everywhere a monetary phenomenon'.

This view can be explained using the Fisher formulation of the **quantity theory of money**:

$$MV \equiv PT$$

where M is the money supply, V is the velocity of circulation of money, P is the price level and T the number of transactions over a period of time. In the short run, increases in M will feed through to higher levels of transactions (i.e. national income will rise and unemployment is likely to fall), and a fall in V. This is known as the monetary **transmission mechanism** (☞ unit 81). But in the long run, with V constant, increases in M over and above the rate of real growth in the economy (the change in T) will feed through to changes in P (☞ unit 71).

The effects of an increase in the money supply can be explained using aggregate demand and aggregate supply analysis (☞ unit 82). An increase in the money supply will lead to an increase in aggregate demand through the transmission mechanism. Consider Figure 93.1. Monetarist or classical economists would argue that the long run aggregate supply curve is vertical. The equilibrium level of output is the full employment level Y_F and the initial price level is P_1. An increase in the money supply shifts the aggregate demand curve to the right from AD_1 to AD_2. Initially the economy moves up the short run aggregate supply curve $SRAS_1$ from K to L. But in the longer run, with increased prices and over-full employment, workers will demand and gain wage rate increases which will push the short run aggregate supply curve up to $SRAS_2$ and then to $SRAS_3$. N is the new long run equilibrium point where aggregate demand is once again equal to long run aggregate supply. Output, having initially risen, has returned to its long run full

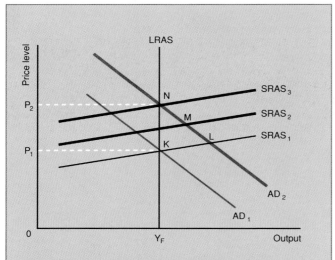

Figure 93.1 *An increase in the money supply*
An increase in the money supply will shift the aggregate demand curve from AD_1 to AD_2. After an initial rise in output, shown by the movement from K to L, the economy will return to long run equilibrium at N. Prices have risen but output remains unchanged.

QUESTION 1
Table 93.1 *The money supply and inflation*

		Percentage change	
	Money supply (£M3)	Real GDP	Prices
1970	9	2.3	6
1971	14	1.4	9
1972	28	3.5	7
1973	27	5.9	9
1974	11	- 0.6	16
1975	6	- 2.1	24
1976	8	4.0	17
1977	9	2.2	16
1978	15	3.5	8

Source: adapted from CSO, *Economic Trends Annual Supplement*.

(a) How do monetarists account for the causes of inflation?
(b) To what extent do the data support this view?

employment level. But prices have risen from P_1 to P_2.

Keynesian analysis suggests that the transmission mechanism is very weak. Rises in the money supply have little effect on aggregate demand and hence they have little impact on the price level. This is not to say that extremely large increases in the money supply will not cause serious inflation. But it makes little difference to inflation whether the money supply grows by, say, 10 per cent a year or 12 per cent a year.

Demand-pull inflation

Monetarists stress that inflation is a **monetary phenomenon**. Keynesians have traditionally argued that inflation occurs because of changes in **real** variables in the economy. One important Keynesian theory is that inflation is caused by excess demand in the economy. The DEMAND-PULL THEORY of inflation says that inflation will result if there is too much money chasing too few goods in the economy.

Figure 93.2 shows the Keynesian 45° line diagram. The economy is at full employment at income Y_F. Planned aggregate expenditure now rises from E_1 to E_2, establishing a new, higher level of equilibrium national income. But the rise in income from Y_F to Y_G cannot be a rise in real income because the economy is already at full employment. It must be a rise in nominal income caused by an increase in prices. This rise in prices can only be prevented by reducing planned expenditure by the size of the **inflationary gap** AB. Inflation is therefore caused by excessive spending by households on consumption, by government on public expenditure or by foreigners on exports.

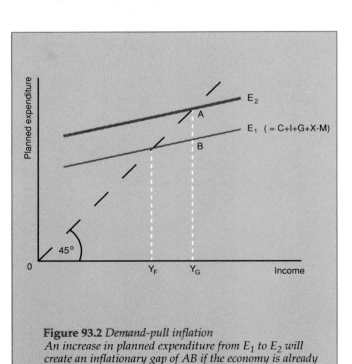

Figure 93.2 *Demand-pull inflation*
An increase in planned expenditure from E_1 to E_2 will create an inflationary gap of AB if the economy is already at full employment. Excess demand pulls up prices leaving real income unchanged.

QUESTION 2
Table 93.2 *Excess demand and inflation*

	Real GDP % change	Unemployment %	Inflation %
1970	2.3	2.6	6
1971	1.4	2.6	9
1972	3.5	2.9	7
1973	5.9	2.0	9
1974	-0.6	2.1	16
1975	-2.1	3.1	24
1976	4.0	4.2	17
1977	2.2	4.4	16
1978	3.5	4.4	8

Source: adapted from CSO, *Economic Trends Annual Supplement*.

(a) Outline a demand-pull theory of inflation.
(b) To what extent do the data support a demand-pull theory of inflation?

Cost-push inflation

A second Keynesian theory of inflation is the COST-PUSH theory of inflation. This states that inflation is caused by increases in costs of production. There are four major sources of increased costs.

■ Wages and salaries. They account for about 70 per cent of national income and hence increases in wages are normally the single most important cause of increases in costs of production.

■ Imported goods. An increase in the price of finished manufactured imports, such as television sets or cars, will lead directly to an increase in the price level. An increase in the price of imported semi-manufactured goods and raw materials, used as component parts of domestically produced manufactured goods, will feed through indirectly via an increase in the price of domestically produced goods.

■ Profits. Firms can raise their prices to increase their profit margins. The more price inelastic the demand for their goods, the less will such behaviour result in a fall in demand for their products.

■ Taxes. Government can raise indirect tax rates or reduce subsidies, thus increasing prices. It can also order nationalised industries to raise their prices more than they might have wished to otherwise. This represents a 'hidden' tax.

There are a number of occasions in the past when there has been a significant rise in prices due to an increase in one of these costs. For instance, all Western economies suffered sharp rises in prices after the four-fold increase in the price of oil in 1973-4.

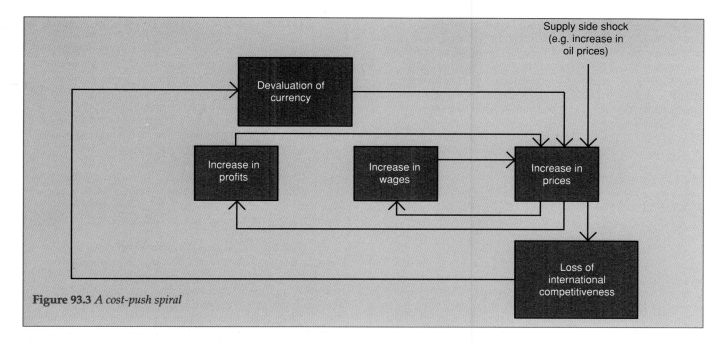

Figure 93.3 *A cost-push spiral*

However, Keynesian economists have argued that a cost-push spiral can develop which leads to a long term cycle of inflation. Consider a developed economy with zero inflation and few natural resources. International commodity prices of products such as oil, gas and coal increase by 50 per cent in one year. Domestic prices rise by 10 per cent as a result. Workers will now be 10 per cent worse off in real terms. So they will press for higher wages. If in the past they have become accustomed to receive a 2 per cent increase in real wages per year, they will be prepared to settle for 12 per cent. Firms pay the 12 per cent and pass on the increase in their costs in the form of higher prices. This fuels inflation. The following year, trade unions will once again fight for pay increases of 2 per cent plus the rate of inflation. In the meantime, the profits of firms will have been declining in real terms. So firms are likely to attempt to increase their profit margins in money terms, again fuelling inflation. This process, shown in Figure 93.3, is called a WAGE-PRICE SPIRAL or sometimes a COST-PUSH SPIRAL.

Keynesian economists differ in their views of whether the spiral is explosive, with inflation increasing over time, or whether inflation will decrease over time. They also differ as to the causes of the cost-push inflation. Some point out that, for the UK for instance, all the major bouts of inflation since 1918 have been started by large increases in the price of imports. Others say that increases in trade union militancy can cause the initial supply side shock which starts the inflationary spiral. Others argue that cost-push inflation is inevitable in a modern economy because of the struggle between workers and capitalists. Both wish to increase their share of national income. Workers force firms to give inflationary pay increases whilst firms increase prices so as to increase their profit margins. There is no solution to this struggle and therefore inflation is bound to be endemic in a modern industrialised society.

QUESTION 3
Table 93.3 *Costs and prices*

	Percentage change		
	Average weekly earnings	Import prices	Retail Price Index
1970	12	4	6
1971	11	5	9
1972	13	5	7
1973	14	28	9
1974	18	46	16
1975	27	14	24
1976	16	22	17
1977	9	16	16
1978	13	4	8

Source: adapted from CSO, *Economic Trends Annual Supplement.*

(a) Outline a theory of cost-push inflation.
(b) To what extent do the data support the view that inflation is mainly cost-push in origin?

Monetary accommodation

Keynesians tend to argue that whilst hyper-inflations are caused by excessive increases in the money supply, the creeping inflation experienced in recent decades in the industrialised world has been caused mainly by changes in real variables. Either there has been excessive spending (demand-pull inflation) or there have been supply side shocks which have increased costs of production. Monetarists would not deny that a supply side shock like the four-fold increase in oil prices in 1973-4 increased prices. But they would argue that this was a once-and-for-all increase, rather like a seasonal increase in the price of tomatoes. It was an increase in prices but it was not inflationary (i.e. it did not in itself cause a general and sustained increase in prices).

Consider Figure 93.4. An increase in oil prices has shifted the short run aggregate supply curve from $SRAS_1$ to $SRAS_2$. The economy has moved from full employment at A to below full employment at B and prices have risen. The economy is now in a position of STAGFLATION or SLUMPFLATION with both price increases and unemployment. Keynesian theory would suggest that workers will now demand higher wage increases to compensate them for increases in prices. But monetarists would question where the money to pay these inflationary wage increases is going to come from. If the money supply is fixed, the aggregate demand curve cannot shift. Wage increases for some workers must be compensated for by wage losses for others. Some workers will 'price themselves out of jobs' as the short run aggregate supply curve rises to $SRAS_3$. Unemployment therefore increases. Eventually workers will start to accept cuts in their wages and this will start to shift the short run aggregate supply curve downwards. Eventually the economy will return to full employment at A at the original price level. So a supply side shock will only be inflationary in the long run if the government allows the money supply to rise to ACCOMMODATE the inflationary pressures within the economy. Accommodation is a very attractive political solution in the short run. Faced with unemployment and inflation, a government can at least reduce unemployment by increasing the money supply and thus increasing aggregate demand. But in the long run such a policy is simply inflationary. What is more, monetarist economists argue that the economy would have returned to full employment anyway through the process of real wage cuts.

The same argument applies to increases in aggregate demand. Assume that firms increase investment when the economy is already at full employment, thus increasing aggregate demand. Prices rise slightly. An increase in investment will almost certainly result in an increase in the demand for borrowed funds. This will increase interest rates. Consumption will fall, whilst on the foreign exchanges there will be an inflow of money from abroad which will finance an increase in imports. Hence domestic aggregate demand will fall to its original level. The expansion in demand is said **not** to have been VALIDATED if the money supply is not increased. If the money supply had been expanded, firms would have reacted by bidding up the price of labour, shifting the short run aggregate supply curve upwards, producing a potential inflationary spiral.

So monetarists argue that demand and supply side shocks cannot cause inflation. It is only if the money supply is allowed to increase that inflation will ensue.

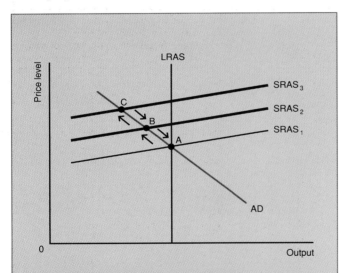

Figure 93.4 *Monetary accommodation*
A supply side shock which shifts the short run aggregate supply curve from $SRAS_1$ to $SRAS_2$ may lead workers to demand inflation-compensating wage increases, shifting the short run aggregate supply curve even farther upward and to the left. But the economy will return to the original point A so long as the government does not accommodate the price rise (i.e. does not increase the money supply which would have the effect of shifting the aggregate demand schedule to the right).

QUESTION 4

(a) Distinguish between monetary accommodation and monetary validation.
(b) Consider the data in Tables 93.1, 93.2 and 93.3. Is there any evidence to suggest that monetary accommodation or validation occurred in the period 1970 to 1978?

Key terms

Applied economics

Inflation in the Lawson boom, 1986-1989

In the first half of the 1980s, the inflation rate fell from 18.0 per cent in 1980 to 4.6 per cent in 1983. Inflation then hovered in the 5 per cent range for the next five years but in mid-1988 it began to increase again. By the end of 1990, the annual growth of the Retail Price Index was over 10 per cent. Why was there this doubling of the inflation rate?

From a monetarist view, the increase in inflation in 1988 can be linked to the jump in the rate of growth of the money supply from 1986. In the early part of the 1980s, the money supply, whether measured as M1, M2, M3 or M4, had grown considerably faster than the level of nominal GDP (i.e. faster than PT in the Fisher equation). As Table 93.4 shows, the annual rate of growth of M4 increased from below 15 per cent per annum to over 15 per cent in 1986 and by 1988 was averaging over 17 per cent. This increase was sufficient to produce the increase in inflation from the middle of 1988. It would suggest that there was a one to two year time lag between initial increases in the rate of growth of the money supply and subsequent increases in the inflation rate at the time.

Keynesians too can provide an explanation of the increase in inflation. As can be seen from Table 93.4, the rate of growth of real GDP increased from a rate of about 3 per cent per annum between 1983 and 1986 to over 4 per cent from the last quarter of 1986. By the first quarter of 1988, annual growth was an unsustainable 5.1 per cent. This very fast growth quickly reduced unemployment from over 3 million in the first half of the 1980s to 1.6 million by the last quarter of 1989, with areas such as the South East of England suffering severe shortages of many types of labour. In Keynesian terms, it could be argued that an inflationary gap had opened, leading to demand-pull inflation.

Table 93.4 *Inflation and its possible determinants*

		Percentage change over previous 12 months				Millions
		Inflation	Money supply	Real GDP	Average earnings	Unempl-oyment
1983	Q1	4.9	14.7	3.2	8.8	3.2
1984	Q1	5.2	11.7	3.4	6.1	3.2
1985	Q1	5.4	14.0	2.3	7.5	3.3
1986	Q1	5.0	13.7	3.1	8.4	3.4
	Q2	2.8	15.3	2.4	8.1	3.3
	Q3	2.7	15.6	3.3	7.4	3.3
	Q4	3.5	15.9	4.0	8.0	3.2
1987	Q1	3.9	14.6	3.7	7.2	3.2
	Q2	4.2	14.1	4.2	7.5	3.1
	Q3	4.3	15.4	5.1	7.9	2.9
	Q4	4.1	16.2	5.1	8.4	2.8
1988	Q1	3.3	16.8	5.4	8.8	2.7
	Q2	4.3	16.9	4.4	8.3	2.5
	Q3	5.5	18.6	4.0	8.4	2.3
	Q4	6.5	17.6	3.5	9.6	2.1
1989	Q1	7.8	18.0	2.9	9.3	2.1
	Q2	8.2	18.6	2.1	9.3	1.9
	Q3	7.7	17.6	1.8	9.9	1.8
	Q4	7.6	18.3	1.7	8.7	1.6

Source: adapted from CSO, *Economic Trends Annual Supplement*; CSO, *Monthly Digest of Statistics*.

Table 93.4 also shows figures for the rate of increase in earnings. Wages are the most significant cost for employers on average. From 1984, there was a gradual increase in the rate of growth of earnings. In the first quarter of 1984, it was 6.1 per cent per annum, but by 1989 it was nearly 10 per cent. This could provide evidence for a cost-push explanation of the rise in inflation.

In fact, it is likely that the increased inflation from 1988 onwards was due to a combination of the above factors. Most economists would accept that aggregate demand increased from 1986 relative to aggregate supply. The increase in the money supply came about, partly because of lower interest rates, but also because of deregulation in the financial markets. In particular, the second half of the 1980s saw the aggressive selling of mortgages as building societies, freed from many of their previous constraints, encouraged customers to borrow money. Banks too entered the mortgage market in an aggressive manner. People moving houses tended to borrow more than they needed to cover the cost of the house purchase and used the cash to buy everything from carpets and curtains to new cars. Increased lending also led to rapid increases in house prices. This encouraged home owners to borrow money secured against the increase in value of their houses.

The consequent increase in consumption then led to increased investment by industry at a time when export sales were growing fast too. Extra spending which led to increased output meant that unemployment fell. With increased tightness in the labour market, workers were able to secure higher wage increases, which led to pressures on costs and prices.

Between 1986 and the middle of 1988, the government **accommodated** the increase in demand by allowing the money supply to rise. However, between 1988 and 1989, in a bid to curb inflation, it doubled interest rates. It takes time for policy to work. The economy began to slow down in 1989 and by 1991 was in recession. Paradoxically, the increases in interest rates, designed to curb inflation, led in the short term to increases in the Retail Price Index (☞ unit 92), which may well have led to increased wage demands by workers attempting to prevent the erosion of their real wage levels. However, by 1991, inflation was beginning to fall.

Data question

MITTERAND, THE MONETARIST

When Francois Mitterand was elected President of France in 1980, he quickly reflated the French economy to tackle rising unemployment. By 1983, the French current account on the balance of payments was in deficit and inflation was not falling fast enough following the second oil crisis of 1978-80. His policy had become unsustainable, especially since the French franc was locked into the Exchange Rate Mechanism (ERM) with low inflation Germany.

In a policy U-turn, the French government deflated the economy with the aim of reducing French inflation rates to those of its German rivals. Growth in GDP fell to less than 2 per cent per annum whilst unemployment rose from 8.3 per cent in 1983 to 10.4 per cent in 1987. Broad money grew by only 53 per cent between 1983 and 1989 compared to 142 per cent in the UK, and inflation fell from 9.6 per cent in 1983 to 2.7 per cent in 1988 and has remained at that level since. Compare this with the increase in the UK inflation rate from 4.6 per cent in 1983 to over 10 per cent by 1990.

The 1990s are likely to see higher economic growth for France, lower unemployment and continued low inflation. By 1990, unemployment had fallen 9 per cent whilst growth had risen to nearly 3 per cent. In the UK, in contrast, unemployment in 1990 was rising with output stagnating as the government attempted to curb inflation.

1. **Suggest reasons why the French inflation rate fell rapidly after 1983.**
2. **Why did the UK not experience a similar fall in inflation?**
3. **Explain why France may enjoy higher rates of economic growth than the UK in the early 1990s.**

Summary

1. The Phillips curve shows the relationship between the rate of change of money wages and unemployment. High unemployment is associated with a low rate of change of money wages, whilst low unemployment is associated with a high rate of change of money wages.
2. Following publication of Phillips's findings in 1958, a view developed that there was a trade-off between unemployment and inflation.
3. From the mid-1960s, the Phillips curve relationship broke down in the UK. The most widely accepted explanation of this is that the original Phillips curve shows the short run adjustment process of the economy assuming money illusion on the part of workers. From the mid-1960s onwards, workers ceased to have money illusion.

4. Classical economists argue that the long run Phillips curve is vertical. Unemployment will always return to its natural rate. The Phillips curve trade off exists only in the short run.
5. A government which increases demand in the economy will succeed in reducing unemployment at the cost of high inflation in the short run, but in the long term unemployment will return to its natural rate at a higher rate of inflation.
6. Policies which succeed in reducing inflation will create unemployment in the short run. Keynesians tend to argue that the unemployment cost will be severe and prolonged. At the other extreme, new classical economists argue that the unemployment cost will be negligible and that the short run adjustment process is rapid.

The original Phillips curve

In 1958, Professor A W Phillips at the London School of Economics published *The Relation between Unemployment and the Rate of Change of Money Wage Rates, 1861-1957*. He showed that there was a remarkably stable relationship between the rate of change of money wages and the level of unemployment. As can be seen from Figure 94.1, high rates of unemployment were associated with low (and even negative) rates of change of money wage rates whilst low rates of unemployment were associated with high rates of change of money wage rates. The line of best fit came to be called the PHILLIPS CURVE.

This relationship provides a useful insight into the causes of inflation. Changes in money wage rates are a

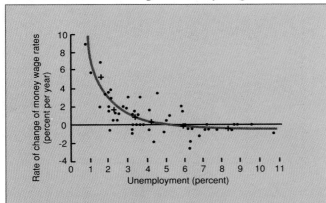

Figure 94.1 *The Phillips curve*
The original Phillips curve was derived from data from the period 1861 to 1913. Phillips then showed that the curve predicted the relationship between the rate of change of money wage rates and unemployment in the period 1913 to 1957.

QUESTION 1

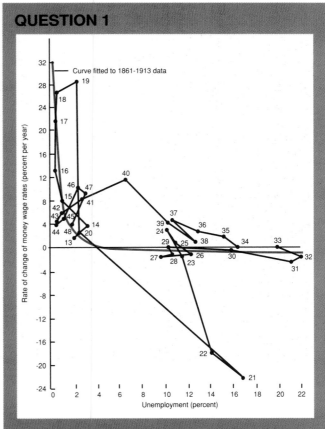

Figure 94.2 *Phillips curve data, 1913-1948*

To what extent do the data shown in Figure 94.2 support the view that there is a stable relationship between unemployment and the rate of change of money wage rates?

key component in changes in prices. Assume money wage rates rise by 10 per cent whilst all other factors remain constant. If 70 per cent of a firm's costs are wages, then its costs will rise by 7 per cent. It is likely to pass these costs on in the form of higher prices. These higher prices will feed through to higher costs for other firms or directly into the inflation rate (for instance, the Retail Price Index in the UK). The higher the rate of change of money wages, the higher the likely rate of inflation. Hence the Phillips curve hypothesis can be altered slightly to state that there is an inverse relationship between inflation and unemployment. When unemployment is low, inflation will be high. When unemployment is high, inflation will be low or even negative (i.e. prices will be falling).

The initial importance of the Phillips curve

The article was important initially for two reasons. Firstly, it helped Keynesians to develop a more sophisticated theory of inflation. In the simplest Keynesian model, the aggregate supply curve is shaped as in Figure 94.3.

Up to the full employment level of income, the supply curve is horizontal. Any increase in aggregate demand will increase output without causing inflation. At full employment, the supply curve is vertical. Any increase in aggregate demand will increase prices without increasing output. But the evidence of the 1950s suggested that the aggregate supply curve was upward sloping near the full employment level of output. Changes in aggregate demand affected **both** output and inflation.

Secondly, policy makers (and particularly

governments) changed their views about how the economy might be managed. Many became convinced that there was a trade-off between unemployment and inflation. Zero inflation (i.e. price stability) could be achieved but only by keeping unemployment at what for the time seemed a relatively high level. On the other hand lower unemployment could be achieved by accepting higher levels of inflation. But it was impossible to set both the rate of unemployment and the rate of inflation.

The breakdown of the simple Phillips curve relationship

Following publication of Phillips' article, a great deal of work was done in the UK and abroad to test the relationship between unemployment and inflation. In general, the relationship seemed to be true in other countries too. In the early 1960s the relationship continued to hold true in the UK. Then from 1966 onwards, it broke down completely. Year after year, points to the right of the original Phillips curve were recorded as shown in Figure 94.7. Even more serious was the fact that no new pattern seemed to emerge. Some economists argued that the original Phillips curve never existed anyway. The accepted theory today is that the Phillips curve as originally plotted was a special case and can be understood only in the wider context of aggregate demand and aggregate supply analysis.

The short run Phillips curve

Assume that prices are stable and that there is an increase in aggregate demand. Perhaps planned investment has increased, or the government wishes to increase its

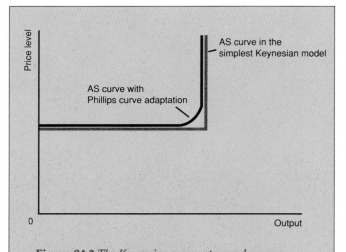

Figure 94.3 *The Keynesian aggregate supply curve The simplest Keynesian model assumes that the aggregate supply curve is horizontal at less than full employment levels of output and then vertical at full employment. With a Phillips curve relationship introduced into the model, the aggregate supply curve becomes upward sloping before reaching full employment output.*

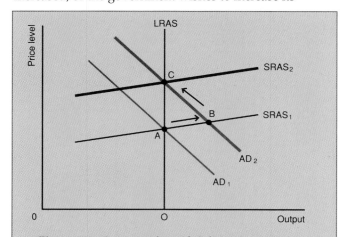

Figure 94.4 *Aggregate demand and aggregate supply An increase in aggregate demand from AD_1 to AD_2 will increase prices. It will also increase output and therefore reduce unemployment. This movement from A to B shows the short run Phillips curve relationship. In the long run the economy moves back to C. There is no trade off in the long run between unemployment and inflation.*

expenditure. This will shift the aggregate demand curve to the right in Figure 94.4. The economy moves along its short run aggregate supply curve from A to B. Note that the movement involves an increase in output and an increase in the price level. An increase in output is usually associated with a fall in unemployment. The increase in the price level is of course inflation. Hence the move from A to B shows the Phillips curve trade-off: higher inflation for lower unemployment. The relationship would be no different if aggregate demand fell, shifting the aggregate demand curve to the left except that lower inflation would be traded off for higher unemployment. So the Phillips curve as originally plotted by Phillips shows what happens when the economy adjusts in the short run to a **demand-side shock**.

The long run Phillips curve with zero inflation

On classical assumptions, point B in Figure 94.4 is not a long run equilibrium point (☞ unit 82). Given that the economy is at full employment at the point A, the economy has moved to a position of over-full employment at B. In the labour market, workers will be able to bid up wage rates, shifting the short run aggregate supply curve upwards. The economy will only return to equilibrium at the point C where aggregate demand once again equals long run aggregate supply. The movement from B to C involves a rise in measured unemployment whilst inflation falls back to zero again when the economy reaches the point C (remember we assumed that the economy had no inflation at A and once the economy reaches C there are no forces which will increase prices any more). In the long run therefore there is no trade-off between inflation and unemployment.

The vertical long run Phillips curve

Over the past 40 years, the UK has suffered from persistent inflation. Up to the mid-1960s, inflation rates were very low, typically in the range 0 to 2 per cent per annum. Since then inflation rates have been very much higher, the peak being nearly 25 per cent in 1975. Households, workers and firms are likely to react very differently to the low creeping inflation seen up to the mid-1960s and the much higher rates experienced since then. Up to the mid-1960s, it is likely that economic agents in the UK suffered from MONEY ILLUSION. This is the belief that prices are stable when in fact they are not. For instance, if a worker received a money wage increase of 2 per cent, she may believe that she is 2 per cent better off. However, if inflation is also running at 2 per cent then she is in fact no better off. She is said to be suffering from money illusion. Her real wage has not changed.

From the mid-1960s, inflation has never been very far away from the main news in the UK. Workers became aware that rises in prices eroded their real standard of

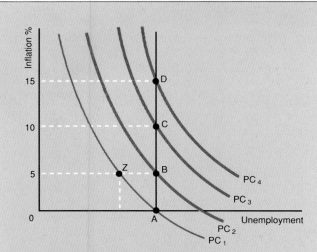

Figure 94.5 *The long run Phillips curve*
In the long run, the Phillips curve is vertical. Attempts by government to reduce unemployment below the natural rate of unemployment OA will be successful in the short run, for instance moving the economy from A to Z. But in the long run the only result will be higher inflation.

living. So they started to negotiate in real terms. Instead of negotiating for a pay increase of 2 per cent, they would negotiate for 2 per cent plus the expected rate of inflation. This affected the position of the short run Phillips curve. In Figure 94.5, the original Phillips curve is PC_1. Workers and firms assume that there will be no price changes and the economy is in equilibrium at the point A. The government now increases aggregate demand, pushing the economy to the point Z on the short run Phillips curve PC_1, reducing unemployment and increasing inflation to 5 per cent. If workers suffer from money illusion, the economy will eventually return to the point A as explained above. But assume that they are more sophisticated and expect inflation to continue at 5 per cent per annum. Workers will bargain for even higher money wages which further push up prices. Hence real wages fall and workers drop out of the labour market. Unemployment will return to a level of OA but a 5 per cent inflation rate will become permanent. The short run

QUESTION 2 In April 1990, the year on year increase in prices was 9.5 per cent. A month later, in May 1990, the National Union of Railwaymen accepted a 9.3 per cent pay offer, having rejected an offer of 8 per cent the month previously. The union stressed that an offer over 9 per cent was necessary if railwaymen were to keep pace with inflation and with current average wage settlements.

(a) Why do the data support the existence of a family of short run Phillips curves?
(b) Would the railwaymens' decision to accept the offer be likely to have been different if inflation had been running at 15 per cent and why?

Phillips curve will have shifted to PC$_2$ and the economy will be at B. If the government attempts again to reduce unemployment, inflation will rise, say to 10 per cent on PC$_2$. In the long run the economy will return to unemployment OA but on a higher Phillips curve PC$_3$.

The natural rate of unemployment

In Figure 94.5, why does the economy keep tending back towards the same level of unemployment, OA? OA is known as the **natural rate of unemployment** (☞ unit 79). It is the rate of unemployment which exists when the economy is in long run equilibrium (i.e. where aggregate demand equals long run aggregate supply). It was explained in unit 80 that the economy, based on classical assumptions, tends towards its long run equilibrium level through changes in wages and prices. If the economy is below the natural rate of unemployment, then aggregate demand is above long run aggregate supply, as at the point B in Figure 94.4. Workers will be able to bid up wage rates, and the short run aggregate supply curve will shift upwards till long run equilibrium is once again re-established. If unemployment is above its natural rate, aggregate demand is less than long run aggregate supply. Unemployment will force workers to accept wage cuts. Firms will then take on more labour, expanding output and lowering unemployment to its natural level.

If the economy is in long run equilibrium, the labour market will also be in equilibrium. So another definition of the natural rate of unemployment is that it is the rate of unemployment which occurs when the demand for labour equals the supply of labour.

In the long run, the economy will always tend towards its natural rate of unemployment. Hence the long run Phillips curve is vertical. It is the line ABCD in Figure 94.5. There is no long run trade-off between unemployment and inflation. A government can reduce unemployment below its natural rate in the short run but, in the long run, unemployment will climb back up again and inflation will be higher.

Reducing inflation

Yet another way of defining the natural rate of unemployment is that it is the rate of unemployment which can be sustained without a change in the inflation rate. Sometimes it is called the NAIRU - THE NON-ACCELERATING INFLATION RATE OF UNEMPLOYMENT. To understand why, consider what happens if the government attempts to reduce inflation. In Figure 94.6, the government wishes to reduce the inflation rate from 10 per cent to 5 per cent. It can only do this by travelling down the short run Phillips curve from the point A to the point B, increasing unemployment in the short term from 1½ million to 3 million. The economy will now slowly return to its natural rate of unemployment of 1½ million at the point C. So to reduce inflation, the government must accept higher unemployment in the short run. If it is not prepared to

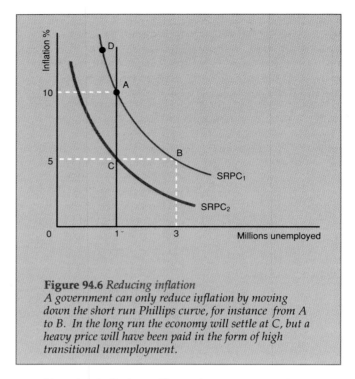

Figure 94.6 *Reducing inflation*
A government can only reduce inflation by moving down the short run Phillips curve, for instance from A to B. In the long run the economy will settle at C, but a heavy price will have been paid in the form of high transitional unemployment.

pay this price, inflation will remain constant at 10 per cent with 1½ million unemployed.

An increase in the inflation rate above 10 per cent can only come about through an increase in aggregate demand over and above what it would otherwise have been. This increase will again move the economy off the point A, this time up the short run Phillips curve to D.

So the labour market can be in equilibrium at the natural rate of unemployment (at the NAIRU) with any inflation rate. Hence, once again the long run Phillips curve is vertical.

The only way to reduce the NAIRU (i.e. push the vertical long run Phillips curve to the left), according to classical economists, is to adopt supply side policies (☞ units 98 and 99).

Keynesians, monetarists and classical economists

The theory that the Phillips curve was vertical in the long run was put forward by the founder of modern monetarism, Milton Friedman. It was he too who suggested that workers might not suffer from money illusion. Hence his theory is sometimes called the **expectations-augmented Phillips curve hypothesis** or **adaptive-expectations hypothesis**.

Many Keynesians doubt the existence of a natural rate of unemployment. This is because they believe that it takes a very long time for labour markets to clear if there is mass unemployment. In Figure 94.6, a government which creates unemployment of CB in order to reduce inflation may well find that the economy gets stuck with an unemployment level of 3 million. Unless it is prepared to wait perhaps a decade or more, it can only reduce unemployment by expanding demand again and accepting higher inflation.

On the other hand, New Classical economists, led in the UK by Professor Patrick Minford of Liverpool University, have suggested that the short run Phillips curve does not exist. In their theory of **rational expectations** they argue that economic agents, such as workers, trade unions and employers, are able to see whether inflation and unemployment are likely to rise or fall in the future. If the government states that it is prepared to accept a rise in unemployment in order to reduce inflation, workers will immediately moderate their wage demands in order to avoid unemployment. Inflation therefore falls

immediately. So the conclusion is that the economy will always be on the vertical long run curve because economic agents perfectly adapt their expectations in the light of economic news.

Key terms

> **The Phillips curve** - the line which shows that higher rates of unemployment are associated with lower rates of change of money wage rates and therefore inflation and vice versa.
> **Money illusion** - when economic agents such as workers believe that changes in money values are the same as changes in real values despite inflation (or deflation) occurring at the time.
> **NAIRU, the non-accelerating inflation rate of unemployment** - the natural rate of unemployment, the level of unemployment which can be sustained with a change in the inflation rate.

QUESTION 3

Table 94.1 *Unemployment and inflation*

		Per cent
	Unemployment	Inflation
1979	4.1	13
1980	5.1	18
1981	8.1	12
1982	9.6	9
1983	10.5	5
1984	10.7	5
1985	10.9	6
1986	11.1	3
1987	10.0	4
1988	8.1	5
1989	6.5	8

Source: adapted from CSO, *Economic Trends Annual Supplement.*

In 1979, the government of Margaret Thatcher was elected with a promise to bring down the rate of inflation.
(a) Using a diagram, explain why reducing the rate of inflation might increase the rate of unemployment.
(b) Do the data suggest that counter-inflation policies in the 1980s had an unemployment cost?

Applied economics

The Phillips curve, 1963-1989

Between 1957, the date of publication of Phillips' original article, and 1965 the UK economy behaved in a way that the original Phillips curve would have predicted. In Figure 94.7, the points for 1963, 1964 and 1965 lie on the original Phillips curve. However, from 1967 combinations of unemployment and inflation rates moved to the right of the original curve. Indeed, rising inflation became associated with rising unemployment, contrary to the predictions of the Phillips curve which suggests a negative correlation between the two variables.

The expectations-augmented Phillips curve hypothesis would suggest that the downward sloping short run Phillips curve had shifted to the right because workers had increased their expectations of future inflation rates. They no longer suffered from money

illusion and hence they took into account future price rises when bargaining for wage increases. Is there any evidence to suggest that workers ceased to suffer from money illusion from the mid-1960s onwards?

One factor must be that inflation from 1964 onwards was much higher than it had been over the previous 40 years. Apart from a brief period during the Korean War in the early 1950s, inflation had at worst been 1 or 2 per cent per annum. Therefore it was a reasonable assumption on the part of workers that money wage increases would roughly equal real wage increases. However, from 1964 onwards, inflation increased substantially, and by 1975 had peaked at 24.1 per cent. It would be surprising if workers had not lost their money illusion after 1964 given these trends.

Another factor must be that 1965 saw the

implementation of the first statutory prices and incomes policy (☞ unit 95). The Labour government of Harold Wilson announced that no wage increases could be awarded for a period of six months in order to curb rising inflation. This ensured that inflation and its control became a central issue in British politics. Workers could not help but become aware that inflation was important for the purchasing power of their wage packets.

The Edward Heath government of 1970-1974 positively encouraged trade unions in 1972-3 to settle for index-linked pay deals with employers as part of its prices and incomes policy. It believed that inflation would fall in the short term and that therefore such deals would produce lower pay rises than if unions had bargained on the basis of the current rate of inflation. In fact, rising world commodity prices, particularly of oil, made these deals inflationary.

Today, it could be argued that trade unions bargain on the basis of 'RPI +'. If inflation is currently running at 10 per cent, then trade unions negotiate on the basis of securing 10 per cent plus a real pay increase. Hence, if government attempts to reduce inflation by increasing interest rates, which in the short term have the effect of increasing the RPI, this could further fuel inflation in the short term, raising the base level from which unions are prepared to negotiate.

If UK inflation falls to German levels in the 1990s, averaging perhaps 1 or 2 per cent per annum, the expectations-augmented Phillips curve hypothesis would suggest that the short run Phillips curve will return to roughly the position that Phillips originally plotted from data for 1861-1957.

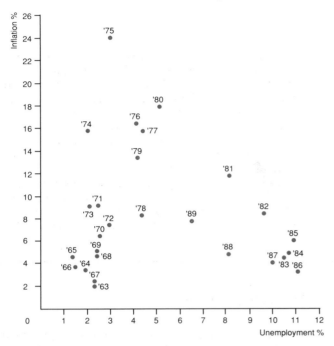

Source: adapted from CSO, *Economic Trends Annual Supplement*.

Figure 94.7 *Phillips curve data, 1963-1989*

WAGE-PRICE SPIRAL FEARS GROW

Fears of a wage-price spiral at the height of the wage-bargaining season have been reawakened by increases in both the rate of average earnings growth and the inflation rate. According to official figures published on Thursday, the annual underlying increase in average earnings rose a quarter of a per cent in February to 9.5 per cent, the first increase in four months. Other figures showed the annual inflation rate reaching 8.1 per cent in March against 7.5 per cent the previous month.

The figures could deal a blow to government and employers' hopes of restraining pay increases; union negotiators will be taking both into account in formulating pay claims, and April is a particularly heavy month for annual pay settlements.

Adding to the problems facing the government and employers is the strong expectation that the Retail Prices Index for April, to be published next month, will show the annual rate of inflation going well over 9 per cent as the community charge or poll tax and Budget increases in excise duties come to be reflected in the figures.

Source: adapted from the *Financial Times*, 14.4.1990.

1. Explain what is meant by a 'wage-price spiral'? Illustrate your answer from the passage.
2. What support does the article give to the expectations-augmented Phillips curve hypothesis?

Summary

1. Economists disagree over the causes of inflation. Monetarists argue that inflation is caused solely by increases in the money supply. Keynesians tend to emphasise that inflation is caused by changes in real variables, in particular excess demand or supply side shocks.
2. If inflation is caused by excessive increases in the money supply, then it can only be curbed by reducing the rate of growth of the money supply through monetary policy. However, a reduction in inflation will necessitate transitional costs of higher unemployment and lower growth.
3. The operation of monetary policy will tend to be more effective if government borrowing is low and if the central bank is independent of government control.
4. Keynesian economists argue that the money supply is endogenous and therefore difficult if not impossible to control. They argue that inflation can only be controlled through control of real variables in the economy. Aggregate demand can be manipulated via fiscal policy. Micro-economic fiscal policies can also be used to break wage-price spirals.
5. Maintaining a stable exchange rate is likely to help in the fight against inflation.
6. Keynesians advocate prices and incomes policies as a possible way of reducing the inflationary impact of supply side shocks. However, it is inappropriate to use them to control inflation caused by excess demand in the economy.

The causes of inflation

A rise in prices is caused either by a rise in aggregate demand or a fall in aggregate supply or some combination of both (☞ unit 82). Any single rise in prices is not necessarily 'inflationary' because inflation is defined as a sustained rise in prices. For inflation to occur, therefore, there must be a **sustained** rise in aggregate demand or fall in supply.

Economists disagree about the fundamental causes of such a sustained rise in prices. Monetarists argue that a rise can only be sustained if there is a sustained rise in the money supply over and above the rise in the level of output. Hence inflation is a monetary phenomenon. Keynesians would not disagree with part of this analysis. For inflation to occur, rises in aggregate demand must be **validated** by a rise in the money supply. The same is true of aggregate supply. A fall in aggregate supply is only inflationary if supply side shocks are **accommodated** by increases in the money supply (☞ unit 93). However Keynesians stress that the inflation seen in the post-war era in Western industrialised economies has been caused by changes in real variables.

The emphasis placed on a particular cause of inflation will influence the choice of policy used to control it. Monetarists would argue that the control of the money supply is the only effective means of regulating inflation. Real variables will find their own value through the market mechanism. Keynesians argue that the control of real variables, such as aggregate demand and aggregate supply, would be more effective in controlling inflation. Put another way, monetarists argue that inflation can only be controlled through **monetary policy** (☞ units 72 and 73). Keynesians argue that monetary policy is ineffective. Inflation is best controlled through policies such as fiscal policy (☞ unit 77) and **incomes policy** (☞ below).

Monetary policy

The monetarist view According to monetarists, monetary policy is the only effective tool available to control inflation. Assume that a government wishes to eliminate inflation from the economy. To do this, it must restrict the growth of the money supply. The link between a fall in the money supply (or a moderation in its rate of growth) is known as the monetary **transmission mechanism** (☞ unit 81 and summarised in Figure 95.1). A restrictive monetary policy will result in a fall in the supply of money relative to the demand for money (i.e. households and firms now hold less money than they desire). They will react by attempting to increase their holdings of money. They will sell some of their non-money financial assets such as stocks and shares, or they will borrow money. They may also reduce their expenditure on goods and services thus enabling them to hold more money in their pockets or accounts. Sales of financial assets, or increasing demand for borrowed funds, will force up the rate of interest (☞ unit 70) which in turn will lead to a reduction in both consumption and investment. So both directly and via the interest rate mechanism, restrictive monetary policy will moderate the growth of aggregate demand or even reduce it. This leads to a fall in inflation.

Note that the government may choose to attempt to restrict the money supply by raising interest rates (☞ unit 72). This is what the UK government did in the late 1980s to reduce inflation. High interest rates, as just described, lead to a fall in consumption and investment and therefore aggregate demand, which in turn leads to a fall in inflation.

Political considerations If it is so easy to reduce inflation, why then is inflation such a persistent problem in many economies such as the UK? Monetarists would

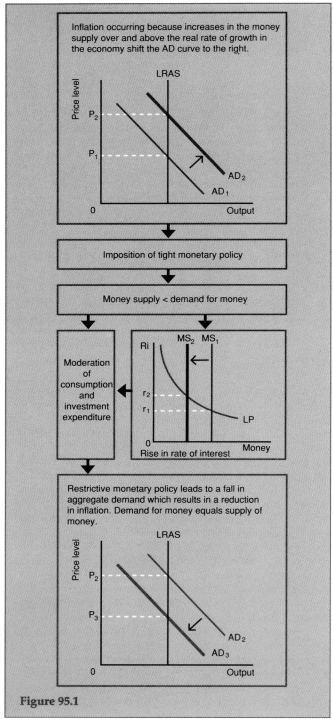

Inflation occurring because increases in the money supply over and above the real rate of growth in the economy shift the AD curve to the right.

Imposition of tight monetary policy

Money supply < demand for money

Moderation of consumption and investment expenditure

Restrictive monetary policy leads to a fall in aggregate demand which results in a reduction in inflation. Demand for money equals supply of money.

Figure 95.1

popularity by **increasing** the rate of growth of the money supply. Votes can be won by cutting taxes and raising public spending. If this is financed not by genuine borrowing but by resorting to the printing presses, then interest rates will fall. This will stimulate consumer and investment spending and reduce unemployment. The government has created an artificial boom. In the long run the economy must return to its **natural rate of unemployment**, but the price level will have risen in the process of adjustment.

The greatest danger, according to monetarists, is that governments will become more and more afraid of tackling inflation because of the consequences for unemployment and output in the short term. To avoid short term political unpopularity, government will continually validate (i.e. print the money to finance) ever increasing rates of inflation. The higher the rate of inflation, the more severe is likely to be the slump needed to return the economy to a low inflation point.

Regulations and rules Monetarists tend to be deeply suspicious of government intervention. They argue that there are ways of ensuring that governments are restricted in their power to print money. One way is to limit the amount that government can borrow in any one year. Government borrowing in the UK is known as the PSBR (Public Sector Borrowing Requirement). The larger the PSBR, the higher will need to be the rate of interest in the economy (☞ unit 73) if the PSBR is financed by genuine borrowing. High interest rates are politically unpopular. Therefore the higher the PSBR, the more tempted governments will be to finance their borrowing by resorting to printing the money.

Secondly, monetarists tend to support the creation of independent central banks whose duty is to maintain price stability. In an economy like the UK, the central bank is effectively controlled by the government. Therefore there is no institution which can resist inflationary policies. In Germany and the USA, central banks are independent and are free to pursue counter-inflationary monetary policy without the need to worry about short term political pressures.

The Keynesian view Keynesians do not deny that controlling the money supply will lead to a reduction in inflation. But they are sceptical of the efficacy of monetary policy. The problem according to Keynesians is that governments cannot control the growth of the money supply directly. The money supply is determined not by the central bank but by the banking system. The money supply is not **exogenous** but **endogenous** (☞ unit 73).

Moreover, there is no precise relationship between the money supply and inflation. Keynesians would not dispute that an annual growth rate of the money supply of 1 000 per cent will increase prices by roughly 1 000 per cent. But as recent evidence from the UK economy shows, the money supply can grow by anything up to 20 per cent a year and inflation can still be very low.

Raising interest rates might be effective in reducing aggregate demand, but it is an inefficient policy. It disproportionately affects demand for durable goods

argue that it is because governments lack the political will to control inflation. In the short run, a reduction in the rate of growth of the money supply, which in turn leads to a fall in aggregate demand, will lead to a fall in output and a rise in unemployment. This is the short run Phillips curve relationship (☞ unit 94). Unemployment and low growth is politically unpopular and governments are often swayed not by what is best for the economy in the long run but by short term electoral considerations.

Moreover, governments can gain short term political

traditionally bought on credit, and those with large mortgages. High interest rates also reduce investment. Raising income tax spreads the burden across far more individuals and far more sectors of industry and works far quicker.

Keynesians would also question the priority given to the control of inflation. It is not obvious that creating millions of unemployed people in the short term is worth a long term reduction in inflation. Moreover, the labour market is highly inflexible. The 'short term' could be five, ten, fifteen or even twenty years (☞ unit 79). Validating or accommodating inflation by increasing the money supply could lead to less loss of economic welfare than the slump that occurred for instance in the early 1980s in the UK.

One final point is that a tight monetary policy causes increased inflation in the short term. Higher interest rates mean higher mortgage repayments which in the UK are a component part of the Retail Price Index. This is likely to lead to higher wage claims which make the process of adjustment to a lower inflation rate a more difficult and longer process.

QUESTION 1 In the UK it has long been taken for granted that the government has the right to use public resources to purchase elections ... Since the Second World War, growth in the UK has tended to peak at around the time of an election, with inflation duly following a year or two thereafter ... A government that wishes to increase public expenditure or lower taxes will find it politically more effective to do so by increasing its borrowing than raising taxes or cutting spending. In time, a larger deficit will usually result in monetary expansion and so inflation ... The solution is to tie the government's hands ... Mrs Thatcher should sacrifice political control and choose an independent Bank of England that would be as good as the German Bundesbank.

Source: adapted from an article by Martin Wolf in the *Financial Times*, 19.10.1989.

(a) Explain why there might be a link between elections and inflation.
(b) Why would giving independence to the Bank of England help break this link?

Fiscal policy

Keynesians tend to argue that fiscal policy can play a crucial role in controlling inflation. If inflation is demand-pull in nature, then an inflationary gap (☞ unit 77) can be controlled by a reduction in government spending or a rise in taxation. In the 1950s, 1960s and 1970s, changes in income tax were widely used in the UK to affect the level of government borrowing. Reducing the PSBR or increasing the PSDR (Public Sector Debt Repayment) will reduce the growth of aggregate demand and therefore reduce the growth of inflation.

Governments can also influence wage-push spirals by

artificially manipulating indirect tax rates. In a wage-push spiral, workers press for wage increases which are equal to a real increase plus the rate of inflation. For instance, if workers want a 2 per cent real increase and the expected inflation rate is 8 per cent, then they will press for a 10 per cent pay rise. But if the inflation rate is 18 per cent they will press for a wage rise of 20 per cent. Governments can reduce the expected rate of inflation by not raising indirect taxes in money terms. For instance, in the UK excise duties tend to be raised each Budget in order to maintain the real value of the tax. Fully indexing all excise duties tends to add about 1 per cent to the Retail Price Index each year. If the Chancellor chooses not to raise duties, the expected rate of inflation will fall, thus moderating pay claims.

If the government owns key industries, like the railways or the Post Office, it can again reduce expected inflation by not raising prices in line with inflation. The result is that these industries make lower profits or even losses, but this may be a small price to pay for lower inflation.

Lower taxes paid by industry will reduce industry's costs. Reducing corporation tax or employers' National Insurance contributions may therefore help break a cost-push spiral. It would be foolish for a government to lower taxes and leave government spending unchanged if the aim were to reduce inflation. It would replace an element of cost-push inflation with more demand-pull inflation. So real public expenditure must be reduced too. One way of reducing real public expenditure is to keep public sector pay below the rate of inflation. This has the added counter-inflationary bonus that government can set an example to private sector workers of what might be the 'going-rate' of pay increase. If the government sets a ceiling of 4 per cent instead of 8 per cent on public sector pay increases when the rate of inflation is 8 per cent, then private sector workers may be prepared to accept 9 per cent wage increases instead of 10 per cent.

Monetarists see all such measures as futile. Tinkering around with indirect taxes to achieve an artificially low rate of inflation can only be a short term measure. It fails to tackle the underlying cause of inflation which is too high a rate of growth of the money supply. As for demand side measures, they only work because the government is simultaneously reducing the rate of growth of the money supply. If the government raised taxes and reduced public spending but allowed the money supply to continue to grow, inflation would still continue. Fiscal austerity only works if its implementation involves monetary austerity.

QUESTION 2 Each year, the Chancellor in his Budget is faced with the choice of whether or not to increase excise duties on alcohol, tobacco and petrol.
(a) Explain why, on cost-push grounds, increasing duties would increase inflationary pressures in the economy.
(b) Why, on demand-pull grounds, might increasing duties reduce inflationary pressures?

Exchange rate policy

In an open economy like the UK, exchange rate policy can be an important component of any counter-inflationary package. Put simply, any devaluation or depreciation of the currency will raise the price of imports (☞ unit 100). Hence devaluation or depreciation can be a source of cost-push inflation. Maintaining the value of the currency, for instance through buying and selling on the foreign exchange markets or increasing domestic interest rates could therefore, according to Keynesians, play an important part in keeping inflation under control.

Some monetarists, too, favour exchange rate stability but for different reasons. A fall in inflation, according to monetarists, can only arise if there is a fall in the rate of growth of the money supply. It can be very difficult to control the money supply directly, so central banks wishing to impose a tight monetary policy may well resort to raising interest rates. (A rise in interest rates with a stable demand for money must be the result of a fall in the money supply.) A rise in interest rates will curb domestic spending and reduce inflationary pressures. Higher interest rates will also attract inflows of financial capital from abroad. The result will be a rise in the exchange rate. This will help reduce inflation because the price of imports will fall. It will also make domestically produced goods less competitive against imported goods, forcing domestic producers to cut costs if they wish to stay in the market.

However, the price of a fall in inflation will be unemployment and loss of output, as implied by the short run Phillips curve. To avoid part of this cost, some monetarists argue that it would be far better for a currency to be pegged to a low inflation currency. An example would be the pegging of the pound to the deutschmark via the EMS (the European Monetary System ☞ unit 102). The free market mechanism would then set to work to reduce inflation. If inflation in the UK continued to be higher than in Germany, UK goods would become less competitive in relation to German goods. UK imports would rise and UK exports would fall. This would impose a deflationary effect on the UK economy. Unemployment would rise and firms would be unable to offer inflationary pay rises to their workers without going out of business. Pay settlements would moderate, the growth in the demand for money would slow and hence

inflation would fall. But the unemployment costs would be lower than if the exchange rate were allowed to rise.

So some monetarists believe that pegging the currency is a way of controlling the money supply. Other monetarists argue that the only way to control the money supply effectively is to control the money supply itself. But it should be remembered that economists disagree about whether or not this is possible.

Prices and incomes policies

PRICES AND INCOMES POLICY is a policy designed to limit the growth of prices and incomes directly. For instance, a government could impose a price freeze and/or an incomes freeze. This means that prices and incomes are not allowed to rise. The government, however, could just control incomes, limiting their growth to 2 per cent for instance, or allowing them to rise only in line with inflation.

Incomes policies became fashionable in the 1960s when it was hoped that their introduction could push the short run Phillips curve to the left. This would enable a government to run the economy with a given level of unemployment at a lower rate of inflation than would otherwise be the case. Unfortunately this displayed a lack of understanding of the economics behind the Phillips curve.

Incomes policies can help reduce inflation caused by supply side factors. Assume that there is a sharp rise in the price of imports which in turn leads to a sharp rise in the Retail Price Index. Workers increase their wage demands, threatening to set off a wage-price spiral. The government could react by tightening monetary policy, allowing the economy to fall into recession and purging the economy of inflation through increased unemployment. An incomes policy offers a less harsh solution. By imposing maximum pay increases, the government breaks the cost-push spiral and helps the economy return to price stability at much lower cost in terms of unemployment.

However, prices and incomes policies cannot be used to repress inflation caused by demand side factors indefinitely. If government continues to allow aggregate demand to exceed aggregate supply, for instance through its own excessive spending or through excessive money supply expansion, then prices will rise sharply following the ending of an incomes policy to what they would have been without the policy. Indeed the excess demand will tend to contribute to the breakdown of the incomes policy. Firms will know that they could charge higher prices for their products because there is excess demand in the economy. Therefore they will be more prepared to award higher wage rises to workers than if there were no excess demand. Workers will realise that firms are prepared to pay higher wages and will be prepared to fight, for instance by taking industrial action. The incomes policy collapses leading to a surge of inflationary wage increases.

An incomes policy may help curb inflation in the short

QUESTION 3 'The exchange rate is the link between one country's price level and another's. If sterling is linked to a non-inflationary currency such as the D-Mark, there is no way in which the movement of prices in traded goods and services in Britain can diverge from that of Germany's in the long run; and a link with the D-Mark becomes a partial substitute for the Gold Standard anchor.'

Source: Samuel Brittan, *Financial Times*, 22.6.1989.

Explain why Samuel Brittan argues that UK inflation can be reduced if it is linked to the deutschmark.

QUESTION 4
Table 95.1

	1974	1975	1976	1977	1978
Change in money supply (£M3) %	11	6	8	9	15
Change in prices %		16	24	17	16	8

Source: adapted from CSO, *Economic Trends Annual Supplement*.

In 1973-4, the UK economy suffered a severe supply side shock arising from large increases in the price of imported commodities, particularly oil. Import prices rose 46 per cent in 1974. In 1975, the Wilson government negotiated an incomes policy with the trade unions which was to last till 1979. However, by 1978, workers were becoming increasingly frustrated with low pay increases. In the winter of 1978/9, the 'winter of discontent', key groups of workers succeeded in breaking the pay guidelines.

(a) Why might the incomes policy described in the passage have helped reduce inflationary pressures?
(b) Why might the changes in the money supply shown in Table 95.1 help explain why workers found it possible to break the incomes policy in 1978/9?

run if inflation is caused by supply side factors. But there is considerable debate about whether an incomes policy has any place in the long run management of an economy. Any guidelines or maximum levels of pay imposed by a policy tend to become norms - every worker receives the government set pay increase. Pay differentials between workers therefore do not change. But pay differentials would change over time if all markets were free. This creates grave problems. In expanding industries for instance, employers would probably like to pay their workers more in order to recruit labour, whilst in declining industries employers might want to pay their workers less, unworried that they might then lose workers. Firms and workers therefore become increasingly resentful of the operation of the incomes policy and have an ever increasing incentive to break it.

Key terms

Prices and incomes policy - a policy designed to limit the growth of prices and incomes directly.

Applied economics

Prices and incomes policies

Prices and incomes policies have been used three times in the post-war era in an attempt to control inflation.

1966-1970 under the Labour administration of Harold Wilson The first prices and incomes policy evolved as a response to rising inflation in the mid-1960s, at a time when the overriding government priority was to secure exchange rate stability and an equilibrium on the current account (☞ unit 100). As shown in Table 95.2, the government initially imposed a prices and incomes freeze in August 1966. The policy was **statutory** (i.e. legally enforceable), which meant that it was illegal either for firms to raise prices or award pay increases. Gradually the policy was relaxed, so that by 1969-70, the target was for a maximum 3.5 per cent increase in wages.

1972-1974 under the Conservative administration of Edward Heath Faced with rising inflation in 1972, the Heath government imposed a statutory incomes policy in November of that year. Again, it started off with a wage and price freeze, followed by a gradual relaxation of policy.

Table 95.2

Time	Measure	Target wage increase per annum %
8.66 - 12.66	Statutory freeze	0.0
1.67 - 6.67	Severe restraint	1.0
7.67 - 3.68	'Nil norm'	3.0
4.68 - 3.69	Ceiling (first year)	3.5
4.69 - 3.70	Ceiling (second year)	3.5
11.72 - 1.73	Statutory wage and price freeze	0.0
1.73 - 4.73	Phase 1, extension of freeze	0.0
4.73 - 9.73	Phase 2, £1 + 4 per cent	average 7.3
10.73 - 2.74	Phase 3, £2.25 per week or 7 per cent	7.5 - 10
74 - 8.75	'Social Contract', voluntary restraint	
8.75 - 8.76	£6 per week	10
8.76 - 8.77	£2.50 - £4.50 or 5 per cent	10
8.77 - 8.78	Maximum 10 per cent plus productivity	10
8.78 - 79	Maximum 5 per cent plus productivity	5

1975-1979 under the Labour administration of Harold Wilson and James Callaghan The Labour government elected into office in 1974 had negotiated a 'Social Contract' with the trade unions. The Labour Party had offered to increase pensions, repeal anti-union laws and take other measures which would favour trade union members if the trade unions restrained their wage demands. The Social Contract had no effect at all on pay bargaining and so in 1975 the Labour government negotiated a more binding voluntary agreement with the trade unions. The trade unions agreed to accept a maximum £6 a week pay increase, with nothing for those earning over £8 500 a year from August 1975. A loosening of pay policy occurred until 1978 when Denis Healey, the Chancellor, proposed to reduce the maximum pay increase from 10 per cent in 1977-8 to 5 per cent in 1978-9. The unions effectively refused to endorse this and in the autumn and winter of 1978-9 there were a series of important and crippling strikes. The government had no legal power to force private sector employers to keep to the 5 per cent guideline. In the public sector, workers were eventually bought off by a promise to set up a commission to consider pay comparability (these pay awards came to be called 'Clegg awards' after the Chairman of the Commission set up to judge the claims). However, the incomes policy had been broken and the 'winter of discontent' was an important factor in causing the Labour Party defeat and Conservative election victory in June 1979.

Incomes policy was used in each case to stem rising inflation. Inflation initially fell but then economic forces were too strong for the government of the day to prevent the incomes policy being broken by powerful trade unions. In each case, the government paid for its failure by losing an election. In 1974, Edward Heath called an election on the issue of whether the miners, who were on strike and crippling the economy, should be allowed to break the incomes policy - he lost. In 1978-9, the 'winter of discontent' paved the way for a Conservative election victory.

In retrospect, it is clear that an incomes policy cannot be successful if the government is allowing aggregate demand to rise at a faster rate than aggregate supply. 1973-4 and 1978-9 were both boom periods for the UK economy - times when it could be expected that inflationary pressures would be particularly high.

Many economists argue that prices and incomes policies only work if the underlying monetary and fiscal policies are bearing down on inflation. An incomes policy is essentially cosmetic, although it might be useful for breaking inflationary expectations to some extent. Other economists argue that incomes policies can be a useful tool in managing the economy so long as they are not used in isolation to bring down rising inflation. Richard Layard, for instance, has argued the case for an incomes policy based upon taxing firms which grant pay increases above a norm. The extra taxes paid by firms paying above the norm would be redistributed to all firms, leaving the total corporate tax burden unchanged. However, firms paying above the norm would be penalised in comparison with those paying below the norm. This would provide a powerful incentive for firms to hold down wage settlements.

Layard's proposals remain untried, and with the UK moving towards closer European integration, it is possible that responsibility for the control of inflation will pass from the UK government to a European central bank and Brussels.

ECONOMY RESPONDING TO TIGHT MONETARY POLICY

John Major, then Chief Secretary to the Treasury, claimed in April 1989 that the economy was responding to the government's tight monetary regime. He said that it would not 'happen overnight' but evidence that the government's policies were working was accumulating gradually. House price rises and turnover had slowed and that in turn was feeding through to lower consumer spending on household durables.

'Recent statistics on retail sales and M0 confirm that consumer spending growth is slowing down in response to the tightening of monetary policy against a background of a Budget surplus', he said. Inflation would be defeated he claimed.

Source: adapted from the Financial Times, 28.4.1989.

1. **Explain, using illustrations from the passage, how a tight monetary policy might lead to a fall in inflation.**

96 Unemployment

Summary

1. Unemployment is a stock concept, measuring the number of people out of work at a point in time.
2. Unemployment will increase if the number of workers losing jobs is greater than the number of people gaining jobs.
3. The costs of unemployment include financial costs to the unemployed, to taxpayers, and to local and national economies. They also include non-financial costs such as possible increased vandalism or increased suicides.

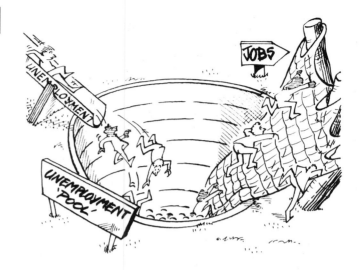

The measurement of unemployment

Unemployment, the number of people out of work, is measured at a point in time. It is a **stock concept** (☞unit 111). However, the level of unemployment will change over time. Millions of people seek jobs each year in the UK. Young people leave school, college or university seeking work. Former workers who have taken time out of the workforce, for instance to bring up children, seek to return to work. Workers who have lost their jobs, either because they have resigned or because they have been made redundant, search for new jobs. Equally, millions of workers lose their jobs. They may retire, or leave work to look after children or they may resign or be made redundant from existing jobs.

Unemployment in an economy with a given labour force will increase if the number of workers losing jobs is greater than the number of people gaining jobs. In 1990, for instance, between 200 000 and 350 000 workers a month either gained or lost jobs. However, the numbers gaining a job were slightly lower per month than the numbers losing jobs. The result was a net rise in unemployment over the year. This flow of workers into or out of the stock of unemployed workers is summarised in Figure 96.1.

Unemployment will also increase if there is a rise in the number of people seeking work but the number of jobs in the economy remains static. During most years in the 1970s and 1980s, there was a rise in the number of school leavers entering the job market as well as more women wanting a job in the UK. It can be argued that at least some of the increase in unemployment in these two decades was a reflection of the inability of the UK

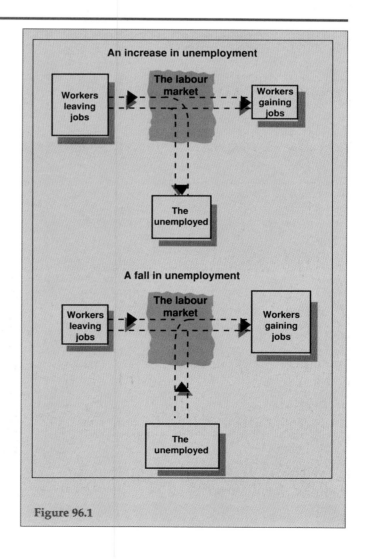

Figure 96.1

economy to provided sufficient new jobs for these extra workers in the labour force.

The costs of unemployment

Long term unemployment is generally considered to be a great social evil. This is perhaps not surprising in view of the following costs of unemployment.

Costs to the unemployed and their dependants The people who are likely to lose the most from unemployment are the unemployed themselves. One obvious cost is the loss of income that could have been earned had the person been in a job. Offset against this is the value of any benefits that the worker might receive and any value placed on the extra leisure time which an unemployed person has at his or her disposal. For most unemployed it is likely that they will be net financial losers.

The costs to the unemployed however do not finish there. Evidence suggests that unemployed people and their families suffer in a whole number of other ways. One simple but very important problem for them is the stigma of being unemployed. Unemployment is often equated with failure both by the unemployed themselves and by society in general. Many feel degraded by the whole process of signing on, receiving benefit and not being able to support themselves or their families. Studies suggest that the unemployed suffer from a wide range of social problems including above average incidence of stress, marital breakdown, suicide, physical illness, mental instability and that they have higher death rates.

Costs to local communities Costs to local communities are more difficult to establish. Some have suggested that unemployment, particularly amongst the young, leads to increased crime, violence on the streets and vandalism. Areas of high unemployment tend to become run down. Shops go out of business. Households have no spare money to look after their properties and their gardens. Increased vandalism further destroys the environment.

Costs to taxpayers The cost to the taxpayer is a heavy one. On the one hand, government has to pay out increased benefits. On the other hand, government loses revenue because these workers would have paid taxes if they had been employed. For instance, they would have paid income tax and National Insurance contributions on their earnings. They would also have paid more in VAT and excise duties because they would have been able to spend more. So taxpayers not only pay more taxes to cover for increased government spending but they also have to pay more because they have to make up the taxes that the unemployed would have paid if they had been in work.

Costs to the economy as a whole Taxpayers paying money to the unemployed is not a loss for the economy as a whole. It is a **transfer payment** (☞ unit 57) which redistributes existing resources within the economy. The actual loss to the whole economy is two-fold. Firstly there is the loss of output which those workers now unemployed could have produced had they been in work. The economy could have produced more goods and services which would then have been available for consumption. Secondly there are the social costs such as increased violence and depression which are borne by the unemployed and the communities in which they live.

Applied economics

Unemployment

Measures of unemployment

In economic theory, the unemployed are defined as those without a job but who are seeking work at current wage rates. Measuring the number of unemployed in an economy, however, is more difficult than economic theory might suggest. There are two basic ways in which unemployment can be calculated.

- Government can undertake a survey of the population to identify the employed and the unemployed. This is the approach taken in countries such as the USA, Japan and Sweden. The UK government also does an annual survey of the workforce, called the Labour Force Survey, but this does not provide the main unemployment statistic for the UK economy.
- The government can count all those who register as unemployed. In some countries, a register of the unemployed is kept by trade unions because unemployment benefit is linked with union membership. In the UK, before 1982, the official monthly unemployment count was based on the numbers who had signed on at Jobcentres. The count was then changed to those who were

claiming benefit for being unemployed from the Department of Health and Social Security (now the Department of Social Security, DSS).

How many unemployed?

Underestimation The way in which unemployment is calculated is very important because the method used to some extent determines the number of people officially counted as unemployed. For instance, during the 1980s, the UK government made a number of important changes in the method of calculating the numbers unemployed. Critics would argue that these changes mean that the unemployment figures in the UK now underestimate the number of unemployed.

In 1979, anyone registered with a Jobcentre as seeking work and not in paid employment was counted as unemployed. Registration at a Jobcentre was a condition for receiving any form of unemployment benefits.

- In November 1981, males over 60 were offered higher supplementary benefit rates to induce them to declare themselves as retired rather than claim unemployment benefit which would have put them

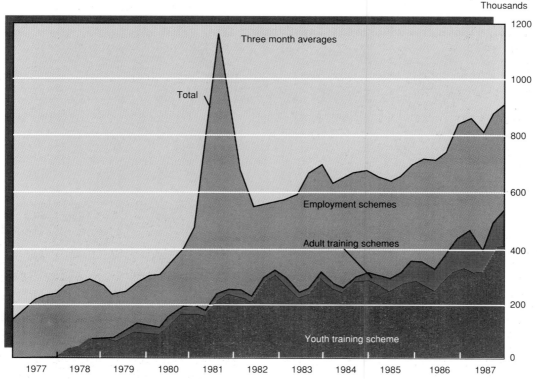

Source: adapted from CSO, *Social Trends*.

Figure 96.2 *Employment and training measures. Numbers of people supported (Great Britain)*

on the register of the unemployed. This cut the numbers unemployed by an estimated 37 000.

- In October 1982, the count was transferred from Jobcentres to the DHSS. There was a 190 000 fall in the numbers unemployed. Most of these will have been women who had registered at Jobcentres because they were seeking work but were unable to claim benefits because their husbands were earning too much and because they were unable to claim National Insurance benefits in their own right.
- In March 1983, another 162 000 non-working males over 60 left the count when they no longer had to register as unemployed in order to be given free contributions to the National Insurance Fund.
- In March 1986, 50 000 disappeared from the register when a two week time lag in counting the unemployed was introduced.
- In July 1986, the government changed the method of calculating the percentage unemployment rate. Before 1986, the total number unemployed was divided by the numbers of employed and unemployed. After May 1986, the percentage unemployment rate was calculated by dividing the unemployed by the total of employed, unemployed, self-employed and HM Forces. By making the denominator larger, the government cut the percentage unemployment rate by 1.5 per cent.
- A further 50 000 disappeared in September 1988 when no youngster under the age of 18 was allowed to register as unemployed. It was argued that any unemployed 16 or 17 year old could not be genuinely unemployed because all were guaranteed a place on the Youth Training Scheme.

In the late 1980s, it was argued that the government put greater pressure on the long term unemployed either to join a training scheme or to go on the Enterprise Allowance Scheme (☞ unit 55). They did this by threatening to withdraw unemployment benefits from those who refused. Exactly how many joined government schemes unwillingly is impossible to estimate. However, Figure 96.2 gives the number of workers on various government schemes during the 1980s. Most of these workers would probably have been unemployed if they had not been on a scheme.

The official UK count also does not capture a large number of hidden unemployed workers. These are mostly women who never signed on at Jobcentres or who now are not eligible for benefit but who would accept employment if offered. The size of this hidden unemployment can be gauged from the fact that 220 000 workers disappeared from the workforce between 1980 and 1983 at a time when unemployment rose from 1.6 million to 3.1 million. Yet between 1983 and 1986 the workforce rose by 1.2 million and the number of females in employment rose by 700 000 at a time when unemployment hovered at just above the 3 million level.

Overestimation Some economists argue that the official UK count vastly overestimates the numbers unemployed. They argue that more accurate figures could be obtained if the following were removed from the official count.

- They argue that there are a large number of officially unemployed workers not actively seeking work and who therefore cannot be called 'unemployed'.
- The severely disabled and the mentally or physically handicapped are unemployable and therefore again should be stripped out of any calculation of unemployment.
- Some workers have jobs in the black economy but continue to claim benefits.
- Workers who are between jobs, for instance those workers out of work for four weeks or less, should not be included as part of the unemployment total as they may not actually be 'unemployed'.

A true level of unemployment Table 96.2 contrasts the two viewpoints that the benefit count in the UK is an accurate measure of unemployment. On the left, it is suggested that the official UK count underestimated the true level of unemployment by 1.45 million in 1988. On the right, the true level of unemployment is estimated at just 900 000.

Table 96.2 *Two measures of unemployment, 1988*

Underestimation		Overestimation	
Unemployed excluded by statistical changes in the 1980s	700 000	Claimants not looking for jobs	500 000
Government schemes	250 000	Unemployed workers e.g. the handicapped	150 000
Unregistered unemployed	500 000	Job changers - out of work for four weeks or less	350 000
		Black economy workers claiming benefit	250 000
Total underestimate	1 450 000	Total overestimate	1 250 000
Official unemployment count	2 150 000	Official unemployment count	2 150 000
Total unemployment	3 600 000	Total unemployment	900 000

Source: adapted from *The Daily Telegraph*.

There are two other measures of unemployment available for the UK. The annual Labour Force Survey defines the unemployed as those seeking work in the last week and who have not done any work whatsoever in the last week before the Survey. In 1989, 590 000 were seeking work but were not counted as officially unemployed because they were not entitled to claim benefit. On the other hand, there were 510 000 registered unemployed who were not looking for work or who were not available for work even though they were claiming benefit. This would suggest that the benefit-based UK count gave a reasonable estimate of unemployment (excluding those on government schemes) even if the method of arriving at the figure was rather dubious.

The OECD (Organisation for Economic Co-operation and Development) also publishes unemployment figures for the UK based upon a count of those seeking work in the last four weeks and who have not done any work during that period. Their estimate is slightly above the official UK count. In July 1990, the OECD figure for the rate of unemployment was 6.2 per cent, compared with a 5.7 per cent figure from the official UK count.

MILLION JOBLESS 'LOST' FROM TALLY

More than a million people have been removed from the unemployment count by an elaborate system of recycling and reclassification, according to a Labour Party report based on unpublished government statistics.

The report, due out later this month, said the fall in unemployment coincided with the introduction four years ago of Restart, the government scheme under which claimants receive a compulsory interview every six months. If they accept a training place, they are removed from the count.

In this time, 7 million interviews have taken place. Evidence in the report supports a Bank of England report which showed that between the introduction of Restart and the last part of 1988, the changes had the effect of reducing the unemployment count by 750,000.

Restart was devised by the then Employment Secretary Lord Young as a way of reducing unemployment figures to below 3 million before the 1987 election. Restart interviewees returning to the count become fresh claims, and are no longer long-term unemployed.

Henry McLeish, Labour's employment spokesman, last night accused the government of 'perpetrating a massive fraud on the British public'. He declared: 'It is one of the most elaborate conspiracies of the past 10 years. Simply by using Restart, the Government has been able to whisk away a large chunk of the population, allowing them to live on benefit'.

Mr McLeish challenged Michael Howard, the Employment Secretary, to publish figures of people leaving the claimant count, and of people who found proper work after Restart. An internal civil service report suggested that between July 1986 - June 1989, of 608,000 referred for jobs only 6,000 secured one.

However, the Department of Employment said it was difficult to comply with such a request, and '...it is impossible to monitor the success of the process.'

The report accuses the government of 'a catalogue of partial truths and incomplete facts'. It says there has been a progressive mystification of the real trends in unemployment, linked to an increasingly; coercive and punitive social security system.

The figures show the unemployed have not gone into jobs created by the government, but were mainly women returners to work. The fall in male unemployment appears to be linked to Restart, and increasingly stringent availability-for-work tests. The report says growing numbers of adult workers now say they are 'economically inactive'.

Government statistics show that between 1979-1988, there was a 773 per cent rise in the number of men who did not need or want employment; while the number of men who believe no jobs are available rose by 457 per cent. In the same period, the number of economically inactive people increased by 4.4 per cent but by 23.9 per cent for men.

The report concludes: 'The government's rhetoric on unemployment does not stand up to scrutiny. It claims it is saving the taxpayer by flushing out those not generally available for work, but it has simply replaced one form of dependency culture with another'.

Source: *The Guardian*, 8.6.1990.

1. **What was 'Restart' and why might it have reduced the number of people officially counted as unemployed?**
2. **How might the Restart programme have affected the costs of unemployment (a) to the unemployed and (b) to the government?**

Summary

1. Unemployment can be classified into different types. These include frictional, search, seasonal, structural, cyclical and classical unemployment.
2. Frictional, search, seasonal, structural and classical unemployment are examples of voluntary unemployment. The unemployed could obtain work if they were prepared to work for lower real wages.
3. Cyclical unemployment is involuntary. Workers are prepared to accept the existing wage rate but are unable to find employment.

Types of unemployment

Economists classify unemployment into types or categories. One system of classification divides unemployment according to the causes of unemployment.

Frictional and search unemployment Most workers who lose their jobs move quickly into new ones. This short-term unemployment is called FRICTIONAL UNEMPLOYMENT. There will always be frictional unemployment in a free market economy and it is not regarded by most economists as a serious problem. The amount of time spent unemployed varies. The higher the level of unemployment benefits or redundancy pay, the longer workers will be able to afford to search for a good job without being forced into total poverty. Equally, the better the job information available to unemployed workers through newspapers, Jobcentres, etc. the shorter the time workers should need to spend searching for jobs. Hence SEARCH UNEMPLOYMENT will be lower.

Seasonal unemployment Some workers, such as construction workers or workers in the tourist industry, tend to work on a seasonal basis. SEASONAL UNEMPLOYMENT tends to rise in winter when some of these workers will be laid off, whilst unemployment falls in summer when they are taken on again. There is little that can be done to prevent this pattern occurring in a market economy where the demand for labour varies through the year.

Structural unemployment Far more serious is the problem of STRUCTURAL UNEMPLOYMENT. This occurs when the demand for labour is less than its supply in an individual labour market in the economy. One example of structural unemployment is **regional unemployment**. Throughout the post-war period, the South of England has tended to be at full employment while regions such as Northern Ireland have consistently suffered unemployment. This has occurred because of a lack of mobility of factors of production between the regions (☞ unit 50). Another example is **sectoral unemployment**. The steel and shipbuilding industries in the UK declined sharply in the late 1970s and early 1980s leaving a considerable number of skilled workers unemployed. Unfortunately their skills were no longer needed in the economy and without retraining and possible relocation, they were unable to adapt to the changing demand. **Technological unemployment** is another example of structural unemployment. Groups of workers across industries may be put out of work by new technology. Again, without retraining and geographical mobility these workers may remain unemployed.

Cyclical or demand-deficient unemployment When an economy goes into recession, unemployment rises

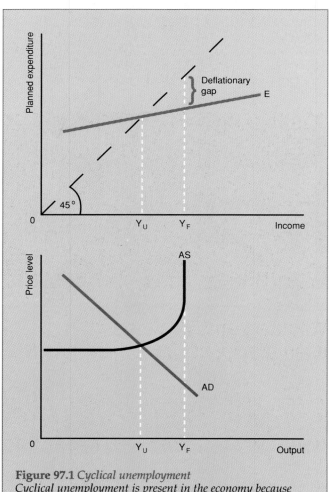

Figure 97.1 *Cyclical unemployment*
Cyclical unemployment is present in the economy because equilibrium income Y_U is below full employment income Y_F.

because there is insufficient demand within the economy. It is not just labour which becomes unemployed. Factories, machines, mines, offices and farms (i.e. land and capital) become unemployed too. CYCLICAL or DEMAND-DEFICIENT UNEMPLOYMENT is also sometimes called KEYNESIAN UNEMPLOYMENT because it was Keynes who argued in the 1930s that the Great Depression was caused by a lack of demand within the economy. In the simple Keynesian model developed in units 74-77, cyclical unemployment occurs when equilibrium income is below full employment income. A **deflationary gap** is then said to be present and this is shown in the 45° line diagram in Figure 97.1. An alternative analysis using aggregate demand and supply curves is shown in the second graph in Figure 97.1. Cyclical unemployment exists here because the equilibrium level of income Y_U is below full employment income Y_F. When there is demand-deficient unemployment in the economy, unemployed workers are prepared to work for existing wage rates. The problem is that there are insufficient jobs on offer for all workers to be re-employed.

Classical unemployment CLASSICAL UNEMPLOYMENT or REAL WAGE UNEMPLOYMENT exists when the real wage rate is above that needed to clear the labour market. Jobs exist but workers choose not to take them because they are not prepared to accept the wages which need to be offered to achieve full employment (☞ unit 79 for a fuller explanation of this view).

unit 79

QUESTION 1 Explain how you would classify each of the following by type of unemployment:
(a) a professional cricketer claiming unemployment benefit in the winter;
(b) an unemployed worker at the height of the Great Depression of the 1930s;
(c) a worker made redundant within the past 7 days;
(d) an unemployed 32 year old who turns down a job because he receives more in benefits than the wage offered;
(e) a worker unemployed in Northern Ireland for the past 5 years.

Voluntary and involuntary unemployment

Another way of categorising unemployment is to split it into two types: **voluntary unemployment** and **involuntary unemployment**. Voluntary unemployment exists when workers refuse opportunities of work at existing wage rates. Involuntary unemployment exists when there are insufficient jobs in the economy at existing wage rates. The percentage of workers who are voluntarily unemployed is known as the **natural rate of unemployment**. The economy is said to be at **full employment** when there is no involuntary unemployment

in the economy. The rate of unemployment which exists at the full employment level is the natural rate of unemployment (☞ unit 79).

Frictional, search, seasonal, structural and classical unemployment can be classified as voluntary unemployment. Workers between jobs could take the first job offered rather than search for a more desirable one. Seasonal workers could find odd jobs, such as working in pubs or cleaning, to fill in the months when they are out of work from their main occupation. Those suffering from structural unemployment could get a job if they were prepared to accept a lower rate of pay or worse conditions of work. For instance, unemployed workers in Northern Ireland could come to the South of England to find jobs. Redundant steel workers could become bar attendants or security guards. Classical unemployment is voluntary by the very definition of the term. Demand-deficient or cyclical unemployment on the other hand is involuntary. Cyclical unemployment means there are insufficient jobs at the current wage rate for all unemployed workers to take.

The extent to which unemployment is voluntary or involuntary is a major controversy in economics. Keynesian economists have argued that most of the unemployment in the two great depressions of the 1930s and 1980s, for instance, was demand-deficient in nature. At the other extreme are classical economists of the rational expectations school of thought who argue that

---

QUESTION 2

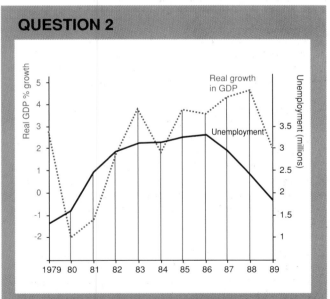

Source: adapted from CSO, *Economic Trends Annual Supplement*.

Figure 97.2 *Rate of growth of GDP and unemployment*

(a) What is meant by a 'recession' and a 'boom' in the economy?
(b) To what extent does the evidence suggest that the high unemployment of the first half of the 1980s was cyclical in nature, given that the average annual rate of growth of GDP since 1960 has been 2 per cent?

labour markets will adjust immediately to large rises in unemployment. Wage rates will fall and the labour market will clear. According to this view, there were plenty of jobs around in the 1930s and the 1980s but workers refused to take them. Hence there was no involuntary unemployment. All the unemployment in these two depressions was voluntary and unemployment stayed at its natural rate throughout the depression years.

Key terms

Frictional unemployment - when workers are unemployed for short lengths of time between jobs.
Search unemployment - when workers spend time searching for the best job available.
Seasonal unemployment - when workers are unemployed at certain times of the year, such as building workers in winter, or agricultural workers at harvest time in summer.
Structural unemployment - when the pattern of demand and production changes leaving workers unemployed in labour markets where demand has shrunk. Examples of structural unemployment are regional unemployment, sectoral unemployment or technological unemployment.
Cyclical, demand-deficient or Keynesian unemployment - when there is insufficient demand in the economy for all workers who wish to work at current wage rates to obtain a job.
Classical or real-wage unemployment - when real wages are kept at such a high level that the demand for labour is greater than the supply of labour.

Applied economics

Types of unemployment

To what extent can recent UK unemployment be classified as frictional, structural or cyclical?

Unemployment statistics collected by the government do not correspond exactly to the classification presented in economic theory. However, Figure 97.3 can give some clues as to the relative importance of

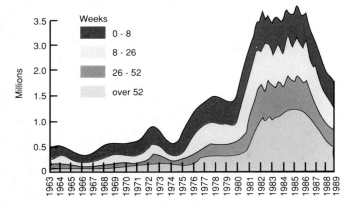

Note: There is a discontinuity in 1982.
Source: adapted from Department of Employment.
Figure 97.3 *Unemployment by duration, UK*

each type of unemployment. The graph shows the number of workers unemployed by duration (i.e. by how long a worker has been out of a job). What can be seen is that when unemployment does increase, there tends to be some increase in unemployment up to 52 weeks, but the single largest increase tends to be in the numbers of unemployed over 52 weeks.

Frictional unemployment Frictional unemployment covers those workers who are between jobs, moving fairly quickly from one employment to another. In the 1960s, for instance, there were about 250 000 workers who were unemployed for 8 weeks or less. Even in the worst period of unemployment in the 1980s, this number did not exceed much more than half a million. In the 1960s, about half of all workers unemployed were in the 0-8 week category. By the 1980s this had fallen to about 20 per cent of total unemployment. This suggests that other types of unemployment were much higher in the 1980s than they were in the 1960s.

Cyclical unemployment Unemployment patterns correspond closely to movements in the trade cycle. Unemployment tends to lag behind the other main indicators such as changes in GDP. This is because firms try to avoid making workers redundant in a recession in the hope that it will not be too pronounced. In a boom, firms are reluctant to take on new staff because they fear that the boom may not last. The major recessions of the 1970s and 1980s can be seen in Figure 97.3: 1971-2, 1974-6 and 1980-82. During the 1980s, unemployment rose from 1.3 million at the start of the decade to a peak of nearly 3.4 million before falling to 1.8 million at the end. This would suggest that most of the rise in unemployment in the 1980s was cyclical in nature. At its worst, there were perhaps between 1½ and 2 million workers on the official count who were out of work because of a lack of aggregate demand.

Structural unemployment From the late 1960s onwards, unemployment tended to rise over time. This would suggest that there was an increase in structural unemployment in the 1970s and 1980s. It is not difficult to find factors which might have caused this. In the late 1960s and 1970s, there were significant increases in the ratio of unemployment benefits to average earnings (the replacement ratio ☞ unit 99), thus increasing the attractiveness of remaining unemployed. There was also a significant increase in the numbers of school leavers entering the working population. Evidence suggests that the economy was not sufficiently flexible to provide work places for all these youngsters. New technologies resulted in net job losses. Some of those jobs, particularly in manufacturing, went abroad to more efficient producers such as the Japanese and the Germans. The loss of jobs in manufacturing industries hit regions in the 'North' of Britain, such as the West Midlands, Wales and Scotland, far more than the 'South' of Britain because of the concentration of manufacturing in the 'North'. For instance, unemployment in the South East rose from 2.4 per cent in the first quarter of 1980 to a peak of 8.4 per cent in the third quarter of 1986, a rise of 6 per cent. In Scotland over the same period, unemployment rose from 5.9 per cent to 13.4 per cent, a rise of 7.5 per cent.

Data question

INNER CITY UNEMPLOYED FEEL THE STRAIN

ANTI - POLL TAX posters were yesterday peeling off the dingy exterior walls of the unemployment benefit office at Stratford in the east London borough of Newman, where unemployment rose by 115 last month on the previous month's 10 206. The increase was part of a 3 300 rise to 199 800 in Greater London.

The downturn in construction in London was cited by two claimants as the cause of their unemployment. Mr Robert Quinn, 24, had been unemployed for two months after being laid off from his labouring job. 'I think the firm was short of money', he said. He could not find any jobs and his marriage had broken up.

Mr David Kimber, 26 and originally from Liverpool, became unemployed three weeks ago when his contract as a tower crane driver expired. 'I have been promised contracts but jobs are being put back.'

Among the steady stream of claimants yesterday, those who had signed on as unemployed over the past couple of months gave several reasons, other than redundancy, for their status.

Mr Kirpal Singh, 24 and single, quit two months ago after two years as a computer operator for Harrods, the department store some 10 miles away. 'It was just too far to travel every day,' he said. He was optimistic about getting another job and said he was being called for second interviews.

Ms Susan Morrison, 19, was pessimistic about getting another job in word processing. She left one job in January after a month when she was told she was 'not the right person' for the job. She previously resigned from British Telecom because she believed she was the lowest paid person in her office.

Several people gave the lack of opportunity for career development as the principal reason for leaving their jobs.

Ms Patricia Jones, 24, a former deputy catering officer at a large London further-education establishment, said: 'There was no career development being offered. I have got all the qualifications to progress in catering so I want a good job with a salary in five figures.'

Mr Peter Vass, 24, a former merchandiser with Maples, the furniture group, resigned because 'I was paid about £8 000 a year and it just was not enough.' Unemployed for 13 weeks he was optimistic about getting a new job.

Source: *Financial Times*, 18.4.1990.

1. **How might an economist classify each of the unemployed workers in the data?**

Summary

1. Demand management techniques can be used to fill a deflationary gap if there is cyclical unemployment in the economy.
2. Increasing aggregate supply is likely to increase output and reduce unemployment.
3. Supply side economics is the study of how aggregate supply can be increased and, in particular, what economic policies a government should pursue to achieve it.
4. Supply side economics has tended to be associated with classical economists who argue in favour of free markets.

5. In particular, supply side economics has been associated with the view that increasing competition in markets and reducing marginal tax rates on income will increase aggregate supply.
6. Some economists are critical of the claims of supply side economics. They dispute whether the economic relationships assumed by supply side economists exist. They point out that there are many examples of market failure and question whether increased efficiency is not gained at the expense of greater inequity.

Demand management

Unemployment can be classified into 5 types (☞ unit 97). If unemployment is Keynesian, or demand-deficient in nature (i.e. caused by too little spending in the economy), then it may be appropriate for government to use policies which lead to an increase in aggregate demand.

During the 1950s and 1960s, successive British governments used **demand management** techniques (☞ unit 77) to keep unemployment at extremely low levels by historical standards. If the economy were below full employment, the government intervened to fill the existing deflationary gap. It would increase its budget deficit either by spending more or reducing taxes, or some combination of the two (i.e. increasing the PSBR). It would also loosen monetary policy, mainly by relaxing controls on the availability of credit in the economy (☞ unit 72). Similarly, if there were excess demand in the economy and inflationary pressures built up, the government would eliminate the inflationary gap by reducing the PSBR and tightening credit controls.

The change in the budget deficit or surplus did not need to be of the same magnitude as the deflationary gap. This was because of the **multiplier** effect. For instance, if the deflationary gap were £10 000 million and the multiplier were 2, then the government would only need to increase its spending by £5 000 million to fill the deflationary gap.

The deflationary gap could even be filled if the government's budget deficit remained unchanged. If the government increased both government spending and taxation by the same amount, then aggregate demand would rise because of the **balanced budget multiplier effect** (☞ unit 77).

The effects of demand management policies can be seen in Figure 98.1. A Keynesian aggregate supply curve is assumed. The economy is initially at A, below the full

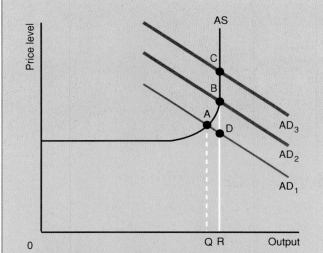

Figure 98.1 *Demand management*
According to Keynesians, expansionary fiscal or monetary policy can shift the AD curve to the right. If the economy is at A, at less than full employment, then an increased budget deficit could move the economy to B. If the economy is already at B, fiscal expansion will be purely inflationary.

employment level of output of OR. An increase in aggregate demand from AD_1 to AD_2 will restore the economy to full employment, albeit at some cost in terms of higher prices. However, a further increase in aggregate demand, from AD_2 to AD_3, will be purely inflationary, since the economy is already at full employment.

Classical economists argue that the long run aggregate supply curve is vertical (☞ unit 80). The economy will always revert to its full employment level. Demand management policies are therefore at best unnecessary and at worst seriously damaging to the economy. If nothing else, expansionary policy will always lead to higher inflation than would otherwise be the case. In Figure 98.1, with an aggregate demand curve of AD_1 and the economy initially at A, there would be a movement back to full employment at D if there were no government intervention. Active demand management, which shifts the aggregate demand curve to AD_2, results in the same output level but higher prices at B.

QUESTION 1 In his 1959 budget, the Chancellor of the Exchequer, Heathcoat Amory, substantially reduced taxes. He justified this in the following words: 'The prospect for home production as I have set it out does not represent a full enough use of the capital resources which have been created in recent years. Nor can we be content with the possibility that unemployment might continue at around the present levels ... (However) we must at all costs make it our business not to return to an overload on the economy, which would make a resumption of inflation inevitable. At the present time, however, this is clearly not an immediate danger.'

(a) Using an aggregate demand and supply diagram, explain why the Chancellor cut taxes.
(b) Would his policy have been any different if inflation had been rising at the time?
(c) The economy grew very strongly in the second half of 1959 and in 1960. Over the next three years the government was to restrict the growth of demand both through fiscal and monetary policies. Using a diagram, suggest why the government adopted deflationary policies.

Supply side economics

Keynesian economists believe that demand-deficient unemployment can be reduced through policies which affect the demand side of the economy. But both Keynesian and classical economists believe that frictional, seasonal, structural and classical unemployment are best reduced by SUPPLY SIDE government policies.

Economists have been studying supply side economics since the foundation of the discipline. Adam Smith's *The Wealth of Nations* (1776) looked at the conditions necessary for increasing output in 18th century Britain and attacked government policy of the day for discouraging competition in the market place. Growth theory (☞ unit 63) is largely based upon the study of supply side factors. Economists of all schools of thought have always argued that national income is likely to rise if aggregate supply increases.

However the phrase, 'supply side economics' is relatively new and dates only from the late 1970s. It tends to be used in a very narrow sense. Supply side economics is associated with the beliefs that:
- changing aggregate supply is a very powerful way of influencing the level of economic activity in an economy;

- changes in aggregate supply come about through changes in individual markets, for instance through changes in levels of physical and human capital;
- competition and incentives play a key role in expanding aggregate supply in a market;
- government attempts to change aggregate demand, for instance through the use of fiscal policy, will be at best ineffective and at worst seriously damaging to the economy in the long run;
- the prime aim of government economic policy, apart from maintaining stable prices, must be to create as free a market as possible through micro-economic policies.

'Supply side economists' tend to be economists working within a classical or neo-classical framework who believe strongly in the power of free market forces to achieve optimal resource allocation and maximum economic growth. Therefore they believe the less government intervention in the economy, the better.

QUESTION 2 The government want to encourage efficient, flexible markets, capable of responding quickly and effectively to changing economic conditions. With a better performance on the supply side, we can have more growth and jobs without inflation.

Source: The Treasury, *Economic Progress Report*, October 1987.

(a) What is meant by the 'supply side' of the economy?
(b) Explain the link between the efficient functioning of markets and growth, jobs and inflation.

Aggregate supply and unemployment

Classical economists claim that increasing aggregate supply is the only way to lower **measured** unemployment without increasing inflation. Consider Figure 98.2. The economy is at full employment at output level OA. Unemployment is therefore at its natural rate (so there will be some measured unemployment in the economy). An increase in aggregate demand, shown by a shift upwards in the AD curve, will only result in higher prices. However, an increase in aggregate supply which shifts the aggregate supply curve from $LRAS_1$ to $LRAS_2$ will both increase output and reduce prices. At OA, the economy is at full employment. The workers who are officially counted as unemployed are therefore voluntarily unemployed (☞ unit 97). The shift in aggregate supply should enable some of these workers to get jobs. Both measured unemployment and the natural rate of unemployment will therefore decline.

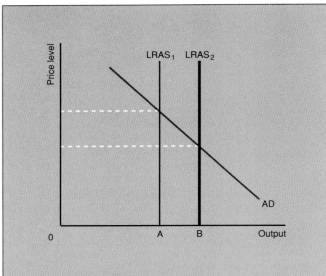

Figure 98.2 *Supply side policies*
An increase in aggregate supply from LRAS₁ to LRAS₂ will increase output and reduce prices. The increase in output should result in a fall in both measured unemployment and the natural rate of unemployment if there is a large pool of voluntary unemployed workers at OA.

Competition

One way of stimulating the supply side of the economy is to encourage competition in individual markets. If **consumer sovereignty** exists in the market (☞ unit 40), consumers will be free to spend their money as they wish. Producers then have to compete for these spending 'votes' cast by consumers. If they produce the goods and services consumers want to buy, they will survive and make a profit. If they don't attract enough 'votes' they will go out of business. Consumers are therefore offered the greatest value for money - a wide range of products of the best possible quality at the lowest price.

If the market were controlled by a monopolist, such as the health service or gas supply in the UK, consumers would have little or no choice. Producers are free to charge whatever they like. Private producers are likely to maximise profit, resulting in higher prices and lower output than would be the case in a competitive industry. Public sector producers, on the other hand, are likely to have higher costs because there is no incentive to be efficient.

Increasing competition will therefore lead to a better use of resources. Because monopoly production is **productively inefficient** (i.e. production is not necessarily at lowest cost), increased competition will lead to more being produced from the same amount of resources. Aggregate supply will therefore increase. Moreover, because monopoly production is also **allocatively inefficient** (e.g. consumers are not being given a large enough choice of products, quality is not as high as it could be, output is less than it would be if the industry were perfectly competitive ☞ unit 37), increased

competition will increase economic efficiency even if aggregate supply does not increase.

In factor markets, such as the labour market, market imperfections lead to reduced output and reduced employment. For instance, powerful trade unions can raise the wages of their members but as a consequence employers employ fewer workers. Workers 'price themselves out of jobs' (☞ unit 49). So reducing market imperfections will increase the employment of factors and increase aggregate supply in the economy.

> **QUESTION 3** Explain why competition in the UK amongst retailers in the grocery trade, such as supermarkets and local corner shops, helps promote efficiency in this market.

Fiscal policy

Another way in which governments can influence aggregate supply is through fiscal policy. High marginal rates of tax on incomes discourage economic activity. A tax on cigarettes leads to fewer cigarettes being bought. A tax on work (income tax) leads to people working less. A tax on profits (corporation tax) is a disincentive to firms to make profits. Lowering certain taxes will therefore raise the level of economic activity and increase aggregate supply.

Supply side economists believe that the supply of labour is relatively elastic. A reduction in marginal tax rates on income will lead to a significant increase in 'work'. This could mean individuals working longer hours, being more willing to accept promotion, being more geographically mobile, or simply being prepared to join the workforce. Work is, arguably, an inferior good, whilst leisure, its alternative, is a normal good. The higher an individual's income, the less willing he or she is to work. So a cut in marginal tax rates will have a negative income effect at the margin (i.e. the worker will be less willing to work). However, a cut in marginal tax rates will have a positive substitution effect because the relative price of work to leisure has changed in favour of work (i.e. the worker will be more willing to work; ☞ unit 47 for a fuller explanation). Supply side economists believe that the substitution effect of a tax cut is more important than the income effect and hence tax cuts increase incentives to work. If cutting marginal income tax rates encourages people to work harder and earn more, then in theory it could be that tax revenues will increase following a tax cut. For instance, if 10 workers, each earning £10 000 a year, pay an average 25 per cent tax, then total tax revenue is £25 000 (10 x £10 000 x 0.25). If a cut in the tax rate to 20 per cent were to make each worker work harder and increase earnings to, say, £15 000, tax revenues would increase to £30 000 (10 x £3 000). This is an example of the LAFFER CURVE effect, after Professor Arthur Laffer who popularised the idea in the late 1970s. Figure 98.3 shows a Laffer curve, which plots tax revenues against tax rates. As tax rates

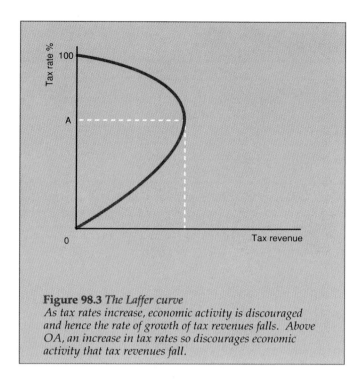

Figure 98.3 *The Laffer curve*
As tax rates increase, economic activity is discouraged and hence the rate of growth of tax revenues falls. Above OA, an increase in tax rates so discourages economic activity that tax revenues fall.

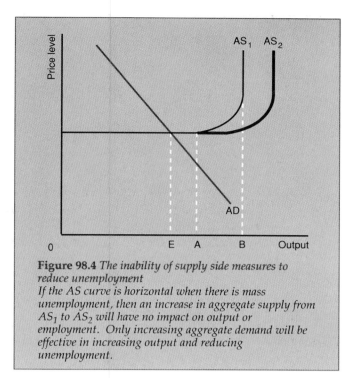

Figure 98.4 *The inability of supply side measures to reduce unemployment*
If the AS curve is horizontal when there is mass unemployment, then an increase in aggregate supply from AS_1 to AS_2 will have no impact on output or employment. Only increasing aggregate demand will be effective in increasing output and reducing unemployment.

increase, the rate of growth of tax revenue falls because of the disincentive effects of the tax. OA shows the maximum revenue position of the tax. At tax rates above OA, an increase in the tax rate so discourages economic activity that tax revenues fall.

QUESTION 4 A top executive earning £40 000 is 'headhunted' by another firm. An increase in salary of £20 000 a year is offered if she will change jobs. The new post would carry far more responsibility and be considerably more stressful than her current post.

Consider whether her decision would be any different if her current marginal rate of tax were 40 per cent than if it were 60 per cent.

A critique of supply side economics

Supply side economics has come to be associated with a belief in the beneficial power of free market forces. All economists would agree that increasing aggregate supply is essential if economies are to grow over time. In that sense, all economists are 'supply side economists'. However, many economists are critical of the supply side economics arguments discussed above.

Mass unemployment Keynesian economists would argue that, faced with the mass unemployment of the 1930s or the early 1980s, policies which increased aggregate supply would not increase either output or

employment. Figure 98.4 shows a Keynesian aggregate supply curve. The equilibrium level of income OE is well below full employment income of OB. Increasing aggregate supply from AS_1 to AS_2 will not change the equilibrium level of income. Only if income is greater than OA will supply side measures have an impact on equilibrium income. Supply side measures only work, according to Keynesian economists, if the economy is at or near full employment, within the income range OA to OB.

Equity Many supply side measures might result in greater economic efficiency. But there may be a conflict with equity considerations. Greater flexibility in labour markets may, for instance, lead to falls in the wages of workers, particularly low paid workers. It is likely that the implementation of supply side policies will leave at least some worse off.

The environment Greater freedom for industry could perhaps result in damage to the environment. The reason why planning controls, for instance, are implemented in all industrialised economies is because there is a recognition that industry, left to itself, would misallocate resources within the economy.

Economic evidence Many supply side measures depend crucially upon assumptions about how markets and individual economic decision makers operate. For instance, central to supply side economics is the belief that lower marginal tax rates will increase incentives to work. Yet many studies show that there is little or no link between tax rates and hours worked.

QUESTION 5 Before 1989 it was illegal for 16-18 year olds (but not older workers) to work for more than 48 hours a week and for more than 9 hours a day in manufacturing industry. They were also legally entitled to minimum meal breaks, rest breaks and holidays. The Employment Act 1989 abolished these 'rights' or 'restrictions'.

(a) Will abolition make 16-18 year olds more or less attractive to employers, particularly small manufacturing companies?
(b) Explain, using a diagram, the likely effect of abolition on the aggregate supply schedule of the UK economy.
(c) To what extent do you think that abolition will increase or reduce economic welfare?

Key terms

Supply side economics - the study of how changes in aggregate supply will affect variables such as national income; in particular how government micro-economic policy might change aggregate supply through individual markets.

Applied economics

The 1980s: a supply side miracle?

1979 marked an important date in post-war British economic history. The Conservative government elected into office believed that demand management was both ineffective and damaging to the economy, and that supply side policies were central to the future prosperity of the economy.

It could be argued that the main elements of the government's supply side policies were:
■ the control of inflation and the elimination of the stop-go cycle to provide a stable environment within which business could prosper;
■ the removal of obstacles to market forces, such as trade unions, to make labour markets more flexible;
■ deregulation and privatisation to extend market forces within the economy;
■ the creation of incentives to work and earn profits through cuts in taxes and welfare benefits;
■ improved training and education, to create a more productive workforce.

By 1987-8, some economists were claiming that there had been a 'supply side miracle'. How does more recent evidence help us evaluate this claim?

One way of making a judgement is to consider anecdotal evidence. For instance, there is little doubt that companies such as British Steel and British Airways became far more efficient in the 1980s: by 1990, British Steel had lower costs and higher productivity than many Japanese steel producers. In the field of industrial relations, trade unions are less powerful than they were in the 1960s and 1970s. Managers in general seem to feel that they have far more scope to manage as they see fit today than they did in 1979. Successful entrepreneurs such as Richard

Table 98.1 *Output per person employed in the seven major industrialised countries (average annual % change)*

	Manufacturing			Whole economy		
	1961-70	1971-80	1981-88	1961-70	1971-80	1981-88
UK	3.0	1.6	5.2	2.4	1.3	2.5
US	3.5	3.0	4.0	2.0	0.4	1.2
Japan	8.8	5.3	3.1	8.9	3.8	2.9
Germany	4.1	2.9	2.2	4.4	2.8	1.8
France	5.4	3.2	3.1	4.6	2.8	2.0
Italy	5.4	3.0	3.5	6.3	2.6	2.0
Canada	3.4	3.0	3.6	2.4	1.5	1.4
G7 average	4.5	3.3	3.6	3.5	1.7	1.8

Source: HM Treasury, *Economic Progress Report*, April 1989.

Branson have been held up as examples of how hard work and willingness to take risks can create economic prosperity for all. All major political parties now agree that the market mechanism is the most efficient way to produce many goods and services in the economy.

Anecdotal evidence, however, if it is to prove anything, needs to be substantiated by evidence of change across the whole economy. A key statistic cited in the debate in the late 1980s was the change in labour productivity. If the aggregate supply curve is to shift to the right, there must an increase in labour productivity (output per worker) given a stable workforce. Table 98.1 shows trends in labour productivity for the G7 group of countries (the 7 largest industrial economies in the world). It shows that in the 1960s and 1970s, the UK lagged well behind its industrial competitors. In the 1980s, it topped the league in manufacturing and came second behind Japan for the whole economy. However, there are two points to consider.

Firstly, UK productivity growth fell in 1989 and 1990. The increase in manufacturing productivity, for instance, was 3.6 per cent in 1989 and only an estimated 1 per cent in 1990. It could be argued that if there was a productivity miracle in the 1980s, it has not been sustained.

Secondly, the increase in productivity has not necessarily led to higher output. The UK economy, measured by change in real GDP, grew by an average 2.7 per cent in the nine years between 1981 and 1989, still below the average for our major industrial competitors and little better than average growth rate in the 1960s and 1970s. In manufacturing, output was only 12.4 per cent higher in 1989 than in 1979. In key industries (man made fibres, metal goods, mechanical engineering, drink and tobacco, textiles, motor vehicles and parts, and clothing and footwear), manufacturing output in 1989 was lower than in 1979.

If labour productivity increased at a much faster rate than output, it would give an indication that supply side policies have failed to stimulate historically low investment rates in the UK. In manufacturing, investment in the 1980s has been poor as Table 98.2 shows. For the decade between 1980 and 1989, net manufacturing fixed investment (gross investment minus depreciation) was **minus** £1 485m at 1985 prices (although these figures do not take into account an increase in the leasing of equipment to manufacturing industry by the financial sector). Net manufacturing investment was less in 1989 than in 1979. Whilst it increased substantially in the second half of the 1980s,

Table 98.2 *Net domestic fixed capital formation*

		£ million at 1985 prices
	Manufacturing	Whole economy
1979	2 058	21 250
1980	487	16 999
1981	- 1 792	10 673
1982	- 2 040	12 171
1983	- 1 990	13 604
1984	- 631	17 118
1985	249	18 470
1986	8	18 625
1987	588	23 621
1988	1 608	32 275
1989	2 028	36 370

Source: adapted from CSO, *United Kingdom National Accounts (Blue Book)*.

preliminary evidence for 1990 suggests net manufacturing investment will fall in 1990 and 1991 and so it could be argued once again that the investment boom has not been sustained.

Another indicator of a supply side revolution might be the international competitiveness of the UK. There are many measures of international competitiveness but they all tend to tell the same story. Between 1979 and 1981, UK competitiveness fell (for instance, the normalised IMF index of relative unit labour costs increased from 81.7 in the first quarter of 1979 to 92.3 in the third quarter of 1979 and by the first quarter of 1981 stood at 122.2). Then competitiveness increased from 1981 to 1986 (the IMF index fell to a low of 90.4 in the fourth quarter of 1986) but has subsequently fallen again (rising to 99.2 in the second quarter of 1990).

As for the balance of payments, if the UK had out-performed her industrial competitors in the 1980s, then the balance of payments difficulties which beset it for most of the post-war period should have largely disappeared. Again the evidence is mixed. Import penetration has increased markedly in the 1980s. After record surpluses on current account in the early 1980s, caused in part by the effect of North Sea oil, the current balance had moved into deficit as early as 1986. By 1989, the current account deficit was a record £19 000 million, totally unsustainable and one of the factors which caused the government to deflate the economy from late 1988 onwards. If there had been a supply side miracle, the high economic growth of the second half of the 1980s should not have led to such a massive current account deficit.

Finally, supply side policies should have had an effect on unemployment with both the measured rate and the natural rate of unemployment falling. Unemployment in 1979, a boom year for the UK economy, was 1.3 million. After climbing to 3.2 million by 1986, it fell to 1.7 million in 1990 before rising again. So measured unemployment fell by over 1.5 million between 1986 and 1990 - the supply side 'miracle' - but was still 0.4 million higher in 1990 than in 1979. Measured unemployment does not equal 'natural' unemployment. However, critics would argue that it is unlikely that the natural rate has fallen since 1979 when the measured rate has risen.

There is no doubt that the British economy is in many ways in better shape today than it was in 1979. Supply side policies have probably been effective in raising labour productivity for instance. However, the rise in inflation and huge balance of payments deficits of the late 1980s, followed by recession, low growth and the low productivity increases of the early 1990s, would suggest that supply side reforms have a long way to go before it can truly be claimed that there has been a 'supply side miracle'.

THE COAL INDUSTRY

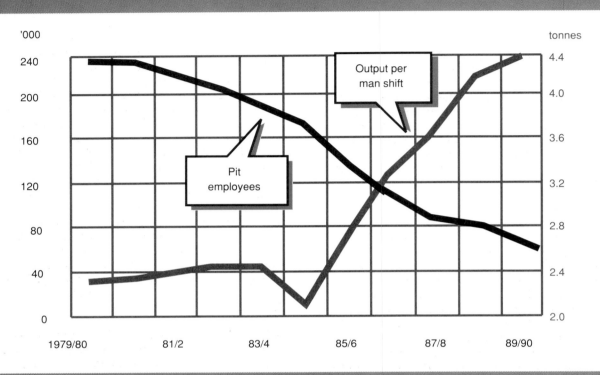

Figure 98.5 *Britsh coal industry*

Source: adapted from the *Financial Times*, 12.11.90.

Following the end of the miners' strike in 1985, the government, through National Coal, imposed two unwritten broad policy objectives on the industry: firstly that the industry should become profitable and secondly that it should be able to compete against imported coal. As Figure 98.5 shows, by 1989/90 the number of workers in the industry had fallen to 70 000, whilst productivity (output per miner) increased dramatically as the number of pits fell from 191 to under 90. As a result, despite producing slightly less coal, the industry had reduced its losses below the £374 million in 1983, the last year before the miners' strike.

Even then, British Coal was selling coal at a higher price than international competitors - in 1988 an average £46 a tonne compared to £27 a tonne for imported coal.

1. What are meant by 'supply side policies'?
2. How does the recent history of the coal industry in the UK illustrate (a) the operation and (b) the success of such policies?
3. What social costs might have arisen as British Coal pursued its goal of making a private profit?

99 Supply side measures

Applied economics

Supply side policies

Supply side policies are government policies which lead to an increase in the efficiency of markets and hence the supply side of the economy. Successful supply side policies will shift the aggregate supply curve to the right, increasing output and possibly reducing the natural rate of unemployment. This unit will consider the range of policies advocated by supply side economists and their implementation in the context of the UK economy, concentrating mainly on the period 1979-1990.

The labour market

Reducing trade union power The purpose of a trade union is to organise workers into one bargaining unit. The trade union then becomes a monopsonist, a sole seller of labour, and prevents workers from competing amongst themselves in the job market. Economic theory predicts that if trade unions raise wage rates for their members, then employment and output will be lower in otherwise competitive markets. They therefore have the effect of shifting the aggregate supply curve to the left. So a government committed to supply side policies must curb the power of trade unions, for instance by reducing their ability to strike.

In the 1970s, trade unions, if anything, increased their legal rights and therefore their power. After 1979, however, a number of Acts were passed which radically changed the face of industrial relations in the UK. In particular, secondary picketing was effectively made illegal as firms gained the power to sue trade unions involved in secondary picketing for damages. Any industrial action approved by a trade union now had to be sanctioned by its membership through secret ballots. Secret ballots were also made compulsory for elections of trade union leaders. Closed shops became more difficult to maintain or enforce. The government also took an extremely hard line with strikes in the public sector, refusing to give in to union demands. The breaking of strikes, such as the miners' strike of 1983-5, increased the confidence of private employers to resist trade union demands.

Reducing state welfare benefits Supply side economists argue that the unemployed are discouraged from working if they can receive as much or almost as much in state benefits as if they were in work. Hence, if these people are to take jobs, it is necessary to increase the gap between wage rates and benefit rates.

The ratio between the wage a worker could receive and the benefits actually received is known as the **replacement ratio**. If the ratio were 1.0, then the unemployed would receive exactly the same from working as from being unemployed. If the ratio were 0.5, the unemployed would be twice as well off working as on the dole. One way of increasing the replacement ratio and giving the unemployed a greater incentive to take a job is to cut welfare benefits.

Within two years of coming to office in 1979, the government abolished earnings-related unemployment benefit and also abolished the index linking of benefits to the rise in average earnings. Benefits since that time have only been indexed to the RPI, the inflation rate. Unemployment benefit was also made subject to income tax. In 1988, a major change in the social security system was implemented. One of its effects was to make low paid workers in jobs slightly better off, whilst making unemployed workers on average worse off (i.e. the replacement ratio was lowered).

Abolishing minimum wage legislation In the UK, wages councils have set minimum wages for low paid workers. However, micro-economic theory suggests that minimum wages set above market equilibrium rates lead to unemployment (☞ unit 50). The higher the wage, the lower the demand for workers by employers. Unemployment would fall and aggregate supply would rise if workers protected by minimum wage legislation could be paid less. Hence repealing minimum wage legislation will increase aggregate supply.

After 1979, the government signalled its intention to abolish wages councils. In 1986, young workers were removed from the scope of legislation and in December 1988 the government issued a consultative document containing proposals to scrap the councils. However, opposition to this, not least from large employers in industries concerned, has meant that no legislation has been put forward to date.

Repealing legislation which limits the use of labour Legislation was passed during the 19th and early 20th centuries which protected the rights of women and children in the workplace in the UK. For instance, workers under the age of 18 were not allowed to work more than 48 hours a week or for more than 9 hours a day. Much of this legislation was still in force in 1979, although working conditions had changed considerably. The legislation was said to restrict the ability of employers to use young workers or women flexibly in the workplace and therefore discouraged their employment. The 1989 Employment Act repealed much of this legislation effectively removing the special protection given in law to female and young workers.

Making the housing market more efficient In the UK, unemployment tends to be concentrated in the 'North' whereas the 'South' experiences labour shortages. Shifting workers from the North to the South would reduce unemployment and raise aggregate supply. The single most important obstacle to this happening today is, arguably, the housing market. Workers in the North cannot move to the South either because they cannot obtain rented accommodation or because they cannot afford to buy houses in the South. Encouraging more people to buy their own homes, and raising rents in subsidised council houses, reduces the difference between housing markets in the North and the South. Abolishing legal rent and tenancy controls, designed to protect the rights of tenants, and subsidising private landlords through tax concessions, will encourage greater provision of private rented accommodation.

After 1979, the extension of a 'property owning democracy' was a central feature of government policy. The two most important ways in which this was achieved were granting council tenants the right to buy their own homes (contained in the Housing Act 1980), and imposing tight restrictions on the building of new council houses. The Housing Act 1980 also attempted to revive the private rented market by making it possible for landlords to charge a market rent and repossess property at the end of a short tenancy period.

More flexible pension arrangements Another obstacle to workers moving jobs is pension arrangements. Many employers in the UK provide pension schemes for their workers. The standard way of calculating the pension is for it to be a percentage of the final salary of the worker times the number of years worked. This system discriminates severely against workers who move job several times during their working life. Pensions from previous jobs are almost worthless because they are based on the salary last paid to the worker in that job - a salary which will be a fraction of current earnings because of the ravages of inflation. It also means that a worker who, for instance, moved job half-way through her career will only be entitled to half a pension from her last job. Introducing 'portable' pensions, pensions which are not based on final salary but on how much has been saved over the working life of the employee, would help some of these problems.

Encouraging training A better educated and trained workforce should be a more productive workforce. Investment in education and training should therefore

result in an increase in aggregate supply. Full time education is arguably the responsibility of government. However, vocational training is best left to employers at a local level, who are more capable than government of perceiving current training needs. Policies to encourage training should therefore work through the market mechanism rather than in opposition to it.

Various employment schemes for the unemployed have been used to encourage training. The Youth Training Scheme, for instance, a six month placement in 1979 for 16-17 year olds, was by 1989 a guaranteed two year course for 16 year olds and a one year course for 17 year olds with a greater emphasis placed upon training. The government also launched the Employment Training Scheme in 1988, designed to provide a year's training for any unemployed adult. In the early 1990s, the government intends to establish a national network of 100 Training and Enterprise Councils (TECs). Unlike previous training programmes, which were a partnership between trade unions, employers and government at a national level, the new TECs will be dominated by employers at a local level. Local groups of employers are being invited to submit proposals for setting up local TECs. Having agreed training strategies with government, the TECs would then be responsible for delivering training programmes. It is expected that most help will be provided to support training in small rather than large firms, given that large firms are more able to deliver effective training by themselves.

In the field of education, the government announced in 1988 that it would implement a national curriculum in schools from 1989 onwards, with the aim of raising standards of education and providing a better educated workforce in the future. A large number of other small scale measures, such as the establishment of city technology colleges, have also been implemented.

Reducing marginal rates of tax Cuts in marginal rates of tax will, according to supply side economists, increase incentives. Cutting income tax will make workers work longer and harder (because the substitution effect of an income tax cut is greater than the income effect ☞ unit 98) and so aggregate supply will increase. Cutting capital taxes will encourage workers to work harder and save more. Cutting taxes on employment will encourage firms to employ more workers. Cutting taxes on profits will encourage risk taking and entrepreneurship.

Cutting direct tax rates was high on the list of government priorities after 1979. The basic rate of income tax was cut from 33 per cent in 1979 to 25 per cent by 1988, whilst the highest rate of tax on earned income fell from 83 per cent to 40 per cent. Personal allowances, the amount of money a worker is able to earn before paying tax, increased by approximately 25

per cent in real terms over the same period. Capital gains tax and inheritance tax (formerly capital transfer tax) were reformed, reducing the tax burden and making it easier for people to pass on their wealth. National Insurance contributions were lightened. In particular the National Insurance Surcharge, a tax of 33½ per cent on company wages paid by employers, was abolished in 1984.

The capital market

Increasing competition in capital markets is beneficial in two senses. Firstly, choice is extended, whether for the couple seeking a mortgage, an individual wanting to save, or for firms wishing to raise finance for new investment. Secondly, small firms are more likely to be able to raise finance for expansion in a competitive market. Eliminating obstacles to a free financial market will encourage efficiency and increase aggregate supply.

Deregulation of the capital and money markets For instance, Big Bang in 1986 swept away the restrictive practices found in the City of London and particularly the Stock Exchange, making money and capital markets more competitive. The Building Societies Act 1986 gave Building Societies the power to compete with banks in offering a wide range of financial services. The abolition of exchange controls in 1979 allowed free movement of financial capital in and out of the UK.

Tax privileges for saving The tax system in the UK has traditionally favoured group savings schemes, such as pensions and assurance policies. It has therefore discouraged individuals from lending money directly to industrial companies, or buying shares in businesses. The government after 1979 wished to see a far more 'level playing field', where tax privileges are evened out between different types of saving. In particular, it has sought to establish a **share owning democracy**. Wider share ownership has been encouraged particularly through the privatisation proramme and through Personal Equity Plans (PEPS), a scheme whereby investors in shares gain tax relief. At the same time, assurance companies have lost some of their tax privileges.

Reduction of public sector borrowing If government spends more than it receives, it will need to borrow the money. But if the government borrows the money, and the money supply is fixed, that means that there will less money for firms to borrow (i.e. there will be financial **crowding-out**). Eliminating the PSBR or even repaying government debt will make it easier for firms to borrow money for investment purposes. The PSBR fell during the 1980s: between 1987 and 1990 there was a PSDR, (Public Sector Debt Repayment). As a consequence, by 1990 long term interest rates were lower than short term interest rates, and it was hoped that companies would use this opportunity to borrow more through issues of debentures (☞ unit 22), reducing the need for short term financing, and encouraging long term investment.

Entrepreneurship

The development of an 'enterprise culture' is at the heart of supply side economics. Entrepreneurs provide competition and develop new products in the market place. They therefore increase the productive and allocative efficiency of the economy. Moreover, some of today's small entrepreneurial firms will become the big successful businesses of tomorrow. Since 1979, the government has encouraged entrepreneurship through a variety of measures.

Reduction of marginal tax rates The small companies' rate of corporation tax was reduced from 42 per cent in 1979 to 27 per cent in 1989, whilst income tax rates were reduced as described above.

Freeing of labour markets Reductions in the power of trade unions and the repeal of restrictive employment legislation has helped create a free labour market for small businesses.

More efficient capital markets The government has attempted to increase the amount of capital available to small companies. The Business Expansion Scheme, set up in 1983, encourages investment in small companies by giving investors tax relief. The Enterprise Allowance Scheme provides unemployed people with £40 a week for a year while they set up their own businesses.

Reduction of government 'red tape' Planning controls, health and safety legislation, pollution controls and other such legal requirements prevent the entrepreneur from being as 'enterprising' as he or she might otherwise be. Since 1979, the government has attempted to reduce this red tape, particularly for small businesses. For instance, the burden of VAT administration has been reduced by various means.

The goods market

It is argued that competition increases both productive and allocative efficiency. Markets should therefore be made as competitive as possible. Encouraging competition was central to government policy after 1979.

Deregulation and privatisation The government has concentrated on measures to make the public sector more competitive. A significant number of public corporations, like British Telecom and British Gas, have been privatised. Central government departments and local authorities have been encouraged to put such services as waste collection or cleaning to tender rather than employing staff directly to provide the service. Many controls have been abolished, one of which was the ending of some of the legal restrictions on pub opening hours. The government also attempted, but failed, to remove legislation governing Sunday trading in 1988.

Elimination of state subsidies to inefficient producers If industries are making losses, this is a clear signal from the market place that the products of those industries are no longer wanted in such large quantities. Government propping up loss-making industries just to prevent unemployment results in a misallocation of resources. That money could be better used in growing industries in the economy. Hence, after 1979 government attempted to make all nationalised industries profitable (in the sense of private profit). In the case of industries like coal or shipbuilding, this has necessitated radical cuts both in plant and manpower. The government has refused to come to the help of declining industries in the private sector, despite calls for subsidies.

Encouragement of international free trade Fierce foreign competition results in a domestic industry which has to be efficient in order to survive. The government has had little sympathy for industrialists who have called for protectionist measures to save them from the effects of what they might call 'unfair'

competition. In contrast to most other EC countries, the government has also welcomed inward investment, for instance from Japanese companies. The government argued that, not only did these companies create wealth and jobs in the UK, but they also set competitive standards for existing UK firms to reach.

Regional and industrial policy

Before 1979, the main focus of supply side policies was regional and industrial policy. Since the time when manufacturing industry began to decline, arguably from the 1920s onwards, the UK government provided a variety of incentives to encourage firms to locate themselves in high unemployment areas. A variety of incentives have been used at different times:
- grants for new investment;
- tax relief on new investment;
- subsidies on employment;
- expenditure on infrastructure, such as motorways or factory buildings then available for subsidised rent;
- a requirement for firms to obtain permission from government to set up or expand in a low unemployment area of the UK (permissions called Industrial Development Certificates).

In the 1970s and early 1980s, the main incentive used was grants for new investment. It was felt that this was not only costly to the Exchequer, but also encouraged the siting of capital intensive manufacture rather than labour intensive manufacture or service industries in high unemployment areas. It was calculated, for instance, that the average cost between 1972 and 1983 to the government of creating an extra job in the assisted regions was £35 000 (at 1982 prices), whilst a total of 500 000 jobs had been created over the period (K Hartley and N Hooper, 1990).

In 1984, government implemented a new system of more selective regional assistance. The areas eligible for assistance were substantially reduced, and were graded into two levels: development areas and intermediate areas. Firms creating new jobs in development areas were automatically eligible for a regional development grant (RDG) of 15 per cent of investment expenditure up to a ceiling of £3 000 per new job created. Regional selective assistance (RSA) was made available to firms creating jobs or safeguarding jobs in both development and intermediate areas, but was discretionary. The Department of Industry attempted to provide the minimum financial support needed to secure the creation of new jobs.

In addition, the EC provided regional grants, but these were not necessarily tied to specific job creation. They were provided for new road building or land reclamation, as well as the building of factories.

There have also been a large number of measures

aimed at revitalising inner cities. The creation of Enterprise Zones, where companies setting up were offered tax incentives, reduced government 'red tape' and possibly subsidised premises, is one example of how government has attempted to regenerate old industrial areas.

Data question

UK VOCATIONAL TRAINING COULD CREATE 'SEMI-LITERATE UNDERCLASS'

In a report published today, the National Institute of Economic and Social Research argues that British vocational training policies for people under 18 are in danger of producing a 'certificated semi-literate underclass'. Ms Valerie Jarvis and Professor Sig Prais, authors of the report, studied differences between French and British approaches to training for retailing. In France they found that the numbers qualifying on retailing courses had doubled during the last decade. Training is based on two to three year courses. Half of those qualifying are pupils in full-time vocational secondary schools and the rest are on apprentice schemes with day-release provision.

In the UK, the number gaining these qualifications is only about one ninth of the French figure. The Youth Training Scheme has expanded the availability of short courses, but these aim only at an introductory level, substantially below that acceptable as a vocational qualification in France or West Germany. The basic levels of vocational qualification are mainly skill based and exclude the broader educational objectives aimed at in France. The authors also question the relatively small amount of externally-examined written tests used in British qualifications.

This approach could result in 'a certificated semi-literate underclass - a section of the workforce inhibited in job flexibility, and inhibited in the possibilities of progression.'

Source: adapted from the *Financial Times*, 1.7.1988.

1. Explain why the UK approach to training in retailing might inhibit 'job flexibility and ... possibilities of progression'.

2. What are the implications of the report for a government committed to implementing supply side policies?

Summary

1. The balance of payments is likely to be in disequilibrium if the value of exports and imports differs over a long period of time.
2. One policy weapon available to governments to tackle a current account deficit is to devalue the currency or allow it to depreciate. The Marshall-Lerner condition states that devaluation will be successful if the combined elasticities of demand for exports and imports exceed unity.
3. In the short term, devaluation is likely to lead to a deterioration in the current account position because of the J curve effect. In the longer term, the competitive benefits of devaluation may be eroded by cost-push inflation.
4. Deflationary policies will act to reduce imports because of the fall in total demand in the economy.

Raising interest rates is one way of implementing a deflationary policy.
5. Raising interest rates is also likely to lead to a rise in the value of the currency in the short term as speculative funds are attracted into the country.
6. Protectionist measures can reduce imports but the ability of governments to implement such policies today is severely limited by international agreements.
7. Supply side policies should lead to an increase in international competitiveness over long periods of time.
8. In the short term, a country may choose to impose currency controls, restricting the supply of its currency for use in international transactions.

Balance of payments equilibrium

The balance of payments can be said to be in **equilibrium** when there is no tendency for it to change. This is most likely to occur in the short to medium term if exports are equal to imports and hence both the current and the capital account are in balance. However, equilibrium could also exist if:

■ imports are greater than exports and the country is using borrowed foreign money to develop its economy as the USA did in the early part of the 19th century;

■ exports are greater than imports and the country is investing the money abroad in order to finance increased imports in the future. It can be argued that Japan is in this position today given that it faces a sharp decline in its workforce and a sharp rise in the number of pensioners in the next 30 years.

In the long term, countries are unlikely to be able to continue as substantial net borrowers because other countries will refuse to lend to countries which get deeper and deeper into debt (as has happened with many Third World countries during the 1980s). In the long term, therefore, equilibrium will occur when exports equal imports.

If the balance of payments is in equilibrium there will

be no tendency for the exchange rate to change. If, on the other hand, a country tends to export more than it imports over long periods, its exchange rate will tend to rise. The demand for the country's currency to pay for its exports will continually exceed the supply of currency offered for sale to pay for imports. Speculation may cause the exchange rate to fluctuate randomly in the short term if exchange rates are floating but the exchange rate trend is likely to be upward in the long term. If the country runs a persistent current account deficit, its exchange rate will tend to fall.

If the current account is in persistent deficit (or surplus), what measures can government take to rectify this situation? How can governments keep exchange rates up when there is persistent selling pressure from the markets?

Devaluation and revaluation

One possible way of curing a current account deficit is for the government to DEVALUE the currency. This means that it lowers the value of the currency against other currencies. Devaluation affects exports and imports because it changes their relative prices and thus affects their international competitiveness. The opposite of devaluation is REVALUATION, an increase in the value of the currency.

Devaluation assumes that the government pegs the value of its currency against other currencies. (This is done by European countries within the Exchange Rate Mechanism or ERM, for instance.) However, exchange rates may **float**, which means that governments allow free market forces to determine the value of the currency. A fall in the value of the currency is then called a DEPRECIATION of the currency. The opposite of depreciation is APPRECIATION of the currency. In what follows, it will be assumed that the government does control the value of the currency and therefore the term devaluation' rather than 'depreciation' will be used. However, devaluation and depreciation have the same effects, as do revaluation and appreciation.

The effects of devaluation

Assume that the pound falls in value against other currencies by 20 per cent. The price of imports will therefore rise in pounds sterling. With an exchange rate of 10F = £1, a French car sold to UK importers for 100 000 francs would have cost £10 000 in pounds sterling. With a 20 per cent devaluation of the pound, the new exchange rate will be 8F = £1. So the cost of a 100 000 franc car will be £12 500. At the new price, demand is likely to fall. The effect on the total value of imports will depend upon the elasticity of demand for French cars. If demand is elastic, the percentage rise in the price of French cars will be more than offset by a percentage fall in the demand for cars. Hence the total sterling value of imported French cars will fall. (This is an application of the relationship between elasticity and revenue ☞ unit 9). If demand is price inelastic, a rise in price will lead to a rise in expenditure on French cars and hence a rise in the sterling value of French car imports.

In summary, a devaluation of the pound will:
- leave the French franc **price** unchanged but increase the sterling price of imported goods;
- result in a fall in **import volumes**;
- lead to a fall in the **total sterling value** of imports assuming that domestic demand for imports is elastic; if demand is inelastic, there will be a rise in the sterling value of imports.

Devaluation of the pound should have no effect on the sterling price of exports. A £10 000 car exported to France will still be £10 000 after devaluation. But the price will have fallen in French francs. If the value of the pound falls from 10F = £1 to 8F = £1, the £10 000 car will fall in price in France from 100 000 francs to 80 000 francs. This should lead to a rise in demand for UK cars.

A devaluation will therefore:
- leave the **sterling price** of exports unchanged but reduce the price in foreign currency terms;
- lead to a rise in **export volumes**;
- increase the **total sterling value** of exports.

Devaluation and elasticity

Overall, devaluation of the pound will increase the sterling value of exports but may or may not lead to a fall in the value of imports depending upon the elasticity of demand for imports. It is likely that, even if import values increase, export values will increase even more. Hence devaluation will result in an improved current account position. The MARSHALL LERNER condition states that, given very stringent conditions, devaluation will result in an improvement on current account if the combined elasticities of demand for exports and imports are greater than 1. If the combined elasticities for exports and imports are less than 1, then the correct policy response to a current account deficit should be a currency **revaluation**.

Devaluation and pricing strategies

So far it has been assumed that UK exporters will choose to keep the sterling price of the products constant and change the foreign currency price whilst importers will choose to keep the foreign currency price of their goods the same and change the sterling price. However, exporters and importers may choose a different strategy. Jaguar, for instance, may price a model at $40 000 in the USA. If the value of the pound is $2 = £1, it will receive £20 000 per car. If the pound is now devalued to $1 = £1, Jaguar has a choice of strategies. It could keep the sterling price constant at £20 000 and reduce the dollar price to $20 000. However, a fall in price of a luxury car may give the wrong signals to US car buyers. They may assume that Jaguar cars are no longer luxury cars. They may think that Jaguar is not doing well in the US and is having to reduce prices in order to maintain sales. The fall in the dollar price may generate few extra sales. So Jaguar is likely to hold constant the dollar price of $40 000 and consequently increase its profit margins. When the value of the pound rises against the dollar, Jaguar may again choose to hold constant the dollar price. A rise in the dollar price may lead to large falls in sales if Jaguar is in a competitive market with other luxury car manufacturers.

If both exporters and importers adopt the strategy of leaving the prices they charge to their customers unchanged, devaluation will still improve the current account position. Assume the pound is devalued.

■ The sterling value of exports will rise because exporters have chosen to increase the sterling price of exported goods rather than reduce their foreign currency price. Export volumes will remain unchanged because the foreign currency price has remained unchanged. Therefore sterling export values will increase because of the sterling price increase.

■ The sterling value of imports will stay the same. Foreign firms have chosen to keep the sterling price of their goods constant. Hence volumes will not change. Neither, therefore, will the sterling value of imports.

With export values increased and import values unchanged, there will be an improvement in the current account position.

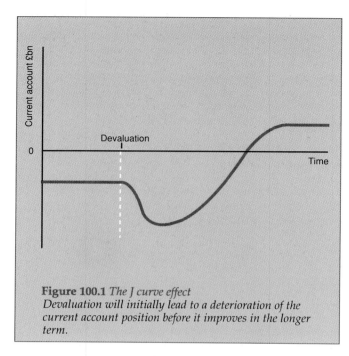

Figure 100.1 *The J curve effect*
Devaluation will initially lead to a deterioration of the current account position before it improves in the longer term.

QUESTION 2 Managers at Imperial Chemical Industries, Britain's biggest manufacturing company, have watched the currency fluctuation of the past two days with mixed feelings.

While the stock market, and some sections of industry, have viewed with concern the pound's fall through the psychologically important DM3 barrier, it benefits ICI in the short term because, like most European chemical companies, ICI sells its products in Western Europe at prices expressed in D-Marks.

For every 10 pfennig increase in the value of the D-Mark against the pound averaged over the year, ICI's profits increase by £25m.

Source: adapted from the *Financial Times*, 11.10.1989.

(a) Why should an increase in the value of the D-Mark lead to an increase in ICI's profits?
(b) Suggest reasons why ICI does not change the short term D-Mark price of its products when the value of the pound changes.

Problems associated with devaluation

There are two major problems with using devaluation as a policy weapon.

The J curve The current account following devaluation is likely to get worse before it gets better. This is known as the J CURVE EFFECT and it is shown in Figure 100.1.

Assume the UK has a current account deficit and attempts to devalue its currency. In the short run the demand for exports and imports will tend to be inelastic. Although the foreign currency price of UK exports will fall, it takes time before other countries react to the change. Hence, the volume of exports will remain the same in the short term, before increasing in the longer term. This means that in the short term, there will be no increase in sterling export values.

Similarly, although the sterling price of imports rises, in the short term UK buyers may be stuck with import contracts they signed before devaluation. Alternatively, there may be no alternative domestic suppliers and hence firms may have to continue to buy imports. Hence, in the short term, sterling import values will rise. In the longer term, contracts can be revised and domestic producers can increase supply, thus leading to a reduction in import volumes.

Overall, in the short term, import values will rise but export values will remain constant, thus producing a deterioration in the current account. In the longer term, export values will rise whilst import values might fall, producing an improvement in the current account position.

Cost-push inflation Devaluation generates imported inflation. This is not serious if there is a once and for all increase in prices. But if it starts up or fuels a **cost-push inflationary spiral**, then the increased competitiveness achieved by the devaluation will be quickly eroded. Keynesian economists have become increasingly sceptical of the value of devaluation as a policy weapon to cure a balance of payments deficit unless it is part of a much wider package of measures designed to increase the competitiveness and performance of a deficit economy.

QUESTION 3 Less inflation today entails more inflation tomorrow. The lesson of the 1980s is that you cannot cure inflation by clobbering industry; you merely postpone it.

It would be better to let the pound sterling fall, and accept that progress in reducing inflation in the short term will be slower, than to prop it up and exacerbate the problem of reducing the longer term underlying inflation rate. The UK government's aims, 'to bring inflation decisively down and keep it down' cannot be achieved by high interest rates and a strong pound.

Source: extract from a letter from Brian Reading, to the *Financial Times*, 5.12. 1989.

Explain the possible costs and benefits (i) in the short term and (ii) in the long term of maintaining a high value of the pound through a high interest rate policy.

Deflation

Devaluation results in **expenditure switching**. Foreigners buy more of our exports and less of their own and other countries' production, whilst domestic consumers buy fewer imports and more domestically produced goods. An alternative approach to curing a current account deficit is **deflation**. This is an **expenditure reducing** policy. If the government reduces aggregate demand in the economy, for instance by raising interest rates or increasing taxes, people have less money to spend so they reduce their consumption of domestically produced goods and imported goods. Imports therefore decline. Exports may also rise if domestic firms switch sales from the depressed domestic market to foreign markets.

For the UK, deflation has proved very successful in reducing imports, particularly because the UK has a very high **marginal propensity to import** in manufactured goods. The effect on exports has been less noticeable. Firms may well choose to reduce output in response to a recession in the economy rather than seek export orders.

One important policy advantage of deflation is that it is likely to reduce inflationary pressures in the economy, assuming those pressures come from the demand side of the economy. On the other hand, it also reduces growth and increases unemployment, both undesirable in themselves. In the long term, the economy must increase its international competitiveness unless the economy is to remain permanently below full employment.

Interest rates

Increased interest rates will initially bolster the value of the currency. They attract speculative inflows into the country, raising the demand for the currency. In the longer term, a rise in interest rates which must have been generated by a fall in the supply of money (☞ unit 73) will lead to a fall in aggregate demand through the **transmission mechanism** (☞ unit 81). Higher interest rates deflate the economy, leading to a fall in imports and hence an improvement in the current account.

QUESTION 4 In 1988, with a worsening balance of payments situation and rising inflation, the UK government raised interest rates. Bank base rates between 1988 and 1990 rose from 7½ per cent to 15 per cent.

Explain how a rise in domestic interest rates might lead to an improvement in the balance of payments current account position.

Protectionism

Increasing tariffs or quotas or other protectionist measures will reduce imports thus improving the current account position. Tariffs and quotas can both have a significant impact in the short term. However, protectionism is not much favoured by economists. Firstly, the country is likely to find itself becoming even more internationally uncompetitive in the long run as its domestic industries have no incentive to improve their efficiency. Secondly, protectionism in one country invites retaliation from its trading partners. The country could find that the gains on current account from reduced imports are more than matched by losses of exports as a result of retaliation (☞ unit 85).

Increased protectionist measures are also forbidden except under certain specific circumstances by GATT (the General Agreement on Trade and Tariffs). Membership of a trading bloc like the European Community severely limits the ability of individual countries to limit imports through protectionist policies.

Currency controls

A government may choose to impose or tighten currency controls. These are controls on the purchase of foreign currency by domestic citizens and firms. In the late 1960s, for instance, the UK government limited the amount of currency that could be taken abroad on holiday to £50 per person. Governments could equally restrict finance for investment abroad or even for imports. The government abolished exchange controls in 1979, and today, the UK government is unable to impose currency controls because of its membership of the European Community.

Supply side policies

One way of making domestically produced goods more competitive is through devaluation: altering the relative price of exports and imports. However, there are many other ways in which domestic industry can become more competitive internationally. **Supply side policies** (☞ units 98 and 99) aimed at reducing unit labour costs, increasing investment, increasing the skills of the labour force and improving the quality and design of products should lead to increased exports and reduced imports. Supply side policies tend to be long term policies. They cannot cure a current account deficit within, for instance, 12-24 months.

QUESTION 5 In February 1990, the government of Bangladesh, faced with a swelling of the country's current account deficit, tightened its currency controls. Importers were required to provide a 50 per cent cash deposit when opening new letters of credit.

A letter of credit is a type of loan common in export/import trade. Explain why the government measure outlined in the passage could lead to (a) an improvement in the current account position and (b) a rise in the value of the Bangladesh currency, the Taka.

Key terms

Devaluation and revaluation - a fall or rise in the value of the currency when the currency is pegged against other currencies.
Depreciation or appreciation - a fall or rise in the value of the currency when the currency is floating and market forces determine its value.
Marshall Lerner condition - devaluation will lead to an improvement in the current account so long as the combined price elasticities of exports and imports are greater than 1.
J curve effect - in the short term a devaluation is likely to lead to a deterioration in the current account position before it starts to improve.

Applied economics

Deflation and devaluation

Policy alternatives

In October 1990, the UK joined the Exchange Rate Mechanism (ERM) of the European Monetary System (EMS). Many economists argued that the exchange rate at which it joined, 2.95 deutschmarks to the pound, was too high. The UK was already suffering a huge current account deficit on its balance of payments - an estimated £14 000 million in 1990. With UK inflation rates higher than its European competitors, critics of the entry rate saw little chance of the current account returning to balance in the foreseeable future. If this were true, then one of two things should happen. Either the UK government would have to continue deflating the economy, as it had been since 1988, to reduce imports, or it would be forced to devalue the pound.

Table 100.1 *The current account balance and the PSBR*

	Current account balance	PSBR
1966	128	947
1967	- 281	1 844
1968	- 264	1 252
1969	482	- 534
1970	821	- 51
1974	- 3 186	6 451
1975	- 1 526	10 161
1976	- 963	8 899
1977	- 175	5 419

Source: adapted from CSO, *Economic Trends Annual Supplement*.

Deflation

Deflation has possibly been the most effective short term response to current account deficits in the post-war era in the UK. For instance, governments responded to the current account crises of both the mid-1960s and the mid-1970s by deflating the economy. As can be seen from Table 100.1, the government cut its budget deficit (the PSBR) in 1968 and 1969 to produce the turnaround in the current balance. Similarly, the budget deficit was cut in 1976 and 1977 to produce the return to balance on the current account.

One of the problems with deflation is that it causes unemployment. Keynesian economists would argue that there is a serious danger that deflationary policies to tackle the possible overvaluation of the pound on entry to the ERM will lead to permanently high unemployment. The only way that the UK will be able to sustain a fixed exchange rate will be to have unemployment at a higher rate than her continental partners, just as the price that Northern Ireland pays for a fixed exchange rate against the rest of the UK is permanently higher unemployment. Classical economists, however, would argue that any unemployment will be short lived. Unemployment will force down wages in the labour market and workers will then price themselves back into work.

Devaluation

An alternative to deflation is devaluation. France and Italy both devalued against the deutschmark on several occasions in the early 1980s after joining the ERM in 1979. Economists disagree about the effectiveness of devaluation. Some believe that devaluation results in cost-push inflation induced by the rise in import prices. This inflation erodes the competitive advantage of the initial devaluation. It can be argued that this is what happened following the 1967 devaluation of sterling. Initially, coupled with the deflationary measures adopted by the government, it increased UK competitiveness and produced a turn around in the current account. However, inflation continued to rise in the late 1960s and by the early 1970s, the competitive advantage gained had been eroded. For instance, the normalised IMF index of relative unit labour costs (a measure of international competitiveness based on relative labour costs) fell for the UK from 89.0 in the third quarter of 1967 to 77.6 in the first quarter of 1968 following devaluation in November 1967, but subsequently rose until it stood at 90.0 in the first quarter of 1972.

Others argue that devaluation can be effective if used in conjunction with other policy instruments. There is some evidence to suggest that devaluation affects, for instance, export volumes significantly. In 1968, following devaluation in November 1967, there was a jump of 14 per cent in export volumes, compared to the 2.5 per cent increase over the two years 1965-67. Similarly, when the sterling exchange rate index increased from 107.0 in 1979 to 119.0 in 1981, export volumes only increased 1 per cent in 1980 and fell 1 per cent in 1981. So export volumes are sensitive to price to some extent, although it is difficult to gauge how price elastic UK exports and imports are overall.

Data question

Sir,

Mr Douglas Jay appears to confuse causality with coincidence (when he argued in an article that the rise in sterling from 1979 to 1981 hit exporters hard).

The slump of the early 1980s was indeed preceded by a strong appreciation of sterling. However, applying this logic to sterling's fall against the D-Mark between 1985 and 1987, we should have seen a strong UK trade performance against West Germany in the late 1980s. We certainly did not.

The 1967 depreciation ensured that any future balance of payments surpluses were worth less in terms of foreign currencies. In addition, no incentive was given to the traded goods sector to reduce costs. These are the economics of depreciation. Indeed, the 1980s saw D-Mark appreciation and a huge German balance of payments surplus.

It is manifestly untrue to claim that the exchange rate is the only instrument available for curing the UK trade deficit. Higher productivity, innovation and production of desirable, high-quality products with low price elasticities are the way forward. Tinkering with sterling is no panacea for improved trade performance as the last 20 years demonstrate. Improved economic performance must be earned through better industrial performance. It cannot be bought in the currency markets.

W Simon Jacques, Cambridge.

Source: letter in the Financial Times, 13.10.1990.

1. **What evidence does the writer give to suggest that devaluation is not a solution to a balance of payments deficit?**
2. **Evaluate the economic solutions he does put forward for 'improved trade performance'.**

Summary

1. There are a number of different types of exchange rate system - mechanisms for determining the conditions of exchange between one currency and another.
2. The Bretton Woods system was an example of an adjustable peg system. In the short term, currencies were fixed in value against each other. In the longer term, currencies could be devalued or revalued. Currencies were fixed in the short term by central bank intervention - the buying and selling of currency using foreign currency reserves.
3. In a floating exchange rate system, the value of a currency is determined, without central bank intervention, by the forces of demand and supply in foreign currency markets.
4. With a managed or dirty float, the price of a currency is determined by free market forces, but occasionally central banks will intervene using their reserves to steady the price of the currency.
5. The Gold Standard was an example of a fixed exchange rate system. Currencies were pegged in value against gold and therefore they could not change in value against each other.
6. The European Monetary System is an example of a currency bloc. A group of currencies maintain fixed exchange rates against each other, but float against other currencies.

Exchange rate systems

An EXCHANGE RATE SYSTEM is any system which determines the conditions under which one currency can be exchanged for another. In unit 87, it was assumed that exchange rates were determined purely by the free market forces of demand and supply. This type of system is known as a free or floating exchange rate system. In contrast fixed exchange rate systems have existed in the past, where currencies have not been allowed to change in value against each other from year to year. In between, there is a variety of adjustable peg systems which combine elements of exchange rate stability in the short term with the possibility of exchange rate movements in the long term.

The Bretton Woods system

An ADJUSTABLE PEG SYSTEM is an exchange rate system where, in the short term, currencies are fixed or pegged against each other and do not change in value, whilst in the longer term the value of a currency can be changed if economic circumstances so dictate. Between the end of the Second World War and the early 1970s, exchange rates were determined by an adjustable peg system. It was known as the BRETTON WOODS SYSTEM after the town in the USA where the meeting by the Allied powers took place in 1944.

How it worked Under the system, each country fixed its exchange rate against other currencies. For instance, between 1949 and 1967, the pound was valued at US $2.80. This was known as the par value for the currency. The Bank of England guaranteed to maintain prices within a narrow 1 per cent boundary. So the price of the pound could fluctuate on a day to day basis between $2.78 and $2.82. Prices were maintained because central banks bought and sold currency. When the price of pounds threatened to go below $2.78, the Bank of England would intervene in the market and buy pounds. When the price threatened to go over $2.82, the Bank of England would sell pounds.

This is illustrated in Figure 101.1. The free market demand curve for pounds is $D_1 D_1$. In contrast, the demand curve under an adjustable peg system, $D_2 D_2$, is kinked. Above a price of $2.78, the demand curve is the same as the free market demand curve. But at $2.78, the Bank of England is prepared to buy any amount of foreign currency to maintain the value of the pound at this minimum level. Therefore the demand curve for pounds becomes horizontal (i.e. perfectly elastic) at this price.

Assume that the supply curve is initially S_1, resulting in

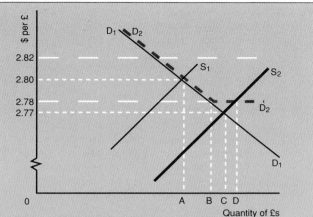

Figure 101.1 *Fixed exchange rate systems*
The pound is pegged at $2.80 but is allowed to fluctuate within a very narrow band from $2.78 to $2.82. If market forces shift the supply curve from S_1 to S_2, the Bank of England will need to buy BD pounds to maintain the minimum price of $2.78.

an equilibrium price of $2.80. OA is bought and sold and the Bank of England does not intervene in the market. Now assume that imports into the UK increase, shifting the supply curve for pounds to the right to, say, S_2. The new free market equilibrium price would be $2.77, below the minimum **intervention price** within the system, with OC currency bought and sold. The Bank of England would react to this by buying pounds with gold or foreign exchange held in its **reserves** (☞unit 86). To restore the exchange rate to the minimum $2.78, it has to buy BD pounds, the difference between the OB pounds demanded by the rest of the market at $2.78 and OD, the quantity supplied for sale.

If the value of the pound threatened to rise above the maximum price of $2.82, the Bank of England would sell pounds on the market, increasing the supply of pounds and thus forcing their price down. Note that on Figure 101.1, the supply curve of sterling under an adjustable peg system would be kinked like the demand curve, becoming horizontal (i.e. perfectly elastic) at a sterling price of $2.82. The Bank of England would be prepared to supply any amount of sterling in exchange for foreign currencies at a price of $2.82.

Adjustment mechanisms Under the Bretton Woods system, countries were committed to two major policy objectives:
- in the short term, to maintaining stable exchange rates;
- in the long term, to maintaining a balance of payments equilibrium (which they would be forced to do anyway by free market forces).

In the short term, exchange rate stability was maintained by buying and selling currencies as explained above. The system was therefore crucially dependent upon the existence of gold and foreign currency reserves held by central banks. In theory, the price of the currency was set at its long term equilibrium level. A run down in reserves caused by the need to buy the domestic currency when the currency was weak would be offset by increases in the reserves at other times when the currency was strong.

However, free market speculation could lead to very rapid depletions of a country's gold and foreign currency reserves. The UK suffered a series of **sterling crises** in the 1950s, 1960s and 1970s as speculators sold pounds believing that the UK government might devalue sterling. Governments had a limited number of options open to them if they wanted to maintain the value of their exchange rate.
- The most likely response to heavy selling pressure on the currency was to raise **interest rates**. This attracted speculative money from abroad, raising the demand for and therefore the price of the currency. In the medium term, a rise in interest rates would have a deflationary impact via the **transmission mechanism** (☞unit 81).
- The government could also attempt to prevent a fall in the value of the currency by introducing **currency controls** (☞unit 100).
- As a last resort, the central bank would turn to the **International Monetary Fund** (IMF). The founders of the system realised that there would be times when an individual country would run out of reserves. So it set up an international fund, the IMF, which would lend money to central banks when needed. Central banks

QUESTION 1

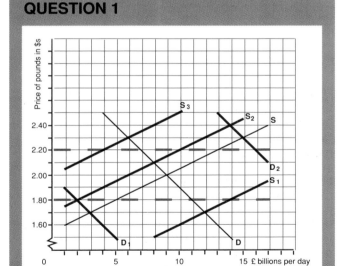

Figure 101.2
D and S are the free market demand and supply curves for pounds in $s. The Bank of England is committed to keeping the dollar price of sterling between $2.20 and $1.80.

(a) What is the free market price of the pound?
(b) With a demand curve D, how much currency (in £) will the Bank of England have to buy or sell per day if the supply curve shifts from S to: (i) S_1; (ii) S_2; (iii) S_3?
(c) With a supply curve S, how much currency (in £) will the Bank of England have to buy or sell per day if the demand curve shifts from D to: (i) D_1; (ii) D_2?

would deposit part of their gold and foreign currency reserves with the IMF and in return would be able to borrow a limited amount of money when in a crisis.

Short term measures were unlikely to satisfy the market for long if speculators were selling a currency because they judged that there was a FUNDAMENTAL DISEQUILIBRIUM on the country's balance of payments. If imports were greater than exports over a long period of time, the central bank of the country would continually be buying its currency and thus running down its reserves. Eventually the reserves, including any money borrowed from the IMF, would be exhausted and the currency would have to fall in value. Governments could adopt a number of long term policies to prevent this happening (☞ unit 100 for more detail).

■ It was intended that governments would officially devalue their currency before markets forced this anyway.

■ In practice, governments tended to deflate their economies, reducing imports and thus restoring a current account balance.

■ Protectionist measures, such as raising tariffs and quotas, were a possibility but were illegal under GATT rules (☞ unit 85). This severely limited their use by major industrialised countries.

■ Supply side policies designed to improve long term competitiveness were also a possibility.

QUESTION 2 In 1952, the ratio of world central bank gold and foreign currency reserves to total world imports stood at 70 per cent. By 1966, this had fallen to 38 per cent.

Suggest reasons why this fall is likely to have contributed to the collapse of the Bretton Woods system in the early 1970s.

Floating exchange rate systems

In a pure FLOATING or FREE EXCHANGE RATE SYSTEM, the value of a currency is determined on a minute by minute basis by free market forces. This is the exchange rate system described in detail in unit 87. Governments, through their central banks, are assumed not to intervene in the foreign exchange markets.

In theory there is no need for intervention because the balance of payments must always balance (☞ unit 86). The balance of payments will look after itself. In practice, governments find it impossible not to intervene because changes in exchange rates can lead to significant changes in domestic output, unemployment and inflation. Moreover, sharp falls in a currency are usually damaging politically and hence governments are tempted at these times to shore up the currency by buying in the market.

A system where the exchange rate is determined by free market forces but governments intervene from time to time to alter the free market price of a currency is known as a MANAGED or DIRTY FLOAT. Governments intervene by buying and selling currency as under the

Bretton Woods system explained above. It is 'managed' by governments. It is 'dirty' because it is a deliberate interference with 'pure' forces of demand and supply.

Adjustment mechanisms Since the collapse of the Bretton Woods system in the early 1970s, world trade has been regulated not under a pure free exchange system but under a system of managed or dirty floats. Governments have used interest rates and their gold and foreign currency reserves to manipulate the value of their currencies. Devaluation, revaluation and deflation have all been used in an attempt to alter current deficits or surpluses. Governments have found it more difficult to pursue openly protectionist policies because of international pressure for greater free trade. Currency controls too have fallen into disfavour as supply side economics has stressed the value of free markets and deregulation in promoting the international competitiveness of economies.

QUESTION 3 The pound ended higher yesterday after the Bank of England intervened consistently throughout the day in support of sterling. By the end of trading in London, sterling was nearly a cent higher against the dollar.

Source: adapted from the *Financial Times*, 30.9.1989.

(a) What is meant by 'intervened consistently'?
(b) Using a diagram, explain why the value of sterling rose against the dollar.

The Gold Standard

How it worked During much of the 19th century and the start of the 20th century exchange rates were determined by the GOLD STANDARD, an example of a FIXED EXCHANGE RATE SYSTEM. The major trading nations made their domestic currencies **convertible** into gold at a fixed rate. For instance, in 1914 a holder of a £1 note could go to the Bank of England and exchange the note for 0.257 ounces of gold. Because French citizens could exchange French francs for a fixed amount of gold, and German citizens the same, and so on, it meant that there was a **fixed exchange rate** between the major trading currencies of the world. The domestic money supply was directly related to the amount of gold held by the central bank. For every extra 0.257 ounces of gold held by the Bank of England, it could issue £1 in paper currency (the currency was backed by gold). On the other hand, a fall in the gold reserves at the Bank of England meant an equivalent fall in the paper money in circulation.

Adjustment mechanisms A deficit on the current account of the balance of payments could not be corrected by devaluation of the currency. By the rules of the Gold standard mechanism, the currency was fixed in value. Imbalances on the current account were corrected instead through deflation and reflation or changes in interest rates.

Assume that the UK is on the Gold Standard and that the current account is in deficit. There is therefore a net outflow of pounds to foreigners. Foreigners have no use for pounds so they will exchange those pounds for gold at the Bank of England. With less gold, the Bank of England will be forced to reduce its issue of notes (the notes handed in by foreigners for gold will effectively be destroyed). The money supply will fall and interest rates will rise. This will produce a deflation in the economy through the **transmission mechanism**. Not only will demand fall, reducing imports, but there will also be a fall in prices (predicted by the **quantity theory of money** ☞ unit 71). Exports will thus become more competitive and imports less competitive. The current account will return to equilibrium. The initial rise in unemployment caused by the fall in demand will be reversed as exports increase, returning the economy to full employment.

Currency blocs

A country may choose to peg its currency against one other currency but allow the currency to fluctuate against all others. This would be a minimal example of a CURRENCY BLOC, a group of currencies fixed in value against each other but floating against all others.

Possibly the most important currency bloc today is the EUROPEAN MONETARY SYSTEM (EMS). Most member countries of the European Community have agreed to keep their currencies within a $2\frac{1}{4}$ per cent band of each other. If a currency threatens to break out of the band, central banks of EMS countries will intervene in the market, buying or selling currency to keep the currency

---

QUESTION 4 The Italian lira remained very firm, at the top of the European Monetary System. In Milan the Bank of Italy bought D-Marks at the fixing and also intervened to support the French franc, as the lira threated to move above its cross rate limit against the franc. At the finish of trading in London the D-mark had rallied against the lira, advancing to L737.95 from L737.70.

Source: *Financial Times*, 9.3.1990.

Using diagrams, explain how intervention by the Bank of Italy affected the value of (a) the D-mark against the lira and (b) the French franc against the lira.

---

within the band. The bloc of currencies floats freely against all other world currencies including the dollar and the yen.

Like the Bretton Woods system, this is an example of a hybrid system, combining elements of fixed and floating exchange rate systems.

Key terms

Exchange rate system - a system which determines the conditions under which one currency can be exchanged for another.
Adjustable peg system - an exchange rate system where currencies are fixed in value in the short term but can be devalued or revalued in the longer term.
Bretton Woods system - an adjustable peg exchange rate system which was used in the post-Second World War period until its collapse in the early 1970s.
Fundamental disequilibrium on the balance of payments - where imports are greater than exports over a long period of time resulting in unsustainable levels of international borrowing.
Free or floating exchange rate system - where the value of a currency is determined by free market forces.
Managed or dirty float - where the exchange rate is determined by free market forces but governments intervene from time to time to alter the free market price of a currency.
The Gold Standard - an exchange rate system under which currencies could be converted into gold at a fixed rate, hence providing a relative price between each currency.
Fixed exchange rate - a rate of exchange between at least two currencies which is constant over a period of time.
Currency bloc - a group of currencies which are fixed in value against each other but which may float freely against other world currencies.
European Monetary System - a currency bloc where the participating currencies are fixed against each other within a $2\frac{1}{4}$ per cent band and where the bloc as a whole fluctuates freely against other currencies.

Applied economics

The Bretton Woods system

The Bretton Woods system first devised in 1944 provided exchange rate stability. Hence it can be argued that it encouraged the growth of world trade during the 1950s and 1960s.

It was intended that governments could choose how

to resolve a current account deficit. They could deflate the economy, creating unemployment, reducing imports and reducing domestic inflation. This was the same adjustment mechanism as present under the Gold Standard. They could also devalue the currency. By changing the relative price of exports and imports, the economy could be made more internationally competitive without creating unemployment. However, there would be some cost in terms of imported inflation.

In practice, countries tended not to devalue except in a crisis. This was because devaluation, wrongly in the view of many economists, came to be associated with economic failure. Deficit countries tended to use deflation as the main policy weapon to deal with balance of payments problems, negating the flexibility of adjusting relative prices built into the system. The burden of adjustment also fell solely on deficit countries. There was little pressure within the system for surplus countries to reduce their surpluses, for instance by revaluing their currencies. The result was that the system became increasingly brittle. Deficit countries like the UK tended to lurch from one foreign exchange crisis to the next whilst surplus countries like West Germany resisted pressures to take any action to reduce their surpluses.

Problems were compounded by the fall in the value of gold and currency reserves as a ratio of world trade over the 1950s and 1960s. To maintain exchange rate stability, central banks bought and sold currency. So long as the central banks were the main buyers and sellers in the market, they could dictate the price of foreign exchange. However, during the 1950s and 1960s world trade expanded at a much faster rate than gold and foreign currency reserves.

In an attempt to inject greater liquidity into the international financial system, the IMF issued **Special Drawing Rights** (SDRs) to member countries in 1969. SDRs are a form of international currency which can only be used by central banks to settle debts between themselves or with the IMF. When a country needs foreign currency to defend its own currency, it can buy it with the SDRs it holds. Whilst SDRs, effectively a handout of 'free' money, increased liquidity in the system at the time, the IMF failed to allocate further SDRs to member countries. The countries which control the IMF, the industrialised nations of the world, particularly the USA, are afraid that further creation of SDRs would encourage countries, particularly in the Third World, to put off dealing with fundamental balance of payments problems by using newly distributed SDRs to finance their large current account deficits. Today, SDRs account for only about 5 per cent of world reserves.

The Vietnam war from 1965 onwards made matters worse. To finance the war the USA ran a large current account deficit and therefore was a net borrower of money on its capital account. Individuals and firms were quite happy to lend their pounds, francs, deutschmarks and other currencies to the US and in exchange receive dollars because exchange rates were fixed to the dollar and dollars were seen to be as safe as gold itself.

By the late 1960s there was a large amount of money, particularly dollars, being held outside its country of origin. Americans were holding pounds, Japanese were holding deutschmarks, Germans were holding dollars, etc. This provided the base for large speculative activity on the foreign exchanges. It had become obvious that the United States would need to devalue the dollar if it were to return to a balance of payments equilibrium. On the other hand, it was obvious that Germany and Japan, two large surplus countries, would have to revalue their currencies. There was persistent selling pressure on the dollar and buying pressure on the D-mark and yen. Central banks found it more and more difficult to match the speculative waves of buying and selling. In the early 1970s, after some traumatic devaluations and revaluations, one country after another announced that it would float its currency.

The Bretton Woods system provided a long period of exchange rate stability during which there was a significant expansion of world trade. The cost of adjustment to current account deficits was probably less than under the Gold Standard. Although deflation was widely used in response to this problem, countries also devalued their currency, trading off slightly higher imported inflation for less unemployment. However, the system was not sufficiently robust to prevent its collapse in the early 1970s.

Data question

G7 AND EXCHANGE RATES

G7 is the Group of Seven, the seven largest industrial economies of the world. They meet on an irregular basis to discuss common problems. In late 1985 its predecessor, the Group of 5, met together and, in what became known as the Plaza Accord, agreed that the dollar should be devalued through central bank intervention in the foreign exchange markets. 2½ years later, meeting in France, the G7 ministers decided that the dollar had fallen far enough and needed supporting. The Louvre Accord informally pegged the dollar within a 5 per cent range of other major currencies. The foreign exchange markets, within a year of the signing of the Louvre Accord, had taken the dollar outside of its target range, but this in part was a reflection of the unwillingness of the G7 countries to intervene sufficiently to support the dollar.

1. **Using diagrams, explain how the G7 central banks could have intervened to change the value of the dollar (a) subsequent to the Plaza Accord and (b) subsequent to the Louvre Accord.**

The advantages and disadvantages of exchange rate systems

Summary

1. An exchange rate system should encourage world trade, particularly through exchange rate stability. Floating exchange rate systems have proved very poor at providing exchange rate stability.
2. Economic costs of adjustment when the balance of payments of a country is in fundamental disequilibrium should be low. Adjustment mechanisms within fixed exchange rate systems, such as the Gold Standard, and to a lesser extent adjustable peg systems, such as the Bretton Woods system and the EMS, tend to create unemployment because they rely upon deflation of the economy. In contrast, floating exchange rate systems tend to give rise to inflation when currencies depreciate following current account deficits.
3. Fixed exchange rate systems and to a lesser extent adjustable peg systems force governments to maintain inflation rates comparable to their industrial competitors.
4. Exchange rate systems should be robust. Free exchange rate systems are the most robust because they require the least government intervention.

Judging between systems

Over the past 200 years, a variety of exchange rate systems have been in operation. This would suggest that no system is without its problems. A number of criteria can be used to judge the relative merits of different exchange rate systems.

Encouragement of world trade

World trade enables countries to specialise in the production of those goods and services in which they have a **comparative advantage** (☞ unit 84). This specialisation increases the total amount of goods available for world consumption. Hence exchange rate systems could be judged upon the extent to which they encourage or discourage world trade.

It has long been argued that exchange rate volatility, such as occurs under free floats or managed floats, discourages trade. If exchange rates fluctuate by large amounts on a day to day basis, exporters and importers will find it impossible to know what price they will receive or have to pay for deliveries in the future. For instance, a UK exporter may agree to sell goods to the US for payment in US dollars in 3 months' time. Built into the $1 million price is a 10 per cent profit margin. Over

the 3 months, the pound falls in value against the dollar by 15 per cent. Not only will the exporter lose its planned profit, but it will also make a loss on the contract of about 5 per cent.

There are ways around this problem in a free or managed float regime. **Futures markets** exist where foreign exchange can be bought at a fixed price for delivery at some point in the future. So the exporter could have bought pounds **forward**. At the time it signs the export agreement, it would have taken out a contract in the foreign exchange markets to buy $1 million worth of pounds in three months' time (which it will pay for using the $1 million gained from the export contract). It now has a guaranteed price in pounds for its contract. Of course the forward price of pounds may be less than the price of pounds today (the spot price). But this is not important in the sense that the UK exporter will have based the export agreement price on the forward rate of the pound, and not on the current spot price. This process of buying currency forward to prevent losses is known as **hedging**.

Unfortunately futures markets are limited in their scope. It is not possible, for instance, to buy a currency for delivery in 5 years' time. So long term contracts need other forms of insurance. This is often provided by government agencies which guarantee prices in the domestic currency for large long term export contracts.

Hedging and insurance cost money and they therefore either discourage trade or raise its cost. Companies that are unable or unwilling to hedge or to insure have to decide whether or not to take the risk of proceeding with the export or import contract.

So in general the less volatile the currency movement, the less likely that international trade will be discouraged. Fixed exchange rate systems, such as the Gold Standard, and adjustable peg systems, such as the Bretton Woods system, are on these criteria considered to be 'better' systems than free or managed float systems.

QUESTION 1 Moves towards European monetary union would lift a heavy burden from the backs of Europe's smaller businesses, most of which lack the expertise to deal with the complexities of foreign exchange markets. Smaller businesses pay a high cost for converting small amounts of foreign currencies, says Ms Jane Waters, a foreign exchange consultant. Banks typically charge 1 per cent on small deals of up to $10 000, but only 0.1 per cent on larger amounts.

Van Halteren, a Dutch meat processor with annual sales of £23m, pays about £25 000 each year to hedge the riskier currencies, such as sterling.

Many small businesses are frightened off from using the textbook exchange hedges - forward transactions or currency option arrangements - because of their perceived complexity and cost. They take evasive action. They invoice customers in their own currency; some delay making transfers of funds until currency rates are favourable; others boost prices to cover the currency risk.

All these manoeuvres carry risks. Better by far, smaller owners argue, to establish a foreign exchange framework which allows companies to get on with their business rather than having to watch currency movements.

Source: adapted from the *Financial Times*, 28.7.1989.

Explain why exchange rate stability might encourage world trade.

Economic costs of adjustment

A country's balance of payments on current account can move into disequilibrium. Different exchange rate systems have different mechanisms for returning the balance of payments to equilibrium. The movement back to equilibrium may involve economic costs, such as increased unemployment or lower economic growth. The larger these transitional costs, the less attractive the exchange rate system.

The main cost of adjustment within a fixed exchange rate system or an adjustable peg system is likely to be increased unemployment. Under the Gold Standard, a current account deficit was automatically eliminated in the long term through a fall in domestic prices. However, economists disagree about the extent to which money wage rates fall quickly in response to unemployment. Keynesian economists tend to argue that wage rate adjustment is slow. Classical or monetarist economists argue that it is a relatively quick process. The slower the adjustment, the higher the cost in terms of unemployment and lost output. Countries abandoned the Gold Standard in the early 1930s because they felt that floating exchange rates would enable their economies to reduce unemployment at a faster rate than if the exchange rate was linked to gold.

Under the Bretton Woods system, countries tended to avoid devaluing their currencies (☞ unit 101). When current accounts moved into deficit, governments tended to deflate their economies, imposing higher taxes or reducing government expenditure. Unemployment therefore rose as the rate of economic growth fell.

One of the main criticisms of floating and managed exchange rate systems is that they encourage inflationary behaviour on the part of governments. Assume that an economy has a higher inflation rate than its major trading partners and that, consequently, the current account is in deficit. Under the Bretton Woods system, governments would have been likely to tackle these two problems through deflating the economy. Under the Gold Standard, deflation would have occurred automatically. Rising unemployment and lost output are politically unpopular as well as costly economically. Under a floating exchange rate system, the exchange rate should fall automatically with a current account deficit. This leads to **imported inflation**. A government can avoid tackling domestic inflation and the current account deficit simply by allowing the exchange rate to fall continually. Hence there is no anti-inflation discipline built into the floating exchange rate system.

Moreover, tackling inflation under a floating exchange rate system can be more costly than under fixed exchange rate systems. Assume that the government reduces the money supply and raises interest rates as part of an anti-inflation package. The rise in domestic interest rates will encourage an inflow of speculative funds on the capital account. This will increase the price of the currency. An increase in the exchange rate will make the economy less internationally competitive. Exports will fall and imports will rise leading to a worsening of the already bad current account deficit. But falling exports and rising imports also lead to a fall in aggregate demand, pushing the economy into recession. This recession is part of the process by which inflation falls and the economy becomes more internationally competitive. The current account will only return to equilibrium when the market exchange rate is approximately equal to the **purchasing power parity rate** (☞ unit 87). It will only stay in equilibrium when the country's inflation rate is equal to that of its trading partners. Lowering inflation is a painful process and will certainly not be politically popular.

QUESTION 2 Throughout the 1980s, the UK exchange rate was determined under a floating exchange rate system, whilst the exchange rate of her main EC trading partners was determined under an adjustable peg system - the ERM. Inflation rates in all EC countries tended to fall in the first half of the 1980s. However, countries which formed part of the ERM saw their inflation rates continue at a low level in the second half of the 1980s, whilst in the UK inflation increased from 1987. In 1990, the UK joined the ERM having already raised interest rates to very high levels in an attempt to curb inflation in the economy. By 1991, the UK economy was in recession.

(a) Why might the choice of exchange rate systems have affected inflation in the UK compared to her EC trading partners?
(b) Explain why recession was necessary if the UK was to maintain a stable exchange rate in the ERM once she had joined in 1990.

Financial disciplines

Today, there are some who argue that inflation is the most important economic problem facing economies and government. Monetarists argue that inflation is caused by excessive increases in the money supply. Under the Gold Standard, governments are unable to expand the money supply unless stocks of gold in the central bank rise first (although countries did issue a fixed amount of notes which were not backed by gold - the **fiduciary issue**; this did not affect the principle that central banks could not increase notes in circulation without corresponding increases in their stocks of gold). Changes in stocks of gold are unlikely to be very large in the short term. Hence the Gold Standard provides an important check on the ability of governments to generate inflation through the creation of money.

Equally, under an adjustable peg system such as the Bretton Woods system, governments could not allow their inflation rates to differ greatly from their industrial competitors because otherwise they would lose international competitiveness, their current account would go into deficit and they would then be likely to deflate to solve this problem.

However, under a floating exchange rate system, as argued above, governments can always solve problems of international competitiveness, caused by domestic inflation, by allowing their currencies to fall in value. There is no financial discipline imposed by the system.

Robustness of the system

Some exchange rate systems are extremely **robust**: that is, they are unlikely to break up when economic conditions are unfavourable. The more likely it is that an exchange rate system will break up under strain, the less attractive the exchange rate system.

Fixed exchange rate systems, or adjustable peg systems, are less robust than free or managed float exchange rate systems. Countries abandoned the Gold Standard in the early 1930s during the Great Depression because they wanted to be able to devalue their currencies in order to gain competitive advantage. By devaluing, they hoped to be able to reduce imports, boost exports and thus reduce domestic unemployment. However, the rest of the 1930s, with a managed float system of exchange rates, saw a series of competitive devaluations with countries trying to export their unemployment. Competitive devaluations are ultimately self-defeating because devaluation by one country, matched by a devaluation by another country simply left exchange rates unchanged.

The unsatisfactory experience of the 1930s led to the creation of the Bretton Woods system. It broke up in the early 1970s, partly because countries failed to devalue and revalue when there was a fundamental disequilibrium on their current accounts and partly because central banks lacked reserves to counter the growing mountain of speculative money which moved so quickly from country to country.

The managed float system of the 1970s and 1980s has had to cope with three oil crises, and in the early 1980s, the worst world slump since the 1930s. Free and managed float systems are extremely robust because governments can allow free market forces to determine the value of the exchange rate without intervening in the market. However, the extreme volatility of exchange rates over the period has led many to advocate a return to some sort of fixed or adjustable peg system. The robustness of the system is less attractive than the exchange rate stability that can be found, for instance, within the European Monetary System.

QUESTION 3 In the early 1970s, the Bretton Woods system of exchange rates broke up. Explain why the system proved insufficiently robust.

Applied economics

European Monetary Union

History

The debate about European Monetary Union (EMU) has a long history in the European Community (EC).

Different currencies within Europe can be argued to be a major obstacle to trade in the same way as tariffs or quotas. In 1970, the Werner Report proposed the creation of a European Monetary Union and for a short period in the early 1970s, the 6 member countries of the EC pegged their currencies against each other. However, the inflationary pressures of the time, culminating in the oil crisis of 1973-4, broke the system as one country after another either devalued or revalued.

The late 1970s saw more stable economic conditions and a fresh start was made in 1979 with the creation of the European Monetary System (EMS), the most important component of which was the Exchange Rate Mechanism (ERM). Member countries agreed to peg their currencies within a 2¼ per cent band of a weighted average of European currencies. This weighted average is called the ECU (the European Currency Unit). Since 1979, there have been 11 **realignments** within the EMS, as countries have devalued or revalued. However, these realignments have been relatively small and the last occurred in 1987. In general, the low inflation, current account surplus countries such as West Germany and Holland have revalued their currencies whilst higher inflation, current account deficit countries such as France and Italy have devalued their currencies.

In 1989, Jacques Delors, President of the EC Commission, presented a radical report suggesting that member countries should move to full European Monetary Union in three stages.

Stage 1 All member countries of the European Community would join the EMS. Controls on financial capital movements between countries would be removed whilst the 1992 'single market' programme would hasten complete freedom of exchange in goods and services.

Stage 2 A European System of Central Banks (ESCB) would be set up, which would co-ordinate monetary policy in the Community, although national central banks would remain in ultimate control of policy for their individual economies. Planning would take place for the next stage.

Stage 3 The ESCB would become the central bank of the European Community, responsible for monetary policy throughout the Community. It would determine exchange rates with third countries such as the US and manage all official reserves. European currencies would be locked together at fixed exchange rates (there would not even be a narrow band in which individual currencies could fluctuate). For monetary policy to be effective, national governments would lose control over their budgets. Rather like local authorities in the UK are set spending limits by Westminster, so Brussels would set spending limits on national governments. Finally, national currencies would be abolished and a single European currency introduced.

The advantages of EMU

The Delors plan is highly controversial. Proponents of the plan argue that it will bring considerable economic benefit to member countries because it will not only increase trade through the elimination of exchange rate fluctuations, but it will also lower costs to industry simply because firms will not have to buy foreign exchange for use within the Community.

Moreover, EMU provides the best way forward to achieve low inflation rates throughout the Community. During the 1980s, high inflation countries, such as France and Italy, have had to reduce their rates of inflation to match the low German rate of inflation. If they had not done this, the franc and the lira would have been periodically devalued (as indeed they were in the early 1980s), negating the fixed exchange rate advantages of the system. Effectively, the German central bank, the Bundesbank, sets inflation targets and therefore monetary policy targets for the rest of the EC.

Why Germany has had a lower inflation rate than her European counterparts in the 1970s and 1980s is a matter of debate. However, it can be argued that the independence from political control of the Bundesbank is the major factor. In countries such as France and the UK, central banks are under the control of governments. If the UK government decides to loosen monetary policy, for instance by reducing interest rates, it can order the Bank of England to carry out this policy on its behalf. There are often very strong pressures, particularly before an election, for governments to loosen the monetary reins and create a boom in the economy. The Bundesbank, in contrast, is independent of government. By law it has a duty to maintain stable prices. It can resist pressures from the German government to pursue reflationary policies if it believes that these will increase inflation within the economy.

The European central bank is likely to be, like the Bundesbank in Germany and the Federal Reserve Bank in the US, independent of government and established with a duty to maintain stable prices in the Community. The hope is that this new central bank will be as successful as the Bundesbank has been in controlling inflation.

There is also a political agenda to EMU. It can be only be achieved by the creation of a central European bank, the complete removal of national control over monetary policy and partial removal over fiscal policy. It will be a considerable step forward towards political union, a United States of Europe.

The disadvantages of EMU

Throughout the 1980s, the UK has been in the forefront of resisting moves towards greater monetary union. It only joined the ERM in 1990, and only after considerable political pressure both within the UK and from its European partners. Throughout the 1980s the government argued that it would be impossible to maintain exchange rate stability within the ERM for a petro-currency like the pound, particularly given the UK's higher inflation rate compared to Germany's (i.e. the system would not be sufficiently robust). There is strong opposition amongst many in the UK to any move towards stages 2 and 3 of the Delors plan.

One argument used against EMU is that the trade advantages have been grossly over-estimated. There is little to be gained from moving from the current ERM, which provides broad exchange rate stability, to a system of fixed exchange rates between countries.

On the political side, it is argued that an independent European central bank is undemocratic. Governments must be able to control the actions of their central banks because governments have been democratically elected by the people, whereas an independent central bank would be controlled by a non-elected body. Moreover, a European central bank would involve considerable loss of sovereignty. Power would be transferred from Westminster to Brussels. This would be highly undesirable because national governments would lose the ability to control policy. It would be one more step down the road towards a Europe where Brussels was akin to Westminster and Westminster was akin to a local authority.

Perhaps the most important economic argument relates to the deflationary tendencies within the system. In the 1980s, France has managed to reduce her inflation rates to German levels at a cost of higher unemployment. The adjustment mechanism in the ERM has acted rather like that of the Gold Standard. Higher French inflation led to French current account balance of payments deficits and downward pressure on the franc. To reduce the deficit, France had to lower its inflation rate by deflating its economy. Exactly the same could well happen to the UK. Reduced inflation will be the result of tight fiscal and monetary policy in the UK. Inevitably, unemployment will rise and real wages will fall. In a pure free market economy, investment would flow out of Germany into the UK to take advantage of cheaper labour whilst industry in the UK would become more competitive than German industry because its labour costs had fallen. The UK would return to full employment at a low inflation rate.

In the real world, such adjustment mechanisms work only very imperfectly. Without a devaluation of sterling within the ERM, unemployment will almost certainly rise in the UK as inflation is squeezed out of the system. But unemployment could then remain stubbornly high, despite wages being lower in the UK than in Germany. The UK won't then have the option of reflating the economy to reduce unemployment because, under stage 1 of the Delors plan, such a reflation would be bound to generate inflation, whilst under stage 3, the UK government would have lost the political power to carry out such a policy to Brussels.

It can be argued that an EMU-type system has long operated within the UK. Wales, Scotland and Northern Ireland have a fixed exchange rate with the UK. Northern Ireland, for instance, cannot devalue against the pound to boost exports and employment. For at least the past 50 years, the South of England has arguably been more prosperous than the rest of the UK. The UK could then become the Northern Ireland of Europe, locked into a low inflation, low wage and high unemployment position. Brussels has long recognised this problem and has consistently advocated strong regional policies to counteract high regional unemployment, as does the Delors plan. But regional policy requires money, and rich German taxpayers are unlikely to look favourably on large increases in their contributions to subsidise their UK counterparts.

ENTRY TO THE ERM

The UK joined the ERM in October 1990 at an exchange rate of DM2.95 to the pound. Many argued that this was far too high an exchange rate for entry. The UK was running a large balance of payments deficit, estimated to be £15bn on current account in 1990. The UK inflation rate was over 7 per cent higher than the German inflation rate and the economy was going into recession as a result of a high interest rate policy. Comparisons were made with 1925, when Winston Churchill put Britain back onto the Gold Standard at too high a level, and with 1980 when the government allowed the pound to soar to record levels. In both instances, the UK subsequently suffered a severe recession.

1. **What might be the economic consequences of Britain's entry into the ERM at an exchange rate of DM2.95?**

103 Economic growth and government policy

Summary

1. Government policy to increase economic growth over the long term should be directed towards increasing labour productivity, either by raising the skills of the labour force or by increasing the quantity or quality of the capital stock.
2. Some economists argue that governments should intervene in the market place if high economic growth is to be achieved. They advocate such policies as increased expenditure on education and training, subsidies for investment, direct government investment in the economy and grants or subsidies for Research and Development.
3. Other economists argue that government is poorly placed to judge how resources should be allocated within an economy. They argue that it is the role of government to liberate markets of restrictions. They advocate the use of supply side policies to increase the rate of economic growth.

The causes of economic growth

Economic growth occurs when there is an increase in the quantity or quality of the factors of production or when they are used more efficiently (☞ unit 63). A government wishing to increase growth in the economy fundamentally must pursue policies which will increase **labour productivity** (i.e. output per worker). There are three main ways to achieve this:

■ the quality of the labour force can increase, meaning that each worker on average can produce more output with an existing stock of capital and an existing state of technology;

■ the quantity of the capital stock can increase, meaning that workers are able to use more capital, thus raising average output;

■ the state of technology can change, meaning that a given capital stock can be more productive with a given labour force.

Government policies to promote growth therefore need to be directed at both the labour and capital markets.

An interventionist approach

Some economists believe that the market mechanism is unlikely to lead to optimal rates of economic growth. There are so many forms of **market failure** (☞ unit 34), that the government must intervene in the market place. For instance, it can be argued that the economic prosperity of countries such as France, Germany and Japan are based upon **interventionist** policies of their governments. There are many ways in which government can act to increase the growth rate of the economy.

Increased public expenditure on education and training The quality of the workforce can be increased if educational standards are raised. This could be achieved if, for instance, more children stay on at school or college after the age of 16, or more people go to university or polytechnic. But a significant increase in the numbers in full time education is likely to require significant increases in the education budgets of government.

Alternatively, employers could provide more training for their staff. But in a free market, firms are under strong cost pressures to spend as little as possible on training. Many firms may find it far cheaper, rather than to train staff directly, to 'poach' trained staff from other firms. The result is market failure - the inability of the free market to provide sufficient training for the country's workforce. Here again there is a crucial role to be played by government. The government could force the private sector to undertake more training, for instance by passing laws which state that firms must pay for at least one day's training a week for all 16 to 18 year olds employed. Or it could encourage training at work by providing generous subsidies to employers with strong training programmes.

QUESTION 1 Britain's low staying-on rate is partly a consequence of schools' failure to motivate children during the compulsory years of education. But it also reflects the type of education available for 16 to 18 year olds. At present, a sharp distinction is drawn between a minority of academic students, who are encouraged to stay on and study for Advanced level examinations, and the non-academic majority, who are expected to leave school and either take a job or seek a place on the government's Youth Training Scheme. The present system serves the interests of neither group.

Source: extract from 'The need to stay the course' by Michael Prowse in the *Financial Times*, 29.11.1989.

(a) Suggest reasons why 'the present system serves the interests of neither group'.
(b) What policies might the government adopt to improve the system?

Subsidising investment Economic theory suggests that firms will invest more if the cost of capital declines (☞ unit 54). So the government could subsidise investment if it wished to increase investment spending in the economy. It has a variety of ways to do this. It could, for instance, provide direct subsidies for new investment, giving a grant for a proportion of any new investment undertaken by a firm, or it could offer tax incentives. Investment could be offset against corporation tax liability. Governments could offer selective assistance to particular industries which it believed would be important in the future. This is known as a policy of 'picking winners'.

Alternatively the government could reduce the cost of capital by lowering interest rates, leading to a move along the **marginal efficiency of capital schedule.** One way of possibly reducing interest rates is to increase the personal savings ratio. The argument here is that actual injections, $I + G + X$ must equal actual withdrawals, $S + T + M$ (☞ unit 78). If G, X, T and M remain constant, an increase in S, total savings, will lead to an increase in I, the level of investment. This occurs through the interest rate mechanism. Hence measures which encourage saving, such as tax allowances, may increase the level of investment.

QUESTION 2

Sir, It is perplexing that in the UK economic debate there is so little focus on the personal sector savings ratio. To raise the underlying rate of growth there must be, in addition to greater risk-taking activity (via lower corporate and income taxes), a higher average rate of investment.

The principal way this can occur is if the personal sector consistently saves a higher proportion of its income, thereby indirectly increasing the amount of borrowing that the corporate sector can undertake whilst maintaining balance of payments equilibrium.

Reasons for a low savings/investment ratio lie not in cultural characteristics but in fiscal incentives. In particular, the combination of mortgage interest tax relief, no capital gains tax on profits from property sales, and taxation on savings/investment income, engenders a low savings ratio.

The UK economy will only be transformed when deferred consumption (savings) becomes the most attractive means of boosting one's asset-based wealth, a la Japan. This could be achieved by imposing a capital gains tax on property profits while making savings income tax free - ensuring that the bulk of funds saved were indeed redirected to the corporate sector.

Jack Brown

Source: Letter in the *Financial Times*, 29.11.1989.

(a) Explain what, in the author's opinion, is the cause of low economic growth in the UK.
(b) How might the measures he advocates increase the growth rate?

Direct government investment Free market forces, even when working in their most efficient way, may still result in a less than socially desirable level of investment in the economy. The government may then be forced to intervene directly, investing in nationalised industries or creating new state owned companies, or investing in infrastructure.

Encouraging Research and Development

Governments can encourage technological progress in a variety of ways. For instance, it can fund universities and polytechnics to engage in fundamental research. It can establish research institutions. It can give grants or tax subsidies to private firms undertaking research and development. It can encourage the widespread dissemination of new inventions and new technologies by subsidising their price, or offering free assistance to firms wanting to know how new technologies might be of benefit to them.

Another way is to encourage the growth of large monopolies and to discourage the existence of small and medium size companies in the market. In the Austrian view(☞ unit 37), large monopolies are the firms which are the most likely to have the money and the incentive to engage in Research and Development. They have the money because they are able to earn abnormal profit. They have the incentive because their monopoly power depends upon their hold over the market with existing technology. In the process of **creative destruction**, monopolies can be destroyed by new competitor firms offering new products to satisfy the same wants. For instance, the monopoly power of the railways of the 19th century was destroyed by the coming of the motor car. On the other hand, firms in perfect competition have no incentive to undertake Research and Development because there is perfect knowledge in the market. Any invention will quickly become common knowledge and will be copied by all firms in the industry.

A free market approach

The alternative approach has a long tradition in economics. Free market economists argue that the market is the most efficient way of allocating resources. Government intervention is at best ineffectual and at worst seriously damaging to the long run economic growth of the economy.

For instance, governments are not best placed to judge what type of training is needed by companies. If companies don't train their workers, it is because the economic rate of return on such training is too small. Companies must be using their scarce resources in more profitable ways (i.e. ways which increase national income more than expenditure on training). Subsidising investment too is economically damaging. It alters the balance between present and future consumption, making future consumption seem more valuable than it is. It encourages capital intensive industry and discriminates against labour intensive industry (because capital intensive industry will receive a large subsidy) without there being any economic justification for this distortion.

As for 'picking winners', government has a long history of throwing money at loss making ventures. Concorde, the shipbuilding industry, and nuclear power, are examples of 'winners' that successive UK governments have picked. Nor has the quality of research in British universities given us a competitive advantage over the Japanese and the Germans.

Free market economists argue that it is government's role to release the power of the market. Cutting taxes, cutting bureaucracy and red tape, privatisation, reducing the power of trade unions, encouraging entrepreneurship, competition and small firms, will all create an **enterprise culture** which in turn will lead to fast economic growth. So free market economists argue that supply side measures (☞ units 98 and 99) are necessary if growth is to be raised.

Applied economics

QUESTION 3 Privatisation of the small Lincolnshire port of Boston, completed earlier this week, marks a turning point for the ports industry. The port was sold by the local council to two local companies for £4.1m.

The sale was made possible by the abolition of the National Dock Labour Scheme in 1989. The scheme, set up by the first post-war Labour government, was intended to end the use of casual labour by placing control of pay and conditions in the hands of local boards of employers and union representatives, and by reserving certain types of work for registered dock workers who were effectively guaranteed jobs for life.

To the employers and to the government, it was an anachronism which restricted growth, limited management initiative, and led to abuses such as 'ghosting', under which overmanning allowed registered dock workers to go home on full pay.

According to the British Ports Federation, abolition of the scheme has led to the redundancy of about 4 000 of the 9 000 former registered dock workers.

Boston, which was losing £100 000 a year under municipal ownership, is expected to move into profit quickly under private ownership as a result of the new manning arrangements.

Source: adapted from the *Financial Times*, 5.1.1990.

How might the abolition of the Dock Labour Scheme lead to faster economic growth for the UK economy?

Industrial policy

In the 1980s, various governments, notably in the UK and the USA, have pursued vigorous free market supply side policies in the belief that economic growth can best be stimulated by reducing government intervention in the market and liberating the energy and dynamism of market forces. This non-interventionist approach has already been discussed at length in units 98 and 99. Here we will consider the alternative strategy of interventionist industrial policy.

It has been argued by some economists that countries such as Japan, Germany and France have experienced higher growth rates than the UK as a direct result of interventionist policies pursued by the governments of these countries. In Japan for instance, the Ministry of International Trade and Industry (MITI) has used a wide range of policies in the post-war period aimed at transforming Japan into a world industrial super-power. Following Japan's defeat after the Second World War, US economists advised Japan to rebuild industries in which it had a comparative advantage, such as textiles and agriculture. This advice was rejected because it was felt that such a development strategy would create a Japan which would always lag behind the USA and Europe in economic development. Instead, through MITI, a number of key industries were identified which would

be the industries of the future. Initially these included ships and steel, and later cars, electrical and electronic goods and computers. MITI then used a battery of policies to stimulate growth in these industries. These included:
■ indicative plans for the whole economy, showing how output was set to grow industry by industry in the future;
■ tax incentives, precisely targeted and withdrawn once a particular goal had been achieved;
■ the creation of state owned companies to undertake research and production in high-risk areas of investment;
■ large scale public funding of research and development programmes;
■ encouraging co-operation between producers where this would enable Japanese companies to compete more successfully in international markets, even if this discouraged domestic competition;
■ encouraging the free exchange of views and ideas between companies, particularly with regard to the fulfilling of state plans for the economy;
■ subsidising investment in key industries;
■ selective use of import controls, particularly to protect emerging industries.

The relationship between MITI and private industry was an informal one. Firms did not need to follow MITI plans. However, the deference to authority within Japanese society meant that Japanese companies on the whole conformed to the plans laid down by the ministry. MITI seems to have been successful at 'spotting winners' - selecting those industries which are likely to have high growth rates in the future.

In France, there have been a succession of state economic plans in the post-war era. Like the Japanese plans, they are indicative plans, showing how the French government expects output to rise over the next five year period. Again, like the Japanese, the French government has been openly interventionist, supporting key industries, particularly high technology industries, through tax incentives, subsidies, tariffs and quotas and the giving of many other forms of support.

The UK has a long history of free trade, dating back to its dominance in trade in manufactures in the 19th century. Industrial policy has been pursued in a much less coherent manner and with far less conviction than in many other industrial countries. One important aspect of UK industrial policy has been **regional policy** (☞ unit 99), but this has been implemented far more to redirect industry to particular locations in the UK than to stimulate industrial growth overall. The Labour government of 1964-1970 has possibly been the government most committed to interventionism in the post-war period. In 1965, it produced a National Plan which was made irrelevant within months of its issue because the government decided to deflate the economy in order to resolve an exchange rate crisis. It also created the Industrial Reorganisation Corporation (IRC), which encouraged key companies to merge in order to be able to exploit economies of scale more fully and be better equipped to compete in international markets. The IRC was abolished by the incoming Conservative administration in the early 1970s. The Labour administration of 1974-1979 created the National Enterprise Board, a holding company for the various relatively small state owned and partially state owned companies in public hands. Lack of funds prevented it from pursuing an aggressive strategy in, for instance, new technologies and it never had a significant impact on the structure of output before it was dissolved by the Conservative administration after 1979. From this evidence, it would be difficult to argue that UK industrial policy has been a key factor in promoting high growth. Advocates of interventionist industrial policy suggest that industrial policy has never really been given a chance to operate in the post-war period in the UK, and this explains its ineffectiveness. Free market economists suggest that it operated but has been ineffective and therefore government intervention in the market should be radically reduced.

INDUSTRY 2000

The Labour Party is constantly taunting the government for its neglect of manufacturing industry. But what would Labour do if it were elected to power?

The crux of the party's alternative strategy is in its newly launched Industry 2 000 policy. According to the document, science-based industries once produced a £3 billion trade surplus but now generate a deficit approaching £6 billion. To remedy this there is a list of detailed proposals to boost technology, including the stimulation of science parks to cross-fertilise with industry, the encouragement of firms from different industries to collaborate and the establishment of nursery units to help advanced technology firms to sprout.

Companies increasing spending on Research and Development would be protected by new takeover procedures which would enable them to invest for the long term, whilst protecting them from being caught by 'corporate raiders' with their share price down.

Source: *The Guardian*, 7.3.1990.

1. **Explain how the Labour Party's proposals outlined in the article might stimulate economic growth.**
2. **What problems may be faced in implementing such proposals in the UK?**

104 The redistribution of income and wealth

Summary

1. Governments redistribute income and wealth because they believe that this will increase economic welfare.
2. They can do this through fiscal means, raising taxes from the relatively well off to spend on services and benefits for the relatively less well off.
3. Governments can also legislate to promote greater equality, for instance through passing equal pay legislation or imposing minimum wages.
4. Some economists argue that redistribution gives rise to large welfare losses. These include lower economic growth and higher unemployment. They conclude that the poor would be better off in the long term without any redistribution of income and wealth by government.
5. Other economists argue that there is little or no evidence to suggest that economies where government redistributes a considerable proportion of income and wealth perform any differently from more free market economies.
6. Critics of the market approach reply that many groups in society, such as the handicapped and the elderly, can only enjoy rising living standards if government deliberately intervenes in their favour.

The distribution of income and wealth

Free market forces give rise to a particular distribution of income and wealth in society. This distribution is unlikely to be either **efficient** or **equitable**. In units 33 to 45, the causes of inefficiency in a market economy were outlined as were the government policies which might correct this **market failure**. This unit outlines how government might intervene to make the distribution of income and wealth in society more equitable.

The current distribution of income and wealth can be seen by government as undesirable for various reasons.

■ **Absolute poverty** (☞ unit 41 for a definition of this and other terms used in this section). Absolute poverty may exist in society. At the extreme, people may be dying on the streets for want of food, shelter or simple medicines.
■ **Relative poverty** may be considered too great. The government may consider the gap between rich and poor in society to be too wide.
■ **Horizontal equity may not exist**. For instance, men may be paid more for doing the same jobs as women. Workers from ethnic minority groups may be discriminated against in employment and housing.
■ The current distribution may be seen to conflict with considerations of **economic efficiency**. For instance, it might be argued that income and wealth differentials need to be increased in order to provide incentives for people to work harder.

The first three of the above arguments suggest that income and wealth differentials should be narrowed. In recent years, however, **supply side economists** (☞ units 98 and 99) have argued strongly that income differentials need to be widened if economic growth is to be increased. How can governments change the distribution of income and wealth in society?

Government expenditure

Government expenditure can be used to alter the distribution of income. One obvious way is for government to provide monetary benefits to those requiring financial support. Social security and national insurance benefits now account for over 30 per cent of UK government expenditure.

However, governments may wish to target help more precisely. For instance, an increase in the old age pension will not necessarily relieve absolute poverty amongst some old people. They may live in houses which are damp and cold and be unable or unwilling to pay considerable sums of money to remedy the situation. So the government may choose to spend money on housing for the elderly, for instance providing low rent housing or offering renovation grants for owner-occupied property. Similarly, governments may choose to help children in need not by increasing child benefit but by offering free clothes or food coupons.

Another important area of government activity is the provision of goods and services which give citizens equality of opportunity in society. The Beveridge Report of 1942 argued that citizens should have access to a minimum standard of health care, housing and education as well as minimum incomes and employment. Some argue that education, housing and health care are no different from cars or holidays. If people have a high income, they should be able to buy better education for their children and better health care for themselves, just as they can buy better cars or more expensive holidays. Others argue that all people should have equal access to the **same** education and health care because these are basic to any standard of living in a modern industrialised economy. Private education and private health care should not be available to those who are capable of affording it.

Taxation

The taxation system plays a crucial role in determining the distribution of income in society. Taxes can be **progressive, regressive or proportional**.
■ Income tax, capital gains tax and inheritance tax are broadly progressive (i.e. the higher the level of earnings of the taxpayer, the higher the proportion of income paid in that tax).
■ VAT is broadly proportional.
■ Excise duties and the poll tax are regressive.
  If there is to be a significant redistribution of income from the rich to the poor, the tax system has to be progressive in nature. The government needs to tax away a higher proportion of income from the well off than from the poor. On the other hand, if the government wishes to widen income and wealth differentials, it should make the tax system less progressive or more regressive.

Legislation

The government may alter the distribution of income directly through its spending and taxation decisions. However, it can also influence the behaviour of private economic agents through legislation. For instance, governments may choose to introduce minimum wage legislation (☞ unit 50), forcing employers to increase rates of pay for the lowest paid workers. They may also choose to make discrimination illegal through measures such as equal pay legislation, or they may force employers to provide benefits such as sickness benefit, pensions, medical care for their employees or redundancy payments. They may attempt to raise the incomes of the low paid and the unemployed through effective retraining or helping workers to be more mobile geographically.

The costs of redistribution

Intervention in the economy may well lead to higher economic welfare for some, but it may also lead to lower economic welfare for others.
  There is an obvious cost to those in society who lose directly from increased taxation. Some economists argue that any taxation results in a loss of freedom. The taxpayer loses the ability to choose how to allocate those scarce resources which are now being expropriated by the state. Therefore in a free society taxation should be kept to an absolute minimum. On the other hand, **the law of diminishing marginal utility** (☞ unit 14) would suggest that taking resources away from an affluent individual to give to a poor person will lead to an increase in the combined utility of the two individuals. The loss of utility by the rich person will be less than the gain in utility by the poor person. It is difficult to show this conclusively because it is not possible to make direct utility comparisons between individuals.
  Classical or supply side economists would suggest that redistribution involves heavy costs in terms of economic growth and employment. Raising income tax rates lowers the incentives of those in employment to work (☞ unit 98) thus reducing the rate at which the aggregate supply curve shifts to the right. Classical economists would also argue that redistribution reduces the incentive of those out of work to find jobs. High unemployment benefits can make it more worthwhile to remain unemployed than to gain employment. This raises the natural rate of unemployment and depresses the level of output in the economy. Minimum wage legislation and equal pay legislation may lead to a loss of employment. Economic theory suggests that if firms are forced to pay higher wages, they will employ fewer staff. High tax rates can lead to a flight of capital and labour from an economy. Individual entrepreneurs may choose to leave the country, taking their money and skills with them. Firms may choose to locate abroad to take advantage of lower tax rates, leading to a loss of domestic jobs and income.

There is also a host of other distortions which become endemic in the system. For instance, some have argued that subsidies to home owners through mortgage income tax relief have led to too great an investment in the housing stock of the country at the expense of investment in wealth-creating industry. Provision of free children's school clothing can lead to some parents selling the clothing immediately and using the money for other purposes. High taxes lead to the growth of tax avoidance and evasion where a considerable amount of resources are devoted to circumventing tax legislation.

QUESTION 3 In the 1980s, a small number of British-born millionaires returned to live in the UK after having gone into tax exile. The reductions of income tax in the 1980s made it far more attractive for these individuals to reside in the UK.

How might a lowering of income tax rates benefit (a) the better off and (b) the less well off?

The role of government

Free market economists argue that the costs of government intervention are extremely large. They are so large in fact that any possible welfare benefits resulting from the redistribution of income from the rich to the poor are far outweighed by the welfare losses which result. They argue that economic growth will increase if taxation is low, if government regulation of the economic activities of the private sector is minimal and if state production of goods and services is kept to the barest minimum. The poor may lose out because there will be little in the way of state benefits. But they will be more than compensated for this through increased economic growth. The wealth generated by the better off in society will trickle down to the less fortunate. For instance, the poor would be better off receiving 10 per cent of a 'national cake' of £20 bn than 15 per cent of a cake of only £10 bn.

The argument that the poor would be better off if income differentials were wider rather than narrower is dependent upon a number of propositions:
- that being better off is a matter of absolute quantities rather than relative quantities;
- it must be true that high marginal income tax rates are a disincentive to work and to enterprise;
- a generous benefit system must act as a disincentive to work;
- there must be a mechanism through which increased wealth in society will benefit not just the rich but also the poor, particularly those who for whatever reason are unable to work.

This could be the case for many employed people but there is no mechanism apart from charity in a free market economy for groups such as the handicapped, the sick and the elderly to benefit from increased prosperity enjoyed by the rest of society.

QUESTION 4 In 1989, the Methodist Conference attacked the government's 'divisive' social and economic policies which victimised the poor. In reply, the Prime Minister, Margaret Thatcher, stated: 'Over the past decade living standards have increased at all points of the income distribution - that includes the poorest.'
'After allowing for inflation, a married man with two children who is in the lowest tenth of earnings has seen his take-home pay go up by 12.5 per cent'.
'Of course some have, through their own endeavours and initiative, raised their living standards further. They are also paying more in taxes, and those who earn most are contributing a higher proportion of the total that government receives from income tax'.
'You equate wealth with selfishness. But it is only through the creation of wealth that poverty can be assisted.'
'Our task is to enlarge opportunity so that more and more people may prosper.'

Over the 1980s, the distribution of income became more unequal. Explain how Margaret Thatcher defended this in her reply to the Methodist Conference.

Applied economics

Redistributive policies in the UK

The Welfare State, whose foundations were laid down by Clement Attlee's Labour administration of 1945-51, should ensure that every citizen of the UK enjoys a minimum standard of living. To achieve this, higher income earners are taxed more than lower income earners and the money is used to provide a variety of benefits in kind and in cash.

Table 104.1 is a CSO (Central Statistical Office)

estimate of how this redistribution affects incomes. It is based on figures from the Family Expenditure Survey, a yearly sample of approximately 7 000 households in the UK. The households have been split into quintile groups (i.e. fifths) according to original incomes of households. For instance, the 1 435 households which form the bottom fifth of households ranked on original income had an original income of

Table 104.1 *Redistribution of income through taxes and benefits, 1986*

United Kingdom   £ per year and numbers

	Quintile groups of households ranked by original income					
	Bottom fifth	Next fifth	Middle fifth	Next fifth	Top fifth	All households
Average per household (£ per year)						
Earnings of main earner	10	1 420	5 980	9 400	16 050	6 570
Earnings of others in the household	-	80	710	2 760	6 720	2 050
Occupational pensions, annuities	50	770	720	480	620	530
Investment income	50	400	480	430	1 180	510
Other income	10	130	130	110	220	120
Total original income	130	2 800	8 030	13 180	24 790	9 790
+ Benefits in cash						
Contributory	1 750	1 880	740	380	270	1 000
Non-contributory	1 620	840	510	490	410	780
Gross income	3 500	5 520	9 280	14 060	25 470	11 570
- Income tax[1] and NIC[2]	- 10[3]	330	1 490	2 710	5 650	2 030
Disposable income	3 510	5 200	7 790	11 350	19 820	9 530
- Indirect taxes	880	1 540	2 280	2 900	4 250	2 370
+ Benefits in kind						
Education	370	450	650	850	850	630
National Health Service	910	870	730	710	720	790
Travel subsidies	50	60	50	50	100	60
Housing subsidy	130	80	50	30	20	60
Welfare foods	50	40	30	20	20	30
Final income	4 130	5 150	7 020	10 120	17 260	8 740
Average per household (numbers)						
Adults	1.4	1.7	1.9	2.2	2.6	2.0
Children	0.4	0.4	0.7	0.8	0.7	0.6
Economically active people	-	0.6	1.2	1.8	2.2	1.2
Retired people	0.8	0.8	0.3	0.1	0.1	0.4
Number of households in sample	1 435	1 436	1 436	1 435	1 436	7 178

1. After tax relief at source on mortgage interest and life assurance premiums.
2. Employees' National Insurance contributions.

Source: CSO, *Social Trends*.

3. Negative average tax payments result largely from imputed tax relief on life assurance premiums paid by those with nil or negligible tax liabilities.

just £130 a year. The top fifth of households, the 1 436 households with an original income of £24 790 per year, earned on average 190 times as much.

These sharp inequalities are reduced through the effects of the tax and benefit system. Benefits in cash, contributory (i.e. National Insurance benefits) and non-contributory benefits increase the incomes of the bottom quintile of income earners from £130 to £3 500 a year. Whilst many benefits are targeted on low income households, some benefits are universal benefits, available to all whatever their income. The most important universal benefit is child benefit.

Benefits have to be paid for by taxes and National Insurance contributions (NICs). The tax system is often considered to be **progressive** in the UK (☞ unit 45). However, as Table 104.2 shows, it is only mildly progressive over the top 60 per cent of the income range if taxes are taken to be direct taxes - income tax and NICs. If indirect taxes are included, then the tax system is regressive over much of the income range. If

income is defined as original income, average tax rates fall from 669 per cent for the bottom fifth of households to 40 per cent for the top fifth. If income is defined as gross income, then the tax system is progressive for the bottom to middle fifth of income earners, but regressive for the middle to top fifth of income earners.

Households receive a variety of benefits in kind. It is commonly believed that the households which most benefit from benefits in kind are low income households. However, Table 104.1 shows this not to be the case. The bottom fifth of households received £1 510 in benefits in kind whilst the top fifth of households received £1 710. In part, this reflects the different composition of households in each quintile. In the bottom fifth, there is a heavy concentration of retired people. Hence, on average whilst the bottom fifth receive more from the NHS, they receive less benefit from education. There are relatively few retired people in the top fifth of households, but there are almost twice the number of children. Hence the top fifth receive less benefit from the health service but more from education.

Overall, whilst the top fifth of households received 190 times the amount of original income compared to the bottom fifth of households, in terms of final income the ratio was only 4.2. Moreover, the top fifth of households contained more people - an average 3.3 compared to 1.8 for the bottom fifth of households. Hence, final income per person in the top fifth of households was £5 230 whilst in the bottom fifth it was £2 294, an income differential of 2.3 times. So it would seem that the Welfare State is successful to some extent in reducing inequalities in society. What the statistics fail to show is a relatively small but growing number of people at the bottom of the income range who during the 1980s seem to have dropped out of the safety net of the Welfare State.

Table 104.2 *Taxes as a proportion of income*

	Bottom fifth	Next fifth	Middle fifth	Next fifth	Top fifth	All house-holds
Tax rate as percentage of original income						
Income tax and NIC	0	12	19	21	23	21
Income tax, NIC and indirect taxes	669	67	47	43	40	45
Tax rate as percentage of gross income						
Income tax and NIC	0	6	16	19	22	18
Income tax, NIC and indirect taxes	25	34	41	40	39	38

Source: adapted from CSO, *Social Trends*.

'SOCIAL GAP GREW IN 1980s,' SAYS INSTITUTE

People living on social security fell 'much further behind the rest of population' during the 1980s, the Institute for Fiscal Studies said yesterday. The Institute's research attempts to update the official series of statistics headed Low Income Families which was dropped by the government two years ago. Information in the final official report stopped at 1985 and the Institute's research carried it on to 1987.

It shows that the number of families receiving supplementary benefit between 1979 and 1987 increased by two-thirds, mainly because of the rise in unemployment during the period. The Institute explained that the value of social security benefits increased a little over the period while average earnings rose much faster. People on benefit in 1987 were therefore much farther behind the rest of the population than in 1979.

The overall picture was one of 'more on low incomes, more people on the minimum safety net benefit and, indeed, more people with incomes below this minimum benefit level', the Institute said. Nearly 2m families had incomes below the supplementary benefit line in 1987, 'despite the fact that it is often assumed that the line is a safety net below which nobody should fall'.

National Children's Bureau, a charity, said the Institute's figures showed that the number of children in families receiving supplementary benefit increased by 115 000 between 1985 and 1987, and those with family incomes below supplementary benefit level rose by 50 000. The bureau was concerned at 'growing evidence that during the 1980s children have borne the brunt of changes that have occurred in economic conditions, demographic structure and social policies in the UK'.

Source: *Financial Times*, 12.10.1990

1. **How, according to the article, have inequalities changed during the 1980s?**
2. **Why have there been changes?**
3. **Evaluate a range of policies which could help relieve poverty in the UK.**

105 The limits of government policy

Summary

1. Government policy is aimed at achieving high growth, low unemployment, price stability and a balance of payments equilibrium.
2. In the Keynesian model, trade-offs exist between high growth and low unemployment, and price stability and a balance of payments equilibrium.
3. Keynesian economists favour the use of fiscal policy to influence the level of aggregate demand in the economy. It can also be used to stimulate investment, training and other supply side variables.
4. Devaluation and prices and incomes policies are also sometimes advocated by Keynesian economists although there are doubts about the long run effectiveness of these policies.
5. Monetarist economists argue that inflation is a monetary phenomenon and can be reduced through control of the money supply.
6. Classical and supply side economists argue that there are no long run trade-offs between macro-economic policy variables. A high economic growth rate can be achieved with price stability and a current account equilibrium if markets are able to adjust to their free market equilibrium levels.

Goals and instruments

It is generally argued that governments have four main macro-economic policy goals:

■ to maintain full employment;
■ to ensure price stability;
■ to achieve a high level of economic growth;
■ to keep the balance of payments in equilibrium.

Sometimes it is also argued that governments have a major responsibility to ensure an equitable distribution of income and wealth, whilst in the 1990s, it is possible that environmental objectives may come to rank in equal importance to these other goals.

Government can achieve these goals by using a wide range of policy instruments, which have been discussed extensively in previous units. These include:

■ fiscal policy - e.g. changing tax rates, the size and distribution of government spending and public borrowing;
■ monetary policy - e.g. controlling the growth of the money supply, changing interest rates, altering terms of credit;
■ exchange rate policy - revaluing or devaluing the currency;
■ supply side policies - some of these, such as lowering marginal tax rates on income, could be classified under fiscal policy, but others include trade union reform, competition policy, privatisation and deregulation, and reform of financial markets.

Demand management policies aim to influence the level of aggregate demand in the economy, whilst supply side policies aim to influence the level of aggregate supply.

Competing economic models of the economy produce radically different policy prescriptions to the problems which beset economies. In this unit, the limitations of government policy will be examined within the framework of the different models outlined in previous units.

The Keynesian model

The Keynesian model of the economy suggests that, in the UK at least, governments face difficult trade-offs between inflation and growth on the one hand and unemployment and balance of payments equilibrium on the other. Figure 105.1 illustrates this. The economy starts off at less than full employment at output level OA. The government decides to reflate the economy by expanding aggregate demand. Traditional demand management techniques would see cuts in taxes and increases in public spending, resulting in an increase in the budget deficit or a reduction in the budget surplus. Cuts in interest rates or relaxations in credit or hire purchase controls might be used to reinforce this. Via the multiplier process, there will be an expansion in aggregate demand, pushing the aggregate demand curve in Figure 105.1 to AD_2.

This shift in the AD curve has returned the economy to full employment at OB. The growth rate in the economy will have increased, simply because GDP will have gone up faster than it would have done if aggregate demand had remained at AD_1 (note that, strictly speaking, this is not economic growth but rather economic recovery - economic growth can only result from increases in aggregate supply, the productive potential of the economy ☞ unit 63). However, the price level will have risen from OE to OF and the current account on the balance of payments will have moved from a surplus of JK to a deficit of KL.

Note that the expansion in demand was greater than the minimum needed to secure full employment. Government only needed to increase aggregate demand to AD_3 to secure its objective of returning the economy to full employment. Keynesian economists have long recognised that it is difficult for governments to 'fine-tune' the economy to an exact position.

On Figure 105.1, it is impossible for the government to

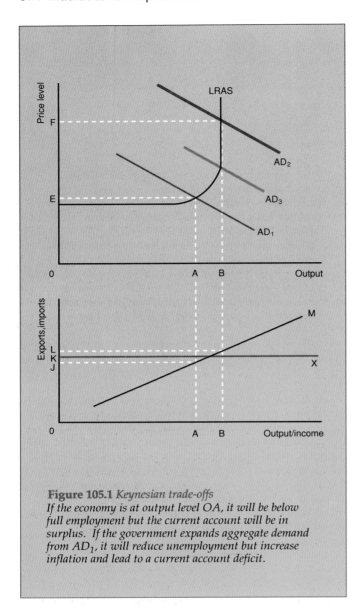

Figure 105.1 *Keynesian trade-offs*
If the economy is at output level OA, it will be below full employment but the current account will be in surplus. If the government expands aggregate demand from AD_1, it will reduce unemployment but increase inflation and lead to a current account deficit.

achieve simultaneously full employment and a current account equilibrium with price stability. The full employment level of income, OB, coincides with a current account deficit and a rise in prices from OE. Keynesian economists have suggested a variety of ways around this possible problem.

Devaluation This would increase exports and reduce imports, returning the economy to equilibrium on the current account. However, as many Keynesian economists would recognise, this in itself produces trade-offs. Devaluation will lead to higher import prices and increased aggregate demand because of increased demand for exports and import substitutes. This in turn will lead to cost-push and demand-pull inflation, eroding the competitive gain from devaluation. Some Keynesians would accept that devaluation is likely to lead to current account gains only in the short to medium term. In the

longer term, say after 5 years, the increased inflation induced by devaluation will have wiped out any competitive gain.

Supply side measures Measures which simultaneously increase output and stimulate exports could be used. For instance, exporters could receive subsidies in the form of cheap loans, foreign exchange insurance, and reduced tax rates. Alternatively, if unemployment was mainly structural rather than cyclical, government could use regional policies or training policies to reduce unemployment, and this could well result in more exports and fewer imports than if the government adopted expansionary demand side policies.

Prices and incomes policies The inflationary impact of an increase in demand could be reduced by the use of prices and incomes policies. Whilst Keynesian economists would accept that the three periods of prices and incomes policy in the 1960s and 1970s in the UK failed in their objective to reduce long term inflation, there are still many Keynesians who believe that a more sophisticated form of incomes policy (for instance, taxing wage increases above a pay norm) would work.

QUESTION 1 In May 1990, the Labour Party issued a campaign document on running the economy. It stated that the Labour Party was committed to exchange rate stability and interest rate stability through membership of the European Exchange Rate Mechanism (ERM).

Increased government spending would be dependent upon economic growth, and would not be financed by increased borrowing. The document states: 'We will not spend, nor will we promise to spend, more than Britain can afford'. However, it would borrow to finance long-term productive investment such as that required in transport and regional investment. It would encourage joint public and private sector capital investment programmes where appropriate. It would also establish a National Investment Bank to help finance new and growing companies and for small and medium-sized regional businesses.

Inflation would be controlled through a variety of policies including ERM membership, checks on the expansion of credit and longer-term supply side measures designed to make industry more competitive. The Party proposes to develop 'regular discussions' between government, employers and trade unions about economic prospects and the competing claims on national output.

Supply side policies would be aimed at increasing investment in the economy and bringing about a 'skills revolution' through improved training for workers.

Source: adapted from the *Financial Times*, 16.5.1990.

(a) To what extent could Labour Party policy outlined in the passage be described as 'Keynesian'?
(b) Suggest why, on economic grounds, the Labour Party has stated that it will only increase government spending in line with general growth in the economy.

Keynesians are generally sceptical of the ability of the labour market, by itself, to restore full employment. Doing nothing, when output is below full employment, at OA in Figure 105.1, might lead eventually to more jobs as workers accept real wage cuts, pricing themselves back into work, but the process is long and difficult. Doing nothing is not an appropriate policy response according to Keynesians.

Equally, whilst they agree that long term growth can only be achieved through supply side growth, they would argue that measures such as cutting marginal tax rates on income or reducing unemployment benefit will have little impact on incentives to work. The key to supply side growth is stimulating greater investment, both in physical and human capital. So using a high interest rate policy to curb inflation is more likely to be damaging to growth because high interest rates discourage investment more than, say, increasing income tax.

Monetarist, classical and supply side models

Just as there are as many Keynesian beliefs as there are Keynesian economists, so too there are many differences in thinking between economists who would classify themselves as 'monetarist', or 'classical' or 'supply siders'. These last three terms refer to three different strands of beliefs amongst non-Keynesian economists.

- Monetarism refers to the belief that inflation is caused by increases in the money supply over and above the real rate of growth in the economy (☞ units 71 and 93).
- Classical economists tend to believe that free markets are highly efficient, whereas government intervention in the market tends to lead to economic inefficiency.
- Supply side economists are economists who believe that increased growth in the economy can only be secured through the freeing of markets from government intervention. This can be achieved through micro-economic policy and not through traditional macro-economic demand management policies popularised by Keynesian economists.

Classical economics and monetarism have a long history. The belief that the duty of government was to protect property rights, maintain a stable currency and provide public goods whilst leaving the production of all other goods and services to free markets was known as **laissez-faire** in the 19th century.

Unemployment Classical economists, faced with the unemployment depicted in Figure 105.1, would argue that the government should not directly intervene. They believe that the long run aggregate supply curve is vertical, as in Figure 105.2. If the economy is below full employment at A, then free market forces will return the economy to equilibrium at B. In the labour market, unemployment will force workers to accept real wage cuts, and thus workers will be priced back into jobs. The cuts in wage rates will mean that the short run aggregate supply (drawn on the assumption of constant wage rates)

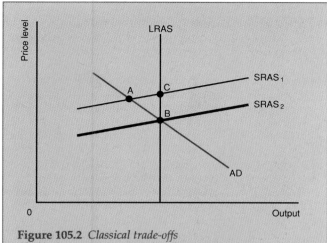

Figure 105.2 *Classical trade-offs*
Classical economists argue that the sort of trade-offs believed to exist by Keynesians are only short run trade-offs. In the long run, the economy will always be at full employment on the long run aggregate supply schedule LRAS.

will shift downwards from SRAS$_1$ to SRAS$_2$. Therefore, there is no long run trade-off between unemployment and inflation as Keynesians would suggest.

Inflation If there is inflation in the economy, this can be reduced through restricting the growth of the money supply. This will have a short run cost. Reducing the rate of growth of the money supply will be initially deflationary. Cuts in money supply growth will, via the transmission mechanism, initially affect output and therefore increase unemployment. But in the longer term, the economy will return to equilibrium with unemployment unaffected at its natural rate. Fiscal policy must be subordinated to monetary policy if the government is to achieve money supply control.

Growth Long term growth can only be raised through increased growth in aggregate supply. If unemployment is considered too high, then again this is a supply side problem. A fall in the natural rate of unemployment and an increase in growth can only be achieved through the successful implementation of supply side policies. Fiscal policy should therefore be used to influence not macro-economic demand as Keynesians suggest, but micro-economic decisions by workers, firms and consumers.

The balance of payments Classical economists argue that the current account can largely be left to itself if, firstly, foreign exchange markets are free and secondly, a current account deficit is not being caused by excess government spending. If foreign exchange markets are free, the currency will find its own level and markets will ensure that undesirable current account deficits are rectified through depreciations. Excess government spending, however, can hamper this. We know that injections must equal withdrawals, so I + G + X = S + M + T. If I and S are roughly equal, then M - X, the current account balance, must equal G - T, the government budget balance. If the government budget is in deficit, this must cause a current account deficit. So the elimination of government budget deficits are important if trade deficits are to be eliminated too.

Trade-offs According to classical economists, the trade-offs which Keynesian economists believe to exist are, if anything, only short term trade-offs. If the economy were at A in Figure 105.2, an increase in aggregate demand would restore the economy to full employment but at the unnecessary cost of higher inflation. Demand management techniques have other limitations.

If the economy is already at B, increased aggregate demand, whilst initially leading to increased output and lower unemployment, will in the longer term be purely inflationary. The economy will return to the natural rate of unemployment at C shown by the vertical long run aggregate supply curve. In the process, government may have increased its share of spending in GDP. This increase in government spending will have resulted from a fall in private sector spending - the process known as **crowding out**.

Demand management will only have its desired effect if the monetary stance of the government changes. For instance, increased government spending which is financed by genuine borrowing will have no effect on aggregate demand. Increased public sector spending will be matched by a reduction in private sector spending resulting from loans by the private sector to the government. The expansionary effect of increased government spending arises only if it is financed by printing the money needed. So fiscal policy cannot be used to influence macro-economic aggregate demand,

whereas monetary policy is dangerously powerful - dangerous because increases in the money supply lead to increases in inflation.

QUESTION 2 The Conservative Party won three successive general elections in 1979, 1983 and 1987. In its election manifestoes, the Party put forward a consistent set of economic policies for the 1980s. It argued that the foremost economic priority was the control of inflation. This could be achieved through the use of monetary policy, either by controlling the growth of the money supply directly or through interest rate policy.

It argued that the rejuvenation of the economy could be achieved through supply side policies which would liberate markets. Specific policies to achieve this included privatisation, reform of trade union and other labour law, a lowering of income tax rates and reform of the benefits system.

It rejected the idea that unemployment could be reduced permanently through increased government spending or increased government borrowing. Permanent jobs in the economy would only be created through investment and the creation of companies.

(a) To what extent could Conservative Party policy outlined in the passage be described as 'classical' or 'monetarist' in its approach?
(b) Explain why, on economic grounds, the Conservative Party rejected using demand management techniques to reduce unemployment.

Applied economics

Boom and bust, 1987-1991

The severe recession of 1979-1981 was followed by a period of relative tranquillity. Although unemployment remained stubbornly high at over 3 million, the current account was in surplus, inflation was low at around 5 per cent and growth averaged 3 per cent per annum during 1982-1986.

However, in 1987, as Table 105.1 shows, the rate of growth of the economy began to increase, and by the fourth quarter, the year on year increase was 5.1 per cent. There then followed a boom in the economy, now called the 'Lawson Boom' after Nigel Lawson, the then Chancellor of the Exchequer. Did the Lawson boom show the traditional short term trade-offs predicted by economic theory?

Table 105.1 shows that:
■ inflation increased from 3.9 per cent in the first quarter of 1987 to 8.1 per cent in the first quarter of 1990;
■ unemployment fell, from 3.2 million in the first quarter of 1987 to 1.6 million by 1990;

■ the current account on the balance of payments slumped seriously into deficit, from being broadly in balance in 1986 to an annual deficit of around £19 000 million in 1989.

By the end of 1990, the economy was going into recession. Growth in output had stagnated, unemployment was rising, but inflation was falling and the current account deficit was falling.

The Lawson boom was unlikely to have been caused by government fiscal policy. The PSBR (Public Sector Borrowing Requirement) was turned into a PSDR (Public Sector Debt Repayment) in 1987. The Budget of 1988 did see cuts in income tax rates from 60 per cent to 40 per cent for higher rate taxpayers, and from 27 per cent to 25 per cent for standard rate taxpayers. However, in Keynesian terms, the budget was still broadly neutral. What it did do perhaps was to encourage people to believe that their incomes would continue to rise at a high level for the foreseeable future, and companies to believe that the boom in spending would continue. This then increased the willingness of both consumers and industry to borrow money to finance consumption and investment.

The most likely cause of the Lawson boom was loose monetary policy (☞ unit 93) in the mid 1980s. This fuelled a consumer spending boom, based on increased borrowing by the personal sector. The most visible effect of this was to send house prices rocketing throughout the country. But everything from car sales to expenditure on carpets and curtains and toys saw record increases as well. By mid-1988, it was apparent that the economy was over-heating and that inflation was on the increase whilst the current account deficit was becoming unsustainable. The Chancellor, Nigel Lawson, responded by doubling interest rates within the next 12 months. Keynesian economists doubted whether raising interest rates would be effective in reducing inflationary pressures. They argued for tax increases. It took some time for high interest rates to work their way through the economy. The immediate effect was to bring the house price spiral to a complete stop. In some areas of the country, such as London and East Anglia, house prices soon began to fall. This brought about a slump in sales of low cost furniture and carpets as fewer people changed houses. By the beginning of 1990, it was clear that the high interest rate policy was reducing growth, and by the end of the year, some economists were predicting a fall in output in 1991.

These events would tend to support those monetarist economists, such as Milton Friedman, who suggest that monetary policy is a powerful weapon, and that the path to lower inflation (the transmission mechanism)

lies in a tightening of monetary policy even though this will create unemployment in the short run.

Table 105.1 *Inflation, unemployment, growth and the current account balance, 1986-1990*

		Percentage change over previous 12 months		Millions	£ millions
		Inflation	Real GDP	Unemployment	Current account balance
1986	Q1	5.0	3.1	3.4	647
	Q2	2.8	2.4	3.3	- 180
	Q3	2.7	3.3	3.3	- 829
	Q4	3.5	4.0	3.2	317
1987	Q1	3.9	3.7	3.2	74
	Q2	4.2	4.2	3.1	- 1 136
	Q3	4.3	5.1	2.9	- 1 605
	Q4	4.1	5.1	2.8	- 1 685
1988	Q1	3.3	5.4	2.7	- 3 439
	Q2	4.3	4.4	2.5	- 3 254
	Q3	5.5	4.0	2.3	- 3 598
	Q4	6.5	3.5	2.1	- 4 669
1989	Q1	7.8	2.9	2.1	- 4 063
	Q2	8.2	2.1	1.9	- 5 025
	Q3	7.7	1.8	1.8	- 6 492
	Q4	7.6	1.7	1.6	- 3 487
1990	Q1	8.1	1.6	1.6	- 5 106

Source: adapted from CSO, *Economic Trends Annual Supplement*; CSO, *Monthly Digest of Statistics*.

THE INSTITUTE OF DIRECTORS' BUDGET SUBMISSION, 1990

In January 1990, the Institute of Directors published their annual Budget proposals for consideration by the Chancellor. They argued that the government should continue its counter-inflationary policy through the use of high interest rates. However, it was vital that the effects of tight monetary policy should be offset by fiscal policies which would encourage savings and business investment in Britain. It therefore proposed that there should be £6bn of tax cuts including:
■ a 1p reduction in the basic rate of income tax to 24p in the pound;
■ two pence off the higher 40p in the pound income tax rate;
■ five pence off the 35p in the pound corporation tax rate;
■ an increase in personal tax allowances by 1 percentage point above inflation;
■ abolition of inheritance tax;
■ no increase in excise duties.

Defending the proposals, the Director General of the Institute of Directors said the ideas were 'clearly focused on the long-term structural needs of the enterprise culture'. He pointed out that the overall burden of tax had risen in the 1988 and 1989 Budgets, and that it now stood at 38 per cent of gross domestic product compared to 33 per cent in 1979.

Source: adapted from the *Financial Times*, 18.1.1990.

1. Taking examples from the passage, distinguish between fiscal, monetary and supply side policies.
2. Using the evidence from Table 105.1 as well as from the passage, outline from the perspective of (a) Keynesian economics and (b) classical, monetarist and supply side economics the possible economic consequences if the Chancellor had implemented the Institute's proposals.

INVESTIGATIONS 9

A. The costs of unemployment

Aims

- To gather data through the use of interviews and desk research on the costs of unemployment to the individual and to the economy as a whole.
- To present the findings of that research in a clear and logical manner.
- To assess the extent to which the information gathered through interviews is typical of the national picture.
- To evaluate policy alternatives to reduce the costs of unemployment.

Research

Your first task is to find one or more unemployed people to interview. This is probably best done as a group task. Someone in the group may have an unemployed relative or acquaintance who would be prepared to be interviewed. Given the sensitive nature of the issue of unemployment, however, it might be better to try and interview someone who is not known to anybody in your group. One possible contact would be the local job club. Alternatively, there may be a number of different voluntary organisations who have people working with them under Youth Training Scheme (YTS) or Employment Training (ET) placements and which could be approached to see if there would be anybody who would be prepared to talk to you. It would be better from the viewpoint of your research and probably for the unemployed people themselves if you could arrange to interview two or three people at the same time in a group interview. Seek permission before the interview to record it on audio tape.

Before the interview, draw up a list of questions. You need to find out what are the costs of unemployment to the individuals being interviewed. Start out by getting them to tell you something about themselves, their education and training and any previous jobs they may have had. Then ask them how unemployment has affected them. Do not be afraid to ask further questions if the information they give you is insufficient for your needs. However, remember to be sensitive at all times - unemployment is never regarded as a success and is usually considered to be a sign of failure on the part of the persons concerned even if they have been made unemployed through no fault of their own. Finally, ask them how they are searching for a new job. You are particularly interested in the costs of that search to the individual. For instance, what monetary costs are there in the process of search? How much time is being spent on the search? To what extent does the search demoralise the individual or give him or her hope and a sense of value?

The second part of your research is to put the cases of the people you have interviewed into a national context. Attempt to make some estimate of the cost of unemployment to the whole economy (☞ unit 96 for an explanation of what costs you need to take into consideration). Average wages, the total numbers unemployed, the numbers receiving different types of benefit for being unemployed (unemployment benefit and income support) and average payments can be found in the *Annual Abstract of Statistics* and the *Monthly Digest of Statistics*, both published by CSO. More detailed figures can be obtained from CSO, *Social Security Statistics*.

Structuring your report

Introduction Outline the aims of your investigation.

National unemployment costs Explain how you attempted to calculate the costs of unemployment nationally. What monetary costs can be placed on current national unemployment? What are the costs on which no monetary value can be placed? Build a picture of the costs for the typical unemployed person.

Case study Present the findings of your interview. Assess the costs of unemployment to the individuals concerned, both financial and non-financial. To what extent were the interviewees typical of the average person unemployed?

Policy alternatives Suggest a variety of ways in which the costs of unemployment could be reduced. Obviously one way would be for the government to reduce unemployment through reflating the economy (i.e. increasing aggregate demand in the economy). However, concentrate here on how unemployment could be reduced through supply side measures, or how the costs of unemployment could be reduced in other ways. Evaluate each policy alternative and suggest a package of measures which you feel would be most suitable and effective.

Sources Outline the sources of information you used. What problems did you encounter in gathering relevant data? What data would you have liked to have obtained but could not? To what extent were the data, particularly the data gathered at the interview, reliable?

Other suggestions

If you are unable to find a suitable interviewee for your investigation on the costs of unemployment, it would be possible to consider the costs of inflation. Consider the costs from the viewpoint of a number of different individuals, such as savers, those with mortgages, workers and pensioners. Then consider the costs from a national viewpoint. For instance, is there any evidence to suggest that inflation leads to lower growth in the economy? The research method, sources and presentation of this investigation are very similar to those outlined above.

B. Current economic problems and government policy

Aims

- To describe the current economic problems facing the economy.
- To discuss the relative importance of these problems using primary research as evidence.
- To outline present government policy and the alternatives to those policies.
- To evaluate the effectiveness of government policy.

Research activity

Your first task is to find out what are the main economic problems currently faced by government. You should be aware, simply through following the news and having studied some economics, what are the main preoccupations of government policy. Use this knowledge to devise a simple questionnaire which asks respondents to state the extent to which they think a problem is important at the moment and to rank in order current economic problems in order of importance. Interview at least 10 adults - parents, relations and other adults you are acquainted with.

Your next task is to survey the current state of the economy. Using *Economic Trends* or the *Monthly Digest of Statistics* (both published by CSO), find out current trends in inflation, the balance of payments, unemployment and economic growth, and any other variables which you consider to be important. Alternatively, use recent newspaper articles which you have collected.

Conduct a newspaper and magazine search for comment about the current economic situation and information and analysis about present government policy. Search through the previous month's issues of the *Financial Times*, other quality newspapers such as the *Independent* and magazines such as the *Economist*. If you wish to pursue your search over a longer time period, use whatever indexes are available in your local large public reference library, such as those produced by individual newspapers and magazines, or a more general index such as the *Research Index*, published by Business Surveys Ltd., which covers articles of financial interest in over 100 newspapers and magazines.

Listen to current affairs programmes on the television and the radio.

Structuring your report

Introduction Outline the aims of your investigation.

Current economic problems Describe the current economic problems facing the economy. Use graphs and tables to illustrate your answer. Assess their relative importance with the help of the results from your questionnaire.

Policy alternatives What policies are the government currently using to solve these problems? For instance, what is the government's monetary policy? How is government using fiscal measures to tackle Britain's problems? What is its exchange rate policy? What other policies could be used instead? Evaluate the range of alternative policies and discuss their relative advantages and disadvantages. What economic policies do you think the government should be pursuing today?

Sources Outline the sources of information you used. What problems did you encounter in gathering relevant data? What data would you have liked to have obtained but could not? To what extent were the data, particularly your questionnaire, reliable?

Other suggestions

The investigation outlined above is very wide ranging. Instead of looking at all the problems facing the UK economy, it would be possible to concentrate on just one. For instance, why is the balance of payments a problem? What is current government policy on the balance of payments? What are the possible policy alternatives and would these, in your opinion, be more effective at resolving the current difficulties?

Alternatively, consider a particular policy weapon, such as interest rates, exchange rates, the PSBR or privatisation. How is government using it to solve Britain's current economic problems? Is it using it effectively? Would other policy weapons be more suitable for resolving the problem?

Summary

1. The function of any economic system is to resolve the basic economic problem.
2. In a command economy, the state allocates resources through a planning mechanism. Some goods and services are provided free at the point of consumption. Others are sold, although goods may be rationed if the price is below the market clearing price.
3. Command economies have mainly been associated with the communist regimes of Eastern Europe and the Soviet Union, although Britain during the Second World War was run very much as a command economy.
4. The command economies of Eastern Europe, whilst possibly reducing inequalities in society, have had relatively low economic growth rates over the past 20 years. Choice and economic freedom has been limited whilst their environmental record has been very poor.

Economic systems

The function of an economy is to resolve the basic **economic problem** - resources are scarce but wants are infinite (☞ unit 1). Resources therefore need to be allocated. This allocation has three dimensions:
■ **what** is to be produced;
■ **how** is it to be produced;
■ **for whom** it is to be produced.

An ECONOMIC SYSTEM is a complex network of individuals, organisations and institutions and their social and legal interrelationships. The function of an economic system is to resolve the basic economic problem. Within an economic system there will be various 'actors'.
■ Individuals. They are consumers and producers. They may own factors of production which they supply for production purposes.
■ Groups. Firms, trade unions, political parties, families and charities are just some of the groups which might exist in an economic system.
■ Government. Government might range from a group of elders in a village, to a local authority to a national or international parliament. One key role of government is to exercise power. It establishes or influences the relationships between groups, for instance through the passing of laws.

Relationships between groups can be regulated by law. In many cases, however, they are regulated by custom - traditional ways of organisation which are accepted by participants within the economic system.

Command economies

In a free market economy (☞ unit 107), economic decision making is decentralised. Millions of economic agents individually make decisions about how resources are allocated. In contrast, in a COMMAND ECONOMY (or PLANNED ECONOMY) resources are allocated by government through a planning process. There are a number of key characteristics of a pure command economy.

The main actors There are three main types of actors within a planned economy: the planners (the government), consumers and workers.

Motivation Consumers, workers and government are all assumed to be selfless, co-operating together to work for the common good. This is in marked contrast with most economic agents in a market economy who are assumed to be motivated only by their own self-interest.

Public ownership All factors of production apart from labour are owned by the state (although labour services can be directed by the state). There is no private property.

Planning Resources are allocated through a planning process. At its most extreme, this means that the state will direct labour into jobs as well as directing consumers what to consume, although it is more likely that they will direct producers what to produce, thus determining the choice of goods available to consumers.

The planning process

Allocating resources through a planning mechanism is a complex operation. Planners have to decide what is to be produced. They have to decide, for instance, how many pairs of shoes, how much alcohol or how many tanks are to be manufactured. They then have to decide how it is to be made. They must decide what techniques of production are to be used and which factors of production are to be employed. Finally decisions about distribution have to be made: which consumers will receive what goods and services.

Planners tend to make use of **input-output analysis** when drawing up their plans. This is a method of charting the flows of resources in an economy. For instance, with a given technology, planners know how many workers, how much iron, how much coal etc. is needed to produce 1 tonne of steel. So they can work out what resources are needed if the economy is to produce, say, 20 million tonnes of steel. Having allocated so many tonnes of coal to steel production, planners now need to work out how many inputs are needed to produce the coal. A complex chart of the economy then arises showing how the factors of production (the inputs) are to be distributed to produce a given quantity of output. Most planned economies have used a mixture of 5, 10 or 15 year plans to outline the growth of their economies in the long term, whilst preparing yearly plans to cover short term planning.

Planning and forecasting is notoriously difficult. Accurate forecasting to produce maximum output assumes that planners know the most efficient way to produce goods and services (i.e. that they have available to them an efficient **production function** for each industry ☞ unit 17). Planners must have accurate statistics about the current state of the economy. There are also many variables which are beyond the control of forecasters. The weather is one important factor which can lead to severe misallocation in the economy.

In practice, planning is so complicated that some choices at least are left to individuals. In all command economies today, workers receive wages. They are then free to choose within limits how to spend this money. Some goods and services, such as education and health care may be provided free of charge to citizens. Others, such as housing, may need to be paid for but there is no free market in the product. Housing is allocated by the state and it is not possible to choose which house to occupy. However, some goods are available for purchase such as food or clothing.

Ideology and the command economy

Command economies have come to be associated with communist (or Marxist) regimes. However, there is no reason why other types of political system should not be associated with a planned economy. Many Third World countries have issued 5 year plans, although they have been to some extent 'indicative' plans because they have relied upon free market forces to deliver much of the output. During the Second World War, the British economy was run very much as a planned economy. Government directed resources and issued output targets to factories. Consumer choice was restricted through a system of rationing.

Moreover, it has been argued that underlying market economies are a complex network of command economies. A firm is a small command economy. With a given number of inputs the firm has to allocate those resources to produce a given quantity of outputs. As in a command economy, firms have to plan how to use those resources and face exactly the same questions of **what** to produce, **how** to produce and **for whom** to produce as a state. The largest firms in the world today, such as General Motors or IBM, have larger outputs than many small developing countries. So even supposedly 'free markets' have an element of planning.

Because communist regimes have tended to organise their economies under command structures, planned economies have tended to be associated with greater equality than under market systems. But again, this need not be the case. Governments could just as well plan to distribute resources in an extremely unequal fashion if they so wished, as is the case in many Third World countries.

The allocation of resources

The planning process determines the allocation of resources within a command economy. However, in practice consumers are given money to spend freely on a limited range of goods and services. There is therefore a type of market mechanism operating in the sale of these products. In a free market, resources are allocated by price. Price rises to the point where demand equals supply. Only those with money can afford to buy the goods. In a planned economy, planners may decide to limit prices so that goods are within the price range of all

---

QUESTION 1 The Belarus tractor factory was a typical example of production in the Soviet Union. It was allocated supplies of raw materials by the state, and in return manufactured approximately 100 000 tractors a year. It was the sole manufacturer of a particular class of tractor in the Soviet Union and the sole supplier of these tractors to state farms. Nearly 25 per cent of the factory's output was exported to other Comecon countries. The management estimate that at current prices, it could sell twice as many tractors as it currently produces if there were a free market in tractors.

Source: adapted from the *Financial Times*, 12.3.1990.

Why is the Belarus tractor factory a 'typical example of production' in a centrally planned economy?

consumers. For instance, planners may set maximum prices for food or clothing. Experience shows however that low prices often result in excess demand. Everyone can afford to buy meat, for instance, but there is insufficient meat in the shops to satisfy consumer demand. There are therefore shortages and resources are usually allocated via a queueing system. When a consignment of goods arrives in a shop, a queue will develop. Those at the front of the queue will be able to buy the goods. Those at the back will be turned away empty-handed.

QUESTION 2 Retail prices are determined centrally in the Soviet Union. Essentials, such as bread and meat, are very cheap; shop prices of bakery products, sugar and vegetable oil were last changed in the Soviet Union in 1955. To travel any distance by metro, bus or trolleybus in Moscow costs only 5 kopecs (5p). Housing rent normally costs only 3 per cent of income. Low prices mean long queues and often poor quality goods. This leads to large secondary and black markets. Anything more than the essentials of life, such as furniture and many articles of clothing, are very expensive and often in short supply. A typical car owner will, for instance, have saved up for seven to eight years to buy a car. However, the system throws up absurdities. For instance, in1984 the Soviet Union, with a population of 275m, produced 740m pairs of shoes. Yet many of these are unsaleable. There are shortages of shoes in various parts of the Soviet Union and sports shoes and sandals command premium prices on the black market.

Source: adapted from the *Financial Times*, 17.9.1986.

How are resources allocated in a command economy? Illustrate your answer with examples from the data.

An evaluation of command economies

Choice In a planned economy, individuals have relatively little choice. As workers, they may be allocated jobs in particular occupations or in particular geographical areas. They may be restricted in their ability to change jobs by state requirements. As consumers, they will have little say about what is provided directly by the state, particularly in non-traded services such as education, health, public transport and housing. What is provided for purchase in shops is likely to be limited. There is no mechanism by which firms compete with each other to provide different types of the same good (what would be called **brands** in a free enterprise economy). So consumers are offered only one make of car, one make of cooker, one type of soap powder, etc.

Subsidies on many essential items such as food and clothing are likely to lead to shortages. Queueing is endemic in many planned economies such as the USSR. Moreover, what is available can often be of poor quality.

In a planned economy, it is difficult to provide sufficient incentives for enterprises and individual workers to produce good quality products. Production targets are often set in volume terms or in value terms. A factory may be told to produce 10 000 cookers. But it is not penalised if these cookers are of poor quality. They will be delivered to state shops which in turn will receive instructions to sell them to consumers.

Income and growth Economic history suggests that, if a country has a relatively low GNP per head, both planned systems and free market systems will deliver comparable rates of economic growth. However, the experience of the past 20 years in Eastern Europe has been that planned economies have consistently failed to match the growth performance of free enterprise and mixed economies. This is perhaps not surprising. As economies grow, they become more complex. The more complex the economy, the more difficult it is to plan the allocation of resources efficiently. Large firms (remember that a firm in itself is a planned economy) in free enterprise economies have faced similar problems. They can experience **diseconomies of scale** (☞ unit 20) because their management structures fail to keep production efficient. Many large firms have responded by decentralising decision making. Parts of the business may become 'profit centres', responsible for attaining profit targets set by headquarters. In some firms, individual production units may even compete with each other for business.

It is not only the problems that arise from inadequate planning that can lead to low economic growth in command economies. There is also little individual incentive for enterprise and innovation. If a firm exceeds its targets for this year, its only 'reward' will be an increased target for the following year, which it might find impossible to achieve. If there are very heavy taxes on high incomes, there is little point in individuals working hard within the state sector. If there is no possibility of ownership of the means of production, there is no incentive for individuals to take risks, establishing new enterprises to do something better than existing firms in the market. There is every incentive for individuals to minimise the amount of effort they put into their official work. They are unlikely to lose their job, nor will they will lose income (although they may be arrested for anti-state activities - which might act as a deterrent). This contrasts with the considerable energy that the same individuals might put into their jobs in unofficial markets. There might be a thriving black market for instance. Or the state may allow people to rent small private plots for production of food.

The distribution of income Planners may choose any particular distribution of resources within a planned economy. In practice, command economies have been associated with socialist or Marxist governments committed to a degree of equality of income. Hence planners have set high priorities on providing all citizens with a minimum standard of living. They have achieved this through subsidising essential goods such as food and providing other essential services such as health care free of charge.

Equally, there is considerable evidence to suggest that those in power (e.g. members of the Communist Party) have used the planning system to their own advantage. For instance, special shops have been set up where a privileged few can purchase a much wider variety of goods than is generally available and without queueing. Housing allocation, or placements at university, have been biased in favour of Party members. Indeed, this is what capitalist, neo-classical economists would predict. Those in power are using that power to maximise their own utility. They are not the disinterested, selfless individuals that the model assumes.

Risk Karl Marx dreamt of creating a society in which each would receive according to their need. A family of four would have a bigger house than a family of two. A sick person would receive medical care. Those no longer able to work would still receive an income. So the risks associated with ill health, injury at work, old age and redundancy would be considerably reduced. Communist planned economies, to some extent, achieved this reduction in risk for the individual. However, it can be argued that removing risk also removes incentives to work and create wealth. If, for instance, a worker knows that he will never be made redundant, then there may be little incentive for him to do his job well. If an enterprise knows that it will always be able to sell its produce because consumers have no choice about what to buy, then it has no incentive to produce high quality goods or to be innovative.

The environment One of the problems with a market economy is that individual producers base their production decisions on **private** rather than **social** costs (☞ unit 35), thus creating negative externalities. However, the environmental record of command economies over the past 50 years is arguably worse than those of market economies. The problem is that planners have been far more interested in securing increased output than in reducing damage to the environment. If environmental objectives are not written into plans, then it is inevitable that damage will be caused to the environment by industrial production.

Political and social costs Command economies can only work if there is a centralised bureaucracy devising and implementing plans. They leave little room for individual freedom. Perhaps not surprisingly, the command economies of Eastern Europe and China have been police states, where the political rights of citizens have, to a very great extent, been taken away. Whether a pure command economy could operate within a political democracy is debatable.

QUESTION 3 The Soviet Union is in the throes of an ecological crisis, compared with which most other global pollution problems pale into insignificance. For instance, the huge Aral Sea, once the world's fourth largest inland water, has effectively ceased to exist. It is now two shrunken salt-poisoned pools in the desert, thanks to the effects of massive and thoughtless irrigation schemes. In the Republic of Byelorussia, one-quarter of all the arable land has been destroyed by the fall-out from the Chernobyl nuclear disaster - contaminated with Caesium 137, which will last for decades to come.

'The most serious problem is in fact the economic system', says academician Mr Alexei Yablokov. 'All the decision making comes from the centre - from the government, the ministries, and the Communist Party', he said. 'The Central committee of the party decides what sort of factory is built where. All the ministries are full of people with the old thinking - more and more production, whatever the price. Their aim is not human happiness, but more production.'

Source: adapted from the *Financial Times*, 12.3.1990.

(a) What ecological problems are highlighted in the passage?
(b) Why might such problems be created in a centrally planned economy?

Key terms

Economic system - a complex network of individuals, organisations and institutions and their social and legal interrelationships.
Command or planned economy - an economic system where government, through a planning process, allocates resources in society.

Applied economics

Central planning in the Soviet Union

The Soviet economy from the 1930s to the late 1980s was the country whose economic system perhaps came closest to the model of a command economy. Overall decisions about economic priorities were taken by the highest political body in the Soviet Union, the Politburo, the central committee of the Communist Party. It would decide whether more resources should be devoted to, say, defence, housing or agriculture. Its decisions would then have to be implemented by the Council of Ministers, who would decide how this could be achieved with the help of **Gosplan**, the State Planning Committee. Gosplan is the major planning body. It constructed input-output matrices for the whole of the Soviet economy and worked out production targets for each region and each industry. Over 20 000 products or groups of products needed to be structured into its plan. Yearly plans were made within the context of successive **five year plans**, the first of which was announced by Stalin in 1928. The five year plan was an attempt to plan the economy in the medium term, because a year was really too short for the achievement of longer term goals.

Production plans would then be communicated to 40 different ministries which, working with Regional Planning Commissions in each Republic of the Soviet Union, would send out orders to hundreds of thousands of production units across the country. At each stage, those lower down the hierarchy had the right to challenge the orders sent to it. Almost invariably, they would be challenged if it was felt that the orders could not be fulfilled. If the challenge was accepted, the plan would have to be modified. There was no need for production units to communicate between themselves. If goods were poor quality, for instance, shops would complain not to the manufacturer but to the planners at the next stage in the hierarchy.

The system arguably worked reasonably well in the 1930s and 1940s. It is true that the transition from a market economy in the 1920s to a command economy in the 1930s was marked by political oppression on a scale which possibly even dwarfed the horrors of Nazi Germany, but this was more a political struggle than an economic necessity. However, by the 1960s the Soviet economy was getting far too large to manage centrally and large diseconomies of scale were emerging.

One key factor became apparent. The incentives within the system discouraged efficient production. For those with a job from which they would be unlikely to be sacked because the right to work was guaranteed, there was an incentive to devote little energy to the official job and take a job on the side to supplement earnings. For managers, the key to success was to negotiate for as many raw material and labour inputs as possible and have as low a production target as possible. Hoarding raw materials too was essential in an economy where supplies were variable. That way, production managers could easily reach and even exceed their production targets.

By the 1980s, many in the Soviet Union felt that if their economy was to be dynamic, it should not be planned centrally. Hence, economic reform to transform the economy into a market economy was begun.

Data question

ROMANIAN AGRICULTURE

Farm No 4 is typical of the 4 000 co-operatives and state farms that were a feature of Romania's command economy. It was the animal section of a 2 500 hectare co-operative which also includes three crop farms.

Farm No 4 suffers from the typical failings of Romania's central planning system - rigid, unrealistic production targets and prices, a complete lack of consideration for local conditions and a fanatical desire to export without importing the necessary inputs. 'They tried to have a large number of animals without having productivity, and there are too many animals for the land', said Mr Stoica, a farm manager. 'There are 700 cows, but only 150 give milk. The initiatives of the people working in the co-operative were not taken into consideration. Everything was ordered by the ministry - what animals to breed and what production to have.'

A similar picture is emerging from the rest of the country. A senior official at the Agriculture Ministry explained how some farmers were ordered by the government to grow maize on steep hillsides; they often harvested less than the seed they had sown. Others are said to have been jailed for feeding grain to their cattle instead of releasing it for export.

Source: adapted from the *Financial Times*, 2.2.1990.

1. **How was agriculture organised in Romania's command economy and what problems resulted?**

Summary

1. In a free market economy, resources are allocated through the spending decisions of millions of different consumers and producers.
2. Resource allocation occurs through the market mechanism. The market determines what is to be produced, how it is to be produced and for whom production is to take place.
3. Government must exist to supply public goods, maintain a sound currency, provide a legal framework within which markets can operate, and prevent the creation of monopolies in markets.
4. Free markets necessarily involve inequalities in society because incentives are needed to make markets work.
5. Free markets provide choice and there are incentives to innovate and for economies to grow.

Characteristics of the system

A MARKET ECONOMY (also called a FREE ENTERPRISE ECONOMY or a CAPITALIST ECONOMY) is an economic system which resolves the basic economic problem mainly through the market mechanism. There are a number of key characteristics of the system.

The main actors The four main types of actors within the system are consumers, producers, owners of private property (land and capital) and government.

Motivation In a pure market economy, consumers, producers and property owners are motivated by pure self-interest. Their decisions are based upon private gain. Consumers aim to maximise their individual welfare or utility (☞ unit 14). Producers aim to maximise profit (☞ unit 24). The owners of the factors of production aim to maximise their wages, rents, interest and profits (☞ units 46-55).

Government on the other hand is assumed to be motivated by considerations of the good of the community and not by self-interest. It seeks to maximise social welfare. (This assumption about government is arguably unrealistic. A great deal of work, beyond the scope of this book, has been done over the past 15 years which assumes that governments pursue sectoral interests.)

Private ownership Nearly all factors of production within the economy are owned mainly by private individuals and organisations. Government has a duty to uphold the rights of citizens to own property. This it does mainly through the legal system.

Free enterprise Owners of the factors of production as well as producers of goods and services have the right to buy and sell what they own through the market mechanism. Government places few limits on what can be bought and sold. Workers can work for whom they want. Homeowners can sell their houses if they so wish. People are free to set up their own businesses. Consumers are free to use their money to buy whatever is offered for sale. Producers are free to sell whatever they wish to sell.

Competition Competition will exist if economic units are free to allocate their resources as they wish. Producers will have to compete for the spending 'votes' of consumers. Workers will have to compete for the spending 'votes' of their employers. Those wishing to borrow money will have to compete with everyone else who wishes to borrow.

Decentralised decision making Because individual economic agents are free to choose how they wish to allocate resources, decision making within a market economy is decentralised. There is no single body which allocates resources within the economy. Rather, the allocation of resources is the result of countless decisions by individual economic agents. This is Adam Smith's **invisible hand** of the market. He argued that, although economic actors pursued their own self interest, the result would be an allocation of resources in the economy which would be in the interests of society as a whole.

QUESTION 1 In a speech in January 1988 to the Centre for Policy Studies, a free market think tank, the Chancellor of the Exchequer, Nigel Lawson, defended the capitalist system on moral and philosophical grounds. He argued that progress and prosperity were best secured through choice and the market rather than through 'big government'. Belief in egalitarianism had been replaced by a conviction that incentives and opportunity were vital. The 'New Britain' created by the Conservatives since 1979 had accepted the 'basic human instinct of self-interest'. This was not immoral. For 'a society based on freedom is inherently stronger, and healthier, than a society based on state coercion'. Whilst capitalism embraced the basic instincts of self-improvement and self-interest, neither need lead to selfishness.

Source: adapted from the *Financial Times*, 20.1.1988.

(a) Identify from the passage the main characteristics of a market economy.
(b) Why does a belief in 'egalitarianism' and 'big government' conflict with a belief in the workings of a market economy?

The market mechanism

Any type of economic system must be capable of allocating resources. In particular, it must be able to provide a mechanism for deciding **what**, **how** and **for whom** production will take place. How are resources allocated under a market mechanism?

What is to be produced? In a pure free market, it is the consumer which determines the allocation of resources. Consumers are **sovereign** (☞ unit 40). Each consumer has a certain amount of money to spend and each £1 is like a spending vote. Consumers cast their spending votes when they purchase goods and services. Firms receive these spending votes and this in turn enables them to buy the factors of production needed to produce goods and services. How firms cast their spending votes on factors of production in turn will determine how much income each individual consumer has to spend. What happens if consumers want to change the composition of the bundle of goods that they are currently buying? Say, for instance, they decide they want to buy more clothes but buy fewer package holidays. The increase in demand for clothes initially will increase the price of clothes. Clothing manufacturers will consequently earn **abnormal profit** (☞ unit 18), profit over and above what is normal in the industry. They will respond to this by increasing production of clothes. New firms too will set themselves up attracted by the high profit levels. Supply will thus expand as will the degree of competition in the industry. This will force down prices to a level where clothing manufacturers are making a high enough profit to stop some going out of business, but a low enough profit to prevent new suppliers from being attracted into the

industry. In the package holiday business, the fall in demand will result in a price war. Profitability will fall. Some firms may even make losses. As a result, firms will scale back the number of the holidays offered and some firms may even go bankrupt. This will continue until package holiday firms once again can earn a sufficiently high level of profit to prevent firms leaving the industry.

Changes in the goods market will then be reflected in the factor markets. Demand for workers, buildings, machines, raw materials etc. will rise in the clothing industry, but fall in the package holiday industry. There will thus be a transfer of resources from one industry to the other.

Notice the key role of profits in this mechanism. Profits act as a signal for what is to be produced. If firms are earning abnormal profits, it is a signal that consumers wish to buy more of a product. If firms are earning insufficient profits or even losses, it must be a signal that consumers wish to see a fall in production in that industry.

How is it to be produced? Producers are in competition with each other. All other things being equal, consumers will buy from the producer which offers the lowest price. So producers must produce at lowest cost if they are to survive in the market place. This then determines how goods are produced. Firms will adopt the lowest cost technique of production. Hence, free markets result in **productive efficiency** (☞ unit 33).

For whom? Consumers spend money. The amount of money they can spend is determined by their wealth and by their income. In a free market economy, this is determined by ownership of the factors of production. Workers receive income from sale of their labour, owners of land receive rents, etc. Those with high incomes and wealth are therefore able to buy large amounts of goods and services. Those with low incomes and little wealth can only buy a few goods and services. In a market economy, the wealthy gain a disproportionate share of what is produced. The poor receive relatively little.

QUESTION 2 In 1989, McDonald's, the US-owned fast food chain, announced that it was to test-market ready-prepared salads to sell alongside its traditional hamburgers in some of its UK outlets. The move is aimed at capitalising on the consumer trend towards more healthy eating and is part of McDonald's defence against the promised onslaught from Burger King, the hamburger chain owned by Grand Metropolitan. Mr David Richards, Burger King's marketing director in the UK was not impressed by the McDonald's salad experiment. He said: 'We don't really think the British consumer wants to buy salads from predominantly burger chains.'

Source: adapted from the *Financial Times*, 18.11.1989.

Explain, using the data to illustrate your answer, how resources are allocated in a market economy.

The role of government

Government has a number of key roles in a market economy.

- Some goods will not be provided by the market mechanism. Examples are defence, the judiciary and the police force. These are known as **public goods** (☞ unit 44). The government therefore has to provide these and raise taxes to pay for them.
- The government is responsible for the issue of money and for the maintenance of its value. In a market economy, the government has a duty to maintain stable prices.
- The government needs to ensure an adequate legal framework for the allocation and enforcement of property rights. It is pointless having a system based upon individual self-interest if citizens are unable to defend what they have gained. For instance, owners of private property need to be protected from the possibility of theft. There need to be laws about contracts of purchase and sale. It must be illegal to willfully destroy other people's property.
- It is equally important that property rights of any value are allocated to an economic unit in society. If they are not, they will treated as a **free good** (a good unlimited in supply) and consumed to the point where marginal utility is zero (☞ unit 14). The atmosphere is one example of an economic resource which in the past has been owned by no one. Producers and consumers have polluted the atmosphere. This would not be important if it weren't for the fact that we now recognise that such pollution can have an adverse impact upon economic units. At worst, it is predicted that the greenhouse effect and the destruction of the ozone layer will wipe out most life on this planet. Contrast this with the care that people show with their own private property.

QUESTION 3 Political 'democracy' that takes half of personal incomes to spend on welfare, or industrial services which give voters as taxpayers little say and less escape, can be as oppressive as communist socialism. Government cannot be depended on to redress market failure. Its electoral short-termism, its ignorance or indifference to individual preference, its vulnerability to pressure groups and its corruption create government failure that is worse than market failure because it is less corrigible. The common people are best empowered by the market. Government should concentrate on the irreducible minimum of goods and services that cannot be supplied in the market. Optimal size of government is unattainable. But it is better to risk having too little government than too much.

Source: adapted from the *Financial Times*, 19.9.1990.

(a) Explain what, according to the article, should be the role of government in an economy.
(b) What arguments can be put forward to justify this position?

- Markets may malfunction for other reasons. In particular, firms or trade unions may seek to gain control over individual markets. Governments therefore need to have powers to break up monopolies, prevent practices which restrict free trade (☞ units 37 to 39) and control the activities of trade unions (☞ unit 49).

The role of government is vital in a market economy. Without government, there would be anarchy. But in a free market economy, the presumption is that government should intervene as little as possible. Government regulation should be the minimum necessary to secure the orderly working of the market economy. Government spending should be confined to the provision of public goods.

An evaluation of free market economies

Choice In a rich free enterprise economy, consumers will be faced with a wide range of choice. Firms will compete with each other either on price if a good is homogeneous, or on a wider range of factors such as quality if the good is non-homogeneous. However, choice is not available to all. Those with high incomes will have a great deal of choice. Those on low incomes will have little. It matters little to low income families, for instance, if there are 100 types of luxury car on the market, or if it is possible to take cruises on even more luxurious liners. In a planned economy, consumers may find it impossible to spend all their income because goods which are priced within the reach of everyone are not in the shops. In a free enterprise economy, there may be plenty of goods in the shops, but they may be out of the price range of the poorest in society.

Quality and innovation One advantage claimed of a free market economy is that there are strong incentives built into the system to innovate and produce high quality goods. Companies which fail to do both are likely to be driven out of business by more efficient firms. However, this assumes that there is consumer sovereignty in the market. In practice, markets tend to be oligopolistic in structure (☞ units 30-32), dominated by a few large producers which manipulate the market through advertising and other forms of marketing in order to exploit the consumer. So whilst choice and innovation are greater than under planned systems, the advantages of free market economies may not be as great as it might at first seem.

Economic growth In a free market economy, there may be considerable dynamism. However, some free market economies have grown at a considerably faster rate than other free market economies. For instance, Japan has grown much faster than the USA over the past 30 years. Many mixed economies too have grown at comparable if not higher rates to the USA. So free markets are not necessarily the key to high economic growth.

Distribution of income and wealth In a pure free market economy, resources are allocated to those with spending power. Individuals with no source of income can pay the ultimate penalty for their economic failure - they die, perhaps from starvation or cold or disease. This fear of economic failure and its price is a major incentive within the free market system for people to take jobs, however poorly paid. One problem with this mechanism is that there are many groups in society who are likely to have little or no income through no fault of their own. The handicapped, orphaned or abandoned children and old people are examples. Free market economists point out that there is a mechanism by which such people can find support - charity. Individuals who earn money can give freely to charities which then provide for the needs of the least well off in society, or individuals can look after their aged relatives, their neighbours and their children within the local neighbourhood community. In practice, it is unlikely that individuals would give enough to charities, or that the better off would provide accommodation for tramps in their homes to fulfil this role. In a free market economy, there is no link whatsoever between need and the allocation of resources. The unemployed can starve, the sick can die for lack of medical treatment, and the homeless can freeze to death on the streets. Income is allocated to those with wealth, whether it is physical, financial or human wealth.

Risk Individuals take great care to reduce the economic risk which lies at the heart of any free market economy. They can overcome the problem of risk by insuring themselves. They take out health insurance. They buy life insurance contracts which pay out to dependants if they should die. Unemployment and sickness can also be insured against. To cope with the problem of old age, individuals ensure that they have pension contracts. However, only a percentage of the population have enough foresight or the income to insure themselves adequately. This then means that many in a free market economy become poor, perhaps unable to support themselves or die through lack of medical attention.

QUESTION 4 Socialism captured the imagination because it offered an enticing conception of social and economic progress. It promised not just a great increase in material wealth, but a world where income would not depend primarily on individuals' arbitrary endowments of financial and genetic capital. It also talked sense about freedom - which can be measured only by the choices individuals have the power to exercise. The range of choice is profoundly influenced by a person's economic means.

Capitalism, whilst offering forever increasing economic output, gives no commitment to increased equality. Quite the contrary: incentives are regarded as an essential motor of growth, and they require inequality. But the commitment to inequality means that poverty will never be eradicated. It will be institutionalised. Once a minimum standard of living is attained, people feel poor if they have less than their neighbours. If a trip to the Asteroids becomes a typical weekend jaunt in the 21st or 22nd century, those who cannot afford extra-terrestrial travel will be considered poor. And they will not be comforted by the thought that they are better off than the poor of 1989.

Source: adapted from the *Financial Times*, 9.6.1989.

(a) Assess the criticisms made in the extract of a capitalist economic system.
(b) What are the causes and nature of poverty in a free market economy?

Key terms

Free market economy, or free enterprise economy or capitalist economy - an economic system which resolves the basic economic problem through the market mechanism.

Applied economics

The USA in the 1980s

The USA is often seen as the greatest free market economy in the world. It is not just that it is the largest free market economy, it is also the richest economy in the world per capita (apart from a few small Gulf states). The average citizen of the United States enjoys a standard of living which is the envy of most in the Third World. However, since 1945, the greatest free market economy in the world has not performed as well as it might. Another free market economy, Japan,

has transformed itself from being a Third World country to an international economic power rivalling the USA. Some of the mixed economies of continental Europe too have grown at a faster rate per annum than the USA.

In 1980, a US president was elected who committed himself to making the 'USA great again', not just in world political terms, but also through revitalising the US economy which he felt had lost its vitality and

Table 107.1 *Real growth of GDP*

| | Year to year percentage changes | | | |
	1960-67	1968-73	1974-79	1980-88
United States	4.5	3.2	2.4	2.8
Japan	10.2	8.7	3.6	4.1
Germany	4.1	4.9	2.3	1.7
France	5.4	5.5	2.8	1.9
United Kingdom	3.0	3.4	1.5	2.2
Italy	5.7	4.5	3.7	2.4
Canada	5.5	5.4	4.2	3.2

Source: adapted from OECD, *Historical Statistics.*

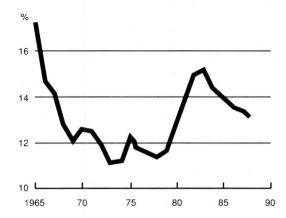

Source: adapted from *US Bureau of Census.*

Figure 107.1 *Percentage of total population below the poverty level*

energy because of too high taxes and too much government interference in the market place. Table 107.1 shows that Ronald Reagan's reforms possibly did stimulate economic growth. The USA, a low growth country amongst the G7 group of countries in the 1960s and 1970s, was the third highest in the 1980s.

However, restoring incentives to the US economy was not without its cost. As Figure 107.1 shows, the first half of the 1980s saw a considerable increase in the percentage of the population below the poverty line. By 1988, nearly 32 million Americans were living below the official poverty line (about $6 000 for a single person) compared with 24.5 million in the late 1970s. Nearly one-fifth of all American children are officially classified as poor. Poverty is particularly concentrated amongst Blacks and Hispanics. In parts of New York, life expectancy at birth is lower than in Bangladesh.

Despite spending 12 per cent of GDP on health care (twice UK spending on the National Health Service), between 31m and 37m Americans are without any health insurance and many more are under-insured, resulting in limited or no access to health care. As Figure 107.2 shows, the poorest 20 per cent of the nation got poorer in the 1980s with a fall in real income as their tax burden increased. The richer you were, the greater the share of increased wealth created in the 1980s, so that the richest 20 per cent saw their real incomes increase by over 30 per cent during the decade. By 1990, the top 5 per cent of US families

Rich and poor in one state of the USA.

received 26.2 per cent of pre-tax income compared with 21.4 per cent in 1980. The bottom 20 per cent's share fell from 4.5 per cent to 3.7 per cent over the period.

Of course, incentives to work, which in effect mean inequalities in income and wealth, are vital to the efficient functioning of a free market economy. However, it can be questioned whether Reaganomics did far more for the rich in America than it did for the nation's overall economic performance. Some critics would argue that it seems strange that in the world's 'richest' economy, part of society is living a Third World existence.

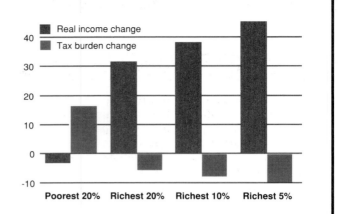

Source: adapted from *House Ways and Means Committee*.

Figure 107.2 *Change in real income and federal tax burden, 1980-1990 (per cent)*

FACE OF AMERICA THAT DESTROYS ITS 'LAND OF THE FREE' MYTH

Data question

Until a year ago, my image of the Unites States was of a wealthy, classless, melting-pot society. That image took a knock when I spent two weeks in Arkansas and Texas recently. There is certainly money. In Houston, mirror-glass skyscrapers soar confidently over immaculate parks. In its fabulously wealthy River Oaks suburb, colonnaded million-dollar mansions exceed the dreams of avarice.

But look again and you see another face of America. Shacks and shanty settlements strung out along the highways. Second-hand cars at a half or even a third of British prices. Wal-Mart supermarkets where a pair of jeans costs a fiver. At first it strikes you as a land of bargains. Then you talk to ordinary Americans and realise that the prices match the wages, and the wages in many cases are desperately low.

One of our coach drivers earned a wretched £4 500 a year - below the official poverty line. The average American family of four earns barely £10 000 and to reach that level both partners invariably work. A woman hotel executive I met in Brownsville returned to work two weeks after giving birth and thought her employers generous for paying her salary during her absence. But she too was benefiting from the system. She could go back to work because she could employ a Mexican maid for £25 a week. In the Land of the Free, there is no free lunch.

Source: adapted from the *Express and Star*, 28.4.1989.

1. How are resources allocated in a free market economy? Illustrate your answer from the passage.
2. To what extent are income differentials desirable in a free market economy?

108 Mixed economies

Summary

1. In a mixed economy, a significant amount of resources are allocated both by government through the planning mechanism, and by the private sector through the market mechanism.
2. The degree of mixing is a controversial issue. Some economists believe that too much government spending reduces incentives and lowers economic growth, whilst others argue that governments must prevent large inequalities arising in society and that high taxation does not necessarily lead to low growth.

Mixed economies

A MIXED ECONOMY, as the name implies, is a mixture of a planned economy and a free enterprise economy. In practice, no **pure** planned economies or free enterprise economies exist in the world. They are **paradigm models** (☞ unit 111). What we call free enterprise economies are economies where most resources are allocated by the market mechanism. What are called planned economies are economies where most resources are allocated by the planning process. Mixed economies are economies where the balance between allocation by the market mechanism and allocation by the planning process is much more equal.

Characteristics

A mixed economy possesses a number of characteristics.

The main actors The four main types of actor within the system are consumers, producers, factor owners and government.

Motivation In the private sector of the economy, consumers, producers and factor owners are assumed to be motivated by pure self-interest. The public sector, however, is motivated by considerations of the 'good' of the community.

Ownership The factors of production are partly owned by private individuals and organisations, but the state also owns a significant proportion.

Competition In the private sector of the economy there is competition. In the state sector, however, resources will be allocated through the planning mechanism. This implies that consumers are offered choice of goods and services within the private sector of the economy but little or no choice within the public sector.

Government Government has a number of important functions. One is to regulate the economic activities of the private sector of the economy. It needs, for instance, to ensure that competition exists and that property laws are upheld. Another function is to provide not just public goods but also **merit goods** (☞ unit 44), like education and health care. These may be provided directly by the state, or provision may be contracted out to private firms (☞ unit 43) but still paid for out of tax revenues. The state may also choose to own key sectors of the economy, such as the railways, postal services and electricity industries. Many of these will be **natural monopolies** (☞ unit 37).

QUESTION 1 From your knowledge of the UK economy, explain to what extent it possesses the characteristics of a mixed economy.

The degree of mixing

There is considerable controversy about the degree of mixing that should take place in a mixed economy. In Sweden, over 60 per cent of GDP is accounted for by public expenditure, compared to an OECD average of 45 per cent, 40 per cent in the UK and approximately 35 per cent in a free market economy like the USA.

In Sweden, there is much greater government spending per capita than, say, in the USA. This means that in Sweden compared to the USA all citizens have access to medical care free at the point of consumption, there are generous state pensions, automatic retraining for those made unemployed and free child care for all working mothers. However, there is a cost. Taxes in Sweden are much higher than in the USA. The fundamental issues concern the following.

■ To what extent should the state ensure that all its citizens enjoy a minimum standard of living? For instance, should the state provide insurance for those who become unemployed? Should they in effect guarantee them a job by training longer term unemployed workers until they succeed in obtaining work? Do citizens have a right to free medical care?

■ To what extent should there be inequalities in society? The degree of inequality in an economy like Sweden is far less than in the USA. During the 1980s, as the UK cut its public expenditure as a proportion of GDP, inequality increased.

■ To what extent should citizens be free to choose how

to spend their money? In Sweden, the effective tax burden is 60 per cent, leaving only 40 per cent of income for individuals and companies to choose how to spend. In Sweden, free child care for mothers is provided whether an individual wants it or not.

■ To what extent are incentives needed to ensure continued high growth? Until the late 1980s, the top rate of income tax in Sweden was 72 per cent, with the ordinary worker paying between 40 and 50 per cent. Tax reforms in the late 1980s have switched the burden of tax from income tax, reducing it to 30 per cent for 85 per cent of workers, but extending the 30 per cent VAT rate to a much wider range of goods and services. The marginal rate of income tax is still much higher, though, than in the USA. Supply side economists would argue that higher rates of tax discourage incentives to work and take risks and that this will lead to lower economic growth (☞ units 98 and 99).

■ To what extent is government an efficient provider of goods and services compared to the private sector (a debate explored at length in units 43 and 44)?

Mixed economies can be judged on the above issues. They could also be evaluated according to their environmental impact. Mixed economies have a better record on the environment than command economies. Indeed, the Scandinavian mixed economies are in the forefront of implementing measures to protect the environment from industrial activity.

Key terms

Mixed economy - an economy where both the free market mechanism and the government planning process allocate significant proportions of total resources.

QUESTION 2 Since 1979, the degree of mixing between public and private sectors in the UK has changed. In 1979, government spending accounted for 46 per cent of GDP, whereas by 1990, it was 39 per cent.

Suggest the possible economic consequences of this shift in resources.

Applied economics

Sweden

In 1932, the Swedish Social Democratic Party gained power and created a model of a mixed economy which has been the envy of left wing economists ever since. The Swedish economy lies at one extreme of the mixed economy model, devoting over 60 per cent of its GDP to public expenditure. As Figure 108.1 shows, the proportion of GDP devoted to public expenditure grew considerably in the 1970s, partly because the Swedish government responded to the unemployment pressures caused by external supply side shocks (such

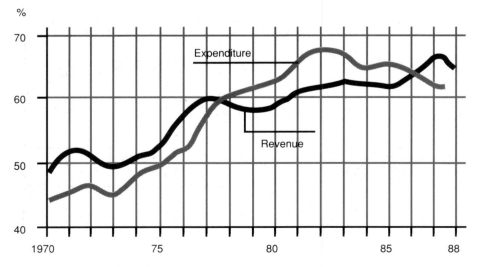

Source: adapted from *Statistics Sweden* and Ministry of Finance.

Figure 108.1 *Public expenditure and revenue as a percentage of GDP*

as the two oil crises) by increasing demand through extra public spending. Since 1982, expenditure as a percentage of GDP has fallen as the Swedes have increasingly debated the extent to which the state rather than the market mechanism should decide how resources should be allocated in the economy.

Sweden provides possibly the most comprehensive welfare state in the world for its citizens with one in three of the workforce employed in the public sector, mainly in education, health or local government. The Swedish attitude to employment and unemployment is typical of the socialist mentality of the country. Governments have been prepared to use demand management techniques (☞ unit 98) to keep unemployment at very low levels by international standards as shown in Figure 108.2, even when demand management became extremely unfashionable in the 1970s and 1980s. So there are relatively few unemployed. Those who do become unemployed can receive benefits of up to 85 per cent of after-tax wages. However, workers are not allowed to stay unemployed for long. A worker who refuses an offer of a job or a training place by the state monopoly labour market office will have all his or her benefits removed. Having said that, the Swedish employment service goes to every length to ensure that unemployed workers obtain a job or a training place which is suited to their abilities. To achieve this, the employment service employs more than 20 times as many general staff and officers per unemployed job-seeker as its counterpart in the UK. This effort to match workers to jobs, if necessary through extensive and expensive retraining, is the supply side counterpart to the demand management policies used by the Swedish government.

Table 108.1 *Real growth of GDP*

| | Year to year percentage changes | | | |
	1960-67	1968-73	1974-79	1980-88
Sweden	4.4	4.5	-0.4	2.2
United States	4.5	3.2	2.4	2.8
Japan	10.2	8.7	3.6	4.1
Germany	4.1	4.9	2.3	1.7
France	5.4	5.5	2.8	1.9
United Kingdom	3.0	3.4	1.5	2.2
Italy	5.7	4.5	3.7	2.4
Canada	5.5	5.4	4.2	3.2

Source: adapted from OECD, *Historical Statistics*.

As supply side economics and the efficiency of the market mechanism have become increasingly fashionable in the 1980s, the Swedes have questioned whether the relatively low growth rates they have experienced in the 1970s and 1980s, shown in Table 108.1, have not been due to excess government spending and very high tax rates. In 1990, a wide-ranging reform of the taxation system was implemented which reduced the standard rate of income tax from 40-50 per cent to 30 per cent, to be paid for by large increases in VAT. There is also general agreement that public expenditure as a percentage of GDP should decline over time, although no party wishes to see large public expenditure cuts in the short term.

The 1980s have also seen the breakdown of a consensus between unions, management and government. In the past, unions and government negotiated an annual pay settlement figure which became the norm for individual pay negotiations. However, low levels of unemployment and consequent

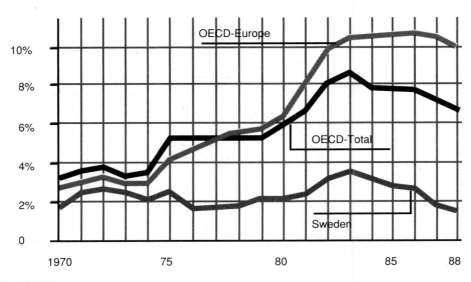

Source: adapted from OECD.

Figure 108.2 *Unemployment*

labour shortages have increasingly meant that unions have felt able to exceed the national norm. The result has been, as Figure 108.3 shows, wage increases and inflation levels above the international average. Given that 30 per cent of GDP is exported, a figure higher than for instance in the UK, the Swedes have been forced to devalue the Krona on a regular basis to maintain international competitiveness. But this has reinforced domestic inflationary pressures and has led Swedish firms to question whether they should not invest in production plants abroad, particularly in their fastest growing market the EC, rather than investing further in Sweden.

Sceptics have predicted that Sweden will look very little different from Germany or France in 50 years time, particularly if it joins the EC as it is likely to do in the next ten years. However, opinion polls show clearly that the Swedes are highly satisfied with their welfare state and have no wish to see it dismantled. But not surprisingly, they would like to enjoy both higher private spending power and receive better public services - like everyone else, they have infinite wants in a world of scarce resources.

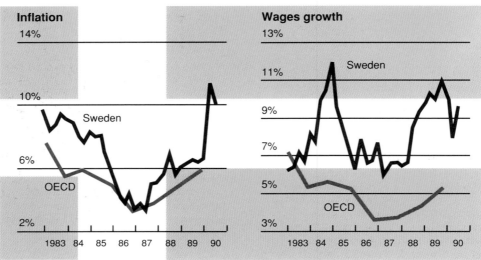

Source: Datastream.

Figure 108.3

A GREEN PIONEER

Sweden's environmental laws, amongst the toughest in the world, have helped prepare the country's industry to exploit opportunities created by the growing 'green' consciousness in the global marketplace.

Long before environmental concerns became fashionable, the nature-conscious Swedes were passing laws enforcing drastic reductions in air and water pollution. They are still playing a pioneering role in Europe. Recent actions include abolishing use of chlorofluorocarbon (CFC) substances by 1994, ahead of the deadline set by the EC. Sweden was the first European country to adopt US standards on the purification of bus and truck exhaust fumes. The use of catalytic converters for new passenger cars has become compulsory. It now plans to classify car models by their environmental safety and tax them accordingly. It has also imposed Europe's first environmental tax on carbon dioxide emissions resulting from the burning of oil, coal, natural gas, petrol and other petroleum products. Other pollution taxes are being levied on the release of nitrogen oxide and sulphur oxide.

Swedish industry has complained that its government's environmental demands are over-ambitious, making it difficult for Swedish companies to compete internationally. On the other hand, Swedish companies will be well placed when stricter environmental standards are imposed in turn on their competitors.

Source: adapted from the *Financial Times*, 3.7.1990.

1. **Explain why, using illustrations from the passage, governments need to intervene in the market.**

2. **Suggest reasons why a mixed economy like Sweden has implemented more environmental protection measures than either a command economy such as the Soviet Union or a free market economy such as the USA.**

Applied economics

The basic economic problem

An economic system is a way of resolving the basic economic problem - scarcity of resources in a world of infinite human wants. The Soviet Union has been a command economy since the early 1930s, following collectivisation of agriculture. Eastern European countries became command economies in the late 1940s and early 1950s following communist takeover of their governments. However, the 1990s are likely to see a return of these economies to a more market orientated system. How can an economy move from being a planned economy to, say, a mixed economy and what costs will be involved in the transition phase?

Output and employment

In 1990, manufacturing output in Eastern Europe fell by approximately 20 per cent according to the United Nations Economic Commission for Europe (ECE) and this was associated with a steep rise in unemployment. It is almost inevitable that a transition from a command structure to a market structure will initially reduce output and create unemployment.

To understand why, consider how resources are allocated in a command economy. Government planners allocate factors of production between differing production units such as factories or farms. So a food factory might be allocated so much in raw materials, say sugar beet, and a given quantity of new physical capital such as new machines. It then has to supply its output to shops in the country.

The state now attempts to introduce reforms to transform the economy into a market economy. The factory is allowed to sell its final product, sugar, to buyers, state shops or private shops. But equally, it now has to buy its inputs such as sugar beet or machinery. It decides that, in view of the economic uncertainties that it faces, it will not buy any new machines that year. This then has repercussions right through the system. The factory manufacturing machines no longer has a guaranteed market for its product. Faced with the cancellation of the order, it will have to reduce output and lay off workers. It will no longer require as much steel and other inputs from other firms in the economy. They too will lay off workers and reduce output.

On the other hand, the sugar factory may have difficulties obtaining raw materials. State farms, freed from restrictions on what to grow, may decide to grow

COMMUNIST
STATE

more wheat and less sugar beet. The sugar factory may also experience problems getting its product to market. In the Soviet Union in the late 1980s, there was considerable chaos on the railways and with road transport. Whole cities may suddenly find that there is no sugar available to be purchased. By 1990, the Soviet government was seriously concerned that the breakdown in supplies occurring as a result of a move towards a free market economy could result in famine in the Soviet Union in 1991.

As Figure 109.1 shows, the cost of change in the Soviet Union in the late 1980s was a fall in output and this was before the substantial economic reforms that the Soviet Union aimed to implement in the 1990s to transform at least part of its economy into a genuine market economy.

Inflation

Economic transformation in Eastern Europe has been associated with very high inflation. A rise in prices is almost inevitable if an economy moves towards a free market system. In a command economy, resources are rationed in a number of different ways, but not through price. In the health service, for instance, health care might be rationed according to need, with

Soviet prices
Annual percentage change estimate

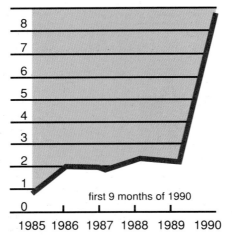

first 9 months of 1990

1985 1986 1987 1988 1989 1990

Soviet industrial production
Annual percentage change estimate

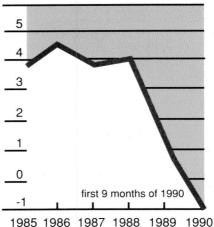

first 9 months of 1990

1985 1986 1987 1988 1989 1990

Source: Goskomstat.

Figure 109.1

criteria decided by doctors. In housing, accommodation might be allocated according to age or length of time on a waiting list. In food, citizens might have ration books, or only a very limited range of foods might be available in shops, discouraging shoppers from making too many purchases. Consumer items such as shoes might be available on a first come, first served basis.

In a market system, resources are allocated by price. The free market price is inevitably above the old state price if consumers have been rationed in the past. So when a market system is introduced, prices rise until demand equals supply. There is no shortage because some consumers have been priced out of the market.

Figure 109.2 shows the results of a *Financial Times* survey in Moscow in March 1990. State prices for goods were on average less than one-fifth the free market price of the same goods. However, products at state prices, sold through state shops, were either unavailable or were rationed in some way. At market prices, they were freely available from private shops or stalls. But the majority of Muscovites could not have afforded a weekly shop at those market prices. Hence demand for free market produce was relatively low.

Higher prices can spark a wage price spiral. Workers in Eastern Europe have reacted to higher prices by demanding higher wages. If firms give higher wages, then employers will need to pass on those higher costs in the form of higher prices which in turn give rise to further wage demands. For the sort of inflation that has been seen in Eastern Europe in the 1980s, it is necessary for the government to **accommodate** those price and wage increases by printing money

(☞ unit 93). If they don't, then firms giving price increases will find that they can't find buyers for their higher priced goods. Lower orders will result in lost production and redundancies. That in turn could mean strikes, riots and civil unrest.

	State	Market
Apples (green)	3.00	15.00
Apples (red)	3.00	8.00
Beef	2.50	12.00
Cabbage	0.16	3.00
Carrots	0.32	1.50
Cucumbers	8.50	15.00
Garlic	1.80	4.00
Grapes	4.00	15.00
Lamb	2.50	15.00
Mandarins	1.00	10.00
Onions	1.00	3.00
Pork	2.50	15.00
Potatoes	0.50	2.00
Tomatoes	3.00	15.00
Veal	2.50	15.00

(average ratio 5.6)

Source: adapted from the *Financial Times*, 12.3.1990.

Figure 109.2 *Price comparisons for state and market prices in Moscow (Roubles per kilogram)*

Ownership and wealth

In a command economy, land and capital is owned by the state. In a free market economy, most land and capital is owned by the private sector. So the move from one type of economy to the other must involve the sale of state assets to private individuals or companies (what would be called 'privatisation' in a UK context). A number of ways of achieving this have been discussed in Eastern Europe in recent years.

- The state could give property and capital away to the individuals or companies currently employing them. For instance, tenants of state housing could be given their accommodation. Factories could be given to their workers. One problem with this is that it is a very arbitrary way of sharing out assets. A worker in a factory which produces goods for export to the West would do far better out of this than a worker whose factory was obsolete.

- The state could put all assets which it proposes to sell into a fund, with each citizen receiving a share allocation in the fund. The fund would sell off assets wherever possible, replacing physical assets with cash. Either the cash would be distributed to shareholders in higher dividends or it could be used to invest in the remaining assets of the fund. Shares in the fund would be tradeable, so citizens could choose either to sell the shares and spend the proceeds now or keep them in the hope of earning dividends and making capital gains.

- The state could sell assets to the highest bidder and use the proceeds to reduce past government debt, pay for increased government spending or reduce current tax levels. Assets could be sold either to domestic individuals or producers, or to foreign companies.

The distribution of resources

There will be a fundamentally different allocation of resources in a mixed economic system to which Eastern European countries are moving than in a command economy. In free markets, resources are allocated to those with spending power. In turn, those with most spending power are likely to be those whose wealth, whether physical, financial or human, is greatest. Currently, few individuals own much of the physical capital, but this could change radically over the next 50 years as fortunes are made in a capitalist market. There are certainly likely to be greater wage differentials even in the short term. This redistribution is likely to take place behind the cloak of inflation, with some workers gaining wage increases above the rate of inflation whilst others will lag behind.

The speed of change

There is widespread disagreement about the speed with which change should be implemented. There are those, like the Polish government in 1989-1990, who believe that the economy should be liberalised as quickly as possible. It is argued that this is vital if the attitudes on the part of planners, workers and consumers are to be changed. They have to change because the result of quick liberalisation is initially economic chaos. Managers now have to operate on a profit basis. Factories, which before had some guarantee of supply of inputs and markets for their products, suddenly have to buy and sell in open markets. Factories which are highly cost inefficient, or produce goods which no one wishes to buy, will close, resulting in a fall in output and unemployment. The rest are likely to operate at less than full capacity as either they cannot get raw material inputs or they cannot find markets for all their products.

Others believe that change should be evolutionary. Markets should be liberalised over a much longer period of time, and only when the market mechanism can lead to constant or perhaps increased output. The advantage claimed is that falling output and increased unemployment is avoided to any great extent. The problem is that there are so many people who stand to lose from liberalisation that a convincing case can always be put that state production should remain at least in the short term, whilst lip service is paid to the need to move to a market economy in the long term.

Special problems

Each country in Eastern Europe faces its own special problems. For instance, in the Soviet Union there is a huge overhang of savings. For years, Russians, unable to buy goods in the shops, have instead chosen to save money. If markets were freed, however, these savings might be liquidated as savers seize the opportunity to buy cars or televisions or whatever else is offered at free market prices. This explosion in spending power would send prices rocketing - too much money would be chasing after too few goods. So the monetary authorities in the Soviet Union need to find a way of neutralising this saving.

The countries of Eastern Europe all face problems with energy supplies. Since 1990, the USSR has demanded payment for oil and gas in hard currency (e.g. US dollars). It has also increased the price of oil from a subsidised price of the equivalent of about $8 a barrel to the world price. Even before the Gulf crisis of 1990, the free market price of oil was about $20 a barrel. This represented a more than doubling in the price of oil for these countries and could be compared to the oil price shocks of 1973-4 and 1978-80 in the First World. Massive price increases in a basic raw material inevitably result in stagflation. Buyers have to cut back their consumption because they cannot afford to buy, and production falls as prices rise. Higher prices for goods then lead to a fall in demand reinforcing the deflationary tendencies.

In East Germany, unification with the West has led to a flood of imports. East Germans no longer want to buy shoddy East German made goods, but do want West German and other western imports. This magnifies the deflationary effect of the movement towards a market economy compared to other countries in Eastern Europe where imports are still controlled to some extent by the state. The unemployment created poses special problems because East Germans are entitled to 'emigrate' to West Germany, whereas Poles or Bulgarians have no right to settle in, say, France or the UK. West Germany has already had difficulties absorbing the hundreds of thousands of East Germans who fled to the West before

unification. Unless the German government can quickly raise East German living standards by securing large scale investment in East Germany, then it will continue to face internal migration problems.

In Romania, unlike its neighbour Hungary, the previous communist government had stifled all initiative in economic affairs. The state was all powerful and there was no entrepreneurial class whatsoever. If there is to be a move to a market economy, everyone needs to 'relearn' the rules of the market place.

In all countries, institutions such as private banks, stock exchanges and commodity exchanges have to be founded if private property is to be traded.

UN ECONOMIC COMMISSION CALLS ON WEST TO PROVIDE SHORT TERM FINANCIAL RELIEF

In November 1990, the United Nations Economic Commission for Europe (ECE) called on western governments and international institutions to give 'immediate attention' to short term financial relief for the countries of Eastern Europe. It warned that, with the people of Eastern Europe and the Soviet Union facing their hardest winter since the end of the war, the reform process could fail with 'incalculable' consequences.

The grim picture of economic developments in the first nine months includes an average 20 per cent collapse in fixed investment in Eastern Europe and 12 per cent decline in the Soviet Union. Inflation is high and accelerating thoughout the region with double-digit annual rates in most, perhaps all, countries. Rough but conservative estimates put the number of registered unemployed at 2.5m in Eastern Europe with a further 2m in the Soviet Union. In Poland alone, the number has climbed from 56 000 in January to more than 1m in October. The ECE secretariat distinguishes two groups of countries. In Poland, Hungary, Czechoslovakia and the former East Germany, the slump reflects the impact of stabilisation policies and efforts to speed economic change. In the Soviet Union, Bulgaria and Romania, the deteriorating situation reflects 'a collapse of central control and a failure to embark on an effective reform programme'.

But the problems of these countries have been exacerbated by a 'multiple energy shock' caused by a five-fold increase in the price of oil caused firstly by the decision of the Soviet Union to charge market prices for

exports of oil and secondly by the Gulf crisis. The breakdown of Comecon trade has also hit countries hard. Czechoslovakia, Hungary and Poland have had limited success in finding new outlets in the West for their products. Hungary managed to offset about a third of the fall in its Comecon exports by boosting deliveries to the West in the first half of 1990. Helped by a large devaluation of the zloty, Poland's exports west grew by 24 per cent in volume. However, against an average increase in volume of around 5 per cent in exports to the West for Eastern Europe as a whole, imports increased sharply by 20 per cent in the first half. The current account deficits of Eastern Europe and even more of the Soviet Union have worsened this year at the same time as the cost of new credit has increased, with Western commercial banks becoming more cautious in their lending. Most countries have had to draw on their official reserves.

Source: adapted from the *Financial Times*, 28.11.1990.

1. **Explain what problems the governments of Eastern Europe and the Soviet Union faced in 1990.**

2. **Why should (a) reform but also (b) lack of reform have led to this situation?**

3. **Suggest how the West could best help the countries of Eastern Europe overcome their current problems.**

Summary

1. Economics is generally classified as a social science.
2. It uses the scientific method as the basis of its investigation.
3. Economics is the study of how groups of individuals make decisions about the allocation of scarce resources.
4. Economists build models and theories to explain economic interactions.
5. Positive economics deals with statements of 'fact' which can either be refuted or not refuted. Normative economics deals with value judgements often in the context of policy recommendations.
6. Models and theories are simplifications of reality.

What is a science?

There are many sciences covering a wide field of knowledge. What links them all is a particular method of work or enquiry called the SCIENTIFIC METHOD. The scientific method at its most basic is relatively easy to understand. A scientist:

■ postulates a THEORY - the scientist puts forward a hypothesis which is capable of refutation (e.g. the earth travels round the sun, the earth is flat, a light body will fall at the same speed as a heavy body);

■ gathers evidence to either support the theory or refute it - astronomical observation gives evidence to support the theory that the earth travels round the sun; on the other hand, data refutes the idea that the earth is flat; gathering evidence may be done through **controlled experiments;**

■ accepts, modifies or refutes the theory - the earth does travel round the sun; a light body will fall at the same speed as a heavy body although it will only do so under certain conditions; the earth is not flat.

QUESTION 1

Table 110.1

£ billion at 1985 prices

Year	Change in consumers' expenditure	Change in personal disposable income
1978	9.9	14.2
1979	7.8	11.8
1980	0.0	3.2
1981	0.0	- 2.6
1982	1.7	- 0.5
1983	8.8	6.2

Source: adapted from CSO, *Economic Trends Annual Supplement.*

Economists suggest that the change in consumer spending varies with changes in the incomes of consumers (their personal disposable income). Does the evidence refute or support this hypothesis?

Theories which gain universal acceptance are often called LAWS. Hence we have the law of gravity, Boyle's law, and in economics the law of diminishing returns.

Economics - the science

Some sciences, such as physics or chemistry, are sometimes called 'hard sciences'. This term doesn't refer to the fact that physics is more difficult than a science such as biology! It refers to the fact that it is relatively easy to apply the scientific method to the study of these subjects. In physics much of the work can take place in laboratories. Observations can be made with some degree of certainty. Control groups can be established. It then becomes relatively easy to accept or refute a particular hypothesis.

This is all much more difficult in social sciences such as economics, sociology, politics and anthropology. In economics it is usually not possible to set up experiments to test hypotheses. It is not possible to establish control groups or to conduct experiments in environments which enable one factor to be varied whilst other factors are kept constant. The economist has to gather data in the ordinary everyday world where many variables are changing over any given time period. It then becomes difficult to decide whether the evidence supports or refutes particular hypotheses. Economists sometimes come to very different conclusions when considering a particular set of data as their interpretations may vary. For example, an unemployment rate of 12 per cent in the North region compared to a national average of 8 per cent may indicate a failure of government policy to help this area. Others may conclude that policy had been a success as unemployment may have been far greater without the use of policy.

It is sometimes argued that economics cannot be a science because it studies human behaviour and human behaviour cannot be reduced to scientific laws. There is an element of truth in this. It is very difficult to understand and predict the behaviour of individuals. However, nearly all economics is based on the study of the behaviour of groups of individuals. The behaviour of groups is often far more predictable than that of individuals. Moreover, we tend to judge a science on its ability to establish laws which are certain and unequivocal. But even in a hard science such as physics, it has become established that some laws can only be stated in terms of probabilities. In economics, much analysis is couched in terms of 'it is likely that' or 'this may possibly happen'. Economists use this type of language because they know they have insufficient data to make firm predictions. In part it is because other variables may change at the same time, altering the course of events. But it is also used because economists know that human behaviour, whilst broadly predictable, is not predictable to the last £1 spent or to the nearest 1 penny of income.

> **QUESTION 2** An important question in economics is 'What determines how much of a good is bought over a period of time?'. Put forward a hypothesis which might be used to answer this question. Give an indication of how you might attempt to test your hypothesis.

Theories and models

The terms 'theory' and MODEL are often used interchangeably. There is no exact distinction to be made between the two. However, an economic theory is generally expressed in looser terms than a model. For instance, 'consumption is dependent upon income' might be an economic theory. '$C_t = 567 + 0.852Y_t$' where 567 is a constant, C_t is current consumption and Y_t current income would be an economic model. Theories can often be expressed in words. But economic models, because they require greater precision in their specification, are often expressed in mathematical terms.

The purpose of modelling

Why are theories and models so useful in a science? The universe is a complex place. There is an infinite number of interactions happening at any moment in time. Somehow we all have to make sense of what is going on. For instance, we assume that if we put our hand into a flame, we will get burnt. If we see a large hole in the ground in front of us we assume that we will fall into it if we carry on going in that direction.

One of the reasons why we construct theories or models is because we want to know why something is as it is. Some people are fascinated by questions such as 'Why do we fall downwards and not upwards?' or 'Why can birds fly?'. But more importantly we use theories and models all the time in deciding how to act. We keep away from fires to prevent getting burnt. We avoid holes in the ground because we don't want to take a tumble.

> **QUESTION 3** Make a list of ten questions in economics which you think are important and to which you would hope to have an answer by the time you have finished your course.

Positive and normative models

These two uses of models - to investigate the world as it is and to use the model as a basis for decision making - lead us to distinguish between two types of economic model.

POSITIVE MODELS and positive economics deal with objective or scientific explanations of the economy. For instance, the model of price determination which states that a rise in price will lead to a fall in the quantity demanded is a positive model. It is capable of refutation (☞ unit 111). It is argued by some economists that positive models are value free.

NORMATIVE MODELS and normative economics attempt to describe what ought to be. A normative statement is one which contains a value judgement. A normative model sets a standard by which reality can be judged. For instance, 'The government has a duty to protect the incomes of everybody in society, not just the well-off' would be a normative statement. It contains a value judgement about the role of government.

For some, the study of economics is fascinating in itself. Studying and constructing positive models is reward enough. But most who study economics are principally interested in the subject because of its normative aspects. They want to know how society can be changed - 'Should society help the poor and disadvantaged?', 'How best might pollution be dealt with?'.

Academic economics has a long tradition of the study of positive economics. But 'political economy', the normative study of economics, has an equally long tradition going back to Adam Smith. In fact it is difficult to separate the two. To know how best to help raise the living standards of the poor (normative economics) we need to know how the economy operates and why people are poor.

Some economists argue that positive economics cannot be distinguished from normative economics because positive economics is subtly value laden. Why, for instance, have economists become so much more

> **QUESTION 4** The government yesterday resisted a last-ditch attempt by peers to strengthen commitments in the Electricity Bill to promote combined heat and power (CHP) generation systems as a means of improving energy efficiency.
>
> Lord Ezra (SLD) said a duty should be placed on the Director-General of Electricity Supply to promote CHP - using waste energy from power stations - to heat homes. He stated during the Bill's third reading that it was one way of reducing environmental damage.
>
> The Earl of Lauderdale (Conservative) said that everyone was 'green' now and CHP was one way of increasing energy efficiency. Lord Peyton of Yeovil (Conservative), however, argued that the government had got its priorities wrong in the bill.
>
> Source: adapted from the *Financial Times*, 19.7.1989.
>
> Which are positive statements and which are normative statements in this quote?

interested in the role of the entrepreneur (the risk-taking small businessman) during the 1980s? Much of the answer must be because Margaret Thatcher and Ronald Reagan made such important claims about the benefits of entrepreneurial activity for an economy.

In practice, all economists make value judgements. But many economists argue that 'good' economics distinguishes between positive and normative aspects. Value judgements are exposed so that we can see whether the analysis can lead to different conclusions if different value judgements are made.

Simplification

One criticism made of economics is that economic theories and models are 'unrealistic'. This is true, but it is equally true of Newton's law of gravity, Einstein's Theory of Relativity or any theory or model. This is because any theory or model has to be a simplification of reality if it is to be useful. Imagine, for instance, using a map which described an area perfectly. To do this it would need to be a full scale reproduction of the entire area which would give no practical advantage. Alternatively, drop a feather and a cannon ball from the top of the leaning tower of Pisa. You will find that both don't descend at the same speed, as one law in physics would predict, because that law assumes that factors such as air resistance and friction don't exist.

If a model is to be useful it has to be simple. The extent of simplification depends upon its use. If you wanted to go from London to Tokyo by air, it wouldn't be very helpful to have maps which were on the scale of your local A to Z. On the other hand, if you wanted to visit a friend in a nearby town it wouldn't be very helpful to have a map of the world with you. The local A to Z is very much more detailed (i.e. closer to reality) than a world map but this does not necessarily make it more useful or make it a 'better' model.

Simplification implies that some factors have been included in the model and some have been omitted. It could even be the case that some factors have been distorted to emphasise particular points in a model. For instance, on a road map of the UK, the cartographer will almost certainly not have attempted to name every small hamlet or to show the geological formation of the area. On the other hand, he or she will have marked in roads and motorways which will appear several miles wide according to the scale of the map. There are a number of reasons why this occurs.

■ Models are constructed in an attempt to present a clear and simple explanation of reality. Trying to include weather and geological information on a large scale road map would make it much more difficult for the motorist to see how to get from A to B. On the other hand, distorting reality by making roads very wide is extremely helpful to a motorist studying a map because it is much easier to read thick lines than thin lines.

■ Models must assume that explanations for much of

what is contained in the model lie elsewhere. For instance a model which explains that consumption varies with income doesn't explain what determines income itself.

■ The creator of a model may not be interested in a particular aspect of reality (which is an example of how normative values can be superimposed on supposedly positive models). The cartographer, for instance, preparing an ordinary road map is not interested in the geology of an area.

■ The model may be constructed deliberately to distort and mislead. For instance, employers might choose to use a model which predicts that minimum wages always increase unemployment, whilst trade unions might construct a different model which showed that minimum wages increased employment.

Models may also omit variables because the author does not believe them to be of importance. This may be a correct premise. On the other hand, it may be false, leading to the model being poorer than it might otherwise be. For instance, few would criticise a weather model which omits the UK rate of inflation from among its variables. On the other hand, a weather model of the UK which omits wind speed is unlikely to perform well.

In conclusion, all subject disciplines simplify and select from a mass of data. This process seems to cause little concern in sciences such as physics and chemistry. However, it is unfortunate for economists that many critics of the subject seem to think that simplification in economics shows that economists have little or no understanding of economic matters. Nothing could be further from the truth!

QUESTION 5 Take any theory with which you are familiar. Explain what simplifications have been made in the construction of the theory.

Key terms

The scientific method - a method which subjects theories or hypotheses to falsification by empirical evidence.
Theory or model - a hypothesis which is capable of refutation by empirical evidence.
Law - a theory or model which has been verified by empirical evidence.
Positive economics - the scientific or objective study of the allocation of resources.
Normative economics - the study and presentation of policy prescriptions involving value judgements about the way in which scarce resources are allocated.

Applied economics

Positive and normative economics

In an advertisement placed in the *Financial Times* on January 20 1989, the Tobacco Advisory Council (TAC), funded by the British tobacco industry, wrote the following.

'Before the last two Budgets we argued that excessive tax on cigarettes makes no economic sense. We explained that high taxes don't make people smoke less. They simply drive smokers to cheaper, imported brands. (Bad for the balance of payments and bad for British jobs.) We also pointed out that the hefty increases some pressure groups demand would add nearly 1 per cent to the inflation rate.

We're grateful our past warnings were not ignored. But this year there's even more of a case for fiscal restraint. Come 1992, the entire European tobacco market will be up for grabs. To stand a chance, the British Tobacco industry needs to maintain its market base. Higher taxes only undermine its position to the advantage of foreign competition.

There were plenty of sound arguments against excessive tax last year. Does it make sense to pile it on this year, now we're offering you an even better case?'

The article makes a number of positive statements which could be tested against economic evidence:
- the quantity of cigarettes smoked is not influenced by the size of the tax on cigarettes;
- an increase in taxes will lead to smokers substituting cheaper brands of cigarettes for the ones they currently smoke;
- these cheaper brands are not manufactured in the UK but are imported;
- these imports lead to a deterioration of the balance of payments position and lead to a loss of jobs, presumably in UK cigarette factories;
- increasing taxes on cigarettes will increase the inflation rate;
- the European Community 1992 programme will increase competition in the European tobacco market;
- companies best placed to survive this increased

competition will be those which have a strong domestic market base.

It also makes a number of normative statements, such as:
- referring to taxes as 'excessive' and labelling the increases in tax demanded by some pressure groups as 'hefty';
- stating that tax on cigarettes makes 'no economic sense';
- arguing that there is 'even more of a case' in 1989 than in previous years.

Overall, the advertisement could be argued to be normative in tone, using value laden terms even when making positive statements. For instance, instead of talking about a 'loss of British jobs', it says 'bad for British jobs', and the whole argument about the effects of 1992 is peppered with phrases such as 'up for grabs', 'stand a chance' and 'undermine their position'.

What the advertisement does not do is consider any alternative case. For instance, if it believes that a raising of taxes merely leads to substitution by consumers, why does it not argue that taxes on cheaper brands of cigarettes be raised by a greater proportion than an increase on dearer cigarettes? If it is concerned about inflation, the effect of a large increase in tobacco duties could be offset by a fall in duties on other goods such as lead free petrol. Does it matter if jobs are lost in the British tobacco industry if those workers are redeployed to other jobs in the economy? The advertisement also says nothing about the health costs of smoking. It avoids raising this issue by implying that nothing can be done to alter the habits of smokers since raising taxes won't affect the level of demand.

As a piece of economic analysis, it is fundamentally flawed, presenting a one-sided viewpoint in value laden terms and making a number of unsubstantiated assertions. As an advertisement, it is intended to sway opinion. We have no evidence to suggest whether or not it succeeds in this aim.

Data question

BAKED BEANS

An economics researcher collects evidence about purchases of canned baked beans. Standing in a supermarket for two hours from 3-5 o'clock on two successive Friday afternoons, she records the following.
- There are only two types of baked beans on sale. One is the supermarket's own label and the other is a well known branded product. The branded product is 15 per cent more expensive than the own label.
- On the first Friday, 55 cans of branded beans are purchased compared to 45 own label cans.

- On the second afternoon, the branded baked beans are on 'special offer'. This has the effect of making them only 5 per cent more expensive than the own label cans. Sales on the second afternoon are 70 cans of branded beans and 40 own label cans.

1. Construct a hypothesis about what determines demand for baked beans.
2. To what extent does this evidence presented above support or refute your hypothesis?

111 Economic models

Summary

1. A good model is one which yields powerful conclusions, is elegant and internally consistent.
2. In addition, a good positive model is one which explains past and present events, can predict future events, is universally applicable and has realistic assumptions.
3. A good positive model must be capable of being refuted whilst a good normative model is one which sets out an ideal or paradigm state of affairs.
4. Models can be distinguished according to whether they are static or dynamic models, equilibrium or disequilibrium models, partial or general models, or micro-economic or macro-economic models.

'Good' models

Many of the units in this book are devoted to one economic model or another. Which of these models are 'good' models? A number of criteria can be used to judge a model.

One important criterion by which a positive economic model may be judged is the extent to which it accurately **explains reality**. Reality exists in three different time periods: **the past, the present and the future**. A very powerful model, such as the model of price determination, is able to explain what happened in the past, explain what is happening today and predict what will happen in the future. Price theory provided an explanation of why the rise in oil prices during the 1970s led to a fall in world wide demand for oil. Today it helps us understand why a restriction in the supply of oil by OPEC leads to a price rise. We can predict with confidence that as world oil reserves diminish over the next 300 years the price of oil will rise.

The simple Keynesian theory of income determination however is not such a good theory. It explains relatively well the workings of the UK economy in the 1950s and 1960s but only gives a partial insight into how the economy performed in the 1970s and 1980s. This is because the simple Keynesian model ignores both changes in the money supply and supply side shocks - reasonable simplifying assumptions in the 1950s and 1960s but very misleading in the context of economic events in the 1970s and 1980s. It may be that the 1970s and 1980s were an exceptional time period and perhaps in the future the simple Keynesian model will once again prove to be a good one.

Macro-economic computer models of the economy, such as the Treasury model, the London Business School (LBS) model or the National Institute of Economic Research (NIESR) model, are judged mainly on their ability to predict the future. They are specifically called **'forecasting models'**. It could be that the best predictor of next year's rate of inflation is this year's rainfall in the Sahara desert. A model which incorporated this would be a good model if we were solely interested in its ability to forecast but it would be a poor model if we wished to understand the causes of inflation in the UK.

There are a number of economic models which are claimed to be good predictors but are not based on **realistic assumptions**. An example is the neo-classical theory of the firm. In the real world there are virtually no industries which conform to the assumptions of either perfect competition or pure monopoly yet these theories are widely taught and discussed. One justification is that although the assumptions are unrealistic the models provide very powerful and clear predictions about the extremes of behaviour of firms. If we know how firms behave at either end of the spectrum of competition then we can predict how firms will behave between these two extremes. Unfortunately these justifications have no logical or empirical validity. The models of perfect competition and monopoly give us little help in understanding the behaviour of firms in the real world, which is why there are so many alternative theories of the firm.

Positive models must be capable of refutation (☞ unit 10). A good model will be one where it is possible to gather data and perhaps perform controlled experiments to refute or support the model.

Normative models need to be judged on different criteria. A normative model does not claim to mirror reality. It attempts to provide a guide as to what is desirable or to be recommended. The neo-classical theory of the firm provides such a **paradigm**. By making a number of assumptions, it is possible to show that efficiency will be maximised in an economy where all firms are perfectly competitive (☞ unit 34). Increasing the degree of competition in industry then becomes an ideal or a goal to be aimed for. Monopoly, on the other hand, is shown to diminish welfare. Therefore the policy goal should be to break up monopolies.

Ultimately it is impossible to judge between competing normative theories. It is impossible to prove or disprove a statement such as 'Citizens should not be economically dependent upon the state'. However, it is possible to expose false reasoning within a normative model. In the 1950s, Lipsey and Lancaster, for instance, proved that greater competition might lead to a loss of welfare in the economy if at least one industry in the economy was not perfectly competitive. This 'theory of the second best' rebutted the general assumption prevalent at the time (and indeed still prevalent amongst certain economists and politicians) that greater competition was always good whilst greater monopoly was always bad.

All models need to be judged on the grounds of internal consistency, and elegance. **Internal consistency** simply means that the logic in the argument is correct and that no mistakes have been made with any mathematics used. An **elegant** model is one which is as simple and as lucid as possible.

Finally, models need to be judged on their power. Price theory is a very **powerful** model. With few assumptions and a minimum of logic, it can be used to explain important events across time and between countries. Aggregate demand and aggregate supply analysis similarly is a powerful model which can show the effects of a variety of demand side and supply side shocks on the price level and output.

QUESTION 1
Table 111.1

	Investment[1] £ billion at 1985 prices	Rate of interest[2] %	Change in national income[3] £ billion at 1985 prices
1984	58.1	11.83	4.9
1985	60.3	11.50	11.2
1986	61.3	10.82	9.2
1987	66.4	10.62	13.2
1988	74.2	10.80	13.1

1. Gross domestic fixed capital formation.
2. Industrial debentures, average yield.
3. Gross domestic product at factor cost.

Source: adapted from CSO, *Economic Trends Annual Supplement*.

To what extent does the data show that (a) the accelerator model and (b) the marginal efficiency of investment model are 'good' models of investment behaviour?

Forms of expression

There are a variety of ways in which models can be expressed.

Verbally A model can be expressed in words. 'Consumption increases when disposable income increases' would be an example. The advantage of using words is that models can be made accessible to a wide variety of readers. On the other hand, the use of jargon, such as 'disposable income', can be a barrier to the non-economist. Words can also be imprecise. In the above statement, we don't know the extent to which the increase is proportional.

Algebraically Over the past twenty years there has been an explosion in the use of algebra in academic economics. It enables relationships to be set down very precisely but is often totally incomprehensible to the non-specialist. It

also presumes that economic relationships are precise. Many economists argue the contrary - that economic relationships, whilst consistent, cannot be expressed so accurately.

Graphically The use of graphs has a long history in economics. It provides a convenient shorthand, encapsulating what would otherwise take many words to explain. Graphs, however, have their limitations. For instance, the fact that they can only be used in two dimensions with any ease limits the number of variables that can be used in a model.

Statistically Statistics are essential for economists if they are to verify hypotheses. They encourage precision, but as with algebra, they can be difficult for the non-specialist to understand and can give a misleading impression of accuracy in economics. **Econometrics**, the empirical testing of economic theories using statistical data, is now an important branch of economics.

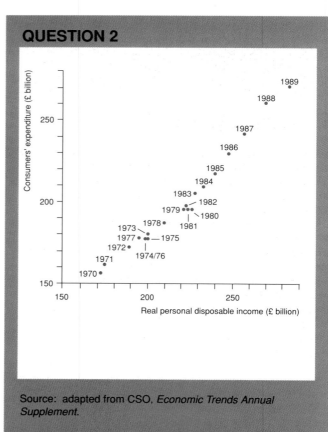

Source: adapted from CSO, *Economic Trends Annual Supplement*.

Figure 111.1 *Consumers' expenditure and personal disposable income at 1985 prices*

This is a scatter diagram.
(a) To what extent does it show that there is a positive correlation between consumers' expenditure and their income?
(b) How might you express the relationship between consumers' expenditure and income (i) verbally and (ii) algebraically?

Exogenous and endogenous variables

Economic models are built with two types of variables. EXOGENOUS VARIABLES are variables whose value is determined outside the model. For instance, in the simple Keynesian model of income determination, investment, government expenditure and exports are exogenous variables. Their values are constant whatever the change in other variables in the model unless it is assumed otherwise. The value of exogenous variables therefore cannot be calculated within the model.

ENDOGENOUS VARIABLES are variables whose value is determined within the model. For instance, in the simple Keynesian model of income determination both consumption and income are endogenous variables. Their value is determined by variables such as income within the consumption function equation. The value of endogenous variables will change if other variables within the model change too.

> **QUESTION 3** What variables would be exogenous and which would be endogenous in marginal efficiency of capital theory?

Static and dynamic

A DYNAMIC model is one which contains time as one of its variables. A STATIC model is one which contains no time element within the model. Nearly all the models explained in this book are static models. For instance, neither the theory of perfect competition nor the Keynesian theory of income determination contain a time variable. Static models can be used to compare two different situations, a technique called **comparative static analysis**. In the theory of perfect competition, it is common to compare one equilibrium situation with another equilibrium situation. For instance, a short run equilibrium position may be compared to the long run equilibrium position. A time element may even be implicitly assumed within the model - it is assumed that the movement from one equilibrium position to another in perfect competition will take place over a period of time rather than instantly at a point in time. However, the model does not explain the path which the industry or the firm will take in the move from one equilibrium position to another. It merely assumes a 'before' and 'after' situation.

The cobweb theory is the only dynamic model explained in this book. It explicitly charts the movement over time of a market in a disequilibrium state.

Dynamic models are in one sense more 'realistic' than static models. Time is a very important variable in the real world. However, as we have already argued, greater realism is not always a desirable characteristic in a model. Dynamic models in economics are more complex and difficult to work with than static models and their

predictions are not necessarily more powerful. For instance, if we wish to know how much revenue a government will raise by increasing taxes on beer, all we need is a static price model comparing the equilibrium situation before and after the imposition of the tax. There is no need to know the exact path that the market takes to get from one equilibrium position to another. Dynamic models are not therefore 'better' or 'worse' than static models - that judgement depends upon the use to which a model is to be put.

Equilibrium and disequilibrium models

Equilibrium is a central feature of all the models studied in this book. In economics, EQUILIBRIUM can be described as a point where expectations are being realised and where no plans are being frustrated. For instance, in the Keynesian model of national income determination, equilibrium national income is the point where planned expenditure equals actual income. In neo-classical price theory the cobweb theory is a disequilibrium model because it charts the behaviour of the market as planned demand and supply differ from actual demand and supply. All static models are equilibrium models because they deal with equilibrium positions.

An equilibrium position may be **stable**. If there is a movement away from equilibrium for some reason, there will be an in-built tendency for equilibrium to be restored. If the equilibrium point is **unstable**, there will be no tendency to move towards an equilibrium point once disequilibrium has been established.

It is easy to make the incorrect assumption that the market (or whatever is being studied) will always return to an equilibrium position; or that the equilibrium point is somehow the optimal or most desirable position. Neither is necessarily true even if economists tend to believe that knowing where is the equilibrium point is helpful in explaining economic events and in making policy recommendations.

Partial and general models

Just as there is no clear distinction between theories and models, so too there is no clear dividing line between a partial and a general model. A GENERAL MODEL can be said to be one which contains a large number of variables. For instance, a model which includes all markets in the economy is a general model. A PARTIAL MODEL is one which contains relatively few variables. A model of the oil market or the demand for money would be partial models.

A partial model will be one in which most variables are assumed to be in the category of CETERIS PARIBUS. Ceteris paribus is Latin for 'all other things being equal' or 'all other things remaining the same'. It is a very powerful simplifying device which enables economists to explain clearly how an economy works. For instance, in neo-classical price theory ceteris paribus is used constantly. When the effect of a change in price on demand is analysed we assume that incomes, the prices of all other goods, and tastes, remain the same. In the Keynesian multiplier model, it is assumed that government spending, exports, the marginal propensity to consume etc. do not change when analysing the effect of a change in investment on national income.

A general model may be realistic because it contains more variables. But again it is not necessarily better than a partial model. If we wish to study the effects of a rise in indirect taxes on the car industry, it is much simpler and easier to use a partial model of price determination than to use a general model. The general model may provide marginally more information but the extra information is unlikely to be worth the time and effort needed to generate it.

Macro-economics and micro-economics

A MACRO-ECONOMIC model is one which models the economy as a whole. It deals with economic relationships at the level of all participants in the economy. A MICRO-ECONOMIC model, on the other hand, deals with the economic behaviour of individuals or groups within society. For instance, the study of the spending decisions of individual consumers or consumers within a particular market such as the market for cars (demand theory) would be micro-economics. The study of consumption patterns for the whole economy (the consumption function) would be an example of macro-economics. The study of the determination of wage rates (wage theory) would be micro-economics. The study of the overall level of wages in the economy (part of national income accounting) would be macro-economics.

QUESTION 4 Consider the following economic models and explain whether they are static or dynamic, equilibrium or disequilibrium, partial or general, and macro-economic or micro-economic models: (a) the Keynesian multiplier model; (b) the accelerator model of investment; (c) the Keynesian consumption function model; (d) the aggregate demand and supply model of income determination; (e) marginal utility theory; (f) the cobweb model; (g) the model of perfect competition; (h) the marginal revenue product theory.

Key terms

Exogenous variables - variables whose value is determined outside the model under consideration.
Endogenous variables - variables whose value is determined within the model being used.
Static and dynamic models - a static model is one where time is not a variable. In a dynamic model, time is a variable explicit in the model.
Equilibrium - the point where what is expected or planned is equal to what is realised or actually happens.
Partial and general models - a partial model is one with few variables whilst a general model has many.
Ceteris paribus - the assumption that all other variables within the model remain constant whilst one change is being considered.
Macro-economics - the study of the economy as a whole.
Micro-economics - the study of the behaviour of individuals or groups within an economy.

Applied economics

Forecasting models

A number of UK macro-economic forecasting models are in current use. They are computer driven, usually relying upon a large number of different relationships to produce predictions about the levels of certain key variables, such as GDP, prices and the balance of payments.

Figure 111.2 shows the main relationships in a version of the Treasury macro-economic model used in the 1970s. The model used over 500 different equations to describe the relationship between different variables. For instance, the consumption function (☞ units 60 and

61) was specified as:

$$C = 160 + dW + eB + fI + gR + J$$

where 160 was autonomous consumption (consumption which did not vary with income), W was net wages and forces pay, B was net current grants to persons (mostly welfare benefits), I was net other personal income (e.g. pensions from private pension schemes), R was the notional value of rent (called imputed rent) from owner-occupied houses and J was the estimated effect on consumers' expenditure of hire purchase regulations in force at the time. The letters d, e, f and g were coefficients. In economic theory terms, they are the marginal propensities to consume. The model assumed that income would be spent over a period of time. For instance, 0.6 of welfare benefits would be spent within the first quarter of receipt, 0.3 within the second quarter and 0.1 within the third quarter. The overall marginal efficiency to consume (MPC) out of benefit income was therefore 1. The MPC out of wages, W, was 0.932 spread over 9 quarters, whilst the MPC out of other personal income, I, was lower still at 0.735 spread over 10 quarters.

Although the consumption function specified in the model is far more complex than that given in units 60 and 61 because precise numbers need to be generated from it, the function is recognisably a Keynesian consumption function. It states that consumption varies with income, there is an autonomous element to consumption and that credit terms can affect consumption.

There are 10 **exogenous** variables in the model, from indirect taxes to interest rates. Figures for these need to be fed into the model before it can generate estimates of the **endogenous** variables such as the current balance, total final expenditure, gross domestic product, the Retail Prices Index and unemployment.

This version of the model is **Keynesian**. All the endogenous variables are real variables. There is no money supply, for instance, in the model. The forecasting models used during the 1980s were far more likely to incorporate the insights of **monetarist theory**.

The Treasury Model in its various forms has in one sense been remarkably accurate. It succeeds in predicting levels of variables such as GDP, prices, exports, imports, unemployment to within 1 or 2 per cent. The problem is that economists and policy makers are not usually very interested in predictions about levels - they are interested in rates of change. A prediction that GDP will be £220 bn next year compared to £200 bn this year with an outturn of £230 bn seems very accurate, but the error in the growth forecast of GDP is 50 per cent. GDP was predicted to grow by 1 per cent (comparing £220 bn with £200 bn), but in fact grew by 1.5 per cent. The average error in forecasts was greater in the 1970s than in the 1960s and 1980s, but this might be expected given the more turbulent economic events of the 1970s which were difficult to predict. The Treasury Model also has performed on average as well as, if not better than, the other forecasting models produced in the UK. However, the fact that its predictions are rarely completely accurate shows the difficulty that economists have in constructing forecasting models.

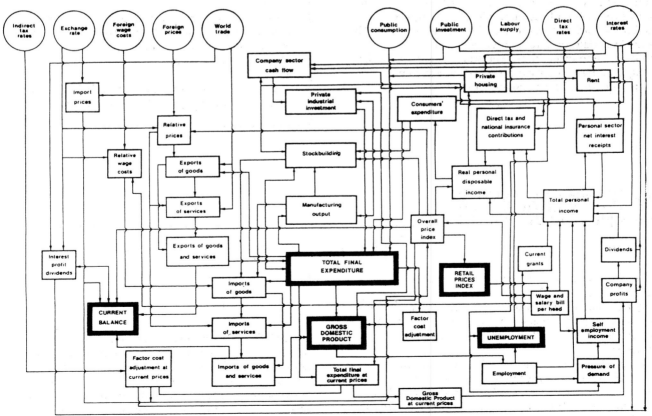

Figure 111.2 *Flow chart of the Treasury macroeconomic model*

INFLATION AND THE RATE OF INTEREST

Table 111.2 *Inflation and the rate of interest*

Per cent

	1980	1981	1982	1983	1984	1985	1986	1987	1988
United States									
Inflation	13.5	10.3	6.1	3.2	4.3	3.5	1.9	3.7	4.1
Rate of interest	11.4	14.0	10.6	8.6	9.5	7.5	6.0	5.8	6.7
Japan									
Inflation	8.0	4.9	2.6	1.8	2.3	2.0	0.4	- 0.2	0.5
Rate of interest	6.3	5.7	5.4	5.3	4.9	4.9	3.6	2.4	2.4
Germany									
Inflation	5.5	6.3	5.3	3.3	2.4	2.2	- 0.1	0.2	1.3
Rate of interest	9.5	12.1	8.9	5.8	6.0	5.4	4.6	4.0	4.3
France									
Inflation	13.6	13.4	11.8	9.6	7.4	5.8	2.7	3.1	2.7
Rate of interest	12.2	15.2	14.6	12.5	11.7	9.9	7.7	8.3	7.9
United Kingdom									
Inflation	18.0	11.9	8.6	4.6	5.0	6.1	3.4	4.2	4.9
Rate of interest	15.0	13.0	11.4	9.6	9.3	11.6	10.3	9.2	9.9
Italy									
Inflation	21.2	17.8	16.6	14.6	10.8	9.2	5.9	4.7	5.0
Rate of interest	16.0	19.8	19.4	17.8	15.3	13.7	11.5	10.7	11.1
Canada									
Inflation	10.2	12.5	10.8	5.8	4.3	4.0	4.2	4.4	4.0
Rate of interest	12.8	17.7	13.6	9.3	11.1	9.4	9.0	8.1	9.5

Source: adapted from OECD, *Historical Statistics*.

1. It has been argued that interest rates will be higher, the higher the rate of inflation. What evidence do the data provide to support this theory?

2. Suggest why the rate of interest and the inflation rate might be linked.

References

Bank of England, *Competition and Credit Control* , (1971)

Bird Associations, *Aluminium Analysis* , (1990)

D. Blanchflower and A. Oswald, 'The wage curve', (1989), cited in M.J. Artis (ed.), *The UK Economy*, Weidenfeld and Nicolson, London, (12th ed., 1989)

B. Burchell and J.Rubery, *Segmented Jobs and Segmented Workers: An Empirical Investigation*, ESRC Social Change and Economic Life Initiative Working Paper 13, (1990)

P. Checchini, *The European Challenge 1992*, Wildwood House, Gower, Aldershot, (1988)

Cmnd. 6527, *Employment Policy*, HMSO, (1944)

K.G. Cowling et al., *Mergers and Economic Performance*, Cambridge University Press, (1980)

A.S. Deaton, 'The Measurement of Income and Price Elasticities', *European Economic Review*, Vol 6, (1975)

Department of Transport, *Central London Rail Study*, HMSO, (1989)

M. Friedman and A. Schwartz, 'Money and business cycles' *Review of Economics and Statistics*, Vol 45 (supplement) (1963)

M. Friedman and A. Schwartz, *A Monetary History of the United States, 1867-1960*, Princeton University Press for National Bureau of Economic Research (1963)

M. Friedman, *Dollars and Deficits*, Prentice Hall (1968)

J.K. Galbraith, *The Affluent Society*, Deutsch, London, (1985)

J.K. Galbraith, *The New Industrial State*, Hamish Hamilton, London, 1967

H. Glennerster and W. Low, 'Education and the Welfare State: does it add up?', in J Hills (ed.) *The State of Welfare*, OUP (1990)

P.E. Hart and R. Clarke, *Concentration in British Industry, 1935-75*, National Institute of Economic and Social Research (1980)

P.E. Hart, *Recent Trends in Concentration in British Industry*, National Institute of Economic and Social Research (1984)

K. Hartley and N. Hooper, 'Industry and Policy', in P.Curwen (ed.) *Understanding the UK Economy*, Macmillan, London, 1990

Institute of Manpower Studies, Sussex University, *The Graduate Labour Market in the 1990s*, (1989)

J.M. Keynes, *The General Theory of Employment, Interest and Money*, Macmillan, London, (1936)

M.C. Kennedy, 'The economy as a whole', in M.J. Artis (ed.), *The UK Economy*, Weidenfeld and Nicolson, London, (12th ed. 1989)

R. Layard and S. Nickell, 'The causes of British unemployment', *National Institute Economic Review*, No 111, February 1985

R. Layard and S. Nickell, 'Unemployment in Britain', in C.Bean, R.Layard and S.Nickell (eds.) *The Rise in Unemployment*, Basil Blackwell, Oxford, (1986)

R.G. Lipsey and K. Lancaster, 'On the General Theory of the Second Best', *Review of Economic Studies*, 1956-7

I. Little, T. Scitovsky, M. Scott, *Industry and Trade in Some Developing Countries*, Oxford University Press, 1970

Low Pay Unit, *Undervalued, Underpaid and Undercut* (1989)

Manchester Business School, Centre for Business Research, *The UK Music Records and Tapes Market*, (1983)

G. Meekes, *Disappointing Marriage: A Study of the Gains from Mergers*, Cambridge University Press, (1977)

Monopolies and Mergers Commission, *The Supply Of Petrol*, HMSO, (1990)

National Consumer Council, *Consumers and the CAP*, HMSO, (1988)

H. Neurberger, *From the Dole Queues to the Sweatshops*, Low Pay Pamphlet No 30, Low Pay Unit (1984)

S. Nickell, 'Few dividends from lashing the unions,' *Financial Times*, February 7 1985

V. Pareto, *Manuel D'Economie Politique*, (1909)

A. W. Phillips, 'The relation between unemployment and the rate of change of money wage rates, 1861-1957', *Economica*, the New Series, Vol 25, November 1958

C.F. Pratten, *Economies of Scale in Manufacturing Industry*, Cambridge University Press, (1971)

E.F. Schumacher, *Small is Beautiful*, Blond and Briggs, London, (1970)

A. Smith, *The Wealth of Nations*, First published 1976, Pelican Books, London, (1970)

M. Stewart, 'Relative earnings and individual union membership in the UK', *Economica*, 50, 111-125 (1983)

L. Tobin, 'Liquidity preference as behaviour toward risk', *Review of Economic Studies*, Vol 25, (1958)

A. Yeats, 'Do African countries pay more for imports?', IMF, *Finance and Development*, Vol 27 number 2, June 1990

Index